MW00781380

HERMETICA

THE ANCIENT GREEK AND LATIN WRITINGS WHICH CONTAIN RELIGIOUS OR PHILOSOPHIC TEACHINGS ASCRIBED TO

HERMES TRISMEGISTUS

From the pavement of Siena Cathedral

See page 32

HERMETICA

THE ANCIENT GREEK AND LATIN WRITINGS WHICH CONTAIN RELIGIOUS OR PHILOSOPHIC TEACHINGS ASCRIBED TO HERMES TRISMEGISTUS

EDITED

WITH ENGLISH TRANSLATION AND NOTES

BY

WALTER SCOTT

VOLUME I

Introduction

Texts and Translation

SHAMBHALA
BOSTON 1985

SHAMBHALA PUBLICATIONS, INC.
314 Dartmouth Street
Boston, Massachusetts 02116

9 8 7 6 5 4 3 2 1
First Shambhala edition

Printed in the United States of America
Distributed in the United States by Random House
and in Canada by Random House of Canada Ltd.

Library of Congress Cataloging in Publication Data
Main entry under title:
Hermetica : the ancient Greek and Latin writings which
contain religious or philosophic teachings ascribed
to Hermes Trismegistus.
Greek and Latin, with English translation.
Reprint. Previously published: Boulder, Colo. :
Hermes House, 1982.
Bibliography: p.
Includes index.
1. Hermetism—Early works to 1800. I. Hermes,
Trismegistus. II. Scott, Walter, 1855-1925.
III. Corpus Hermeticum. English & Greek.
BF1600.H474 1985 299'.93 85-8198
ISBN 0-87773-338-4 (pbk.)
ISBN 0-394-74225-7 (Random House : pbk.)

Cover: Cretan coin from Sybritta displaying a head of Hermes.
Courtesy Hirmer Fotoarchiv Munchen.

HERMETICA

Plan of the Work

Vol. I. Introduction, Texts and Translation.

Vols. II & III. Commentary.

Vol. IV. Testimonia, Appendices and Indices.

INTRODUCTION

THE *Hermetica* dealt with in this book may be described as 'those Greek and Latin writings which contain religious or philosophic teachings ascribed to Hermes Trismegistus'. It does not much matter whether we say 'religious' or 'philosophic';[1] the writers in question taught philosophic doctrines, but valued those doctrines only as means or aids to religion.

There is, besides these, another class of documents, the contents of which are also ascribed to Hermes Trismegistus; namely, writings concerning astrology, magic, alchemy, and kindred forms of pseudo-science.[2] But in the character of their contents these latter differ fundamentally from the former. The two classes of writers agreed in ascribing what they wrote to Hermes, but in nothing else. They had little or nothing to do with one another; they were of very different mental calibre; and it is in most cases easy to decide at a glance whether a given document is to be assigned to the one class or to the other. We are therefore justified in treating the 'religious' or 'philosophic' *Hermetica* as a class apart, and, for our present purpose, ignoring the masses of rubbish which fall under the other head.

By what sort of people, and in what circumstances, were our *Hermetica* written? That question may be answered as follows. There were in Egypt under the Roman Empire men who had received some instruction in Greek philosophy, and especially in the Platonism of the period, but were not content with merely accepting and repeating the cut-and-dried dogmas of the orthodox philosophic schools, and sought to build up, on a basis of Platonic

1 'Theological', if taken in the etymological sense of the word, would perhaps be better; for the *Hermetica* are 'talks about God', or 'discussions concerning God'. But the word *theology*, as now commonly used, has associations that would be misleading.

2 These things might be grouped together under the vague but convenient term '*occult* arts and sciences'.

doctrine, a philosophic religion that would better satisfy their needs. Ammonius Saccas, the Egyptian teacher of the Egyptian Plotinus, must have been a man of this type; and there were others more or less like him.[1] These men did not openly compete with the established schools of philosophy, or try to establish a new school of their own on similar lines; but here and there one of these 'seekers after God' would quietly gather round him a small group of disciples, and endeavour to communicate to them the truth in which he had found salvation for himself. The teaching in these little groups must have been mainly oral, and not based on written texts; it must have consisted of private and intimate talks of the teacher with a single pupil at a time, or with two or three pupils at most. But now and then the teacher would set down in writing the gist of a talk in which some point of primary importance was explained; or perhaps a pupil, after such a talk with his teacher, would write down as much of it as he could remember; and when once written, the writing would be passed from hand to hand within the group, and from one group to another.

Specimens of such writings have come down to us, and these are our *Hermetica*. The *Hermetica* are short records, most of them not many pages in length, of talks such as I have described, or similar talks imagined by the writer, and doubtless modelled on those which actually took place.

But if that is what the *Hermetica* are, how is it that they have been commonly thought to be something very different? That has

[1] Ammonius Saccas died in or about A. D. 243. He is known to us chiefly by what is said of him in Porphyry, *Vita Plotini*, 3: 'Plotinus, in his 28th year (A. D. 233), took to philosophy. He attended the lectures of the teachers who were at that time in high repute in Alexandria; but he came away dejected and sorrowful. A friend, to whom he described his state of mind, understood what his soul desired, and took him to Ammonius, of whose teaching he had not till then made trial. Plotinus went to Ammonius and heard him speak, and thereupon said to his friend, "This is the man I was looking for". And from that day he stuck to Ammonius, and under his instruction became so devoted to philosophy that', &c. (Porphyry says he had heard this told by Plotinus himself.)

There is no external evidence that Ammonius Saccas was in any way connected with the Hermetists; but seeing that (1) Plotinus is known to have been strongly influenced by Ammonius Saccas, and (2) there is much in the teachings recorded in the *Hermetica* that approximates to the philosophic religion of Plotinus, we may fairly put these two facts together, and infer that the Hermetic teachers were men of the same type as Ammonius Saccas. Indeed, it is not impossible that in some few of the extant *Hermetica* we have specimens of the teaching of Ammonius Saccas, set down in writing (and ascribed to Hermes) by one of his pupils. There is no evidence for that; but at any rate we are justified in saying that the teaching of Ammonius Saccas must have closely resembled that which we find in some of the *Hermetica*.

resulted from the fact that in these writings the names given to teacher and pupils are fictitious. The teacher is, in most cases, called Hermes Trismegistus, and the pupil, Tat or Asclepius or Ammon.

What was the reason for that? Why did these writers prefer to call the tractates which they wrote 'Discourses of Hermes Trismegistus', and compose dialogues in which they made Hermes speak as teacher, instead of writing in their own names, and saying in their own persons whatever it was that they wanted to say? The motive must have been similar to that which made a Jew write a Book of Daniel, or a Book of Enoch, instead of a book of his own. In the Hellenistic period, and under the Roman Empire, that vigour of independent thought, which showed itself so conspicuously among the Greeks of earlier centuries, had dwindled away. There was an increasing tendency to lean on the support of authority and tradition; and among those who were interested in philosophy, the man who was 'nullius addictus iurare in verba magistri' became more and more exceptional. It is true that there was at the same time a strong tendency to syncretism; that is to say, men of different philosophic schools were very ready to borrow thoughts from one another; but that, for the most part, meant little more than that a man acknowledged the authority of two or more masters instead of only one, and made some attempt to blend or reconcile the teachings of those masters. The names of the great thinkers of earlier times—Plato, Pythagoras, and others—were held in almost superstitious veneration; and lists were drawn up in which the succession of pupils of those great teachers was set forth, and it was stated that A had learnt from B, and B from C, and so on. Every one must, it was thought, have learnt from some one else whatever wisdom he possessed; it hardly occurred to people that any one could possibly hit on a truth by thinking for himself. And the great masters themselves came to be dealt with in the same way. Plato was commonly held to have learnt from Pythagoras; and there arose a desire to get direct access to the sources from which Plato had drawn his philosophy. In Plato one got the wisdom of Pythagoras at second hand; it would be still better if one could get it at first hand. It must have been chiefly in response to this demand, that there were produced (mostly between 100 B.C. and 100 A.D.) large numbers of pseudonymous writings ascribed to this or that early Pythagorean—or in some cases even to Pythagoras himself, in spite of the recorded fact that Pythagoras had left nothing in writing.[1]

But then again, Pythagoras in turn must have learnt from some one else. From whom did *he* get his wisdom?

An answer to this question was found by Greeks resident in Egypt, or men of Egyptian race who had acquired Greek culture. It had long been accepted as a known historical fact that both Pythagoras and Plato studied in Egypt. They must have studied in the schools of the Egyptian priests. And what was taught in those schools? No one, except the priests themselves, knew what was taught in them; the priests were careful to keep that knowledge to themselves. All that the outside public knew about it was that the priests had in their hands a collection of ancient books, which were said to have been written by the god Thoth,[2] the scribe of the gods and inventor of the art of writing. Some of those books are known to us now—the 'Book of the Dead', for instance, and others of like character; and it may seem to us strange that any one should ever have imagined them to contain a profound philosophy. But in those times none but the priests had access to them; and a Greek, even if he had got access to them, could have made nothing of them, since they were written in a script and language unknown to him. That which was known to so few must, it was thought, be something very high and holy. From all this it was inferred that Pythagoras and Plato got their wisdom from the priests of Egypt, and the priests of Egypt got it from their sacred books, which were the books of Thoth.[3]

Greeks, from the time of Herodotus[4] or earlier, had been accustomed to translate the Egyptian god-name Thoth by the name Hermes. At a later time they distinguished this Egyptian Hermes from the very different Hermes of Greece by tacking on to the name

[1] A long list of these 'Neo-Pythagorean' writings is given by Zeller, *Philos. der Gr.* III. ii (1903), p. 115, n. 3. The author of each of them put forth under a feigned name, and usually in a would-be Doric dialect, his own version of the syncretic Platonism that was current in his time, and sought to make it appear that this was the sort of thing Pythagoras had taught.

[2] A full account of Thoth, based on 'a fairly complete examination of the chief references to the god in Egyptian literature and ritual', is given by P. Boylan, *Thoth, the Hermes of Egypt*, 1922.

[3] We may compare the theory maintained by many Jews and Christians (e.g. by Clement of Alexandria), that the Greek philosophers got their wisdom (or such imperfect wisdom as they had) from Moses.

[4] Herodotus 2. 67 calls the city of Thoth Ἑρμέω πόλις; and in 2. 138 he mentions a temple of 'Hermes' (meaning Thoth) in Bubastis.

a translation of an epithet applied by Egyptians to their god Thoth, and meaning 'very great'; and thenceforward they called this personage (whether regarded by them as a god or as a man) Hermes *τρισμέγιστος*,[1] and the Egyptian books ascribed to him 'the writings of Hermes Trismegistus'.

Hence it was that men such as I have spoken of, little known and almost solitary thinkers, came to choose Hermes Trismegistus as the name best suited for their purpose, and in their writings gave out as taught by Hermes what was really their own teaching. These men were teaching what they held to be the supreme and essential truth towards which Greek philosophy pointed; and it was taken as known that Greek philosophy was derived from the Egyptian books of Hermes, in which that essential truth was taught. Their own teachings therefore must necessarily coincide in substance, if not in words, with the unknown contents of those Egyptian books—that is, with what Hermes himself had taught. That being so, that which they wrote might as well be ascribed to Hermes as to the actual authors; and if that were done, their writings would gain the prestige attached to that great name. A piece of writing to which little attention might be paid if it only bore the name of some obscure Ammonius, would carry more weight if it professed to reveal the secret teaching of Hermes Trismegistus.

[1] In Egyptian texts Thoth is frequently called ꜥꜣ ꜥꜣ, 'great-great' (i.e. 'greatest' or 'very great'), and is also frequently called ꜥꜣ ꜥꜣ *wr*, which probably means 'very great-great'. (For references to the Eg. texts see P. Boylan, *Thoth, the Hermes of Egypt*, pp. 129 and 182). He is called 'five times great' in a text of early Ptolemaic date (see Griffith and Thompson, *Demotic Magical Papyrus*, p. 30, note on l. 26). In an Eg. text published by Griffith, *Stories of the High Priests of Memphis*, p. 58 (Reitzenstein, *Poim.*, p. 118), he appears to be called 'five times great' (if not more than five times); but in this instance the reading is doubtful. In Greek, 'Thoth great-great' is translated Ἑρμῆς ὁ μέγας καὶ μέγας in the *Rosetta Stone* inscr., 196 B.C. (Similarly, in some Fayum inscriptions, the god Souchos is called μέγας μέγας: Mahaffy, *Empire of the Ptolemies*, p. 320. Cf. Ἥρων θεὸς μέγας μέγας on a stele dated 67 B.C.: Perdrizet, *Negotium perambulans in tenebris*, p. 9.) τρίσμεγας also occurs (cf. Zosimus Alchem. i. 9 in *Testim.*: ὁ τρίσμεγας Πλάτων καὶ ὁ μυριόμεγας Ἑρμῆς); but the usual epithet of the Egyptian Hermes in Greek writings is τρισμέγιστος.

There can be no doubt that τρισμέγιστος was meant for a translation of one of the Egyptian epithets of Thoth; but why did the Greeks choose the particular form 'thrice-greatest'? It is most likely that τρισμέγιστος is (as Mr. Boylan is inclined to think) a translation of ꜥꜣ ꜥꜣ *wr*, 'very great-great'; and the word can be best accounted for in this way. The Greek who first invented it rendered ꜥꜣ ꜥꜣ, 'great-great', by μέγιστος, and expressed the meaning of the appended *wr*, 'very', by prefixing τρισ-. A prefixed τρισ- is frequently used in Greek to intensify the meaning of an adjective; e.g. τρίσμακαρ, τρισόλβιος, τρισάγιος (Plutarch, *Is. et Os.* 36, says, τὸ "πολλάκις" εἰώθαμεν καὶ "τρὶς" λέγειν, ὡς τὸ "τρισμάκαρες"). On the other hand, δισ- is not thus used; a Greek would therefore not be disposed to write δίσμεγας or δισμέγιστος.

Some one of the teachers of whom I have spoken must have been the first to hit on this device; others, into whose hands his writings passed, were urged by like motives to follow his example; and before long the Hermetic dialogue or discourse became, in certain circles in Egypt, the established form for writings on these subjects.[1]

It is not necessarily to be assumed that the authors of the *Hermetica* intended to *deceive* their readers, any more than Plato did, when he wrote dialogues in which Socrates was made to say things that Socrates had never said. It may be that the writers, or some of them at least, did not mean or expect to deceive any one, and that, within the narrow circle of readers for which each of these writings was originally intended, no one was deceived. But when the document passed beyond the bounds of that circle, and got into the hands of others, those others at any rate were apt to take it at its face value, and think it to be a genuine and trustworthy record of things that had been said by an ancient sage named Hermes Trismegistus, or a translation into Greek of things that he had written in the Egyptian language. And that is what was commonly thought by people who knew of these writings, for about thirteen hundred years, from the time of Lactantius to that of Casaubon. There may, perhaps, be some who think so still.

What sort of person was this Hermes Trismegistus thought to be? Was he a god or a man? If one of the Hermetic writers had been asked that question, he would, I think, have answered in some such way as this: 'Hermes was a man like you and me—a man who lived in Egypt a very long time ago, in the time of King Ammon. But he was a man who attained to *gnosis* (that is to say, knowledge of God, but a kind of "knowledge" that involves union with God); and he was the first and greatest teacher of *gnosis*. He died, as other men die; and after death he became a god—just as you and I also, if *we* attain to *gnosis*, will become gods after *our* deaths. But in the dialogues which I and others like me write, and in which we make Hermes speak as teacher, we represent him as talking to his pupils at the time when he was living on earth; and at that time he was a man.'

Comparing the *Hermetica* with other writings of the period on

[1] It should be remembered that all the extant *Hermetica* together are probably only a small fraction of the mass of such writings that was once in existence. There were most likely hundreds of Hermetic *libelli* of like character in circulation about A. D. 300.

the same subjects, we find that there are two things that are 'conspicuous by their absence' in these documents. In the first place, the Hermetic writers recognize no inspired and infallible Scripture; and there is, for them, no written text with the words of which all that they say must be made to conform. They are therefore not obliged, as were the Jew Philo, and Christians such as Clement and Origen, to connect their teaching at every step with documents written in other times and for other purposes, and to maintain, as Jews and Christians were driven to do, that when the inspired writer said one thing he meant another. Hence each of the Hermetists was free to start afresh, and think things out for himself—free in a sense in which Jews and Christians were not free, and even the professional teachers of Pagan philosophy, much occupied in expounding and commenting on the writings of Plato or Aristotle or Chrysippus, made comparatively little use of such freedom as they had. Released from this subjection to the past, a Hermetist could go straight to the main point, unhampered by the accumulations of lumber by which others were impeded; and this made it possible for him to pack into the space of a few pages all that he found it needful to write. Hence there is in the *Hermetica* a directness and simplicity of statement such as is not to be found in other theological writings of the time, whether Pagan, Jewish, or Christian. I do not mean to say that there is much that is *original* in the doctrines taught in the *Hermetica*; the writers were ready enough to accept suggestions from others (mostly from the Platonists), and there is little in these documents that had not been thought of by some one else before. But if a Hermetist has adopted his beliefs from others, they are none the less *his own* beliefs; and his writing is not a mere repetition of traditional formulas. He may have accepted the thought from some one else, but he has thought it over afresh, and felt its truth in his own person.[1] Some at least of the Hermetic writers felt themselves to be inspired by God.[2] They speak of the divine νοῦς in much the same way that a Jew or Christian might have spoken of the Spirit

[1] The Hermetic *libelli* differ so much among themselves, that few general statements can be made concerning them to which exceptions may not be found; but I am here describing the impression produced by them as a whole, or for the most part.

[2] A Hermetic teacher might have said, like a Homeric bard (*Od.* 22. 347), αὐτοδίδακτος δ' εἰμί, θεὸς δέ μοι ἐν φρεσὶν οἴμας παντοίας ἐνέφυσεν. The meaning of θεός had changed, but the notion of inspiration was still nearly the same.

of God. It is the divine νοῦς which has entered into the man that tells him what he needs to know; and with that divine νοῦς the man's true or highest self is identical or consubstantial. 'Think things out for yourself', says a Hermetist, 'and you will not go astray.'[1]

And a second thing to be noted is the absence of *theurgia*—that is, of ritualism, or sacramentalism. The notion of the efficacy of sacramental rites, which filled so large a place both in the religion of the Christians and in that of the adherents of the Pagan mystery-cults, is (with quite insignificant exceptions) absent throughout these *Hermetica*. The writer of *Corp.* XI. ii, for instance, says, 'Everywhere God will come to meet you'. He does not say that God will come to meet a man in initiation-rites like those of Isis or Mithras, or in the water of baptism, or the bread and wine of the Christian Eucharist; what he does say is, 'God will come to meet you *everywhere*', in all you see, and in all you do.

At what dates were the *Hermetica* written? This question, together with the closely connected question from what sources were derived the doctrines taught in them, is discussed in detail in the notes on the several *libelli*. I here sum up shortly the conclusions at which I have arrived.

The external evidence (collected in the *Testimonia*) proves that in A. D. 207–13 some *Hermetica* of the same character as ours were already in existence and accessible to Christian readers; and that in or about A. D. 310 most, if not all, of the extant *Hermetica* were in existence, as well as many others that have perished.

From internal evidence I have been able to assign a definite date to one document only. If I am not mistaken, the Greek original of *Ascl. Lat.* III was written within a year or two of A. D. 270.

With respect to all the other *Hermetica*, we have nothing to go upon except the character of the doctrines taught in them.[2] What can be inferred from that?

There was no one system of Hermetic philosophy or theology, no one body of fixed dogmas; each of these numerous writers had his own manner of thinking, and looked at things from his own

[1] *Corp.* XI. ii *fin.*

[2] Perhaps some evidence as to dates might also be got by a close investigation of the *words* and *diction*, dealt with as in lexicons and historical grammars. This I have not attempted; possibly some one else may think it worth while to undertake it.

point of view; and there are wide differences between the teaching of one *libellus* and that of another. But underlying all these differences there is a certain general similarity, such as would naturally result from similar training and a common environment.

In the first place, the influence of Plato—and of the *Timaeus* more than any of Plato's other dialogues—is manifest in almost every page. Most of the Hermetists were probably not much given to reading (that would seem to follow from the fact that they relied on talk much more than on books in their teaching), and it may be that some of them had never read a line of Plato's own writings; but somehow or other, whether by attendance at the public lectures of professional teachers of philosophy, or by private talk with men who knew about these things, they had imbibed the fundamental doctrines of that kind of Platonism which was current in their time.

But this prevailing Platonism is modified, in various degrees, by the infusion of a Stoic ingredient. Terms and conceptions derived from Stoic physics or cosmology are to be found in most of the *libelli*. Now Platonism modified by Stoic influence—the sort of syncretic Platonism that we find in Philo, for instance—was not and cannot have been anywhere in existence much before the first century B. C. There can have been no such blending of doctrines during the period of scepticism in the Platonic school, when Academics such as Carneades[1] were waging war against the dogmatism of the Stoics. It was not until that feud had died down, that the scepticism of the Academy was replaced by a more positive form of Platonic teaching; and it was only then that Platonists began to Stoicize, and Stoics to Platonize. This new departure may be dated, roughly speaking, at about 100 B. C. Among the Stoics who Platonized, the most prominent name is that of Posidonius, who wrote between 100 B. C. and 50 B. C.; and in some of the *Hermetica* the influence of Posidonius can be clearly seen. Any proposal to put the date of the *Hermetica* before 100 B. C. may therefore be disregarded. It is not merely probable, but certain, that the true date is later than that.

But how much later? If we want an answer to that question, we must not be content with talking about the *Hermetica* in general; we must examine the *libelli* one by one, and try to find out, with regard to each of them in turn, what date is indicated by the details

[1] Carneades was in Rome in 155 B. C., and died 129 B. C.

of doctrinal statement that we find in that particular document. That is what I have tried to do. Inferences drawn from *data* of this kind must inevitably be somewhat vague; but the conclusion towards which I have found myself led is this—that the *Hermetica* which have come down to us were most of them, if not all, written in the third century after Christ.[1] Some of them may have been written before the end of the second century;[2] but probably none[3] so early as the first century. And this conclusion, drawn from the doctrinal contents of the documents, agrees with the date A. D. 270, which is indicated by the prophecy in *Ascl. Lat.* III, and does not disagree with the external evidence.

So far, I have spoken only of doctrines derived from Greek philosophy. That includes nearly all that these documents contain; but not quite all. There are, in some of the *libelli*, things that may or must have come from some other source. But these are of quite subordinate importance.

In the first place, it may be asked whether there is anything in the *Hermetica* that is derived from the indigenous religion of Egypt. As far as definite statements of doctrine are concerned, there is very little. With the exception of the mere framework and setting of the dialogues—the names Hermes Trismegistus, Ammon, &c., and mentions of a few supposed facts that are connected with those names—there is hardly anything of which it can be asserted without doubt that it is of native Egyptian origin. Here and there one comes on a form of expression, or a way of putting things, which is not quite that to which we are accustomed in Greek philosophic writings; and in some of these cases it seems *possible* that what the writer says was suggested to him by phrases that were in use in the Egyptian cults. For instance, we find it stated in some of the *Hermetica* that God is self-generated; that God is hidden; that God is nameless, and yet innumerably-named; that God is bisexual; that God is life, and the source or author of all life; and so on. Parallels to these statements can be found in native Egyptian documents; and in each of these cases it is possible that the writer got the notion from an Egyptian source; but then it is also possible that it came to him from some other quarter. And even

[1] The *Isis to Horus* documents, which form a class apart, and differ in some respects from the rest, may possibly be as late as the fourth century.

[2] That is, in or about the time of Numenius, A. D. 150–200.

[3] There may possibly be one or two unimportant exceptions, e. g. *Corp.* III.

if on such points we give Egypt the benefit of the doubt, the Egyptian ingredient in Hermetic doctrine still remains comparatively small in amount; the main bulk of it is unquestionably derived from Greek philosophy.

Egyptian influence may, however, have worked more strongly in another way; it may have affected the spirit or temper of the writers. These men were, some of them certainly, and probably almost all, Egyptians by race, though Greek by education; and there is in some of their writings a fervour and intensity of religious emotion, culminating in a sense of complete union with God, or absorption into God,[1] such as is hardly to be found in Greek philosophic writings, until we come down to Plotinus, who was himself an Egyptian by birth and bringing up. It is true that in Plato himself there was something of 'mysticism', if this mood or state of feeling may be so named; but in him there was so much else beside, that the passages in his writings in which it finds expression are comparatively few and far between. And something of the same sort may be said also of most of the followers of Plato in later times (until we come to Plotinus)—such men as Plutarch, for instance. Numenius (who was a Syrian) may have been more like the Hermetists; but of him we have only short fragments. There may have been something more nearly analogous to the religious fervour of the Hermetic writers in some of the Greek mystery-cults, and still more in foreign mystery-cults adopted by the Greeks, especially that of Isis (which again was of Egyptian origin). But the votaries of those cults stood, for the most part, on a far lower intellectual level than the Hermetists, and their devotion to the gods they worshipped was inextricably intermixed with sacramental rites and quasi-magical operations from which the Hermetic teachers held aloof. And when we compare the Hermetists with the Greek writers on philosophy from whom they got their doctrines, we find that it is just this greater intensity of religious fervour that marks them off as different. I am inclined to think then that it is this tone of feeling that is the distinctively Egyptian element in the *Hermetica*. What we have in them is the effect that was produced by Greek philosophy when it was adopted by men of Egyptian temperament.

Secondly, is there anything of Jewish origin? There is, un-

[1] See, for instance, *Corp.* V. 11.

doubtedly, something of this; but not much. In *Corp.* I (the *Poimandres*), and in the short piece *Corp.* III, knowledge of the beginning of the Book of Genesis is clearly shown. Moreover, *Corp.* I contains a doctrine derived from Jewish speculations about Adam, and shows, in some respects, close resemblances to Philo. The writer of that one document was certainly affected by Jewish influence. But that *libellus* differs widely from the rest of the *Hermetica*; there is no reason to suppose that most of the Hermetists had ever seen or heard of it; and I do not think it was ascribed to Hermes by its author.

In the rest of the *Hermetica* we find hardly more than an isolated term or phrase here and there that seems to be of Jewish origin; hardly more, that is, than any Pagan might have picked up in occasional talks with Jews, or by reading the first chapter of *Genesis*, which was probably known to many Pagans of the time as an interesting specimen of a barbarian cosmogony.

Thirdly and lastly, is there any borrowing from Christians? To this my answer is that I have failed to find anything in the doctrines taught that is of Christian origin—with the possible exception of the doctrine of rebirth in *Corp.* XIII. That is the only extant *libellus* in which the notion of rebirth occurs; and its author (or the author of an earlier *Hermeticum* to which he refers) *may* have got it from a Christian source; but it cannot be said to be certain that he did.

Setting that aside, I can find nothing in the doctrines taught that is derived from Christianity. The Hermetists have no Christ, and no equivalent for Christ.[1] Hermes is nothing of the sort; he is merely a man and a teacher, and differs from other human teachers only in degree. Some of the Hermetists speak of a 'second God', and apply to him phrases resembling some of those applied by Christian theologians to the second Person of the Christian Trinity. But this 'second God' of the Hermetists is the Kosmos (or, in some few cases, Helios); and when Hermetic writers call the Kosmos 'son of God' and 'image of God', they are following a tradition derived from Plato's *Timaeus*, and not from the New

[1] The contrast between the Hermetic teaching and Christianity might be described in another way by saying that, in the view of the Hermetists, every man is (potentially at least) what the Christians held Christ, but Christ alone, to be; for the Hermetists said that each and every man is a being whose origin and home is in the world above, and who has come down to earth and been incarnated for a time, but (if he lives aright on earth) will return to the home above from which he came. That is not Christianity, but Platonism.

Testament. (There are also a *few* Hermetic passages in which a hypostatized λόγος of God occurs; but in those cases the source is Jewish, not Christian.) The 'second God' of the Hermetists differs fundamentally from the Christ of the Christians in this, that he is not a Saviour of mankind. There is in the *Hermetica* no trace of a 'Saviour' in the Christian sense—that is, of a divine or supracosmic Person, who has come down to earth to redeem men, has returned to the world above, and will take up his followers to dwell there with him. Hermetists might speak of salvation; it was salvation that they sought, and held that they had found; but they did not speak of a Saviour such as was worshipped by the Christians. According to their doctrine, it is by the operation of the divine νοῦς in a man [1] that the man is saved; and the divine νοῦς was never incarnated upon earth.[2]

The Hermetic writers must, of course, have known very well that Christianity was there. Some of them may have known little about its inner meaning, and may perhaps have thought of Christians merely as one of the various kinds of people included under the general term ἀσεβεῖς or ἄθεοι; but whether they knew much or little about Christianity, they ignored it in their writings. There is, indeed, one Hermetic document, *Ascl. Lat.* III, the writer of which does speak of Christianity (without naming it); but he speaks of it as of a deadly enemy, and foresees its coming victory over the Pagan cults with intense distress and horror. There is also, in *Corp.* IX, a passing remark which probably refers to Christians, and likewise implies that they are enemies. But these two instances are exceptional; and the Hermetists in general appear to have considered Christianity either a thing too hateful to be spoken of, or a thing too contemptible to be worth mention.

It would almost seem then that, if any borrowing took place,

[1] In this respect the divine νοῦς of the Hermetists is comparable to Christ (or 'the spirit of Christ') indwelling in the individual Christian (not in the Church, for the Hermetists recognized nothing analogous to the Christian Church); but it is in no way comparable to the Christ who lived on earth and died and rose again. For the most part the Hermetic νοῦς corresponds, not to Christ, but to the Jewish and Christian πνεῦμα. But the Hermetic conception of νοῦς was not derived from Jewish or Christian sources; it is wholly of Platonic origin.

[2] Except indeed in the sense that it 'enters into' every man that is worthy to receive it. Sometimes a man might imagine that he heard the divine νοῦς speaking to him, as if with a human voice, and even that he saw it, in a dream or vision (*Corp.* I); or Νοῦς might be represented (merely by a literary artifice?) as a teacher giving instruction to a human pupil (*Corp.* XI); but that is a very different thing from what Christians meant when they spoke of the incarnation of Christ.

it must have been the other way about. Did Christians borrow anything from Hermetists? But 'borrowing' is hardly the right word. It is not to be supposed that the Christian Church took over this or that theological dogma ready made from Hermetists, or from any other Pagans. And yet the Christian Church took over a good deal; for it took over the men themselves. If not the very men by whom our *Hermetica* were written, at any rate most of their sons or grandsons or great-grandsons, and most of their pupils, or the pupils of their pupils, must have turned Christians, as most Pagans did at about that time. Some few of them may have held out, and stuck to Paganism; and the results towards which the teaching of such men tended may be seen in Plotinus and his Neoplatonic successors. But most of them must have turned Christians. And what did that mean? In some respects the change would not be a large one. The Hermetist, when he became a Christian, would not have so very much to unlearn. If one were to try to sum up the Hermetic teaching in one sentence, I can think of none that would serve the purpose better than the sentence 'Blessed are the pure in heart, for they shall see God'. To that extent at least the Hermetist had nothing new to learn from the Christian catechist. He had been accustomed to aspire towards union with God, and to hold that 'to hate one's body'[1] is the first step on the way to the fulfilment of that aspiration; and when we come upon him, a little later on, transformed into a Christian hermit in the Egyptian desert, we find that he is still of the same opinion.[2] On the other hand, the convert would have to accept, *in addition to* the doctrines which he already held, some others that were new and strange to him; he would be told that he must henceforth believe in a Saviour who had 'become flesh'; and he would have to admit the efficacy of certain sacramental rites, and the infallibility of certain writings, and so on.

But we have to consider not only what conversion to Christianity meant for the Hermetists themselves, but also what were the effects produced by their conversion in the body of Christians into which they were incorporated. And it is here, if anywhere, that the influence of the Hermetic teaching on Christianity is to be looked for. However much these men may have been 'born again' in

[1] *Corp.* IV. 6 b.

[2] Cf. *De imitatione Christi*, I. 3: 'Ista est summa sapientia, per contemptum mundi tendere ad regna caelestia.' That might have been said by a Hermetist.

Christian baptism, they must have retained, under altered forms, much of their ingrained ways of thinking and feeling, and must have impressed something of this on those who were henceforth their fellow-Christians. So far as their influence extended, there would be a tendency to emphasize those sides or aspects of Christian doctrine and of Christian life which were most nearly in accord with the Hermetic teaching. And though the Hermetic teachers and their adherents must have been few in number in comparison with the mass of Egyptian Christians, their influence may have been far more than in proportion to their number; for they were the men who had been most in earnest about religion as Pagans, and they would be much in earnest still. Men of the stamp of these Hermetic teachers must have been prominent among those who set the tone in the Christian monasteries which sprang up in Egypt in the fourth century, and took the lead in debates on questions of Christian theology in Alexandria. And in that sense it might be said that in the *Hermetica* we get a glimpse into one of the many workshops in which Christianity was fashioned.

The extant *Hermetica* are:

(1) The *libelli* of the *Corpus Hermeticum.*

(2) The Latin *Asclepius* mistakenly attributed to Apuleius.

(3) The Hermetic excerpts in the *Anthologium* of Stobaeus.

(4) Fragments quoted by Lactantius, Cyril, and other writers.[1]

List of Hermetic Writings.

Hermes to Tat (*a.* γενικοὶ λόγοι; *b.* διεξοδικοὶ λόγοι): Corp. IV, V, VIII, X, XII. i, XII. ii, XIII; Stob. *Exc.* I–XI; Fragm. 12, 30, 32 (?), 33.

Hermes to Asclepius: Corp. II, VI, IX, XIV (epistle); Ascl. Lat. (λόγος τέλειος); Fragm. 23, 24, 31.

Hermes to Ammon: Stob. *Exc.* XII–XVII (XVIII and XIX?).

Hermes (no pupil named): Corp. III; Stob. *Exc.* XVIII–XXII: Fragm. 1–11, 13–22, 25–8, 32, 34–6.

Νοῦς to Hermes: Corp. XI. i, XI. ii.

Agathos Daimon to Hermes: reported by Hermes to Tat in Corp. XII. i.

[1] In this edition, the Hermetic fragments are collected under the heading *Fragmenta*; but each of them is also given, together with the context of the writing in which it is quoted, and with notes, under the heading *Testimonia*.

Agathos Daimon to Osiris: reported by Hermes to Asclepius, Fragm. 31.

Agathos Daimon to an Egyptian τεμενίτης: reported by Hermes, Fragm. 29.

Agathos Daimon: Fragm. 37.

Asclepius to Ammon (epistle): Corp. XVI.

Tat to King (Ammon?): Corp. XVII.

Isis to Horus: Stob. *Exc.* XXIII (*Kore Kosmu*), XXIV–XXVII.

Poimandres to a prophet: Corp. I.

Sermon (preached by the same prophet?): Corp. VII.

[Oration by a *rhetor*: Corp. XVIII.]

[Apophthegm of Hermes: Stob. *Exc.* XXVIII.]

[Verses on the planets: Stob. *Exc.* XXIX.]

CORPUS HERMETICUM

Corpus Hermeticum is the name given by recent commentators to a collection of about seventeen[1] distinct documents, which first makes its appearance (as a collection) in manuscripts of the fourteenth century. In the MSS. the collection as a whole bears no title, but each of the several documents contained in it has a separate heading of its own. The heading of the first document is Ἑρμοῦ τρισμεγίστου Ποιμάνδρης; and Ficinus, who published a Latin translation of the first fourteen documents in 1471, made the mistake of supposing that heading to be meant for a title of the whole collection.[2] Turnebus, who printed the *editio princeps* of the Greek text (1554), followed Ficinus in this mistake, and entitled *Corp.* I–XIV *Mercurii Trismegisti Poemander*. Similarly, Flussas (1574) gives to *Corp.* I–XIV, together with a '*Caput* XV' made up of Hermetic excerpts from elsewhere, the title *Mercurii Trismegisti Pimandras*, distinguishing the several documents as '*Caput* I', '*Caput* II', &c. (He appends '*Caput* XVI' under the different title *Aesculapii ad Ammonem.*) The blunder was corrected by Patrizzi (1591),[3] who uses the name *Poemander* rightly to denote *Libellus* I; but Parthey (1854) reverted to the old mistake, giving the title *Hermetis Trismegisti Poemander* to his edition of *Corp.* I–XIV, and calling the several documents *cap.* 1, *cap.* 2, &c. This is much as if one were to call the New Testament as a whole 'the Gospel according to St. Matthew',

1 By my reckoning, the number of distinct *libelli* in our text of the *Corpus* amounts to nineteen; and if we add a lost *libellus* between I and II, the original number must have been twenty.

2 Ficinus, f. 2 b: 'Est autem huius libri (i.e. of *Corpus* I–XIV) titulus *Pimander*, quoniam ex quattuor personis quae hoc in dyalogo disputant (i.e. in *Corp.* I–XIV regarded as a single "dialogue") primae Pimandro partes attribuuntur. . . . Ordo autem voluminis est, ut in libellos quattuordecim distinguamus, utque primae dialogi partes Pimandro dentur, secundas teneat Trismegistus, tertias Esculapius, quartum locum obtineat Tacius.'

3 Patrizzi says, 'Nostra sententia Poemander ille a Ficino in 14 capita dissectus non unus liber est, sed totidem libelli per se, a Poemandro separati, cui solus primus debetur. Reliqui, cum nullam Poemandri mentionem faciant (he should have added, "with the exception of *Libellus* XIII"), nec ab eo pendeant aut ordine dogmatum aut connexione ulla, Poemandri partes dici non possunt.'

and refer to the Epistle to the Romans, for instance, as 'the sixth chapter of Matthew'. The documents of the *Corpus* differ from one another in the same sort of way as the various writings of the New Testament; it is certain from internal evidence that most of them, if not all, were written by different authors; and there is nothing to show that the majority of the writers had read *Corp.* I, or had ever heard of the name *Poimandres.*

As to the numbering of the documents, there is much discrepancy and confusion. The variations are shown in the appended table.

Present edition	Manuscripts			
	A (I–XIV)	BCDM (I–XVIII)	R (I–XVIII)	*Index capitum* in S
Libellus I	No numbering	No numbering	κε(φάλαιον) α'	α'
— II &c.			— β' &c.	β' &c.
— XI. i	}	}	} — ια'	ια'
— XI. ii				
— XII. i	}	}	} — ιβ'	ιβ'
— XII. ii				
— XIII			{ (XIII. 1–16) ιγ' { (XIII. 17–22) ιδ'	{ ιγ' { ιδ'
— XIV			— ιε'	ιε'
— XVI		} XVI and XVII as one document	} XVI–XVIII as a separate work, in three unnumbered parts, viz. XVI+XVII, XVIII. 1–10, XVIII. 11–16	ιϛ'
— XVII				
— XVIII		{ XVIII. 1–10 { XVIII. 11–16		

By separating the two parts of XI and the two parts of XII, I have increased the number of distinct documents in the *Corpus* from seventeen to nineteen; and if I had been starting afresh, I should have numbered them consecutively from I to XIX. But in order to avoid confusion of references, I have thought it best to retain the numbering of Flussas and Parthey in respect of *Libelli* I–XIV, and that of Flussas and Reitzenstein in respect of XVI, and to follow Reitzenstein in calling the last two documents XVII and XVIII. The 'Caput XV' of Flussas is not a part of

Ficinus (I–XIV)	Turnebus (I–XVIII)	Flussas (I–XVI)	Patrizzi	Parthey (I–XIV)	Reitzenstein, *Poimandres*
No numbering	No numbering	Caput I	The *libelli* of the *Corpus* placed in a different order, with other *Hermetica* interspersed among them.	Cap. I	Kap. I
		— II &c.		— II &c.	— II (III) &c.
		— XI		— XI	— XI (XII)
		— XII		— XII	— XII (XIII)
		— XIII		— XIII	— XIII (XIV)
		— XIV		— XIV	— XIV (XV)
	Three excerpts from Stob. are here appended.	— XV, made up of same three excerpts from Stob. and an extract from Suidas.			
	XVI–XVIII as in R.	— XVI			— XVI
					— XVII
					— XVIII

the *Corpus*; there is therefore no *Libellus* XV in the present edition.

In dividing the text of each *libellus* into sections, I have, for the most part, followed Reitzenstein in the *libelli* edited by him in his *Poimandres* (viz. I, XIII, XVI, XVII, XVIII), and Parthey in the rest of the *Corpus*; and in cases where further subdivision seemed desirable, I have added letters to the number of the section, dividing § 3, for instance, into § 3 a and § 3 b. But I have here and there slightly shifted the point of division between two sections, in order to make it correspond better with a division in the sense.

The manuscripts of the *Corpus* have been carefully investigated by Reitzenstein, to whom I owe most of the information given in the following list. But to the fifteen MSS. mentioned and described by him (*Poim.* pp. 323 ff.) must be added three Oxford MSS. (Bodl. 3388, which I call Q; Bodl. 8827, which I call R; and Bodl. 3037, which I call S), of the existence of which he appears to have been unaware.[1] All the manuscripts reproduce, with slight variations, the text of a common archetype,[2] which was full of corruptions. The first task of an editor is to reconstruct the text of the lost archetype; his second and more difficult task is to infer from this what the author of each document wrote; his third task is to find out what the author meant. And in cases in which it is impossible to recover the precise words which the author wrote, it may still be possible to guess his meaning.

List of MSS. of the *Corpus*.

A: *Laurentianus* 71, 33; 14th cent.; contains *Corp.* I–XIV.

This manuscript was brought from Macedonia to Cosmo de' Medici at Florence, and was by him handed over to Marsiglio Ficino, who made from it the Latin translation which he published in 1471.

From 'a twin-brother of A' (Reitz.) are derived the following three MSS.:

[1] He speaks of Bodl. 16987, but says nothing about the three other *Bodleiani*.

[2] In our MSS. two large pieces are missing. The first of them contained the beginning of our *Corp.* II, together with a lost *libellus* which originally preceded our II (see prefatory note on *Corp.* II); the second contained almost the whole of *Corp.* XVII, of which only a short passage at the end has been preserved. It must be inferred from these omissions that in the archetype of our MSS. some leaves were torn out and lost at each of these two points.

Ottobonianus Graec. 153, 15th cent.
Coislinianus 332, 15th cent.
Parisinus 2518, written by Vergicius, 16th cent.

B: *Parisinus Graec.* 1220; middle of the 14th cent.; contains *Corp.* I–XVIII.

There are numerous corrections by one or more later hands (B[2]); but it appears that these corrections are for the most part conjectural, and not derived from another MS.

C: *Vaticanus Graec.* 237; 14th cent.; contains *Corp.* I–XVIII.

Closely connected with C are:
Parisinus Graec. 2007, 16th cent.
Ottobonianus Graec. 177, 16th cent.

D: *Vindobonensis phil.* 102; 15th cent.; contains *Corp.* I–XVIII. The printed text of Turnebus is a reproduction of a MS. nearly related to D; so that his edition may be treated as equivalent to a MS. of this family.

Palatinus Graec. 53, 15th or 16th cent., was found by Reitzenstein to be closely connected with D.

M: *Vaticanus Graec.* 951; 14th cent.; contains *Corp.* I–XVIII.

Q: *Bodleianus* 3388 (Arch. Seld. B 58); 15th cent. The text breaks off at the foot of fol. 62 b, at the words καὶ τὸ μὲν θνητὸν in *Corp.* XIII. 14; and the following leaves, which presumably contained the rest of the *Corpus* down to the end of XVIII, have been lost. Q is closely connected with D.

Bodleianus 16987 (d'Orville 109, Auct. X. 1. 4. 7); 16th cent.; contains *Corp.* I–XVIII. This MS. is a faithful transcript of Q.[1] There are numerous corrections by a different hand; the corrector must have used another MS.

R: *Bodleianus* 8827 (Misc. 131, Auct. F, infr. 2. 2); 16th cent.: contains *Corp.* I–XVIII.

In *Corp.* I–XIV, R is derived from a MS. hardly distinguishable from A.[2] (In this part of R, there are numerous corrections by

[1] The derivation of Bodl. 16987 from Q is sufficiently proved by the fact that two passages in *Corp.* II and four passages in *Corp.* XII, which have been accidentally omitted in Q, are also omitted in Bodl. 16987 (first hand).

The connexion of Bodl. 16987 with D was recognized by Reitzenstein, who did not know of the existence of Q, the immediate source of Bodl. 16987.

[2] R cannot be derived from A itself, because five small lacunae which occur in

a different hand; these corrections must have been taken from another MS.) The writing of *Corp.* XVI–XVIII is smaller, but similar in character to that of I–XIV, and both parts of the MS. may have been written by the same hand. The text of XVI–XVIII appears to be derived from a MS. closely related to D. (See the readings of R given in the foot-notes to *Corp.* XVI–XVIII.)

S: *Bodleianus* 3037 (Misc. Gr. 36, Auct. E 2. 8): 16th cent. The text of S breaks off at the words *ταῦτά σοι ἀσκληπιὲ ἐνοῦντι* in *Corp.* IX. 10, and the rest is lost; but the prefixed *Index capitum* gives the headings of all the documents in the *Corpus*, including XVI–XVIII. S is closely connected with C.[1]

Reitzenstein mentions three other MSS., viz.: *Parisinus Graec.* 1297; 16th cent.; contains *Corp.* I–XIV; 'much touched up, often agrees with B².' *Vaticanus Graec.* 914; end of 15th cent.; contains *Corp.* I. 1–28. *Parisinus Graec. suppl.* 395; 17th cent.; contains *Corp.* I. 1–21. But these three are of no importance.

It is possible that there may be in existence some MSS. of the *Corpus* which have not yet been discovered;[2] but it is not likely that any future discovery will make any appreciable addition to the material already at our disposal. The known MSS. are more than sufficient to enable us to reconstruct the lost archetype from which they are all derived; the more serious difficulties begin when we try to correct by conjecture the corrupt text of that archetype. Reitzenstein considers that, when the relations of the MSS. to one another and to the printed texts have once been ascertained, an editor need concern himself only with the readings of A, C, and M, and can safely disregard the rest. I have not done precisely that; but I hope that what I have done in this matter does not fall very

the A-text of *Corp.* I. 4, 5, and are indicated by blank spaces in A, do not occur in R. But in all else, R (I–XIV) very closely agrees with A. E.g. I. 3, *φησὶν* om. AR | I. 9, *ὑπάρχων* om. AR | *Ib.*, *ἑπτά τινας* AR: *τινας ἑπτά* cett. | I. 11 b, *νοητὰ* AR: *νηκτὰ* cett. | I. 15, *ὢν* om. AR | I. 21, *καὶ πατὴρ* AR: *καὶ ὁ πατὴρ* cett. | I. 22, *ἐγὼ αὐτὸς* AR: *ἐγὼ* Q Turn.: *αὐτὸς ἐγὼ* cett. | *Ib.*, *ὑμνοῦσι* AR: *ὑμνοῦντες* cett. | I. 26 a, *συγχαίρουσι . . . πατέρα* om. AR (*homoeoteleuton*). | I. 27, *κάλλος* AR: *κλέος* cett. | I. 28, *σπάνῃ* AR: *πλάνῃ* cett.

[1] For instance, S agrees with C, and differs from ABDM, in the following readings: I. 4, *τούτω* CS: *τοῦτο* cett. | I. 5 b, *σῶαβαίνοντος* CS: *ἀναβαίνοντος* cett. | I. 6, *βλέπων καὶ ἀκούων* CS: *βλέπον καὶ ἀκοῦον* cett. | I. 7, *ἀντέπησέ* CS: ex *ἀντέφησέ* corr. *ἀντώπησέ* A: *ἀντώπησέ* cett. | I. 9, *περιέχοντε* CS: *περιέχοντας* cett. | I. 11 a, *ἔτρεψε* CS: *ἔστρεψε* cett. | I. 14, *ὡς τε* C: *ὥστε* S: *ὡς ἅτε* cett.

[2] Reitzenstein says that he was obliged to leave Italy without carrying out his intention of searching for MSS. of the *Corpus* in the smaller libraries of that country.

far short of that which he thinks requisite. In *Corp.* I and XIII, I have given the readings of the MSS. used by Reitzenstein (viz. ABCDM), and of the printed text of Turnebus, and added those of Q. In *Corp.* II–XI, I have given the readings of A, Q, and Turn.; and in II–IX. 10, I have added those of S, using S as a substitute for C, with which it is closely connected. In *Corp.* XII and XIV, not having a collation of A in my hands, I have used R as a substitute for A (to which R, as tested in *Corp.* I and XIII, closely adheres), and have given the readings of Q, R, and Turn. in XII, and those of R and Turn. in XIV. And in *Corp.* XVI–XVIII, I have given the readings of the MSS. used by Reitzenstein (viz. BCDM), and those of Turn., and have added those of R (which, in this part of the *Corpus*, agrees closely with D). It would have been more entirely satisfactory if I could have added the readings of C and M in II–XI, and those of A, C, and M in XII and XIV; but I see no reason to think that, if I had postponed the completion of my work on the text till I could go to Italy to get those readings, the results would have been of sufficient importance to compensate for the delay. The manuscripts differ but slightly from one another and from the text of Turnebus; and it is unlikely that, if I had had before me a complete *conspectus* of the readings of all existing MSS., I should have arrived at a different conclusion as to the meaning of a single clause in the whole *Corpus*.

For the manuscript readings given in my foot-notes to the text of the *Corpus*, my authorities are as follows:

Dr. F. C. Conybeare, to whom my most hearty thanks are due for his generous help, has collated for me the greater part of A (viz. I–XI and XIII. 1, 2), and some specimens of three other MSS. (viz. I. 1–21, XIII. 1–10, and XVIII. 11–16 in C and M, and I. 1–21 in *Palat. Gr.* 53).[1]

Reitzenstein has published the readings of A in *Corp.* I and XIII; those of B, C, D, and M in I, XIII, and XVI–XVIII; and those of A, C, and M in a few short passages in other *libelli*; and I have made use of his published readings.[2]

[1] His collation is my sole authority for the readings of A which are given in my foot-notes to *Corp.* II–XI.

[2] In A, *Libelli* I, XIII, XIV were collated for Reitzenstein by G. Vitelli; in C, *Libelli* I, XIII, XVI–XVIII were collated for him by Dr. De Stefani. Reitzenstein has himself collated the rest of A and C, and the whole of B, D, and M. Thus he has had at his disposal complete collations of ABCDM; but he has published the readings of these MSS. in those parts of the *Corpus* only which are mentioned above.

I have myself collated the whole of Q; *Corp.* I and XII–XVIII in R; and the whole of S and Bodl. 16987.[1]

Parthey used collations of A and B in his edition of *Corp.* I–XIV. But the collation of A, with which he was supplied, was either inaccurate or carelessly employed by him; and his statements as to the readings of B are vitiated by the fact that he makes no distinction between the first hand and B^2. I have therefore deliberately ignored Parthey's report of the readings of A and B.

In the case of MSS. which I have not myself collated, I have expressly named this or that MS. (e.g. A) only when I had before me a positive statement as to its reading, and not when that reading was only to be inferred from the collator's silence. I have used the abbreviation *codd.* to signify the *consensus* of all MSS. of which the readings are known to me in any way, whether from my own collation, or from positive statements of others, or by inference from the silence of the collators.

I have, as a rule, taken no notice of the accents, breathings, and punctuation of the MSS., nor of the presence or absence of ι *subscript* in them.

The notation employed in my text of the *Corpus*, and in that of the other *Hermetica* also, is as follows:

Letters, words, and passages which occur in the MSS., and presumably occurred in the archetype from which our MSS. are derived, but which, in my opinion, were either certainly or probably not present in the text as written by the author, are enclosed by two-angled brackets, thus: [ ].

Letters, words, and passages which do not occur in any MS., but have been inserted by conjecture, are enclosed by one-angled brackets, thus: ⟨ ⟩.

Words and passages transposed by conjecture are (with the exception of a few of the longer passages) printed both at the place where they stand in the MSS., and at the place to which I have transposed them. At the place where they stand in the MSS., they are enclosed by two-angled brackets doubled, thus: [[ ]]. At the place to which I have transposed them, they are enclosed by one-angled brackets doubled, thus: ⟨⟨ ⟩⟩.[2]

[1] I had collated Bodl. 16987 throughout before I discovered its dependence on Q, which makes its readings valueless for our purpose, at least in regard to *Corp.* I–XIII. 14, the part of the text which has been preserved in Q.

[2] In cases in which the alteration indicated by the brackets has been made by

Words and passages which I take to be corrupt, but which I have left standing unaltered, are enclosed between the marks ⌜ ⌝.

Letters substituted by conjecture for others (not always in exactly equal number) given by the MSS. are printed in distinct type.

My object in adopting this notation is to make it manifest where the traditional text (i. e. that which, on the evidence of the MSS., may be inferred to have been the text of the archetype) is given unaltered in the present edition, and where and how much it is altered. If the reader retains the letters, words, and passages which are enclosed by the marks [ ] and [[ ]], omits those enclosed by the marks ⟨ ⟩ and ⟨⟨ ⟩⟩, and, in the case of letters printed in distinct type, substitutes the reading given in the foot-note for that in the text, he will have each document before him in the form in which it has been transmitted to us in the MSS. He will find in it many passages which consist of words without meaning, and which, therefore, cannot have been first written in the shape in which they now stand; and in dealing with every such passage, he will be free to choose whether to treat it as a blank, or to accept the more or less probable guess at what the author wrote that is here offered, or to make another guess (which may very likely be a better one) for himself. The unsightliness of the printed text which results from this procedure may be considered an advantage, because it makes apparent to the eye the extent of the corruptions, and secures the reader against the danger of mistaking the conjectures of a modern editor for readings supported by manuscript authority.

When and by whom was the archetype written? Reitzenstein (*Poim.*, pp. 211, 319, 325 f.) says that a damaged manuscript of the *Corpus* was re-discovered in the eleventh century, and came into the hands of Michael Psellus, the great reviver of Platonic studies in Byzantium[1] (*c.* A. D. 1050); that Psellus wrote or got some one to write[2] a copy of that manuscript; and that the copy written by Psellus, or under his direction, was the archetype from which our MSS. are derived. And he thinks it probable that the traditional text contains glosses and interpolations added by Psellus, and that,

some one else before me, that fact is stated in a foot-note. When there is no such statement in the foot-notes, it is to be understood that it is I that propose this alteration of the text.

[1] See Zervos, *Michel Psellos (un philosophe néoplatonicien du XIe siècle)*, Paris, 1920.

[2] Reitzenstein speaks of the 'Text der Psellosabschrift'.

in *Corp.* XVIII especially, Psellus filled gaps in the text by inserting conjectural supplements. But what evidence is there that Psellus took the part assigned to him by Reitzenstein, or any part at all, in the transmission of the *Corpus*?

In support of his statements,[1] Reitzenstein puts forward only the two following facts. (1) In *Corp.* I. 18, there is inserted in the text of *Cod.* M an anonymous *scholion*,[2] in which it is pointed out that 'this γόης' (i. e. the author of *Corp.* I, who is assumed to be Hermes) must have been acquainted with the Mosaic account of the Creation. And in the margin of *Cod.* B, this same *scholion* is written by a later hand (B^2), with the superscription τοῦ Ψέλλου. (2) In *Cod.* M (which contains several different and unconnected works), the *Corpus Hermeticum* is immediately preceded by two copies of a treatise of Psellus on the *Chaldaean Oracles*, and the second of these two copies is written by the same hand as the *Corpus Hermeticum*.[3]

The second fact is negligible. It does not follow, because two works which appear side by side in a *Codex* of the fourteenth century were written by the same hand in that *Codex*, that the archetype of the one had been written by the hand of the man (of the eleventh century) who was the author of the other, or had ever been in that man's possession.

It seems then that the only evidence[4] that Psellus had a hand in the transmission of the *Corpus* is the fact that a *scholion* on *Corp.* I. 18 is ascribed to Psellus by an unknown person who revised

[1] Reitzenstein says that it was Br. Keil who first called his attention to 'the connexion of the Platonic studies of Psellus with the editing of the *Corpus*'; but I have not met with any published statement of Keil on this subject.

[2] For this *scholion* see Psellus in *Testim.*

[3] Similarly, in Cod. S (which was not known to Reitzenstein), the *Corpus Hermeticum* is immediately preceded by Psellus *In psychogoniam Platonis*, written by the same hand.

[4] Or at least, the only evidence given by Reitzenstein in his *Poimandres*.

From the passages of Psellus which I give under *Testim.* it appears that Psellus had probably read *Corp.* X, and perhaps *Corp.* XI. ii; and if the *scholion* is rightly ascribed to him, he had certainly read *Corp.* I. But that is not enough to prove that the *Corpus* as a collection was known to him. I have not made a thorough search in the writings of Psellus; and it is not unlikely that there are in them other *testimonia* which I have failed to find. Zervos, *Michel Psellos*, p. 191, says that 'plusieurs commentaires théologiques de Psellos ont été tirés des livres orphiques et *hermétiques*', and on this point refers to an unpublished manuscript, Paris, Bibl. Nat. MS. grec, no. 1182, fol. 26 and fol. 265 vo.

Zervos, *ib.* p. 168, says 'Nous ne savons pas le nombre d'ouvrages que Psellos avait composés sur la littérature hermétique. Il n'en reste qu'une scholie sur le *Poemander*' (i.e. the *scholion* on *Corp.* I. 18). But is there any evidence that Psellus 'composed works on the Hermetic literature', or any one such work?

Cod. B. Assuming the truth of this ascription, how much can be inferred from it? It necessarily follows that Psellus had read and reflected on *Corp.* I; and as this *libellus* is not known to have been anywhere in existence in the middle ages except as a part of the *Corpus Hermeticum*, it is probable (but not certain) that Psellus had in his hands a MS. of the whole *Corpus*; that he wrote in the margin of that MS. his *scholion* on I. 18; and that from that MS. were derived both the M-text of the *Corpus*, and the unknown MS. from which the reviser of *Cod.* B got the *scholion*. But it does not follow that Psellus transcribed the *Corpus* with his own hand, or had it transcribed for him, and that all our MSS. are derived from that transcription. And still less does it follow that he added to the corruption of the text by inserting glosses, supplements, or conjectures of his own.

If we take it as established that Psellus had in his hands a MS. of the *Corpus*, it is a legitimate hypothesis that that MS. was the archetype of all our MSS.; and considering the leading part which he is known to have taken in the revival of Platonic studies, it is perhaps more likely that it was so than that it was not so. But as far as I have been able to ascertain, it is a hypothesis only, and not a proved fact.

What was the history of the text before the time of Psellus? Some help towards answering this question may be got from the fact that excerpts from three of the *libelli* of which the *Corpus* is made up[1] occur in the *Anthologium* of Stobaeus (*c.* A. D. 500). The text of these pieces as given by Stobaeus differs from that of the *Corpus*-archetype in many details;[2] but there are some corruptions which are common to Stobaeus and the *Corpus*, and must therefore have got into the text of these three *libelli* before A. D. 500.

At what date was the collection of documents which we call the *Corpus* put together? As far as I know, there is no absolutely cogent proof that it was in existence before the fourteenth century, in which our earliest MSS. were written. But as there must have been a lapse of time between the writing of the *Corpus*-archetype and the loss of some of its leaves,[3] and a further lapse of time

[1] Viz. *Corp.* II. 1–4, 6 b–9, 10–13; IV. 1 b, 10–11 b; X. 7–8 b, 12–13, 16–18, 19, 22 b–25.

[2] At the beginning of *Libellus* II, a passage which is missing in our *Corpus* MSS. has been preserved by Stobaeus.

[3] It is conceivable that the two losses of leaves (that between I and II and that between XVI and XVII) may have taken place independently, and in two different

between the loss of the leaves and the writing of our MSS., it may be considered almost certain that the collection as a whole existed at least as early as the twelfth century. Moreover, it is probable that the *Corpus* as a whole was known to Psellus, and consequently, that the *libelli* of which it is composed had been brought together by about A.D. 1050. That, however, is the earliest date at which any trace of it can be found.

The *Corpus* was almost certainly known to the author of the *Hermippus*,[1] as he shows knowledge of five at least of the *libelli* contained in it,[2] and in some of his borrowings from them, reproduces the corruptions of our *Corpus*-text. But the date of the *Hermippus* is unknown; it may have been written as late as the eleventh century,[3] or even later.

Fulgentius Mythographus (*c.* A. D. 500) refers to *Libellus* I, and quotes a phrase from it;[4] but that is no proof that the collection of *libelli* which we call the *Corpus Hermeticum* existed in his time.

Stobaeus prefixes to his excerpts from *Libellus* X the heading Ἑρμοῦ ἐκ τῶν πρὸς Τάτ, and to those from *Libellus* II the heading Ἑρμοῦ ἐκ τῶν πρὸς Ἀσκληπιόν. (Of his two excerpts from *Libellus* IV, the first has no heading, and the second is headed simply Ἑρμοῦ.) It is to be inferred from this that he found *Libellus* X (and presumably *Libellus* IV also) in a book entitled 'The discourses of

MSS.; and in that case neither of those two MSS. need necessarily have included the whole *Corpus*. One of them, for instance, might have contained I–XIV, and the other XVI–XVIII; and our *Corpus* as a whole might have been brought into being at some later time by putting together these two groups of *libelli*. But that, though not impossible, is unlikely.

1 As to the *Hermippus*, see prefatory note on *Corp.* XVI.

2 Viz. *Corp.* I, IV, X, XIII, XVI. He does not, as far as I have observed, show knowledge of any *Hermetica* not included in the *Corpus*.

3 Kroll, *De oraculis Chaldaicis*, p. 76, points out two passages in the *Hermippus* which show knowledge of the *Chaldaean Oracles*. That fact somewhat increases the probability that the author of the *Hermippus* was in touch with Psellus, who made a collection of the *Chaldaean Oracles*, and wrote about them.

4 See *Corp.* I. 1. Reitzenstein (*Poim.*, p. 210) adds that Fulgentius (Helm, p. 88. 3) quotes, but *ascribes to Plato*, some words of *Corp.* XII. The passage of Fulg. to which Reitz. refers is this: '*illam . . . Platonis antiquam firmantes sententiam, ubi ait*: nus antropinosteos utose anagatosteos euuermenos; *id est: sensus hominis deus est; i si bonus sit, deus est propitius.*' The Greek was probably νοῦς ἀνθρώπινος θεός· οὗτος ἐὰν ἀγαθὸς ⟨ᾖ, ὁ⟩ θεὸς [*euu*? perhaps ἐστιν?] εὐμενής. There is very little resemblance between this and the passages in *Corp.* XII with which Helm compares it, viz. οὗτος δὲ ὁ νοῦς ἐν μὲν ἀνθρώποις ⸢θεός⸣ ἐστι (XII. 1), and ὁ γὰρ νοῦς ψυχῶν ἐστιν εὐεργέτης ἀνθρώπων· ἐργάζεται γὰρ αὐτα[ς ε]ἰς τὸ ἀγαθόν (XII. 2); and I see no reason to think that Fulgentius got his 'ancient saying of Plato' from that document. It is more likely that he got it from some *scholion* or commentary on Pl. *Tim.* 90 A (τὸ κυριώτατον ψυχῆς εἶδος, i. e. τὸν νοῦν) δαίμονα θεὸς ἑκάστῳ δέδωκε.

Hermes to Tat',[1] and *Libellus* II in a book entitled 'The discourses of Hermes to Asclepius'. He shows no knowledge of any collection resembling our *Corpus*, which contains discourses addressed to Tat together with others addressed to Asclepius. Nor is any knowledge of the *Corpus* as a whole shown by Lactantius or Cyril, though both of them quote from or refer to some of the *libelli* included in it.[2]

The alchemist Zosimus (soon after A. D. 300) had read *Libellus* I and *Libellus* IV;[3] but there is no evidence that he had read them in the *Corpus*.

It is possible then that the *Corpus* was first compiled in the time of Psellus; and it is not impossible that Psellus himself was its compiler. On the other hand, it is also possible that this collection of Hermetic documents had been made several centuries before the date of Psellus, and even that, though unknown to Stobaeus, Cyril, and Lactantius, it was already in existence in their time, and had come into being almost immediately after the composition of the latest of the *libelli* contained in it.[4] In short, the *Corpus* may have been put together at any time between A. D. 300 and 1050. Or again, it may not have been put together at any one time, or by any one person, but may have been formed gradually, by appending to *Corp.* I a series of other *libelli* (or small groups of *libelli*) in succession, and at various dates.

Whence were the individual *libelli* taken? To this question also no definite answer can be given. The several *libelli* may have been taken directly from the collections of *Hermetica* known to Stobaeus (the 'Discourses of Hermes to Tat', &c.); though in that case, it is not clear for what reasons the man or men who put them into the *Corpus* selected some of the *libelli* contained in those collections, and rejected others. But it is possible that some of the Hermetic

[1] He gives under this same heading (Ἑρμοῦ ἐκ τῶν πρὸς Τάτ) a number of other passages which come from Hermetic *libelli* not included in the *Corpus*. His *Anthologium* contains also some excerpts from a third book, called 'The discourses of Hermes to Ammon', and some from a collection of Hermetic documents (including the *Kore Kosmu*) in which the teacher is Isis, and the pupil Horus.

[2] Lactantius quotes from *Corp.* XII. ii and *Corp.* XVI; it is more or less probable that he also refers to *Corp.* V, *Corp.* IX, and *Corp.* X. Cyril quotes from *Corp.* XI. ii and *Corp.* XIV. See *Testim.*

[3] See note on *Corp.* I. 2.

[4] The probable date of *Corp.* XVIII is within a year or two of A. D. 300, and there is no reason to think that any of the other *libelli* in the *Corpus* are of later date than this.

libelli included in the collections used by Stobaeus were also in circulation singly; and there may have been others which had never been included in them, but stood alone. If so, a compiler of the *Corpus* may have added each *libellus* in turn to his own collection as he happened to meet with it.

In some of the MSS., the *Corpus* is divided into two distinct parts, the first part (*Corp.* I–XIV) being thought to contain the teachings of Hermes, and the second (*Corp.* XVI–XVIII), the teachings of Asclepius. It is probably a result of this distinction that *Libelli* XVI–XVIII were omitted in A; the transcriber copied only 'the teachings of Hermes', and did not go on to copy 'the teachings of Asclepius', which he considered to be a different work. But we do not know whether this division existed from the first, or was subsequently introduced by some redactor or copyist. As a matter of fact, *Corp.* XVI, in which the teacher is Asclepius, and the surviving fragment of *Corp.* XVII, in which the teacher is Tat, are similar in general character to the majority of the preceding *libelli*, and must have come from similar sources; while *Corp.* XVIII, which the transcribers apparently assumed to be a speech (or two speeches) delivered by Asclepius, has in reality no connexion either with Hermes or with his pupils.

At any rate, it seems to have been by deliberate intention that the three *libelli* in which Hermes does not appear either as teacher or as pupil[1] were placed together, and put at the end of the collection. But in *Corp.* I–XIV, there are few traces of designed arrangement. It is true that *Libellus* I, in which a man (assumed by the transcribers to be Hermes) is taught by God, and sets forth to teach to mankind the *gnosis* which God has taught him, is well suited for its place at the beginning; and the documents which follow may have been regarded as specimens of that teaching of which *Libellus* I describes the origin. But in II–XIV, there is no internal connexion between adjacent documents,[2] and the order in which these *libelli* stand in the *Corpus* appears to be merely accidental.

[1] There are three other *libelli* (I, III, and VII) which, when first written, probably had nothing to do with Hermes; but these three had doubtless been ascribed to Hermes before they were included in the *Corpus*.

[2] It is possible that in two or three instances a redactor of the *Corpus* may have slightly altered the opening words of a *libellus*, in order to make them appear to refer back to the document which immediately precedes it in the collection. (See the first sentences of *Corp.* V, X, and XIV.) But in no case is there any real connexion between the contents of two successive *libelli*, except, perhaps, in XI. i and XI. ii, in both of which the teacher is Νοῦς.

Printed Editions of the *Corpus*, Translations, and Commentaries.[1]

Ficinus, 1471.[2]—*Mercurii Trismegisti Liber de Potestate et Sapientia Dei, e Graeco in Latinum traductus a Marsilio Ficino . . . Tarvisii.* This is a Latin translation of the Greek text of Cod. A, and consequently contains only *Corp.* I–XIV.

In an *Argumentum* prefixed to his translation, Ficino gives the following account of Hermes Trismegistus: 'Eo tempore quo Moyses natus est, floruit Athlas astrologus, Promethei physici frater, ac maternus avus maioris Mercurii; cuius nepos fuit Mercurius Trismegistus. . . . Primus igitur (Merc. Trismegistus) theologiae appellatus est auctor. Eum secutus Orpheus secundas antiquae theologiae partes obtinuit. Orphei sacris iniciatus est Aglaophemus. Aglaophemo successit in theologia Picthagoras; quem Philolaus sectatus est, Divi Platonis nostri praeceptor. Itaque una priscae theologiae undique sibi consona secta ex theologis sex miro quodam ordine conflata est, exordia sumens a Mercurio, a Divo Platone penitus absoluta.'

Ficino's theory of the relation between Hermes Trismegistus and the Greek philosophers was based partly on *data* supplied by early Christian writers, especially Lactantius and Augustine, and partly on the internal evidence of the *Corpus Hermeticum* and the Latin *Asclepius* of Pseudo-Apuleius. He saw—as indeed no competent scholar who had read Plato and the *Hermetica* could fail to see—that the resemblance between the Hermetic doctrines and those of Plato was such as necessarily to imply some historical connexion; but accepting it as a known fact that the author of the *Hermetica* was a man who lived about the time of Moses, he inverted the true relation, and thought that Plato had derived his theology,

[1] See Fabricius, *Bibl. Graec.* (revised by Harles), 1790, vol. i, pp. 52–66. A full list of editions and translations of the *Corpus* is given by G. R. S. Mead, *Thrice-Greatest Hermes*, 1906, vol. i, pp. 8–16. I mention here only those publications which I have found some reason to notice.

[2] Reitzenstein says—on what authority I do not know—that Ficino translated the *Corpus* in 1463. This must mean that he *wrote* his translation in that year. But the earliest printed edition of it is dated thus: 'Finitum. M.CCCC.LXXI. Die XVIII Decemb.' *Tarvisium* is Treviso, near Venice.

Ficino subsequently wrote a *Theologia Platonica* (printed in 1482), and translated Plato (1483–4) and Plotinus (1492). He was one of the most influential promoters of that revival of Platonism in Western Europe which had been started at Florence by Pletho, who resided for a time (from 1438 on) at the court of Cosmo de' Medici.

through Pythagoras, from Trismegistus. And his view was adopted, at least in its main outlines, by all who dealt with the subject down to the end of the sixteenth century.

The publication of Ficino's translation of the *Corpus* excited keen and widespread interest in Hermes Trismegistus and his teaching.[1]

[1] It is an indication of this general interest, that Hermes Trismegistus is depicted in one of the designs with which the pavement of the cathedral of Siena is decorated. (See Frontispiece.) These designs are 'pictures incised in slabs of white marble, and filled in with black or red marble' (Murray's *Handbook*, 1900). The date of the Hermes-group is 1488. 'It is not definitely known who designed' this group, 'but it is generally supposed, with considerable show of reason, to have been Giovanni di Maestro Stefano' (R. H. H. Cust, *The Pavement Masters of Siena*, 1901). The Hermes-design is placed in the middle of the floor at the west end of the Duomo, so that it is the first thing that meets the eye as one enters; and on either side of it are ranged five Sibyls. The designers had doubtless read about Hermes Trismegistus and the Sibyls in Lactantius, and considered them suitable subjects for the decoration of a church, on the ground that they were heathen prophets who, in very ancient times, had borne witness to the truths of Christian theology. (As Ficino says, 'Lactantius (Trismegistum) inter sibyllas ac prophetas connumerare non dubitat'.)

At the foot of the design is the inscription *Hermis Mercurius Trismegistus contemporaneus Moysi.* The group contains three figures. In the middle of the picture stands a man with a long beard, who wears a high pointed hat or mitre. He is handing an open book to a bearded man wearing a turban, who reverentially accepts it from him; and behind the turbaned man stands a beardless man wearing a hood. In the book which the first of the three men is handing to the second, is written *Suscipite o licteras et leges Egiptii.* The word *licteras* is *litteras* misspelt; and the meaning is 'Take up letters and laws, O Egyptians'. This is probably meant for a hexameter (hence the strange position of *O*); though, if so, there are two false quantities, *lĭcteras* and *Egiptĭi*. The words were doubtless suggested by Cic. *Nat. deor.* 3. 56 (quoted by Lactantius, *Div. inst.* 1. 6. 2): *Mercurius . . . quintus* (whom the Egyptians call Theuth) . . . *dicitur . . . Aegyptiis leges et litteras tradidisse.*

The left hand of the man in the pointed hat rests on the upper edge of a slab, on which is inscribed in Latin a saying of Trismegistus (*Deus omnium creator*, &c.). This is a free translation of the Greek original of a passage in *Ascl. Lat.* I. 8. The designer must have got the saying directly or indirectly from Lactantius, who gives this passage in the original Greek.

Who are the persons represented by these three figures? And which of them is Hermes? Mr. Cust (*op. cit.* p. 20) says, 'The principal figure (i. e. the man in the pointed hat) represents . . . Hermes Mercurius Trismegistus, who, as we read below, was *contemporaneus Moysi.* The two (other) men, one old (or middle-aged?) and turbaned, and the other veiled (or rather hooded), may perhaps typify the learned men of the East and West.'

I was at first inclined to think that the 'principal figure' is Moses, and that it is the turbaned man who respectfully receives instruction from him that is meant for Trismegistus, the turban being intended to mark him as an Egyptian. If so, the hooded man who stands behind Trismegistus might be one of his Egyptian pupils (say Asclepius), and the two together would then be the 'Egyptii' whom Moses is addressing; or the hooded man might perhaps be Plato. This interpretation of the design would agree well with the notions which were current at the time; 'Hermes', it was thought, 'learnt his philosophy from Moses, in whose time he lived; from Hermes the doctrine was transmitted to Plato; and so it came about that Plato, in his *Timaeus*, reproduced the teaching of Moses concerning the creation of the world.' But on the other hand, it is Trismegistus that, in Cic. *Nat. deor.*, '*dicitur Aegyptiis leges et litteras tradidisse*'; and if the

Eight editions of Ficino's book appeared before 1500; and Mead enumerates twenty-two editions of it from 1471 to 1641.

Turnebus, 1554.—*Mercurii Trismegisti Poemander, seu de potestate ac sapientia divina. Aesculapii definitiones ad Ammonem regem. . . . Parisiis, M.D.LIIII: apud Adr. Turnebum typographum regium.*

This is the *editio princeps* of the Greek text. It contains the whole *Corpus*, I–XIV under the title *Mercurii Trismegisti Poemander*, and XVI–XVIII under the title *Aesculapii definitiones*. One MS. only was used; and the printed text appears to be an exact reproduction of that MS., which must have been closely related to *Cod.* D. At the end are given about fifty variant readings, which may have been got from the margin of the MS.

The text printed by Turnebus is preceded by a preface, in Greek, written by Vergicius. (This preface is reprinted in Parthey's *Poemander.*) Vergicius says that 'Hermes Trismegistus was an Egyptian by race; but who his father and his mother were, no one can say. He flourished before the time of Pharaoh, as many of the *chronographi* think.[1] Some, among whom is Cicero, suppose that he is the person whom the Egyptians called Thoth. Some reckon him a contemporary of Pharaoh; but I differ from them, for the following reason. . . . He must, therefore, have lived before Pharaoh, and consequently, before Moses also.[2]

'They say that this Hermes left his own country, and travelled all over the world . . .; and that he tried to teach men to revere and worship one God alone, the *demiurgus* and *genetor* of all things; . . . and that he lived a very wise and pious life, occupied in intellectual contemplation (ταῖς τοῦ νοῦ θεωρίαις), and giving no heed to the gross things of the material world (τῶν κατωφερῶν τῆς ὕλης); and that having returned to his own country, he wrote at that time many books of mystical philosophy and theology. Among these writings, there are two of special importance; the one[3] is called *Asclepius*, and the other,[4] *Poimandres*.'

words written in the book were taken from that passage, it follows that the man who is handing the book over (i. e. the 'principal figure' in the pointed hat) must be Trismegistus, and not Moses, and that the turbaned man who receives it from him must represent the Egyptians whom Trismegistus taught. If it is so, the hooded man may be meant to stand for Plato and the Platonists, including, perhaps, Italian scholars such as Ficino.

[1] See Malala, *Testim.*

[2] Vergicius then rejected the opinion, which was held by some, that Trismegistus learnt from Moses.

[3] Viz. the Latin *Asclepius* of Pseudo-Apuleius.

[4] Viz. *Corp.* I–XIV.

Vergicius lays stress on the resemblances between the teaching of the *Corpus Hermeticum* and that of Christianity; and he quotes from Suidas what he calls 'the greatest and most marvellous of all the sayings of Hermes', in which that ancient Egyptian 'expressly teaches the doctrine of the Holy Trinity'.[1] He adds that he has found many other sayings or writings of Hermes in Stobaeus.

In Turnebus's edition, three Hermetic excerpts from Stobaeus (viz. *Exc.* II A, *Exc.* I, and the Greek original of *Ascl. Lat.* III. 27 e) are printed as an appendage to *Corp.* I–XIV, and included under the title *Poimandres.*

Flussas (François Foix de Candalle), 1574.—*Mercurii Trismegisti Pimandras utraque lingua restitutus, D. Francisci Flussatis Candallae industria.... Burdigalae,* ... 1574.

Flussas used no manuscript. His text is based on that of Turnebus. He has made a good many alterations (some of his emendations were suggested or approved by 'Josephus Scaliger, iuvenis illustrissimus', and other scholars); but where his printed text differs from that of Turnebus, he has, with few exceptions, given the Turnebus-reading in his margin. Thus, if we substitute the marginal readings for those of the text, we have in this edition an almost exact reproduction of the MS. from which Turnebus printed. The *Pimandras* of Flussas[2] is to this day, with the exception of the scarce *editio princeps*, the only publication in which is to be found a trustworthy printed text of those parts of the *Corpus* which have not been edited by Reitzenstein—i. e. of *Corp.* II–XII and XIV.

Flussas gives to *Corp.* I–XIV the title *Trismegisti Pimandras*, and calls the several *libelli* 'Caput I', 'Caput II', &c. After XIV he appends, and includes under the title *Pimandras*, a 'Caput XV', which is made up of the same three Stobaeus-excerpts which had been inserted by Turnebus, with the addition of the extract from Suidas which Vergicius had quoted in his preface to the *editio princeps.* After this stands 'Caput XVI' (our *Libellus* XVI), under the title *Aesculapii ad Ammonem.* But Flussas tacitly omits the surviving fragment of *Libellus* XVII, doubtless because he saw that it has nothing to do with *Libellus* XVI, to which, in the MSS. and the *editio princeps*, it is joined on as a part of the same document.

[1] See Suidas, *Testim.*

[2] The latest reprint of the *Pimandras* of Flussas is that which is included in the Cologne edition (1630) of Rossel's commentary. (See below.)

He also omits *Libellus* XVIII, probably because he saw that it could not rightly be ascribed to Asclepius.

In his dedicatory letter, addressed to the Emperor Maximilian II,[1] Flussas says that Hermes attained to a knowledge of divine things surpassing that which was revealed to the Hebrew prophets, and equalling that of the Apostles and Evangelists. 'Nimirum hic (Trismegistus) unus inter eos, qui divinitus inspirati sunt, de omnipotentis dei essentia solerti admodum colloquio quamplura detegit—mundi facturam, hominis ad Dei imaginem ac similitudinem opificium, eiusdem insuper tantae miseriae lapsum, huius denique lapsus amplioris foelicitatis medelam: undique Deum incorporeum ac extra materiam sciscitandum edocet. At si exigua sint haec, et antiquos Divini nutus nuncios nihilo antecellentia, aderunt quamplura, quae a Mose, prophetis, ac quibusvis Christi patefactionem praecedentibus silentio praetermissa sunt, Mercurio huic termaximo patefacta. Qualia sunt, de Triade summa uno Deo sermo:[2] Divinum insuper Verbum Patris filium:[3] ac a Patre et Verbo Spiritum, ignis et spiritus Deum, prolatum, cunctorum operatorem fuisse:[4] Verbum autem unum hominem, Divino nutu regenerandorum hominum ἐνέργειαν extitisse:[5] ab hoc insuper regenerandi solo effectu salutem pendere.[6] Cratere item Spiritu referto sacrosanctum aperit Baptisma.[7] Corporibus officio functis ad sua munia reditum pollicetur.[8] Precationes demum omnipotenti Deo prolatas, per Verbum offerri iubet.'[9] 'What more', asks Flussas, 'is made known to us by those who were instructed by our Saviour himself? And yet this man was anterior in time, not only to the disciples of our Lord, but also to all the prophets and teachers of our Law, and, as the Ancients say, to Moses himself.' He must then, Flussas thinks, have been inspired by God, and more fully inspired than any of the Hebrew Prophets.

In his preface (which is reprinted in Parthey's *Poemander*) Flussas

[1] *Invictissimo Caesari Maximiliano huius nominis quarto.* The man is Maximilian II, who was emperor from 1564 to 1576. What does Flussas mean by calling him 'the *fourth* of that name'? Miss Helen Cam tells me that there were two Saints named Maximilian, one of whom was martyred in A. D. 295 and the other in A. D. 362 (*Biographie Universelle*), and suggests that these two Saints may have been reckoned as the first and second Maximilians.

[2] This refers especially to the extract from Suidas.

[3] *Corp.* I. 6. [4] *Corp.* I. 9. [5] *Corp.* XIII. 4.

[6] *Corp.* XIII *passim.* [7] *Corp.* IV. 4.

[8] *Corp.* III. 4, taken to signify the resurrection of the body.

[9] *Corp.* XIII. 21. Most of these supposed instances of distinctively Christian doctrine in the *Hermetica*, if not all of them, are due to misunderstandings of the text.

mentions, and apparently adopts,[1] the opinion that Trismegistus first put forth his writings in the Egyptian language, and afterwards himself translated them into Greek.

As to the Latin *Asclepius*, Flussas thinks it probable that Apuleius, who is known to have been a very wicked man, inserted idolatrous and impious passages[2] into his translation of the Greek text of Hermes, and then suppressed the Greek original, in order that his fraud might escape detection. Since the *Asclepius* has been thus polluted, Flussas decides not to include it in his edition.

He discusses the date of Trismegistus at some length, and gives reasons for thinking that he flourished about the time of Abraham.

Hannibal Rossel, *Pymander Mercurii Trismegisti*, Cracow, 1585–1590. This is a ponderous commentary, in six volumes, on selected passages of *Corp.* I–VII and the Latin *Asclepius*. The passages taken from the *Corpus* are given in Latin only, and not in Greek. I have merely glanced into Rossel's commentary; but I gather from what others say about it that nothing could possibly be gained by reading it. He appears to use the sayings of Hermes merely as pegs on which to hang his own disquisitions on things in general.[3]

A later edition of Rossel's commentary, with a reprint of Flussas's *Pimandras* prefixed to it, was printed in Cologne in 1630.

Patritius, 1591.—Patrizzi published the *libelli* of the *Corpus Hermeticum*, together with much other matter, in a comprehensive work, which was printed at Ferrara in 1591.[4]

Title-page of the second edition: *Nova de universis philosophia, libris quinquaginta comprehensa: in qua Aristotelico methodo non per motum, sed per lucem et lumina ad primam causam ascenditur. Deinde nova quadam ac peculiari methodo tota in contemplationem venit divinitas. Postremo methodo Platonico rerum universitas a conditore Deo deducitur.*[5] *Auctore Francisco Patritio.... Quibus postremo sunt adiecta | Zoroastris oracula CCCXX, ex Platonicis collecta: | Hermetis*

[1] His language on this point is far from clear, and I am not sure that I have understood him rightly.

[2] He doubtless means especially *Ascl. Lat.* III. 23 b–24 a and 37–38 a, the passages in which it is asserted that 'men make gods'.

[3] The contents of the several volumes are described in the title-pages as follows: Tom. I, '*de S. S. Trinitate*'; Tom. II, '*de Spiritu S. et angelis*'; Tom. III, '*de ente, materia, forma, et rebus metaphysicis*'; Tom. IV, '*de caelo*'; Tom. V, '*de Elementis, et descriptione totius orbis*'; Tom. VI, '*de immortalitate Animae*'.

[4] I have seen the second edition of this work (Venice, 1593), but not the first edition (Ferrara, 1591).

[5] In place of all this (from *Nova de universis* to *Deo deducitur*), the title of the first edition, as given by Fabricius, has only *De aethere ac rebus coelestibus*.

Trismegisti libelli, et fragmenta, quotcumque reperiuntur, ordine scientifico disposita: | *Asclepi discipuli tres libelli:* | *Mystica Aegyptiorum, a Platone dictata, ab Aristotele excepta et perscripta Philosophia:* | *Platonicorum dialogorum novus penitus a Francisco Patritio inventus ordo scientificus:* | *Capita demum multa in quibus Plato concors, Aristoteles vero Catholice fidei adversarius ostenditur.* | *Venetiis*, . . . 1593.[1]

Patrizzi seems to have been impelled by a genuine enthusiasm to take upon himself the task of bringing about a restoration of true religion; and he regarded the *Hermetica* as one of the most effective instruments that could be used in the execution of this design. In his preface, addressed to Pope Gregory XIV, he says: 'In this volume I present to you five philosophies, viz. (1) *nostram recens conditam*,[2] (2) *Chaldaicam Zoroastri*,[3] (3) *Hermetis Trismegisti Aegyptiam*,[4] (4) *Aegyptiam aliam mysticam*,[5] and (5) *aliam Platonis pro-*

[1] Certain parts of Patrizzi's work, including his collection of *Hermetica*, were reissued at London in 1611, in a volume thus entitled: *Hermetis Trismegisti Opuscula, cum fragmentis quotquot reperiuntur, ordine scientifico disposita . . .* | *Item Asclepii discipuli tres libelli.* | *Quibus sunt adiecta* | *Zoroastri oracula CCCXX . . .*: | *Mystica Aegiptiorum a Platone dictata . . . Philosophia.* | *Londini 1611.* | *Illustrissimo . . . D. Johanni Radcliffe . . . admirandum hunc divinae sapientiae thesaurum, grati animi obsequium, L.M.D.C.Q.* In this republication Patrizzi's own system of philosophy is omitted; the *Hermetica* are placed at the beginning of the volume, as being first in importance, and two of Patrizzi's other *adiecta* are appended to them. In the parts thus reissued in 1611 the pages agree, letter for letter, with those of the 1593 edition of Patrizzi.

[2] i. e. a system of philosophy constructed by Patrizzi himself. In Ueberweg's *Hist. of philosophy*, Eng. tr. 1874, ii, pp. 20, 25, 465, Patrizzi's teaching is described as a blend of a theosophy based on Neoplatonism with opinions on natural science which he adopted from his elder contemporary Bernardinus Telesius.

[3] i. e. the extant fragments of the so-called *Chaldaean Oracles*, an exposition, in clumsy Greek hexameters, of a Pagan system of *gnosis*. These *Oracles* were known to Porphyry, and were probably composed about A. D. 200. Scattered fragments of them, preserved by quotation in the writings of Proclus and other Neoplatonists, were collected and commented on by Psellus, from whom Patrizzi got them. See Kroll, *De Oraculis Chaldaicis*, 1894.

[4] i. e. the teaching of Hermes (*Corp.* I–XIV, Stobaeus-excerpts, &c., and the Latin *Asclepius*), and that of his pupil Asclepius (*Corp.* XVI–XVIII). As to the latter, Patr. says, '*De tribus his libellis, primus quidem* (i. e. *Corp.* XVI) *et tertius* (*Corp.* XVIII. 11–16) *digni videntur quibus Hermetis auditor* (Asclepius) *fuerit author. Sed secundus* (*Corp.* XVIII. 1–10), *quamvis ab eo tertius pendere videatur, suppositus possit existimari.*'

[5] The work reprinted by Patrizzi under the title *Mystica Aegyptiorum . . . philosophia* is a Latin version of a treatise entitled 'The *Theologia* of Aristotle', which had been translated from Greek into Arabic about A. D. 840, and was well known and highly esteemed among the Arabs, who supposed it to be a genuine work of Aristotle. The bulk of it is a paraphrase of portions of Plotinus, *Enneads* IV–VI; but in the introductory chapter Aristotle is made to speak in his own person, and refers to 'my earlier book, the *Metaphysics*'. Ueberweg (*Hist. Phil.*, Eng. tr. 1880, i, p. 425) says that it 'was known in a Latin translation to the Scholastics'. Soon after 1500 Franciscus Roseus found an Arabic MS.

priam.[1] . . . In our day, men laugh at philosophers; and it is commonly said "So-and-so is a philosopher, he does not believe in God". The reason of this is, that the only philosophy studied is that of Aristotle, which, as men know and are told, denies the omnipotence and providence of God. Yet Hermes said *sine philosophia impossibile esse summe esse pium.*[2] Reflecting on this saying, I thought that it might be possible to discover a truer philosophy, by which we might return to God who made us. I threw myself into the search for it; . . . and after much toil and resolute effort, I think I have brought it to completion.

'I have appended to my own philosophy the other four (i. e. those numbered (2), (3), (4), and (5) above); for all these alike "propositum sibi finem habent, ut doceant Deum rerum esse conditorem, rectorem, curatorem ac provisorem, et ut homines tum illum, tum seipsos cognoscant, et addiscant, quibus modis ad creatorem Deum animae humanae redeant, aeternaque apud eum beatitudine fruantur".

'I hope', says Patrizzi to the Pope, 'that you and your successors will adopt this new and restored religious philosophy, and cause it to

of it at Damascus, and got Moses Rouas to translate the Arabic text into Italian; the Italian of Rouas was translated into Latin by Petrus Nicolaus ex Castellaniis; and the Latin version thus produced was printed at Rome in 1519, under the patronage of Pope Leo X, with the title *Sapientissimi Aristotelis Stagiritae Theologia sive mistica Philosophia Secundum Aegyptios noviter Reperta et in Latinum Castigatissime redacta.* A revised edition of it, in more polished Latin, was published by Carpentarius at Paris in 1572; but Patrizzi preferred to reproduce the edition of 1519, as more faithfully representing the original. Fr. Dieterici has published the Arabic text (*Die sogenannte Theologie des Aristoteles*, 1882), and a German translation of it (1883). Dieterici says that the Latin version of 1519 (i. e. that which Patrizzi reprinted), 'judged from the present standpoint of Arabic philology, is worthless'.

Patrizzi saw that the doctrine of this treatise is what is commonly called Neoplatonic; yet he contrived to retain his belief that it had been written by Aristotle. His theory about it is as follows. Plato studied for thirteen years under the Egyptian priests at Heliopolis (Strabo 806), and was permitted by them to read the writings of Hermes Trismegistus. After his return to Athens, Plato taught two distinct philosophies—an 'exoteric' philosophy, which is given in his written Dialogues, and an 'esoteric' philosophy, based on the ancient wisdom of Egypt, which he imparted orally to his pupil Aristotle. The latter wrote down day by day the secret teaching which he received from the lips of Plato; and the *Mystica philosophia* consists of the notes which he thus wrote down. Afterwards, Aristotle quarrelled with Plato and his followers, and started a school of his own in opposition to them; and the books commonly known as Aristotle's writings are those which he wrote during that period of his life. But in his old age he returned to the true Platonic faith. The book in which this 'mystic philosophy' was written down by Aristotle was lost, Patrizzi thinks, immediately after his death, but was found again in the time of Ammonius Saccas, the teacher of Plotinus; and the Neoplatonists borrowed from it.

[1] i. e. Plato's 'exoteric' teaching, which is given in his Dialogues.

[2] Herm. *ap.* Stob. *Exc.* II B. 2.

be studied everywhere. Why are those parts alone of Aristotle's philosophy studied which are hostile to God and his Church, while these *piae adiutrices* are disregarded? Assuredly the treatise of Hermes *de pietate ac philosophia*[1] contains more philosophy than all the works of Aristotle taken together. . . . "Poemander (i.e. *Corp.* I) creationem mundi et hominis, cum Mosaica fere eandem, complectitur. Et Trinitatis mysterium longe apertius quam Moses ipse enarrat. Multi apud (Hermetem) et vera pietate et vera philosophia sunt plenissimi libelli, qui pro Aristotelis impiis subrogari et possint et debent."

'Many of Plato's dialogues also may be publicly taught "sine impietatis periculo ullo, pietatis adiumento multo"; especially the Philebus, Timaeus, Sophista, Parmenides, and Phaedo. "Plotini libri omnes sacram quandam continent verius theologiam quam philosophiam." (He mentions with approval Proclus and Damascius also.)

'Almost all the early Fathers, "quia scirent paucis mutatis Platonicos facile Christianos fieri posse, . . . Platonem eiusque sectatores hosce philosophis reliquis omnibus antetulerunt, Aristotelem non nisi cum infamia nominarunt. Quadringentis vero abhinc circiter annis[2] Scholastici Theologi in contrarium sunt annixi, Aristotelicis impietatibus pro fidei fundamentis sunt usi. Excusatos eos habemus, quod cum Graecas litteras nescirent, illos cognoscere non potuerunt. Non vero eos excusamus, quod impietate (-tati?) pietatem adstruere sint conati. . . ."

'I would have you then, Holy Father, and all future Popes, give orders that some of the books which I have named[3] shall be continually taught everywhere, as I have taught them for the last fourteen years at Ferrara. You will thus make all able men in Italy, Spain, and France friendly to the Church; and perhaps even the German protestants will follow their example, and return to the Catholic faith. It is much easier to win them back in this way than to compel them by ecclesiastical censures or by secular arms. You should cause this doctrine to be taught in the schools of the Jesuits, who are doing such good work. If you do this, great glory will await you among men of future times. And I beg you to accept me as your helper in this undertaking.'

[1] i.e. Herm. *ap.* Stob. *Exc.* II B, which Patrizzi has placed at the beginning of his collection of *Hermetica*.

[2] i.e. from about A.D. 1200.

[3] Including the *Hermetica*.

In an introduction to that part of his book which contains the *Hermetica*, Patrizzi says, 'Videtur Hermes hic Trismegistus coetaneus quidem fuisse Mosy, sed paulo senior. . . . Apparebit autem ex hisce Hermetis tum libellis tum fragmentis pia quaedam erga Deum philosophia, fidei dogmatibus ut plurimum consona. Apparebit quoque Graecas philosophias omnes, Pythagoream, Platonicam in divinis ac morum dogmatibus,[1] Aristotelicam autem et Stoicam in physicis, et medicinae etiam prima principia, et ex his et ex aliis qui perierunt eius libris fuisse desumptas.

'Quamobrem (apparebit) longe satius et Christianis hominibus consultius et utilius longe futurum esse, si Hermetis dogmata potius quam Aristotelica, quae ubique magna scatent impietate, in scholis publicis et monachorum Aristoteli nimium addictorum coenobiis aliquando legantur. Quod ut comodius fieri queat, libellos iuxta materiarum, uti diximus, sequellam et seriem in ordinem redegimus.'

He has rearranged the *Hermetica*, and placed them in the following order: Stob. I. 41. 1 (which I have divided into the two distinct excerpts II B and XI): *Corp.* I, III, X, V, VI, XIII, VII, II, XI, XII, IV: *Kore Kosmu*, followed by eight other Stobaeus-excerpts: *Corp.* IX: six Stobaeus-excerpts: *Corp.* VIII: *Corp.* XIV: fragments from Cyril, Stobaeus, &c.: the Latin *Asclepius*. Then follows, as a separate work by a different author, the ὅροι Ἀσκληπιοῦ πρὸς Ἄμμονα (i. e. *Corp.* XVI–XVIII). In regarding the several documents contained in the *Corpus* as unconnected *libelli*, Patrizzi made a decided advance beyond the position of the earlier editors; but there is not much to be said for the order in which he thought fit to arrange the Hermetic writings.

What were the sources from which Patrizzi got his text of the *libelli* of the *Corpus*? He certainly used the printed editions of Turnebus and Flussas. But Reitzenstein has found reason to think that Patrizzi based his text on a MS. other than that used by Turnebus, and that he merely introduced here and there the readings of the earlier editors. The question is, however, of little importance; for as Patrizzi has made many arbitrary alterations in the text, and does not tell us whether the reading which he adopts is derived from some authority or is of his own invention, his edition furnishes no material that can be used as an aid to textual criticism.[2]

[1] i.e. in theology and ethics.

[2] I have noted some signs of a specially close relation between Patrizzi's text of the *Corpus-libelli* and that of Q and Bodl. 16987. But it would be waste of time to investigate the question of Patrizzi's sources more thoroughly.

Casaubon, 1614.—*Isaaci Casauboni . . . Exercitationes XVI. Ad Cardinalis Baronii Prolegomena in Annales. . . . Londini . . . MDCXIIII.* In *Exercit.* I. 10, pp. 70 ff., Casaubon discusses the date and origin of the *Sibyllina* and *Hermetica*; and in this short tractate we find for the first time a view of the Hermetic writings which is, in the main at least, historically sound. As compared with all who had previously written on the subject, from Lactantius to Patrizzi, Casaubon οἶος πέπνυται, τοὶ δὲ σκιαὶ ἀΐσσουσιν. He does not deny that there may have been a man named Hermes Trismegistus who lived before Moses; but he sees that the *Hermetica* cannot have been written by any such person. He says, 'Librum . . . qui sub nomine Mercurii Trismegisti circumferri ab aliquot seculis cepit (i. e. the Corpus Hermeticum) non veremur pronuntiare, et omni asseveratione confirmare, esse ψευδεπίγραφον': and he concludes that it was written about the end of the first century after Christ.[1] 'Nunc probemus certis argumentis . . . librum qui hodieque plerisque doctorum in deliciis et magno pretio est tanquam vere Mercurii Trismegisti, ψευδεπίγραφον esse et merum πλάσμα. . . . Nos igitur . . . affirmamus, in eo libro contineri non Aegyptiacam Mercurii doctrinam, sed partim Graecam e Platonis et Platonicorum libris, et quidem persaepe ipsis eorum verbis, depromptam: partim Christianam[2] e libris sacris petitam.

'Quodnam philosophiae genus in usu olim fuerit apud veteres Aegyptios, a libris Eusebii . . . et aliis priscis scriptoribus potest intelligi. At Pseudomercurii huius diversa est genere toto philosophandi ratio:[3] et res enim et verba scholam Platonis sapiunt, iis dumtaxat exceptis, quae miscet e libris divinis. Ne temere videamur tot doctorum opinioni contraire, paucis demonstremus quod dicimus.' (Here he goes into details, and discusses particular passages in the *Corpus.*)

'Tum autem, si vere Mercurii esset hic liber, oporteret ut vel ipse Graece eum scripsisset, vel ex Aegyptiaco sermone aliquis vertisset. Nos utrumvis horum firmissime negamus esse factum: prius, quia stylus huius libri alienissimus est a sermone illo quo

[1] He puts the date a little too early; most of the *libelli* of the *Corpus* were probably written in the third century, some perhaps in the second century.

[2] He ought rather to have said *Judaicam*. (See *Corp.* I and III.)

[3] More is now known about the modes of thought of the ancient Egyptians; but Casaubon's opinion on this point is confirmed by the results of modern Egyptology. Traces of the influence of indigenous Egyptian thought, if not entirely absent, are rare in the *Hermetica*.

Graeci Hermetis aequales sunt usi. . . . Hic (i. e. in the Hermetica) nullum penitus vestigium antiquitatis: . . . contra, multa hic vocabula, quae ne vetustior quidem Hellenismus agnoscat eo qui vigebat circa nativitatem Domini. . . . Quis priorum dixit ὑλότης, οὐσιότης, et id genus alia?

'Nego etiam ex alia lingua versa haec esse: αὐτοφυῆ esse et Graece primitus scripta pertendo. Nulla unquam versio tam feliciter elaborata fuit, quae peregrinitatem non prae se ferret, et certis indiciis demonstraret. Hic nihil eiusmodi. Omnia γνησίως Graeca, et Hellenismo eius quam designavi aetatis, sua ubique constat ratio . . . .

'Falsum igitur est, immo falsissimum, quod iste planus in Epistola ad Ammonem (*Corp.* XVI) persuadere vult nobis; a Mercurio prius Aegyptiaco sermone ista fuisse conscripta. Falsissimum etiam est, quod docti indocti videntur hactenus credidisse; aut scripta haec fuisse a Mercurio Trismegisto, vetustissimo Aegypti sapiente, aut ex illius scriptis esse versa. Quorum utrumque probavimus esse longe absurdissimum.'

In one important matter, however, Casaubon's view requires correction. He thinks, as his predecessors thought, that the *Corpus* contains distinctively Christian doctrines; and he thence infers that the *Hermetica* were, like the *Oracula Sibyllina*, forged by a Christian ('or rather', he adds, 'a semi-Christian'), with the object of recommending the doctrines of his religion to his Pagan neighbours by making it appear that they were vouched for by the authority of an ancient and venerated name.[1] This is true of some of the *Sibyllina*; but it is not true of the *Hermetica*. The authors of the *libelli* collected in the *Corpus* were Pagans; and apart from a few interpolated words, the resemblances to Christian doctrine which we find in the Hermetic writings are to be accounted for, not by assuming that the writers borrowed from the New Testament or from other Christian sources, but by recognizing the fact that, at the time when the *Hermetica* were written, there were many matters on which Christians and Pagan Platonists thought and spoke alike. We must, therefore, substitute 'a number of Pagan writers' for the 'Christian or semi-Christian' author of whom Casaubon speaks. With this

[1] Casaubon says, 'Neque vero dubitamus id egisse auctorem, ut multa pietatis Christianae dogmata, quae ceu nova et prius inaudita reiiciebantur, probaret ab ultima antiquitate sapientibus fuisse nota, et ab illo ipso Mercurio in literas fuisse relata, quem non solum Aegyptii, sed etiam Graeci propter vetustatem et doctrinae opinionem magnopere suspiciebant.'

correction, his statement of the motive for employing the name of Hermes may be considered to hold good.

Casaubon's opinion as to the period in which the *Hermetica* were written gradually prevailed, and came to be adopted by all competent scholars;[1] and, deprived of the prestige which their supposed antiquity had conferred on them, the Hermetic writings lost their hold on men's interest, and sank into comparative neglect.[2] Translations of the *Corpus* continued to appear from time to time;[3] but from 1630 to 1854, no reprint of the Greek text was issued.

Tiedemann, 1781.—*Hermes Trismegists Poemander oder von der göttlichen Macht und Weisheit, aus dem Griechischen übersetzt . . . von Dieterich Tiedemann. Berlin und Stettin*, . . . 1781. This is a

[1] e.g. T. Gale, in his edition of 'Iamblichus *De mysteriis*', 1678, says, 'Equidem parum tribuo omnibus istis scriptis, quae sub Hermetis nomine extant. Credo nihil esse aliud, quam adumbrationes quorundam locorum ex sacra pagina et antiquioribus philosophis excerptorum.'

[2] The true significance of the *Hermetica*, as documents of primary importance for the history of religion, not in the second millennium before Christ, but in the third century after Christ (the critical period of the struggle between Paganism and Christianity), has been strangely overlooked in the past, and is even now inadequately recognized.

[3] For instance: *The divine Pymander of Hermes Mercurius Trismegistus, in XVII books. Translated formerly out of the Arabick* [this presumably means 'out of the Egyptian'] *into Greek, and thence into Latine, and Dutch, and now out of the Original* [!] *into English: by that Learned Divine Doctor Everard: London . . . 1650.* This is a translation of *Corp.* I-XIV and three Stobaeus-excerpts. The text translated is that of Patrizzi, and the *libelli* are placed in the order in which Patrizzi arranged them. The preface (written, after Everard's death, by some one who signs himself 'J. F.') begins thus: 'This Book may justly challenge the first place for antiquity, from all the Books in the World, being written some hundreds of yeers before Moses his time, as I shall endevor to make good. . . . In this Book, though so very old, is contained more true knowledg of God and Nature, then in all the Books in the World besides, I except onely Sacred Writ.' Everard's translation has been several times reprinted—most recently by the Theosophical Publishing Society in 1893; and doubtless some readers, down to our own time, have accepted it without question as the oldest book in the world.

Des Mousseaux, *La magie au dix-neuvième siècle*, 1860, p. 343, speaking of the passages about 'making gods' in *Ascl. Lat.* III, says, 'Telle est l'antiquité de Trismegiste (whom he assumes to be the author of the *Asclepius*), que beaucoup d'auteurs le prennent pour un fils de Cham ou pour Cham lui-même! Ses ancêtres, dont il nous parle là, seraient donc les chefs *de la magie antédiluvienne!* Quelle date! et combien elle est logique!' Des Mousseaux, a devout Roman Catholic, includes under the term 'magic' both the Pagan cults of antiquity and modern mesmerism and spiritualism, and is convinced that both in ancient oracles, &c., and in the phenomena of contemporary hypnotism and the like (of which he has had much personal experience), the agent who operates is the Devil, or a devil. His book is ably written, and contains much interesting matter.

The time of the Deluge is the earliest time to which I have found the Hermetic teaching assigned in Europe. But Arabic writers dated it still earlier; for they identified Hermes with Enoch, and his teacher Agathos Daimon with Seth, son of Adam.

German translation of the *Corpus*, based on the Greek text of Flussas. Reitzenstein says that Tiedemann gives in his notes 'a whole series of excellent conjectures'. The book is scarce, and I have not seen it.

Parthey, 1854.—*Hermetis Trismegisti Poemander. Ad fidem codicum manu scriptorum recognovit Gustavus Parthey. Berolini, MDCCCLIV.*[1] This is an edition of *Corp.* I–XIV. Parthey says in his preface that, if it meets with a good reception, he intends to edit afterwards *reliqua Hermetis scripta, apud Lactantium, Cyrillum, Stobaeum servata*; but this project was never carried out by him. He says nothing about *Corp.* XVI–XVIII.

Parthey made use of the editions of Turnebus, Flussas, and Patrizzi, and Tiedemann's notes; but he professes to base his text mainly on two MSS., A and B.[2] *Cod.* A had been collated for him by F. de Furia, and *Cod.* B by D. Hamm. But whether through his own carelessness or incompetence, or through that of the collators, his statements as to the readings of A and B are untrustworthy;[3] and for any one who has access, either directly or through the medium of the *Pimandras* of Flussas, to the sounder text of the *editio princeps*, which reproduces without alteration that of a MS., Parthey's edition is useless, if not misleading.

Ménard, 1866.—*Hermes Trismégiste. Traduction complète, précédée d'une étude sur l'origine des livres Hermétiques. Par Louis Ménard. . . . Paris, . . . 1866.* The *Traduction* is a free translation of *Corp.* I–XIV, the Latin *Asclepius*, twenty-six Stobaeus-excerpts, some fragments from Cyril, &c., and *Corp.* XVI–XVIII. Ménard does not stick closely to the (often meaningless) words of the traditional text, but expresses in fluent French what he rightly or wrongly takes to have been the author's meaning. His introductory *Étude* (111 pages) is a sensible and well-written treatise on the *Hermetica*. For those who wish to make acquaintance with the Hermetists, but do not read Greek and Latin, Ménard's book is, I think, to be recommended in preference to any other work on the subject that has yet been published.

Zeller (*Philosophie der Griechen, Theil III, Abth. II*, 4th edition,

[1] An exact reprint of Parthey's *Poemander* of 1854 has been published within the last few years. It would have been better if the *editio princeps*, or the *Pimandras* of Flussas, had been reprinted instead.

[2] 'Codices A et B ita secutus sum, ut nusquam, nisi monito lectore, ab eorum auctoritate recesserim.'

[3] 'Auf keine seiner Angaben ist irgenwelcher Verlass', says Reitzenstein.

1903, pp. 242–54) gives an account of the *Hermetica*, and summarizes the doctrines taught in them. He says that these writings 'seem in their present form to belong to the last *decennia* of the third century after Christ'.

Reitzenstein, 1904.—*Poimandres. Studien zur griechisch-aegyptisehen und früh-christlichen literatur. Von R. Reitzenstein. Leipzig, . . . 1904.* As an appendix to the book is printed Reitzenstein's critical edition of *Corp.* I, XIII, and XVI-XVIII.

The publication of Reitzenstein's *Poimandres* marks the beginning of a fresh stage in the study of the Hermetic writings. Working as a pioneer in what was, for modern scholarship, almost a new and untouched field, he has made some serious mistakes; but he has put the study of the *Hermetica* on a scientific footing, and all later work on this subject must be based on his investigations.

Reitzenstein has also discussed some passages of the *Corpus* in *Die hellenistischen Mysterienreligionen, ihre Grundgedanken und Wirkungen*, 1910.

Among recent publications may be mentioned *Thrice-Greatest Hermes. Studies in Hellenistic Theosophy and Gnosis. Being a Translation of the Extant Sermons and Fragments of the Trismegistic Literature, with Prolegomena, Commentaries, and Notes. By G. R. S. Mead. London and Benares. The Theosophical Publishing Society, 1906* (three volumes). Mr. Mead's point of view is indicated by these words in his preface: 'Along this ray of the Trismegistic tradition we may allow ourselves to be drawn backwards in time towards the holy of holies of the Wisdom of Ancient Egypt. The sympathetic study of this material may well prove an initiatory process towards an understanding of that Archaic Gnosis.'

A strange and quite untenable theory as to the dates of the *Hermetica* has been put forward by Dr. Flinders Petrie, in a paper printed in the *Transactions of the Third Internat. Congress of the History of Religions*, 1908, pp. 196 and 224. He puts the date of the *Kore Kosmu* (which he calls 'the earliest Hermetic document') at 'about 510 B. C., or certainly before 410 B. C.'; that of *Corp.* XVI at 'about 350 B. C.'; and that of the original of the Latin *Asclepius* at 'about 340 B. C.'. And he says that 'if the longest Hermetic writings thus belong to the Persian age' (i. e. to a time before 332 B. C.), 'it is probable that the whole group are not far removed from that period'. In a book entitled *Personal Religion in Egypt before Christianity*, 1909 (ch. 3, 'The dateable Hermetic writings'), he again expresses the same opinion as to the dates of *Kore Kosmu*, *Corp.* XVI, and *Ascl. Lat.*, adding that 'there is nothing incompatible with such a date for Egyptian originals, while the Greek translations may very likely show a later style'. He thinks (*ib.*, pp. 85–91) that *Corp.* II, III, V, VI, VII, VIII, and X, were probably written before the time of Alexander, and between 450 and 350 B.C.; that *Corp.* XII 'must' be earlier than 332 B.C.; that *Corp.* IV 'belongs to about 300 B.C.'; that *Corp.* XIII 'seems to be of the same date or rather later'; and that the date of *Corp.* I, which 'seems to be the last of the longer writings of this class', may very well be about 300–200 B.C. 'The Hermetic books as a whole', he says (p. 102), 'seem to hang together, and to belong to one general period, 500–200 B.C.' If these dates were proved to be right, there would necessarily result from them an astounding *bouleversement* of all commonly accepted views as to the history of Greek thought. But the arguments by which he endeavours to support his datings are not such as to be worth serious attention.[1]

Josef Kroll, *Die Lehren des Hermes Trismegistos*, Münster i. W., 1914. In this book Kroll's aim is 'to trace in detail the connexion of the Hermetic doctrines with Greek or Hellenistic doctrines in general, and to assign to the several notions (which present themselves in the *Hermetica*) their place in the history of religious and philosophic thought'. For that purpose, he arranges the teachings of the *Hermetica* under a series of subject-headings; and in dealing with each subject, he brings together what is said about it in the several Hermetic *libelli*, and quotes or refers to parallels in other writings. He concludes (pp. 386–9) that in the main the doctrines of the *Hermetica* belong to 'the sphere of Hellenistic thought—the general philosophy of the culture-world of that time', and that among the sources from which the Hermetists drew, special importance is to be assigned to Posidonius; that their thoughts have been little, if at all, affected by Egyptian influence; that their doctrines are in many respects similar to those of Philo, and that here and there are to be found in them distinctively Jewish notions; and that there is in the *Hermetica* 'no trace of any influence of Christianity'.[2]

[1] It is to be regretted that a man who has earned a high reputation by good work in other departments has in this case strayed into a field of research in which he does not know his bearings.

[2] These conclusions are in close agreement with those at which I had independently arrived before reading Kroll's book.

As to the dating of the Hermetic writings, Kroll says (p. 389) that, for most of them, any date after the time of Philo is possible, but that there are some pieces, one of which is *Corp.* I, that cannot have been written before the time of Numenius (A. D. 150–200). He adds, 'the dating in detail (of the several *libelli*) must be carried out by some one who undertakes the attractive but difficult task of distinguishing the different strata of the doctrines, and considering each of the different tractates in itself, and their relations to one another'.

That is precisely what I have aimed at doing in the present edition. There was no one Hermetic school or sect, and no one body of Hermetic doctrine. What we have before us is a number of *libelli*, written by a number of different men, each of whom had his distinct and separate point of view and mode of thought. There is in their teachings a certain general similarity, but there is also much divergence; and it is, for most purposes, more profitable to take the Hermetic *libelli* one by one, and investigate the doctrine of each of them separately, than to lump them all together.

C. F. G. Heinrici, *Die Hermes-Mystik und das Neue Testament*, edited by E. von Dobschütz, Leipzig, 1918. Heinrici died leaving the book unfinished, and von Dobschütz published Heinrici's MS. almost unaltered, merely adding some pages of *Nachträge* written by himself.

The purpose of this book is to determine the relation between the teachings of the *Hermetica* and those of primitive Christianity as presented in the New Testament. With that purpose in view, Heinrici, in Part II, examines the Hermetic documents one by one (in that respect his method is preferable to that of J. Kroll), and in each of them looks for similarities in word or thought to things said in the New Testament. In Part III, he arranges the teachings of the *Hermetica* in general under a series of subject-headings, and under each heading compares the teachings of the New Testament on the same subject. His conclusions may be summed up by saying that he finds in the *Hermetica* many passages that are *parallels* to passages in the New Testament, but little that is *borrowed* from the New Testament.[1]

He does not undertake to examine the relations between the *Hermetica* and Greek philosophic writings; his book is intended

[1] As to this, I should differ only by reducing his 'little' to still less, or to nothing.

to be a complement to that of J. Kroll, in which that subject was dealt with.

Heinrici's book contains some useful suggestions; but it does not throw much fresh light on the Hermetic writings. I have found in it mistakes on particular points,[1] some of which are of considerable importance. And taking the book as a whole, Heinrici does not seem to understand rightly the main drift of the Hermetic teaching, and the relations in which it stands to other religious and philosophic movements of the time. The term 'Hermes-*Mystik*', employed by him in the title and throughout the book, is ambiguous. Of 'mysticism' in the sense of aspiration towards union with God, there is much in our *Hermetica*; but of the sacramentalism of the Pagan mystery-cults, and of *theurgia* in general, there is hardly anything; and Heinrici, though he here and there shows some recognition of this fact, is too much inclined to bring the philosophic *Hermetica* into connexion with mystery-cults and magical practices which he includes under the vague term *Mystik*, but with which they have in reality little or nothing in common.[2] He begins by contrasting *Mystik* (which he defines as 'revelation-literature') with philosophy, and coupling together the names Orpheus and Hermes as representative of this *Mystik*. It would be truer to say that the name Hermes (as far as the *libelli* of the *Corpus Hermeticum* and the other documents of the same class are concerned) stands for philosophy, or for a religion based on philosophy, and that of Orpheus (the reputed founder of the mystery-cults, and supposed author of the *Orphica* revered by the later Neoplatonists) stands for *theurgia* as opposed to philosophy. He refers to Plato now and again; but he does not adequately recognize the fact that the doctrines of these *Hermetica* are, in the main, derived from Platonism, and that all the other ingredients together are of comparatively small amount.

[1] Some of the mistakes might perhaps have been corrected if the author had lived to revise his work.

[2] For instance, he includes among the documents with which he deals the pieces printed in Pitra, *Analecta* II, which obviously (with one exception) belong to a different class, and have nothing to do with the philosophic *Hermetica*.

THE LATIN ASCLEPIUS

THE *Asclepius* has come down to us in the form of a Latin dialogue attributed to Apuleius. This Latin dialogue is a translation of a Greek original, which was known to Lactantius and others, but is now lost.

The manuscript tradition of the Latin text has been thoroughly investigated by P. Thomas; and the results of his researches are incorporated in the text which he has published in his edition of the philosophic writings of Apuleius (*Apulei opera quae supersunt vol. III, De philosophia libri, rec. P. Thomas*, Teubner, Lips. 1908). Thomas's edition supersedes all earlier publications of the text; and I have used it as my sole authority for the readings of the manuscripts.

Thomas classifies the more important manuscripts in two groups, as follows:

I. *Codices melioris notae:*

(1) B = Bruxellensis 10054–10056; written early in the eleventh century. Collated by Thomas. This MS. is very decidedly superior to all the rest. The hands of several correctors can be distinguished. One of these, B 2, who made his corrections at or near the end of the eleventh century, seems to have been a well-instructed man. In a few instances he alone gives what is certainly or probably the true reading; but Thomas concludes that his emendations are merely conjectural. The other correctors of B contribute nothing of value.

(2) M = Monacensis 621; twelfth century. Collated by Goldbacher for his edition of Apuleius, 1876, and again by Thomas.

(3) V = Vaticanus 3385; twelfth century. The text of the *Asclepius* contained in this MS. has not yet been collated. But as V very closely resembles M (being, in Goldbacher's opinion, a more carelessly written copy of the same original from which M was copied), it is not likely that its collation will add largely to the material at our disposal for textual restoration. M and V are closely

related to B; but Thomas thinks it probable that they were copied, not directly from B, but from a corrected copy of B.

(4) G = Gudianus 168 Bibliothecae Guelferbytanae; thirteenth century. Collated by Goldbacher.

II. *Codices deteriores:*

Collated by Goldbacher:

(1) P = Parisinus 6634; twelfth century.

(2) L = Laurentianus plut. LXXVI cod. 36; twelfth or thirteenth century.

(3) F = Florentinus, olim Marcianus 284; twelfth century.

Besides these two groups, Thomas mentions a MS. in the British Museum (Add. 11983, twelfth century), which he has found to be of very little value; and a large number of 'interpolated MSS.', which he has deliberately disregarded.

Thomas has reconstructed the text of the archetype from which our MSS. are derived. But that is only the first stage on the road to the discovery of the Hermetic teacher's meaning. The text of the archetype itself was corrupt; and even if we could restore the Latin to the exact form in which it came from the hand of its first writer, we should still be far from the completion of our task. We have to do with a Latin translation of a Greek document. The Greek text was probably already damaged when it came into the translator's hands; the translator was very imperfectly qualified for his work, and it is certain that he has frequently blundered. Our first business is to work back to the Latin text as the translator wrote it; but having done this, we have still to guess what was the Greek which the translator had before him, and thence to infer the meaning which the writer of the lost original intended to convey. Thomas has brought together the results of the previous work of other scholars in the emendation of the text, and has added much of his own that is of high value; but he has still left much to be done. Not only have both the Greek original and the Latin translation been damaged by errors of transcription; but it is evident that either the original or the translation has been mutilated in a quite exceptional way. Some passages have been lost, some have been misplaced, and many words, phrases, and sentences have been transposed from a context in which they made sense to a context in which they make nonsense. If the Latin text had once existed in an intelligible and clearly written form, it is difficult to imagine any process by which it could have been reduced to its present state. The ordinary causes of corruption do not suffice to explain its condition. The facts might perhaps be accounted for by assuming that the translator never wrote out a fair copy of his work, but left it full of erasures and corrections, with words and phrases, representing his second thoughts, scribbled in wherever he could find room for them; and that this confused mass of words was afterwards copied out by some one who mechanically wrote down what he saw before him, without regard for the meaning.

The text which results from my attempts to restore the original order of the words is still very faulty, and I hope that it will be further emended by others; but in spite of the many problems which remain unsolved, I think that it is near enough to the original to enable us to recover the thoughts of the writer (or writers) of the Greek treatise in the main, though not in every detail.

In order that the reader may have before him the continuous text in the traditional arrangement, each word, phrase, or passage which I have transposed (with the exception of a few of the longest of these passages) is printed between doubled rectangular brackets [[ ]] at the place where it stands in the MSS., and repeated between doubled brackets of a different shape ⟨⟨ ⟩⟩ at the place to which I have transferred it.

In the foot-notes to the text, I have adopted the notation employed by Thomas:

ω = *omnium codicum consensus.*
ς = *codices interpolati.*
Ed. Rom. = *editio princeps Romana*, 1469.

In the English translation which faces the Latin text, I have aimed at expressing what I suppose to have been the meaning of the original Greek, rather than the meaning—or, too frequently, the absence of meaning—of the Latin.

The component parts of the ASCLEPIUS. It appears from internal evidence that the dialogue has been made up by putting together three distinct and unconnected documents—which I have named respectively '*Asclepius I* (*De homine*)', '*Asclepius II* (*De origine mali*)', and '*Asclepius III* (*De cultu deorum*)'—and adding a '*prologus*' and an '*epilogus*'.

The contents of ASCLEPIUS *I.* That part of the traditional text which I call *Ascl.* I (viz. chs. 2–14 a) is a well-constructed whole, the parts of which are arranged and linked together with some skill. It is a treatise '*de tota summitate*' (ch. 7 c)—concerning *Deus, Mundus,* and *Homo*, and their inter-relations ;—but the writer deals with this all-embracing subject from a definite point of view, and according to a definite plan. Throughout the discussion, *Man* is the central figure ;[1] and the teacher nowhere loses sight of his practical aim—that of urging men to live the life to which, as men, they are called. To this end he describes man's origin and nature (partly cosmic and partly supracosmic), and his station among and relations to beings of other grades (2–7) ; the twofold function assigned to him in accordance with his twofold nature (7 *fin.*–11 a) ; and the destiny which awaits him according as he fulfils his function or neglects it (11 b–12 *init.*). The subdivisions in the treatment of the theme are clearly marked, and yet are so connected that we pass on from each to the next without a break. There are two subordinate topics on which the writer has a special message to deliver, viz. the call to renounce possessions (11 a), and the mischief of a certain method of philosophic teaching (12 *fin.*–14 a). But each of these topics is introduced without breach of continuity. The renunciation of possessions is spoken of as a thing required with a view to the fulfilment of man's function ; and the corruption of philosophy is coupled with the love of possessions, as one of the hindrances to the realization of man's high destiny. Thus the concluding paragraph, on philosophy, is made to arise naturally out of the main subject ; and so the discourse ends appropriately with a description of that teaching which the writer holds to be the true philosophy, and of which the treatise itself is a specimen.

Asclepius I, then, is a well-ordered whole, complete in itself. There can, I think, be little doubt that the Greek original of *Ascl.* I at first existed as a separate document, of the same type as the *Hermes to Asclepius* libelli preserved in the *Corpus* ; and it may be presumed that it once formed part of the collection of discourses known to Stobaeus as τὰ Ἑρμοῦ πρὸς Ἀσκληπιόν.

The sources of ASCL. *I.* In this treatise, as in most of the *Hermetica*, there is little novelty or originality in the doctrines taught ; and the discourse of Hermes contains few statements to

[1] The subject of this document might be described in the words of Pl. *Theaet.* 174 b : τί δέ ποτ' ἐστὶν ἄνθρωπος, καὶ τί τῇ τοιαύτῃ φύσει προσήκει διάφορον τῶν ἄλλων ποιεῖν ἢ πάσχειν, ζητεῖ (ὁ φιλόσοφος).

which parallels cannot be found in earlier Greek writings. Yet the teaching of *Ascl.* I is not a mere repetition of traditional formulas; the writer's words ring true, and are alive with genuine feeling. If he has adopted his beliefs from others, they are none the less his own.

The influence of Plato is manifest throughout. The fundamental articles of the writer's creed—the doctrine of a supracosmic God, who is the maker and ruler of the universe, and that of a supracosmic element in the human soul—have been transmitted to him from Plato; and verbal echoes of phrases used by Plato may be recognized (see for instance the reminiscences of the *Timaeus* in ch. 8). But there is ample evidence of dependence on Greek writers of later date than Plato. The terms ὕλη and *qualitas* (ποιόν or ποιότης), as employed in *Ascl.* I, did not come into use until after Plato's time. The cosmology of chs. 2–6 is largely Stoic. The notion of a lower and mortal soul which is either composed of fire and air, or inseparably connected with those elements, must have been arrived at by a blending of Platonism with Stoic physics. The terms *quod sursum versus fertur* and *quod deorsum fertur* (τὸ ἀνωφερές, τὸ κατωφερές), ch. 2—*species* (εἶδος) in the sense of an individual, or the group of qualities distinctive of an individual, chs. 2 *fin.*–4—*spiritus* (πνεῦμα), ch. 6—and the statement that plants are ἄψυχα, ch. 4, are of Stoic origin. The phrase (νοῦς) *quae quinta pars soli homini concessa est ex aethere*, ch. 6 *fin.*, seems to have been derived from the Peripatetic Critolaus, perhaps through the syncretic Platonist Antiochus.[1]

The writer of *Ascl.* I says that man has been embodied on earth 'in order that he may tend the things of earth' (ἵνα τὰ ἐπίγεια θεραπεύῃ); and it is in the treatment of this theme, if anywhere, that he shows independence. The earliest Pagan writer in whom I have found this thought expressed is Cicero; and he probably got it from Posidonius. In this part of *Ascl.* I, therefore, the influence of Posidonius may be suspected.

The modification of a fundamentally Platonic system of thought by an intermixture of Stoic physics, such as we find in this document as well as in most of the other *Hermetica*, must have been derived from Antiochus and Posidonius, or from writers subsequent to them and influenced by them.

[1] The passage ⟨*sunt res*⟩ *quaedam quae ante factae sunt*, &c., ch. 5 *init.*, probably comes from Antiochus; but it is doubtful whether this passage existed in the original text of *Ascl.* I.

There seems to be nothing distinctively Egyptian in the doctrine of *Ascl.* I. The religious fervour of the writer is characteristic of his Egyptian nationality; but there is nothing in his dogmas that cannot be derived from Greek philosophy.

There are several phrases which show some resemblance to passages in the first two chapters of *Genesis*. See notes on ch. 3, *mundus . . . praeparatus est a deo* (i. e. ὕλη has been created by God); ch. 7, *pars* (*hominis*, sc. the νοῦς), *quam vocamus divinae similitudinis formam*; ch. 8, καλὸς δὲ (τῷ θεῷ) ἐφάνη ὢν (ὁ κόσμος); *ib.*, *talesque omnes esse praecepit* (which implies the making of a 'first man'); *ib.*, man has been embodied *ut possit . . . gubernare terrena.* There is, then, a possibility that the writer was to some slight extent affected by Jewish influence; but as each of these thoughts may very well have been suggested in some other way, it remains a possibility only.

The writer uses the term ὁ κύριος as a name or title of the supreme God (ch. 8). Is this to be regarded as a result of Jewish influence? The word κύριος (with a dependent genitive) was applied to Zeus by Pindar, *Isthm.* 4 (5). 67: Ζεὺς τά τε καὶ τὰ νέμει, Ζεὺς ὁ πάντων κύριος· and according to Liddell and Scott, κύριος occurs 'in inscriptions, as a name of divers gods, Zeus, Hermes, Kronos, &c., *vide C. I.* Index III; so Κυρία of Artemis, &c., *ib.*' But it was not commonly used by Greek philosophic writers with reference to the supreme God. There is no instance of this use of it in Diels *Fr. Vorsokr.*, in Plato, in Aristotle, or in Diels *Doxogr.*[1] But it was employed by the translators of the LXX as a rendering of the Hebrew name of God; and where it is similarly used by Pagan writers, it may have been taken over by them from Hellenistic Jews. It occurs frequently in the books of magic; e.g. the god is addressed as κύριε in Dieterich *Mithrasliturgie*, pp. 8, 10 (thrice), 14 (twice), and Dieterich *Abraxas*, p. 177, &c. Its use in such cases is comparable to that of the Hebrew names (e.g. Σαβαώθ, *Abraxas* p. 176) employed in magic invocations.

I have failed to find the slightest trace of Christian influence in *Ascl.* I.

Date of the Greek original of ASCL. *I.* The only definite *terminus*

[1] The nearest approaches to it are the following. Aetius, *Doxogr.*, p. 297 (Stoic): τῶν μὲν ἁπάντων τὸ θεῖον κυριώτατον, τῶν δὲ ζῴων ἄνθρωπος κάλλιστον. Hermias, *ib.*, p. 652, in a statement of the doctrine of Anaxagoras: ἀρχὴ πάντων ὁ νοῦς, καὶ οὗτος αἴτιος καὶ κύριος τῶν ὅλων. But in both these instances the word is followed by a genitive.

a quo is that which is given by the fact that the writer mixes Stoic physics with his Platonism. This sort of syncretism began in the time of Antiochus and Posidonius, i. e. in the first half of the first century B.C. It is therefore certain that the treatise cannot have been written before 100 B. C. But it was probably not written until much later.

A *terminus ante quem* may, perhaps, be inferred from the absence of any recognition of the existence of Christianity. The attitude of the writer of *Ascl.* I presents in this respect a contrast to that of the writer of *Ascl.* III. The latter, writing about A. D. 270 (see below), regards the advance of Christianity with horror and dismay; it is already clear to him that the Christians will soon get the upper hand, and that the Pagan cults will be abolished. But the writer of *Ascl.* I, when he asks himself (ch. 12 f.) what is the most serious obstacle in the path of those who seek salvation, finds it in the fact that certain Pagan teachers attach too much importance to the study of mathematics. If he had been aware that the very existence of his religion was threatened by the spread of Christianity, he could hardly have omitted to mention at this point a danger in comparison with which the error of which he speaks would have seemed to him a negligible trifle. This seems a sufficient reason for putting the date of *Ascl.* I earlier than that of *Ascl.* III. *Ascl.* I was probably written at a time when Christianity was not yet strong or aggressive enough to cause grave alarm or distress to the adherents of the old religions; *Ascl.* III was written at a time when it had already become apparent to the writer, not only that a danger was impending, but that the total extinction of Pagan religion was inevitable. For reasons given below, I think that a man in the situation of the writer of *Ascl.* I would not have been likely to ignore this danger at any time later than A.D. 260. We may therefore fix on 100 B.C. and A.D. 260 as the extreme limits between which the date of *Ascl.* I must be placed; and we might with strong probability restrict the range somewhat more narrowly, and say that the date must lie between 50 B.C. and A.D. 250.

I can find no internal evidence which would enable us to fix the date of *Ascl.* I more exactly; but on the ground of considerations which apply to the *Hermetica* in general, I am inclined to think that this *libellus* is not likely to have been written before the second century A. D.; and perhaps we should not be far wrong in conjecturing that the writer was a contemporary of Clement, who was teaching in Alexandria between A. D. 190 and 200.

The circumstances of the writer. The author of *Ascl.* I was probably an Egyptian by race. He can hardly have been a priest; for he takes no interest in theurgic ritual; and the worship of 'daemons' (i.e. temple-gods) is, in his eyes, a comparatively low form of religion, though better than none. It may be inferred that he had not been trained in the schools of the Egyptian priests, but had received a Hellenic education in Alexandria. Perhaps he had attended the lectures of one of the professional teachers of Platonism in that city, and is speaking from his own experience when he complains that such teachers put difficulties in the way of a seeker after God by including in their curriculum a compulsory course of mathematics. But in spite of these difficulties, he succeeded in learning as much of Greek philosophy as he needed for his purpose; and we may suppose that he afterwards retired to some more secluded place, where he could live the contemplative life in companionship with a small group of congenial spirits, at first, perhaps, as a pupil of some older teacher of the *gnosis*, and afterwards as a teacher in his turn. The instruction in these little communities must have been chiefly oral, and carried on, for the most part, by means of colloquies between the master and a single pupil at a time; and when one of the teachers committed his thoughts to writing, no doubt he reproduced, in the form of imaginary dialogues between Hermes and Tat or Asclepius, the method and contents of his own talks with this or that disciple.

If the writer of *Ascl.* I practised what he preached (ch. 11), he must have renounced all private possessions; and it almost necessarily follows from this that the brotherhood to which he belonged, and of which he was perhaps the head, held property in common, and that the produce of their labours was thrown into a common stock, from which the wants of all the members were supplied. They must have divided their time between *cultus terrenorum* and *cultus caelestium*; that is, they must have been occupied partly in tilling the piece of land which they owned collectively, and partly in adoration of the *di caelestes* (especially in the form of hymn-singing, ch. 9), and in drawing near to the supreme God by private prayer and meditation, and by such talk between teacher and pupil as is exemplified in our *Hermetica*. They felt that, in living such a life as this, they were doing the work which God had sent them down to earth to do; and they looked forward with trustful hope to the time when they would be 'released from the bonds of mortality', and, by God's grace, permitted to return to their true home above.

Asclepius II. That part of the composite dialogue which I call *Ascl.* II deals with the origin of evil; the writer seeks to account for the existence of evil by attributing it to the operation of ὕλη. This discussion is not in any way connected either with the contents of *Ascl.* I or with those of *Ascl.* III; and the dualism of *Ascl.* II is irreconcilable with the monism of *Ascl.* I and *Ascl.* III. There can, therefore, be little doubt that the Greek original of *Ascl.* II was in existence before it was made use of to form a part of the *Asclepius.* It appears to be complete in itself; but whether it was an independent *libellus*,[1] or a piece extracted by the compiler of the *Asclepius* from a longer document, we have no means of knowing.

There is no indication of any definite date for the Greek original of *Ascl.* II. We may suppose it to have been written in the same period as the Greek originals of *Ascl.* I and *Ascl.* III, i. e. probably about A. D. 150–270; and this supposition is to some extent confirmed by the resemblance between the teaching of *Ascl.* II and that of Numenius and Hermogenes (A. D. 150–200) on the same subject.

The contents of ASCLEPIUS *III.* That part of the traditional text which I have named *Ascl.* III presents, at first sight, a mere chaos of passages not only unconnected with *Ascl.* I and *Ascl.* II, but also unconnected with one another. But this confusion may be in part, if not wholly, a result of the mutilated and disordered state in which the Latin text has come down to us; and it seems probable that the Greek original of *Ascl.* III existed as a single document before the composite dialogue was compiled.

It appears that a number of passages were somehow severed from their context, but were preserved as detached fragments; and that these fragments were collected into two blocks (27 b–29 b and 33–6), which have been inserted into the text at the two places at which we find them. I have transposed these passages to what I conjecture to have been their original positions; and the contents of *Ascl.* III, as rearranged by me, may be tabulated as follows:

[1] It would be a short *libellus*, but not shorter than some other *Hermetica* which may perhaps have been written as independent *libelli*, and meant to stand alone, e. g. *Corp.* VIII and *Corp.* III.

α { 16 b, 17 a c, ⟨⟨33 a c, 34 a⟩⟩: *Ratio mundanorum*; a short account of the constituents of the material universe, viz. ὕλη, μορφαί, and πνεῦμα.

18 b, 19 a, ⟨⟨34 b⟩⟩, 19 b ⟨⟨27 c b⟩⟩,[1] 19 c, ⟨⟨34 c, ⟨⟨17 b⟩⟩, 35, 36⟩⟩: *Ratio divinorum*; a discussion of νοητά.

* * * * * * * * * * *

β { 20, 21: *Alia ratio divinorum*; on procreation.

22, 23 a: the gift of reason bestowed by God on man.

23 b, 24 a: man's power of making gods.

24 b–26 a: *the Prophecy*; Hermes predicts the extinction of the national religion of Egypt.

26 b, 27 a, 29 c–32 a, ⟨⟨40 b⟩⟩: the eternity of God and the time-process of the Kosmos.

32 b: the three kinds of νοῦς (divine, cosmic, and human).

* * * * * * * * * * *

γ { 37, ⟨⟨27 d⟩⟩, 38 a: gods made by men (i. e. terrestrial gods).

38 b–40 a: functions of terrestrial and celestial gods; Heimarmene.

* * * * * * * * * * *

δ { ⟨⟨27 e–29 a⟩⟩: *de inmortali et mortali*: on the life after death. (The latter part of this passage is lost.)

⟨⟨29 b⟩⟩[2]: the happiness of the pious in this life.

In the portion marked β (i. e. chs. 20–32 b, omitting the misplaced fragments 27 b–29 b), the discourse of Hermes runs on without a break. The portion marked γ (i. e. chs. 37–40 a), which is also continuous in itself, begins with a reference back to 23 b (*homo fictor est deorum*), and is thereby shown to have been intended by its writer to form part of the same treatise with β. As to the rest, there is much that remains doubtful; but the portion marked α, as conjecturally reconstructed, seems suitable for the beginning of the treatise; and the portion marked δ may very well have stood at or near the end of it.

Even in that part of the text which is undoubtedly continuous (viz. β, chs. 20–32 b), there is a lack of orderly and systematic arrangement; the writer seems to stray at random from one topic to another, as each in succession happens to occur to him. (In this

[1] It is doubtful whether the passage 19 b ⟨⟨27 c b⟩⟩ (i. e. the list of οὐσιάρχαι) is rightly placed here.

[2] It is uncertain where the fragment 29 b ought to stand.

respect, *Ascl.* III stands in marked contrast to *Ascl.* I.) The treatise as a whole has little unity; and it is difficult to describe its subject in a single phrase. But every part of it contributes in some way to the exposition of what the writer holds to be the true religion; and in some parts at least he is occupied in explaining what gods are to be worshipped, and how men ought to worship them. In the Prophecy he laments the impending abandonment of the old cults; his repeated assertion that men make gods (23 b, 37) is a defiant justification of the usages of Pagan worship in the face of Christian hostility; and the passage on time and eternity (26 b–32) leads up to a mention of that vision of the Eternal in which all worship culminates. Perhaps then the loosely connected discussions of which *Ascl.* III is composed may be fairly comprehended under the title *De cultu deorum.*

The sources of Asclepius *III.* The influence of Plato is manifest throughout. The fundamental conceptions of the writer—that of a supracosmic God, and that of an incorporeal *νοῦς*—are derived from Plato. The notion of eternity (26 b–32) is Platonic; and the use of the word *aeternitas* (*αἰών*) to express this notion comes from the *Timaeus.* The doctrine of *νοητὰ* and *εἴδη* contained in chs. 17 b, 18 b, 19 a c, 34 b–36, is based on the teaching of Plato; and the distinction between *νοητὰ εἴδη* and *αἰσθητὰ εἴδη* (17 b and 35) belongs to a stage of Platonism which can hardly have been reached before the time of Antiochus (first century B.C.). The daemonology of 27 e–29 a must have been taken over from some Platonic authority. The use of the term *ὕλη* (17 a) originated among the pupils of Plato. In 16 b, the Kosmos is described as *sensibilis deus* (*αἰσθητὸς θεός*, Pl. *Tim.*).

To Stoic influence must be ascribed the use of the term *spiritus* (*πνεῦμα*) in 16 b, 17 a, 18 b, and the doctrine of *εἱμαρμένη* in 39, 40 a. The definition of *vox* (*φωνή*) in 20 a is Stoic. In the words *quod dicitur extra mundum,* 33 a, the writer refers to the Stoic doctrine of a void outside the Kosmos. The statement that no two individuals are alike (ch. 35) is derived from the Stoics of the second century B.C., who maintained this doctrine in opposition to the Academics; and the astral explanation of individual differences (*ib.*) would hardly have been found in the writings of any Stoic earlier than Posidonius. The terms *ἀποκατέστησεν* and *regenitura* (*παλιγγενεσία*) in the last paragraph of the Prophecy, 26 a, are Stoic, and the contents of this paragraph are probably derived in part from a Stoic source. In the account of the life after death, 27 e–29 a, the assumption that all souls alike, on their separation from the body, ascend into the atmosphere is of Stoic origin; and the division of the atmosphere into two distinct strata, and the purgation of impure souls in the lower stratum, are derived from Posidonius.

The statement that νοῦς is *divina pars mundi*, ch. 22 b, is due to the influence of Stoic materialism, but may perhaps have been transmitted to the writer by the Peripatetic Critolaus and the Platonist Antiochus. The remarks on circular movement in 31 *fin.* and 40 b may perhaps have been derived from Aristotle.

The contents of chs. 20, 21 (God is ἀνώνυμος or παντώνυμος—God is ἀρσενόθηλυς) may possibly be derived from native Egyptian sources. The views expressed in connexion with the statement that man makes gods (23 b, 24 a, and 37, 38) are Egyptian rather than Hellenic. In these passages, the writer formulates certain beliefs of his countrymen; he is here speaking of things familiar to him by direct and personal knowledge, and has no occasion to borrow from earlier writers.

In the list of οὐσιάρχαι (19 b, 27 c), the notion of a system of departmental gods, and the names *Zeus*, *Heimarmene*, indicate a Stoic source; but the terms ⟨*Decani*⟩, *Horoscopi*, and *Pantomorphos* are derived rather from the astral religion of Hellenistic Egypt. The combination of Stoic and Egyptian ingredients in this passage might be accounted for by the assumption that the scheme of οὐσιάρχαι has been borrowed from the Egyptian Stoic Chaeremon.

The form of the Prophecy, 24 b–26 a, may have been suggested by earlier apocalypses, Egyptian or Jewish; but its contents, so far as it refers to contemporary events, must be original.

Analogies to Jewish teaching may be found in the exaltation of human procreation, ch. 21 (cf. Gen. i. 28, αὐξάνεσθε καὶ πληθύνεσθε); in the statement that man is made *ex parte corruptiore mundi et ex divina*, ch. 22 (cf. Gen. ii. 7, ἔπλασεν ὁ θεὸς τὸν ἄνθρωπον χοῦν ἀπὸ τῆς γῆς κ.τ.λ.); and in the application of the term *summus* (ὕψιστος) to the supreme God (*summus qui dicitur deus*, 16 b); but there is no proof that the writer was in any way affected by Jewish influences.

There is not the slightest reason to think that any part of the doctrine of *Ascl.* III has been derived from Christian sources. On the other hand, the writer's attitude is to a large extent determined by his repugnance to Christianity. This repugnance finds direct expression in the Prophecy, and underlies his treatment of the topics of god-making and procreation.

Date of the Greek original of ASCLEPIUS *III.* A consideration of the sources from which the doctrine of *Ascl.* III is derived makes it certain that the treatise must have been written after the time of Antiochus and Posidonius, i. e. at some time later than 100 B.C. At no earlier period could Stoic conceptions have been blended with Platonism as we find them blended in this document. And if the writer has borrowed from Chaeremon, the date must be later than A.D. 50.

But the Prophecy, ch. 24 f., contains references to contemporary events; and by examining these references, it may be possible to determine the date more exactly. The contents of the Prophecy may be summarized thus: 'Cruel and impious foreigners will invade the land of Egypt, and slaughter a large part of the inhabitants; thereupon, the Egyptians themselves will become cruel and impious, and the national religion will die out.' At what date were these predictions written? It is evident that the writer is describing, under the form of a prophecy uttered by Trismegistus, things which had recently taken place, or were taking place before his eyes. If, therefore, we can identify the events of which he speaks, we shall obtain an approximate date for the writing of chs. 24–6 at least, if not for the whole treatise.

Let us consider first the predicted abandonment of the national religion.

Under the rule of the Persians and the Greeks, and under the earlier Roman empire, the Egyptian religion had maintained itself, not indeed unchanged, but unimpaired in strength, and unshaken by any sudden or violent transformation; and at no time could it be thought to be in danger of perishing, until it was threatened with extinction by the advance of Christianity.[1]

[1] Under the Ptolemies and the early Roman emperors, the only declared opponents of Paganism in Egypt were the Jews; and they were never numerous or influential enough to cause such a feeling of impending and inevitable doom as is expressed by our Hermetist. (On the Jewish rising under Trajan, see below.)

An illustration of the attitude of the Jews towards the Egyptian religion is to be found in *Orac. Sibyll.* 5. 484–503, written by an Alexandrian Jew of unknown date (possibly about the time of Trajan or Hadrian):

Ἶσι, θεὰ τριτάλαινα, μενεῖς ἐπὶ χεύμασι Νείλου
μούνη, μαινὰς ἄναυδος ἐπὶ ψαμάθοις Ἀχέροντος,
κοὐκέτι σου μνεία γε μενεῖ κατὰ γαῖαν ἅπασαν.
καὶ σύ, Σάραπι, λίθους ἀργοὺς ἐπικείμενε πολλούς,
κείσῃ πτῶμα μέγιστον ἐν Αἰγύπτῳ τριταλαίνῃ·

What, then, is the earliest date at which Christianity was powerful and aggressive enough in Egypt to give rise to such gloomy anticipations as are expressed in chs. 24–5 of the *Asclepius*? Harnack, *Mission und Ausbreitung des Christentums*, Book IV, has collected the evidences of the spread of Christianity down to A.D. 325. Celsus[1] (A.D. 176–80) speaks as if Christianity had been almost extirpated. Doubtless he exaggerates the success of the repressive measures of Marcus Aurelius; but he could not have spoken thus if the Christians were numerous enough to cause serious alarm. In his time, Pagans regarded Christianity with hatred and contempt, but not with fear.

Tertullian[2] (A.D. 197–213) speaks in a tone which foreshadows the coming danger to Paganism. But allowance must be made for his rhetorical style; he greatly exaggerates the numbers and power of the Christians.

ὅσσοι δ' Αἰγύπτου πόθον ἤγαγον εἴς σε, ἅπαντες
κλαύσονταί σε κακῶς, θεὸν ἄφθιτον ἐν φρεσὶ θέντες·
γνώσονταί σε τὸ μηδέν, ὅσοι θεὸν ἐξύμνησαν.
καὶ ⟨τότε⟩ τῶν ἱερέων τις ἐρεῖ, λινόστολος ἀνήρ·
"δεῦτε, θεοῦ τέμενος καλὸν στήσωμεν ἀληθοῦς·
δεῦτε, τὸν ἐκ προγόνων δεινὸν νόμον ἀλλάξωμεν,
τοῦ χάριν οἱ λιθίνοις καὶ ὀστρακίνοισι θεοῖσιν
πομπὰς καὶ τελετὰς ποιούμενοι οὐκ ἐνόησαν.
στρέψωμεν ψυχὰς θεὸν ἄφθιτον ἐξυμνοῦντες
τὸν πρύτανιν πάντων, τὸν ἀληθέα, τὸν βασιλῆα,
ψυχοτρόφον γενετῆρα, θεὸν μέγαν αἰὲν ἐόντα."

The Jewish Sibyllist here predicts the conversion of the Egyptians, as the writer of Isaiah ch. 19 had predicted it before him; but it is hardly to be thought that an Egyptian idolater would at any time have admitted that the conversion of the whole nation to Judaism was even possible, much less that it was inevitable.

[1] Celsus, in Origen *contra Cels.* 8. 69: ὑμῶν δὲ (sc. of you Christians) *κἂν πλανᾶταί τις ἔτι λανθάνων, ἀλλὰ ζητεῖται πρὸς θανάτου δίκην.* (The dates of the books here cited are taken from Harnack, *Chronol. der Altchrist. Litt.*, 1897–1904.)

[2] Tertull. *Apolog.* 2 (A.D. 197) 'Obsessam vociferantur civitatem, in agris, in castellis, in insulis Christianos, omnem sexum, aetatem, condicionem, etiam dignitatem transgredi ad hoc nomen'. *Ib.* 37 'Si et hostes exertos, non tantum vindices occultos agere vellemus, deesset nobis vis numerorum et copiarum? . . . Hesterni sumus, et vestra omnia implevimus. . . . Cui bello non idonei, non prompti fuissemus, etiam impares copiis, qui tam libenter trucidamur, si non apud istam disciplinam magis occidi liceret quam occidere? . . . Si enim tanta vis hominum in aliquem orbis remoti sinum abrupissemus a vobis, suffudisset utique dominationem vestram tot qualiumcumque civium amissio, immo etiam et ipsa destitutione punisset. . . . Plures hostes quam cives vobis remansissent. Nunc etiam pauciores hostes habetis prae multitudine Christianorum, paene omnium civitatium paene omnes cives Christianos habendo.' Tertull. *adv. Judaeos* (A.D. 198–203) 'In quem alium universae gentes crediderunt nisi in Christum?' Tertull. *adv. Marc.* 3. 20 (A.D. 198–209) 'Aspice universas nationes de voragine erroris humani exinde emergentes. . . . Christus totum iam orbem evangelii sui fide cepit.' Tertull. *ad Scapulam* 2 (A.D. 212–13) 'Tanta hominum multitudo, pars paene maior civitatis cuiusque, in silentio et modestia agimus'. See also Minucius Felix 9 (A.D. 222–50).

Origen[1] (A. D. 246–9), speaking the language of sober truth, supplies the necessary corrective to Tertullian's exaggerations. He admits that there are still many people, even in the Roman empire, whose ears the preaching of Christianity has not yet reached; and that the Christians are still 'very few' as compared with the Pagans. He looks forward with confident assurance to the ultimate prevalence of good over evil, either in this world or in the world to come; but he doubts whether the universal acceptance of the true religion is possible on earth.

Harnack (*op. cit.*, p. 376) concludes that 'as regards the stages in the history of the mission-work, the great advances, after the time of Paul, were made (1) in the epoch of Commodus (A. D. 180–92) and his next successors, and (2) in the years 260–303; and it was in the latter period that the progress was most rapid'.[2]

From the time of the edict of toleration issued at Milan by Constantine and Licinius in A. D. 313, the victory of the new religion was assured. Eusebius,[3] about A. D. 325, describes the Christians as 'the most numerous of all the nations'; and Firmicus Maternus, some twenty years later, speaks of Paganism as almost extinct.[4]

[1] Origenes, *ad Matth.* 24. 9 (A. D. 246–9) 'Multi enim non solum barbararum, sed etiam nostrarum gentium usque nunc non audierunt Christianitatis verbum'. Orig. *contra Cels.* 3. 29 (A. D. 246–8) ὁ δε πέμψας τὸν Ἰησουν θεὸς . . . ἐποίησε πανταχοῦ τῆς οἰκουμένης ὑπὲρ τῆς τῶν ἀνθρώπων ἐπιστροφῆς καὶ διορθώσεως κρατῆσαι τὸ εὐαγγέλιον Ἰησοῦ, καὶ γενέσθαι πανταχοῦ ἐκκλησίας ἀντιπολιτευομένας ἐκκλησίαις δεισιδαιμόνων καὶ ἀκολάστων καὶ ἀδίκων. *Ib.* 8. 69 εἴπερ "ἂν δύο συμφωνῶσιν" ἐξ ἡμῶν . . . "γενήσεται αὐτοῖς παρὰ τοῦ ἐν τοῖς οὐρανοῖς πατρός," . . . τί χρὴ νομίζειν, εἰ μὴ μόνον ὡς νῦν πάνυ ὀλίγοι συμφωνοῖεν, ἀλλὰ πᾶσα ἡ ὑπὸ Ῥωμαίων ἀρχή; *Ib.* 8. 68 ἥτις (*sc.* ἡ τῶν Χριστιανῶν θρησκεία) καὶ μόνη ποτὲ κρατήσει, τοῦ λόγου ἀεὶ πλείονας νεμομένου ψυχάς. *Ib.* 8. 72 εὐχήν τινα εἰπὼν (*sc.* Celsus) τὴν "Εἰ γὰρ δὴ οἷόν τε εἰς ἕνα συμφρονῆσαι νόμον τοὺς τὴν Ἀσίαν καὶ Εὐρώπην καὶ Λιβύην κατοικοῦντας Ἕλληνας καὶ βαρβάρους ἄχρι περάτων νενεμημένους", ἀδύνατον τοῦτο νομίσας εἶναι, ἐπιφέρει ὅτι "ὁ τοῦτο οἰόμενος οἶδεν οὐδέν". εἰ δὲ χρὴ καὶ τοῦτ' εἰπεῖν, λελέξεται ὀλίγα . . . εἰς τὸ φανῆναι οὐ μόνον δυνατόν, ἀλλὰ καὶ ἀληθὲς τὸ λεγόμενον περὶ τοῦ εἰς ἕνα συμφρονῆσαι νόμον πᾶν τὸ λογικόν . . . πάντων γὰρ τῶν ἐν τῇ ψυχῇ κακῶν δυνατώτερος ὢν ὁ λόγος, καὶ ἡ ἐν αὐτῷ θεραπεία, προσάγει κατὰ βούλησιν θεοῦ ἑκάστῳ αὐτήν· καὶ τὸ τέλος τῶν πραγμάτων ἀναιρεθῆναί ἐστι τὴν κακίαν . . . καὶ τάχα ἀληθῶς ἀδύνατον μὲν τὸ τοιοῦτον τοῖς ἔτι ἐν σώματι, οὐ μὴν ἀδύνατον καὶ ἀπολυθεῖσιν αὐτοῦ.

[2] See Euseb. *Hist. Eccl.* 5. 21. 1; 6. 36. 1; 8. 1. 1; 9. 9.

[3] Euseb. *H. E.* 1. 4. 2 πάντων τῶν ἐθνῶν πολυανθρωπότατον.

[4] Firmicus Maternus, *de Err. Prof. Relig.* 20 (A. D. 346–7) 'Licet adhuc in quibusdam regionibus idololatriae morientia palpitent membra, tamen in eo res est ut a Christianis omnibus terris pestiferum hoc malum funditus amputetur'. But this is an exaggeration. Paganism died slowly; and the reaction under Julian, A. D. 361–3, gave it a fresh lease of life. Firmicus himself, ch. 13, admits that the cult of Sarapis in Alexandria was still openly carried on at the time when he wrote. During the youth of Augustine, about A. D. 372, festivals of the Magna Mater and Attis were publicly celebrated in Carthage (Aug. *De civ. dei* 2. 4 and

From the evidence of the authors so far cited, we may form some notion of the stages by which Christianity advanced in the Roman empire as a whole. Our present purpose would be better served if we could trace the progress made in Egypt. The history of Christianity in Egypt down to A. D. 180 is almost a blank;[1] concerning that period we know only that some early Christian documents were probably written there; that a 'Gospel according to the Egyptians' was in circulation; and that Basilides, Valentinus, and other Christian Gnostics taught in Egypt. About 180, we find a vigorous Christian Church established in Alexandria, and the Christian 'Catechetical School' already at work. In the time of Clement (from A. D. 190 onwards), that School was attended by Pagans as well as Christians; and if Clement's words[2] may be taken as specially applying to Egypt, they imply that Christianity had gained a firm footing among the people of the country. Eusebius (*Hist. Eccl.* 6. 1, 2) says that in the persecution of Septimius Severus, A. D. 202, a large number of Christians 'from all (Lower) Egypt and all the Thebaid' suffered martyrdom in Alexandria.[3] Harnack (*op. cit.*, p. 454) says that 'from the fragments of the letters of Dionysius Alex., bishop of Alexandria (A. D. 247–65), and from the accounts of the persecutions (A. D. 250–60), we get the impression that the number of Christians in Alexandria was large, and that Christianity had spread to a considerable extent in the towns and villages of the country. After the middle of the third century, Lower Egypt was certainly one of the regions in which the Christians were especially numerous. . . . At the time of the persecution of Decius (A. D. 250) there were already Christians holding public offices in Alexandria, and many wealthy men were Christians (Euseb.

7. 26; Boissier, *Fin du paganisme,* i, p. 347). Libanius, *De templis,* about A. D. 384–7, speaks of Pagan cults as still practised (Boissier, *ib.*, ii, p. 341); the edict of Theodosius in A. D. 392 (*Cod. Theodos.* 16. 10. 12) shows that the need of fresh enactments against them was still felt at that time; and even Theodosius II (*Cod. Theod.* 16. 10. 22) issued an edict against *paganos qui supersunt, quamquam iam nullos esse credamus.* In A. D. 398, Claudian (*De quarto cons. Honorii* 570 sqq.; Otto, *Priester und Tempel,* ii. 281 and i. 404) describes a procession of statues of the gods in Memphis.

[1] Harnack, *Mission und Ausbreitung des Chr.*, p. 448.

[2] *Strom.* 6. 18. 167 ὁ δέ γε τοῦ διδασκάλου τοῦ ἡμετέρου λόγος . . . ἐχύθη . . . ἀνὰ πᾶσαν τὴν οἰκουμένην, πείθων Ἑλλήνων τὲ ὁμοῦ καὶ βαρβάρων κατὰ ἔθνος καὶ κώμην καὶ πόλιν πᾶσαν, οἴκους ὅλους καὶ ἰδίᾳ ἕκαστον τῶν ἐπακηκοότων, καὶ αὐτῶν γε τῶν φιλοσόφων οὐκ ὀλίγους ἤδη ἐπὶ τὴν ἀλήθειαν μεθίστας.

[3] Eusebius here speaks of 'a myriad' of martyrs: *μυρίων ὅσων τοῖς κατὰ τὸ μαρτύριον ἀναδουμένων στεφάνοις.* But *μυρίοι* in Euseb. merely means 'a good many'. Origen, *c. Celsum* 3. 8, says: ὀλίγοι κατὰ καιροὺς καὶ σφόδρα εὐαρίθμητοι ὑπὲρ τῆς Χριστιανῶν θεοσεβείας τεθνήκασι.

6. 41 ; 7. 11)'. The descriptions of the persecution of Diocletian (A. D. 303) prove that there were at that time large numbers of Christians in the Thebaid. Dionysius Alex. (Euseb. *Hist. Eccl.* 6. 41) speaks of Christians among the native Egyptian population as well as among the Greeks; and the translation of the Bible into Coptic was probably begun, in Upper Egypt, in the second half of the third century. 'It is certain', says Harnack, 'that at the time of the persecution of Diocletian the Christians in Egypt had long outnumbered the Jews; at the beginning of the fourth century their number probably exceeded a million.'

What, then, is the earliest date at which it would be possible for an adherent of Paganism in Egypt to foresee and lament the coming extinction of his religion? To this question no exact and certain answer can be given; but we may conclude that chapters 24–5 can hardly have been written before the renewed expansion of Christianity which followed on the close of the period of persecution under Decius, Gallus, and Valerian (A. D. 250–3 and 257–60). Thus from what we know of the progress of Christianity, we might fix on the year 260 as the *terminus a quo* for the Greek original of chs. 24–6. A *terminus ante quem* is given by Lactantius's quotation from the Greek original of ch. 26 in his *Div. Inst.*, written within a few years of A. D. 310. The prophecy, then, was probably written at some time in the half-century A. D. 260–310.

But we may hope to fix the date more exactly by identifying the particular events referred to. The prophecy speaks of an invasion of Egypt by *alienigenae*, and an immigration of 'Scythians or Indians or some such barbarians'. Who are these *alienigenae*? The term cannot be meant to apply to Greeks or Jews; for Greeks and Jews had been resident in Egypt in large numbers ever since the time of Alexander, and the invasion spoken of is evidently recent. Nor can the Roman conquest be meant; for we are told that the foreigners will 'fill the land'; but the Roman conquest caused no large and sudden influx of foreigners; indeed, Italians were at no time numerous in Egypt. And neither Greek, Jew, nor Italian can be described as 'Scythes aut Indus'.

We are also told of a vast slaughter, or series of slaughters, in which a large part of the population of Egypt perishes. The earliest incident to which this description could possibly be supposed to apply is the insurrection of the Jews under Trajan.[1] But though

[1] Mommsen, *Provs. of Rom. Empire*, Eng. tr., 1886, ii, p. 221: 'In the year

the Jewish insurgents, during their short-lived success, may have dealt harshly with the Egyptian idolaters, there is no reason to suppose that any large proportion of the Egyptians abandoned the religion of their fathers; and no one at that date could anticipate the total extinction of Egyptian Paganism. Besides, there is nothing in that incident to account for the mention of *alienigenae*[1] and *Scythes aut Indus*. It is therefore certain that the event referred to cannot be the Jewish insurrection of A. D. 116.

The next incident to which the prophecy of slaughter might seem to be applicable[2] is the massacre of Alexandrians by order of Caracalla[3] in A. D. 215. But the words *alienigenis terram complentibus* and *inhabitabit Aegyptum Indus aut Scythes* cannot be made to apply to Caracalla's soldiers.

It would seem that after this disaster Alexandria never fully recovered its former prosperity; and from this time onward, things went from bad to worse in Egypt. In A. D. 252 we first hear of a pestilence which ravaged the empire in successive outbreaks during a space of fifteen years, and by which large numbers of Egyptians perished. But it was especially during the troubled years which followed the capture of Valerian by the Persians in 260, that calamities fell thick and fast upon the land. We have a contemporary description of the situation in Egypt between A. D. 261 and 265,[4] in the letters written by Dionysius, bishop of Alexandria.

116, the Jews of the eastern Mediterranean rose against the imperial government.' The chief seats of the rising were Cyrene, Cyprus, and Egypt; it was 'directed to the expulsion of the Romans as well as of the Hellenes, and apparently to the establishment of a separate Jewish state'. The Jews for a time got the upper hand in Egypt; 'they killed those (Greeks and Romans) whom they seized'; but 'in Alexandria, which does not itself appear to have fallen into the hands of the Jews, the besieged Hellenes slew whatever Jews were then in the city'. The insurrection was suppressed by an army and fleet sent by Trajan. Appian says that Trajan annihilated the Jews in Alexandria.

[1] The insurgent Jews in Egypt, though they may have been reinforced by contingents from elsewhere, must have been in the main Egyptian residents, and not invaders.

[2] It is certainly not applicable to the insurrection of the Βουκόλοι in Egypt in the time of Marcus Aurelius (Dio Cass. 71. 4).

[3] Schiller, *Gesch. der röm. Kaiserzeit*, i. 747: 'A rising in Egypt summoned Caracalla to that land, and Alexandria was severely punished; the town was given up to the soldiers to be plundered, and a great part of the inhabitants were killed.' Dio 77. 22, 23; Herodian 4. 8. 6–9 and 9; Spartianus, *Vita Caracall.* 6. 2. 3. The details are uncertain, but the fact that a great slaughter took place cannot be doubted. 'The subjection of Egypt' is depicted on a Roman coin struck at this time.

[4] Euseb. *H. E.* 7. 21 ff. The persecution of the Christians was stopped by order of Gallienus (Euseb. *H. E.* 7. 13); and as, after the capture of Valerian in 260, the rule of Macrianus was for a time recognized in Egypt, the order of

'When persecution had ceased', says Eusebius, 'Dionysius returned to Alexandria. There, civil strife and war broke out; and as the Christians were divided between the two factions, it was not possible for him to visit in person all the brethren in the city. He, therefore, at the Easter festival, communicated with them by letter, writing to them as if from beyond the borders, though he was in Alexandria.'

What was the *στάσις καὶ πόλεμος* of which Eusebius is speaking? The only recorded disturbance in Egypt which can be assigned to this time is the insurrection of Aemilianus.[1] It may be presumed, then, that one part of Alexandria was held by the troops and partisans of Aemilianus, and another part by those of the Roman commander Theodotus.[2]

Dionysius writes thus: 'I am obliged to communicate by letter with the members of my own church; and how my letter is to be conveyed to them, I do not know. For it would be easier to go

Gallienus cannot have taken effect there before 261. Dionysius died in 265 (Euseb. 7. 28. 3). The letters must therefore have been written between 261 and 265.

Mommsen's account of these events is self-contradictory. He rightly says that Dionysius died in 265 (*Rom. Emp.*, ii, p. 250, n. 2), and that the Palmyrene invasion of Egypt did not take place until after the death of Odaenathus in 266-7 (*ib.* pp. 106, 107); and yet he speaks of the incidents described by Dionysius as if they arose out of the Palmyrene invasion (*ib.* p. 250).

[1] Trebellius Pollio, *Vita Gallieni*, 4. 1: 'Per idem tempus (i. e. not far from the time of the death of Macrianus, A. D. 262) Aemilianus apud Aegyptum sumpsit imperium. Sed hunc dux Gallieni Theodotus conflictu habito cepit.' *Ib.* 5. 6; 6. 4; 9. 1. *Tyrann. Trig.* 22: the Alexandrian mob attacked the house 'Aemiliani ducis': . . . 'Aemilianus sumpsit imperium. . . . Consenserunt ei Aegypti totius exercitus, maxime in Gallieni odium. Nec eius ad regendam remp. vigor defuit; nam Thebaidem totamque Aegyptum peragravit, et, quatenus potuit, barbarorum gentes (Blemmyes and Saracens?) forti auctoritate summovit. . . . Misso Theodoto duce, Gallieno iubente, dedit poenas.' *Ib.* 26. 4 (whence it appears that Theodotus was an Egyptian by birth). This 'Aemilianus dux' may be identical with the Αἰμιλιανὸς διέπων τὴν ἡγεμονίαν in Egypt, before whom Dionysius was summoned during the persecution of 257–60, Euseb. *H. E.* 7. 11. 6.

Mommsen, *Rom. Emp.*, ii. 251, n. 1, rejects the evidence of Trebellius Pollio, and doubts the existence of the alleged usurper Aemilianus. But this is surely an excess of scepticism. At any rate, the contemporary evidence of Dionysius makes it certain that either Aemilianus, or some person whose name we do not know, raised 'civil strife and war' in Egypt between 261 and 265.

As the Easter letter written by Dionysius during the *στάσις* is followed by another Easter letter written by him when fighting had ceased and pestilence was raging, and that again by others written 'when the city was at peace again', the *στάσις* may be assigned with probability, if not with certainty, to the year 262.

[2] We shall find a similar situation recurring a few years later in the 'siege of Brucheion'. We are told that Caracalla, after his massacre in 215, had ordered a wall to be built, by which the city was divided into two parts; Dio 77. 23, τὴν Ἀλεξάνδρειαν διατειχισθῆναί τε καὶ φρουρίοις ⸤διατειχισθῆναι⸥ ἐκέλευσεν, ὅπως μηκέτ' ἀδεῶς παρ' ἀλλήλους φοιτῷεν. It would seem that this fortification was still in existence, and was utilized by the combatants, in the time of Dionysius.

into a foreign country, or even to traverse the world from East to West, than to pass from one part of Alexandria to the other. The principal street of the city is more impassable than the desert of Sinai; and the harbours of Alexandria have become like the Red Sea, for they have many times been reddened with bloodshed. The river which waters the city[1] was at one time drier than the desert;[2] at another time it overflowed its banks and flooded all the ways and lands around the city; and it is continually polluted with blood and slayings and drownings. As in the days of Moses, "the waters have been turned to blood, and the river stinks".[3] The air is turbid with noisome vapours; earth and sea, river and harbour reek with foul exhalations; corpses lie rotting everywhere,[4] and the dew is corrupted by their fetid juices. And yet men wonder what is the cause of these incessant pestilences! And they ask whence comes this great and manifold destruction of mankind,[5] and why it is that the inhabitants of our great city, young and old together, are fewer in number than the elderly persons[6] alone were in times gone by. For though all from fourteen to eighty years of age have now been included in the list of those entitled to receive the public corn-dole, they are less numerous than the people from forty to seventy years of age used to be in those times.[7] Men see the human race continually diminishing and wasting away, and yet they do not tremble, though the course of things is tending more and more towards their total destruction.'

In another letter, written (apparently in the following year) when the war is ended, but the pestilence is at its height, Dionysius says, 'There is lamentation and mourning everywhere; the city resounds with cries of woe by reason of the multitude of the dead, and of those that are dying day by day;[5] for "there is not a house where

[1] i.e. the canal by which the water of the Nile was brought to Alexandria.

[2] The regulation of the water-supply was probably neglected during the disturbances, and the water may have been purposely cut off by the besiegers.

[3] Exod. vii. 20, 21. Cf. *Ascl. Lat.* 24 b: 'Torrenti sanguine plenus usque ad ripas erumpes, undaeque divinae non solum polluentur sanguine, sed totae corrumpentur.'

[4] *Ib.* 'Tunc terra ista . . . sepulcrorum erit mortuorumque plenissima'.

[5] *Ascl. Lat.* 24 b: 'Vivis multo maior erit numerus sepulchrorum.'

[6] ὠμογέροντας, i.e. old, but still vigorous.

[7] Dionysius does not tell us of what earlier time he is speaking; it may have been any time before the massacre of Caracalla. It appears that, for the purpose of the corn-dole, a maximum limit of number was maintained unaltered. In the time of greatest prosperity the full number had been made up by entering on the roll those between forty and seventy alone; as the population decreased, the names of younger and older persons were added to the register.

there is not one dead "[1]—and would that there were not more than one. Even before this, many terrible things had befallen us; first, the persecution of the Christians;[2] . . . then, war[3] and famine, which we Christians endured together with the Pagans, sharing the evils which they inflicted on each other; . . . and then, after short respite to us and them, there came on us this pestilence, a thing most terrible to them, and the most cruel of all disasters.' The Christians, Dionysius says, tenderly nursed the sick, and buried the dead; and many of them, in so doing, caught the infection and died themselves. 'But with the Pagans, it is far otherwise; they thrust away from them people who were sickening; they fled from their nearest and dearest; they flung them out into the streets when they were dying; and they cast forth corpses unburied, like offal.'

There is a striking resemblance between the situation depicted in these letters and that predicted by Trismegistus; and it seems probable enough that the writer of the prophecy had lived through the events which Dionysius describes. As yet, however, we have met with no trace of the *alienigenae.* But Egypt was invaded by foreigners a few years later. Odaenathus of Palmyra, who ruled over the provinces of Syria and Arabia, and some adjacent countries,[4] nominally as *Dux Orientis* under Gallienus, but in practical independence, was murdered between August 29, 266, and August 29, 267. His widow Zenobia claimed the succession for her son Vaballathus, and ruled in his name; and, shortly after her husband's death,[5] she sent an army under her general Zabdas to occupy Egypt, professedly on behalf of the Roman emperor. The fullest and most trustworthy account of the Palmyrene invasion is that given by Zosimus. He says (1. 44 ff.) that, after the first Gothic campaign of Claudius, 'Zenobia, seeking to extend her power, sent Zabdas to Egypt, which Timagenes, a native of the country, was endeavouring to bring under the rule of the Palmyrenes. The invading army was composed of Palmyrenes, Syrians, and barbarians, and amounted to the number of 70,000 men. The Egyptians met them with a force of 50,000, and a great battle took place. The Palmyrenes were

[1] Exod. xii. 30.
[2] A. D. 257-61.
[3] i. e. the στάσις of the first letter.
[4] 'Possibly Armenia, Cilicia, and Cappadocia,' says Mommsen, *Rom. Emp.*, ii. 107.
[5] Apparently in the year 268; for Zosimus and Trebellius Pollio (*Vita Claud.* 11) agree that the Palmyrene invasion of Egypt took place in the reign of Claudius. Claudius succeeded Gallienus in 268, and there would hardly be room for the subsequent events if we placed the invasion later than that year.

victorious in the war; they placed a garrison of 5,000 men in the country, and withdrew. Probus, who had been appointed by the emperor (Claudius) to clear the sea of the (Gothic) pirates, hearing that Egypt was occupied by the Palmyrenes, proceeded thither with his force, and being joined by those Egyptians who were not of the Palmyrene faction, attacked the garrison and drove it out.[1] The Palmyrenes[2] once more marched against Egypt; Probus got together an army of Egyptians and Libyans to oppose them; the Egyptians (under Probus) got the upper hand, and were driving the Palmyrenes out of the country. Probus took up a position on the mountain near Babylon,[3] meaning to bar the passage of the enemy there as they marched towards Syria; but Timagenes, making use of his knowledge of the locality, occupied the summit of the mountain with 2,000 Palmyrenes, and surprised and destroyed the Egyptian force. Probus was caught with the rest, and killed himself. Thus Egypt became subject to the Palmyrenes.'[4]

[1] It appears that Probus, in treating the Palmyrene invaders as enemies of Rome, acted on his own responsibility, without waiting for instructions from the emperor; and Claudius, being too much occupied with the Goths to be willing to involve himself in a simultaneous war in the East, afterwards acquiesced in the *fait accompli*, and recognized Vaballathus as governor of Egypt in his name.

[2] i. e. probably the main army, recalled, in the course of its homeward march, by the news of the defeat of the garrison.

[3] Babylon is the fortress of 'Old Cairo', on the eastern bank of the Nile. (See A. J. Butler, *Babylon of Egypt*, p. 23.) The most convenient route from Alexandria to Syria passes round the apex of the Delta, from which Cairo is only a few miles distant up the river; and if the Palmyrenes, at the time of their retreat from Alexandria, still held the fortress of Babylon, they would naturally choose the point guarded by it for their crossing of the Nile. 'The mountain near Babylon' must mean some spur of the desert heights to the north-east of Babylon, i. e. east of the modern town of Cairo. (The citadel of Cairo stands on such a spur, and its site may be the very place.) Probus posted his force here, apparently with the intention of attacking the Palmyrenes in flank as they marched northward from Babylon after crossing the river. While the attention of Probus was fixed on the river-valley below him, Timagenes stole round behind, over the desert tableland, and came down upon him from above.

[4] These events are summarized by Trebellius Pollio, *Vita Claud.* 11, as follows: 'Dum haec a divo Claudio aguntur, Palmyreni ducibus Saba et Timagene contra Aegyptios bellum sumunt, atque ab his Aegyptia pervicacia et indefessa pugnandi continuatione vincuntur. Dux tamen Aegyptiorum Probatus Timagenis insidiis interemptus est: Aegyptii vero omnes se Romano imperatori dederunt, in absentis Claudii verba iurantes.' Trebellius Pollio has omitted to say that Timagenes was an Egyptian; but his account, as far as it goes, agrees in the main with that of Zosimus. But who is Probatus? Schiller, *röm. Kaiserzeit*, i. 859, says that 'near the end of the reign of Gallienus, Egypt had revolted under a usurper Probatus. On the accession of Claudius II . . . Zenobia . . . caused the land to be reconquered for the Roman empire by her general Zabda.' But there is no evidence for the existence of Probatus except this passage of Trebell. Poll.; and Mommsen (ii. 107, n. 1) is undoubtedly right in identifying the 'dux Aegyptiorum Probatus' of Trebell. Poll. with the Probus of Zosimus, who was not a usurper, but a Roman commander opposing the Palmyrenes in the interest of the empire.

The war of conquest must have lasted for at least a large part of a year (A. D. 268–9). How long did the Palmyrenes hold the country they had conquered? Zosimus (i. 50) says that Aurelian, after his accession (early in 270), spent some time in settling affairs in Italy and Paeonia, and then 'was purposing to make war on the Palmyrenes, who by this time were masters of the inhabitants of Egypt, and of all the East as far (westward) as Ancyra in Galatia'. Aurelian probably set out on his expedition to the East in 271, captured Zenobia and received the surrender of Palmyra in the spring of 272, and, on the renewed revolt at Palmyra, destroyed that city in the spring of 273.[1] At what stage in the war did he recover possession of Egypt? Zosimus does not tell us. Vopiscus says that Egypt was reconquered for Aurelian by the future emperor Probus,[2] but gives no date. The most probable date seems to be

The *insidiae Timagenis* by which he perished must mean the fight near Babylon. What pretext, if any, Zenobia put forward to justify her occupation of Egypt, we do not know; but if there was any disturbance in the country which might be represented as calling for her interference, no record of it has come down to us; and Probus evidently regarded the invasion as an act of war against Rome, though Claudius subsequently found it convenient to recognize the Palmyrene as legitimate governor of Egypt in his name.

The last sentence of Trebell. Poll., 'Aegyptii vero . . . verba iurantes', must be taken to mean that the Egyptians submitted to Vaballathus, accepting him, however, not as an independent ruler, but as viceregent of the Roman emperor Claudius.

1 Bury on Gibbon, i. 462.

2 *Vita Probi* 5. 9 '(Probus) pugnavit etiam contra Palmyrenos Odenati et Cleopatrae (i. e. Zenobiae) partibus Aegyptum defendentes, primo feliciter, postea temere, ut paene caperetur; sed postea refectis viribus Aegyptum et orientis maximam partem in Aureliani potestatem redegit'. The earlier part of this passage (as Mommsen has noted) suspiciously resembles the account of the conquest of Egypt by the Palmyrenes in 268–9. In that war another Probus had fought against the Palmyrenes in Egypt; and according to Zosimus's account, it might be said of him that he had fought 'primo feliciter, postea temere, ut caperetur'. It seems probable, therefore, that Vopiscus has erroneously taken as referring to the more famous Probus something that he had read about the doings of the other. The statement which follows, that the future emperor Probus reconquered Egypt for Aurelian, may none the less be correct; but the evidence is open to suspicion.

Mommsen (ii, p. 108) says, 'Egypt was already, *at the close of the year* 270, brought back to the empire . . . by Probus'; and he adds, 'The determination of the date depends on the fact that the usurpation-coins of Vaballathus cease entirely in the fifth year of his Egyptian reign' (by which must be understood the fifth year from the death of his father Odaenathus, not from his acquisition of Egypt), 'i. e. Aug. 29, 270—Aug. 29, 271; the fact that they are very rare speaks for the beginning of the year'. But this merely negative evidence is hardly conclusive; and the cessation of the coins may be otherwise accounted for, by the supposition that Vaballathus died in 270–1 (Schiller, i. 864).

Mommsen, *ib.*, p. 250, says, 'When Probus, the general *sent by Claudius*, at length gained the upper hand', &c. Is this a slip of the pen? Or has Mommsen, like Vopiscus, here confused the one Probus with the other? It is certain that the Roman war against the Palmyrenes did not begin till after the death of Claudius.

271; so that we may conclude that Egypt was under the dominion of the Palmyrenes for about two years.

An incident in this war of reconquest[1] is described by Eusebius (*H. E.* 7. 32), who speaks of it as occurring 'in the course of the siege of Piruchion[2] at Alexandria'. The Roman commander held one part of the city, and was blockading the Palmyrene faction (including, it would seem, the bulk of the inhabitants), who were cooped up in the other part, and were dying of hunger. The besieged Alexandrians were under the rule of a council (*βουλή*, *συνέδριον*). An influential Christian who was amongst them induced the council to grant permission to the starving non-combatants to pass the lines and go over to the Romans, and at the same time, communicating with a friend on the other side who had access to the Roman commander, obtained from the latter a promise to spare the lives of all who came over to him. By so doing, he saved from death not only the aged, the women, and the children, but also a large number of able-bodied men, who took the opportunity to escape from the blockaded quarter, disguised in women's clothes.

The Palmyrene faction was conquered for the time, but it was not yet extinguished. Even before the invasion, there had been in Egypt a party, headed by Timagenes, which sought to place the land under the rule of the Palmyrenes; and some two years after the reconquest of the country by Aurelian's force, this party (no

[1] Schiller (i. 865) speaks of the siege of Brucheion as taking place in the course of the suppression of the subsequent revolt of Firmus in 273. But against this view it may be argued (1) that we are told that Aurelian suppressed that revolt 'statim' (Vopiscus), *σὺν τάχει* (Zosimus), and this is not consistent with a prolonged blockade; and (2) Eusebius's mention of an unnamed 'Roman commander' (*τοῦ Ῥωμαίων στρατηλάτου, τὸν Ῥωμαίων στρατηγόν*) implies that Aurelian was not present in person, whereas it is stated that, in the suppression of the revolt of Firmus, Aurelian himself was in command.

[2] According to Mommsen, ii. 108, the Prucheion (Piruchion, or Brucheion) 'was no part of the city, but a locality close by the city on the side of the great oasis; Hieronymus, *vit. Hilarionis, c.* 33, 34, vol. ii, p. 32 Vall.' *Ib.*, p. 250, 'the strong castle of Prucheion in the immediate neighbourhood of the city'. Eusebius, however, was of a different opinion; for his narrative clearly implies that the place besieged was a part of the city itself—presumably one of the two parts into which the city was divided by the wall of Caracalla. The two statements may be reconciled by assuming that, in consequence of the devastation of this part of the city by Aurelian, and the subsequent dwindling of the population, the Brucheion ceased to be inhabited. It was a part of the Alexandria known to Eusebius; it was outside the Alexandria known to Jerome. Cf. Ammianus 22. 16. 15 'Alexandria, . . . Aureliano imperium agente, civilibus iurgiis ad certamina interneciva prolapsis dirutisque moenibus amisit regionis maximam partem, quae Bruchion appellabatur'. Eusebius, *Chron.*, mentions the siege of Brucheion, but puts it in the first year of Claudius, 268. Is this a mistake? Or does it refer to a distinct event which occurred at the time of the Palmyrene invasion in that year?

doubt strengthened by foreign immigrants who had settled there during the Palmyrene supremacy) once more asserted itself. About the time of the final revolt of Palmyra in 273, and probably in connexion with it, the Palmyrene faction in Egypt rose in insurrection, under the lead of a rich Egyptian merchant named Firmus,[1] who called in the Blemmyes [2] and Saracens as his allies. Aurelian, shortly after his return from Palmyra, proceeded to Egypt in person, promptly suppressed the insurrection, and inflicted punishment on Alexandria.[3] But he was unable to expel the Blemmyes, or at any rate, to prevent their return; and they continued to hold a large part of Upper Egypt until driven out by the emperor Probus in A.D. 279.[4]

[1] Vopiscus, *Vita Aurelian.* 32 'Firmus quidam extitit, qui sibi Aegyptum sine insignibus imperii, quasi ut esset civitas libera, vindicavit. (As to *civitas libera* cf. the *συνέδριον* spoken of by Eusebius in his account of the siege of Brucheion.) Ad quem continuo Aurelianus revertit (from Europe, shortly after his return from Palmyra in 273). Nec illic defuit felicitas solita; nam Aegyptum statim recepit.' Vopiscus xxix, *Vita Firmi*, 2–6: 'Firmum, qui Aureliani temporibus Aegyptum occupaverat. . . . Illum et purpura usum et percussa moneta Augustum esse vocitatum. . . . (Firmus), Zenobiae amicus et socius, qui Alexandriam Aegyptiorum incitatus furore pervasit, et quem Aurelianus . . . contrivit. . . . Idem et cum Blemmyis societatem maximam tenuit et cum Saracenis. . . . Hic ergo contra Aurelianum sumpsit imperium ad defendendas partes quae supererant Zenobiae. Sed Aureliano de Thraciis redeunte superatus est.' *Ib.*, c. 5, dispatch of Aurelian: 'Firmum etiam, latronem Aegyptium, barbaricis motibus (*sc.* of Blemmyes and Saracens) aestuantem, et feminei propudii (*sc.* Zenobiae) reliquias colligentem, . . . fugavimus, obsedimus, cruciavimus, et occidimus.'

Mommsen, *Rom. Emp.*, ii. 111, n. 1, and 251, n. 1, rejects the evidence of Vopiscus concerning Firmus as worthless; and he says that 'the so-called description of the life of Firmus is nothing else than the sadly disfigured catastrophe of Prucheion' (i.e. the reconquest of the country by Probus for Aurelian at an early stage of the war against Zenobia). Vopiscus is not a Thucydides; but it is difficult to believe that he can have created *ex nihilo* the story of this insurrection. What motive could he or his informant have for such audacious lying? Moreover, Mommsen ignores the corroborative evidence of Zosimus, who speaks of the suppression of a revolt in Egypt by Aurelian at the time in question. Zos. 1. 61 (Aurelian destroyed Palmyra), *σὺν τάχει δὲ καὶ Ἀλεξανδρέας στασιάσαντας καὶ πρὸς ἀπόστασιν ἰδόντας παραστησάμενος, θρίαμβον εἰς τὴν Ῥώμην εἰσαγαγὼν κ.τ.λ.*

[2] The Blemmyes lived in the mountain country to the south-east of Egypt. They harried Egypt with frequent raids from this time onward to the Arab conquest.

[3] We are told that he destroyed all buildings in the Brucheion that might harbour insurgents, and increased the dues paid to Rome by the Egyptians. *Vita Aurel.* 45. 1. Zosimus 1. 61.

[4] Mommsen, ii, 250–1. To complete the list of the calamities of Egypt during the third century, I quote from Mommsen (*ib.*): 'Under the government of Diocletian, we do not know why or wherefore, as well the native Egyptians as the burgesses of Alexandria rose in revolt against the existing government. . . . The revolt lasted from three to four years, the towns Busiris in the Delta and Coptos not far from Thebes were destroyed by the troops of the government, and ultimately under the leading of Diocletian in person in the spring of 297 the

It appears, then, that it is impossible to find any time to which the prophecy of Trismegistus could refer, except the time of the Palmyrene occupation of Egypt; and that the events of that time—i. e. of the five years 268–73—correspond exactly with the indications given in the prophecy.

We are told that the invading army, 70,000 in number, was composed of Palmyrenes, Syrians, 'and barbarians'. These barbarians were, no doubt, contingents sent by countries subject or allied to Zenobia, and adventurers attracted by the prospect of pay and plunder. Among them were certainly Saraceni (Bedouin Arabs), probably Armenians, perhaps Iberians, and possibly Persians.[1] A patriotic Egyptian might naturally enough describe a body thus composed by the contemptuous phrase 'Scythes aut Indus aut aliquis talis de vicina barbaria'. It should be remembered that the trade-route between Egypt and India traversed the Red Sea, and consequently the inhabitants of the southern coast-lands of the Red Sea—Arabes Eudaemones and Axomitae, and perhaps Blemmyes also—were, from the point of view of an Egyptian, neighbours of the Indians;[2] while the Armenians, Iberians, and Persians were neighbours of the Scythians. Moreover, the conquest of the country would probably give occasion for a large influx of Arab and other immigrants in addition to the armed forces; and if to these we add the hordes of the Blemmyes pouring in over the

capital was reduced after an eight months' siege.' This, however, cannot be the event referred to in the prophecy; for there was at this time no fresh invasion of *alienigenae*.

[1] During the siege of Palmyra in 272, Zenobia was expecting succour from Persia. Letter of Zenobia in Vopiscus, *Vita Aurelian.* 27: 'Nobis Persarum auxilia non desunt, quae iam speramus; pro nobis sunt Saraceni, pro nobis Armenii.' Letter of Aurelian in Trebell. Poll. *Trig. Tyrann.* 30. 7: 'Possum adserere tanto apud Orientales et Aegyptiorum populos timori mulierem fuisse, ut se non Arabes, non Saraceni, non Armenii commoverent.' Vopiscus, *Vita Aurelian.* 33, describing Aurelian's triumph at Rome after his conquest of Palmyra, mentions the attendance of deputations from the Blemmyes, Axomitae (Abyssinians), Arabes Eudaemones, Indi, Bactrani, Hiberi, Saraceni, Persae. It is implied that all these races had been so far concerned in or affected by the struggle, that they found it expedient to show respect to the conqueror; and with the exception of the Indi, all the nations named may have given some support to Zenobia. Cf. the hyperbolical encomium quoted in *Vita Aurelian.* 41. 9: '(Aurelianus) Persas ... fudit, fugavit, oppressit: illum Saraceni, Blemmyes, Axomitae, Bactrani, Seres (!), Hiberi, Albani, Armenii, populi etiam Indorum veluti praesentem paene venerati sunt deum.'

[2] In Josephus, *Bell. Jud.* 2. 385, Agrippa describes Egypt as ὅμορος τῆς Ἰνδικῆς. In a Coptic document, quoted by E. O. Winstedt in *Classical Quarterly*, July, 1909, p. 218, the Axomitae, the Adulitae, the Homeritae (of south-west Arabia), and other dwellers in that region (including a tribe which Mr. Winstedt identifies with the Blemmyes) are called Indians.

southern frontier, there is quite enough to account for the words 'Alienigenis terram istam complentibus'.

The loss of life caused by war and insurrection during these five years, and by the famine and disease that war brought with it, must have been enormous; and scenes such as those described by Dionysius a few years earlier must have recurred again and again. It might well be said that 'the land was filled with corpses', and 'the waters were polluted with blood', and even (if we make some allowance for a prophet's rhetoric) that 'the dead were far more in number than the survivors'.

The inhabitants were divided into two factions, the one siding with the Palmyrenes, and the other opposing them. Thus the horrors of civil war were added to those of foreign invasion; 'Egypt itself was infected with yet worse plagues' than those inflicted by the barbarian invader, and 'set an example of cruelty to the world'.

And lastly, the national religion was dying out. As we have already seen, the power which Christianity had acquired by A.D. 260, and its rapid growth from that time onward, were enough to give a worshipper of the gods of Egypt cause to anticipate the total defeat and overthrow of his religion; and the violent disturbance of native traditions caused by the shock of the Palmyrene invasion must have further promoted that general abandonment of the old cults which was already in progress. The invaders and immigrants, who at this time 'filled the land', were doubtless worshippers of many different gods,[1] but all of them alike must have been strangers to the national religion of Egypt, and little disposed to venerate its rites. The Palmyrene rulers, if they did not directly promote the spread of the new faith, were at any rate not hostile to it;[2] and a devout Egyptian might well feel, when his land fell under their dominion, that Egypt was forsaken by the gods, and that the national religion, already much impaired by the encroachments of Christianity, was now indeed doomed to perish.

[1] There must have been Christians among them. Harnack, *Mission und Ausbreitung des Chr.*, p. 440: 'It is established that before 190 A.D. Christianity was strong in Edessa and the vicinity, and that (soon after the year 201, or even earlier?) the royal family of Edessa had gone over to the Church.' (Edessa was one of the principal cities within the dominion of Zenobia.) In the kingdom of Armenia, Christianity was the officially established religion by the beginning of the fourth century: Harnack, *ib.*, p. 472; Euseb. *H. E.* 9. 8. 2.

[2] Paulus of Samosata, the bishop of Antioch described in Euseb. *H. E.* 7. 30, is said to have been favoured by Zenobia. Harnack, *ib.*, p. 430. On the other hand, the Pagan Longinus was one of her counsellors. The Palmyrene invaders may perhaps have plundered temples, or confiscated temple endowments.

I think then that we may take it as established that the prophecy in chs. 24–6 of the *Asclepius* was written under the impression produced by the Palmyrene invasion of Egypt and the events connected with it. And as there is in the prophecy no hint that the foreigner will be expelled or dispossessed, and it seems to be assumed that his occupation of the land will be permanent ('inhabitabit Aegyptum'), it may be inferred that the passage was written either before the reconquest of the country for Aurelian in 271, or at any rate, before the final suppression of the Palmyrene faction in 273. The writing of the prophecy then (with the exception of two sentences added after A.D. 353) must be assigned to the years 268–73.

It remains to be considered whether *Asclepius* III as a whole is of the same date. It is conceivable that the prophecy might have been inserted into an already existing document. But as ch. 26, which is closely connected with the preceding predictions, passes on without a break into the main current of the treatise, I do not think this hypothesis can be admitted. It is also conceivable that different parts of the prophecy itself might be of different dates—i.e. that the prediction of the extinction of the national religion (in chs. 25 and 26) might have formed part of an *Ascl.* III which was in existence before 268, and that the references to the Palmyrene invasion ('Alienigenis enim . . . videbitur alienus', if my rearrangement of the sentences is accepted) might have been subsequently inserted in 268–73. But against this it may be said, first, that the latter passage, if not absolutely needed for continuity, at any rate fits perfectly with its context, and supplies a cause for that decay of religion of which the writer goes on to speak; and secondly, that, since we have already found reason to think the writer's conviction of the impending doom of the national religion could hardly have arisen before A.D. 260, the dates of the two portions of the prophecy could in any case be separated by no more than a few years at most. I conclude therefore that this hypothesis also must be rejected, and consequently, that the Greek original of *Ascl.* III as a whole was written in A.D. 268–73.

Circumstances of the writer of ASCLEPIUS III. The author of *Ascl.* III must have been an Egyptian by race; he regards Egypt as his country, and his Hellenic education has not diminished the intensity of his national patriotism (ch. 24 b). Seeing that he localizes the cult of the god Asclepius (ch. 37) and the ancient cult of the Egyptian kings (ch. 27 d) at Arsinoe-Crocodilopolis, it seems probable that he resided in or near the Fayum. His keen interest in the national temple-cults, and his grief at the prospect of their suppression, suggest that he may have been an Egyptian priest. His approval of marriage (ch. 21) makes it unlikely that he was a member of a monastic brotherhood such as that to which the writer of *Ascl.* I presumably belonged. He shows a less unworldly disposition than that writer; he values the mundane benefits which the temple-gods confer; and his hearty love and admiration of the material universe (ch. 25) seems hardly consistent with the *contemptus mundi*, and aspiration to escape from the body, which his principles required him to profess. We may imagine him then to have been a priest attached to the temple of one of the local deities of the Fayum; and we may suppose that he had assimilated the Hermetic doctrine without ceasing to discharge his priestly functions and to take his part in social life, and that he found in that doctrine a justification of the worship in which his interests centred, and a means of defending it against the attacks of the Christians.

Date of the composite Λόγος τέλειος. The Greek original of the Latin *Asclepius* as a whole was known to Lactantius, under the title Λόγος τέλειος, about A.D. 310. The redactor who joined together the Greek *Ascl.* I, *Ascl.* II, and *Ascl.* III to make a single dialogue must therefore have done his work at some time between A.D. 270 and 310. But *Corp.* IX announces itself as a sequel to the Λόγος τέλειος; and if, as seems probable, this title was given only to the composite document, and not to any of its component parts before they were joined together,[1] the redactor's work must have been done before *Corp.* IX was written. We may conjecture then that the Λόγος τέλειος was compiled about A.D. 280–90, and that *Corp.* IX was written about A.D. 290–300. It is possible that the same person who compiled the composite Λόγος τέλειος proceeded to write *Corp.* IX as a sequel to it; if so, the date of both might be about A.D. 290.

It may be doubted whether the concluding prayer of the *Asclepius* (41 b) formed part of the original *Ascl.* III (written about A.D. 270), or was added by the compiler of the Λόγος τέλειος. This prayer has been borrowed by the sorcerer who wrote one of the magic incantations preserved in the *Papyrus Mimaut* (Reitzenstein, *Poimandres*, pp. 151, 156). Wessely (*Denkschr. der kais. Akad. der Wissensch.*

[1] See notes on *Ascl. Lat. init.*

xxxvi, Wien, 1888, Abth. 2, p. 36) says that the *Papyrus Mimaut* was written in the fourth century A.D.; but Reitzenstein (*Arch. für Rel.*, 1904, p. 397) is inclined to assign it to the third century rather than the fourth. Thus the prayer may have been first written about A.D. 270–90, and borrowed by a sorcerer a little later.

Date of the Latin translation. The Latin *Asclepius* has come down to us among the works of Apuleius. Now Apuleius was born about A.D. 125, and wrote under Antoninus Pius and Marcus Aurelius, i. e. before A.D. 180. If, therefore, any good reason could be shown for attributing the translation to Apuleius, it would be necessary to reconsider our conclusion as to the date of the Greek original of *Ascl.* III.

Hildebrand (*Apuleii Opera*, 1842, vol. i, pp. xlix ff.) discusses the question whether the translation was written by Apuleius, dealing with it mainly on the ground of Latin style, and states his conclusion thus: 'hunc dialogum ab Apuleio confectum esse persuasum mihi quidem est. . . . Demonstrasse mihi videor, dicendi rationem quae in hoc dialogo cognoscitur ab Apuleiana non esse alienam, ac pluribus locis cum ea concordare. Inde quamquam colligi per se nequit Apuleium revera huius dialogi esse auctorem, tamen cum accedat manuscriptorum auctoritas, qui optimi quique Apuleii nomen in fronte habent, non intelligo cur nostro scriptori hic liber abiudicandus sit.'

But the incompetence shown by our translator[1] is a strong argument against identifying him with Apuleius, who would surely have done the work better. Moreover, the method of translation in the *Asclepius* differs widely (as Hildebrand admits) from that of Apuleius in his version of the Aristotelian *De mundo*.[2] In the *De mundo*, the translation is free and fluent; in the *Asclepius*, it is literal[3] and clumsy.

It may be considered certain that Augustine, who knew our translation, did not suppose it to have been written by Apuleius. In quoting from it,[4] he says 'Huius Aegyptii verba, *sicut in nostram*

[1] The quality of his work as a translator can be judged from the fragments of the Greek original which have been preserved, as well as from the numerous difficulties in the text which can only be explained on the assumption that he has misunderstood or inadequately rendered the meaning of the Greek.

[2] That the translator of the *De mundo* was Apuleius is attested by Augustine, *Civ. Dei* 4. 2: 'quae . . . Apuleius breviter stringit in eo libello quem de mundo scripsit.'

[3] e.g. we find a Greek genitive (gen. abs. or gen. after a comparative) represented by a Latin genitive, where Latin grammar demands an ablative.

[4] *Civ. Dei* 8. 23 ff.

linguam interpretata sunt, ponam', without naming the translator. But in the same passage Augustine speaks of Apuleius, and contrasts the view of Apuleius with that of 'Hermes' (i. e. that expressed in the *Asclepius*); if therefore he had thought the Latin *Asclepius* to be the work of Apuleius, he would have mentioned the fact—as he does elsewhere in the case of the *De mundo.*

I can therefore see no reason to dissent from Goldbacher,[1] who says, 'Asclepi dialogum . . . iniuria inter Apulei opera referri mihi persuasum (est)'. After speaking of the passage in Augustine, Goldbacher continues, 'Quo cum accedant aliae res gravissimae, quas Bernaysius[2] . . . exposuit, haud quemquam fore putaverim, qui hunc dialogum ab Apuleio e Graeco in Latinum conversum esse existimet'. The Latin *Asclepius* was, no doubt, attributed to Apuleius in the archetype of our MSS.: but that attribution was an error. Consequently, there is nothing to set against the conclusion at which we have already arrived, namely, that the Greek original of *Ascl.* III was written in A. D. 268–73; and the Latin translation must have been written at some time after that date.

The *terminus ante quem* for the Latin translation is given by the fact that Augustine quotes from it in his *De civ. Dei,* about A.D. 413–26. If the references to penal laws against Pagan worship are contemporary with the rest of the Latin text,[3] the translation must be dated between 353 and 426. If those references have been subsequently interpolated into the Latin text, any date between about 280 and 426 is possible for the translation.

Who was the translator? That question cannot be answered with certainty; but the only man known to us to whom the translation might with some probability be attributed is C. Marius Victorinus. Hieronymus *Vir. illustr.* 101: 'Victorinus, natione Afer, Romae sub Constantio principe (A. D. 350–61) rhetoricam

[1] *Apulei Opuscula quae sunt de Philosophia,* 1876, p. xv.

[2] Bernays, *Gesammelte Abhandlungen,* vol. i, p. 340: 'tritt hierdurch zu der inneren Unmöglichkeit, das ein stilistischer Künstler mit gelehrte Bildung wie Apuleius der Urheber unserer holperichten und zuweilen schnitzerhaften Uebersetzung sei, noch ein äusseres Anzeichen, da Lactantius eine durch Apuleius' Namen empfohlene Arbeit schwerlich unbenutzt gelassen hätte.'

[3] Boissier, *La Fin du Paganisme,* ii, p. 229, speaking of the Latin *Asclepius,* says: 'L'ouvrage original était composé avant la victoire du christianisme, mais le traducteur, qui écrivait pendant que l'ancien culte était persécuté, n'a pu s'empêcher d'ajouter au texte quelques allusions à ces lois, . . . qui proscrivent la piété et en font un crime capital.' The two references to penal laws are certainly of later date than the rest of the prophecy; and it is probable that one of them at least was inserted by the translator.

docuit, et in extrema senectute Christi se tradens fidei[1] scripsit adversus Arium libros more dialectico valde obscuros, qui nisi ab eruditis non intelleguntur, et commentarios in apostolum' (*sc.* Paulum).[2] Hieron. *Praef. comm. in Ep. ad. Galat.*: 'Non quia ignorem C. Marium Victorinum, qui Romae me puero[3] rhetoricam docuit, edidisse commentarios in apostolum, sed quod occupatus ille eruditione saecularium litterarum omnino sanctas ignoraverit.'[4] Hieron. *Chron.*, ad ann. 2370:[5] 'Victorinus rhetor et Donatus grammaticus praeceptor meus Romae insignes habentur; e quibus Victorinus etiam statuam in foro Traiani meruit.' August. *Confess.* 8. 2: 'legisse me quosdam libros Platonicorum, quos Victorinus quondam rhetor urbis Romae, quem Christianum defunctum esse audieram, in Latinam linguam transtulisset.[6] . . . Ille doctissimus

[1] The conversion of Victorinus to Christianity is spoken of at greater length by Augustine, *Confess.* 8. 1–5; and we are there told that he was already a Christian at the time when, by Julian's edict (A. D. 362), Christians were prohibited from holding posts as public teachers. He may have been converted about A. D. 356.

[2] Christian writings ascribed to Victorinus are printed in Migne, *Patr. Lat.* 8. 993–1310. Those which may be accepted as certainly authentic are (1) *De generatione Verbi divini, ad Candidum Arianum*; (2) *IV libri contra Arium*; (3) *De ὁμοουσίῳ recipiendo*; (4) *Hymni tres de Trinitate*; (5) *Commentarii in Apostolum* (*Gal.*, *Philipp.*, and *Eph.*). In these writings Victorinus maintains the Nicaean ὁμοούσιον-formula in opposition to the Arians. Their contents are discussed by Gore, *C. Marius Victorinus Afer*, in Smith and Wace, *Dict. of Christian Biography*, 1887; G. Geiger, *C. Marius Victorinus, ein neuplatonischer Philosoph*, Landshut, 1888; and R. Schmid, *Marius Victorinus Rhetor und seine Beziehungen zu Augustin*, Kiel, 1895. Victorinus's treatment of the question is a blending of Christian doctrine with a Neoplatonic system closely resembling that of Plotinus. (In that respect his position is similar to that of Augustine about the time of his baptism, A. D. 387. See P. Alfaric, *L'évolution intellectuelle de S. Augustin*, i. 515–27: 'S'il (*sc.* Augustin) était mort après avoir rédigé les *Soliloques* (written at Cassiciacum, A. D. 387) ou le traité *De la quantité de l'âme* (written at Rome, A. D. 387–8), on ne le considérerait que comme un Néoplatonicien convaincu, plus ou moins teinté de Christianisme.')

These writings are rightly described by Jerome as *valde obscuri.* It is, as Gore says, 'matter of astonishment that one who had Victorinus's reputation as a rhetorician should have been so wholly incapable of giving clear expression to his thought'; and since his style, as shown in his Christian treatises, so little deserves the reward of a public statue, we must suppose that he gained that honour rather by his influence as a teacher of the Plotinian philosophy, and perhaps by personal qualities which won for him the respect and affection of his senatorial pupils.

[3] Jerome was born about A. D. 340; *me puero* therefore agrees with the other evidence, which indicates that Victorinus held the post of *rhetor* at Rome during the years A. D. 350–62.

[4] Victorinus's frequent quotations from the Bible in his Christian writings show that, at the time when he wrote them, he was not '*wholly* ignorant of sacred literature'; but he lived to old age in the study of Pagan philosophy before he became a Christian.

[5] A. D. 354, Teuffel; A. D. 358, Gore.

[6] Alfaric, *L'évolution intell. de S. Augustin*, i. 374 sqq., says that among the *libri Platonicorum*, of which Latin translations by Victorinus were read by

senex et omnium liberalium doctrinarum peritissimus, quique philosophorum tam multa legerat et diiudicaverat, doctor tot nobilium senatorum, qui etiam ob insigne praeclari magisterii . . . statuam in Romano foro meruerat et acceperat.' Boethius, *In Isagogen Porphyrii*, Brandt (*Editionis primae*), 1. 1: 'id quod Victorinus, orator sui temporis ferme doctissimus, Porphyrii per Isagogen, id est per introductionem in Aristotelis Categorias, dicitur transtulisse.' Boethius *ib.* (*Editionis secundae*), 5. 24: 'huius libri seriem primo quidem ab rhetore Victorino, post vero a nobis Latina oratione conversam.' Boethius found Victorinus's translation of the *Isagoge* to be inaccurate,[1] and for that reason wrote a fresh translation of it for himself.

Victorinus then, in the course of a long life which ended soon after A. D. 362, was much occupied in the study of Pagan philosophy; he translated into Latin (presumably for the use of his pupils at Rome) 'books of Platonists', among which were some of the writings of Plotinus and Porphyry; and his translations were read by Augustine, who, since he did not read Greek, was dependent on them for his knowledge of Neoplatonism. Such a man would almost necessarily become acquainted with the Hermetic Λόγος τέλειος, and might very well think it worth while to translate a document which contained doctrines so closely related to those of his Neoplatonic creed; and the fact, made known to us by Boethius, that he sometimes misunderstood his Greek original, and made mistakes in translation, adds to the probability of the hypothesis that our Latin *Asclepius* is his work. There is no positive evidence that it was so; but it may safely be said that the translator was either Victorinus or some one who had much in common with him.

Augustine, were probably Plotinus, *Enn.* i, 2, 3, 4, 6; iii, 2; and v, 1; and perhaps also Porphyry, *De reditu animae ad Deum* and *Sententiae ad intellegibilia ducentes* (Ἀφορμαὶ πρὸς τὰ νοητά).

[1] e. g. Boeth. *ib.* 2. 6: *quod Victorinus scilicet intellexisse minus videtur: nam quod Porphyrius* ἀνάλογον *dixit, id est proportionale, ille* (*sc. Victorinus*) *sic accepit quasi* ἄλογον *diceret, id est irrationale.*

THE *HERMETICA* IN THE *ANTHOLOGIUM* OF STOBAEUS

JOANNES STOBAEUS, at some date not far from A. D. 500,[1] compiled a large collection of extracts from Pagan Greek writers. The collection was divided into four books, and was entitled ἐκλογῶν, ἀποφθεγμάτων, ὑποθηκῶν βιβλία τέσσαρα. It seems to have been made up by putting together the contents of earlier collections of extracts, and adding to them passages extracted by Stobaeus himself from books which he had read. He arranged the extracts in chapters according to subjects, and placed at the head of each chapter a superscription stating the subject of the extracts contained in it.

Photius (*c.* A. D. 850) read this *anthologium* in a copy differing little from the original as written by Stobaeus; and in his *Bibliotheca*, p. 112 a, 16 ff., he describes it as a work in two volumes (τεύχη), consisting of four books (βιβλία), and gives the superscriptions of the 208 chapters into which the four books were divided.

Our MSS. of Stobaeus are derived from an archetype closely resembling the MS. used by Photius, if not from that very MS. But at some time not far from A. D. 1000, the two volumes of which the archetype consisted were separated; the two parts passed into different hands, and thenceforward, each of them was copied and recopied separately. Hence the first part (Bks. I and II) has come down to us in one set of MSS., and the second part (Bks. III and IV) in another set of MSS. The two parts consequently came to be edited separately, as if they were two different works; and the editors gave to Bks. I and II the title *Eclogae physicae et ethicae*, and to Bks. III and IV the title *Florilegium*. Either the term *Eclogae* or the term *Florilegium* might serve as a title for the whole (each extract, whether in Bks. I and II or in Bks. III and IV, is an

[1] The latest writer quoted by Stobaeus is the Neoplatonist Hierocles, a contemporary of Proclus (A. D. 410–85). The fact that Stobaeus ignores all Christian writings makes it improbable that he lived much later than Hierocles (Christ, *Gesch. der gr. Litt.*, p. 848).

ecloga, and the four Books are collectively a *florilegium*); but the assignment of the title *Eclogae* to one part of the collection and the title *Florilegium* to the other is arbitrary and groundless, and Wachsmuth and Hense, the latest editors, have rightly rejected these titles. In their edition, what had hitherto been called *Stob. Ecl.* is called *Stobaei Anthologii libri duo priores*, and what had hitherto been called *Stob. Floril.* is called *Stobaei Anthologii libri duo posteriores*; and their correction will doubtless be henceforth accepted by all scholars.

After the separation of the two parts of the *Anthologium*, the first part (Bks. I and II) was reduced to smaller compass by an epitomator, who had a preference for philosophical writings. He copied out almost in full Bk. I, chs. 1–30; but from that point onward as far as his handiwork can be traced (i. e. down to Bk. II, ch. 9), he omitted nearly all extracts except those from Plato, Aristotle, Archytas, Porphyry, and (fortunately for our present purpose) Hermes. The last part of his *epitome* (Bk. II, chs. 10–46) is lost. It is only this mutilated *epitome* of Bks. I and II, and not the full text of these two books as read by Photius, that has come down to us in the MSS. of Stobaeus. Some of the missing passages have, however, been recovered from a *gnomologium*, partially preserved in a cod. Laurentianus (fourteenth century), the compiler of which borrowed largely from the four Books of Stobaeus at a time when they were still complete; and from that source Wachsmuth has been able to print the text of Stob., Bk. II, chs. 15, 31, 33, and 46.

Stobaeus seems to have got his *Hermetica* from (1) a collection of Ἑρμοῦ λόγοι πρὸς Τάτ; (2) a collection of Ἑρμοῦ λόγοι πρὸς Ἀσκληπιόν; (3) a collection of Ἑρμοῦ λόγοι πρὸς Ἄμμωνα; and (4) a collection of Ἑρμοῦ λόγοι Ἴσιδος πρὸς Ὧρον. The total number of Hermetic excerpts in his *Anthologium* is forty-two,[1] if we include *Exc.* [XXVIII] and [XXIX], and count as separate excerpts the two parts of Stob. 1. 41. 1 (which I call *Exc.* II B and *Exc.* XI), and the two parts of Stob. 1. 41. 6 (which I call *Exc.* IV B and *Exc.* III). Of these, ten are taken from *libelli* which have been preserved in the *Corpus Hermeticum* (*Corp.* II, IV, and X); and one (Stob. 4. 52. 47)

[1] There may perhaps have been some more *Hermetica* in chs. 10–46 of Bk. II, which are missing in our MSS. of Stobaeus; ch. 11, for instance, the superscription of which was Ὅτι χρὴ σέβειν τὸ θεῖον, may very likely have contained some Hermetic extracts.

is an extract from the Greek original of the Latin *Asclepius*. The remaining thirty-one are given in the present edition as Excerpts I, II A, II B, III, IV A, IV B, V—[XXIX]. I have arranged and numbered them, grouping together the *Hermes to Tat* Excerpts (I–XI), the *Hermes to Ammon* Excerpts (XII–XVII), the Excerpts in which there is no indication of the pupil's name (XVIII–XXII), and the *Isis to Horus* Excerpts (XXIII–XXVII); and I have divided the longer Excerpts into numbered sections.

Twenty-seven of these 'Excerpts', as well as all the ten extracts from *libelli* which are extant in the *Corpus*, occur in Stob. Bk. I, and two (*Exc.* I and *Exc.* XVIII) in what remains of Stob. Bk. II. There are only two Hermetic extracts (*Exc.* II A and *Exc.* XXVII) in Stob. Bk. III, and only one (the extract from the original of *Ascl. Lat.*) in Stob. Bk. IV. But by an accident which must have happened before the separation of the two parts of the *Anthologium*, the leaf of Bk. II on which *Exc.* I was written in the archetype was, together with two other leaves, shifted from its place, and inserted in Bk. IV; and the contents of these three leaves have consequently been transmitted as part of the text of Bk. IV. For the text of *Exc.* I therefore we are dependent on the MSS. of Bks. III and IV (the so-called *Florilegium*), and not on the MSS. of Bks. I and II (the so-called *Eclogae*). Wachsmuth has now restored these misplaced passages to their original positions in Bk. II, chs. 1, 4, and 2.

Of the MSS. which contain the extant remains of Stob. Bks. I and II, two only need be taken into account, as all the other MSS. are derived from them. These two are

cod. Farnesinus (F), fourteenth century;
cod. Parisinus (P), fifteenth century.

F and P then are our only sources for the text of all the Hermetic extracts except four. F is much the better of the two; but the evidence of P also is of some value. There are in P numerous corrections by two or three later hands; but these corrections (marked P^2) are conjectural.

The other four Hermetic extracts (viz. *Excerpts* I, II A, XXVII, and the fragment of the Greek original of *Ascl. Lat.*) have come down to us in the MSS. of Stob. Bks. III and IV. Of these, the earliest and best is cod. Vindobonensis (S), written soon after A.D. 1000. The *editio princeps* of Bks. III and IV by Trincavelli

(Tr.) faithfully reproduces the text of a cod. Marcianus (fifteenth or sixteenth century) closely related to S, if not wholly derived from it, and is useful chiefly as a substitute for certain missing parts of S. There are two other MSS. which are of some value, as representing a text of different descent, viz. cod. Escurialensis (M), *c.* A. D. 1100, and cod. Parisinus (A), fourteenth century. Hense has also made use of the cod. Laurentianus (L) mentioned above, which contains extracts from Stob. Bks. III and IV as well as from Stob. Bks. I and II, and of another *gnomologium*, preserved in cod. Bruxellensis (Br.), fourteenth or fifteenth century, which likewise contains borrowings from Stob. Thus our sources for these four Hermetic extracts are S (with Tr.) and MA, supplemented by L and Br.

The chief printed editions of Stobaeus are the following:—

Bks. I and II: Canter (*ed. princeps*), Antwerp, 1575; Heeren, 1792–1801; Gaisford, 1850; Meineke, 1860–3; and Wachsmuth, Berlin, 1884.

Bks. III and IV: Trincavelli (*ed. princeps*), Venice, 1535–6; Gesner, 1st edition 1543, 2nd ed. 1549, 3rd ed. 1559; Gaisford, 1822; Meineke, 1860–3; and Hense, Berlin, 1894–1912.

Wachsmuth and Hense have investigated the MSS. far more thoroughly than any of the previous editors; and the edition of the *Anthologium* of Stobaeus which they have produced by their combined labours supersedes all earlier publications of the text. Their edition is my sole authority for the readings of the MSS. in the Hermetic extracts.

In my text of the *Excerpts*, and in my textual notes on them, I have used the same notation as in the *libelli* of the *Corpus Hermeticum*.[1] The readings of P^2 I have treated as conjectures.

The task which Wachsmuth and Hense have set themselves in their edition, and which they may be considered to have accomplished, as far as its accomplishment is possible, is that of restoring the text of the *Anthologium* as written by Stobaeus.[2] There remains

[1] In passages based on F and P alone, I have sometimes marked as P a reading of that MS. which I have inferred from a statement of Wachsmuth concerning F, or vice versa.

[2] Wachsmuth, vol. i, p. xxxi, says: 'Ex his igitur codicibus recognovi Stobaei verba; cui fundamento certo speramus fore ut iam multi suam emendandi operam superstruant; nam permultos philosophorum potissimum locos etiamnunc medicina egere nemo me melius intellegit. Quodsi in hac editione non improbabiliter emendationem incohatam esse confido, id prorsus debetur amicitiae Hermanni Useneri. . . . In afferendis verbis eorum scriptorum, quorum libri ipsi aetatem tulerunt (e.g. in the extracts from *libelli* which are extant in the *Corpus*

the further task of emending the more or less corrupt text of each extract as read by Stobaeus, and so recovering, as nearly as may be, the original text of the passage as written by its author. For the performance of this task also, Wachsmuth and Hense have given valuable help; but much remains to be done; and it is this that, as far as the Hermetic extracts are concerned, I have aimed at doing in the present edition. Starting from the text of the archetype of the Stobaeus-MSS., as reconstructed by Wachsmuth and Hense, I have tried to discover or guess, firstly, what words the author of each Hermetic passage wrote, and secondly, what he meant by the words he wrote. When one has concluded that a phrase is corrupt, the best way to deal with it is usually to attack the second of these two problems first; i. e. to infer from the context, and from parallels in other writings, what the author must have meant, and thence, if possible, to infer what words he used to express his meaning. In a matter of this kind, complete success is unattainable; but there is much that can be done, and it is to be hoped that the process of recovering the thoughts of the Hermetic writers, to which I have tried to contribute, will be taken up and carried farther by others.

Hermeticum), hanc normam tenui, ut non ea quae ipsos scripsisse probabile esset, sed ea tantum quae in exemplo suo Stobaeus legisse videretur restituerem.'

Hense, vol. iii, p. lxv, says: 'Mihi quid in hac editione propositum fuerit, iam puto elucere. Ad librorum manuscriptorum fidem reversus id operam dedi, ut et ordo eclogarum et contextus ab illorum archetypo abesset quam proxime.'

TESTIMONIA

The earliest evidence for the existence of writings of similar character to our religious and philosophic *Hermetica* is that of Athenagoras, A. D. 177–80. But that evidence is not quite free from doubt; for the statement which Athenagoras apparently ascribes to Hermes, viz. that he was descended from 'gods' who were men (i. e. from men who were held to have become gods after death), might have occurred in any sort of document the teaching of which was attributed to Hermes, e. g. in a dialogue dealing with astrology or magic.

Tertullian, *De an.* 33, quotes a passage from a writing of the same kind as our *Hermetica*. His obscure style makes it difficult to be sure what he means in the three passages in which he mentions Hermes Trismegistus without quoting him; but it may be inferred from *Adv. Valentin.* 15 and *De an.* 2 that he knew of writings of which Hermes was supposed to have been the author, and which contained doctrines resembling those of Greek philosophers, and especially those of Plato. His evidence proves then that in A. D. 207–13 some *Hermetica* similar to ours were in existence, and were accessible to Christian readers; but it does not prove that at that time any of the extant *Hermetica* had yet been written.

In the writings of Clement of Alexandria,[1] there is no mention of any Greek *Hermetica*. What is to be inferred from this fact? Large parts of Clement's *Stromateis* are occupied with discussions of the relation between Greek philosophy and 'barbarian' philosophy (by which he usually means the teaching of Moses and the Hebrew prophets). He seeks to prove that the Greek philosophers were later in date than the Hebrew writers, and 'stole' from them. If he had known our *Hermetica*, and believed them to contain the

[1] Clement taught in the Catechetical School of Alexandria from about A. D. 190 to 202 or 203. At the latter date he quitted Egypt; he was residing in Asia Minor about A. D. 211, and he died in or about A. D. 216. The dates of his chief writings are probably *Protrept.*, A. D. 190–200; *Strom.* i–iv, *Paedag.*, *Strom.* v–vii (in this order), A. D. 203–16 (Harnack, *Chronol.*, ii. 3–18).

teachings of an ancient Egyptian sage, he could not possibly have omitted to speak of them in the course of these discussions. He could not have failed to notice the resemblance between the Hermetic doctrines and those of Plato; and he would have said, as others did, 'Plato borrowed from Hermes'.[1] His silence concerning the Greek *Hermetica* can therefore be accounted for only by assuming either that they were not yet in existence; or that they were in existence but unknown to him; or that he knew them, but knew them to be of recent date, and therefore had no more reason to speak of them than of other recent writings. Now the hypothesis that no such writings were yet in existence is excluded by the evidence of Clement's contemporary, Tertullian, who quotes from a philosophic *Hermeticum*; and if writings of this character were known to Tertullian, it is most unlikely that they were unknown to Clement, whose work as a teacher in Alexandria must have brought him into contact with thinkers of all kinds that were to be found in Egypt, Pagans as well as Christians. It is therefore probable that Clement knew of the existence of some Greek *Hermetica* of the same character as ours, but knew them to have been composed by men of his own time, and therefore to have no bearing on the question what sort of doctrines were taught in Egypt before the beginnings of Greek philosophy.

Arguments *ex silentio* are often of little weight; but in the case of Clement, the force of this argument will, I think, be evident to any one who reads the following passages. *Strom.* 1. 15. 66–73 (a long list of Greek philosophers who were either barbarian by race or pupils of barbarian teachers). *Strom.* 1. 21. 134 (an item in a long list of Pagan prophets): ἀλλὰ καὶ τῶν παρ' Αἰγυπτίοις ἀνθρώπων ποτέ, γενομένων δὲ ἀνθρωπίνῃ δόξῃ θεῶν, Ἑρμῆς τε ὁ Θηβαῖος καὶ Ἀσκληπιὸς ὁ Μεμφίτης.[2] *Strom.* 5. 5. 29: καὶ ὅλως ὁ Πυθαγόρας καὶ οἱ ἀπ' αὐτοῦ σὺν καὶ Πλάτωνι μάλιστα τῶν ἄλλων φιλοσόφων

[1] Moreover, if he had read our *Hermetica* with attention, he would have noticed in *Corp.* I and elsewhere certain resemblances to *Genesis*, and would consequently have added, as some others did, 'Hermes borrowed from Moses'. But we have no proof that any of the *extant* Hermetica were in existence in Clement's time.

[2] The conjunction of these two names might perhaps be thought to indicate a knowledge of dialogues in which Hermes and Asclepius were speakers. But Clement cannot here have been thinking of any writings resembling our *Hermetica.* The context shows that he means by 'prophets' men who predict future events (see § 135); but in our *Hermetica* Hermes does not speak as a prophet in that sense (except in the 'Prophecy' in *Ascl. Lat.* iii, and in a few *obiter dicta* elsewhere).

σφόδρα τῷ νομοθέτῃ ὡμίλησαν (i. e. read the Books of Moses), ὡς ἔστιν ἐξ αὐτῶν συμβαλέσθαι τῶν δογμάτων. Why did not Clement mention the much more evident resemblance between the doctrines of Plato and the Greek *Hermetica*? *Strom.* 5. 12. 78: Clement quotes Pl. *Tim.* 28 C (τὸν γὰρ πατέρα . . . ἐξειπεῖν ἀδύνατον), and says that Plato got this thought from *Exod.* xix, where it is shown that God is ἀόρατος καὶ ἄρρητος; and he compares some verses of Orpheus, who, he says, got the same truth from the same source. Why did he not rather adduce Herm. *ap.* Stob. *Exc.* I (which is much more like the passage in Plato), if it was known to him? *Strom.* 6. 4. 35–8: εὕροιμεν δ' ἂν καὶ ἄλλο μαρτύριον εἰς βεβαίωσιν τοῦ τὰ κάλλιστα τῶν δογμάτων τοὺς ἀρίστους τῶν φιλοσόφων παρ' ἡμῶν (i. e. from our Hebrew Scriptures) σφετερισαμένους ὡς ἴδια αὐχεῖν, τὸ καὶ παρὰ τῶν ἄλλων βαρβάρων (i. e. from others besides the Hebrews) ἀπηνθίσθαι τῶν εἰς ἑκάστην αἵρεσιν συντεινόντων τινά, μάλιστα δὲ Αἰγυπτίων τά τε ἄλλα καὶ τὸ περὶ τὴν μετενσωμάτωσιν τῆς ψυχῆς δόγμα.[1] μετίασι γὰρ οἰκείαν τινὰ φιλοσοφίαν Αἰγύπτιοι· αὐτίκα τοῦτο ἐμφαίνει μάλιστα ἡ ἱεροπρεπὴς αὐτῶν θρησκεία. (Here follows a list of the different orders of Egyptian priests, and of the subjects dealt with in the 'Books of Hermes' which priests of the several orders were required to study.) δύο μὲν οὖν καὶ τεσσαράκοντα αἱ πάνυ ἀναγκαῖαι τῷ Ἑρμῇ γεγόνασι βίβλοι· ὧν τὰς μὲν τριάκοντα ἕξ, τὴν πᾶσαν Αἰγυπτίων περιεχούσας φιλοσοφίαν, οἱ προειρημένοι (priests) ἐκμανθάνουσι, τὰς δὲ λοιπὰς ἓξ οἱ παστοφόροι, ἰατρικὰς οὔσας . . . καὶ τὰ μὲν Αἰγυπτίων, ὡς ἐν βραχεῖ φάναι, τοιαῦτα· Ἰνδῶν δὲ ἡ φιλοσοφία κ.τ.λ. Clement evidently means by 'Books of Hermes' books written in the Egyptian language, and ascribed to Thoth, which were used in the schools of the priests. He must have got the

[1] Clement thought that the doctrine of *metensomatosis*, taught by Pythagoras and Plato, was of Egyptian origin. But there is no need to suppose that he was here thinking of Greek *Hermetica* in which that doctrine was taught; he may have got his mistaken notion from Herodotus 2. 123. The notion that the Egyptians believed in *metensomatosis* was probably a false inference drawn by Greeks, in or before the time of Herodotus, from the observed fact that Egyptians reverenced certain kinds of animals, and thought it wicked to kill and eat them. A Greek, knowing that Pythagoreans abstained from the flesh of animals, would be apt to think that the reason for these strange Egyptian usages must be the same that Pythagoreans gave for their abstention, viz. that they believed that a human soul was or might be incarnated in the animal. Moreover, Greeks would be told by Egyptians that in each of the individual animals worshipped in the temple-cults (e. g. the Apis-bull) some god (e. g. Osiris), who had once reigned as a king on earth, was incarnated; and this might easily seem to the Greek visitor to be merely a particular instance of the doctrine of *metensomatosis* taught by Pythagoras.

list of books, directly or indirectly, from a native Egyptian; and he knew nothing about their contents, beyond the meagre information which he gives at second hand. If he had believed any Greek *Hermetica* known to him to be translations or paraphrases of ancient and genuine 'books of Hermes', he would necessarily have referred to them here, as the best evidence accessible to him and his readers concerning the character of the 'Egyptian philosophy', instead of talking of the books studied by the priests, books which he could not read, and about which he knew very little.

We must conclude then that Clement either did not know of any Greek *Hermetica* such as ours, or else, as seems more likely, knew of some such writings (not necessarily any of those which have come down to us), but knew that they were of recent date, and that their contents could not be rightly attributed to the ancient teacher Hermes.[1]

Did Origen (A.D. 185–255) know any philosophic or religious *Hermetica*? No quotations from or references to Hermetic documents have been found in his writings. Origen, like his teacher and predecessor Clement, repeatedly asserts that Moses and the Hebrew prophets were prior in time to the Greek philosophers, and says that, as far as there was any borrowing, it must have been the Greeks that borrowed from the Hebrews; but he does not discuss this question at length and in detail, as Clement does; and I do not know of any passages in Origen's works in which the course of his argument is such that, if he had known any Greek *Hermetica* and thought the teachings contained in them to be Egyptian and of ancient date, it would have been *necessary* for him to speak of them.[2]

[1] Clement assumed without question the authenticity of pseudonymous writings such as those ascribed to Orpheus and the Sibyl; and he would hardly have been capable of discovering the true character and date of *Hermetica* merely by examining their contents (as Casaubon did at a later time). But he may have known something about the authors of Greek *Hermetica* by direct information; indeed, it is not impossible that he was personally acquainted with some of them.

[2] There are passages in which a mention of the *Hermetica* would have been appropriate; e.g. Orig. *c. Cels.* I. 12: *οἱ μὲν Αἰγυπτίων σοφοὶ κατὰ τὰ πάτρια γράμματα πολλὰ φιλοσοφοῦσι περὶ τῶν παρ' αὐτοῖς νενομισμένων θείων* (*al.* *θεῶν*)· *οἱ δὲ ἰδιῶται, μύθους τινὰς ἀκούσαντες ὧν τοὺς λόγους* (meanings or explanations) *οὐκ ἐπίστανται, μέγα ἐπ' αὐτοῖς φρονοῦσιν.* Origen here goes on to say that the only men who know this secret wisdom of the Egyptians, and from whom it might be learnt, are the priests. (That however is merely an *obiter dictum.*)

Ib. 4. 39: 'Some think that Plato, while staying in Egypt, met Jewish philosophers (*τοῖς τὰ Ἰουδαίων φιλοσοφοῦσι*), and learnt some things from them.' That notion is not so absurd as it might seem at first sight; there were Jews in Egypt before the time of Alexander, and it is not quite impossible that some

It may however be said of Origen, with even more confidence than of Clement, that if any such writings were current in his time, he must have been aware of their existence. Origen was born and brought up in Alexandria, and lived and taught there as head of the Catechetical School (with some intermissions) from A. D. 203 to 230, after which he migrated to Palestine. He had a wide and thorough knowledge of Pagan philosophic writings, and especially of those of the Platonists, down to and including Numenius. Some have thought that he was for a time a pupil of Ammonius Saccas, and a fellow-pupil with Plotinus (who was junior to him by about eighteen years). Statements to that effect seem to have arisen out of a confusion between the Christian Origen and a Pagan Platonist of the same name. But be that as it may, the fact remains that he was living in Egypt at the same time as Ammonius Saccas and Plotinus; that he *may* have been personally acquainted with one or both of them; and that he *must* have got his Platonism from the same sources that they did, or from similar sources. Among the sources from which he got it, were any *Hermetica* included? That question we have no means of answering. There are in his writings many passages which, in the thoughts expressed, closely resemble passages in our *Hermetica*; but I have found no instances of verbal resemblance of a kind that could be held to prove direct borrowing; and the resemblances in thought prove nothing more than that both Origen and the Hermetists were familiar with Platonism.

In any case, Origen's writings are of special significance for the study of the *Hermetica*, because he lived at the very time during which we have reason to think that most of the earlier of our extant *Hermetica* were written. He was a Platonist as well as a Christian.[1] The Platonism that is to be found in his writings is intermixed with allegorical interpretations of Bible texts, but it can, for the most part, be disentangled from them without much difficulty;[2] and we

report of the Jewish account of the Creation may have reached Plato by that route, and may have been borne in mind by him (together with much else) when he was writing the *Timaeus*. But to any one who knew our *Hermetica*, and thought them to be ancient, it would have seemed much more evident that Plato had learnt some things from *them*.

[1] Just as Philo was a Platonist as well as a Jew.

[2] See, for instance, Orig. *De principiis*, I. I. 5-7, pp. 31-9 Lommatzsch (concerning the incorporeality of God and mind). That passage might, without change of a single word, have been written by a Pagan Platonist; and if it had come down to us as a *libellus* ascribed to *Hermes*, we should have found in it nothing incongruous with that ascription.

have it in a specimen of the kind of Platonism that was current in Egypt at that time, i.e. after Numenius, and before the publication of the teachings of Plotinus.

The date of the sentence concerning Hermes in Cyprian (?) *Quod idola* is so uncertain, that no inference can safely be drawn from it.

The author of the *Cohortatio ad Graecos* (probably A. D. 260–302) quotes Herm. *ap*. Stob. *Exc.* I; and if the conjecture Ἀγαθοῦ δαίμονος for Ἄκμωνος is accepted, he also knew a Hermetic dialogue in which Agathos Daimon was the teacher.

The earliest Pagan *testimonium* is that of Porphyry, who, in his *Letter to Anebo*, written in the latter part of the third century, said that he had met with some philosophic *Hermetica* (*Abammonis resp.* 8. 4 a: ἐν τοῖς συγγράμμασιν οἷς λέγεις περιτετυχηκέναι . . . τὰ μὲν γὰρ φερόμενα ὡς Ἑρμοῦ κ.τ.λ.).

It might perhaps be argued that the Greek *Hermetica* may have been for some considerable time kept secret (as is enjoined in some of them), that is, may have been passed from hand to hand within the small groups of men for whose instruction they were written, but concealed from all others; and that they may therefore have been in existence long before they became known to outsiders. But that seems improbable. Among 'seekers after God', such as were the authors of our *Hermetica* and their pupils, conversions to Christianity must have been frequent; and a Hermetist who had become a Christian would no longer have any motive for concealing the writings which he had previously held sacred. There was therefore nothing to prevent these documents from becoming widely known soon after they were written.

We find then that the external evidence agrees with and confirms the conclusion to which the internal evidence points, namely, that most of the extant *Hermetica* were written in the course of the third century after Christ, and that few of them, if any, can have been written long before A. D. 200.

That most of them, if not all, were in existence at the end of the third century, is proved by the evidence of Lactantius.

The treatise of Lactantius *De opificio dei*, his larger work *Divinae institutiones*, and his treatise *De ira dei* were written between A. D. 303 and 311.[1] The contents of the *Divinae institutiones* are

[1] See Harnack, *Chronol. der altchrist. Litt.*, ii. 415 ff., and Bardenhewer, *Patrologie*, pp. 178–80.

repeated in an abridged form, with some variations and additions, in the *Epitome div. inst.*, which was written by Lactantius some years later, perhaps about A. D. 315. For the text of Lactantius, my authority is Brandt's edition, *Corp. script. eccl. Lat.* vol. xix (1890) and vol. xxvii (1893–7).[1]

In the *De opif. dei* (*c.* A. D. 304), there is no mention of Hermes. In *Div. inst.* 2. 10. 14 f., speaking of the making of the human body by God, Lactantius mentions Hermes, together with the Stoics and Cicero, as having dealt with the subject, and adds, 'I pass over this topic now, because I have recently written a book (viz. the *De opif. dei*) about it'. But he does not there say that he made use of any Hermetic document when he was writing the *De opif. dei*; and it is possible that the Hermetic passage (probably *Corp.* V. 6) to which he refers in *Div. inst. l. c.* was not known to him until after the *De opif. dei* was finished.

Brandt, *Über die Quellen von Lactanz' Schrift De opificio dei* (*Wiener Studien* 13, 1891, pp. 255–92), tries to prove that one of the two main sources of the *De opif. dei* was a Hermetic document—probably, he thinks, the *Aphrodite*, of which Herm. *ap.* Stob. *Exc.* XXII is a fragment. His argument may be summarized as follows: 'Lactantius, throughout *De opif. dei* cc. 2–13, insists on the *beauty* of man's bodily structure even more than on its *utility*. Now that is exceptional; in most other writings on the same topic (e. g. in Cic. *Nat. deor.* 2. 133–53) the utility of the bodily organs is spoken of, but not their beauty. Lactantius must therefore have drawn from a source other than Cicero and Varro, and other than the Stoic writings of which Cicero and Varro made use. And as Lactantius in *Div. inst.* 2. 10. 13 says that Hermes had dealt with the subject, the peculiar source from which Lactantius drew in the *De opif. dei* must have been a *Hermeticum*. In that *Hermeticum*, beauty must have been spoken of side by side with utility. The only extant Hermetic passage in which the construction of the human body by God is dealt with is *Corp.* V. 6; and that', says Brandt (mistakenly, as it seems to me), 'cannot be the passage referred to in *Div. inst. l. c.*, because it speaks only of the beauty of the bodily organs, and not of their utility. The *Hermeticum*

[1] The chief MSS. of *Div. inst.* are *B*, sixth or seventh century; *R*, ninth century; *H*, tenth century; *S*, twelfth century; *P*, ninth century; *V*, tenth or eleventh century; and (for the passages quoted in Greek by Lactantius) *Sedulius*, ninth century.

of which Lactantius made use in the *De opif. dei* must therefore have been a *libellus* which is now lost; and it may very likely have been the *Aphrodite*. From it are derived those parts of the *De opif. dei* in which either the utility and the beauty of the bodily organs are spoken of together, or their beauty is spoken of alone; viz. *cap.* 2, *cap.* 5. 13, nearly the whole of *cap.* 7, much in *cap.* 8. 1–8, much in *cap.* 10, and most of *cap.* 13.'

If that were established, it might be said that a large part of the contents of a lost Hermetic *libellus* has been preserved in the *De opif. dei*. But Brandt's argument does not appear to me to be convincing.[1] Beauty as well as utility is spoken of in this connexion by Minucius Felix, *Octavius* 17. 11: 'formae nostrae pulchritudo deum fatetur artificem: . . . nihil in homine membrorum est, quod non et necessitatis causa sit et decoris.' The passages of Lact. *De opif. dei* which Brandt thinks to be of Hermetic origin are an expansion of that statement. Minucius Felix shows no knowledge of Hermetic writings. His *Octavius* was certainly known to Lactantius; and the passages in the *De opif. dei* of which Brandt speaks may have been suggested to Lactantius either by that passage of Minucius Felix, or by some Stoic treatise which was known to both of them.[2] We must conclude then that there is no evidence that anything in the *De opif. dei* of Lactantius comes from a Hermetic source. But Hermes is many times spoken of and quoted in the *Div. inst.*, and is once referred to in the *De ira dei*.

Lactantius knew of 'many' writings ascribed to Hermes that were of the same character as our *Hermetica* ('libros, et quidem multos, ad cognitionem divinarum rerum pertinentes', *Div. inst.* 1. 6. 4). He had read the Greek original of *Ascl. Lat.*, which he calls Λόγος τέλειος; and as he refers to three different parts of it (*Ascl. Lat.* I. 8; III. 24 b–26 a; *Epilogus* 41 a under that same title—*Div. inst.* 4. 6. 4; 7. 18. 4; 6. 25. 1) there can be no doubt that the compilation

[1] Brandt's conclusion is rejected by Gronau, *Poseidonios und die jüdisch-christl. Genesisexegesis*, 1914, p. 162.

[2] Gronau, *op. cit.*, p. 162, points out the resemblance between Lact. *De opif. dei* 2. 7 (*si homini ferinos dentes aut cornua aut ungues aut ungulas aut caudam aut varii coloris pilos addidisset, quis non sentiat quam turpe animal esset futurum?*) and Gregory of Nyssa, *De hominis opificio* 141 B (*εἰ . . . οὕτως δυνάμεως εἶχεν ὁ ἄνθρωπος, ὡς τῇ μὲν ὠκύτητι παρατρέχειν τὸν ἵππον, ἄτριπτον δὲ ὑπὸ στερρότητος ἔχειν τὸν πόδα, ὁπλαῖς τισιν ἢ χηλαῖς ἐρειδόμενον, κέρατα δὲ καὶ κέντρα καὶ ὄνυχας ἐν ἑαυτῷ φέρειν, . . . θηριώδης τις ἂν ἦν καὶ δυσάντητος*). A large part of the contents of Gregory's *De hom. opif.*, as Gronau has shown, must have been derived directly or indirectly from Posidonius; and a large part of the contents of Lact. *De opif. dei* may have been derived from the same source.

of that composite dialogue was already completed, and that it was known to him in a form differing little from that in which it has come down to us in the Latin translation. There is positive proof that he knew also *Corp.* XII. ii (*Div. inst.* 6. 25. 10), *Corp.* XVI (*Div. inst.* 2. 15. 7), Herm. *ap.* Stob. *Exc.* I (*Epit.* 4. 5 and *De ira dei* 11. 11), and *Exc.* II A (*Div. inst.* 2. 12. 5); and there is probably, if not certainly, a reference to *Corp.* V in *Div. inst.* 2. 10. 14. It is possible, but not certain, that *Corp.* X is referred to in *Div. inst.* 1. 11. 61, and *Corp.* IX in *Div. inst.* 2. 15. 6. Lactantius also quotes or refers to several passages in Hermetic writings which were known to him but are not now extant (*Div. inst.* 1. 6. 4; 4. 7. 3; 7. 13. 3; 1. 7. 2; 4. 8. 5; 7. 9. 11).

It may be inferred then from the evidence of Lactantius that nearly all the extant *Hermetica*,[1] as well as a considerable number of Hermetic *libelli* that are now lost, were written before A. D. 311 at the latest, and probably before A. D. 300.

From the time of Lactantius onward, the existence of religious or philosophic *Hermetica*, and the resemblance of the doctrines taught in them to those of Platonism, were widely known among the Christians. In the course of the Arian controversy of the fourth century, disputants on both sides referred to these documents. (See Marcellus of Ancyra and Ps.-Anthimus.) They were read by Didymus (A. D. 380–93), and by Cyril of Alexandria (A. D. 435–41). Augustine (A. D. 413–26) read *Ascl. Lat.* in the translation which has come down to us, but does not appear to have read any other *Hermetica*. He did not read Greek; and the Λόγος τέλειος was probably the only *Hermeticum* that had in his time been translated into Latin. Lactantius, Augustine, and Cyril took for granted the antiquity and authenticity of the *Hermetica*; and it does not appear that any doubt on that point arose among Christians thenceforward down to the time of Casaubon.

The Pagan Neoplatonists paid little attention to the *Hermetica*. Porphyry spoke of them in his *Letter to Anebo*, but there is no reference to them in any of his extant writings. The author of *Abammonis responsum* shows knowledge of them in his reply to Porphyry. Iamblichus is said by Proclus *In Tim.* 117 D to have cited a statement of 'Hermes'; and Proclus makes use of that statement to show that a certain doctrine was taught by 'the

[1] There is no proof that any of the *Isis to Horus* documents were known to Lactantius.

tradition of the Egyptians'. But with these exceptions, the *Hermetica* are ignored in Neoplatonic literature.[1] Seeing that the doctrines set forth in the Hermetic writings are closely connected with those taught by Plotinus and his successors, we might have expected the Neoplatonists to be keenly interested in these documents. Why did they neglect them, and prefer to accept as inspired scriptures the *Oracula Chaldaica* and the *Orphica*, which would seem to us far less suitable for their purpose? Probably because they knew that the attribution of the *Hermetica* to the ancient prophet Hermes was an error. Porphyry was too good a scholar and critic to be misled in this matter; he must have seen them to be what in fact they are, namely, documents written by Egyptian Platonists in his own time, or very shortly before it. The author of *Abammonis resp.* knew at least that they were not written by Hermes (that is implied by his phrase τὰ φερόμενα ὡς Ἑρμοῦ, 8. 4 a, which he may have taken over from Porphyry); though he mistakenly thought that they correctly reproduced the meaning of doctrines taught in books written by ancient Egyptian priests. The later Neoplatonists, if they were aware that the *Hermetica* were of recent date, would have little reason to refer to them; for all that was acceptable to them in the teaching of the *Hermetica* was to be found more fully worked out in Plotinus.

Some of our *Hermetica* were known to the alchemist Zosimus (A. D. 300–50?). Stobaeus, *c.* A. D. 500, had access to the whole mass of *Hermetica*, and made copious extracts from them. About the same time Fulgentius happened to meet with *Corp.* I; and the Λόγος τέλειος, and at least one other *Hermeticum*, were read by Lydus, *c.* A. D. 550. From that time onward the Greek *Hermetica*

[1] Malalas (Migne, tom. 97, col. 512) says that in A. D. 367–83 Θέων ὁ σοφώτατος φιλόσοφος (that is, no doubt, Theon of Alexandria, the father of Hypatia) ἐδίδασκε καὶ ἡρμήνευε τὰ ἀστρονομικά, καὶ τὰ Ἑρμοῦ τοῦ τρισμεγίστου συγγράμματα, καὶ τὰ Ὀρφέως. (See note on Herm. *ap.* Stob. *Exc.* [XXIX].) But we are not told that 'the writings of Hermes Trismegistus' on which Theon commented were philosophic or religious; they may have been writings on astrology or some other kind of 'occult' science.

Cyril of Alexandria (Migne, tom. 76, col. 548 B; see *Testim.*) says that some man, whom he does not name, 'composed at Athens the fifteen books entitled Ἑρμαικά'; and he quotes from the first book of that work (which seems to have been written in the form of a dialogue) a passage, put into the mouth of an Egyptian priest, in which it is said that Hermes was the founder of Egyptian civilization and science. But we do not know how long before Cyril's time the work called *Hermaica* was written; we know nothing about its contents except the extract quoted by Cyril; and in that extract nothing is said of Hermes as a teacher of philosophy or religion.

seem to have been little known and seldom read, until they were brought to light again in the revival of learning which took place at Constantinople under the lead of Psellus. In that interval (A.D. 550–1050) most of them perished; and (apart from extracts and quoted fragments) those only survived which were, at some date unknown to us, put together to form the *Corpus Hermeticum*. The Latin *Asclepius* may have owed its preservation to the fact that it was mistakenly ascribed to Apuleius, and handed down together with his writings.

But while the reputation of Hermes as a philosopher and teacher of religion dwindled in Europe, it lasted on undiminished in another region. The centre in which it most strongly maintained itself, and from which it spread afresh, was Harran,[1] an important city in northern Mesopotamia, situated on the main road between Babylonia and the West. When Christianity, in the course of the fourth century, became the dominant religion in the neighbouring regions of the Roman empire, the majority of the Harranians refused to be converted, and continued to worship in their heathen temples as before;[2] so that Harran came to be spoken of by Christians as a 'city of Pagans' (Ἑλλήνων πόλις).[3] When Syria and Mesopotamia were invaded and conquered by the Arabs (A.D. 633–43), a large part of the Harranians were still Pagans; and under Moslem rule they adhered to their religion with the same pertinacity. We hear little of them for nearly two centuries; but they emerge into light again in the reign of the Abbasid caliph al-Ma'mún (son of Hárún ar-Rashíd). In A.D. 830, al-Mamun, setting out from Bagdad, his

[1] The evidence of Arabic writers concerning the Pagans of Harran has been collected and very thoroughly discussed by D. Chwolsohn, *Die Ssabier und der Ssabismus*, St. Petersburg, 1856 (a work in two volumes, which contains large stores of material, exasperatingly ill arranged). Chwolsohn's main conclusions are accepted by more recent authorities, e.g. Carra de Vaux, *Avicenne*, 1900, pp. 61–71, and E. G. Browne, *Lit. Hist. of Persia*, 1902, pp. 302–6. (It is very likely that my transliterations of Arabic names will be found inaccurate or inconsistent. In writing the names I usually omit diacritical marks, except at the first place where each name occurs.)

[2] Northern Mesopotamia was the chief battle-ground in the long series of wars between the Romans and the Persians. It was therefore of great importance to the Roman government to retain the loyalty and goodwill of the inhabitants of Harran, which was one of the chief strongholds of that region; and it may have been for this reason that Paganism was connived at there when it was forcibly suppressed in other places.

[3] Chwolsohn, i, pp. 303 and 438. (He refers to *Acta Conciliorum*, t. ix, ed. Paris, 1644, pp. 34 and 37.) Procopius, *Bell. Pers.* 2. 13, says that in A.D. 540 the Persian king Chosroes showed exceptional favour to Harran 'because its inhabitants were mostly Pagans' (ὅτι δὴ οἱ πλεῖστοι οὐ Χριστιανοί, ἀλλὰ δόξης τῆς παλαιᾶς τυγχάνουσιν ὄντες).

capital, on a campaign against the Byzantines, passed through Harran,[1] and noticing, among those who there presented themselves before him, some people strangely dressed, asked them, 'To which of the peoples protected by law[2] do you belong?' They answered, 'We are Harranians'. 'Are you Christians?' 'No.' 'Jews?' 'No.' 'Magians?' 'No.' 'Have you a holy scripture or a prophet?' To this question they gave an evasive answer. 'You are infidels and idolaters then', said the caliph, 'and it is permitted to shed your blood. If you have not, by the time when I return from my campaign, become either Moslems or adherents of one of the religions recognized in the Koran, I will extirpate you to a man.'[3] Under this threat, many of them, in outward profession

[1] This story is quoted by an-Nadím, *Fihrist* (A. D. 987), Bk. 9, cap. 2 (Chwolsohn, ii, pp. 14 sqq.), from a book called *The disclosure of the doctrine of the Harranians, who are in our time known under the name of Ṣabians,* which was written (probably *c.* A. D. 900) by a Christian named Abú-Júsuf Abshaa'al-Qathíí.

[2] According to Mohammedan law, 'Peoples of a Book', i. e. non-Moslems whose religion was founded on a scripture containing truths revealed by God to one whom Moslems recognized as a prophet, were entitled to toleration, on condition of payment of a fixed tax. This law was based on certain passages in the Koran in which Jews, Christians, and 'Sabians' were favourably spoken of. (*Koran* 2. 59: 'The believers, be they Jews, Christians, or Sabians, if only they believe in God and the last day, and do what is right, will find reward in the presence of their Lord; neither fear nor sorrow shall torment them.' See also *Koran* 5. 73 and 22. 17.)

According to Chwolsohn, the people called 'Sabians' by Mohammed were the Mandaeans, a sect residing in the marsh-lands near the head of the Persian Gulf. (See Brandt, *Mandäische Religion,* 1889, and *Mandäische Schriften,* 1893.) These people called themselves Mandaeans, a name derived from *mandâ,* which means ἡ γνῶσις; but their neighbours called them Ṣabians, a Semitic word meaning 'people who wash themselves', or 'baptists'. A few thousands of Mandaeans were still to be found in the neighbourhood of Basra in the nineteenth century; but they are probably by this time almost, if not quite, extinct. The sect may have been in existence as early as the second century A. D. Their scriptures are written in an Aramaic dialect, and contain a mixture of Babylonian, Jewish, and Zoroastrian ingredients, slightly modified by Christian influence. These writings, in the form in which they are now extant, may perhaps have been composed about the seventh or eighth century A. D., but were doubtless compiled out of documents of earlier date. In the ninth century, so little was generally known about this sect, that it was possible for the Pagans of Harran, who had no connexion whatever with them, to claim the name of Sabians without fear of contradiction, and thereby to get for themselves a legal status similar to that of Jews, Christians, and Magians (i. e. Zoroastrians) under Moslem rule.

There is, however, some doubt whether Chwolsohn was right in identifying the 'Sabians' of the Koran with the Mandaeans. De Goeje (*Actes du 6me congrès international des Orientalistes,* Pt. ii, section 1, Leyden, 1885, p. 289) says that the people called Sabians in the Koran were 'a Christian sect strongly impregnated with Pagan elements, the Elkasaites, who existed in Babylonia, and who, while having much resemblance to the Mandaeans, are not identical with them, as Chwolsohn thought they were'. But whether the sect denoted by the name Sabians before A. D. 830 was that of the Mandaeans or some other, it was in any case a sect with which the Pagans of Harran had nothing to do.

[3] Ameer Ali, *A Short History of the Saracens,* 1921, p. 274, says: 'In his

at least, went over to Islam, and others to Christianity. But some of them held out, and consulted a Moslem jurist, who, in return for a large fee, gave them this advice: 'When al-Mamun comes back, say to him, "We are Sabians"; for that is the name of a religion of which God speaks in the Koran.' Al-Mamun never came back (he died two or three years later, while still at war); but the Harranian Pagans acted on the advice of the jurist. They called themselves Sabians, and were thenceforward officially recognized by the Moslem government as entitled to toleration under that name.[1]

But in order to make good their claim to this legal status, it was necessary for them not merely to call themselves by a new name, but also to put forward a Book on which it could be said that their religion was based, and a Prophet or Prophets to whom the contents of that Book had been revealed. The sacred books of the sect which had hitherto been denoted by the name Sabians were probably unknown and inaccessible at Harran; and if they had been known there, it would have been evident that those books had nothing to do with the religion of the Harranians. It was therefore

sagacious tolerance, Mamun recognized no distinction of creed or race; all his subjects were declared eligible for public offices, and every religious distinction was effaced. . . . Liberty of conscience and freedom of worship had been always enjoyed by non-Moslems under the Islamic *régime*; any occasional variation in this policy was due to the peculiar temperament of some local governor. Under Mamun, however, the liberality towards other religions was large-hearted and exemplary.' This seems hardly consistent with the story told above. But the discrepancy is to be explained in this way; Mamun's tolerance of non-Moslem religions was genuine as far as it went, but it extended only to those religions which were recognized by law.

Carra de Vaux, *Avicenne*, p. 30, tells a story (reported by Masudi) of a group of Manichaeans arrested and put to death as heretics by Mamun's order.

[1] Hence, from A. D. 830 onward, the name Sabians had a new and different meaning. Some Arabic writers were aware that there were people 'in the marshes' near the head of the Persian Gulf who were called Sabians; but the name was henceforward more commonly used to denote the Harranian Pagans. And since these were the only Pagans with whom the Moslem Arabs of the Bagdad region were directly or personally acquainted, the name Sabians came to be habitually used (from about A. D. 1000 onward) to signify Pagan polytheists or 'star-worshippers' in general. (The Arabs were inclined to think that all Pagans were star-worshippers; this notion they probably got by generalizing from what was known to them about the local cults of Harran.) An Arabic writer says, for instance, that Constantine was converted from 'Sabism' to Christianity; and another says that Pharaoh was a 'Sabian'.

The name 'Sabians' then had three different meanings. (1) Before A. D. 830, it meant the Mandaeans, or some other sect of similar character. (2) From A. D. 830 to about 1000, it meant the Harranian Pagans. (3) From about A. D. 1000 onward, it meant Pagans in general, of all places and all times. But most Moslems were not aware of these distinctions; and it is often difficult to decide whether an Arabic writer is using the name in the second or the third sense.

necessary to choose some other writings, which would serve the purpose better.

Now the religion of the Pagan Harranians of the ninth century was the indigenous religion of heathen Syria, more or less modified by Hellenic and perhaps by Persian and other influences. For the mass of the people, religion must have been, there as elsewhere, a matter of cult far more than of doctrine. Of the local cults of Harran some descriptions have come down to us in Arabic writings; but these are mostly vague and meagre, and some of the more definite statements are evidently due either to gross misunderstanding or to malicious invention. We learn from them, however, that there was at Harran a temple of the Moon-god Sîn,[1] and that among the deities worshipped by the Harranians the seven planet-gods were prominent; and there are also descriptions of a cult[2] which seems to show some resemblances to Mithraism.

But there were among the Pagans of Harran learned men who were well acquainted with Greek philosophy; and in those times Greek philosophy meant a religious philosophy founded on Plato and Aristotle—that is, in one word, Neoplatonism.[3] The religion

[1] The cult of the Moon-god Sin must have been firmly rooted at Harran ever since what may be vaguely called 'the time of Abraham'; and this Harranian cult was in high repute under the Roman empire. We hear of it, for instance, in the time of Caracalla; and in A.D. 363, Julian, halting at Harran on his way to war against the Persians, worshipped in the temple of the Moon-god (Amm. Marcell. 23. 3. 1). This worship seems to have continued without intermission under Moslem rule, until the temple of Sin at Harran was finally destroyed, either in A.D. 1032, or according to another authority, at the time of the Tartar invasion in A.D. 1230.

[2] We are told (Chwolsohn, i. 496, 513, and ii. 319–64) that in one of the temples at Harran was worshipped a god named *Shemâl*, 'the lord of the genii (or daemons), the highest God, the God of the mysteries'; and that underneath this temple there were crypts, in which were idols, and in which mysteries were celebrated. Boys were admitted into a crypt, and were there terrified by weird sounds and voices. Women were excluded from the rites. There was a sacrament in which cakes were eaten (we are told that these cakes were made of meal mixed with the blood of a slaughtered baby; but that is doubtless a calumny, like similar accusations against the early Christians; and in both cases alike, the accusation may have been based on a too literal interpretation of symbolic actions and metaphorical phrases used in the ritual); and there was also a sacramental drinking of some liquid out of seven cups.

In this description there is much that reminds one of Mithraism. It must have been in some region not far distant from northern Mesopotamia that the Mithraic cult which spread over the Roman empire first took shape; and after it had spread westward, it might have been brought back to that same region and revived there by Roman soldiers and merchants.

[3] Roughly speaking, it may be said that the Neoplatonists made use of Aristotle as their chief authority for logic, but Plato for philosophy in the stricter sense. But they habitually tried to explain away the differences between Plato and Aristotle, and to show that one and the same philosophy was taught by both. The

of these men must have been related to that of the uneducated mass of worshippers of Sin and the planet-gods in the same sort of way that the religion of Iamblichus was related to that of uneducated Pagans in the Roman empire. And when the Pagan Harranians were required, on pain of death or merciless persecution, to name a Book on which their religion was based, it would necessarily fall to the learned men among them to find an answer to the question, and to speak on behalf of the whole body. They might have said with some truth that their religion (i. e. the philosophic religion of these learned men themselves, though not the religion of the mass of Pagans) was based on Plato's Dialogues; but they preferred to name what were believed to be the more ancient writings from which Plato had derived his wisdom—that is, the Greek *Hermetica*. 'Our Scriptures', they must have said to the Moslem officials, 'are the Hermetic writings; and our Prophets are those whose teaching is recorded in those writings, namely, Hermes Trismegistus, and his teacher Agathos Daimon.'[1]

The Moslems did not set any fixed limit to the number of 'prophets' acknowledged by them (among those whom they recognized as prophets were Adam, Seth, Enoch, Noah, Abraham, &c., and we are told by one authority that the total number of prophets amounted to 313, Chw. i. 626); and there might be no great difficulty in adding two more to the list; but it would be easier to get these two accepted if they could be identified with prophets already well known to Mohammedans. It was probably for this reason, and at the suggestion of Harranians, that Agathodaimon came to be identified with Seth son of Adam, and Hermes with Idrís, whom Moslems held to be identical with Enoch (*Koran* 19. 57 and 21. 85).

The fact that the Harranian Pagans, when required to name a Scripture, chose the *Hermetica*, proves that in A. D. 830 a collection of *Hermetica* was known and read in Syria; and the fact that they named Agathodaimon as a prophet together with Hermes proves that their collection included some dialogues (now lost, and known

'Aristotle' of the Arabs meant Aristotle as interpreted by Neoplatonic commentators, and included, *inter alia*, the so-called *Theologia of Aristotle*, which is a paraphrase of Plotinus.

[1] An Arabic writer, who died in A. D. 898, describes the doctrine of the 'Sabians' (i. e. Harranian Pagans) as a philosophy, and says that their teachers are Agathodaimon and Hermes, and that they have a writing of the latter (Chwolsohn, i. 196).

to us only by a few fragments and references), in which Hermes was the pupil, and Agathos Daimon the teacher. It may be inferred from the occurrence of the names Tat, Asclepius, and Ammon in conjunction with that of Hermes in Arabic writings,[1] that these Harranians had in their possession Hermetic *libelli* in which the pupils were so named; and among these were presumably some that are now lost, as well as those which have come down to us.

In the ninth century, Hermetic documents were most likely known to some scholars at Harran in the original Greek; but the *Hermetica* had probably been translated into Syriac long before that time, and were doubtless usually read in Syriac by Harranians and their neighbours at Edessa and elsewhere.[2]

[1] 'Tat son of Hermes' is repeatedly spoken of in Arabic writings; and Asclepius is mentioned as one of the prophets recognized by the Harranians (Chwolsohn, i. 229, ii. 523, &c.), and is called a follower of Hermes (Chw., i. 243). Of Ammon there is at least one mention; al-Qifthi, A. D. 1248 (Chw., i, p. 787, and ii, p. 533), wrote a book containing, *inter alia*, biographies of Idris (i. e. Hermes), *King Amon*, Asclepius, Empedocles, and Plato.

[2] We know from Ephraim Syrus (see *Testim.*) that *Hermetica* were known in Syria *c.* A. D. 365, and that at that time a Syrian who probably did not read Greek had some knowledge of their contents (but perhaps only at second hand). De Boer, *Geschichte der Philosophie im Islam*, 1901, says that translation of profane writings from Greek into Syriac began in or about the fourth century. In the fifth century, there was in Edessa a flourishing academy, furnished with a large library of Greek and Syriac books (Chw., i. 172–4), and there can be little doubt that among those books were the *Hermetica*. We hear of works of Aristotle translated into Syriac in the fifth century (Chw., *ib.*). The school at Edessa, having become infected with Nestorianism, was suppressed by the emperor Zeno in A. D. 489 (C. de Vaux, *Avicenne*, p. 41), and there seems to have been thenceforward no one central seat of learning for Syrian Christians; but the work which had been centred at Edessa was still carried on in other Syrian cities (e. g. at Nisibis). Meanwhile, Harran was the chief seat of learning for Syrian Pagans, and continued to be so down to the end of the ninth century. The Arabs got their knowledge of Greek science and philosophy partly from Syrian Christians (orthodox, Monophysite, and Nestorian), but (from A. D. 830 onward, if not before) partly also from Syrian Pagans of Harran.

Masudi (*ap.* C. de Vaux, *Avic.*, p. 38) reports from a lost work of al-Farabi (who died in A. D. 950) the following sketch of the history of learning: 'The chief seat of human knowledge was transferred from Athens to Alexandria in Egypt. The emperor Augustus, after destroying Cleopatra, established two centres of teaching, Alexandria and Rome; the emperor Theodosius put a stop to the teaching at Rome, and brought back the whole of it to Alexandria. Under Omar son of Abd-el-Aziz (A. D. 705–10), the chief seat of teaching was transferred from Alexandria to Antioch; and later on, in the reign of Mutawakkil, it was transferred to Harran.' The caliph Mutawakkil, 'the Nero of the Arabs', was a drunken debauchee, and a rigidly orthodox Mohammedan (Ameer Ali, *Short Hist.*, p. 288). Why is he, of all people, mentioned in this connexion? Apparently because it was in his reign (A. D. 847–61) that the learning of the Harranians first became widely known among the Arabs. From the time of the Arab conquest until A. D. 830, the date at which their religion was granted legal recognition, the learned Pagans of Harran had been forced to remain in concealment.

From that time onward, for about two centuries (A. D. 850–1050), we hear much of the Harranian Pagans. Some of them rose to positions of high eminence, and played an important part in the intellectual life of Bagdad.

The most famous of them is Thabit ibn Qurra,[1] who was born A. D. 835, and died *c.* A. D. 901. During the earlier part of his life he resided in Harran, as a money-changer. But shortly before A. D. 872, there was a schism in the community[2] of 'Sabians', as the Harranian Pagans were now called; Thabit's party was defeated, and he was expelled, and forced to leave the city. After some years he settled at Bagdad, was introduced to the caliph, and attained to high favour at court; and he got the government to recognize him and his companions as a separate and independent community of 'Sabians', with a head of its own.[3] Most of the learned men of Harran probably migrated to Bagdad and joined him. The community thus established at Bagdad must have been a sort of school of Pagan Neoplatonism,[4] in some respects analogous to the school of Pagan Neoplatonism which had flourished at Athens until suppressed by Justinian about 350 years before.[5] But there

[1] Chw., i. 546 sqq., 482 sqq., 177, 516, &c.

[2] When the Harranian Pagans obtained a legal status, it would necessarily follow that they became, like Jews and Christians under Moslem rule, a definitely organized body, with an official head or primate, through whom the government would communicate with them.

We are not told what the quarrel was about; but it may be conjectured that the learned men and students of philosophy differed so widely in their views from the uneducated vulgar, that it was found impossible for the two parties to act together.

[3] Chwolsohn (i. 488) says that this Sabian community in Bagdad was probably founded under the caliph Mutadhid, A. D. 892–902.

[4] One result of the migration must have been to diminish the importance of cult for these men, and increase the comparative importance of philosophy. The Harranians who had migrated to Bagdad might still take a theoretic interest in the local cults of Harran, but would henceforth be debarred from practising them; and there were in Bagdad no Pagan temples in which they could worship.

Masudi calls the Sabians (meaning the Harranian Pagans of Bagdad) 'eclectic philosophers' (Chw., i. 543); and Avicenna (†1037) speaks of them as having a philosophic theory of religion (Chw., i. 225).

[5] We are not told that any of the teachers and students who quitted Athens at that time settled at Harran; but it seems not unlikely that some of them did so. The heads of the Athenian schools who, when forbidden to teach at Athens, migrated to Persia in the expectation of finding ideal happiness there under the rule of a philosopher-king, and returned disillusioned a few years later, most likely passed through Harran, both on their way to Persia and on their way back. A. Stahr, in Smith's *Dict. Biogr.*, says that Damascius, who was the professor of Platonic philosophy at Athens when Justinian closed the Pagan schools there in A. D. 529, and who was one of those that migrated to Persia, 'appears to have returned to the West' in A. D. 533; but that 'we have no further particulars of the life of Damascius; we only know that he did not, after his return, found any

were doubtless considerable differences; and one of the differences was this, that whereas the Neoplatonists of Athens had ignored the *Hermetica*, the Harranian Neoplatonists of Bagdad recognized the *Hermetica* as their 'Scripture', and regarded the Hermetic teaching as the source whence their philosophy was derived.

Thabit lived on at Bagdad, occupied in teaching and writing, till his death about A. D. 901. We are told that towards the end of his life he was forced to become a Mohammedan; but his sons remained Pagans, and the Pagan community which he had founded in Bagdad continued its activities after his death.

Thabit's work as a writer extended over a wide range of subjects. He is spoken of as highly distinguished in mathematics, astronomy, logic, and medicine, as well as in philosophy. His mother tongue was Syriac, but he knew also the Greek and Arabic languages. Barhebraeus says that Thabit wrote about 150 works (translations included?) in Arabic, and 16 in Syriac. He translated Greek writings, and corrected earlier translations made by others; and according to an Arabic writer, it was said that 'no one would have been able to get any benefit from the philosophic writings of the Greeks, if they had not had Thabit's translations'.[1] Among his writings on philosophy and logic were the following: a *Tractatus de argumento Socrati ascripto*; a *Tractatus de solutione mysteriorum in Platonis Republica obviorum*; a translation of part of Proclus's commentary on the *Aurea carmina* of Pythagoras; an *Isagoge in logicam*; commentaries on Aristotle's Περὶ ἑρμηνείας, and a part of Aristotle's Φυσικὴ ἀκρόασις; extracts from Arist. *Cat.*, *Anal. prior.*, and Περὶ ἑρμ. But he was, like the Neoplatonists of Athens, interested in Pagan cults (more especially, perhaps, but not exclusively, the local cults of Harran), as well as in philosophy; and under this head may be placed the following titles given in the list of his writings: *Liber de lege et canonibus* (ceremonial law and ritual?) *ethnicorum*; *Liber de sepultura mortuorum*; *Liber de confirmatione religionis ethnicorum*; *Liber de munditie et immunditie*;

school either at Athens or at any other place'. Is it certain that Damascius did not settle down at Harran and teach there? He could hardly find any other place where he would feel so much at home as in that 'city of Pagans'. He was a Syrian, born at Damascus, whence he got his name.

[1] This agrees with what is said by Carra de Vaux, *Avicenne*, p. 37: 'Translation into Arabic began under al-Mansur (A. D. 753–74); but philosophic writings were not at first included among those translated, and the Arabs had not sufficiently perfect translations of Aristotle into Arabic until the time of al-Farabi, at the beginning of the fourth century of the *Hegira*' (i. e. *c.* A. D. 912, a few years after Thabit's death).

Liber de animalibus sacrificio aptis; *Liber de horis precum*; *Liber de lectionibus recitandis ad singulas septem planetas accommodatis*; *Liber de poenitentia et deprecatione*; *Liber de religione Sabiorum*; *Liber de legibus* (ceremonial regulations?) *Hermetis, et de orationibus* (prayers) *quibus utuntur ethnici.* From one of these books (perhaps the *Liber de confirmatione religionis ethnicorum*) must have been taken the following passage, quoted from Thabit by Barhebraeus: 'We are the heirs and propagators of Paganism. . . . Happy is he who, for the sake of Paganism, bears the burden (of persecution?) with firm hope. Who else have civilized the world, and built the cities, if not the nobles and kings of Paganism? Who else have set in order the harbours and the rivers? And who else have taught the hidden wisdom? To whom else has the Deity revealed itself,[1] given oracles, and told about the future, if not to the famous men among the Pagans? The Pagans have made known all this. They have discovered the art of healing the soul; they have also made known the art of healing the body. They have filled the earth with settled forms of government, and with wisdom, which is the highest good. Without Paganism the world would be empty and miserable.'

Thabit seems to have also dabbled in the 'occult' sciences; he paid some attention to astrology, and he wrote a commentary on a 'Book of Hermes' concerning *doctrina litterarum et nominum*—probably a treatise dealing with the cryptic significance or magic efficacy of letters of the alphabet.[2] It is very likely that he knew other books also on such subjects (e.g. on astrology) that were ascribed to Hermes, and assumed them to have been written by the same Hermes that he believed to be the author of the teachings recorded in the religious and philosophic *Hermetica*.

Thabit's son Sinán was a physician of high repute, and held by official appointment the position of head of the medical profession in Bagdad. Masudi says that Sinan had a thorough knowledge of mathematics, astronomy, logic, metaphysic, and the philosophic systems of Socrates, Plato, and Aristotle.

Chwolsohn (i. 577 sqq.) enumerates twenty-seven other 'Sabians' (i.e. Harranian Pagans) whose names have been preserved. One of them, al-Battáni (A.D. 877–918), was a famous astronomer and mathematician, known as Albategnus in medieval Europe.[3]

[1] An audacious thing to write under a Mohammedan government.

[2] See F. Dornseiff, *Das alphabet in Mystik und Magie*, Teubner, 1922.

[3] C. de Vaux says, 'It is thought that al-Battani knew Greek; he commented

It appears that the 'Sabians' lived on at Bagdad, and continued to be known there as a separate sect, for about 150 years after the death of Thabit (A. D. 900–1050). At that time the 'Golden Age' of the great caliphs (al-Mansur, ar-Rashid, and al-Mamun, A. D. 754–833) was past, and the vast empire over which they had ruled had fallen to pieces. The decline may be said to have begun in the reign of Mutawakkil, *c.* A. D. 850. There was a period of confusion, in the course of which caliphs at Bagdad were helpless in the hands of Turkish praetorians, and provincial governors made themselves independent and established local dynasties. But shortly before A. D. 950 one of these local rulers, a son of Buwayh, who had got possession of a large part of Persia, made himself master of Bagdad; and thenceforward (until the coming of the Seljuks in 1055) the Buwayhids governed there as 'Mayors of the Palace', and the caliphs, reduced to impotence, retained only a shadowy dignity as pontiffs. Thus during the greater part of the century A. D. 950–1050 Bagdad was under a tolerably firm and settled government, and though shorn of much of its earlier glory, was still the chief city of a considerable dominion (Mesopotamia, Iraq, and western Persia).

During these political changes, students pursued their work without intermission, some at Bagdad, and others at the place of residence of this or that local dynast; and it was not until after the political decline had begun that Arabic learning reached its highest level.

In the intellectual activity of A. D. 900–1050 the Sabians of Bagdad took their part. During that time, or at least during the earlier part of it, there was still under Moslem rule much freedom of thought; and non-Moslems, though subject to occasional ill-usage or annoyance, were often well received at court, and found the highest careers open to them. But from about A. D. 1050 we hear no more of these Sabians; and their disappearance is probably to be accounted for as the result of a gradual increase in the strictness with which Mohammedan orthodoxy was enforced.

Among 'the two and seventy jarring sects' of Islam, there were, and had been from the first, two main tendencies in conflict. There was a school of theologians (the 'orthodox' theologians as they may be called) who relied wholly and solely on the authority of

on the *Tetrabiblos* of Ptolemy, and revised the *Almagest* and several works of Archimedes'.

revelation—i. e. on what God had revealed to Mohammed—and refused to diverge from this or go beyond it; and opposed to them there was a school of 'liberal' theologians, who, while accepting the authority of the Koran, claimed a right to the use of human reason in the interpretation of the sacred text, and exercised that right to a varying extent. In the ninth century, when the Arabs had got access to Greek learning, there arose, side by side with the two schools of theologians, a third school, that of the 'philosophers'.[1] Philosophy meant, for the Arabs, not a search for truth in any direction, but adherence to those philosophic doctrines which they had learnt from the Greeks—that is, to Neoplatonism; so that the 'philosophers' were, in fact, a sect among other sects. They were professedly Mohammedans (differing in this from the Sabians, who were not Mohammedans in any sense), and they did not openly reject the Koran; but they disregarded it as far as they could with safety, and when obliged to take notice of it, contrived some sort of compromise between their Neoplatonic doctrines and those of Moslem theology. Meanwhile, the liberal theologians also read the philosophic writings, and got from them arguments which they employed in their controversies with the more rigidly orthodox. Thus the 'orthodox theologians' and the 'philosophers' came to stand opposed to one another as the two extremes, while the 'liberal theologians' held an intermediate position between them.

Under the great caliphs, the liberal theologians had, on the whole, the upper hand, and men of all ways of thinking could express their opinions openly. But as time went on, the orthodox party grew in strength, and asserted itself more and more. The tenets of this party, or of a comparatively moderate section of it, were formulated by al-Ashari (who died A. D. 935, i. e. about half a century after the founding of the Sabian community in Bagdad); and his followers, known as 'the Asharites', carried on the struggle until they brought it to a victorious conclusion. From the school of the Asharites issued Ghazali (A. D. 1058–1111), who 'crushed the philosophers', and finally established the system of Mohammedan orthodoxy which has, in the main, been in force from his time down to our own day.

[1] Among the numerous Oriental Arabs who taught philosophy in their writings, there are three whose names stand out conspicuously, viz. al-Kindi, who died about A. D. 873 (of his writings only small remnants have been preserved); al-Farabi, who died A. D. 950; and ibn-Sina (Avicenna), who died A. D. 1037.

What is here said about the religious parties and disputes of the Moslem Arabs is taken chiefly from de Boer, *Gesch. der Philosophie im Islam*, 1901, and Carra de Vaux, *Avicenne* and *Gazali*.

Thus, about A.D. 1050, the forces hostile to freedom of thought were already prevailing. Men such as the Sabians of whom I have been speaking could no longer venture to speak out; they could escape ill-treatment only by remaining in obscurity; and they were probably soon absorbed into the mass of orthodox Moslems.

Now the time at which the Sabians disappear at Bagdad (*c.* A.D. 1050) is just about the time at which documents of the *Corpus Hermeticum*, after an interval of five centuries during which nothing has been heard of them in Europe, reappear at Constantinople, in the hands of Psellus. Is there not something more than chance in this? It may be that one of the Sabians of Bagdad, finding that his position under Moslem rule was becoming unendurable, migrated to Constantinople, and brought in his baggage a bundle of Greek *Hermetica*—and that our *Corpus* is that bundle. If so, the line along which the *libelli* of the *Corpus* have been transmitted to us from Egypt runs through Harran and Bagdad. This is merely an unproved hypothesis; but it is one that agrees well with the facts known to us. The Pagans of Harran almost certainly possessed the whole collection of *Hermetica* (including many documents that are not now extant) in Greek, at the time when they adopted these writings as their Scriptures, in A.D. 830; and there can be little doubt that Thabit, who was a good Greek scholar, still had a copy of them in Greek at the end of the ninth century. During the 150 years which had since elapsed, knowledge of Greek must have almost, if not quite, died out at Bagdad, and the *Hermetica* must have been now read only, or almost only, in Syriac or Arabic translations. But a man such as the Sabian I am supposing would, even if he did not himself know the Greek language, have good reason to preserve with care, and to take with him when he migrated to a place where Greek was spoken, any portions of his Scriptures, in the original Greek, that had chanced to escape destruction and to come into his hands; and it is just such a chance collection of specimens that we have in the *Corpus*.

Moreover, if we choose to indulge in yet further conjectures, there is nothing to prevent us from supposing that it was the arrival in Constantinople of a few such Sabian Neoplatonists from Bagdad, and the writings which they brought with them, that first started that revival of Platonic study in which Psellus[1] took the leading

[1] Psellus might be called a Byzantine Cicero. A modern Plutarch would be able to show that the lives of Cicero and Psellus are curiously parallel in some

part. This would be very much like what took place four centuries later, when Neoplatonism, conveyed by Greeks who migrated westward, passed on from Constantinople to Florence, and again carried with it the *Corpus Hermeticum*.

It is almost surprising that no extracts or quotations from the *Hermetica* (except the insignificant scrap which I call Fragment 37) have been found in Arabic writings. Possibly some such passages may yet be discovered. There may be in existence unpublished MSS. containing treatises on philosophic or religious subjects, written by Thabit b. Qurra or by other Sabians of Bagdad; and it might be expected that these men would sometimes quote from the documents which were regarded as their Scriptures.[1]

Al-Kindi (who died about A.D. 873, i.e. before the Sabian community in Bagdad was founded) said that he had seen a book 'the teaching of which is accepted by' the Pagans of Harran, and which consisted of treatises 'which Hermes wrote for his son' (i.e. a collection of *Hermes to Tat* documents); but he does not quote from these documents, and he tells us little about their contents, except that they teach 'the unity of God'.

Shahrastani (†A.D. 1153), Katibi (†A.D. 1276), and other Arabic writers give summaries of the philosophic teaching of the Harranian Sabians; and the contents of these summaries are probably derived (either directly or through Moslem intermediaries) from some of the writings of Thabit and his associates. The doctrines which these Arabic writers ascribe to the Harranian Sabians are for the most part such as are to be found in our *Hermetica*, or might have been found in *Hermetica* now lost; but we have no means of knowing whether the Sabian writers got them from the *Hermetica*, or from Platonic sources of the same kind as those from which the Hermetists drew.

Among the Arabic writers whose *testimonia* are known to me, the only one who shows any considerable knowledge of the contents of the Greek *Hermetica* is the mystic Suhrawardi (†A.D. 1191). This man says he 'finds himself in agreement' with Hermes as well as with Plato; and this implies that he knew writings which contained philosophic or religious teachings ascribed to Hermes,

respects; and one of the things in which the two men were alike is that each of them did much to make philosophy known to his countrymen.

[1] It would be worth while to examine for this purpose a document entitled *Gubernatio animarum*, written by Sinan son of Thabit (British Museum *Cod. Arab.* MS. Add. 7473 Rich, foll. 26–31).

and saw that these teachings resembled those of Plato. He says 'it can be proved' of Hermes (as well as of Plato) that he 'saw the spiritual world' (i. e. τὰ νοητά); and he must have found his proof of this in passages of the *Hermetica* in which Hermes speaks of 'seeing' God or things incorporeal 'with the eye of the mind'. He says that Hermes (as well as Pythagoras, Plato, and others) taught 'transmigration of souls', and the doctrine 'that the spheres of heaven give forth sounds'; these statements must be based on particular passages in the *Hermetica*.

It appears then that Suhrawardi had the same sort of knowledge of the philosophic *Hermetica* that he had of the writings of Plato, and of the doctrines ascribed to Pythagoras by Greek tradition; and hence it may be inferred that he had either himself read some of the *Hermetica* (in a Syriac or Arabic translation), or got information about their contents from the writings of Sabians or Moslems who had read them. We know from Barhebraeus (*Testim.*) that a Syriac translation of a collection of *Hermes to Tat* dialogues was extant in and after Suhrawardi's time.

The statements of Arabic writers concerning Hermes show that, down to the twelfth century and later, his name was widely known among them, and was held in high repute as that of a teacher of philosophic religion; but they add nothing to our knowledge of the Greek *Hermetica*. There has come down to us, however, one document which may be called an Arabic *Hermeticum*; namely, *Hermes de castigatione animae*, a translation of which is given at the end of the *Testimonia*. There are many passages in it which contain teaching that closely resembles that of some of the Greek *Hermetica*. It seems probable that most of these passages are extracts from the writings of men who knew the Greek *Hermetica* (or Syriac or Arabic translations of them), and that some of them have been translated, with little alteration, from Greek originals. It is possible that some of these Greek originals were *Hermetica*; but it cannot be said with certainty of any passage in the *Castig. an.* that it is a translation of a Greek *Hermeticum*.

A collection of 'Sayings of Hermes' is given by Honein ibn Isháq,[1] *Dicta philosophorum* (Loewenthal, 1896). This book con-

[1] Honein ibn Ishaq (†A. D. 873) was a Nestorian Christian. He took a leading part in the translation of Greek writings into Arabic, and was assisted in the work by his son and nephew. He resided mostly at Bagdad, but travelled in Byzantine territory, where he remained for two years, and brought back thence a collection

tains a *gnomologium* in which are reported *dicta* of several sages (Socrates, Plato, Aristotle, &c.), one of whom is Hermes. Among the thirty-six sayings ascribed by him to Hermes are the following: 'Desire is slavery; renunciation is freedom.' 'He who publicly reprimands any one deserves blame and contempt.' 'Let nothing of the advantages which the Creator has given you be small in your eyes, that you may not lose that which is already given.' 'Leave the liar and his company, for you get nothing that is of use from him; he is like the mirage in the desert, which shines, but does no quench your thirst.' 'He who scorns another on account of his sins finds no forgiveness.' 'For the merciful, the repentance of the offender is a sufficient advocate.' 'Death is like an arrow (that is already) in flight, and your life lasts only until it reaches you.' 'The height of magnanimity is to be merciful to fools.' Gnomic sayings such as these have nothing to do with the Greek *Hermetica.* It is evident that the name Hermes has here been employed at random, and it is a mere chance that these sayings are ascribed to him, and not to Socrates or some other sage. This document therefore is, for our present purpose, significant only as showing that in the ninth century Hermes was, in the circle to which Honein belonged, reputed a 'wise man' in the same sense as the chief Greek philosophers.

Bardenhewer, in his introduction to the *Castig. an.*, says that there is an unpublished writing of Mubashshiri b. Fatik (*Cat. bibl. Acad. Lugd.-Bat.* iii, p. 342) which contains a *collectio acute dictorum* (doubtless a *gnomologium* resembling that of Honein), and in which *Hermes gravem agit personam*; and that there are other similar and partly identical Arabic collections of gnomic sayings.

of Greek writings. But as far as one can judge from the book translated by Loewenthal, he appears to have been surprisingly ignorant of Greek life and thought, and can hardly have been capable of understanding the writings which he translated.

TEXTS AND TRANSLATION

CORPVS HERMETICVM

LIBELLVS I

[‘Ερμοῦ τρισμεγίστου] Ποιμάνδρης.

1 ’Εννοίας μοί ποτε γενομένης περὶ τῶν ὄντων, καὶ μετεωρι-
σθείσης μὲν τῆς διανοίας σφόδρα, ⟨⟨ὕπνῳ⟩⟩ ⟨δὲ⟩ κατασχεθει-
σῶν μου τῶν σωματικῶν αἰσθήσεων, ⟨οὐ μέντοι⟩ καθάπερ
⟨τ⟩οῖ⟨ς⟩ [[ὕπνῳ]] βεβαρημένοι⟨ς⟩ ἐκ κόρου τροφῆς ἢ ἐκ κόπου
σώματος, ἔδοξά τινα ὑπερμεγέθη μέτρῳ ἀπεριορίστῳ ⟨ἐν⟩-
τυγχάνοντα καλεῖν μου τὸ ὄνομα, καὶ λέγειν [τα] μοι·
Τί βούλει ἀκοῦσαι καὶ θεάσασθαι, καὶ νοήσας μαθεῖν καὶ
2 γνῶναι;—φημὶ ἐγώ· Σὺ γὰρ τίς εἶ;—’Εγὼ μέν, φησίν,
εἰμὶ ὁ Ποιμάνδρης, ὁ τῆς αὐθεντίας νοῦς. [[οἶδα ὃ βούλει
3 καὶ σύνειμί σοι πανταχοῦ.]]—φημὶ ἐγώ· Μαθεῖν θέλω τὰ
ὄντα καὶ νοῆσαι τὴν τούτων φύσιν, καὶ γνῶναι τὸν θεόν.
⟨περὶ τοῦ⟩των, ἔφην, ἀκοῦσαι βούλομαι.—φησὶν ἐμοὶ πάλιν·
⟨⟨Οἶδα ὃ βούλει, ⟨ὃς⟩ καὶ σύνειμί σοι πανταχοῦ·⟩⟩ ἔχε νῷ
σῷ ὅσα θέλεις μαθεῖν, κἀγώ σε διδάξω.—
4 οὕτως εἰπόν⟨τος⟩, ἠλλάγη ⟨⟨εὐθέως πάντα μοι⟩⟩ τῇ ἰδέᾳ
καὶ [[εὐθέως πάντα μοι]] ἤνοικτο ῥοπῇ. καὶ ὁρῶ θέαν
ἀόριστον, φῶς [δὲ] πάντα γεγενημένα ἤπιόν τε καὶ ἱλαρόν·
καὶ ἠράσθην ἰδών. καὶ μετ’ ὀλίγον, σκότος κατωφερὲς ἦν
ἐν μέρει ⟨τινὶ⟩ γεγενημένον, φοβερόν τε καὶ στυγνόν,
⌜σκολιῶς πεπειραμένον⌝ [ὡς εἰκάσαι με]. ⟨ . . . ⟩ εἶδον
μεταβαλλόμενον τὸ σκότος εἰς ὑγράν τινα φύσιν ἀφάτως
τεταραγμένην, καὶ καπνὸν ἀποδιδοῦσαν ὡς ἀπὸ πυρός. καί
τινα ἦχον ⌜ἀποτελοῦσαν⌝ ἀνεκλάλητον γοώδη· [εἶτα] βοὴ ⟨γὰρ⟩

In Libello I, codicum ABCDMQ et Turnebi lectiones adhibui. O = codicum ABCDM prima manus teste Reitzenstein.

1 ‘Ερμοῦ τοῦ τρισμεγίστου DM Turnebus: ‘Ερμοῦ Τρισμεγίστου cett. 2 *μοί ποτε* AMQ Turn.: *μηποτε* C 3 *μὲν* scripsi: *μοι* codd., Turn. 4 *καθάπερ* A: *ὥσπερ* CDQ Turn. 5 *τοῖς βεβαρημένοις* scripsi: *οἱ ὕπνω βεβαρημένοι* A: *οἱ ἐν ὕπνῳ βεβαρημένοι* CDQ Turn. 5–6 Fulgentius *Myth.* p. 26. 18 Helm: ‘*Hermes in Opimandrae libro ait*: eccurutrofes et cufusomatos (*ἐκ κό[υ]ρου τροφῆς* ⟨ἢ⟩ *ἐκ κούφου σώματος*): *id est, absque instructione escae et vacuo corpore*’ 6 Fortasse *τινα* [ ] *μέτρῳ ἀπεριόριστον*

CORPVS HERMETICVM

LIBELLVS I

The Poimandres [of Hermes Trismegistus].

1
Once on a time, when I had begun to think about the things that are, and my thoughts had soared high aloft, while my bodily senses had been put under restraint by sleep,—yet not such sleep as that of men weighed down by fullness of food or by bodily weariness,—methought there came to me a Being of vast and boundless magnitude, who called me by my name, and said to me, 'What do you wish to hear and see, and to learn and come to
know by thought?' 'Who are you?' I said. 'I,' said he, 'am 2
Poimandres, the Mind of the Sovereignty.' 'I would fain learn,' 3
said I, 'the things that are, and understand their nature, and get knowledge of God. These,' I said, 'are the things of which I wish to hear.' He answered, 'I know what you wish, for indeed I am with you everywhere; keep in mind all that you desire to learn, and I will teach you.'

4
When he had thus spoken, forthwith all things changed in aspect before me, and were opened out in a moment. And I beheld a boundless view; all was changed into light, a mild and joyous light; and I marvelled when I saw it. And in a little while, there had come to be in one part a downward-tending darkness, terrible and grim. . . . And thereafter I saw the darkness changing into a watery substance, which was unspeakably tossed about, and gave forth smoke as from fire; and I heard it making an indescribable sound of lamentation; for there was sent forth

7 *μου* om. Turn.: *μου* ex *με* corr. A | *λέγειν* Tiedemann: *λέγοντά* codd., Turn. 13 *περὶ τούτων* scripsi: *πῶς* OQ Turn. | *φησὶν* om. A | *ἐμοὶ* Flussas: *ἐμὲ* OQ Turn. 15 *ἐγώ* CDQ: *κἀγώ* cett. 16 *οὕτως εἰπόντος* scripsi: *οὗτος εἰπὼν* Turn.: *τούτω εἰπὼν* C: *τοῦτο εἰπὼν* cett. 18 *ἤπιόν* scripsi: *ἥδιόν* OQ Turn.: *εὔδιόν* Plasberg 19 *ἠγάσθην* Keil: *ἠράσθην* OQ Turn. 20 *φοβερόν τι καὶ* Q 20–21 *φοβερόν . . . πεπειραμένον* om. C. Fortasse *σκότος [κατωφερὲς] ἦν . . . δυσκόλως ἐπαιρόμενον* 21 *εἶδον* scripsi: *εἰδότα* OQ Turn.: *ἰδόντα* B[2] 24 *ἀποτελοῦσαν* codd., Turn.: fortasse *ἀφιείσης ἤκουσα* | *ἀνεκλάλητον* om. A, vacuo relicto xi litterarum spatio | *βοὴ γὰρ* scripsi: *εἶτα βοὴ* codd. (*εἶτα βοὴν* M)

ἐξ αὐτῆς ἀσύναρθρος ἐξεπέμπετο. [[ὡς εἰκάσαι φωνὴν
5a φωτός.]] ἐκ δὲ ⟨τοῦ⟩ φωτὸς π⟨ροελθὼν⟩ λόγος ἅγιος ἐπέβη
τῇ ⟨ὑγρᾷ⟩ φύσει, ⟨⟨ὡς εἰκάσαι ⟨με⟩ φωνὴν ⟨εἶναι τοῦ⟩ φωτός.⟩⟩
[[5 b καὶ πῦρ ἄκρατον . . . πνευματικὸν λόγον.]]
6 [[εἰς ἀκοὴν]] ὁ δὲ Ποιμάνδρης ⟨⟨εἰς ἀκοὴν⟩⟩ ἐμοὶ Ἐνόησας,
φησί, τὴν θέαν ταύτην ὅ τι καὶ βούλεται; — ⟨ . . . ⟩ καὶ
γνώσομαι, ἔφην ἐγώ.—Τὸ φῶς ἐκεῖνο, ἔφη, ἐγώ, νοῦς, ὁ πρῶτος
θεός, ὁ πρὸ φύσεως ὑγρᾶς τῆς ἐκ σκότους φανείσης· ὁ δὲ ἐκ
[νοὸς] φωτ[ειν]ὸς λόγος υἱὸς θεοῦ.—Τί οὖν; φημί.—Οὕτω
γνῶθι, τὸ ἐν σοὶ βλέπων [καὶ ἀκούων]· ⟨ἐπεὶ καὶ ἐν σοὶ ὁ⟩
λόγος [κυρίου] ⟨υἱός⟩, ὁ δὲ νοῦς πατήρ [θεός]. οὐ γὰρ
διίστανται ἀπ' ἀλλήλων· ἕνωσις γὰρ τούτων ἐστὶν ἡ ζωή.—
Εὐχαριστῶ σοι, ἔφην ἐγώ.—
7 Ἀλλὰ δὴ νόει τὸ φῶς, καὶ γνώριζε τοῦτο.—εἰπὼν τοσ-
[τ]αῦτα, ἐπὶ πλείονα χρόνον ἀντώπησέ μοι, ὥστε με τρέμειν
αὐτοῦ τὴν ἰδέαν. ἀνανεύσα[ντο]ς δέ, θεωρῶ ἐν τῷ νοΐ μου
τὸ φῶς ἐν δυνάμεσιν ἀναριθμήτοις ὄν, καὶ κόσμον ἀπεριόριστον
γεγενημένον. [[καὶ περισχέσθαι τὸ πῦρ δυνάμει μεγίστῃ
καὶ στάσιν ἐσχηκέναι κρατούμενον.]] ταῦτα δὲ ἐγὼ διενοήθην
8a ὁρῶν διὰ τὸν τοῦ Ποιμάνδρου λόγον. ὡς δὲ ἐν ἐμπλήξει μου
ὄντος, φησὶ πάλιν ἐμοί· Εἶδες ἐν τῷ νῷ τὸ ἀρχέτυπον εἶδος,
τὸ προάρχον τῆς ἀρχῆς, τὸ ἀπέραντον.—ταῦτα ὁ Ποιμάνδρης
ἐμοί.
8b Τί οὖν; ἐγώ φημι· ⟨τὰ⟩ στοιχεῖα τῆς φύσεως πόθεν
ὑπέστη;—πάλιν ἐκεῖνος πρὸς ταῦτα· Ἐκ βουλῆς θεοῦ, ἥτις
[[λαβοῦσα τὸν λόγον]] [καὶ] ἰδοῦσα τὸν καλὸν κόσμον ἐμιμή-
σατο. ⟨ἡ γὰρ ὑγρὰ φύσις⟩ ⟨⟨λαβοῦσα τὸν λόγον⟩⟩ ⟨ἐ⟩κοσμο-
ποιήθη, δια⟨κριθέν⟩των ἐ⟨ξ⟩ αὐτῆς ⟨τῶν⟩ στοιχείων, ⟨ἐξ ὧν⟩
5b καὶ ⟨τὸ⟩ γέννημα τῶν ⟨ἐμ⟩ψύχων. ⟨⟨καὶ ⟨γὰρ⟩ πῦρ ἄκρατον

1 ἀσύναρθρος ἐξεπέμπετο Reitz.: ἀσυνάρθρως ἐξεμπέμπετο BCDMQ Turn.: om. A, vacuo relicto xx litterarum spatio 2 φωτὸς προελθὼν λόγος scripsi: φωτὸς τί λόγος BCDMQ Turn.: φωτὸς (spatium vi litt.) λόγος A 4 § 5 b (καὶ πῦρ . . . πνευματικὸν λόγον) hinc transposui: vide post § 8 b 6 Fortasse ⟨Σύ μοι φράσον⟩ 7 ὁ πρῶτος θεός scripsi: ὁ σὸς θεός codd., Turn. (σὸς ex ᾱος factum esse conicio) 10 βλέπων καὶ ἀκούων C: βλέπων καὶ ἀκοῦον Q: βλέπον καὶ ἀκοῦον cett. 11 γὰρ (post οὐ) om. CDQ 13 σοι om. CDQ 14–15 εἰπὼν τοσαῦτα scripsi: εἰπόντος ταῦτα codd., Turn. (τοῦτο φησίν, καὶ εἰπὼν ταῦτα B[2]) 15 ἀντέπησέ CQ: ἀντέφησέ (ἀντώπησέ corr. man. pr.) A | ὥστε μοι A: ὥστε με cett. 17 ὂν Turn.: ὄντος OQ | κόσμου DQ et man. pr. C 18–19 καὶ . . . κρατούμενον hinc ad § 5 b transposui 22 τὸ ἀπέραντον scripsi: τῆς ἀπεράντου codd., Turn. 24 Τὰ οὖν, ἐγώ φημι, στοιχεῖα codd., Turn.: ‘vielleicht τί οὖν;

from it an inarticulate cry. But from the Light there came forth 5 a
a holy Word,[1] which took its stand upon the watery substance;
and methought this Word[1] was the voice of the Light.

And Poimandres spoke for me to hear, and said to me, 'Do 6
you understand the meaning of what you have seen?' 'Tell me
its meaning,' I said, 'and I shall know.' 'That Light,' he said,
'is I, even Mind, the first God, who was before the watery substance which appeared out of the darkness; and the Word which came forth from the Light is son of God.' 'How so?' said I. 'Learn my meaning,' said he, 'by looking at what you yourself have in you; for in you too, the word[1] is son, and the mind is father of the word. They are not separate one from the other; for life is the union of word[1] and mind.' Said I, 'For this I thank you.'

'Now fix your thought upon the Light,' he said, 'and learn to 7
know it.' And when he had thus spoken, he gazed long upon
me, eye to eye, so that I trembled at his aspect. And when I raised my head again, I saw in my mind that the Light consisted of innumerable Powers, and had come to be an ordered world, but a world without bounds.[2] This I perceived in thought, seeing it by reason of the word which Poimandres
had spoken to me. And when I was amazed, he spoke again, 8 a
and said to me, 'You have seen in your mind the archetypal
form, which is prior to the beginning of things, and is limitless.'
Thus spoke Poimandres to me.

'But tell me,' said I, 'whence did the elements of nature[3] 8 b
come into being?' He answered, 'They issued from God's
Purpose, which beheld that beauteous world[4] and copied it. The watery substance, having received the Word, was fashioned into an ordered world, the elements being separated out from it; and from the elements came forth the brood of living creatures.
Fire unmixed leapt forth from the watery substance, and rose up 5 b

[1] Or 'Speech'.

[2] The 'world' here spoken of is the 'intelligible world', as opposed to the 'sensible world'.

[3] I.e. the elements of the material or sensible world.

[4] I.e. the intelligible world.

ἐγώ φημι, ⟨τὰ⟩ στοιχεῖα' Reitz. 27–28 ἐκοσμοποιήθη scripsi: κοσμοποιηθεῖσα codd., Turn. 28 διακριθέντων ἐξ αὐτῆς τῶν στοιχείων scripsi: διὰ τῶν ἑαυτῆς στοιχείων codd., Turn. 28–29 ἐξ ὧν καὶ τὸ γέννημα τῶν ἐμψύχων scripsi: καὶ γεννημάτων ψυχῶν codd., Turn. 29 § 5 b (καὶ πῦρ . . . πνευματικὸν λόγον) huc transposui

ἐξεπήδησεν ἐκ τῆς ὑγρᾶς φύσεως ἄνω εἰς ὕψος· κουφὸν δὲ ἦν καὶ ὀξύ, δραστικόν τε. ἅμα ⟨δὲ⟩ καὶ ὁ ἀήρ, ἐλαφρὸς ὤν, ἠκολούθησε τῷ πυρί, ἀναβαίνων [τοσοῦτον] μέχρι τοῦ πυρὸς ἀπὸ γῆς καὶ ὕδατος, ὡς δοκεῖν κρέμασθαι αὐτὸν ἀπ' αὐτοῦ. ⟨⟨καὶ περι⟨ε⟩σχέθη τὸ πῦρ δυνάμει μεγίστῃ, καὶ στάσιν ἔσχ[ηκ]ε[ναι] κρατούμενον.⟩⟩ γῆ δὲ καὶ ὕδωρ ἔμενε καθ' ἑαυτὰ συμμεμιγμένα, ὡς μὴ ⌜θεωρεῖσθαι⌝ [ἀπὸ] [[τοῦ ὕδατος]]· κινούμενα δὲ ἦν διὰ τὸν ⟨ἐπάνω⟩ ⟨⟨τοῦ ὕδατος⟩⟩ ἐπιφερόμενον πνευματικὸν λόγον.⟩⟩

9 ὁ δὲ νοῦς ὁ πρῶτος, [[ἀρρενόθηλυς ὤν,]] ⟨ὁ⟩ ζωὴ καὶ φῶς ὑπάρχων, ⟨⟨ἀρρενόθηλυς ὤν,⟩⟩ ἀπεκύησε⟨ν⟩ [λόγῳ] ἕτερον νοῦν δημιουργόν, ὃς Δεύτερος [τοῦ] [[πυρὸς καὶ πνεύματος]] ὢν ἐδημιούργησε⟨ν ἐκ⟩ ⟨⟨πυρὸς καὶ πνεύματος⟩⟩ διοικήτ⟨ορ⟩άς τινας ἑπτά, ἐν κύκλοις περιέχοντας τὸν αἰσθητὸν κόσμον· καὶ ἡ διοίκησις αὐτῶν εἱμαρμένη καλεῖται.

10 ἐπήδησεν εὐθὺς ἐκ τῶν κατωφερῶν στοιχείων ⟨⟨τῆς φύσεως⟩⟩ [τοῦ θεοῦ] ὁ τοῦ θεοῦ λόγος εἰς τὸ καθαρὸν [[τῆς φύσεως]] δημιούργημα, καὶ ἡνώθη τῷ δημιουργῷ νῷ· ὁμοούσιος γὰρ ἦν· καὶ κατελείφθη [τὰ] ἄλογα τὰ κατωφερῆ τῆς φύσεως στοιχεῖα, ὡς εἶναι ὕλην μόνην.

11 a ὁ δὲ δημιουργὸς νοῦς σὺν τῷ λόγῳ, [ὁ] περιίσχων τοὺς κύκλους καὶ δινῶν ῥοίζῳ, ἔστρεψε τὰ ἑαυτοῦ δημιουργήματα, καὶ εἴασε στρέφεσθαι ἀπ' ἀρχῆς ἀορίστου εἰς ἀπέραντον τέλος· ἄρχεται γὰρ οὗ λήγει ἡ [δὲ] τούτων περιφορά.

11 b ⟨ἡ δὲ φύσις,⟩ καθὼς ἠθέλησεν ὁ νοῦς, ἐκ τῶν κατωφερῶν στοιχείων ζῷα ἤνεγκεν ἄλογα· οὐ γὰρ ἔτι εἶχε τὸν λόγον. ἀὴρ δὲ πετεινὰ ἤνεγκε, καὶ τὸ ὕδωρ νηκτά,—διεκεχώριστο δὲ

1 ἐξεπήδησεν om. A, vacuo relicto xvi litt. spatio | κουφὸν δὲ om. A, vacuo relicto viii litt. spatio 2 δραστικόν τε DQ Turn. : δραστικὸν δὲ ABCM 3 πυρί Reitz. : πν̄ι vel πνεύματι OQ Turn. | ἀναβαίνων [τοσοῦτον] scripsi : ἀναβαίνοντος (σῶα βαίνοντος C) αὐτοῦ codd. 5–6 καὶ . . . κρατούμενον huc a § 7 transposui 5 περιεσχέθη scripsi : περισχέσθαι OQ Turn. 6 ἔσχε scripsi : ἐσχηκέναι codd., Turn. 8 ἐπιφερόμενον om. BC 10 πρῶτος (i.e. ᾱος) scripsi : θεός codd., Turn. 11 ὑπάρχων om. A | λόγῳ seclusit Reitz. Fortasse ἀπεκύησε ⟨πρὸς τῷ⟩ λόγῳ 12 δεύτερος (i.e. β̄ος) scripsi : θεὸς codd., Turn. 14 ἑπτά τινας A : τινας ἑπτά cett. | περιέχοντε C 17 τοῦ θεοῦ seclusit Tiedemann | εἰς τὸ τῆς θαρὸν BC 18 δημιούργημος C 19 τὰ (ante ἄλογα) seclusit Reitz. 21 ὁ περιίσχων DQ Turn. : ὁ περι ἴσχων M : ὅπερ ἴσχων C : ὁ περιέχων AB | ἔτρεψε C 23 ἀόριστον CDM | δὲ seclusit Reitz. 25 ἡ δὲ φύσις hic addidi : ἄρχεται γὰρ . . . περιφορά, καθὼς θέλει ὁ Νοῦς. ⟨ἡ δὲ φύσις⟩ ἐκ τῶν Reitz. | ἠθέλησεν AB : ἤθελε C[2] : θέλει CDMQ Turn. | Fortasse ὁ ⟨δημιουργὸς⟩ νοῦς | ὁ νοῦς, καὶ ἐκ Turn. 26 'Vielleicht ἔτι εἶχε'

aloft; the fire was light and keen, and active. And therewith the air too, being light, followed the fire, and mounted up till it reached the fire, parting from earth and water; so that it seemed that the air was suspended from the fire. And the fire was encompassed by a mighty power, and was held fast, and stood firm. But earth and water remained in their own place, mingled together, so as not to be . . . ;[1] but they were kept in motion, by reason of the breath-like[2] Word which moved upon the face of the water.

And the first Mind,—that Mind which is Life and Light,— 9
being bisexual, gave birth to another Mind, a Maker of things; and this second Mind made out of fire and air seven Administrators,[3] who encompass with their orbits the world perceived by sense; and their administration is called Destiny.

And forthwith the Word of God leapt up from the downward- 10
tending elements of nature to the pure body which had been made,[4] and was united with Mind the Maker;[5] for the Word was of one substance with that Mind. And the downward-tending elements of nature were left devoid of reason,[6] so as to be mere matter.

And Mind the Maker worked together with the Word, and 11 a
encompassing the orbits of the Administrators, and whirling them round with a rushing movement, set circling the bodies he had made, and let them revolve, travelling from no fixed starting-point to no determined goal; for their revolution begins where it ends.

And Nature, even as Mind the Maker willed, brought forth 11 b
from the downward-tending elements animals devoid of reason; for she no longer had with her the Word.[7] The air brought forth birds, and the water, fishes,—earth and water had by this

[1] Perhaps, 'so that they could not be distinguished'.

[2] Or 'wind-like', or 'airy'. (Not 'spiritual', but perhaps 'of the nature of vital spirit'.)

[3] I.e. the seven planets.

[4] This 'pure body' is heaven, or the highest sphere of heaven.

[5] I.e. the second Mind.

[6] Earth and water were left 'devoid of reason', because 'the Word', which here signifies 'reason', departed from them.

[7] Or 'Reason'.

Reitz.: ἐπεῖχε codd., Turn. 27 νοητά A: νηκτά cett. | διεκεχώριστο scripsi: διακεχώρισται codd. (-ρησται Q), Turn.

ἀπ' ἀλλήλων ἥ τε γῆ καὶ τὸ ὕδωρ [καθὼς ἠθέλησεν ὁ νοῦς],—
καὶ ἐξήνεγκεν ⟨ἡ γῆ⟩ [ἀπ' αὐτῆς ἃ εἶχε] ζῷα τετράποδα ⟨καὶ⟩
ἑρπετά, θηρία ἄγρια καὶ ἥμερα.
12 ὁ δὲ πάντων πατὴρ [[ὁ]] νοῦς, ⟨⟨ὁ⟩⟩ ὢν ζωὴ καὶ φῶς,
ἀπεκύησεν ἄνθρωπον αὐτῷ ⟨ὅμ⟩οιον. οὗ ἠΓάσθη ὡς ἰδίου
τόκου· περικαλλὴς γὰρ ⟨ἦν⟩, τὴν τοῦ πατρὸς εἰκόνα ἔχων.
εἰκότως [γ]ἄρ⟨α⟩ [καὶ] ὁ θεὸς ἠΓάσθη τῆς ἰδίας μορφῆς· καὶ
παρέδωκε⟨ν⟩ [[τὰ]] [ἑ]αὐτῷ πάντα ⟨⟨τὰ⟩⟩ δημιουργήματα.
13a ⟨ὁ δέ,⟩ ⟨⟨γενόμενος ἐν τῇ δημιουργικῇ σφαίρᾳ,⟩⟩ ⟨⟨κατενόησε
τοῦ ἀδελφοῦ τὰ δημιουργήματα⟩⟩ ⟨⟨τοῦ ἐπικειμένου ἐπὶ τοῦ
πυρός·⟩⟩ [καὶ] κατανοήσας δὲ τὴν τοῦ δημιουργοῦ κτίσιν ἐν
τῷ πΥρί, ἠβουλήθη καὶ αὐτὸς δημιουργεῖν· καὶ συνεχωρήθη
ὑπὸ τοῦ πατρός. [[γενόμενος ἐν τῇ δημιουργικῇ σφαίρᾳ]] [ἐξ
ὧν τὴν πᾶσαν ἐξουσίαν] [[κατενόησε τοῦ ἀδελφοῦ τὰ δημιουρ-
γήματα]] ⟨ . . . ⟩ ⟨⟨πᾶσαν ἐνέργειαν ἐν ἑαυτῷ ἔχοντα τῶν
διοικητόρων·⟩⟩ οἱ δὲ ἠΓάσθησαν αὐτοῦ, ἕκαστος δὲ μετεδίδου
τῆς ἰδίας [τάξεως] ⟨φύσεως⟩.
13b καὶ καταμαθὼν τὴν τούτων οὐσίαν, καὶ μεταλαβὼν τῆς
[ἑ]αὐτῶν φύσεως, ἠβουλήθη ἀναρρῆξαι τὴν περιφέρειαν τῶν
κύκλων [καὶ τὸ κράτος] [[τοῦ ἐπικειμένου ἐπὶ τοῦ πυρὸς]]
14 [κατανοῆσαι]· καὶ [ὁ τοῦ τῶν θνητῶν κόσμου καὶ τῶν ἀλόγων
ζῴων ἔχων πᾶσαν ἐξουσίαν] διὰ τῆς ἁρμονίας παρέκυψεν,
ἀναρρήξας τὸ κΎτος, καὶ ἔδειξε τῇ κατωφερεῖ φύσει τὴν
καλὴν τοῦ θεοῦ μορφήν. ἡ[ν] ⟨δέ⟩, ἰδοῦσα ⟨τὸ⟩ [[ἀκόρεστον]]
κάλλος [[πᾶσαν ἐνέργειαν ἐν ἑαυτῷ ἔχοντα τῶν διοικητόρων]]
τῆϲ [τε] μορφῆϲ τοῦ θεοῦ, ἐμειδίασεν ἔρωτι ⟨⟨ἀκορέστῳ⟩⟩ ⟨⟨τοῦ
ἀνθρώπου⟩⟩, [ἅτε] τῆς καλλίστης μορφῆς [[τοῦ ἀνθρώπου]] τὸ
εἶδος ἐν τῷ ὕδατι ⟨ἀναδ⟩ιδοῦσα, καὶ τὸ σκίασμα ἐπὶ τῆς γῆς.
ὁ δέ, ἰδὼν τὴν ὁμοίαν αὐτῷ μορφὴν [ἐν ἑαυτῷ] οὖσαν ἐν
⟨τῇ γῇ καὶ⟩ τῷ ὕδατι, ἐφίλησε, καὶ ἠβουλήθη αὐτοῦ οἰκεῖν.

2 ἡ γῆ addidi (καὶ ἡ γῆ ἐξήνεγκεν Patritius) | καὶ (ante ἑρπετά) addidit Reitz. 4 ὁ (ante νοῦς) om. DQ | φῶς AB Turn. : φύσις CDMQ 5 ὅμοιον Patr. : ἴσον codd., Turn. | ἠγάσθη scripsi : ἠράσθη codd., Turn. 6 ἦν addidit Patr. 7 εἰκότως ἄρα scripsi : ὄντως γὰρ καὶ codd., Turn. | ἠγάσθη scripsi : ἠράσθη codd., Turn. | Fortasse ἠγάσθη, τῆς ἰδίας ⟨ἀγάμενος⟩ μορφῆς 7–8 καὶ παρέδωκεν αὐτῷ scripsi : παρέδωκέ τε ἑαυτοῦ A : καὶ παρέδωκε τὰ ἑαυτοῦ DQ Turn. : καὶ παρέδωκεν αὐτῷ τὰ ἑαυτοῦ B² 10–11 τοῦ ἐπικειμένου ἐπὶ τοῦ πυρός huc a § 13 b transposui 11 κτίσιν Turn. : κτῆσιν OQ 12 πυρί scripsi : πατρί codd., Turn. 13 ὑπὸ Q : ἀπὸ cett. 15–16 πᾶσαν . . . διοικητόρων huc a § 14 transposui 15 ἔχοντα Turn. : ἑκόντα ABDMQ 16 ἠγάσθησαν scripsi : ἠράσθησαν codd., Turn. 19 αὐτῶν B² : ἑαυτῶν O Turn. 20 τοῦ . . . πυρὸς hinc ad § 13 a transposui | τοῦ (ante πυρὸς) om. A 21 κόσμου om. CDQ 21–22 καὶ τῶν ἀλόγων ζῴων

time been separated from one another,—and the earth brought forth four-footed creatures and creeping things, beasts wild and tame.

But Mind the Father of all, he who is Life and Light,[1] gave 12
birth to Man, a Being like to Himself. And He took delight in Man, as being His own offspring; for Man was very goodly to look on, bearing the likeness of his Father. With good reason then did God take delight in Man; for it was God's own form that God took delight in. And God delivered over to Man all things that had been made.

And Man took station in the Maker's sphere,[2] and observed 13 a
the things made by his brother,[3] who was set over the region of fire; and having observed the Maker's creation in the region of fire, he willed to make things for his own part also; and his Father gave permission. . . . having in himself all the working of the Administrators;[4] and the Administrators took delight in him, and each of them gave him a share of his own nature.

And having learnt to know the being of the Administrators, 13 b
and received a share of their nature, he willed to break through
the bounding circle of their orbits; and he looked down through 14
the structure of the heavens, having broken through the sphere,[5] and showed to downward-tending Nature[6] the beautiful form of God. And Nature, seeing the beauty of the form of God,[7] smiled with insatiate love of Man, showing the reflection of that most beautiful form in the water, and its shadow on the earth. And he, seeing this form, a form like to his own, in earth and water, loved it, and willed to dwell there. And the deed followed

[1] I.e. the first Mind.

[2] I.e. in the highest sphere of heaven, which was the abode of Mind the Maker.

[3] 'His brother' is Mind the Maker. 'The things made by his brother' are the planets.

[4] I.e. of the planets.

[5] It must be the lowest sphere of heaven (i.e. the lunar sphere) that he broke through.

[6] 'Downward-tending Nature' is the force which works in the 'downward-tending elements', earth and water. This force is here personified.

[7] Seeing Man, who 'bore the likeness of God', she saw in him 'the form of God'.

ἔχων A : *ζῴων καὶ τῶν ἀλόγων ἔχων* C Turn. **23** *κύτος* scripsi : *κράτος* codd. | *τῇ κατωφερεῖ φύσει* B² Flussas : *τὴν κατωφερῆ φύσιν* AM Turn. : *τὴν κατοφερῆ φύσιν* Q : *τὴν κατοροφῆ φύσιν* C **24** *ἡ δὲ* Reitz. : *ἣν* OQ : *ὃν* Turn. **25** *πᾶσαν . . . διοικητόρων* hinc ad § 13 a transposui **26** *τῆς μορφῆς* scripsi : *τήν τε μορφὴν* codd., Turn. **27** *ἅτε* Turn. : *ὥς τε* C : *ὡς ἅτε* codd. cett. **28** *ἀναδιδοῦσα* scripsi : *ἰδοῦσα* codd., Turn. **30** *αὐτῷ* vel *αὐτῷ* CDQ Turn. : *αὐτοῦ* cett.

ἅμα δὲ τῇ βουλῇ ἐγένετο ἐνέργεια, καὶ ᾤκησε τὴν ἄλογον ⌜μορφήν⌝. ἡ δὲ φύσις λαβοῦσα τὸν ἐρώμενον περιεπλάκη ὅλη, καὶ ἐμίγησαν· ἐρώμενοι γὰρ ἦσαν.

15 καὶ διὰ τοῦτο παρὰ πάντα τὰ ἐπὶ γῆς ζῷα διπλοῦς ἐστιν ὁ ἄνθρωπος, θνητὸς μὲν διὰ τὸ σῶμα, ἀθάνατος δὲ διὰ τὸν οὐσιώδη ἄνθρωπον. ἀθάνατος γὰρ ὤν, καὶ πάντων τὴν ἐξουσίαν ἔχων, τὰ θνητὰ πάσχει, ὑποκείμενος τῇ εἱμαρμένῃ. ὑπεράνω ⟨γὰρ⟩ [οὖν] ὢν τῆς ἁρμονίας, [ἐναρμόνιος] ⟨εἱμαρμένης⟩ γέγονε δοῦλος· ἀρρενόθηλυς δὲ ὢν ἐξ ἀρρενοθήλεος ὄν⟨τος τοῦ⟩ πατρός, καὶ ἄυπνος ἀπὸ ἀύπνου, ⟨ὑπ᾽ ἔρωτος καὶ λήθης⟩ κρατεῖται.—

16 καὶ μετὰ ταῦτα ⟨ἔφην ἐγώ· Καὶ τὰ λοιπά, ὦ⟩ νοῦ[ς], ⟨φράσον⟩ [ὁ ἐ]μοι· καὶ αὐτὸς γὰρ ἐρῶ τοῦ λόγου.—ὁ δὲ Ποιμάνδρης εἶπε· Τοῦτο ἔστι τὸ [[κεκρυμμένον]] μυστήριον ⟨τὸ⟩ μέχρι τῆσδε τῆς ἡμέρας ⟨⟨κεκρυμμένον⟩⟩. ἡ γὰρ φύσις ἐπιμιγεῖσα τῷ ἀνθρώπῳ ἤνεγκέ τι θαῦμα θαυμασιώτατον. ἔχοντος γὰρ αὐτοῦ ⟨ἀπὸ⟩ τῆς ἁρμονίας τῶν ἑπτὰ τὴν φύσιν, οὓ⟨ς⟩ ἔφην σοι ἐκ πυρὸς καὶ πνεύματος ⟨γεγονέναι⟩, οὐκ ἀνέμεινεν ἡ φύσις, ἀλλ᾽ εὐθὺς ἀπεκύησεν ἑπτὰ ἀνθρώπους πρὸς τὰς φύσεις τῶν ἑπτὰ διοικητόρων, ἀρρενοθήλε[ι]ας καὶ μεταρσίους.—καὶ μετὰ ταῦτα ⟨ἔφην ἐγώ⟩· Ὦ Ποιμάνδρη, εἰς μεγάλην γὰρ νῦν ἐπιθυμίαν ἦλθον, καὶ ποθῶ ἀκοῦσαι, μὴ ἔκτρεχε.—καὶ ὁ Ποιμάνδρης εἶπεν· Ἀλλὰ σιώπα· οὔπω γάρ σοι ἀνήπλωσα τὸν πρῶτον λόγον.—Ἰδοὺ σιωπῶ, ἔφην ἐγώ.—

17 Ἐγένετο οὖν, [ὡς] ἔφη[ν], τῶν ἑπτὰ τούτων ἡ γένεσις τοιῷδε τρόπῳ. ⟨⟨ἐξήνεγκεν ἡ φύσις τὰ σώματα·⟩⟩ θηλυκὴ γὰρ ἦν ⟨ἡ γῆ⟩, καὶ ⟨τὸ⟩ ὕδωρ ὀχευτικόν· [τὸ δὲ ἐκ πυρὸς πέπειρον·] ἐκ δὲ αἰθέρος τὸ πνεῦμα ἔλαβο⟨ν⟩. [καὶ] [[ἐξήνεγκεν ἡ φύσις τὰ σώματα]] ⟨. . .⟩ πρὸς τὸ εἶδος τοῦ ἀνθρώπου· ὁ δὲ ἄνθρωπος ἐκ ζωῆς καὶ φωτὸς ἐγένετο εἰς ψυχὴν καὶ νοῦν, ἐκ μὲν ζωῆς ψυχήν, ἐκ δὲ φωτὸς νοῦν. καὶ ἔμεινεν οὕτω τὰ

1 βουλῇ codd.: fortasse βουλήσει 2 μορφήν codd.: fortasse ὕλην 7 τὰ θνητὰ OQ Turn.: τὰ θνητῶν B²: τὰ θνητοῦ Reitz. | πάσχειν AB: πάσχει cett. | ὑποκείμενος Casaubon: ὑποκείμενα OQ Turn. 8 γὰρ Reitz.: οὖν OQ Turn. 9 ἐξ ἀρρενοθήλυος AMQ Turn.: ἐξ ἀρρενοθήλεος cett. 9–10 ὄντος τοῦ scripsi: ὢν codd. (om A) et Turn. 12–13 μετὰ ταῦτα ἔφην ἐγώ· Καὶ τὰ λοιπά, ὦ νοῦ, φράσον μοι scripsi: μετὰ ταῦτα νοῦς ὁ ἐμός codd., Turn.: μετὰ ταῦτα ⟨ἐγώ· Δίδαξόν με πάντα⟩, νοῦς ὁ ἐμός Reitz. 18 οὓς Keil: οὗ OQ Turn. | πυρὸς Reitz.: πρ̄ς (i. e. πατρὸς) OQ: πατρὸς Turn. 19 ἀνέμειν εν CDQ: ἀνέμενεν codd. cett., Turn. 20 ἀρρενοθήλεας Reitz.: ἀρρενοθηλείας AM: ἀρρενοθήλυας BDQ Turn. 21 ἔφην ἐγὼ

close on the design; and he took up his abode in matter devoid of reason. And Nature, when she had got him with whom she was in love, wrapped him in her clasp, and they were mingled in one; for they were in love with one another.

And that is why man, unlike all other living creatures upon 15
earth, is twofold. He is mortal by reason of his body; he is immortal by reason of the Man of eternal substance. He is immortal, and has all things in his power; yet he suffers the lot of a mortal, being subject to Destiny. He is exalted above the structure of the heavens; yet he is born a slave of Destiny. He is bisexual, as his Father is bisexual, and sleepless, as his Father is sleepless; yet he is mastered by carnal desire and by oblivion.'

Thereafter I said, 'Tell me the rest, O Mind; for I too am 16
mastered by desire to hear your teaching.' And Poimandres said, 'This is the secret which has been kept hidden until this day. Nature, mingled in marriage with Man, brought forth a marvel most marvellous. Inasmuch as Man had got from the structure of the heavens the character of the seven Administrators, who were made, as I told you, of fire and air, Nature tarried not, but forthwith gave birth to seven Men, according to the characters of the seven Administrators; and these seven Men were bisexual and . . . .'[1] And thereupon I said, 'Now indeed, Poimandres, my desire is strong, and I long to hear; do not swerve aside.' 'Nay, be silent,' said Poimandres; 'I have not yet finished explaining this first thing.' 'See, I am silent,' said I. 'These seven Men then,' said he, 'were generated in 17
this wise. Nature brought forth their bodies; earth was the female element,[2] and water the male element; and from the aether[3] they received their vital spirit. ⟨But their incorporeal part was made⟩ after the form of Man;[4] and the Man in them changed from Life and Light into soul and mind, soul from Life,

[1] Perhaps, 'and stood erect (upon the earth)', in contrast to the beasts.
[2] *Sc.* in the generating of their bodies.
[3] 'Aether' seems to mean here either air, or air and fire together.
[4] I. e. in the likeness of the first Man, their father.

---

add. B[2] 24 *ἀνεπλήρωσα* Turn.: *ἀνήπλωσα* codd. 25 *ἔφη* scripsi: *ὡς ἔφην* codd., Turn. 26–27 *θηλυκὴ γὰρ ἦν ἡ γῆ* scripsi: *θηλυκὴ γὰρ ἦν* codd., Turn.: *θηλυκὴ γῆ ἦν* B[2] Flussas: 'denkbar wäre: *θηλυκὸν γὰρ ἡ γῆ*' Reitz. 28 *ἔλαβον* scripsi: *ἔλαβε* codd., Turn. 29 Fortasse ⟨*τὸ δὲ ἀσώματον αὐτῶν ἐγεννήθη*⟩

πάντα [τοῦ αἰσθητοῦ κόσμου] μέχρι περιόδου τέλους [ἄρχων γενῶν].

18 ἄκουε λοιπὸν ὃν ποθεῖς λόγον ἀκοῦσαι. τῆς περιόδου πεπληρωμένης, ἐλύθη ὁ πάντων σύνδεσμος ἐκ βουλῆς θεοῦ· πάντα γὰρ τὰ ζῷα, ἀρρενοθήλεα ὄντα, διελύετο ἅμα τῷ ἀνθρώπῳ, καὶ ἐγένετο τὰ μὲν ἀρρενικὰ ἐν μέρει, τὰ δὲ θηλυκὰ ὁμοίως. ὁ δὲ θεὸς εὐθὺς εἶπεν ἁγίῳ λόγῳ· "Αὐξάνεσθε ἐν αὐξήσει καὶ πληθύνεσθε ἐν πλήθει πάντα τὰ κτίσματα καὶ δημιουργήματα. καὶ ἀναγνωρισάτω ὁ ἔννους 〈ἄνθρωπος〉 ἑαυτὸν ὄντα ἀθάνατον, καὶ τὸν αἴτιον τοῦ θανάτου ἔρωτα [καὶ πάντα τὰ] ὄντα. 〈ὁ δὲ ἀναγνωρίσας ἑαυτὸν
19 εἰς τὸ ἀγαθὸν χωρεῖ.〉" τοῦτο εἰπόντος, ἡ πρόνοια διὰ τῆς εἱμαρμένης καὶ ἁρμονίας τὰς μίξεις ἐποιήσατο καὶ τὰς γενέσεις κατέστησε· καὶ ἐπληθύνθη κατὰ γένος τὰ πάντα. καὶ ὁ ἀναγνωρίσας ἑαυτὸν ἐλήλυθεν εἰς τὸ 〈ὑ〉περ[ι]ούσιον ἀγαθόν· ὁ δὲ ἀγαπήσας [[τὸ]] ἐκ πλάνης ἔρωτος 〈〈τὸ〉〉 σῶμα, οὗτος μένει ἐν τῷ σκότει πλανώμενος ⌜αἰσθητῶς⌝, πάσχων τὰ τοῦ θανάτου.—

20 Τί τοσοῦτον ἁμαρτάνουσιν, ἔφην ἐγώ, οἱ ἀγνοοῦντες, ἵνα στερηθῶσι τῆς ἀθανασίας;—Ἔοικας, ὦ οὗτος, [τοῦ] μὴ πεφροντικέναι ὧν ἤκουσας. οὐκ ἔφην σοι νοεῖν;—Νοῶ καὶ μιμνήσκομαι, εὐχαριστῶ δὲ ἅμα.—Εἰ ἐνόησας, εἰπέ μοι, διὰ τί ἄξιοί εἰσι τοῦ θανάτου οἱ ἐν [τῷ θανάτῳ] 〈ἀγνοίᾳ〉 ὄντες;—Ὅτι προκατάρχεται τοῦ ⌜οἰκείου⌝ σώματος τὸ στυγνὸν σκότος, ἐξ οὗ ἡ ὑγρὰ φύσις, ἐξ ἧς τὸ σῶμα συνέστηκεν· 〈 . . . 〉 ἐν
21 τῷ αἰσθητῷ κόσμῳ, ἐξ οὗ θάνατος ἀρ[δε]ύεται.—Ἐνόησας ὀρθῶς, ὦ οὗτος. κατὰ τί δὲ "ὁ [νοήσας] 〈ἀναγνωρίσας〉 ἑαυτὸν εἰς 〈τὸ〉 ἀγαθὸν χωρεῖ," ὥ〈σ〉περ ἔχει ὁ τοῦ θεοῦ λόγος; —φημὶ ἐγώ· Ὅτι ἐκ φωτὸς καὶ ζωῆς συνέστηκεν ὁ πατὴρ

1–2 ἄρχων γενῶν OQ : om. Turn. 5 ἀρρενοθήλεα B²: ἀρρενοθῆλυ OQ Turn. 7 Post ὁμοίως add. M ἔοικεν ὁ γόης . . . πολλοῖς ἀποδέδεικται (i.e. Pselli scholion : vide Psellum in *Testim.*) 9 ὁ Turn. : om. codd. | ἄνθρωπος addidit Reitz. (ἄνος pro ἔννους B²) 11–12 Vide § 21 *init.* 12 ὑπόντος Q : εἰπόντος cett. 13 Nescio an delendum sit aut εἱμαρμένης καὶ aut καὶ ἁρμονίας 15 ὑπερούσιον scripsi : περιούσιον codd., Turn. 16 τὸ transposuit Reitz. 17 πλανώμενος, αἰσθητῶς πάσχων Reitz. 20 τοῦ OQ Turn. : om. B² 20–21 μὴ πεφορτικέναι BC : μη . . . . . τικέναι A, vacuo relicto v litterarum spatio 24 προκατάρχεται Reitz. : προκατέρχεται ABCMQ Turn. : προκατέχεται D | οἰκείου OQ Turn. : ὑλικοῦ Reitz. : fortasse ἐπιγείου 25 ἐξ ἧς τὸ σῶμα Reitz. : ἐξ οὗ τὸ σῶμα OQ Turn. 26 ἀρύεται Reitz. : ἀρδεύεται OQ Turn. : ἀρτύεται Keil 27 ὁ ἀναγνωρίσας scripsi : ὁ νοήσας Reitz. : ἐνόησας OQ Turn. 28 εἰς τὸ ἀγαθὸν scripsi : εἰς αὐτὸν codd., Turn. | χωρεῖν Turn. : χωρεῖ cett. | ὥσπερ scripsi : ὅπερ codd., Turn.

and mind from Light. And all things remained so until the end
of a period.

And now I will tell you that which you have been longing to 18
hear. When the period was completed, the bond by which all
things were held together was loosed, by God's design; all living
creatures, having till then been bisexual, were parted asunder,
and man with the rest; and so there came to be males on the
one part, and likewise females on the other part. And thereon
God spoke thus in holy speech: "Increase and multiply abundantly, all ye that have been created and made. And let the
man that has mind in him recognize that he is immortal, and
that the cause of death is carnal desire.[1] And he who has
recognized himself[2] enters into the Good." And when God had 19
thus spoken, his Providence, by means of Destiny and the
structure of the heavens,[3] brought about the unions of male and
female, and set the births going; and all creatures multiplied after
their kinds. And he who has recognized himself has entered into that
Good which is above all being; but he who, being led astray by
carnal desire, has set his affection on the body, continues wandering in the darkness of the sense-world, suffering the lot of death.'

'But what great sin,' said I, 'do those who are in ignorance 20
commit, that they should be deprived of immortality?' 'O man,'
said he, 'it seems you have not heeded what you heard. Did
I not bid you mark my words?' 'I do so,' said I, 'and I keep
in memory what you have told me, and moreover I am thankful
for it.' 'If then you have marked my words,' said he, 'tell me
why those who are in ignorance deserve death.' I answered, 'It
is because the source from which the material body has issued is
that grim darkness, whence came the watery substance of which
the body is composed; . . . in the sensible world,[4] from which
is drawn the draught of death.' 'O man,' said he, 'you have 21
understood aright. But why is it that "he who has recognized
himself enters into the Good", as it was said in God's speech?'
I answered, 'It is because the Father of all consists of Light and

[1] Carnal desire causes souls to be incarnated in mortal bodies, and thereby causes death.

[2] I.e. he who has become aware that one part of him is incorporeal and immortal, and has recognized that this part of him is his true self.

[3] Perhaps, 'by means of [ ] the structure of the heavens' (i.e. by the working of astral influences).

[4] Perhaps, '⟨and therefore those who have set their affection on the body are deservedly held captive⟩ in the sensible world', &c.

τῶν ὅλων, ἐξ οὗ γέγονεν ὁ ἄνθρωπος.—Εὖ φῄς [λαλῶν ⟨ὅτι⟩ φῶς καὶ ζωή ἐστιν ὁ θεὸς καὶ πατήρ, ἐξ οὗ ἐγένετο ὁ ἄνθρωπος]. ἐὰν οὖν, [[μάθῃς ἑαυτὸν]] ἐκ ζωῆς καὶ φωτὸς ὤν, [τα καὶ] ⟨⟨μάθῃς ἑαυτὸν⟩⟩ ὅτι ἐκ τούτων τυγχάνεις, εἰς ζωὴν ⟨καὶ φῶς⟩ πάλιν χωρήσεις.—ταῦτα ὁ Ποιμάνδρης εἶπεν.

Ἀλλ' ἔτι μοι εἰπέ, [[πῶς εἰς ζωὴν χωρήσω]] ⟨ἔφην⟩ ἐγώ· [[ἔφην ὦ νοῦς ἐμός]] φησὶ γὰρ ὁ θεὸς "ὁ ἔννους ἄνθρωπος ἀναγνωρισάτω ἑαυτόν"· οὐ πάντες γὰρ ἄνθρωποι νοῦν
22 ἔχουσιν;—⟨⟨ἔφη[ν] ὁ νοῦς ἐμοί·⟩⟩ Εὐφήμ⟨ε⟩ι, ὦ οὗτος [λαλῶν]. παραγίνομαι ἐγὼ ὁ νοῦς τοῖς ὁσίοις καὶ ἀγαθοῖς καὶ καθαροῖς καὶ ἐλεήμοσι [τοῖς εὐσεβοῦσι], καὶ ἡ παρουσία μου γίνεται ⟨αὐτοῖς⟩ βοήθεια, καὶ εὐθὺς τὰ πάντα γνωρίζουσι, καὶ τὸν πατέρα ἱλάσκονται ἀγαπητικῶς, καὶ εὐχαριστοῦσιν εὐλογοῦντες καὶ ὑμνοῦντες, τετα[γ]μένοι πρὸς αὐτὸν τῇ στοργῇ. καὶ πρὸ τοῦ παραδοῦναι τὸ σῶμα ⟨τῷ⟩ ἰδίῳ θανάτῳ μυσάττονται τὰς αἰσθήσεις, εἰδότες αὐτῶν τὰ ἐνεργήματα. μᾶλλον δὲ οὐκ ἐάσω αὐτὸς ὁ νοῦς τὰ προσπίπτοντα ἐνεργήματα τοῦ σώματος ἐκτελεσθῆναι· πυλωρὸς ⟨γὰρ⟩ ὢν ἀποκλείσω τὰς εἰσόδους τῶν κακῶν καὶ αἰσχρῶν ἐνεργημάτων, τὰς ἐνθυμήσεις
23 ἐκκόπτων. τοῖς δὲ ἀνοήτοις καὶ κακοῖς καὶ πονηροῖς καὶ φθονεροῖς καὶ πλεονέκταις καὶ φονεῦσι καὶ ἀσεβέσι πόρρωθέν εἰμι, τῷ τιμωρῷ ἐκχωρήσας δαίμονι, ὅστις τὴν ὀξύτητα τοῦ πυρὸς προσβάλλων ⟨τὸν⟩ ⟨⟨τ⟨οι⟩οῦτον βασανίζει⟩⟩, θράσσων αὐτὸν αἰσθητικῶς, καὶ μᾶλλον ἐπὶ τὰς ἀνομίας αὐτὸν ὁπλίζει, ἵνα τύχῃ μείζονος τιμωρίας. καὶ οὐ παύεται ⟨⟨σκοτομαχῶν⟩⟩, ἐπ' ὀρέξεις ἀπλέτους ⟨ . . . ⟩, τὴν ἐπιθυμίαν ἔχων ἀκόρεστον, [[σκοτομαχῶν]] [καὶ] [[τοῦτον βασανίζει]] καὶ ἐφ' αὐτὸν ⟨τὸ⟩ πῦρ ἐπὶ πλεῖον αὐξάνει.—

24 Εὖ με πάντα, ὡς ἐβουλόμην, ἐδίδαξας, ὦ νοῦ[ς]. ἔτι δέ μοι εἰπὲ ⟨περὶ⟩ τῆς ἀνόδου τῆς γινομένης, ⟨⟨πῶς εἰς ζωὴν χωρήσω.⟩⟩—πρὸς ταῦτα ὁ Ποιμάνδρης εἶπε· Πρῶτον μὲν ἐν τῇ ἀναλύσει τοῦ σώματος τοῦ ὑλικοῦ παραδίδως[ιν] αὐτὸ τὸ

1 φῄς Reitz.: φημὶ OQ Turn. 2 καὶ πατήρ A: καὶ ὁ πατήρ CDMQ Turn. 3 ὤν scripsi: ὄντα καὶ codd., Turn. 5 χωρήσῃς BCM 6 πῶς εἰς ζωὴν χωρήσω hinc ad § 24 transposui 9 Εὐφήμει B² Reitz.: εὖ φημι OQ Turn. 10 ἐγὼ ὁ νοῦς Q Turn.: ἐγὼ αὐτὸς ὁ νοῦς A: αὐτὸς ἐγὼ ὁ νοῦς cett. | ἰδίοις DQ: ὁσίοις cett. 11 τοῖς εὐσεβῶς βιοῦσι Q Turn.: τοῖς εὐσεβοῦσι cett. 12 τὰ πάντα codd.: fortasse τὰ ὄντα 14 καὶ ὑμνοῦντες om. Q: καὶ ὑμνοῦσι A | τεταμένοι Reitz.: τεταγμένως OQ Turn. 15 παραδοῦναι τὸ D Turn.: παραδοῦναι τῷ Q: παραδοῦ τὸ A: παραδῶ τὸ BCM 15–16 μυσάττονται Turn.: μυσάττοντες A: μυσάσσοντες B: μουσάσσοντες CD¹MQ 18 γὰρ add. B² 20 καὶ (post κακοῖς) om. CDMQ

Life, and from him Man has sprung.' 'You are right,' said he
'If then, being made of Life and Light, you learn to know that
you are made of them, you will go back into Life and Light.'
Thus spoke Poimandres.

'But tell me this too,' said I. 'God said, "Let *the man who
has mind in him* recognize himself;" but have not all men
mind?' 'O man,' said Mind to me, 'speak not so. I, even 22
Mind, come to those men who are holy and good and pure and
merciful; and my coming is a succour to them, and forthwith
they recognize all things,[1] and win the Father's grace by loving
worship, and give thanks to him, praising and hymning him with
hearts uplifted to him in filial affection. And before they give up
the body to the death which is proper to it, they loathe the
bodily senses, knowing what manner of work the senses do. Nay,
rather I myself, even Mind, will not suffer the workings of the
body by which they are assailed to take effect; I will keep guard
at the gates, and bar the entrance of the base and evil workings
of the senses, cutting off all thoughts of them. But from men 23
that are foolish and evil and wicked and envious and covetous
and murderous and impious I keep far aloof, and give place to
the avenging daemon. And he brings to bear on such a man the
fierce heat of fire, and tortures him, tossing him about in the
tumult of the senses; and he equips the man more fully for his
lawless deeds, that so he may incur the greater punishment.
And that man ceases not to struggle blindly; he gives way to
boundless appetites, his desire being insatiable; and so by his
own doing he makes the fire yet hotter for his torment.'

'Full well have you taught me all, O Mind,' said I, 'even as 24
I wished. But tell me furthermore of the ascent by which men
mount; tell me how I shall enter into Life.' Poimandres
answered, 'At the dissolution of your material body, you first

[1] Perhaps, 'they come to know the things that are'.

---

23 *τὸν τοιοῦτον βασανίζει* addidi (vide *καὶ τοῦτον βασανίζει* infra): *τοῦτον βασανίζει καὶ ἐπ' αὐτὸν πῦρ ἐπὶ τὸ πλέον αὐξάνει* huc transposuit Reitz. | *θράσσων* scripsi: *θράσσει* Keil: *θρώσκει* OQ Turn.: ⟨*καὶ*⟩ *θρώσκει* Reitz. 26 *ἀπλάτους* BC: *ἀπλέτους* cett. | *ἀκόρεστον* scripsi: *ἀκορέστως* OQ Turn. 27 *καὶ τοῦτον βασανίζει* ABCM: *καὶ τοῦτον ἀφανίζει καὶ ἐπὶ πλέον βασανίζει* DQ Turn.: seclusi | *ἐφ' αὐτὸν* scripsi: *ἐπ' αὐτὸν* O Turn.: *ἐτὸν* Q | *τὸ* add. B^2 28 *ἐπὶ πλεῖον* DQ Turn.: *ἐπὶ τὸ πλεῖον* ABCM. Fortasse *ἔτι πλεῖον* 29 *εὖ με* Turn.: *εὖ μοι* codd. 30 *περὶ* add. B^2 Turn. 30–31 *πῶς εἰς ζωὴν χωρήσω* huc a § 21 transposui 32 *παραδίδως* Tiedemann: *παραδίδωσιν* OQ Turn.

σῶμα εἰς ἀλλοίωσιν, καὶ τὸ εἶδος ὃ εἶχες ἀφανὲς γίνεται. καὶ τὸ ⌜ἦθος⌝ τῷ †δαίμονι⌝ ἀνενέργητον παραδίδως· καὶ αἱ αἰσθήσεις τοῦ σώματος εἰς τὰς ἑαυτῶν πηγὰς ἐπανέρχονται, μέρη ⟨τοῦ κόσμου⟩ γινόμεναι, καὶ πάλιν συνιστάμεναι εἰς [τὰς] ⟨ἑτέρας⟩ ἐνεργείας. [καὶ ὁ θυμὸς καὶ ἡ ἐπιθυμία
25 εἰς τὴν ἄλογον φύσιν χωρεῖ.] καὶ οὕτως ὁρμᾷ λοιπὸν ἄνω ⟨ὁ ἄνθρωπος⟩ διὰ τῆς ἁρμονίας. καὶ τῇ πρώτῃ ζώνῃ δίδωσι τὴν αὐξητικὴν ἐνέργειαν καὶ τὴν μειωτικήν, καὶ τῇ δευτέρᾳ τὴν μηχανὴν τῶν κακῶν δόλων [ἀνενέργητον], καὶ τῇ τρίτῃ τὴν ἐπιθυμητικὴν ἀπατὴν [ἀνενέργητον], καὶ τῇ τετάρτῃ τὴν ἀρχοντικὴν ⟨ὑ⟩π⟨ε⟩ρηφανίαν [ἀπλεονέκτητον], καὶ τῇ πέμπτῃ τὸ θράσος τὸ ἀνόσιον καὶ τῆς τόλμης τὴν προπέτειαν, καὶ τῇ ἕκτῃ τὰς ἐφορμὰς τὰς κακὰς τοῦ πλούτου [ἀνενεργήτους], καὶ
26a τῇ ἑβδόμῃ [ζώνῃ] τὸ ἐνεδρεῦον ψεῦδος. καὶ τότε, γυμνωθεὶς ἀπὸ τῶν τῆς ἁρμονίας ἐνεργημάτων, γίνεται ἐπὶ τὴν ὀγδοαδικὴν φύσιν, τὴν ἰδίαν δύναμιν ἔχων, καὶ ὑμνεῖ σὺν τοῖς ⟨ἐκεῖ⟩ οὖσι τὸν πατέρα· συγχαίρουσι δὲ οἱ παρόντες τῇ τούτου παρουσίᾳ. καὶ ὁμοιωθεὶς τοῖς συνοῦσιν, ἀκούει καὶ τῶν δυνάμεων, ὑπὲρ τὴν ὀγδοαδικὴν φύσιν οὐσῶν, φωνῇ τινι ἰδίᾳ ὑμνουσῶν τὸν θεόν. καὶ τότε τάξει ἀνέρχονται πρὸς τὸν πατέρα· [[καὶ αὐτοὶ]] εἰς ⟨γὰρ τὰς⟩ δυνάμεις ἑαυτοὺς παραδιδόασι, καὶ δυνάμεις ⟨⟨καὶ αὐτοὶ⟩⟩ γινόμενοι, ἐν θεῷ γίνονται. τοῦτό ἐστι τὸ ἀγαθόν, ⟨τοῦτο τὸ⟩ τέλος τοῖς γνῶσιν ἐσχηκόσι [θεωθῆναι].
26b λοιπόν, τί μέλλεις; οὐχ ὡς πάντα παραλαβὼν καθοδηγὸς γίνῃ τοῖς ἀξίοις, ὅπως τὸ γένος τῆς ἀνθρωπότητος διὰ σοῦ ὑπὸ θεοῦ σωθῇ;—ταῦτα εἰπὼν ἐμοὶ ὁ Ποιμάνδρης ἐμίγη ταῖς δυνάμεσιν.

[[27–29 ἐγὼ δὲ εὐχαριστήσας . . . τὴν ἰδίαν κοίτην.]]

1 Fortasse πρῶτον μὲν ἐν τῇ ἀλλοιώσει [ ] παραδίδως αὐτὸ τὸ σῶμα ⟨τῇ φύσει⟩ εἰς ἀνάλυσιν 2 Fortasse τὸ πνεῦμα τῷ ἀέρι | παραδίδως codd. : παραδίδωσι Turn. 4 συνιστάμεναι DQ Turn. : συνανιστάμεναι codd. cett. 6 καὶ (ante οὕτως) om. Q Turn. | οὗτος BM : οὕτως cett. 7 ὁ ἄνθρωπος addidit Keil 9 δόλων M : δόλον codd. cett., Turn. 11 ὑπερηφανίαν B[2]: προφανίαν OQ Turn. 13 ἐφορμὰς scripsi : ἀφορμὰς codd., Turn. | ἀνενεργήτους Turn. : ἀνενέργητον OQ 15 ὀγδοαδικὴν Reitz. : ὀγδοατικὴν OQ Turn. 17–20 συγχαίρουσι δὲ . . . ἀνέρχονται πρὸς τὸν πατέρα om. A 18 τῶν DQ Turn. : τηνῶν M : τινων codd. cett. 19 ὀγδοαδικὴν Reitz. : ὀγδοατικὴν BCDMQ Turn. | ἰδίᾳ DQ Turn. : ἡδείᾳ BCM 21 παραδιδόασι ADMQ Turn. : παραπέμπουσι BC 22 γινόμενοι DQ : γενόμενοι codd. cett., Turn. 23 ἐσχηκέναι A : ἐσχηκόσι cett. 26 εἰπὼν ἐμοὶ ὁ Ποιμάνδρης DMQ Turn. : εἰπὼν ὁ Ποιμάνδρης ἐμοὶ codd. cett. 28 §§ 27–29 (ἐγὼ δὲ . . . ἰδίαν κοίτην) hinc transposui : vide post § 32

yield up the body itself to be changed,[1] and the visible form you
bore is no longer seen. And your . . . you yield up to the . . .,[2]
so that it no longer works in you; and the bodily senses go back
to their own sources, becoming parts of the universe, and entering
into fresh combinations to do other work. And thereupon the 25
man mounts upward through the structure of the heavens. And
to the first zone of heaven[3] he gives up the force which works
increase and that which works decrease; to the second zone,[4]
the machinations of evil cunning; to the third zone,[5] the lust
whereby men are deceived; to the fourth zone,[6] domineering
arrogance; to the fifth zone,[7] unholy daring and rash audacity;
to the sixth zone,[8] evil strivings after wealth; and to the seventh
zone,[9] the falsehood which lies in wait to work harm. And 26a
thereupon, having been stripped of all that was wrought upon
him by the structure of the heavens, he ascends to the substance
of the eighth sphere,[10] being now possessed of his own proper
power; and he sings, together with those who dwell there, hymning
the Father; and they that are there rejoice with him at his
coming. And being made like to those with whom he dwells,
he hears the Powers, who are above the substance of the eighth
sphere, singing praise to God with a voice that is theirs alone.
And thereafter, each in his turn, they[11] mount upward to the
Father; they give themselves up to the Powers, and becoming
Powers themselves, they enter into God. This is the Good;
this is the consummation, for those who have got *gnosis*.[12]

And now, why do you delay? Seeing that you have received 26 b
all, why do you not make yourself a guide to those who are
worthy of the boon, that so mankind may through you be saved
by God?' And when Poimandres had thus spoken to me, he
mingled with the Powers.[13]

[1] Perhaps, 'When the time comes for you to be changed, you first yield up the body itself to nature for dissolution.'

[2] MSS.: 'your moral character you yield up to the daemon.' But it ought rather to be, 'your vital spirit you yield up to the atmosphere'.

[3] I.e. the sphere of the Moon.

[4] That of the planet Mercury.

[5] That of the planet Venus.

[6] That of the Sun.

[7] That of the planet Mars.

[8] That of the planet Jupiter.

[9] That of the planet Saturn.

[10] I.e. the sphere of the fixed stars, the highest or outermost of the spheres of heaven.

[11] I.e. the men who have ascended to the eighth sphere.

[12] I.e. knowledge of God, and of the relation between man's true self and God.

[13] I.e. he departed to the incorporeal world, in which the Powers reside.

30 ἐγὼ δὲ τὴν εὐεργεσίαν τοῦ Ποιμάνδρου ἀνεγραψάμην εἰς ἐμαυτόν, καὶ πληρωθεὶς ὧν ἤθελον ἐξηυφράνθην. ἐγένετο γὰρ ὁ τοῦ σώματος ὕπνος τῆς ψυχῆς νῆψις, καὶ ἡ κάμμυσις τῶν ὀφθαλμῶν ἀληθινὴ ὅρασις, καὶ ἡ σιωπή μου ἐγκύμων τοῦ ἀγαθοῦ, καὶ ἡ τοῦ λόγου ἀφορ⟨ί⟩α γέννημα[τα] ⌜ἀγαθῶν⌝. τοῦτο δὲ συνέβη μοι λαβόντι ἀπὸ [τοῦ νοός μου] [[τουτέστι]] τοῦ Ποιμάνδρου, ⟨⟨τουτέστι⟩⟩ τοῦ τῆς αὐθεντίας ⟨νοός, τὸν . . .⟩ λόγον, ⟨ὅθεν⟩ θεόπνους γενόμενος ⟨ . . . ⟩ τῆς ἀληθείας ἦλθον.

διὸ δίδωμι ἐκ ψυχῆς καὶ ἰσχύος ὅλης εὐλογίαν τῷ πατρὶ θεῷ.

31 Ἅγιος ὁ θεὸς καὶ πατὴρ τῶν ὅλων, (ὁ πρὸ) ἀρχῆ(ς ὤν)·
ἅγιος ὁ θεός, οὗ ἡ βουλὴ τελεῖται ἀπὸ τῶν ⌜ἰδίων⌝ δυνάμεων·
ἅγιος ὁ θεός, ὃς γνωσθῆναι βούλεται, καὶ γινώσκεται τοῖς ἰδίοις.

ἅγιος εἶ, ὁ λόγῳ συστησάμενος τὰ ὄντα·
ἅγιος εἶ, ὃν ἡ φύσις οὐκ ἠμαύρωσεν·
ἅγιος εἶ, οὗ πᾶσα φύσις εἰκὼν ἔφυ.

ἅγιος εἶ, ὁ πάσης δυναστείας ἰσχυρότερος·
ἅγιος εἶ, ὁ πάσης ὑπεροχῆς μείζων·
ἅγιος εἶ, ὁ κρείττων ⟨πάν⟩των ἐπαίνων.

δέξαι λογικὰς θυσίας ἁγνὰς ἀπὸ ψυχῆς καὶ καρδίας πρὸς σὲ ἀνατεταμένης, ἀνεκλάλητε, ἄρρητε, σιωπῇ φωνούμενε.

32 αἰτουμένῳ τὸ μὴ σφαλῆναι τῆς γνώσεως τῆς κατ' οὐσίαν ἡμῶν ἐπίνευσόν μοι· καὶ ἐνδυνάμωσόν με, ⟨ἵνα⟩ [καὶ] τῆς χάριτος ταύτης ⟨τυχὼν⟩ φωτίσω τοὺς ἐν ἀγνοίᾳ τοῦ γένους μου, ἀδελφοὺς ⟨ἐμούς⟩, υἱοὺς δὲ σοῦ.

§§ 31, 32 (ἅγιος ὁ θεὸς . . . τὴν πᾶσαν ἐξουσίαν): Papyrus Berol. 9764; Berliner Klassikertexte, Heft VI (1910), *Altchristliche Texte* (C. Schmidt und W. Schubart), pp. 110 ff.

2 ἐξηυφράθην A 5 ἀφορία scripsi: ἐκφορὰ codd., Turn. | γεννήματα ἀγαθῶν codd., Turn.: fortasse γέννημα ἁγίων ⟨νοημάτων⟩ 6 μοι λαβόντι μοι BCDMQ 7–8 τοῦ τῆς αὐθεντίας λόγου OQ Turn.: τὸν τῆς αὐθεντίας λόγον Reitz. 8 ὅθεν add. Flussas | ⟨ἐπὶ τὸν κύκλον⟩ τῆς Ἀληθείας Reitz. Fortasse ⟨ἐπὶ τὸ πεδίον⟩ τῆς ἀληθείας: cf. Pl. *Phaedr.* 248 B 10 Fortasse ἔδωκα 12 Ante ἅγιος add. Pap. ἅγιος (ὁ θεός, ὁ ὑποδ)είξας μοι ἀπὸ τοῦ νιος ζωὴν καὶ φ(ῶς) | θεὸς κ(αὶ πατὴρ τῶ)ν Pap.: θεὸς ὁ πατὴρ τῶν codd. Corp. | Post ὅλων add. Pap. ἅγιος εἶ | . . . αρχη . . . Pap.: om. codd. Corp.: (ὁ πρὸ) ἀρχῆ(ς ὤν) scripsi: (ὁ ἀπ') ἀρχῆ(ς ὤν) Schmidt et Schubart 13 ἰδίων codd.: fortasse εἰδικῶν | ο(ὗ ἐπιτελεῖ)ται ἀπὸ τῶν ἰδίω(ν δυνάμεων ἡ βουλή) Pap. (Reitz.) 14 γινώσκεται τοῖς ἰδίοις codd. Corp: γινώσ(κεται τοῖς) εἰ(δίοις) Pap. (Reitz.) 16 ἅγιος εἶ (ante ὁ λόγῳ) codd. Corp.: om. Pap. 17–18 ἅγιος εἶ, ὃ(ν) ἡ φύσις οὐκ ἐμαύρωσεν· ἅγιος εἶ, οὗ πᾶσα φ(ύσις

And I inscribed in my memory the benefaction of Poimandres; and I was exceeding glad, for I was fed full with that for which I craved. My bodily sleep had come to be sober wakefulness of soul; and the closing of my eyes, true vision; and my silence, pregnant with good; and my barrenness of speech, a brood of . . .[1] And this befell me, in that I received from Poimandres, that is, from the Mind of the Sovereignty, the teaching of . . . ; whereby, becoming God-inspired, I attained to the abode of Truth. 30

Therefore with all my soul and with all my strength did I give praise to God the Father, saying:

'Holy is God the Father of all, who is before the first beginning;[2] 31
holy is God, whose purpose is accomplished by his several Powers;
holy is God, who wills to be known, and is known by them that are his own.

Holy art Thou, who by thy word hast constructed all that is;
holy art Thou, whose brightness nature[3] has not darkened;
holy art Thou, of whom all nature is an image.

Holy art Thou, who art stronger than all domination;
holy art Thou, who art greater than all pre-eminence;
holy art Thou, who surpassest all praises.

Accept pure offerings of speech from a soul and heart uplifted to thee, Thou of whom no words can tell, no tongue can speak, whom silence only can declare.

I pray that I may never fall away from that knowledge of thee which matches with our being; grant Thou this my prayer. And put power into me, that so, having obtained this boon, I may enlighten those of my race who are in ignorance, my brothers and thy sons. 32

[1] Perhaps, 'a brood of holy thoughts'.
[2] I.e. who was before the world began to be.
[3] 'Nature' here means the material world, which issued from the 'grim darkness' spoken of in § 4.

εἰκὼν ἔ)φυ Pap.: ἅγιος εἶ, οὗ πᾶσα φύσις εἰκὼν ἔφυ (ἔφη A)· ἅγιος εἶ, ὃν ἡ φύσις (φύσεις A) οὐκ ἐμόρφωσεν codd. Corp. 19 δυναστείας scripsi: δυνάστεως Pap.: δυνάμεως codd. Corp. 20 ὁ πάσης ὑπεροχῆς μείζων codd. Corp.: ὁ (τῆς? ὑπεροχῆς) μείζων Pap. 21 πάντων Plasberg: τῶν codd. Corp. et Pap. 22 δέξαι λογικὰς θυσίας ἁγνὰς codd. Corp.: δέξαι λο(γικὰς ἁγ)νὰς Pap. (Reitz.) ἁγνὰς secludendum? An scribendum ἁγνῆς? 23 ἀνατεταμένης codd. Corp. (ἀνατεταμένας Q Turn.): ἀνατεταγμένας Pap. 24–25 τῆς κατ' οὐσίαν ἡμῶν codd. Corp.: τῆς κατὰ ὕφος ἡμῶν αὐτῶν (fortasse τῆς κατὰ τὸ ὕψος ἡμῶν) Pap. 25 μοι (post ἐπίνευσόν) codd. Corp. (om. A): με Pap. | ἐνδυνάμωσόν μοι C 26 φώτισον Q Turn.: φωτίσω codd. Corp. cett., Pap. | ἀγνοίᾳ codd. Corp.: εὐνοίᾳ Pap. 27 Post υἱοὺς δὲ σοῦ add. Pap. τὸ γὰρ πνεῦμά μου τῷ θείῳ πνεύματι

⟨. . .⟩ διὸ πιστεύω καὶ μαρτυρῶ ⟨ὅτι⟩ εἰς ζωὴν καὶ
φῶς χωρῶ.
εὐλογητὸς εἶ, πάτερ· ὁ σὸς ἄνθρωπος συναγιάζειν σοι
βούλεται, καθὼς παρέδωκας αὐτῷ τὴν πᾶσαν ἐξουσίαν.—
27 ⟨⟨ἐγὼ δέ, εὐχαριστήσας καὶ εὐλογήσας τὸν πατέρα τῶν
ὅλων, ἀνείθην ὑπ' αὐτοῦ δυναμωθείς, καὶ διδαχθεὶς τοῦ
παντὸς τὴν φύσιν, καὶ τὴν μεγίστην ⟨θεασάμενος⟩ θέαν.
καὶ ἤργμαι κηρύσσειν τοῖς ἀνθρώποις τὸ τῆς εὐσεβείας καὶ
γνώσεως κάλλος· "Ὦ λαοί, ἄνδρες γηγενεῖς, οἱ μέθῃ καὶ
ὕπνῳ ἑαυτοὺς ἐκδεδωκότες [[καὶ]] τῇ ἀγνωσίᾳ τοῦ θεοῦ,
νήψατε, παύσασθε δὲ κραιπαλῶντες ⟨⟨καὶ⟩⟩ θελγόμενοι ὕπνῳ
28 ἀλόγῳ." οἱ δὲ ἀκούσαντες παρεγένοντο ὁμοθυμαδόν. ἐγὼ
δέ φημι· "Τί ἑαυτούς, ὦ ἄνδρες [γηγενεῖς], εἰς θάνατον
ἐκδεδώκατε, ἔχοντες ἐξουσίαν τῆς ἀθανασίας μεταλαβεῖν;
μετανοήσατε, οἱ συνοδεύσαντες τῇ πλάνῃ καὶ συγκοινωνή-
σαντες τῇ ἀγνοίᾳ· ἀπαλλάγητε τοῦ σκότ[ειν]ου⟨ς, ἅψασθε
τοῦ⟩ φωτός· μεταλάβετε τῆς ἀθανασίας, καταλείψαντες τὴν
φθοράν."
29 καὶ οἱ μὲν αὐτῶν καταφλυαρήσαντες ἀπέστησαν, τῇ τοῦ
θανάτου ὁδῷ ἑαυτοὺς ἐκδεδωκότες· οἱ δὲ παρεκάλουν διδαχ-
θῆναι, ἑαυτοὺς πρὸ ποδῶν μου ῥίψαντες· ἐγὼ δέ, ἀναστήσας
αὐτούς, καθοδηγὸς ἐγενόμην τοῦ γένους, τοὺς λόγους διδάσκων,
πῶς καὶ τίνι τρόπῳ σωθήσονται. καὶ ἔσπειρα ⟨ἐν⟩ αὐτοῖς
τοὺς τῆς σοφίας λόγους, καὶ ἐτράφη[σαν] ⟨τὸ σπαρὲν⟩ ἐκ τοῦ
ἀμβροσίου ὕδατος. ὀψίας δὲ γενομένης, καὶ τῆς τοῦ ἡλίου
αὐγῆς ἀρχομένης δύεσθαι, ὅλοις ἐκέλευσα αὐτοῖς εὐχαριστεῖν
τῷ θεῷ. καὶ ἀναπληρώσαντες τὴν εὐχαριστίαν ἕκαστος
ἐτράπη εἰς τὴν ἰδίαν κοίτην.⟩⟩

1 εἰς codd. Corp.: ης Pap. 3 Fortasse ὁ σὸς υἱὸς 4 παρέδωκας αὐτῷ τὴν πᾶσαν ἐξουσίαν codd. Corp.: παρέδωκας τὴν πᾶσαν ἐξουσίαν αὐτῷ Pap. | Post ἐξουσίαν αὐτῷ add. Pap. ε(ἴ)η σοι δόξα καὶ νῦν καὶ ⟨ἀ⟩εὶ καὶ εἰς τοὺς σ(ύ)μπαντα(ς αἰ)ῶνας τ(ῶ)ν αἰώνων. (ἀ)μήν 5–28 §§ 27–29 (ἐγὼ δέ . . . ἰδίαν κοίτην) huc transposui 6 ἀνείθην OQ: ἀνέστην Turn. | Fortasse ἐνδυναμωθείς 9 κάλλος A: κλέος BCDMQ Turn. 15 σπάνῃ A: πλάνῃ cett. 16–17 ἀπαλλάγητε τοῦ σκότους, ἅψασθε τοῦ φωτός scripsi

. . . Wherefore I believe and bear witness that I enter into Life and Light.

Blessed art thou, Father; thy Man[1] seeks to share thy holiness, even as Thou hast given him all authority.'

And when I had given thanks and praise to the Father of all, 27
I was sent forth by him, having had power given me, and having
been taught the nature of all that is, and seen the supreme
vision. And I began to preach to men the beauty of piety and of
the knowledge of God, saying: 'Hearken, ye folk, men born of
earth, who have given yourselves up to drunkenness and sleep in
your ignorance of God; awake to soberness, cease to be sodden
with strong drink and lulled in sleep devoid of reason.' And 28
when they heard, they gathered round me with one accord.
And I said, 'O men, why have you given yourselves up to death,
when you have been granted power to partake of immortality?
Repent, ye who have journeyed with Error, and joined company
with Ignorance; rid yourselves of darkness, and lay hold on the
Light; partake of immortality, forsaking corruption.'

And some of them mocked at my words, and stood aloof; for 29
they had given themselves up to the way of death. But others
besought me that they might be taught, and cast themselves
down at my feet. And I bade them stand up; and I made myself
a guide to mankind, teaching them the doctrine, how and in what
wise they might be saved. And I sowed in them the teachings
of wisdom; and that which I sowed was watered with the water
of immortal life. And when evening was come, and the light of
the sun was beginning to go down, I bade them all with one
accord give thanks to God. And when they had accomplished
their thanksgiving, they betook them every man to his own bed.

[1] Perhaps, 'thy son' or 'Man, (who is) thy son'.

ἀπαλλάγητε τοῦ σκοτεινοῦ φωτός codd., Turn. **22** *ἐγινόμην* M **24** *ἐτράφη τὸ σπαρὲν* scripsi: *ἐτράφησαν* codd., Turn. **25** *ἀβρωσίου* Q **26** *ὅλοις* scripsi: *ὅλης* codd., Turn.

LIBELLVS II

⟨Ἑρμοῦ τρισμεγίστου πρὸς Ἀσκληπιόν.⟩

1 Πᾶν τὸ κινούμενον, ὦ Ἀσκληπιέ, οὐκ ἔν τινι κινεῖται, καὶ
ὑπό τινος;—Μάλιστα.—Οὐκ ἀνάγκη δὲ μεῖζον εἶναι ⟨τὸ⟩ ἐν
ᾧ κινεῖται ⟨ἢ⟩ τὸ κινούμενον;—Ἀνάγκη.—[Ἰσχυρότερον ἄρα
τὸ κινοῦν τοῦ κινουμένου.—Ἰσχυρότερον γάρ.—] Ἐναντίαν
δὲ ἔχειν φύσιν ἀνάγκη τὸ ἐν ᾧ κινεῖται τῇ τοῦ κινουμένου.—
Καὶ πάνυ.—
2 Μέγας οὖν οὗτος ⟨ὁ⟩ κόσμος, οὗ μεῖζον οὐκ ἔστι σῶμα.—
Ὡμολόγηται.—Καὶ στιβαρός· πεπλήρωται γὰρ ἄλλων σωμάτων μεγάλων πολλῶν, μᾶλλον δὲ πάντων ὅσα ἔστι
σωμάτων.—Οὕτως ἔχει.—Σῶμα δὲ ὁ κόσμος;—Σῶμα.—
3 Καὶ κινούμενον;—Μάλιστα.—Πηλίκον οὖν δεῖ τὸν τόπον
εἶναι ἐν ᾧ κινεῖται, καὶ ποταπὸν τὴν φύσιν; οὐ πολὺ μείζονα,
ἵνα δυνηθῇ δέξασθαι τῆς φορᾶς τὴν συνέχειαν, καὶ μὴ
θλιβόμενον τὸ κινούμενον ὑπὸ τῆς στενότητος ἐπίσχῃ τὴν
4a κίνησιν;—Παμμέγεθές τι χρῆμα, ὦ Τρισμέγιστε.—Ποταπῆς
δὲ φύσεως; ⟨⟨ἆρα⟩⟩ ⟨οὐ⟩ τῆς ἐναντίας [[ἄρα]], ὦ Ἀσκληπιέ;
σώματι δὲ ἐναντία φύσις τὸ ἀσώματον.—Ὡμολόγηται.—
Ἀσώματος οὖν ὁ τόπος.
4b τὸ δὲ ἀσώματον ἢ θεῖόν ἐστιν || ἢ ὁ θεός. τὸ δὲ θεῖον
λέγω νῦν οὐ τὸ γεννητόν, ἀλλὰ τὸ ἀγέννητον. ἐὰν μὲν οὖν
ᾖ θεῖον, οὐσιῶδές ἐστιν· ἐὰν δὲ ᾖ ⟨ὁ⟩ θεός, καὶ ἀνουσίαστον
5 γίνεται ⟨. . .⟩. ἄλλως δὲ νοητὸς ὁ τόπος· νοητὸς γὰρ

In Libellis II–IX, codicum AQS et Turnebi lectiones adhibui.

II. 1–4b: Stobaei *Anthologium* 1. 18. 2, vol. i, p. 157 Wachsmuth (*Ecl.* I. 384 Heeren): Ἑρμοῦ ἐκ τῶν πρὸς Ἀσκληπιόν. Πᾶν τὸ κινούμενον, ὦ Ἀσκλ. . . . ἀλλὰ τὸ ἀγέννητον.

II. 6b–9: Stob. 1. 19. 2, vol. i, p. 163 W (*Ecl.* I. 398 H): Ἑρμοῦ ἐκ τοῦ πρὸς Ἀσκληπιόν. Πᾶν τὸ κινούμενον οὐκ ἐν . . . δύο σώματα φέρῃ.

II. 10–13: Stob. 1. 18. 3, vol. i, p. 158 W (*Ecl.* I. 386 H): Ἐν ταὐτῷ (sc. Ἑρμοῦ ἐκ τῶν πρὸς Ἀσκληπιόν). Οὐδὲ ἓν τῶν ὄντων . . . ἑνὶ ἑκάστῳ τῶν ὄντων πάντων.

Codices Stob.: F (Farnesinus, saec. xiv), P (Parisinus, saec. xv).

Tit.: Ἑρμοῦ πρὸς τῶτ λόγος καθολικός A: Ἑρμοῦ τοῦ (om. τοῦ Turn.) τρισμεγίστου πρὸς Τὰτ λόγος καθολικός QS Turn. In codicibus Corp. Herm. desunt §§ 1–4b *init.* (Πᾶν τὸ κινούμενον . . . ἢ θεῖόν ἐστιν), ita ut incipiat dialogus a verbis ἢ θεὸς τὸ θεῖον λέγω

3 τὸ add. Patritius 4 ἢ add. Patr. 6 τὸ Wachsmuth: τὴν FP 8 ὁ add. Patr. 11 σωμάτων scripsi: σώματα codd. 17 τῆς ἐναντίας ἆρα Wachsm.: τῆς ἐναντίας ἄρα FP 20 ἢ θεῖόν FP: ἢ τὸ θεῖόν Meineke | ἢ ὁ θεός Stob. F: ἢ θεός Stob. P: ᾗ θεός AQ: η θεὸς S Turn. | τὸ δὲ

LIBELLVS II

A discourse of Hermes Trismegistus to Asclepius.

Hermes. Is it not true of everything which is moved, Asclepius, 1
that it is moved *in* something, and is moved *by* something?—
Asclepius. Assuredly.—*Herm.* And is not that in which the thing
is moved necessarily greater than the thing moved?—*Ascl.* Yes.—
Herm. And that in which the thing is moved must be of opposite
nature to the thing moved.—*Ascl.* Certainly it must.—

Herm. Now this Kosmos is great; there is no body greater 2
than the Kosmos.—*Ascl.* Agreed.—*Herm.* And it is massive;
for it is filled with many other great bodies, or rather, with all the
bodies that exist.—*Ascl.* It is so.—*Herm.* And the Kosmos is
a body, is it not?—*Ascl.* Yes.—*Herm.* And a thing that is
moved?—*Ascl.* Assuredly.—*Herm.* Of what magnitude then 3
must be the space in which the Kosmos is moved? And of
what nature? Must not that space be far greater, that it may
be able to contain the continuous motion of the Kosmos, and
that the thing moved may not be cramped through want of
room, and cease to move?—*Ascl.* Great indeed must be that
space, Trismegistus.—*Herm.* And of what nature must it be, 4a
Asclepius? Must it not be of opposite nature to the Kosmos?
And of opposite nature to body is the incorporeal.—*Ascl.*
Agreed.—*Herm.* That space then is incorporeal.

Now that which is incorporeal is either something that apper- 4b
tains to God, or else it is God himself. (By 'a thing that
appertains to God' I mean, not a thing that comes into being,
but a thing without beginning.) If then the incorporeal thing
is something that appertains to God, it is of the nature of eternal
substance; but if it is God himself, it must be distinct from
substance, ⟨. . .⟩.[1] Space is an object of thought, but not in the 5

[1] The text of §§ 4b–6a is badly corrupted, and the restoration of it that is here proposed is very doubtful. What the author meant might perhaps be expressed by writing as follows: 'It must be distinct from substance, ⟨and distinct from objects of thought. It is true that God is, in one sense, an object of thought, for he is not an object of sense-perception;⟩ but Space is an object of thought in a different sense', &c.

θεῖον codd. Stob.: τὸ θεῖον AQS Turn. 22 καὶ (post θεός) AQS: om. Turn. 22–23 Fortasse hoc fere modo supplendum: καὶ ἀνουσίαστον (an ἀνούσιον?) γίνεται ⟨καὶ ἀνόητον. οὐ μὴν ἀλλὰ πῇ μὲν νοητὸς ὁ θεός· οὐ γὰρ ⟨⟨αἰσθήσει ὑποπίπτει ὁ θεός⟩⟩.⟩ ἄλλως δὲ νοητὸς ὁ τόπος 23 νοητὸς ὁ τόπος scripsi: νοητῷ οὕτω A: νοητὸν οὕτως QS: νοητὸς οὕτω Turn.

πρώτως ὁ θεός ἐστιν ⟨ἑαυτῷ, ὁ δὲ τόπος⟩ ἡμῖν, οὐχ ἑαυτῷ. τὸ γὰρ νοητὸν τῷ νοοῦντι ⟨νοητόν ἐστιν⟩· [αἰσθήσει ὑποπίπτει ὁ θεός] οὐκοῦν οὐχ ἑαυτῷ νοητός ⟨ὁ τόπος⟩,—οὐ γὰρ [ἄλλο τι ὢν τοῦ νοουμένου] ὑφ' ἑαυτοῦ νοεῖται,—ἡμῖν δέ. [[ἄλλο τί
6a ἐστι]] [διὰ τοῦτο ἡμῖν νοεῖται] εἰ δὲ νοητὸς ὁ τόπος οὐχ ⟨ὡς⟩ ὁ θεός, [ἀλλ' ὁ τόπος] [εἰ δὲ καὶ ὁ θεὸς οὐχ ὡς τόπος] ἀλλ' ὡς ἐνέργεια χωρητική, ⟨⟨ἄλλο τί ἐστι⟩⟩ ⟨τοῦ θεοῦ ὁ τόπος⟩.
6b πᾶν δὲ τὸ κινούμενον οὐκ ἐν κινουμένῳ κινεῖται, ἀλλ' ἐν ἑστῶτι. καὶ τὸ κινοῦν δὲ ἕστηκεν· ἀδύνατον γὰρ αὐτὸ συγκινεῖσθαι.

—Πῶς οὖν, ὦ Τρισμέγιστε, τὰ ἐνθάδε ⟨κινοῦντα⟩ συγκινεῖται τοῖς κινουμένοις; τὰς γὰρ σφαίρας ἔφης τὰς πλανωμένας κινεῖσθαι ὑπὸ τῆς ἀπλανοῦς σφαίρας.—Οὐκ ἔστιν αὕτη, ὦ Ἀσκληπιέ, συγκίνησις, ἀλλ' ἀντικίνησις· οὐ γὰρ ὁμοίως κινοῦνται, ἀλλ' ἐναντίως ἀλλήλαις. ἡ δὲ ἐναντίωσις ⟨⟨τῆς κινήσεως⟩⟩ τὴν ἀντέρεισιν [[τῆς κινήσεως]] ἔχει ἑστῶσαν·
7 ἡ γὰρ ἀντιτυπία στάσις φορᾶς. αἱ οὖν πλανώμεναι σφαῖραι, ἐναντίως κινούμεναι τῇ ἀπλανεῖ, ⌜ὑπ' ἀλλήλων τῇ ἐναντίᾳ ὑπαντήσει περὶ τὴν ἐναντιότητα αὐτὴν ὑπὸ τῆς ἑστώσης κινοῦνται.⌝ καὶ ἄλλως ἔχειν ἀδύνατον. τὰς γὰρ ἄρκτους ταύτας, ἃς ὁρᾷς μήτε δυνούσας μήτε ἀνατελλούσας, [περὶ δὲ τὸ αὐτὸ στρεφομένας,] οἴει κινεῖσθαι ἢ ἑστάναι;—Κινεῖσθαι, ὦ Τρισμέγιστε.—Κίνησιν ποίαν, ὦ Ἀσκληπιέ;—Τὴν περὶ τὸ αὐτὸ στρεφομένην.—Ἡ δὲ περιφορὰ ἡ περὶ τὸ αὐτὸ κίνησίς ἐστιν ὑπὸ στάσεως κατεχομένη· τὸ γὰρ περὶ ⟨τὸ⟩ αὐτὸ κωλύει τὸ ὑπὲρ αὐτό, κωλυόμενον δὲ τὸ ὑπὲρ αὐτὸ ⌜εἰ ἕστη⌝ εἰς τὸ περὶ ⟨τὸ⟩ αὐτό. οὕτω καὶ ἡ ἐναντία φορὰ
8a ἕστηκεν ἑδραία, ὑπὸ τῆς ἐναντιότητος στηριζομένη. παράδειγμα δέ σοι τοῖς ὀφθαλμοῖς ἐΜπῖπτον φράσω, τὰ ἐπίγεια ⟨⟨λέγω⟩⟩ ζῷα. οἷον τὸν

1 πρώτως scripsi: πρῶτος codd. 3–4 τι ὦ τοῦ S: τι ὢν τοῦ cett. 4 ὑφ' ἑαυτῆς S: ὑφ' ἑαυτοῦ cett. 4–5 ἡμῖν δέ . . . ἡμῖν νοεῖται om. S | ἄλλο τί ἐστι hinc ad § 6a transposui 5–6 εἰ δὲ νοητὸς . . . ἀλλ' ὁ τόπος om. Q 6 εἰ δὲ καὶ ὁ θεὸς QS: εἰ δὲ καὶ ὡς θεὸς Turn. 8 δὲ codd. Corp.: om. codd. Stob. 9–10 ἀδύνατον γὰρ αὐτὸ συγκ. scripsi: ἀδύνατον γὰρ αὐτῷ συγκ. codd. Corp.: ἀδύνατον συγκ. codd. Stob. 11 συγκινεῖσθαι S: συγκινεῖται cett. 11–12 τοῖς κινουμένοις codd. Corp.: τοῖς κινοῦσιν codd. Stob. 12 ὑπὸ τοὺς S: ὑπὸ τῆς cett. 13 συγκίνησις codd. Stob.: κίνησις codd. Corp. 13–14 ἀλλ' ἀντικίνησις codd. Corp. et Stob. F: om. Stob. P 14 ἀλλ' ἐναντίως codd. Stob.: ἀλλ' ἐναντίαι codd. Corp. 14–15 ἡ δὲ ἐναντίωσις codd. Corp.: ἡ δὲ ἐναντίως codd. Stob. 15 ἔχει ἑστῶσαν Turn.: ἔχει (om ἑστῶσαν) QS: ἑστῶσαν ἔχει (codd. Stob.?) Wachsm. 16 στάσις φορᾶς codd. Stob.: στάσεως ἐστι φορά (φωρὰ S) codd. Corp. | αἱ οὖν πλανώμεναι codd. Corp.: διὸ καὶ πλανώμεναι Stob. FP[1]: διὸ καὶ αἱ πλανώμεναι Stob. P[2] 17 τῇ ἀπλανῆ S 17–18 περὶ τὴν ἐναντιώτητα QS 18 αὐτὴν ὑπὸ τῆς ἑστώσης κινοῦνται codd. Corp.: ἑστῶσαν αὐτὴν ὑπ' αὐτῆς ἕξει codd. Stob. | καὶ ἄλλως ἔχειν ἀδύνατον om. codd. Stob. 20 περὶ . . . στρεφομένας seclusi: περὶ δὲ τὸ αὐτὸ στρεφομένας A et codd. Stob.: περὶ δὲ αὐτὸ στρεφομένας QS: περὶ δὲ τὸ αὐτὸ ἀντιστρεφομένας

same sense that God is; for God is an object of thought primarily to himself, but Space is an object of thought to us, not to itself. That which is an object of thought is such to him who contemplates it in thought; Space therefore is an object of thought, not to itself (for it is not contemplated by itself), but to us. And if 6a
Space is an object of thought, not as God is, but as the working of a power by which things are contained, then Space is something other than God.

Moreover, everything that is moved is moved, not in something 6b
that is itself moved, but in something that stands fast. And the mover too stands fast; it is impossible that that which moves a thing should be moved together with the thing it moves.

Ascl. How is it[1] then, Trismegistus, that the things which in our world move other things are moved together with the things they move? For I have heard you say that the planet-spheres are moved by the sphere of the fixed stars; ⟨and surely that sphere is itself moved.⟩—*Herm.* In that instance, Asclepius, the two things are not moved together. Their movements are contrary; for the sphere of the fixed stars is not moved in the same way as the planet-spheres, but in the opposite direction. And the contrariety of the two movements keeps the fulcrum stationary; for motion is stayed by resistance. The planet-spheres 7
then, being moved in the opposite direction to the sphere of the fixed stars, . . . It cannot be otherwise. Look at the Great Bear and the Little Bear. As you see, they neither set nor rise; are they moved, think you, or do they stand fast?—*Ascl.* They are moved, Trismegistus.—*Herm.* And of what kind is their movement?—*Ascl.* It is a movement which circles round one point.—*Herm.* Yes, and their revolution round one point is a movement that is held fast by immobility. For revolution round one point prevents departure from the orbit; and the prevention of departure from the orbit results in revolution round one point. And even so it is that movement in contrary directions is steadfast and stable, being kept stationary by the contrariety. I will give you 8a
an example which you can see with your own eyes. Take the case of some

[1] This passage ('How is it . . . makes the matter clear, Trismegistus', §§ 6b–8a) is obscure, and appears to have been inserted by some one who misunderstood the meaning of the *libellus*.

Turn. | οἴει Stob. P[2] : ἢ οἴει codd. Corp. : ποιεῖ Stob. FP[1] | κινεῖσθαι ἢ ἑστάναι codd. Corp. (om. S) et Stob. P[2] : κινεῖσθαι καὶ ἑστάναι Stob. FP[1] **21** τὴν περὶ τὸ αὐτὸ Parthey : τὴν περὶ αὐτὸ codd. Corp. : τὴν περὶ τὰ αὐτὰ codd. Stob. **21–22** στρεφομένην codd. Corp. : ἀναστρεφομένην codd. Stob. **22** περιφορὰ ἡ περὶ τὸ αὐτὸ codd. Stob. : περιφορὰ τὸ αὐτὸ καὶ ἡ περὶ αὐτὸ codd. Corp. | κίνησίς ἐστιν ὑπὸ codd. Stob. : κίνησις ὑπὸ codd. Corp. **23** κωλύει τὸ περὶ (ὑπὲρ suprascr.) αὐτό A : κωλύει τὸ ὑπὲρ αὐτό cett. **23–24** κωλυόμενον . . . περὶ ⟨τὸ⟩ αὐτό om. codd. Stob. | δὲ τὸ Turn. : δὲ τοῦς τὸ A : δὲ τοὺς τὸ QS (κωλυόμενον δὲ τοὺς τὸ ὑπὲρ αὐτὸ bis scriptum S). Fortasse κωλυομένου δὲ τοῦ **24** εἰ ἕστη codd. : 'fortasse ἐνίσταται' Wachsm. **25** ἕστηκεν codd. Stob. : ἕστη ἢ AQ Turn. : ἐστιν ἢ S | Post δέ σοι add. ἐπίγειον codd Stob. **26** ἐμπῖπτον Patr. : ἐπιπίπτον codd. Stob. : πίπτον codd. Corp. | ἐπίγεια codd. Corp. : ἐπίκηρα codd. Stob.

ἄνθρωπον [[λέγω]] θεώρει νηχόμενον· φερομένου γὰρ τοῦ ὕδατος ἡ ἀντιτυπία τῶν ποδῶν καὶ τῶν χειρῶν στάσις γίνεται τῷ ἀνθρώπῳ τοῦ μὴ συγκατενεχθῆναι τῷ ὕδατι.—Σαφὲς τὸ παράδειγμα, ὦ Τρισμέγιστε.—

πᾶσα οὖν κίνησις ἐν στάσει καὶ ὑπὸ στάσεως κινεῖται.

8 b ⟨. . .⟩ ἡ οὖν κίνησις τοῦ κόσμου, καὶ παντὸς δὲ ζῴου ὑλικοῦ, οὐχ ὑπὸ τῶν κατεκτὸς τοῦ σώματος συμβαίνει γίνεσθαι, ἀλλ' ὑπὸ τῶν ἐντὸς εἰς τὸ κατεκτός, ἤτοι ψυχῆς [ἢ πνεύματος] ἢ ἄλλου τινὸς ἀσωμάτου. σῶμα γὰρ ἔμψυχον οὐ⟨χ ὑπὸ σώματος⟩ κινεῖ⟨ται⟩· ἀλλ' οὐδὲ τὸ σύνολον σῶμα, κἂν ᾖ

9 ἄψυχον.—Πῶς τοῦτο λέγεις, ὦ Τρισμέγιστε; τὰ οὖν ξύλα καὶ τοὺς λίθους καὶ τὰ ἄλλα πάντα ἄψυχα οὐ σώματά ἐστι τὰ κινοῦντα;—Οὐδαμῶς, ὦ Ἀσκληπιέ· τὸ γὰρ ἔνδον τοῦ σώματος, τὸ κινοῦν τὸ ἄψυχον, οὐ σῶμά ⟨ἐστιν⟩. ἐκεῖνό ἐστι τὸ ἀμφότερα κινοῦν, καὶ τὸ τοῦ βαστάζοντος ⟨σῶμα⟩ καὶ τὸ τοῦ βασταζομένου· ⟨⟨ἐπεὶ⟩⟩ [διόπερ] ⟨τὸ⟩ ἄψυχον ⟨αὐ⟩τὸ καθ' ⟨αὑτὸ⟩ οὐδὲν [[ἐπεὶ]] κινεῖ. ὁρᾷς γοῦν καταβαρυνομένην τὴν ψυχήν, ὅταν μόνη δύο σώματα φέρῃ. ⟨ὥστε⟩ καὶ [ὅτι μὲν] ἐν τίνι κινεῖται τὰ κινούμενα, καὶ ὑπὸ τίνος, δῆλον.—

10 Ἐν κενῷ δὲ ⟨οὐ⟩ δεῖ κινεῖσθαι τὰ κινούμενα, ὦ Τρισμέγιστε; —Εὐφήμ⟨ει⟩, ὦ Ἀσκληπιέ. οὐδὲ ἓν τῶν ὄντων ἐστὶ κενόν· μόνον δὲ τὸ μὴ ὂν κενόν ἐστι. ⟨⟨τὸ γὰρ ὑπάρχον⟩⟩ τῷ τῆς ὑπάρξεως λόγῳ ⟨⟨κενὸν οὐδέποτε γενέσθαι δύναται·⟩⟩ τὸ δὲ ὂν οὐκ ἂν ἠδύνατο εἶναι ὄν, εἰ μὴ μεστὸν τῆς ὑπάρξεως ἦν. [[τὸ γὰρ ὑπάρχον]] [[κενὸν οὐδέποτε γενέσθαι δύναται.]]—Οὐκ ἔστιν οὖν κενά τινα, ὦ Τρισμέγιστε, τοιαῦτα, οἷον κάδος

1 θεώρει (θεωρία A) νηχόμενον (νηχώμενον S) codd. Corp.: νηχόμενον θεώρησον codd. Stob. | φερομένου γὰρ τοῦ codd. Corp: φερόμενον τοῦ γὰρ codd. Stob. 2 τοῦ μὴ codd. Stob.: μὴ (om. τοῦ) codd. Corp. 3 συγκατανεχθῆναι S | Post ὕδατι add. Patr. (ex codice aliquo?) μήτε δῦναι ὑπ' αὐτό | σαφὲς τὸ παράδειγμα codd. Stob.: σαφέστατον παράδειγμα εἶπες codd. Corp. 4 ὑπὸ στάσεως Turn.: ὑποστάσει A: ὑπὸ στάσει QS: ὑποστάσεως codd. Stob. | κινεῖται codd.: fortasse γίνεται 5 κόσμου codd. Stob. et QS: ζῴου A Turn. | δὲ codd. Corp.: om. codd. Stob. 6 σώματος codd. Stob.: κόσμου Turn. 6–7 τοῦ σώματος συμβαίνει . . . εἰς τὸ κατεκτός om. QS 7 εἰς τὸ κατεκτός secludit Wachsm. | ἤτοι codd. Corp.: τῶν νοητῶν codd. Stob. | ἢ πνεύματος seclusi: ἢ τοῦ πνεύματος Stob. F: ἢ σώματος QS 8–9 σῶμα γὰρ ἔμψυχον οὐχ ὑπὸ σώματος κινεῖται scripsi: σῶμα γὰρ σῶμα ἔμψυχον οὐ κινεῖ codd Corp.: σῶμα γὰρ ἔμψυχον οὐ κινεῖ codd. Stob. 9 ᾖ codd. Stob.: om. codd. Corp. 11 ἄλλα codd. Corp.: om. codd. Stob. | ἄψυχα codd. Stob.: ἔμψυχα codd. Corp. 12 τὰ κινοῦντα codd. Corp.: om. codd. Stob. | οὐδαμῶς ὦ Ἀσκληπιέ QS Turn.: οὐδαμῶς om. A: ὦ om. codd. Stob. 13 τὸ κινοῦν Turn.: τοῦ κινοῦντος QS et codd. Stob. 14 βαστάζοντος codd. Corp.: βαστάζοντα Stob. F: βαστάζοντος (*os* in *a* corr.) Stob. P 15–16 ἐπεὶ τὸ ἄψυχον αὐτὸ καθ' αὑτὸ οὐδὲν κινεῖ scripsi: διόπερ ἔμψυχον (ex ἄψυχον corr. ἔμψυχον S) τὸ καθεῦδον

animal on earth; look at a man, for instance, swimming. The water flows; but the resistance made by the swimmer's hands and feet keeps him stationary, so that he is not borne away down stream.—*Ascl.* That example makes the matter clear, Trismegistus.—

All movement then takes place *within* something that stands fast, and is caused *by* something that stands fast. . . .

The movement of the Kosmos then, and of every living being 8 b
that is material, is caused, not by things outside the body, but by things within it, which operate outwards from within; that is to say, either by soul or by something else that is incorporeal. For the body which contains a soul is not moved by a body; indeed, body cannot move body at all, even if the body moved be soulless.—*Ascl.* What mean you, Trismegistus? When logs and 9
stones and all other soulless things are moved, are they not moved by bodies?—*Herm.* Certainly not, Asclepius. That which is within the body, and which moves the soulless thing, is not a body; and that is what moves both the body of him who carries a thing and the body of the thing carried; for a soulless thing cannot of itself move anything. Thus it is that you see the soul distressed by the weight of its burden, when it bears two bodies at once.

I have now explained to you what is that *by* which things are moved, as well as what is that *in* which things are moved.—

Ascl. But surely, Trismegistus, it must be in void that things 10
are moved.—*Herm.* You ought not to say that, Asclepius. Nothing that is, is void; it is only that which is not, that is void. That which exists can never come to be void; (this is implied in the very meaning of the word 'existence';) and that which is could not be a thing which is, if it were not filled with something existent.—*Ascl.* But what would you say, Trismegistus,

ἐπεὶ κινεῖ codd. Corp. (pro *καθεῦδον* coni. *καθεαυτόν* Flussas): *διόπερ ἄψυχον οὐκ ἄψυχον κινήσει* codd. Stob. **16** *γοῦν* (codd. Stob.?) Wachsm.: *οὖν* codd. Corp. | *καταβαρυνομένην* Patr.: *καταβαρουμένην* codd. Corp.: *καὶ βαρυνομένην* codd. Stob. **17** *μόνη* codd. Corp.: om. codd. Stob. | *σώματα* codd. Stob. et AS: *σώματε* Q Turn. | *φέρῃ* vel *φέρη* codd. Corp. et Stob. P[2]: *φέρει* Stob. FP[1] **17–18** *ὥστε καὶ ἐν τίνι . . . καὶ ὑπὸ τίνος* scripsi: *καὶ ὅτι μὲν ἔν τινι . . . καὶ ὑπό τινος* codd. (*καὶ ὑπό τινος . . . κινεῖσθαι τὰ κινούμενα* om. QS) **19** *ἐν κενῷ* Flussas: *ἐν ἐκείνῳ* A Turn. **20** *εὖ φῂς* codd., Turn.: 'legendum videtur **Εὐφήμει**' Parthey **20–23** *οὐδὲ ἓν τῶν ὄντων ἐστὶ κενὸν τῷ τῆς ὑπάρξεως λόγῳ· τὸ δὲ ὂν οὐκ ἂν ἠδύνατο εἶναι ὄν, εἰ μὴ μεστὸν τῆς ὑπάρξεως ἦν* codd. Stob.: *οὐδὲν δὲ τῶν ὄντων ἐστὶ κενόν· μόνον δὲ τὸ μὴ ὂν κενόν ἐστι ξένον τῆς ὑπάρξεως* codd. Corp. (ante *ξένον* add. *καὶ* Turn.: *ὑπάρξεως* ex *ὑπερτάξεως*, ut videtur, corr. man. pr. A) **25** *οὖν κενά τινα* codd. Stob.: *οὖν τινὰ* codd. Corp. | *τοιαῦτα* scripsi: *ἔστι τοιαῦτα* codd. Corp.: om. codd. Stob.

κενὸς καὶ κέραμος καὶ ⌜ποταμὸς ὅλος⌝ καὶ ληνὸς καὶ τὰ
ἄλλα πάντα τὰ παραπλήσια;—Φεῦ τῆς πολλῆς πλάνης,
ὦ Ἀσκληπιέ. τὰ μᾶλλον πληρέστατα καὶ μεστότατα ὄντα,
11 ταῦτα κενὰ ἡγῇ εἶναι;—Πῶς λέγεις, ὦ Τρισμέγιστε;—Οὐ
σῶμά ἐστιν ὁ ἀήρ;—Σῶμα.—Τοῦτο δὲ τὸ σῶμα οὐ διὰ πάντων
διήκει τῶν ὄντων, καὶ πάντα διῆκον πληροῖ; σῶμα δὲ οὐκ ἐκ
τῶν τεσσάρων σωμάτων κεκραμένον συνέστηκε; μεστὰ οὖν
πάντα ἐστίν, ἃ σὺ φῄς κενά, τοῦ ἀέρος, εἰ δὲ τοῦ ἀέρος, καὶ
τῶν τεσσάρων σωμάτων· καὶ συμβαίνει ὁ ἐναντίος λόγος
ἐκφαίνεσθαι, ὅτι ἃ σὺ φῂς μεστά, ταῦτα πάντα κενά ἐστι
τοῦ ἀέρος, ἐκείνων ὑπ' ἄλλων σωμάτων στενοχωρουμένων, καὶ
μὴ ἐχόντων τόπον δέξασθαι τὸν ἀέρα. ταῦτα οὖν, ἃ σὺ φῂς
εἶναι κενά, κοῖλα δεῖ ὀνομάζειν, οὐ κενά· ὑπάρξεως γὰρ
μεστά ἐστιν [ἀέρος καὶ πνεύματος].—Ἀναντίρρητος ὁ λόγος,
ὦ Τρισμέγιστε.—

12a Τὸν οὖν τόπον τὸν ἐν ᾧ τὸ πᾶν κινεῖται τί εἴπομεν;
ἀσώματον, ὦ Ἀσκληπιέ.—Τὸ οὖν ἀσώματον ⟨τοῦτο⟩ τί ἐστι;—
Νοῦς ὅλος ἐξ ὅλου ἑαυτὸν ἐμπεριέχων, ἐλεύθερος σωματικῆς
[α]πλάνης, ἀπαθής, ἀναφής, αὐτὸς ἐν ἑαυτῷ ἑστώς, [[συγ]]-
χωρητικὸς ⟨⟨συμ⟩⟩πάντων καὶ σωτήριος τῶν ὄντων, ⟨τὸ⟩ ⟨⟨τῆς
ψυχῆς⟩⟩ ⟨φῶς⟩.—

12b ⟨⟨Τί οὖν φῄς⟩⟩ ⟨⟨τὸ ἀγαθόν⟩⟩;—⟨⟨Τὸ ἀρχέτυπον φῶς⟩⟩, οὗ
ὥσπερ ἀκτῖνές εἰσι⟨ν⟩ [[τὸ ἀγαθὸν]] ⟨ὅ τε νοῦς καὶ⟩ ἡ ἀλήθεια.
[[τὸ ἀρχέτυπον φῶς]] [τὸ ἀρχέτυπον] [[τῆς ψυχῆς]]—

1 *κάδος κενὸς καὶ κέραμος* scripsi: *κάδδος κενὸς καὶ κέραμος κενὸς* codd. Corp. (ante *κέραμος* om. *καὶ* A): *κάδος καὶ κέραμος κενὸς* Stob. F: *κάδος καὶ κέραμος* Stob. P | *καὶ ποταμὸς ὅλος* AQS Turn. (etiam MC teste Reitz.): om. codd. Stob.: *καὶ ποτήριον* Reitz. | *καὶ ληνὸς* codd. Stob.: om. codd. Corp. **2** *πάντα* codd. Corp.: om. codd. Stob. | *σπάνης* Stob. F: *πλάνης* cett. **3** *ὦ* om. codd. Stob. | *καὶ μᾶλλον* QS: *τὰ μᾶλλον* cett. **3–4** *μεστότατα ὄντα, ταῦτα* scripsi: *μεστότατα ταῦτα* codd. Stob.: *μέγιστα ὄντα ταῦτα* codd. Corp. **4–5** *οὐ σῶμά ἐστιν* codd. Stob.: *σῶμά ἐστιν* (om. *οὐ*) codd. Corp. **5** *σῶμα* (post *ἀήρ;*) codd. Stob.: om. codd. Corp. **6** *δὲ* om. A **7** *τῶν τεσσάρων σωμάτων* scripsi: *τῶν τεσσάρων* codd. Stob.: *τῶν σωμάτων* codd. Corp. | *κεκραμμένον* S | *συνέστηκε* codd. Stob.: om. codd. Corp. | *μεστὰ* codd. Corp., Stob. F: *δὲ μετὰ* Stob. P **8** *ἐστι πάντα, ἃ φῂς* A: *πάντα ἐστίν, ἃ σὺ φῄς* cett. | *εἰ δὲ τοῦ ἀέρος, καὶ* codd. Stob.: *εἰ δὲ τοῦ ἀέρος* (om. *καὶ*) QS: om. Turn.: *εἰ δὲ τοῦ ἀέρος . . . δέξασθαι τὸν ἀέρα* om. A **10** *μεστὰ* QS Turn.: *μετὰ* codd. Stob. **11** *ἐκείνων* codd. Stob.: om. QS Turn. | *στενοχορουμένων* S **12** *τόπον* (ex B marg.) Wachsm.: *τοῦτον* codd. Stob.: om. QS Turn. | Post *ἀέρα* add. *ἐν τόπῳ αὐτῶν* QS Turn. **13** *εἶναι κενὰ* AQS Turn.: om. codd. Stob. **13–14** *ὑπάρξεως γὰρ μεστά* scripsi: *ὑπάρξει γὰρ μεστά* codd. Stob.: *ὑπάρχει γὰρ καὶ μεστά* AQS Turn. **14** *ἐναντίρρητος* P[1]: *ἀναντίρητος* A | *ὁ* om. A **15** Post *τρισμέγιστε* add. AQ Turn. verba *σῶμά ἐστιν ὁ ἀὴρ τοῦτο δὲ . . . πάντα διῆκον πληροῖ* e § 11 *init.* repetita. (S habet verba *ὁ ἀὴρ τοῦτο δὲ . . . πάντα διῆκον πληροῖ*, omissis

of an empty jar, or pot, or . . .,[1] or trough, and the like? Are not such things void?—*Herm.* How far you are in error, Asclepius! Do you suppose these things to be void? The truth is rather that they are completely full.—*Ascl.* What do 11
you mean, Trismegistus?—*Herm.* Is not air a body?—*Ascl.* Yes.—*Herm.* And does not that body permeate all things that are, and fill them by its permeation? And are not bodies composed of a mixture of the four elements? All things that you call void then are filled with air; and if with air, they are filled with all four elements. Thus we are led to a conclusion opposite to what you said; we must say that all those things which you call full are void of air, because the presence of other bodies in them leaves no space unoccupied, and so they have no room to admit the air. Hence the things which you call void ought to be called hollow, not void; for they are full of something that exists.—*Ascl.* There is no gainsaying that, Trismegistus.—

Herm. Now what was it that we said[2] of that Space in which 12 a
the universe is moved? We said, Asclepius, that it is incorporeal.—*Ascl.* What then is that incorporeal thing?—*Herm.* It is Mind, entire and wholly self-encompassing, free from the erratic movement of things corporeal; it is imperturbable, intangible, standing firm-fixed in itself, containing all things, and maintaining in being all things that are; and it is the light whereby soul is illuminated.—

Ascl. Tell me then, what is the Good?—*Herm.* The Good is 12 b
the archetypal Light; and Mind and Truth[3] are, so to speak, rays emitted by that Light.—

[1] Perhaps, 'mortar' (ὄλμος). [2] See § 4a. [3] Or 'Reality'.

---

verbis ἀέρος καὶ πνεύματος . . . σῶμά ἐστιν quae in ceteris Corp. Herm. codicibus praecedunt) **16** τόπον τὸν ἐν ᾧ κινεῖται codd. Corp.: τόπον ἐν ᾧ κινεῖται τὸ πᾶν codd. Stob. | εἴπομεν codd. Stob.: εἴπωμεν codd. Corp. **17** ᾧ om. codd. Stob. | τί codd. Corp.: om. codd. Stob. **18** νοῦς ὅλος codd. Stob.: νοῦς, λόγος codd. Corp. **18–19** ἐλεύθερος σωματικῆς πλάνης scripsi: ἐλεύθερος σώματος παντός, ἀπλανής codd. Stob.: ἐλεύθερον σώματος παντός· ἀπλανὴς codd. Corp. **19** Post ἀπαθὴς add. σώματι καὶ codd. Corp. | ἀναφὴς codd. Corp.: ἀφανὴς codd. Stob. | ἐν om. codd. Corp. **20** χωρητικὸς συμπάντων scripsi: χωρητικὸς τῶν πάντων codd. Corp.: συγχωρητικὸς πάντων Stob. F: χωρητικὸς πάντων Stob. P **20–21** τὸ τῆς ψυχῆς φῶς addidi (vide § 12 b *fin.*) **22** τί οὖν φῂς huc a § 13 *fin.* transposui **22–23** οὗ ὥσπερ codd. Stob.: οὗπερ codd. Corp. **23** ἔκτινες S: ἀκτῖνες cett. **24** τὸ ἀρχέτυπον φῶς codd. Corp.: τὸ ἀρχέτυπον πνεύματος codd. Stob. | τῆς ψυχῆς (τῆς om. Stob. F) hinc ad § 12 a *fin.* transposui

13 Ὁ οὖν θεὸς τί ἐστιν;—Ὁ μηδέ⟨τερ⟩ον τούτων ὑπάρχων,
ὧν δὲ καὶ ⟨⟨τούτοις⟩⟩ τοῦ εἶναι [[τούτοις]] αἴτιος, καὶ πᾶσι καὶ
ἑνὶ ἑκάστῳ τῶν ὄντων πάντων· οὐδὲ γὰρ οὐδὲν ὑπέλιπε, πλὴν
τὸ μὴ ὄν. πάντα δέ ἐστι τὰ ⟨γινόμενα⟩ ἐκ τῶν ὄντων γινόμενα,
οὐκ[ι μὴ] ἐκ τῶν μὴ ὄντων· τὰ γὰρ μὴ ὄντα οὐ φύσιν ἔχει
τοῦ δύνασθαι γενέσθαι ⟨τι⟩, ἀλλὰ τοῦ μὴ δύνασθαί τι [τὸ]
γενέσθαι· καὶ πάλιν τὰ ὄντα οὐ φύσιν ἔχει [τοῦ μηδέποτ'
εἶναι] [[τί οὖν φῄς]] τοῦ μὴ εἶναί ποτε. ὁ οὖν θεὸς οὐ νοῦς
ἐστιν, αἴτιος δὲ τοῦ ⟨νοῦν⟩ εἶναι. [οὐδὲ πνεῦμα, αἴτιος δὲ τοῦ
εἶναι πνεῦμα,] [οὐδὲ φῶς, αἴτιος δὲ τοῦ φῶς εἶναι.]
14 ὅθεν τὸν θεὸν δυσὶ ταύταις ταῖς προσηγορίαις σέβεσθαι
δεῖ, ταῖς μόνῳ αὐτῷ προσῳκειωμέναις καὶ ἄλλῳ οὐδενί. οὔτε
γὰρ τῶν ἄλλων λεγομένων θεῶν οὔτε ἀνθρώπων οὔτε δαιμόνων
τις δύναται κἂν καθ' ὁποσονοῦν ἀγαθὸς εἶναι, ἢ μόνος ὁ θεός·
[[καὶ τοῦτό ἐστι μόνον, καὶ οὐδὲν ἄλλο·]] τὰ δὲ ἄλλα πάντα
⟨ἀ⟩χώρητά ἐστι τῆς τοῦ ἀγαθοῦ φύσεως. σῶμα γάρ ἐστι καὶ
ψυχὴ τόπον οὐκ ἔχοντα χωρῆσαι δυνάμενον τὸ ἀγαθόν·
15 τοσοῦτον γάρ ἐστι τοῦ ἀγαθοῦ τὸ μέγεθος, ὅσον ἐστὶν ⟨ἡ⟩
ὕπαρξις πάντων τῶν ὄντων, καὶ σωμάτων καὶ ἀσωμάτων,
καὶ αἰσθητῶν καὶ νοητῶν. ⟨⟨καὶ⟩⟩ τοῦτο ἔστι ⟨⟨μόνον⟩⟩ ὁ θεός,
⟨⟨καὶ οὐδὲν ἄλλο⟩⟩. μὴ οὖν εἴπῃς ἄλλο τι ἀγαθὸν ⟨ἢ μόνον
τὸν θεόν⟩, ἐπεὶ ἀσεβ⟨ήσ⟩εις· ἢ ἄλλο τί ποτε τὸν θεὸν ἢ
16 μόνον τὸ ἀγαθόν, ἐπεὶ πάλιν ἀσεβ⟨ήσ⟩εις. λόγῳ μὲν οὖν ὑπὸ
πάντων λέγεται τὸ ἀγαθόν, οὐ νοεῖται δὲ τί ποτέ ἐστιν ὑπὸ
πάντων· διὰ τοῦτο οὐδὲ ⟨ὁ⟩ θεὸς νοεῖται ὑπὸ πάντων· ἀλλ'
ἀγνοίᾳ καὶ τοὺς θεοὺς καί τινας τῶν ἀνθρώπων ἀγαθοὺς
ὀνομάζουσι, μηδέποτε δυναμένους μήτε εἶναι μήτε γενέσθαι ἄν.

1 ὁ οὖν θεὸς τί ἐστιν AQS : ὁ οὖν θεός ἐστιν Turn. : ταῦτ' οὖν τί ἐστιν codd. Stob. | μηδέτερον scripsi : μηδὲν S : μηδὲ ἓν codd. cett. **1–2** ὑπάρχων, ὧν δὲ codd. Corp. : ὤν, ὧν δὲ codd. Stob. **2** τούτοις αἴτιος codd. Stob. : τούτων αἴτιος codd. Corp. | Post αἴτιος add. ὧν codd. Stob. | καὶ πᾶσι om. QS **3** ἑνὶ Patr. : ἓν codd. Stob. : ἐπὶ codd. Corp. | Post ἑκάστῳ add. μέρει ἐφ' ἕκαστον τούτων codd. Corp. | ὑπέλιπε, πλὴν scripsi : ὑπέλιπε πλέον QS Turn. : ὑπέλειπε πλεῖον A **4** ὄντων γενόμενα S : ὄντων γινόμενα cett. **5** οὐκ scripsi : οὐχὶ μὴ codd., Turn. | φησὶ (ν suprascr.) ἔχειν S : φύσιν ἔχει cett. **6** τὸ δύνασθαι QS : τοῦ δύνασθαι cett. | γενέσθαι ἀλλὰ τοῦ μὴ δύνασθαι om. S **6–7** τι γενέσθαι Parthey : τι τὸ γενέσθαι codd. **8** τί οὖν φῂς hinc ad § 12 b transposui | οὐ νοῦς QS Turn. : ὁ νοῦς A **9–10** αἴτιος δὲ τοῦ εἶναι πνεῦμα AQS : om. Turn. **12** αὐτῷ om. S | καὶ ἄλλο S : καὶ ἄλλῳ cett. **13** ἄλλων λεγομένων codd. : fortasse ἀγαθῶν λεγομένων | θεῶν οὔτε secludendum? Sed vide § 16 **14** καθ' ὁποσονοῦν scripsi : καταποσονοῦν codd., Turn. **15** μόνον om. S | καὶ τοῦτο . . . ἄλλο seclusi (vide § 15) | Fortasse ἢ μόνος ὁ θεός. ⟨⟨ὁ γὰρ θεὸς ἀγαθός ἐστιν, ὡς ἅπαντα διδοὺς καὶ μηδὲν λαμβάνων·⟩⟩ τὰ δὲ ἄλλα κ.τ.λ. (vide § 16 *fin.*) **16** ἀχώρητά scripsi : χώρητά

Ascl. What then is God?—*Herm.* God is He that is neither 13
Mind nor Truth,[1] but is the cause to which Mind and Truth,[1] and all things, and each several thing that is, owe their existence. Nothing is left over, except that which is not. And all things that come into being come out of things that are, not out of things that are not. For not such is the nature of things which are not, that they can come to be something; their nature is such that they cannot come to be anything. And not such is the nature of things which are, that they can ever cease to be. God is not Mind then, but the cause to which Mind owes its being.

And so, in our worship of God, we ought to call him by 14
these two names;[2] they belong to Him alone, and to none beside him. None of the other beings called 'gods', nor any man or daemon,[3] can be good in any degree. God alone is good; all other things[4] are incapable of containing such a thing as the Good. Neither body nor soul has room enough in it to contain
the Good; for such is the greatness of the Good, that it is 15
coextensive with the existence of all things that are, things corporeal and things incorporeal, objects of sense and objects of thought together. And God is the Good, and nothing but the Good.[5] Call nothing else good then, nothing but God; it would be impious. And never call God anything but the Good; that
also would be impious. All men speak of the good, but some 16
do not understand what the Good is; and hence it is that some do not understand what God is. And in their ignorance they call the gods good, and they call certain men good; whereas gods and men can never be good, and cannot possibly become good.

[1] Or 'Reality'.

[2] Viz. 'God' and 'the Good'. But the writer of § 17 a took the two names to be 'the Good' and 'the Father'.

[3] Perhaps, 'None of the other beings, whether men or daemons, that are called good'.

[4] Perhaps, 'can be good in any degree, but God alone. ⟨⟨God is good, inasmuch as he gives all things and receives nothing;⟩⟩ but all other things', &c.

[5] Or perhaps, 'And God alone (*μόνος*), and nothing but God, is the Good'.

---

codd., Turn. | *γάρ εἰσι* QS : *γάρ ἐστι* cett. **20–21** *καὶ τοῦτο ἔστι μόνον ὁ θεός, καὶ οὐδὲν ἄλλο* scripsi (vide § 14) : *τοῦτό ἐστιν ὁ θεός* Turn. : *τοῦτό ἐστι τὸ ἀγαθόν· τοῦτό ἐστιν ὁ θεός* AQS **21** *εἴπεις* QS **22–23** *ἀσεβήσεις* (bis) scripsi : *ἀσεβεῖς* codd., Turn. **25** *διὰ τοῦτο . . . ὑπὸ πάντων* fortasse secludendum **26** *καὶ τοὺς θεοὺς* secludendum ? | Post *ἀγαθοὺς* add. et eras. *εἶναι* man. pr. A **27** *μήτε εἶναι* om. QS

ἀλλοτριώτατον γάρ ἐστι ⟨τούτων τὸ ἀγαθόν⟩, ⟨⟨καὶ⟩⟩ τοῦ θεοῦ [[καὶ]] ἀχώριστον, ὡς αὐτὸς ὁ θεὸς ὄν. θεοὶ μὲν οὖν οἱ ἄλλοι πάντες [ἀθάνατοι] ⟨ἀγαθοὶ λέγονται⟩, τετιμημένοι τῇ τοῦ θεοῦ προσηγορίᾳ· ὁ δὲ θεὸς τὸ ἀγαθὸν ⟨λέγεται⟩ οὐ κατὰ τιμήν, ἀλλὰ κατὰ φύσιν· μία γὰρ ἡ φύσις τοῦ θεοῦ ⟨τῇ⟩ το⟨ῦ⟩ ἀγαθοῦ [καὶ ἓν γένος ἀμφοτέρων, ἐξ οὗ τὰ γένη πάντα]. [ὁ γὰρ ⟨θεὸς⟩ ἀγαθός ⟨⟨ἐστι⟨ν⟩⟩⟩, ⟨ὡς⟩ ἅπαντα [[ἐστι]] διδοὺς καὶ μηδὲν λαμβάνων.] [ὁ οὖν θεὸς πάντα δίδωσι καὶ οὐδὲν λαμβάνει.] ὁ οὖν θεὸς ⟨τὸ⟩ ἀγαθόν, καὶ τὸ ἀγαθὸν ὁ θεός.

17 a ἡ δὲ ἑτέρα προσηγορία ἐστὶν ἡ τοῦ πατρὸς πάλιν, διὰ τὸ ποιητικὸν πάντων· πατρὸς γὰρ τὸ ποιεῖν. διὸ καὶ μεγίστη ⟨τῶν⟩ ἐν τῷ βίῳ σπουδὴ καὶ εὐσεβεστάτη τοῖς εὖ φρονοῦσίν ἐστιν ἡ παιδοποιία· καὶ μέγιστον ἀτύχημα καὶ ἀσέβημά ἐστιν ἄτεκνόν τινα ἐξ ἀνθρώπων ἀπαλλαγῆναι· ⟨⟨ὅπερ ἐστὶ κατηραμένον ὑπὸ τοῦ ἡλίου.⟩⟩ καὶ δίκην οὗτος δίδωσι μετὰ θάνατον τοῖς δαίμοσιν. ἡ δὲ τιμωρία ἐστὶν ἥδε, τὴν τοῦ ἀτέκνου ψυχὴν εἰς σῶμα καταδικασθῆναι μήτε ἀνδρὸς μήτε γυναικὸς φύσιν ἔχον. [[ὅπερ ἐστὶ κατηραμένον ὑπὸ τοῦ ἡλίου.]] τοιγαροῦν, ὦ Ἀσκληπιέ, μηδενὶ ὄντι ἀτέκνῳ συνησθῇς, τοὐναντίον δὲ ἐλέησον τὴν συμφοράν, ἐπιστάμενος οἵα αὐτὸν μένει τιμωρία.

17 b τοσαῦτά σοι καὶ τοιαῦτα λελέχθω, ὦ Ἀσκληπιέ, προγνωσία τις τῆς πάντων φύσεως.

LIBELLVS III

Ἑρμοῦ τοῦ τρισμεγίστου λόγος ἱερός.

⟨ὅτι⟩ πρῶτος ἁπάντων ὁ θεός, καὶ θεῖον ⟨τὸ πᾶν⟩, καὶ ⟨ἡ⟩ φύσις θεία.

1 a Ἀρχὴ τῶν ὄντων ὁ θεός, καὶ νοῦ[ς] καὶ φύσεως καὶ ὕλη⟨ς⟩, σοφία⟨ς⟩ εἰς δεῖξιν ⟨ποιήσας πάντ⟩α, πάντων ὢν ἀρχή· ⟨⟨καὶ⟩⟩ το⟨ῦ⟩ θε[ι]οῦ [[καὶ]] ⟨⟨ἐνέργεια⟩⟩ ἡ φύσις [καὶ] [[ἐνέργεια]], κατ' ἀνάγκη⟨ν⟩ καὶ τέλος καὶ ἀνανέωσιν ⟨ἐνεργοῦσα⟩.

2 ὄν Reitz. : ὤν AQS (etiam MC teste Reitz.) Turn. | οὖν om. Q : καὶ S pro οὖν 4 τεμὴν S : τιμὴν cett. 5–6 τῇ τοῦ ἀγαθοῦ scripsi : τὸ ἀγαθὸν codd., Turn. 6 γένος QS Turn. : γενόμενος A. 9 τὸ addidi (τἀγαθόν Patr.) 16 φύσιν om. QS | ἔχον QS Turn. : ἔχοντες A 23 πρῶτος ἁπάντων scripsi : δόξα πάντων codd., Turn. ; quod ex ᾱος (= πρῶτος) ἁπάντων factum esse conicio 24–25 θεία ἀρχὴ A : θεία· καὶ ἀρχὴ QS Turn. 25 νοῦ καὶ φύσεως καὶ ὕλης scripsi : νοῦς καὶ φύσις καὶ ὕλη codd., Turn. 26 σοφίας εἰς δεῖξιν ποιήσας πάντα, πάντων ὢν ἀρχή scripsi : σοφία εἰς δεῖξιν ἁπάντων ὤν· ἀρχὴ codd., Turn. 26–27 καὶ τοῦ θεοῦ ἐνέργεια ἡ φύσις scripsi : τὸ θεῖον καὶ

For the Good is utterly alien to gods and men;[1] but it is inseparable from God, for it is God himself. All the other gods are called good merely because men have sought to honour them by giving them a title which belongs to God; but God is called the Good not by way of honouring him, but because that is his nature; for the nature of God is one and the same with the nature of the Good. God then is the Good, and the Good is God.

And[2] the other name of God is 'Father'. He is called the Father, because he is the maker or begetter of all things; for it is the part of a father to beget. And for this reason the begetting of children is held by those who think aright to be the most weighty concern in human life, and the most pious of deeds. That a man should depart from life and leave no child is a great misfortune, and a great sin; it is a thing accursed in the sight of the Sun. Such a one is punished by the daemons after death; and the punishment is this, that the soul of the man who has no child is condemned to enter a body that is neither that of a man nor that of a woman. Therefore, Asclepius, never be glad on behalf of any man that he is childless, but pity his misfortune, knowing what manner of punishment awaits him. **17 a**

Let this suffice. What I have taught you to-day, Asclepius, **17 b** is a beginning of knowledge of the nature of all things.

LIBELLVS III

A holy discourse of Hermes Trismegistus.[3]

That God is the first of all things, and the universe is divine,[4] *and nature is divine.*[4]

God is the source of all that is; He is the source of mind, and **1 a** of nature, and of matter. To show forth his wisdom has He made all things; for He is the source of all. And nature is a force by which God works; nature operates in subjection to necessity, and her work is the extinction and renewal of things.

[1] Perhaps, 'they call [ ] certain men good; whereas [ ] men can never', &c., and 'is utterly alien to [ ] men'.

[2] § 17 a was probably added by another person.

[3] The text of Libellus III, as given in the MSS., is almost entirely meaningless, and sense can be made of it only by altering it largely.

[4] I.e. derived from God, or dependent on God.

ἡ (ἡ om. A) φύσις καὶ ἐνέργεια codd., Turn. 27–28 κατ' ἀνάγκην scripsi : καὶ ἀνάγκη codd., Turn. 28 ἀνανέωσιν ἐνεργοῦσα scripsi : ἀνανέωσις codd., Turn.

1b *ἦν γὰρ σκότος [[ἄπειρον]] ἐν ἀβύσσῳ, καὶ ὕδωρ ⟨⟨ἄπειρον⟩⟩,
καὶ πνεῦμα λεπτὸν νοερόν, δυνάμει θείᾳ ⟨. . . .⟩ον τὰ ἐν χάει.
⟨⟨ἀδιορίστων δὲ ὄντων ἁπάντων καὶ ἀκατασκευάστων,⟩⟩ ἀνείθη
δὴ φῶς ἅγιον· [[καὶ ἐπάγη ὑπ' ἄμμῳ ἐξ ὑγρᾶς οὐσίας]] ⟨καὶ
ἐγένετο τὰ⟩ στοιχεῖα [καὶ θεοὶ πάντες]. [[καταδιαιροῦσι φύσεως
2a ἐνσπόρου]] [[ἀδιορίστων δὲ ὄντων ἁπάντων καὶ ἀκατασκευά-
στων]] ⟨⟨τῶν ⟨γὰρ⟩ ὅλων διορισθέντων⟩⟩ ἀπεχωρίσθη τὰ ἐλαφρὰ
εἰς ὕψος, ⟨⟨ἀνακρεμασθέντος ⟨τοῦ πυρὸς τῷ⟩ πνεύματι
ὀχεῖσθαι·⟩⟩ καὶ τὰ βαρέα ⟨κατηνέχθη, καὶ⟩ ἐθεμελιώθη ὑφ'
ὑγρᾷ ⟨οὐσίᾳ⟩ ἄμμος, ⟨⟨καὶ ἐπάγη ⟨ἡ ξηρὰ⟩ [ὑπ' ἄμμῳ] ἐξ
ὑγρᾶς οὐσίας.⟩⟩ [πυρὶ] [[τῶν ὅλων διορισθέντων]] [καὶ]
[[ἀνακρεμασθέντων πνεύματι ὀχεῖσθαι]].
2b ⟨⟨καὶ διηρθρώθη ⟨ἡ πυρίνη οὐσία⟩ σὺν τοῖς ἐν αὐτῇ θεοῖς·⟩⟩
καὶ ὤφθη ὁ οὐρανὸς ἐν κύκλοις ἑπτά, καὶ θεοὶ [ταῖς] ἐν ἄστρων
ἰδέαις ὀπτανόμενοι σὺν τοῖς αὐτῶν σημείοις ἅπασι· [[καὶ
διηρθρώθη σὺν τοῖς ἐν αὐτῇ θεοῖς]] καὶ περιε⟨ι⟩λίχθη τὸ
[περικύκλιον] α⟨ἰθ⟩έρι⟨ον⟩ κυκλίῳ δρομήματι, πνεύματι θείῳ
ὀχούμενον.*
3a *ἀνῆκε δὲ ἕκαστος θεὸς διὰ τῆς ἰδίας δυνάμεως τὸ προσταχθὲν
αὐτῷ· καὶ ἐγένετο θηρία τετράποδα καὶ ἑρπετὰ καὶ ἔνυδρα
καὶ πτηνά, [καὶ πᾶσα σπορὰ ἔνσπορος] καὶ χόρτος καὶ ἄνθους
παντὸς χλόη, ⟨⟨κατὰ διαίρεσι⟨ν⟩ φύσεων ἔνσπορα,⟩⟩ τὸ σπέρμα
τῆς παλιγγενεσίας ἐν ἑαυτοῖς [ε]σπερμογονοῦντα[ς].*
3b *⟨. . .⟩ τε γενέσεις τῶν ἀνθρώπων, [εἰς ἔργων θείων γνῶσιν,
καὶ φύσεως ἐνεργούσης μαρτυρίαν, [καὶ πλῆθος ἀνθρώπων]
καὶ πάντων τῶν ὑπ' οὐρανὸν δεσποτείαν, καὶ ἀγαθῶν ἐπίγνωσιν]
εἰς τὸ αὐξάνεσθαι ἐν αὐξήσει καὶ πληθύνεσθαι ἐν πλήθει.
καὶ πᾶσαν ἐνσαρκ⟨ο⟩ῖ ψυχὴν διὰ δρομήματος θεῶν ἐγκυκλίων,
παρασκευάσας εἰς κατοπτ⟨ε⟩ίαν οὐρανοῦ [καὶ δρομήματος
οὐρανίων θεῶν] ⟨⟨καὶ πάντων τῶν ὑπ' οὐρανὸν δεσποτείαν⟩⟩,
καὶ ⟨⟨εἰς γνῶσιν θείας δυνάμεως⟩⟩ [ἔργων θείων] καὶ φύσεως*

1 *ἐν* codd., Turn.: fortasse *ἐπ'* | *ἀφυσσω* Q: *ἀβύσσῳ* cett. 2 *θείᾳ ὄντα ἐν* codd., Turn.: fortasse *θείᾳ ⟨διῆκ⟩ον τὰ ἐν* 3 *ἀδιορίστων . . . ἀκατασκευάστων* huc a § 2 a *init.* transposui 4 *καὶ ἐπάγη . . . οὐσίας* hinc ad § 2 a *fin.* transposui | *ὑφ' ἄμμω* QS | *ὑγρὰ* S: *ὑγρᾶς* cett. 5 *καταδιαιροῦσι* Turn.: *καταδιερῶσι* A: *καταδιαιρῶσι* QS: *καταδ. . . . ἐνσπόρου* hinc ad § 3 a transposui 7 *ἀπεχωρίσθη* scripsi: *ἀποδιωρίσθη* codd., Turn. 9 *ἐφ'* QS: *ὑφ'* cett. 10 *ὑγρᾷ οὐσίᾳ ἄμμος* scripsi: *ὑγρᾷ* (*ὑγρὰ* S) *ἄμμῳ* codd., Turn. 10–11 *καὶ ἐπάγη . . . οὐσίας* huc a § 1 b transposui 14 *ἐν* (ante *ἄστρων*) om. S 16 *περιειλίχθη* scripsi: *περιελήγη* A: *περιελήγει* QS: *περιλήγει* Turn. 17 *αἰθέριον* scripsi: *ἀέρι* codd., Turn. | *κυκλί* S: *κυκλίῳ* cett. 20 *θηρία* om. S | *καὶ ἑρπετὰ* om. S 21 *καὶ . . . ἔνσπορος* seclusi: fortasse *κατὰ πᾶσαν σπορὰν ἔνσπορα* 22 *κατὰ κ.τ.λ.* huc a § 1 b *fin.*

There was darkness in the deep,[1] and water without form; and 1 b
there was a subtle breath,[2] intelligent, which permeated[3] the
things in Chaos with divine power. Then, when all was yet
undistinguished and unwrought, there was shed forth holy light;
and the elements came into being. All things were divided one 2 a
from another, and the lighter things were parted off on high,
the fire being suspended aloft, so that it rode upon the air; and
the heavier things sank down, and sand was deposited beneath
the watery substance, and the dry land was separated out from the
watery substance, and became solid.

And the fiery substance was articulated,[4] with the gods therein; 2 b
and heaven appeared, with its seven spheres, and the gods, visible
in starry forms, with all their constellations. And heaven
revolved,[5] and began to run its circling course, riding upon the
divine air.

And each god,[6] by his several power, put forth that which he 3 a
was bidden to put forth. And there came forth four-footed
beasts and creeping things and fishes and winged birds, and
grass and every flowering herb, all having seed in them according
to their diverse natures; for they generated within themselves
the seed by which their races should be renewed.

⟨. . .[7] And God ordained the⟩ births of men, and bade mankind 3 b
increase and multiply abundantly. And He implants each soul
in flesh by means of the gods who circle in the heavens. And to
this end did He make men, that they might contemplate heaven,
and have dominion over all things under heaven, and that they
might come to know God's power, and witness nature's workings,

[1] Or perhaps, 'upon the deep'.

[2] Or 'a fine airy substance', or 'a subtle spirit'.

[3] Or perhaps, 'which was moving upon'.

[4] Or 'was organized'; that is, the mass of fire was fashioned into an ordered whole made up of distinct and interdependent parts.

[5] Or 'was wrapped round (the world)'.

[6] The 'gods' here spoken of are earth, water, and air, i.e. three of the four elements. (Fire, the fourth element, has already been dealt with.)

[7] The making of man must have been here described in a passage now lost.

---

transposui | *κατὰ διαίρεσιν φύσεων ἔνσπορα* scripsi : *καταδιαιροῦσι* (*-διαιρῶσι* QS, *-διερῶσι* A) *φύσεως ἐνσπόρου* codd., Turn. 23 *ἑαυτοῖς* A : *αὐτοῖς* QS Turn. | *σπερμογονοῦντα* scripsi : *ἐσπερμολόγουν· τὰς* codd., Turn. 24–26 *εἰς ἔργων . . . ἀγαθῶν ἐπίγνωσιν* seclusi : haec duplicantur infra, vv. 31–2 inf. 24 *θείων γνῶσιν* QS Turn. : *γνῶσιν θείων* A 25 *ἐνεργούσης* scripsi : *ἐνεργοῦσαν* codd., Turn. 27 *εἰς τὸ* codd., Turn. : fortasse ⟨*ἐκέλ*⟩*ευσέ τε* vel *εἶπέ τε* 28 *ἐνσαρκοῖ* scripsi : *ἐν σαρκὶ* codd., Turn. 29 *παρασκευάσας* scripsi : *τερασπορίας* codd., Turn. 30 *καὶ πάντων . . . δεσποτείαν* addidi (vide supra) 31 *φύσεως* QS Turn. : *φύσεων* A

ἐνεργείας ⟨⟨μαρτυρίαν⟩⟩, εἴς τε σημείω⟨σιν⟩ ἀγαθῶν [[εἰς γνῶσιν θείας δυνάμεως]], μοίρας ⌜ὀχλουμένης⌝ γνῶναι ἀγαθῶν καὶ φαύλων, καὶ πᾶσαν [ἀγαθῶν] δαιδαλουργίαν εὑρεῖν.

4 *⟨ὑπ⟩άρχε⟨ι⟩ τε αὐτοῖς βιῶσαί τε καὶ ἀφ⟨αν⟩ισθῆναι πρὸς μοῖραν δρομήματος ⟨ἐγ⟩κυκλίων θεῶν, καὶ ἀναλυθῆναι εἰς ⌜ὃ⌝ ⟨. . . . καὶ οἱ μὲν ὀνομαστοὶ⟩ ἔσονται, μεγάλα ἀπομνημονεύματα τεχνουργημάτων ἐπὶ τῆς γῆς καταλιπόντες· ⟨τῶν δὲ πολλ⟩ῶν ⟨τὰ⟩ ὀνόματα ⟨ὁ⟩ χρόνος ἀμαυρώσει. καὶ πᾶσαν γένεσιν ἐμψύχου σαρκὸς καὶ καρποῦ σπορᾶς [καὶ πάσας τεχνουργίας] ⟨διαδέξεται φθορά⟩· τὰ ⟨δὲ⟩ ἐλαττούμενα ἀνανεωθήσεται [ἀνάγκῃ] [καὶ ἀνανεώσει] θεῶν [καὶ φύσεως] ⟨ἐγ⟩κυκλίων ἐναριθμίῳ δρομήματι. το⟨ῦ⟩ γὰρ θε[ι]οῦ ⟨ἐκκρέμαται⟩ ἡ πᾶσα κοσμικὴ σύγκρασις, φύσει ἀνανεουμένη· ἐν γὰρ τῷ θε[ι]ῷ καὶ ἡ φύσις καθέστηκεν.*

LIBELLVS IV

Ἑρμοῦ πρὸς Τάτ.

ὁ κρατήρ. [ἡ μονάς.]

* * * *

1a *[[ἐπειδὴ τὸν πάντα κόσμον ἐποίησεν ὁ δημιουργὸς]] [οὐ χερσὶν ἀλλὰ λόγῳ] [[ὥστε οὕτως ὑπολάμβανε, ὡς τοῦ παρόντος καὶ ἀεὶ ὄντος καὶ πάντα ποιήσαντος καὶ ἑνὸς μόνου, τῇ δὲ αὐτοῦ θελήσει δημιουργήσαντος τὰ ὄντα.]]*

1b *⟨. . .⟩ τ⟨οι⟩οῦτο γάρ ἐστι τὸ ⟨ἀ⟩σώμα⟨τον⟩ [[ἐκείνου]], οὐχ ἁπτόν, οὐδὲ ὁρατόν, οὐδὲ μετρητόν, οὐδὲ διαστατόν, οὐδὲ ἄλλῳ τινὶ ὅμοιον. οὔτε γὰρ πῦρ ἐστιν ⟨⟨ἐκεῖνος⟩⟩, οὔτε ὕδωρ, οὔτε ἀήρ, οὔτε πνεῦμα· ἀλλὰ πάντα ⟨ταῦ⟩τα ὑπ' αὐτοῦ ⟨γέγονεν⟩.*

1 *μαρτυρίαν* addidi (vide supra) | *σημείωσιν* scripsi : *σημεῖα* codd., Turn. 2 *μοίρας* S Turn. : *μοίρης* AQ | *ὀχλουμένης* AQS Turn. : fortasse *κεχωρισμένας* | Fortasse ⟨*δια*⟩*γνῶναι* 4 *ὑπάρχει τε αὐτοῖς* scripsi : *ἄρχεται αὐτῶν* AQS Turn. | *βιῶσητὲ καὶ* S | *ἀφανισθῆναι* scripsi : *σοφισθῆναι* codd., Turn. 5 *εἰς ὃ* codd., Turn. : fortasse *εἰς τὰ στοιχεῖα* 6 *ἔσονται* Turn. : *ἔσται* AQS 7–8 *τῶν δὲ πολλῶν τὰ ὀνόματα ὁ χρόνος ἀμαυρώσει* scripsi : *ἐν ὀνόματι χρόνων ἀμαύρωσιν* codd., Turn. 9 *ἐμψύχου* QS Turn. : *ἔμψυχον* A | *πάσας* scripsi : *πάσης* codd., Turn. 11–12 *θεῶν ἐγκυκλίων ἐναριθμίῳ δρομήματι* scripsi : *θεῶν καὶ φύσεως κύκλου ἐναριθμίου δρομήματι* codd., Turn. 12–13 *τοῦ γὰρ θεοῦ ἐκκρέμαται ἡ* scripsi : *τὸ γὰρ θεῖον ἡ* codd., Turn. 31 *ἀνανεουμένη* A : *ἀναθεωρουμένη* QS Turn. 14 *θεῷ* scripsi : *θείῳ* codd., Turn. | *καθέστηκεν* QS : *συνέστηκεν* (suprascr. *καθ* pr. man.) A : *συγκαθέστηκεν* Turn.

and that they might mark what things are good, and discern the diverse natures of things good and bad, and invent all manner of cunning arts.

And it is the lot of men to live their lives[1] and pass away 4
according to the destiny determined by the gods who circle in the heavens, and to be resolved into the elements. And some there are whose names will live on, because they have left upon the earth mighty memorials of their handiwork; but the names of the many time will hide in darkness. And every birth of living flesh, even as every growth of crop from seed, will be followed by destruction; but all that decays will be renewed by the measured courses of the gods who circle in the heavens. For the whole composition of the universe is dependent on God, being ever renewed by nature's working; for it is in God that nature has her being.

LIBELLVS IV

A discourse of Hermes to Tat.

The Basin.

* * * * * *

Hermes. . . .[2] For the incorporeal is not a thing perceptible 1 b
by touch or sight; it cannot be measured; it is not extended in space; it is like nothing else. God is not fire, nor water, nor air, nor breath; but all these things have been made by him.

[1] Perhaps, 'to ⟨be born and⟩ live their lives'.

[2] It must have been said in the lost passage which preceded, that God is invisible to us, because he is incorporeal.

IV. 1 b, 2 *init.*: Stob. I. 1. 30, vol. i, p. 38 Wachsmuth (deest lemma): *τοῦτο γάρ ἐστι . . . γῆν κοσμῆσαι.*

IV. 10–11 b *init.*: Stob. I. 10. 15, vol. i, p. 127 W.: Ἑρμοῦ. *ἡ γὰρ μονάς . . . ὑπογέγραπται τοῦ θεοῦ εἰκών.* Codices Stob.: FP.

15 Ερμου προς τατ A: Ερμου του τρισμεγιστου προς τον εαυτου υιον τατ λογος S Turn. **16** *ἡ μονάς* scripsi: *ἣ μονάς* AQS: *η μονας* Turn. **17** *ἐπειδὴ . . . δημιουργὸς* hinc ad § 2 *init.* transposui **18–20** *ὥστε . . . τὰ ὄντα* hinc ad § 1 b transposui **19** ex *ζῶντος* corr. *ὄντος* S **21** *τοιοῦτο* Heeren: *τοῦτο* codd. | *ἀσώματον* scripsi: *σῶμα ἐκείνου* codd. **22** *οὔτε ὁρατόν* Stob. F **22–23** *ἄλλο τινὶ* QS **23** *τινὶ ὅμοιον* codd. Corp.: *τινὶ σώματι ὅμοιον* codd. Stob. **24** *πάντα ταῦτα ὑπ' αὐτοῦ γέγονεν* scripsi: *πάντα τὰ ὑπ' αὐτοῦ* codd. Corp.: *πάντα ἀπ' αὐτοῦ* codd. Stob.

⟨⟨ὥστε οὕτως ὑπολάμβανε, ὡς ⟨αὐ⟩τοῦ προόντος, καὶ ἀεὶ ὄντος, καὶ πάντα ποιήσαντος [[καὶ]] ἑνὸς ⟨⟨καὶ⟩⟩ μόνου, τῇ δὲ αὐτοῦ θελήσει δημιουργήσαντος τὰ ὄντα.⟩⟩ ἀγαθὸς γὰρ ὤν, ⌜μόνῳ ἑαυτῷ τοῦτο ἀναθεῖναι⌝.

2 ⟨⟨ἐπεὶ δὲ τὸν πάντα κόσμον ἐποίησεν ὁ δημιουργός,⟩⟩ ἠθέλησε καὶ τὴν γῆν κοσμῆσαι· κόσμον δὲ θείου σώματος κατέπεμψε τὸν ἄνθρωπον, ⟨εἰκόνα⟩ ζῴου ἀθανάτου ζῷον θνητόν. [[καὶ ὁ μὲν κόσμος τῶν ζῴων ἐπλεονέκτει τοῦ ζῴου καὶ τοῦ κόσμου τὸν λόγον καὶ τὸν νοῦν.]] ⟨. . .⟩ θεατὴς γὰρ [[ἐγένετο]] τῶν ἔργων τοῦ θεοῦ ὁ ἄνθρωπος· καὶ ⟨ἐπὶ τοῦτο ⟨⟨ἐγένετο⟩⟩, τὸ τὸν κόσμον⟩ [ἐ]θαυμάσαι, καὶ [ἐ]γνωρίσαι τὸν ποιήσαντα.

3 ⟨⟨καὶ ὁ μὲν κόσμος ⟨. . .· ὁ δὲ ἄνθρωπος⟩ τῶν ⟨ἄλλων⟩ ζῴων [ἐ]πλεονεκτεῖ [τοῦ ζῴου καὶ τοῦ κόσμου] τὸν λόγον καὶ τὸν νοῦν.⟩⟩ τὸν μὲν οὖν λόγον, ὦ Τάτ, [ἐν] πᾶσι τοῖς ἀνθρώποις ἐμέρισε, τὸν δὲ νοῦν οὐκέτι, οὐ φθονῶν τισιν· ὁ γὰρ φθόνος οὐκ οὐραν⟨ό⟩θεν ἄρχεται, κάτω δὲ συνίσταται ταῖς τῶν νοῦν μὴ ἐχόντων ἀνθρώπων ψυχαῖς.—Διὰ τί οὖν, ὦ πάτερ, οὐ πᾶσιν ἐμέρισε τὸν νοῦν ὁ θεός;—Ἠθέλησεν, ὦ τέκνον, τοῦτον
4 ἐν μέσῳ ταῖς ψυχαῖς ὥσπερ ἆθλον ἱδρῦσθαι.—Καὶ ποῦ αὐτὸν ἱδρύσατο;—Κρατῆρα μέγαν πληρώσας τούτου κατέπεμψε, δοὺς κήρυκα, καὶ ἐκέλευσεν αὐτῷ κηρύξαι ταῖς τῶν ἀνθρώπων καρδίαις τάδε· "Βάπτισον σεαυτὴν ἡ δυναμένη εἰς τοῦτον τὸν κρατῆρα, ⟨⟨γνωρίζουσα ἐπὶ τί γέγονας,⟩⟩ ⟨καὶ⟩ [ἡ] πιστεύουσα ὅτι ἀνελεύσῃ πρὸς τὸν καταπέμψαντα τὸν κρατῆρα [ἡ] [[γνωρίζουσα ἐπὶ τί γέγονας]]." ὅσοι μὲν οὖν συνῆκαν τοῦ κηρύγματος, καὶ ἐβαπτίσαντο τοῦ νοός, οὗτοι μετέσχον τῆς γνώσεως, καὶ τέλειοι ἐγένοντο ἄνθρωποι, τὸν νοῦν δεξά-

1–3 ὥστε . . . τὰ ὄντα huc a § 1 a transposui 1 αὐτοῦ προόντος scripsi: τοῦ παρόντος codd. 3–4 ἀγαθὸς γὰρ ὤν, μόνῳ ἑαυτῷ τοῦτο ἀναθεῖναι (ἀναθῆναι F) codd. Stob.: ἀγαθὸς ὤν. μόνῳ γὰρ τούτῳ ἀνατέθεικεν codd. Corp. Fortasse ἀγαθὸς γὰρ ὢν (μόνος αὐτός?), ⟨ἠβουλήθη πάντα⟩ ἀγαθ⟨ὰ⟩ εἶναι (cf. Pl. *Tim.* 30 A) 5 ἐπεὶ . . . δημιουργός huc a § 1 a transposui 6 κοσμήσας QS: κοσμῆσαι cett. 7 κατέπεμψε QS Turn.: καὶ κατέπεμψε A | ἀθανάτου, καὶ ζῷον S 8–9 καὶ ὁ μὲν . . . τὸν νοῦν hinc ad § 3 *init.* transposui 8 κόσμος τοῦ ζώου QS 10 τῶν ἔργων QS Turn.: τοῦ ἔργου A 11 θαυμάσαι καὶ γνωρίσαι scripsi: ἐθαύμασε καὶ ἐγνώρισε codd., Turn. 13 Fortasse ὁ μὲν κόσμος ⟨ζῷον θεῖον⟩ 14 πλεονεκτεῖ scripsi: ἐπλεονέκτει codd., Turn. 16 οὐ φθονῶν τισίν· ὁ γὰρ φθόνος Turn.: οὐ φθονῶν· τισὶ γὰρ ὁ φθόνος AQS 17 οὐρανόθεν scripsi: ἔνθον S: ἔνθεν codd. cett., Turn. | Fortasse ⟨ἐν⟩ ταῖς | τῶν Q Turn.: τὸν AS 19 τοῦτον A: τούτων QS Turn. 21 μέγαν A: μὲν γὰρ QS Turn. | κατέπεμψε codd.: fortasse κατέστησε 23 κύρικα Q: κήρυκα cett. | ex αὐτῷ corr. αὐτὸν S | κηρύξαι om. QS

You must understand then that God is pre-existent, and ever-existent, and that He, and He alone, made all things, and created by his will the things that are. For inasmuch as He is good, . . .[1]

And when the Creator had made the ordered universe, he 2
willed to set in order[2] the earth also; and so he sent down man,
a mortal creature made in the image of an immortal being,[3] to be
an embellishment of the divine body.[4] . . . For it is man's
function to contemplate the works of God; and for this purpose
was he made, that he might view the universe with wondering
awe, and come to know its Maker.

The Kosmos . . . ;[5] but man has this advantage over all other 3
living beings, that he possesses speech and mind. Now speech,
my son, God imparted to all men; but mind he did not impart
to all. Not that he grudged it to any; for the grudging temper
does not start from heaven above, but comes into being here
below, in the souls of those men who are devoid of mind.—
Tat. Tell me then, father, why did not God impart mind to all
men?—*Hermes.* It was his will, my son, that mind should be
placed in the midst as a prize that human souls may win.—
Tat. And where did he place it?—*Hermes.* He filled a great 4
basin with mind, and sent it down to earth;[6] and he appointed
a herald, and bade him make proclamation to the hearts of men:
'Hearken, each human heart; dip yourself in this basin, if you
can,[7] recognizing for what purpose you have been made, and
believing that you shall ascend to Him who sent the basin
down.'[8] Now those who gave heed to the proclamation, and
dipped themselves in the bath of mind, these men got a share of
gnosis;[9] they received mind, and so became complete men. But

[1] Perhaps, 'inasmuch as He is good, He willed that all things should be good'.
[2] Or, 'to embellish'.
[3] The 'immortal being' is the Kosmos.
[4] This 'divine body' is the earth.
[5] Perhaps, 'is a divine being'.
[6] Or perhaps, 'and set it among men'.
[7] Perhaps, 'if you will'.
[8] Perhaps, 'Him who sent you down (to earth)'.
[9] I. e. knowledge of God.

---

23 δυναμένη codd.: fortasse βουλομένη 24–25 ἡ πιστεύουσα . . . τὸν κρατῆρα om. QS 25 Fortasse πρὸς τόν ⟨σε⟩ καταπέμψαντα [τὸν κρατῆρα] 27 μετέχον S : μετέσχον cett.

μενοι· ὅσοι δὲ ἥμαρτον τοῦ κηρύγματος, οὗτοι ⟨⟨οἱ⟩⟩ ⟨τὸν⟩
μὲν [[οἱ]] λόγ[ικ]ον ⟨ἔχοντες⟩, τὸν ⟨δὲ⟩ νοῦν μὴ προσειληφότες.
5 ⟨καὶ οὗτοι μέν⟩, ἀγνοοῦντες ἐπὶ τί γεγόνασι καὶ ὑπὸ τίνος,
[αἱ δὲ αἰσθήσεις τούτων ταῖς τῶν ἀλόγων ζῴων παραπλήσιαι]
[καὶ ἐν θυμῷ καὶ ἐν] ὀργῇ [τὴν] ⟨καὶ ἀ⟩κρασίᾳ ⟨συν⟩έχονται,
[οὐ] θαυμάζοντες ⟨⟨τὰ⟩⟩ οὐ [[τὰ]] θέας ἄξια, ταῖς [δὲ] τῶν
σωμάτων ἡδοναῖς καὶ ὀρέξεσι προσέχοντες, καὶ διὰ ταῦτα τὸν
ἄνθρωπον γεγονέναι πιστεύοντες. ὅσοι δὲ τῆς ἀπὸ τοῦ θεοῦ
δωρεᾶς μετέσχον, οὗτοι, ὦ Τάτ, κατὰ σύγκρισιν τῶν ἑτέρων
ἀθάνατοι ἀντὶ θνητῶν εἰσί· πάντα ⟨γὰρ⟩ ἐμπεριλαβόντες τῷ
ἑαυτῶν νοΐ, τὰ ἐπὶ γῆς, τὰ ἐν οὐρανῷ, καὶ εἴ τί ἐστιν ὑπὲρ
οὐρανόν, τοσοῦτον ἑαυτοὺς ὑψώσαντες εἶδον τὸ ἀγαθόν, καὶ
ἰδόντες, συμφορὰν ἡγήσαντο τὴν ἐνθάδε διατριβήν, ⟨καὶ⟩
καταφρονήσαντες πάντων τῶν σωματικῶν [καὶ ἀσωμάτων],
6a ἐπὶ τὸ ἓν καὶ μόνον ⟨ἀγαθὸν⟩ σπεύδουσιν. αὕτη, ὦ Τάτ,
ἡ τοῦ νοῦ ἐστὶν ⟨ἐνέργεια⟩, ἐπιστήμη⟨ς⟩ τῶν θείων εὐπορία
καὶ [ἡ] τοῦ θεοῦ κατανοήσεως [θείου ὄντος] [[τοῦ κρατῆ-
ρος]].—
6b Κἀγὼ ⟨⟨τοῦ κρατῆρος⟩⟩ βαπτισθῆναι βούλομαι, ὦ πάτερ.—
Ἐὰν μὴ πρῶτον τὸ σῶμα μισήσῃς, ὦ τέκνον, σεαυτὸν φιλῆσαι
οὐ δύνασαι· φιλήσας δὲ σεαυτόν, νοῦν ἕξεις, καὶ τὸν νοῦν
ἔχων, καὶ τῆς ἐπιστήμης μεταλήψῃ.—Πῶς ταῦτα λέγεις,
ὦ πάτερ;—Ἀδύνατον γάρ ἐστιν, ὦ τέκνον, περὶ ἀμφότερα
γίνεσθαι, τὰ θνητὰ δηλαδὴ καὶ τὰ θεῖα. δύο γὰρ ὄντων τῶν
ὄντων, σώματος καὶ ἀσωμάτου, ἐν οἷς τὸ θνητὸν καὶ τὸ θεῖον,
ἡ αἵρεσις θατέρου καταλείπεται τῷ ἑλέσθαι βουλομένῳ.
οὐ γὰρ [ἐστιν] ἀμφότερα [ἐν] οἷό⟨ν⟩ τε [ἡ ἐξαίρεσις] κατα-
λαβεῖν· τὸ δὲ ἕτερον ἐλαττωθὲν τὴν τοῦ ἑτέρου ἐφανέρωσεν
7 ἐνέργειαν. ἡ μὲν οὖν [ἐνέργεια] τοῦ κρείττονος αἵρεσις [[οὐ
μόνον]] τῷ ἑλομένῳ καλλίστη τυγχάνει, ⟨⟨οὐ μόνον⟩⟩ τὸν
ἄνθρωπον ἀποσώζουσα, ἀλλὰ καὶ τὴν πρὸς ⟨τὸν⟩ θεὸν εὐσέβειαν
ἐπιδεικνῦσα. ἡ δὲ τοῦ ἐλάττονος τὸν μὲν ἄνθρωπον ἀπώλεσεν,

1–2 οὗτοι οἱ τὸν μὲν λόγον ἔχοντες, τὸν δὲ νοῦν scripsi (αὐτοὶ μὲν τὸν λόγον, τὸν δὲ νοῦν Flussas): αὐτοὶ μὲν οἱ λογικὸν τὸν νοῦν Turn.: αὐτοὶ μὲν οἱ λογικοὶ τὸν νοῦν AQS 3 τίνος scripsi: τίνων codd., Turn. 4 ταῖς om. QS 5 ὀργῇ καὶ ἀκρασίᾳ συνέχονται scripsi: καὶ ἐν θυμῷ καὶ ἐν ὀργῇ (κ. ἐ. θ. καὶ ὀργῇ QS) τὴν κρᾶσιν ἔχοντες codd., Turn. 8 τοῦ QS Turn.: om. A 9 μετέσχοις S | τοῦτο QS: οὗτοι cett. | σύγκρησιν QS | ἑτέρων scripsi: ἔργων codd., Turn. 11 ἑαυτῶνοῒ S | ἐπὶ γῆς A: ἐπὶ τῆς γῆς QS Turn. 13 καὶ (ante καταφρον.) addidit Reitz. 14 τῶν om. S 16–17 ἐπιστήμης τῶν θείων εὐπορία καὶ τοῦ θεοῦ κατανοήσεως scripsi: ἐπιστήμη, τῶν θείων ἐντορία, καὶ ἡ τοῦ θεοῦ κατανόησις codd., Turn. 17 τοῦ (ante

those who failed to heed the proclamation, these are they who
possess speech indeed, but have not received mind also. And 5
these, inasmuch as they know not for what purpose they have
been made, nor by whom they have been made, are held under
constraint by anger and incontinence; they admire the things
that are not worth looking at;[1] they give heed only to their
bodily pleasures and desires, and believe that man has been
made for such things as these. But as many as have partaken of
the gift which God has sent,[2] these, my son, in comparison with
the others, are as immortal gods to mortal men. They embrace
in their own mind all things that are, the things on earth and the
things in heaven, and even what is above heaven, if there is
aught above heaven; and raising themselves to that height, they
see the Good. And having seen the Good, they deem their
sojourn here on earth a thing to be deplored; and scorning all
things corporeal, they press on to reach that which alone is good.
Such, my son, is the work that mind does; it throws open the 6a
way to knowledge of things divine, and enables us to apprehend
God.—

Tat. I too, father, would fain be dipped in that basin.— 6b
Hermes. If you do not first hate your body, my son, you cannot
love yourself;[3] but if you love yourself, you will have mind; and
having mind, you will partake of knowledge also.—*Tat.* What
mean you, father?—*Hermes.* It is not possible, my son, to attach
yourself both to things mortal and to things divine. There are
two sorts of things, the corporeal and the incorporeal; that which
is mortal is of the one sort, and that which is divine is of the
other sort; and he who wills to make his choice is left free to
choose the one or the other. It is not possible to take both;
and when the one is slighted, then the working of the other
becomes manifest. The choice of the better is glorious for the 7
chooser; for it not only saves the man from perdition, but also
shows him to be pious towards God. The choice of the worse is

[1] I. e. material things. [2] This 'gift' is mind.
[3] That is, your true self, which is incorporeal.

κρατῆρος) om. QS 20 *σῶμα μισήσῃς* Q: *σῶμα μισήσας* S: *σῶμά σου μισήσῃς* cett. 22 *μεταλήψῃ* QS Turn.: *καταλήψῃ* A | *λέγῃς* S: *λέγεις* cett. 24 *γίνεσθαι, τὰ θνητὰ δηλαδὴ καὶ* Turn.: *γίνεσθαι, περὶ τὰ θνητὰ καὶ* AQS 25 *τὸ* (ante *θεῖον*) om. S 27–28 *οἷόν τε καταλαβεῖν* scripsi: *ἐν οἷς τε ἡ* (*ἐν οἷς ἡ* S) *ἐξαίρεσις καταλείπεται* codd., Turn. 28 *τὴν τοῦ* om. QS 31 *ἀποσώζουσα* scripsi: *ἀποθεῶσαι* codd., Turn. 32 *ἐπιδεικνῦσα* scripsi: *ἐπιδείκνυσιν* codd., Turn.

οὐδὲν δὲ ⟨ἧττοι⟩ εἰς τὸν θεὸν ἐπλημμέλησεν [ἢ τοῦτο μόνον]·
ὅτι καθάπερ αἱ πομπαὶ μέσον παρέρχονται, μήτε αὐταὶ
ἐνεργῆσαί τι δυνάμεναι, τοὺς δὲ ἐμποδίζουσαι, τὸν αὐτὸν
τρόπον καὶ οὗτοι μόνον πομπεύουσιν ἐν τῷ κόσμῳ, παραγ[εν]ό-
8 a μενοι ὑπὸ τῶν σωματικῶν [ἡδονῶν]. τούτων δὲ οὕτως ἐχόντων,
ὦ Τάτ, τὰ μὲν παρὰ τοῦ θεοῦ ἡμῖν [τε] ὑπῆρξε καὶ ὑπάρξει,
τὰ δὲ ἀφ' ἡμῶν ἀκολουθησάτω, καὶ μὴ ὑστερησάτω· ἐπεὶ
ὁ μὲν θεὸς ἀναίτιος, ἡμεῖς δὲ αἴτιοι τῶν κακῶν, ταῦτα προ-
κρίνοντες τῶν ἀγαθῶν.
8 b ⟨. . .⟩ ὁρᾷς, ὦ τέκνον, πόσα ἡμᾶς δεῖ σώματα ⟨⟨κατὰ
συνέχειαν⟩⟩ διεξελθεῖν, καὶ πόσους χοροὺς δαιμόνων [[καὶ
συνέχειαν]] καὶ δρόμους ἀστέρων, ἵνα πρὸς τὸν ἕνα καὶ μόνον
θεὸν σπεύσωμεν. ⟨. . . ἀ⟩διάβατον γὰρ τὸ ἀγαθόν, καὶ
ἀπέραντον, καὶ ἀτελές, αὐτῷ δὲ καὶ ἄναρχον, ἡμῖν δὲ δοκοῦν
9 ἀρχὴν ἔχειν τὴν γνῶσιν. οὐκ αὐτοῦ ⟨γ⟩οῦν ⟨⟨τοῦ γνωσθη-
σομένου⟩⟩ ἀρχὴ γίνεται ἡ γνῶσις, ἀλλ' ἡμῖν τὴν ἀρχὴν
παρέχεται [[τοῦ γνωσθησομένου]]. λαβώμεθα οὖν τῆς ἀρχῆς,
καὶ ὁδεύσωμεν τάχει ἅπαντι. πάνυ γάρ ἐστι ⟨δύ⟩σκολ[ι]ον
τὸ τὰ συνήθη καὶ παρόντα καταλιπόντα ἐπὶ τὰ παλαιὰ καὶ
ἀρχαῖα ἀνακάμπτειν· τὰ μὲν γὰρ φαινόμενα τέρπει, τὰ δὲ
ἀφανῆ δυσπιστίαν ποιεῖ. φανερώτερα δέ ἐστι τὰ κακά·
τὸ δὲ ἀγαθὸν ἀφανὲς τοῖς φανεροῖς· οὐ γὰρ μορφὴ οὔτε τύπος
ἐστὶν αὐτῷ. ⟨⟨ἀδύνατον γὰρ ἀσώματον σώματι φανῆναι⟩⟩ διὰ
τοῦτο, ⟨ὅτι⟩ αὐτῷ μέν ἐστιν ὅμοιον, τοῖς δὲ ἄλλοις πᾶσιν
ἀνόμοιον. [[ἀδύνατον γὰρ ἀσώματον σώματι φανῆναι.]] [αὕτη
διαφορὰ τοῦ ὁμοίου πρὸς τὸ ἀνόμοιον, καὶ τῷ ἀνομοίῳ ὑστέρημα
πρὸς τὸ ὅμοιον.]
10 ⟨. . .⟩ [[ἡ γὰρ μονάς, πάντων οὖσα ἀρχὴ καὶ ῥίζα]] ⟨ὁ γὰρ
θεὸς⟩ ἐν πᾶσίν ἐστιν ὡς ἂν ῥίζα καὶ ἀρχή. ἄνευ δὲ ἀρχῆς
οὐδέν· αὐτὴ δὲ ⟨ἡ ἀρχὴ⟩ ἐξ οὐδενὸς ἀλλ' ἢ [ἐξ] αὑτῆς, εἴ γε

1 δὲ (post οὐδὲν) om. S | ἐπλημμέλησεν S 2 αὐταὶ Reitz.: αὗται AQS (etiam MC teste Reitz.) et Turn. 4 πομπτεύουσιν S 4-5 παραγόμενοι Patr.: παραγενόμενοι AQS (etiam MC teste Reitz.) et Turn. 7 ἡμῶν QS Turn.: ὑμῶν A 10 ἡμεῖς S: ἡμᾶς cett. 11 χωροὺς S: χοροὺς cett. 12 δρόμους QS Turn.: δρόμον A 13 θεὸν om. QS | Fortasse τὸ ἓν καὶ μόνον ἀγαθὸν (vide § 5 *fin.*) 15 ἔχειν QS Turn.: ἔχει A | αὐτοῦ A: αὐτῷ QS Turn. | γοῦν scripsi: οὖν codd., Turn. 17 λαβόμεθα QS: λαβώμεθα cett. 18 ἅπαντι scripsi: ἅπαντα codd., Turn. | δύσκολον scripsi: σκολιὸν AQS Turn. 20 ἀνακάπτω S: ἀνακάμπτειν cett. 21 δυσπιστίαν scripsi: δυσπιστεῖν codd., Turn. | φανερώτερα QS Turn.: φανερώτατα A 23 αὐτῷ QS Turn.: αὐτοῦ A 26 ἀνομίω S: ἀνομοίῳ cett. 28 πάντων οὖσα QS Turn.: οὖσα πάντων A, codd. Stob.

perdition to the man, and is likewise an offence against God; for
as processions pass through the midst of the people, but can do
nothing themselves, and obstruct the way for others, even so
these men merely pass in procession in the Kosmos, led along
by things corporeal. This being so, my son, God has done his 8 a
part towards us, and will do it; it is for us to do our part
accordingly, and not to fall short. For God is blameless; it is
we that are to blame for our evils, if we choose the evils in
preference to the goods.

. . . You see, my son, through how many bodily things in 8 b
succession we have to make our way, and through how many
troops of daemons and courses of stars, that we may press on to
the one and only God.[1] . . .[2] For we can never reach the
farther boundary of the Good; it is limitless, and without end;
and in itself, it is without beginning, though to us it seems to
begin when we get knowledge of it. For the thing to be known 9
does not itself begin to be when we get knowledge of it; it is
only for us that our knowledge makes it begin. Let us then lay
hold on this beginning, and make our way thither with all speed;
for it is hard for us to forsake the familiar things around us, and
turn back to the old home whence we came.[3] Things seen
delight us, and things unseen give rise to disbelief. Now the
things that are evil are more manifest to sight; but the Good
cannot be seen by things manifest;[4] for it has no form or shape.
It is impossible that an incorporeal thing should be manifested
to a thing that is corporeal; because the incorporeal is like to
itself, but unlike to all else.[5]

. . . God is in all things, as their root and the source of 10
their being. There is nothing that has not a source; but the
source itself springs from nothing but itself, if it is the source

[1] Perhaps, 'to Him who alone is good', or 'to that which alone is good'.

[2] Perhaps, '⟨But when we have once attained to the Good, it will never fail us⟩'.

[3] I.e. to the world of the 'incorporeal' and 'divine', whence we were 'sent down' to earth.

[4] I.e. by our bodily eyes.

[5] The writer assumes that a thing can be seen or known only by that which is like it.

29 ἐν πᾶσίν ἐστιν ὡς ἂν ῥίζα codd. Stob.: om. codd. Corp. | καὶ ἀρχή, ἄνευ δὲ codd. Stob.: καὶ ἀρχὴ οὖσα· ἄνευ δὲ codd. Corp. 30 αὐτὴ δὲ ἡ ἀρχὴ scripsi: ἀρχὴ δὲ codd. | οὐδενὸς ἀλλ' ἢ αὐτῆς scripsi: οὐδενός, ἀλλ' ἐξ αὐτῆς codd. Stob.: οὐδενὸς ἢ ἐξ αὐτῆς codd. Corp. | εἴ γε codd. Stob.: ἐπεὶ codd. Corp.

ἀρχή ἐστι τῶν ἑτέρων. [αὐτὴ γὰρ ⟨αὑτῆς⟩ ἐστιν ⟨⟨ἀρχή⟩⟩, ἐπεὶ μὴ ἄλλης ἀρχῆς ἔτυχεν] [οὖσα]. μονάδι οὖν ⟨ἔοικεν ὁ θεός⟩ [[ἀρχή]]. ⟨⟨ἡ γὰρ μονάς, πάντων οὖσα ⟨ἀριθμῶν⟩ ἀρχὴ καὶ ῥίζα,⟩⟩ πάντα ἀριθμὸν ἐμπεριέχει, ὑπὸ μηδενὸς ἐμπεριεχομένη, καὶ πάντα ἀριθμὸν γεννᾷ, ὑπὸ μηδενὸς γεννωμένη ἑτέρου ἀριθμοῦ.

11 a πᾶν δὲ τὸ γεννώμενον ἀτελές, καὶ διαιρετόν, καὶ αὐξητὸν καὶ μειωτόν· τῷ δὲ τελείῳ οὐδὲν τούτων γίνεται. [καὶ τὸ μὲν αὐξητὸν αὐξάνεται ἀπὸ τῆς μονάδος, ἁλίσκεται δὲ ὑπὸ τῆς αὐτοῦ ἀσθενείας, μηκέτι δυνάμενον τὴν μονάδα χωρῆσαι.]

11 b αὕτη σοι, ὦ Τάτ, κατὰ τὸ δυνατὸν ὑπογέγραπται τοῦ θεοῦ εἰκών· ἣν ἀκριβῶς εἰ θεάσῃ [καὶ νοήσεις] τοῖς τῆς καρδίας ὀφθαλμοῖς, πίστευσόν μοι, τέκνον, εὑρήσεις τὴν πρὸς τὰ ἄνω ὁδόν· μᾶλλον δὲ αὐτή σε ἡ [εἰκὼν] ⟨θέα⟩ ὁδηγήσει. ἔχει γάρ τι ἴδιον ⌜ἡ θέα⌝· τοὺς φθάσαντας θεάσασθαι κατέχει, καὶ ἀνέλκει καθάπερ φασὶν ἡ Μαγνῆτις λίθος τὸν σίδηρον.

LIBELLVS V

Ἑρμοῦ πρὸς Τὰτ υἱόν.

ὅτι ἀφανὴς ⟨ . . . ⟩ θεὸς φανερώτατός ἐστι.

1 a *Καὶ* τόνδε σοι τὸν λόγον, ὦ Τάτ, διεξελεύσομαι, ὅπως μὴ ἀμύητος ᾖς τοῦ κρείττονος θεοῦ ὀνόματος. σὺ δὲ νόει πῶς ⟨λέγω· νοοῦντι γὰρ⟩ τὸ δοκοῦν τοῖς πολλοῖς ἀφανὲς φανερώτατόν σοι γενήσεται.

1 b ⟨ . . . ⟩ ⌜οὐ γὰρ ἂν ἦν εἰ ἀφανὲς ἦν.⌝ πᾶν γὰρ τὸ φαινόμενον γεννητόν· ἐφάνη γάρ. τὸ δὲ ἀφανὲς ἀεὶ ἔστι· τοῦ γὰρ φανῆναι οὐ χρῄζει. ⟨ . . . ⟩ ἀεὶ γὰρ ἔστι· καὶ τὰ ἄλλα πάντα φανερὰ ποιεῖ, αὐτὸς ἀφανὴς ὤν, ὡς ἀεὶ ὤν.

1–2 αὕτη γάρ ἐστιν, ἐπεὶ μὴ ἄλλης ἀρχῆς ἔτυχεν οὖσα codd. Corp. : om. codd. Stob. 2–3 μονάδι οὖν ἔοικεν ὁ θεός scripsi : μονὰς οὖν ἀρχὴ A : μονὰς οὖν ἡ ἀρχὴ QS Turn. : μονὰς οὖσα οὖν ἀρχὴ codd. Stob. 4 πάντα ἀριθμὸν ἐμπ. codd. Stob. : καὶ πάντα ἀριθμὸν ἐμπ. codd. Corp. 5–6 γενομένη A : γεννωμένη cett. 7 διαιρετὸν codd. Stob. : ἀδιαίρετον AQS Turn. | τῷ δὲ τελείῳ codd. : fortasse τῷ δὲ ἀγεννήτῳ 8–10 καὶ τὸ μὲν αὐξητὸν . . . χωρῆσαι codd. Corp. : om. codd. Stob. 11 σοι codd. Corp. : οὖν codd. Stob. | δυνατὸν codd. Corp. : δυνατόν σοι codd. Stob. 14 ἔχει δέ QS : ἔχει γάρ cett. 15 ἡ θέα (post. ἴδιον) codd. : fortasse τὸ θεῖον vel τὸ ἀγαθόν 16 λίθος om. QS

of all else. God then is like the unit of number. For the unit, being the source of all numbers, and the root of them all, contains every number within itself, and is contained by none of them; it generates every number, and is generated
by no other number. Now everything that is generated is II a
incomplete, and divisible, and subject to increase and decrease; but that which is complete[1] is subject to none of these things.

In these outlines, my son, I have drawn a likeness of God for II b
you, so far as that is possible; and if you gaze upon this likeness with the eyes of your heart, then, my son, believe me, you will find the upward path; or rather, the sight itself will guide you on your way. For the . . .[2] has a power peculiar to itself; it takes possession of those who have attained to the sight of it, and draws them upward, even as men say the loadstone draws the iron.

LIBELLVS V

A discourse of Hermes to his son Tat.

That God is hidden from sight, and yet is most manifest.

This doctrine also, Tat, I will expound to you, that you may I a
not remain uninitiated in the mysteries of Him who is too mighty to be named God. Grasp the meaning of my words; for if you grasp it, that which seems to the many to be hidden will become most manifest to you.

. . . .[3] For all that is manifest has been brought into being; I b
for it has been manifested. But that which is hidden is ever-existent; for it has no need to be manifested. . . .; for God is ever-existent; and He makes manifest all else, but He himself is hidden, because He is ever-existent. He manifests all

[1] Perhaps, 'that which is not generated'.
[2] Perhaps, 'that which is divine', or 'the Good'.
[3] Perhaps, 'for it would not have been ever-existent, if it had not been hidden'.

---

17 Ἑρμοῦ πρὸς Τὰτ υἱόν A: Ἑρμοῦ τοῦ τρισμεγίστου πρὸς τὸν ἑαυτοῦ υἱὸν Τάτ QS Turn. 18 Fortasse ὅτι ⟨πῇ μὲν⟩ ἀφανὴς ⟨ὁ⟩ θεός, ⟨πῇ δὲ⟩ φανερώτατός ἐστι 20 ἀμύνητος S: ἀμύητος cett. 22 γένηται QS 23 Fortasse οὐ γὰρ ἂν ⟨ἀεὶ⟩ ἦν εἰ ⟨μὴ⟩ ἀφανὲς ἦν 24 ἀφὲς S: ἀφανὲς cett.

⟨πάντα οὖν⟩ φανερῶν, αὐτὸς οὐ φανεροῦται, οὐκ αὐτὸς γεννώμενος ἐν φαντασίᾳ, [[δὲ]] πάντα ⟨⟨δὲ⟩⟩ φαντασιῶν. ἡ γὰρ φαντασία μόνων τῶν γεννητῶν ἐστίν· οὐδὲν γάρ ἐστιν ἢ φαντασία ἡ γένεσις. ὁ δὴ εἷς ἀγέννητος ⟨ὢν⟩ δῆλον ὅτι καὶ ἀφαντασίαστος· ⟨εἰ δὲ ἀφαντασίαστος,⟩ καὶ ἀφανής.

2 τὰ δὲ πάντα φαντασιῶν, διὰ πάντων φαίνεται, καὶ ἐν πᾶσι· καὶ μάλιστα οἷς ἂν αὐτὸς βουληθῇ φανῆναι. σὺ οὖν, ὦ Τὰτ τέκνον, εὖξαι πρῶτον τῷ κυρίῳ καὶ πατρί, [καὶ] ⟨τῷ⟩ μόνῳ καὶ [οὐχ] ἑνὶ ⟨ἀγαθῷ⟩ [ἀλλ' ἀφ' οὗ ὁ εἷς], ἵλεω τυχεῖν, [[ἵνα δυνηθῇς τὸν τηλικοῦτον θεὸν νοῆσαι,]] καὶ ἀκτῖνά σοι κἂν μίαν αὐτοῦ τῇ σῇ διανοίᾳ ἐλλάμψαι, ⟨⟨ἵνα δυνηθῇς τὸν τηλικοῦτον [θεὸν] νοῆσαι.⟩⟩ νόησις γὰρ μόνη ὁρᾷ τὸ ἀφανές, ὡς καὶ αὐτὴ ἀφανὴς οὖσα· ⟨⟨εἰ δὲ καὶ τὸ ἐν σοὶ ἀφανές ἐστί σοι, πῶς αὐτὸς ἐν ἑαυτῷ ⟨ὢν⟩ διὰ τῶν ὀφθαλμῶν σοι φανήσεται;⟩⟩ εἰ ⟨δὲ⟩ δύνασαι τοῖς τοῦ νοῦ ὀφθαλμοῖς ⟨⟨ἰδεῖν⟩⟩, φανήσεται, ὦ Τάτ· ἀφθόνως γὰρ ὁ κύριος φαίνεται διὰ παντὸς τοῦ κόσμου [νόησιν] [[ἰδεῖν]]· ⟨⟨καὶ τὴν εἰκόνα τοῦ θεοῦ θεάσασθαι⟩⟩ καὶ λαβέσθαι αὐτῆς ταῖς χερσὶ δύνασαι [[καὶ τὴν εἰκόνα τοῦ θεοῦ θεάσασθαι]]. [[εἰ δὲ καὶ τὸ ἐν σοὶ ἀφανές ἐστί σοι, πῶς αὐτὸς ἐν σαυτῷ διὰ τῶν ὀφθαλμῶν σοι φανήσεται;]]

3 εἰ δὲ θέλεις αὐτὸν ἰδεῖν, νόησον τὸν ἥλιον, νόησον τὸν σελήνης δρόμον, νόησον τῶν ἀστέρων τὴν τάξιν. τίς ὁ τὴν τάξιν τηρῶν; [τάξις γὰρ πᾶσα] [[περιώρισται ἀριθμῷ καὶ τόπῳ.]] ὁ ἥλιος [[θεὸς]] μέγιστος τῶν κατ' οὐρανὸν θεῶν, ᾧ πάντες εἴκουσιν οἱ οὐράνιοι θεοὶ ὡσανεὶ βασιλεῖ καὶ δυνάστῃ· καὶ οὗτος ὁ τηλικοῦτος ⟨⟨θεός⟩⟩, ὁ μείζων γῆς καὶ θαλάττης, ἀνέχεται ὑπὲρ ἑαυτὸν ἔχων ἑαυτοῦ μικροτέρους πολεύοντας ἀστέρας· τίνα αἰδούμενος, ἢ τίνα φοβούμενος, ὦ τέκνον; ἕκαστος τούτων τῶν ἀστέρων ⟨⟨περιώρισται ἀριθμῷ καὶ τόπῳ⟩⟩· ⟨διὰ τί⟩ οὐ⟨χ⟩ [[τὸν]] ὅμοιον ἢ ἴσον ⟨⟨τὸν⟩⟩ δρόμον ποιοῦνται ⟨πάντες οἱ⟩ ἐν οὐρανῷ ὄντες; τίς ὁ ἑκάστῳ τὸν
4 τ[ρ]όπον καὶ τὸ μέγεθος τοῦ δρόμου ὁρίσας; ⟨ἡ⟩ ἄρκτος, ⟨⟨ἡ⟩⟩ αὐτὴ [[ἡ]] περὶ αὐτὴν στρεφομένη, καὶ τὸν πάντα

3–4 ἡ φαντασία ἡ scripsi : ἡ φαντασία ἢ codd., Turn. 4 δὴ scripsi : δὲ codd., Turn. 6 φαίνονται S : φαίνεται cett. 7 φανῆναι A : φανεῖται QS Turn. 8 ὦ Τὰτ τέκνον QS Turn. : τέκνον τὰτ A 10 τῶν S : τὸν cett. | καὶ scripsi : κἂν codd., Turn. 11 μία S : μίαν cett. | ἐλλάμψαι scripsi : ἐκλάμψαι codd., Turn. 14 αὐτὸς Turn. : αὐτὸν A : ἑαυτὸν QS | ἐν ἑαυτῷ ὢν scripsi : ἐν σαυτῷ codd., Turn. 16 ἀφθόνως scripsi : ἄφθονος codd., Turn. 17 ἰδεῖν AQS : λαβεῖν Turn. 18 αὐτῆς scripsi :

things, but is not manifested; He is not himself brought into being in images presented through our senses, but He presents all things to us in such images. It is only things which are brought into being that are presented through sense; coming into being is nothing else than presentation through sense.[1] It is evident then that He who alone has not come into being cannot be presented through sense; and that being so, He is hidden from our sight.

But He presents all things to us through our senses, and thereby 2
manifests himself through all things, and in all things; and especially, to those to whom He wills to manifest himself. Begin then, my son Tat, with a prayer to the Lord and Father, who alone is good; pray that you may find favour with him, and that one ray of him, if only one, may flash into your mind, that so you may have power to grasp in thought that mighty Being. For thought alone can see that which is hidden, inasmuch as thought itself is hidden from sight; and if even the thought which is within you is hidden from your sight, how can He, being in himself, be manifested to you through your bodily eyes? But if you have power to see with the eyes of the mind, then, my son, He will manifest himself to you. For the Lord manifests himself ungrudgingly through all the universe; and you can behold God's image[2] with your eyes, and lay hold on it with your hands.

If you wish to see Him, think on the Sun, think on the course 3
of the Moon, think on the order of the stars. Who is it that maintains that order? The Sun is the greatest of the gods in heaven;
to him, as to their king and over-lord, all the gods of heaven
yield place; and yet this mighty god, greater than earth and sea,
submits to have smaller stars circling above him. Who is it then,
my son, that he obeys with reverence and awe? Each of these
stars too is confined by measured limits, and has an appointed
space to range in. Why do not all the stars in heaven run like
and equal courses? Who is it that has assigned to each its place,
and marked out for each the extent of its course? The Bear, who 4
revolves upon herself, and carries round with her the whole

[1] Or, 'presentation through sense is nothing else than coming into being'.
[2] I e. the Kosmos.

αὐταῖς codd., Turn. 22 αὐτοῦ S: αὐτὸν cett. 24 τυρῶν QS: τηρῶν cett. 25 τύπῳ S: τόπῳ cett. 29 πολεύοντας A Turn.: πολιτεύοντας QS Flussas 30 Fortasse τούτων ἕκαστος τῶν ἀστ. 31 οὐχ ὅμοιον ἢ ἴσον τὸν δρόμον scripsi: οὐ τὸν ὅμοιον ἢ ἴσον δρόμον codd., Turn. 32 ποιοῦντα S: ποιοῦνται cett. 33 τόπον scripsi: τρόπον codd., Turn. 34 στρεφομένην S: στρεφομένη cett.

κόσμον συμπεριφέρουσα, ⟨. . .· τίς ὁ . . . ; ὁ ἀὴρ . . .·⟩ τίς ὁ τοῦτο κεκτημένος τὸ ὄργανον; τίς ὁ τῇ θαλάσσῃ τοὺς ὅρους περιβαλών; τίς ὁ τὴν γῆν ἑδράσας; ἔστι γάρ τις, ὦ Τάτ, ὁ τούτων πάντων ποιητὴς καὶ δεσπότης· ἀδύνατον γὰρ ἢ τόπον ἢ ἀριθμὸν ἢ μέτρον φυλαχθῆναι χωρὶς τοῦ ποιήσαντος. πᾶσα γὰρ τάξις ⟨ποιητή, μόνη δὲ ἡ⟩ ἀτοπία καὶ ἀμετρία ἀποίητος. ἀλλ' οὐκ ἀδέσποτος οὐδὲ αὕτη, ὦ τέκνον· καὶ γὰρ εἴ τι ἄτακτόν ἐστιν, ⌜ἐνδεὲς ὅτε κατέχει τοῦτό ἐστι τὸν τρόπον τῆς τάξεως·⌝ καὶ ⟨γὰρ ἡ ἀταξία⟩ ὑπὸ τὸν δεσπότην ἐστί, τὸν μηδέπω αὐτῇ τὴν τάξιν τάξαντα.

5 εἴθε δυνατόν σοι ἦν πτηνῷ γενομένῳ ἀναπτῆναι εἰς τὸν ἀέρα, καὶ μέσον ἀρθέντα [τῆς] γῆς καὶ οὐρανοῦ ἰδεῖν γῆς μὲν τὸ στερεόν, θαλάσσης δὲ τὸ κεχυμένον, ποταμῶν δὲ τὰ ῥεύματα, ἀέρος τὸ ἀνειμένον, πυρὸς τὴν ὀξύτητα, ἄστρων τὸν δρόμον, οὐρανοῦ τὴν ταχύτητα τῆς περὶ ταῦτα περιβάσεως. ὦ θέας ἐκείνης, τέκνον, εὐτυχεστάτης, ὑπὸ μίαν ῥοπὴν πάντα ταῦτα ⟨φερόμενα ἰδόντα⟩ θεάσασθαι τὸν ἀκίνητον διὰ ⟨τῶν κινητῶν⟩ κινούμενον, καὶ τὸν ἀφανῆ φαινόμενον δι' ὧν ποιεῖ.

6 αὕτη ἡ τάξις τοῦ κόσμου [καὶ οὗτος ὁ κόσμος τῆς τάξεως]. εἰ ⟨δὲ⟩ θέλεις καὶ διὰ τῶν θνητῶν ⟨αὐτὸν⟩ θεάσασθαι τῶν ἐπὶ γῆς καὶ τῶν ἐν βυθῷ, ⟨. . .⟩. νόησον, ὦ τέκνον, δημιουργούμενον ἐν τῇ γαστρὶ τὸν ἄνθρωπον, καὶ τοῦ δημιουργήματος ἀκριβῶς τὴν τέχνην ἐξέτασον, καὶ μάθε τίς ὁ δημιουργῶν τὴν καλὴν ταύτην καὶ θείαν [τοῦ ἀνθρώπου] εἰκόνα. τίς ὁ τοὺς ὀφθαλμοὺς περιγράψας; τίς ὁ τὰς ῥῖνας καὶ τὰ ὦτα τρυπήσας; τίς ὁ τὸ στόμα διανοίξας; τίς ὁ τὰ νεῦρα ἐκτείνας καὶ δεσμεύσας; τίς ὁ ὀχετεύσας τὰς φλέβας; τίς ὁ τὰ ὀστέα στερροποιήσας; τίς ὁ ⟨τὸ⟩ δέρμα τῇ σαρκὶ περιβαλών; τίς ὁ τοὺς δακτύλους διελών; τίς ὁ τοῖς ποσὶ ⟨τὴν⟩ βάσιν πλατύνας; τίς ὁ διορύξας τοὺς πόρους; [[τίς ὁ τὸν σπλῆνα ἐκτείνας;]] τίς ὁ τὴν καρδίαν πυραμοειδῆ ποιήσας, ⟨καὶ⟩ [τίς ὁ] τὰ νεῦρα ⟨αὐτῇ⟩ συνθείς; τίς ὁ τὸ ἧπαρ πλατύνας;

2 ὁ τῇ θαλάσσῃ Turn.: ὁ θαλάσσῃ QS: ὁ τῆς θαλάσσης A 6 τάξις QS Turn.: τάξις ἀμετρία (sed ἀμετρία eras. man. pr.) A 6–7 ἀτοπία καὶ ἀμετρίᾳ A: ἀτοπίᾳ, καὶ ἀμετρίᾳ Turn. 7 οὐδὲν S: οὐδὲ cett. 8 εἴ τι scripsi: εἰ τὸ codd., Turn. 8–9 Fortasse ⟨οὐκ⟩ ἐνδεές ⟨⟨ἐστι⟩⟩ ⟨τοῦ τάξοντος⟩ εἴ τι κατέχε⟨τα⟩ι τοῦτο⟨ν⟩ [[ ]] τὸν τρόπον τῇ ⟨ἀ⟩ταξίᾳ 10 τὸν (ante δεσπότην) QS Turn.: om. A 15 τῆς . . . περιβάσεως scripsi: τὴν . . . περίβασιν codd., Turn. 17–18 διὰ τῶν κινητῶν κινούμενον scripsi: διακινούμενον codd., Turn. 19 αὕτη codd.: fortasse τοιαύτη 20–21 ἐπὶ γῆς A: ἐπὶ τῆς γῆς QS Turn. 24 τὴν καλὴν

Kosmos, ⟨. . . ; who is it that has . . . ? The air . . . ;⟩[1] who is it that owns this instrument? Who is it that has confined the sea within its bounds, and fixed the earth firm in its seat? Some one there must be, my son, who is the Maker and the Master of all these; it could not be that place and limit and measure should be observed by all, if there were not one who has made them. For all order must have been made; it is only that which is out of place and out of measure that has not been made. And yet, my son, even that which is out of place and out of measure is not without a master. If there is aught that is in disorder, . . . ;[2] for disorder also is subject to the Master, but he has not yet imposed order upon it.

Would that it were possible for you to grow wings, and soar 5 into the air! Poised between earth and heaven, you might see the solid earth, the fluid sea and the streaming rivers, the wandering air, the penetrating fire, the courses of the stars, and the swiftness of the movement with which heaven encompasses all. What happiness were that, my son, to see all these borne along with one impulse,[3] and to behold Him who is unmoved moving in all that moves, and Him who is hidden made manifest through his works!

Such is the order of the universe. But if you wish to see Him 6 through mortal creatures also, both those on earth and those in the depths of the sea, ... Think, my son, how man is fashioned in the womb; investigate with care the skill shown in that work, and find out what craftsman it is that makes this fair and godlike image. Who is it that has traced the circles of the eyes, that has pierced the orifices of the nostrils and the ears, and made the opening of the mouth? Who is it that has stretched the sinews out and tied them fast, and dug out the channels of the veins? Who is it that has made the bones hard, and covered the flesh with skin? Who is it that has separated the fingers, and shaped the broad surface of the soles of the feet? Who is it that has bored the ducts? Who is it that has shaped the heart into a cone, and joined the sinews to it, that has made the liver broad,

[1] Perhaps, '⟨. . . ; who is it that has imposed this task upon her? The air is the instrument by which life is conveyed to all creatures upon earth;⟩'.

[2] Perhaps, 'it is not without one who will bring it to order, if there is anything that is thus possessed by disorder'.

[3] Or, 'to see all these in one moment of time'.

ταύτην QS Turn.: *ταύτην τὴν καλὴν* A 26 *ἀνοίξας* S: *διανοίξας* cett. 30 *τοὺς* (ante *πόρους*) om. QS | *τὴν σπλῆνα* QS

⟨⟨τίς ὁ τὸν σπλῆνα ἐκτείνας;⟩⟩ τίς ὁ τὸν πνεύμονα σηραγγώσας;
τίς ὁ τὴν κοιλίαν εὐρύχωρον ποιήσας; τίς ὁ τὰ τιμιώτατα
7 εἰς τὸ φανερὸν ἐκτυπώσας, καὶ τὰ αἰσχρὰ κρύψας; ἴδε
πόσαι τέχναι μίας ὕλης, καὶ πόσα ἔργα ⟨ἐν⟩ μιᾷ περιγραφῇ·
καὶ πάντα περικαλλῆ, καὶ πάντα μεμετρημένα, πάντα δὲ ἐν
διαφορᾷ. τίς πάντα ταῦτα ἐποίησε; ποία μήτηρ, ποῖος
πατήρ, εἰ μὴ ὁ ἀφανὴς θεός, ⟨ὁ⟩ τῷ ἑαυτοῦ θελήματι πάντα
8 δημιουργήσας; καὶ ἀνδριάντα μὲν ἢ εἰκόνα χωρὶς ἀνδριαν-
τοποιοῦ ἢ ζωγράφου οὐδείς φησι γεγονέναι· τοῦτο δὲ τὸ
δημιούργημα χωρὶς δημιουργοῦ γέγονεν; ὢ τῆς πολλῆς
τυφλότητος, ὢ τῆς πολλῆς ἀσεβείας, ὢ τῆς πολλῆς ἀγνω-
μοσύνης. μηδέποτε, ὦ τέκνον Τάτ, ἀποστερήσῃς τοῦ
δημιουργοῦ τὰ δημιουργήματα· μᾶλλον δὲ ⟨. . .⟩.
9 [⌈κρείττων ἐστὶν ὅσος κατὰ θεὸν ὀνόματος τοσοῦτος.⌉]
⟨τίς γὰρ ἄλλος⟩ ἐστὶν ὁ πάντων πατήρ; ἢ γὰρ ⟨οὐ⟩ μόνος
οὗτος; καὶ τοῦτο αὐτῷ τὸ ἔργον ἐστί, ⟨τὸ⟩ πατέρα εἶναι.
εἰ δέ τί με καὶ τολμηρότερον ἀνάγκη[ζεις] εἰπεῖν, τούτου
ἐστὶν ⟨ἡ⟩ οὐσία τὸ κινεῖν πάντα καὶ ποιεῖν· καὶ ὥσπερ χωρὶς
τοῦ ποιοῦντος ἀδύνατόν ἐστι γενέσθαι τι, οὕτω καὶ τοῦτον
δεῖ μὴ εἶναι, εἰ μὴ πάντα ἀεὶ ποιοῦντα, ἐν οὐρανῷ, ἐν ἀέρι,
ἐν γῇ, ἐν βυθῷ, ἐν παντὶ τοῦ κόσμου ⟨μέρει⟩, ἐν παντὶ [τοῦ
παντὸς] τῷ ὄντι καὶ τῷ μὴ ὄντι. οὐδὲν γάρ ἐστιν ἐν παντὶ
ἐκείνῳ ὃ οὐκ ἔστιν αὐτός. ἔστιν αὐτὸς καὶ τὰ ὄντα καὶ τὰ
μὴ ὄντα· τὰ μὲν γὰρ ὄντα ἐφανέρωσε, τὰ δὲ μὴ ὄντα ἔχει ἐν
ἑαυτῷ.
10 a οὗτος ὁ θεοῦ ὀνόματος κρείττων. οὗτος ὁ ἀφανής, οὗτος
ὁ φανερώτατος. οὗτος ὁ τῷ νοῒ θεωρητός, οὗτος ὁ τοῖς
ὀφθαλμοῖς ὁρατός. οὗτος ὁ ἀσώματος, ⟨οὗτος⟩ ὁ πολυσώματος,
μᾶλλον δὲ παντο[ς]σώματος. οὐδέν ἐστιν [[οὗτος]] ὃ οὐκ
ἔστι⟨ν⟩ ⟨⟨οὗτος⟩⟩· πάντα γὰρ ⟨ἃ⟩ ἔστι καὶ οὗτός ἐστι. καὶ
διὰ τοῦτο αὐτὸς ὀνόματα ἔχει ἅπαντα, ὅτι ἑνὸς ⟨αὐτοῦ πάντα⟩
ἐστὶ πατρός· καὶ διὰ τοῦτο αὐτὸς ὄνομα οὐκ ἔχει, ὅτι πάντων
ἐστὶ πατήρ.

1 σηραγγώσας Flussas : συραγγώσας Q Turn. : συρραγγώσας S : σιραγγώσας A 2 τίς τὴν κοιλίαν (om. ὁ) QS Turn. : ὁ τὴν κοιλίαν (om. τίς) A 5–6 ἐνδιάφορα Q : ἐνδιαφορὰ S : ἐν διαφορᾷ cett. 12 ἀποστερήσῃς Q Turn. : -σεις A : ex -σεις corr. -σῃς S 14 καὶ κρείττων Turn. : καὶ κρειττόν Q : κρεῖττόν (om. καὶ) AS | ὅσος Q Turn. : ὁσὸς S : ὅσον A | κρείττων . . . τοσοῦτος seclusi. Fortasse [κρείττων ἐστὶν οὗτος κα⟨ὶ⟩ τοῦ θεοῦ ὀνόματος· [τος] οὗτος ⟨. . .⟩] : vide § 10 a *init.* 16 αὐτῷ QS Turn. : αὐτὸ A 17 ἀνάγκη scripsi : ἀναγκάζεις codd., Turn. 18 κινεῖν scripsi : κύειν codd., Turn.

and the spleen long, and hollowed out the cavities of the lungs, and made the belly capacious? Who is it that has so fashioned the most honourable parts that all may see them, and concealed
the parts that are unseemly? See how many crafts have been 7
employed on one material, and how many works of art are enclosed within one compass! All are beautiful, all true to measure, yet all are diverse one from another. Who produced all these? What mother, or what father? Who but the hidden
God, who has wrought all things by his own will? No one says 8
that a statue or a portrait has come into being without a sculptor or a painter; and has such a work as this come into being without a Maker? How blind men are! How impious, how obtuse! Never, my son, deprive the things made of their Maker; but rather . . . .

For who else is the Father of all? Surely, He alone; and it is 9
his work to be father. Nay, if I needs must speak with some boldness, I will even say that it is his very being to set all things in motion,[1] and to make all things; and as it is impossible for anything to come into being without a maker, so too it needs must be that He does not exist, if he is not ever making all things, in heaven, in air, on earth, and in the deep, in every part of the Kosmos, in all that is and in all that is not. For in all this there is nothing that He is not. He is both the things that are and the things that are not; for the things that are He has made manifest, and the things that are not He contains within himself.

Such is He who is too great to be named God. He is hidden, 10 a
yet most manifest. He is apprehensible by thought alone, yet we can see Him with our eyes. He is bodiless, and yet has many bodies, or rather, is embodied in all bodies. There is nothing that He is not;[2] for all things that exist are even He. For this reason all names are names of Him, because all things come from Him, their one Father; and for this reason He has no name, because He is the Father of all.

[1] MSS.: 'to give birth to all things.'
[2] Or, 'that is not He'.

---

20 δεῖ scripsi : ἀεὶ codd., Turn. 20–21 ἐν ἀέρι ἐν γῇ AQS : ἐν γῇ, ἐν ἀέρι Turn. 21–22 ἐν παντὶ τοῦ παντὸς om. QS 23 ὄντα καὶ Turn. : ὄντα· αὐτὸς καὶ AQS 24 μὴ ὄντα QS Turn. : μὴ ἔχοντα A 26 θεοῦ QS Turn. : θεὸς A 26–28 ὁ (sexies) secludendum? 29 παντοσώματος scripsi : παντὸς σώματος codd., Turn. 30 ἃ add. Flussas 31 αὐτὸς Turn. : om. AQS

10 b τίς οὖν σε εὐλογῆσαι ὑπέρ σου ἢ πρός σε δύναιτο;

ποῦ δὲ καὶ βλέπων εὐλογήσω σε, ἄνω, κάτω, ἔσω, ἔξω; σὺ γὰρ ⟨ὁ⟩ τ[ρ]όπος ⟨⟨τῶν ὄντων⟩⟩· οὐ τόπος ἐστὶ⟨ν⟩ ⟨⟨ἄλλο⟨ς⟩ οὐδεὶς⟩⟩ παρὰ σέ [οὐδὲ] [[ἄλλο οὐδὲν]] [[τῶν ὄντων]], πάντα δὲ ἐν σοί.

⟨. . .⟩ πάντα ἀπὸ σοῦ· πάντα δίδως, καὶ οὐδὲν λαμβάνεις· πάντα γὰρ ἔχεις, καὶ οὐδὲν ὃ οὐκ ἔχεις.

11 πότε δέ σε ὑμνήσω; οὔτε γὰρ ὥραν ⟨χωρίς⟩ σου οὔτε χρόνον καταλαβεῖν δυνατόν.

ὑπὲρ τίνος δὲ καὶ ὑμνήσω ⟨σε⟩; ὑπὲρ ὧν ἐποίησας, ἢ ὑπὲρ ὧν οὐκ ἐποίησας; ὑπὲρ ὧν ἐφανέρωσας, ἢ ὑπὲρ ὧν ἔκρυψας;

διὰ τί⟨νος⟩ δὲ καὶ ὑμνήσω σε; ὡς ἐμαυτοῦ ὤν; ὡς ἔχων τι ἴδιον; ὡς ἄλλος ὤν; σὺ γὰρ εἶ ὃ [ε]ὰν ὦ, σὺ εἶ ὃ ἂν ποιῶ, σὺ εἶ ὃ ἂν λέγω. σὺ γὰρ πάντα εἶ, καὶ ἄλλο οὐδὲν ἔστιν ὃ μὴ σὺ εἶ. σὺ εἶ πᾶν τὸ γενόμενον, σὺ τὸ μὴ γενόμενον. νοῦς μὲν ⟨εἶ⟩, νοούμενος· πατὴρ δέ, δημιουργῶν· θεὸς δέ, ἐνεργῶν· ἀγαθὸς δέ, [καὶ] πάντα ποιῶν.

[ὕλης μὲν γὰρ τὸ λεπτομερέστερον ἀήρ, ἀέρος δὲ ψυχή, ψυχῆς δὲ νοῦς, νοῦ δὲ θεός.]

LIBELLVS VI

Ἑρμοῦ τοῦ τρισμεγίστου.

ὅτι ἐν μόνῳ τῷ θεῷ τὸ ἀγαθόν ἐστιν, ἀλλαχόθι δὲ οὐδαμοῦ.

1 a Τὸ ἀγαθόν, ὦ Ἀσκληπιέ, [ἐν οὐδενί ἐστιν εἰ μὴ ἐν μόνῳ τῷ θεῷ. μᾶλλον δὲ τὸ ἀγαθὸν αὐτός ἐστιν ὁ θεός [ἀεί]. εἰ δὲ οὕτως,] οὐσίαν εἶναι δεῖ πάσης κινήσεως καὶ γενέσεως ἔρημον [δὲ οὐδέν ἐστιν], αὐτὴν ⟨⟨δὲ⟩⟩ περὶ [[δὲ]] αὐτὴν στατικὴν ἐνέργειαν ἔχουσα⟨ν⟩, ἀνενδεῆ καὶ ⟨παθῶν⟩ ἀπείρητον,

1 *τί* QS : *τίς* cett. | *δύναιτο* Turn. : om. AQS 2 *καὶ* om. S 3 *σὺ γὰρ ὁ τόπος τῶν ὄντων* scripsi : *οὐ γὰρ τρόπος* codd., Turn. 3–4 *ἐστὶν ἄλλος οὐδεὶς παρὰ σέ* scripsi : *ἐστὶ περί σε* codd., Turn. 6 Fortasse ⟨*τίνα δέ σοι πέμψω θυσίαν;*⟩ *πάντα* ⟨*γὰρ*⟩ *ἀπὸ σοῦ* 11 *ὧν* (ante *ἔκρυψας*) om. S 12 *τίνος* scripsi : *τί* codd., Turn. 13 *ἐὰν* AQS (etiam MC teste Reitz.), Turn. : *ἂν* Reitz. | *σὺ εἶ ὃ ἂν ποιῶ* om. S 14 *εἶ, καὶ ἄλλο* AS : *εἶ, τὸ ἄλλο* Q Turn. 15 *ὃ μὴ σὺ εἶ. σὺ εἶ πᾶν* scripsi : *ὃ μή ἐστι. σὺ εἶ πᾶν* QS Turn. : *ὃ μή ἐστιν σύ εἶ· σύ πᾶν* A 17 *καὶ* seclusit Reitz. 18–19 *ὕλης . . . θεός* secluserunt edd. recentiores 18 *τὸ* om. Q 19 *δὲ θεός* QS : *δὲ ὁ θεός* cett.

Who then can speak of Thee or to Thee, and tell Thy praise? 10 b
Whither shall I look when I praise Thee? Upward or downward, inward or outward? For Thou art the place in which all
things are contained; there is no other place beside Thee; all
things are in Thee.

⟨And what offering shall I bring Thee? For⟩ all things are from Thee. Thou givest all, and receivest nothing; for Thou hast all things, and there is nothing that Thou hast not.

And at what time shall I sing hymns to Thee? For it is 11
impossible to find a season or a space of time that is apart from
Thee.

And for what shall I praise Thee? For the things Thou hast made, or for the things Thou hast not made? For the things Thou hast made manifest, or for the things Thou hast concealed?

And wherewith shall I sing to Thee? Am I my own, or have I anything of my own? Am I other than Thou? Thou art whatsoever I am; Thou art whatsoever I do, and whatsoever I say. Thou art all things, and there is nothing beside Thee, nothing that Thou art not. Thou art all that has come into being, and all that has not come into being. Thou art Mind, in that Thou thinkest; and Father, in that Thou createst; and God, in that Thou workest; and Good, in that Thou makest all things.

LIBELLVS VI

A discourse of Hermes Trismegistus.

That the Good is in God alone, and nowhere else.

The Good, Asclepius, must be a thing that is devoid of all 1 a
movement and all becoming, and has a motionless activity that is
centred in itself; a thing that lacks nothing, and is not assailed by
perturbations;[1] a thing that is wholly filled with supplies ⟨of all

[1] Or 'passions'.

---

21 τῷ om. S 24 Pro εἶναι fortasse νοεῖν | δεῖ om. QS 25 αὐτὴν δὲ περὶ αὐτὴν scripsi: αὐτῆς· περὶ δὲ αὐτὴν codd., Turn. 26 ἔχουσαν scripsi: ἔχουσα codd., Turn. | παθῶν ἀπείρητον scripsi: ἀπείριτον A Turn.: ἀπέριττον QS Flussas

πληρεστάτην χορηγ⟨ημάτ⟩ων. [[ἐν δὲ ἀρχῇ πάντων]] πᾶν γὰρ τὸ χορηγοῦν ἀγαθὸν [ὅταν] λέγεται· ⟨⟨ἐν δὲ ἀρχῇ πάντων,⟩⟩ καὶ πάντα καὶ ἀεὶ ⟨χορηγοῦν, τὸ⟩ ἀγαθόν ἐστι.

1 b τοῦτο δὲ [ἐν] οὐδενὶ ἄλλῳ πρόσεστιν εἰ μὴ μόνῳ τῷ θεῷ. οὔτε γὰρ ἐνδεής ἐστί τινος, ἵνα ἐπιθυμήσας αὐτὸ κτήσασθαι κακὸς γένηται· οὔτε τῶν ὄντων οὐδὲν ἀπόβλητόν ἐστιν αὐτῷ, ὃ ἀποβαλὼν λυπηθήσεται· [λύπη γὰρ κακίας μέρος·] οὔτε κρεῖττον αὐτοῦ ἐστὶν οὐδέν, ὑφ' οὗ ⟨⟨ἀδικηθεὶς⟩⟩ πολεμήσει· οὔτε σύζυγόν ἐστιν αὐτῷ, [τὸ [[ἀδικηθῆναι]] καὶ διὰ τοῦτο] [αὐτ]οῦ ἐρασθήσεται· οὔτε ἀνήκοον, ᾧ ὀργισθήσεται· οὔτε σοφώτερον, ὃ ζηλώσει. τούτων δὲ μὴ ⟨ἐν⟩όντος τῇ οὐσίᾳ ⟨αὐτοῦ⟩ μηδενός, τί ὑπολείπεται ἢ μόνον τὸ ἀγαθόν;

2a ὥσπερ ⌜γὰρ⌝ οὐδὲν τῶν ⟨κακῶν⟩ ἐν τῇ τοιαύτῃ οὐσίᾳ, οὕτως ἐν οὐδενὶ τῶν ἄλλων τὸ ἀγαθὸν εὑρεθήσεται. ἐν πᾶσι γὰρ τοῖς ἄλλοις πάντα ἐστὶ ⟨κακά⟩, καὶ ἐν τοῖς μικροῖς καὶ ἐν τοῖς μεγάλοις, καὶ ἐν τοῖς καθ' ἓν[α] καὶ ἐν αὐτῷ τῷ ζῴῳ τῷ πάντων μείζονι καὶ δυνατωτάτῳ. παθῶν γὰρ πλήρη τὰ γενητά, αὐτῆς τῆς γενέσεως παθητῆς οὔσης. ὅπου δὲ πάθος, οὐδαμοῦ τὸ ἀγαθόν· ὅπου δὲ τὸ ἀγαθόν, οὐδαμοῦ οὐδὲ ἓν πάθος. ὅπου γὰρ ἡμέρα, οὐδαμοῦ νύξ· ὅπου δὲ νύξ, οὐδαμοῦ ἡμέρα. ὅθεν ἀδύνατον ἐν γενέσει εἶναι τὸ ἀγαθόν, ἐν μόνῳ δὲ τῷ ἀγεννήτῳ.

2b ὥσπερ δὲ μετουσία πάντων ἐστὶν ἐν τῇ ὕλῃ δεδομένη, οὕτω καὶ τοῦ ἀγαθοῦ. τοῦτον τὸν τρόπον ἀγαθὸς ὁ κόσμος, καθὰ καὶ αὐτὸς πάντα ποιεῖ, ⟨ὡς⟩ ἐν τῷ μέρει τοῦ ποιεῖν ἀγαθὸς εἶναι. ἐν δὲ τοῖς ἄλλοις πᾶσιν οὐκ ἀγαθός· καὶ γὰρ παθητός ἐστι [καὶ κινητὸς] καὶ παθητῶν ποιητής.

3a [[ἐν δὲ τῷ ἀνθρώπῳ κατὰ σύγκρισιν τοῦ ἀγαθοῦ τὸ κακὸν τέτακται· τὸ γὰρ μὴ λίαν κακὸν ἐνθάδε τὸ ἀγαθόν]] [ἐστι.] [[τὸ δὲ ἐνθάδε ἀγαθὸν μόριον τοῦ κακοῦ τὸ ἐλάχιστον.]] ἀδύνατον οὖν [τὸ ἀγαθὸν] ⟨τὰ⟩ ἐνθάδε καθαρεύειν τῆς κακίας·

1 *χορηγημάτων* scripsi: *χορηγόν* codd., Turn. | *ἐν δὲ ἀρχῇ* (*ἀρχη* A) *πάντων* AQS : *ἐν δὲ ἀρχῇ πάντως* Turn. 2 *γὰρ τὸ χορηγοῦν* AQS : *γὰρ χορηγοῦν* Turn. Fortasse *γὰρ τὸ ⟨ὁτιοῦν⟩ χορηγοῦν* | *λέγεται* scripsi : *λέγω* codd., Turn. 3 *καὶ πάντα* AQS : *καὶ πάντως* Turn. 4 *τούτω* QS : *τοῦτο* cett. 5 Fortasse *τινος ⟨ὁ θεός⟩* 6 *κακὸς γένηται* Parthey : *κακὸς γενέσθαι* A : *κακῶς κέκτηται* QS : *κακὸς κέκτηται* Turn. | *οὔτε τῶν* AQS : *οὐδὲ τῶν* Turn. 8 *ὑφ' οὗ ἀδικηθεὶς πολεμήσει* scripsi : *ὑφ' οὗ πολεμηθήσεται* codd., Turn. 9 *οὔτε σύζυγόν* scripsi : *οὐδὲ σύζυγόν* codd., Turn. 10 *οὗ* scripsi : *αὐτοῦ* codd., Turn. 11 *ἐνόντος* scripsi : *ὄντων* codd., Turn. 13 Fortasse *δὲ* | *κακῶν* add. Flussas 15 *τοῖς ἄλλοις* scripsi : *τὰ ἄλλα* codd., Turn. 16 *ἓν* scripsi : *ἕνα* codd., Turn. | *αὐτῶ* A : *ταυτῷ* QS Turn. 17 Fortasse *δυνατωτέρῳ* 18 *ὅπο δὲ πάθος* S 19–20 *οὐδὲ*

that is desired⟩. Everything that furnishes any sort of supply is called good; but the Good is the one thing which is the source of all things, and supplies all things at all times.

And this belongs to none save God alone. There is nothing 1 b
that God lacks, so that he should desire to gain it, and should thereby become evil. There is nothing that God can lose, and at the loss of which he might be grieved. There is nothing stronger than God, to do him wrong, and so provoke him to quarrel. God has no consort, to excite in him the passion of love; no disobedient subject, to rouse anger in him; there is none wiser than God, to make him jealous. And since his being admits of none of these passions, what remains, save only the Good?

But as no evil can be found in such a being, even so the Good 2 a
cannot be found in any other. In all other things all is evil, in things small and great alike, in each thing severally, and in the one living being that is greater than all, and mightiest of all.[1] For all things that come into being are full of perturbations, seeing that the very process of coming into being involves perturbation. But wherever there is perturbation, there the Good cannot be, and wherever the Good is, there no perturbation at all can be; even as wherever day is, night cannot be, and wherever night is, day cannot be. Hence the Good cannot be in things that come into being, but only in that which is without beginning.[2]

Yet as participation in all ⟨the ideal archetypes of things⟩ is 2 b
distributed in the world of matter, so also participation in the
Good. And in this way the Kosmos too is good, in that the
Kosmos also makes all things,[3] and so, is good in respect of its
function of making things. But in all other respects the Kosmos
is not good; for it is subject to perturbation, and the things
which it makes are subject to perturbation. It is impossible then 3 a
for things in this world to be pure from evil; and that which is

[1] Viz. the Kosmos.

[2] Or, 'only in Him who is without beginning'. In either case, the meaning is 'in God'.

[3] The Kosmos 'makes things', i.e. produces living organisms, working in subordination to God, who is the supreme 'Maker'.

ἓν πάθος A: *οὐδὲν πάθος* QS: *οὐδὲ ἓν τὸ πάθος* Turn. **21–24** Didymus *De Trinitate* 2. 3 (*Testim.*): *ὅθεν εἴρηται καὶ τῷ Ἑρμῇ τῷ ἐπίκλην Τρισμεγίστῳ· "ἀδύνατον ἐν γενέσει . . . οὕτω καὶ τοῦ ἀγαθοῦ"* **23** *ἐν* om. Didymus | *δεδομένη* codd. Corp., Turn., Didymus: fortasse *διαδεδομένη* **25** *ὡς* add. Flussas **27** *γὰρ* om. QS **28–29** *ἐν δὲ . . . ἐνθάδε τὸ ἀγαθόν* hinc ad § 3 b transposui

⟨⟨τὸ δὲ ἐνθάδε ἀγαθόν, ⟨ᾧ⟩ μόριον τοῦ κακοῦ [τὸ] ἐλάχιστον·⟩⟩
κακοῦται γὰρ ἐνθάδε τὸ ἀγαθόν. [κακούμενον γὰρ οὐκέτι
ἀγαθὸν μένει· μὴ μεῖναν δέ, κακὸν γίνεται.]
3 b ἐν μόνῳ ἄρα τῷ θεῷ τὸ ἀγαθόν ἐστιν [ἢ αὐτός ἐστιν ὁ θεὸς
τὸ ἀγαθόν]. ⟨⟨ἐν δὲ τῷ ἀνθρώπῳ κατὰ σύγκρισιν τοῦ κακοῦ
τὸ ἀγαθὸν λέλεκται· τὸ γὰρ μὴ λίαν κακὸν ἐνθάδε [τὸ]
ἀγαθὸν⟩⟩ ⟨προσείρηται⟩. μόνον οὖν, ὦ Ἀσκληπιέ, τὸ ὄνομα
τοῦ ἀγαθοῦ ἐν ἀνθρώποις, τὸ δὲ ἔργον οὐδαμοῦ· ἀδύνατον
γάρ. οὐ γὰρ χωρεῖ σῶμα ὑλικόν, τὸ πάντοθεν ἐσφιγμένον
κακίᾳ, καὶ πόνοις καὶ ἀλγηδόσι, καὶ ἐπιθυμίαις καὶ ὀργαῖς,
καὶ ἀπάταις καὶ δόξαις ἀνοήτοις. καὶ τὸ πάντων κάκιστόν
ἐστιν, ὦ Ἀσκληπιέ, ὅτι ἕκαστον τούτων τῶν προειρημένων
[εμ]πεπίστευται ἐνθάδε [τὸ] μέγιστον εἶναι ἀγαθόν, τὸ μᾶλλον
ἀνυπέρβλητον κακόν. [ἡ γαστριμαργία] [ἡ] τῶν κακῶν
πάντων χορηγὸς ἡ πλάνη ⟨αὕτη⟩ [ἡ [[ἀπουσία]] ἐνθάδε τοῦ
4 a ἀγαθοῦ] ἐστί. κἀγὼ δὲ χάριν ἔχω τῷ θεῷ, τῷ εἰς νοῦν μοι
βαλόντι κἂν περὶ τῆς [γνώσεως] ⟨⟨ἀπουσία⟨ς⟩⟩⟩ τοῦ ἀγαθοῦ,
ὅτι ἀδύνατόν ἐστιν αὐτὸ ἐν τῷ κόσμῳ εἶναι. ὁ γὰρ κόσμος
πλήρωμά ἐστι τῆς κακίας, ὁ δὲ θεὸς τοῦ ἀγαθοῦ [ἢ τὸ ἀγαθὸν
τοῦ θεοῦ].
4 b ⟨ . . . ⟩ ⌜αἱ γὰρ ἐξοχαὶ τῶν καλῶν περὶ αὐτήν εἰσι τὴν
οὐσίαν φαίνονται καὶ καθαρώτεραι καὶ εἰλικρινέσταται τάχα
που καὶ αὗται αἱ οὐσίαι ἐκείνου.⌝ τολμητέον γὰρ εἰπεῖν,
ὦ Ἀσκληπιέ, ὅτι ἡ οὐσία τοῦ θεοῦ, εἴ γε οὐσίαν ἔχει, τὸ
καλόν ἐστι [τὸ δὲ καλὸν] καὶ ⟨τὸ⟩ ἀγαθόν. ⟨ὑπὸ δὲ τούτων⟩
οὐδὲν ἔστι καταλά⟨μ⟩πεσθαι τῶν ἐν τῷ κόσμῳ. πάντα γὰρ
τὰ ὀφθαλμῷ ὑποπίπτοντα εἴδωλά ἐστι, καὶ ὥσπερ σκιαγραφίαι·
τὰ δὲ μὴ ὑποπίπτοντα ⟨ . . . ⟩, μάλιστα δὲ ἡ τοῦ καλοῦ καὶ
τοῦ ἀγαθοῦ ⟨ . . . ⟩. καὶ ὥσπερ ὀφθαλμὸς οὐ δύναται τὸν
θεὸν ἰδεῖν, οὕτως οὐδὲ τὸ καλὸν καὶ τὸ ἀγαθόν. ταῦτα γὰρ
μέρη τοῦ θεοῦ ἐστιν, [[ὁλόκληρα,]] ἴδια αὐτοῦ μόνου, οἰκεῖα,
ἀχώριστα, ⟨⟨ὁλόκληρα,⟩⟩ ἐρασμιώτατα, ὧν [ἢ] αὐτὸς ὁ θεὸς
5 ἐρᾷ [ἢ αὐτὰ τοῦ θεοῦ ἐρᾷ]. εἰ δύνασαι νοῆσαι τὸν θεόν,
νοήσεις τὸ καλὸν καὶ ⟨τὸ⟩ ἀγαθόν, [τὸ ὑπέρλαμπρον] τὸ
⌜ὑπερλαμπόμενον⌝ ὑπὸ τοῦ θεοῦ. ἐκεῖνο γὰρ τὸ κάλλος

2 ἔνθα δὲ τὸ ἀγαθὸν κακούμενον Q | γὰρ om. QS 5–6 τοῦ κακοῦ τὸ ἀγαθὸν Flussas: τοῦ ἀγαθοῦ τὸ κακὸν AQS Turn. 6 λέλεκται scripsi: τέτακται AQS Turn. 7 προσείρηται addidi. Cf. Didymus *l. c.*: κατὰ σύγκρισιν δὲ τοῦ κακοῦ τὸ ἀγαθὸν . . . τέτακται· τὸ γὰρ μὴ λίαν κακὸν . . . ἀγαθὸν ἐνθάδε προσείρηται 9 ἃ γὰρ S: οὐ γὰρ cett. | Fortasse χωρεῖ ⟨αὐτὸ⟩ 13 πεπίστευται scripsi: ἐμπεπίστευται codd., Turn. 14 ἀνυπέρ-

good in this world is that which has the smallest share of evil; for in this world the good becomes evil.

The Good then is in God alone. In man, that which is called 3 b
good is so called in comparison with evil; for that which is not evil beyond measure is named good. Thus in men, Asclepius, it is only the name of the Good that is present; the thing itself is nowhere to be found. It is impossible; for there is not room for the Good in a material body, hemmed in and gripped as such a body is by evil,—by pains and griefs, desires and angry passions, delusions and foolish thoughts. And what is worst of all, Asclepius, each of these things of which I have spoken is in this world believed to be the greatest good, whereas it is rather an evil than which none is greater. This error it is that leads the train of[1] all the evils. And for my part, I thank God for this very 4 a
thought that he has put into my mind, even the thought that the Good is absent, and that it is impossible for it to be present in the Kosmos. For the Kosmos is one mass of evil, even as God is one mass of good.

. . . For we need not fear to say, Asclepius, that the very being 4 b
of God, if 'being' can be ascribed to God, is the Beautiful and the Good. But it is not possible that the light of the Beautiful and the Good should shine on anything in the Kosmos. For all things which the eye can see are mere phantoms, and unsubstantial outlines; but the things which the eye cannot see are the realities, and above all, the ideal form of the Beautiful and the Good. And as the eye cannot see God, so it cannot see the Beautiful and the Good. For the Beautiful and the Good are parts of God; they are properties of God alone; they belong to God, and are inseparable from him; they are without blemish, and most lovely, and God himself is in love with them. If you 5
are able to apprehend God, then you will apprehend the Beautiful and the Good, ...[2] For that Beauty is incomparable, and that

[1] Or, 'supplies' or 'furnishes'.

[2] Perhaps, 'which are the light that God sheds forth around him'.

βλυτον S | τῶν κῶν S : τῶν κακῶν cett. **17** βαλλόντι S : βαλόντι cett. **22** εἰλικρινέστατται A : εἰλικρινέστεραι cett. **23** αἱ οὖσαι Q : αἱ οὖσαι S : αἱ οὐσίαι cett. **25** ἐστι καὶ τὸ ἀγαθόν scripsi : ἐστι· τὸ δὲ καλὸν καὶ ἀγαθόν codd., Turn. **26** καταλάμπεσθαι scripsi : καταλαβέσθαι codd., Turn. **26–27** γὰρ τὰ QS : γὰρ τῷ cett. : fortasse γὰρ τὰ τῷ **27** σκιαγραφίαι S : σκιογραφίαι Q Turn. **28** Fortasse ⟨ἀληθῆ⟩ **29** Fortasse ⟨ἰδέα⟩ **30** οὐδὲ scripsi : οὔτε codd., Turn. **30-31** γὰρ μέρη AQ : γὰρ μέρει S : γὰρ τὰ μέρη Turn. **34** τὸ ὑπέρλαμπρον QS Turn. : τὸ ὑπέρλαμπον A.

ἀσύγκριτον, καὶ ἐκεῖνο τὸ ἀγαθὸν ἀμίμητον, ὥσπερ καὶ αὐτὸς ὁ θεός. ὡς οὖν τὸν θεὸν νοεῖς, οὕτω καὶ τὸ καλὸν καὶ ⟨τὸ⟩ ἀγαθὸν νόει. ἀκοινώνητα γὰρ ταῦτα τοῖς ἄλλοις [τῶν ἄλλων ζῴων] ἐστί, διὰ τὸ ἀχώριστα εἶναι τοῦ θεοῦ. ἐὰν περὶ τοῦ θεοῦ ζητῇς, καὶ περὶ τοῦ καλοῦ ζητεῖς. μία γάρ ἐστιν εἰς αὐτὸ ἀποφέρουσα ὁδὸς ἡ μετὰ γνώσεως εὐσέβεια.

6 *ὅθεν οἱ ἀγνοοῦντες, καὶ μὴ ὁδεύσαντες τὴν [περὶ] τῆς εὐσεβείας ὁδόν, καλὸν καὶ ἀγαθὸν τολμῶσι λέγειν ἄνθρωπον, μηδὲ ὄναρ θεασάμενον εἴ τί ἐστιν ἀγαθόν, ἀλλὰ παντὶ κακῷ περιειλημμένον, καὶ τὸ κακὸν πιστεύσαντα ἀγαθὸν εἶναι, καὶ οὕτως αὐτῷ χρώμενον ἀκορέστως, καὶ φοβούμενον αὐτοῦ στερηθῆναι, πάντα δὲ ἀγωνιζόμενον ἵνα μὴ μόνον ἔχῃ, ἀλλὰ καὶ ἐπαύξῃ. τοιαῦτα τὰ ἀνθρώπεια ἀγαθὰ καὶ [τὰ] καλά, ὦ Ἀσκληπιέ, ἃ οὔτε φυγεῖν δυνάμεθα οὔτε μισῆσαι· τὸ γὰρ πάντων χαλεπώτατον, ὅτι χρείαν αὐτῶν ἔχομεν, καὶ ζῆν τούτων χωρὶς οὐ δυνάμεθα.*

LIBELLVS VII

[Ἑρμοῦ τοῦ τρισμεγίστου.]

ὅτι μέγιστον κακὸν ἐν τοῖς ἀνθρώποις ἡ περὶ τοῦ θεοῦ ἀγνωσία.

1a *Ποῖ φέρεσθε, ὦ ἄνθρωποι, μεθύοντες, τὸν τῆς ἀγνωσίας ἄκρατον [λόγον] ἐκπιόντες; ὃν οὐδὲ φέρειν δύνασθε, ἀλλ' ἤδη αὐτὸν καὶ ἐμεῖτε. στῆτε νήψαντες, ἀναβλέψαντες τοῖς τῆς καρδίας ὀφθαλμοῖς, καὶ εἰ μὴ πάντες δύνασθε, οἵ γε καὶ δυνάμενοι.*

1b *ἡ γὰρ τῆς ἀγνωσίας κακία ἐπικλύζει πᾶσαν τὴν γῆν, καὶ συνφθείρει τὴν ἐν τῷ σώματι κατακεκλεισμένην ψυχήν, μὴ ἐῶσα ἐνορμίσασθαι τοῖς τῆς σωτηρίας λιμέσι. μὴ*

1 Post *ἀσύγκριτον* add. S *καὶ ἐκεῖνο τὸ κάλλος ἀσύγκριτον* | *ἀγαθὸν ἀμίμητον* QS Turn.: *ἀγαθὸν τὸ ἀμίμητον* A: fortasse *ἀγαθὸν ἀλάλητον* 5 *ζητῇς* Turn.: *ζητεῖς* QS: *ζητῇς* ex *ζητεῖς* corr. man. pr. A | *ἐστιν εἰς* A: *ἐστιν ἡ εἰς* QS Turn. 5–6 Fortasse *περὶ τοῦ καλοῦ ⟨καὶ τοῦ ἀγαθοῦ⟩ ζητεῖς. μία γάρ ἐστιν εἰς αὐτά* 9–10 *μηδὲ ὄναρ . . . κακῷ προειλημμένον* bis scriptum Q 10 *περιειλημμένον* scripsi: *προειλημμένον* codd., Turn. 14 *μισῆσε* QS: *μισῆσαι* cett.

18 *ὑπερὶ* S: *ἡ περὶ* cett. 22 *ἐκεῖτε* S: *ἐμεῖτε* cett. | *νήψοντες* S: *νήψαντες* cett. 22–23 *τοῖς τῆς καρδίας ὀφθαλμοῖς* QS Turn.: *τοῖς ὀφθαλμοῖς*

Good is inimitable,[1] even as God himself is. As then you apprehend God, even so you must apprehend the Beautiful and the Good. For they are incommunicable to all other things, because they are inseparable from God. If you seek knowledge of God, you are also seeking knowledge of the Beautiful.[2] For there is one road alone that leads to the Beautiful,[2] and that is piety joined with knowledge of God.

Hence those who have not that knowledge, and have not 6
travelled on the road of piety, are not afraid to call a man 'beautiful and good';[3] and that, though the man has never even in dream seen anything that is good, but is encompassed by every kind of evil, and has come to believe that the evil is good, and in this belief, is insatiable in his dealings with evil, and fears to be deprived of it, and strives with all his might not only to keep it, but to increase it. Such, Asclepius, are the things which men deem good and beautiful. And we cannot shun these things nor hate them; for the hardest thing of all is this, that we have need of them, and cannot live without them.

LIBELLVS VII

That ignorance of God is the greatest evil in men.

O men, whither are you being swept away? You are drunken; 1 a
you have drunk up the strong drink of ignorance;[4] it has overpowered you, and now you are even vomiting it forth. Stand firm; turn sober; look upward with the eyes of the heart,—if you cannot all, yet those at least who can.

This evil of ignorance floods all the land; its current sweeps 1 b
along the soul which is penned up in the body, and prevents it from coming to anchor in the havens of salvation. Suffer not

[1] Perhaps, 'is unspeakable'.
[2] Perhaps, 'the Beautiful ⟨and the Good⟩'.
[3] Among the Greeks, the phrase 'beautiful and good', applied to a man, was in frequent use, and meant something like 'a gentleman'.
[4] I.e. ignorance of God, which implies estrangement from God.

τῆς καρδίας A **23** *καὶ εἰ μὴ πάντες δύνασθε* secludendum? | *καὶ* (post *οἵ γε*) om. QS **26** *συσσύρει* scripsi: *συμφθείρει* codd., Turn. **27** *μὴ* (ante *ἐῶσα*) QS Turn.: *καὶ μὴ* A | *ἐνορμίσασθαι* scripsi: *ἐνορμίζεσθαι* codd., Turn.

2a συγκατενεχθῆτε τοιγαροῦν τῷ πολλῷ ῥεύματι· ἀναρροίᾳ δὲ χρησάμενοι, οἱ δυνάμενοι λαβέσθαι τοῦ [τῆς σωτηρίας] λιμένος, ἐνορμισάμενοι τούτῳ, ζητήσατε χειραγωγόν, τὸν ὁδηγήσοντα ὑμᾶς ἐπὶ τὰς τῆς γνώσεως θύρας, ὅπου ἐστὶ τὸ λαμπρὸν φῶς, τὸ καθαρὸν σκότους· ὅπου οὐδὲ εἷς μεθύει, ἀλλὰ πάντες νήφουσιν, ἀφορῶντες τῇ καρδίᾳ εἰς τὸν ⟨οὕτως⟩ ὁραθῆναι θέλοντα· οὐ γάρ ἐστιν ἀκουστός, οὐδὲ λεκτός, οὐδὲ ὁρατὸς ὀφθαλμοῖς, ἀλλὰ νῷ καὶ καρδίᾳ.

2b πρῶτον δὲ δεῖ σε περιρρήξασθαι ὃν φορεῖς χιτῶνα, ⟨⟨τὸν σκοτεινὸν περίβολον,⟩⟩ τὸ τῆς ἀγνωσίας ὕφασμα, τὸ τῆς κακίας ⌜στήριγμα⌝, τὸν τῆς φθορᾶς δεσμόν, [[τὸν σκοτεινὸν περίβολον,]] τὸν ζῶντα θάνατον, τὸν αἰσθητ⟨ικ⟩ὸν νεκρόν, τὸν περιφόρητον τάφον, τὸν ἔνοικον λῃστήν, ⟨⟨⟨τὸν⟩ ἐχθρὸν⟩⟩ τὸν [δι'] ὧν ⟨ἐ⟩φίεσαι μισοῦντα καὶ [δι'] ὧν ⟨ἐπιθυ⟩μ⟨ε⟩ῖς ⟨σ⟩οι
3 φθονοῦντα. τοιοῦτός ἐστιν ὃν ἐνεδύσω [[ἐχθρὸν]] χιτῶν[α], ἄγχων σε κάτω πρὸς αὐτόν, ἵνα μὴ ἀναβλέψας καὶ θεασάμενος τὸ κάλλος τῆς ἀληθείας, καὶ τὸ ἐ[γ]κεῖ μένον ἀγαθόν, μισήσῃς τὴν τούτου κακίαν, νοήσας αὐτοῦ τὴν ἐπιβουλὴν ἣν ἐπεβούλευσέ σοι, τὰ [δοκοῦντα καὶ μὴ] νομιζόμενα αἰσθητήρια ἀναίσθητα ποιῶν, τῇ πολλῇ ὕλῃ αὐτὰ ἀποφράξας, καὶ μυσαρᾶς ἡδονῆς ἐμπλήσας, ἵνα μήτε ἀκούῃς περὶ ὧν ἀκούειν σε δεῖ, μήτε βλέπῃς [περὶ ὧν] ⟨ἃ⟩ βλέπειν σε δεῖ.

* * * *

1 Ex συγκαταχεῖτε corr. συγκατεχεῖτε S: συγκατενεχθῆτε cett. 2–3 οἱ δυνάμενοι . . . ἐνορμισάμενοι om. S 3 ζητήσετε S: ζητήσατε cett. 4 ὁδηγήσοντα Turn.: ὁδηγήσαντα AQS 6 τὸν QS Turn.: τὸ A 7 ὁρασθῆναι S 10–11 τὸ . . . στήριγμα codd.: fortasse τὸν . . . στήμονα 11 τὸ τῆς φθορᾶς S: τὸν τῆς φθορᾶς cett. 12 αἰσθητὸν QS Turn., man. pr. A: αἰσθητικὸν man. post. A, Flussas | νεαρὸν S: νεκρόν cett. 13–14 τὸν ὧν ἐφίεσαι μισοῦντα scripsi: τὸν δι' ὧν φιλεῖ μισοῦντα codd., Turn. 14–15 καὶ ὧν ἐπιθυμεῖς σοι φθονοῦντα scripsi: καὶ δι' ὧν μισεῖ

yourselves then to be borne along down stream by the strong
current, but avail yourselves of a backflow, those of you who are 2 a
able to reach the haven, and cast anchor there, and seek a guide
to lead you to the door of the House of Knowledge.[1] There you
will find the bright light which is pure from darkness; there none
is drunken, but all are sober, and they look up and see with the
heart Him whose will it is that with the heart alone He should be
seen. For He cannot be known by hearing, nor made known by
speech; nor can He be seen with bodily eyes, but with mind and
heart alone.

But first you must tear off this garment[2] which you wear,--this 2 b
cloak of darkness, this web of ignorance, this ⌈prop⌉ of evil, this
bond of corruption,—this living death, this conscious corpse, this
tomb you carry about with you,—this robber in the house, this
enemy who hates the things you seek after, and grudges you the
things which you desire. Such is the garment in which you have 3
clothed yourself; and it grips you to itself and holds you down,
that you may not look upward and behold the beauty of the
Truth,[3] and the Good that abides above, and hate the evil of this
thing, discovering its ill designs against you. For it makes senseless what men deem to be their organs of sense, stuffing them up
with the gross mass of matter, and cramming them with loathly
pleasures, so that you may neither hear of the things you ought to
hear of, nor see the things you ought to see.

* * * *

[1] I.e. knowledge of God, which implies union with God.
[2] I.e. the body.
[3] Or 'of Reality'.

φθονοῦντα codd., Turn. **15** *χιτών* scripsi : *χιτῶνα* codd., Turn. **17** *ἐκεῖ μένον* scripsi : *ἐγκείμενον* codd., Turn. **19** *δοκοῦντα καὶ μή* A : *δοκοῦντα ἐμοὶ* QS : *δοκοῦντά μοι καὶ* Turn.

LIBELLVS VIII

Ἑρμοῦ τοῦ τρισμεγίστου.

ὅτι οὐδὲν τῶν ὄντων ἀπόλλυται, ἀλλὰ τὰς μεταβολὰς ἀπωλείας καὶ θανάτους πλανώμενοι λέγουσιν.

1 a Περὶ ψυχῆς καὶ σώματος, ὦ παῖ, νῦν λεκτέον, τρόπῳ μὲν ποίῳ ἀθάνατος ἡ ψυχή, ἐνεργείᾳ δὲ ποταπῇ ⟨ . . . ⟩ ἐστι συστάσεως σώματος καὶ διαλύσεως.

1 b ⟨ . . . ⟩ περὶ οὐδὲν γὰρ αὐτῶν ὁ θάνατος· ἀλλὰ ⟨ὄ⟩νο[η]μά ἐστιν Ἡ θανάτου προσηγορία[ς ἢ] κενὸν ἔργογ. [ἢ κατὰ στέρησιν τοῦ πρώτου γράμματος λεγόμενος θάνατος ἀντὶ τοῦ ἀθάνατος.] ὁ γὰρ θάνατος ἀπώλειά[ς] ἐστιν, οὐδὲν δὲ τῶν ἐν τῷ κόσμῳ ἀπόλλυται. εἰ γὰρ δεύτερος θεὸς ὁ κόσμος, καὶ ζῷον ἀθάνατον, ἀδύνατόν ἐστι τοῦ ἀθανάτου ζῴου μέρος τι ἀποθανεῖν· πάντα δὲ τὰ ἐν τῷ κόσμῳ μέρη ἐστὶ τοῦ κόσμου. [μάλιστα δὲ ⟨ἀθάνατος⟩ ὁ ἄνθρωπος, τὸ λογικὸν ζῷον.]

2 πρῶτος γὰρ πάντων, ⟨⟨καὶ⟩⟩ ὄντως [[καὶ]] ἀΐδιος καὶ ἀγέννητος, [καὶ] ⟨ὁ⟩ δημιουργὸς τῶν ὅλων θεός· δεύτερος δὲ ὁ κατ' εἰκόνα αὐτοῦ ὑπ' αὐτοῦ γενόμενος, καὶ ὑπ' αὐτοῦ συνεχόμενος καὶ τρεφόμενος, ⟨⟨ἀείζωο⟨ς ὤ⟩ν, ὡς⟩⟩ ἀθανατιζόμενος [ὡς] ὑπὸ ἀιδίου ⟨ὄντος τοῦ⟩ πατρός [[ἀείζωον ὡς]] [ἀθάνατος]. τὸ γὰρ ἀείζωον τοῦ ἀιδίου διαφέρει. ὁ μὲν γὰρ ⟨πατὴρ⟩ ὑπὸ ἑτέρου οὐκ ἐγένετο· εἰ δὲ καὶ ἐγένετο, ὑφ' ἑαυτοῦ· ⟨μᾶλλον δὲ⟩ οὔποτε ἐγένετο, ἀλλ'· ἀεὶ ⟨ἔστιν· ὁ δὲ κόσμος ἀεὶ⟩ γίνεται. τὸ γὰρ αἴτιον ⟨τ⟩οῦ [ἀΐδιόν ἐστι] ⟨εἶναι⟩ τὸ πᾶν ⟨ὁ πατήρ⟩· ὁ δὲ πατὴρ αὐτὸς ἑαυτοῦ αἴτιος. ὁ δΗ κόσμος ὑπὸ τοῦ πατρὸς ἀιδί⟨ου ὄντ⟩ος [καὶ] ἀθάνατος γέγονε.

3 καὶ ὅσον ἦν τῆς ὕλης ὑποκείμενον τῷ ἑαυτοῦ ⟨θελήματι⟩,

3 *θανάτους* QS Turn. : *θανάτου* A | *λέγουσιν* A : *λέγουσιν οἱ ἄνθρωποι* QS Turn. 5–6 Fortasse *ἐνεργείᾳ δὲ ποταπῇ ⟨συνίσταται τὰ σώματα καὶ διαλύεται· γένεσις γὰρ καὶ φθορὰ ὀνόματά⟩ εἰσι συστάσεως σώματος καὶ διαλύσεως* 7 *αὐτὸς ὁ* S : *αὐτῶν ὁ* cett. 7–8 *ὄνομά ἐστιν ἡ θανάτου προσηγορία κενὸν ἔργου* scripsi : *νόημά ἐστιν ἀθανάτου προσηγορίας ἢ κενὸν ἔργον* codd., Turn. 10 *ἀπώλειά ἐστιν* scripsi : *ἀπωλείας ἐστίν* codd., Turn. | Post *τῶν* add. *μὲν* S 11 *τῷ* (ante *κόσμῳ*) om. A 18 *ἀθανατιζόμενος* Turn. : *καὶ ἀθανατιζόμενος* AQS 19 *ἀιδίου* Turn. : *ἰδίου* codd., Flussas 20 *φέρει* QS : *διαφέρει* cett. 23 *τὸ γὰρ αἴτιον τοῦ εἶναι τὸ πᾶν ὁ πατήρ* scripsi : *τὸ γὰρ ἀίδιον οὗ*

LIBELLVS VIII

A discourse of Hermes Trismegistus.

That nothing that exists perishes, but men are in error when they call the changes which take place 'destructions' and 'deaths'.

Hermes. We have now to speak, my son, of soul and body; 1 a
I must explain in what way the soul is immortal, and by the working of what sort of force . . . of the composition and dissolution of a body.[1]

. . . For death has nothing to do with any of them.[2] The 1 b
word 'death' is a mere name, without any corresponding fact. For death means destruction; and nothing in the Kosmos is destroyed. For seeing that the Kosmos is the second God, and an immortal being, it is impossible that a part of that immortal being should die; and all things in the Kosmos are parts of the Kosmos.

First of all things, and in very truth eternal and without 2
beginning, is God, who is the Maker of the universe; and second is the Kosmos, which has been made by God in his image, and is kept in being and sustained by God. The Kosmos is ever-living; for it is made immortal by the Father, who is eternal. 'Ever-living' is not the same as 'eternal'. The Father has not been made by another; if he has been made at all, he has been made by himself; but it ought rather to be said that he has never been made, but ever is. But the Kosmos is ever being made. For the cause of the existence of the universe is the Father; but the Father is the cause of his own existence. The Kosmos then has been made immortal by the Father, who is eternal.

The Father took all that part of matter which was subject to his 3

[1] Perhaps, 'by the working of what sort of force ⟨bodies are composed and dissolved; for birth and destruction are names which men give to⟩ the composition and dissolution of a body'.

[2] I.e. any of the things in the Kosmos.

ἀΐδιόν ἐστι τὸ πᾶν codd., Turn. **24** αἴτιος scripsi : ἀΐδιος codd., Turn. | δὴ scripsi : δὲ codd., Turn. **25** ἀιδίου ὄντος scripsi : ἀΐδιος καὶ codd., Turn. **26** ὑποκείμενον A : ἀποκείμενον QS Turn.

τὸ πᾶν ὁ πατὴρ σωματοποιήσας καὶ ὀγκώσας ἐποίησε σφαιροειδές, τοῦτο αὐτῷ τὸ ποιὸν περιθείς, οὖσαν καὶ αὐτὴν ἀθάνατον, καὶ ἔχουσαν ἀίδιον τὴν ὑλότητα. πλέον δέ, τῶν ζῴων τὰ ποιὰ ὁ πατὴρ ἐγκατασπείρας τῇ σφαίρᾳ ὥσπερ ἐν ἄντρῳ κατέκλεισε, πάσῃ ποιότητι κοσμῆσαι βουλόμενος τὸ μετ' αὐτοῦ ⟨ἄ⟩ποιον. τῇ δὲ ἀθανασίᾳ περι⟨έ⟩βαλε τὸ πᾶν σῶμα, ἵνα μὴ ⟨ἡ⟩ ὕλη, [καὶ] τῆς τούτου συστάσεως θελήσασα ἀποστῆναι, διαλυθῇ εἰς τὴν ἑαυτῆς ἀταξίαν. ὅτε γὰρ ἦν ἀσώματος ἡ ὕλη, ὦ τέκνον, ἄτακτος ἦν· ἔχει δὲ καὶ ἐνθάδε ⟨ἄτακτόν⟩ τι περὶ τὰ [ἄλλα] μικρὰ [ποιὰ] ⟨ζῷα⟩ εἱλούμενον, τὸ τῆς αὐξήσεως καὶ [τὸ τῆς] μειώσεως [ὃν θάνατον οἱ ἄνθρωποι
4 καλοῦσιν]. αὕτη δὲ ἡ ἀταξία ⟨π⟩ερὶ τὰ ἐπίγεια ζῷα γίνεται. τῶν γὰρ οὐρανίων τὰ σώματα μίαν τάξιν ἔχει, ἣν εἴληχεν ἀπὸ τοῦ πατρὸς τὴν ἀρχήν· τηρεῖται δὲ αὕτη ὑπὸ τῆς ἑκάστου ἀποκαταστάσεως ἀδιάλυτος. ἡ δὲ ἀποκατάστασις τῶν ἐπιγείων σωμάτων ⟨διαλυθείσης γίνεται τῆς⟩ συστάσεως· ⟨τ⟩ῇ δὲ διαλύσει ⟨τ⟩αύτῃ ἀποκαθίσταται εἰς τὰ ἀδιάλυτα σώματα, τουτέστι τὰ ἀθάνατα· καὶ οὕτω στέρησις γίνεται τῆς αἰσθήσεως, οὐκ ἀπώλεια ⟨⟨ζωῆς⟩⟩ [τῶν σωμάτων].

5 τὸ δὲ τρίτον [[ζῷον]] ὁ ἄνθρωπος, κατ' εἰκόνα τοῦ κόσμου γενόμενος, ⟨ν⟩οῦ⟨ν⟩ κατὰ βούλησιν τοῦ πατρὸς ἔχων παρὰ τὰ ἄλλα ἐπίγεια ζῷα, οὐ μόνον πρὸς τὸν δεύτερον θεὸν συμπάθειαν ἔχων, ἀλλὰ καὶ ἔννοιαν τοῦ πρώτου. τοῦ μὲν γὰρ αἰσθάνεται ὡς σώματος, τοῦ δὲ ἔννοιαν λαμβάνει ὡς ἀσωμάτου

2 τοῦτο scripsi : τούτῳ codd., Turn. | αὐτῷ om. S **3** ἀθανάτου S : ἀθάνατον cett. **4** ζῴων scripsi : ἰδεῶν codd., Turn. | τὰ om. S **6** ἄποιον scripsi : ποιόν codd., Turn. | περιέβαλε scripsi : περιβαλὼν codd., Turn. **9–10** ἐνθάδε ἄτακτόν τι περὶ τὰ μικρὰ ζῷα εἱλούμενον scripsi : ἐνθάδε τὴν περὶ τὰ ἄλλα μικρὰ ποιὰ εἱλουμένην AQS Turn. **12** περὶ Flussas : ἐπὶ codd., Turn. **16–17** τῇ δὲ διαλύσει ταύτῃ scripsi : ἡ δὲ διάλυσις αὐτὴ codd., Turn. **19** ἀπώλει S : ἀπώλεια cett. **21** νοῦν Flussas : οὐ AQS Turn. **23** πρώτου QS Turn. : πρ̅ςύτου (id est πατρὸς ⟨α⟩ὐτοῦ) prima manu, ut videtur, ex πρώτου corr. A **24** αἰσθάνεται Turn. : αἴσθεται AQS

will, and made it into a body, and gave it bulk, and fashioned it into a sphere.[1] This quality[2] the Father imposed on the matter; but matter is of itself immortal, and its materiality is eternal. Moreover, the Father implanted within this sphere[3] the qualities of all kinds of living creatures, and shut them up in it, as in a cave; for he willed to embellish[4] with all manner of qualities the matter which existed beside him, but was hitherto devoid of qualities. And he enveloped the whole body with a wrapping of immortality,[5] that the matter might not seek to break away from the composite structure of the universe, and so dissolve into its primal disorder. For when matter was not yet formed into body, my son, it was in disorder; and even in our world, it retains something of disorder, which besets the small living creatures;[6] for the process of growth and decay is a remnant of disorder.
But it is only the living creatures upon earth that are involved in 4
this disorder. The bodies of the celestial gods[7] keep without change that order which has been assigned to them by the Father in the beginning; and that order is preserved unbroken by the reinstatement of each of them in its former place.[8] But the reinstatement of the terrestrial bodies is brought about by the dissolution of their composition; and through this dissolution, they are reinstated by absorption into the bodies which are indissoluble,[9] that is, immortal. When this takes place, consciousness ceases, but life is not destroyed.

And the third being is man, who has been made in the image 5
of the Kosmos. Man differs from all other living creatures upon earth, in that he possesses mind, for so the Father has willed; and not only does man find himself to be in union with the second God,[10] but he also apprehends by thought the first God. He perceives the second God as a body; he apprehends the first

[1] I.e. out of this part of matter he made the sphere of heaven.
[2] Viz. spherical shape.
[3] I. e. in the sublunar world.
[4] Or, 'to set in order'.
[5] That is, he enclosed the world within the immortal sphere of heaven.
[6] The creatures which live in the sublunar world are here called 'small', in contrast to the Kosmos itself, which is 'the great living creature', and to the heavenly bodies.
[7] I.e. the heavenly bodies.
[8] That is, by the cyclic movement of the heavenly bodies, which brings each of them back to the same point again when it has travelled round its orbit.
[9] 'The indissoluble bodies' are the cosmic elements, earth, water, air, and fire.
[10] I.e. he feels himself to be a part of the Kosmos, and to be organically connected with every other part of it.

[καὶ νοῦ τοῦ ἀγαθοῦ].—Τοῦτο οὖν οὐκ ἀπόλλυται τὸ ζῷον;—Εὐφήμησον, ὦ τέκνον, καὶ νόησον τί θεός, τί κόσμος, τί ζῷον ἀθάνατον, τί ζῷον διάλυτον. καὶ [νόησον ὅτι] ὁ μὲν κόσμος ὑπὸ τοῦ θεοῦ καὶ ἐν τῷ θεῷ, ὁ δὲ ἄνθρωπος ὑπὸ τοῦ κόσμου καὶ ἐν τῷ κόσμῳ· ἀρχὴ δὲ καὶ περιοχὴ καὶ σύστασις πάντων ὁ θεός.

LIBELLVS IX

Ἑρμοῦ τοῦ τρισμεγίστου.

περὶ νοήσεως καὶ αἰσθήσεως [καὶ ὅτι ἐν μόνῳ τῷ θεῷ τὸ καλὸν καὶ τὸ ἀγαθόν ἐστιν, ἀλλαχόθι δὲ οὐδαμοῦ].

1a Χθές, ὦ Ἀσκληπιέ, τὸν τέλειον ἀπ[οδ]έδωκα λόγον· νῦν δὲ ἀναγκαῖον ἡγοῦμαι ἀκόλουθον ἐκείνῳ καὶ τὸν περὶ αἰσθήσεως λόγον διεξελθεῖν.

1b αἴσθησις γὰρ καὶ νόησις διαφορὰν μὲν δοκοῦσιν ἔχειν, ὅτι ἡ μὲν ὑλική ἐστιν, ἡ δὲ οὐσιώδης· ἐμοὶ δὲ δοκοῦσιν ἀμφότεραι ἡνῶσθαι καὶ μὴ διαιρεῖσθαι, ἐν ἀνθρώποις λέγω· ἐν γὰρ τοῖς ἄλλοις ζῴοις ἡ αἴσθησις τῇ φύσει ἥνωται, ἐν δὲ ἀνθρώποις ⟨τ⟩ῇ νοήσει.

1c νοήσεως δὲ ὁ νοῦς διαφέρει τοσοῦτον ὅσον ὁ θεὸς θειότητος. ἡ μὲν γὰρ θειότης ὑπὸ τοῦ θεοῦ γίνεται, ἡ δὲ νόησις ὑπὸ τοῦ νοῦ, ἀδελφὴ οὖσα τοῦ λόγου. καὶ ὄργανα ⟨ταῦτα⟩ ἀλλήλων· οὔτε γὰρ ὁ λόγος [[ἐκφωνεῖται]] ⟨ . . . ⟩ χωρὶς νοήσεως, οὔτε ἡ νόησις [φαίνεται] ⟨⟨ἐκφωνεῖται⟩⟩ χωρὶς λόγου.

2 ἡ οὖν αἴσθησις καὶ ἡ νόησις ἀμφότεραι εἰς τὸν ἄνθρωπον συνεπεισρέουσιν ἀλλήλαις, ὥσπερ συμπεπλεγμέναι· οὔτε γὰρ χωρὶς αἰσθήσεως δυνατὸν νοῆσαι, οὔτε αἰσθέσθαι χωρὶς νοήσεως [δυνατὸν δὲ νόησιν]. ⟨ . . . ⟩ χωρὶς αἰσθήσεως νοεῖσθαι, καθάπερ οἱ διὰ τῶν ὀνείρων φανταζόμενοι ὁράματα·

8 κινήσεως QS: νοήσεως cett. 10 ἀπέδωκα scripsi: ἀποδέδωκα codd., Turn. 13 νόησις Flussas: κίνησις AQS Turn. 15 λέγω Flussas: λόγῳ AQS Turn. 16 ἄλλοι S: ἄλλοις cett.: fortasse ἀλόγοις 17 τῇ νοήσει scripsi: ἡ νόησις codd., Turn. 18 δὲ (post νοήσεως) Turn.: om. AQS 20 νοῦ QS Turn.: ἀν̄'ου (i.e. ἀνθρώπου) A | ἀδελφὴ QS Turn.: ἀδελφὸς A 21 ἐκφονεῖται Q | Fortasse ⟨καταλαμβάνεται⟩ χωρὶς 23 ἡ γοῦν QS: ἡ οὖν cett. 24 συνεπειρέουσιν S 25 δυνατὸν Q Flussas:

God as bodiless.—*Tat.* Do you say then that this living creature[1] does not perish?—*Hermes.* Speak not of man as perishing, my son. Think what God is, and what the Kosmos is, and what is meant by a living creature that is immortal, and a living creature that is dissoluble. The Kosmos is made by God, and is contained in God; man is made by the Kosmos, and is contained in the Kosmos; and it is God that is the author of all, and encompasses all, and knits all things together.

LIBELLVS IX

A discourse of Hermes Trismegistus.
Concerning thought and sense.

Yesterday, Asclepius, I delivered my crowning discourse;[2] 1a
and to-day I think it necessary, by way of sequel to that discourse, to expound the doctrine of sense.

Men think that there is a difference between sense and thought, 1b
in that sense is connected with matter, and thought with incorporeal and eternal substance. But I hold that sense and thought are united, and cannot be separated,—that is to say, in the case of men. In the lower animals, sense is united with instinct; in men, sense is united with thought.

Mind differs from thought to the same extent that God differs 1c
from divine influence.[3] Divine influence is put forth by God; and thought is put forth by mind, and is sister to speech. Thought and speech are instruments of one another; speech cannot be understood without thought, and thought cannot be uttered without speech.

Sense and thought are infused into a man together, being 2
intertwined with one another, so to speak; for a man can neither think without perceiving, nor perceive without thinking. It is sometimes said that men may think without sense-perception, as when one sees imaginary things in dreams; but I hold rather that

[1] Viz. man.

[2] The Greek original of the Latin *Asclepius* was entitled 'The Crowning Discourse of Hermes'.

[3] 'Divine influence' probably means God's operation in a man, i.e. divine inspiration.

δύναται cett. 25–26 *δυνατὸν νοῆσαι . . . χωρὶς νοήσεως* om. S 25 *αἰσθέσθαι* Turn.: *αἰσθῆναι* AQ 26 Fortasse ⟨*καίτοι λέγονται ἄνθρωποι ἐνίοτε*⟩ *χωρὶς*

ἐμοὶ δὲ δοκεῖ ⟨. . .⟩ τὸ γεγονέναι ἀμφοτέρας τὰς ἐνεργείας ἐν τῇ τῶν ὀνείρων ὄψει· ἐγρηγοροῦσι γὰρ ⟨. . .⟩ αἰσθήσει. διῄρηται γά⟨ρ ἡ αἴσθησις⟩ εἴς τε τὸ σῶμα καὶ εἰς τὴν ψυχήν· καὶ ὅταν ἀμφότερα τὰ μέρη τῆς αἰσθήσεως πρὸς ἄλληλα συμφωνήσῃ, τότε ⟨συμβαίνει⟩ τὴν νόησιν ἐκφαίνε[ι]σθαι, ἀποκυηθεῖσαν ὑπὸ τοῦ νοῦ.

3 ὁ γὰρ νοῦς κύει πάντα τὰ νοήματα, ἀγαθὰ μέν, ὅταν ὑπὸ τοῦ θεοῦ τὰ σπέρματα λάβῃ, ἐναντία δέ, ὅταν ὑπό τινος τῶν δαιμόν[ι]ων, [μηδενὸς μέρους τοῦ κόσμου κενοῦ ὄντος δαίμονος,] ⟨⟨ὅστις ὑπεισελθὼν⟩⟩ τῷ ⟨μὴ⟩ ὑπὸ τοῦ θεοῦ πεφωτισμένῳ [δαίμονι] [[ὅστις ὑπεισελθὼν]] ἔσπειρε τῆς ἰδίας ἐνεργείας τὸ σπέρμα, καὶ ἐκύησεν ὁ νοῦς τὸ σπαρέν, μοιχείας, φόνους, πατροτυπίας, ἱεροσυλίας, ἀσεβείας [ἀγχόνας, κατὰ κρημνῶν
4a καταφοράς, καὶ ἄλλα πάντα ὅσα δαιμόνων ἔργα]. τοῦ γὰρ θεοῦ τὰ σπέρματα ὀλίγα, μεγάλα μέν⟨τοι⟩ καὶ καλὰ καὶ ἀγαθά, ἀρετὴ καὶ σωφροσύνη καὶ εὐσέβεια. εὐσέβεια δέ ἐστι θεοῦ γνῶσις· ὃν ὁ ἐπιγνούς, πλήρης γενόμενος πάντων τῶν ἀγαθῶν, τὰς νοήσεις θείας ἴσχει, καὶ οὐ τοῖς πολλοῖς ὁμοίας.

4b διὰ τοῦτο οἱ ἐν γνώσει ὄντες οὔτε τοῖς πολλοῖς ἀρέσκουσιν, οὔτε οἱ πολλοὶ αὐτοῖς· μεμηνέναι δὲ δοκοῦσι, καὶ γέλωτα ὀφλισκάνουσι, μισούμενοί τε καὶ καταφρονούμενοι, καὶ τάχα που καὶ φονευόμενοι. τὴν γὰρ κακίαν ἐνθάδε δεῖν οἰκεῖν εἶπον, ἐν τῷ ἑαυτῆς χωρίῳ οὖσαν· χωρίον γὰρ αὐτῆς ἡ γῆ, οὐχ ὁ κόσμος, ὡς ἔνιοί ποτε ἐροῦσι βλασφημοῦντες. ὁ μέντοι θεοσεβὴς πάντα ὑποστήσει ἀ⟨ντ⟩ισχόμενος τῆς γνώσεως. πάντα γὰρ τῷ τοιούτῳ, κἂν τοῖς ἄλλοις ⟨ᾖ⟩ [τὰ] κακά, ἀγαθά ἐστι· καὶ ἐπιβουλευόμενος πάντα ἀναφέρει εἰς τὴν γνῶσιν, καὶ τὰ κακὰ μόνος ἀγαθοποιεῖ.

5 ἐπάνειμι πάλιν ἐπὶ τὸν τῆς αἰσθήσεως λόγον. ἀνθρώπινον οὖν τὸ κοινωνῆσαι αἴσθησιν νοήσει· οὐ πᾶς δὲ ἄνθρωπος, ὡς προεῖπον, ἀπολαύει τῆς νοήσεως· [ἀλλ' ὁ μὲν ὑλικός, ὁ δὲ

1 Fortasse ἐμοὶ δὲ δοκεῖ ⟨μᾶλλον εὔλογον εἶναι⟩ | τὸ (ante γεγονέναι) AQS: τῷ Turn. 2 ἐγρηγοροῦσι AQS: ἐγρηγορόσι Turn. | Fortasse ⟨συνέζευκται ἀεὶ νόησις⟩ αἰσθήσει 3 διῄρηται γὰρ ἡ αἴσθησις scripsi: διῄρηταί γε codd., Turn. | εἰς (post καὶ) om. QS 5 ἐκφαίνεσθαι scripsi: ἐκφωνεῖσθαι codd., Turn. 8 τοῦ om. S | ὑπό τινος QS Turn.: ὑπὸ τίνων A 9 δαιμόνων scripsi: δαιμονίων codd., Turn. | κενοῦ QS Turn. et man. post. A: καινοῦ man. pr. A 15 μέντοι scripsi: μὲν QS Turn.: δὲ A 17 ὁ om. A | πλήρεις QS: πλήρης cett. 23 δεῖ S: δεῖν cett. 24 εἶπον, ἐν scripsi: εἴπομεν codd., Turn. 26 ἀντισχό-

both thought and sense-perception have taken place in the dream-
vision; for when we are awake, thought is always combined with
sense-perception. Sense belongs in part to the body, and in part
to the soul; and when the body-sense and the soul-sense are in
accord, then it results that thought manifests itself, being brought
forth as offspring by the mind.[1]

For all man's thoughts are brought forth by his mind,—good 3
thoughts, when the mind is impregnated by God, and bad
thoughts, when it is impregnated by some daemon, who enters
into the man that has not been illuminated by God, and deposits
in his mind the seed of such thoughts as it is the special work of
that daemon to beget; and the mind brings forth those things
which spring from this seed,—adulteries, murders, acts of
parricide and sacrilege, and all manner of impious deeds.
But the seeds which God deposits in the mind are few in number, 4a
but potent, and fair, and good; they are virtue, and self-control,
and piety. Now piety is the knowledge of God; and he who has
come to know God is filled with all things good; his thoughts are
divine, and are not like those of the many.

Hence it is that those who have attained to the knowledge 4b
of God are not pleasing to the many, nor the many to them.
They are thought mad, and are laughed at; they are hated and
despised, and perhaps they may even be put to death. For evil,
as I have told you before, must needs dwell here on earth, where
it is at home; for the home of evil is the earth, and not the whole
universe, as some will blasphemously say in days to come. But
the pious man will endure all things, cleaving to his knowledge of
God. For to such a man all things are good, even though they
be evil to others. When men devise mischief against him, he
sees all this in the light of his knowledge of God; and he, and
none but he, changes things evil into good.

But let us return to the doctrine of sense. It is a property of 5
man that sense in him is joined with thought; but as I have
already told you, it is not every man that profits by his power of

[1] The text of § 2 is badly damaged, and this attempt to give the meaning of what the author wrote is largely conjectural.

μενος scripsi: αἰσθόμενος codd., Turn. 30 τῆς A: om. QS Turn.
31 αἴσθησιν scripsi: ἄνθρωπον codd., Turn.

οὐσιώδης.] ὁ μὲν γὰρ μετὰ κακίας [ὑλικός] ⟨νοεῖ⟩, ὡς ἔφην, ἀπὸ τῶν δαιμόνων τὸ σπέρμα τῆς νοήσεως ἴσχων, οἱ δὲ μετὰ τοῦ ἀγαθοῦ [οὐσιωδῶς], ὑπὸ τοῦ θεοῦ σωζόμενοι. ὁ μὲν γὰρ θεός, πάντων δημιουργὸς [δημιουργ] ὤν, πάντα ποιεῖ [μὲν] ἑαυτῷ ὅμοια, ταῦτα δ', ἀγαθὰ γενόμενα, ἐν τῇ χρήσει τῆς ἐνεργείας ⌜αφορα⌝· ἡ γὰρ κοσμικὴ φορά, τρέπουσα τὰς γενέσεις, ποιὰς ποιεῖ, τὰς μὲν ῥυπαίνουσα τῇ κακίᾳ, τὰς δὲ καθαίρουσα τῷ ἀγαθῷ.

6 καὶ γὰρ ὁ κόσμος, ὦ Ἀσκληπιέ, αἴσθησιν ἰδίαν καὶ νόησιν ἔχει, οὐχ ὁμοίαν τῇ ἀνθρωπείᾳ, οὐδὲ ⟨οὕτ⟩ως ποικίλην, ἀλλ⟨ὰ⟩ [ως δὲ] κρείττω καὶ ἁπλουστέραν. ἡ γὰρ αἴσθησις καὶ νόησις τοῦ κόσμου μία ἐστί, τὸ πάντα ποιεῖν καὶ εἰς ἑαυτὸν ἀποποιεῖν, ὄργανον ⟨⟨ὄντα⟩⟩ τῆς τοῦ θεοῦ βουλήσεως, καὶ [[ὄντως]] ⟨ἐπὶ τοῦτο⟩ [ὀργανο] ποιηθέν⟨τα⟩, ἵνα πάντων ⟨τῶν⟩ παρ' ἑαυτῷ ἀπὸ τοῦ θεοῦ λαβὼν τὰ σπέρματα ⟨καὶ⟩ φυλάττων ἐν ἑαυτῷ πάντα ποιῇ ἐνεργῶς. ⟨⟨φερόμενος δὲ πάντα ζωοποιεῖ·⟩⟩ καὶ διαλύων πάντα, ἀνανεοῖ [καὶ] ⟨τὰ⟩ δια-[τοῦτο]-λυθέντα, ὥσπερ ἀγαθὸς [ζωῆς] γεωργὸς τῇ καταβολῇ ἀνανέωσιν αὐτοῖς [φερόμενος] παρέχων. οὐκ ἔστιν ὃ μὴ ζωογονεῖ· [[φερόμενος δὲ πάντα ζωοποιεῖ·]] καὶ ὁμοῦ τόπος ἐστὶ καὶ δημιουργὸς ζωῆς.
7 τὰ δὲ σώματα ἀπὸ ὕλης, ἐν διαφορᾷ· [τὰ μὲν γάρ ἐστιν ἐκ γῆς, τὰ δὲ ἐξ ὕδατος, τὰ δὲ ἐξ ἀέρος, τὰ δὲ ἐκ πυρός·] πάντα δέ ἐστι σύνθετα, καὶ τὰ μὲν μᾶλλον, τὰ δὲ ἁπλούστερα· μᾶλλον μὲν τὰ βαρύτερα, ἧττον δὲ τὰ κουφότερα. τὸ δὲ τάχος αὐτοῦ τῆς φορᾶς τὴν ποικιλίαν τῶν [ποιῶν] γενέσεων ἐργάζεται. πνοὴ γάρ, οὖσα πυκνοτάτη, προτείνει τὰ ποιὰ
8 τοῖς σώμασι μετὰ ἑνὸς πληρώματος τῆς ζωῆς. [πατὴρ μὲν οὖν ὁ θεὸς τοῦ κόσμου, ὁ δὲ κόσμος τῶν ἐν τῷ κόσμῳ· καὶ ὁ μὲν κόσμος υἱὸς τοῦ θεοῦ, τὰ δὲ ἐν τῷ κόσμῳ ⟨υἱοὶ⟩ [ὑπὸ] τοῦ κόσμου.] καὶ εἰκότως κόσμος κέκληται· κοσμεῖ⟨ται⟩ γὰρ

1 μὲν om. A | ὑλικός codd., Turn. : fortasse ὑλικῶς 2 ἴσχων scripsi : ἴσχει codd., Turn. 4 ὤν scripsi : δημιουργῶν codd., Turn. 6 ἀφορᾷ codd., Turn. : fortasse ⟨ἐκβαίνει δι⟩άφορα | τρέπουσα scripsi : τρίβουσα codd., Turn. 7 ποιὰς codd., Turn. : fortasse ποι⟨κίλ⟩ας 9 ἰδίαν QS Turn. : ἰδία A | νόησιν Flussas; κίνησιν AQS Turn. 10 οὕτως scripsi : ὡς codd., Turn. 10–11 ἀλλὰ scripsi : ἄλλως δὲ codd., Turn. 12 τὸ πάντα scripsi : τῷ πάντα codd., Turn. | ἑαυτὸν scripsi : ἑαυτὴν codd., Turn. 13–14 καὶ ἐπὶ τοῦτο ποιηθέντα scripsi : καὶ ὄντως ὀργανοποιηθὲν codd., Turn. 14 πάντων τῶν scripsi : πάντα codd., Turn. 16 ποιεῖ S : ποιῇ cett. | ἐνεργῶς A : ἐναργῶς QS Turn. 17 τὰ διαλυθέντα scripsi : καὶ διὰ τοῦτο λυθέντα codd., Turn. 18 αὐτοῖς suprascr. prima (?) man. A 19 παρέχων scripsi : παρέχει AQS Turn. | οὐκ Turn. : om. AQS : fortasse οὐ γὰρ 21 An ἐνδιάφορα? 21–22 ἐκ γῆς QS Turn. : ἐκ τῆς γῆς A 23 Pro

thought; for one man's thoughts are combined with evil, as I said, because he has got from the daemons the seed from which his thinking springs, and other men's thoughts are combined with good, because they are kept safe by God. God is the Maker of all things, and makes all things like to himself;[1] but though good when first made, they . . .[2] when the cosmic force works on them;[3] for the movement of the Kosmos varies the births of things, and gives them this or that quality; it fouls with evil the births of some things, and purifies with good the births of others.

The Kosmos also, Asclepius, has sense and thought; but its 6
sense and thought are of a kind peculiar to itself, not like the sense and thought of man, nor varying like his, but mightier and less diversified. The sense and thought of the Kosmos are occupied solely in making all things, and dissolving them again into itself. The Kosmos is an instrument of God's will; and it was made by him to this end, that, having received from God the seeds of all things that belong to it, and keeping these seeds within itself, it might bring all things into actual existence. The Kosmos produces life in all things by its movement; and decomposing them, it renews the things that have been decomposed; for, like a good husbandman, it gives them renewal by sowing seed. There is nothing in which the Kosmos does not generate life; and it is both the place in which life is contained, and the
maker of life. The bodies of all living beings are made of matter. 7
They are diversely made, but all are composite, in greater or less degree; the heavier bodies are more composite, and the lighter less. It is the swiftness of the movement of the Kosmos that causes the diversity of the births. For the cosmic life-breath, working without intermission, conveys into the bodies a succession of qualities, and therewith makes the universe one mass of
life. [ ][4] And rightly is the Kosmos so named;[5] for all 8

[1] I. e. makes all things good.

[2] Perhaps, 'they come to vary in quality' (i.e. some of them become bad).

[3] Or 'when they come into action'? The phrase is obscure, and perhaps corrupt.

[4] ['God then is the father of the Kosmos, and the Kosmos is the father of the things contained in it; the Kosmos is son of God, and the things contained in it are sons of the Kosmos.']

[5] The word *κόσμος* means (1) order, (2) ornament, (3) the ordered universe.

ἁπλούστερα fortasse *ἧττον* 27 *πληρόματος* S | *τῆς ζωῆς* Turn.: *τοῦ τῆς ζωῆς* AQS 29 *τά τε* S: *τὰ δὲ* cett. 29–30 *ὑπὸ τοῦ κόσμου καὶ εἰκότως κόσμος* om. S 30 *κοσμεῖται* scripsi: *κοσμεῖ* codd., Turn.

τὰ πάντα τῇ ποικιλίᾳ τῆς γενέσεως, καὶ τῷ ἀδιαλείπτῳ τῆς ζωῆς, καὶ ⟨τῷ⟩ ἀκοπιάστῳ τῆς ἐνεργείας, καὶ τῷ τάχει ⟨τῆς φορᾶς, καὶ τῷ ἀτρέπτῳ⟩ τῆς ἀνάγκης, καὶ τῇ συστάσει τῶν στοιχείων, καὶ τῇ τάξει τῶν γινομένων. ὁ αὐτὸς οὖν κόσμος καὶ ⌜ἀναγκαίως⌝ καὶ οἰκείως καλοῖτο.

9 πάντων οὖν τῶν ζῴων ἡ αἴσθησις καὶ νόησις ἔξωθεν ἐπεισέρχεται, εἰσπνέουσα ἀπὸ τοῦ περιέχοντος· ὁ δὲ κόσμος, ἅπαξ λαβὼν ἅμα τῷ γενέσθαι, ἀπὸ τοῦ θεοῦ λαβὼν ἔχει. ὁ δὲ θεὸς οὐχ ὥσπερ ἐνίοις δόξει ἀναίσθητός ἐστι καὶ ἀνόητος· ὑπὸ γὰρ δεισιδαιμονίας βλασφημοῦσι. ⟨⟨καὶ τοῦτο ἔστιν ἡ αἴσθησις καὶ νόησις τοῦ θεοῦ, τὸ τὰ πάντα ἀεὶ κινεῖν.⟩⟩ πάντα γὰρ ὅσα ἔστιν, ὦ Ἀσκληπιέ, ταῦτα ἐν τῷ θεῷ ἐστι, καὶ ὑπὸ τοῦ θεοῦ γινόμενα, καὶ ἐκεῖθεν ἠρτημένα, τὰ μὲν διὰ σωμάτων ἐνεργοῦντα, τὰ δὲ διὰ οὐσίας ψυχικῆς κινοῦντα, τὰ δὲ διὰ πνεύματος ζωοποιοῦντα, τὰ δὲ τὰ κεκμηκότα ὑποδεχόμενα. [καὶ εἰκότως.] [[μᾶλλον δὲ λέγω ὅτι οὐκ αὐτὸς αὐτὰ ἔχει, ἀλλὰ τὸ ἀληθὲς ἀποφαίνομαι, αὐτὸς ἅπαντά ἐστιν]] [οὐκ ἔξωθεν αὐτὰ προσλαμβάνων, ἔξω δὲ ἐπιδιδούς.] [[καὶ τοῦτό ἐστιν ἡ αἴσθησις καὶ νόησις τοῦ θεοῦ, τὸ τὰ πάντα ἀεὶ κινεῖν.]] καὶ οὐκ ἔσται ποτὲ χρόνος ὅτε ἀπολειφθήσεταί τι τῶν ὄντων· [ὅταν δὲ λέγω τῶν ὄντων, λέγω τοῦ θεοῦ·] τὰ γὰρ ὄντα ὁ θεὸς ἔχει, καὶ οὔτε αὐτοῦ οὐδὲν ἐκτὸς οὔτε αὐτὸς οὐδενός. ⟨⟨μᾶλλον δὲ λέγω ὅτι οὐκ αὐτὸς αὐτὰ ἔχει, ἀλλὰ τὸ ἀληθὲς ἀποφαίνομαι, αὐτὸς ἅπαντά ἐστιν.⟩⟩

10 ταῦτά σοι, Ἀσκληπιέ, ἐννοοῦντι ⟨μὲν⟩ ἀληθῆ δόξειεν ἄν, ⟨μὴ ἐν⟩νοοῦντι δὲ ἄπιστα· τῷ γὰρ νοῆσαι ἕπεται τὸ πιστεῦσαι, τὸ ἀπιστῆσαι δὲ τῷ μὴ νοῆσαι. ὁ γὰρ λόγος [μ] οὐ φθάνει μέχρι τῆς ἀληθείας· ὁ δὲ νοῦς μέγας ἐστί, καὶ ὑπὸ τοῦ λόγου μέχρι τινὸς ὁδηγηθείς, φθάνει μέχρι τῆς ἀληθείας· καὶ

1 τὰ (ante πάντα) om. S 3 τῇ συστάσει Flussas : τῇ συσκιάσει A Turn. : τῇ σκιάσει QS 4 δόξει S : τάξει cett. 4–5 ὁ αὐτὸς . . . καλοῖτο secludendum? 5 ἀναγκαῖος QS : ἀναγκαίως cett. : fortasse ἀναλόγως | οἰκεῖος S : οἰκείως cett. 6 καὶ ἡ νόησις S : καὶ νόησις cett. 7 ἀπὸ scripsi : ὑπὸ codd., Turn. 8 τῷ (post ἅμα) om. S | ἀπὸ scripsi : ὑπὸ codd., Turn. 13 καὶ (ante ἐκεῖθεν) om. QS 13–14 διὰ σωμάτων A : διὰ τῶν σωμάτων QS Turn. 15 τὰ (ante κεκμηκότα) om. QS 18 προσλαμβάνων S 19 καὶ ἡ νόησις Q : καὶ νόησις cett. 20 ἀπολειφθείσεται S 22 οὐδὲν ἐκτὸς om. S 22–23 αὐτὸς οὐδενός Turn. : αὐτοῦ οὐδενός AQS 23 Fortasse λέγω οὐχ ὅτι 25 ἐνοῦντι S. — Desinit S in verbis ἀσκληπιὲ ἐνοῦντι 25–26 δόξειεν ἄν, μὴ ἐννοοῦντι scripsi : δόξειεν, ἀγνοοῦντι codd., Turn. 26 τῷ γὰρ νοῆσαι ἕπεται scripsi : τὸ γὰρ νοῆσαί ἐστι codd., Turn. 27 τὸ (ante ἀπιστῆσαι) om. A | τῷ μὴ scripsi : τὸ μὴ codd., Turn. | οὐ

things in it are wrought into an ordered whole by the diversity of births and the incessant continuance of life, and by its unwearied activity, and the swiftness of its movement, and the immutable necessity that rules in it, and by the combining of the elements, and the fit disposal of all things that come into being. Thus the name 'Kosmos' may be applied to it in a secondary sense as well as literally.

Now the sense and thought of all living creatures enter into 9
them from without, being breathed into them from the atmosphere; but the Kosmos received sense and thought once for all when it first came into being, and has got them from God. God is not devoid of sense and thought, as in time to come some men will think he is; those who speak thus of God blaspheme through excess of reverence. And the sense and thought of God consist in this, that he is ever moving all things. For all things that exist, Asclepius, are in God, and are made by God, and are dependent on him, whether they be things that put forth activity by means of their bodies,[1] or things that effect movement by means of soul-stuff,[2] or things that generate life by means of vital breath,[3] or things that receive into themselves the bodies that life has quitted.[4] And there will never come a time when anything that exists will cease to be; for God contains all things, and there is nothing which is not in God, and nothing in which God is not. Nay, I would rather say, not that God *contains* all things, but that, to speak the full truth, God *is* all things.

What I have told you, Asclepius, you will deem true if you 10
apply your thought to it; but if not, you will not believe it; for belief follows on thinking, and disbelief follows on want of thinking. Speech does not attain to truth; but mind has mighty power, and when it has been led some distance on its way by speech,[5] it attains to truth; and having thought over all things,

[1] This probably means vegetables.

[2] This probably means animals (including men).

[3] I.e. by being drawn into the body of a man or beast in the process of breathing. These things are probably the two lighter elements, fire and air.

[4] Probably the two heavier elements, earth and water.

[5] I.e. when the pupil's thoughts have been started in the right direction by the teacher's words.

---

scripsi : *μου* A : *μοι* Q Turn. 29 *φθάνει μέχρι* Reitz.: *φθάνειν ἔχει* codd., Turn. | *φθάνει . . . ἀληθείας* secludendum ?

περινοήσας τὰ πάντα, καὶ εὑρὼν σύμφωνα τοῖς ὑπὸ τοῦ λόγου ἑρμηνευθεῖσιν, ἐπίστευσε, καὶ τῇ καλῇ πίστει ἐπανεπαύσατο. τοιγ⟨αρ⟩οῦν [[τὰ προειρημένα]] [ὑπὸ τοῦ θεοῦ] νοήσασι μὲν πιστὰ ⟨⟨τὰ προειρημένα⟩⟩, μὴ νοήσασι δὲ ἄπιστα.

ταῦτα καὶ τοσαῦτα περὶ νοήσεως καὶ αἰσθήσεως λεγέσθω.

LIBELLVS X

Ἑρμοῦ τοῦ τρισμεγίστου.

Κλείς.

1a Τὸν χθὲς λόγον, ὦ Ἀσκληπιέ, σοὶ ἀνέθηκα· τὸν δὲ σήμερον δίκαιόν ἐστι τῷ Τὰτ ἀναθεῖναι, ἐπεὶ καὶ τῶν ⟨γ⟩ενικῶν λόγων τῶν πρὸς αὐτὸν λελαλημένων ἐστὶν ἐπιτομή.

1b ὁ μὲν οὖν θεὸς καὶ πατήρ, καὶ τὸ ἀγαθόν, ὦ Τάτ, τὴν αὐτὴν ἔχει φύσιν, μᾶλλον δὲ [καὶ] ἐνέργειαν. ἡ μὲν γὰρ φύσ⟨ις γενέσ⟩εως καὶ αὐξήσεώς ἐστι προσηγορία, ἅπερ ἐστὶ περὶ τὰ μεταβλητὰ καὶ κινητά· ⟨ἡ δὲ τοῦ θεοῦ ἐνέργεια περὶ τὰ ἀμετάβλητα⟩ καὶ ἀκίνητα, τουτέστι τὰ θεῖα [τε], ⟨⟨ὧν⟩⟩ καὶ ⟨τὰ⟩ ἀνθρώπεια [[ὧν]] αὐτὸς βούλεται εἶναι. ἀλλαχοῦ δὲ ⟨περὶ⟩ ἐνεργειῶν [[καθὼς καὶ ἐπὶ τῶν ἄλλων]] ἐδιδάξαμεν θείων τε καὶ ἀνθρωπίνων· ἃ δεῖ νοεῖν ἐπὶ τούτου ⟨⟨καθὼς καὶ ἐπὶ τῶν ἄλλων⟩⟩.

2 ἡ γὰρ τούτου ἐνέργεια ἡ θέλησίς ἐστι· καὶ ἡ οὐσία αὐτοῦ τὸ θέλειν πάντα εἶναι. τί γάρ ἐστι⟨ν ὁ⟩ θεὸς καὶ πατὴρ [καὶ τὸ ἀγαθὸν] ἢ τὸ τῶν πάντων εἶναι οὐκέτι ὄντων; ἀλλὰ ὕπαρξις αὕτη τῶν ὄντων. τοῦτο ὁ θεός, τοῦτο ὁ πατήρ. τούτῳ ⟨δὲ πρόσεστι⟩ τὸ ἀγαθόν, ⟨τοιοῦτο ὂν⟩ ὃ μηδεν⟨ὶ⟩ πρόσ-

3 **τοιγαροῦν** scripsi: *τοῖς οὖν* codd., Turn. 5 *καὶ αἰσθήσεως* in A et C abesse testatur Reitz.

In Libellis X et XI, codicum AQ et Turnebi lectiones adhibui.

X. 7–8 b:—Stobaei *Anthol.* I. 49. 48, vol. i, p. 416 Wachsmuth (*Ecl.* I. 1000 Heeren): Ἑρμοῦ ἐκ τῶν πρὸς Τάτ. *Οὐκ ἤκουσας ἐν τοῖς γενικοῖς . . . αὕτη κακία ψυχῆς.*

X. 12, 13:—Stob. I. 47. 9, vol. i, p. 305 W. (*Ecl.* I. 770 H.): Ἑρμοῦ ἐκ τῶν πρὸς Τάτ. *Ὁ μὲν ἄνθρωπος τὸ δεύτερον ζῷον μετὰ τὸν κόσμον, πρῶτον δὲ τῶν θνητῶν.—ψυχὴ δὲ ἀνθρώπου ὀχεῖται . . . ὁ θάνατος τοῦ σώματος.*

X. 16–18:—Stob. I. 48. 3, vol. i, p. 310 W. (*Ecl.* I. 774 H.): Ἑρμοῦ. *Πῶς τοῦτο λέγεις, ὦ πάτερ . . . ἀνθρώπινος ὢν τῇ οἰκήσει.*

X. 19 a, b:—Stob. I. 49. 49, vol. i, p. 417 W. (*Ecl.* I. 1002 H.): Τοῦ αὐτοῦ (*sc.* Ἑρμοῦ). *Ψυχὴ δὲ ἀνθρωπίνη . . . τῆς τοιαύτης ὕβρεως.*

X. 22 b–25:—Stob. I. 47. 8, vol. i, p. 303 W. (*Ecl.* I. 764 H.): Ἑρμοῦ ἐκ τῶν πρὸς Τάτ. *Κοινωνία δέ ἐστι ψυχῶν . . . ὑπὸ δὲ τοῦ ἑνὸς πάντα.*

and found all to be in accord with that which has been expounded to it by speech, the mind believes, and finds rest in that goodly belief. And so, if men grasp with their thought what I have said, they will believe it; but if they do not grasp it with their thought, they will not believe it.

Concerning thought and sense, let this suffice.

LIBELLVS X

A discourse of Hermes Trismegistus.

The Key.

Hermes. The teaching which I gave yesterday, Asclepius, I dedicated to you; and it is only right that I should dedicate to Tat that which I am about to give to-day; for it is an abridgement of the General Discourses which I have addressed to him. 1 a

Know then, Tat, that God the Father is of one nature with the Good; or rather, the working of God the Father is one with the working of the Good. 'Nature' is a term applied to birth and growth, and birth and growth have to do with things subject to change and movement; but God's working has to do with things free from change and movement, that is, with things divine; and it is God's will that what is human should be divine. Of forces at work, divine and human, I have spoken elsewhere; and in dealing with our present topic, as well as in other matters, you must bear in mind what I have taught you concerning them. 1 b

The force with which God works is his will; and his very being consists in willing the existence of all things. What else is God the Father but the being of all things when as yet they are not? It is this[1] that constitutes the existence of all things that are. Such then is God, such is the Father. And to him appertains the Good; for the Good is a thing that can appertain to none 2

[1] Viz. God's will.

---

7 τὸ δὲ Q: τὸν δὲ cett. 8 γενικῶν Patritius: ἐνικῶν codd. (etiam MC teste Reitz.), Turn. 10 Fortasse [καὶ] τῷ ἀγαθῷ 12 φύσις γενέσεως scripsi: φύσεως codd., Turn. 16 περὶ ἐνεργειῶν scripsi: ἐνέργειαν codd., Turn. 21 ἢ τὸ Turn.: εἰ τοῦ Q, man. pr. A: ἢ τοῦ man. post. A 22 ὕπαρξις αὐτὴ Turn.: ὕπαρξιν αὐτῶν (αυτη ex αὐτῶν corr. man. post.) A: ὕπαρξιν αὐτὴν Q 23 τούτῳ δὲ πρόσεστι τὸ ἀγαθόν scripsi: τοῦτο τὸ ἀγαθόν codd., Turn. | ὃ μηδενὶ scripsi: ᾧ μηδὲν codd., Turn.

εστι τῶν ἄλλων. ὁ μὲν γὰρ κόσμος [καὶ ὁ ἥλιος] τῶν κατὰ
μετουσίαν ⟨ἀγαθῶν⟩ καὶ αὐτὸς πατήρ, οὐκέτι δὲ τοῦ ἀγαθοῦ
τοῖς ζῴοις ἴσως αἴτιός ἐστιν· οὐδὲ ⟨γὰρ⟩ τοῦ ζῆν· εἰ δέ [τοῦτο
οὕτως ἔχει], πάντως μέντοι ἀναγκαζόμενος ὑπὸ τοῦ [ἀγαθοῦ]
θελήματος ⟨τοῦ θεοῦ⟩, οὗ χωρὶς οὔτε εἶναί ⟨τι⟩ οὔτε γενέσθαι
3 δυνατόν. αἴτιος δέ, ὡς πατὴρ τοῖς τέκνοις, καὶ τῆς σπορᾶς
καὶ τῆς τροφῆς, ⟨παρὰ τοῦ θεοῦ⟩ τὴν ⟨χ⟩ορηγίαν λαβὼν τοῦ
ἀγαθοῦ [διὰ τοῦ ἡλίου]. τὸ γὰρ ἀγαθόν ἐστι τὸ ποιητικόν·
τοῦτο δὲ οὐ δυνατὸν ἐγγενέσθαι ἄλλῳ τινὶ ἢ μόνῳ ἐκείνῳ, τῷ
μηδὲν μὲν λαμβάνοντι, πάντα δὲ θέλοντι εἶναι. οὐ γὰρ ἐρῶ,
ὦ Τάτ, ποιοῦντι· ὁ γὰρ ποιῶν ἐλλιπής ἐστι πολλῷ χρόνῳ,
⌜ἐν ᾧ⌝ ὅτε μὲν ποιεῖ, ὅτε δὲ οὐ ποιεῖ. καὶ ποιότητας καὶ
ποσότητας ⟨ποιεῖ⟩· ποτὲ μὲν γὰρ ποσὰ καὶ ποιὰ ⟨ποιεῖ⟩, ὅτε
δὲ τὰ ἐναντία. ὁ δὲ θεὸς [καὶ πατὴρ καὶ τὸ ἀγαθὸν] τῷ
4a ⟨θέλειν⟩ εἶναι τὰ πάντα ⟨πάντων πατήρ⟩. [[οὕτως ἄρα]]
[ταῦτα] [[τῷ δυναμένῳ ἰδεῖν]] καὶ γὰρ ταῦτα θέλει εἶναι, καὶ
⟨⟨οὕτως ἄρα⟩⟩ ἔστι καὶ αὐτά. μάλιστα δὲ αὐτὸ ⟨⟨ἔστι τὸ
ἀγαθόν, ὦ Τάτ⟩⟩· καὶ γὰρ τὰ ἄλλα πάντα διὰ τοῦτο ἔστιν.
4b ⟨. . .⟩ ἴδιον γὰρ τοῦ ἀγαθοῦ τὸ γνωρίζεσθαι [[ἐστὶ τὸ
ἀγαθὸν ὦ Τὰτ]] ⟨⟨τῷ δυναμένῳ ἰδεῖν⟩⟩.—Ἐπλήρωσας ἡμᾶς,
ὦ πάτερ, τῆς ἀγαθῆς καὶ καλλίστης θέας· καὶ ὀλίγου δεῖν
⟨ἐπ⟩εσκιάσθη μου ὁ τοῦ νοῦ ὀφθαλμὸς ὑπὸ τῆς τοιαύτης
⌜θέας⌝.—Οὐ γὰρ ὥσπερ ἡ τοῦ ἡλίου ἀκτὶς πυρώδης οὖσα
καταυγάζει καὶ μύειν ποιεῖ τοὺς ὀφθαλμούς, οὕτω καὶ ἡ τοῦ
ἀγαθοῦ θέα· τοὐναντίον δὲ ἐκλάμπει [καὶ] ἐπὶ τοσοῦτον, ἐφ'
ὅσον δύναται ὁ θεώμενος δέξασθαι τὴν ἐπεισροὴν τῆς νοητῆς
λαμπηδόνος. ὀξυτέρα μὲν γάρ ἐστιν εἰς τὸ καθικνεῖσθαι,
5 ἀβλαβὴς δέ, καὶ πάσης ἀθανασίας ἀνάπλεως. ⟨καὶ μ⟩ὴν οἱ
δυνάμενοι πλέον τι ἀρύσασθαι τῆς θέας κατακοιμίζονται

5–6 γενέσθαι δυνατόν A: ἔσται δυνατόν Q: γενέσθαι ἔσται δυνατόν Turn. 6 ὡς πατὴρ τοῖς τέκνοις scripsi: ὁ πατὴρ τῶν τέκνων codd., Turn. 7 χορηγίαν scripsi: ὄρεξιν codd., Turn. 10 μὲν A: om. Q Turn. 12 ἐν ᾧ codd., Turn.: fortasse ὅς γε 12–13 ποιότητας καὶ ποσότητας ποιεῖ scripsi: ποιότητος καὶ ποσότητος codd., Turn. 16 τῷ δυναμένῳ ἰδεῖν hinc ad § 4 b transposui | γὰρ ταῦτα scripsi: γὰρ τοῦτο codd., Turn. 17 καὶ αὐτά scripsi: καὶ αὐτῷ Q: καὶ αὐτὸ cett. | δὲ αὐτὸ AQ: δὲ αὐτῷ Turn. 17–18 ἔστι τὸ ἀγαθόν, ὦ Τάτ huc a § 4 b transposui 18 τοῦτο Q: τοῦτον cett. 19 Fortasse γνωρίζεσθαι ⟨θέλειν⟩ 21 ἀγαθῆς καὶ secludendum? 22 ἐπεσκιάσθη scripsi: ἐσεβάσθη codd., Turn. 22–23 τοιαύτης θέας codd., Turn.: fortasse τοιαύτης μαρμαρυγῆς 23 πυρρώδης Q 25 δὲ Turn.: om. A: ο (?) eras. Q | ἐκλάμπειν A: ἐκλάμπει cett. 26 θεώμενος scripsi: δυνάμενος codd., Turn. 27 καθικνεῖσθαι Turn.: κατικνεῖσθαι AQ 28 δὲ καὶ

save God alone. It is true that the Kosmos also is father of
things which are good in so far as they partake of the Good; but
the Kosmos is not, in like measure with God, the author of what
is good in living creatures; for the Kosmos is not the author of
their life; or if it acts as an author of life, it does so only under
the compulsion imposed on it by God's will, without which nothing
can be or come into being. The Kosmos is to the things within 3
it as a father to his children, in that it is the author of their
generation and nutrition; but it has received from God its supply
of good.[1] It is the Good that is the creative principle; and it is
impossible that the creative principle should come to be in any
save God alone,—God, who receives nothing, but wills the
existence of all things. I will not say '*makes* all things'; for he
who 'makes' things falls short of the fulfilment of his function
during long intervals of time, in that he is sometimes making, and
at other times not making. And moreover, he who 'makes'
things makes only qualities and magnitudes;[2] for he makes things
have certain magnitudes and qualities at one time, and contrary
magnitudes and qualities at another time. But God makes by his
will the very existence of all things; and it is in this sense that he
is the Father of all things. For God wills things to be, and, in 4a
that way,[3] these things also have existence. But the Good itself,
my son, exists in the highest degree; for it is by reason of the
Good that all other things exist.

. . . For it is a property of the Good that it becomes known[4] 4b
to him who is able to see it.—*Tat.* Father, you have given me my
fill of this good and most beautiful sight; and my mind's eye is
almost blinded by the splendour of the vision.—*Hermes.* Nay, the
vision of the Good is not a thing of fire, as are the sun's rays;
it does not blaze down upon us and force us to close our eyes;
it shines forth much or little, according as he who gazes on it is
able to receive the inflow of the incorporeal radiance. It is more
penetrating than visible light in its descent upon us; but it cannot
harm us; it is full of all immortal life. Even those who are able 5
to imbibe somewhat more than others of that vision are again and

[1] I. e. of life, or power to give life to things.

[2] Qualities and magnitudes, *but not substances*. That is, a 'maker' works on something that already exists, and merely makes some change in it.

[3] I. e. as being willed by God. [4] Perhaps, 'that it wills to become known'.

πάσης ἀθανασίας Turn. : *δὲ πάσης καὶ ἀθανασίας* AQ | *ἀνάπλεως· καὶ μὴν οἱ* scripsi : *ἀνάπλεως ἦν. οἱ* codd., Turn. 29 *ἀρρύσασθαι* A

πολλάκις δή ὑπὸ τοῦ σώματος· ⟨ἀπολυθέντες δὲ τοῦ σώματος⟩ εἰς τὴν καλλίστην ὄψιν ⟨ἐνέτυχον⟩, ὥσπερ Οὐρανὸς καὶ Κρόνος, οἱ ἡμέτεροι πρόγονοι, ἐντετυχήκασιν.—Εἴθε καὶ ἡμεῖς, ὦ πάτερ.—Εἴθε γάρ, ὦ τέκνον· νῦν δὲ ἔτι ἀτονοῦμεν πρὸς τὴν ὄψιν, καὶ οὕτως οὐκ ἰσχύομεν ἀναπετάσαι ἡμῶν τοὺς τοῦ νοῦ ὀφθαλμούς, καὶ θεάσασθαι τὸ κάλλος τοῦ ἀγαθοῦ, ἐκεῖνο[υ] τὸ ἄφθαρτον, τὸ ⟨ἀλ⟩άλη[π]τον. τότε γὰρ αὐτὸ ὄψει, ὅταν μηδὲν περὶ αὐτοῦ ἔχῃς εἰπεῖν· ἡ γὰρ γνῶσις αὐτοῦ βαθεῖα σιωπή ἐστι, καὶ καταργία πασῶν τῶν αἰσθήσεων.
6 οὔτε γὰρ ἄλλο τι δύναται νοῆσαι ὁ τοῦτο νοήσας, οὔτε ἄλλο τι θεάσασθαι ὁ τοῦτο θεασάμενος, οὔτε περὶ ἄλλου τινὸς ἀκοῦσαι, οὔτε τὸ σύνολον τὸ σῶμα κινῆσαι· πασῶν γὰρ τῶν σωματικῶν αἰσθήσεών τε καὶ κινήσεων ἐπιλαθόμενος ἀτρεμεῖ· περιλάμψαν δὲ [πάντα] τὸν νοῦν, [καὶ] τὴν ὅλην ψυχὴν ἀναλαμβ⟨άν⟩ει καὶ ἀνέλκει διὰ τοῦ σώματος, καὶ ὅλον αὐτὸν εἰς οὐσίαν μεταβάλλει. ἀδύνατον γάρ, ὦ τέκνον, ψυχὴν ἀποθεωθῆναι ἐν σώματι ἀνθρώπου ⟨μένουσαν· ἀλλὰ χρὴ μεταβληθῆναι αὐτήν, καὶ οὕτω δὴ⟩ θεασαμένην τοῦ ἀγαθοῦ ⟨τὸ⟩ κάλλος [τῷ] ἀποθεωθῆναι.—
7 Πῶς λέγεις, ὦ πάτερ;—Πάσης ψυχῆς, ὦ τέκνον, διαιρετῆς μεταβολαὶ ⟨πολλαὶ⟩ δή.—Πῶς πάλιν διαιρετῆς;—Οὐκ ἤκουσας ἐν τοῖς γενικοῖς, ὅτι ἀπὸ μιᾶς ψυχῆς τῆς τοῦ παντὸς πᾶσαι αἱ ψυχαί εἰσιν αὗται ⟨⟨ὥσπερ ἀπονενεμημέναι⟩⟩, ⟨αἱ⟩ ἐν τῷ παντὶ κόσμῳ κυλινδούμεναι [[ὥσπερ ἀπονενεμημέναι]]; τούτων τοίνυν τῶν ψυχῶν πολλαὶ αἱ μεταβολαί, τῶν μὲν ἐπὶ τὸ εὐτυχέστερον, τῶν δὲ ἐπὶ τὸ ἐναντίον. αἱ μὲν γὰρ ἑρπετώδεις οὖσαι εἰς ἔνυδρα μεταβάλλουσιν, αἱ δὲ ἔνυδροι εἰς χερσαῖα, αἱ δὲ χερσαῖαι εἰς πετεινά, αἱ δὲ ἀέριαι εἰς ἀνθρώπους· αἱ δὲ ἀνθρώπειαι, ἀρχὴν ἀθανασίας [ι]σχοῦσαι, εἰς δαίμονας

1 δή scripsi: δὲ codd., Turn. | ὑπὸ Q Turn.: ἀπὸ A 2 ὥσπερ scripsi: ὅπερ Q Turn.: ὅσπερ (A ?) Flussas 3 ἐντετυχήκασιν A: ἐκτετυχήκασιν Q Turn. 4 δὲ om. Q 5 οὐκ Turn.: om. AQ 7 ἐκεῖνο scripsi: ἐκείνου codd., Turn. | ἀλάλητον scripsi: ἄληπτον codd., Turn. 9 βαθεῖα scripsi: καὶ θεία AQ (etiam MC teste Reitz.) Turn. 11 ἄλλου codd., Flussas: ἀνθρώπου (id est ἀν̅ο̅υ) Turn. 12 τὸ (ante σῶμα) Q (et M teste Reitz.) Turn.: om. A (et C teste Reitz.) 13 ἐπιλαθόμενος Reitz.: ἐπιλαβόμενος codd. (etiam MC teste Reitz.), Turn. 14–15 ἀναλαμβάνει scripsi: ἀναλάμπει codd., Turn. 19 τὸ (ante κάλλος) addidit Reitz. 20 διαιρετὰς (?) Q 21 πολλαὶ δή scripsi: om. Q: δὲ cett. 23 εἰσιν αὗται αἱ ἐν Heeren: εἰσιν αὗται ἐν codd. Stob.: εἰσιν αἵ τε ἐν codd. Corp., Turn. | τῷ (ante παντὶ) Q Turn., codd. Stob.: om. A 24 ἀπονεμημένε Q 25 αἱ (post πολλαὶ) codd. Stob.: om. codd. Corp., Turn. 25–26 ἐπὶ bis codd. Corp., Turn.: εἰς bis codd. Stob. 26 γὰρ codd. Stob.: οὖν

again sunk in blind sleep by the body; but when they have been released from the body, then they attain to full fruition of that most lovely sight, as Uranos and Kronos, our forefathers, have attained to it.—*Tat.* Would that we too, my father, might attain to it.—*Hermes.* Would that we might, my son. But in this life we are still too weak to see that sight; we have not strength to open our mental eyes, and to behold the beauty of the Good, that incorruptible beauty which no tongue can tell. Then only will you see it, when you cannot speak of it; for the knowledge of
it is deep silence, and suppression of all the senses. He who has 6
apprehended the beauty of the Good can apprehend nothing else; he who has seen it can see nothing else; he cannot hear speech about aught else; he cannot move his body at all; he forgets all bodily sensations and all bodily movements, and is still. But the beauty of the Good bathes his mind in light, and takes all his soul up to itself, and draws it forth from the body, and changes the whole man into eternal substance. For it cannot be, my son, that a soul should become a god while it abides in a human body; it must be changed, and then behold the beauty of the Good, and therewith become a god.—

Tat. What do you mean, father, by saying that the soul 'must 7
be changed'?—*Hermes.* Every separated soul, my son, passes through many changes.—*Tat.* And what is a 'separated' soul?—*Hermes.* Have you not heard me say in my General Discourses, that all these souls which shift about from place to place throughout the Kosmos are, so to speak, parted off and portioned out from one soul, even the soul of the universe? Now these souls undergo many changes, by which some of them pass to a happier lot, and others to a worse lot. Souls of the nature of creeping things change into things which dwell in the waters; souls which dwell in the waters change into beasts which dwell on land; souls which dwell on land change into birds of the air; souls which fly in air change into men. And human souls, when they have attained to a beginning of immortal life, change into daemons,

---

codd. Corp., Turn. 27 *μεταβάλλουσιν* codd. Stob. : *μεταβάλλονται* codd. Corp., Turn. | *ἔνυδροι* codd. Stob. : *τῶν ἐνύδρων* codd. Corp., Turn. 28 *πετεινά* codd. Stob. : *πτηνά* codd. Corp., Turn. 28–29 *αἱ δὲ ἀνθρώπειαι . . . σχοῦσαι* scripsi : *αἱ δὲ ἀνθρώπιναι ἀρχὴν ἀθανασίας ἴσχουσιν* codd. Stob. : *αἱ δὲ ἀνθρώπειαι αἱ ἀθανασίας ἔχουσαι* A : *αἱ δὲ ἀνθρώπειαι ἀθανασίας ἔχουσαι* Q Turn.

μεταβάλλουσιν, εἶθ' οὕτως εἰς τὸν τῶν θεῶν χορὸν χωρ[ευ]οῦσι·
[χοροὶ δὲ δύο θεῶν, ὁ μὲν τῶν πλανωμένων, ὁ δὲ τῶν ἀπλανῶν·]
8a καὶ αὕτη ψυχῆς ἡ τελειοτάτη δόξα. ψυχὴ δὲ εἰς ἀνθρώπου
σῶμα εἰσελθοῦσα, ἐὰν κακὴ μείνῃ, οὐ[τε] γεύεται ἀθανασίας,
[οὔτε τοῦ ἀγαθοῦ μεταλαμβάνει,] παλίσσυρτος δὲ τὴν ὁδὸν
ὑποστρέφει τὴν ἐπὶ τὰ ἑρπετά· ⟨⟨καὶ ἡ κακοδαίμων, ἀγνοήσασα
ἑαυτήν, δουλεύει σώμασιν ἀλλοκότοις καὶ μοχθηροῖς.⟩⟩ καὶ
αὕτη καταδίκη ψυχῆς κακῆς.
8b κακία δὲ ψυχῆς ἀγνωσία· ψυχὴ γὰρ μηδὲν γνοῦσα τῶν
ὄντων, μηδὲ τὴν τούτων φύσιν, μηδὲ τὸ ἀγαθόν, τυφλώττουσα
δέ, ἐντινάσσε⟨τα⟩ι τοῖς σωματικοῖς πάθεσι, [[καὶ ἡ κακοδαίμων
ἀγνοήσασα ἑαυτὴν δουλεύει σώμασιν ἀλλοκότοις καὶ μοχθηροῖς,]] ὥσπερ φορτίον βαστάζουσα τὸ σῶμα, καὶ οὐκ ἄρχουσα,
9 ἀλλ' ἀρχομένη. αὕτη κακία ψυχῆς. τοὐναντίον δὲ ἀρετὴ
ψυχῆς γνῶσις· ὁ γὰρ γνοὺς καὶ ἀγαθὸς καὶ εὐσεβής, καὶ
ἤδη θεῖος.—Τίς δέ ἐστιν οὗτος, ὦ πάτερ;—Ὁ μὴ πολλὰ
λαλῶν, μηδὲ πολλὰ ἀκούων. ὁ γὰρ διαλόγοις σχολάζων καὶ
ἀκοαῖς, ὦ τέκνον, σκιαμαχεῖ· ὁ γὰρ θεὸς καὶ πατὴρ [καὶ τὸ
ἀγαθὸν] οὔτε λέγεται οὔτε ἀκούεται. [[τούτου δὲ οὕτως
ἔχοντος ἐν πᾶσι τοῖς οὖσιν]] ⌜αἱ αἰσθήσεις εἰσί⌝ [[διὰ τὸ μὴ
10a δύνασθαι εἶναι χωρὶς αὐτοῦ]]. γνῶσις δὲ αἰσθήσεως πολὺ
διαφέρει. αἴσθησις μὲν γὰρ γίνεται τοῦ ⟨ὑλικοῦ⟩ ἐπικρα-
τοῦντος, ⟨ὀργάνῳ χρωμένη τῷ σώματι,⟩ ⟨⟨διὰ τὸ μὴ δύνασθαι
εἶναι χωρὶς αὐτοῦ·⟩⟩ γνῶσις δὲ [ἐστιν ἐπιστήμης τὸ τέλος,
ἐπιστήμη δὲ δῶρον τοῦ θεοῦ· πᾶσα γὰρ ἐπιστήμη] ἀσώματος,
ὀργάνῳ χρωμένη αὐτῷ τῷ νοΐ· ὁ δὲ νοῦς τῷ σώματι ⟨ἐναντίος⟩.
ἀμφότερα οὖν χωρεῖ εἰς σῶμα ⟨εἰσδῦσα ψυχή⟩, τά τε νοητὰ
καὶ τὰ ὑλικά. ⟨⟨καὶ τοῦτο ἄλλως εἶναι ἀδύνατον·⟩⟩ ἐξ ἀντι-
θέσεως γὰρ καὶ ἐναντιότητος δεῖ τὰ πάντα συνεστάναι. [[καὶ

1 μεταβάλλουσιν Meineke: μεταβάλλουσαι codd. Stob.: μεταβάλλονται codd. Corp., Turn. | εἶθ' AQ: εἰ δ' Turn.: εἴτἀν codd. Stob. | τῶν (ante θεῶν) codd. Stob., Turn.: om. AQ | χορὸν χωροῦσι scripsi: χορὸν χορεύουσι AQ: χορὸν ἀπλανῶν χορεύουσι Turn.: χῶρον (om. χορεύουσι) codd. Stob. 2 χοροὶ codd. Corp., Turn.: χῶροι Stob. P²: χῶρον Stob. FP¹ | ἀφανῶν Q: ἀπλανῶν cett. 3 δὲ (post ψυχὴ) codd. Stob.: om. codd. Corp., Turn. 3–4 εἰς ἀνθρώπου σῶμα εἰσελθοῦσα codd. Corp., Turn.: εἰς ἀνθρώπους ἐλθοῦσα codd. Stob. 4 οὐ γεύεται scripsi: οὔτε γεύεται codd. Corp., Turn.: οὔποτε τεύξεται codd. Stob. 5 οὔτε τοῦ ἀγαθοῦ μεταλαμβάνει codd. Corp., Turn.: om. codd. Stob. | παλίσσυρτος A Turn.: παλίσυρτος Q: παλίσσυτος codd. Stob. | δὲ om. A 6 ὑποστρέφει codd. Corp., Turn.: ὑποστρέψει codd. Stob. | ἐπὶ codd. Stob.: εἰς codd. Corp., Turn. 6–7 καὶ ἡ . . . μοχθηροῖς huc a § 8 b transposui 7 καὶ (ante αὕτη) secludendum? 9 ψυχῆς ἀγνωσία codd. Stob.: ψυχῆς ἡ ἀγνωσία Q:

and thereafter pass on into the choral dance of the gods;[1] [ ][2]
that is the crowning glory of the soul. But if a soul, when it has 8 a
entered a human body, persists in evil, it does not taste the sweets of immortal life, but is dragged back again; it reverses its course, and takes its way back to the creeping things; and that ill-fated soul, having failed to know itself, lives in servitude to uncouth and noxious bodies.[3] To this doom are vicious souls condemned.

And the vice of the soul is lack of knowledge. A soul that has 8 b
gained no knowledge of the things that are, and has not come to know their nature, nor to know the Good, but is blind,—such a soul is tossed about among the passions which the body breeds; it carries the body as a burden, and is ruled by it, instead of
ruling it. That is the vice of the soul. On the other hand, the 9
virtue of the soul is knowledge. He who has got knowledge is good and pious; he is already divine.—*Tat.* And who is such a one, my father?—*Hermes.* One who does not speak many words, nor listen to much talk. He who spends his time in disputations and in listening to men's words is beating the air, my son; for knowledge of God the Father cannot be taught by speech, nor learnt by hearing. . . . Knowledge differs greatly from sense-perception. Sense-perception takes place when that which is material has the mastery; and it uses the body as its organ, for it cannot exist apart from the body. But knowledge [ ][4] is incorporeal; the organ which it uses is the 10 a
mind itself; and the mind is contrary to the body. A soul then, when it has entered into a body, admits into itself both things of the mind and things material. It cannot be otherwise; for all things must needs be composed of opposites

[1] I. e. the troop of the star-gods, who circle in the heavens.

[2] ['There are two choral groups of gods; the one is that of the planets, and the other is that of the fixed stars'].

[3] I.e. it undergoes a series of reincarnations in the bodies of irrational animals.

[4] ['is the perfection of science, and science is a gift of God; for all science'].

ψυχῆς ἐστὶν ἡ ἀγνωσία cett. | *γνοῦσα* codd. Corp., Turn.: *ἐπιγνοῦσα* codd. Stob. **10** *τούτου* Q: *τούτων* cett. | *μηδὲ τὴν . . . τὸ ἀγαθόν* secludendum? **11** *δὲ* codd. Stob.: om. codd. Corp., Turn. | *ἐντινάσσεται* Tiedemann: *ἐκτινάσσει* Q: *ἐντινάσσει* codd. cett., Turn. **13** *ὥσπερ . . . καὶ* secludendum? | *οὐκ ἄρχουσα* codd. Corp., Turn.: *οὐ κατάρχουσα* codd. Stob. (*οὐκέτ' ἄρχουσα* Meineke) **17** *διαλόγοις* scripsi: *δύο λόγοις* codd., Turn. **18** *σκιομαχεῖ* Q **19–20** *τούτου . . . οὖσιν* hinc ad § 10 a transposui **26** *χρωμένους* Q: *χρωμένη* cett. **27** *εἰς σῶμα εἰσδῦσα ψυχή, τά τε* scripsi: *εἰς σώματά τε* codd., Turn. **28** *τὰ* (ante *ὑλικά*) Q Turn.: om. A

τοῦτο ἄλλως εἶναι ἀδύνατον.]] ⟨⟨τούτου δὲ οὕτως ἔχοντος ἐν
πᾶσι τοῖς οὖσιν,⟩⟩ ⟨. . .⟩—
10 b Τί[ς] οὖν ὁ ὑλικὸς θεὸς ὁδί, ⟨ὁ κόσμος⟩;—Ο⟨ὐ⟩ κακὸς
⟨ὁ⟩ κόσμος, οὐκέ[σ]τι δὲ ἀγαθός· ὑλικὸς γάρ, καὶ [ευ]παθητός.
καὶ πρῶτος μὲν πάντων παθητῶν, δεύτερος δὲ τῶν ὄντων, [καὶ
αὐτοδεὴς] καὶ αὐτὸς [ποτὲ μὲν γενόμενος] ἀεὶ [δὲ] ὤν, ὢν δὲ
ἐν γενέσει, καὶ γινόμενος ἀεὶ ⟨τῇ⟩ γενέσει τῶν ποιῶν καὶ τῶν
ποσῶν. κινητὸς [γ]ἄρ⟨α⟩· πᾶσα γὰρ ⟨⟨γένεσις⟩⟩ ὑλικὴ κίνησίς
11 [[γένεσις]] ἐστιν. ἡ δὲ νοητὴ στάσις κινεῖ τὴν ὑλικὴν κίνησιν
τὸν τρόπον τοῦτον. ἐπεὶ ὁ κόσμος σφαῖρά ἐστι, τουτέστι
κεφαλή, [κεφαλῆς δὲ οὐδὲν ὑπεράνω ὑλικόν, ὥσπερ οὐδὲ ποδῶν
οὐδὲν νοητὸν ὑποκάτω, πᾶν δὲ ὑλικόν,] [⌜νοῦς δὲ κεφαλὴ
αὕτη⌝ σφαιρικῶς κινουμένη, τοῦτο ἔστι κεφαλικῶς,] ὅσα οὖν
προσήνωται τῷ ὑμένι τῆς κεφαλῆς ταύτης, ⟨ἐν ᾧ . . .⟩ ἐστὶν
ἡ ψυχή, ἀθάνατα πέφυκεν, [ὥσπερ] [[ἐν ψυχῇ δὲ σώματος
πεποιημένου]] [καὶ] πλείω τοῦ σώματος τὴν ψυχὴν ἔχοντα·
τὰ δὲ πόρρω τοῦ ὑμένος θνητά, πλέον ἔχοντα τῆς ψυχῆς τὸ
σῶμα. [[πᾶν δὲ ζῷον]] ὥστε τὸ πᾶν ἔκ τε ὑλικοῦ καὶ νοητοῦ
συνέστηκεν. ⟨⟨ἐμψύχου δὲ ⟨τοῦ⟩ σώματος πεποιημένου,⟩⟩
⟨τὸ⟩ ⟨⟨πᾶν δὴ ζῷον.⟩⟩
12 καὶ ὁ μὲν κόσμος πρῶτον ⟨⟨τῶν ἄλλων ζῴων⟩⟩· ὁ δὲ
ἄνθρωπος δεύτερον ζῷον μετὰ τὸν κόσμον, πρῶτον δὲ τῶν
θνητῶν [[τῶν [μὲν] ἄλλων ζῴων]] [τὸ ἔμψυχον ἔχει]. οὐκέτι
δὲ [[μόνον]] οὐκ ἀγαθὸς ⟨⟨μόνον⟩⟩, ἀλλὰ καὶ κακός, ὡς θνητός.
ὁ μὲν γὰρ κόσμος οὐκ ἀγαθός, ὡς κινητός, οὐ κακὸς δέ, ὡς
ἀθάνατος· ὁ δὲ ἄνθρωπος καὶ ὡς κινητὸς ⟨οὐκ ἀγαθός⟩, καὶ
13 ὡς θνητὸς κακός. ψυχὴ δὲ ἀνθρώπου ὀχεῖται τὸν τρόπον
τοῦτον, ὁ νοῦς [ἐν τῷ λόγῳ, ὁ λόγος] ἐν τῇ ψυχῇ, ἡ δὲ ψυχὴ
ἐν τῷ πνεύματι· τὸ ⟨δὲ⟩ πνεῦμα, διῆκον διὰ ⟨τῶν⟩ [φλεβῶν

1–2 τούτου . . . οὖσιν huc a § 9 transposui 3 Τί scripsi: τίς codd., Turn. | ὁδί Turn.: ὅδε AQ 3–4 Οὐ κακὸς ὁ κόσμος scripsi (vide § 12): ὁ καλὸς κόσμος AQ (etiam MC teste Reitz.), Turn. 4 οὐκέτι scripsi: οὐκ ἔστι codd., Turn. | παθητός scripsi: εὐπάθητος codd., Turn. 5 πάντων A: om. Q Turn. 6 ποτὲ μὲν γενόμενος Turn.: μὲν ποτὲ μὲν γενόμενος Q: μέν ποτε γενόμενος A 7 τῇ γενέσει scripsi: γένεσιν Q: γένεσις cett. 8 κινητὸς ἄρα scripsi: κινητός ἐστι Q: κινητὸς γάρ cett. 11 κεφαλῆς δὲ Turn.: κεφαλῇ δὲ Q: κεφαλὴ δὲ A 12 οὐδὲν νοητὸν Q Turn.: οὐδὲ νοητὸν A 12–13 Fortasse ⟨ἔν⟩νους δὲ ⟨ἡ⟩ κεφαλὴ αὕτη 13 κεφαλικὸς Q 14 ἐν ᾧ addidit Flussas: fortasse ἐν ᾧ μάλιστα ἵδρυται ἡ ψυχή 16 πεποιημένου Q Turn.: πεποιημένον (sed σ supra -ον) A | πλείω scripsi: πλεῖν Q: πλὴν εἰ A: πλήρη Turn. 17 τὰ δὲ Turn.: τὸ δὲ AQ | θνητά scripsi: ἐν ᾗ τὸ AQ: ἐν ᾧ τὸ Turn. 18 ὥστε Turn.: ὥσπερ οὖν AQ.

and contraries. And seeing that this is so in all things that exist, . . .—

Tat. What then are we to think of this material God, the 10 b
Kosmos?—*Hermes.* The Kosmos is not indeed evil, but it is not good, as God is; for it is material, and subject to perturbation. It is first among all things that are subject to perturbation, but second among things that are. The Kosmos also [1] is ever-existent; but it exists in process of becoming; it is ever becoming, in that the qualities and magnitudes of things are ever coming into being. It is therefore in motion; for all becoming is material movement.
That which is incorporeal and motionless [2] works the material 11
movement; and it does so in the following way. The Kosmos is a sphere, that is to say, a head; and so, all things that are united to the cerebral membrane [3] of this head,—the membrane in which the soul is chiefly seated,—are immortal, for they have in them more soul than body; but the things which are at a distance from the cerebral membrane [4] are mortal, for they have in them more body than soul. Thus the universe is composed of a part that is material and a part that is incorporeal; [5] and inasmuch as its body is made with soul in it, the universe is a living creature.

The Kosmos is first among all living creatures; man, as a living 12
creature, ranks next after the Kosmos, and first among those which are mortal. Man is not merely not-good; he is evil, inasmuch as he is mortal. The Kosmos is not-good, as being subject to movement; but it is not-evil, as being immortal. Man, on the other hand, is both not-good, as being subject to movement, and evil, as being mortal. And the soul of man is vehicled thus. 13
The mind has for its vehicle the soul; the soul has for its vehicle the vital spirit; and the vital spirit, traversing the arteries together

[1] I.e. as well as God. [2] Viz. the soul of the Kosmos.
[3] The 'cerebral membrane' or *meninx* of the Kosmos is the outermost sphere of heaven; and 'the things which are united to it' are the fixed stars and planets.
[4] I.e. all sublunar things. [5] I.e. of body and soul.

Fortasse ὥσπερ οὖν ⟨ὁ ἄνθρωπος, οὕτω καὶ⟩ **19** συνέστηκεν Q: συνέστηκε cett. **21** πρῶτον Flussas: πρῶτος AQ (etiam MC teste Reitz.), Turn. | ὁ δὲ AQ Turn.: ὁ μὲν codd. Stob. **22** ἄνθρωπος τὸ δεύτερον codd. Stob. | πρῶτον δὲ A Turn.: πρῶτος δὲ Q Flussas **26** οὐκ ἀγαθός addidit Reitz. **27–28** τὸν τρόπον . . . δὲ ψυχὴ fortasse secludendum **28** δὲ (post ἡ) codd. Stob.: om. AQ Turn. **29** πνεύματι Turn., codd. Stob.: σώματι AQ | Post πνεύματι add. τὸ πνεῦμα ἐν τῷ σώματι Turn. | δὲ (post τὸ) add. Parthey | διῆκον Stob. F: διοίκον Stob. P: διήκει AQ Turn.

καὶ] ἀρτηριῶν [καὶ] ⟨μετὰ τοῦ⟩ αἵματος, κινεῖ τὸ [ζῷον] ⟨σῶμα⟩ καὶ ὥσπερ φόρτον τινὰ βαστάζει. διὸ καί τινες τὴν ψυχὴν αἷμα ἐνόμισαν εἶναι, σφαλλόμενοι τῆς φύσεως, οὐκ εἰδότες ὅτι πρῶτον δεῖ [[τοῦ πνεύματος ἀναχωρήσαντος εἰς]] ⟨ἐξελθεῖν⟩ τὴν ψυχήν, καὶ τότε, ⟨⟨τοῦ πνεύματος ἀναχωρήσαντος εἰς⟩⟩ ⟨τὸ περιέχον⟩, τὸ αἷμα παγῆναι κατὰ τὰς φλέβας, καὶ τὰς ἀρτηρίας κενωθείσας [τὸ ζῷον] καταλ[ε]ιπεῖν. καὶ τοῦτο ἔστιν ὁ θάνατος τοῦ σώματος.

14 a *ἐκ μιᾶς δὲ ἀρχῆς τὰ πάντα ἤρτηται, ἡ δὲ ἀρχὴ ἐκ τοῦ ἑνὸς καὶ μόνου. καὶ ἡ μὲν ἀρχὴ κινεῖται, ἵνα πάντων ἀρχὴ γένηται· τὸ δὲ ἓν μόνον ἕστηκεν, καὶ οὐ κινεῖται.*

14 b *[καὶ] τρία τοίνυν ταῦτα, ὁ θεός [καὶ πατὴρ καὶ τὸ ἀγαθόν], καὶ ὁ κόσμος, καὶ ὁ ἄνθρωπος· καὶ τὸν μὲν κόσμον ὁ θεὸς ἔχει, τὸν δὲ ἄνθρωπον ὁ κόσμος. καὶ γίνεται ὁ μὲν κόσμος τοῦ θεοῦ υἱός, ὁ δὲ ἄνθρωπος τοῦ κόσμου ⟨υἱός, καὶ τοῦ θεοῦ⟩*

15 a *ὥσπερ ἔγγονος. οὐκ ἄρ⟨α⟩ ἀγνοεῖ τὸν ἄνθρωπον ὁ θεός, ἀλλὰ καὶ πάνυ γνωρίζει, καὶ θέλει γνωρίζεσθαι. τοῦτο μόνον σωτήριον ἀνθρώπῳ ἐστίν, ἡ γνῶσις τοῦ θεοῦ· αὕτη εἰς τὸν Ὄλυμπον ἀνάβασις· τούτῳ μόνῳ ἀγαθὴ ⟨⟨γίνεται⟩⟩ ψυχή.*

15 b *⟨. . .⟩ καὶ οὐδέποτε ἀγαθὴ ⟨μένει⟩, κακὴ δὲ [[γίνεται]] κατ' ἀνάγκην γίνεται.—Πῶς τοῦτο λέγεις, ὦ τρισμέγιστε;—Ψυχὴν παιδὸς θέασαι, ὦ τέκνον, [ε]αὐτὴν διάλυσιν αὐτῆς μηδέπω ἐπιδεχομένην, τοῦ σώματος αὐτῆς ἔτι ὀλίγ⟨ου⟩ ὄν⟨τος⟩ καὶ μηδέπω τὸ πᾶν ὠγκωμένου, πῶς καλὴ[ν μὲν] βλέπειν πανταχοῦ, μηδέπω[τε δὲ] τεθολωμένη[ν] ὑπὸ τῶν τοῦ σώματος παθῶν, ἔτι σχεδὸν ἠρτημένη τῆς τοῦ κόσμου ψυχῆς. ὅταν δὲ ὀγκωθῇ τὸ σῶμα, καὶ κατασπάσῃ αὐτὴν εἰς τοὺς [τοῦ σώματος] ὄγκους, ⟨⟨ἐγγεννᾷ λήθην·⟩⟩ διαλύσασα δὲ ἑαυτὴν*

2 *φόρτον* Usener: *τρόπον* codd., Turn. 3 *ἐνόμισαν* codd. Corp., Turn.: *νομίζουσιν* codd. Stob. | *τῆς φύσεως* scripsi: *τὴν φύσιν* codd., Turn. 4 *δεῖ* codd. Corp., Turn.: *δὴ* codd. Stob. | *τοῦ πνεύματος ἀναχωρήσαντος* codd. Stob.: *τὸ πνεῦμα ἀναχωρῆσαι* codd. Corp., Turn. 5 *καὶ τότε* AQ Turn.: om. codd. Stob. 6 *τὸ* (ante *αἷμα*) om. A | *κατὰ* scripsi: *καὶ* codd., Turn. | *τὰς* (ante *ἀρτηρίας*) om. A 7 *κενωθείσας καταλιπεῖν* scripsi: *κενωθείσας τὸ ζῷον καταλείπειν* codd. Stob.: *κενωθῆναι, καὶ τότε τὸ ζῷον καθελεῖν* codd. Corp., Turn. 7–8 *ἔστιν ὁ θάνατος* codd. Stob.: *ἐστι θάνατος* codd. Corp., Turn. 9 Fortasse *ἀρχῆς ⟨τοῦ νοῦ⟩* | *καὶ μόνου* secludendum? 10 *πάντων* scripsi: *πάλιν* codd., Turn. | *ἓν μόνω* Q: *ἓν μόνον* cett.: fortasse *ἓν ⟨καὶ⟩ μόνον* 11 *καὶ* (ante *οὐ*) Turn.: om. AQ 13 *μὲν* (post *τὸν*) om. Q 16 *ἔγγονος* scripsi: *ἔκγονος* codd., Turn. | *οὐκ ἄρα* scripsi: *οὐ γὰρ* codd., Turn. 19 *ὄλυμπον ἀνάβασις* A: *ὄλυμπόν ἐστιν ἀνάβασις* Q Turn. | *τούτῳ μόνῳ* Turn.: *οὕτω μόνω* AQ | *γίνεται* huc a § 15 b *init.* transposui | *ἀγαθῇ ψυχῇ* (dat.) Q 20 Fortasse ⟨*φύσει*

with the blood, moves the body, and carries it like a burden. Hence some have thought that the soul is the blood. But those who think this are mistaken as to its nature; they do not know that at death the soul must quit the body first, and then, when the vital spirit has withdrawn into the atmosphere, the blood must coagulate along the course of the veins, and leave the arteries emptied. This is the death of the body.

All things[1] are dependent on one first cause;[2] and that first cause is depen- 14 a
dent on the One and Only. The first cause is moved, that it may come to be first cause of all things; the One alone stands fast, and is not moved.

There are these three then,—God, Kosmos, Man. The Kosmos 14 b
is contained by God, and man is contained by the Kosmos. The Kosmos is son of God; man is son of the Kosmos, and grandson,
so to speak, of God. God then does not ignore man, but 15 a
acknowledges him to the full, and wills to be acknowledged by him. And this alone, even the knowledge of God, is man's salvation; this is the ascent to Olympus; and by this alone can a soul become good.

. . . and it never remains good,[3] but becomes evil by 15 b
necessity.—*Tat.* What do you mean, thrice-greatest one?—*Hermes.* Look at the soul of a child, my son, a soul that has not yet come to accept its separation from its source; for its body is still small, and has not yet grown to its full bulk. How beautiful throughout is such a soul as that! It is not yet fouled by the bodily passions; it is still hardly detached from the soul of the Kosmos. But when the body has increased in bulk, and has drawn the soul down into its material mass, it generates oblivion; and so the soul separates itself from the Beautiful and Good,

[1] § 14 a was probably not written by the author of Libellus X.
[2] Viz. Mind?
[3] Perhaps, '⟨The soul is good by nature; but when it has entered a body, it is corrupted⟩, and no longer remains good'.

μὲν γὰρ ἀγαθὴ ἡ ψυχή· ἐνσωματωθεῖσα δὲ μολύνεται,⟩ καὶ οὐκέτι ἀγαθὴ ⟨μένει⟩ | *δὲ* AQ: om. Turn. **21** *ἀνάγκην γίνεται* AQ: *ἀνάγκην δὲ γίνεται* Turn. **22** *αὐτὴν* Flussas: *ἑαυτὴν* AQ Turn. **23** *ὀλίγου ὄντος* scripsi (*ὀλίγου* Flussas): *ὀλίγον* Turn.: *ὀλίγον ὄγκωτο* A: *ὀλίγον ὤγκωτο* Q **24** *ὠγκωμένου* Turn.: *ὀγκωμένον* A: *ὀγκουμένου* Q | *πῶς καλὴ* scripsi: *πῶς καλὴν μὲν* AQ: **Πῶς. Καλὴν** *μὲν* Turn. | *βλέπει* Q: *βλέπειν* cett.: fortasse *ἐμβλέπειν* **25** *μηδέπω* scripsi: *μηδέποτε δὲ* codd., Turn. | *τεθολωμένη* scripsi: *θολωμένην* Q: *τεθολωμένην* cett. **26** *ἠρτημένη* Q: *ἠρτημένην* cett. **28** *διαμύσασα* Q

[[ἐγγεννᾷ λήθην]] [καὶ] τοῦ καλοῦ καὶ ἀγαθοῦ, οὐ⟨κέτι τούτου⟩ μεταλαμβάνει, ⟨τ⟩ῇ δὲ λήθῃ κακὴ γίνεται.

16 τὸ δὲ [αὐτὸ] ⟨ἐναντίον⟩ συμβαίνει [καὶ] τοῖς τοῦ σώματος ἐξιοῦσιν. ἀναδραμοῦσα γὰρ ἡ ψυχὴ εἰς ⟨τὰ⟩ ἑαυτῆς ⟨τοῦ πνεύματος χωρίζεται, καὶ ὁ νοῦς τῆς ψυχῆς⟩· [[συστέλλεται τὸ πνεῦμα εἰς τὸ αἷμα, ἡ δὲ ψυχὴ εἰς τὸ πνεῦμα]] ὁ δὲ νοῦς καθαρὸς γενόμενος τῶν ἐνδυμάτων, θεῖος ὢν φύσει, σώματος πυρίνου ⟨ἐπι⟩λαβόμενος περιπολεῖ πάντα τόπον, καταλιπὼν τὴν ψυχὴν κρίσει καὶ τῇ κατ' ἀξίαν δίκῃ.—Πῶς τοῦτο λέγεις, ὦ πάτερ, ⟨ὅτι⟩ ὁ νοῦς τῆς ψυχῆς χωρίζεται [καὶ ἡ ψυχὴ τοῦ πνεύματος], [σοῦ εἰπόντος ἔνδυμα εἶναι τοῦ μὲν νοῦ
17 τὴν ψυχήν, τῆς δὲ ψυχῆς τὸ πνεῦμα];—Συννοεῖν δεῖ, ὦ τέκνον, τὸν ἀκούοντα τῷ λέγοντι [καὶ συμπνεῖν], καὶ ὀξυτέραν ἔχειν τὴν ἀκοὴν τῆς τοῦ λέγοντος φωνῆς. ἡ σύνθεσις [τῶν ἐνδυμάτων] τούτων ἐν σώματι γηίνῳ γίνεται. ἀδύνατον γὰρ τὸν νοῦν ἐν γηίνῳ σώματι γυμνὸν αὐτὸν καθ' ἑαυτὸν ἑδράσ⟨ασθ⟩αι· οὔτε γὰρ τὸ γήινον σῶμα δυνατόν ἐστι τηλικαύτην ἀθανασίαν ἐνεγκεῖν, οὔτε τὴν τοσαύτην ἀρετὴν ἀνέχεσθαι συγχρωτιζόμενον αὐτῇ παθητὸν σῶμα. ἔλαβεν οὖν ὥσπερ περιβολὴν τὴν ψυχήν· ἡ δὲ ψυχή, καὶ αὐτὴ θεία τις οὖσα, καθαπερεὶ περι⟨βολῇ⟩ τῷ πνεύματι χρῆται, τὸ δὲ πνεῦμα τὸ [ζῷον] ⟨σῶμα⟩ διοικεῖ· ⟨⟨συστέλλεται ⟨γὰρ⟩ τὸ ⟨μὲν⟩ πνεῦμα εἰς τὸ αἷμα, ἡ δὲ ψυχὴ εἰς τὸ πνεῦμα.⟩⟩

18 ὅταν οὖν ὁ νοῦς ἀπαλλαγῇ τοῦ γηίνου σώματος, τὸν ἴδιον εὐθὺς ἐνεδύσατο χιτῶνα, τὸν πύρινον, ὃν οὐκ ἠδύνατο ἔχων εἰς τὸ γήινον σῶμα κατοικῆσαι. γῆ γὰρ πῦρ οὐ βαστάζει· πᾶσα γὰρ φλέγεται καὶ ὑπὸ ὀλίγου σπινθῆρος· καὶ διὰ τοῦτο καὶ τὸ ὕδωρ περικέχυται τῇ γῇ, ὥσπερ ἔρυμα καὶ τεῖχος ἀντέχον πρὸς τὴν τοῦ πυρὸς φλόγα. νοῦς δέ, ὀξύτατος ὢν πάντων τῶν [θείων] νοη[μα]τῶν, καὶ τὸ ὀξύτατον πάντων τῶν

1 οὐκέτι τούτου scripsi: οὐ codd., Turn. 2 τῇ δὲ λήθῃ κακὴ scripsi: ἡ δὲ λήθη κακία codd., Turn. 4 τὰ ἑαυτῆς scripsi: ἑαυτὴν codd., Turn. 5-6 συστέλλεται . . . , πνεῦμα hinc ad § 17 *fin.* transposui 7 βύσει Q: φύσει cett. 11 ἔνδυμα codd. Corp., Turn.: δύναμιν codd. Stob. 12 ὦ om. codd. Stob. 13 καὶ συμπνεῖν codd. Stob.: καὶ συμπνέειν codd. Corp., Turn. 15 Post τούτων add. ὦ τέκνον codd. Corp., Turn.: om. codd. Stob. 17 ἑδράσασθαι scripsi: ἑδράσαι codd., Turn. | Post ἐστι add. τὴν codd. Stob. 18 τοσαύτην AQ, codd. Stob.: τοιαύτην Turn. 19 ἀνέχεσθαι codd. Corp., Turn.: ἀνασχέσθαι codd. Stob. | συγχρωτιζόμενον codd. Stob.: συγχρωματιζόμενον (-ζώμενον Q) codd. Corp., Turn. | αὐτῇ Wachsmuth: αὐτῇ codd. Stob.: αὐτῷ codd. Corp., Turn. | Fortasse συγχρωτιζομένην παθητῷ σώματι 20 οὖν codd. Corp., Turn.: om. codd. Stob. | περιβολὴν codd. Corp., Turn.: περιβόλαιον codd. Stob.

and no longer partakes of that; and through this oblivion the soul becomes evil.

But when men quit the body, the process is reversed. The 16
soul ascends to its own place, and is separated from the vital
spirit; and the mind is separated from the soul. Thus the mind,
which is divine by nature, is freed from its integuments; and
taking to itself a body of fire, it ranges through all space, leaving
the soul to be judged and punished according to its deserts.—
Tat. What do you mean, father, by saying that the mind is
separated from the soul?—*Hermes.* My son, the learner ought to 17
share in his teacher's thought; he should be quicker in his
listening than the teacher is in his speaking. It is in an earthy
body only that the mind and the soul are joined together. The
mind cannot, naked and alone, take up its abode in an earthy
body; a body of earth could not endure the presence of that
mighty and immortal being, nor could so great a power submit to
contact with a body defiled by passion. And so the mind takes
to itself the soul for a wrap; the soul,—for the soul also is in
some measure divine,—uses as its wrap the vital spirit; and the
vital spirit controls the body. For the vital spirit is enveloped in
the blood, and the soul in the vital spirit. The mind then, when 18
it departs from the earthy body, clothes itself forthwith in its own
proper vesture, that is, a vesture of fire, which it could not retain
when it took up its abode in the earthy body. For earth cannot
sustain fire; even a little spark is enough to set it all in a blaze;
and it is for this very reason that the earth is encompassed by
water, which serves as a barrier and defence to protect it from the
flaming heat of the fire.[1] But mind, which is the keenest of all
things incorporeal, has for its body fire, the keenest of all the

[1] I. e. the fire of heaven, or the heat emitted by the heavenly bodies.

20–21 *αὔτη θεία τις* codd. Corp., Turn. : *αὐτή τις θεία* codd. Stob. 21 *καθαπερεὶ περιβολῇ* scripsi (*καθάπερ περιβολῇ* Parthey): *καθάπερ οἱ περὶ* AQ: *καθαπερεὶ πυρὶ* Turn.: *καθάπερ ὑπηρέτου* Stob. P[1] (*κ. ὑπηρέτη* P[2]): *καθάπερ ὑπηρέτις* Stob. F 22–23 *συστέλλεται . . . εἰς τὸ πνεῦμα* huc a § 16 transposui 24 *οὖν* codd. Corp., Turn.: om. codd. Stob. 25 *ἠδύνατο ἔχων* codd. Stob.: *ἐδύνατο ἔχων* Q Turn.: *ἐδύνατο ἔχον* A 27 *γὰρ φλέγεται* codd. Corp., Turn.: *γὰρ γῇ φλέγεται* codd. Stob. | *καὶ* (ante *διὰ*) codd. Corp., Turn.: om. codd. Stob. 28 *καὶ* (ante *τὸ*) codd. Stob.: om. codd. Corp., Turn. 29 *νοῦς δὲ ὀξύτατος* codd. Stob.: *νοῦς ὀξύτατος* Q Turn.: *ὃς ὀξύτατος* A | *ὢν* AQ Turn.: om. codd. Stob. 30 *πάντων τῶν νοητῶν* scripsi: *πάντων τῶν θείων νοημάτων* codd. Stob.: *πάντων θείων νοημάτων* A: *πάντων νοημάτων θείων* Q Turn. | *καὶ τὸ ὀξύτατον* codd. Stob.: *καὶ ὀξύτερος* codd. Corp., Turn.

στοιχείων ἔχει σῶμα, τὸ πῦρ. δημιουργὸς γὰρ ὢν [πάντων] ὁ νοῦς ὀργάνῳ τῷ πυρὶ πρὸς τὴν δημιουργίαν χρῆται. καὶ ὁ μὲν τοῦ παντὸς τῶν πάντων ⟨δημιουργός⟩, ὁ δὲ τοῦ ἀνθρώπου τῶν ἐπιγείων μόνον· γυμνὸς γὰρ ὢν τοῦ πυρὸς ὁ ἐν ἀνθρώπῳ νοῦς ἀδυνατεῖ τὰ θεῖα δημιουργεῖν, ἀνθρώπινος ὢν τῇ οἰκήσει.

19a *ψυχὴ δὲ ἀνθρωπίνη, οὐ πᾶσα μέν, ἡ δὲ εὐσεβής, δαιμονία τίς ἐστι καὶ θεία· καὶ ἡ τοιαύτη ψυχή, [[μετὰ τὸ ἀπαλλαγῆναι τοῦ σώματος]] τὸν τῆς εὐσεβείας ἀγῶνα ἀγωνισαμένη, —ἀγὼν δὲ εὐσεβείας τὸ γνῶναι τὸν θεὸν καὶ μηδένα ἀνθρώπων ἀδικῆσαι,—ὅλη νοῦς γίνεται· ⟨καὶ⟩ ⟨⟨μετὰ τὸ ἀπαλλαγῆναι τοῦ σώματος,⟩⟩ ⟨⟨ὅταν δαίμων γένηται, πυρίνου τυχεῖν σώματος τέτακται πρὸς τὰς τοῦ θεοῦ ὑπηρεσίας.⟩⟩ ἡ δὲ ἀσεβὴς ψυχὴ μένει ἐπὶ τῆς ἰδίας οὐσίας, ὑφ' ἑαυτῆς κολαζομένη, καὶ γήινον σῶμα ζητοῦσα εἰς ὃ εἰσέλθῃ.*

19b ἀνθρώπινον δέ· ἄλλο γὰρ σῶμα οὐ χωρεῖ ἀνθρωπίνην ψυχήν. οὐδὲ θέμις ἐστὶν εἰς ἀλόγου ζῴου σῶμα ψυχὴν ἀνθρωπίνην καταπεσεῖν· θεοῦ γὰρ νόμος οὗτος, φυλάσσειν ψυχὴν ἀνθρωπίνην ἀπὸ τῆς τοιαύτης ὕβρεως.

20 —Πῶς οὖν κολάζεται, ὦ πάτερ, ἀνθρωπίνη ψυχή;—Καὶ τίς ἐστι μείζων κόλασις [ἀνθρωπίνης ψυχῆς], ὦ τέκνον, ἢ ἡ ἀσέβεια; ποῖον πῦρ τοσαύτην φλόγα ἔχει ὅσην ἡ ἀσέβεια; ποῖον δὲ δακετὸν θηρίον ⟨τοσοῦτον ἰσχύει⟩ [ὥστε] λυμᾶναι ⟨τὸ⟩ σῶμα, ὅσον αὐτὴν τὴν ψυχὴν ἡ ἀσέβεια; ἢ οὐχ ὁρᾷς ὅσα κακὰ πάσχει ψυχὴ ἡ ἀσεβής, βοώσης αὐτῆς καὶ κεκραγυίας "καίομαι, φλέγομαι· τί εἴπω, τί ποιήσω οὐκ οἶδα· διεσθίομαι ἡ κακοδαίμων ὑπὸ τῶν κατεχόντων με κακῶν. [οὔτε βλέπω οὔτε ἀκούω.]" αὗται αἱ φωναὶ οὐ κολαζομένης εἰσὶ ψυχῆς; ἢ ὡς οἱ πολλοὶ δοκοῦσι καὶ σὺ δοξάζεις, ὦ τέκνον, ὅτι ψυχὴ ἐξελθοῦσα τοῦ
21 σώματος θηριάζεται; ὅπερ ἐστὶ πλάνη μεγίστη. ψυχὴ γὰρ κολάζεται τοῦτον τὸν τρόπον. ὁ γὰρ νοῦς, [[ὅταν δαίμων γένηται, πυρίνου τυχεῖν σώματος τέτακται πρὸς τὰς τοῦ θεοῦ ὑπηρεσίας,]] [καὶ] εἰσδὺς εἰς τὴν ἀσεβῆ ψυχήν, αἰκίζεται αὐτὴν ταῖς τῶν ἁμαρτημάτων μάστιξιν, ὑφ' ὧν μαστιζομένη [ἀσεβὴς ψυχὴ] ⟨κολάζεται⟩· τρέπεται ⟨γὰρ⟩ ἐπὶ ⟨⟨βλασφημίας, καὶ⟩⟩ φόνους καὶ ὕβρεις καὶ [[βλασφημίας καὶ]] βίας ποικίλας δι'

1 *σῶμα τὸ πῦρ* codd. Corp., Turn. : *τὸ πῦρ σῶμα* codd. Stob. 1–2 *γὰρ ὢν ὁ νοῦς ὀργάνῳ* scripsi : *γὰρ ὢν ὁ νοῦς τῶν πάντων ὀργάνῳ* codd. Stob. : *γὰρ ὢν πάντων τῶν οὐρανῶν* AQ : *γὰρ ἁπάντων τῶν οὐρανῶν* Turn. 4 *τῶν ἐπὶ γῆς μόνον* codd. Stob. : *τῶν ἐπιγείων πάντων* codd. Corp., Turn. | *ἀνθρώπῳ* codd. Corp., Turn. : *ἀνθρώποις* codd. Stob. 5 *ἀνθρώπινος* (*ἀνῖος* Q) codd. Corp., Turn. : *ἀνθρώπου* codd. Stob. | *οἰκήσει* codd. Stob. : *διοικήσει* codd. Corp., Turn. 6 *οὐ* codd. Corp., Turn. : om. codd. Stob. 7 *τοιαύτη ψυχὴ* codd. Corp., Turn. : *τοιαύτη καὶ* (om. *ψυχή*) codd. Stob. 8 *ἀγωνισαμένη* codd. Stob. : *ἠγωνισμένη θεὸς γίνεται* codd. Corp., Turn. 9 *τὸν θεὸν* codd.

material elements. Mind is the maker of things, and in making things it uses fire as its instrument. The mind of the universe is the maker of all things; but the human mind is a maker of earthly things alone; for the mind which is in man is stripped of its vesture of fire, and therefore cannot make divine things, being merely human, by reason of its place of abode. Now the human 19 a
soul,—not indeed every human soul, but the pious soul,—is daemonic and divine. And such a soul, when it has run the race of piety,—and this means, when it has come to know God, and has wronged no man,—becomes mind throughout; and it is ordained that after its departure from the body, when it becomes a daemon, it shall receive a body of fire, so that it may work in God's service. But the impious soul retains its own substance unchanged; it suffers self-inflicted punishment, and seeks an earthy body into which it may enter.

But it can enter a human body only;[1] for no other kind of body can contain 19 b
a human soul. It is not permitted that a human soul should fall so low as to enter the body of an irrational animal; it is a law of God that human souls must be kept safe from such outrage as that.—*Tat.* Tell me then, father, how 20
are human souls punished?—*Hermes.* Why, what greater punishment can there be, my son, than impiety? What fire burns with so fierce a flame as impiety? What ravenous beast has such power to mangle the body, as impiety has to mangle the very soul? See you not what tortures the impious soul endures? It cries and shrieks 'I am burning, I am all on fire; I know not what to say or what to do; wretch that I am, I am devoured by the miseries that have hold on me.' Are not such cries as these the outcries of a soul that is suffering punishment? Or do you too, my son, suppose, as most men do, that a soul, when it quits the body, is turned into a beast? That is a very great error. Souls are punished thus: the mind, when it has entered an impious soul, 21
torments it with the scourges of its sins, and by these scourgings it is punished; it is impelled to blasphemies against God, and murders and outrages and

[1] This passage (§§ 19 b–22 a) contradicts what is said elsewhere in Libellus X, and cannot have been written by the same person.

Corp., Turn.: τὸ θεῖον codd. Stob. 10 ὅλη codd. Stob.: ἣ δὴ Turn.: ἤδι Q 11–12 ὅταν . . . ὑπηρεσίας huc a § 21 transposui 13 ἀσεβὴς codd. Corp., Turn.: ἀσεβοῦς codd. Stob. 14–15 εἰς δ εἰσέλθῃ ἀνθρώπειον om. δέ) Q Turn.: εἰς ὃ εἰσέλθῃ ἀνθρώπινον A: εἰσελθεῖν, εἰς ἀνθρώπινον δέ codd. Stob. 15 σῶμα om. man. pr. A 17 φυλάσσει Stob. P: φυλάσσειν cett. 18 ἀνθρωπίνη ψυχή Q Turn.: ψυχὴ ἀνθρωπίνη A 19 ἢ ἡ Turn.: ἢ om. Q: ἡ om. A 19–20 ποῖον πῦρ . . . ἀσέβεια om. Q 22 ἡ Q Turn.: om. A 28–29 ὅταν . . . ὑπηρεσίας hinc ad § 19 a transposui 29 εἰσδὺς Turn.: εἰσδύνεται A: εἰσδύνασα Q 30 ἀσεβῆ scripsi: ἀσεβεστάτην codd., Turn. | ἁμαρτημάτων scripsi: ἁμαρτανόντων codd., Turn. | μάστιξιν Q Turn.: μάστιξ A 31 ἀσεβὴς ψυχὴ A: ἡ ἀσεβὴς ψυχὴ Q Turn. 32 Fortasse βλασφημίας ⟨δι' ὧν ὁ θεὸς ἀσεβεῖται⟩, καὶ

ὧν ἄνθρωποι ἀδικοῦνται. εἰς δὲ τὴν εὐσεβῆ ψυχὴν ὁ νοῦς ἐμβὰς ὁδηγεῖ αὐτὴν ἐπὶ τὸ τῆς γνώσεως φῶς· ἡ δὲ τοιαύτη ψυχὴ κόρον οὐδέποτε ἴσχει ⟨τὸν θεὸν⟩ ὑμνοῦσα εὐφημοῦσά τε, ⟨καὶ⟩ πάντας ἀνθρώπους καὶ λόγοις καὶ
22 a ἔργοις πάντα εὖ ποιοῦσα, μιμουμένη αὐτῆς τὸν πατέρα. διό, ὦ τέκνον, εὐχαριστοῦντα τῷ θεῷ δεῖ εὔχεσθαι καλοῦ τοῦ νοῦ τυχεῖν.

εἰς μὲν οὖν τὸ κρεῖττον ψυχὴ μεταβαίνει· εἰς δὲ τὸ ἔλαττον ἀδύνατον.

22 b κοινωνία δέ ἐστι ψυχῶν· καὶ κοινωνοῦσι⟨ν⟩ ⟨⟨αἱ⟩⟩ μὲν [[αἱ]] τῶν θεῶν ταῖς τῶν ἀνθρώπων, αἱ δὲ τῶν ἀνθρώπων ταῖς τῶν ἀλόγων. ἐπιμελοῦνται δὲ οἱ κρείττονες τῶν ἐλαττόνων, θεοὶ μὲν ἀνθρώπων, ἄνθρωποι δὲ τῶν ἀλόγων [ζῴων], ὁ δὲ θεὸς πάντων· πάντων γὰρ οὗτος κρείττων [καὶ πάντα αὐτοῦ ἐλάττονα]. ὁ μὲν οὖν κόσμος ὑπόκειται τῷ θεῷ, ὁ δὲ ἄνθρωπος τῷ κόσμῳ, τὰ δὲ ἄλογα τῷ ἀνθρώπῳ· ὁ δὲ θεὸς ὑπὲρ πάντα καὶ περὶ πάντα. καὶ τοῦ μὲν θεοῦ καθάπερ ἀκτῖνες αἱ ἐνέργειαι· τοῦ δὲ κόσμου [ἀκτῖνες] αἱ φύσεις· τοῦ δὲ ἀνθρώπου, αἱ τέχναι καὶ ἐπιστῆμαι. καὶ αἱ μὲν ἐνέργειαι, διὰ τοῦ κόσμου ἐνεργοῦσ⟨α⟩ι, καὶ ἐπὶ τὸν ἄνθρωπον ⟨διήκουσι⟩ διὰ τῶν τοῦ κόσμου φυσικῶν ἀκτίνων· αἱ δὲ φύσεις διὰ τῶν στοιχείων. [οἱ δὲ ἄνθρωποι διὰ τῶν τεχνῶν καὶ ἐπιστημῶν.]

23 καὶ αὕτη ἡ τοῦ παντός ἐστι διοίκησις, ἠρτημένων ⟨πάντων⟩ ἐκ τῆς ἑνὸς ⟨τοῦ θεοῦ⟩ φύσεως, καὶ διοικουμένων δι' ἑνὸς τοῦ νοῦ· ⟨οὗ⟩ οὐδέν ἐστι θειότερον καὶ ἐνεργέστερον, καὶ ἑνωτικώτερον ἀνθρώπων μὲν πρὸς θεούς, θεῶν δὲ πρὸς ἀνθρώπους. οὗτός ἐστιν ὁ ἀγαθὸς δαίμων· μακαρία ψυχὴ ἡ τούτου πλήρης, κακοδαίμων δὲ [ψυχὴ] ἡ τούτου κενή. — Πῶς τοῦτο πάλιν λέγεις, ὦ πάτερ; — Οἴει οὖν, ὦ τέκνον, ὅτι πᾶσα ψυχὴ νοῦν ἔχει; [τὸν ἀγαθόν· περὶ γὰρ τούτου νῦν ὁ λόγος, οὐ τοῦ ὑπηρετικοῦ περὶ οὗ ἔμπροσθεν εἰρήκαμεν, τοῦ κατα-

2 ἴσχει Q Turn.: ἔχει A 3 ὑμνοῦσα Flussas: ὑπνοῦσα AQ Turn. | εὐφημοῦσά τε Turn.: εὐφημοῦσα δὲ AQ 3–4 λόγοις καὶ ἔργοις Q Turn.: ἔργοις καὶ λόγοις A 4 εὖ ποιοῦσα Flussas: ἐμποιοῦσα AQ Turn. 9–11 αἱ δὲ τῶν ἀνθρώπων . . . τῶν ἀλόγων ζῴων codd. Stob.: om. codd. Corp., Turn: ζῴων seclusit Meineke 12–13 πάντων γὰρ . . . αὐτοῦ ἐλάττονα codd. Corp., Turn.: om. codd. Stob. 14–15 ὑπὲρ πάντα codd. Corp., Turn.: ὑπὲρ ἅπαντα Stob. P: ὑπεράπαντα Stob. F 15 καθάπερ ἀκτῖνες codd. Corp., Turn.: καθάπερ αἱ ἀκτῖνες codd. Stob.: καθαπερεὶ ἀκτῖνες Meineke 16 ἀκτῖνες (post κόσμου) codd. Corp., Turn.: αἱ ἀκτῖνες codd. Stob.: seclusit Wachsmuth 17 καὶ ἐπιστῆμαι codd. Corp., Turn.: καὶ αἱ ἐπιστῆμαι codd. Stob. 18 ἐνεργοῦσαι scripsi: ἐνεργοῦσι codd., Turn. 21 παντός ἐστι codd. Corp., Turn.: παντὸς (om. ἐστι) codd. Stob. | ἠρτημένων πάντων scripsi: ἠρτημένη codd., Turn. 22 τῆς ἑνὸς τοῦ θεοῦ φύσεως scripsi: τῆς ἑνὸς φύσεως codd. Stob.: τῆς τοῦ ἑνὸς φύσεως codd. Corp., Turn. | καὶ διοικουμένων scripsi: καὶ διήκουσα codd. Corp., Turn., Stob. F: καὶ ἡ διοίκουσα

manifold deeds of violence by which men are wronged. But when the mind
has entered a pious soul, it leads that soul to the light of knowledge; and such
a soul is never weary of praising and blessing God, and doing all manner of
good to all men by word and deed, in imitation of its Father. Therefore, my 22 a
son, when you are giving thanks to God, you must pray that the mind assigned
to you may be a good mind.

A soul then may rise to a higher grade of being, but cannot sink to a lower grade.

There is communion between soul and soul. The souls of the 22 b
gods are in communion with those of men, and the souls of men
with those of the creatures without reason. The higher have the
lower in their charge; gods take care of men, and men take care
of creatures without reason. And God takes care of all; for He
is higher than all. The Kosmos then is subject to God; man is
subject to the Kosmos; the creatures without reason are subject
to man; and God is above all, and watches over all. The divine
forces are, so to speak, radiations emitted by God; the forces that
work birth and growth are radiations emitted by the Kosmos; the
arts and crafts are radiations emitted by man. The divine forces
operate by means of the Kosmos, and their operation reaches
man by means of the cosmic radiations to which birth and
growth are due; and the forces that work birth and growth
operate by means of the material elements. Thus is the 23
universe administered. All things are dependent on the
being of God alone, and are administered by means of mind
alone. There is nothing more divine than mind, nothing more
potent in its operation, nothing more apt to unite men to gods,
and gods to men. Mind is 'the good daemon'[1]; blessed is
the soul that is filled with mind, and ill-fated is the soul that is
devoid of it.—*Tat.* Again I ask you, father, what do you mean by
that?[2]—*Hermes.* Do you think then, my son, that every soul has

[1] I.e. the author of a man's happiness.
[2] I.e. by speaking of souls 'devoid of mind'.

Stob. P | δι' codd. Corp., Turn.; τοῦ (om. δι') codd. Stob. 23 οὐ add. Flussas | οὐδὲν codd. Corp., Turn. : ὁ δὲ νοῦς codd. Stob. 24 πρὸς θεούς codd. Stob. : πρὸς τοὺς θεοὺς codd. Corp., Turn. | δὲ om. A | πρὸς ἀνθρώπους codd. Stob.: πρὸς τοὺς ἀνθρώπους AQ Turn. 25 μακαρία codd. Corp., Turn.: οὗ ἂν μακαρία codd. Stob. | ἡ (post μακαρία ψυχὴ) codd. Corp., Turn.: ᾗ codd. Stob. 26 πλήρης scripsi: πληρεστάτη codd., Turn. | κενή codd. Corp., Turn.: κενωτάτη codd. Stob. 27 λέγεις πάλιν A: πάλιν λέγεις cett. 28 ἔχει τὸ ἀγαθόν A: ἔχει τὸν ἀγαθόν cett. | τούτου νῦν ὁ λόγος Heeren: τούτου ὁ νῦν λόγος codd. Stob.: τούτου ἐστὶν ἡμῖν ὁ λόγος codd. Corp., Turn. 29 οὐ τοῦ ὑπηρετικοῦ περὶ οὗ codd. Stob.: οὐ περὶ τοῦ ὑπηρετικοῦ οὗ codd. Corp., Turn.

24 a πεμπομένου ὑπὸ τῆς δίκης.] [[ψυχὴ γὰρ χωρὶς νοῦ οὔτε τι εἰπεῖν οὔτ' ἔρξαι δύναται.]] πολλάκις γὰρ ἐξίσταται ὁ νοῦς τῆς ψυχῆς· καὶ ἐν ἐκείνῃ τῇ ὥρᾳ οὔτε βλέπει ἡ ψυχὴ οὔτε ἀκούει, ἀλλ' ἀλόγῳ ζῴῳ ἔοικε· ⟨⟨ψυχὴ γὰρ χωρὶς νοῦ "οὔτε τι εἰπεῖν οὔτ' ἔρξαι δύναται."⟩⟩ τηλικαύτη δύναμίς ἐστι τοῦ νοῦ. ἀλλ' οὐδὲ νωθρᾶς ψυχῆς ἀνέχεται, ἀλλὰ καταλείπει τὴν [ἐν] τῷ σώματι προσηρτημένην καὶ ὑπ' αὐτοῦ ἀγχομένην κάτω. ἡ δὲ τοιαύτη ψυχή, ὦ τέκνον, νοῦν οὐχ ἔχει· ὅθεν οὐδ' ἄνθρωπον ἡγεῖσθαι δεῖ τὸν τοιοῦτον.

24 b ὁ γὰρ ἄνθρωπος ζῷόν ἐστι θεῖον, καὶ τοῖς ἄλλοις ζῴοις οὐ συγκρίνεται τοῖς ἐπιγείοις, ἀλλὰ τοῖς ἐν οὐρανῷ [ἄνω λεγομένοις] θεοῖς· μᾶλλον δέ, εἰ χρὴ τολμήσαντας εἰπεῖν τὸ ἀληθές, καὶ ὑπὲρ ἐκείνους ἐστὶν ὁ ὄντως ἄνθρωπος, ἢ πάντως

25 γε ἰσοδυναμοῦσιν ἀλλήλοις. οὐδεὶς μὲν γὰρ τῶν οὐρανίων θεῶν ἐπὶ γῆν κατελεύσεται, οὐρανοῦ τὸν ὅρον καταλιπών· ὁ δὲ ἄνθρωπος καὶ εἰς τὸν οὐρανὸν ἀναβαίνει, καὶ μετρεῖ αὐτὸν [καὶ οἶδε ποῖα μέν ἐστιν αὐτοῦ ὕψηλα, ποῖα δὲ ταπεινά, καὶ τὰ ἄλλα πάντα ἀκριβῶς μανθάνει]· καὶ τὸ πάντων μεῖζον, οὐδὲ τὴν γῆν καταλιπὼν ἄνω γίνεται· τοσοῦτον τὸ μέγεθός ἐστιν αὐτῷ τῆς ἐκτάσεως. διὸ τολμητέον εἰπεῖν τὸν μὲν ⟨⟨ἐπίγειον⟩⟩ ἄνθρωπον [[ἐπίγειον]] εἶναι θνητὸν θεόν, τὸν δὲ οὐράνιον θεὸν ἀθάνατον ἄνθρωπον.

διόπερ διὰ τούτων τὰ πάντα διοικεῖται τῶν δύο, κόσμου καὶ ἀνθρώπου, ὑπὸ δὲ [[τοῦ]] ἑνὸς ⟨⟨τοῦ⟩⟩ ⟨θεοῦ⟩ τὰ πάντα.

1 *χωρὶς νοῦ* codd. Stob.: *χωρὶς τοῦ νοῦ* codd. Corp., Turn. 2 *οὔτ' ἔρξαι* codd. Stob.: *οὔτέ τι εἶρξαι* codd. Corp., Turn. | *ἐξίσταται* Meineke: *ἐξίπταται* codd. Stob.: *ἐξέστη* codd. Corp., Turn. 3 *ἡ* codd. Stob.: om. codd. Corp., Turn. 6 *ἀλλ' οὐδὲ . . . ἀνέχεται* codd. Stob.: om. codd. Corp., Turn. | Fortasse *νωθρᾷ ψυχῇ σ⟨υνὼν⟩* 7 *τὴν ἐν* codd. Stob.: *τὴν τοιαύτην ψυχὴν* codd. Corp., Turn. | *προσηρτημένην* codd. Corp., Turn.: *προσκειμένην* codd. Stob. | *καὶ ὑπ' αὐτοῦ* Q Turn.: *καὶ πρὸς* (suprascr. *ὑπ'* man. pr.) *αὐτοῦ* A: *κατὰ πάντα* codd. Stob. 8 *ἡ δὲ τοιαύτη* codd. Corp., Turn.: *ἡ τοιαύτη δὲ* codd. Stob. ('An *δὴ*?' Wachsmuth) | *ὦ* codd. Stob.: om. codd. Corp., Turn. 9 *ἡγεῖσθαι δεῖ* codd. Stob.: *δεῖ λέγεσθαι* codd. Corp., Turn. 10 *ζῷόν ἐστι θεῖον* codd. Corp., Turn.: *θεῖον ζῷόν ἐστι* codd. Stob. 10–11 *καὶ τοῖς ἄλλοις ζῴοις οὐ συγκρίνεται* codd. Corp., Turn.: *καὶ οὐδὲ τοῖς ἄλλοις ζῴοις συγκρινόμενον* codd. Stob.: fortasse *κ. τ. ἀ. ζ. οὐ σύγκριτον* 11 *τοῖς ἐπιγείοις* scripsi: *τῶν ἐπιγείων* codd. Corp., Turn.: *τῶν ἐπιγείων τισίν* codd. Stob. | *ἐν οὐρανῷ ἄνω* codd. Corp., Turn.: *ἄνω ἐν οὐρανῷ* codd. Stob. 12 *εἰ χρὴ* codd. Corp., Turn.: *ἐχρῆν* codd. Stob. | *τολμήσαντας* codd.

mind? [ ][1] Oftentimes the mind quits the soul; and at such 24 a
times, the soul can neither see nor hear, but is like a beast
devoid of reason. For a soul without mind 'can neither say
aught nor do aught'[2]; so great is the power of mind. Nor does
mind endure a torpid soul; it abandons the soul which is fastened
to the body, and held down in the grip of the body. Such a soul,
my son, has no mind in it; and therefore such a one ought not
to be deemed a man.

For man is a being of divine nature; he is comparable, not to 24 b
the other living creatures upon earth, but to the gods in heaven.
Nay, if we are to speak the truth without fear, he who is indeed a
man is even above the gods of heaven, or at any rate he equals
them in power. None of the gods of heaven will ever quit 25
heaven, and pass its boundary, and come down to earth; but
man ascends even to heaven, and measures it; and what is
more than all beside, he mounts to heaven without quitting the
earth; to so vast a distance can he put forth his power. We
must not shrink then from saying that a man on earth is a mortal
god, and that a god in heaven is an immortal man.

All things then are administered through these two, the Kosmos and Man; but all things are governed by God alone.

[1] ['That is, the good mind; for it is of the good mind that I am now speaking, and not of that mind of which I spoke before, namely, the mind which is employed in service, and is sent down by penal justice.']

[2] A quotation from Theognis, l. 177 Bergk.

Stob.: *τολμήσαντα* codd. Corp., Turn. 12–13 *τὸ ἀληθές* secludendum? 13 *καὶ* codd. Corp., Turn.: om. codd. Stob. 14 *γε* codd. Corp., Turn.: om. codd. Stob. 14 *οὐδεὶς* codd. Stob.: *ὅστις* codd. Corp., Turn. 15 *θεῶν* codd. Corp., Turn.: om. codd. Stob. | *γῆν* scripsi: *γῆς* codd., Turn. | *καταλείπει* Turn.: *καταλιπών* cett. 16 *καὶ* (ante *εἰς*) codd. Stob.: om. codd. Corp., Turn. 17–18 *καὶ οἶδε . . . ἀκριβῶς μανθάνει* codd. Corp., Turn.: om. codd. Stob.: fortasse retinendum *καὶ* [ ] *ἀκριβῶς μανθάνει* 17 *ἐστιν αὐτοῦ* Q: *ἐστιν αὐτῷ* Turn.: *αὐτῶ ἐστιν* A 20 *τὸ* (ante *μέγεθός*) codd. Stob.: om. codd. Corp., Turn. | *αὐτῷ* codd. Corp., Turn.: *αὐτοῦ* codd. Stob. | *ἐκτάσεως* codd. Corp., Turn.: *ἐκστάσεως* codd. Stob. 21 *εἰπεῖν* codd. Stob.: *ἐστὶν εἰπεῖν* codd. Corp., Turn. 22 *οὐράνιον θεὸν* Wachsm.: *οὐρανὸν θεὸν* codd. Stob.: *οὐράνιον* (*οὐρανὸν* (?) Q) *εἶναι θεὸν* codd. Corp., Turn. 23 *διοικεῖται* codd. Corp., Turn.: om. codd. Stob. 24 *τὰ* codd. Corp., Turn.: om. codd. Stob.

LIBELLVS XI. (i)

Νοῦ πρὸς Ἑρμῆν

1 a [[κατάσχες οὖν τοῦ λόγου, ὦ τρισμέγιστε Ἑρμῆ, καὶ μέμνησο τῶν λεγομένων.

1 b ὡς δέ μοι ἐπῆλθεν εἰπεῖν οὐκ ὀκνήσω. ἐπεὶ πολλὰ πολλῶν καὶ ταῦτα διάφορα περὶ τοῦ παντὸς καὶ τοῦ θεοῦ εἰπόντων ἐγὼ τὸ ἀληθὲς οὐκ ἔμαθον, σύ μοι περὶ τούτου, δέσποτα, διασάφησον· σοὶ γὰρ ἂν καὶ μόνῳ πιστεύσαιμι τὴν περὶ τούτου φανέρωσιν. [ὁ χρόνος.] ἄκουε, ὦ τέκνον, ὡς ἔχει ὁ θεὸς καὶ τὸ πᾶν.]]

2 ⟨ὁ⟩ θεός, ὁ αἰών, ὁ κόσμος, ὁ χρόνος, ἡ γένεσις.

ὁ θεὸς ⟨τὸν⟩ αἰῶνα ποιεῖ,
ὁ αἰὼν δὲ τὸν κόσμον,
ὁ κόσμος δὲ τὸν χρόνον,
ὁ χρόνος δὲ τὴν γένεσιν.

τοῦ δὲ θεοῦ [ὥσπερ] οὐσία ἐστὶ τὸ ἀγαθόν, [τὸ καλόν, ἡ εὐδαιμονία, ἡ σοφία,]
τοῦ δὲ αἰῶνος, ἡ ταυτότης,
τοῦ δὲ κόσμου, ἡ τάξις,
τοῦ δὲ χρόνου, ἡ μεταβολή,
τῆς δὲ γενέσεως, ἡ ζωή [καὶ ὁ θάνατος].

ἐνέργειαι δὲ τοῦ θεοῦ νοῦς καὶ ψυχή,
τοῦ δὲ αἰῶνος, ἀθανασία καὶ διαμονή,
τοῦ δὲ κόσμου, ἀποκατάστασις καὶ ἀνταποκατάστασις,
τοῦ δὲ χρόνου, αὔξησις καὶ μείωσις,
τῆς δὲ γενέσεως, ποιότης ⟨καὶ ποσότης⟩.

ὁ οὖν αἰὼν ἐν τῷ θεῷ,
ὁ δὲ κόσμος ἐν τῷ αἰῶνι,
ὁ δὲ χρόνος ἐν τῷ κόσμῳ,
ἡ δὲ γένεσις ἐν τῷ χρόνῳ.

1 νοῦ Q: νοῦς A Turn. 2–9 κατάσχες . . . τὸ πᾶν hinc transposui; vide post § 6 a 10 ὁ κόσμος Q Turn.: om. A | ὁ χρόνος om. Q 13 τὸν (ante χρόνον) Q Turn.: om. A 14 τὴν Q Turn.: om. A 21 ἐνέρ-

LIBELLVS XI. (i)

A discourse of Mind to Hermes

God, Aeon,[1] Kosmos, Time, Coming-to-be. 2
God makes the Aeon,
the Aeon makes the Kosmos,
the Kosmos makes Time,
and Time makes Coming-to-be.

The essence of God is the Good,
the essence of the Aeon is sameness,
the essence of the Kosmos is order,
the essence of Time is change,
and the essence of Coming-to-be is life.

The workings of God are mind and soul,
the workings of the Aeon are immortality and duration,
the workings of the Kosmos are reinstatement in identity and reinstatement by substitution,
the workings of Time are increase and decrease,
and the workings of Coming-to-be are quality and quantity.

The Aeon then is in God,
the Kosmos is in the Aeon,
Time is in the Kosmos,
and Coming-to-be is in Time.

[1] Or 'Eternity'.

γειαι Turn. : ἐνέργεια AQ 22 ἀθανασία καὶ διαμονή scripsi : διαμονὴ καὶ ἀθανασία Turn.

καὶ ὁ μὲν αἰὼν ἕστηκε περὶ τὸν θεόν,
ὁ δὲ κόσμος κινεῖται ἐν τῷ αἰῶνι,
ὁ δὲ χρόνος περαιοῦται ἐν τῷ κόσμῳ,
ἡ δὲ γένεσις γίνεται ἐν τῷ χρόνῳ.

3 *πηγὴ μὲν οὖν πάντων ὁ θεός, [οὐσία δὲ ὁ αἰών, ὕλη δὲ ὁ κόσμος,] δύναμις δὲ τοῦ θεοῦ ὁ αἰών, ἔργον δὲ τοῦ αἰῶνος ὁ κόσμος, γενόμενος οὔποτε, καὶ ἀεὶ γινόμενος ὑπὸ τοῦ αἰῶνος. διὸ οὐδὲ φθαρήσεταί ποτε· αἰὼν γὰρ ἄφθαρτος. οὐδὲ ἀπολεῖταί τι τῶν ἐν τῷ κόσμῳ, τοῦ κόσμου ὑπὸ τοῦ αἰῶνος ἐμπεριεχομένου. [ἡ δὲ τοῦ θεοῦ [[σοφία]] ⟨οὐσία⟩ τί[ς] ἐστι; τὸ ἀγαθὸν καὶ τὸ καλόν.] [καὶ ἡ ⟨⟨σοφία⟩⟩ εὐδαιμονία καὶ*
4 a *[ἡ] πᾶσα ἀρετή.] καὶ ὁ αἰὼν κοσμεῖ [οὖν] τὴν ⟨ὕλην⟩, ἀθανασίαν καὶ διαμονὴν ἐνθεὶς τῇ ὕλῃ· [ἡ γὰρ ἐκείνης γένεσις] [[ἤρτηται ἐκ τοῦ αἰῶνος, καθάπερ καὶ ὁ αἰὼν ἐκ τοῦ θεοῦ·]] ἡ γὰρ γένεσις [καὶ ὁ χρόνος ἐν οὐρανῷ καὶ ἐν γῇ εἰσιν ὄντες] διφυής, ἐν μὲν οὐρανῷ ἀμεταβλήτων καὶ ἀφθάρτων, ἐν δὲ γῇ μεταβλητῶν καὶ φθαρτῶν. ⟨ὁ κόσμος οὖν⟩ ⟨⟨ἤρτηται ἐκ τοῦ αἰῶνος, καθάπερ καὶ ὁ αἰὼν ἐκ τοῦ θεοῦ·⟩⟩ καὶ τοῦ μὲν αἰῶνος ⌜ἡ ψυχή⌝ ὁ θεός, τοῦ δὲ κόσμου ὁ αἰών [τῆς δὲ γῆς ὁ οὐρανός].*

4 b *[καὶ ὁ μὲν θεὸς ἐν τῷ νῷ, ὁ δὲ νοῦς ἐν τῇ ψυχῇ, ἡ δὲ ψυχὴ ἐν τῇ ὕλῃ.] [πάντα δὲ ταῦτα διὰ τοῦ αἰῶνος.] τὸ δὲ πᾶν τοῦτο σῶμα, ἐν ᾧ τὰ πάντα ἐστὶ σώματα, ⟨ψυχῆς πλῆρές ἐστιν· ἡ δὲ⟩ ψυχὴ πλήρης τοῦ νοῦ, καὶ ⟨ὁ νοῦς⟩ τοῦ θεοῦ. ⟨ψυχὴ δὲ⟩ ἐντὸς μὲν αὐτὸ πληροῖ, ἐκτὸς δὲ περιλαμβάνει, ζωοποιοῦσα τὸ πᾶν, ἐκτὸς μὲν τοῦτο τὸ μέγα καὶ τέλειον ζῷον [τὸν κόσμον], ἐντὸς δὲ πάντα τὰ ζῷα, καὶ ἄνω μὲν ἐν τῷ οὐρανῷ διαμένουσα ⟨ἐν⟩ τῇ ταυτότητι, κάτω δὲ ἐπὶ τῆς γῆς ⟨ἅμα⟩ τῇ γενέσει μεταβάλλουσα.*

5 *συνέχει δὲ τοῦτο ⟨τὸ πᾶ⟩ν ὁ αἰών,—εἴτε [δι'] ἀνάγκην, εἴτε πρόνοιαν, εἴτε φύσιν, [καὶ] εἴ⟨τε⟩ τι ἄλλο οἴεται ἢ οἰηθήσεταί τις,—τοῦτο ἔστι [πᾶ]ν, ὁ θεὸς ἐνεργῶν. ἡ δὲ ἐνέργεια ⟨τοῦ⟩ θεοῦ δυνάμει [οὖσα] ἀνυπέρβλητος, ᾗ οὔτε τὰ ἀνθρώπεια οὔτε τὰ θεῖα παραβάλλοι ἄν τις. διό, ⟨ὦ⟩ Ἑρμῆ, μή[δεπο]τε τῶν κάτω μήτε τῶν ἄνω ὅμοιόν τι ἡγήσῃ τῷ θεῷ·*

1 *τῶν θεῶν* Q : *τὸν θεόν* cett. 10 *τί* scripsi : *τίς* (vel *τις*) codd., Turn. 11 *ἡ* (ante *εὐδαιμονία*) Turn. : om. AQ 13 *ἐνθεὶς τῇ ὕλῃ* Q : *ἐνθεὶς ὁ αἰὼν τῇ ὕλῃ* cett. : fortasse *ἐνθεὶς ἐκείνῃ* 14 *γένεσις* om. Q 16 *διφυής* scripsi : *διφυεῖς* codd., Turn. 16–17 *ἀμεταβλήτων καὶ ἀφθάρτων . . . μετα-*

The Aeon stands fast in connexion with God,
the Kosmos moves in the Aeon,
Time passes in the Kosmos,
and Coming-to-be takes place in Time.

God then is the source of all things; the Aeon is the power of 3
God; and the work of the Aeon is the Kosmos, which never
came into being, but is ever coming into being by the action of
the Aeon. And so the Kosmos will never be destroyed; for the
Aeon is indestructible. Nor will anything in the Kosmos perish;
for the Kosmos is encompassed by the Aeon. And the Aeon 4 a
imposes order on matter, putting immortality and duration[1] into
matter. For things come into being in two different ways; the
things that come into being in heaven are immutable and
imperishable, but those that come into being on earth are
mutable and perishable. The Kosmos then is dependent on
the Aeon, as the Aeon is dependent on God; the Aeon's source
of being is God, and that of the Kosmos is the Aeon.

And this whole body,[2] in which all bodies are contained, is filled 4 b
with soul; soul is filled with mind; and mind is filled with God.
Soul fills the whole body within, and encompasses it without,
giving life to the universe; without, it gives life to this great and
perfect living creature,[3] and within, to all the living creatures.
In heaven above, soul persists in sameness; on earth below, it
changes as things come into being.

That which holds this universe together[4] is the Aeon; (some 5
perhaps think, or will think in time to come, that it is Necessity,
or Providence, or Nature, or something else;) that is to say, it is
God at work. And God's working is unsurpassable in power;
nothing human or divine can be compared to it. Deem not
then, Hermes, that anything on earth below or in heaven above is

[1] I. e. *finite* duration, as opposed to immortality.
[2] I. e. the body of the Kosmos. [3] Viz. the Kosmos.
[4] Or 'keeps the universe in existence'.

βλητῶν καὶ φθαρτῶν scripsi: *ἀμετάβλητοι καὶ ἄφθαρτοι . . . μεταβλητοὶ καὶ φθαρτοί* codd., Turn. **18–19** Fortasse *τοῦ μὲν αἰῶνος ἀρχή* **21** *τῇ* (ante *ψυχῇ*) om. Q **23–24** *ψυχῆς . . . ἡ δὲ* addidit Reitz. **29** *ἅμα τῇ γενέσει* scripsi: *τὴν γένεσιν* codd., Turn. **30** *τοῦτο τὸ πᾶν* scripsi: *τοῦτον* codd., Turn. **31** *εἴτε πρόνοιαν* AQ: *εἴτε διὰ πρόνοιαν* Turn. **32** *ἔστιν* scripsi: *ἔστι πᾶν* codd., Turn. **33** *δυνάμει* scripsi: *δύναμις οὖσα* codd., Turn. **35** *μήτε* (ante *τῶν κάτω*) scripsi: *μηδέποτε* codd., Turn.

ἐπεὶ τῆς ἀληθείας ἐκπεσῇ· οὐδὲν γὰρ ὅμοιον τῷ [ἀνομοίῳ καὶ] μόνῳ καὶ ἑνί. [καὶ] μηδὲ ἄλλῳ τινὶ ἡγήσῃ τῆς δυνάμεως ἐκχωρεῖν· τίς γὰρ κατ' ἐκεῖνον; ⟨τίς ἄλλος αἴτιος⟩ [εἴτε] ζωῆς, καὶ ἀθανασίας καὶ μεταβολῆς ποιητής; τί δὲ αὐτοῦ ἄλλο ⟨ἔργον ἢ⟩ τὸ ποιεῖν; οὐ γὰρ ἀργὸς ὁ θεός· ἐπεὶ πάντα ἂν ἦν ἀργά· ἅπαντα γὰρ πλήρη τοῦ θεοῦ. ἀλλ' οὐδὲ ἐν τῷ κόσμῳ ἐστὶν ἀργία οὐδαμοῦ [οὐδὲ ἔν τινι ἄλλῳ]· ἀργία γὰρ ὄνομα κενόν ἐστι, καὶ τοῦ ποιοῦντος καὶ τοῦ γινομένου.

6 a πάντα δὲ δεῖ γίνεσθαι καὶ ἀεὶ καὶ καθ' ἕκαστον τόπον [ῥοπήν]. ὁ γὰρ ποιῶν ἐν πᾶσίν ἐστιν, οὐκ ἔν τινι ἱδρυμένος, οὐδὲ ἕν τι ποιῶν, ἀλλὰ πάντα, ⟨πανταχοῦ⟩ ⟨⟨ὢν ἐνεργής⟩⟩. δύναμις γὰρ [[ὢν ἐνεργὴς]] οὐκ αὐτάρκης ἐστὶ τοῖς γινομένοις, ἀλλὰ τὰ γινόμενα ὑπ' αὐτῷ.

1 a ⟨⟨κατάσχες οὖν τοῦ λόγου, ὦ τρισμέγιστε Ἑρμῆ, καὶ μέμνησο τῶν λεγομένων.⟩⟩

LIBELLVS XI. (ii)

⟨Νοῦ πρὸς Ἑρμῆν⟩

1 b ⟨⟨. . . ὡς δέ μοι ἐπῆλθεν εἰπεῖν οὐκ ὀκνήσω. ἐπεὶ πολλὰ πολλῶν καὶ ταῦτα διάφορα περὶ τοῦ παντὸς καὶ τοῦ θεοῦ εἰπόντων ἐγὼ τὸ ἀληθὲς οὐκ ἔμαθον, σύ μοι περὶ τούτου, δέσποτα, διασάφησον· σοὶ γὰρ ἂν καὶ μόνῳ πιστεύσαιμι τὴν περὶ τούτου φανέρωσιν.—

[ὁ χρόνος] Ἄκουε, ὦ τέκνον, ὡς ἔχει ὁ θεὸς καὶ τὸ πᾶν.⟩⟩

6 b θέασαι δὴ δι' ἐμοῦ τὸν κόσμον ὑποκείμενον τῇ σῇ ὄψει, [τό τε κάλλος αὐτοῦ ἀκριβῶς κατανόησον,] σῶμα [μὲν] ἀκήρατον, καὶ οὗ παλαιότερον οὐδέν ἐστ[α]ι, διὰ παντὸς δὲ

7 ἀκμαῖον καὶ νέον [καὶ μᾶλλον ἀκμαιότερον]. ἴδε καὶ τοὺς ὑποκειμένους ἑπτὰ κόσμους, κεκοσμημένους τάξει αἰωνίῳ, καὶ

1 οὐ Q: οὐδὲν cett. 3 ἐκχωρεῖν scripsi: ἐγχωρεῖν codd., Turn. | κατ' scripsi: μετ' codd., Turn. 4 καὶ (ante μεταβολῆς) Turn.: om. AQ | ποιητής scripsi: ποιότητος codd., Turn. 4–5 αὐτοῦ ἄλλο ἔργον ἢ τὸ ποιεῖν scripsi: αὐτὸς ἄλλο τι ποιήσειεν codd., Turn. 8 κενόν man. pr. Q Turn.: καινόν A, man. post. Q 9 ἕκαστον τόπον scripsi: ἑκάστου τόπου codd., Turn. 10 ῥοὴν Q: ῥοπήν cett. 11 οὐδὲ ἔν τινι ποιῶν Q: οὐδὲ ἕν τι ποιῶν cett. 14–15 § 1 a huc transposui. 15 Fortasse λελεγμέναν
17–22 § 1 b huc transposui 23 δὴ scripsi: δὲ codd., Turn. 25 οὐδέν ἐστι scripsi: οὐδὲν ἔσται codd., Turn. 27 ἑπτὰ om. Q

like to God; else you will err from the truth; for nothing can be like to the One and Only. And deem not that God resigns aught of his power to another; for who is as God is? Who else is the author of life, and the maker both of immortality and of the changing life of mortals? And what is God's work, if not to make things?[1] God is not idle; if he were, then all things would be idle; for all things are full of God. Nay, in the Kosmos also there is no idleness anywhere; idleness, whether of the Maker or
of that which he makes, is a word devoid of meaning. It needs 6a
must be that all things come into being, and that things are coming into being always and everywhere. For the Maker is in all things; his abode is not in some one place, nor does he make some one thing; no, he makes all things, and everywhere he is at work. The things that come into being have no independent power; to God is subject all that comes into being.

Grasp this my teaching then, thrice-greatest Hermes, and keep 1a
in memory what I tell you.

LIBELLVS XI. (ii)

A discourse of Mind to Hermes

Hermes. . . . But I will not shrink from speaking as the 1b
thought has come to me. Many men have told me many and diverse things concerning the universe and God, and yet I have not learnt the truth. I ask you therefore, Master, to make this matter clear to me. You, and you alone, I shall believe, if you will show me the truth about it.

Mind. Hearken then, my son, and I will tell you how things are, as to God and the universe.

Look upon things through me,[2] and contemplate the Kosmos 6b
as it lies before your eyes, that body which no harm can touch, the most ancient of all things, yet ever in its prime, and ever
new. See too the seven subject worlds,[3] marshalled in ever- 7
lasting order, and filling up the measure of everlasting time as

[1] I.e. to make living creatures, or in other words, to put life into the universe and all things in it.
[2] I.e. 'with the eye of the mind'; for it is Mind that is speaking.
[3] I.e. the seven planets.

δρόμῳ διαφόρῳ τὸν αἰῶνα ἀναπληροῦντας. φωτὸς δὲ πάντα
πλήρη, πῦρ δὲ οὐδαμοῦ ⟨. . . τ⟩ῇ γὰρ φιλίᾳ ⟨⟨τῶν ἐναν-
τίων⟩⟩ καὶ ⟨τ⟩ῇ συγκράσει [[τῶν ἐναντίων]] [καὶ] τῶν ἀνομοίων
⟨τὸ πῦρ⟩ φῶς γέγονε, καταλαμπόμενον ὑπὸ τῆς τοῦ [θεοῦ]
⟨ἡλίου⟩ ἐνεργείας, ⟨τοῦ⟩ παντὸς ἀγαθοῦ γεννήτορος, καὶ πάσης
τάξεως ἄρχοντος, καὶ ἡγεμόνος τῶν ἑπτὰ κόσμων. σελήνην
⟨ἴ⟩δε, ἐκείνων πρόδρομον πάντων, ὄργανον τῆς φύσεως, τὴν
κάτω ὕλην μεταβάλλουσαν· τήν τε γῆν, μέσην τοῦ παντὸς
⟨⟨ἱδρυμένην⟩⟩, ὑποστάθμην τοῦ καλοῦ κόσμου [[ἱδρυμένην]],
τροφὸν καὶ τιθήνην τῶν ἐπιγείων. θέασαι δὲ καὶ τὸ πλῆθος
τῶν ἀθανάτων ζῴων ὅσον ἐστί, καὶ τὸ τῶν θνητῶν, μέσην δὲ
ἀμφοτέρων [τῶν τε ἀθανάτων καὶ τῶν θνητῶν] τὴν σελήνην
8a περιπορευομένην. πάντα δὲ πλήρη ψυχῆς, καὶ πάντα κινούμενα, τὰ μὲν περὶ τὸν οὐρανόν, τὰ δὲ περὶ τὴν γῆν. [καὶ
μήτε τὰ δεξιὰ ἐπὶ τὰ ἀριστερὰ μήτε τὰ ἀριστερὰ ἐπὶ τὰ δεξιά,
μήτε τὰ ἄνω κάτω μήτε τὰ κάτω ἄνω.]

8b καὶ ὅτι πάντα ταῦτα γεννητά, ὦ φίλτατε Ἑρμῆ, οὐκέτι
ἐμοῦ χρῄζεις μαθεῖν. καὶ γὰρ σώματά ἐστι, καὶ ψυχὴν ἔχει,
⟨ᾗ⟩ καὶ κινεῖται· ταῦτα δὲ εἰς ἓν συνελθεῖν ἀδύνατον χωρὶς
τοῦ συναγόντος. δεῖ οὖν ⟨τοιοῦτόν⟩ τινα εἶναι, ⟨⟨καὶ⟩⟩ τοῦτον
9 [[καὶ]] πάντως ἕνα. [ἐν] διαφόρων γὰρ καὶ πολλῶν οὐσῶν
τῶν κινήσεων, καὶ τῶν σωμάτων οὐχ ὁμοίων, μιᾶς δὲ κατὰ
πάντων τάξεως τετα[γ]μένης, ἀδύνατον δύο ἢ πλείους ποιητὰς
εἶναι. μία γὰρ ἐπὶ πολλῶν οὐ τηρεῖται τάξις· ζῆλος δὲ τοῖς
πολλοῖς παρέψεται, ⟨. . .⟩ τοῦ κρείττονος, καὶ ἐριοῦσι. καὶ
εἰ ἕτερος ἦν ὁ ποιητὴς τῶν μεταβλητῶν [ζῴων] καὶ θνητῶν,
ἐπεθύμησεν ἂν καὶ ἀθανάτους ποιῆσαι, ὥσπερ καὶ ὁ τῶν
ἀθανάτων θνητούς. φέρε δέ, εἰ καὶ δύο εἰσί, μιᾶς οὔσης τῆς
ὕλης καὶ μιᾶς τῆς ψυχῆς, παρὰ τίνι [ἂν] αὐτῶν ἡ χορηγία
[τῆς ποιήσεως]; εἰ δὲ καὶ παρὰ ἀμφοτέροις, παρὰ τίνι τὸ

2 Fortasse οὐδαμοῦ ⟨γῆς⟩ vel οὐδαμοῦ ⟨κάτω⟩: vel πῦρ δ' ἐ⟨ν⟩ οὐρανῷ ⟨μόνῳ⟩ 2–4 τῇ γὰρ φιλίᾳ τῶν ἐναντίων καὶ τῇ συγκράσει τῶν ἀνομοίων scripsi : ἡ γὰρ φιλία καὶ ἡ σύγκρασις τῶν ἐναντίων καὶ τῶν ἀνομοίων codd., Turn. 6 ἄρχοντος καὶ ἡγεμόνος Turn. : ἄρχων καὶ ἡγεμὼν AQ 7 ἴδε scripsi : δὲ codd., Turn. 8 μεταβάλλουσαν Q Turn. : μεταβάλλουσα A 9 τοῦ καλοῦ codd., Turn. : fortasse ὅλου τοῦ 10 τροφὴν Q, τροφὸν cett. 11 ὅσον om. Q | τὸ (ante τῶν θνητῶν) eras. man. post. A 11–12 Fortasse μέσης [δὲ] ἀμφοτέρων [ ] τῆς σελήνης περιπορευομένης 17 γενητὰ Q | ὦ A : om. Q Turn. 21 ἐνδιαφόρων? 22 τῶν κινήσεων Q Turn. : τῶν κινήσεως A 23 τάξεως τεταμένης scripsi : ταχύτητος τεταγμένης codd., Turn. 25 παρέψεται Q Turn. : παρέπεται A | fortasse ⟨ἐχθρὸς γὰρ ἔσται ὁ ἥττων⟩ τοῦ κρείττονος | ἐριοῦσι Turn. : ἐρῶσι A : ἐρῶ σοι Q 27–28 ἀθανάτους ποιῆσαι . . . θνητούς AQ Turn. : ἀθάνατα ποιῆσαι . . . θνητά Flussas 28 εἰ Turn. :

they run their diverse courses. And all things are filled with
light; but nowhere is there . . . fire;[1] for by the friendship of
contraries, and the blending of things unlike, the fire of heaven
has been changed into light, which is shed on all below by the
working of the Sun; and the Sun is the begetter of all good, the
ruler of all ordered movement, and governor of the seven worlds.
Look at the Moon, who outstrips all the other planets in her
course,[2] the instrument by which birth and growth are wrought,[3]
the worker of change in matter here below. Look at the Earth,
firm-seated at the centre, the foundation[4] of this goodly universe,[5]
the feeder and nurse of all terrestrial creatures. See too how
great is the multitude of living beings, both those which are
immortal and those which are mortal; and note how the Moon,
as she goes her round, divides the immortals from the mortals.
And all are filled with soul, and all are in movement, immortals 8 a
in heaven, and mortals upon earth.

Now all these have been made. There is no need for me to 8 b
tell you that, dear Hermes. It must be so, because they are
bodies with soul in them;—it is the soul that moves them;—and
body and soul cannot meet in one, unless there is some one who
brings them together. There must then be such a one; and he
must needs be one. The movements are diverse and many, and 9
the bodies differ one from another, but there is one ordered
system which extends through all; therefore, there cannot be two
or more makers. Where there are many makers, one order cannot be maintained; there will be rivalry among the many; the weaker will hate the stronger, and they will be at strife. And if the maker of mutable and mortal creatures had been another than the maker of immortals, he would have wanted to make immortals also; and the maker of immortals would have wanted to make mortals. Yes, and if there are two makers, then, seeing that matter is one and soul is one, to which of the two does the supply of matter and soul belong? Or if it belongs to both, to

[1] The meaning must have been 'nowhere, except in heaven, is there a region of unmixed fire'.

[2] The moon's movement (relatively to the fixed stars) is more rapid than that of any other planet.

[3] Or 'the instrument by means of which Nature works'.

[4] Or 'sediment'.

[5] Perhaps, 'of the whole Kosmos'.

ὅτι AQ 30 τῆς ποιήσεως codd.: fortasse εἰς τὴν ποίησιν | παρὰ (ante ἀμφοτέροις) Q Turn.: περὶ A

10 πλεῖον μέρος; οὕτω δὲ νόει, ὡς παντὸς σώματος ζῶντος ἐξ ὕλης καὶ ψυχῆς τὴν σύστασιν ἔχοντος, καὶ τοῦ ἀθανάτου καὶ τοῦ θνητοῦ, καὶ τοῦ ⟨λογικοῦ καὶ τοῦ⟩ ἀλόγου. πάντα γὰρ σώματα ζῶντα ἔμψυχα, τὰ δὲ μὴ ζῶντα ὕλη [πάλιν] καθ' ἑαυτήν ἐστι· καὶ ψυχὴ ὁμοίως καθ' ἑαυτήν, τῷ ποιητῇ παρακειμένη, τῆς ζωῆς οὐσία. [[τῆς δὲ ζωῆς πᾶς αἴτιος ὁ τῶν ἀθανάτων.]] πῶς οὖν [[καὶ τὰ θνητὰ ζῷα]] ⟨ἡ τῶν ἀθανάτων ζωὴ⟩ ἄλλη ⟨τῆς⟩ τῶν θνητῶν; πῶς δὲ ⟨εὔλογον τὸν⟩ τὰ ἀθάνατα [καὶ ἀθανασίαν] ποιοῦντα ζῷα μὴ ⟨⟨καὶ τὰ θνητὰ ζῷα⟩⟩ ποιεῖν; ⟨⟨τῆς δὴ ζωῆς πάσ⟨ης⟩ αἴτιος ὁ ⟨τῆς⟩ τῶν ἀθανάτων.⟩⟩

11 καὶ ὅτι μὲν ἔστι τις ὁ ποιῶν ταῦτα, δῆλον. ὅτι δὲ καὶ εἷς, φανερώτατον· καὶ γὰρ μία ψυχή, καὶ μία ζωή, καὶ μία ὕλη. τίς δὲ οὗτος; τίς δὲ ἂν ἄλλος ⟨εἴη⟩, εἰ μὴ εἷς ὁ θεός; τίνι γὰρ ἂν ἄλλῳ πρέποι [ζῷα] ἔμψυχα ποιεῖν, εἰ μὴ μόνῳ τῷ θεῷ; [εἷς οὖν θεός. γελοιότατον.] καὶ τὸν μὲν κόσμον ὡμολόγησας ἕνα εἶναι, καὶ τὸν ἥλιον ἕνα, καὶ τὴν σελήνην μίαν, καὶ [θειότητα] ⟨τὴν γῆν⟩ μίαν· αὐτὸν δὲ τὸν θεὸν πόστον εἶναι θέλεις; [πάντα οὖν αὐτὸς ποιεῖ.] εἰ πολλοί,
14 b γελοιότατον. ⟨⟨εἷς ἄρα καὶ ὁ θεός. καὶ πάλιν, εἰ πάντα ζῷά ἐστι, καὶ τὰ ἐν οὐρανῷ καὶ τὰ ἐν τῇ γῇ, μία δὲ κατὰ πάντων ζωή, ⟨ζωὴ δὲ⟩ ὑπὸ τοῦ θεοῦ γίνεται, [καὶ αὕτη ἐστὶ θεός,] ὑπὸ τοῦ θεοῦ ἄρα γίνεται πάντα.⟩⟩

12 a καὶ τί μέγα τῷ θεῷ [ζωὴν καὶ ψυχὴν] καὶ ἀθανασίαν καὶ μεταβολὴν ποιεῖν, σοῦ τοσαῦτα ποιοῦντος; καὶ γὰρ βλέπεις, καὶ λαλεῖς, καὶ ἀκούεις, καὶ ὀσφραίνῃ, καὶ ἅπτῃ, καὶ περιπατεῖς, καὶ νοεῖς, καὶ πνεῖς. καὶ οὐχ ἕτερος μέν ἐστιν ὁ βλέπων, ἕτερος δὲ ὁ ἀκούων, ἕτερος δὲ ὁ λαλῶν, ἄλλος δὲ ὁ ἁπτόμενος, ἄλλος δὲ ὁ ὀσφραινόμενος, ἄλλος δὲ ὁ περιπατῶν, καὶ ἄλλος ὁ νοῶν, καὶ ἄλλος ὁ ἀναπνέων· ἀλλὰ εἷς ὁ ταῦτα πάντα ⟨ποιῶν⟩.

1 ὡς Q Turn.: οὐ A 3 λογικοῦ καὶ τοῦ addidi. (An secludendum καὶ τοῦ ἀλόγου?) 6 οὐσία scripsi: αἰτία codd., Turn. 8 ἄλλη scripsi: ἄλλα codd., Turn. 8-9 τὰ ἀθάνατα scripsi: τὸ ἀθάνατον codd., Turn. 9 ποιοῦντα ζῷα scripsi: ποιοῦντα, ζωῶν A: ποιοῦν, τὰ ζώων Q: ποιοῦν, ζῶον Turn. 10 ποιεῖν AQ: ποιεῖ Turn. 12 δῆλον. ὅτι δὲ καὶ scripsi: δηλονότι δὲ καὶ Q Turn.: δηλονότι καὶ A 13 καὶ μία ζωή secludendum? 14 εἷς Q Turn.: om. A 15 ἄλλω ἂν A: ἂν ἄλλῳ cett. 16 εἷς οὖν θεός· γελοιότατον AQ Turn.: γελοιότατον. εἷς οὖν θεός Flussas 17 ὡμολόγησας ἕνα εἶναι Turn.: ὡμολόγησεν ἀεὶ εἶναι AQ | ἕνα (post ἥλιον) Q Turn.: ex ἀεὶ corr. ἕνα A 19 εἰ πολλοί scripsi: ἐν πολλῷ AQ Turn. 20 ζῶα codd., Turn.: fortasse ζῶντα 25-30 Fortasse καὶ γὰρ [ ] λαλεῖς καὶ

which of the two does it belong in larger measure? You must understand that every living body, be it immortal or mortal, rational or irrational, is composed of matter and soul. All living bodies have soul in them; things which are not alive are matter apart by itself; and there is likewise soul by itself, laid up in the Maker's keeping; for soul is the substance of which life is made. How then can the life which is in the immortals be other than the life which is in mortal creatures? And how can it be maintained that the maker of those living beings which are immortal is not the maker of those which are mortal also? He therefore is the author of all life, who is the author of the life of the immortals. **10**

It is clear that there is some one who makes these things. And it is manifest that the maker is one; for soul is one, and life is one, and matter is one. And who is that maker? Who else can he be but God alone? To whom save God alone should it belong to put soul into things? You have agreed that the Kosmos is one, and that the Sun is one, and the Moon is one, and the Earth is one; and would you have it that God himself is but one among many? It would be absurd to suppose that there are many Gods. God also then is one. Moreover, if all things, **11**
both those in heaven and those on earth, are alive, and there is one life in them all, and life is made by God, it follows that all things are made by God. **14 b**

And why should it be thought strange[1] for God to make both what is immortal and what is mutable, when you yourself do[2] so many different things? You see; you speak and hear; you smell, and feel by touch; you walk; you think; you breathe. It is not one that sees, another that hears, and another that speaks; it is not one that feels by touch, another that smells, another that walks, another that thinks, and another that breathes;[3] but he who does all these things is one. **12 a**

[1] Or 'a hard task'.

[2] The Greek verb here translated 'do' is the same that is translated 'make' in the preceding clause.

[3] Perhaps, 'You speak and hear, you walk and breathe. It is not one man that hears and another that speaks, nor one that walks and another that breathes'.

ἀκούεις [ ] καὶ περιπατεῖς [ ] καὶ ⟨ἀνα⟩πνεῖς. καὶ οὐχ ἕτερος μέν ἐστιν [ ] ὁ ἀκούων, ἕτερος δὲ ὁ λαλῶν, [ ] ἄλλος δὲ ὁ περιπατῶν, [ ] καὶ ἄλλος ὁ ἀναπνέων

12 b ἀλλὰ οὐδὲ δυνατὸν [[ἐκεῖνα]] χωρὶς τοῦ ⟨⟨ἐκεῖνα⟩⟩ ⟨ποιεῖν
τὸν⟩ θεὸν εἶναι. ὥσπερ γάρ, ἂν τούτων καταργηθῇς, οὐκέτι
ζῷον εἶ, οὕτως, [οὐδ'] ἂν ἐκείνων καταργηθῇ, ὁ θεός, ὃ μὴ
13 a θέμις ἐστὶν εἰπεῖν, οὐκέτι ἐστὶ θεός. εἰ γὰρ ἀποδέδεικται
μηδὲν ⟨ποιῶν ἄνθρωπος οὐ⟩ δυνάμενος εἶναι, πόσῳ μᾶλλον
ὁ θεός; εἰ γάρ τι ἐστὶν ὃ μὴ ποιεῖ, καὶ ⟨ὁ θεός⟩, ὃ μὴ θέμις
εἰπεῖν, ἀτελής ἐστιν· εἰ δὲ μή τι ἀργός ἐστι, τέλειος. ⟨ὁ θεὸς⟩
[δὲ] ἄρα πάντα ποιεῖ.
13 b πρὸς ὀλίγον δ' ἄν μοι σεαυτὸν ἐπίδῷς, ὦ Ἑρμῆ, ῥᾴδιον
νοῆσαι τὸ τοῦ θεοῦ ἔργον ἓν ὄν, ἵνα πάντα γίνηται [τὰ γινόμενα, ἢ τὰ ἅπαξ γεγονότα, ἢ τὰ μέλλοντα γίνεσθαι]· [[ἔστι
δὲ τοῦτο, ὦ φίλτατε, ζωή·]] [τοῦτο δέ ἐστι τὸ καλόν,] τοῦτο δέ
17 c ἐστι τὸ ἀγαθόν. [τοῦτο ἔστιν ὁ θεός.] ⟨⟨ὥσπερ γὰρ ὁ
ἄνθρωπος χωρὶς [ζωῆς] ⟨πνοῆς⟩ οὐ δύναται ζῆν, οὕτως οὐδὲ
ὁ θεὸς δύναται ⟨εἶναι⟩ μὴ ποιῶν τὸ ἀγαθόν· ⟨⟨ἔστι δὲ τοῦτο,
ὦ φίλτατε, ζωή.⟩⟩ τοῦτο γὰρ ὥσπερ [ζωὴ καὶ ὥσπερ κίνησις]
⟨οὐσία⟩ ἐστὶ τοῦ θεοῦ, ⟨τὸ⟩ κινεῖν τὰ πάντα καὶ ζωοποιεῖν.⟩⟩
14 a εἰ δὲ καὶ ἔργῳ αὐτὸ θέλεις νοῆσαι, ἴδε τί σοὶ ἐγγίνεται
θέλοντι γεννῆσαι. ἀλλ' οὐκ ἐκείνῳ τοῦτο ὅμοιον· ἐκεῖνος
⟨γ⟩ὰρ [α] οὐχ ἥδεται· οὐδὲ γὰρ ἄλλο ἔχει συνεργόν. αὐτ-
ουργὸς [γ] ἄρ⟨α⟩ ὤν, ἀεί ἐστιν ἐν τῷ ἔργῳ, αὐτὸς ὢν ὃ ποιεῖ.
εἰ γὰρ χωρισθείη αὐτοῦ, πάντα μὲν συμπεσεῖσθαι, πάντα δὲ
τεθνήξεσθαι ἀνάγκη, ὡς μὴ οὔσης ζωῆς. εἰ δὲ πάντα ζῷα,
[μία δὲ καὶ ἡ ζωή,] ⟨. . .⟩.
14 b [[εἷς ἄρα καὶ ὁ θεός. καὶ πάλιν, εἰ πάντα ζῷά ἐστι, καὶ
τὰ ἐν οὐρανῷ καὶ τὰ ἐν τῇ γῇ, μία δὲ κατὰ πάντων ζωὴ ὑπὸ
τοῦ θεοῦ γίνεται, καὶ αὕτη ἐστὶ θεός, ὑπὸ τοῦ θεοῦ ἄρα
γίνεται πάντα.]]
14 c [ζωὴ δέ ἐστιν ἕνωσις [νοῦ] ⟨σώματος⟩ καὶ ψυχῆς. θάνατος
δὴ οὐκ ἀπώλεια τῶν συναχθέντων, διάλυσις δὲ τῆς ἑνώσεώς
ἐστι.]
15 a [τοίνυν εἰκὼν τοῦ θεοῦ ὁ αἰών,
τοῦ δὲ αἰῶνος ὁ κόσμος,
τοῦ δὲ κόσμου ὁ ἥλιος,
τοῦ δὲ ἡλίου ὁ ἄνθρωπος.]
15 b ⟨. . .⟩ τὴν δὲ μεταβολὴν θάνατόν φασιν εἶναι, διὰ τὸ τὸ

1 δυνατὸν scripsi : δυνατὰ codd., Turn. | ἐκεῖνα ante χωρὶς suprascr. man. pr. A 2 θεὸν scripsi : θεοῦ codd., Turn. 3 εἶ Q Turn. : ᾖ A 4 Fortasse οὐκέτι ἔσται 5 δυνάμενος scripsi : δυνάμενον codd., Turn.

Nay, it is not possible for God to exist without doing what 12 b
I said he does. You, if you cease to do the things I spoke of,
are no longer a living being; and even so, God, if he ceases to do
his work, is no longer God,—a thing which none may dare to say.
I have shown that a man cannot exist and yet be doing nothing; 13 a
and still more does this hold good of God. If there is anything
which God does not make, then God himself is incomplete,—
a thing which none may dare to say; but if he is idle in nothing,
then he is perfect. God then makes all things.

And if you give yourself up to me,[1] Hermes, for a little while, 13 b
you will find it easy to understand that God's work is this, and
this alone, to bring all things into being; and this[2] is the good.
For as a man cannot live without breathing, even so God cannot 17 c
exist without making that which is good; and that, dear Hermes,
is life. For it is, so to speak, God's very being to generate
movement and life in all things. If you wish to understand this 14 a
by your own experience, note what takes place in you when you
desire to beget offspring. Yet what God does is not like what
you do; for God does not find carnal pleasure in it; he has no
consort to work with him. He works alone then; and he is ever
at his work, and is himself that which he makes.[3] If what he
makes were separated from him, all things would of necessity
collapse and die; for there would be no life in them. But seeing
that all things are alive, ... [ ][4] [ ][5].

. . . But men call the change 'death', because, when it takes 15 b

[1] I.e. 'if you think a little'. To 'give oneself up to Mind' is to think.

[2] Viz. the coming-into-being of all things.

[3] Perhaps, 'and he himself is in that which he makes'.

[4] [§ 14 c. 'But life is the union of body and soul. Death then is not the destruction of the things which have been brought together (viz. body and soul), but the dissolution of their union.']

[5] [§ 15 a. 'The Aeon then is an image of God; the Kosmos is an image of the Aeon; the Sun is an image of the Kosmos; and Man is an image of the Sun.']

---

6 *ποιεῖ, καὶ ὁ θεός, ὃ μὴ* scripsi: *ποιεῖ, καὶ εἰ μὴ* Turn.: *ποιεῖ εἰ μὴ* AQ 7 *μή τι* scripsi: *μήτε* codd., Turn. 9 *ἐπίδῳς* Turn.: *ἐπίδος* AQ 10 *νοῆσαι* scripsi: *νοήσεις* codd., Turn. | *γίνηται* Q Turn.: *γίνεται* A 11–12 *ἔστι . . . ζωή* hinc ad § 17 c transposui 12 *δέ* (ante *ἔστι τὸ ἀγαθόν*) AQ: om. Turn. 20 *γὰρ οὐχ* scripsi: *ἄρα οὐχ* codd., Turn. | *ἄλλο* Turn.: *ἄλλον* Flussas 21 *ἄρα ὤν* scripsi: *γὰρ ὤν* codd., Turn. | *ὃ ποιεῖ* codd., Turn.: fortasse *ἐν ᾧ ποιεῖ* 23 *ζῶα* codd., Turn.: fortasse *ζῶντα* 25–28 § 14 b hinc transposui: vide post § 11 36 *τὸ* (post *διὰ*) om. Q

μὲν σῶμα διαλύεσθαι, τὴν δὲ ζωὴν εἰς τὸ ἀφανὲς χωρεῖν [τὰ διαλυόμενα].

τούτῳ τῷ λόγῳ, φίλτατέ μοι Ἑρμῆ, καὶ τὸν κόσμον [δεισιδαίμων ὡς] ⟨δι' αἰῶνός⟩ [ἀκούεις] φημι μεταβάλλεσθαι, διὰ τὸ γίνεσθαι μέρος ⟨τι τῆς ζωῆς⟩ αὐτοῦ καθ' ἑκάστην ἡμέραν ἐν τῷ ἀφανεῖ, μηδέποτε ⟨δὲ⟩ διαλύεσθαι. καὶ ταῦτά
ἐστι τὰ τοῦ κόσμου πάθη, ⌜δινήσεις τε καὶ κρύψεις· καὶ ἡ
16 a μὲν δίνησις στροφή, ἡ δὲ κρύψις ἀνανέωσις⌝. ⟨. . .⟩
παντόμορφος δέ ἐστιν, οὐ τὰς μορφὰς ἐγκειμένας ἔχων ἐν ἑαυτῷ, [[δὲ]] αὐτὸς ⟨⟨δὲ⟩⟩ μεταβάλλων.

16 b ἐπεὶ οὖν ὁ κόσμος παντόμορφος γέγονεν, ὁ ποιήσας τί ἂν εἴη; ἄμορφος μὲν γὰρ μὴ γένοιτο· εἰ δὲ καὶ αὐτὸς παντόμορφος, ὅμοιος ἔσται τῷ κόσμῳ. ἀλλὰ μίαν ἔχων μορφήν, κατὰ τοῦτο ἐλάττων ἔσται τοῦ κόσμου. τί οὖν φῶμεν αὐτὸν εἶναι; μὴ εἰς ἀπορίαν τὸν λόγον περιστήσωμεν· οὐδὲν γὰρ ἄπορον περὶ τοῦ θεοῦ νοουμένοις. μίαν οὖν ἔχει ἰδέαν, [εἴ τις
ἔστιν αὐτοῦ ἰδέα,] ἥτις ταῖς ὄψεσιν οὐχ ὑποσταίη· ἀσώματος
17 a ⟨γάρ⟩. [καὶ πάσας διὰ τῶν σωμάτων δείκνυσι.] καὶ μὴ
θαυμάσῃς εἰ ἔστι τις ἀσώματος ἰδέα· ἔστι γάρ· ὥσπερ [ἡ τοῦ λόγου] καὶ ἐν ταῖς γραφαῖς ἀκρώρειαι ὁρῶνται μὲν [γὰρ] πάνυ ἐξέχουσαι, λεῖαι δὲ τῇ φύσει καὶ ὁμαλαί εἰσι παντελῶς.

17 b ἐννοήσας δὲ τὸ λεγόμενον τολμηρότερον, ἀληθέστερον [δὲ]
17 c ⟨⟨νοήσεις τὸν περιέχοντα τὰ πάντα⟩⟩. [[ὥσπερ γὰρ ὁ ἄνθρωπος χωρὶς ζωῆς οὐ δύναται ζῆν, οὕτως οὐδὲ ὁ θεὸς δύναται μὴ
ποιῶν τὸ ἀγαθόν. τοῦτο γὰρ ὥσπερ ζωὴ καὶ ὥσπερ κίνησίς
18 ἐστι τοῦ θεοῦ, κινεῖν τὰ πάντα καὶ ζωοποιεῖν.]] ἔνια δὲ τῶν
λεγομένων ἰδίαν ἔννοιαν ἔχειν ὀφείλει, οἷον ὃ λέγω ⟨νῦν⟩ [νόησον]. πάντα ⟨γάρ⟩ ἐστιν ἐν τῷ θεῷ, οὐχ ὡς ἐν τόπῳ κείμενα· ὁ μὲν γὰρ τόπος [καὶ] σῶμά ἐστι, καὶ ⟨πᾶν⟩ σῶμα ⟨κινητόν· τὸ δὲ ἀσώματον⟩ ἀκίνητον, καὶ τὰ ⟨ἐν αὐτῷ⟩ κείμενα κίνησιν οὐκ ἔχει· κεῖται γὰρ ἄλλως ἐν ἀσωμάτῳ [φαντασίᾳ]. [[νόησον τὸν περιέχοντα τὰ πάντα.]] καὶ [νόησον ὅτι] τοῦ ἀσωμάτου οὐδέν ἐστι περιοριστικόν, [οὐδὲ ταχύτερον, οὐδὲ δυνατώτερον,] αὐτὸ δὲ πάντων ⟨περιοριστικόν⟩,

3 τούτῳ Q Turn. : τοῦτο A   8 κρύψεις Q : κρύψις cett.   14 φῶμεν scripsi : φαμὲν codd., Turn. | αὐτὸν om. A   16 νοουμένοις scripsi : νοούμενον codd., Turn. | ἰδέαν Turn. : εἰ δὲ ἂν AQ | εἴ τις A : εἴη τις Q : ἥτίς Turn.   17 ἰδέα scripsi : ἰδία codd., Turn. | τ' ὄψεσιν

place, the body is decomposed, and the life departs and is no longer seen.

And speaking in this way, dear Hermes, I say that the Kosmos
also is changing through all time, inasmuch as day by day a part
of its life passes away out of our sight, but that it is never decomposed. And the things that befall the Kosmos are . . . . And 16 a
the Kosmos assumes all forms; it does not contain the forms as
things placed in it, but the Kosmos itself changes.

Now if the Kosmos is so made that it assumes all forms, what 16 b
is to be said of its Maker? Shall we say that he is formless?
Surely not that! Yet if he too assumes all forms, he will be like
the Kosmos; and if he has but one form, he will in that respect
be inferior to the Kosmos. What then are we to say of him?
We must not let the discussion end in unsolved doubt; for in our
thoughts of God, no question is insoluble. We will say then that
God has one form, and one alone, but it is a form that no eye can
see; for it is incorporeal. And marvel not that there is an 17 a
incorporeal form. Such things there are; for instance, in pictures
we see mountain-tops standing out high, though the picture itself
is quite smooth and flat.

And if you boldly grasp this conception,[1] you will get a truer 17 b
notion of Him who contains all things. There are terms which 18
must be taken in a sense peculiar to the thing spoken of; and of
this, what I am now saying is an instance. All things are in God; but things are not situated in God as in a place. A place is a body,[2] and all bodies are subject to movement; but that which is incorporeal is motionless, and the things situated in it have no movement; for it is in a different sense that things 'are situated in' what is incorporeal. And the incorporeal[3] cannot be enclosed by anything; but it can itself enclose all things; it is the quickest

[1] Viz. the conception of incorporeal form, or incorporeality.
[2] Perhaps, 'is something which contains bodies'.
[3] 'The incorporeal', in this passage, means mind or soul.

Q: *ταῖς ὄψεσιν* cett. **20–21** Fortasse *ὁρῶνται μὲν* ⟨*τῇ φαντασίᾳ*⟩: vide [*φαντασίᾳ*], § 18 **23** *ἐννοήσας* scripsi: *ἐννόησον* codd., Turn. **24** *νοήσεις . . . πάντα* huc a § 18 transposui. *νοήσεις* scripsi: *νόησον* codd., Turn. **24–27** § 17 c (*ὥσπερ . . . ζωοποιεῖν*) hinc transposui; vide post § 13 b **28** *ὃ λέγων* Q: *ὃ λέγω* cett. **30** *σῶμά* (ante *ἐστι*) codd., Turn.: fortasse *σωμα*⟨*τικός*⟩ vel *σωμά*⟨*των περιεκτικός*⟩ **30–31** *καὶ πᾶν σῶμα κινητόν· τὸ δὲ ἀσώματον ἀκίνητον* scripsi: *καὶ σῶμα ἀκίνητον* AQ: *καὶ ἀκίνητον* Turn. **33** *νόησον . . . πάντα* hinc ad § 17 b transposui **34** *οὐδέν ἐστι* Turn.: *οὐδέ ἐστι* AQ

19 [καὶ ἀπεριόριστον καὶ] ταχύτατον ⟨ὂν⟩ καὶ δυνατώτατον. καὶ ⟨τ⟩οῦτο νόησον ἀπὸ σεαυτοῦ. [καὶ] κέλευσόν σου τῇ ψυχῇ εἰς ἣν δὴ καὶ ⟨βούλει γῆν⟩ πορευθῆναι, καὶ ταχύτερόν σου τῆς κελεύσεως ἐκεῖ ἔσται. μετελθεῖν δὲ αὐτῇ κέλευσον ἐπὶ τὸν ὠκεανόν, καὶ οὕτως ἐκεῖ πάλιν ταχέως ἔσται, οὐχ ὡς μεταβᾶσα ἀπὸ τόπου εἰς τόπον, ἀλλ᾽ ὡς ἐκεῖ οὖσα. κέλευσον δὲ αὐτῇ καὶ εἰς τὸν οὐρανὸν ἀναπτῆναι, καὶ οὐδὲ πτερῶν δεηθήσεται· ἀλλ᾽ οὐδὲ αὐτῇ οὐδὲν ἐμπόδιον, οὐ τὸ τοῦ ἡλίου πῦρ, [οὐχ ὁ αἰθήρ,] οὐχ ἡ ⟨τῶν ἀστέρων⟩ δίνη [οὐχὶ τὰ τῶν ἄλλων ἀστέρων σώματα]· πάντα δὲ διατεμοῦσα ἀναπτήσεται μέχρι τοῦ ἐσχάτου σώματος. εἰ δὲ βουληθείης καὶ αὐτὸ ⟨τὸ⟩ ὅλον διαρρήξασθαι, καὶ τὰ ἐκτός, εἴ γέ τι ἐκτὸς τοῦ κόσμου,
20a θεάσασθαι, ἔξεστί σοι. ἴδε ὅσην δύναμιν, ὅσον τάχος ἔχεις. εἶτα σὺ μὲν δύνασαι ταῦτα, ὁ θεὸς δὲ οὔ; τοῦτον οὖν τὸν τρόπον νόησον τὸν θεόν, ὥσπερ νοήματα, πάντα ἐν ἑαυτῷ ἔχειν, τὸν κόσμον, ἑαυτόν, ⟨τὸ⟩ ὅλον.

20b ἐὰν οὖν μὴ σεαυτὸν ἐξισάσῃς τῷ θεῷ, τὸν θεὸν νοῆσαι οὐ δύνασαι· τὸ γὰρ ὅμοιον τῷ[ν] ὁμοίῳ[ν] νοητόν. ⟨⟨παντὸς σώματος ἐκπηδήσας⟩⟩ συναύξησον σεαυτὸν τῷ ἀμετρήτῳ μεγέθει [[παντὸς σώματος ἐκπηδήσας]], καὶ πάντα χρόνον ὑπεράρας αἰών⟨ιος⟩ γενοῦ, καὶ νοήσεις τὸν θεόν. μηδὲν ἀδύνατον σεαυτῷ ὑπόστησαι· σεαυτὸν ἥγησαι ἀθάνατον, καὶ πάντα δυνάμενον νοῆσαι, πᾶσαν μὲν τέχνην, πᾶσαν δὲ ἐπιστήμην. παντὸς ζῴου ἦθος ⟨. . .⟩, παντὸς δὲ ὕψους ὑψηλότερος γενοῦ, καὶ παντὸς βάθους ταπεινότερος· πάσας δὲ τὰς ἀντιθέσεις τῶν ποι⟨οτ⟩ήτων σύλλαβε ἐν σεαυτῷ, [πυρός, ὕδατος,] ⟨θερμοῦ καὶ ψυχροῦ,⟩ ξηροῦ καὶ ὑγροῦ· καὶ ὁμοῦ πανταχῇ ⟨νόησον⟩ εἶναι, ἐν γῇ, ἐν θαλάττῃ, ἐν οὐρανῷ· μηδέπω γεγεν⟨ν⟩ῆσθαι, ἐν τῇ γαστρὶ εἶναι, νέος, γέρων, τεθνηκέναι, τὰ μετὰ τὸν θάνατον· καὶ ταῦτα πάντα ὁμοῦ νοήσας, χρόνους, τόπους, πράγματα, ποιότητας, ποσό-
21a τητας, δύνασαι νοῆσαι τὸν θεόν. ἐὰν δὲ κατακλείσῃς σου τὴν ψυχὴν ἐν τῷ σώματι, καὶ ταπεινώσῃς ἑαυτόν, καὶ εἴπῃς

2 τοῦτο scripsi : οὕτω codd., Turn. 3 εἰς ἣν δὴ καὶ βούλει γῆν πορευθῆναι scripsi : εἰς ἣν δὲ καὶ πορευθῆναι AQ : ἐκεῖσε πορευθῆναι Turn. 4 ἐκεῖ Q Turn. : om. (sed μετ (?) erasum) A 5 καὶ (ante οὕτως) A : om. Q Turn. 5–6 μεταβᾶσα ἀπὸ τόπου εἰς τόπον, ἀλλ᾽ om. A 8 τὸ (ante τοῦ ἡλίου) om. A 10 ἀναπτήσεται Turn. : ἀνατεπτήσεται A : ἀναπτήσσεται Q 11 βουληθείης Q Turn. : βουληθείη A 12 τοι ἐκτὸς Q : τι ἐκτὸς cett. 18 τῷ ὁμοίῳ scripsi : τῶν ὁμοίων codd., Turn. 21 αἰώνιος scripsi : αἰὼν codd., Turn. 22 σεαυτῷ (post ἀδύνατον) Q : ἐν σεαυτῷ cett. | ὑπόστησαι

of all things, and the mightiest. Think of yourself, and you will 19
see that it is so. Bid your soul travel to any land you choose, and sooner than you can bid it go, it will be there. Bid it pass on from land to ocean, and it will be there too no less quickly; it has not moved as one moves from place to place, but it *is* there. Bid it fly up to heaven, and it will have no need of wings; nothing can bar its way, neither the fiery heat of the sun, nor the swirl of the planet-spheres; cleaving its way through all, it will fly up till it reaches the outermost of all corporeal things.[1] And should you wish to break forth from the universe itself, and gaze on the things outside the Kosmos (if indeed there is anything outside the Kosmos), even that is permitted to you. See what 20 a
power, what quickness is yours. And when you yourself can do all this, cannot God do it? You must understand then that it is in this way that God contains within himself the Kosmos, and himself, and all that is; it is as thoughts which God thinks, that all things are contained in him.

If then you do not make yourself equal to God, you cannot 20 b
apprehend God; for like is known by like. Leap clear of all that is corporeal, and make yourself grow to a like expanse with that greatness which is beyond all measure; rise above all time, and become eternal; then you will apprehend God. Think that for you too nothing is impossible; deem that you too are immortal, and that you are able to grasp all things in your thought, to know every craft and every science; find your home in the haunts of every living creature; make yourself higher than all heights, and lower than all depths; bring together in yourself all opposites of quality, heat and cold, dryness and fluidity; think that you are everywhere at once, on land, at sea, in heaven; think that you are not yet begotten, that you are in the womb, that you are young, that you are old, that you have died, that you are in the world beyond the grave; grasp in your thought all this at once, all times and places, all substances and qualities and magnitudes together; then you can apprehend God. But if you shut up your 21 a
soul in your body, and abase yourself, and say 'I know nothing,

[1] I.e. the outermost sphere of heaven.

scripsi: *ὑποστησάμενος* codd., Turn. **24** *ἤθη* scripsi: *ἦθος* (ex corr. A) codd., Turn. **25** *ὑψηλότατος* Q **26** *ἀντιθέσεις τῶν ποιοτήτων* scripsi: *αἰσθήσεις τῶν ποιητῶν* codd., Turn. **31** *νοήσας* Turn.; *νοήσεις* AQ **33** *ἑαυτόν* scripsi; *ἑαυτήν* A: *αὐτὴν* Q Turn.

“ Οὐδὲν νοῶ, οὐδὲν δύναμαι· φοβοῦμαι ⌐γῆν ⟨καὶ⟩ θάλασσαν· εἰς τὸν οὐρανὸν ἀναβῆναι οὐ δύναμαι· οὐκ οἶδα τίς ἤμην, οὐκ οἶδα τίς ἔσομαι·” τί σοι καὶ τῷ θεῷ; οὐδὲν γὰρ δύνασαι τῶν καλῶν καὶ ἀγαθῶν ⟨⟨νοῆσαι⟩⟩, φιλοσώματος ὢν καὶ κακὸς [[νοῆσαι]].

21 b ἡ γὰρ τελεία κακία τὸ ἀγνοεῖν τὸ⟨ν⟩ θε[ι]όν· τὸ δὲ δύνασθαι γνῶναι, καὶ θελῆσαι, καὶ ἐλπίσαι, ὁδός ἐστιν εὐθὺ [ἰδία] τοῦ ἀγαθοῦ φέρουσα, καὶ ῥᾳδία ὁδεύοντι [[σοι]]. πανταχοῦ συναντήσει ⟨⟨σοι⟩⟩ ⟨ὁ θεός⟩, καὶ πανταχοῦ ὀφθήσεται, ὅπου καὶ ὅτε οὐ προσδοκᾷς, γρηγοροῦντι κοιμωμένῳ, πλέοντι ὁδεύοντι, νυκτὸς ἡμέρας, λαλοῦντι σιωπῶντι· οὐδὲν γάρ ἐστιν

22 a ὃ οὐκ ἔστιν [εἰκόνι] ⟨ἐκεῖνος⟩. εἶτα φῂς “ ἀόρατος ὁ θεός ”; εὐφήμησον. καὶ τίς αὐτοῦ φανερώτερος; δι' αὐτὸ τοῦτο πάντα πεποίηκεν, ἵνα διὰ πάντων αὐτὸν βλέπῃς. [τοῦτο ἔστι τὸ ἀγαθὸν] [[τοῦ θεοῦ,]] τοῦτο ἡ ⟨⟨τοῦ θεοῦ⟩⟩ ἀρετή, τὸ αὐτὸν φαίνεσθαι διὰ πάντων. οὐδὲν γὰρ ⟨ἀ⟩όρατον, οὐδὲ τῶν ἀσωμάτων· ⟨ὁ⟩ νοῦς ὁρᾶται ἐν τῷ νοεῖν, ὁ θεὸς ἐν τῷ ποιεῖν.

22 b ταῦτά σοι ἐπὶ τοσοῦτον πεφανέρωται, ὦ τρισμέγιστε. τὰ δὲ ἄλλα πάντα ὁμοίως κατὰ σεαυτὸν νόει, καὶ οὐ διαψευσθήσῃ.

LIBELLVS XII. (i)

Ἑρμοῦ τοῦ τρισμεγίστου περὶ νοῦ ⌐κοινοῦ¬ πρὸς Τάτ

1 Ὁ νοῦς, ὦ Τάτ, ἐξ αὐτῆς τῆς τοῦ θεοῦ οὐσίας ἐστίν, εἴ γέ τις ἔστιν οὐσία θεοῦ· καὶ ποία τις οὖσα τυγχάνει, αὐτὸς μόνος ἀκριβῶς [αὐτὸν] οἶδεν. ὁ νοῦς οὖν οὐκ ἔστιν ἀπο-

1 *γῆν καὶ θάλασσαν* scripsi : *τὴν θάλασσαν* codd., Turn. 4 *φιλοσώματος ὢν καὶ κακὸς* A : *φιλοσώματος καὶ κακὸς ὢν* Q Turn. 6 *τὸν θεόν* scripsi : *τὸ θεῖον* codd., Turn. 7 *εὐθὺ τοῦ* scripsi : *εὐθεῖα, ἰδία τοῦ* codd., Turn. 8 *ἀγαθοῦ φέρουσα* A : *ἀγαθοῦ, καὶ φέρουσα* Q Turn. 9 *καὶ* (ante *πανταχοῦ*) A (etiam C teste Reitz.) : om. Q Turn. 9–10 *ὅπου καὶ* AQ : *ὅπου τε καὶ* Turn. 10 *γρηγοροῦντι κοιμωμένῳ* Q Turn. : *γρηγορητὶ κοιμωμένῳ* MC teste Reitz. : om. spatio relicto A 12 *ὃ* codd., Turn. : fortasse ⟨*ἐν*⟩ *ᾧ* | *ἔστιν ἐκεῖνος* scripsi : *ἔστιν εἰκόνι* AQ : *ἔστιν ἐν εἰκόνι* Turn. 12–16 Cyrillus *c. Iulianum* 2. 52, Migne 76. 580 B : *εἶτα φῂς . . . φαίνεσθαι διὰ πάντων* 12 *εἶτά φησιν* (*εἶτα φύσιν* Aub., ‘*deinde inquit*’ Oec.) Cyril. : *ταφῇς* codd. Corp., Turn. 13

I can do nothing; I am afraid of earth and sea, I cannot mount to heaven; I know not what I was, nor what I shall be'; then, what have you to do with God? Your thought can grasp nothing beautiful and good, if you cleave to the body, and are evil.

For it is the height of evil not to know God; but to be capable 21 b
of knowing God, and to wish and hope to know him, is the road which leads straight to the Good; and it is an easy road to travel. Everywhere God will come to meet you, everywhere he will appear to you, at places and times at which you look not for it, in your waking hours and in your sleep, when you are journeying by water and by land, in the night-time and in the day-time, when you are speaking and when you are silent; for there is nothing which is not God.[1] And do you say 'God is invisible'? 22 a
Speak not so. Who is more manifest than God? For this very purpose has he made all things, that through all things you may see him. This is God's goodness, that he manifests himself through all things. Nothing is invisible, not even an incorporeal thing; mind is seen in its thinking, and God in his working.

So far, thrice-greatest one, I have shown you the truth. Think 22b
out all else in like manner for yourself, and you will not be misled.

LIBELLVS XII. (i)

A discourse of Hermes Trismegistus to Tat, concerning mind in men.

Hermes. Mind, my son Tat, is of the very substance of God, if 1
indeed there is a substance of God; and of what nature that substance is, God alone knows precisely. Mind then is not severed

[1] Perhaps, 'for there is nothing in which God is not'.

φανερώτερος Cyril.: *φανερώτατος* codd. Corp., Turn. **13–14** *δι' αὐτὸ τοῦτο πάντα ἐποίησεν* codd. Corp., Turn.: *διὰ τοῦτο πεποίηκεν* Cyril. **14** *αὐτὸν βλέπῃς* codd. Corp., Turn.: *τις αὐτὸν βλέπῃ* Cyril. **15** *τοῦτο ἡ τοῦ θεοῦ ἀρετή* scripsi: *τοῦ* (*τὸ τοῦ* Q) *θεοῦ, τοῦτο δὲ αὐτοῦ ἀρετή* codd. Corp., Turn.: *τοῦ θεοῦ, τοῦτο ἡ ἀρετή* Cyril. **16** *ἀόρατον* scripsi: *ὁρατόν* codd., Turn. **18** *ἐπὶ* om. A

In Libellis XII. i et XII. ii, codicum QR et Turnebi lectiones adhibui.

21 Fortasse *περὶ νοῦ ἀ̄νίνου* (i. e. *ἀνθρωπίνου*) **24** *αὐτὸς* scripsi: *οὗτος* QR Turn.

τετμημένος τῆς οὐσιότητος τοῦ θεοῦ, ἀλλ' ὥσπερ ἡπλωμένος,
καθάπερ τὸ τοῦ ἡλίου φῶς. οὗτος δὲ ὁ νοῦς ἐν μὲν ἀνθρώποις ⸢θεός⸣ ἐστι· διὸ καί τινες τῶν ἀνθρώπων θε⟨ῖ⟩οί εἰσι,
καὶ ἡ ⟨τ⟩ούτων ἀνθρωπότης ἐγγύς ἐστι τῆς θεότητος· καὶ
γὰρ ὁ Ἀγαθὸς Δαίμων τοὺς μὲν θεοὺς ⟨ἀνθρώπους⟩ εἶπεν
ἀθανάτους, τοὺς δὲ ἀνθρώπους θεοὺς θνητούς. ἐν δὲ τοῖς
2 ἀλόγοις ζῴοις ⟨. . .⟩ ἡ φύσις ἐστίν. ὅπου γὰρ [ψυχή, ἐκεῖ
καὶ νοῦς ἐστιν, ὥσπερ ὅπου καὶ] ζωή, ἐκεῖ καὶ ψυχή ἐστιν·
ἐν δὲ τοῖς ἀλόγοις ζῴοις ἡ ψυχὴ [ζωή] ἐστι κενὴ τοῦ νοῦ.
ὁ γὰρ νοῦς ψυχῶν ἐστιν εὐεργέτης ἀνθρώπων· ἐργάζεται
γὰρ αὐτα⟨ῖ⟩ς [εἰς] τὸ ἀγαθόν. καὶ τοῖς μὲν ἀλόγοις τῇ
⟨ἰ⟩δί⟨ᾳ⟩ ἑκάστου φύσει συνεργεῖ, ταῖς δὲ τῶν ἀνθρώπων
ἀντιπράσσει. ψυχὴ γὰρ πᾶσα, ἐν σώματι γενομένη, εὐθέως
ὑπό τε τῆς λύπης καὶ τῆς ἡδονῆς κακίζεται· σώματος γὰρ
συνθέτου ὥσπερ χυμοὶ ζέουσιν ἥ τε λύπη καὶ ἡ ἡδονή, εἰς ἃς
3 ἐμβᾶσα ἡ ψυχὴ βαπτίζεται. ὅσαις ἂν οὖν ψυχαῖς ὁ νοῦς
ἐπιστατήσῃ, ταύταις φαίνει ἑαυτοῦ τὸ φέγγος, ἀντιπράσσων
αὐτῶν τοῖς προλήμμασιν. ὥσπερ ⟨γὰρ⟩ ἰατρὸς ἀγαθὸς λυπεῖ
τὸ σῶμα προειλημμένον ὑπὸ νόσου καίων ἢ τέμνων, τὸν αὐτὸν
τρόπον καὶ ὁ νοῦς ⟨τὴν⟩ ψυχὴν λυπεῖ, ἐξυφαιρῶν αὐτῆς τὴν
ἡδονήν, ἀφ' ἧς πᾶσα νόσος ψυχῆς γίνεται. νόσος δὲ μεγάλη
ψυχῆς ἀθεότης· ἐπεὶ τα⟨ῖς τῶν ἀθέων⟩ δόξα[ε]ις πάντα τὰ
κακὰ ἐπακολουθεῖ, καὶ ἀγαθὸν οὐδέν. ἆρ' οὖν ὁ νοῦς, ἀντιπράσσων αὐτῇ, τὸ ἀγαθὸν περιποιεῖται τῇ ψυχῇ, ὥσπερ καὶ
4 ὁ ἰατρὸς τῷ σώματι τὴν ὑγίειαν. ὅσαι δὲ ψυχαὶ ἀνθρώπιναι
οὐκ ἔτυχον κυβερνήτου τοῦ νοῦ, τὸ αὐτὸ πάσχουσι ταῖς τῶν
ἀλόγων ζῴων. συνεργὸς γὰρ αὐταῖς γενόμενος, καὶ ἀνέσας
τὰς ἐπιθυμίας, ⟨. . .⟩ εἰς ἃς φέρονται τῇ ῥύμῃ τῆς ὀρέξεως,
πρὸς τὸ ἄλογον συντείνουσαι. καὶ ὥσπερ τὰ ἄλογα τῶν
ζῴων, ἀλόγως θυμούμεναι καὶ ἀλόγως ἐπιθυμοῦσαι οὐ παύον-
ται, οὐδὲ κόρον ἔχουσι τῶν κακῶν· θυμοὶ γὰρ καὶ ἐπιθυμίαι
ἄλογοι κακίαι ὑπερβάλλουσαι. ταύταις δὲ ὥσπερ τιμωρὸν
καὶ ἔλεγχον ὁ θεὸς ἐπέστησε τὸν νόμον.—

1 Fortasse ἐξηπλωμένος 3 θεῖοί scripsi : θεοί QR Turn. 4 τούτων scripsi : αὐτοῦ QR Turn. 5 ἀνθρώπους addidit Reitz. 7 Fortasse ⟨ἀντὶ νοῦ⟩ ἡ φύσις ἐστίν 8 καὶ ψυχή ἐστιν Q Turn. : καὶ ἡ ψυχή (om. ἐστιν) R 10 Fortasse ψυχῶν . . . ἀνθρωπίνων 11 γὰρ (post ἐργάζεται) om. Q | αὐταῖς scripsi : αὐτὰς εἰς QR Turn. 12 ἰδίᾳ scripsi : δι' QR Turn. 17 τὸ φέγγος Q Turn. R^2 : om. man. pr. R 18 προσλήμμασιν Q 20 ψυχὴν Q Turn. R^2 : om. man. pr. R 20–21 αὐτῆς τὴν ἡδονήν Q Turn. R^2 : αὐτὴν τῆς ἡδονῆς man. pr. R 22 ἐπεὶ ταῖς τῶν ἀθέων δόξαις scripsi : ἔπειτα

from the substantiality of God, but is, so to speak, spread abroad
from that source, as the light of the sun is spread abroad. In men,
this mind is . . .[1] Hence some men are divine, and the humanity
of such men is near to deity; for the Agathos Daimon said 'gods
are immortal men, and men are mortal gods'. But in the irrational
animals, there is instinct in place of mind. Wherever there is life, 2
there is soul; but in the irrational animals, the soul is devoid of
mind. Mind is a benefactor to the souls of men; it produces good
for them. In the case of the irrational animals, mind co-operates
with the special form of instinct which belongs to each several kind
of beast; but in men, mind works against the natural instincts.
Every soul, as soon as it has been embodied, is depraved by pain
and pleasure; for pain and pleasure belong to a composite body,
and seethe like juices in it, and the soul steps into them and
is plunged in them. Those souls then of which mind takes 3
command are illuminated by its light, and it counteracts their
prepossessions; for as a good physician inflicts pain on the body,
burning or cutting it, when disease has taken possession of it,
even so mind inflicts pain on the soul, ridding it of pleasure, from
which spring all the soul's diseases. And godlessness is a great
disease of the soul; for the beliefs of the godless bring in their train
all kinds of evils, and nothing that is good. Clearly then, mind,
inasmuch as it counteracts this disease, confers good on the soul,
just as the physician confers health on the body. But those 4
human souls which have not got mind to guide them are in the
same case as the souls of the irrational animals. For mind
co-operates with them, and gives free course to their desires; and
such souls are swept along by the rush of appetite to the gratification of their desires, and strive towards irrational ends; and like the irrational animals, they cease not from irrational anger and irrational desire, and are insatiable in their craving for evils; for irrational angers and desires are passions that exceed all else in evil. And to punish and convict such souls as these, God has established penal law.—

[1] Perhaps, 'this mind is productive of divinity'.

δόξα εἰς QR Turn. 25 *ὁ* (ante *ἰατρὸς*) om. R | *ὑγείαν* Q 27 Fortasse *γενόμενος ⟨ὁ νοῦς⟩* 28 *τὰς ἐπιθυμίας* Q Turn.: *ταῖς ἐπιθυμίαις* R 29 *συντείνουσαι* scripsi: *συντεινούσας* QR Turn. | *καὶ* (ante *ὥσπερ*) QR: om. Turn. | *τὰ ἄλογα* scripsi: *τὸ ἄλογον* QR Turn. 31 *οὐδὲ* R: *οὐδὲν* Q: *καὶ οὐδὲν* Turn. 33 *ἐπέστησε* Q Turn., man. post. R: *μετέστησε* man. pr. R

5 Ἐνταῦθα, ὦ πάτερ, ὁ περὶ τῆς εἱμαρμένης λόγος, ὅ⟨ν⟩
ἔμπροσθέν μοι ⟨δι⟩εξελήλυθας, κινδυνεύει ἀνατρέπεσθαι. εἰ
γὰρ πάντως εἵμαρται τῷδέ τινι μοιχεῦσαι, ἢ ἱεροσυλῆσαι, ἢ
ἄλλο τι κακὸν δρᾶσαι, διὰ τί κολάζεται ὁ [ἐξ] ἀναγκ⟨ασάσ⟩ης
τῆς εἱμαρμένης δράσας τὸ ἔργον; εἱμαρμένης γὰρ πάντα τὰ
ἔργα.—⟨. . . ,⟩ ὦ τέκνον, καὶ χωρὶς ἐκείνης οὐδὲν [τι] τῶν
σωματικῶν, οὔτε ἀγαθὸν οὔτε κακόν, γενέσθαι συμβαίνει·
εἵμαρται δὲ καὶ ⟨τὸν⟩ τὸ κακὸν ποιήσαντα [τὸ] ⟨κακὸν⟩ παθεῖν·
6 καὶ διὰ τοῦτο δρᾷ, ἵνα πάθῃ ὃ πάσχει ὅτι ἔδρασε. τὸ δὲ νῦν
ἔχον, ο⟨ὐ⟩ περὶ κακίας καὶ εἱμαρμένης ⟨ὁ⟩ λόγος· ἐν ἄλλοις
μὲν ⟨γὰρ⟩ περὶ τούτων εἰρήκαμεν, νῦν δὲ περὶ νοῦ ἐστιν ἡμῖν
ὁ λόγος, τί δύναται νοῦς, καὶ πῶς ἐνδιάφορός ἐστιν, ἐν μὲν
ἀνθρώποις τοιόσδε, ἐν δὲ τοῖς ἀλόγοις ζῴοις ἠλλαγμένος· καὶ
πάλιν, ὅτι ἐν μὲν τοῖς ἀλόγοις ζῴοις οὐκ ἔστιν εὐεργετικός,
⟨ἐν δὲ τοῖς ἀνθρώποις ἀγαθὸν ἐργάζεται,⟩ ἀλλ' ἀνομοίως,
⟨οὐκ⟩ ἐν πᾶσι τό τε θυμικὸν καὶ τὸ ἐπιθυμητικὸν σβεννύων.
καὶ τούτων τοὺς μὲν ἐλλογίμους [ἄνδρας] δεῖ νοεῖν, τοὺς δὲ
ἀλόγους. πάντες δὲ οἱ ἄνθρωποι εἱμαρμένῃ ὑπόκεινται, ⟨ἐπεὶ⟩
καὶ γενέσει καὶ μεταβολῇ· ἀρχὴ γὰρ καὶ τέλος ταῦτα εἱμαρ-
7 μένης. καὶ πάντες μὲν ἄνθρωποι πάσχουσι τὰ εἱμαρμένα·
οἱ δὲ ἐλλόγιμοι, ὧν ἔφαμεν τὸν νοῦν ἡγεμονεύειν, οὐχ ὁμοίως
τοῖς ἄλλοις πάσχουσιν, ἀλλὰ τῆς κακίας ἀπηλλαγμένοι· οὐ
⟨γὰρ⟩ κακοὶ ὄντες πάσχουσι.—Πῶς πάλιν λέγεις, ὦ πάτερ;
ὁ μοιχὸς οὐ κακός; ὁ φονεὺς οὐ κακός, καὶ οἱ ἄλλοι πάντες;
—Ἀλλ' ὁ ἐλλόγιμος, ὦ τέκνον, οὐ μοιχεύσας πείσεται, ἀλλ'
ὡς ⟨ὁ⟩ μοιχεύσας, οὐδὲ φονεύσας, ἀλλ' ὡς ⟨ὁ⟩ φονεύσας. καὶ
⌜ποιότητα⌝ μεταβολῆς ἀδύνατόν ἐστι διεκφυγεῖν, ὥσπερ καὶ
8 γενέσεως· κακίαν δὲ τῷ νοῦν ἔχοντι διεκφυγεῖν ἔστι. [διὸ]
καὶ τοῦ Ἀγαθοῦ Δαίμονος, ὦ τέκνον, ἐγὼ ἤκουσα λέγοντος ἃ
εἰ καὶ [εἰ] ἐγγράφως ⟨ἐξ⟩εδεδώκει, πάνυ ἂν τὸ τῶν ἀνθρώπων
γένος ὠφελήκει· ἐκεῖνος γὰρ μόνος, ὦ τέκνον, [[ἀληθῶς]] ὡς

1–2 ὅν . . . διεξελήλυθας scripsi : ὁ . . . ἐξεληλυθὼς QR Turn. 4 διὰ τί κολάζεται ὁ Turn. : καὶ κολάζεται ἢ ὁ QR | ἀναγκασάσης scripsi : ἐξ ἀνάγκης QR Turn. 6 τι R Turn. : ἐστι Q 8 καὶ τὸν τὸ κακὸν ποιήσαντα κακὸν παθεῖν scripsi : καὶ τὸ κακὸν ποιήσαντα, τὸ παθεῖν Turn. : καὶ τὸν καλὸν ποιήσαντα τὸ παθεῖν QR²: καὶ τὸ καλὸν ποιήσαντα παθεῖν man. pr. R 9 Fortasse διὰ τοῦτο ⟨εἵμαρται αὐτὸν⟩ δρᾶ⟨ν⟩ 10 οὐ scripsi : ὁ QR Turn. 13 ζῴοις (ante ἠλλαγμένος) QR : om. Turn. 14 ἀλόγοις (post μὲν τοῖς) Q Turn. : ἄλοις R 15 ἀνομοίως scripsi : ἀνόμοιος QR Turn. 18 οἱ (ante ἄνθρωποι) om. Q 22–23 πάσχουσιν, ἀλλὰ . . . κακοὶ ὄντες om. Q 26 οὐδὲ φονεύσας om. Q 29–30 λέγοντος ἃ εἰ καὶ ἐγγράφως scripsi : λέγοντος ἀεί·

Tat. But if that is so, father, it would almost seem that the 5
doctrine of destiny which you have explained to me before is
overthrown. If a man is inevitably destined to commit adultery,
or sacrilege, or some other crime, why is punishment inflicted on
one who has been compelled by destiny to do the deed? It is
destiny that has committed all these crimes.—*Hermes.* It is true,
my son, that . . ., and that nothing, whether good or bad, which
has to do with the body, can come to pass apart from destiny.
But it is destined also that he who has done evil shall suffer evil;
and to this end he does it,[1] that he may suffer the penalty for
having done it. But for the present, we are not discussing evil- 6
doing and destiny. Of those matters I have spoken elsewhere;
but we are now concerned with mind, and the questions we have
to consider are these,—what mind can do, and how it admits of
differences, being of one sort in men, and of another sort in the
irrational animals. And further, we have to consider that in the
irrational animals mind does not work good, whereas in men it
works good, but not alike in all men; for not in all men does it
quench the passions of anger and desire. The one sort of men
we must hold to be rational, and the other sort irrational. Now
all men are subject to destiny, inasmuch as all are subject to birth
and death;[2] for a man's destiny begins at his birth, and ends at his
death. And all men undergo what destiny has appointed for 7
them; but rational men (that is, those who, as I said, are governed
by mind) do not undergo it in the same way as the irrational.
They are freed from wickedness; they undergo what is destined,
but they are not wicked.—*Tat.* Once more, father, what do you
mean? The adulterer, and the murderer, and all the rest, are
they not wicked?—*Hermes.* Nay, my son, the rational man has
not committed adultery or murder, yet he must undergo what is
destined, as the adulterer and the murderer undergo it. It is
impossible for a man to escape from his destined death, just as it
is impossible for him to escape from his destined birth; but from
wickedness a man can escape, if he has mind in him. I will tell 8
you, my son, what I heard the Agathos Daimon say. If he had
put forth in writing what he said, he would have conferred a great
benefit on the human race; for being the first-born god, he alone,

[1] Perhaps, 'to this end he is destined (or compelled) to do it'.
[2] Literally, 'birth and change'; but 'change' here means 'death'.

καὶ εἰ ἐγγράφως QR Turn. 30 *ἐξεδεδώκει* scripsi: *ἐκδεδώκει* R (etiam MC teste Reitz.): *ἐδεδώκει* Q Turn. (etiam A teste Reitz.)

πρωτόγονος θεός, τὰ πάντα κατιδών, θείους ⟨⟨ἀληθῶς⟩⟩ λόγους
ἐφθέγξατο. ἤκουσα γοῦν αὐτοῦ ποτε λέγοντος ὅτι ⌜ἕν ἐστι
τὰ πάντα, καὶ μάλιστα νοητὰ σώματα· ζῶμεν δὲ δυνάμει καὶ
ἐνεργείᾳ καὶ αἰῶνι. καὶ ὁ νοῦς τούτου ἀγαθός ἐστιν, ὅπερ ἐστὶν
αὐτοῦ καὶ ψυχή· τούτου δὲ τοιούτου ὄντος, οὐδὲν διαστατὸν
τῶν νοητῶν· ὡς οὖν δυνατὸν νοῦν, ἄρχοντα πάντων, καὶ
9 ψυχὴν ὄντα τοῦ θεοῦ, ποιεῖν ὅπερ βούλεται⌝. σὺ δὲ νόει,
καὶ τὸν λόγον τοῦτον ἀνένεγκαι πρὸς τὴν πεῦσιν ἣν ἐπύθου
μου ἐν τοῖς ἔμπροσθεν, λέγω δὲ περὶ τῆς εἱμαρμένης [τοῦ
νοῦ]. ἐὰν γὰρ τοὺς ἐριστικοὺς λόγους ἀκριβῶς ἀφέλῃ, ὦ
τέκνον, εὑρήσεις ὅτι ἀληθῶς πάντων ἐπικρατεῖ ὁ νοῦς [ἡ τοῦ
θεοῦ ψυχή], καὶ εἱμαρμένης, καὶ νόμου, καὶ τῶν ἄλλων
πάντων· καὶ οὐδὲν αὐτῷ ἀδύνατον, οὔτε εἱμαρμένης ὑπεράνω
θε⟨ῖναι⟩ [νοῦν] ψυχὴν ἀνθρωπίνην, οὔτε ἀμελήσασαν, ἅπερ
συμβαίνει, ὑπὸ τὴν εἱμαρμένην ⟨θ⟩εῖναι. καὶ ταῦτα μὲν ἐπὶ
τοσοῦτον λελέχθω. [τὰ τοῦ Ἀγαθοῦ Δαίμονος ἄριστα.]—
Καὶ θείως, ὦ πάτερ, ταῦτα, καὶ ἀληθῶς καὶ ὠφελίμως.
10 ἐκεῖνο δέ μοι ἔτι διασάφησον· ἔλεγες γὰρ τὸν νοῦν ἐν τοῖς
ἀλόγοις ζῴοις φύσεως δίκην ἐνεργεῖν, συνεργοῦντα αὐτῶν
ταῖς ὁρμαῖς. αἱ δὲ ὁρμαὶ τῶν ἀλόγων ζῴων, ὡς οἶμαι, πάθη
εἰσίν· εἰ δὲ καὶ ὁ νοῦς συνεργεῖ ταῖς ὁρμαῖς, αἱ δὲ ὁρμαὶ
πάθη, καὶ ὁ νοῦς ἄρα παθ⟨ητ⟩ός ἐστι, συγχρω[μα]τίζων τοῖς
πάθεσιν.—Εὖγε, ὦ τέκνον· γενναίως πυνθάνῃ, δίκαιον δὲ
11 κἀμὲ ἀποκρίνασθαι. πάντα, ὦ τέκνον, τὰ ἐν σώματι [[ἀσώ-
ματα]] παθητά. καὶ κυρίως ⟨μὲν⟩ αὐτά ἐστι ⟨⟨⟨τ⟩ὰ σώματα⟩⟩
παθη⟨τά⟩· ⟨⟨καὶ τὰ ἀσώματα δὲ⟩⟩ ⟨. . .⟩. πᾶν γὰρ τὸ
κινοῦν ἀσώματον, πᾶν δὲ τὸ κινούμενον σῶμα· [[καὶ τὰ
ἀσώματα δὲ]] [κινεῖται ὑπὸ τοῦ νοῦ·] [κίνησις δὲ πάθος·]
πάσχει οὖν ἀμφότερα, καὶ τὸ κινοῦν καὶ τὸ κινούμενον, τὸ
μὲν ἄρχον, τὸ δὲ ἀρχόμενον. ⟨ὥστε καὶ ὁ νοῦς, ἐν σώματι
μὲν ὤν, παθητός ἐστιν,⟩ ἀπαλλαγεὶς δὲ τοῦ σώματος, ἀπηλ-
λάγη καὶ τοῦ πάθους. ⌜μᾶλλον δέ ποτε, ὦ τέκνον, οὐδὲν
ἀπαθές, πάντα δὲ παθητά. διαφέρει δὲ πάθος παθητοῦ.
τὸ μὲν γὰρ ἐνεργεῖ, τὸ δὲ πάσχει· τὰ δὲ σώματα καὶ καθ'
αὑτὰ ἐνεργεῖ. ἢ γὰρ ἀκίνητά ἐστιν ἢ κινεῖται· ὁπότερον δὲ

2 αὐτοῦ ποτὲ Q Turn.: ποτὲ αὐτοῦ R 4 ὅπέρ ἐστιν QR: ὅπέρν ἐστι (typographi, ut videtur, errore) Turn. 7 βύλεται Turn. 8–9 ἐπίθου μοι man. pr. R: γρ'. ἐπύθου μου R² 13–14 ὑπεράνω θεῖναι Flussas: ὑπεράνωθεν οὖν QR (etiam MAC teste Reitz.) Turn. 15 θεῖναι Flussas: εἶναι QR (etiam A teste Reitz.), Turn.: οὖν MC teste Reitz. 18 διάφησον

my son, had seen all things, and spoke words that are in very truth divine. I once heard him say '. . .'[1]. Think on these 9
words, and apply this teaching to the question which you asked me just now, that is, the question about destiny. For if you are careful to put aside contentious arguments, my son, you will find that in very truth mind is master of all things,—master of destiny, and of penal law, and of all else; and for mind nothing is impossible, neither to exalt a human soul above destiny, nor, if the soul, as sometimes happens, gives no heed, to make it subject to destiny. As to destiny then, let this suffice.—

Tat. This teaching, father, is divine; it is both true and helpful. But there is yet another thing which I must ask you to 10
explain. You said that in the irrational animals mind works in the way of instinct, co-operating with their impulses. Now the impulses of the irrational animals are passive affections,[2] I suppose; and if mind co-operates with the impulses, and the impulses are passive affections, then mind also must be passively affected, being polluted by contact with the passive affections.—*Hermes.* Well said, my son! Your question shows the right spirit, and it is only fair that I should answer it. All things that are in a body, 11
my son, are subject to passive affection. It is the bodies themselves that are subject to passive affection in the primary sense of the term; but the incorporeals[3] also. . . .[4] For everything that moves something is incorporeal, and everything that is moved is body; both the mover then and that which is moved are passively affected, the one being the ruler, and the other that which is ruled. And so, mind, as long as it is in a body, is subject to passive affection; but when it is freed from the body, it is freed from the passive affection also. . . .[5] You must not let yourself

[1] The saying of the Agathos Daimon, as given in the MSS., is meaningless.

[2] πάθη, here and throughout the paragraph, might also be translated 'perturbations'.

[3] The 'incorporeals' spoken of in this passage are, or include, mind and soul.

[4] Perhaps, 'are passively affected under certain conditions' (that is, when they are in a body).

[5] The passage here omitted is meaningless as given in the MSS.

---

man. pr. R: διασάφησον cett. **21** συνεργεῖ Turn.: συνεργεῖται QR **22** παθητός scripsi: πάθος QR Turn. | συγχρωτίζων scripsi: συγχρωματίζων QR Turn.: fortasse συγχρωτιζόμενος **26** παθητά scripsi: πάθη QR Turn. **29** καὶ τὸ κινοῦν Q Turn.: τὸ κινοῦν τε R **34–35** τὸ δὲ πάσχει . . . καθ' αὑτὰ ἐνεργεῖ om. Q | καὶ καθ' αὑτὰ Turn.: καὶ καὶ καθ' ἑαυτὰ R

ἂν ᾖ, πάθος ἐστί. τὰ δὲ ἀσώματα ἀεὶ ἐνεργεῖται, καὶ διὰ τοῦτο παθητά ἐστι.⌉ μὴ οὖν σε αἱ προσηγορίαι ταραττέτωσαν· ⌈ἡ τὲ γὰρ ἐνέργεια καὶ τὸ πάθος ταὐτόν ἐστιν·⌉ εὐφημοτέρῳ δὲ τῷ ὀνόματι χρήσασθαι οὐ λυπεῖ.—Σαφέστατα, ὦ πάτερ, τὸν λόγον ἀποδέδωκας.—

12 Κἀκεῖνο δὲ ὅρα, ὦ τέκνον, ὅτι δύο ταῦτα τῷ ἀνθρώπῳ ὁ θεὸς παρὰ πάντα τὰ θνητὰ ζῷα ἐχαρίσατο, τόν τε νοῦν καὶ τὸν λόγον, ἰσότιμα τῇ ἀθανασίᾳ· [τὸν δὲ προφορικὸν ⟨λ⟩έγει·] τούτοις δὲ εἴ τις χρήσαιτο εἰς ἃ δεῖ, οὐδὲν τῶν ἀθανάτων διοίσει, μᾶλλον δὲ ⟨τῷ ἐν σώματι εἶναι μόνον διοίσει,⟩ καὶ ἐξελθὼν ἐκ τοῦ σώματος, ὁδηγηθήσεται ὑπὸ
13 a ἀμφοτέρων εἰς τὴν τῶν θεῶν καὶ μακάρων χορόν.—Τὰ γὰρ ἄλλα ζῷα λόγῳ οὐ χρῆται, ὦ πάτερ;—Οὔ, τέκνον, ἀλλὰ φωνῇ. πάμπολυ δὲ διαφέρει λόγος φωνῆς· ὁ μὲν γὰρ λόγος κοινὸς πάντων ἀνθρώπων, ἰδία δὲ ἑκάστου φωνή ἐστι γένους ζῴου.—Ἀλλὰ καὶ τῶν ἀνθρώπων, ὦ πάτερ, ἕκαστον κατὰ ἔθνος διάφορος ὁ λόγος.—Διάφορος μέν, ὦ τέκνον, ⟨ἡ διάλεκτος,⟩ εἷς δὲ ὁ ἄνθρωπος, οὕτω καὶ ὁ λόγος εἷς ἐστι· καὶ μεθερμηνεύεται, καὶ ὁ αὐτὸς εὑρίσκεται καὶ ἐν Αἰγύπτῳ καὶ Περσίδι καὶ Ἑλλάδι. ⟨. . .⟩ ⟨⟨ὁ οὖν λόγος ἐστὶν εἰκὼν ⟨τοῦ νοῦ⟩, καὶ ⟨ὁ⟩ νοῦς τοῦ θεοῦ.⟩⟩
13 b ὁ γὰρ μακάριος θεὸς Ἀγαθὸς Δαίμων ψυχὴν μὲν ἐν σώματι ἔφη εἶναι, νοῦν δὲ ἐν ψυχῇ, [λόγον] ⟨θεὸν⟩ δὲ ἐν τῷ νῷ.
14 a [τὸν οὖν θεὸν τούτων πατέρα.] [[ὁ οὖν λόγος ἐστὶν εἰκὼν καὶ νοῦς τοῦ θεοῦ]] [καὶ τὸ σῶμα δὲ τῆς ἰδέας, ἡ δὲ ἰδέα τῆς ψυχῆς.] ἔστιν οὖν τῆς μὲν ὕλης τὸ λεπτομερέστατον ἀήρ, ἀέρος δὲ ψυχή, ψυχῆς δὲ νοῦς, νοῦ δὲ θεός. καὶ ὁ μὲν θεὸς περὶ πάντα καὶ διὰ πάντων, ὁ δὲ νοῦς περὶ τὴν ψυχήν, ἡ δὲ ψυχὴ περὶ τὸν ἀέρα, ὁ δὲ ἀὴρ περὶ τὴν ὕλην.

1–2 Fortasse τὰ δὲ [α]σώματα ἀεὶ ἐνεργεῖται, καὶ διὰ τοῦτο ⟨ἀεὶ⟩ παθητά ἐστι **1** ἀσώματα Q Turn. : σώματα (γρ'. ἀσώματα man. post.) R | καὶ διὰ Q Tnrn. R²: τὸ διὰ man. pr. R **7** παρὰ QR Turn. : περὶ C teste Reitz. | θνητὰ ζῷα Q Turn. R²: ἔθνη τῶν ζώων man. pr. R **9** λέγει scripsi : ἔχει QR Turn. | τις ex τι corr. R **12–13** γὰρ ἄλλα ζῷα λόγῳ οὐ Q Turn. R²: γὰρ ζῷα οὐ man. pr. R **13** χρῆται Turn. : χρᾶται QR **15–16** ἑκάστου φωνή ἐστι γένους ζώου. ἀλλὰ καὶ Q Turn. : ἑκάστου γένους ζώου φωνή ἐστι καλή, καὶ man. pr. R : post καλή add. ἀλλὰ R² **17** ὁ (ante λόγος) om. R **18** δὲ (post εἷς) Q Turn. : μὲν R

be confused by the use of these terms; . . .[1] but there is no
harm in using the better-sounding word.[2]—*Tat.* You have explained the matter most clearly, father.—

Hermes. There is another thing to be considered, my son. 12
There are two gifts which God has bestowed on man alone, and
on no other mortal creature. These two are mind and speech;
and the gift of mind and speech is equivalent to that of immortality. If a man uses these two gifts rightly, he will differ in
nothing from the immortals; or rather, he will differ from them
only in this, that he is embodied upon earth; and when he quits
the body, mind and speech will be his guides, and by them he
will be brought into the troop of the gods and the souls that have
attained to bliss.—*Tat.* But do not the other living creatures use 13 a
speech, father?—*Hermes.* No, my son; they have voice, but not
speech; and speech is very different from voice. All men have
speech in common; but each kind of living creatures has its special
sort of voice.—*Tat.* But among men also, father, each nation
has a different speech.—*Hermes.* Languages differ, my son, but
mankind is one; and speech likewise is one. It is translated
from tongue to tongue, and we find it to be the same in Egypt,
Persia, and Greece. . . . Speech then is an image of mind; and
mind is an image of God.

That blessed god, the Agathos Daimon, said 'soul is in body, 13 b
mind is in soul, and God is in mind'. The rarest part of matter 14 a
then is air; the rarest part of air is soul; the rarest part of soul
is mind; and the rarest part of mind is God. And God deals
with all things, and permeates all things; mind deals with soul;
soul deals with air; and air deals with gross matter.

[1] 'These terms' are probably 'working actively' and 'passively affected', both of which are applicable to embodied mind. The author's meaning might perhaps be expressed by writing here 'for it is one and the same thing (viz. embodied mind) that both works actively and is passively affected'.

[2] I.e. there is no harm in saying that embodied mind 'works actively', and omitting to say that it is 'passively affected'.

---

20 καὶ ἐν ἑλλάδι R **20–21** ὁ οὖν . . . θεοῦ huc a § 14 a *init.* transposui **21** τοῦ νοῦ addidit Flussas **25** ἡ δὲ ἰδέα Q Turn. R[2]: ἡδέα man. pr. R **27** θεὸς (post ὁ μὲν) Q Turn. R[2]: om. man. pr. R

LIBELLVS XII. (ii)

⟨Ἑρμοῦ πρὸς Τάτ.⟩

14 b ⟨. . .⟩ ἀνάγκη δὲ καὶ [ἡ] πρόνοια καὶ [ἡ] φύσις ὄργανά ἐστι
⟨τῆς διοικήσεως⟩ τοῦ κόσμου, καὶ τῆς τάξεως τῆς ὕλης.
14 c καὶ τῶν μὲν νοητῶν ἕκαστόν ἐστιν ⟨ἕν⟩ [οὐσία], οὐσία δὲ αὐτῶν ἡ
ταυτότης· τῶν δὲ τοῦ παντὸς σωμάτων ἕκαστον πολλά ἐστιν. ⟨⟨καὶ
ἡ ὕλη μία·⟩⟩ ἔχετα⟨ι⟩ γὰρ τῆς ταυτότητος τὰ ⟨ἀ⟩σύνθετα σώματα, καὶ
τὴν μεταβολὴν εἰς ἄλληλα ποιούμενα, ἀεὶ τῆς ταυτότητος τὴν ἀφθαρσίαν
σώζει. ἐν δὲ τοῖς [ἄλλοις] συνθέτοις πᾶσι σώμασιν ἀριθμὸς ἑκάστου
15 a ἐστί· χωρὶς γὰρ ἀριθμοῦ σύστασιν ἢ σύνθεσιν [ἢ διάλυσιν] ἀδύνατον
γενέσθαι. αἱ δὲ ἑνάδες τὸν ἀριθμὸν γεννῶσι καὶ αὔξουσι, καὶ πάλιν
διαλυόμενον εἰς ἑαυτὰς δέχονται. [[καὶ ἡ ὕλη μία.]]

15 b ὁ δὲ σύμπας κόσμος οὗτος, ὁ μέγας θεός, καὶ τοῦ μείζονος
εἰκών, καὶ ἡνωμένος ἐκείνῳ, καὶ σώζων τὴν τάξιν κατ⟨ὰ τὴν⟩
βούλησιν τοῦ πατρός, πλήρωμά ἐστι τῆς ζωῆς· καὶ οὐδέν
ἐστιν ἐν τούτῳ, διὰ παντὸς τοῦ αἰῶνος ⟨⟨ἀπὸ⟩⟩ τῆς πρώτης
[[ἀπο]]καταστάσεως, οὔτε τοῦ παντὸς οὔτε τῶν κατὰ μέρος,
ὃ οὐχὶ ζῇ. νεκρὸν γὰρ οὐδὲ ἓν οὔτε γέγονεν οὔτε ἐστὶν οὔτε
ἔσται ἐν ⟨τῷ⟩ κόσμῳ. ζῷον γὰρ ἠθέλησεν ὁ πατὴρ αὐτὸ⟨ν⟩
16 εἶναι ἔστ' ἂν συνεστήκῃ· διὸ καὶ θεὸν εἶναι ἀνάγκη. πῶς ἂν
οὖν δύναιτο, ὦ τέκνον, ἐν τῷ θεῷ, ἐν τῇ τοῦ πατρὸς εἰκόνι, ἐν
τῷ τῆς ζωῆς πληρώματι, νεκρὰ εἶναι; ἡ γὰρ νεκρότης φθορά
ἐστιν, ἡ δὲ φθορὰ ἀπώλεια. πῶς οὖν μέρος τι δύναται
φθαρῆναι τοῦ ἀφθάρτου, ἢ ἀπολέσ⟨θ⟩αι τι τοῦ θεοῦ;—Οὐκ
ἀποθνήσκει οὖν, ὦ πάτερ, τὰ ἐν αὐτῷ ζῷα, ὄντα αὐτοῦ μέρη;
—Εὐφήμησον, ὦ τέκνον, πλανώμενος τῇ προσηγορίᾳ τοῦ γινομένου.
οὐ γὰρ ἀποθνήσκει, ὦ τέκνον, ἀλλ' ὡς σύνθετα
σώματα διαλύεται. ἡ δὲ διάλυσις οὐ θάνατός ἐστιν, ἀλλὰ

2 *ἐστι* Q Turn. : *εἶναι* R **5–6** *καὶ ἡ ⟨μὲν ?⟩ ὕλη μία* huc a § 15 a *fin.* transposui **6** *ἔχεται γὰρ τῆς ταυτότητος* scripsi : *ἔχοντα γὰρ τὴν ταυτότητα* QR Turn. | *τὰ* om. Q | *ἀσύνθετα* scripsi : *σύνθετα* QR Turn. **11** *διαλυόμενον* scripsi : *διαλυόμεναι* QR Turn. **13** *σώζων* man. pr. R (*σῴζων* A teste Reitz.) : *σύσωζων* QR[2] Turn. (*συσσώζων* CM teste Reitz.) **13–14** *κατὰ τὴν βούλησιν* scripsi : *καὶ βούλησιν* QR Turn. **14** *τῆς ζωῆς* Q Turn. : *τῆς πρ͂ς ζωῆς* R **15–16** *τοῦ αἰῶνος . . . οὔτε τοῦ παντὸς* om. Q | *αἰῶνος ἀπὸ τῆς πρώτης καταστάσεως* scripsi : *αἰῶνος, τῆς πατρῴας ἀποκαταστάσεως* Turn. : *αἰῶνος τῆς ἀποκαταστάσεως* R **18** *ζῷον . . . αὐτὸν* scripsi : *ζῶον . . . αὐτὸ* QR : *ζῶον . . . αὐτῷ* Turn. : *ζωὴν . . . αὐτῷ* Flussas **19** *συνεστήκῃ* scripsi : *συνέστηκε* Q Turn. : *συνέστηκεν* R **20** *πατρὸς* scripsi :

LIBELLVS XII. (ii)

A discourse of Hermes to Tat.

Hermes. . . . And necessity[1] and providence and nature are 14 b
instruments by means of which the Kosmos is governed, and by
means of which matter is set in order.

Each of the intelligibles[2] is one, and sameness is their essence; but each of 14 c
the bodies contained in the universe is many. And matter is one; for the
incomposite bodies[3] cleave to sameness, and though they change into one
another, they maintain their sameness unimpaired for ever. But in every com- 15 a
posite body there is number; for there cannot be combination or composition
unless there is number. And the units generate number and increase it, and
receive it back into themselves when it is broken up.

Now this whole Kosmos,—which is a great god, and an image 15 b
of Him who is greater, and is united with Him, and maintains its
order in accordance with the Father's will,—is one mass of life;
and there is not anything in the Kosmos, nor has been through
all time from the first foundation of the universe, neither in the
whole nor among the several things contained in it, that is not
alive. There is not, and has never been, and never will be in
the Kosmos anything that is dead. For it was the Father's will
that the Kosmos, as long as it exists, should be a living being;
and therefore it must needs be a god also. How then, my son, 16
could there be dead things in that which is a god, in that which
is an image of the Father, in that which is one mass of life?
Deadness is corruption, and corruption is destruction. How then
can any part of that which is incorruptible be corrupted, or any
part of that which is a god be destroyed?—*Tat.* Is it not true
then, father, that the living creatures in the Kosmos die? And
are they not parts of the Kosmos?—*Hermes.* Say not so, my son.
You are misled by the terms that men apply to that which takes
place.[4] The living creatures do not die, my son; but they are
composite bodies, and as such, they undergo dissolution. Dissolution is not death; it is only the separation of things which

[1] Perhaps, '⟨destiny⟩ and necessity'; see § 21.
[2] I. e. incorporeal things. [3] I. e. the four cosmic elements.
[4] I. e. by the common use of the word 'death'.

παντὸς QR Turn. 23 ἀπολέσθαι Parthey : ἀπολέσαι QR Turn. 27 διαλύονται R : διαλύεται cett.

*κράματος ⸢διάλυσις⸣· διαλύεται δὲ οὐχ ἵν' ἀπόληται, ἀλλ'
ἵνα νέα γένηται. ἐπεὶ τίς τῆς ζωῆς ἐστιν ἡ ἐνέργεια; οὐχὶ
κίνησις; τί οὖν ἐν τῷ κόσμῳ ἀκίνητον; οὐδέν, ὦ τέκνον.—*
17 *Οὐδ' ἡ γῆ ἀκίνητός σοι δοκεῖ, ὦ πάτερ;—Οὔ, τέκνον, ἀλλὰ
καὶ πολυκίνητος μόνη ἥδε καὶ στάσιμος. πῶς οὐκ ἂν γελοῖον
εἴη τὴν τροφὸν πάντων ἀκίνητον εἶναι, τὴν φύουσαν καὶ
γεννῶσαν τὰ πάντα; ἀδύνατον γὰρ χωρὶς κινήσεως φύειν τι
[τὸν φύοντα]. γελοιότατον δὲ ἐπύθου, εἰ τὸ τέταρτον μέρος
ἀργόν ἐστ[α]ι· οὐδὲν γὰρ ἕτερον σημαίνει τὸ ἀκίνητον σῶμα*
18 *ἢ ἀργίαν. πᾶν τοίνυν ἴσθι καθολικῶς, ὦ τέκνον, τὸ ὂν ἐν
κόσμῳ κινούμενον [ἢ κατὰ μείωσιν ἢ αὔξησιν]· τὸ δὲ κινούμενον καὶ ζῇ. τὸ δὲ ζῶ[ο]ν πᾶν οὐκ ἀνάγκη τὸ αὐτὸ ⟨ἀεὶ⟩
εἶναι· ὢν γὰρ ὁμοῦ σύμπας ὁ κόσμος ἀμετάβλητος, ὦ τέκνον,
ἐστί, τὰ δὲ μέρη αὐτοῦ πάντα μεταβλητά, οὐδὲν δὲ φθαρτὸν
ἢ ἀπολλύμενον· αἱ δὲ προσηγορίαι τοὺς ἀνθρώπους ταράτ-
τουσιν. οὐ γὰρ ἡ γένεσίς ἐστι ζωῆ⟨ς ἀρχή⟩, ἀλλ' [ἡ]
αἰσθήσεως· οὐδὲ ἡ μεταβολὴ θάνατος, ἀλλὰ λήθη. τούτων
τοίνυν οὕτως ἐχόντων, ἀθάνατα πάντα ⟨⟨ἐξ ὧν πᾶν ζῷον
συνέστηκε⟨ν⟩⟩⟩, ἡ ὕλη [ζωή], τὸ πνεῦμα [ὁ νοῦς], ⟨ἡ⟩ ψυχή
[[ἐξ οὗ πᾶν ζῷον συνέστηκε]]· πᾶν ἄρα ζῷον ἀθάνατον δι⟨ὰ
τὴν ἀθανασίαν⟩ αὐτῶν.*
19 *πάντων δὲ μᾶλλον ⟨ἀθάνατος⟩ ὁ ἄνθρωπος, ὁ καὶ τοῦ θεοῦ
δεκτικὸς καὶ τῷ θεῷ συνουσιαστικός. τούτῳ γὰρ μόνῳ τῷ
ζώῳ ὁ θεὸς ὁμιλεῖ, νυκτὸς μὲν δι' ὀνείρων, ἡμέρας δὲ διὰ
συμβόλων, καὶ διὰ πάντων αὐτῷ προλέγει τὰ μέλλοντα, διὰ
ὀρνέων, διὰ σπλάγχνων, διὰ πνεύματος, διὰ δρυός· διὸ καὶ
ἐπαγγέλλεται ὁ ἄνθρωπος ἐπίστασθαι τὰ προγεγενημένα καὶ*
20 a *ἐνεστῶτα καὶ μέλλοντα. κἀκεῖνο δὲ ὅρα, ὦ τέκνον, ὅτι ἕκαστον
τῶν ζῴων ἑνὶ μέρει ἐπιφοιτᾷ τοῦ κόσμου, τὰ μὲν ἔνυδρα τῷ
ὕδατι, τὰ δὲ χερσαῖα τῇ γῇ, τὰ δὲ μετάρσια τῷ ἀέρι· ὁ δὲ*

1 *διάλυσις* codd., Turn.: fortasse *διάκρισις* 2 *τίς* om. man. pr. R | *τῆς ζωῆς ἐστιν ἡ ἐνέργεια* Turn.: *τῆς ζωῆς ἐστιν ἐνέργεια* Q: *τῆς ζωῆς ἡ ἐνέργεια* (post *ἐνέργεια* add. *ἐστὶ* man. post.) R 4 *ἀκίνητός σοι* Q Turn.: *σοι ἀκίνητος* R 5 *μόνη* R Turn.: *μόνον* Q: *γρ'. μόνον* man. post. R | *στασίμη* Q 7 *φύειν τι* Turn.: *φῦναί τι* Q: *φυῆναί τι* R 8 *γελοιότερον* R 9 *ἀργόν ἐστι* scripsi: *ἀργὸν ἔσται* QR Turn. 11 *ἢ* (ante *κατὰ*) Q Turn.: *ἤτοι* R 12 *ζῶν* scripsi: *ζῶον* QR Turn. 13 *ὦ τέκνον* om. R 16–17 *ζωῆς ἀρχή, ἀλλ' αἰσθήσεως* scripsi: *ζωή, ἀλλ' ἡ αἴσθησις* QR Turn. 17 *ἡ* (post *οὐδὲ*) om. R 18 *ἐχώντων* R 19 *τὸ πνεῦμα, ἡ ψυχή* scripsi: *τὸ πνεῦμα, ὁ νοῦς, ψυχὴ* Q Turn.: *τὸ πνεῦμα, ψυχὴ, ὁ νοῦς* R 20 *ἐξ ὧν* Flussas: *ἐξ οὗ* QR Turn. 20–21 *διὰ τὴν ἀθανασίαν αὐτῶν* scripsi: *δι' αὐτόν* QR Turn. 27 *ἐπαγγέλεται* R | *τὰ*

were combined; and they undergo dissolution, not to perish, but to be made new. Why, wherein does life manifest its force? Surely, in movement. And what is there in the Kosmos that is
motionless? Nothing, my son.—*Tat.* Do you think then, father, 17
that not even the earth is motionless?—*Hermes.* No, my son, not even the earth; but the earth, alone of all things, is both in motion in manifold ways, and at the same time stationary. Would it not be absurd to say that the nurse of all things [1] is motionless, she who brings forth and generates all things? Without motion, it is impossible to bring forth anything. And it is utterly absurd to ask, as you did, whether the fourth part of the universe is idle; for if you say that a body is motionless, that
means nothing else than that it is idle. Know then, my son, 18
that everything which exists in the Kosmos, everything without exception, is in motion; and that which is in motion must be alive. But it is not necessary that in every case it should be one and the same thing that is alive at all times. Considered as one whole, my son, the Kosmos is exempt from change; but all its parts are subject to change. But there is nothing in it that suffers corruption or destruction; if men think otherwise, their thoughts are confused by the terms in use. Birth is not a beginning of life, but only a beginning of consciousness; and the change to another state is not death, but oblivion. And this being so, all the things of which every living creature is composed, —gross matter, and vital spirit, and soul,—are immortal; and so, by reason of their immortality, every living creature is immortal.

But more than all the rest, man is immortal; for he can 19
receive God, and hold intercourse with God. With man alone of living creatures God associates. God speaks to man by dreams at night, and by signs in the daytime; God foretells the future to him in manifold ways, by the flight of birds, by the inward parts of beasts, by inspiration, or by the whispering of an oak-tree. And so man can boast that he knows things past,
things present, and things future. Mark this too, my son; each 20 a
of the other kinds of living creatures haunts but one part of the Kosmos; fishes live in the water, beasts on the earth, and birds

[1] I.e. the earth.

γεγενημένα R cett. 28 κἀκεῖνος R 29 μὲν γὰρ ἔνυδρα R: μὲν ἔνυδρα

ἄνθρωπος τούτοις πᾶσι χρῆται, γῇ, ὕδατι, ἀέρι [πυρί]· ὁρᾷ δὲ καὶ οὐρανόν, ἅπτεται δὲ καὶ τούτου αἰσθήσει.
20 b ⟨. . .⟩ [ὁ δὲ θεὸς καὶ περὶ πάντα καὶ διὰ πάντων.]
⌜ἐνέργεια γάρ ἐστι δύναμις.⌝ καὶ οὐδὲν δύσκολόν ἐστι
νοῆσαι τὸν θεόν, ὦ τέκνον, εἰ δὲ θέλεις, [[αὐτὸν]] καὶ θεω-
21 ρῆσαι ⟨⟨αὐτόν⟩⟩. ἴδε τὴν τάξιν τοῦ κόσμου [καὶ τὴν εὐκοσμίαν τῆς τάξεως]· ἴδε τὴν ἀνάγκην τῶν φαινομένων, καὶ τὴν πρόνοιαν τῶν γεγονότων τε καὶ γινομένων· ἴδε τὴν ὕλην πληρεστάτην οὖσαν ζωῆς· ⟨ἴδε⟩ τὸν τηλικοῦτον θεὸν κινούμενον μετὰ πάντων ⟨τῶν ἐνόντων⟩ [ἀγαθῶν καὶ καλῶν] [θεῶν τε καὶ δαιμόνων καὶ ἀνθρώπων].—Ἀλλ' αὗται, ὦ πάτερ, ἐνέργειαι ὅλως εἰσίν.—Εἰ οὖν ἐνέργειαί [ὅλως] εἰσιν, ὦ τέκνον, ὑπὸ τίνος [οὖν] ἐνεργοῦνται [ὑπὸ] ἄλλου ⟨ἢ τοῦ⟩ θεοῦ; ἢ ἀγνοεῖς ὅτι ὥσπερ τοῦ κόσμου μέρη εἰσὶν οὐρανὸς καὶ γῆ καὶ ὕδωρ καὶ ἀήρ, τὸν αὐτὸν τρόπον μέρη ἐστὶ ⟨τοῦ⟩ θεοῦ [ζωὴ καὶ ἀθανασία καὶ] εἱμα⟨ρμένη⟩ καὶ ἀνάγκη καὶ πρόνοια καὶ φύσις [καὶ ψυχὴ καὶ νοῦς]; [καὶ τούτων πάντων ἡ διαμονὴ] [τὸ λεγόμενον ἀγαθόν.] καὶ οὐκ [ἔτι] ἔστι τι τῶν γινομένων ἢ
22 τῶν γεγονότων ὅπου οὐκ ἔστιν ὁ θεός.—Ἐν τῇ ὕλῃ οὖν, ὦ πάτερ;—Ἡ γὰρ ὕλη, ὦ τέκνον, χωρὶς θεοῦ ⟨τί⟩ ἐστιν, ἵνα τόπον αὐτῇ ἀπομερίσῃς [τόπον]; τί δὲ [ουσ] ἂν ἢ σωρὸν αὐτὴν οἴει εἶναι, μὴ ἐνεργουμένην; εἰ δὲ ἐνεργεῖται, ὑπὸ τίνος ἐνεργεῖται; τὰς γὰρ ἐνεργείας ἔφαμεν εἶναι μέρη τοῦ θεοῦ. ὑπὸ τίνος οὖν ζωοποιεῖται τὰ πάντα ζῷα; ὑπὸ τίνος ἀθανατίζεται τὰ ἀθάνατα; ὑπὸ τίνος μεταβάλλεται τὰ μεταβλητά; εἴτε δὲ ὕλην; εἴτε σῶμα, εἴτε οὐσίαν φῄς, ἴσθι καὶ ταύτας οὔσας ἐνεργείας τοῦ θεοῦ· ⟨ὁ γὰρ θεὸς⟩ καὶ ⟨τῆς⟩ ὕλη⟨ς⟩ ἐνεργεῖ τὴν ὑλότητα, καὶ τῶν σωμάτων ⟨τὴν⟩ σωματότητα, καὶ ⟨τ⟩ῇ⟨ς⟩ οὐσία⟨ς⟩ τὴν οὐσιότητα. καὶ τοῦτο ἔστιν ὁ θεός, τὸ πᾶν·
23 a ἐν δὲ τῷ παντὶ οὐδέν ἐστιν ὃ μὴ ἔστιν. ὅθεν οὔτε μέγεθος οὔτε τόπος οὔτε ποιότης οὔτε σχῆμα οὔτε χρόνος παρὰ τὸν

1 τούτοις πᾶσι Q Turn. : πᾶσι τούτοις R | ὁρᾷ QR² Turn. : ὁρᾶται man. pr. R 3 καὶ (post θεὸς) om. man pr. R 4 ἐστι καὶ δύναμις Q : ἐστι δύναμις cett. 8 γινομένων scripsi : γενομένων Turn. 10 ἀγαθὸν Q : ἀγαθῶν cett. 12 ὅλως (post πάτερ, ἐνέργειαι) om. Q | Εἰ οὖν . . . εἴσιν om. R 13 ἐνεργοῦντος man pr. R : ἐνεργοῦνται cett. 14 ὥσπερ τοῦ κόσμου μέρη εἰσὶν οὐραι ὸς QR² Turn. : ὥσπερ ἐστὶν ὁ οὐρανὸς man. pr. R 14–15 γῆ καὶ ὕδωρ Q Turn. : ὕδωρ καὶ γῆ R 15 μέρη scripsi : μέλη QR Turn. | θεοῦ om. Q 16 εἱμαρμένη scripsi : αἷμα QR Turn. 18 οὐκ ἔστι τι scripsi : οὐκ ἔτι ἐστί τι Turn. : οὐκ ἔτι τί Q | γενομένων R : γινομένων cett. 19 ἐστι θεός R : ἔστιν ὁ θεός cett. 21 τόπον scripsi : ποιὸν QR Turn.

in the air; but man makes use of all these elements, earth, water, air; yes, and heaven[1] too he beholds, and grasps that also with his sense of sight.

. . . And it is not difficult, my son, to contemplate God in **20b**
thought, or even, if you will, to see him. Look at the order of **21**
the Kosmos; look at the necessity which governs all that is presented to our sight, and the providence shown in things that have been, and in things that come to be; look at matter filled to the full with life, and see this great god[2] in movement, with all things that are contained in him.—*Tat.* But these, father, are nothing but forces at work.—*Hermes.* If they are forces at work, my son, who is it that works them? Is it not God? Do you not know that, just as heaven and earth and water and air are parts of the Kosmos, even so destiny and necessity and providence and nature are parts of God? And there is nothing that comes to be
or has come to be, in which God is not.—*Tat.* Is God in **22**
matter then, father?—*Hermes.* Why, what is matter apart from God, my son, that you should assign a place to it? What else but an inert mass do you suppose matter would be, if it were not worked upon? And if it is worked upon, who is it that works upon it? I have told you that the forces at work are parts of God; who is it then that puts life into all living creatures? Who is it that gives immortal beings their immortality? Who is it that works change in things subject to change?[3] And whether you speak of matter, or body, or substance, know that these also are manifestations of God's working; for it is God that by his working makes matter material, and bodies corporeal, and substance substantial. God is the All; and there is nothing that is
not included in the All. Hence there is neither magnitude nor **23a**
place nor quality nor shape nor time[4] beside God; for God

[1] Heaven consists of fire, the fourth element.

[2] Viz. the Kosmos.

[3] I. e. brings to pass what are commonly called deaths and fresh births in the case of mortal beings.

[4] Perhaps, 'nor shape nor colour'.

| ἂν scripsi : οὖσαν QR Turn. | Fortasse σορὸν 22 οἴει Q Turn. : ἢ R | γρ'. ἀπὸ man. post. R : ὑπὸ cett. 26 ὕλη R : ὕλην cett. 27 οὔσας scripsi : αὐτὰς QR Turn. | καὶ τῆς ὕλης scripsi : καὶ ὕλη QR Turn. | ἐνεργεῖ τὴν Turn. : ἐνέργεια τὴν QR 28–29 καὶ τῶν σωμάτων . . . οὐσιότητα R^2 Turn. : om. Q et man. pr. R | τῆς οὐσίας scripsi : ἡ οὐσία Turn. 31 χρόνος QR Turn. : fortasse χρῶμα | παρὰ scripsi : περὶ QR Turn.

θεόν ἐστι· πᾶν γάρ ἐστι, τὸ δὲ πᾶν διὰ πάντων καὶ περὶ πάντα.

23 b τοῦτον [τὸν λόγον], ὦ τέκνον, προσκύνει καὶ θρήσκευε. θρησκεία δὲ τοῦ θεοῦ μία ἐστί, μὴ εἶναι κακόν.

LIBELLVS XIII

Ἑρμοῦ τοῦ τρισμεγίστου πρὸς τὸν υἱὸν Τὰτ [ἐν ὄρει] λόγος ἀπόκρυφος περὶ παλιγγενεσίας [καὶ σιγῆς ἐπαγγελίας]

1 Ἐν τοῖς γενικοῖς, ὦ πάτερ, αἰνιγματωδῶς καὶ οὐ τηλαυγῶς ἔφρασας, περὶ θειότητος διαλεγόμενος· [[οὐκ ἀπεκάλυψας]] φάμενος ⟨γὰρ⟩ μηδένα δύνασθαι σωθῆναι πρὸ τῆς παλιγγενεσίας, ⟨⟨οὐκ ἀπεκάλυψας·⟩⟩ ἐμοῦ τε σοῦ ἱκέτου γενομένου ⌜ἐπὶ τῆς τοῦ ὄρους μεταβάσεως⌝ μετὰ τὸ σὲ ἐμοὶ διαλεχθῆναι [πυθομένου] τὸν τῆς παλιγγενεσίας λόγον μαθεῖν, ὅτι τοῦτον παρὰ πάντα μόνον ἀγνοῶ, ⟨οὔπω ἠξίωσας⟩ ⟨⟨παραδιδόναι μοι,⟩⟩ καὶ ἔφης "ὅταν μέλλῃς ⟨τοῦ⟩ κόσμου ἀπαλλοτριοῦσθαι [[παραδιδόναι μοι]] ⟨παραδώσω." ἐγὼ δὲ ἤδη⟩ ἕτοιμος ἐγενόμην, καὶ ἀπηλλοτρίωσα τὸ ἐν ἐμοὶ φρόνημα ἀπὸ τῆς τοῦ κόσμου ἀπάτης· σὺ δέ μου καὶ τὰ ὑστερήματα ἀναπλήρωσον, ὡς ἔφης μοι, παλιγγενεσίαν παραδοῦναι προθέμενος [ἐκ φωνῆς ἢ κρυβήν]. ἀγνοῶ, ὦ τρισμέγιστε, ἐξ οἵας μήτρας
2 ἄνθρωπος ⟨ἀν⟩αγεννηθ⟨εί⟩η ⟨ἄν⟩, σπορᾶς δὲ ποίας.—Ὦ τέκνον, σοφία ⟨ἡ⟩ μήτρα, ἐν σιγῇ ⟨κύουσα⟩, καὶ ἡ σπορὰ τὸ ἀληθινὸν ἀγαθόν.—Τίνος σπείραντος, ὦ πάτερ; τὸ γὰρ σύνολον ἀπορῶ.—Τοῦ θελήματος τοῦ θεοῦ, ὦ τέκνον.—⟨⟨Λέγε μοι καὶ τοῦτο· τίς ἐστι τελεσιουργὸς τῆς παλιγγενεσίας;—[ὁ τοῦ] Θεοῦ παῖς ἄνθρωπος εἷς, θελήματι θεοῦ⟩⟩ ⟨ὑπουργῶν⟩.—Καὶ

1 περὶ (ante πάντα) om. Q 3–4 Lactantius *Div. inst.* 6. 25. 10: 'Trismegistus . . . sic locutus est: *Hoc verbum, o fili, adora et cole: cultus autem dei unus est, malum non esse.*' Fortasse ⟨κατὰ⟩ τοῦτον τὸν λόγον, ὦ τέκνον, ⟨τὸν θεὸν⟩ προσκύνει

In Libello XIII, codicum ABCDMQ et Turnebi lectiones adhibui. O = codicum ABCDM prima manus teste Reitzenstein.

5 τοῦ D Turn.: om. codd. cett. 5–6 ἐν ὄρει λόγος ἀπόκρυφος om. A 9 θειότητος Turn.: θειότητος cett. | οὐκ ABDM: καὶ οὐκ CQ Turn. 13 πυθομένου OQ: καὶ πυθομένου Turn., B[2] 14 παρὰ πάντα Q Turn.: περὶ πάντα ACM 17 ἀπηλλοτρίωσα Turn.: ἀπηνδρίωσα OQ | ἐνὸν

is all, and the All permeates all things, and has to do with all things.

This God, my son, I bid you worship and adore.[1] And there 23 b
is but one way to worship God; it is to be devoid of evil.

LIBELLVS XIII

A secret discourse of Hermes Trismegistus to his son Tat, concerning Rebirth.

Tat. In your general discourses, father, you spoke in riddles, 1
and did not make your meaning clear, when you were discussing the divinity of man. You said that no one can be saved until he has been born again; but you did not make known to me what you meant by this. After your talk with me . . ., I besought you to let me learn the doctrine of Rebirth, as this was the one part of your teaching that I did not know; but you did not think fit to transmit it to me at that time; you said, 'When you are ready to alienate yourself from the world, then I will teach it to you'. I am now prepared to receive it; I have alienated the thoughts of my heart from the world's deceptions; and I entreat you to supply what is yet lacking to me, as you said you would, when you promised to transmit the Rebirth to me. I know not, thrice-greatest one, from what womb a man can be born again, nor from what
seed.—*Hermes.* My son, the womb is Wisdom, conceiving in 2
silence; and the seed is the true Good.—*Tat.* And who is it, father, that begets? I am wholly at a loss.—*Hermes.* The Will of God, my son, is the begetter.—*Tat.* Tell me this too; who is the ministrant by whom the consummation of the Rebirth is brought to pass?—*Hermes.* Some man who is a son of God, working in subordination to God's will.—*Tat.* And what manner of

[1] Or perhaps, 'Let your worship and adoration of God, my son, be in accordance with this my teaching'.

ἐμοὶ A : *ἐν ἐμοὶ* cett. | *φρόνημα καὶ ἀπὸ* D Turn. 18 *μοι* Q Turn. : *μου* cett. 19 *ὡς* scripsi : *οἷς* codd., Turn. | *παλιγγενεσίαν* MQ Turn. : *παλιγγενεσίας* cett. 21 *ἀναγεννηθείη ἂν* scripsi : *ἐγεννήθη* O Turn. : *ἐγενήθη* man. pr. Q 22 *σοφία ἡ μήτρα, ἐν σιγῇ κύουσα* scripsi : *σοφία νοερὰ* (*σοφίαν νοερὰν* D) *ἐν σιγῇ* codd., Turn. 24–26 *Λέγε μοι . . . θελήματι θεοῦ* huc a § 4 transposui 25 *τελεσιουργὸς* scripsi : *γενεσιουργὸς* codd., Turn. 26 Fortasse *εἷς* ⟨*τις*⟩

ποταπὸς ὁ γεννώμενος, ὦ πάτερ; [[ἄμοιρος γὰρ τῆς ἐν ἐμοὶ
οὐσίας καὶ τῆς νοητῆς]]—Ἄλλος [ἔσται] ὁ γεννώμενος, θεοῦ
θεὸς παῖς, τὸ πᾶν, ἐν παντί· 〈〈ἄμοιρος γάρ 〈ἐστι〉 τῆς ⌜ἐν
ἐμοὶ⌝ οὐσίας, καὶ τῆς νοητῆς〉〉 〈μοῖραν ἔχει〉, ἐκ πασῶν
δυνάμεων συνεστώς.—Αἴνιγμα μοι λέγεις, ὦ πάτερ, καὶ οὐχ
ὡς πατὴρ υἱῷ διαλέγῃ.—Τοῦτο τὸ γένος, ὦ τέκνον, οὐ
διδάσκεται, ἀλλ' [[ὅταν θέλῃ]] ὑπὸ τοῦ θεοῦ, 〈〈ὅταν θέλῃ,〉〉
3 ἀναμιμνήσκεται.—Ἀδύνατά μοι λέγεις, ὦ πάτερ, καὶ βεβια-
σμένα. ὅθεν πρὸς ταῦτα ὀρθῶς ἀντειπεῖν ἔχω "〈ἆρ'〉 ἀλλότριος
[υἱὸς] πέφυκα τοῦ πατρικοῦ γένους;" μὴ φθόνει μοι, πάτερ·
γνήσιος υἱός εἰμί· διάφρασόν μοι τῆς παλιγγενεσίας τὸν
τρόπον.—Τί εἴπω, ὦ τέκνον; 〈〈τὸ πρᾶγμα τοῦτο οὐ διδάσκεται, οὐδὲ τῷ πλαστῷ τούτῳ ⌜στοιχείῳ⌝, δι' οὗ 〈σὺ ὁρᾷς〉,
ἐστιν ἰδεῖν.〉〉 οὐκ ἔχω λέγειν πλὴν τοῦτο· ὁρῶ[ν] τι〈ν'〉 ἐν
ἐμοὶ ἄπλαστον ἰδέαν γεγενημένην ἐξ ἐλέου θεοῦ, καὶ ἐμαυτὸν
〈δι〉εξελήλυθα εἰς ἀθάνατον σῶμα· καί εἰμι νῦν οὐχ ὁ πρίν,
ἀλλ' 〈ἀν〉εγεννήθην ἐν νῷ, [[τὸ πρᾶγμα τοῦτο οὐ διδάσκεται
οὐδὲ τῷ πλαστῷ τούτῳ στοιχείῳ δι' οὗ ἐστιν ἰδεῖν]] καὶ
διαλέλυταί μοι τὸ πρῶτον [σύνθετον] εἶδος. οὐκέτι κεχρω-
〈μάτ〉ισμαι καὶ ἁφὴν ἔχω καὶ μέτρον, ἀλλότριος δὲ τούτων
εἰμὶ νῦν, [ὁρᾷς με ὦ τέκνον ὀφθαλμοῖς] 〈καὶ πάντων〉 ὅσα
[δὲ] κατανοεῖς ἀτενίζων σωματικῇ ὁράσει. οὐκ ὀφθαλμοῖς
4 τ〈οι〉ούτοις θεωροῦμαι νῦν, ὦ τέκνον.—Εἰς μανίαν με οὐκ
ὀλίγην καὶ οἴστρησιν φρενῶν ἐνεσείσας, ὦ πάτερ. ἐμαυτὸν
γὰρ νῦν οὐχ ὁρῶ;—Εἴθε, ὦ τέκνον, καὶ σὺ σεαυτὸν διεξεληλύθεις, 〈ἵνα εἶδες, μὴ〉 ὡς οἱ ἐν ὕπνῳ ὀνειροπολούμενοι, 〈ἀλλὰ〉
χωρὶς ὕπνου.—[[Λέγε μοι καὶ τοῦτο· τίς ἐστι γενεσιουργὸς
τῆς παλιγγενεσίας;—Ὁ τοῦ θεοῦ παῖς ἄνθρωπος εἷς θελή-
5 ματι θεοῦ.—]] Νῦν τὸ λοιπόν, ὦ πάτερ, εἰς ἀφασίαν με
ἠνέγκας. [[τῶν πρὶν ἀπολειφθεὶς φρενῶν]]. τὸ γὰρ μέγεθος
βλέπω τὸ σὸν τὸ αὐτό, ὦ πάτερ, σὺν τῷ χαρακτῆρι.—Καὶ ἐν

3–4 ἐν ἐμοὶ codd., Turn.: ἐναίμου? σωματικῆς? 5 συνεστός DQ Turn. 9 ἔχω scripsi: θέλω codd., Turn. 13 Fortasse τῷ πλαστῷ τούτῳ 〈ἐκ〉 στοιχείω〈ν ὀργάνῳ〉 | σὺ ὁρᾷς addidi (ὁρᾷς add. Reitz.) 14 ὁρῶ τιν' Flussas: ὁρῶν τι ABCDQ Turn.: ὁρῶντι M 15 ἰδέαν scripsi: θέαν codd., Turn. 16 διεξελήλυθα Reitz.: ἐξελήλυθα codd., Turn. 17 'Vielleicht ἀνεγεννήθην' Reitz.: ἐγεννήθην codd., Turn. 19 διαλέλυταί scripsi: διὸ (δι' οὗ D) ἠμέληται OQ Turn.: διαμεμέλισται Keil | οὐκέτι Keil: οὐχ ὅτι OQ Turn. 19–20 κεχρωμάτισμαι scripsi: κεχρωΐσμαι Q: κέχρωσμαι cett. 21 καὶ πάντων ὅσα scripsi: ὅτε δὲ A (O?): ὅτι δὲ Q: ὅτε δὴ Turn. 22 σωματικῇ scripsi: σώματι καὶ O Turn. 23 τοιούτοις scripsi: τούτοις codd., Turn. | μανίην Q | μοι AB: με cett. 25–26 διεξεληλύθεις scripsi: διεξελή-

man is he that is brought into being by the Rebirth?—*Hermes.*
He that is born by that birth is another; he is a god, and son of
God. He is the All, and is in all; for he has no part in corporeal
substance; he partakes of the substance of things intelligible,[1]
being wholly composed of Powers of God.—*Tat.* Your words
are riddles, father; you do not speak to me as a father to his son.
—*Hermes.* This sort of thing cannot be taught, my son; but
God, when he so wills, recalls it to our memory.[2]—*Tat.* But 3
what you say is impossible, father; it does violence to common
sense. When you treat me thus, I have good reason to ask, 'Am
I an alien to my father's race?' Do not grudge me this boon,
father; I am your true-born son; explain to me what manner of
thing the Rebirth is.—*Hermes.* What can I say, my son? This
thing cannot be taught; and it is not possible for you to see it
with your organs of sight, which are fashioned out of material
elements. I can tell you nothing but this; I see that by God's
mercy there has come to be in me a form which is not fashioned
out of matter, and I have passed forth out of myself, and entered
into an immortal body. I am not now the man I was; I have
been born again in Mind, and the bodily shape which was mine
before has been put away from me. I am no longer an object
coloured and tangible, a thing of spatial dimensions; I am now
alien to all this, and to all that you perceive when you gaze with
bodily eyesight. To such eyes as yours, my son, I am not now
visible.—*Tat.* Father, you have driven me to raving madness. 4
Will you tell me that I do not at this moment see my own self?
—*Hermes.* Would that you too, my son, had passed forth out of
yourself, so that you might have seen, not as men see dream-
figures in their sleep, but as one who is awake.—*Tat.* Now 5
indeed, father, you have reduced me to speechless amazement.
Why, I see you, father, with your stature unchanged, and your
features the same as ever.—*Hermes.* Even in this you are

[1] I. e. incorporeal and divine.

[2] I. e. knowledge of these things comes to us only through reminiscence of our ante-natal state; and it is God that calls up the reminiscence in us.

λυθας codd., Turn. **27–29** λέγε μοι . . . θελήματι θεοῦ hinc ad § 2 transposui **29** ἀθανασίαν C: ἀφ?σίαν ex ἀθανασίαν corr. man. pr. B: ἀφασίαν codd. cett., Turn. **30** τῶν . . . φρενῶν hinc ad § 6 transposui **31** βλέπω τὸ σὸν τὸ αὐτὸ DMQ Turn.: βλέπω τὸ αὐτὸ codd. cett. | Fortasse σὲ γὰρ βλέπων τὸ μέγεθος ὁρῶ τὸ αὐτὸ ὄν

τούτῳ ψεύδη· τὸ γὰρ θνητὸν εἶδος καθ' ἡμέραν ἀλλάσσεται· χρόνῳ γὰρ τρέπεται εἰς αὔξησιν καὶ μείωσιν, ὡς ψεῦδος ⟨ὄν⟩.

6 —Τί οὖν ἀληθές ἐστιν, ὦ τρισμέγιστε;—Τὸ μὴ θολούμενον, ὦ τέκνον, τὸ μὴ ⟨πε⟩ριοριζόμενον, τὸ ἀχρώματον, τὸ ἀσχημάτιστον, [[τὸ ἄτρεπτον,]] τὸ γυμνόν, τὸ φα[ι]νόν, τὸ αὐτῷ καταληπτόν, ⟨⟨τὸ ἄτρεπτον,⟩⟩ τὸ ἀναλλοίωτον, τὸ ἀγαθόν [[τὸ ἀσώματον]].—Μέμηνα ὄντως, ὦ πάτερ, ⟨⟨τῶν πρὶν ἀπολειφθεὶς φρενῶν·⟩⟩ δοκοῦντος γάρ μου ὑπὸ σοῦ σοφοῦ γεγονέναι, ἐνεφράχθησαν αἱ αἰσθήσεις ⟨προβληθέντος⟩ τούτου μοι τοῦ νοήματος.—Οὕτως ἔχει, ὦ τέκνον. τὸ μὲν ἀνωφερὲς [ὡς πῦρ] καὶ κατωφερὲς [ὡς γῆ] καὶ ὑγρὸν [ὡς ὕδωρ] καὶ σύμπνοον [ὡς ἀὴρ] ⟨αἰσθήσει ὑποπίπτει· τὸ δὲ τούτοις ἀνόμοιον⟩ πῶς αἰσθητῶς οὕτω νοήσεις, τὸ μὴ σκληρόν, τὸ μὴ ὑγρόν, τὸ ⌜ἀσφίγγωτον⌝, τὸ μὴ διαλυόμενον, τὸ μόνον δυνάμει [καὶ ἐνεργείᾳ] νοούμενον, δεόμενον δὲ τοῦ δυναμένου νοεῖν

7a ⟨⟨τὸ ἀσώματον⟩⟩ [τὴν ἐν θεῷ γένεσιν];—ἀδύνατος οὖν εἰμι, ὦ πάτερ;—Μὴ γένοιτο, ὦ τέκνον. ἐπίσπασαι εἰς ἑαυτόν, καὶ ἐλεύσεται· θέλησον, καὶ γίνεται. κατάργησον τοῦ σώματος τὰς αἰσθήσεις, καὶ ἔσται ἡ γένεσις τῆς θεότητος.

7b ⟨. . . δεῖ⟩ καθᾶραι σεαυτὸν ἀπὸ τῶν ἀλόγων τῆς ὕλης τιμωριῶν.—Τιμωροὺς γὰρ ἐν ἐμαυτῷ ἔχω, ὦ πάτερ;—Οὐκ ὀλίγους, ὦ τέκνον, ἀλλὰ καὶ φοβεροὺς καὶ πολλούς.—Ἀγνοῶ, ὦ πάτερ.—Μία αὕτη, ὦ τέκνον, τιμωρία, ἡ ἄγνοια.

δευτέρα λύπη·
τρίτη ἀκρασία·
τετάρτη ἐπιθυμία·
πέμπτη ἀδικία·
ἕκτη πλεονεξία·
ἑβδόμη ἀπάτη·
ὀγδόη φθόνος·

1 ψεύδη B^1C : ψευδῆ MDQ : ψεύδει B : ψευδεῖ A Turn. | θνητῶν BCD Turn. 4 περιοριζόμενον scripsi : διοριζόμενον codd., Turn. 5 φανόν scripsi : φαῖνον codd., Turn. | αὐτὸ Q : αὐτῷ cett. 6 τὸ (ante ἀγαθόν) DQ Turn. : om. cett. 7-8 τῶν . . . φρενῶν huc a § 5 transposui 9-10 τούτου μοι scripsi : τούτου μου codd., Turn. 11 καὶ κατωφερὲς ABC : τὸ δὲ κατωφερὲς DQ Turn. 12-13 αἰσθήσει ὑποπίπτει· τὸ δὲ τούτοις ἀνόμοιον addidi (αἰσθήσει ὑποπίπτει· ὃ δὲ χωρὶς τούτων addidit Reitz.) 13 αἰσθητῷ D : αἰσθητῶς cett. | οὕτω scripsi : αὐτὸ codd., Turn. 14 ἀσφίγγωτον codd., Turn. : fortasse ἀσύνθετον | διαλυόμενον Parthey : διαδυόμενον OQ Turn. 15 δεόμενον man. post. B (om. man. pr. B) : δεομένου codd. cett., Turn. 16 οὖν μοι man. pr. B : οὖν εἰμι cett. 17 αὐτὸν man. pr. B : ἑαυτὸν codd. cett., Turn. : σεαυτὸν Parthey 17-18 καὶ καὶ ἐλεύσεται

mistaken. The mortal form changes day by day; it is altered by
lapse of time, and becomes larger and smaller; for it is an
illusion.—*Tat.* What then is real, thrice-greatest one?—*Hermes.* 6
That which is not sullied by matter, my son, nor limited by boundaries, that which has no colour and no shape, that which is without integument, and is luminous, that which is apprehended by itself alone, that which is changeless and unalterable, that which is good. —*Tat.* I must indeed have gone mad, father; I have lost the wits I had. I thought your teaching had made me wise; but when you put this thought before me, my senses are stopped up.[1]—*Hermes.* It is even so, my son. The fire which rises, and the earth which sinks, the liquid water, and the air we breathe, are perceived by the senses; but how can you perceive by mere sense a thing of other nature, a thing that is neither rigid nor fluid, that is incomposite and indissoluble, a thing which can be apprehended only by divine power, and demands one who has power to apprehend
the incorporeal?—*Tat.* Is it then beyond my power, father?— 7 a
Hermes. Heaven forbid, my son. Draw it into you, and it will come; will it, and it comes to be. Stop the working of your bodily senses, and then will deity be born in you.

But if you would be born again, you must cleanse yourself 7 b
from the irrational torments of matter.[2]—*Tat.* What, father, have I torturers within me?—*Hermes.* Yes, my son, and not a few; they are terrible, and they are many. *Tat.* I do not know them, father.—*Hermes.* This very ignorance, my son, is one of the torments.

The second is Grief;[3]
the third is Incontinence;
the fourth is Desire;
the fifth is Injustice;
the sixth is Covetousness;
the seventh is Deceitfulness;[4]
the eighth is Envy;

[1] I. e. I find myself unable to apprehend it.

[2] I. e. get rid of the evil passions which arise from the material body and from material objects of desire.

[3] The passages printed in smaller type were probably not written by the author of the Libellus, but subsequently added by some one else.

[4] Or 'Being deceived', i. e. Error.

Q: fortasse *καὶ κατελεύσεται* **18** *γίνεται* codd., Turn.: fortasse *γενήσεται* **19** *ἔσται* Turn.: *εἴτε* OQ | *ἡ* om. Q **20** *κάθαιρε* A: *κάθαραι* codd. cett., Turn. (*καθάραι* ex *κάθαραι* corr. man. pr. B) **21** *τιμωριῶν* codd.: *τιμωρῶν* Turn. | *ἑαυτῷ* ADQ Turn.: *ἐμαυτῷ* cett. **22–23** *ἀλλὰ καὶ . . . Μία αὕτη, ὦ τέκνον* om. man. pr. M **24** *δευτέρα δὲ λύπη* Q Turn.

ἐνάτη δόλος·
δεκάτη ὀργή·
ἑνδεκάτη προπέτεια·
δωδεκάτη κακία.

εἰσὶ δὲ καὶ

αὗται τὸν ἀριθμὸν δώδεκα, ὑπὸ δὲ ταύταις

πλείονες ἄλλαι, ὦ τέκνον, ⟨αἳ⟩ διὰ της [[το δεσμωτηρίου τοῦ σώματος]] αἰσθήσεως πάσχειν ἀναγκάζουσι τὸν ἐν ⟨⟨τῷ δεσμωτηρίῳ τοῦ σώματος⟩⟩ δεδε⟨μ⟩ένον ἄνθρωπον. ἀφίστανται δὲ αὗται [οὐκ] ἀθρόως ἀπὸ τοῦ ἐλεηθέντος ὑπὸ τοῦ θεοῦ, καὶ οὕτω συνίσταται ὁ ⟨⟨λόγος⟩⟩. ⟨οὗτος ὁ⟩ τῆς παλιγγενεσίας τρόπος [καὶ] [[λόγος]].

8a λοιπὸν σιώπησον, ὦ τέκνον, καὶ εὐφήμησον· ⌜καὶ διὰ τοῦτο οὐ καταπαύσει⌝ τὸ ἔλεος εἰς ἡμᾶς ἀπὸ τοῦ θεοῦ.

8b χαῖρε λοιπόν, ὦ τέκνον, ἀνακαθαιρόμενος ταῖς τοῦ θεοῦ δυνάμεσιν· ⟨πάρεισι γὰρ⟩ εἰς συνάρθρωσιν τοῦ λόγου. ἦλθεν ἡμῖν γνῶσις θεοῦ· ταύτης ἐλθούσης, ὦ τέκνον, ἐξηλάθη ἡ ἄγνοια.

8c ἦλθεν ἡμῖν [γνῶσις] χαρά[ς]· παραγενομένης ταύτης, ὦ τέκνον, ἡ λύπη φεύξεται εἰς τοὺς χωροῦντας αὐτήν.

9 ⟨τρίτην⟩ δύναμιν καλῶ ἐπὶ χαρᾷ τὴν ἐγκράτειαν. ὦ δύναμις ἡδίστη· προσλάβωμεν αὐτήν, ὦ τέκνον, ἀσμενέστατα. πῶς ἅμα τῷ παραγενέσθαι ἀπώσατο τὴν ἀκρασίαν.

τετάρτην δὲ νῦν καλῶ καρτερίαν, τὴν κατὰ τῆς ἐπιθυμίας δύναμιν. ⟨. . .⟩

ὁ βαθμὸς οὗτος, ὦ τέκνον, δικαιοσύνης ἐστὶν ἕδρασμα. [[χωρὶς γὰρ κτίσεως]] ἰδὲ πῶς τὴν ἀδικίαν ἐξήλασεν· ⟨⟨χωρὶς γὰρ κρίσεως⟩⟩ ἐδικαιώθημεν, ὦ τέκνον, ἀδικίας ἀπούσης.

ἕκτην δύναμιν καλῶ εἰς ἡμᾶς τὴν κατὰ τῆς πλεονεξίας, ⟨τὴν⟩ κοινωνίαν. ἀποστάσης δὲ ⟨τῆς πλεονεξίας . . .

ἑβδόμην⟩ ἐπικαλῶ τὴν ἀλήθειαν. φεῦγε[ι] ἀπάτη· ἀλήθεια παραγίνεται.

ἰδὲ πῶς τὸ ἀγαθὸν πεπλήρωται, ὦ τέκνον, παραγενομένης τῆς ἀληθείας. φθόνος γὰρ ἀφ' ἡμῶν ἀπέστη ⟨καὶ αἱ λοιπαὶ τιμωρίαι⟩.

5 καὶ Q Turn., om. cett. 6 ταύτας ACM : ταύτας ex ταύταις B 7–9 αἳ διὰ τῆς αἰσθήσεως πάσχειν ἀναγκάζουσι τὸν ἐν τῷ δεσμωτηρίῳ τοῦ σώματος δεδεμένον ἄνθρωπον scripsi : διὰ τοῦτο δεσμωτηρίου τοῦ σώματος αἰσθητικῶς πάσχειν ἀναγκάζουσι τὸν ἐνδιάθετον ἄνθρωπον codd., Turn. 8 Fortasse ⟨κακὰ⟩ πάσχειν 10 οὐκ seclusi : ⟨μόνον⟩ οὐκ Reitz. | τοῦ (ante θεοῦ) om. A 14 καταπαύσει DQ Turn. : καταπαύσω ACM : καταπαύσεται Reitz. | Fortasse καὶ

the ninth is Fraud;
the tenth is Anger;
the eleventh is Rashness;
the twelfth is Vice.[1]

These are twelve in number; and under them There are many others also, my son; and by means of the senses they force the man who is bound in the prison of the body to suffer what they inflict. But when God has had mercy on a man, they depart from him together, one and all; and then is reason[2] built up in him. Such is the manner of the Rebirth.

And now, my son, speak not, but keep solemn silence; so will 8 a
the mercy come down on us from God.

Rejoice now, my son; you are being cleansed by the Powers 8 b
of God; for they have come to build up in you the body of reason.[3] The knowledge of God has come to us; and at its coming, my son, ignorance has been driven out.

Joy has come to us; and at her coming, my son, Grief will flee away, to 8 c
enter into those in whom there is room for her.

And after Joy, I summon a third Power, even Continence. O sweetest 9
Power! Let us receive her, my son, most gladly. See how, at the instant of her coming, she has pushed Incontinence away.

And now I summon the fourth Power, Endurance, the opponent of Desire. . . .

And this, my son, is the tribunal on which Justice sits enthroned. See how she has driven out Injustice. We have been justified, my son, without being brought to judgement; for Injustice is no longer here.

As the sixth Power, I call to us Unselfishness, the opponent of Covetousness. And when Covetousness has departed, ...

As the seventh, I invoke Truth. Flee away, Deceit; for Truth has come.

See, my son, how, on the coming of Truth, the Good is completed; for Envy has departed from us, ⟨and the other torments also⟩.

[1] Or 'Malice'. [2] Or 'the Word (of God)'.

[3] Or 'of the Word (of God)'. The Logos is an organism, of which the several Powers of God are the constituent parts; and this organism is built up in the reborn man, as the body is built up out of the several members.

οὕτω κατελεύσεται 17 *γνῶσις τοῦ θεοῦ* A Turn. | *ταύτης δὲ ἐλθούσης* DQ Turn. 19 *χαρά* scripsi: *γνῶσις χαρᾶς* codd., Turn. 21 *τρίτην* addidit Reitz. | *ἐπὶ χαρὰν* A 22 *αὐτὴν ὦ τέκνον* DMQ Turn.: *ὦ τέκνον, αὐτὴν* cett. 23 *ἀπώσεται* D 25 Lacunam significavit Reitz. 27 *κρίσεως* Parthey: *κτίσεως* OQ Turn. 28 *ἀπούσης* AQ Turn.: *ἀπούσης* ex *ἀπρύτης* corr. man. pr. B: *ἀτρύτης* CM: *ἀπάσης* D 29 *κατ' αὐτῆς* D: *κατὰ τῆς* cett. | *τὴν* (ante *κοινωνίαν*) addidit Reitz. 31 *ἐπικαλῶ* scripsi: *ἔτι καλῶ* codd., Turn. | *φεῦγε* Plasberg: *φεύγει* AB: *καὶ φεύγει* CDMQ Turn. 33 *πεπλήρωκα* D: *πεπλήρωμα* Q | *παραγενομένης* Patritius: *παραγινομένης* codd., Turn.

τῇ δὲ ἀληθείᾳ καὶ τὸ ἀγαθὸν ἐπεγένετο ἅμα ζωῇ καὶ φωτί.
καὶ οὐκέτι ἐπῆλθεν οὐδεμία τοῦ σκότους τιμωρία, ἀλλ'
10 ἐξέπτησαν [νικηθεῖσαι] ῥοίζῳ. [[ἔγνωκας, ὦ τέκνον, τῆς
παλιγγενεσίας τὸν τρόπον]]

[τῆς δεκάδος παραγινομένης]

⟨οὕτω δή⟩, ὦ τέκνον, συνετέθη ⟨ἡ⟩ νοερὰ [γένεσις] ⟨οὐσία⟩,

[καὶ τὴν δωδεκάτην ἐξελαύνει,]

καὶ ἐθεώ[ρη]θημεν τῇ ⟨ταύτης⟩ γενέσει. ὅστις οὖν ἔτυχε κατὰ
τὸ ἔλεος τῆς κατὰ θεὸν γενέσεως, τὴν σωματικὴν αἴσθησιν
καταλιπὼν ἑαυτὸν γνωρίζει ἐκ [τούτων] ⟨δυνάμεων⟩ συνιστά-
μενον, καὶ ⟨γνωρίσας⟩ εὐφραίνεται.—
11 a ⟨Οὐσί⟩α καινὴ[ς] γενόμενος ὑπὸ τοῦ θεοῦ, ὦ πάτερ, φαντά-
ζομαι οὐχ ὁράσει ὀφθαλμῶν, ἀλλὰ τῇ [διὰ δυνάμεων] νοητικῇ
13 a ἐνεργείᾳ.—⟨⟨Αὕτη ἐστὶν ἡ παλιγγενεσία, ὦ τέκνον, τὸ
μηκέτι φαντάζεσθαι [εἰς] τὸ σῶμα τὸ τριχῇ διαστατόν,⟩⟩
⟨ἀλλὰ τὸ ἀσώματον.⟩—⟨⟨Πάτερ, τὸ πᾶν ὁρῶ [καὶ] ἐμαυτὸν
11 b ⟨ὄντα⟩, ἐν τῷ νοΐ⟩⟩ ⟨ὁρῶν⟩. ἐν οὐρανῷ εἰμι, ἐν γῇ, ἐν ὕδατι,
ἐν ἀέρι· ἐν ζῴοις εἰμί, ἐν φυτοῖς· ἐν γαστρί, πρὸ γαστρός,
μετὰ γαστέρα· πανταχοῦ ⟨πάρειμι⟩.—⟨⟨Ἔγνωκας, ὦ τέκνον,
τῆς παλιγγενεσίας τὸν τρόπον.⟩⟩—
11 c ['Αλλ' ἔτι τοῦτό μοι εἰπέ, πῶς αἱ τιμωρίαι τοῦ σκότους, οὖσαι ἀριθμῷ
δώδεκα, ὑπὸ δέκα δυνάμεων ἀπωθοῦνται. τίς ὁ τρόπος, ὦ τρισμέγιστε;
12 —Τὸ σκῆνος τοῦτο, [[καὶ]] ὦ τέκνον, ὃ ⟨⟨καὶ⟩⟩ διεξεληλύθαμεν, ἐκ τοῦ
ζῳοφόρου κύκλου συνέστη, [[καὶ τούτου συνεστῶτος ἐξ ἀριθμῶν δώδεκα
ὄντων τὸν ἀριθμόν,]] ⟨γεννῶντος⟩ φύσεως μιᾶς παντομόρφου⟨ς⟩ ἰδέας εἰς
πλάνην τοῦ ἀνθρώπου· ⟨⟨καὶ τούτου συνεστῶτος ἐκ ζῳδίων δώδεκα ὄντων
τὸν ἀριθμόν,⟩⟩ διαζυγ⟨ί⟩αι ἐν αὐταῖς εἰσιν, ὦ τέκνον, ⟨δώδεκα.⟩ ⟨⟨εἰσὶ δὲ
καὶ ἀδιορίστοι,⟩⟩ ἡνωμέναι ἐν τῇ πράξει· ἀχώριστος ⟨γάρ⟩ ἐστιν ἡ προ-
πέτεια τῆς ὁρμῆς. [[εἰσὶ δὲ καὶ ἀδιόριστοι]] εἰκότως οὖν [[κατὰ τὸν ὄρθον
λόγον]] τὴν ἀπόστασιν ποιοῦνται, καθὼς ⟨εἶπον, ἀθρόως⟩. καὶ ⟨⟨κατὰ [τὸν
ὄρθον] λόγον⟩⟩ ἀπὸ δέκα δυνάμεων ἐλαύνονται, τουτέστιν ἀπὸ τῆς δεκάδος·

1 Fortasse (post ἐξηλάθη ἡ ἄγνοια, § 8 b), ⟨παρεγένετο ἡ ἀλήθεια·⟩ τῇ δὲ ἀληθείᾳ κ.τ.λ. 3 κινηθεῖσαι B: νικηθεῖσαι cett. 3–4 ἔγνωκας . . . τρόπον hinc ad § 11 b *fin.* transposui 5–8 τῆς δεκάδος παραγινομένης, ὦ τέκνον, ἣ τὴν δωδεκάδα ἐξελαύνει, συνετέθη ἡ νοερὰ γένεσις, καὶ ἐθεώθημεν Reitz. 6 ἡ addidit Reitz. 8 ἐθεώθημεν Reitz.: ἐθεωρήθημεν OQ Turn. | γενέσει codd., Turn.: fortasse συνθέσει 10 Fortasse ἐκ ⟨ζωῆς καὶ φωτός⟩ συνιστάμενον 10–11 ἑαυτὸν γνωρίζει ⟨ἐκ φωτὸς καὶ ζωῆς τυγχάνοντα, καὶ⟩ ἐκ τούτων συνιστάμενος [καὶ] εὐφραίνεται coni. Reitz. | συνιστάμενον scripsi: συνιστάμενος codd., Turn. 12 οὐσία καινὴ scripsi: ἀκλινὴς codd.,

Truth[1] has come to us, and on it has followed the Good, with Life and Light. No longer has there come upon us any of the torments of darkness; they have flown away with rushing wings.

Thus, my son, has the intellectual being[2] been made up in us; 10
and by its coming to be, we have been made gods. Whoever then has by God's mercy attained to this divine birth, abandons bodily sense; he knows himself to be composed of Powers of God, and knowing this, is glad.—

Tat. Father, God has made me a new being, and I perceive 11 a
things now, not with bodily eyesight, but by the working of mind.—*Hermes.* Even so it is, my son, when a man is born 13 a
again; it is no longer body of three dimensions that he perceives, but the incorporeal.—*Tat.* Father, now that I see in mind,
I see myself to be the All. I am in heaven and in earth, in 11 b
water and in air; I am in beasts and plants; I am a babe in the womb, and one that is not yet conceived, and one that has been born; I am present everywhere.—*Hermes.* Now, my son, you know what the Rebirth is.—

[*Tat.* But tell me further; how is it that the torments of darkness, which are 11 c
twelve in number, are driven off by ten Powers? How does this come about,
thrice-greatest one?—*Hermes.* This earthly tabernacle,[3] my son, out of which 12
we have passed forth, has been put together by the working of the Zodiac, which produces manifold forms of one and the same thing[4] to lead men astray; and as the Signs of which the Zodiac consists are twelve in number, the forms produced by it, my son, fall into twelve divisions. But at the same time they are inseparable, being united in their action; for the reckless vehemence of irrational impulse is indivisible. It is with good reason then that they all depart together, as I said before. And it is also in accordance with reason that they are driven out by ten Powers, that is, by the Decad; for the Decad, my son, is

[1] Or 'Reality'.

[2] I. e. that which was previously called the Logos.

[3] I. e. the body.

[4] These 'manifold forms' are the several 'torments', i. e. the twelve different kinds of evil passion.

Turn. | τοῦ om. BCDMQ **16–17** Fortasse Πάτερ, ἐν τῷ νοΐ ὁρῶν, τὸ πᾶν ὁρῶ ἐμαυτὸν ὄντα **19–20** ἔγνωκας . . . τρόπον huc a § 10 transposui **23** ὦ τέκνον, ὃ καὶ scripsi (ὃ καί, ὦ τέκνον Keil) : ὦ τέκνον Turn. : καὶ ὦ τέκνον AB : καὶ ὃ τέκνον C : ὃ τέκνον DQ : ὃ (corr. ex ὦ) τέκνον M **24** ζωηφόρου Turn. **25** παντομόρφους scripsi : παντομόρφου codd., Turn. **26** ἐκ ζῳδίων scripsi (γράφεται ἐκ ζωδίων B² in marg.): ἐξ ἀριθμῶν OQ Turn. **27** διαζυγίαι scripsi : διαζυγαὶ codd., Turn. **29** ὁρμῆς scripsi : ὀργῆς codd., Turn. | ἀόριστοι DQ Turn. : ἀδιόριστοι cett. **30** εἶπον, ἀθρόως addidi (vide § 7 b *fin.*) **31** ἐλαύνονται scripsi : ἐλαύνομαι B : ἐλαυνόμεναι cett.

ἡ γὰρ δεκάς, ὦ τέκνον, ἐστὶ ψυχογόνος. ζωὴ δὲ καὶ φῶς ἡνωμέναι εἰσὶν ἑνάς· ὁ ⟨δὲ⟩ τῆς ἑνάδος ἀριθμὸς πέφυκε τοῦ [πνεύματος] ⟨τῆς δεκάδος ἀρχή⟩. ἡ ἑνὰς οὖν κατὰ λόγον τὴν δεκάδα ⟨ἐμπερι⟩έχει [καὶ ἡ δεκὰς τὴν ἑνάδα].]

13 a [[*Πάτερ, τὸ πᾶν ὁρῶ καὶ ἐμαυτὸν ἐν τῷ νοΐ.*]] [[*Αὕτη ἐστὶν ἡ παλιγγενεσία, ὦ τέκνον, τὸ μηκέτι φαντάζεσθαι εἰς τὸ σῶμα τὸ τριχῇ διαστατόν.*]]

13 b [[*διὰ τὸν λόγον τοῦτον τὸν περὶ τῆς παλιγγενεσίας εἰς ὃν ὑπεμνηματισάμην, ἵνα μὴ ὦμεν διάβολοι τοῦ παντὸς εἰς τοὺς πολλούς, εἰς οὓς ὁ θεὸς αὐτὸς θέλει.*]]

14 *Εἰπέ μοι, ὦ πάτερ, τὸ σῶμα τοῦτο τὸ ἐκ δυνάμεων συνεστὸς λύσιν ἕξει ποτέ;—Εὐφήμησον, καὶ μὴ ἀδύνατα φθέγγου, ἐπεὶ [ἁμαρτήσεις καὶ] ἀσεβή⟨σεις. μὴ ἐσβέσ⟩θη [σεται] σου ὁ ὀφθαλμὸς τοῦ νοῦ; τὸ αἰσθητὸν τῆς φύσεως σῶμα πόρρωθέν ἐστι [τῆς] ⟨τοῦ⟩ οὐσιώδους [γενέσεως]· τὸ μὲν γάρ ἐστι διαλυτόν, τὸ δὲ ἀδιάλυτον, καὶ τὸ μὲν θνητόν, τὸ δὲ ἀθάνατον. ἀγνοεῖς ὅτι θεὸς πέφυκας καὶ τοῦ ἑνὸς παῖς, ὃ κἀγώ;—*

15 *Ἐβουλόμην, ὦ πάτερ, τὴν διὰ τοῦ ὕμνου εὐλογίαν ⟨μαθεῖν⟩, ἥν, ⟨⟨καθὼς⟩⟩ ἔφης, ἐπὶ τὴν ὀγδοάδα γενομένου σου ἀκού-σ⟨εσθ⟩αί ⟨σε⟩ τῶν δυνάμεων [[καθὼς]] [ὀγδοάδα] ὁ Ποιμάνδρης ἐθέσπισε.—⟨Ὦ⟩ τέκνον, καλῶς σπεύδεις· ⟨⟨κεκάθαρσαι γάρ,⟩⟩ λυσάμ⟨ενος⟩ τὸ σκῆνος [[κεκαθαρμένος γάρ.]] ὁ Ποιμάνδρης, ὁ τῆς αὐθεντίας νοῦς, πλέον μοι τῶν ἐγγεγραμμένων οὐ παρέδωκεν, εἰδὼς ὅτι ἀπ' ἐμαυτοῦ δυνήσομαι πάντα νοεῖν, καὶ ἀκούειν ὧν βούλομαι, καὶ ὁρᾶν τὰ πάντα· καὶ ἐπέτρεψέ μοι ἐκεῖνος ⌈ποιεῖν τὰ καλά.⌉ διὸ [κ] αἱ ἐν πᾶσι[ν αἱ] δυνάμεις καὶ ἐν ἐμοὶ ᾄδουσι.—Θέλω, πάτερ, ἀκοῦσαι ⟨⟨ταῦτα⟩⟩,*

16 *καὶ βούλομαι [[ταῦτα]] νοῆσαι.—Ἡσύχασον, ὦ τέκνον, καὶ τῆς ἁρμοζούσης ⟨⟨τῇ παλιγγενεσίᾳ⟩⟩ νῦν ἄκουε εὐλογίας τὸν*

2 ἑνάς scripsi: ἔνθα codd., Turn. 3 ἐμπεριέχει scripsi: ἔχει codd., Turn. | καὶ ἡ DMQ Turn.: ἡ δὲ cett. 5–7 Πάτερ . . . νοΐ et Αὕτη . . . διαστατόν hinc transposui: vide post § 11 a 8–10 διὰ τὸν . . . θέλει hinc transposui: vide post § 22 b 10 εἰς οὓς αὐτοὺς θέλει ὁ θεός DQ Turn.: εἰς οὓς ὁ θεὸς αὐτὸς θέλει codd. cett. 11 Fortasse Ἀλλ' ἔτι τοῦτό μοι εἰπέ (vide § 11 c) | τὸ (ante σῶμα) om. Turn. | τὸ (ante ἐκ) om. AB | δυνάμεως AB 11–12 συνεστὼς BCDMQ 12 ἕξει scripsi: ἔχει D: ἴσχει codd. cett., Turn. 13 ἀσεβήσεις. μὴ ἐσβέσθη scripsi: ἀποσβεσθήσεταί Reitz.: ἀσεβηθήσεταί ABCMQ Turn. | σου ex σοι A: μου BC: σου cett. 14 ὁ om. Turn. 14–15 πόρρωθέν ἐστι ⟨τοῦ ἐκ⟩ τῆς οὐσιώδους γενέσεως Reitz. | Fortasse τὸ αἰσθητὸν σῶμα πόρρωθέν ἐστι τῆς τοῦ οὐσιώδους φύσεως 16 Desinit Q in verbis τὸ μὲν θνητὸν 17 τοῦ ἑνὸς codd., Turn.: fortasse τοῦ

the number by which soul is generated. Life and Light united are a Unit; and the number One is the source of the Decad. It is reasonable then that the Unit contains in itself the Decad.[1]—]

Tat. Tell me, father, will this body which is composed of 14
divine Powers[2] ever suffer dissolution?—*Hermes.* Hush! Speak not of a thing that cannot be; it would be impious to say that. Has the eye of your mind been blinded? The physical body, which is an object of sense, differs widely from that other body, which is of the nature of true Being. The one is dissoluble, the other is indissoluble. The one is mortal, the other is immortal. Do you not know that you have become a god, and son of the One,[3] even as I have?—

Tat. Father, I would fain be taught that hymn of praise which, 15
as you have told us, Poimandres predicted that you would hear the Powers sing when you had ascended to the eighth sphere of heaven.—*Hermes.* My son, you do well to seek that; for you are purified, now that you have put away from you the earthly tabernacle. Poimandres, the Mind of the Sovereignty, told me no more than stands written in the book;[4] for he knew that I should be able of myself to apprehend all things, and to hear what I would, and to see all; and he left it to me . . . .[5] And so the Powers which are in all things sing within me also.—*Tat.* Father, I would fain hear that song; I wish to make it mine
in thought.—*Hermes.* Be still then, my son, and listen to the 16

[1] The conclusion implied is that the *ten* Powers act *as one* in driving out the evil passions.

[2] That is, the new self of the man who is reborn.

[3] Perhaps, 'son of God'.

[4] I. e. in Corp. I, which the author of Corp. XIII takes to have been written by Hermes.

[5] 'to think out what he did not tell me'?

θεοῦ **18** *πάτερ, διὰ τὴν τοῦ* B | *εὐλογίαν* D Turn.: *ἀλογίαν* C: *ἀλαλογίαν* A: *ἀναλογίαν* ex *ἀλογίαν* corr. man. pr. B | *μαθεῖν* addidi (*μανθάνειν* add. Reitz.) **19** *σου* Reitz.: *μου* O Turn. **19–20** *ἀκούσεσθαί σε* scripsi: *ἀκοῦσαι* codd., Turn. **21–22** *σπεύδεις· κεκάθαρσαι γάρ, λυσάμενος τὸ σκῆνος* scripsi: *σπεύδεις λῦσαι τὸ σκῆνος, κεκαθαρμένος γάρ* codd., Turn. **23** *ἐγγραμμένων* BC **26** *ποιεῖν τὰ καλά* codd.: fortasse *νοεῖν τὰ ἄλλα* **26–27** *αἱ ἐν πᾶσι δυνάμεις καὶ ἐν ἐμοὶ* scripsi: *καὶ ἐν πᾶσιν αἱ δυνάμεις καὶ ἐν ἐμοὶ* codd.: *καὶ ἐν πᾶσιν καὶ αἱ δυνάμεις αἱ ἐν ἐμοὶ* Turn.

ὕμνον [[τῆς παλιγγενεσίας]], ὃν οὐκ ἔκρινα οὕτως εὐκόλως ἐκφάναι ⟨⟨σοι⟩⟩ [[εἰ μὴ [[σοι]] ἐπὶ τέλει τοῦ παντός]].

[ὅθεν τοῦτο οὐ διδάσκεται, ⟨⟨εἰ μὴ ἐπὶ τέλει τοῦ παντός,⟩⟩ ἀλλὰ κρύπτεται ἐν σιγῇ.] [οὕτως οὖν, [ὦ τέκνον,] στὰς ἐν ὑπαίθρῳ τόπῳ, νότῳ ἀνέμῳ ἀποβλέπων, περὶ καταφορὰν ἡλίου [δύνοντος] προσκύνει· ὁμοίως ⟨δὲ⟩ καὶ ἀνιόντος πρὸς ἀπηλιώτην.] [ἡσύχασον, ὦ τέκνον.]

17 [ὑμνῳδία κρυπτή.]

⟨⟨Ἀνοιγήτω μοι πᾶς μοχλὸς ⟨τοῦ⟩ ⟨⟨κόσμου⟩⟩·
πᾶσα φύσις [[κόσμου]] προσδεχέσθω τοῦ ὕμνου τὴν ἀκοήν.
ἀνοίγηθι γῆ, [[ἀνοιγήτω μοι πᾶς μοχλὸς]] [ὄμβρου], τὰ δένδρα μὴ σείεσθε·
ὑμνεῖν μέλλω τὸν [τῆς κτίσεως κύριον] καὶ τὸ πᾶν καὶ τὸ ἓν ⟨ὄντα⟩.
ἀνοίγητε οὐρανοί, ἄνεμοί τε στῆτε·
ὁ κύκλος ὁ ἀθάνατος [τοῦ θεοῦ] προσδεξάσθω μου τὸν λόγον.
μέλλω γὰρ ὑμνεῖν τὸν κτίσαντα τὰ πάντα,
τὸν πήξαντα τὴν γῆν καὶ οὐρανὸν κρεμάσαντα,
[καὶ] ⟨τὸν⟩ ⌜ἐπιτάξαντα⌝ ἐκ τοῦ ὠκεανοῦ τὸ γλυκὺ ὕδωρ εἰς τὴν οἰκουμένην [καὶ ἀοίκητον],
ὑπάρχειν εἰς διατροφὴν [καὶ κτίσιν] πάντων ⌜ἀνθρώπων⌝,
[τὸν] ⟨καὶ⟩ ἐπιτάξαντα πῦρ φανῆναι
εἰς πᾶσαν πρᾶξιν θεοῖς τε καὶ ἀνθρώποις.
δῶμεν πάντες ὁμοῦ αὐτῷ τὴν εὐλογίαν,
τῷ ἐπὶ τῶν οὐρανῶν μετεώρῳ, τῷ πάσης φύσεως κτίστῃ.
18 οὗτός ἐστιν ὁ τοῦ νο⟨ός⟩ μου ὀφθαλμός·
[καὶ] δέξαιτο τῶν δυνάμεών μου τὴν εὐλογίαν.
αἱ δυνάμεις αἱ ἐν ἐμοί, ὑμνεῖτε τὸ ἓν καὶ τὸ πᾶν·
συνᾴσατε τῷ θελήματί μου, πᾶσαι αἱ ἐν ἐμοὶ δυνάμεις.
γνῶσις ἁγία, φωτισθεὶς ἀπὸ σοῦ,
διὰ σοῦ τὸ νοητὸν φῶς ὑμνῶ[ν].
⟨. . .⟩ χαίρω ἐν χαρᾷ νοῦ·
πᾶσαι δυνάμεις [ὑμνεῖτε] ⟨χαίρετε⟩ σὺν ἐμοί.
καὶ σύ μοι, ἐγκράτεια, ὕμνει·
⟨καρτερία . . .⟩·
δικαιοσύνη μου, τὸ δίκαιον ὕμνει δι' ἐμοῦ·

4 στὰς ex τὰς corr. man. pr. B : τὰς ACDM Turn. 5 ἀποβλέπων om. A 5–6 καταφορὰν ἡλίου D Turn. : καταφορὰν τοῦ ἡλίου codd. cett. 8 ὑμνῳδία A : υμνωδια κρυπτη Turn. : ὑμνῳδία κρυπτὴ λόγος δ' BCDM 9 μυχὸς B²:

hymn of praise which is appropriate to the Rebirth. I had not meant to make it known to you so readily. [ ][1]

Let every bar[2] of the universe be flung open to me; 17
and let all nature[3] receive the sound of my hymn.
Be thou opened,[4] O Earth, and ye trees, wave not your boughs;
I am about to sing the praise of Him who is both the All and the One.
Be ye opened,[4] ye heavens, and ye winds, be still;
let the immortal sphere of heaven receive my utterance.
For I am about to sing the praise of Him who created all things,
who fixed the earth, and hung heaven above;
who made the sweet water flow from Ocean into the lands wherein men dwell,
that it might serve for the sustenance of all mankind,[5]
and gave command that fire should come forth,
to be used by gods and men in all their works.
Let us all with one accord give praise to Him,
who is seated high upon the heavens, creator of all that is.
It is He that is the eye of my mind; 18
may He accept the praise sung by my Powers.
Ye Powers that are within me, praise ye the One and the All;
sing ye in concord with my will, all ye Powers that are within me.
O holy Knowledge, by thee am I illumined,
and through thee do I sing praise to the incorporeal Light.[6]
. . . I rejoice in joy of mind;
rejoice with me, all ye Powers.
And do thou, O Continence, sing praise;
⟨and thou, Endurance;⟩
and thou, my Justice, praise the Just through me;

[1] ['This hymn therefore is not taught, except at the end of all, but is kept hidden in silence.'] ['You must take your stand then in a place open to the sky, and worship thus, facing to the South, at the hour of sunset; and you must worship in like manner at sunrise, facing to the East.']
[2] Perhaps, 'every recess'.
[3] Or 'each several thing (in the physical world)'.
[4] Perhaps, 'Be silent'.
[5] Perhaps, 'of all living creatures'.
[6] Literally, 'the Light which mind (alone) can apprehend'.

μοχλὸς cett. **12** Fortasse σίγησον ἡ γῆ **16** ἀνοίγετε AB: fortasse σιγᾶτε | τε om. AB **17** τοῦ θεοῦ codd.: fortasse τοῦ αἰθέρος **19** τὰ πάντα om. D: τὰ om. Turn. **21** ἐπιτάξαντα codd.: fortasse ὀχετεύσαντα **23** καὶ κτίσιν O: καὶ κτῆσιν Turn.: 'scheint καὶ κτ. späterer Zusatz' Reitz. | πάντων τῶν ἀνθρώπων A: fortasse πάντων τῶν ζωὴν ἐχόντων **28** νοός μου Reitz.: νόμου DM: νοῦ ABC Turn. **29** μου om. AB **33** ὑμνῶ scripsi: ὑμνῶν codd., Turn.

κοινωνία ἡ ἐμή, τὸ πᾶν ὕμνει δι' ἐμοῦ·
ὕμνει ἀλήθεια τὴν ἀλήθειαν.
τὸ ἀγαθόν, ἀγαθὸν ⟨τὸ ἐν ἐμοί,⟩ ὕμνει·
ζωὴ καὶ φῶς, ἀφ' ὑμῶν εἰς ὑμᾶς χωρεῖ ἡ εὐλογία.
εὐχαριστῶ σοι, πάτερ, ἐνέργεια τῶν δυνάμεών ⟨μου⟩·
εὐχαριστῶ σοι, θεέ, ⌈δύναμις τῶν ἐνεργειῶν μου⌉.
[[ὁ σὸς λόγος δι' ἐμοῦ ὑμνεῖ σέ·]]
[[δι' ἐμοῦ]] [δέξαι ⌈τὸ πᾶν λόγῳ⌉ λογικὴν θυσίαν.]
19 ταῦτα βοῶσαι αἱ δυνάμεις αἱ ἐν ἐμοὶ [[τὸ πᾶν ὑμνοῦσι]] τὸ σὸν θέλημα τελοῦσι·
⟨⟨τὸ πᾶν ὑμνοῦσ⟨α⟩ι⟩⟩ ⟨. . . τῇ⟩ σῇ βουλῇ ⟨. . .⟩ [[ἀπὸ σοῦ ἐπὶ σὲ τὸ πᾶν.]]
⟨⟨ὁ σὸς λόγος δι' ἐμοῦ ὑμνεῖ σέ·⟩⟩
⟨⟨λόγον γὰρ τὸν ἐμὸν ποιμαίνει⟨ς σὺ⟩ ὁ νοῦς.⟩⟩
⟨⟨δι' ἐμοῦ⟩⟩ δέξαι ἀπὸ πάντων λογικὴν θυσίαν·
τὸ πᾶν ⟨γὰρ⟩ ⟨⟨ἀπὸ σοῦ, ⟨καὶ⟩ ἐπὶ σὲ τὸ πᾶν.⟩⟩
⟨τὸν νοῦν⟩ τὸ⟨ν⟩ ἐν ἡμῖν [[σῶζε ζωή]] φώτιζε φῶς·
⟨τὴν ψυχὴν . . .⟩ ⟨⟨σῶζε ζωή⟩⟩.
[⌈πνεῦμα θεέ⌉ [[λόγον γὰρ τὸν σὸν ποιμαίνει ὁ νοῦς]]
⌈πνευματοφόρε δημιουργέ, σὺ εἶ ὁ θεός.⌉]
20 ὁ σὸς ἄνθρωπος ταῦτα βοᾷ [διὰ πυρός, δι' ἀέρος, διὰ γῆς, διὰ ὕδατος,] [διὰ πνεύματος,] διὰ τῶν κτισμάτων σοῦ,
ἀπὸ τοῦ αἰῶνος ⟨τὴν⟩ εὐλογίαν εὑρών.
[καὶ] ὃ ζητῶ ⟨⟨εἶδον⟩⟩·
βουλῇ τῇ σῇ ἀναπέπαυμαι [[εἶδον]]·
θελήματι τῷ σῷ ⟨ἀνεγεννήθην⟩.—

21 Τὴν εὐλογίαν ταύτην λέγων, ὦ πάτερ, τέθεικα⟨ς⟩ καὶ ἐν κόσμῳ τῷ ἐμῷ—"Ἐν τῷ νοητῷ" λέγε, τέκνον.—Ἐν τῷ νοητῷ, ὦ πάτερ, δύναμιν ἐκ τοῦ σοῦ ὕμνου, καὶ ⟨διὰ⟩ τῆς σῆς εὐλογίας ἐπιπεφώτισταί μου ὁ νοῦς. πλὴν θέλω κἀγὼ πέμψαι ἐξ ἰδίας φρενὸς εὐλογίαν τῷ θεῷ.—Ὦ τέκνον, μὴ ἀσκόπως.—

Ἐν τῷ νῷ, ὦ πάτερ, ἃ θεωρῶ λέγω.

1 ἡ ἐμοὶ Turn.: ἡ ἐμή cett. 4 ὑμῶν Reitz.: ἡμῶν O Turn. | ἡμᾶς D: ὑμᾶς ex ἡμᾶς corr. man. pr. M 5 μου addidit Reitz. 7 διὰ σοῦ D: δι' ἐμοῦ cett. 9 βοῶσαι scripsi: βοῶσιν codd., Turn. 11 τῇ σῇ βουλῇ scripsi: σὴ βουλὴ codd.: ἡ σὴ βουλὴ Turn. 14 ἐμὸν scripsi: σὸν codd., Turn. | ποιμαίνεις σὺ ὁ νοῦς scripsi: ποιμαίνει ὁ νοῦς codd., Turn. 19–20 Fortasse ⟨τὸ⟩ πνεῦμα ⟨ἔμπνει⟩, θεέ· [[ ]] πνεύματος γὰρ δημιουργὸς σὺ εἶ μόνος 21 ὁ σὸς ἄνθρωπος codd., Turn.: fortasse ὁ σὸς παῖς 23 ἀπὸ

thou, my Unselfishness, praise the All through me;
O Truth, sing praise to Truth.
O Good that is in me, praise the Good;
O Life and Light, from you comes the song of praise, and to you does it go forth.
I give thanks to thee, O Father, who workest in my Powers;
I give thanks to thee, O God, ...
Thus crying, the Powers that are in me accomplish thy will; 19
praising the All, they fulfil thy purpose.
It is thy Word that through me sings thy praise;
for by thee, O Mind, is my speech shepherded.
Through me accept from all an offering of speech;
for the All is from thee, and to thee returns the All.
O Light, illumine thou the mind that is in us;
O Life, keep my soul alive.
Thy man[1] cries thus to thee by means of the things thou hast made;[2] 20
but he has got from thine eternity[3] the praises which he utters.
I have seen that which I seek;
I have found rest according to thy purpose;
by thy will I am born again.—

Tat. Father, by your song of praise to God you have put into 21
my world also ——[4] *Hermes.* Nay, my son, say rather 'my *incorporeal* world'.—*Tat.* By your hymn you have put fresh power into my incorporeal world, and through your song of praise my mind has been further illumined. But now I too wish to present to God an offering of praise of my own devising.—*Hermes.* My son, venture not heedlessly.—*Tat.* Nay, father, it is that which I behold in Mind that I would utter in speech.

[1] Perhaps, 'Thy son', or 'The man, thy son'.
[2] I. e. by means of his corporeal organs.
[3] I. e. from the incorporeal world. It is the divine Mind that puts into him the thoughts which his lips utter.
[4] Tat's sentence is here interrupted by Hermes, but is resumed and completed after the interruption. Tat's 'world' is Tat himself, regarded as a microcosm; and his 'incorporeal world' is his mind.

τοῦ Patr.: *ἀπὸ σοῦ* codd., Turn.: *ἀπὸ τοῦ σοῦ* Reitz. | *εὑρών* scripsi: *εὗρον* codd., Turn. 27 *λέγων* scripsi: *λέγομεν* B: *λεγομένην* cett. | *τέθεικας* scripsi: *τέθεικα* codd., Turn. 29 *δύναμιν* scripsi: *δύναμαι* codd., Turn. | *διὰ* addidi (*ἐκ* add. Reitz.) 30 *πλὴν* Turn.: *πλέον* codd. 33–1 *infra*: *λέγω. σοί* Reitz: *λέγε σὺ* D: *λέγω σοι* codd. cett., Turn.

Σοὶ ⟨ἐγώ, ὦ⟩ γενάρχα τῆς γενεσιουργίας,
Τὰτ θεῷ πέμπω λογικὰς θυσίας.
θεέ, σὺ ⟨ὁ⟩ πατήρ·
[σὺ ὁ] κύριε, σὺ ὁ νοῦς.
δέξαι ⟨εὐ⟩λογί[κ]ας ἃς θέλεις ἀπ' ἐμοῦ·
σοῦ γὰρ βουλομένου πάντα ⟨μοι⟩ τελεῖται.—

Εὖ, ὦ τέκνον· ⟨ἔ⟩πεμψας δεκτὴν θυσίαν τῷ πάντων πατρὶ θεῷ. ἀλλὰ καὶ πρόσθες, ὦ τέκνον, "διὰ τοῦ λόγου."—Εὐχαριστῶ σοι, πάτερ [⟨ὅτι⟩ ταῦτά μοι αἰνεῖς εὐξαμένῳ].—

22 a Χαίρω, τέκνον, ⟨ὡς⟩ καρποφορήσοντος ⟨σου . . .⟩ ἐκ τῆς ἀληθείας [τὰ ἀγαθὰ] τὰ ἀθάνατα ⟨⟨τῆς ἀρετῆς⟩⟩ γεννήματα· ⟨ἐπεὶ⟩ ⟨⟨νοερῶς ἔγνως σεαυτὸν καὶ τὸν πατέρα τὸν ἡμέτερον.⟩⟩

22 b τοῦτο μαθὼν παρ' ἐμοῦ, [[τῆς ἀρετῆς]] σιγὴν ἐπάγγειλαι, ⟨ὦ⟩ ⟨⟨τέκνον,⟩⟩ μηδενὶ [[τέκνον]] ἐκφα[ι]νεῖν τῆς παλιγγενεσίας τὴν παράδοσιν, ἵνα μὴ ὡς διάβολοι ⟨τοῦ παντὸς⟩ λογισθῶμεν. ⟨. . .⟩ ἱκανῶς γὰρ ἕκαστος ἡμῶν ⟨ἑαυτοῦ⟩ ἐπεμελήθη, ἐγώ τε [ὁ] λέγων σύ τε [ὁ] ἀκούων. [[νοερῶς ἔγνως σεαυτὸν καὶ τὸν πατέρα τὸν ἡμέτερον.]]

13 b ⟨⟨ ⟨ἰ⟩δίᾳ τὸν λόγον τοῦτον τὸν περὶ τῆς παλιγγενεσίας [εἰς ὃν] ⟨⟨εἰς οὓς ὁ θεὸς αὐτὸς θέλει⟩⟩ ὑπεμνηματισάμην, ⟨οὐκ⟩ ⟨⟨εἰς τοὺς πολλούς,⟩⟩ ἵνα μὴ ⟨λογισθ⟩ῶμεν διάβολοι τοῦ παντός. [[εἰς τοὺς πολλούς]] [[εἰς οὓς ὁ θεὸς αὐτὸς θέλει.]]⟩⟩

1 Fortasse τελεσιουργίας 3 σὺ ὁ πατήρ scripsi : σὺ πάτερ O Turn. 4 κύριε scripsi : σὺ ὁ κύριος codd., Turn. 5 εὐλογίας scripsi : λογικὰς codd., Turn. | Fortasse ἃς ⟨σὺ⟩ θέλεις 6 Fortasse πάντα μοι τετέλεσται 7 εὖ, ὦ τέκνον, ἔπεμψας Keil : σύ, ὦ τέκνον, πέμψον codd., Turn. 8 Fortasse διὰ τοῦ ⟨σοῦ⟩ λόγου 9 ὅτι ταῦτά μοι αἰνεῖς scripsi : ταῦτά μοι αἰνεῖν codd., Turn. 10 καρποφορήσοντος scripsi : καρποφορήσαντος codd., Turn. 12 Fortasse νοερὸς ⟨γενόμενος⟩ | ἔγνων D : ἔγνως cett. 13 ἐπάγγειλαι Flussas : ἐπάγγειλε ACDM Turn. : ἐπήγγειλε B 14 ἐκφανεῖν scripsi : ἐκφαίνων codd., Turn. 16 Fortasse ⟨τοσαῦτα ἡμῖν εἰρήσθω·⟩ ἱκανῶς γὰρ 19 ἰδίᾳ scripsi : διὰ codd., Turn. 19–20 Fortasse [[διὰ]] τὸν λόγον τοῦτον τὸν περὶ τῆς παλιγγ. ⟨⟨ἰδίᾳ⟩⟩ εἰς οὓς ὁ θεὸς αὐτὸς θέλει ὑπεμν. 21 λογισθῶμεν scripsi : ὦμεν codd., Turn.

O thou first author of the work by which the Rebirth has been
wrought in me,
to thee, O God, do I, Tat, bring offerings of speech.
O God, thou art the Father;
O Lord, thou art Mind.
From me accept praises such as thou willest;
for by thy will it is that all is accomplished for me.[1]—

Hermes. Good, my son; you have presented an offering acceptable to God the Father of all. But add, my son, 'by thy Word'. —*Tat.* I thank you, father.—

Hermes. I rejoice, my son, that you are like to bring forth **22 a** fruit. Out of the Truth will spring up in you the immortal brood of virtue;[2] for by the working of mind[3] you have come to know yourself and our Father.

Now that you have learnt this from me, my son, you must **22 b** promise to keep silence, and not to reveal to any one how the Rebirth is transmitted, that we may not be deemed maligners of the universe.

And now, no more; for we have both of us done enough to satisfy our wants, I as teacher, and you as learner.

This discourse about the Rebirth[4] I have set down in writing **13 b** privately, to be read by those to whom God himself wills it to be made known, and not by the many, that we may not be deemed maligners of the universe.

[1] I. e. that I am born again.
[2] The 'brood of virtue' probably means good deeds.
[3] Perhaps, 'now that you have got mind'.
[4] This sentence is not spoken by Hermes; it is an appended note, in which the writer of the dialogue speaks in his own person

LIBELLVS XIV

Ἑρμοῦ τοῦ τρισμεγίστου Ἀσκληπιῷ εὖ φρονεῖν.

1 Ἐπεὶ ὁ υἱός μου Τὰτ ἀπόντος σου τὴν τῶν ὄντων ἠθέλησε φύσιν μαθεῖν, ὑπερθέσθαι δέ μοι οὐκ ἐπέτρεπεν, ὡς [υἱὸς] [[καὶ]] νεωτέρῳ ⟨⟨καὶ⟩⟩ ἄρτι παρελθόν⟨τι⟩ ἐπὶ τὴν γνῶσιν [τῶν] περὶ ἑνὸς ἑκάστου ἠναγκάσθην πλείονα εἰπεῖν, ὅπως εὐπαρακολούθητος αὐτῷ γένηται ἡ θεωρία. σοὶ δὲ ἐγὼ τῶν λεχθέντων τὰ κυριώτατα κεφάλαια ἐκλεξάμενος δι' ὀλίγων ἠθέλησα ἐπιστεῖλαι [μυστικώτερον αὐτὰ ἑρμηνεύσας], ὡς ἂν τηλικούτῳ καὶ ἐπιστήμονι τῆς φύσεως.

2 εἰ τὰ φαινόμενα πάντα γέγονε καὶ γίνεται, [τὰ δὲ γεννητὰ
οὐχ ὑφ' ἑαυτοῦ ἀλλ' ὑφ' ἑτέρου γίνεται,]—πολλὰ δὲ [γεννητά,
μᾶλλον δὲ πάντα] τὰ φαινόμενα, καὶ πάντα [τὰ] διάφορα καὶ
οὐχ ὅμοια,—γίνεται δὲ ὑφ' ἑτέρου τὰ γινόμενα, ἔστι τις ὁ
ταῦτα ποιῶν· καὶ οὗτος ἀγέννητος, ἵν' ᾖ πρεσβύτερος τῶν
γεννητῶν. τὰ γὰρ γεννητά φημι ὑφ' ἑτέρου γίνεσθαι· τῶν
δὲ γεννητῶν ὄντων ἀδύνατόν τι πρεσβύτερον πάντων εἶναι ἢ
3 μόνον τὸ ἀγέννητον. οὗτος δὲ ⟨⟨εἷς, καὶ⟩⟩ ⟨πάντων⟩ κρείττων,
καὶ [[εἷς καὶ]] μόνος ὄντως σοφὸς τὰ πάντα, ὡς μὴ ἔχων
μηδὲν πρεσβύτερον· ἄρχει γὰρ καὶ τοῦ πλήθους ⟨⟨τῶν γινο-
μένων⟩⟩ [καὶ] τῷ μεγέθει, καὶ τῇ⟨ς⟩ διαφορᾷ⟨ς⟩ [[τῶν γενο-
μένων]] [καὶ] τῇ συνεχείᾳ τῆς ποιήσεως. ἐπεὶ [τα] δὲ τὰ
γεννητὰ ὁρώμενά ἐστι, κἀκεῖνος δὴ [α] ὁρατός· διὰ τοῦτο γὰρ
ποιεῖ, ἵνα [α] ὁρατὸς ᾖ. ἀεὶ οὖν ποιῶν, ἀ⟨εὶ⟩ ὁρατός [τοιγα-
ροῦν] ἐστιν.

4 οὕτως ἄξιόν ἐστι νοῆσαι, καὶ νοήσαντα θαυμάσαι, καὶ θαυμάσαντα ἑαυτὸν μακαρίσαι ⟨ὡς⟩ τὸν πατέρα γνωρίσαντα·

In Libello XIV, codicis R et Turnebi lectiones adhibui.

1 Ἑρμοῦ τοῦ τρισμεγίστου Ἀσκληπιῷ εὖ φρονεῖν Turn. (etiam MC teste Reitz.) : Ἑρμοῦ πρὸς Ἀσκληπιόν R (etiam A teste Reitz.) 3 ὄντων Turn. : ὅλων R (etiam MC teste Reitz.) 4 ἐπέτρεπεν R Turn. : ἔπρεπεν M[1] teste Reitz. | ὡς υἱὸς Turn. : ὁ υἱὸς man. pr. R (etiam AC teste Reitz.): ὡς ὁ υἱὸς R[2] : υἱὸς seclusi 5 νεωτέρῳ καὶ ἄρτι παρελθόντι scripsi: καὶ νεώτερος ἄρτι παρελθὼν R Turn. 6 τῶν seclusit Reitz. 12 οὐχ ὑφ' ἑτέρου (om. ὑφ' ἑαυτοῦ ἀλλ') man. pr. R: οὐχ ὑφ' ἑαυτῶν οὐχ ὑφ' ἑτέρου R[2] 13 τὰ (ante φαινόμενα) om. R 18–19 οὗτος δὲ εἷς, καὶ πάντων κρείττων, καὶ μόνος scripsi : οὗτος δὲ κρείττων, καὶ εἷς, καὶ μόνος Turn. : οὗτος καὶ κρείττω, καὶ εἷς καὶ μόνως R 20–21 τοῦ πλήθους τῶν γινομένων τῷ scripsi :

LIBELLVS XIV

Hermes Trismegistus writes to Asclepius, wishing him health of mind.

In your absence, my son Tat desired to be taught the nature of 1
things, and would not let me postpone his instruction; and as he
was young, and had only just begun to learn the *gnosis*, I was
obliged to discourse to him on each several matter at some length,
in order to make it easy for him to understand the doctrine. But
since you are older, and have knowledge of the nature of things,
I have thought fit to select and send to you in writing, in the
form of a short summary, the most important of the truths
I taught him.

The things presented to our sight are many, and all different, 2
and not like to one another; and seeing that all these things have
come into being, and are ever coming into being, and that things
which come into being are brought into being by another, there
must be one who makes these things. And he who makes them
cannot have been generated; for he must be prior to the things
that are generated. These things, as I said, are brought into
being by another; and it is impossible that anything should be
prior to them all, save only that which has not been generated.
And the Maker is one; he is mightier than all, and he alone is 3
truly wise in all things, for there is nothing that is prior to him.
He rules over the multitude of things made, in virtue of his
greatness; and he rules over all their differences, because he
makes things without intermission. And inasmuch as the things
generated are seen, the Maker also can be seen; for to this end
he makes them, that he may be seen. Since then he is at all
times making things, he can be seen at all times.

Thus is it meet for us to think, and thus thinking, to marvel, 4
and marvelling, to deem ourselves blest, in that we have come to

τῷ πλήθει, καὶ τῷ R Turn. **21–22** *τῆς διαφορᾶς τῇ* scripsi : *τῇ διαφορᾷ τῶν γενομένων καὶ τῇ* R Turn. **22** *ἐπεὶ* scripsi : *ἔπειτα* R Turn. **23** *ἐστι, κἀκεῖνος δὴ ὁρατός* scripsi: *ἐστιν, ἐκεῖνος δὲ ἀόρατος* R Turn. **24** *ὁρατὸς ᾖ* scripsi : *ἀόρατος ᾖ* R Turn. **24-25** *ποιῶν, ἀεὶ ὁρατός ἐστιν* scripsi : *ποιεῖ. ἀόρατος τοιγαροῦν* (*τιγαροῦν* Turn.) *ἐστιν* R Turn. **26** *ἄξιόν ἐστι* Turn. : *ἐστὶν ἄξιος* R

τί γὰρ γλυκύτερον πατρὸς γνησίου; τίς οὖν ἐστιν οὗτος, καὶ πῶς αὐτὸν γνωρίσωμεν; ἢ ⟨γὰρ⟩ τούτῳ τὴν τοῦ θεοῦ προσηγορίαν μόνον δίκαιον ἀνακεῖσθαι, ἢ τὴν τοῦ ποιητοῦ, ἢ τὴν τοῦ πατρός; ἢ καὶ τὰς τρεῖς, θεὸν μὲν διὰ τὴν δύναμιν, ποιητὴν δὲ διὰ τὴν ἐνέργειαν, πατέρα δὲ διὰ τὸ ἀγαθόν. δυνάμει γάρ ἐστι διάφορος τῶν γινομένων, ἐνεργεῖ[α] δὲ ἐν τῷ πάντα γινέσθαι, ⟨ἀγαθὸς δέ ἐστι . . .⟩.

5 διὸ τῆς πολυλογίας τε καὶ ματαιολογίας ἀπαλλαγέντας χρὴ νοεῖν δύο ταῦτα, τὸ γινόμενον καὶ τὸν ποιοῦντα· μέσον γὰρ τούτων οὐδέν, οὐδὲ τρίτον τι. πάντα οὖν νοῶν, καὶ πάντα ἀκούων, τῶν δύο τούτων μέμνησο, καὶ ταῦτα εἶναι νόμιζε τὰ πάντα, μηδὲν ἐν ἀπορίᾳ ⟨⟨ἢ ἐν μυχῷ⟩⟩ τιθέμενος, μὴ τῶν ἄνω, μὴ τῶν κάτω, μὴ τῶν θείων, μὴ τῶν μεταβλητῶν [[ἢ [τῶν] ἐν μυχῷ]]· δύο γάρ ἐστι τὰ πάντα, τὸ γινόμενον καὶ τὸ ποιοῦν. καὶ διαστῆναι τὸ ἕτερον ἀπὸ τοῦ ἑτέρου οὐ δύναται· οὔτε γὰρ τὸν ποιοῦντα χωρὶς τοῦ γινομένου δυνατὸν εἶναι, ⟨οὔτε τὸ γινόμενον χωρὶς τοῦ ποιοῦντος.⟩ ἑκάτερον γὰρ αὐτῶν αὐτὸ τοῦτό ἐστι· διὸ οὐκ ἔστι τὸ ἕτερον τοῦ ἑτέρου

6 χωρισθῆναι, [ἀλλ'] ⟨ὥσπερ οὐδὲ⟩ αὐτὸ ἑαυτοῦ. εἰ γὰρ ὁ ποιῶν ἄλλο οὐδέν ἐστιν ἢ τὸ ποιοῦν μόνον, ἁπλοῦν, ἀσύνθετον, ποιεῖν ἀνάγκη ⸢τοῦτο αὐτὸ ἑαυτῷ ᾧ γένεσίς ἐστι τὸ ποιοῦν τοῦ ποιοῦντος⸣. καὶ πᾶν τὸ γινόμενον ἀδύνατον ὑφ' ἑαυτοῦ γινόμενον εἶναι, γινόμενον δέ, ὑφ' ἑτέρου ἀνάγκη γίνεσθαι· τοῦ δὲ ποιοῦντος ἄνευ τὸ γεννητὸν οὔτε γίνεται οὔτε ἔστι. τὸ γὰρ ἕτερον τοῦ ἑτέρου ἄνευ ἀπώλεσε τὴν ἰδίαν φύσιν [στερήσει τοῦ ἑτέρου]. εἰ τοίνυν δύο ὡμολόγηται τὰ ὄντα, τὸ γινόμενον καὶ τὸ ποιοῦν, ἕν ἐστι τῇ ἑνώσει, τὸ μὲν προηγούμενον, τὸ δὲ ἑπόμενον, προηγούμενον μὲν ὁ ποιῶν θεός, ἑπόμενον δὲ τὸ γινόμενον, ὁποῖον ἂν ᾖ.

7 καὶ μὴ διὰ τὴν ποικιλίαν τῶν γινομένων φυλάξῃ, φοβούμενος μὴ ταπεινότητα καὶ ἀδοξίαν τῷ θεῷ περιάψῃς. μία γάρ ἐστιν αὐτῷ δόξα, τὸ ποιεῖν τὰ πάντα, καὶ τοῦτο ἔστι τοῦ

1–2 καὶ πῶς αὐτὸν om. R **2** γνωρίσωμεν scripsi: γνωρίσομεν R Turn. | ἢ γὰρ τούτῳ scripsi: ἢ τούτῳ R Turn. **3** μόνον Flussas: μόνῳ R Turn. **6** δυνάμει scripsi: δύναμις R Turn. | γινομένων scripsi: γενομένων R Turn. | ἐνεργεῖ scripsi: ἐνέργεια R Turn. **10** οὐδὲ (ante τρίτον) Turn.: οὐδὲν R **15** ἀπὸ Turn. R²: om. man. pr. R **15–16** οὐ δύναται. οὔτε Turn.: ἀδύνατον. οὐδὲ R **17** ἑκάτερον scripsi: ἑκάτερος R Turn. **21** ᾧ γένεσίς ἐστι Turn.: ὡς γένεσις δὲ R **26** εἰ τοίνυν δύο . . . οὔτε τὸν ῥύπον οἱ γεννήσαντες (§ 7) citat Cyrillus *c. Iulianum* 2. 63, Migne *Patrol.* tom. 76, 597 D (vide *Testim.*) **27** τὰ ὄντα Cyril.: om. R Turn. | τὸ (ante γινόμενον) R

recognize our Father; for what is dearer to a son than his true father? Who is he then, and how are we to recognize him? Are we to say that it is right that the name of God alone should be assigned to him, or that of Maker, or that of Father? Nay, all three names are his; he is rightly named God by reason of his power, and Maker by reason of the work he does, and Father by reason of his goodness. In power he surpasses the things that come into being; he is at work in bringing all things into being; ⟨and his goodness is shown in . . .⟩.

We ought therefore to get rid of superfluous and idle talk, and 5
keep our thoughts fixed upon these two, the thing made and
the Maker. Between them there is nothing; there is no third.
In all your thoughts then, and in all that you are told, keep in
mind these two, and hold them to be all that is, making no
difficulty or mystery about anything in heaven above or here
below, divine or mutable. All things are but two, that which
is made and that which makes. And the one cannot be separated
from the other; the Maker cannot exist apart from the thing
made, nor the thing made, apart from the Maker. Each of them
is just that and nothing else; and so the one can no more be
parted from the other than it can be parted from itself. For 6
if the Maker is nothing else but that which makes, and that alone,
simple and incomposite, he must of necessity make .... And
again, what is made cannot be made by itself; if it is made, it
must of necessity be made by another; without the Maker, the
thing made can neither come into being nor exist. If the one is
wanting, the other ceases to be itself. If then it is admitted that
there are two things, that which is made and that which makes,
these two are one in virtue of their union, the one of them going
before, and the other following after. It is the Maker, that is,
God, that goes before: and it is the thing made, whatsoever it be,
that follows after.

And if the things made vary in quality, do not for that reason 7
hesitate through fear of degrading God, or impairing his glory.
For God's glory is this, and this alone, that he makes all things;

Turn.: *τό τε* Cyril. 28 *μὲν* (ante *ὁ ποιῶν*) om. R 29 *ὁποῖον* R Turn.: *ὅ τι* Cyril. | *ἂν* ex *ἐὰν* corr. R 30–31 *φυλάξῃ, φοβούμενος* Cyril.: *φυλάξῃ ὁ φοβούμενος* R Turn. 31 *μὴ* Turn.: om. R Cyril. | *τῷ* (ante *θεῷ*) om. Cyril. | *περιάψῃς* Turn.: *περιάψῃ* R: *περιγράψαι* Cyril. 32 *γάρ ἐστιν αὐτῷ* R Turn.: *γὰρ αὐτῷ ἐστι* Cyril. | *τὰ* (ante *πάντα*) om. Cyril | *ἐστι τοῦ* R Turn.: *ἐστι τὸ τοῦ* Cyril.

θεοῦ ὥσπερ οὐσία, ἡ ποίησις· αὐτῷ δὲ τῷ ποιοῦντι οὐδὲν
κακὸν οὐδ' αἰσχρὸν νομιστέον. ταῦτα γάρ ἐστι τὰ πάθη
[τὰ] τῇ γενέσει παρεπόμενα, ὥσπερ ὁ ἰὸς τῷ χαλκῷ, καὶ
ὁ ῥύπος τῷ σώματι· ἀλλ' οὔτε τὸν ἰὸν ὁ χαλκουργὸς ἐποίησεν,
οὔτε τὸν ῥύπον ὁ ⟨τὸ σῶμα⟩ γεννήσα[ντε]ς [[γεγέννηκεν]].
οὐδὲ τὴν κακίαν ⟨⟨γεγέννηκεν⟩⟩ ὁ θεός, ἡ δὲ τῆς γενέσεως
διαμονὴ καθάπερ ἐξανθεῖν ποιεῖ. καὶ διὰ τοῦτο ἐποίησε τὴν
μεταβολὴν ὁ θεός, ὥσπερ ἀνακάθαρσιν τῆς γενέσεως.
8 εἶτα τῷ μὲν αὐτῷ ζωγράφῳ ἔξεστι καὶ οὐρανὸν ποιῆσαι
καὶ γῆν καὶ θάλασσαν, καὶ θεοὺς καὶ ἀνθρώπους καὶ τὰ
ἄλογα πάντα καὶ τὰ ἄψυχα, τῷ δὲ θεῷ οὐ δυνατὸν πάντα
ποιεῖν; ὢ τῆς πολλῆς ἀνοίας καὶ ἀγνωσίας τῆς περὶ τὸν
θεόν. τὸ γὰρ πάντων καινότατον πάσχουσιν οἱ τοιοῦτοι·
τὸν γὰρ θεὸν φάσκοντες εὐλογεῖν τῷ μὴ τὴν τῶν πάντων
ποίησιν αὐτῷ ἀνατιθέναι, οὔτε τὸν θεὸν ἴσασι, πρὸς δὲ τῷ μὴ
εἰδέναι, καὶ τὰ μέγιστα εἰς αὐτὸν ἀσεβοῦσι, πάθος αὐτῷ
περιτιθέντες, ὑπεροψίαν ἢ ἀδυναμίαν. εἰ γὰρ μὴ πάντα
ποιεῖ, ἢ ὑπερηφανῶν οὐ ποιεῖ, ἢ μὴ δυνάμενος· ὅπερ ἐστὶν
9 ἀσεβές. ὁ γὰρ θεὸς ἓν μόνον ἔχει πάθος, τὸ ἀγαθόν· ὁ δὲ
ἀγαθὸς οὔτε ὑπερήφανος οὔτε ἀδύνατος. [[τοῦτο γάρ ἐστιν
ὁ θεός, τὸ ἀγαθόν· ᾧ πᾶσα δύναμις τοῦ ποιεῖν πάντα.]] πᾶν
δὴ τὸ γεννητὸν ὑπὸ τοῦ θεοῦ γέγονεν, ὅπερ ἐστίν, ὑπὸ τοῦ
ἀγαθοῦ καὶ [τοῦ] πάντα δυναμένου ποιεῖν. ⟨⟨τοῦτο γάρ ἐστιν
ὁ θεός, τὸ ἀγαθόν· ⟨τῷ δὲ ἀγαθ⟩ῷ πᾶσα δύναμις τοῦ ποιεῖν
πάντα.⟩⟩
10 εἰ δὲ πῶς μὲν αὐτὸς ποιεῖ, πῶς δὲ τὰ γινόμενα γίνεται
βούλει μαθεῖν, ἔξεστί σοι ἰδεῖν εἰκόνα καλλίστην καὶ ὁμοιο-
τάτην. ἴδε γεωργὸν σπέρμα καταβάλλοντα εἰς γῆν, ὅπου μὲν
πυρόν, ὅπου δὲ κριθήν, ὅπου δὲ ἄλλο τι τῶν σπερμάτων· ἴδε

1 οὐσία scripsi : σῶμα R Turn. : τὸ σῶμα Cyril. | δὲ Turn., Cyril. : δὴ R 2 νομιστέον scripsi : νομιζόμενον R Turn., Cyril. 2–3 τὰ πάθη τὰ τῇ Turn., Cyril. : τὰ παθητὰ τῇ R 3 ὁ (ante ἰὸς) Cyril. : om. R Turn. 4 οὔτε ἰὸν ὁ χαλκουργὸς R Turn. : οὔτε ὁ χαλκουργὸς τὸν ἰὸν Cyril. 5 ὁ τὸ σῶμα γεννήσας scripsi : οἱ γεννήσαντες Cyril. : ὁ ποιητὴς γεγέννηκεν R Turn. 6 οὐδὲ scripsi : οὔτε R Turn. 7 ἐπιδιαμονὴ R : διαμονὴ cett. 9 εἶτα τῷ μὲν αὐτῷ ζωγράφῳ . . . ἐν δὲ τῷ παντὶ ζωὴν καὶ κίνησιν (§ 10) citat Cyrillus *c. Iulianum* 2. 64, Migne 76. 600 A (vide *Testim.*) 9–10 ποιῆσαι καὶ γῆν Cyril. : ποιῆσαι καὶ θεοὺς καὶ γῆν R Turn. 10 θάλασσαν καὶ R Turn. : θάλασσαν ταῦτα καὶ Cyril. | θεοὺς καὶ Cyril. : om. R Turn. 10–11 καὶ τὰ ἄλογα πάντα καὶ τὰ ἄψυχα R Turn. : καὶ πάντα τὰ ἄλογα καὶ ἄψυχα Cyril. 11 οὐ δυνατὸν πάντα Cyril. : ἀδύνατον ταῦτα Turn. 12 τῆς (ante πολλῆς) Turn. : om. Cyril. 12–13 ὢ τῆς . . . τὸν θεὸν om. man. pr. R 13 καινότατον R Turn. : δεινότατον Cyril. 14 φάσκοντες εὐλογεῖν R Turn. :

and the making of things is, so to speak, God's very being. In relation to the Maker himself, nothing is to be deemed evil or foul. Evil and foulness are accidents which follow on the making of things, just as rust forms on metal, or dirt collects on a man's body; but the metal-worker did not make the rust, nor did the father who begot the body make the dirt. And even so, God is not the author of evil; but it is the lasting on of the things made that causes evil to break out on them. And that is why God has subjected things to change; for by transmutation the things made are purged of evil.

The same painter can make heaven and earth and sea, gods 8
and men, and beasts of every kind, and things without life; and is it impossible for God to make all things? What fools men are! How little they know of God! It is a strange mistake; such men profess to honour God by refusing to ascribe to him the making of all things; but they know not God, and not only that, but they are guilty of the worst impiety against him; for they attribute a bad quality to God; they make him out to be either disdainful or incapable. If God does not make all things, it must be either because he disdains to make things, or because he
is not able; and it is impious to say that. God has one quality, 9
and one alone, the quality of goodness; and he who is good is neither disdainful nor incapable. All that has come into being then has been brought into being by God, that is, by him who is good, and is able to make all; for God is the Good, and the Good has all power to make all.

And if you wish to know how God makes things, and how the 10
things made come into being, you may see an image of it,—a goodly sight, and very like. Look at a husbandman sowing seed, here wheat, there barley, and elsewhere some other kind of

φάσκοντες εὐσεβεῖν τε καὶ εὐλογεῖν Cyril. | τῶν (ante πάντων) R Turn. : om. Cyril. 15 αὐτῷ ἀνατιθέναι R Turn.: ἀνατιθέναι αὐτῷ Cyril. | οὔτε R Turn.: οὐδὲ Cyril. | ἴσασι Cyril. : οἴδασι Turn. : οἴδασιν R | πρὸς δὲ τὸ R : πρὸς δὲ τῷ cett. 16 πάθος Cyril. (Aub.): πάθη Turn. 17 εἰ γὰρ μὴ R Cyril. : εἰ μὴ γὰρ Turn. 18 ἢ (post πάντα ποιεῖ) R Turn. : om. Cyril. (Aub.) | ὑπερηφανῶν οὐ ποιεῖ Cyril.: ὑπερήφανός ἐστιν R Turn. 19 πάθος secludendum? 22 δὴ scripsi: δὲ R Turn., Cyril. | ἐστὶν ὑπὸ τοῦ Cyril. : ἐστὶ τοῦ R Turn. 23 πάντα Cyril. : τὰ πάντα R Turn. 24 τὸ ἀγαθόν Cyril. : τὸ γὰρ ἀγαθὸν R Turn. | τῷ δὲ ἀγαθῷ πᾶσα scripsi : ᾧ πᾶσα Cyril.: ᾗ πᾶσα R Turn. 24–25 ποιεῖν πάντα Cyril.: ποιεῖν τὰ πάντα R Turn. 26 εἰ δὲ Cyril. : ἴδε R Turn. 26–27 γίνεται, βούλει Cyril.: γίνεται, καὶ εἰ βούλει R Turn. 27 ἔξεστί σοι ἰδεῖν εἰκόνα R Turn.: ἔξεστί σοι. ἴδε εἰκόνα Cyril. 28 ἴδε R Turn. : om. Cyril. | καταβαλόντα R | εἰς γῆν Turn. : εἰς τὴν γῆν R Cyril.

τὸν αὐτὸν ἄμπελον φυτεύοντα καὶ μηλέαν καὶ τὰ ἄλλα τῶν δένδρων. οὕτω καὶ ὁ θεὸς ἐν μὲν οὐρανῷ ἀθανασίαν σπείρει, ἐν δὲ γῇ μεταβολήν, ἐν δὲ τῷ παντὶ ζωὴν καὶ κίνησιν. [ταῦτα δὲ οὐ πολλά ἐστιν, ἀλλ' ὀλίγα καὶ εὐαρίθμητα· τὰ γὰρ πάντα τέσσαρα.] ⟨δύο γάρ⟩ ἐστιν, αὐτὸς ὁ θεὸς καὶ ἡ γένεσις, ἐν οἷς τὰ ὄντα ἐστίν.

LIBELLVS XVI

[ὅροι] Ἀσκληπιοῦ πρὸς Ἄμμωνα βασιλέα

[περὶ θεοῦ, περὶ ὕλης, περὶ κακίας, περὶ εἱμαρμένης, περὶ ἡλίου, περὶ νοητῆς οὐσίας, περὶ θείας οὐσίας, περὶ ἀνθρώπου, περὶ οἰκονομίας τοῦ πληρώματος, περὶ τῶν ἑπτὰ ἀστέρων, περὶ τοῦ κατ' εἰκόνα ἀνθρώπου.]

1a μέγαν σοι ⟨τοῦτον⟩ τὸν λόγον, ὦ βασιλεῦ, διεπεμψάμην,
πάντων τῶν ἄλλων ὥσπερ κορυφὴν καὶ ὑπόμνημα, οὐ κατὰ
τὴν τῶν πολλῶν δόξαν συγκείμενον, ἔχοντα δὲ πολλὴν
ἐκείνοις ἀντίλε[ι]ξιν. ⌜φανήσεται γάρ σοι καὶ τοῖς ἐμοῖς
1b ἐνίοις λόγοις ἀντίφωνος.⌝ ⟨. . .⟩ Ἑρμῆς μὲν γὰρ ὁ διδά-
σκαλός μου πολλάκις μοι διαλεγόμενος καὶ ἰδίᾳ καὶ τοῦ Τὰτ
ἐνίοτε παρόντος ἔλεγεν ὅτι δόξει τοῖς ⟨. . .⟩ ἐντυγχάνουσί μου
τοῖς βιβλίοις ἁπλουστάτη εἶναι ἡ σύνταξις καὶ σαφής, ἐκ δὲ
τῶν ἐναντίων ⟨ὁρμωμένοις διαβληθήσεται ὡς⟩ ἀσαφὴς οὖσα,
καὶ κεκρυμμένον τὸν νοῦν τῶν λόγων ἔχουσα. καὶ ἔτι ἀσα-
φεστέρα ⟨φανήσεται⟩ τῶν Ἑλλήνων ὕστερον βουληθέντων
τὴν ἡμετέραν διάλεκτον εἰς τὴν ἰδίαν μεθερμηνεῦσαι, ὅπερ
ἔσται τῶν γεγραμμένων μεγίστη διαστροφή τε καὶ ἀσάφεια.
2 ὁ δὲ λόγος τῇ πατρῴᾳ διαλέκτῳ ἑρμηνευόμενος ἔχει σαφῆ

2 οὕτω καὶ ὁ Cyril. : οὕτως ὁ R Turn. 5 ἐστιν, αὐτὸς scripsi : ἐστι, καὶ αὐτὸς R Turn.

In Libellis XVI–XVIII, codicum BCDMR et Turnebi lectiones adhibui. O = codicum BCDM prima manus teste Reitzenstein.

7 Ἄμμωνα B : Ἄμμονα cett. 8 περὶ κακίας om. DR Turn. 10 περὶ (ante τῶν ἑπτὰ) om. DR Turn. 12 τὸν om. DR Turn. 15 ἀντίλεξιν scripsi : ἀντίδειξιν codd., Turn. 16 γὰρ DR Turn. : om. BC 16–17 ὁ ἐμὸς διδάσκαλος DR Turn. : ὁ διδάσκαλός μου cett. 18 τοῖς om. man. pr. M | Fortasse ⟨εὐσεβῶς⟩ 21 λόγον R : λόγων cett. | ἔχουσα ex ἔχοντα corr. R 21–22 ἀσαφεστάτη codd., Turn. : 'vielleicht ἀσαφεστέρα' Reitz. 24 ἐστι B : ἔσται cett. 25–8 *infra* : ὁ δὲ λόγος τῇ πατρῴᾳ διαλέκτῳ ἑρμηνευόμενος ἔχει . . . ἔχει τὴν ἐνέργειαν τῶν λεγομένων. ὅσον οὖν δυνατόν ἐστί σοι . . . ὀνομάτων φράσιν codd. Corp. Apud

seed. Look at him planting now a vine, and now an apple-tree, and trees of other kinds; the same man plants them all. And even so, God sows immortality in heaven, and change on earth, and in all the universe, life and movement. For in these two,—God, and the world of things made,—is comprised all that exists.

LIBELLVS XVI

An epistle of Asclepius to King Ammon.

Of weighty import is this discourse which I send to you, my 1 a
King; it is, so to speak, a summing up of all the other discourses,
and a reminder of their teaching. It is not composed in accordance with the opinion of the many; it contains much that
contradicts their beliefs. . . . For my teacher[1] Hermes often used 1 b
to say in talk with me when we were alone, and sometimes when
Tat was with us, that those who read my[2] writings . . .[3] will think
them to be quite simply and clearly written, but those who hold
opposite principles to start with will say that the style is obscure,
and conceals the meaning. And it will be thought still more
obscure in time to come, when the Greeks think fit to translate
these writings from our tongue[4] into theirs. Translation will
greatly distort the sense of the writings, and cause much obscurity.
Expressed in our native language,[5] the teaching conveys its mean- 2

[1] Perhaps, '⟨And some people will find it difficult to understand.⟩ For my teacher', &c.

[2] Perhaps, 'his', or 'our'. [3] Perhaps, 'with a devout mind'.

[4] I. e. from the Egyptian language.

[5] 'Expressed in our native language . . . the cogent force of the words.' This passage is quoted in a different form by Nicephorus Gregoras. According to him, it runs thus: 'As far as it is in your power, my King, keep ⟨untranslated⟩ the teaching which I have transmitted to you, in order that secrets so holy may not be revealed to Greeks, and that the disdainful mode of speech of the Greeks, with its showy tricks of style, may not reduce to impotence the impressive strength of the language, and the cogent force of the words. For such teachings, when expressed in our native language, convey their meaning clearly; for the very quality of the sounds, and the power of the Egyptian words, have in it (i.e. in our native language?) the efficacy of the things signified; but when distorted (by translation), these teachings become obscure and ineffectual.'

Nicephorum Gregoram (vide *Testim.*) inverso ordine legitur *ὅσον δυνατόν ἐστί σοι . . . ὀνομάτων φράσιν. οἱ γὰρ τοιοῦτοι λόγοι τῇ πατρῴᾳ διαλέκτῳ ἑρμηνευόμενοι ἔχουσι . . . τὴν τῶν λεγομένων ἐνέργειαν ἔχουσι* | Post *ἐνέργειαν ἔχουσι* add. Niceph. *διαστρεφόμενοι δὲ ἀσαφεῖς τε γίνονται καὶ ἀνενέργητοι*

τὸν τῶν λόγων νοῦν· καὶ γὰρ αὐτὸ τὸ τῆς φωνῆς ποιὸν ⟨. . .⟩, καὶ ἡ τῶν Αἰγυπτίων ὀνομάτων ⌜δύναμις⌝ ἐν ἑαυτῇ ἔχει τὴν ἐνέργειαν τῶν λεγομένων. ὅσον οὖν δύνατόν ἐστί σοι, βασιλεῦ,—πάντα δὲ δύνασαι,—τὸν λόγον διατήρησον ἀνερμήνευτον, ἵνα μήτε εἰς Ἕλληνας ἔλθῃ τοιαῦτα μυστήρια, μήτε ἡ τῶν Ἑλλήνων ⌜ὑπερήφανος⌝ φράσις καὶ ἐκλελυμένη καὶ ὥσπερ κεκαλλωπισμένη ἐξίτηλον ποιήσῃ τὸ σεμνὸν καὶ στιβαρὸν καὶ τὴν ἐνεργητικὴν τῶν ὀνομάτων φράσιν. Ἕλληνες γάρ, ὦ βασιλεῦ, λόγους ἔχουσι κενοὺς ἀποδείξεων [ἐνεργητικούς]· καὶ αὕτη ἐστὶν ⟨ἡ⟩ Ἑλλήνων φιλοσοφία, λόγων ψόφος. ἡμεῖς δὲ οὐ λόγοις χρώμεθα, ἀλλὰ φωναῖς με[γι]σταῖς [τῶν] ἔργων.

3 ἄρξομαι δὲ τοῦ λόγου ἔνθεν, τὸν θεὸν ἐπικαλεσάμενος τὸν τῶν ὅλων δεσπότην καὶ ποιητὴν καὶ πατέρα καὶ περίβολον, [καὶ πάντα ὄντα] τὸν [ἕνα] καὶ ἕνα ὄντα ⟨καὶ⟩ τὰ πάντα, [[τῶν πάντων γὰρ τὸ πλήρωμα ἕν ἐστι]] [καὶ ἐν ἑνί] οὐ ⌜δευτεροῦντος⌝ τοῦ ἑνός, ἀλλ' ἀμφοτέρων ἑνὸς ὄντος· ⟨⟨τῶν πάντων γὰρ τὸ πλήρωμα ἕν ἐστι.⟩⟩ καὶ τοῦτόν μοι τὸν νοῦν διατήρησον, ὦ βασιλεῦ, παρ' ὅλην τὴν τοῦ λόγου πραγματείαν. ἐὰν γάρ τις ἐπιχειρήσῃ τὰ πάντα [καὶ ἓν ⌜δοκοῦντι⌝ καὶ ταὐτὸν εἶναι] τοῦ ἑνὸς χωρίσαι, ἐκδεξάμενος τὴν τῶν πάντων προσηγορίαν ἐπὶ πλήθους, οὐκ ἐπὶ πληρώματος, [[ὅπερ ἐστὶν ἀδύνατον,]] τὸ πᾶν τοῦ ἑνὸς λύσας ἀπολέσει τὸ πᾶν· ⟨⟨ὅπερ ἐστὶν ἀδύνατον.⟩⟩ πάντα γὰρ ἓν εἶναι δεῖ, εἴ γε [ἓν] ἔστιν,—ἔστι δέ, καὶ οὐδέποτε παύεται [ἓν] ὄντα,—ἵνα μὴ τὸ πλήρωμα λυθῇ.

4 ἴδοις ἂν ἐν τῇ γῇ πολλὰς πηγὰς ὑδάτων καὶ ἀέρος ἀναβρυούσας ἐν τοῖς μεσαιτάτοις μέρεσι, καὶ ἐν τῷ αὐτῷ τὰς τρεῖς φύσεις ὁρωμένας ἀέρος καὶ ὕδατος καὶ γῆς, ἐκ μιᾶς ῥίζης ἠρτημένας. ὅθεν καὶ ⟨ἡ γῆ⟩ πάσης ὕλης πεπίστευται εἶναι ταμιεῖον· καὶ ἀναδίδωσι μὲν αὐτῆς τὴν χορηγίαν,
5 ἀνταπολαμβάνει δὲ τὴν ἄνωθεν ὕπαρξιν. οὕτω γὰρ οὐρανὸν

1 τῶν λόγων secludendum? 2 δύναμις Turn. et Niceph.: om. codd. Corp. (συνθήκη B[2]): φράσις Reitz. | αὐτῇ B: ἑαυτῇ codd. Corp. cett.: αὐτῷ Niceph. 4 πάντα δὲ δύνασαι om. Niceph. | τὸν λόγον codd. Corp.: τὸν ὑφ' ἡμῶν παραδεδομένον σοι λόγον Niceph. 4–5 ἀνερμήνευτον om. Niceph. 6 ἡ om. Turn. 6–7 καὶ ἐκλελυμένη καὶ ὥσπερ om. Niceph. 9 κενοὺς B[2]: καινοὺς BCMR Turn.: καὶ νοῦς D 9–10 ⟨οὐδὲ⟩ ἀποδείξεων ἐνεργητικοὺς Reitz. 10 ἡ addidit Reitz. 12 μεσταῖς Tiedemann: μεγίσταις OR: μεγίστας Turn. 14 τῶν (ante ὅλων) om. B | ὅλλων R 14–15 περίβολον καὶ πάντα ὄντα [τὸν ἕνα] καὶ ἕνα [ὄντα τὰ πάντα] Reitz.

ing clearly; for the very quality of the sounds . . .; and when the Egyptian words are spoken, the force of the things signified works in them. Therefore, my King, as far as it is in your power, (and you are all-powerful,) keep the teaching untranslated, in order that secrets so holy may not be revealed to Greeks, and that the Greek mode of speech, with its . . .,[1] and feebleness, and showy tricks of style, may not reduce to impotence the impressive strength of the language, and the cogent force of the words. For the speech of the Greeks, my King, is devoid of power to convince; and the Greek philosophy is nothing but a noise of talk. But *our* speech is not mere talk; it is an utterance replete with workings.

I will begin by invoking God, the Master and Maker and 3
Father and Encompasser of all, who is both One and all things; not that the One is two, but that these two[2] are one; for the whole which is made up of all things is one. And I beg you to keep this in mind, my King, throughout your study of my teaching. For if any one attempts to separate all things from the One, taking the term 'all things' to signify a mere plurality of things, and not a whole made up of things, he will sever the All from the One, and will thereby bring to naught the All; but that is impossible. It needs must be that all things are one, if they exist, (and they do exist, and never cease to exist,) in order that the whole which is made up of them may not be dissolved.

You can see that in the earth there gush forth many springs of 4
water and of air in its midmost parts, and that these three things, air, water, and earth, are found in the same place, being attached to one single root. Hence we believe that the earth is the storehouse of all matter; it gives forth the supply of matter, and in
return receives that thing which comes from above.[3] For in this 5

[1] MSS., 'arrogance' or 'disdainfulness'.
[2] Viz. 'the One' and 'all things'.
[3] Viz. light, which is the vehicle of life.

---

15 *καὶ πάντα τὰ ὄντα* B : *καὶ πάντα ὄντα* cett. | *καὶ τὰ* scripsi : *τὰ* Turn. : *τὸν* codd. **16** *τὸ* (ante *πλήρωμα*) om. R **17** *δευτεροῦντος* codd., Turn. : *δευτέρου ὄντος* Reitz. : fortasse *δύο ὄντος* **18** *μου* D : *μοι* cett. **19** *διατήρισον* R **20** *τὰ* scripsi : *τῷ* OR : *τὸ* Turn. | *δοκοῦντι* OR : *δοκοῦν τε* Turn. **21** *χωρίσαι* MR Turn. : *χωρῆσαι* BD : *χωρίσαι* ex *χωρῆσαι* corr. man. pr. C **23** *ἀπολέσει* Turn. : *ἀπολέσεις* CMR : *ἀπολέσῃς* D **24–26** Fortasse *πάντα γὰρ ἓν εἶναι δεῖ* [*εἴ γε . . . ὄντα*], *ἵνα μὴ τὸ πλήρωμα λυθῇ* **25** *ἓν* (post *εἴ γε*) seclusit Reitz. | *εἴγε ἔνεστιν* BR | *μὴ* om. DR Turn. **27** *ἴδοις ἂν ἐπὶ* Turn. : *ἴδῃς οὖν ἐπὶ* DR : *ἰδὲ οὖν ἐν* cett. | *ἀέρος* scripsi (vide § 8) : *πυρὸς* codd., Turn. **29** *ἀέρος* scripsi : *πυρὸς* codd., Turn.

καὶ γῆν ⟨συν⟩ά⟨γ⟩ει ὁ δημιουργός, λέγω δὴ ὁ ἥλιος, τὴν μὲν
οὐσίαν κατάγων, τὴν δὲ ὕλην ἀνάγων· καὶ περὶ αὐτὸν ⟨. . .⟩,
καὶ εἰς αὐτὸν ⌜τὰ πάντα⌝ ἕλκων, καὶ ἀπὸ ἑαυτοῦ ⌜πάντα⌝
διδούς· πᾶσι γὰρ τὸ φῶς ἄφθονον χαρίζεται. αὐτὸς γάρ
ἐστιν, οὗ ἀγαθαὶ ἐνέργειαι οὐ μόνον ἐν οὐρανῷ [καὶ ἀέρι],
ἀλλὰ καὶ ἐπὶ γῆς ⟨. . ., καὶ⟩ εἰς τὸν κατώτατον βυθὸν [καὶ
6 ἄβυσσον] διήκουσιν. ⟨. . .⟩ ⟨⟨ἐστιν ὁ τούτου ὄγκος·⟩⟩ εἰ δέ
τις ἔστι καὶ νοητὴ οὐσία, ⟨τ⟩αύτη⟨ς⟩ [[ἐστὶν ὁ τούτου ὄγκος]]
[ἧς] ὑποδοχὴ ἂν εἴη τὸ τούτου φῶς. πόθεν δὲ αὕτη συνίσταται
ἢ ἐπιρρεῖ, αὐτὸς μόνος οἶδεν ⟨ὁ θεός. ὁ δὲ ἥλιος,⟩ [ἢ] καὶ τῷ
τόπῳ καὶ τῇ φύσει ἐγγὺς ὢν ⟨ἡμῶν, ὄψιν⟩ ἑαυτοῦ ⟨παρέχει.
καὶ ὁ μὲν θεὸς ἀφανής,⟩ μὴ ὑφ' ἡμῶν ὁρώμενος, στοχασμῷ δὲ
7 βιαζομένων νοούμ⟨ενος⟩· ἡ δὲ τούτου θέα οὐκ ἔστι στοχά-
ζοντος, ἀλλ' αὐτῇ ⟨τ⟩ῇ ὄψει ⟨ὁρᾶται⟩. λαμπρότατα ⟨γὰρ⟩
περιλάμπει πάντα τὸν κόσμον τὸν ὑπερκείμενον καὶ ὑποκεί-
μενον· μέσος γὰρ ἵδρυται, στεφανηφορῶν τὸν κόσμον.
⟨⟨ἀφῆκεν οὖν φέρεσθαι ⟨αὐτὸν⟩ οὐ πόρρωθεν ἑαυτοῦ, ἀλλ' εἰ
χρὴ τὸ ἀληθὲς εἰπεῖν, σὺν ἑαυτῷ,⟩⟩ [καὶ] καθάπερ ἡνίοχος
ἀγαθός, τὸ τοῦ κόσμου ἅρμα ἀσφαλισάμενος καὶ ἀναδήσας
εἰς ἑαυτόν, μή πως ἀτάκτως φέροιτο· εἰσὶ δὲ αἱ ἡνίαι ⟨. . .⟩
[ζωὴ καὶ ψυχὴ καὶ πνεῦμα] [καὶ ἀθανασία καὶ γένεσις].
[[ἀφῆκεν οὖν φέρεσθαι οὐ πόρρωθεν ἑαυτοῦ, ἀλλ' εἰ χρὴ τὸ
8 ἀληθὲς εἰπεῖν, σὺν ἑαυτῷ.]] καὶ τοῦτον τὸν τρόπον δημιουργεῖ τὰ[ι α]πάντα, τοῖς μὲν ἀθανάτοις τὴν ἀίδιον διαμονὴν
ἀπονέμων, καὶ τῇ ἀνωφερείᾳ [τῇ] τοῦ φωτὸς [ε]αὐτοῦ, ὅσον
ἀναπέμπει ἐκ τοῦ θατέρου μέρους τοῦ πρὸς οὐρανὸν βλέ-
ποντος, τὰ ἀθάνατα μέρη τοῦ κόσμου τρέφων[τος], τῷ δὲ
κατα[λαμ]βαλλομένῳ, καὶ περιλάμποντι τὸ πᾶν ὕδατος καὶ
γῆς καὶ ἀέρος κύτος, ⟨⟨τὰ ἐν τούτοις τοῖς μέρεσι τοῦ κόσμου⟩⟩
ζωοποιῶν καὶ ἀνακινῶν ⟨εἰς⟩ γένεσιν, καὶ μεταβολαῖς [[τὰ ἐν

1 *συνάγει* scripsi : *ἀεὶ* codd. (om. R), Turn. : *ἄγει* Flussas 2 Fortasse *περὶ αὐτὸν ⟨τὸν κόσμον διοικεῖ⟩* 3 *καὶ* (ante *εἰς*) om. R 3–4 *πάντα διδοὺς πᾶσι [καὶ τὸ φῶς ἄφθονον χαρίζεται]* Reitz. | Fortasse *πᾶσι ζωὴν διδούς* 4 *γὰρ* (ante *τὸ φῶς*) scripsi : *καὶ* codd., Turn. 5 *οὗ ἀγαθαὶ αἱ ἐνέργειαι* D : fortasse *οὗ αἱ ἐνέργειαι* 7 Fortasse *⟨τῆς γὰρ αἰσθητῆς τοῦ φωτὸς οὐσίας πηγή⟩ ἐστιν ὁ τούτου ὄγκος* 8–9 *ταύτης ὑποδοχὴ* scripsi : *αὕτη ἐστιν ὁ τούτου ὄγκος ἧς ὑποδοχὴ* codd., Turn. 11 *φύσι* R | *ἐγγὺς ὢν ἑαυτοῦ ⟨τὴν ὄψιν . . .⟩* Reitz. 12 *μὴ* om. B | *στοχασμῶν* B Turn. 13 *νοούμενος* scripsi : *νοεῖν* codd. : *νοεῖ* Turn. 14 *αὐτῇ τῇ ὄψει ὁρᾶται* scripsi : *αὐτὴ ἡ ὄψις* codd., Turn. 15–16 *καὶ ὑποκείμενον* om. DR Turn. 23–24 *δημιουργεῖ τὰ πάντα* Reitz. : *δημιουργεῖται ἅπαντα* OR : *δημιουργεῖ τὰ ἅπαντα* Turn. 25 *τῇ ἄνω περιφερείᾳ* DR Turn. | *αὐτοῦ* Reitz. : *ἑαυτοῦ* BMR Turn. :

way the Demiurgus (that is, the Sun) brings together heaven and
earth, sending down true being[1] from above, and raising up
matter from below. And he . . .[2] in connexion with himself, both
drawing . . . to himself, and giving forth . . . from himself; for he
lavishes light on all things without stint.[3] For the Sun is he
whose beneficent workings operate not only in heaven, but also
upon earth, and penetrate even to the lowest depths. The 6
material body of the Sun is . . . ;[4] and if there is such a thing as
a substance not perceptible by sense,[5] the light of the Sun must
be the receptacle of that substance. But of what that substance
consists, or whence it flows in, God only knows. The Sun, being
near to us in position, and like to us in nature, presents himself to
our sight. God does not manifest himself to us; we cannot see
him, and it is only by conjecture, and with hard effort, that we can
apprehend him in thought. But it is not by conjecture that we 7
contemplate the Sun; we see him with our very eyes. He shines
most brightly on all the universe, illuminating both the world
above and the world below; for he is stationed in the midst, and
wears the Kosmos as a wreath around him. And so he lets the
Kosmos go on its course, not leaving it far separated from himself, but, to speak truly, keeping it joined to himself; for like
a skilled driver, he has made fast and bound to himself the
chariot of the Kosmos, lest it should rush away in disorder. And
the reins are . . .[6]

In this wise he makes all things.[7] He assigns to the immortals 8
their everlasting permanence, and with that part of his light which
tends upwards (that is, the light which he sends forth from that
side of him which faces heaven), he maintains the immortal parts
of the Kosmos;[8] but with the light which is shed downward, and
illuminates all the sphere of water, earth, and air, he puts life into
the things in this region of the Kosmos, and stirs them up to

[1] I. e. light, or life.
[2] Perhaps, 'And he orders all things'.
[3] The sense required by the context is 'both drawing life to himself and giving forth life from himself'.
[4] Perhaps, 'composed of visible light', or 'the source of visible light'.
[5] Literally, 'intelligible substance'.
[6] Perhaps, 'And the reins with which he controls it are his light-rays'.
[7] I. e. gives life to all things.
[8] I. e. the heavenly bodies.

ἑαυτῷ D 27 *τρέφων* Tiedemann: *τρέφοντος* OR Turn. 28 *καταβαλλομένῳ* Keil: *καταλαμβανομένῳ* OR Turn. 30 *μεταβολὰς* Turn.

τούτοις τοῖς μέρεσι τοῦ κόσμου]] ⟨τὰ⟩ ζῷα [ἕλικος τρόπον]
9 μεταποιῶν καὶ μεταμορφῶν ⌜εἰς ἄλληλα γένη γενῶν καὶ εἴδη
εἰδῶν ἀντικαταλλασσομένης τῆς εἰς ἄλληλα μεταβολῆς,
καθάπερ καὶ ἐπὶ τῶν μεγάλων σωμάτων ποιεῖ δημιουργῶν.⌝
παντὸς γὰρ σώματος διαμονὴ μεταβολή, καὶ τοῦ μὲν ἀθανάτου ἀδιάλυτος, τοῦ δὲ θνητοῦ μετὰ διαλύσεως· καὶ αὕτη ἡ
διαφορά ἐστι τοῦ ἀθανάτου πρὸς τὸ θνητὸν [καὶ ἡ τοῦ θνητοῦ
10 a πρὸς τὸ ἀθάνατον]. ὥσπερ δὲ τὸ φῶς αὐτοῦ πυκνόν, οὕτω
καὶ ἡ ζωογονία αὐτοῦ πυκνή τις καὶ ἀδιάλειπτος ⌜τῷ τόπῳ
καὶ τῇ χορηγίᾳ⌝.

10 b καὶ γὰρ δαιμόνων χοροὶ περὶ αὐτὸν πολλοὶ καὶ ποικίλαις στρατ[ε]ιαῖς
ἐοικότες, οἳ ⌜σύνοικοι καὶ τῶν ἀθανάτων οὐκ εἰσὶ πόρρω ἐνθένδε.⌝
⟨οὗτοι,⟩ λαχόντες τὴν ⟨μεταξὺ⟩ [τούτων] χώραν, τὰ τῶν ἀνθρώπων
ἐφορῶσι, τὰ δὲ ὑπὸ τῶν θεῶν ἐπιταττόμενα ἐνεργοῦσι, θυέλλαις καὶ
καταιγίσι καὶ πρηστῆρσι καὶ μεταβολαῖς ἀέρος καὶ σεισμοῖς ἔτι δὲ λιμοῖς
11 καὶ πολέμοις ἀμυνόμενοι τὴν ⟨⟨εἰς θεοὺς⟩⟩ ἀσέβειαν. αὕτη γὰρ ἀνθρώποις [[εἰς θεοὺς]] ἡ μεγίστη κακία. [θεῶν μὲν γὰρ τὸ εὖ ποιεῖν,
[ἀνθρώπων δὲ τὸ εὐσεβεῖν,] δαιμόνων δὲ τὸ ⟨τοῖς θεοῖς⟩ ἐπαμύνειν.] τὰ
γὰρ ἄλλα τὰ ὑπ' ἀνθρώπων τολμώμενα ἢ πλάνῃ [ἢ] τολμᾶ⟨ται⟩ ἢ ἀνάγκῃ
[ἣν καλοῦσιν εἱμαρμένην] ἢ ἀγνοίᾳ· ⟨καὶ⟩ ταῦτα πάντα παρὰ θεοῖς ἀνεύ-
θυνα, μόνη δὲ ἡ ἀσέβεια δίκῃ ὑποπέπτωκε.

12 σωτὴρ δὴ καὶ τροφεύς ἐστι παντὸς γένους ὁ ἥλιος· καὶ
ὥσπερ ὁ νοητὸς κόσμος, τὸν αἰσθητ[ικ]ὸν κόσμον περιέχων,
πληροῖ [αυ]τὸν ὄγκον [ταῖς] ποικίλαις καὶ παντομόρφοις ἰδέαις,
οὕτω καὶ ὁ ἥλιος πάντα ⟨τὰ⟩ ἐν τῷ κόσμῳ [περιέχων] ⟨. . .⟩
ὀγκοῖ ⌜πάντων τὰς γενέσεις⌝ καὶ ἰσχυροποιεῖ, καμόντων δὲ καὶ
ῥευσάντων ⟨. . .⟩ ὑποδέχεται.

13 ὑπὸ τούτῳ δὲ ἐτάγη ὁ τῶν δαιμόνων χορός, μᾶλλον δὲ
χοροί· πολλοὶ γὰρ οὗτοι καὶ ποικίλοι, ὑπὸ τῇ τῶν ἀστέρων
[[πλινθίδας]] ⟨ἡγεμονίᾳ⟩ τεταγμένοι, ἑκάστῳ τούτων ἰσάριθμοι.
διατεταγμένοι οὖν ⟨κατὰ⟩ ⟨⟨πλινθίδας⟩⟩ ὑπηρετοῦσιν ἑκάστῳ
τῶν ἀστέρων, ἀγαθοὶ καὶ κακοὶ ὄντες τὰς φύσεις, τουτέστι

2 ἄλληλα γένη Turn. : ἀλληλογενῆ OR 3 ἀντιτασσομένης DR Turn. : ἀντικαταλλασσομένης cett. 8–9 Fortasse ὥσπερ δὲ τὸ φῶς αὐτοῦ πυκνὸν ⟨⟨τῇ χορηγίᾳ⟩⟩, οὕτω καὶ ἡ ζωογονία αὐτοῦ πυκνή τις καὶ ἀδιάλειπτος 9 ἀδιάλυπτος R : ἀδιάλειπτος codd. cett. : ἀδιάλυτος Turn. 11 Fortasse αὐτοὺς (*sc.* τοὺς θεούς) | στρατίαις R : στρατείαις O Turn. 12 οἳ ⟨τοῖς θνητοῖς ὄντες⟩ σύνοικοι Reitz. 13 οὗτοι λαχόντες τὴν μεταξὺ χώραν scripsi : λαχόντες τὴν τούτων χώραν DR Turn. : λαχόντες τούτων χώραν codd. cett. : ⟨ἀλλ'⟩ ἐνθένδε λαχόντες ⟨μέχρι⟩ τούτων χώραν Reitz. 15 ἀέρος scripsi : πυρὸς codd., Turn. : πνεύματος (= ἀέρος) conj. Reitz. 17 ποιεῖ R : ποιεῖν

birth, and by successive changes remakes the living creatures and
transforms them.... For the permanence of every kind of body is 9
maintained by change. Immortal bodies undergo change without dissolution, but the changes of mortal bodies are accompanied by dissolution; that is the difference between immortals and mortals.
And as the light of the Sun is poured forth continuously, so his 10 a
production of life also is continuous and without intermission . . .

For[1] about him[2] are many troops of daemons, like to armies of divers sorts. 10 b
. . .[3] To them is assigned the intermediate region. They watch over the affairs of men, and execute the orders of the gods. By means of storms and hurricanes and fiery blasts, and corruptions of the air,[4] and earthquakes, and
famines also and wars, they punish men's impiety. For impiety is the supreme 11
wickedness of men. All men's other sins are committed either by reason of misleading, or under compulsion, or through ignorance, and for all these the gods do not call them to account; impiety alone is subject to punishment.

The Sun then is the preserver and maintainer of every kind of 12
living beings; and as the intelligible Kosmos, encompassing the sensible Kosmos, fills its material mass with manifold forms of every shape, so the Sun also . . . all things in the Kosmos . . . gives mass and strength to . . ., and when they fail and sink away, receives . . . into itself.[5]

And to the Sun is subject the troop of daemons,—or rather, 13
troops; for there are many and diverse troops of them, placed under the command of the planets, an equal number of daemons being assigned to each planet. Thus marshalled in separate corps, the daemons serve under the several planets. They are both good and bad in their natures, that is, in their workings;

[1] This passage (§§ 10 b–11) cannot have been written by the author of *Corp.* XVI; it must have been inserted by a transcriber.

[2] Perhaps, 'about them' (*sc.* the planet-gods).

[3] Perhaps, 'They dwell with us mortals, and yet are not far separated from the immortals'.

[4] I. e. pestilences.

[5] Perhaps, 'so the Sun also fills all things in the Kosmos with his light, and makes them live. And the Earth, supplying matter for the births of things, gives mass and strength to all things, and when they fail and sink away, receives the matter back into herself'.

---

cett. 19 *ἄλλα τὰ* om. DR Turn. | *πλάνῃ τολμᾶται* scripsi : *πλάνῃ ἢ τόλμῃ* codd., Turn. 20 *ἄγνοιαν* R 22 *δὴ* scripsi : *δὲ* codd., Turn. 23 *αἰσθητὸν Hermippus* : *αἰσθητικὸν* OR Turn. 24 *τὸν ὄγκον* scripsi : *αὐτὸν ὀγκῶν* codd., Turn. (*ἐν τῷ κόσμῳ πάντα Hermippus*) 25–27 Fortasse *οὕτω καὶ ὁ ἥλιος πάντα τὰ ἐν τῷ κόσμῳ ⟨τῷ φωτὶ πληρῶν ζωοποιεῖ. ἡ δὲ γῆ ὕλην παρέχουσα εἰς⟩ ⟨⟨τὰς γενέσεις⟩⟩ ὀγκοῖ πάντα* [[ ]] *καὶ ἰσχυροποιεῖ, καμόντων δὲ καὶ ῥευσάντων ⟨τὴν ὕλην⟩ ὑποδέχεται* 28 *τούτων* R : *τούτῳ* cett. 29 *τῇ* scripsi : *τὰς* codd., Turn. 31 *διατεταγμένον* R Turn.

τὰς ἐνεργείας· δαίμονος γὰρ οὐσία ἐνέργεια. [εἰσὶ δέ τινες
14 αὐτῶν κεκραμένοι ἐξ ἀγαθοῦ καὶ κακοῦ.] οὗτοι, πάντων τῶν
ἐπὶ γῆς πραγμάτων τὴν ἐξουσίαν κεκληρωμένοι, ⟨. . . . αἴτιοι
δέ⟩ εἰσι καὶ τῶν ἐπὶ γῆς θορύβων, καὶ ποικίλην ταραχὴν
ἐργάζονται καὶ κοινῇ ταῖς πόλεσι καὶ τοῖς ἔθνεσι καὶ ἰδίᾳ
ἑκάστῳ. ἀναπλάττονται γὰρ καὶ ἀνθέλκουσι τὰς ψυχὰς
ἡμῶν εἰς ἑαυτούς, ἐγκαθήμενοι ἡμῶν νεύροις καὶ μυελοῖς καὶ
φλεψὶ καὶ ἀρτηρίαις [καὶ αὐτῷ τῷ ἐγκεφάλῳ], διήκοντες
15 μέχρι καὶ αὐτῶν τῶν σπλάγχνων. γενόμενον γὰρ ἡμῶν
ἕκαστον καὶ ψυχωθέντα παραλαμβάνουσι δαίμονες οἱ κατ'
ἐκείνην τὴν ⟨σ⟩τι⟨γ⟩μὴν τῆς γενέσεως ὑπηρέται, οἳ ⟨ὑπ⟩-
ετάγησαν ἑκάστῳ τῶν ἀστέρων· οὗτοι γὰρ κατὰ στιγμὴν
ἐναλλάσσονται, οὐχ οἱ αὐτοὶ ἐπιμένοντες, ἀλλ' ἀνακυκλού-
μενοι. οὗτοι οὖν εἰς τὰ δύο ⟨ἄλογα⟩ μέρη τῆς ψυχῆς δύντες
διὰ τοῦ σώματος στροβοῦσιν αὐτὴν ἕκαστος πρὸς τὴν ἰδίαν
ἐνέργειαν. τὸ δὲ λογικὸν μέρος τῆς ψυχῆς ἀδέσποτον τῶν
16 δαιμόνων ἕστηκεν, ἐπιτήδειον εἰς ὑποδοχὴν τοῦ θεοῦ. ⟨ὅ⟩τῳ
οὖν ἐν τῷ λογικῷ ἀκτὶς ἐπιλάμπει [διὰ τοῦ ἡλίου] ⟨ἀπὸ τοῦ
θεοῦ⟩, [[οὗτοι δὲ πάντες ὀλίγοι εἰσί,]] τούτῳ[ν] καταργοῦνται
οἱ δαίμονες· οὐδεὶς γὰρ οὐδὲν δύναται οὔτε δαιμόνων οὔτε
θεῶν πρὸς μίαν ἀκτῖνα τοῦ θεοῦ. ⟨⟨οὗτοι δὲ πάντως ὀλίγοι
εἰσί⟨ν⟩·⟩⟩ οἱ δὲ ἄλλοι πάντες ἄγονται καὶ φέρονται καὶ τὰς
ψυχὰς καὶ τὰ σώματα ὑπὸ τῶν δαιμόνων, ἀγαπῶντες καὶ
στέργοντες τὰς ἐκείνων ἐνεργείας· καὶ ὁ λόγον οὐκ ⟨ἔχων⟩
ἔρως ⟨. . .⟩ ἐστίν, ὁ πλανώμενος καὶ πλανῶν. τὴν οὖν
ἐπίγειον ⌜διοίκησιν⌝ ταύτην πᾶσαν διοικοῦσι δι' ὀργάνων τῶν
ἡμετέρων σωμάτων. ταύτην δὲ τὴν διοίκησιν Ἑρμῆς εἱμαρμένην ἐκάλεσεν.

17 ἤρτηται οὖν ὁ νοητὸς κόσμος τοῦ θεοῦ [ὁ δὲ αἰσθητὸς τοῦ
νοητοῦ]· ὁ δὲ ἥλιος διὰ τοῦ νοητοῦ [καὶ αἰσθητοῦ] κόσμου τὴν
ἐπιρροὴν ἀπὸ τοῦ θεοῦ χορηγεῖται τοῦ ἀγαθοῦ, τουτέστι τῆς

1 *οὐσία ἡ ἐνέργεια* B **2** *κεκραμμένοι* BDR | *πάντων* Reitz. : *πάντες* OR Turn. **3–4** *αἴτιοι δέ* addidi (*αἴτιοί* addidit Reitz.) **6** *ἀνθέλκουσι* scripsi : *ἀνεγείρουσι* codd., Turn. | *ταῖς ψυχαῖς* B : *τὰς ψυχὰς* cett. **7** *ἑαυτοὺς* B : *αὐτοὺς* CDMR Turn. **9** *σπλάγχων* CD | *γενόμενον* ex *γενομένων* (?) corr. R **11** *στιγμὴν* Reitz. : *τιμὴν* OR Turn. **11–12** *ὑπετάγησαν* scripsi : *ἐτάγησαν ἐν* R Turn. : *ἐτάγησαν* codd. cett. : *ἐτάγησαν ὑφ'* Reitz. **14** *ἄλογα* addidi. Fortasse *εἰς τὰ ἄλογα μέρη* **17** *ὅτῳ* Keil : *τῷ* CDMR Turn. : *τῶν* B **19** *τούτῳ* scripsi : *τούτων* codd., Turn. **24–25** *ὁ λόγον οὐκ*

for the being of a daemon consists in his working. To these 14
daemons is given dominion over all things upon earth, . . . They are also the authors of the disturbances upon earth, and work manifold trouble both for cities and nations collectively and for individual men. For they mould our souls into another shape, and pull them away to themselves, being seated in our nerves[1] and marrow and veins and arteries, and penetrating even to our inmost organs. For at the time when each one of us is born and 15
made alive, the daemons who are at that moment on duty as ministers of birth take charge of us,—that is, the daemons who are subject to some one planet. For the planets replace one another from moment to moment; they do not go on working without change, but succeed one another in rotation. These daemons then make their way in through the body, and enter into the two irrational parts[2] of the soul; and each daemon perverts the soul in a different way, according to his special mode of action. But the rational part of the soul remains free from the dominion of the daemons, and fit to receive God into itself. If 16
then the rational part of a man's soul is illumined by a ray of light from God,[3] for that man the working of the daemons is brought to naught; for no daemon and no god[4] has power against a single ray of the light of God. But such men are few indeed; and all others are led and driven, soul and body, by the daemons, setting their hearts and affections on the workings of the daemons. This is that love which is devoid of reason, that love which goes astray and leads men astray. The daemons then govern all our earthly life, using our bodies as their instruments; and this government Hermes called 'destiny'.

The intelligible Kosmos then is dependent on God; and the 17
Sun receives from God, through the intelligible Kosmos, the influx of good (that is, of life-giving energy), with which he is

[1] Or 'sinews'.

[2] Viz. the part which feels desire, and the part which feels repugnance.

[3] The 'light' here spoken of is not the visible sunlight, but the divine and incorporeal light of Mind.

[4] I. e. no planet-god. Such a man is freed from astral influences, or in other words, is not subject to Heimarmene.

ἔχων ἔρως scripsi: ὁ λόγος οὐκ ἔρως codd., Turn. | Fortasse ⟨οὗτός⟩ ἐστιν 26 διοίκησιν codd., Turn.: fortasse διαγωγὴν | διοικοῦσι καὶ δι' R Turn.

δημιουργίας. περὶ δὲ τὸν ἥλιον αἱ ὀκτώ εἰσι σφαῖραι, τούτου
ἠρτημέναι, ἥ τε τῶν ἀπλανῶν καὶ ⟨αἱ⟩ ἓξ τῶν πλανωμένων
καὶ ἡ μία περίγειος. τούτων δὲ τῶν σφαιρῶν ἤρτηνται οἱ
δαίμονες, τῶν δὲ δαιμόνων οἱ ἄνθρωποι· καὶ οὕτω πάντα
18 τε καὶ πάντες ἀπὸ τοῦ θεοῦ εἰσιν ἠρτημένοι. διὸ πατὴρ μὲν
πάντων ὁ θεός, δημιουργὸς δὲ ὁ ἥλιος· ὁ δὲ κόσμος ὄργανον
τῆς δημιουργίας. καὶ ⌜οὐρανὸν μὲν ἡ νοητὴ οὐσία διοικεῖ,
οὐρανὸς⌝ δὲ θεούς, δαίμονες δὲ θεοῖς ὑποτεταγμένοι ἀνθρώπους
19 διοικοῦσιν. αὕτη ἡ θεῶν καὶ δαιμόνων στρατιά. ⟨πάν⟩τα δὲ ὁ
θεὸς ποιεῖ διὰ τούτων ἑαυτῷ, καὶ μόρια τοῦ θεοῦ πάντα ἐστίν·
εἰ δὲ πάντα μόρια, πάντα ἄρα ὁ θεός. πάντα οὖν ποιῶν
ἑαυτὸν ποιεῖ· καὶ οὐκ ἄν ποτε παύσαιτο ⟨ποιῶν⟩, ἐπεὶ καὶ
αὐτὸς ἄπαυστος. [καὶ ὥσπερ ὁ θεὸς οὐ τέλος ἔχει, οὕτως
οὐδὲ ἡ ποίησις αὐτοῦ [ἀρχὴν ἢ] τέλος ἔχει].

LIBELLVS XVII

*   *   *   *

εἰ δὲ νοεῖς, ἔστιν, ὦ βασιλεῦ, καὶ σωμάτων ⟨εἴδωλα⟩ ἀσώματα. —Ποῖα; ἔφη ὁ βασιλεύς.—Τὰ ἐν τοῖς ἐσόπτροις φαινόμενα [σώματα] οὐ δοκεῖ σοι ἀσώματα εἶναι;—Οὕτως ἔχει, ὦ Τάτ, [θείως νοεῖς,] ὁ βασιλεὺς εἶπεν.—Ἔστι δὲ καὶ ἀσώματα ἄλλα· οἷον αἱ ἰδέαι οὐ δοκοῦσί σοι ἀσώματοι εἶναι, ὅ[υ]σαι ἐν σώμασι φαίνονται οὐ μόνον τῶν ἐμψύχων, ἀλλὰ καὶ τῶν ἀψύχων;—Εὖ λέγεις, ὦ Τάτ.—⟨. . .,⟩ οὕτως ἀντανακλάσεις εἰσὶ τῶν ἀσωμάτων πρὸς τὰ σώματα, [καὶ τῶν σωμάτων πρὸς τὰ ἀσώματα, τουτέστι τοῦ αἰσθητοῦ πρὸς τὸν νοητὸν κόσμον,] καὶ τοῦ νοητοῦ ⟨κόσμου⟩ πρὸς τὸν αἰσθητόν. διὸ προσκύνει τὰ ἀγάλματα, ὦ βασιλεῦ, ὡς καὶ αὐτὰ ἰδέας ἔχοντα ἀπὸ τοῦ [αἰσθητοῦ] ⟨νοητοῦ⟩ κόσμου.—

1 *διμηουργίας* R : *διμιουργίας* Turn. 2 *καὶ αἱ ἓξ* scripsi : *καὶ ἓξ* Turn. : *ἓξ* codd. : *αἵ τε ἓξ* Reitz. 4–6 *τῶν δὲ δαιμόνων . . . ὁ δὲ κόσμος* om. R 7–8 Fortasse *καὶ ἥλιον μὲν ὁ θεὸς διὰ τῆς νοητῆς οὐσίας διοικεῖ, ἥλιος δὲ τοὺς ἄλλους θεούς* 9 *δοκοῦσιν* B : *διοικοῦσιν* cett. | *πάντα δὲ* Reitz. : *τὰ δὲ* O : *τάδε* Turn.

15 *εἴδωλα* addidi (‘Ergänze: *εἴδωλα* oder *εἴδη* oder *εἰκονίσματα* oder dergl.’ Reitz.) 16 *ἐνόπτροις* DR Turn. 17 *εἶναι* DR Turn. : *οὖν* BCM 19 *δοκοῦσί σοι* scripsi : *δοκεῖ οὖν σοι* codd. | *ἀσώματι* D | *εἶναι, ὅσαι* scripsi : *εἶναι* R : *εἶναι οὖσαι* cod. Bodl. 16987 : *οὖσαι* cett. 19–20 An *ἀσώματοι εἶναι οὐσ⟨ί⟩αι, ⟨αἱ⟩ ἐν σώμασι φαινόμεναι*? 20 *σώμασι* Reitz. : *σώματι* OR Turn. | *φαίνονται* scripsi : *φαινόμεναι* codd. | *μόνων* R : *μόνον* cett.

supplied. And round about the Sun, and dependent on the Sun, are the eight spheres, namely, the sphere of the fixed stars, and the six planet-spheres, and the sphere which surrounds the earth;[1] and the daemons are dependent on these spheres; and men are dependent on the daemons. Thus all things and all persons are
dependent on God. God then is the Father of all; the Sun is 18
the Demiurgus;[2] and the Kosmos[3] is the instrument by means of which the Demiurgus works . . . The . . . governs the gods;[4] and the daemons are subject to the gods, and govern men. Thus
is marshalled the army of gods and daemons. Working through 19
gods and daemons, God makes all things for himself; and all things are parts of God. And inasmuch as all things are parts of him, God is all things. Therefore, in making all things, God makes himself. And it is impossible that he should ever cease from making; for God himself can never cease to be.

LIBELLVS XVII

* * * *

'... And if you think of it, my King, there are incorporeal images of bodies also.'—'What sort of things do you mean?' asked the King.—'Do you not think that the images seen in mirrors are incorporeal?'—'Yes, Tat, it is so,' said the King.—'And there are other things also that are incorporeal; for instance, do you not think that the forms which are seen not only in the bodies of living beings, but also in those of lifeless things, are incorporeal?'—'Yes, Tat, you are right.'—'⟨Well then, as bodies are reflected in mirrors,⟩ so incorporeal things are reflected in bodies, and the intelligible Kosmos is reflected in the sensible Kosmos. Therefore, my King, worship the statues of the gods, seeing that these statues too have in them forms which come from the intelligible Kosmos.'—

[1] I. e. the atmosphere.

[2] I. e. Maker of things; but for this writer, 'making things' means giving life to them.

[3] I. e. the system of spheres which has just been described.

[4] The sense required by the context is: 'God, by means of the intelligible substance, governs the Sun, and the Sun governs the other gods (i. e. the gods who preside over the eight spheres)'.

20-21 ἀλλὰ καὶ τῶν ἀψύχων om. D   21 Fortasse ⟨οὐκοῦν ὥσπερ . . .,⟩ οὕτως | ἀνακλάσεις R   26 αἰσθητοῦ OR Turn. : νοητοῦ B², Reitz.

ὁ οὖν βασιλεὺς ἐξαναστὰς ἔφη· Ὥρα ἐστίν, ὦ προφῆτα, περὶ τὴν τῶν ξένων ἐπιμέλειαν γενέσθαι· τῇ δὲ ἐπιούσῃ περὶ τῶν ἑξῆς θεολογήσομεν.

LIBELLVS XVIII

[περὶ τῆς ὑπὸ τοῦ πάθους τοῦ σώματος ἐμποδιζομένης ψυχῆς.]

1 τοῖς τῆς παμμούσου μελῳδίας τὴν ἁρμονίαν ἐπαγγελλομένοις εἰ κατὰ τὴν ἐπίδειξιν ἐμπόδων τῇ προθυμίᾳ γένηται ἡ τῶν ὀργάνων ἀναρμοστία,

[καταγέλαστον τὸ ἐπιχείρημα· τῶν γὰρ ὀργάνων ἐξασθενούντων πρὸς τὴν χρείαν, τὸν μουσουργὸν ἀνάγκη παρὰ τῶν θεωρῶν ἐπιτωθάζεσθαι.]

[ὁ μὲν γὰρ ἀκάματον [εὐγνωμόνως] ἀποδίδωσι τὴν τέχνην, τῶν δὲ τὸ ἀσθενὲς καταμέμφεται ⟨. . .⟩.]

[[ὁ γάρ τοι κατὰ φύσιν μουσικὸς θεὸς καὶ τῶν ᾠδῶν ἁρμονίαν οὐ μόνον ἐργαζόμενος ἀλλὰ καὶ ἄχρι τῶν κατὰ μέρος ὀργάνων τῆς οἰκείας μελῳδίας τὸν ῥυθμὸν παραπέμπων ἀκάματός ἐστιν]] [ὁ θεός· οὐ γὰρ πρὸς θεοῦ τὸ κάμνειν.]

2 [εἰ δέ ποτε θελήσαντι τῷ τεχνίτῃ ὡς[περ] μάλιστα ἐναγωνίζεσθαι περὶ μουσικήν]

[ἄρτι μὲν [καὶ] σαλπιγκτῶν τὴν [αὐτὴν] ἐπίδειξιν τῆς ἐπιστήμης ποιησαμένων, ἄρτι δὲ καὶ αὐλητῶν τοῖς μελικοῖς ὀργάνοις τὸ [τῆς μελῳδίας] λιγυρὸν ἐργασαμένων, ⟨τῶν δὲ⟩ καὶ καλάμῳ καὶ πλήκτρῳ [τῆς ᾠδῆς] τὴν μολπὴν ἐπιτελούντων,] οὐ τῷ πνεύματι τοῦ μουσικοῦ τις ἀναπέμπεται τὴν αἰτίαν, [οὐ τῷ κρείττονί ⟨τις ἀναπέμπεται⟩ τὴν αἰτίαν, ἀλλὰ τῷ μὲν ἀποδίδωσι πρέπον τὸ σέβας,] τὴν δὲ τοῦ ὀργάνου καταμέμφεται σαθρότητα, ὅτι δὴ τοῖς μάλιστα καλοῖς ἐμποδὼν κατέστη, τῷ μὲν μουσουργῷ πρὸς τὴν μελῳδίαν ⌜ἐμποδίσασ⟨α⟩⌝, τῶν δὲ ἀκροατῶν τὴν λιγυρὰν ᾠδὴν συλήσασ⟨α⟩.
3 οὑτωσὶ δὲ καὶ ἡμῶν τῆς περὶ τὸ σῶμα ἀσθενείας χάριν μή τις τῶν θεωρῶν καταμέμψηται ⟨τὴν τέχνην⟩· [εὐσεβῶς] [[τὸ ἡμέτερον γένος]], ἀλλὰ γινωσκέτω ὡς ἀκάματον μὲν [ἐστι] ⟨τὸ⟩ πνεῦμα ⟨. . .⟩ ὁ θεὸς ⟨εἰς⟩ ⟨⟨τὸ ἡμέτερον γένος⟩⟩. ⟨⟨ὁ γάρ τοι ⟨⟨θεός⟩⟩, κατὰ φύσιν μουσικὸς [[θεὸς]] ⟨ὑπάρχων⟩, καὶ

1 ὥρα B : ἄρα CDR : ἆρα Turn. 2 γίνεσθαι codd., Turn. : γενέσθαι B²

Thereupon the King rose from his seat, and said, 'Prophet, it is time for me to see to the entertainment of my guests;[1] but to-morrow we will continue our discussion about the gods, and deal with the next part of the subject.'

LIBELLVS XVIII

When musicians undertake to make harmonious melody, then, 1
if in the performance their good intent is thwarted by the discordance of their instruments, [ ][2] one does not impute the blame 2
to the musician's inspiration, but one ascribes the fault to the unsoundness of the instrument; it is this, we say, that has made the music fall short of perfect beauty, obstructing the musician in his rendering of the melody, and depriving the audience of the joy of hearing the clear sweet strain. And even so, let no man 3
who is present at this festival find fault with my art by reason of my personal defects; but be it known that the spirit which God breathes into men of my sort is unfailing. For God, who is by nature a musician, and not only works harmony in the universe at

[1] I. e. 'it is dinner-time; I must go'.

[2] [' The writer's argument is absurd; for when the instruments are defective, and fail to do what is required of them, the musician is bound to be jeered at by the audience.'] This must be a note written by a dissentient reader.

4–5 *περὶ . . . ψυχῆς* seclusit Reitz. **7** Fortasse *γένοιτο* **10** *περὶ* C : *παρὰ* cett. **13** Fortasse *καταμέμφεται* ⟨*ὁ ἀκροατής*⟩ **14–17** *ὁ γάρ . . . ἀκάματός ἐστιν* hinc ad § 3 transposui **17** *πρὸς θεῶν* Turn. **18** *εἰ δὲ τότε* BCMR **23–24** Fortasse *ἐπιτελεσάντων* **25** *οὐ τῷ κρείττονι τὴν αἰτίαν* seclusit Reitz. **26–27** *τὴν . . . σαθρότητα* scripsi : *τῇ . . . σαθρότητι* codd., Turn. **28–29** *ἐμποδίσασα* Reitz. : *ἐμποδίσας* OR Turn. : fortasse *ἐνοχλήσασα* **29** Fortasse *τοὺς δὲ ἀκροατὰς* | *συλήσασα* Reitz. : *συλήσας* OR Turn. **30–31** *μόγις* DR Turn. : *μή τις* cett. **31** *καταμέμψεται* Turn. **33** ⟨*χορηγεῖ*⟩ *ὁ θεός*? **33–3** *infra* : *ὁ γὰρ . . . ἀκάματός ἐστιν* huc a § 1 transposui

[τῶν ᾠδῶν] ἁρμονίαν οὐ μόνον ⟨ἐν τῷ παντὶ⟩ ἐργαζόμενος, ἀλλὰ καὶ ἄχρι τῶν κατὰ μέρος [ὀργάνων] τῆς οἰκείας μελῳδίας τὸν ῥυθμὸν παραπέμπων, ἀκάματός ἐστιν,⟩⟩ ἀεὶ [δὲ καὶ] ὡσαύτως ἔχων τῆς [οἰκείας] ἐπιστήμης, [διηνεκὴς δὲ ταῖς εὐδαιμονίαις,] εὐεργεσίαις δὲ ταῖς αὐταῖς διὰ παντὸς κεχρη-
4 μένος. εἰ δὲ μάλιστα [τῷ Φειδίᾳ] τῷ δημιουργῷ οὐχ ὑπήκουσεν ἡ τῆς ὕλης χρεία πρὸς ἐντελῆ τὴν ποικιλίαν ⟨. . . τοιγαροῦν εἴ ποτε . . .,⟩ διήρκεσε δὲ αὐτὸς ὁ μουσουργὸς κατὰ δύναμιν, μὴ εἰς αὐτὸν τὴν αἰτίαν ἀναφέρωμεν, τῆς δὲ χορδῆς καταμεμφώμεθα τὴν ἀσθένειαν, ὅτι δὴ τὸν τόνον ὑποχαλάσασα [ὅτι δὴ τὸν τόνον ὑπαραιώσασα] τῆς εὐμουσίας τὸν ⌜ῥυθμὸν⌝ ἠφάνισεν.

5 [ἀλλὰ δὴ] [τοῦ συμπτώματος περὶ τὸ ὄργανον γεγενημένου οὐδείς ποτε τὸν μουσουργὸν ᾐτιάσατο, ἀλλ' ὅσῳπερ τὸ ὄργανον ἐκάκισε, τοσούτῳ τὸν μουσουργὸν ηὔξησεν ⌜ὁπότε τῆς κρούσεως πολλάκις πρὸς τὸν τόνον ἐμπεσούσης⌝· καὶ τὸν ἔρωτα οἱ ἀκροαταὶ πλείονα εἰς ἐκεῖνον [τὸν μουσουργὸν] ἀναφέρονται.]

[καὶ ὅμως οὐκ ἔσχον [τὴν] κατ' αὐτοῦ αἰτίασιν.]

[οὕτω καὶ ἡμεῖς, ὦ τιμιώτατοι]

[⌜ἔνδον πάλιν⌝ τῷ μουσουργῷ τὴν οἰκείαν ἐναρμόσασθαι λύραν.]

6 ἀλλὰ δὴ ὁρῶ τινα τῶν τεχνιτῶν [καὶ χωρὶς τῆς κατὰ λύραν ἐνεργείας], εἴ ποτε πρὸς μεγαλοφυῆ ὑπόθεσιν εἴη παρεσκευασμένος, [ὥσπερ αὐτῷ πολλάκις ὀργάνῳ κεχρημένον] [καὶ τὴν τῆς νευρᾶς θεραπείαν] ⟨τὴν λύραν⟩ δι' ἀπορρήτων ἐναρμοσάμενον, ὡς ἂν τὸ χρειῶδες εἰς τὸ μεγαλοπρεπὲς θεμένου οἱ ἀκροαταὶ ὑπερεκπλήττοιντο. [λέγεται μὲν δὴ ⟨ὡς⟩ καί τινος τεχνίτου κιθαρῳδίαν διαγωνιζομένου, τῆς νευρᾶς ῥαγείσης, ὑπὸ τοῦ κρείττονος] λέγεται μὲν δή τινα κιθαρῳδόν, τὸν τῆς μουσουργίας ἔφορον θεὸν ἔχοντα εὐμενῆ, ἐπειδὴ ἐναγώνιον τὴν κιθαρῳδίαν ποιουμένῳ [ἡ] νευρὰ ῥαγεῖσα πρὸς ἐμπόδιον τῆς ἀθλήσεως αὐτῷ γεγένηται, ⟨. . .⟩ [τὸ παρὰ τοῦ κρείττονος εὐμενὲς ⟨. . .⟩ τὴν νευρὰν ἀνεπλήρωσεν αὐτῷ, καὶ τῆς εὐδοκιμήσεως πάρεσχε τὴν χάριν.] ἀντὶ μὲν γὰρ τῆς νευρᾶς αὐτῷ τέττιγα κατὰ πρόνοιαν τοῦ κρείττονος ἐφιζάνοντα ἀναπληροῦν τὸ μέλος, [καὶ τῆς νευρᾶς φυλάττειν τὴν χώραν,] τὸν κιθαρῳδὸν δὲ [τῇ τῆς νευρᾶς ἰάσει] τῆς λύπης παυσά-

4 ἔχον CD : ἔχων cett. | ἰδίας DR Turn. : οἰκείας cett. 7–8 Lacunam

large, but also transmits to individuals the rhythm of his own music,—God, I say, can never fail; there is no variation in his skill, and his bounties[1] are the same for ever. And even if the 4
matter which the craftsman has to use does not yield such obedience to his hand as would bring the work of art to perfection, ... If then ..., but[2] the musician has done his part as far as it is in his power, we must not lay the blame on *him*, but we must charge the fault to the shortcoming of the lyre-string, for that it has lowered the pitch of the note, and so has marred the beauty of true music.

But I see that it sometimes comes to pass that, when an artist 6
has made ready to deal with a noble theme, he gets his lyre put in tune by mysterious means,[3] in such wise as to bring its deficiency to a glorious issue, to the amazement of his hearers. It is told of a certain lute-player, one that enjoyed the favour of the god who presides over music, that when he was playing the lute for a prize, and was hindered in his competition by the breaking of a string, ... For by God's providence, a cicala settled on his lute, and made good the defect in the music; and so the lute-player's grief was stayed, and he won the honour of

[1] I.e. his gifts of 'spirit' to men.
[2] Perhaps, 'it is not he that is at fault. If then the music goes amiss, but', &c.
[3] I.e. by God's help.

(post ποικιλίαν) significavit Reitz. 9 ἀναφέρομεν CM 11 ὅτι...ὑπαραιώσασα (ὑπεραιώσασα C) seclusit Reitz. 15 τοσοῦτο D: τοσοῦτον R | τῶν μουσουργῶν R: τὸν μουσουργὸν cett. 17–18 ἀναφέρεται R 19 ὅμως codd.: ὅλως Reitz. | οὐκ ἔσχον κατ' αὐτοῦ τὴν αἰτίασιν Reitz. 20 ἡμεῖς DR Turn.: ὑμεῖς BCM 21 τῷ μουσουργῷ ex τὸν μουσουργὸν corr. B: τῷ μουσουργῷ cett. | ἐναρμόσασθε BCM Turn. 25 αὐτῷ πολλάκις ⟨⟨ὥσπερ⟩⟩ ὀργάνῳ κεχρημένον Reitz. 25–26 κεχρημένος κατὰ DR Turn.: κεχρημένον καὶ cett. 27 ἐναρμονησάμενον R Turn. 28 θεμένου Keil: θέμενοι OR Turn.: fortasse θεμένου ⟨τοῦ κρείττονος⟩ 28–30 λέγεται ... κρείττονος om. Turn.: seclusit Reitz. 29 Fortasse κιθαρῳδίᾳ 33 Fortasse γεγένητο | περὶ BC: παρὰ cett. 34 εὐσεβὲς D: εὐμενὲς cett. | Lacunam significavit Reitz. | καὶ om. B 35 ἀντὶ Reitz.: ἄρτι OR Turn.

7a μενον τῆς νίκης ἐσχηκέναι τὴν εὐδοκίμησιν. οὕτως οὖν καὶ αὐτὸς αἰσθάνομαι πάσχειν, ὦ τιμιώτατοι. ἄρτι μὲν γὰρ τὴν ἀσθένειαν καθωμολόγησα [[ἔοικα]], [καὶ πρὸ βραχέος ἀρρώστως διακεῖσθαι,] ἐν δυνάμει δὲ τοῦ κρείττονος ὥσπερ ἀναπληρωθείσης τῆς [περὶ τὸν βασιλέα] μελῳδίας ⟨προσηνῶς⟩ ⟨⟨ἔοικα⟩⟩ μουσουργ⟨ήσ⟩ειν.

7b τοιγάρτοι τὸ πέρας τῆς ⌜ὠφελείας⌝ ἐστ[α]ὶ βασιλέων εὔκλεια, καὶ ⟨⟨ἐκ⟩⟩ τῶν [[ἐξ]] ἐκείνων τροπαίων ἡ τοῦ λόγου προθυμία. ἄγε δὴ ἴωμεν· τοῦτο γὰρ [[ὁ μουσουργὸς]] ⟨ὁ θεὸς⟩ βούλεται· [ἄγε δὴ σπεύσωμεν· τοῦτο γὰρ ὁ μουσουργὸς θέλει,] [καὶ πρὸς τοῦτο τὴν λύραν ἥρμοσται·] καὶ ⟨⟨ὁ μουσουργὸς⟩⟩ λιγυρώτερον μελῳδήσει, [καὶ προσηνέστερα μουσουργήσει,] ὅσῳπερ τὰ τῆς ὑποθήκης μείζονα [τὴν ᾠδὴν] ἔχει.

8 ἐπειδὴ οὖν εἰς βασιλέας αὐτῷ μάλιστα τὰ τῆς λύρας ἐνήρμοσται, καὶ τῶν ἐγκωμίων τὸν τόνον ἔχει, [καὶ τὸν σκοπὸν εἰς βασιλικοὺς ἐπαίνους,] διήγειρε πρῶτον ἑαυτὸν εἰς τὸν ὕπατον βασιλέα τῶν ὅλων [ἀγαθὸν θεόν], καὶ [ὑψόθεν ἀρξάμενος τῆς ᾠδῆς] δευτέρᾳ τάξει πρὸς τοὺς κατ' εἰκόνα ἐκείνου τὴν σκηπτουχίαν ἔχοντας καταβαίνει· ἐπειδὴ καὶ αὐτοῖς τοῖς βασιλεῦσι φίλον τὸ ὕψοθεν κατὰ βαθμὸν τὰ τῆς ᾠδῆς καθήκειν, καὶ ὅθενπερ αὐτοῖς τὰ τῆς νίκης πεπρυτάνευται, ἐκεῖθεν καὶ τὰ τῶν ⌜ἐλπίδων⌝ κατ' ἀκολουθίαν παρά-
9 γεσθαι. ἡκέτω τοίνυν ὁ μουσουργὸς πρὸς τὸν μέγιστον βασιλέα [τῶν ὅλων θεόν], ὃς ἀθάνατος μέν ἐστι [διὰ παντὸς] [ἀίδιός τε] καὶ ἐξ ἀιδίου τὸ κράτος ἔχων, καλλίνικος ⟨δὲ⟩ πρῶτος, ἀφ' οὗ πᾶσαι αἱ νῖκαι εἰς τού⟨ς⟩ ἑξῆς φέρονται [διαδεξάμενοι τὴν νίκην].

15 ⟨⟨οὕτω μὲν δὴ τὸν θεὸν εὐφημήσωμεν· ἀλλὰ δὴ καταβαίνομεν καὶ ἐπὶ τοὺς δεξαμένους παρ' ἐκείνου τὰ σκῆπτρα. δεῖ γὰρ [ἀπὸ τῶν βασιλέων ἀρξαμένους καὶ] ἀπὸ τούτων ἀσκουμένους [[καὶ]] ἤδη ⟨⟨καὶ⟩⟩ συνεθίζειν ἑαυτοὺς [εἰς ἐγκώμια] καὶ ⟨γ⟩υμν⟨άζ⟩ειν ⟨εἰς⟩ τὴν πρὸς τὸ κρεῖττον εὐσέβειαν. [καὶ τὴν μὲν πρώτην καταρχὴν τῆς εὐφημίας ἀπὸ τούτου ἐνασκεῖν, τὴν δὲ ἄσκησιν διὰ τούτου γυμνάζειν] [ἵνα ἐν ἡμῖν ᾖ καὶ ἡ γυμνασία τῆς πρὸς τὸν θεὸν εὐσεβείας καὶ ἡ πρὸς τοὺς βασιλέας εὐφημία.]⟩⟩

10 ἐπὶ ⟨τοὺς τούτων⟩ ἐπαίνους τοίνυν ἡμῖν καταβαίνει ὁ λόγος

2 αὐτὸς αἰσθάνομαι Turn.: αὐτὸς ὥσπερ αἴσθομαι cett. 3 καθωμολόγησα scripsi: καθομολογεῖν ἔοικα codd., Turn. | βραχέως CD: βραχέος cett. 6 μουσουργήσειν scripsi: μουσουργεῖν codd., Turn. 7 ὠφελείας codd., Turn.: fortasse ἐπαγγελίας | ἐστὶ scripsi: ἔσται codd., Turn. 8 καὶ

the victory. And even so I feel it is with me, most honoured 7a
Sirs. Just now I confessed my weakness; but by God's power methinks the defect in the melody has been made good, and I am like to make right pleasant music.

The aim of my endeavour is the glory of kings; and it is the 7b
trophies which our kings have won that make me eager to speak. Onward then! for so God wills; and the melody that the musician makes will sound the sweeter by reason of the greatness of his theme.

Since then his lyre is tuned to treat of kings, and is set to the 8
right pitch for songs of praise, he first uplifts his voice to laud the supreme King of the universe, and comes down thereafter to those who hold their sovereignty after His likeness. For this our kings themselves would wish, that the song should come down step by step from heaven above, and that our praise of them should be derived in due succession from the Power that has
conferred on them their victories. Let the musician then address 9
his song to that most mighty King, who is immortal, and reigns from all eternity; that primal Victor, from whom all victories come to those who follow after.

Thus let us praise God; but from Him we will pass down to 15
those who have received the sceptre from his hand. For we must practise ourselves by praising earthly kings, and so habituate
and train ourselves for adoration of the Deity. My discourse 10

ἐκ τῶν scripsi: καὶ ⟨γὰρ⟩ ἐκ τῶν Reitz.: καὶ τῶν ἐξ OR Turn. **11** πρὸς τούτῳ BM: πρὸς τοῦτο cett. | καὶ om. man. pr. B **12** λιγυρότερον R **14–15** Fortasse ἐπειδὴ οὖν εἰς βασιλέωΝ ⟨ἐγκώμιον⟩ αὐτῷ τὰ τῆς λύρας ἐνήρμοσται [καὶ τῶν ἐγκωμίων τὸν τόνον ἔχει] **17** ἀγαθὸν seclusit Reitz. **19** καταβαίνειν C **20** φίλον τῷ ὕψοθεν CM **22** ἐλπίδων codd., Turn.: fortasse εὐλογιῶν **22-23** παράγεσθαι Reitz.: περιάγεσθαι BCM: ἄγεσθαι DR Turn. **24** ἀθάνατος codd., Turn.: fortasse ἀίδιος **25** ἐξ om. Turn. | δὲ addidit Reitz. **26** τοὺς Reitz.: τὸν OR Turn. **27** διαδεξάμενοι BM: διαδεξάμεναι CDR Turn. **28–35** § 15 (οὕτω . . . εὐφημία) huc transposui **28** Fortasse εὐφημήσαμεν **28–29** καταβαίνομεν OR: καταβαίνωμεν Turn. **30** τῶν (ante βασιλέων) DR Turn.: om. cett **31** καὶ transposuit Keil **31–32** γυμνάζειν Reitz.: ὑμνεῖν OR Turn. **33** τούτου (post ἀπὸ) Turn.: τοῦ OR **34** ἵνα καὶ ἡ γυμνασία ἐν ἡμῖν ᾖ D **34–35** Fortasse ἵνα γυμνασία ἡμῖν ᾖ τῆς πρὸς τὸν θεὸν εὐσεβείας ἡ πρὸς τοὺς βασιλέας εὐφημία **35** τὸν (ante θεὸν) om. B **36** καταβαίνει BR: καταβαίνειν cett.

[[ἐπείγεται]], καὶ πρὸς τοὺς τῆς κοινῆς ἀσφαλείας καὶ εἰρήνης πρυτάνεις ⟨⟨ἐπείγεται⟩⟩ βασιλέας, οἷς [πάλαι] μάλιστα τὸ κῦρος παρὰ τοῦ κρείττονος [θεοῦ] κεκορύφωται, οἷς ἡ νίκη πρὸς τῆς ἐκείνου δεξιᾶς πεπρυτάνευται, οἷς τὰ βραβεῖα καὶ πρὸ τῆς ἐν πολέμοις [ἀρρωστίας] ⟨ἀριστείας⟩ προευτρέπισται, ὧν τὰ τρόπαια καὶ πρὸ τῆς συμπλοκῆς ἵσταται, [οἷς οὐ τὸ βασιλεύειν μόνον ἀλλὰ καὶ τὸ ἀριστεύειν συντέτακται,] οὓς καὶ πρὸ τῆς

16 κινήσεως ἐκπλήττεται τὸ βάρβαρον. ⟨⟨δεῖ γὰρ καὶ τούτοις ἀποδιδόναι τὰς ἀμοιβάς, τοσαύτης ἡμῖν εἰρήνης εὐετηρίαν ἁπλώσασι. βασιλέως δὲ ἀρετὴ ⟨. . .⟩, καὶ τοὔνομα μόνον εἰρήνην βραβεύει· βασιλεὺς γὰρ διὰ τοῦτο εἴρηται, ἐπειδὴ [τῇ] βάσ⟨ε⟩ι λείᾳ ταῖ⟨ς⟩ κορυφαῖς[τητι] [κατ]ἐπεμβαίνει, καὶ ⟨διὰ⟩ τοῦ λόγου [τοῦ εἰς εἰρήνην] κρατεῖ· [καὶ ὅτι γε ὑπερέχειν πέφυκε [τῆς βασιλείας] τῆς βαρβαρικῆς·] ὥστε καὶ τοὔνομα σύμβολόν ⟨ἐστιν⟩ εἰρήνης. [τοιγάρτοι καὶ ἐπηγορία βασιλέως πολλάκις εὐθὺς τὸν πολέμιον [ἀναστέλλειν πέφυκεν] ⟨ἀνέστειλεν⟩.] ἀλλὰ μὴν καὶ οἱ ἀνδριάντες οἱ τούτου τοῖς μάλιστα χειμαζομένοις ὅρμοι τυγχάνουσιν [εἰρήνης]· ἤδη δὲ καὶ μόνη εἰκὼν φανεῖσα βασιλέως [ἐνήργησε τὴν νίκην καὶ] τὸ ἄτρομον [τε καὶ ἄτρωτον] προυξένησε [τοῖς ἐνοικοῦσιν].⟩⟩

* * * *

14 b ⟨⟨οὐκ ἔστιν οὖν ⟨τοῖς⟩ ἐκεῖσε πρὸς ἀλλήλους διαφορά, [οὐκ ἔστι τὸ ἀλλοπρόσαλλον ἐκεῖσε,] ἀλλὰ πάντες ἓν φρονοῦσι⟨ν⟩, [μία δὲ πάντων πρόγνωσις,] εἷς αὐτοῖς νοῦς [ὁ πατήρ], μία αἴσθησις [δι' αὐτῶν ἐργαζομένη]· τὸ ⟨γὰρ⟩ εἰς ἀλλήλους φίλτρον ἔρως ὁ αὐτός, μίαν ἐργαζόμενος ἁρμονίαν τῶν πάντων.⟩⟩

* * * *

11 [περὶ εὐφημίας τοῦ κρείττονος, καὶ ἐγκώμιον βασιλέως.]

ἀλλὰ σπεύδει ὁ ⌜λόγος⌝ εἰς τὰς ἀρχὰς καταλῦσαι τὸ τέρμα, καὶ εἰς εὐφημίαν τοῦ κρείττονος [ἔπειτα δὲ καὶ τῶν

3 θεοῦ seclusi ('vielleicht zu tilgen' Reitz.) | πρὸς R Turn. : πρὸ O 4 πρὸ τοῖς ἐν BR : πρὸ τῆς ἐν cett. 5 ἀριστείας Reitz. : ἀρρωστίας codd., Turn. 8 νικήσεως B : κινήσεως cett. 8–20 § 16 (δεῖ γὰρ . . . τοῖς ἐνοικοῦσιν) huc transposui 8 τούτων DR Turn. : τούτοις cett. 9 Fortasse τοσαύτην ἡμῖν | εὐετηρίαν DR Turn. : εὐκτηρίαν BC 10 Fortasse ἀρετὴ ⟨ἐν τῷ εἰρηνοποιεῖν φανεροῦται⟩ 11 ἐπειδὴ βάσει λείᾳ Reitz. : ἐπειδὴ τῇ βασιλείᾳ OR Turn. 12 ταῖς κορυφαῖς scripsi : καὶ κορυφαιότητι O : καὶ τῇ κορυφαιότητι R Turn. | ἐπεμβαίνει scripsi : κατεπεμβαίνει codd., Turn. 13 καὶ τῆς εἰρήνης DR Turn. : τοῦ εἰς εἰρήνην codd. cett. 18 χειμαζόμενοι D 21–26 § 14 b (οὐκ ἔστιν . . . τῶν πάντων) huc transposui 22 εὖ φρονοῦσι

comes down then to the praise of those who rule on earth, and hastens on to these our kings, whose rule provides safety and peace for all; these to whom God has given the topmost height of sovereignty, and on whom victory has been conferred by God's right hand; for whom the prizes have been made ready even before they win them by their prowess in the wars; whose trophies are set up even before the armies meet in battle; who strike terror into the barbarians even before the troops march
forth to fight. For we must make requital to our kings, for that 16
they have spread abroad among us the prosperity which comes of this great peace.[1] The virtue of a king is shown in making peace; nay, the very name of *king* confers peace; for the king is so called for this cause, that *with smooth tread*[2] he plants his feet upon the topmost heights, and prevails by means of reason;[3] so that this name is in itself a token of peace. Moreover, even the statues of the king serve as havens to men tossed by the fiercest storms; and it has come to pass ere now that the sight of a mere image of the king has given protection from all fears.

* * * *

Among those then who dwell in that world above[4] there is no 14 b
disagreement; all have one purpose; there is one mind, one feeling in them all; for the spell which binds them one to another is Love, the same in all,[5] and by it all are wrought together into one harmonious whole.

* * * *

But now the speaker hastens on to end as he began, and to 11

[1] Or perhaps, 'this great prosperity which comes of peace'.

[2] The writer assumes that the word βασιλεύς (king) means by derivation *one who treads smoothly*. It is as if one took the English word *sovereign* to be derived from *softly treading*.

[3] I. e. by reason and not by force; or by persuasive words and not by deeds of violence.

[4] I. e. among the celestial gods, or in other words, the heavenly bodies.

[5] I. e. their common love of God, or of the Good.

DR Turn. : ἐν φρονοῦσι cett. **23** μίαν R : μία cett. | ὁ πατήρ seclusit Reitz. **24** γὰρ addidit Reitz. **25** φίλτρον ὁ ἔρως DR Turn. **27** περὶ . . . βασιλέως seclusit Reitz. **28** εἰς τὰς ἀρχὰς B: εἰς ἀρχὰς cett. | καταλῦσαι codd.: fortasse ἀνακλάσαι

θειοτάτων βασιλέων τῶν εἰρήνην ἡμῖν βραβευόντων] περα-
τῶσαι τὸν λόγον. [ὥσπερ γὰρ ἐκ τοῦ κρείττονος [καὶ τῆς
ἄνω δυνάμεως] ἠρξάμεθα, οὕτως εἰς αὐτὸ πάλιν τὸ κρεῖττον
ἀντανακλάσομεν τὸ πέρας.] καὶ ⟨γὰρ⟩ ὥσπερ ὁ ἥλιος,
τρόφιμος ὢν πάντων τῶν βλαστημάτων, αὐτὸς [πρῶτος
ἀνασχὼν] τῶν καρπῶν τὰς ἀπαρχὰς καρποῦται, χερσὶ μεγί-
σταις [ὥσπερ] [εἰς ἀπόδρεψιν τῶν καρπῶν χρώμενος] ταῖς
ἀκτῖσι [καὶ χεῖρες αὐτῷ αἱ ἀκτῖνες] τὰ τῶν φυτῶν ἀμβροσιω-
δέστατα [πρῶτον] ἀποδρεπόμενος, οὕτω δὴ καὶ ἡμῖν, [ἀπὸ τοῦ
κρείττονος ἀρξαμένοις καὶ] τῆς ἐκείνου σοφίας τὴν ἀπόρροιαν
δεξαμένοις [καὶ ταύτην] εἰς τὰ [ἡμέτερα] τῶν ψυχῶν [ὑπερ]-
ουράνια φυτά, καταχρωμένοις πάλιν εἰς αὐτὸ⟨ν⟩ [γυμναστέον
τὰ τῆς εὐφημίας] [ἧς αὐτὸς ἡμῖν ἐπομβρήσει] τὴν βλάστην
ἅπασαν ⟨. . .⟩.
12 *θεῷ μὲν ⟨οὖν⟩, [πανακηράτῳ καὶ] ⟨τῷ⟩ πατρὶ τῶν ἡμετέρων*
ψυχῶν, πρὸς μυρίων στομάτων καὶ φωνῶν τὴν εὐφημίαν
ἀναφέρεσθαι πρέπει, κἂν εἰ μὴ [τὸ] πρὸς ἀξίαν ἔστιν εἰπεῖν,
ἐφαμίλλους οὐκ ὄντας τῷ λέγειν. οὐδὲ γὰρ οἱ ἀρτιγενεῖς
ὄντες τὸν πατέρα πρὸς ἀξίαν ὑμνεῖν ἔχουσι, τὰ δὲ κατὰ
δύναμιν αὐτοῖς πρεπόντως ἀποδιδόασι [καὶ συγγνώμην ἔχουσιν]
[ἐνταῦθα]. μᾶλλον δὲ αὐτὸ τοῦτο εὔκλεια τῷ θεῷ, τὸ μείζονα
αὐτὸν εἶναι ⟨τοῦ⟩ τῶν ἑαυτοῦ γεννημάτων ⟨ἐπαίνου⟩· καὶ τὰ
προοίμια [καὶ τὴν χάριν] καὶ μέσ[οτητ]α καὶ τέλος τῶν
εὐφημιῶν τὸ ὁμολογεῖν τὸν πατέρα ἀπειροδύναμον ⟨εἶναι⟩ καὶ
13 *⌜ἀπειροτέρμονα⌝. [οὑτωσὶ δὲ καὶ τὰ βασιλέως] [φύσει γὰρ*
ἡμῖν τοῖς ἀνθρώποις, ὥσπερ ἐκγόνοις [ἀπ'] ἐκείνου τυγχάνουσι,
τὰ τῆς εὐφημίας ἔνεστιν.] αἰτητέον δὲ τὰ τῆς συγγνώμης,
εἰ καὶ τὰ μάλιστα ταῦτα πρὸ τῆς αἰτήσεως παρὰ τοῦ πατρὸς
⟨τὰ τέκνα⟩ τυγχάνει· ⟨⟨καὶ⟩⟩ ὥσπερ [[καὶ]] τοὺς [ἀρτιτόκους
καὶ] ἀρτιγενεῖς ⟨εἰκός⟩ ⟨⟨ἐστι⟨ν⟩⟩⟩ οὐχ ὅπως [[ἐστὶ]] τῆς ἀδυνα-
μίας ⟨χάριν⟩ ἀποστρέφεσθαι τὸν πατέρα, ἀλλὰ καὶ χαίρειν
ἐπὶ τῆς ἐπιγνώσεως, οὕτω[σι δὲ] καὶ ⟨ἡμᾶς . . .⟩. ⌜ἡ γνῶσις
τοῦ παντὸς ἥπερ ζωὴν πᾶσι πρυτανεύει⌝ ⌜καὶ τὴν εἰς θεὸν
14 a *εὐφημίαν ἣν ἡμῖν ἐδωρήσατο.⌝ ὁ θεὸς γάρ, ἀγαθὸς ὑπάρχων*
[καὶ ἀειφεγγής], καὶ ἐν ⟨ἑ⟩αυτῷ [διὰ παντὸς] τῆς οἰκείας

1 *τῶν εἰρήνην* DR Turn. : *τῶν τὴν εἰρήνην* cett. 4 *ὁ* (ante *ἥλιος*) om. M 5 *πρῶτος* codd. : 'Vielleicht *πρῶτον*' Reitz. 6 *ἀρχὰς* R : *ἀπαρχὰς* cett. 9 *ἀποδρεπόμενος* man. post. C : *ἀποδρεπόμενα* BC : *ἀπο-δρεπόμεναι* cett. 9–13 Fortasse *οὕτω δὴ καὶ ἡμῖν*, [ ] *τῆς ἐκείνου σοφίας*

conclude his speech with praise of God. For as the Sun, who nurtures all vegetation, also gathers the first-fruits of the produce with his rays, as it were with mighty hands, plucking the sweetest odours of the plants; even so we too, having received into our souls (which are plants of heavenly origin) the efflux of God's wisdom, must, in return, use in his service all that springs up in us . . . .[1]

To God then, the Father of our souls, it is fitting that praise 12
should rise from countless tongues and voices, even though our
words cannot be worthy of him, seeing that it is a task beyond
our power to tell of him. Even so, little children are not able
worthily to sing their father's praise; but they do what is fitting
when they render to him such honour as they can. Nay, this
very thing redounds to God's glory, that his greatness transcends
the praises of his offspring; and the beginning and middle and
end of our praise is to confess that our Father is infinite in
power, and . . . . But we must beseech him to pardon us;[2] though 13
his children do indeed get pardon from their Father even before
they ask it; and just as it is to be looked for that a father, so far
from turning his face away from his babes because they can do so
little, should be glad when they acknowledge him, even so . . . .[3]
For God, inasmuch as he is good, and has in himself the only 14 a

* * * *

[1] Perhaps, 'must, in return, send up to him hymns of praise, using in his service all the growth that he has fostered in us with his showers'.

[2] *Sc.* for the inadequacy of our praise of him.

[3] Perhaps, 'even so does God take pleasure in our praises'.

τὴν ἀπόρροιαν [[ ]] [ ] *εἰς τὰ* [ ] *τῶν ψυχῶν οὐράνια φυτὰ* ⟨⟨*δεξαμένοις*⟩⟩, [[ ]] ἀΝΟΙ*στέον τὰ τῆς εὐφημίας*, ⟨⟨*καταχρωμένοις πάλιν εἰς αὐτό*⟨*ν*⟩⟩⟩ [[ ]] *τὴν βλάστην ἅπασαν* ⟨⟨ἣΝ *αὐτὸς ἡμῖν ἐπώμβρισε*Ν⟩⟩. **10** *τοῖς ἐκείνου* BC : *τῆς ἐκείνου* cett. | *ἀπορείαν* D : *ἀπόρροιαν* cett. **11–12** *οὐράνια* scripsi : *ὑπερουράνια* codd., Turn. **12** *αὐτὸν* scripsi : *αὐτὸ* codd., Turn. **13** *ἐπομβρήσῃ* D Turn. : *ἐπομβρήσει* cett. **14** *ἅπασα* B : *ἅπασαν* cett. **15** *οὖν* addidit Reitz. **16** *μυρίων* DMR Turn. : *μυστηρίων* BC **17** *κἂν* scripsi : *καὶ* codd., Turn. **20** *ἀποδίδωσι* R **21–22** *εὔκλεια . . . γεννημάτων* om. R **23** *μέσα* scripsi : *μεσότητα* codd., Turn. **28** *τὰ* (ante *μάλιστα*) B(C ?)M : om. cett. **29** *καὶ* (ante *τοὺς*) om. B **32–33** Fortasse *ἡ γνῶσις τοῦ πατρὸς ὅσπερ* **33–34** Fortasse *τὴν τῆς εὐφημίας δύναμιν* **34** *ἡμεῖς ἐδορήσατο* R : *ἡμῖν ἐδωρήσατο* cett. **35** *καὶ ἀειφεγγής* om. R Turn | *αὐτῷ* vel *αὑτῷ* OR Turn.

ἀριπρεπείας ἔχων τὸ πέρας, ἀθάνατος δὲ ὤν, καὶ [ἐν ἑαυτῷ] τὴν ἀτελεύτητον λῆξιν [περιέχων] [καὶ διὰ παντὸς] [[ἀένναος]] ἀπὸ τῆς [ἐκεῖσε] ⟨⟨ἀεν[ν]άου⟩⟩ ἐνεργείας καὶ εἰς τόνδε τὸν κόσμον παρέχων, ⌜τὴν ἐπαγγελίαν εἰς διασωστικὴν εὐφημίαν⌝ ⟨. . .⟩.

*   *   *   *

14 b [[οὐκ ἔστιν οὖν . . . ἁρμονίαν τῶν πάντων.]] Vide ante § 11.

15 [[οὕτω μὲν δὴ . . . βασιλέας εὐφημία.]] Vide post § 9.

16 [[δεῖ γὰρ καὶ . . . τοῖς ἐνοικοῦσιν.]] Vide post § 10.

1 ἀριπρεπείας scripsi : ἀειπρεπείας codd., Turn. | ἐν ἑαυτῷ BCM : ἐν αὐτῷ (vel ἐν αὑτῷ) cett. 3 καὶ (ante εἰς τόνδε) om DR Turn. 4 ἀπαγγελίαν R Turn. : ἐπαγγελίαν cett.

limit of his own pre-eminence,[1] and inasmuch as he is immortal, and from his everlasting energy supplies to this world also its appointed lot of endless duration, ...

* * * *

[1] I. e. God is limited by nothing other than himself.

ASCLEPIUS

Ἑρμοῦ τρισμεγίστου βίβλος ἱερὰ πρὸς Ἀσκληπιὸν προσφωνηθεῖσα

⟨*Prologus*⟩

1 a ⟨*Trismegistus loquitur*:⟩ 'Deus, deus te nobis, o Asclepi, ut divino sermoni interesses, adduxit, eoque tali, qui merito omnium antea a nobis factorum, vel nobis divino numine inspiratorum, videatur esse religiosa pietate divinior. Quem si intellegens ⟨deum⟩ videris, eris omnium bonorum tota mente plenissimus, si tamen multa sunt bona, et non unum, in quo sunt omnia. Alterum enim alterius consentaneum esse dinoscitur [omnia unius esse aut unum esse omnia]; ita enim sibi est utrumque conexum, ut separari alterum ab *al*t⟨e⟩ro non possit. Sed de futuro sermone hoc diligenti intentione cognosces.

1 b Tu vero, o Asclepi, procede paululum, Tatque, nobis qui intersit, evoca.' Quo ingresso, Asclepius et Hammona[m] interesse suggessit. Trismegistus ait: 'Nulla invidia Hammona prohibet a nobis; etenim ad eius nomen multa meminimus a nobis esse conscripta, sicuti etiam ad Tat amantissimum et carissimum filium multa physica ⟨di⟩exo*d*icaque quam plurima. Tractatum hunc autem tuo ⟨in⟩scribam nomine. Praeter Hammona nullum vocassis alterum, ne tantae rei religiosissimus sermo multorum interventu praesentiaque violetur. Tractatum

1 *Post titulum addunt* asclepius iste pro sole mihi est *codices*: *seclusit Ménard* 12 altero *scripsi*: utro *BM*: utroque *cett.* 14 tatque (*sed priore* t *eraso*) *B*: atque *cett.* 18 Tat *Thomas*: tativ̄ (*i.e.* Tatium) *B*: *om. cett.* 19 diexodicaque *scripsi*: '*fortasse* diexodicaque' *Thomas*: exoticaque *ω*

ASCLEPIUS

A holy book of Hermes Trismegistus, addressed to Asclepius.[1]

Prologue

Trismegistus. 'It is God that has brought you to me, Asclepius, **1 a**
to hear a teaching[2] which comes from God. My discourse will be of such a nature, that by reason of its pious fervour it will be rightly[3] deemed that there is in it more of God's working[4] than in all that I have spoken before,—or rather, that God's power has inspired me to speak. And if you understand[5] my words, and thereby come to see God, your mind will be wholly filled with all things good,—if indeed there are many goods, and not rather one Good, in which all goods are comprised. For we find that these two things agree with one another; they are so linked together that it is impossible to part them. But this you will learn from my discourse to-day, if you listen with earnest attention.

But go forth for a moment, Asclepius, and summon Tat to **1 b**
join us.' When Tat had entered, Asclepius proposed that Ammon also should be present. Trismegistus replied, 'I do not grudge permission to Ammon to be with us; for I bear in mind that many of my writings have been addressed to him, as again many of my treatises on nature,[6] and a very large number of my explanatory[7] writings, have been addressed to Tat, my dear and loving son. As for our discussion to-day, I will inscribe on it your name, Asclepius. You may call Ammon; but summon no one else, lest a discourse which treats of the loftiest of themes, and breathes the deepest reverence, should be profaned by the

[1] This document was also called Λόγος τέλειος, 'the *Crowning Discourse* of Hermes Trismegistus'.

[2] *Sermo* = λόγος.

[3] *Merito* = εἰκότως.

[4] *Omnium divinior* = πάντων θειότερος.

[5] *Intellegens* = νοήσας.

[6] φυσικά, probably substituted for γενικά.

[7] διεξοδικά.

enim tota numinis maiestate plenissimum inreligiosae mentis est multorum conscientia publicare.'

Hammone etiam adytum ingresso, sanctoque illo quattuor virorum religione et divina [dei] completo praesentia, conpetenti venerabiliter silentio [[ex ore Hermu]] animis singulorum mentibusque pendentibus, ⟨⟨ex ore Hermu⟩⟩ divinus Cupido sic est orsus dicere.

⟨*Asclepius I*⟩

2a *Trism.* O Asclepi, omnis humana inmortalis est anima: sed non uniformiter cunctae, sed aliae alio more [vel tempore] ⟨creatae sunt animae⟩; non enim [o Trismegiste] omnis unius qualitatis est anima.—⟨*Ascl.* Non enim, o Trismegiste, . . . ?⟩—*Trism.* O Asclepi, ut celeriter de vera⟨e⟩ rationis continentia decidisti! Non enim hoc dixi, omnia unum esse et unum omnia, utpote quae in creatore fuerint omnia, antequam creasset omnia? Nec inmerito ipse dictus est omnia, cuius membra sunt omnia. Huius itaque, qui est unus omnia, vel ipse est creator omnium, in tota hac disputatione curato meminisse.

2b De caelo cuncta ⟨. . .⟩ in terram et in aquam, et in aera ignis. Solum quod sursum versus fertur vivificum; quod deorsum, ei deserviens. At vero quicquid de alto descendit generans est; quod sursum versus emanat, nutriens. Terra, sola in se ipsa consistens, omnium est ⟨⟨gener⟨anti⟩um⟩⟩ receptrix, omniumque [[generum]] quae accepit restitutrix. Hoc ergo totum, sicut meministi, quod est omnium vel omnia, ⟨constat ex anima et mundo⟩. Anima et mundus a natura conprehensa agitantur, ita

9–12 *In codd. et in edd. prioribus sic legitur*: (Trism.:) '. . . alio more vel tempore.' (Ascl.:) 'Non enim, o Trismegiste . . . est anima?' (Trism.:) 'O Asclepi, ut celeriter . . .' 12 verae *Rohde*: vera *ω* 14 utpote quae *ed. Rom.*: utpote que *G*: utpote qui *codd. cett.* 24 omnium *ω*: '*fortasse* unum' *Thomas*

entrance and presence of a throng of listeners. For it would be impiety to make public through the presence of many witnesses a discussion which is replete with God in all his majesty.' Then Ammon also entered the sanctuary; and the place was made holy[1] by the pious awe of the four men, and was filled with God's presence. And the hearers listened in fitting silence, and with heart and soul each of them hung[2] on the words in reverence, as through the lips of Hermes the divine Eros[3] thus began to speak.

Asclepius I

Trism. All human souls, Asclepius, are immortal. But souls 2 a
are not all of one kind;[4] different souls have been created in different fashions; for souls differ in quality.—⟨*Ascl.* But tell me, Trismegistus, is not . . . ?⟩[5]—*Trism.* How quickly, Asclepius, you have lost your hold on the true doctrine![6] Have I not told you this before, that all things are one, and the One is all things, seeing that all things were in the Creator[7] before he created them all? And rightly[8] has it been said of him that he is all things; for all things are parts[9] of him. Throughout our discussion then, be careful to remember him, the One who is all things,—him who is the creator of all things.

From heaven are derived all . . . . ⟨Air⟩ enters into earth and 2 b
water; and fire enters into air. That only which tends upward[10] is life-giving;[11] and that which tends downward[12] is subservient to it.[13] Moreover, all that descends from on high is generative;[14] and that which issues upward from below is nutritive.[15] Earth, which alone stands fast in its own place, receives all that is generative into itself, and renders back all that it has received. This whole then, which is made up of all things, or is all things, consists, as you have heard me say before, of soul and corporeal substance.[16] Soul and corporeal substance together are embraced by nature,[17]

[1] *Sancto illo* = ἁγιασθέντος ἐκείνου (*sc.* τοῦ ἀδύτου)?
[2] *Pendentibus* = αἰωρουμένων?
[3] *Divinus Cupido* = ὁ θεῖος ἔρως, i e. the yearning for God which is implanted in men by God.
[4] *Uniformiter* = ὁμοειδῶς, which may perhaps be a misreading for ὁμοειδεῖς.
[5] Possibly, 'are not souls uncreated?'
[6] *Ratio* = λόγος. [7] *Creator* = δημιουργός, or ποιητής?
[8] *Non inmerito* = οὐκ ἀπεικότως. [9] *Membra* = μόρια.
[10] *Quod sursum versus fertur* = τὸ ἀνωφερές, i.e. fire and air.
[11] *Vivificum* = ζωοποιόν or ζωτικόν.
[12] *Quod deorsum fertur* = τὸ κατωφερές, i.e. earth and water.
[13] *Ei deserviens* = ὑπηρετικόν. [14] *Generans* = γεννητικόν.
[15] *Nutriens* = θρεπτικόν. [16] *Mundus* = ὕλη. [17] *Natura* = φύσις.

omnium multiformi imaginum [ae]qualitate variata, ut infinitae qualitatum ex intervallo species [esse] n*a*scantur, adunatae tamen
3 a ad hoc, ut totum unum et ex uno omnia esse videantur. Totus itaque quibus formatus est mundus, elementa sunt quattuor, ignis, aqua, terra, aer: mundus unus, anima una, et deus unus.

3 b Nunc mihi adesto totus, quantum mente vales, quantum calles astutia. Divinitatis etenim ratio, divina sensus intentione noscenda, torrenti simillima est fluvio e summo in pronum praecipiti rapacitate currenti[s]; quo efficitur ut intentionem nostram, non solum audientium, verum tractantium ipsorum, celeri velocitate praetereat.

3 c Caelum ergo, sensibilis deus, administrator est omnium corporum; quorum augmenta detrimentaque sol et luna sortiti sunt. Caeli vero et ipsius [[animae]] et omnium quae [mundo] insunt ipse gubernator est ⟨⟨deus⟩⟩; qui est ⟨⟨omnium generum et omnium specierum per naturam rerum⟩⟩ effector [[deus]]. A supradictis enim omnibus, quorum idem gubernator deus omnium, ⟨⟨animae⟩⟩ frequentatio fertur influens per mundum [et per animam] [[omnium generum et omnium specierum per rerum naturam]]. Mundus autem praeparatus est a deo receptaculum omniformium specierum; natura autem, per species imaginans mundum per quattuor elementa, ad caelum usque
4 p*ro*ducit cuncta dei visibus placitura. Omnia autem ⟨. . .⟩ desuper pendentia in species dividuntur hoc quo dicturus sum ⟨modo⟩ [genere]. Genera rerum omnium sua*e* species sequuntur, ut sit [ita] ⟨specierum⟩ soliditas genus, species generis particula.

1 qualitate *edd. vett.*: aequalitate ω 2 nascantur *scripsi*: noscantur ω 5 et deus unus *secludendum?* 9 currenti *edd.*: currentis ω 22 producit *scripsi*: perducit ω | Omnia autem ⟨vivifica⟩? 24 suae *Kroll*: suas ω 25 ita *seclusit Thomas*

and are by nature's working kept in movement;[1] and by this
movement, the manifold qualities of all things that take shape[2]
are made to differ among themselves, in such sort that there come
into existence individual things of infinitely numerous forms,[3] by
reason of the differences of their qualities,[4] and yet all individuals
are united to the whole; so that we see that the whole is one, and
of the one are all things. The elements through which all matter 3 a
has been indued with form[5] are four in number,—fire, water,
earth, and air; but matter is one, soul is one, and God is one.

And now give me your whole attention, exerting to the utmost 3 b
your power of thought and keenness of intelligence. For the
doctrine[6] which teaches of God's being needs for its apprehension
such effort of thought[7] as man cannot make save by God's help.
It is like a torrent plunging downward with headlong rush, so that
in its swiftness it outstrips the man who strives to follow it, and
leaves behind not only the hearers, but even the teacher himself.

To Heaven, a god perceptible by sense,[8] is committed the 3 c
administration[9] of all bodies; and the growth and decay of
bodies fall under the charge of Sun and Moon. But Heaven
itself, and all things in it, are governed[10] by God; and he, working
through nature,[11] is the maker[11] of all general and individual forms
of living things. For by all the heavenly bodies, which all alike
are governed by God, there is poured into all matter an uninter-
rupted stream[13] of soul. Matter[14] has been made ready by God
beforehand to be the recipient of individual forms of every
shape;[15] and nature, fashioning matter in individual forms[16] by
means of the four elements, brings into being, up to the height of
heaven, all things that will be pleasing in God's sight. All . . .[17] 4
are dependent on the powers above, and are distributed among
individuals in the way that I will now describe. The individuals
of each kind are fashioned in accordance with[18] the form of their
kind. The kind is the whole[19] made up of the individuals; the

1 *Agitantur* = κινοῦνται. 2 *Imagines* = σχήματα? 3 *Species* = εἴδη.
4 *Qualitatum ex intervallo* = ἐκ τῆς τῶν ποιοτήτων (or ποιῶν) διαστάσεως?
5 *Formatus est mundus* = μεμόρφωται ἡ ὕλη? 6 *Ratio* = λόγος.
7 *Sensus* = νόησις? 8 *Sensibilis deus* = αἰσθητὸς θεός.
9 *Administrator* = ἐπίτροπος? 10 *Gubernator* = κυβερνήτης.
11 *Per naturam rerum* = διὰ τῆς φύσεως. 12 *Effector* = ποιητής or δημιουργός.
13 *Frequentatio* = πυκνότης or πύκνωσις. 14 *Mundus* = ὕλη.
15 *Receptaculum* = ὑποδοχή: *species* = εἴδη: *omniformes* = παντόμορφα.
16 *Per species imaginans* = εἰδοποιοῦσα?
17 'All portions of soul' or 'of vital spirit'?
18 *Sequuntur* = ἀκολουθοῦσι. 19 *Soliditas* = τὸ ὅλον.

Genus ergo deorum ex se deorum faci[e]t species; daemonum genus aeque; hominum similiter, volucrum, et omnium quae in se mundus habet, sui[s] similes species generat genus. Est et aliud animalis genus, sine anima quidem, et tamen non carens sensibus, unde et beneficiis gaudet, et adversis ⟨dolet quibus⟩ minuitur atque vitiatur: omnium dico quae in terra radicum incolumitate vivescunt: qu*o*rum species per totam sparsae sunt terram. Ipsud caelum plenum est [deo] ⟨diis: eorum inmortales sunt species⟩. Supradicta autem genera inhabitant usque ad loca [specierum] ⟨deorum⟩; quarum omnium rerum [in]mortales sunt species. Species enim pars est generis, ut homo humanitatis; quam necesse est sequi qualitatem generis sui. Unde efficitur ut, quamvis omnia genera inmortalia sint, species non omnes sint inmortales. Divinitatis enim genus et ipsum et species inmortales sunt. Reliquorum genera [[quorum aeternitas est generis]], quamvis per species occida⟨n⟩t, nascendi fecunditate servantur: ideoque species mortales sunt ⟨⟨quorum aeternitas est generis⟩⟩; ut homo mortalis sit, inmortalis humanitas.

5 ⟨⟨Sunt omnes simillimae generibus suis species;⟩⟩ omnibus tamen generibus omnium generum species miscentur.

⟨Sunt res⟩ quaedam quae ante factae sunt, quaedam quae de his quae factae sunt fiunt. Haec itaque quae fiunt aut ab diis *et* daemonibus ⟨fiunt⟩, aut ab hominibus. [[Sunt omnes simillimae generibus suis species.]] Corpora enim inpossibile est ⟨ad genus⟩ conformari sine nutu divino, ⟨in⟩ species figurari sine adiutorio daemonum; inanimalia institui et coli sine hominibus non possunt.

Quicunque ergo daemonum, a genere suo defluentes [in speciem], alicuius speciei generis divini proximitate et consortio ⟨generi divino⟩ fortuito coniuncti sunt, diis similes habentur. Quorum vero daemonum species *in* qualitate sui generis perse-

1 facit *scripsi*: faciet ω 3 sui *ed. Rom.*: suis ω 7 quorum *scripsi*: quarum ω 10 'quarum *vix sanum*: *fortasse* quare non' *Thomas* 14 sint *man.* 2 *B*: *om. cett.* 16 occidant *scripsi*: occidat ω 17 servantur ς: servatur *cett.* 21 his quae factae *G*, *man.* 2 *B*: his factae *cett.* 22 et *scripsi*: aut ω 29 in *Kroll*: sunt ω

individual is a part of the kind. Thus the god-kind produces individual gods, and the daemon-kind produces individual daemons. And so too the kind or race of men, and that of birds, and those of all beings which the universe contains, generate individuals of like form to their kind. And there is yet another kind of living beings,[1] which are devoid of soul[2] indeed, yet not without sensation,[3] so that they are gladdened by all that does them good, and suffer pain from all that impairs and harms them. This kind consists of all things which are implanted in the soil, and spring into life with firm-fixed[4] roots; and the individuals of this kind are spread abroad over all the earth. Heaven itself is filled with gods; and the gods are individually immortal. The other kinds of which I have spoken dwell in the space which extends from earth to the abode of the gods; and in all these kinds, the individuals are mortal. For the individual is a part of the kind,—as a man, for instance, is a part of mankind,—and must necessarily agree in quality with the kind of which it is a part. Hence, though all kinds are immortal, not all individuals are immortal. In the case of the gods, both the kind and the individuals are immortal. All other kinds, though they perish in their individuals, are kept in being by their reproductive fertility.[5] Thus the individuals are mortal, but the kind is everlasting;[6] so that men are mortal, but mankind is immortal.

But though all individuals exactly resemble the type of their 5
kind, yet individuals of each kind intermingle[7] with all other kinds. [ ][8]. All daemons who have dissociated themselves[9] from their own kind, and have come to be[10] united to the god-kind through close connexion and fellowship with some individual of the god-kind, are held to be 'godlike daemons';[11] individuals of the daemon-kind who maintain unchanged the character of their own

[1] *Animalis* = τοῦ ζῶντος or ζωὴν ἔχοντος. *Sine anima* = ἄψυχον.
[3] *Sensus* = αἰσθήσεις. [4] *Incolumitas* = ἀσφάλεια.
[5] *Nascendi* = γεννήσεως.
[6] *Species . . . generis* = θνητὰ τὰ εἴδη ὧν ἀΐδιον τὸ γένος.
[7] *Miscentur* = ἐπιμίγνυνται?
[8] ['There are things which have been made before (viz. the four elements), and other things which are made out of those which have been made before. The things which are made are made either by gods and daemons, or by men. Organic bodies cannot receive their generic forms save by the fiat of the gods; nor can they be fashioned into their individual shapes without the ministration of daemons. Inanimate things cannot be constructed and kept in order save by the hands of men.'] *Quaedam . . . quaedam* = τὰ μὲν . . . τὰ δέ.
[9] *Defluentes* = ἀπορρέοντες? [10] *Fortuito* = ἔτυχον.
[11] *Diis similes* = θεοειδεῖς.

verant, ⟨. . . . Qui vero . . .,⟩ ii amantes hominum ⟦ratio⟧ daemones nuncupantur. Similis est et hominum ⟨⟨ratio⟩⟩, et eo amplior. Multiformis enim variaque generis humani species, et ipsa ⌜a praedictae⌝ desuper veniens, consortio [omnium] aliarum specierum multas et prope omnium ⟨generum⟩ per necessitatem coniunctiones facit. Propter quod et prope deos accedit qui se mente, qua diis iunctus est, divina religione diis iunxerit, et daemonum, qui his iunctus est: humani vero, qui medietate generis sui contenti sunt: et reliquae hominum species his similes erunt, quorum se generis speciebus adiunxerint.

6a Propter haec, o Asclepi, magnum miraculum est homo, animal adorandum atque honorandum. Hoc enim in naturam dei transit, quasi ipse sit deus: hoc daemonum genus novit, utpote qui [cum] isdem se ortum esse cognoscat: hoc humanae naturae partem in se ipse despicit, alterius partis divinitate confisus. O hominum quanto est natura temperata felicius! Diis cognata divinitate coniunctus est: partem sui, qua terrenus est, intra se despicit: cetera omnia, quibus se necessarium esse caelesti dispositione cognoscit, nexu secum caritatis adstringit. Suspicit caelum: ⟨⟨colit terram⟩⟩. Sic ergo feliciore loco medietatis est positus, ut quae infra se sunt diligat, ipse a se superioribus diligatur. ⟦Colit terram.⟧ ⟦Elementis velocitate miscetur.⟧ ⟨⟨Omnia illi licent:⟩⟩ acumine mentis in maris profunda descendit; ⟦omnia illi licent;⟧ non caelum videtur altissimum, quasi e proximo enim animi sagacitate metitur. ⟨⟨Elementis velocitate miscetur:⟩⟩ intentionem animi eius nulla aeris caligo

1 ratio *BM*: rationem *vel* ratione *cett.* 1–2 ratio *transposuit Thomas* 4 praedicto *L*: praedictae *cett.* 16 quanta *BM*: quanto *cett.* 22 elementis *codd.*: caelo mentis *Diels* (*Elementum* p. 75) *dubitanter* 23 *Fortasse* omnia illi ⟨adire⟩ lice⌜n⌝t

kind are called . . .; and those who associate with men are called 'daemons friendly to man'.[1] And the like is to be said of men; indeed, the range of men is yet wider than that of the daemons. The individuals of the human kind are diverse, and of many characters. They, like the daemons, come from above; and entering into fellowship with other individuals, they make for themselves many and intimate connexions with almost all other kinds. Accordingly, the man who, in virtue of the mind[2] in him, through which he is akin to the gods,[3] has attached himself to them by pious devotion, becomes like to the gods; he who has attached himself to daemons becomes like to the daemons;[4] those who are content with the intermediate station[5] of their kind remain mere men and nothing more; and all other individuals of the human kind, according as they have attached themselves to individuals of this kind or that, will resemble the beings to which they have attached themselves.

Man is a marvel then, Asclepius; honour and reverence to **6 a**
such a being! Man takes on him the attributes of a god, as though he were himself a god; he is familiar with[6] the daemon-kind, for he comes to know that he is sprung from the same source as they; and strong in the assurance of that in him which is divine, he scorns the merely human part of his own nature. How far more happily blended are the properties of man than those of other beings! He is linked to the gods, inasmuch as there is in him a divinity akin to theirs; he scorns that part of his own being which makes him a thing of earth; and all else with which he finds himself connected[7] by heaven's ordering, he binds to himself by the tie of his affection. He raises reverent eyes to heaven above; he tends the earth below. Blest in his intermediate station, he is so placed that he loves all below him, and is loved by all above him. He has access to all; he descends to the depths of the sea by the keenness of his thought; and heaven is not found too high for him, for he measures it by his sagacity, as though it were within his reach. With his quick wit[8] he penetrates the elements; air cannot blind his mental vision with its

[1] *Amantes hominum* = φιλάνθρωποι. [2] *Mens* = νοῦς.
[3] *Diis iunctus est* = τοῖς θεοῖς συγγενής ἐστι.
[4] *Et prope deos accedit . . . et daemonum* = καὶ τῶν θεῶν ἐγγίζει . . . καὶ τῶν δαιμόνων.
[5] *Medietas* = μεσότης. [6] *Novit* = ἔγνωκε.
[7] *Necessarius* = ἀναγκαῖος. [8] *Velocitas* = ταχύνοια?

confundit, non densitas terrae operam eius inpedit, non aquae altitudo profunda despectum eius obtundit. Omnia idem est, et ubique idem est.

6 b Horum omnium generum, quae sunt animalia desuper deorsum radices pervenientes habent: inanimali*a* autem de imo in superna ⌈viva⌉ radice silvescunt. Quaedam autem duplicibus aluntur alimentis, quaedam simplicibus. Alimenta autem sunt bina anim*ae* et corporis, e quibus animalia constant. Anima ⟨ignis et aeris, superiorum⟩ mundi ⟨elementorum,⟩ inquieta semper agitatione nutritur: corpora ex aqua et terra, inferiori⟨bu⟩s mundi *ele*mentis, augescunt. [Spiritus, quo plena sunt omnia, permixtus cunctis cuncta vivificat.] Sensu⟨s⟩ [addito ad hominis intellegentiam], quae quinta pars soli homini concessa est ex aethere, [sed] de animalibus cunctis humanos tantum sensus ad divinae rationis intellegentiam exornat, erigit, atque sustollit.

6 c Sed quoniam de sensu commoneor dicere, paulo post et huius rationem vobis exponam: est enim sanctissima et magna, et non minor quam ea quae est **7 a** divinitatis ipsius. Sed nunc vobis expediam quae coeperam. Dicebam enim [in ipso initio rerum] de coniunctione deorum, qua homines soli eorum dignatione perfruuntur, quicumque etenim hominum tantum felicitatis adepti sunt, ut illum intellegentiae divin*ae* perciperent sensum, qui sensus est divinior in solo deo et in humana intellegentia.—*Ascl.* Non enim omnium hominum, o Trismegiste, uniformis est sensus?—*Trism.* Non omnes, o Asclepi, intellegentiam veram adepti sunt, sed imaginem temerario inpetu nulla vera inspecta ratione sequentes decipiuntur, quae in mentibus malitiam parit, et transformat optimum animal in naturam ferae moresque beluarum. De sensu autem et de omnibus similibus, quando et de spiritu, tunc totam vobis praestabo rationem.

7 b Solum enim animal homo duplex est; et eius una pars simplex,

5 inanimalia *scripsi*: inanimalium ω 8 animae *scripsi*: animi ω 10–11 inferioribus mundi elementis *scripsi*: inferioris mundi alimentis ω 12 sensus *scripsi*: sensu ω 13 soli *G et man.* 2 *B*: sola *cett.* 21 divinae *scripsi*: divinum ω

thickest darkness; dense earth cannot impede his work; the deepest water cannot blur his downward gaze. Man is all things; man is everywhere.

Now of all the different kinds or races, those which possess 6 b
soul[1] have roots extending downward to them from above; and those which are soulless sprout from roots which reach upward from below. The one sort[2] are nourished with two kinds of food; the other sort, with food of one kind only. Animals are composed of soul and body; and their food is of two kinds,—food for the soul and food for the body. The soul is nourished by the ceaseless movement of fire and air, the higher elements; the growth of bodies is supplied from water and earth, the lower elements. Mind,[3] a fifth component part, which comes from the aether, has been bestowed on man alone; and of all beings that have soul, man is the only one whose faculty of cognition[4] is, by this gift of mind,[3] so strengthened, elevated, and exalted, that he can attain to knowledge of the truth concerning God.[5]

As[6] I have been led to speak of mind,[3] I will later on expound to you the 6 c
true doctrine concerning mind also; for it is a high and holy doctrine, and one
no less sublime than that which treats of God himself. But for the present,
I will continue the explanation I have begun. I was speaking of that attach- 7 a
ment to the gods which men, and men alone, are by the grace of the gods permitted to enjoy,—that is to say, such men as[7] have attained to the great happiness of acquiring that divine faculty of apprehending truth, that diviner sort of mind, which exists only in God and in the intellect of man.[8]—*Ascl.* But tell me then, Trismegistus, is not the mind of all men of one quality?—*Trism.* Not all men, Asclepius, have attained to true knowledge.[9] Many men, yielding to reckless impulse, and seeing nothing of the truth,[10] are misled by illusions;[11] and these illusions breed evil in their hearts, and transform man, the best of living beings, into a wild and savage beast. But concerning mind and the like I will fully set forth the truth to you later on, when I come to treat of spirit also.

Man, and man alone of all beings that have soul, is of twofold 7 b
nature. Of the two parts of which he is composed, the one is

[1] *Animalia* = ἔμψυχα, i.e. animals: *inanimalia* = ἄψυχα, i.e. vegetables.
[2] *Quaedam . . . quaedam* = τὰ μὲν . . . τὰ δέ.
[3] *Sensus* = νοῦς, which might be translated 'mind' or 'intellect' or 'reason'.
[4] *Sensus* = αἴσθησις?
[5] *Divinae rationis intellegentia* = ἡ τοῦ θείου λόγου (i.e. θεολογίας) γνῶσις?
[6] This passage (chs. 6 c, 7 a) was probably absent in the original text of *Ascl.* I; it may have been added by the compiler of the composite *Asclepius*.
[7] *Quicumque etenim* = ὅσοι δή.
[8] Perhaps, 'in God and in those men who have *gnosis*.'
[9] *Intellegentia* = γνῶσις?
[10] *Vera ratio* = ὁ ἀληθὴς λόγος.
[11] *Imago* = φαντασία?

quae, ut Graeci aiunt, οὐσιώδης, quam vocamus divinae similitudinis formam; est autem ⟨altera pars⟩ quadruplex, quod ὑλικόν Graeci, nos mundanum dicimus, [e quo factum est corpus,] quo circumtegitur illud quod in homine divinum esse iam diximus, in quo mentis divinitas tecta sola cum cognatis suis, id est mentis purae sensibus, secum ipsa conquiescat tamquam muro corporis saepta.—

7c *Ascl.* Quid ergo oportuit, o Trismegiste, hominem in mundo constitui, et non in ea parte, qua deus est, eum in summa beatitudine degere?—*Trism.* Recte quaeris, o Asclepi: et nos enim deum rogamus, tribuat nobis facultatem reddendae rationis istius. Cum enim omnia ex eius voluntate dependeant, tum illa vel maxime, quae de tota summitate tractantur, quam rationem
8 praesenti disputatione conquirimus. Audi ergo, Asclepi. Dominus et omnium conformator, quem recte dicimus deum, quo⟨niam⟩ a se secundum fec[er]it ⟨deum⟩ qui videri et sentiri possit;—

13 maxime *G*: maxima *cett.* 15 quoniam *Goldberg*: quo *ω* 16 fecit deum qui *scripsi*: fecerit qui *ω* | videri et sentiri *G*: viderit et viderten possit *B*: viderit et videre (t *eras.*) possit *M*

---

c. 8 *init.*—Lactant. *Div. inst.* 4. 6. 4 (vide *Testim.*): 'Hermes in eo libro qui Λόγος τέλειος inscribitur his usus est verbis:

"ὁ κύριος καὶ τῶν πάντων ποιητής, ὃν θεὸν καλεῖν νενομίκαμεν, ἐπεὶ τὸν δεύτερον ἐποίησε, θεὸν ὁρατὸν καὶ αἰσθητόν, —αἰσθητὸν δέ φημι οὐ διὰ τὸ αἰσθάνεσθαι αὐτόν, περὶ γὰρ τούτου, πότερον αὐτὸς αἰσθάνεται ⟨ἢ μή, εἰσαῦθις ῥηθήσεται⟩, ἀλλὰ ὅτι εἰς αἴσθησιν ὑποπίπτει καὶ εἰς ὅρασιν,—ἐπεὶ οὖν τοῦτον ἐποιησε πρῶτον καὶ μόνον καὶ ἕνα, καλὸς δὲ αὐτῷ ἐφάνη ⟨ὢν⟩ καὶ πληρέστατος πάντων τῶν ἀγαθῶν, ἠγάσθη τε καὶ πάνυ ἐφίλησεν ὡς ἴδιον τόκον."'

Lactant. *Epit. div. inst.* 37. 4: 'Plato de primo ac secundo deo ... locutus est, fortasse in hoc Trismegistum secutus; cuius verba de Graecis conversa subieci:

"Dominus et factor universorum, quem deum vocare existimavimus, secundum fecit deum visibilem et sensibilem. Sensibilem autem dico non quod ipse sensum accipiat, sed quod in sensum mittat et visum. Cum ergo hunc fecisset primum et solum et unum, optimus ei apparuit et plenissimus omnium bonorum."'

Ps.-Augustin. *c. quinque haereses* 3: 'Hermes . . . scripsit librum qui Λόγος τέλειος appellatur, id est verbum perfectum. . . . Audiamus quid loquatur

single and undivided; this part is incorporeal and eternal, and we call it 'that which is formed in the likeness of God'. The other part of man is fourfold, and material; and within it is enclosed that part of him which I just now called divine, to the end that, sheltered therein, the divine mind,[1] together with the thoughts[2] of pure mind, which are cognate to it, secluded from all else, may dwell at rest, fenced in by the body, as it were by a wall.—

Ascl. But what need was there, Trismegistus, that man should 7c
be placed in this material world? Why might he not have dwelt in the region where God is, and there enjoyed perfect happiness? —*Trism.* You are right, Asclepius, in asking that question; and I pray God to give me power to answer it. For on his will depend all things, and above all else, the investigation of that which is highest and most comprehensive; and such is that with which our present inquiry is concerned. Listen then, Asclepius. When 8
the Master, the Maker of all things, whom by usage we name God, had made him who is second,[3] a god visible and sensible;

[1] *Mens* = νοῦς. [2] *Sensus* = νοήματα? [3] Viz. the Kosmos.

Mercurius de verbo perfecto: "Dominus" inquit "et omnium factor deorum secundum fecit dominum" ('deum *scribendum*?' *Brandt*). Et post pauca, ut ostenderet quid dixerit, repetiit et dixit: "Quoniam ergo hunc fecit primum et solum et unum, bonus autem ei visus est et plenissimus omnium bonorum, . . . laetatus est et valde dilexit tanquam unigenitum suum."'

In tabula Mercurium Trismegistum docentem ostendente, quae in pavimento aedis Senensis insculpta est (A.D. 1488), leguntur in tabella inscripta verba haec: 'Deus omnium creator secum* deum fecit visibilem et hunc fecit primum et solum quo oblectatus est et valde amavit proprium filium qui appellatur sanctum verbum.' (* secum *perperam scriptum est pro* secundum.)

Pseudo-Anthimus *Ad Theodorum* (vide *Testim.*) §§ 10, 11:

φάσκει γὰρ οὕτως (*sc.* Ἑρμῆς ὁ Τρισμέγιστος) πρὸς Ἀσκληπιὸν τὸν ἰατρόν· "ἄκουε τοιγαροῦν, Ἀσκληπιέ. ὁ κύριος καὶ τῶν πάντων ποιητής, ὃν καλεῖν θεὸν νενομίκαμεν, ἔτι τὸν δεύτερον ἐποίησε θεὸν ὁρατὸν καὶ αἰσθητόν." . . . εἶτα πάλιν ὁ Τρισμέγιστός φησιν· "ἐπεὶ οὖν τοῦτον ἐποίησε πρῶτον καὶ μόνον καὶ ἕνα, κάλλι⟨στ⟩ος δὲ αὐτῷ ἐφάνη καὶ πληρέστατος πάντων τῶν ἀγαθῶν, ἠγάσθη τε καὶ πάνυ ἐφίλησεν ὡς ἴδιον τόκον."

eu*m* de⟨u⟩m secundum sensibilem [ita] dixerim non ideo, quod ipse sentiat, (de hoc enim, an ipse sentiat an non, alio dicemus tempore,) sed eo, quoniam videntium sensus incurrit;—quoniam ergo hunc fecit ex se primum et a se secundum, visusque ei pulcher, utpote qui sit omnium bonitate plenissimus, amavit eum ut divinitatis part*u*m suae. Ergo, ut ⌜tantus et⌝ bonus, esse[t] voluit alium, qui illum, quem ex se fecerat, intueri potuisset, simulque et rationis ⟨suae⟩ imitatorem et diligentiae fecit hominem. Voluntas etenim dei ipsa est summa perfectio, utpote cum voluisse et perfecisse uno eodemque temporis puncto conpleat. Cum itaque eum οὐσιώδη ⟨fecisset⟩, et animadverteret eum non posse omnium rerum esse diligentem nisi eum mundano integimento contegeret, texit eum corporea domo, talesque omnes esse praecepit [[ex utraque natura in unum confundens miscensque quantum satis esse debuisset]]. Itaque hominem conformat ex animi et corporis, id est, ex aeterna atque mortali natura, ⟨⟨ex utraque natura in unum confundens miscensque quantum satis esse⟨t⟩ [debuisset],⟩⟩ ut animal ita conformatum utraeque origini suae satisfacere possit, et mirari atque ⟨ad⟩orare caelestia, et [in]colere atque gubernare terrena. ⟨Terrena⟩ [[modo]] autem dico [mortalia] non ⟨⟨modo⟩⟩ aquam et terram, quae duo de quattuor elementis subiecit natura hominibus, sed ea quae ab hominibus aut in his aut de his fiunt, [a]ut ipsius terrae cultus, pascuae, aedificatio, portus, navigationes, communicationes, commodationes alternae, quae est humanitatis inter se firmissimus

1 eum deum *scripsi*: eundem ω | ita *seclusit Kroll* 4 facit *B*: fecit *cett.* 6 partum *Kroll*: partem ω | esse *Kroll*: esset ω 8 fecit *F*: facit *cett.* 9 dei ipsa *F*: de ipsa *cett.* 11 fecisset *addidi* (creasset *addidit Koziol*) 18 esset *scripsi*: esse debuisset ω 19 adorare *Rohde*: orare ω 23 ut *edd. vett.*: aut ω (*sed* a *exp. B*)

—and I call him 'sensible', not because he perceives things by sense, (for the question whether he perceives things by sense or not, we will discuss later on,) but because he can be perceived by sense and sight;—when, I say, God had made this being, his first and one and only creation,[1] and when he saw that the being he had made was beautiful, and wholly filled with all things good, he rejoiced in him, and loved him dearly, as being his own offspring. Therefore, being ⟨wise⟩ and good himself, he willed that there should be another who might look upon the being whom he had begotten; and in that act of willing,[2] he made man, to be an imitator of his wisdom[3] and his fostering care.[4] For with God, to will[5] is to accomplish, inasmuch as, when he wills, the doing is completed in the self-same moment as the willing. And so, having made man as an incorporeal and eternal being, and perceiving that the man whom he had made could not tend all things ⟨on earth⟩ unless he enclosed him in a material[6] envelope, God gave him the shelter of a body to dwell in, and ordained that all men should be formed in like manner. Thus he fashioned man of the substance of mind[7] and the substance of body,—of that which is eternal and that which is mortal,—blending and mingling together portions of either substance in adequate measure, to the end that the creature so fashioned might be able to fulfil the demands of both sources of his being, that is to say, to venerate and worship the things of heaven, and at the same time to tend[8] and administer the things of earth. And when I say 'the things of earth', I do not mean merely the two elements, water and earth, which nature has placed in subjection to men; I mean all things that men do on land and water, or make out of earth and water, as for instance tillage and pasture, building, harbour-works and navigation, and intercourse and mutual service, that strong bond by which the members of the human race are linked together. ⟨For to man is given the charge⟩ of that part of the

[1] In the earliest form of the text, this sentence probably ran as follows: *ὁ κύριος καὶ τῶν πάντων ποιητής, ὃν θεὸν καλεῖν νενομίκαμεν, ἐπεὶ τὸν δεύτερον ἐποίησε, θεὸν ὁρατὸν καὶ αἰσθητὸν [ ] πρῶτον καὶ μόνον καὶ ἕνα, καλὸς δὲ αὐτῷ ἐφάνη ὢν καὶ πληρέστατος πάντων τῶν ἀγαθῶν, ἠγάσθη τε καὶ πάνυ ἐφίλησεν ὡς ἴδιον τόκον.* 'When the Master . . . had made him who is second, the first and one and only visible and sensible god, and when he saw that,' &c.

[2] *Simul* = ἅμα ⟨βουλόμενος⟩?

[3] *Ratio* = λογισμός?

[4] *Diligentia* = θεραπεία.

[5] *Voluntas* = βούλησις or θέλημα.

[6] *Mundanus* = ὑλικός.

[7] *Animus* = νοῦς?

[8] *Colere* = θεραπεύειν.

nexus. ⌜Et⌝ ⟨. . .⟩ mundi partis quae est aquae et terrae; quae pars terrena mundi artium disciplinarumque cognitione atque usu servatur, sine quibus mundum deus noluit esse perfectum. [Placitum enim dei necessitas sequitur, voluntatem comitatur effectus.] [Neque enim credibile est deo displiciturum esse quod placuit, cum et futurum id et placiturum multo ante sciverit.]

9 Sed, o Asclepi, animadverto ut celeri mentis cupiditate festines audire quomodo homo caeli vel quae in eo sunt dilectum possit habere vel cultum. Audi itaque, o Asclepi. Dilectus [dei] caeli cum his quae insunt omnibus una est obsequiorum frequentatio. Hanc aliud animal non f*a*cit nec divinorum nec *mort*alium, nisi solus homo. Hominum enim admirationibus, adorationibus, laudibus, obsequiis caelum caelestesque delectantur. Nec inmerito in hominum coetum Musarum chorus est a summa divinitate demissus, scilicet ne terrenus mundus videretur incultior, si modorum dulcedine caruisset, sed potius ut musicatis hominum cantilenis concelebraretur laudibus qui solus omnia aut pater est omnium, atque ita caelestibus laudibus nec in terris harmoniae suavitas defuisset. Aliqui ergo, ipsique paucissimi, pura mente praediti, sortiti sunt caeli suspiciendi venerabilem curam. Quicunque autem ex duplici⟨s⟩ naturae suae confusione ⟨in⟩ in*f*eriorem intellegentiam mole corporis resederunt, curandis elementis hisque inferioribus sunt praepositi. Animal ergo homo ⟨ex parte mortale⟩; non quod is eo minor, quod ex parte mortalis sit, sed ⟨⟨mortalitate auctus esse videatur⟩⟩, e*a* *s*orte aptius efficaciusque conpositus ad certam rationem [[mortalitate auctus esse videatur]]. Scilicet quoniam utrumque nisi ex utraque materia sustinere non

9 dei *seclusit Koziol* **11** facit *scripsi*: fecit *ω* (*sed* facit *corr. B*) | mortalium *Kroll*: animalium *ω* **17** laudibus '*fortasse delendum*' *Thomas* **19** ergo ipsique *Thomas*: ipsique ergo *ω* (*sed cum traiectionis signo B*) **21** duplicis *scripsi*: duplici *ω* | in inferiorem *Koziol*: interiorem *ω* **24** non quod is *MG*: non quo dis *B* **25** ea sorte *scripsi*: eo forie *B*: eo forte *cett.*

universe[1] which consists of earth and water; and this earthly part of the universe is kept in order[2] by means of man's knowledge and application of the arts and sciences.[3] For God willed that the universe should not be complete until man had done his part. [ ] [ ][4]

But I see, Asclepius, that you are eager and impatient to be 9
told how man can tend[5] heaven or the things in heaven. Listen then, Asclepius. Tendance of heaven and of all things that are therein is nothing else than constant[6] worship;[7] and there is no other being, divine or mortal, that worships, but man alone. For in the reverence and adoration, the praise and worship of men, heaven and the gods of heaven find pleasure. And not without good reason[8] has the supreme Deity sent down the choir of the Muses to dwell among mankind. The earthly part of the universe would have seemed but rude and savage, if it had been wanting in sweet melody; and lest this should be, God sent the Muses down, to the intent that men might adore with hymns of praise Him who is all things in one, the Father of all, and that thus sweet music might not be lacking upon earth, to sound in concord with the singing of his praise in heaven. To some men then, but to very few, men who are endowed with mind uncontaminate,[9] has fallen the high task of raising reverent eyes to heaven. But to all who, through the intermingling of the diverse parts of their twofold being, are weighed down by the burden of the body, and have sunk to a lower grade of intelligence,[10]—to all such men is assigned the charge of tending the elements, and the things of this lower world. Thus man is a being ⟨partly divine, and partly mortal⟩; not that he is to be thought the lower because he is mortal in part; we ought rather to regard him as exalted by his mortality, in that he is by such a lot more fitly and effectively constituted for a purpose pre-ordained. For since he could not have met the demands of both his functions if he had not been

[1] *Mundus* = κόσμος.

[2] *Servatur* = φυλάσσεται.

[3] *Disciplinarum* = ἐπιστημῶν.

[4] ['For that must needs be, which it has pleased God to ordain. He wills, and it is done.'] ['For it cannot be thought that what it has once pleased God to ordain will ever be displeasing in his sight, inasmuch as he knew long before, both that it would come to pass, and that it would be pleasing to him.']

[5] *Dilectum vel cultum* = θεραπείαν.

[6] *Frequentatio* = πύκνωσις or πυκνότης.

[7] *Obsequium* = θρησκεία?

[8] *Nec inmerito* = οὐκ ἀπεικότως.

[9] *Pura mens* = νοῦς καθαρός.

[10] *Intellegentia* = νόησις?

potuisset, ex utraque formatus est, ut et terrenum cultum et divinitatis posset habere dilectum.

10 Rationem vero tractatus istius, o Asclepi, non solum sagaci intentione, verum etiam cupio te animi vivacitate percipere. Est enim ratio plurimis incredibilis, integra autem et vera percipienda sanctioribus mentibus. Itaque hinc exordiar. Aeternitatis dominus deus primus est, secundus est mundus, homo est tertius. Effector mundi deus et eorum quae insunt omnium simul cuncta gubernando [[cum]] homine⟨m⟩ ⟨⟨cum⟩⟩ ipso gubernatore⟨m⟩ conpos*uit*. Quod totum suscipiens homo, id est curam propriam diligentiae suae, efficit ut sit ipse et mundus uterque ornamento sibi; ut ex hac ⟨h⟩om⟨i⟩nis divina conpositione mundus (Graece rectius κόσμος) dictus esse videatur. Is novit se, novit et mundum, scilicet ut meminerit quid partibus conveniat suis, quae sibi utenda, quibus sibi inserviendum sit recognoscat, laudes gratesque maximas agens deo, eius imaginem venerans, non ignarus se etiam secundam esse imaginem dei: cuius sunt imagines duae mundus et homo, [[unde efficitur ut]] quoniam est ⟨et⟩ ipsius una conpago. ⟨⟨Nam ut homo ex utraque parte possit esse plenissimus, quaternis eum utriusque partis elementis animadverte esse formatum :⟩⟩ ⟨⟨unde efficitur ut⟩⟩ parte ⟨⟨divin*a*⟩⟩, quae ex anim*o* et sensu, spiritu atque ratione [[divinus]] est, velut ex elementis superioribus, inscendere posse videatur in caelum, parte vero mundana, quae constat ex igne et aqua ⟨et terra⟩ et aere, mortalis

9–10 hominem cum ipso gubernatorem conposuit *scripsi* : in homine ipso gubernatorem conposuit '*ex PL* (?) *proposuit Kroll*': cum homine ipso gubernatore conpositi *cett.* **12** hominis *ed. Rom.* : omnis ω **17** secundam *G* : secundum *cett.* | sint *M* : sunt *cett.* **19–21** nam ut . . . esse formatum *huc a cap.* 11 a *transposui* **21** quae *B* : qua *cett.* | animo *scripsi* : anima ω **24** igne et aqua *G*δ : igne aqua *cett.*

made of both kinds of substance, he was fashioned out of both, to the end that he might be able both to tend the earth and to do service to the Deity.

10 And now, Asclepius, I desire you to listen with a strong effort of thought, as well as with keen penetration, to that which I am about to expound to you.[1] It is a doctrine which the many[2] do not believe, but which should be accepted as sound and true by men of saintlier mind. Thus I begin. God, the Master of eternity,[3] is first; the Kosmos is second; man is third. God, the maker of the Kosmos and of all things that are therein, governs all things, but has made man as a composite being to govern in conjunction with him. And if man takes upon him in all its fullness the function assigned to him, that is, the tendance which is his special task, he becomes the means of right order[4] to the Kosmos, and the Kosmos to him;[5] so that it seems the Kosmos (that is, the ordered universe) has been rightly so named, because man's composite structure has been thus ordered[6] by God. Man knows[7] himself, and knows the Kosmos also, provided that he bears in mind what action is suited to the part he has to play, and recognizes what things he is to use for his own ends, and to what things he in turn is to do service, rendering praise and thanks in full measure to God, and revering God's image (the Kosmos), not unaware that he himself is a second image of God. For there are two images of God; the Kosmos is one, and man is another, inasmuch as he, like the Kosmos, is a single whole built up of diverse parts. For you must note that man, in order that he may be fully equipped on both sides, has been so fashioned that each of his two parts is made up of four elements; and so, in respect of the divine part of him, which is composed of other and higher 'elements', so to speak, namely, mind, intellect, spirit, and reason,[8] he is found capable of rising to heaven; but in respect of his material[9] part, which consists of fire, water, earth, and air, he is mortal, and remains on earth, that he may not leave

[1] *Ratio* = λόγος: *istius* = τοῦδε, pointing forward to what follows.

[2] *Plurimis* = τοῖς πλείστοις.

[3] *Aeternitatis dominus* = ὁ τοῦ αἰῶνος κύριος.

[4] *Ornamentum* = κόσμησις.

[5] *Sibi* = ἑαυτοῖς, in the sense of ἀλλήλοις.

[6] *Compositio* = συγκόσμησις?

[7] *Novit* = ἔγνωκε.

[8] *Animus* = διάνοια? *Sensus* = νοῦς. *Spiritus* = πνεῦμα (but in a different sense from that in which the word is used in ch. 6 b). *Ratio* = λόγος.

[9] *Mundanus* = ὑλικός.

resistat in terra, ne curae omnia suae mandata vidua desertaque dimittat. Sic enim humanitas, ex parte divina, ex alia parte
11 a effecta mortalis est, in corpore consistens. Est autem mensura eius utriusque, id est hominis, ante omni*a* religio, quam sequitur bonitas. Ea demum tunc videtur esse perfecta, si contra cupiditatem ⟨⟨virtute munita⟩⟩ alienarum omnium rerum sit despectus [[virtute munita]]. Sunt ab omnibus cognationis divinae partibus aliena omnia, quaecunque terrena corporali cupiditate possidentur; quae merito [possessionum nomine nuncupantur], quoniam non nata nobiscum, sed postea a nobis possideri coeperunt, idcirco etiam possessionum nomine nuncupantur. Omnia ergo huiusmodi ab homine aliena sunt, etiam corpus, ut et ea quae adpetimus, et illud, ex quo adpetentiae nobis est vitium, despiciamus. Ut enim meum animum rationis ducit intentio, homo hactenus esse debuit, ut contemplatione divinitatis partem quae sibi [[iuncta mortalis est]] mundi in*f*erioris necessitate servandi ⟨⟨iuncta mortalis est⟩⟩ despiciat atque contemnat. [[Nam ut homo ex utraque parte possit esse plenissimus, quaternis eum utriusque partis elementis animadverte esse formatum,]] [manibus et pedibus utrisque binis, [aliisque] corporis membris, quibus inferiori, id est terreno, mundo deserviat, illis vero partibus quattuor animi, ⟨⟨ratione⟩⟩, sensu[s], memoria[e], atque providentia[e], quarum [[ratione]] ⟨usu⟩ cuncta divina norit atque suspiciat.]

[Unde efficitur ut rerum diversitates, qualitates, effectus, quantitates suspiciosa indagatione sectetur, retardatus vero gravi⟨s⟩ [et] nimi*um* corporis vitio has naturae rerum causas quae verae sunt proprie pervidere non possit.]

11 b Hunc ergo sic effectum conformatumque et tali ministerio obsequioque praepositum a summo deo, eumque [conpetenter] munde mundum servando, deum pie colendo, digne et conpetenter in utroque dei voluntati parentem, talem quo munere credis esse munerandum,—siquidem, cum dei opera sit mundus,

4 omnia *scripsi*: omnis ω 16 inferioris *Koziol*: interioris ω 17–19 Nam ut . . . formatum *hinc ad cap.* 10 *transposui* 22–23 sensu memoria atque providentia *scripsi*: sensus memoriae atque providentiae ω 26–27 gravis nimium *scripsi*: gravi et nimio ω 28 possit *GL*[1]: possunt *cett.* 30 competenter *seclusit Kroll*

forsaken and abandoned all things that are entrusted to his keeping. Thus it is that man, though in part divine, has been made mortal also in part, being placed in a body. Now the right regulation[1] of the two parts, that is, of the whole man, consists first and chiefly in piety;[2] and piety is accompanied by goodness.[3] But goodness is to be seen in its perfection only when man's virtue[4] is fortified against desire,[5] and he scorns all things that are alien to him. Now all earthly things which man holds in his possession to gratify his bodily desires are alien to all that part of his nature which is akin to God;[6] and these things are rightly called 'possessions',[7] for this reason, that they were not born with us, but we began to get possession[8] of them at a later time. All such things then are alien to man; yes, and the body too we must regard as alien, that so we may scorn not only the objects of our greed, but also that[9] which is the source of the vicious greed within us. For according to the view to which my thinking[10] leads me, it is man's duty not to acquiesce in his merely human state, but rather, in the strength of his contemplation of things divine,[11] to scorn and despise that mortal part which has been attached to him because it was needful that he should keep and tend[12] this lower world. [ ] [ ][13] 11 a

Seeing then that man has been thus made and fashioned, and has been appointed by the supreme God to such tasks of service and of worship,[14] what, think you, should be his reward, if by a well-ordered life of labour in the world committed to his charge,[15] and by honouring God with pious observance, in both respects 11 b

1 *Mensura* = μέτρον.
2 *Religio* = εὐσέβεια. 3 *Bonitas* = ἀγαθότης.
4 *Virtus* = ἀρετή. 5 *Cupiditas* = ἐπιθυμία.
6 Or, 'are alien to all members of God's family'?
7 *Possessiones* = κτήματα. 8 *Possidere* = κτᾶσθαι. 9 Viz. the body.
10 *Rationis intentio* = διανοίας (or λογισμοῦ) ἐπιβολή?
11 *Contemplatio divinitatis* = ἡ τοῦ θείου θεωρία.
12 *Servare* = φυλάσσειν.
13 ['Man has a pair of hands and a pair of feet, as bodily members, that he may therewith do service to the lower and earthly part of the universe; and he has four mental parts, namely, reason (λόγος), intellect (νοῦς), memory (μνήμη), and foresight (πρόνοια), that he may therewith know and reverence all things divine.']

['Hence it comes to pass that men investigate with anxious search the differences of things, their qualities, their workings (ἐνεργείας), and their dimensions, but being hampered by the evil influence of a body which weighs them down, they cannot adequately understand the true causes of all that takes place in the world.']
14 *Ministerium* = ὑπηρεσία? *Obsequium* = θρησκεία or λατρεία?
15 *Munde mundum servando* = τῷ τὸν κόσμον κοσμίως φυλάσσειν.

eius pulchritudinem qui diligentia servat atque auget, operam suam cum dei voluntate coniungit, cum speciem, quam ille divina intentione formavit, adminiculo sui corporis diurno opere curaque conponit,—nisi eo, quo parentes nostri munerati sunt, quo etiam nos quoque munerari, si f*ueri*t divinae pietati conplacitum, optamus piissimis votis, id est, ut emeritos atque exutos mundana custodia, nexibus mortalitatis absolutos, naturae superioris partis, id est divinae, puros sanctosque restituat?—

12 a *Ascl.* Iuste et vere dicis, o Trismegiste.—*Trism.* Haec est enim merces pie sub deo, diligenter cum mundo viventibus. Secus enim inpieque qui vixerint, et reditus denegatur in caelum, et constituitur in corpora alia, indigna animo sancto, [et] foeda migratio.—*Ascl.* Ut iste rationis sermo processit, o Trismegiste, futurae aeternitatis spe animae in mundana vita periclitantur.—*Trism.* Sed aliis incredibile, aliis fabulosum, aliis forsitan videatur esse deridendum. Res enim dulcis est in hac corporali vita qui capitur de possessionibus fructus: quae res animam obtorto, ut aiunt, detinet collo, ut in parte sui qua mortalis est inhaereat.

12 b Nec sinit partem divinitatis agnoscere invidens inmortalitat*e* malignitas. Ego enim tibi quasi praedivinans dixero nullum post nos habiturum dilectum simplicem [qui est] philosophiae, quae sola est in cognoscenda divinitate frequens obtutus et sancta

5 fuerit *scripsi* : foret ω 9–4 *infra*: '*quae in hoc capite leguntur inter personas sic fere mihi distribuenda videntur*: As. Iuste . . . o Trismegiste. Tr. Haec est enim . . . migratio. As. Ut iste . . . malignitas. Tr. Ego enim . . . confundunt. As. Ut iste . . . malignitas. Tr. Ego enim . . . confundunt. As. Quomodo ergo . . . confundunt? *cuius distributionis aliquot vestigia in G et al. extant*' *Thomas. Ego, quod ad cetera pertinet ei consentiens, verba* sed aliis . . . malignitas *Trismegisto attribui.* 17 quae res *B* : quare *cett.* 20 inmortalitate *scripsi*: inmortalitati ω

alike he worthily and fittingly obeys God's will? For since the world is God's handiwork, he who maintains and heightens its beauty by his tendance is co-operating with the will of God, when he contributes the aid of his bodily strength, and by his care and labour day by day makes things assume that shape and aspect which God's purpose has designed. What shall be his reward? Shall it not be that which our fathers have received, and which we pray with heartfelt piety that we too may receive, if God in his mercy[1] is pleased to grant it? And that is, that when our term of service is ended, when we are divested of our guardianship[2] of the material world, and freed from the bonds of mortality, he will restore us, cleansed and sanctified, to the primal condition of
that higher part of us which is divine.—*Ascl.* Right and true, 12 a
Trismegistus.—*Trism.* Yes, such is the reward of those who spend their lives in piety to God above, and in tendance[3] of the world around them. But those who have lived evil and impious lives are not permitted to return to heaven. For such men is ordained a shameful transmigration into bodies of another kind,[4] bodies unworthy to be the abode of holy mind.—*Ascl.* According to your teaching[5] then, Trismegistus, souls have at stake in this earthly life their hope of eternity[6] in the life to come.—*Trism.* Yes. But some cannot believe this; and some regard it as an empty tale; and to some, perhaps, it seems a thing to mock at. For in our bodily life on earth, the enjoyment derived from possessions is a pleasant thing; and the pleasure which they yield grips the soul by the throat, so to speak, and holds it down to earth, compelling it to cleave to man's mortal part.

Moreover, there are some whose ungenerous temper grudges[7] 12 b
men the boon of immortality, and will not suffer them to get knowledge of that in them which is divine. For speaking as a prophet speaks, I tell you that in after times none will pursue philosophy in singleness of heart. Philosophy is nothing else than striving through constant contemplation[8] and saintly piety to attain to knowledge of God;[9] but there will be many who will

[1] *Pietas* = ἔλεος? [2] *Custodia* = φυλακή or φρουρά.
[3] *Diligenter viventes* = θεραπευτικῶς ζῶντες?
[4] I.e. the bodies of beasts. [5] *Rationis sermo* = λόγος?
[6] *Aeternitas* = αἰωνιότης?
[7] *Invidens inmortalitate* = φθονοῦσα αὐτοῖς τῆς ἀθανασίας.
[8] *Frequens obtutus* = πυκνὴ θεωρία.
[9] *Cognoscere divinitatem* = τὸν θεὸν (or τὸ θεῖον) γιγνώσκειν.

religio. Multi etenim ⟨⟨inconprehensibilem philosophiam effi-
ci*e*nt⟩⟩, et eam multifaria ratione confund*e*nt.—*Ascl.* Quomodo
ergo [multi [[inconprehensibilem philosophiam efficiunt]], aut
13 quemadmodum eam multifaria ratione confundunt]?—*Trism.*
O Asclepi, hoc modo: in varias disciplinas nec conprehensibiles
eam callida commentatione miscentes, ἀριθμητικὴν et musicen et
geometriam. Puram autem philosophiam, eamque ⟨e⟩ divina
tantum religione pendentem, tantum intendere in reliquas oporte-
bit, ut apocatastasis astrorum, stationes praefinitas cursu⟨u⟩mque
commutation*e*s numeris constare miretur; terrae vero dimensiones,
[[qualitates, quantitates,]] maris profunda, ⟨aeris . . . ⟩, ignis vim,
et horum omnium ⟨⟨qualitates, quantitates,⟩⟩ effectus natura*s*que
cognoscens miretur, adoret atque conlaudet artem mentemque
divinam. Musicen vero nosse nihil aliud es*t* nisi cunctarum
[omnium] rerum ordinem scire, quaeque sit ⟨omnes res⟩ divina
ratio sortita: ordo enim rerum singularum in unum omnium
artifici ratione conlata⟨rum⟩ concentum quendam melo divino
14 a dulcissimum verissimumque confici[e]t. Qui ergo homines post
nos erunt, sophistarum calliditate decepti, a vera, pura sanctaque
philosophia avertentur. Simplici enim mente et anima divinitatem
colere eiusque facta venerari, agere etiam dei voluntati gratias,
quae est bonitatis sola plenissima, haec est nulla animi inportuna
curiositate violata philosophia.

⟨*Asclepius II*⟩

14 b [Et de his sit hucusque tractatus: de spiritu vero et de his similibus hinc sumatur exordium.]

Fuit deus et ὕλη ⌜quem Graece credimus mundum⌝. [Et mundo comitabatur spiritus, vel inerat mundo spiritus, sed non similiter ut deo: nec deo ⟨. . .⟩.] Haec, de quibus mundus, idcirco non erant, qu⟨i⟩a n⟨a⟩ta non erant; sed in eo iam tunc

2 et (*ante* eam) *om. G* | eam *GL*: ea *cett.* 7 e *addidit Thomas* 8–9 oporterit *BM*: oportuerit M^2 9–10 cursuumque commutationes *scripsi*: cursumque commutationis ω 12 naturasque *scripsi*: naturamque ω 14 est *edd. vett.*: esse ω 15 omnium *om. G* 17 conlata ω: conlatus *ed. Rom.*: '*fortasse* conlatarum' *Thomas* 18 conficit *scripsi*: conficiet ω 19 pura *om. BM* 22 nulla *GL*: nulli *cett.* 23 violenta *BM*

29 quia nata *Thomas*: quanta *BMP*: quando *GLF*

make philosophy hard to understand, and corrupt it with manifold
speculations.[1]—*Ascl.* How so?—*Trism.* In this way, Asclepius; 13
by a cunning sort of study, in which philosophy will be mixed
with diverse and unintelligible sciences, such as arithmetic, music,
and geometry. Whereas the student of philosophy undefiled,
which is dependent on devotion to God, and on that alone, ought
to direct his attention to the other sciences only so far as he may
thereby learn to see and marvel how the returns of the heavenly
bodies to their former places, their halts [2] in pre-ordained positions,
and the variations of their movements, are true to the reckonings
of number; only so far as, learning the measurements of the
earth, the depth of the sea, ⟨the . . . of air,⟩ the force of fire, and
the properties, magnitudes, workings, and natures of all material
things, he may be led to revere, adore, and praise God's skill and
wisdom. And to know the science of music is nothing else than
this,—to know how all things are ordered, and how God's design [3]
has assigned to each its place; [4] for the ordered system in which
each and all by the supreme Artist's skill are wrought together
into a single whole yields a divinely musical harmony, sweet and
true beyond all melodious sounds. I tell you then that the men 14 a
of after times will be misled by cunning sophists, and will be
turned away from the pure and holy teachings of true philosophy.
For to worship God in thought and spirit with singleness of heart,
to revere God in all his works, and to give thanks to God,
whose will, and his alone, is wholly filled with goodness,—this is
philosophy unsullied by intrusive cravings for unprofitable
knowledge.[5]

Asclepius II

[Here let the discussion of these things end; and let us now 14 b
begin to speak of spirit and the like.]

Trism. In the beginning were [6] God and Matter. The elements of which the universe [7] is composed were not then in existence, because they had not yet come into being; [8] but

[1] *Ratio* = λογισμός? [2] *Stationes* = στάσεις.
[3] *Ratio* = λόγος.
[4] *Sit sortita* = κεκλήρωκε.
[5] *Curiositas* = περιεργία, or πολυπραγμοσύνη?
[6] *Fuit* = ἦν.
[7] *Mundus* = ὁ κόσμος.
[8] *Nata non erant* = οὔπω ἐγεγόνει.

erant unde nasci habuerunt. [Non enim ea sola non nata dicuntur quae necdum nata sunt, sed ea ⟨etiam quae . . .⟩. ⟨. . .⟩ quae carent fecunditate generandi, ita ut ex his nihil nasci possit.]

Quaecunque ergo sunt quibus inest natura generandi, haec et generabilia sunt: de quibus nasci potest ⟨aliquid⟩, tametsi ea ex se nata sunt. Neque enim dubitatur ex his quae ex se nata sunt facile nasci posse ⟨. . .⟩. ⟨. . .⟩ de quibus cuncta nascuntur.

Deus ergo sempiternus, deus aeternus: nec nasci potest nec potuit: hoc est, hoc fuit, hoc erit semper. Haec ergo est, quae ex se tota est, natura dei.

ὕλη autem (vel mundi natura) [et spiritus], quamvis nata non videa[n]tur, a principio tamen in se nascendi procreandique vim posside[n]t atque naturam. Fecunditatis etenim initium in qualitate [naturae] ⟨materiae⟩ est, quae et conceptus et partus in se possidet vim atque [materiam] ⟨naturam⟩. Haec itaque sine alieno conceptu est sola generabilis, ⟨⟨qu*ae* utique in se vim totius naturae habet.⟩⟩

15 At vero ea, quae vim solam concipiendi habent ex alterius commixtione naturae, ita discernenda sunt, ut ⟨. . .⟩. *S*ic locus mundi cum his quae in se sunt vide[a]tur esse non natus [[qui utique in se vim totius naturae habet]]: locum autem dico in quo sint omnia. Neque enim haec omnia esse potuissent, si locus deesset qui omnia sustinere potuisset. Omnibus enim rebus quae fuerint praecavendum est loco: nec qualitates etenim nec

13 videatur *scripsi*: videantur ω 14 possidet *scripsi*: possident ω 17–18 quae utique . . . habet *huc a cap.* 15 *transposui* 17 quae *scripsi*: qui ω 20 Sic *scripsi*: hic ω 21 videtur *scripsi*: videatur ω 24 qui (*post* deesset) *ex* quo *corr. M*: quo *B*: qui *cett.*

they were already in that from which they were to be generated.[1]

Now all things which possess the faculty of generating are generative;[2] and it is possible for something else to be generated from them, even if they are self-generated.[3] For there is no doubt that from things self-generated can easily be generated . . . . from which all things come into being.

God is everlasting, God is eternal.[4] That he should come into being, or should ever have come into being, is impossible. He is, he was, he will be for ever. Such is God's being; he is wholly self-generated.[5]

Matter,[6] though it is manifestly ungenerated,[7] yet has in itself from the first[8] the power of generating;[9] for an original[10] fecundity is inherent in the properties of matter, which possesses in itself the power of conceiving things and giving birth to them. Matter then is generative by itself, without the help of anything else.[11] It undoubtedly contains in itself the power of generating[12] all things.

On the other hand, we must class apart from matter those 15
things which are enabled to conceive only when something else is intermingled with them; though ⟨such things also may be ungenerated⟩. Thus the space[13] in which is contained the universe[14] with all things that are therein[15] is manifestly ungenerated. (By 'space' I here mean that in which all things are contained.) For the existence of all things that are would have been impossible, if space had not existed as an antecedent condition of their being.[16] For if anything is to exist, space for it must be provided beforehand; if things were nowhere,[17] their

[1] Perhaps ἐνῆν ἤδη ἐν τῷ ἐξ οὗ (or ἐν τοῖς ἐξ ὧν?) ἔμελλε γενήσεσθαι.
[2] *Generabilia* = γεννητικά. [3] *Ex se nata* = αὐτογέννητα.
[4] *Sempiternus* = ἀΐδιος: *aeternus* = αἰώνιος.
[5] Perhaps τοιαύτη ἡ τοῦ θεοῦ φύσις, αὐτογέννητος ὅλη οὖσα.
[6] *Vel mundi natura*: added by the translator, as an explanation of ὕλη.
[7] ἀγέννητος οὖσα φαίνεται, rather than ἀγέννητος εἶναι δοκεῖ.
[8] *A principio* = ἐξ ἀρχῆς.
[9] *Nascendi procreandique* = γεννήσεως? *Vim atque naturam* = δύναμιν?
[10] *Initium* = ἀρχή.
[11] *Sine alieno conceptu* = ἄνευ συλλήψεως ἀλλοτρίας.
[12] *Naturae* = γεννήσεως? [13] *Locus* = τόπος, or χώρα.
[14] *Mundi* = τοῦ κόσμου.
[15] *In se* = ἐν αὐτῷ, which the translator read as ἐν αὑτῷ.
[16] *Omnia sustinere* = πᾶσιν ὑπόκεισθαι?
[17] *Earum rerum quae nusquam sunt* = τῶν μηδαμοῦ ὄντων. The translator may perhaps have written *sunt*, though he ought rather to have written *essent*.

quantitates nec positiones nec effectus dinosci potuissent earum rerum quae nusquam sunt.

Sic ergo et mundus quamvis natus non sit, in se tamen omnium naturas habet, utpote qui his omnibus ad concipiendum fecundissimos sinus praestet.

Hoc est ergo totum qualitatis ⟨diversae, prout natura est⟩ materiae, quae creabilis est, tametsi creata non est. Sicuti enim [in] natura materiae [qualitas] ⟨bonitatis⟩ fecunda est, sic et malignitatis eadem est aeque fecunda.

16 a Ne ergo dix⟨er⟩i⟨tis⟩, o Asclepi et ⟨Tat et⟩ Hammon, quod a multis dicitur: ⟨⟨dicunt enim [ipsi] deum debuisse omnifariam mundum a malitia liberare.⟩⟩ [[Non poterat deus incidere atque avertere a rerum natura malitiam.]] Quibus respondendum nihil omnino est: vestri tamen causa et haec prosequar quae coeperam, et rationem reddam. ⟨⟨Non poterat deus incidere atque avertere a rerum natura malitiam⟩⟩: [[dicunt enim ipsi deum debuisse omnifariam mundum a malitia liberare:]] ita enim in mundo est, ut quasi membrum ipsius esse videatur. Provisum cautumque est, quantum rationabiliter potuisset, a summo deo, tunc cum sensu, disciplina, intellegentia mentes hominum est munerare dignatus. Hisce enim rebus, quibus ceteris antestamus animalibus, solis possumus malitiae fraudes, dolos, vitiaque vitare. Ea enim qui, antequam his inplicitus est, ex aspectu vitarit, is homo est divina intellegentia prudentiaque munitus: fundamentum est enim disciplinae in summa bonitate consistens. [Spiritu autem ministrantur omnia et vegetantur in mundo] [[qui quasi organum vel machina summi dei voluntati subiectus est.]]

[Itaque ⟨haec⟩ hactenus a nobis intellegantur.]

⟨*Asclepius III*⟩

16 b Mente sola intellegibilis, summus qui dicitur, deus rector gubernatorque est sensibilis dei eius, qui in se circumplectitur

10 dixeritis *scripsi*: dixi ω   21 solis ω: *fortasse* soli   26–27 qui quasi . . . subiectus est *hinc ad cap.* 17 a *transposui*   28 haec *addidit Thomas*

properties, magnitudes, positions, and operations[1] could not be discerned.[2]

Matter[3] then, though it is likewise[4] ungenerated, yet contains in itself the births of all things, inasmuch as it presents a womb[5] most fertile for the conception of all things that come into being.

This sum of things therefore is of diverse quality,[6] in accordance with the varying action of the generative power of matter,[7] which, though uncreated, is creative. For as the generative power of matter is productive of good, so it is equally productive of evil[8] also.

You must not then, my pupils, speak as many do, who say that **16 a**
God ought by all means[9] to have freed the world[10] from evil. To those who speak thus, not a word ought to be said in answer; but for your sake I will pursue my argument, and therewith explain this. It was beyond God's power to put a stop to evil, and expel it from the universe; for evil is present in the world[11] in such sort that it is manifestly an inseparable part[12] thereof. But the supreme God provided and guarded against evil as far as he reasonably[13] could, by deigning to endow the minds of men with intellect, knowledge, and intuition.[14] It is in virtue of these gifts that we stand higher than the beasts; and by these, and these alone,[15] are we enabled to shun the traps and deceptions and corruptions of evil. If a man shuns them when he sees them from afar, before he is entangled in them, it is by God's wisdom and forethought[16] that he is protected from them; for man's knowledge is based on the supreme goodness of God.

[On this topic then, let this explanation suffice.]

Asclepius III

Trism. He whom we name God supreme,[17] a God apprehen- **16 b**
sible by thought alone,[18] is the ruler and director[19] of that god

[1] *Effectus* = ἐνέργειαι.
[2] *Dinosci* = διακρίνεσθαι?
[3] *Mundus* = ὕλη.
[4] I. e. as space also is.
[5] *Sinus* = κόλπον.
[6] I. e. partly good and partly bad.
[7] *Materiae* = ὕλης.
[8] *Bonitatis* = ἀγαθοῦ : *malignitatis* = κακοῦ.
[9] *Omnifariam* = πάντως.
[10] *Mundum* = τὸν κόσμον.
[11] *In mundo* = ἐν τῷ κόσμῳ.
[12] *Membrum* = μόριον.
[13] *Rationabiliter* = εὐλόγως?
[14] *Sensus* = νοῦς : *disciplina* = ἐπιστήμη : *intellegentia* = γνῶσις?
[15] Or perhaps, reading *soli*, 'by these gifts we alone (as opposed to the beasts) are enabled'.
[16] *Divina intellegentia prudentiaque* = τῇ τοῦ θεοῦ φρονήσει καὶ προνοίᾳ?
[17] *Summus* = ὕψιστος.
[18] *Mente sola intellegibilis* = νοητός, or νοήσει μόνῃ καταληπτός.
[19] *Rector gubernatorque* = διοικητὴς καὶ κυβερνήτης?

[omnem locum] omnem rerum substantiam totamque [[gignentium creantiumque]] materiam, et omne quicquid est, quantumcumque
17 a est, ⟨⟨gignentium creantiumque⟩⟩. Spiritu vero, ⟨⟨qui quasi organum vel machina summi dei voluntati subiectus est,⟩⟩ agitantur sive gubernantur omnes in mundo species, unaquaeque secundum naturam suam a deo distributam sibi. ὕλη autem (vel mundus) omnium est ⟨formarum⟩ receptaculum; omniumque agitatio atque frequentatio ⟨. . .⟩. Quorum deus gubernator, dispensans omnibus [[quantum]] rebus mundanis ⟨⟨quantum⟩⟩ unicuique necessarium *est*: spiritu vero inplet omnia, ut cuiusque naturae qualitas est inaltata.

17 b [[Est enim cava mundi rotunditas in modum sphaerae, ipsa sibi qualitatis vel formae suae causa invisibilis tota; quippe cum quemcumque in ea summum subter despiciendi causa delegeris locum, ex eo, in imo quid sit, videre non possis: propter quod multis loci[s] instar qualitatemque habere creditur. Per formas enim solas specierum, quarum imaginibus videtur insculpta, quasi visibilis creditur, cum depicta monstratur: re autem vera est sibi ipsi invisibilis semper. Ex quo eius imum, vel pars ⟨ima⟩, si locus ⟨imus⟩ est in sphaera, Graece Ἅιδης dicitur, siquidem ἰδεῖν Graece videre dicatur, quo⟨d⟩ visu imum sphaerae careat. Unde et ideae dicuntur species, quod sint visibiles formae. Ab eo itaque quod visu priventur, Graece Ἅιδης, ab eo quod in imo sphaerae sint, Latine inferi nuncupantur.]]

17 c Haec ergo sunt principalia et antiquiora et quasi capita (vel initia) omnium, qu*ia* sunt in his aut per haec aut de his ⟨⟨mundana, ut ita dixerim,⟩⟩ omnia.

18 a [[Haec ergo ipsa ut dicis quae est o Trismegiste]] [[mundana ut ita dixerim]] [[specierum omnium quae insunt uniuscuiusque sicuti est tota substantia.]]

33 a ⟨⟨De inani vero, quod etiam magnum videtur esse quam pluri-

3–4 qui quasi . . . subiectus est *huc a cap.* 16 a *transposui* **9** quantum *transposuit Hildebrand*: omnibus rebus humanis quantum *F* **10** est *scripsi*: sed (vel est *man.* 2) *B*: *om. GF* **11** inaltata *BM*: inalata *F*: *om. GPL* **12–24** *Cap.* 17 b (est enim . . . inferi nuncupantur) *hinc transposui: vide post cap.* 34 c (p. 326) **26** quia *scripsi*: quae ω **26–27** mundana ut ita dixerim *huc a cap.* 18 a *transposui* **26–29** (Trism. :) '. . . aut de his.'—(Ascl. :) 'Omnia haec ergo ipsa . . . o Trismegiste?'—(Trism. :) 'Mundana ut ita dixerim . . .' *ω et edd. prior.* **28** Haec ergo . . . Trismegiste *hinc ad cap.* 19 a (p. 322) *transposui* | aut *BM* (*sed* a *exp. B*): ut *cett.* **29–30** specierum . . . substantia *hinc ad cap.* 17 b (p. 328) *transposui* **31** *sqq.*: *cap.* 33 a–34 a (de inani . . . hominum signa) *huc transposui* **31** quod iam *BM*: quod etiam *cett.*: quod tam *Vulcanius*

perceptible by sense,[1] who embraces within himself all substances[2] and all matter, and all things without exception that have to do
with birth and production.[3] Spirit,[4] which is subject to the will of 17 a
the supreme God, and serves him as his instrument,[5] is that by means of which are moved or directed[6] all kinds of beings[7] in the universe, each in accordance with the special character assigned to it by God. Matter[8] is the recipient[9] of all forms;[10] and the changes and unbroken successions[11] of the forms ⟨are wrought by means of spirit⟩. The process is directed by God, who distributes ⟨life⟩ to all things in the universe, giving to each one of them as much as it needs. Into all things he infuses spirit, assigning it to each in larger measure, in proportion as the thing stands higher in the scale of being.[12]

These[13] then are the primary things, the prior things, the heads 17 c
or first principles[14] of all things in the universe; for all cosmic[15] things are contained in them, or wrought by means of them, or made of them.

But as to Void,[16] which most people think to be a thing of great 33 a

[1] *Sensibilis deus* = ὁ αἰσθητὸς θεός (i.e. ὁ κόσμος).
[2] *Substantia* = οὐσία.
[3] Perhaps, something like πάντα ὅσα δή ποτ' οὖν τὰ γενέσεως μετέχοντα.
[4] πνεῦμα, in the sense of 'vital spirit', a gaseous substance.
[5] *Organum vel machina* = ὄργανον.
[6] *Agitantur* = κινοῦνται : *gubernantur* = κυβερνῶνται.
[7] *Species* = εἴδη.
[8] *Vel mundus*, added by the translator.
[9] *Receptaculum* = ὑποδοχή.
[10] *Formae* = μορφαί.
[11] *Agitatio et frequentatio* = κίνησις καὶ πύκνωσις.
[12] *Naturae qualitas* = ἡ τῆς φύσεως ποιότης.
[13] Viz. ὕλη, μορφαί, and πνεῦμα.
[14] *Principalia* = τὰ προηγούμενα? *Antiquiora* = τὰ πρότερα. *Capita* = κεφάλαια? *Initia* = ἀρχαί? But *vel initia* may have been added by the translator.
[15] *Mundana* = κοσμικά. *Ut ita dixerim* probably added by the translator.
[16] *Inane* = κενόν.

mis, sic sentio: inane nec esse aliquid nec esse potuisse nec futurum umquam. Omnia enim mundi sunt membra plenissima [[ut ipse mundus sit plenus atque perfectus]] corporibus qualitate formaque diversis et speciem suam habentibus et magnitudinem, ⟨⟨ut ipse mundus sit plenus atque perfectus⟩⟩. Quorum unum est alio maius, aut alio [aliud] minus, et validitate et tenuitate diversa. Nam et quaedam eorum validiora facilius videntur, sicuti et maiora: minora vero aut tenuiora aut vix videri aut omnino non possunt: quas [[solum]] *re*s esse adtrectatione ⟨⟨solum⟩⟩ cognoscimus. Unde contigit multis credere haec non esse corpora, et esse inanes locos; quod est inpossibile. [Sicuti enim] ⟨⟨Nec istud enim⟩⟩ quod dicitur extra mundum, si tamen est aliquid, [[nec istud enim]] ⟨inane⟩ ⟨⟨esse⟩⟩ credo, sic a*d*eo plenum [[esse]] intellegibilium rerum, id est divinitati suae similium: ut hic etiam sensibilis mundus qui dicitur sit plenissimus corporum et animalium naturae suae et qualitati convenientium. Quorum facies non omnes videmus ⟨pares⟩, sed quasdam ultra modum grandes, quasdam brevissimas, ⟨cum⟩ [aut] propter spatii interiecti longitudinem [aut quod acie sumus obtunsi] tales nobis esse videantur; ⟨quaedam⟩ aut⟨em⟩ omnino propter nimiam brevitatem ⟨aut tenuitatem non videmus, ut⟩ multis non esse credantur.

33 b [[Dico nunc daemonas quos credo commorari nobiscum, et heroas, quos inter aeris purissimam partem supra nos et in terram, ubi nec nubilis locus est nec nubibus, nec ex signorum aliquorum agitatione commotio.]]

33 c Propter quod, Asclepi, inane nihil dixeris, nisi cuius rei sit inane hoc, quod dicis inane, praedixeris, ut inane ab igni, ab aqua, et his similibus; quod, etsi contigerit videri quid ⟨inane, quod⟩

9 res esse *H. Stephanus*: eas esse ω **10** contingit *B*: contingitur *M* **13** adeo *scripsi*: habeo *M*: abeo *cett.* | plenum eum esse *B corr.*, *M* **18** cum *addidit Thomas* **20** quaedam autem *scripsi*: aut ω **22–25** *Cap.* 33 b (dico nunc . . . commotio) *hinc transposui: vide post cap.* 29 a (p. 368) **28** quid inane, quod inane *scripsi*: quod inane *L*: quid inane *cett.*

importance,[1] I hold that no such thing as void exists, or can have existed in the past, or ever will exist. For all the several parts[2] of the Kosmos are wholly filled with bodies of various qualities and forms,[3] each having its own shape[4] and magnitude; and thus the Kosmos as a whole is full and complete.[5] Of these bodies, some are larger, some are smaller; and they differ in the greater or lesser firmness[6] of their substance. Those of them which are of firmer substance[7] are more easily seen, as are also those which are larger; whereas smaller bodies, and those which are of less firm substance, are almost or quite invisible, and it is only by the sense of touch[8] that we are made aware of their existence. Hence many people have come to think that these bodies do not exist,[9] and that there are void spaces; but that is impossible. And[10] the like holds good of what is called 'the extramundane', if indeed any such thing exists; for I hold that not even the region outside the Kosmos is void, seeing that it is filled with things apprehensible by thought alone, that is, with things of like nature with its own divine being. And so our Kosmos also,—the sensible universe, as it is called,—is wholly filled with bodies, and living bodies, suited to its character. The shapes[11] presented by these bodies to our sight differ in magnitude; some[12] of these shapes are very large; others are very small, when the distance of the objects makes them appear small to us; and some things, on account of their extreme minuteness or tenuity, are wholly invisible to us, and are consequently supposed by many people to be non-existent.

And so, Asclepius, you must not call anything void, without 33 c
saying what the thing in question is void of, as when you say that a thing is void of fire or water or the like. For[13] it is possible for

[1] *Quod etiam . . . quam plurimis* = ὃ καὶ μέγα τι τοῖς πλείστοις δοκεῖ εἶναι.

[2] *Membra* = μόρια.

[3] *Qualitate formaque diversis* = τῇ ποιότητι καὶ τῇ μορφῇ διαφέρουσι.

[4] *Speciem* = εἶδος, or σχῆμα.

[5] *Perfectus* = τέλειος

[6] *Validitas* = στιβαρότης, or στερεότης, or στερεμνιότης. *Tenuitas* = μανότης, or ἀραιότης, or λεπτομέρεια.

[7] *Quaedam eorum validiora* = τὰ μὲν στιβαρώτερα αὐτῶν.

[8] *Attrectatio* = ἁφή.

[9] Or 'that these things are not bodies'.

[10] I assume the original to have been something of this sort: οὐδὲ γὰρ ἐκεῖνο τὸ ἐκτὸς τοῦ κόσμου λεγόμενον, εἴ γέ τι ἐστί, κενόν μοι δοκεῖ εἶναι, οὕτω γε πλῆρες ὂν νοητῶν, τοῦτ' ἔστι τῇ θειότητι αὐτοῦ ὁμοίων. ὥστε καὶ ὁ αἰσθητὸς κόσμος κ.τ.λ.

[11] *Facies* = σχήματα?

[12] *Quasdam . . . quasdam* = τὰ μὲν . . . τὰ δέ.

[13] The Greek may have been somewhat as follows: ἣν γὰρ καὶ συμβῇ φαίνεσθαί τι κενὸν εἶναι,—τῶν γὰρ τοιούτων κενὸν εἶναι δυνατόν,—ὅμως πνεύματός γε καὶ ἀέρος κενὸν οὐκ ἂν δύναιτο οὐδὲ τὸ ἐλάχιστον εἶναι τῶν φαινομένων εἶναι κενῶν.

inane possit esse a rebus huiusmodi, ⟨⟨spiritu tamen et aere,⟩⟩ quamvis sit breve [vel magnum] quod inane videtur, [[spiritu tamen et aere]] vacuum esse non possit.

34 a Similiter vero de loco dicendum est; quod vocabulum solum intellectu caret. Locus enim ex eo cuius est quid sit apparet: principali enim dempto, nominis significatio mutilatur. Quare aquae locus, ignis locus, aut his similium, recte dicemus. Sicuti enim inane esse aliquid inpossibile est, sic et locus solus quid sit dinosci non potest. Nam si posueris locum sine eo cuius est, inanis videbitur locus; quem in mundo esse non credo. Quod si inane nihil est, nec per se quid sit locus apparet. [[nisi ei aut longitudinis aut latitudinis aut altitudinis addideris ut corporibus hominum signa.]]⟩⟩

18 b ⟨. . .⟩ Mundus itaque nutrit corpora, animas spiritus. Sensus autem ⟨his accedit⟩, quo dono caelesti sola felix sit humanitas; neque enim omnes, sed pauci, quorum ita mens est, ut tanti beneficii capax esse possit. Ut enim sole mundus, ita mens humana isto clarescit lumine, et eo amplius. Nam sol quicquid inluminat, aliquando terrae interiectu interveniente nocte eius privatur lumine: sensus autem cum semel fuerit animae commixtus humanae, fit una ex bene coalescente commixtione [materia] ⟨natura⟩, ita ut numquam huiusmodi mentes caliginum impediantur erroribus.

Unde iuste sensu*m* deorum animam dixerunt. Ego vero nec eorum dico omnium, sed magnorum quorum*dam* et principalium.

6 nomini(s) *B corr.*: nominis *M*: nomine *cett.* **11–13** nisi ei . . . hominum signa *hinc ad cap.* 34 b (p. 322) *transposui* **12** longitudinis aut latitudinis aut altitudinis (*sed* -is *in* -es *ubique corr. man. post.*) *B*: longitudines aut latitudines aut altitudines *cett.* **19** terrae et interiectu (*sed* et *expunct.*) *B*: terrae et lunae interiectu *cett.* **24** sensum *Thomas*: sensus *ω* **25** quorumdam *scripsi*: quorumque *ω*

a thing to be void of such things as these, and it may consequently come to *seem* void; but the thing that seems void, however small it be, cannot possibly be empty of spirit[1] and of air.

And the like must be said of Space.[2] The word 'space' is 34 a
unmeaning when it stands alone; for it is only by regarding something which is in space, that we come to see what space is; and apart from the thing to which it belongs,[3] the meaning of the term 'space' is incomplete. Thus we may rightly speak of the space occupied by water, and fire, and so on, ⟨but not of space alone.⟩ For as there cannot be a void, so it is impossible to determine what space is, if you regard it by itself. For if you assume a space apart from something which is in it, it will follow that there is a void space; and I hold that there is no such thing as that in the universe. If void has no existence,[4] then it is impossible to find any real thing answering to the word 'space' taken by itself.

... Gross matter[5] then is the nutriment[6] of bodies, and spirit[7] 18 b
is the nutriment of souls.[8] But besides these, there is mind,[9] which is a gift from heaven, and one with which mankind alone are blessed,—not indeed[10] all men, but those few whose souls[11] are of such quality as to be capable of receiving so great a boon. By the light of mind the human soul[11] is illumined,[12] as the world is illumined by the sun,—nay, in yet fuller measure. For all things on which the sun shines are deprived of his light from time to time by the interposition of the earth, when night comes on; but when mind has once been interfused with the soul of man, there results from the intimate blending of mind with soul a thing[13] that is one and indivisible, so that such men's thought is never obstructed by the darkness of error.[14]

Hence it has been rightly said that the souls of gods consist wholly of mind. But for my part, I hold that, even as regards

[1] Or 'of wind' (πνεῦμα). [2] *Locus* = τόπος.

[3] *Principali dempto*: *lit.* 'when the primary thing is taken away'. Perhaps ἀπόντος τοῦ προηγουμένου.

[4] *Nihil* = μὴ ὄν.

[5] *Mundus* = ὕλη (which must here be taken to mean the two grosser elements, earth and water).

[6] *Nutrit* = τρέφει.

[7] *Spiritus* = πνεῦμα (which consists of the two finer elements, air and fire).

[8] *Animas* = ψυχάς. [9] *Sensus* = νοῦς ('mind' or 'intellect' or 'reason').

[10] *Neque enim* = οὐ μήν, or οὐ μὲν οὖν? [11] *Mens* = ψυχή?

[12] *Clarescit* = φωτίζεται. [13] *Natura* = φύσις.

[14] *Caliginum erroribus* = τῷ σκότῳ τῆς πλάνης?

19 a —*Ascl.* Quos dicis [vel rerum capita vel initia primordiorum], o Trismegiste?—*Trism.* Magna tibi pando, et divina nudo mysteria, cuius rei initium facio exoptato favore caelesti. Deorum genera multa sunt, eorumque omnium pars intellegibilis, alia vero sensibilis. Intellegibiles dicuntur non ideo, quod putentur non subiacere sensibus nostris; magis enim ipsos sentimus quam eos quos visibiles nuncupamus, sicuti disputatio perdocebit, et tu, si intendas, poteris pervidere. Sublimis etenim ratio [[eoque]] divin[i]or⟨um⟩, ⟨⟨eoque⟩⟩ ultra hominum mentes intentionesque consistens, si non attentiore aurium obsequio verba loquenti*s* acceperi*s*, transvolabit et transfluet, aut magis refluet suique se fontis liquoribus miscebit.—

⟨⟨*Ascl.* Haec ergo ipsa ⟨divinorum⟩, ut dicis, ⟨ratio⟩ quae est,
34 b o Trismegiste?⟩⟩—⟨⟨*Trism.* [His ergo sic se habentibus] O Asclepi [et vos qui adestis], scito[te] intellegibilem mundum, id est, qui mentis sol*um* obtutu dinoscitur, esse incorporalem, nec eius naturae misceri aliquid posse corporale, id est, quod possit qualitate, quantitate, numerisque dinosci: in ipso enim nihil tale consistit,⟩⟩ ⟨⟨nisi ei aut longitudinis aut latitudinis aut altitudinis addideris, ut corporibus [hominum], signa.⟩⟩

19 b ⟨. . .⟩ Sunt ergo omnium ⌜specierum⌝ principes dii ⟨intellegibiles⟩, ⟨⟨quorum est [princeps] ⟨appellatio⟩ οὐσιά⟨ρχαι⟩.⟩⟩ Hos consecuntur dii [[quorum est princeps οὐσία]] hi sensibiles, utriusque originis consimiles suae, qui per sensibilem naturam

6 ipsos δ: ipse *B*: ipsa *M*: *om.* *G* 8–9 ratio divinorum, eoque ultra *scripsi*: ratio eoque divinior ultra ω 9 mentes intentionesque ω: *fortasse* mentis intentionem 10 loquentis *Thomas*: loquentias *B*: loquentia *cett.* 11 acceperis *Thomas*: acceperit ω 13–14 haec ergo . . . Trismegiste *huc a cap.* 18 a *transposui* 14–19 *Cap.* 34 b (his ergo . . . tale consistit) *huc transposui* 15 scito *scripsi*: scitote ω 16 solum *scripsi*: solo ω 19–20 nisi ei . . . signa *huc a cap.* 34 a *transposui* 21 *Fortasse* omnium ⟨substantiae⟩ specierum 23 consecuntur *B*: sequuntur *cett.* 24 virisque *BM*: utriusque *cett.*

the gods, this cannot be said of all, but of certain great and chief
gods only.—*Ascl.* And which are they, Trismegistus?—*Trism.* It **19 a**
is a weighty secret that I am about to disclose, a holy mystery that
I am about to reveal to you;[1] and I pray for the grace[2] of Heaven
to aid me as I speak. There are many kinds of gods; some of
them are apprehensible by thought alone, and others are perceptible by sense.[3] The gods apprehensible by thought are so called,
not because it is held that they are not subject to our perception;
for we perceive[4] them[5] more truly than we perceive those gods
whom we call visible,[6] as my discourse will show, and as you will
be able to see for yourself,—but only if you exert[7] to the uttermost your powers of thought. For so lofty[8] is the doctrine of
things divine,[9] that it is beyond the reach of any effort of merely
human thought; and if you do not hearken to my words with
keen attention, my teaching will wing its way beyond you, and
flow past you, or rather, will flow back thither whence it came,
and mingle with its source.—*Ascl.* And what then, Trismegistus,
is this doctrine of things divine, of which you speak?—*Trism.* Be **34 b**
it known to you that the intelligible[10] Kosmos, that is to say, that
Kosmos which is discerned by thought alone,[11] is incorporeal,[12]
and that nothing corporeal can be mingled with its being,—
nothing, that is, which admits of determination by quality,[13]
magnitude, or number; for nothing of this kind exists in it.
You cannot measure it as you would measure a body, affixing
marks of length and breadth and height.

. . . There are then certain gods apprehensible by thought **19 b**
alone, who preside over all departments of the world, and are
called 'Rulers over material things';[14] and subordinate to them
are the gods perceptible by sense. These sensible gods bear the
likeness of both the sources of their being; and these are they

[1] *Tibi*, singular. [2] *Favor* = χάρις.

[3] *Pars intellegibilis, alia vero sensibilis* = οἱ μὲν νοητοί, οἱ δὲ αἰσθητοί.

[4] *Sensibus* = αἰσθήσει, and *sentimus* = αἰσθάνομεθα? Or, *sensibus* = θεωρίᾳ, and *sentimus* = θεωροῦμεν?

[5] *Ipsos* = αὐτούς. [6] *Visibiles* = ὁρατούς.

[7] *Intendere* = ἐντείνειν, or ἐπιβάλλειν? [8] *Sublimis* = ὕψηλος.

[9] *Ratio divinorum* = ὁ τῶν θείων λόγος. [10] *Intellegibilis* = νοητός.

[11] *Qui mentis solum obtutu dinoscitur* = νοήσει θεωρητός.

[12] *Incorporalem* = ἀσώματον: *corporale* = σωματικόν.

[13] *Qualitas* = ποιότης or ποιόν.

[14] Literally, either 'rulers of substances' (ἄρχοντες οὐσιῶν) or 'sources or causes of substances' (ἀρχαὶ οὐσιῶν). The Greek may perhaps have been εἰσὶν οὖν θεοί τινες νοητοί, πάντων τῶν τῆς οὐσίας εἰδῶν ἄρχοντες, ὧν προσηγορία οὐσιάρχαι.

conficiunt omnia, alter per alterum, unusquisque opus suum inluminans.

Caeli, vel quidquid est quod eo nomine conprehenditur, *οὐσιάρχης* est Iuppiter ⟨*ὕπατος*⟩; per caelum enim Iuppiter omnibus praebet vitam.

[Solis *οὐσιάρχης* lumen est; bonum enim luminis per orbem nobis solis infunditur.]

⟨Decanorum⟩ [[xxxvi quorum vocabulum est Horoscopi]], id est, eodem loco semper defixorum siderum ⟨⟨xxxvi quorum vocabulum est Horoscopi⟩⟩, horum *οὐσιάρχης* (vel princeps) est quem *Παντόμορφον* (vel Omniformem) vocant, qui [diversis] speciebus ⟨singulis⟩ diversas formas facit.

Septem sphaerae quae vocantur habent *οὐσιάρχην*, id est sui principe*m*, quam Fortunam dicunt aut *Εἱμαρμένην*, ⟨a⟩ qu*a* inmutantur omnia lege naturae, stabilitate firmissima sempiterna agitatione variata.

Aer vero organum est vel machina omnium, per quam omnia fiunt; est autem *οὐσιάρχης* huius secundus ⟨vitae⟩

27 c ⟨⟨dispensator, qui [est] inter caelum et terram obtinet locum, quem Iovem ⟨*νέατον*⟩ vocamus.

Terrae vero et mari dominatur Iuppiter Plutonius; et hic nutritor est animantium mortalium et fructiferarum ⟨ar⟩*b*orum omnium, ⟨cuius⟩ viribus fructus [arbusta et] terra⟨e⟩ vegetantur.

Aliorum vero vires et effectus per omnia quae sunt distribuuntur.⟩⟩

27 b ⟨⟨[Ac per hoc] Deus, supra verticem summi caeli consistens, ubique est, omniaque circum inspicit: *hu*ic est enim ultra caelum locus, sine stellis, ab omnibus rebus corpulentis alienus.⟩⟩

13–14 *οὐσιάρχην* . . . principem *scripsi*: *οὐσιάρχας* . . . principes *ω* **14** a qua *scripsi*: quibus *ω* **15** lege *GL*: leges *cett.* | stabilitate *F*: stabilitateque *cett.* **17** quam *B*: quem *cett.* **19–25** *Cap.* 27 c (dispensator . . . distribuuntur) *huc transposui* **22** arborum *scripsi*: horum *ω* **23** terrae *scripsi*: terra *ω* **24–25** distribuuntur *F*: distribuentur *cett.* **26–28** *Cap.* 27 b (ac per hoc deus . . . alienus) *huc transposui* **27** huic *scripsi*: sic *ω*

13–15. Lydus *De mensibus* (Wuensch) 4. 7: *ὅτι τὸ τῆς τύχης καὶ εἱμαρμένης ἐπὶ τῆς γενέσεως προβέβληται ὄνομα· καὶ μάρτυς Ἑρμῆς, ἐν τῷ καλουμένῳ τελείῳ λόγῳ οὕτως εἰπών·*

αἱ καλούμεναι ἑπτὰ σφαῖραι ἔχουσιν ⟨οὐσι⟩άρχην τὴν καλουμένην τύχην ἢ εἱμαρμένην, ἥτις πάντα ἀλλοιοῖ [καὶ ἐπὶ τῶν αὐτῶν οὐκ ἐᾷ μένειν].

(*ἔχουσιν οὐσιάρχην scripsi*: *ἔχουσιν ἀρχὴν Wuensch*)

who make all things throughout the sensible world, working one through another, each pouring light[1] into the things he makes.

The Ruler of Heaven, or of whatsoever is included under the name 'Heaven', is Zeus ⟨Hypatos[2]⟩; for life is given to all beings by Zeus through the medium of Heaven.

The Ruler of the Decani,—that is, the thirty-six fixed stars which are called Horoscopi,—is the god named Pantomorphos;[3] he it is that gives to the individuals of each kind their diverse forms.

The seven spheres, as they are called, have as their Ruler the deity called Fortune or Destiny, who changes all things according to the law of natural growth, working with a fixity which is immutable, and which yet is varied by everlasting movement.

The air is the instrument[4] with which all these gods work, and by means of which all is done. The Ruler of the air is the
subordinate distributor[5] of life; to him belongs the region **27 c**
between heaven and earth; and we call him Zeus ⟨Neatos[6]⟩.

Earth and sea are ruled by Zeus Chthonios;[7] he it is that supplies nutriment to all mortal beings that have soul,[8] and to all trees that bear fruit; and it is by his power[9] that the fruits of the earth are produced.

And there are other gods beside, whose powers and operations[10] are distributed through all things that exist.

But God, who dwells above the summit of the highest heaven, **27 b**
is present everywhere, and from all around he watches all things; his abode is beyond heaven, in a starless region, far removed from all things corporeal.

1 Or 'the light of life'. *Illuminans* = φωτίζων; and φῶς here implies ζωή.
2 I.e. 'highest'.
3 I.e. 'giver of all manner of forms'.
4 *Organum vel machina* = ὄργανον.
5 *Dispensator* = ταμίας.
6 I.e. 'last' or 'lowest'.
7 I.e. 'of the underworld'.
8 *Animantium* = ἐμψύχων, i.e. animals.
9 *Viribus* = δυνάμει.
10 *Effectus* = ἐνέργειαι.

19 c ⟨Hoc modo coniuncta sunt in⟩mortalibus mortalia [et his similia], ⟨⟨sensibiliaque insensibilibus adnexa sunt; summa vero gubernationis summo illi domino paret.⟩⟩ His ergo ita se habentibus, ab imo ad summum se admoventibus sic sibi conexa sunt omnia, pertinentia ad se, [at de mortalibus mortalia] [[sensibiliaque insensibilibus adnexa sunt; summa vero gubernationis summo illi domino paret]] [vel] ⟨ut videantur⟩ esse non multa, aut potius unum. Ex uno etenim cuncta pendentia ex eoque defluentia, cum distantia videntur, creduntur esse quam plurima, adunata vero, unum. [vel potius duo, unde fiunt omnia, et a quo fiunt, id est, de materia qua fiunt, et ex eius voluntate cuius nutu efficiuntur.]

34 c ⟨⟨Hic ergo sensibilis qui dicitur mundus receptaculum est omnium sensibilium specierum ⟨⟨vel⟩⟩ qualitatum [[vel]] corporum; quae omnia sine deo vegetari non possunt. Omnia enim deus, et ab eo omnia, et eius omnia voluntatis ⟨⟨et pruden*tiae* inimitabil*is*⟩⟩. Quod totum est bonum ⟨et⟩ decens, [[et prudens inimitabile]] et ipsi soli sensibile atque intellegibile: et sine hoc nec fuit aliquid nec est nec erit. Omnia enim ab eo et in ipso et per ipsum, et variae et multiformes qualitates, et magnae quantitates et omnes mensuras excedentes magnitudin*i*s, et omniformes species. Qua*e* si intellexeris, o Asclepi, gratias acturus es deo.

Sin totum animadvertes, vera ratione perdisces mundum ipsum sensibilem et quae in eo sunt omnia a superiore illo mundo quasi
17 b [ex] vestiment*um* esse conte*x*ta.⟩⟩ ⟨⟨Est enim ⟨ὕλη⟩

> cava mundi rotunditas in modum spherae

ipsa sibi qualitatis vel formae suae causa invisibilis tota:

> quippe cum quemcumque in ea summum subter despiciendi causa delegeris locum, ex eo, in imo quid sit, videre non possis:

propter quod multis loci[s] instar qualitatemque habere creditur.

4 atmoventibus *B*: admoventibus *MG*: id moventibus *PL*: moventibus *F* 5 omni *B*: omnia *cett.* | at de *B*: ac de *MGP*: et de *L*: ac (*om.* de) *F* 6 gubernationis *G*: gubernatoris *cett.*: gubernatori *Thomas* 12–24 *Cap.* 34 c (hic ergo . . . esse contexta) *huc transposui* 20 magnitudinis *scripsi*: magnitudines ω 21 quae *scripsi*: qua(s) (*corr. man. post.*) *B*: quas *cett.* 22 sin *G*: si in *cett.* 23–24 quasi vestimentum esse contexta *scripsi*: quasi ex vestimento esse contecta ω (contexta *corr. man. recent. B*) 24–11 *infra*: *cap.* 17 b (est enim . . . inferi nuncupantur) *huc transposui* 29 loci *Thomas*: locis ω

Thus mortal things are joined to things immortal, and things 19 c
perceptible by sense are linked to things beyond the reach of sense;[1] but the supreme control is subject to the will of the Master[2] who is high above all. And this being so, all things are linked together, and connected one with another in a chain extending from the lowest to the highest; so that we see that they are not many, or rather, that all are one. For inasmuch as all things hang on the One and flow from the One, we think indeed that they are many when we look at them apart, but when we regard them as united,[3] we hold them to be one.

This sensible[4] Kosmos then is the recipient[5] of all the sensible 34 c
forms[6] or qualities of bodies; and all bodies can receive life only from God. For God is all things; from him are all things; and all things are dependent on his will, and on his inimitable wisdom.[7] And this whole sum of things is good and beautiful,[8] and is apprehensible by sense and thought to God alone. Without God nothing has been or is or will be; from God and in God and through God are all things,—all the various and multiform qualities, the vast and measureless magnitudes, and the forms of every aspect.[9] If you learn to understand this, Asclepius, you will render thanks to God.

And if you consider the whole, you will learn that in truth[10] the sensible Kosmos itself, with all things that are therein, is
woven like a garment by that higher Kosmos.[11] For matter,[12] 17 b
having no quality or form of its own to make it visible, is in itself[13] wholly invisible;[14] and for that reason many people think that it is like space, and has the properties of space. It is only by

[1] *Sensibilia* = αἰσθητά: *insensibilia* = ἀναίσθητα (i.e. νοητά).
[2] *Dominus* = κύριος, or δεσπότης.
[3] *Adunata* = ἡνωμένα.
[4] *Sensibilis* = αἰσθητός.
[5] *Receptaculum* = ὑποδοχή.
[6] *Sensibiles species* = τὰ αἰσθητὰ εἴδη.
[7] *Prudentia inimitabilis* = ἡ ἀμίμητος πρόνοια or σοφία.
[8] *Bonum et decens* = ἀγαθὸν καὶ καλόν.
[9] *Omniformes species* = παντόμορφα εἴδη.
[10] *Vera ratione* = κατὰ τὸν ἀληθῆ (or ὀρθὸν) λόγον.
[11] I. e. the intelligible Kosmos.
[12] This translation of cap. 17 b gives what I suppose to have been the meaning of the passage as originally written. In the traditional Latin text, cap. 17 b has been altered, by interpolations, into a statement to the effect that 'one cannot see into the depths of the earth, because it is a solid globe'.
[13] *Sibi ipsi* = αὐτὴ καθ' αὑτήν.
[14] More literally, 'matter is in itself wholly invisible, as far as depends on any quality or form of its own'. *Causa* = ἕνεκα.

Per formas enim solas specierum, quarum imaginibus videtur ⟨⟨quasi⟩⟩ insculpta, [[quasi]] visibilis creditur:

cum depicta monstratur:

re autem vera est sibi ipsi invisibilis semper,

ex quo eius imum, vel pars ⟨ima⟩, si locus est ⟨imus⟩ in sphaera, Graece Ἅιδης dicitur, siquidem ἰδεῖν Graece videre dicatur, quo⟨d⟩ visu imum sphaerae careat: unde et ideae dicuntur species,

quod *su*nt visibiles formae ⟨⟨[specierum omnium] quae ⟨omnibus⟩ insunt uniuscuiusque, sicuti est, tota substantia.⟩⟩

Ab eo itaque quod visu priventur, Graece Ἅιδης, ab eo quod in imo sphaerae sunt, Latine inferi nuncupantur.⟩⟩

⟨. . .⟩ ⟨⟨Species enim, quae divina est, incorporalis est, *u*t quicquid mente conprehenditur.

Cum itaque haec duo, ex quibus constant [forma et] corpora, incorporalia sint,⟩⟩ ⟨. . .⟩.

35 ⟨⟨Unumquodque enim [genus] animal[ium], o Asclepi, ⟨generis⟩ cuiuscunque, vel mortalis vel inmortalis, vel rationalis ⟨vel inrationalis⟩, sive sit animans sive sine anima sit, prout cuique est genus, sic singula generis sui imagines habent. Et quamvis unumquodque animal[is genus] omnem generis sui possideat formam, in eadem forma singula tamen sui dissimilia sunt: ut hominum genus quamvis sit uniforme, ut homo dinosci ex aspectu possit, singuli tamen in eadem forma sui dissimiles sunt. [[Species enim, quae divina est, incorporalis est, et quicquid mente conprehenditur. Cum itaque haec duo ex quibus constant forma et corpora incorporalia sint,]] ⟨Etenim⟩ inpossibile est formam unamquamque alteri simillimam nasci horarum et climatum distantibus punctis; sed inmutantur totiens, quot hora momenta habet circuli circumcurrentis, in quo est ille Omniformis quem diximus deus. Species ergo permanet, ex se totiens pariens imagines tantas tamque diversas, quanta habet conversio mundi momenta;

5 vel pars ima, si locus est imus in *scripsi*: vel pars (par *M*) si locus est in ω: vel pars ⟨. . .⟩ si locus est in *Goldbacher*: vel pars ⟨infera⟩, s. l. e. i. *Koziol*: '*fortasse* ex quo eius imum [vel pars], ⟨imo⟩ si locus est in' *Thomas* **6** quod *Thomas*: quo ω **8** quod sunt *scripsi*: quod sint *man.* 2 *B*, *ed. Rom.*: quo sint *cett.* **8–9** specierum . . . substantia *huc a cap.* 18 a *transposui* **12–15** Species enim . . . incorporalia sint *huc a cap.* 35 *transposui* **12** ut *Thomas*: et ω **14–15** *Fortasse* Cum itaque haec duo ex quibus constant ⟨⟨corpora⟩⟩, forma et ⟨ὕλη⟩ [[ ]], incorporalia sint (= ἀσωμάτων οὖν ὄντων τῶν δύο τούτων ἐξ ὧν συνέστηκε σώματα, τῆς μορφῆς καὶ τῆς ὕλης) | Cum itaque haec duo, ex quibus constant formae, corpora ⟨et⟩ incorporalia sint *Thomas* **16** *sqq.*: *cap.* 35 *et* 36 (unumquodque enim . . . splendore reddentium) *huc transposui* **16** animal *scripsi*: genus animalium ω **17–18** vel inrationalis *addidit Goldbacher* **20** animal *scripsi*: animalis genus ω

reason of the shapes[1] derived from those ideal forms[2] in the likeness of which we see it carved, so to speak, that men suppose it to be visible; but in reality, matter in itself is ever invisible; for the substance[3] of each thing, in so far as the thing is actually existent, consists wholly of the visible shapes which are present in all things.

. . . For the ideal form,[4] which is divine, is incorporeal, as are all things apprehensible by thought alone.

Since therefore the two constituents of which bodies consist (namely, form and matter) are incorporeal, ...

For every living being,[5] Asclepius, whatever be its kind,[6] and 35
whether that kind be mortal or immortal, rational or irrational,[7] endowed with soul or devoid of soul,[8] bears the likeness[9] of its kind, according as the character of that kind may be. But though each living being has in all respects the form[10] which is proper to its kind, the individuals, while one and all have the same form, yet differ among themselves. For instance, though the human race has a common form, so that we can know from a man's appearance[11] that he is a man, at the same time individual men, for all their sameness of form, yet differ one from another. For it is impossible that any single form should come into being which is exactly like a second, if they originate at different points of time, and at places differently situated; but the forms change at every moment in each hour of the revolution of that celestial circle[12] in which resides the god whom we have named Pantomorphos. Thus the type[13] persists unchanged, but generates at successive instants copies of itself as numerous[14] and different as are the moments in the revolution of the sphere of heaven;[15]

[1] *Formae* = μορφαί (or σχήματα?). [2] *Species* = εἴδη or ἰδέαι.
[3] *Substantia* = οὐσία (or ὑπόστασις, or ὕπαρξις?).
[4] *Species* = εἶδος or ἰδέα. [5] *Animal* = ζωὴν ἔχον. [6] *Genus* = γένος.
[7] *Rationalis* = λογικός: *inrationalis* = ἄλογος.
[8] *Animans* = ἔμψυχος: *sine anima* = ἄψυχος.
[9] *Imago* = εἰκών (or μίμημα). [10] *Forma* = μορφή, or εἶδος?
[11] *Aspectus* = ὄψις.
[12] I. e. the Zodiac, over which presides 'the god who gives all forms'.
[13] Or 'the generic form'. [14] *Tantas* . . . *quanta* = τοσαύτας . . . ὅσα.
[15] *Mundus* = οὐρανός, or κόσμος in the sense of οὐρανός.

qui⟨a⟩ mundus in conversione mutatur, species vero nec mutatur nec convertitur. Sic generum [[singulorum]] formae sunt permanentes, ⟨⟨singul*a*⟩⟩ in eadem [[sua]] forma ⟨⟨su*i*⟩⟩ dissimil*ia*.—

36 *Ascl.* Et mundus speciem mutat, o Trismegiste?—*Trism.* Vides ergo, o Asclepi, tibi omnia quasi dormienti esse narrata. Quid est enim mundus, aut ex quibus constat, nisi ex omnibus natis? Ergo hoc vis dicere de caelo, terra, et elementis. Nam quae alia magis frequenter mutantur in species? Caelum umescens vel arescens, vel frigescens vel ignescens, vel clarescens vel sordescens, in una caeli specie hae sunt quae saepe alternantur species. Terra vero speciei suae multas inmutationes habet semper, et cum parturit fruges, et cum eadem partus nutricat suos, fructuum omnium cum reddit varias diversasque qualitates et quantitates [[atque stationes aut cursus]], et ante omni*a* arborum ⟨⟨qualitates⟩⟩, florum, bacarum [[qualitates]] odores, sapores [[species]]. ⟨⟨A[t]qu*a* stationes aut cursus⟩⟩ ⟨mutat.⟩ Ignis facit conversiones plurimas, atque divinas ⟨recipit⟩ ⟨⟨species⟩⟩. Solis etenim et lunae omniformes imagines sunt; sunt enim quasi speculorum nostrorum similes, imaginum similitudines aemulo splendore reddentium.—⟩⟩

⟨ * * * * * * ⟩

20 a *Ascl.* Alia haec iterum ratio quae est, o Trismegiste?—*Trism.* Talis, o Asclepi. Deus etenim vel pater vel dominus omnium quocumque [alio] nomine [[ab hominibus sanctius religiosiusque]] nuncupatur [quod] inter nos intellectus nostri causa, ⟨⟨ab hominibus sanctius religiosiusque⟩⟩ debet esse sacratum tanti [[etenim]] numinis contemplatione: nullo ⟨⟨etenim⟩⟩ ex his nominibus eum definite nuncupabimus. Si enim vox hoc est, ex aere spiritu percusso sonus, declarans omnem hominis ⌜voluntatem vel sensum⌝

1 quia *Kroll*: qui ω **3** dissimilia *scripsi*: dissimiles ω **14** omnia *scripsi*: '*fortasse* omnia' *Thomas*: omnis ω **17** et *post* lunae *add. MPL*: et ⟨omnium stellarum⟩ *Koziol* **19–20** reddentium ω: *fortasse* reddentes **21** Alia *Asclepio attribui. Edd. priores verba sic dividunt*: *cap.* 19 c *fin.*: (Trism.) '. . . nutu efficiuntur alia.' *cap.* 20 a *init.*: (Ascl.) 'Haec iterum ratio . . .' **22** rialis *BM*: talis *cett.* **22–23** omnium quocumque *BM*: omnium vel quocumque *cett.*

for the sphere of heaven changes as it revolves, but the type neither changes nor revolves. Thus the generic forms persist unchanged, but the individuals, for all their sameness of generic form, yet differ one from another.—

Ascl. And does the Kosmos also, Trismegistus, change its **36**
forms?[1]—*Trism.* Why, you must have been asleep, Asclepius; you cannot have heard what I have been telling you all this while. What is the Kosmos, and of what is it composed, if not of things which have all come into being?[2] When you speak of the Kosmos then, you are speaking of sky, and earth, and the elements.[3] And do not these change their forms as often as anything that exists? The sky[4] is moist and dry, cold and hot, bright and obscured by turns; these are the rapidly alternating ⟨sensible⟩ forms included under the one ⟨ideal or universal⟩ form of the sky. The earth is ever passing through many changes of form; it generates produce, it nourishes the produce it has generated, it yields all manner of crops, with manifold differences of quality and quantity; and above all, it puts forth many sorts of trees, differing in the scent of their flowers and the taste of their fruits. Water takes different forms, now standing and now running. Fire undergoes many changes, and assumes godlike forms; thus the aspects[5] of the sun and moon pass through all manner of forms; they are like our mirrors, and reproduce ⟨the ideal or universal form⟩ in visible copies with rival brilliance.

* * * * * *

Ascl. And what is this other doctrine,[6] Trismegistus?— **20 a**
Trism. It is this, Asclepius. Whether he of whom I speak be called God, or Father, or Master of all, whatever be the name by which we name him to convey our meaning in our talk one with another, it is for men to hallow the name[7] with a higher sanctity by contemplation of his supreme divinity; for his being cannot be accurately[8] described by any of the names we call him. For if a word is but a sound made by the impact of our breath[9] upon the air, whereby a man makes known any thought which has

[1] *Species* here = *μορφή* or (*αἰσθητὸν*) *εἶδος* in the sense of *forma visibilis.*
[2] *Ex omnibus natis* = *ἐκ πάντων γεν(ν)ητῶν.*
[3] *Elementa* = *στοιχεῖα* (including the heavenly bodies).
[4] *Caelum* = *τὸ περιέχον*, or *οὐρανός* in the sense of *τὸ περιέχον*, i.e. the atmosphere, and not the region of the stars.
[5] *Imagines* = *ὄψεις*?
[6] *Alia . . . quae est* = *ὁ δ' ἄλλος αὖ λόγος οὗτος τίς ἐστιν;*
[7] *Debet esse sacratum* = *χρὴ ἁγιάζεσθαι τὸ ὄνομα.*
[8] *Definite* = *διοριστικῶς*?
[9] *Spiritus* = *πνεῦμα* or *πνοή.*

quem forte ex sensibus mente perceperit, cuius nominis tota substantia paucis conposita syllabis definita atque circumscripta est, ut esset in homine necessarium vocis auriumque commercium, simul etiam et sensus et spiritus et aeris ⟨nomina⟩ et omni*a* in his aut per haec aut *de* his nomen est totum dei. Non enim spero totius maiestatis effectorem omniumque rerum patrem vel dominum uno posse quamvis e multis conposito nuncupari nomine, hunc vero innomine⟨m⟩ vel potius omninomine⟨m⟩ ⟨⟨esse⟩⟩, siquidem is sit unus [et] omnia, ut sit necesse aut omnia [[esse]] eius nomine, aut ipsum omnium nominibus nuncupari.

20 b Hic ergo, solus [ut] omni[a] utr*ius*que sexus fecunditate plenissimus, semper *boni*tatis praegnans suae, parit semper quicquid voluerit procreare. Voluntas eius ⟨⟨eadem⟩⟩ est bonitas omnis. Haec [[eadem]] bonitas omnium rerum est ex divinitate eius nata [natura], uti sint omnia ⟨fecunda⟩ [[sicuti sunt et fuerunt]], et futuris omnibus dehinc ⟨⟨sicuti sunt et fuerunt⟩⟩ natura[m] ex se nascendi sufficiat. Haec ergo ratio, o Asclepi, tibi sit reddita,
21 quare et quomodo fiant omnia ⟨utriusque sexus⟩.—*Ascl.* Utriusque sexus ergo deum dicis, o Trismegiste?—*Trism.* Non deum solum, Asclepi, sed omnia animalia et inanimalia. Inpossibile est enim aliquid eorum quae sunt infecundum esse: fecunditate enim dempta ex omnibus quae sunt, inpossibile erit semper esse quae sunt. Ego enim et ⌜in naturam et sensum et naturam⌝, et mundum dico in se continere naturam et nata omnia conservare. Procreatione enim uterque plenus est sexus, et eius utriusque conexio aut, quod est verius, unitas inconprehensibilis est; quem sive Cupidinem sive Venerem sive utrumque recte poteris nuncu-

4 omnia *scripsi*: omnium ω 5 aut de his *Thomas*: autem his *B*: his autem *MG*: aut cum his δ: *fortasse* aut ex his 8 innominem *Hildebrand*: innomine *BMF*: in nomine *GP*: uno nomine *L* | omninominem *Hildebrand*: omnomine *BPF*: soninomine *M*: omni nomine *G*: omnium nomine *L* | esse *huc transposuit Thomas* 11 solus omni utriusque *scripsi*: solus ut omnia utraque ω 12 bonitatis *scripsi*: voluntatis ω 16 natura *Reitzenstein*: naturam ω 18–19 (Trism.:) '. . . quomodo fiant omnia.'—(Ascl.:) 'Utriusque sexus ergo . . .' *Kroll et Thomas*: (Trism.:) '. . . quomodo fiant omnia utriusque sexus.'—(Ascl.:) 'Ergo . . .' *edd. priores* 20 enim ut *BMP* (*sed* ut *eras. M*): enim *cett.* 23 in (*ante* naturam) *B*: *om. cett.* | *Fortasse* Ego enim et ⟨deum⟩ . . .

entered his mind through his senses, whenever he wills to do so;[1] and if a name is nothing more than a few syllables, and is restricted in length, so as to render possible the indispensable intercourse of man with man by speech and hearing;—if this is so, the full name of God must include the names of sense, and breath, and air, and all names that are contained in sense and breath and air,[2] or are uttered by means of them, or are composed of them. For I deem it impossible that he who is the maker of the universe in all its greatness, the Father or Master of all things, can be named by a single name, though it be made up of ever so many others; I hold that he is nameless, or rather, that all names are names of him.[3] For he in his unity is all things; so that we must either call all things by his name, or call him by the names of all things.

He, filled with all the fecundity of both sexes in one, and ever **20 b**
teeming with his own goodness,[4] unceasingly brings into being all that he has willed to generate; and all that he wills is good. From his divine being has sprung the goodness of all things in this world below; and hence it is that all things are productive, and that their procreative power is adequate to ensure that all shall hereafter be as it is now, and as it has been in the past. Take this, Asclepius, as my answer to the question why and how it comes to pass that all kinds of beings are male and female.[5]—
Ascl. You say then, Trismegistus, that God is bisexual?— **21**
Trism. Yes, Asclepius; and not God alone, but all kinds of beings, whether endowed with soul or soulless.[6] Nothing that exists can be barren; for if all things that now exist are deprived of fertility, it will be impossible for the now existing races to endure for ever. I tell you ⟨that God eternally generates the Kosmos,⟩ and that the Kosmos possesses generative power, and thereby maintains all races that have come into being. For either sex is filled with procreative force; and in that conjunction of the two sexes, or, to speak more truly, that fusion of them into one,[7] which may be rightly named Eros, or Aphrodite, or both at

[1] *Declarans omnem . . . mente perceperit*: perhaps something like δηλοῖ πάντα ὅσα βούλεται, εἴ τι φαντασιωσάμενος τυγχάνει. (*Vel* may have been added by the translator.) *Sensum* perhaps = φαντασίαν: *ex sensibus* = ἐκ τῶν αἰσθήσεων.

[2] *Omnia in his* = πάντα τὰ ἐν τούτοις.

[3] *Innominem* = ἀνώνυμον: *omninominem* = παντώνυμον.

[4] *Bonitas* = ἀγαθότης or ἀγαθόν.

[5] *Utriusque sexus* = ἀρσενόθηλυς.

[6] *Animalia* = ἔμψυχα: *inanimalia* = ἄψυχα.

[7] *Unitas* = ἕνωσις.

pare. Hoc ergo omni vero verius manifestiusque mente per-c*i*p⟨i⟩to,quod ex ⟨d⟩om⟨i⟩n*o* illo totius naturae deo hoc sit cunctis in aeternum procreandi inventum tributumque mysterium, cui summa caritas, laetitia, hilaritas, cupiditas, amorque divinus innatus est. Et dicendum foret quanta sit eius mysterii vis atque necessitas, nisi ex sui contemplatione unicuique ex intimo sensu nota esse potuisset. Si enim illud extremum temporis ⟨⟨animadvertas⟩⟩, quo ex crebro adtritu ⟨eo⟩ pervenimus ut utraque in utramque ⟨se⟩ fundat natura, progeniem [[animadvertas]] ut altera ⟨emittat⟩, avide alter*a* rapiat interiusque recondat, denique eo tempore ex commixtione communi *e*t virtutem feminae marum adipiscuntur, et mares femineo torpore lassescunt. Effectus itaque huius tam blandi necessariique mysterii in occulto perpetratur, ne vulgo inridentibus inperitis utriusque naturae divinitas ex commixtione sexus cogatur erubescere, multo magis etiam si visibus inreligiosorum hominum subicia[n]tur.

22 a Sunt autem non multi, aut admodum pauci, ita ut numerari etiam ⟨⟨possint⟩⟩, in mundo [[possint]] religiosi, [[unde contingit in multis remanere malitiam,]] defectu prudentiae scientiaeque rerum omnium quae sunt, ⟨⟨unde contingit in multis remanere malitiam⟩⟩. Ex intellectu enim rationis divinae, qua constituta sunt omnia, contemptus ⟨⟨mundi totius⟩⟩ medelaque nascitur vitiorum [[mundi totius]]: perseverante autem inperitia atque inscientia, vitia omnia convalescunt, vulnerantque animam insanabilibus ⌜vitiis⌝; quae infecta isdem atque vitiata quasi venenis tumescit, nisi eorum quorum animarum disciplina et intellectus summa curatio est.

22 b Si solis ⟨his⟩ ergo et paucis hoc proderit, dignum est hunc

1–2 percipito *Hildebrand*: percepto ω 2 domino *Kroll*: omni ω: *seclusit Thomas* | deo esti cunctis *B*: deo est cunctis *M*: deo hoc sit cunctis *cett.* 8 crebro *MG*: cerebro *B* | adtritu *MG*: adtritum *B*: ad ritum δ | perveniamus (a *eras.*) *B*: pervenimus *cett.* 10 altera *scripsi*: alterius ω 11 communi et *Thomas*: communiat (vel et *superscript. man.* 2) *B*: communi (*om.* et) *cett.* 14 nec *BM*: ne *cett.* 16 subiciatur *scripsi*: subiciantur ω 18 contingit *BMF*: contigit *GPL* 22 medelaque *ed. Rom.*: medullaque ω (vel medela *superscript. man.* 2 *B*) 25 vitiis ω: '*fortasse* malis' *Thomas*

once, there is a deeper meaning than man can comprehend. It is a truth to be accepted as sure and evident above all other truths, that by God, the Master of all generative power, has been devised and bestowed upon all creatures this sacrament of eternal reproduction, with all the affection, all the joy and gladness, all the yearning and the heavenly love that are inherent in its being. And there were need that I should tell of the compelling force with which this sacrament binds man and woman together, were it not that each one of us, if he directs his thought upon himself, can learn it from his inmost feeling. For if you note that supreme moment when, through interaction [1] without pause, we come at last to this, that either sex infuses itself into the other, the one giving forth its issue, and the other eagerly taking hold on it and laying it up within, you will find that at that moment, through the intermingling of the two natures, the female acquires masculine vigour, and the male is relaxed in feminine languor. And so this sacramental act, sweet as it is, and a thing that must needs be done, is done in secret, lest, if it were done openly, the ignorant should mock, and thereby the deity manifested in either sex through the mingling of male and female should be put to the blush,—and the more so, if the act is exposed to the eyes of impious men.

Now there are not many pious men in the world,—nay, there are **22 a**
so few that they could easily be numbered; [2] for men lack wisdom and knowledge of all truth,[3] and hence it is that in the many [4] vice persists. For if a man understands the design of God [5] by which all things are ordained, he will despise all material things, and his vices will be healed; but when folly and ignorance [6] continue, all the vices grow in strength, and lacerate the soul with incurable sores; and infected and corrupted by the poison, the soul breaks out in tumours, so to speak, save in the case of those whose souls are cured [7] by the sovereign remedy of knowledge and intelligence.[8]

If then my words are likely to be profitable only to such men **22 b**

[1] *Ex crebro adtritu* = διὰ πυκνῆς παρατριβῆς.

[2] *Ita ut numerari etiam possint* = εὐαρίθμητοι.

[3] *Prudentia* = φρόνησις? *Scientia rerum omnium quae sunt* = ἡ πάντων τῶν ὄντων ἐπιστήμη (or γνῶσις)?

[4] *In multis* = ἐν τοῖς πολλοῖς.

[5] *Ex intellectu rationis divinae* = ἐκ τοῦ τὸν θεῖον λόγον νοεῖν.

[6] *Imperitia atque inscientia* = ἀμαθία καὶ ἄγνοια (or ἀγνωσία).

[7] *Curatio* = θεραπεία.

[8] *Disciplina* = ἐπιστήμη : *intellectus* = γνῶσις or νόησις?

persequi ⟨⟨tractatum⟩⟩, atque expedire [[tractatum]] quare solis hominibus intellegentiam et disciplinam divinitas suam sit inpertire dignata. Audi itaque. Deus pater et dominus cum post deos homines efficeret, ex parte corruptiore mundi et ex divina pari lance conponderans, vitia contigit mundi, corporibus commixta, remanere, et alia propter cibos ⟨intrare⟩ victumque quem necessario habemus cum omnibus animalibus communem; quibus de rebus necesse est cupiditatum desideria et reliqua mentis vitia animis humanis insidere. Diis vero, utpote ex mundissima parte *m*at*er*⟨i⟩ae effectis, et nullis indigentibus rationis disciplinaeque adminiculis, quamvis inmortalitas et unius semper aetatis vigor ipse sit eis ⟨omni efficacior⟩ prudentia et disciplina, tamen [[propter unitatem rationis]] pro disciplina et pro intellectu [[ne ab his essent alieni]] ordinem necessitatis lege conscriptum aeterna [lege] constituit: homine*s* ex animalibus cunctis [de] sol*os* ratione disciplinaque ⟨indigere⟩ cognoscens, per quae vitia corporum [homines] avertere atque abalienare potuissent, ⟨⟨propter⟨ea his comm⟩unitatem rationis⟩⟩ ⟨dedit, simul⟩ ips*i*s, ⟨⟨ne a *di*is essent alieni,⟩⟩ [ad] inmortalitatis spem intentionemque protendens. Denique et ⌜bonum⌝ hominem et qui posset inmortalis esse ex utraque natura conposuit, divina atque mortali: et sic conpositum ⟨⟨hominem⟩⟩ per voluntatem dei [[hominem]] constitutum est esse meliorem et diis, qui sunt ex sola inmortali natura formati, et omnium mortalium, Propter quod homo, diis cognatione coniunctus, ipsos religione et sancta mente veneratur, diique etiam pio affectu humana omnia respiciunt atque custo-
23 a diunt. Sed de hominibus istud dictum paucis sit pia mente

8 cupiditatem *B*: cupiditatum *cett.*: '*fortasse* cupiditates' *Thomas* 10 materiae *scripsi*: naturae ω 15 lege *seclusit Thomas* | homines *scripsi*: hominem ω 16 solos *scripsi*: de sola ω 17–18 propterea his communitatem *scripsi*: propter unitatem ω 18 ipsis *scripsi*: ipsos ω | a diis *scripsi*: ab his ω 20 bonum ω: *fortasse* terrenum 22 conpositum per *F*: conpositum est per *cett.* (conpositum et per *corr. B*) 23 est *F*: *om. cett.*

as these, few though they be,[1] it is worth while[2] to pursue this discussion, and explain why God has deigned to impart his intelligence[3] and knowledge to men alone. Listen then. Since God, the Father and Master, after he had made the gods, made man of ingredients weighed out in equal measure from the more corrupt part of matter[4] and from that part which is divine, it came to pass that evils inherent in matter were intermingled with the human body, and so persisted, while other evils enter in by reason of the eating of food, in which we must needs take part together with all living creatures; whence it necessarily results that lustful appetites and all other evil passions find place in the human soul. But the gods[5] are made of the purest part of matter, and have no need of reason and knowledge[6] to aid them; and accordingly, though their immortality and the vigour of their everlasting youth are mightier than any wisdom or knowledge, yet in place of knowledge and intelligence[7] God appointed for them an ordered movement determined by necessity and prescribed by eternal law. On the other hand, God saw that of all living creatures men alone had need of reason and knowledge, whereby they might repel and put away from them the evil passions inherent in their bodies; and for this cause he imparted to them the gift of reason; and at the same time, to the end that they might not be severed from the gods, he held out to them the hope of immortality, and gave them power to strive towards it. Willing then that man should be at once . . .[8] and capable of immortality, God compacted him of these two substances, the one divine, the other mortal; and in that he is thus compacted, it is ordained by God's will that man is not only better than all mortal beings,[9] but also better than the gods, who are made wholly of immortal substance. Hence man, being joined to the gods by kinship, worships them with piety and holy thoughts; while the gods on their side regard and watch over all the concerns of men
with loving mercy. But you must take this as said only of the **23 a**
few who are endowed with piety. Of the vicious it is better to

[1] *Et paucis* = καὶ σπανίοις οὖσι.
[2] *Dignum* = ἄξιον.
[3] *Intellegentia* = γνῶσις, or νοῦς?
[4] *Mundus* = ὕλη.
[5] I.e. the 'celestial gods' (*viz.* sun, moon, and stars).
[6] *Ratio* = λογισμός or διάνοια (*discursive* reason)? *Disciplina* = ἐπιστήμη.
[7] *Intellectus* = διάνοια?
[8] Perhaps 'a thing of earth'.
[9] *Meliorem . . . omnium mortalium* = βελτίονα πάντων τῶν θνητῶν.

praeditis: de vitiosis vero nihil dicendum est, ne sanctissimus sermo eorum contemplatione violetur.

23 b Et quoniam de cognatione et consortio hominum deorumque nobis ind*u*citur sermo, potestatem hominis, o Asclepi, vimque cognosce. Dominus et pater vel, quod est summum, deus ut effector est deorum caelestium, ita homo fictor est deorum qui in templis sunt humana proximitate contenti; et non solum inlumina[n]tur, verum etiam inlumina[n]t, nec solum ad deum proficit, verum etiam conformat deos. Miraris, o Asclepi, an numquid et tu diffidis, ut multi?—*Ascl.* Confundor, o Trismegiste: sed tuis verbis libenter adsensus, felicissimum hominem iudico, qui sit tantam felicitatem consecutus.—*Trism.* Nec inmerito miraculo dignus est, qui est omnium maximus. Deorum genus ⟨caelestium⟩ omnium conf*es*⟨s⟩ione manifestum est de mundissima parte *m*at*e*r⟨i⟩ae esse prognatum, signaque eorum sola quasi capita pro omnibus esse. Species vero deorum quas conformat humanitas ex utraque natura conformatae sunt, ex divina, quae est purior multoque ⌜divinior⌝, et ex ea quae in*f*ra homines est, id est ex materia qua fuerint fabricatae; et non solum capitibus solis, sed membris omnibus totoque corpore figurantur. Ita humanitas, semper memor naturae et originis suae, in illa divinitatis imitatione perseverat, ut, sicuti pater ac dominus, ut sui similes essent, deos fecit aeternos, ita humanitas deos suos ex sui vultus similitudine
24 a figuraret.—*Ascl.* Statuas dicis, o Trismegiste?—*Trism.* Statuas, o Asclepi. Videsne quatenus tu ipse diffidas? Statuas animatas sensu et spiritu plenas, tantaque facientes et talia, statuas futurorum

3–7 Et quoniam . . . proximitate contenti *citat Augustinus De civ. dei* 8. 23 4 inducitur *scripsi*: indicitur ω *et Augustinus* 7–8 inluminatur *Thomas* 8 inluminat *Thomas* 9 conformat *Goldbacher*: confirmat ω (*sed* o *superscript. B*) | deos δ *et M ex corr.*: deus *BG* 14 confessione *Rohde*: confusione ω 15 materiae *scripsi*: naturae ω 17 conformatae sunt *man.* 2 *B*: conformata est *cett.* | purior *B*: prior *cett.* 18 divinior ω: *fortasse* superior | infra *scripsi*: intra ω 20–10 *infra*: Ita humanitas . . . (*cap.* 24 b) sedula religione servasse *citat August. De civ. dei* 8. 23

say nothing, lest by turning our thoughts on them we should profane the high sanctity of our discourse.[1]

And now that the topic of men's kinship and association with 23 b
the gods has been introduced,[2] let me tell you, Asclepius, how great is the power and might of man. Even as the Master and Father, or, to call him by his highest name, even as God is the maker of the gods of heaven, so man is the fashioner of the gods who dwell in temples and are content to have men for their neighbours. Thus man not only receives the light of divine life, but gives it also;[3] he not only makes his way upward to God,[4] but he even fashions gods. Do you wonder at this, Asclepius? Or do you too doubt it, as many do?—*Ascl.* I am amazed, Trismegistus; but I gladly give assent to what you say, and deem man most highly blest, in that he has attained to such felicity.[5]—*Trism.* Yes, you may well hold man to be a marvel; he surpasses all other creatures. As to the celestial gods, it is admitted by all men that they are manifestly generated from the purest part of matter, and that their astral forms[6] are heads, as it were, and heads alone, in place of bodily frames. But the gods whose shapes[7] are fashioned by mankind are made of both substances, that is, of the divine substance, which is purer and far nobler, and the substance which is lower than man, namely, the material of which they are wrought; and they are fashioned[8] not in the shape of a head alone, but in the shape of a body with all its members. Mankind is ever mindful of its own parentage[9] and the source whence it has sprung, and steadfastly persists in following God's example; and consequently, just as the Father and Master made the gods of heaven eternal, that they might resemble him who made them, even so do men also
fashion their gods in the likeness of their own aspect.—*Ascl.* Do 24 a
you mean statues, Trismegistus?—*Trism.* Yes, Asclepius. See how even you give way to doubt! I mean statues, but statues living and conscious,[10] filled with the breath of life,[11] and doing many[12] mighty works; statues which have foreknowledge, and

[1] *Sermo* = λόγος. [2] *Inducitur* = εἰσάγεται.
[3] οὐ φωτίζεται μόνον, ἀλλὰ καὶ φωτίζει. [4] Perhaps, 'to the gods'.
[5] *Felicissimum iudico* = σφόδρα μακαρίζω: *felicitatem* = εὐτυχίαν?
[6] *Signa* = σημεῖα. [7] *Species* = σχήματα?
[8] *Figurantur* = σχηματίζονται. [9] *Natura* = γένεσις?
[10] *Sensus* = αἴσθησις. [11] *Spiritus* = πνεῦμα.
[12] *Tanta* = τόσαδε.

praescias, eaque sorte, vate, somniis, multisque aliis rebus praedicentes, inbecillitates hominibus facientes easque curantes, tristitiam laetitiamque pro meritis ⟨dispensantes⟩.

24 b An ignoras, o Asclepi, quod Aegyptus imago sit caeli, aut, quod est verius, ⟨. . .⟩ translatio aut descensio omnium quae gubernantur atque exercentur in caelo? Et si dicendum est verius, terra nostra mundi totius est templum. Et tamen, quoniam praescire cuncta prudentes decet, istud vos ignorare fas non est: futurum tempus est, cum adpareat Aegyptios incassum pia mente divinitatem sedula religione servasse; et omnis ⟨d⟩eorum sancta veneratio in inritum casura ⟨est, vel⟩ frustrabitur. E terris enim est ad caelum recursura divinitas, linqueturque Aegyptus, terraque, sedes religionum quae fuit, viduata numinum praesentia destituetur. Alienigenis enim regionem istam terramque complentibus, non solum neglectum religionum ⟨. . .⟩

sed, quod est durius, quasi de legibus a religione, pietate, cultuque divino statuetur praescripta poena prohibitio.

⟨⟨et inhabitabit Aegyptum Scythes aut Indus aut aliquis talis [i]de[st] vicina barbaria.⟩⟩ Tunc terra ista sanctissima, sedes delubrorum atque templorum, sepulcrorum erit mortuorumque plenissima. [[O Aegypte, Aegypte, religionum tuarum solae supererunt fabulae, eaeque incredibiles posteris tuis, solaque supererunt verba lapidibus incisa tua pia facta narrantibus]] [[et inhabitabit Aegyptum Scythes aut Indus aut aliquis talis, id est vicina barbaria.]] [Divinitas enim repetet caelum, deserti homines toti morientur, atque ita Aegyptus deo et homine viduata deseretur.] Te vero appello, sanctissimum flumen, tibique futura praedico: torrenti sanguine plenus adusque ripas erumpes, undaeque divinae non solum polluentur sanguine, sed totae ⟨cor⟩rumpentur. [[Et vivis multo maior numerus erit sepulchro-

1 eaque *August.*: easque ω (*sed* s *expunct. man. post. B*) | sorte *B et August.*: forte *cett.* | vate, somniis *August.*: vatas omnes (*corr.* somniis) *B*: fata somnis *ex* vatas omnis *corr. M*: vates ominis *G* **3** tristitiam laetitiamque *August.*: tristitiamque ω | '*Post* pro meritis *participium expectes, v.g.* dispensantes' *Thomas* **5** *Fortasse* ⟨in Aegyptum facta sit⟩ translatio **6** et ω: ac *August.* **8** prudentes ω: prudentem *August.* **10** divinitatem et sedula *man.* 2 *B* | deorum *Bernays*: eorum ω **11–12** enim est *man.* 2 *B*: enim (*om.* est) *F*: enim et *cett.* **14** religionem *B*: regionem *cett.* **15** neglectus *ed. Rom.* **19** id est ω: e *Bernays*: '*malim* de' *Thomas* **19–21** Tunc terra . . . plenissima *citat August. De civ. dei* 8. 26 **21–23** O Aegypte . . . narrantibus *hinc ad cap.* 25 *transposui* **25** repetet *G et man. post. B*: repetit *cett.* **30** corrumpentur *Bernays*: rumpentur ω **30–2** *infra*: et vivis . . . alienus *hinc ad cap.* 25 *transposui* **30–1** *infra*: sepultorum *unus* ϛ *et ed. Rom.*: sepulchrorum *cett.*

predict future events by the drawing of lots, and by prophetic inspiration, and by dreams, and in many other ways; statues which inflict diseases[1] and heal[2] them, dispensing sorrow and joy according to men's deserts.

Do you not know, Asclepius, that Egypt is an image of heaven, **24 b**
or, to speak more exactly, in Egypt all the operations of the powers which rule and work in heaven have been transferred[3] to earth below? Nay, it should rather be said that the whole Kosmos dwells in this our land as in its sanctuary. And yet, since it is fitting that wise men should have knowledge of all events before they come to pass, you must not be left in ignorance of this: there will come a time when it will be seen that in vain have the Egyptians honoured[4] the deity with heartfelt piety and assiduous service; and all our holy worship will be found bootless and ineffectual. For the gods will return from earth to heaven; Egypt will be forsaken, and the land which was once the home of religion will be left desolate, bereft of the presence of its deities. This land and region will be filled with foreigners; not only will men neglect the service of the gods, but . . . ;[5] and Egypt will be occupied by Scythians or Indians, or by some such race from the barbarian countries thereabout. In that day will our most holy land, this land of shrines and temples, be filled with funerals and corpses.[6] To thee, most holy Nile, I cry, to thee I foretell that which shall be; swollen with torrents of blood, thou wilt rise to the level of thy banks, and thy sacred waves will be not only stained, but utterly fouled

[1] *Inbecillitates* = ἀσθενείας. [2] *Curare* = θεραπεύειν.
[3] *Translatio* = μετάθεσις: *descensio* = κατάβασις.
[4] *Servare* = *observare* = θεραπεύειν.
[5] MSS.: 'but, what is harder still, there will be enacted so-called laws' (*quasi* = δῆθεν) 'by which religion and piety and worship of the gods will be forbidden, and a penalty prescribed'. This must have been added at a later date.
[6] *Sepulcrorum mortuorumque* = ταφῶν καὶ νεκρῶν.

rum; superstes vero qui foret, lingua sola cognoscetur Aegyptius,
25 actibus vero videbitur alienus.] Quid fles, o Asclepi? Et his amplius multoque deterius ipsa Aegyptus suadebitur, inbueturque peioribus malis; quae sancta quondam, divinitatis amantissima, deorum in terra suae religionis merito sola deductio, sanctitatis et pietatis magistra, erit maximae crudelitatis exemplum: ⟨⟨et vivis multo maior numerus erit sepulchrorum; superstes vero qui fuerit, lingua sola cognoscetur Aegyptius, actibus vero videbitur alienus.⟩⟩ ⟨⟨O Aegypte, Aegypte, religionum tuarum solae supererunt fabulae, eaeque incredibiles posteris tuis, solaque supererunt verba lapidibus incisa tua pia facta narrantibus.⟩⟩ Et tunc taedio hominum non admirandus videbitur mundus nec adorandus. Hoc totum bonum, quo melius nec fuit nec est nec erit quod videri possit, periclitabitur, eritque grave hominibus, ac per hoc contemnetur; nec diligetur totus hic mundus, dei opus inimitabile, gloriosa constructio, bonum multiformi imaginum varietate conpositum, machina voluntatis dei in suo opere absque invidia ⟨homini⟩ suffragantis, in unum omnium, quae venerari, laudari, amari denique a videntibus possunt, multiformis adunata congestio. Nam et tenebrae praeponentur lumini, et mors vita utilior iudicabitur; nemo suspiciet caelum; religiosus pro insano, inreligiosus putabitur prudens, furiosus fortis, pro bono habebitur pessimus. Anima enim et omnia circum eam, quibus aut inmortalis nata est aut inmortalitatem se consecuturam esse praesumit, secundum quod vobis exposui, non solum risui, sed etiam putabitur vanitas.

Sed mihi credite, et capitale periculum constituetur in eum qui se mentis religioni dederit. Nova constituentur iura, lex nova.

5 terras *B*: terra *cett.* 8 fuerit *scripsi*: foret ω 10 tuis *edd. cum uno* ς: suis *codd. cett.* 17 dei suo operi *G*: dei in suo opere *cett.* | invia *BMP*: invidia *cett.*

with gore. Do you weep at this, Asclepius? There is worse 25
to come; Egypt herself will have yet more to suffer;[1] she will fall into a far more piteous plight, and will be infected with yet more grievous plagues; and this land, which once was holy, a land which loved the gods, and wherein alone, in reward for her devotion, the gods deigned to sojourn[2] upon earth, a land which was the teacher of mankind in holiness and piety,—this land will go beyond all in cruel deeds. The dead will far outnumber the living; and the survivors will be known for Egyptians by their tongue alone, but in their actions they will seem to be men of another race. O Egypt, Egypt, of thy religion nothing will remain but an empty tale, which thine own children in time to come will not believe; nothing will be left but graven words, and only the stones will tell of thy piety. And in that day men will be weary of life, and they will cease to think the universe worthy of reverent wonder and of worship. And so religion, the greatest of all blessings,—for there is nothing, nor has been, nor ever shall be, that can be deemed a greater boon,—will be threatened with destruction; men will think it a burden, and will come to scorn it. They will no longer love this world around us, this incomparable work of God, this glorious structure which he has built, this sum of good made up of things of many diverse forms, this instrument[3] whereby the will of God operates in that which he has made, ungrudgingly favouring man's welfare, this combination and accumulation of all the manifold things that can call forth the veneration, praise, and love of the beholder. Darkness will be preferred to light, and death will be thought more profitable than life; no one will raise his eyes to heaven; the pious will be deemed insane, and the impious wise; the madman will be thought a brave man, and the wicked will be esteemed as good. As to the soul, and the belief that it is immortal by nature, or may hope to attain to immortality, as I have taught you,—all this they will mock at, and will even persuade themselves that it is false.[4] No word of reverence or piety, no

[1] *Suadebitur* = πείσεται, fut. of πάσχω (Bernays).

[2] *Deductio* = καταγωγή.

[3] *Machina* = ὄργανον.

[4] Here follows in the MSS.: 'But believe me, it will even be decreed that he who shall have devoted himself to the religion of mind shall be liable to the penalty of death; there will be ordained new law and a new statute.' This also must have been added later.

Nihil sanctum, nihil religiosum nec caelo nec caelestibus dignum audietur aut mente credetur.

⟨. . .⟩ Fit deorum ab hominibus dolenda secessio: soli nocentes angeli remanent, qui humanitate commixti ad omnia audaciae mala miseros manu iniecta compellunt, in bella, in rapinas, in fraudes et in omnia quae sunt animarum naturae contraria. Tunc nec terra constabit, nec navigabitur mare, nec caelum astrorum cursibus ⟨. . .⟩, nec siderum cursus constabit in caelo; omnis vox divina necessaria taciturnitate mutescet; fructus terrae conrumpentur, nec fecunda tellus erit, et aer ipse maesto torpore
26 a languescet. Haec et talis senectus veniet mundi; inreligio, inordinatio, inrationabilitas, bonorum omnium ⟨. . .⟩.

Cum haec cuncta contigerint, o Asclepi, tunc ille dominus et pater, deus primipotens et ⌜unius gubernator dei⌝, intuens in mores factaque [voluntaria], voluntate sua, quae est dei benignitas, vitiis resistens et corruptelae omnium, errorem revocans, malignitatem omnem vel inluvione diluens, vel igne consumens, vel morbis pestilentibus iisque per diversa loca dispersis finiens,

3 fi(e)t (*'corr. man.* I, *ut videtur' Thomas*) *B*: fit *cett.* 4 remane(bu)nt (*corr. man.* 2) *B*: remanent *cett.* 5 conpellunt *man.* I *B et cett.*: conpellent *man.* 2 *B* 8 *Fortasse* cursibus ⟨subsistet⟩ 9 mutescit *in* mutescet *corr. man. post. B*: mutescet *cett.* 11 linguescit *man.* I *B*: languescit *MP*: languescet *man.* 2 *B et cett.* 12 *Fortasse* omnium ⟨defectio⟩ 15 voluntaria *seclusit Bernays* 16 corruptelae *F*: corruptela *cett.* 18 pestilentiisque *ex* pestilentibus iisque *corr. B*: pestilentibus usque *cett.*: pestilentibus iisque *Bernays*

Cap. 26 a: 'Cum haec . . . revocabit.' *Lactantius Div. Inst.* 7. 18. 3 sq. (*Brandt*): 'Sed et illut non sine daemonum fraude subtractum[a], missuiri a patre tunc filium dei, qui deletis omnibus malis pios liberet. Quod Hermes tamen non dissimulavit: in eo enim libro qui λόγος τέλειος inscribitur, post enumerationem malorum de quibus diximus subiecit haec:—

ἐπὰν δὴ ταῦτα γένηται, ὦ Ἀσκληπιέ, τότε ὁ κύριος καὶ πατὴρ καὶ θεὸς καὶ ⌜τοῦ πρώτου καὶ ἑνὸς[b] θεοῦ⌝ δημιουργός, ἐπιβλέψας τοῖς γενομένοις, καὶ τὴν ἑαυτοῦ βούλησιν, τοῦτ' ἔστιν τὸ ἀγαθόν, ἀντερείσας τῇ ἀταξίᾳ, καὶ ἀνακαλεσάμενος τὴν πλάνην, καὶ τὴν κακίαν ἐκκαθάρας, πῇ μὲν ὕδατι πολλῷ κατακλύσας, πῇ δὲ πυρὶ ὀξυτάτῳ διακαύσας, ἐνίοτε δὲ πολέμοις καὶ λοιμοῖς ἐκπαίσας,[c] ἤγαγεν ἐπὶ τὸ ἀρχαῖον καὶ ἀποκατέστησεν τὸν ἑαυτοῦ κόσμον.'

utterance worthy of heaven and of the gods of heaven, will be heard or believed.

And so the gods will depart from mankind,—a grievous thing!—and only evil angels will remain, who will mingle with men, and drive the poor wretches by main force into all manner of reckless crime, into wars, and robberies, and frauds, and all things hostile to the nature of the soul. Then will the earth no longer stand unshaken, and the sea will bear no ships; heaven will not support the stars in their orbits, nor will the stars pursue their constant course in heaven; all voices of the gods will of necessity be silenced and dumb; the fruits of the earth will rot; the soil will turn barren, and the very air
will sicken in sullen stagnation. After this manner will old age **26 a**
come upon the world. Religion will be no more; all things will be disordered and awry;[1] all good will disappear.

But when all this has befallen, Asclepius, then the Master and Father, God, the first before all, the maker of that god who first came into being,[2] will look on that which has come to pass, and will stay the disorder by the counterworking of his will, which is the good. He will call back to the right path those who have gone astray; he will cleanse the world from evil, now washing it away with waterfloods, now burning it out with fiercest fire, or again expelling it by war and pestilence. And thus he

[1] *Inordinatio* = ἀταξία : *inrationabilitas* = ἀλογία.
[2] *Deus primipotens et unius gubernator dei*: perhaps, ὁ θεὸς ὁ πρωτάρχης καὶ τοῦ πρωτογόνου θεοῦ (*sc.* τοῦ κόσμου) δημιουργός.

---

[a] *Sc. subtractum ab Hystaspis vaticinatione, quam superius citat Lactantius.*
[b] τοῦ πρώτου καὶ ἑνὸς *Brandt, codicum indicia secutus*: τοῦ πρωτογενοῦς *coni. Davis.* 'dominus et pater et deus et primi et unius dei creator' *interpretatio Lat. in B et P.*
[c] ἐκπαίσας *Brandt*: ЄΚΙΤЄϹΑϹ ('malitia . . . percussa' *interpret. Lat.*) *B*: ecpesas *H*: ΗΚΠϹΑϹ *P*: ЄΚΠΗϹΑϹ ('excutiens' *interpret. Lat.*) *Sedulius*: ἐκπιέσας *Bernays.*

ad antiquam faciem mundum revocabit, ut et mundus ipse adorandus videatur atque mirandus, et tanti operis effector et restitutor deus ab hominibus, qui tunc erunt, frequentibus laudum praeconiis benedictionibusque celebretur. Haec enim mundi ⟨re⟩genitura: cunctarum reformatio rerum bonarum, et naturae ipsius sanctissima et religiosissima restitutio, per[co]acta temporis cursu ⟨dei voluntate⟩, quae est [[et fuit sine initio]] sempiterna.

26 b Voluntas enim dei caret initio, quae eadem est ⟨semper⟩, et, sicuti est, [sempiterna] ⟨⟨et fuit sine initio.⟩⟩ Dei enim natura consilium est [[voluntatis]] bonita⟨ti⟩s.—*Ascl.* ⟨⟨Voluntatis⟩⟩ summa consilium, o Trismegiste?—*Trism.* Voluntas, o Asclepi, consilio nascitur, et ipsum velle e voluntate. Neque enim ⌜inpense⌝ aliquid vult, qui est omnium plenissimus; [[et ea vult quae habet]] vult autem omnia bona. Et habet omnia quae vult, ⟨⟨et ea vult quae habet;⟩⟩ omnia autem bona et cogitat et vult.

27 a Hoc est autem deus: eius imago mundus, boni ⟨bonus⟩.—*Ascl.* Bonus, o Trismegiste?—*Trism.* Bonus, o Asclepi, ut ego te docebo. Sicuti enim deus omnibus speciebus vel generibus, quae in mundo sunt, dispensator distributorque est bonorum, id est sensus, animae, et vitae, sic et mundus tributor est et praestitor omnium quae mortalibus videntur bona, id est alternationis partuum temporalium, fructuum nativitatis, augmentorum, et maturitatis, et horum similium.

27 b [[ac per hoc deus, supra verticem summi caeli consistens, ubique est, omniaque circum inspicit. Sic est enim ultra caelum locus, sine stellis, ab omnibus rebus corpulentis alienus.]]

27 c [[dispensator qui est, inter caelum et terram obtinet locum, quem Iovem vocamus. Terrae vero et mari dominatur Iuppiter Plutonius; et hic nutritor est animantium mortalium et fructiferarum. Horum omnium viribus fructus, arbusta, et terra vegetantur. Aliorum vero vires et effectus per omnia quae sunt distribuentur.]]

27 d [[⌜Distribuentur⌝ vero qui terrae dominantur, et conlocabuntur in

5 regenitura *Bernays*: genitura ω 6–7 peracta temporis cursu *Kroll*: per coacta temporis cursu *BMPF*: per coactum temporis cursum *GL* 7 dei *addidit Thomas*: voluntate *prius addiderat Goldbacher* 10 (Trism.): '. . . consilium est voluntatis.'—(Ascl.:) 'Bonitas summa consilium, o Trismegiste?' *codd. et edd. pr.* 16 mundus boni *ex* mundus bonus *corr. B* | bonus *addidit Kroll* 20 sensus *F*: sensibus *cett.* 20–21 praestator *B*: praestitor *cett.* 21–22 id est alternationis *GF*: id est et alternationis *cett.* 24–32 *Cap.* 27 b *et* 27 c *hinc transposui*: *vide post cap.* 19 b (p. 324) 33–4 *infra*: *cap.* 27 d *hinc transposui*: *vide post cap.* 37 (p. 360)

will bring back his world to its former aspect, so that the Kosmos will once more be deemed worthy of worship and wondering reverence, and God, the maker and restorer of the mighty fabric, will be adored by the men of that day with unceasing hymns of praise and blessing. Such is the new birth[1] of the Kosmos; it is a making again[2] of all things good, a holy and awe-striking restoration[3] of all nature; and it is wrought in the process of time by the eternal[4] will of God.

For God's will[5] has no beginning; it is ever the same, and **26 b**
as it now is, even so it has ever been, without beginning. For it is the very being of God to purpose[6] good.—*Ascl.* Is 'will' then, Trismegistus, summed up in 'purpose'?—*Trism.* Will, Asclepius, issues from purpose; and from will issues each several act of will.[7] Not without effect[8] does God will a thing, for he is fully supplied with all things; and all things that he wills are good. He has all things which he wills, and wills the things which he has; and all that he purposes[9] and wills is good.

Such is God. The Kosmos is God's image; and since God is
good, the Kosmos also is good.—*Ascl.* Do you say, Trismegistus, **27 a**
that the Kosmos is good?—*Trism.* Yes, Asclepius; and I will show you that it is so. God dispenses and distributes goods, namely, sense, soul, and life,[10] to all kinds of beings[11] in the Kosmos; and in like manner, the Kosmos gives and supplies all things which seem good to mortals, namely, the succession of births in time,[12] the formation, growth, and ripening of the

[1] *Regenitura* = παλιγγενεσία. [2] *Reformatio* = ἀνανέωσις.

[3] *Restitutio* = ἀποκατάστασις, or ἐπανόρθωσις. *Religiosissima* = εὐσεβεστάτη? But in what sense?

[4] *Sempiternus* = ἀίδιος (or αἰώνιος?).

[5] *Voluntas* = βούλησις.

[6] *Consilium* = βουλή.

[7] *Velle* = τὸ βούλεσθαι.

[8] In place of *inpense*, some word equivalent to μάτην or ἀπράκτως seems to be needed.

[9] *Cogitat* = βουλεύεται.

[10] *Sensus* = αἴσθησις: *anima* = ψυχή: *vita* = ζωή.

[11] *Speciebus vel generibus*: probably the translator's alternatives for a single Greek word, which may have been either εἴδεσι or γένεσι.

[12] Or, reading *partium*, 'the alternation of the seasons'.

civitate in summo initio Aegypti, quae a parte solis occidentis condetur, ad quam terra marique festinabit omne mortale genus.—*Ascl.* Modo tamen hoc in tempore ubi isti sunt, o Trismegiste?—*Trism.* Conlocati sunt in maxima civitate in monte Libyco.]]

27e–29b [[Et haec usque eo narrata sint. De inmortali vero aut de mortali modo disserendum est. Multos enim . . . stellas inluminat.]]

29c Secundum etenim deum hunc crede, o Asclepi, omnia gubernantem [omniaque mundana inlustrantem] animalia, sive animantia sive inanimantia. Si enim animal mundus vivensque semper et fuit et est et erit, nihil in mundo mortale est. Viventis etenim semper uniuscuiusque partis [quae] est sicuti est; [in] ipsoque mundo semper uno, eoque animali semperque vivente, in eo nullus est mortalitatis locus. Ergo vitae aeternitatisque debet esse plenissimus, si semper eum necesse est vivere.

[Sol ergo, sicuti mundus sempiternus est, sic et ipse semper gubernator vitalium vel totius vivacitatis eorumque frequentator vel dispensator est.]

Deus ergo viventium vel vitalium, in mundo quae sunt, sempiternus gubernator est, ipsiusque vitae dispensator aeternus. Semel autem dispensa[vi]t⟨a⟩ vita vitalibus cunctis aeterna lege

30 praestatur hoc more, quo dicam. In ipsa enim aeternitatis vivacitate mundus agitatur, et in ipsa vitali aeternitate locus est mundi: propter quod nec stabi⟨t a⟩liquando nec conrumpetur, sempiternitate vivendi circumvallatus et quasi constrictus. Ipse mundus vitae dispensator est his omnibus quae in se sunt, et locus est omnium quae sub sole gubernantur. Et commotio mundi ipsius ex duplici constat effectu: ipse extrinsecus vivificatur ab aeternitate, vivificatque ea quae intra se sunt omnia, differens numeris et temporibus statutis atque infixis cuncta per solis effectum stellarumque discursum. Omni[a] ⟨⟨autem⟩⟩ temporaria ratione divina lege conscripta, terrenum [[autem]] tempus aeris qualitate, aestuum frigorisque varietate dinoscitur, caeleste

5–7 *Cap.* 27 e–29 b *hinc transposui: vide post cap.* 40 c (p. 364) **10** si enim *GLF*: sive enim *BMP* | mundus *GL*: mundum *BMPF* **12** in *seclusit Thomas* **21** dispensata *Thomas*: dispensavit ω | vita *B*: vitam *cett.* | cuncta *BM*: cunctis *cett.* **24** stabit aliquando *Zink*: stabili quando ω (*totum locum refinxit F*) **31** omni *Thomas*: omnia ω

fruits of the earth, and the like. For you must deem the Kosmos **29 c**
a second god, Asclepius, a god who governs all living things, both those which have souls and those which are soulless.[1] For if the Kosmos has been and is and will be a living and ever-living being,[2] nothing in the Kosmos is mortal. It is the everlasting life of each of its several parts[3] that makes the Kosmos what it is; and seeing that the Kosmos is ever one,[4] and is a living and ever-living being, mortality can have no place in it. It must therefore be filled with life, and with eternal life, if it needs must live for ever.

It is God then that everlastingly[5] governs all the sources of life[6] in the Kosmos; he is the eternal dispenser[7] of life itself. But when life has once been dispensed to all the (intracosmic) sources of life, the supply of it is maintained in accordance with eternal law; and the manner of its maintenance I will proceed
to explain. The Kosmos moves[8] within the very life of eternity,[9] **30**
and is contained in that very eternity whence all life issues;[10] and for this reason it is impossible that it should at any time come to a stand, or be destroyed, since it is walled in and bound together, so to speak, by eternal life.[11] And the Kosmos is itself the dispenser of life to all things in it[12] here below, and the place in which are contained all things which are subject to control beneath the sun. The movement[13] of the Kosmos itself consists of a twofold working;[14] life is infused into the Kosmos from without by eternity;[15] and the Kosmos infuses life into all things that are within it, distributing all things according to fixed and determined relations of number and time, by the operation of the sun and the movements of the stars. The process of time is wholly determined by God's law; but the lapse of terrestrial time is marked by the changing states of the atmosphere, and the variations of heat and cold; while that of celestial time

[1] *Animalia* = τὰ ζωὴν ἔχοντα : *animantia* = ἔμψυχα : *inanimantia* = ἄψυχα.
[2] *Animal vivensque semper* = ζῷον καὶ ἀείζωον.
[3] *Viventis semper uniuscuiusque partis* = ζῶντος ἀεὶ ἑκάστου τῶν μερῶν, gen. abs.
[4] *Ipsoque mundo semper uno* = καὶ αὐτοῦ τοῦ κόσμου ἑνὸς ἀεὶ ὄντος, gen. abs.
[5] *Sempiternus* = ἀΐδιος? [6] *Viventium vel vitalium* = ζωτικῶν?
[7] *Aeternus* = αἰώνιος : *dispensator* = ταμίας. [8] *Agitatur* = κινεῖται.
[9] *In ipsa aeternitatis vivacitate* = ἐν αὐτῇ τῇ τοῦ αἰῶνος ζωῇ?
[10] *In ipsa vitali aeternitate* = ἐν αὐτῷ τῷ ζωτικῷ αἰῶνι?
[11] *Sempiternitas vivendi* = ἀΐδιος (or αἰώνιος) ζωή?
[12] *In se* = ἐν αὐτῷ. [13] *Commotio* = κίνησις.
[14] *Effectus* = ἐνέργεια. [15] *Ab aeternitate* = ὑπὸ (or ἀπὸ?) τοῦ αἰῶνος.

vero reversionibus siderum ad eadem loca temporaria conversione currentium. Et mundus est receptaculum temporis, cuius cursu et agitatione vegetatur. Tempus autem ordinatione servatur: ordo et tempus innovationem omnium rerum, quae in mundo sunt, per alternationem faciunt. Cunctis ergo ita se habentibus, nihil stabile, nihil fixum, nihil inmobile [nec] nascentium, nec caelestium nec terrenorum. Solus deus ⟨stabilis⟩, et merito [solus]; ipse enim in se est, et a se est, et circum se totus est, plenus atque perfectus, isque sua firm*us* stabilita*te* est, nec alicuius inpulsu [nec] loco moveri potest, cum in eo sunt omnia et in omnibus ipse est solus; nisi aliquis audeat dicere ipsius commotionem in aeternitate esse: sed magis et ipsa inmobilis ⟨est⟩ aeternitas, in quam omnium temporum agitatio remeat, et ex
31 qua omnium temporum agitatio sumit exordium. Deus ergo stabilis fuit, semperque similiter cum eo aeternitas constitit, mundum non natum, quem recte ⟨in⟩sensibilem dicimus, intra se habens. Huius [dei] imago hic effectus est mundus, aeternitatis imitator. Habet autem tempus, ⟨⟨quamvis semper agitetur,⟩⟩ stabilitatis suae vim atque naturam [[quamvis semper agitetur]], ea ipsa in se revertendi necessitate. Itaque quamvis sit aeternitas stabilis, inmobilis, atque fixa, tamen quoniam temporis, quod mobile est, in aeternitatem semper revocatur agitatio, [[eaque mobilitas ratione temporis vertitur,]] efficitur ut et ipsa aeternitas, inmobilis

1–2 conversione *F*: conversatione *cett.* **2** recurrentium *F* **6** nec (*post* inmobile) *abesse malit Kroll* **9** firmus stabilitate *scripsi*: firma stabilitas ω **10** nec *seclusit Kroll* **12** commonitionem *BM*: commotionem *cett.* **13–14** remeat . . . agitatio *om. BM* **15** consistit (*sed* is *ex corr.*) *B*: constitit *cett.* **16** insensibilem *scripsi*: sensibilem ω **22–23** eaque . . . vertitur *hinc ad cap.* 40 b *fin.* (p. 354) *transposui*

is marked by the return of the heavenly bodies to their former
positions[1] as they move in their periodic revolutions. The
Kosmos is that in which time is contained;[2] and it is by the
progress and movement of time that life is maintained in
the Kosmos. The process of time is regulated by a fixed order;[3]
and time in its ordered course[4] renews[5] all things in the Kosmos
by alternation. All things being subject to this process, there
is nothing that stands fast,[6] nothing fixed, nothing free from
change,[7] among the things which come into being, neither among
those in heaven nor among those on earth. God alone stands
unmoved, and with good reason;[8] for he is self-contained, and
self-derived,[9] and wholly self-centred,[10] and in him is no deficiency
or imperfection.[11] He stands fast in virtue of his own immobility,
nor can he be moved by any force impinging on him from
without, seeing that in him are all things, and that it is he alone
that is in all things; unless indeed one should presume to say
that he moves (not in time, but) in eternity.[12] But it should
rather be said that eternity also is motionless; into eternity all
movements of time go back,[13] and from eternity all movements
of time take their beginning. God then stands unmoved;[14] 31
and eternity likewise is ever changeless, containing in itself
a Kosmos which is without beginning,[15] even that Kosmos which
we rightly call 'imperceptible to sense'.[16] This (sensible) Kosmos
has been made in the image of that other Kosmos, and reproduces
eternity in a copy. Now time, though it is ever in movement,
possesses a faculty of stability peculiar to itself,[17] in that its return
into itself is determined by necessity. And accordingly, though
eternity is stable, fixed, and motionless, yet since time is mobile,
and its movement ever goes back into[18] eternity, it results from
this that eternity also, though motionless in itself, appears to be

[1] *Reversiones ad eadem loca* = ἀποκαταστάσεις.
[2] *Receptaculum* = ὑποδοχή.
[3] *Ordinatio* = διάταξις?
[4] *Ordo* = τάξις.
[5] *Innovatio* = ἀνανέωσις.
[6] *Stabilis* = ἑστώς.
[7] *Inmobilis* = ἀκίνητος.
[8] *Merito* = εἰκότως.
[9] *A se est*: he is αὐτογέννητος.
[10] *Circum se totus est* = αὐτὸς περὶ αὑτὸν ὅλος ἐστί.
[11] *Plenus atque perfectus* = πλήρης καὶ τέλειος ὤν.
[12] *In aeternitate* = ἐν αἰῶνι.
[13] *Remeat* = ἀναφέρεται?
[14] *Stabilis fuit* = ἕστηκε. *Constitit* also presumably represents a Greek perfect.
[15] *Non natum* = ἀγέννητον.
[16] *Insensibilem* = νοητόν, or ἀναίσθητον in the sense of νοητόν.
[17] *Vim atque naturam* = δύναμιν: *stabilitatis* = στάσεως: *suae* = ἰδίας.
[18] *Revocatur in* = ἀναφέρεται εἰς?

quidem sola, ⟨⟨videatur agitari⟩⟩ per tempus, in quo ipsa est, et est in eo omnis agitatio [[videatur agitari]]. Sic efficitur ut et aeternitatis stabilitas moveatur, et temporis mobilitas stabilis fiat fixa lege currendi. Sic et deum agitari credibile est in se ipsum eadem inmobilitate. Stabilita[s] etenim ipsius [in] magnitudine est inmobilis agitatio; ipsius enim magnitudinis inmobili⟨ta⟩s lex est. Hoc ergo, quod est tale quod non subicitur sensibus, ⟨⟨sive deus, sive aeternitas, sive uterque, sive alter in altero sive uterque in utroque sunt⟩⟩, indefinitum, inconprehensibile, inaestimabile est; nec sustineri etenim nec ferri nec indagari potest. Ubi enim et quo et unde, et quomodo aut quale sit, incertum est. Fertur enim in summa stabilitate, et in ipso ⟨fertur⟩ stabilitas sua [[sive deus, sive aeternitas, sive uterque, sive alter in altero sive uterque in utroque sunt]]. Propter quod aeternitas sine definitione est temporis: tempus autem, quod definiri potest [vel] numero, [vel] alternatione vel [alterius] per ambitionem reditus aeternum est. Utrumque ergo infinitum, utrumque videtur aeternum: ⟨aeternitatis autem⟩ stabilitas [enim], utpote defixa, quo sustinere quae agitabilia sunt possit ⟨⟨habendo inmobilem firmitatem⟩⟩, beneficio firmitatis merito obtinet principatum.

32 a Omnium ergo, quae sunt, primordia deus est et aeternitas. Mundus autem, quod sit mobilis, non habet principatum; praevenit enim mobilitas eius stabilitatem suam in lege agitationis sempiternae, ⟨⟨aeternitas quae secunda est⟩⟩ [[habendo inmobilem

40 b firmitatem]]. ⟨⟨Haec ergo est aeternitas ⟨⟨in omnibus ⟨quibus⟩ mundus iste perfectus est⟩⟩; [[quae nec coepit esse nec desinet]]

5 stabilita etenim *scripsi*: stabilitatis etenim *B*: stabilis etenim *M*: stabilistas enim *G*: stabilitates ⟨*an* -is ?⟩ enim *P*: stabilitas enim *L* | stabilitatis in magnitudine enim ipsius *F* 6 inmobilitas *scripsi*: inmobilis ω 11 et quomodo *MG*: aut quomodo *B* 13 sive deus *om.* *BM* 15 definiri non potest *GL*: definiri potest *cett.* 16 reditu *F*: reditus *cett.* 19 quo *F*, '*fortasse recte*' *Thomas*: quod *cett.* 19–20 habendo inmobilem firmitatem *huc a cap.* 32 a *transposui* 23 lege *L*: legem *cett.* 24 aeternitas quae secunda est *huc a cap.* 32 b (p. 356, v. 6) *transposui* 25–7 *infra*: cap 40 b (Haec ergo . . . et sequi) *huc transposui* 25–26 in omnibus . . . perfectus est *huc a cap.* 39 (p. 362, v. 21) *transposui*

in motion, on account of its relation to time; for eternity enters into time, and it is in time that all movement takes place. Hence it follows that on the one hand eternity, stable though it be, is also mobile, and on the other hand, time, mobile though it be, is rendered stable by the immutability of the law by which its movement is determined. And in this way it is possible to hold that God also moves within himself,[1] though God, like eternity, is motionless; for the movement of God, being made stable by his greatness, is no movement, inasmuch as his greatness is necessarily motionless.[2] The being, then, of which I speak,—whether it is to be called God, or eternity, or both, and whether God is in eternity, or eternity in God, or each in the other,—this being, I say, is imperceptible by sense;[3] it is infinite, incomprehensible, immeasurable;[4] it exceeds our powers, and is beyond our scrutiny. The place of it, the whither and the whence, the manner and quality of its being, are unknown to us. It moves[5] in absolute stability, and its stability moves within it. Eternity then is not limited by the conditions of time; and time, which admits of numerical limitations, is eternal in virtue of its cyclic recurrence.[6] Thus time as well as eternity is infinite, and is thought to be eternal. But eternity is rightly[7] held to rank above time, in virtue of[8] its fixity; for it is firmly fixed, so as to be able, by its rigid immobility, to sustain those things
which are in motion.[9] God and eternity then are the first **32 a**
principles of all things which exist.[10] The Kosmos does not hold the first and highest place, because it is mobile; for its mobility takes precedence of the immutability with which it obeys the law of its everlasting movement, which is a secondary sort
of eternity. It is this sort of eternity that enters into all the **40 b**
parts of which the Kosmos is composed.[11] For the Kosmos,

[1] *Agitari in se ipsum* = αὐτὸν ἐν αὐτῷ κινεῖσθαι.

[2] *Stabilita . . . lex est*: perhaps, ἐν γὰρ τῷ μεγέθει αὐτοῦ καθεστῶσα ἀκίνητός ἐστιν ἡ κίνησις· τοῦ γὰρ μεγέθους αὐτοῦ νόμος ἐστὶν ἡ ἀκινησία. (Or, retaining *inmobilis*, ὁ γὰρ τοῦ μεγέθους αὐτοῦ νόμος ἐστὶν ἀκίνητος.)

[3] *Quod est tale quod non subicitur sensibus* = τοιοῦτον ὂν οἷον μὴ ὑποπίπτειν ταῖς αἰσθήσεσιν?

[4] *Indefinitum* = ἀόριστον: *incomprehensibile* = ἀκατάληπτον: *inaestimabile* = ἀμέτρητον?

[5] *Fertur* = φέρεται.

[6] *Alternatione vel per ambitionem reditus* = τῇ ἀνακυκλήσει?

[7] *Merito* = εἰκότως.

[8] *Beneficio* = χάριν.

[9] *Quo sustinere quae agitabilia sunt possit* = ἵνα ὑφεστάναι δύνηται τοῖς κινητοῖς.

[10] *Omnium . . . aeternitas* = πάντων οὖν τῶν ὄντων ἀρχαί εἰσιν ὁ θεὸς καὶ ὁ αἰών.

[11] *Quibus mundus iste perfectus est* = ἐξ ὧν ὁ κόσμος οὗτος ἀποτετέλεσται?

qu*i*, fixa inmutabili⟨s⟩ lege currendi, sempiterna commotione versatur, ⟨⟨quae nec coepit esse nec desinet,⟩⟩ oriturque et occidit alternis [[saepe]] per membra, ita ut variatis temporibus ⟨⟨saepe⟩⟩ isdem quibus occiderat membris oriatur. Sic est enim rotundita⟨ti⟩s volubilis ratio, ut ita sibi coartata sint cuncta, ut initium quod sit volubilitatis ignores, cum omnia se semper et praecedere videantur et sequi :⟩⟩ ⟨⟨eaque mobilita⟨ti⟩s ratione temp*us* vertitur.⟩⟩

32 b Omnis ergo sensus divi⟨nus aeter⟩nitatis similis. Inmobilis ipse, in stabilitate se commovet sua : sanctus et incorruptus et sempiternus est, et si quid potest melius nuncupari dei summi in ipsa veritate consistens aeternitas, plenissimus omnium ⟨in⟩sensibilium et totius disciplinae, consistens, ut ita dixerim, cum deo. Sensus vero mundanus receptaculum est sensibilium omnium specierum et disciplinarum. Humanus vero ⟨sensus . . .⟩ ex memoriae tenacitate, quod memor sit omnium quas gesserit rerum. Usque ad humanum enim animal sensus divinitas descendendo pervenit : deus enim summu*s* divinum sensum

1 qui *scripsi* : quae ω | inmutabilis *scripsi* : inmutabili ω 2 occidit *GF* : occidet *cett.* 4–5 rotunditatis *scripsi* : rotunditas ω 5–6 initium sit quod sit *BMP* (aliter ut quod sit inicium volubilitatis ignores *superscript. man. recent. B*) : initium quod sit *cett* : initium, si quod sit, *Thomas* 7–8 eaque . . . vertitur *huc a cap.* 31 *transposui* 7 mobilitatis *scripsi* : mobilitas ω | tempus *scripsi* : temporis ω 9 divinus aeternitatis *scripsi* : divinitatis ω : '*fortasse* ⟨divinus⟩ divinitatis' *Thomas* 11 et si *om. BM* 12–13 insensibilium *scripsi* : sensibilium ω 15 *lacunam post* vero *significavit Goldbacher* : pendet *supplevit Brakman* 17 divinitas (vel tis *superscript. man.* 2) *B* : divinitatis *F* 18 summus *Thomas* : summum ω (vel suum *superscript. man.* 2 *B*)

changeless in virtue of the unalterable law by which its motion is determined, revolves with an everlasting movement. That movement has had no beginning, and will have no end; it manifests itself and disappears by turns in the several parts of the Kosmos, and that in such fashion that again and again in the chequered course of time it manifests itself anew in those same parts in which it disappeared before. Such is the nature of circular movement; all points in the circle are so linked together, that you can find no place at which the movement can begin; for it is evident that all points in the line of movement both precede and follow one another for ever. And it is in this manner that time revolves.

The divine mind[1] is wholly of like nature with eternity. It is 32 b
motionless in itself, but though stable, is yet self-moving; it is holy, and incorruptible, and everlasting,[2] and has all attributes yet higher, if higher there be, that can be assigned to the eternal life of the supreme God, that life which stands fast in absolute reality.[3] It is wholly filled with all things imperceptible to sense,[4] and with all-embracing knowledge;[5] it is, so to speak, consubstantial[6] with God.

The cosmic mind[7] is the recipient[8] of all sensible forms[9] and of all kinds of knowledge of sensible things.

The (merely) human mind[10] is . . ., and is dependent on the retentiveness of man's memory, that is, on his remembrance of all his past experiences.[11]

The divine mind[12] descends in the scale of being as far as man, but no farther; for the supreme God willed not that the divine

[1] Or 'intellect'. *Sensus divinus* = ὁ θεῖος νοῦς.
[2] *Incorruptus* = ἄφθαρτος: *sempiternus* = ἀΐδιος.
[3] *Veritas* = ἀλήθεια.
[4] *Plenissimus omnium insensibilium* = πλήρης (or πλήρωμα) ἐστὶ πάντων τῶν νοητῶν.
[5] *Totius disciplinae* = ὅλης ἐπιστήμης? Or τῆς τοῦ ὅλου ἐπιστήμης?
[6] *Consistens* = συνυφεστώς?
[7] *Sensus mundanus* = ὁ κοσμικὸς νοῦς, or ὁ τοῦ κόσμου νοῦς.
[8] *Receptaculum* = ὑποδοχή.
[9] *Sensibiles species* = τὰ αἰσθητὰ εἴδη, or αἱ αἰσθηταὶ μορφαί.
[10] *Humanus sensus* = ὁ ἀνθρώπειος νοῦς.
[11] *Omnium quas gesserit rerum* = πάντων τῶν πεπραγμένων.
[12] *Sensus divinitas* = ὁ θεῖος νοῦς, or ἡ τοῦ νοῦ θειότης in the sense of ὁ θεῖος νοῦς.

cunctis confundi noluit, ne erubesceret aliorum commixtione animantium. Intellegentia enim sensus humani, qualis aut quanta sit, tota in memoria est praeteritorum: per eam enim memoriae tenacitatem et gubernator effectus est terrae. Intellectus autem naturae et qualitat*is* sensus mundi ex omnibus quae in mundo sensibilia sunt poterit p*ro*videri. [[aeternitas quae secunda est]] [ex sensibili mundo sensus ⟨mundi⟩ *n*atu*ra* qualitasque dinoscitur.] At intellectus qualitatis sensus summi dei sola veritas est, cuius veritatis in mundo nequidem extrema linea umbra⟨ve⟩ dinoscitur. Ubi enim quid temporum dimensione dinoscitur, *i*bi sunt mendacia; ubi geniturae, *i*bi errores videntur. [[Vides ergo, o Asclepi, in quibus constituti quae tractemus, aut quae audeamus adtingere. Sed tibi, deus summe, gratias ago, qui me videndae divinitatis luminasti lumine. Et vos, o Tat et Asclepi et Hammon, intra secreta pectoris divina mysteria silentio tegite et taciturnitate celate.]]

Hoc autem differt intellectus a sensu, quod intellectus noster ad qualitatem sensus mundi intellegendam et dinoscendam mentis pervenit intentione, ⌜intellectus autem mundi⌝ pervenit ad aeternitatem et deos noscendos qui supra se sunt. Et sic contingit hominibus ut quasi per caliginem quae in caelo sunt videamus, quantum possibile est per condicionem sensus humani. Haec autem intentio p*rae* videndis tantis angustissima est nobis; latissima vero, cum viderit, felicita*s* e⟨st⟩ conscientiae. ⟨⟨Vides ergo, o Asclepi, in quibus constituti quae tractemus, aut quae audeamus adtingere. Sed tibi, deus summe, gratias ago, qui me videndae divinitatis luminasti

1 cunctis confundi *BMPF*: cunctis animantibus confundi *cett.* 5 enim *GL*: autem *cett.* | et qualitatis *Thomas*: et qualitate *BM*: ex qualitate *GPL*: qualitate et *F* 6 provideri *scripsi*: pervideri ω 6–7 aeternitas quae secunda est *hinc ad cap.* 32 a *transposui* 7–8 ex sensibili ... dinoscitur *seclusi* 7 natura *scripsi*: datus ω 8 intellectus qualitatis sensus *scripsi*: intellectus qualitatisque sensus *BM*: intellectus qualitatis qualitasque sensus *cett.* 10 umbra ω, *sed* ve *add. man.* 2 *B* 11 ibi sunt *Goldbacher*: ubi sunt ω | ibi errores *Goldbacher*: ubi errores (ergo res *B*) ω | videtur *B*: videntur *cett.* 23 prae videndis *Kroll*: pervidendis ω | bonis (nobis *superscript. man. post.*) *B*: nobis *cett.* (angustissima est pervidendis tantis bonis latissima *F*) 24 felicitas est *Kroll*: felicitate ω 26 tuae *post* divinitatis *add. F*

mind should be interfused with all things, lest it should be put to shame by mingling with the lower animals.

The knowledge which corresponds to the character and extent of the human mind[1] is based wholly on man's memory of the past; it is the retentiveness of his memory that has given him dominion over the earth. The knowledge which corresponds to the nature and character of the cosmic mind[2] is such as can be procured[3] from all the sensible things in the Kosmos.[4] But the knowledge which corresponds to the character of the supreme God's mind,[5]—this knowledge, and this alone, is truth;[6] and of this truth not the faintest outline or shadow is discernible in the Kosmos. For where things are discerned at intervals of time, there is falsehood; and where things have an origin in time,[7] there errors arise.

Thought,[8] however, differs from mind[9] in this respect, that our thought[8] attains by mental effort[10] to the kind of knowledge which corresponds to the character of the cosmic mind;[11] and having come to know cosmic things, it furthermore attains to a knowledge of eternity and the supracosmic[12] gods. And thus it comes to pass that we men see, as through dark mist, the things of heaven,[13] so far as this is compatible with the conditions of the human mind.[9] Our powers, when we aspire to the sight of things so high, are limited by narrow bounds; but great is man's happiness when he has seen that vision. You see, Asclepius, how lowly is our station, and how lofty are the things of which we treat; but to thee, O God supreme, I give my thanks, that thou hast shed on me the light[14] whereby I see that which

[1] *Intellegentia sensus humani, qualis aut quanta sit* = ἡ γνῶσις ἡ κατὰ τὸ τοῦ ἀνθρωπείου νοῦ ποιὸν καὶ ποσόν?

[2] *Intellectus naturae et qualitatis sensus mundi* = ἡ γνῶσις ἡ κατὰ τὸ ποιὸν τοῦ κοσμικοῦ νοῦ?

[3] *Provideri* = πορίζεσθαι?

[4] I.e. 'can be acquired by observation or investigation of all things perceptible by sense' (?).

[5] *Intellectus qualitatis sensus summi dei* = ἡ γνῶσις ἡ κατὰ τὸ ποιὸν τοῦ νοῦ τοῦ ὑψίστου θεοῦ?

[6] *Veritas* = ἀλήθεια.

[7] *Geniturae* = γενέσεις.

[8] *Intellectus* = διάνοια?

[9] Or 'intellect'. *Sensus* = νοῦς.

[10] *Mentis intentione* = τῇ τῆς νοήσεως ἐπιτάσει?

[11] *Ad qualitatem sensus mundi intellegendam et dinoscendum pervenit* = φθάνει μέχρι τῆς γνώσεως τῆς κατὰ τὸ ποιὸν τοῦ κοσμικοῦ νοῦ?

[12] *Deos qui supra se sunt* = τοὺς ὑπὲρ αὐτὸν θεούς.

[13] *Quae in caelo sunt* = τὰ ἐπουράνια?

[14] *Luminasti* = ἐφώτισας.

lumine. [Et vos, o Tat et Asclepi et Hammon, intra secreta pectoris divina mysteria silentio tegite et taciturnitate celate.]⟩⟩

33a–34a [[De inani vero . . . corporibus hominum signa.]] *Vide post cap.* 18 a (pp. 316–320).

34 b [[His ergo sic se habentibus . . . in ipso enim nihil tale consistit.]] *Vide post cap.* 19 a (p. 322).

34 c [[Hic ergo sensibilis qui dicitur mundus . . . quasi ex vestimento esse contecta.]] *Vide post cap.* 19 c (p. 326).

35, 36 [[Unumquodque enim genus animalium . . . imaginum similitudines aemulo splendore reddentium.]] *Vide post cap.* 17 b (pp. 328–330).

37 Sed iam de talibus sint satis dicta talia. Iterum ad hominem rationemque redeamus, ex quo divino dono homo animal dictu*s* est rationale. Minus enim miranda, etsi miranda sunt, quae de homine dicta sunt ⟨cetera⟩; omnium enim mirabilium vincit admirationem, quod homo divinam potuit invenire naturam, eamque efficere. Quoniam ergo proavi nostri multum errabant circa deorum naturam, increduli et non animadvertentes ad cultum religionemque divinam, invenerunt artem qua efficerent deos ⟨⟨de mundi natura conveniente[m]⟩⟩; cui inventae adiunxerunt virtutem [[de mundi natura convenientem]] ⟨⟨per qua*m* idola et bene faciendi et male vires habere potuissent⟩⟩, eamque misc*uerunt*: quoniam ⟨enim⟩ animas facere non poterant, evocantes animas daemonum vel angelorum, eas indiderunt imaginibus sanctis divinisque mysteriis [[per quas idola et bene faciendi et male vires habere potuissent]]. Avus enim tuus, Asclepi, medicinae primus inventor, cui templum consecratum est in monte Libyae circa litus crocodillorum, in quo eius iacet mundanus homo, id est corpus,—reliquus enim, vel potius totus, si est homo totus in sensu vitae, [melior] remeavit in caelum,—omnia etiamnunc hominibus adiumenta praesta*t* infirmis numine nunc suo, quae ante solebat medicinae arte praebere. Hermes, cuius avitum mihi nomen est, nonne in sibi cognomine patria consistens omnes

12–8 *infra*: sed iam . . . nominibus nuncupentur *citat Augustinus De civ. dei* 8. 24 *et* 26 **13** dictus *scripsi*: dictum ω *Aug.* **15** vicit *B* (*man.* 1) *et Aug.*: vincit *cett.* **17** que *post* eam *om. B* (*man.* 1) *et M* **20** conveniente *scripsi*: convenientem ω *Aug.* **21** per quam *scripsi*: per quas ω *Aug.* **22** miscuerunt *scripsi*: miscentes ω *Aug.* **31** praestat *scripsi*: praestans ω *Aug.* | nunc *om. F* **32** ante *om. Aug.* | solebat *GF*: solet *BMPL*: solent *Aug.* | praeberi *Aug.* **33** nonne *Aug.*: non ω (*om. F*) | patria *Aug.*: patriam ω

is divine.[1] [And you, Tat and Asclepius and Ammon, I bid you keep these divine mysteries hidden in your hearts, and cover them with the veil of silence.]

But as to these matters, let this suffice; and let us now return 37
to the topic of man, and that divine gift of reason,[2] in virtue of which man is called a rational animal.[3] Marvellous is all that I have told you of man; but one thing there is, more marvellous than all the rest; for all marvels are surpassed by this, that man has been able to find out how gods can be brought into being,[4] and to make them. Our ancestors were at first far astray[5] from the truth about the gods; they had no belief in them,[6] and gave no heed to worship and religion. But afterwards, they invented the art of making gods out of some material substance[7] suited for the purpose. And to this invention they added a supernatural force whereby the images might have power to work good or hurt, and combined it with the material substance;[8] that is to say, being unable to make souls, they invoked[9] the souls of daemons,[10] and implanted[11] them in the statues by means of certain holy and sacred rites. We have an instance in your grandfather, Asclepius, who was the first inventor of the art of healing, and to whom a temple has been dedicated in the Libyan mountain, near the shore of crocodiles.[12] There lies the material man,[13] that is, the body; but the rest of him,—or rather, the whole of him, if it is conscious life[14] that constitutes a man's whole being,—has returned to heaven. And to this day he renders to the sick by his divine power all the aid which he used to render to them by his medicinal art. Again, there is my grandfather Hermes, whose name I bear. Has he not taken up his abode in his native city, which is named after him,[15] and does he not help and safeguard all mortal men who come to him

[1] *Videndae divinitatis* = τοῦ τὸ θεῖον ἰδεῖν.

[2] *Ratio* = λογισμός? [3] *Animal rationale* = λογικὸν ζῷον.

[4] *Divinam invenire naturam* = θεῶν γένεσιν εὑρεῖν?

[5] *Quoniam errabant* = ἐπεὶ (or ἐπειδὴ) πεπλανημένοι ἦσαν.

[6] *Increduli* = ἄπιστοι ὄντες.

[7] *Mundi natura* = ὑλική τις φύσις.

[8] *Cui inventae . . . . eamque miscuerunt.* Perhaps something like this: τούτῳ δὲ τῷ εὑρήματι προσέθεσαν ἀρετήν (or δύναμίν) τινα δι' ἧς ἔμελλε τὰ εἴδωλα ἰσχὺν ἕξειν τοῦ εὖ τε καὶ κακῶς ποιεῖν, καὶ ταύτην συνεκέρασαν· ἐπεὶ γὰρ κ.τ.λ.

[9] *Evocantes* = ἐκκαλέσαντες?

[10] *Daemonum vel angelorum* = δαιμόνων? [11] *Indiderunt* = ἐνέθεσαν?

[12] That is, in the Fayum.

[13] *Mundanus homo* = ὁ ὑλικὸς ἄνθρωπος.

[14] *Sensus vitae* = ἡ ζωτικὴ αἴσθησις? [15] Viz. Hermopolis.

mortales undique venientes adiuvat atque conservat? Isin vero Osiri⟨di⟩s quam multa bona praestare propitiam, quantis obesse scimus iratam! Terrenis etenim diis atque mundanis facile est irasci, utpote qui sint ab hominibus ex utraque natura facti atque conpositi. Unde contigit ab Aegyptiis haec sancta animalia nuncupari, colique per singulas civitates eorum animas, quorum sunt consecrata ⟨quasi imagines⟩ viventes, ita ut et eorum legibus incolantur et eorum nominibus nuncupentur. Per hanc causam, o Asclepi, quod ⟨⟨quae⟩⟩ aliis [[quae]] colenda videntur atque veneranda, apud alios dissimiliter habentur, [ac] propterea bellis
27 d se lacessere Aegyptiorum solent civitates. ⟨⟨*Consecrabu*ntur vero qui terrae dominantur, et conlocabuntur in civitate in summo initio Aegypti, quae a parte solis occidentis condetur, ad quam terra marique festinabit omne mortale genus.—*Ascl.* Modo tamen hoc in tempore ubi isti sunt, o Trismegiste?—*Trism.* Conlocati sunt in maxima civitate in monte Libyco.—⟩⟩

38 a *Ascl.* Et horum, o Trismegiste, deorum, qui terreni habentur, ⟨evocatio⟩ cuiusmodi est [qualitas]?—*Trism.* Constat, o Asclepi, de herbis, de lapidibus, et de aromatibus divinitatis naturam in se habentibus. Et propter hanc causam sacrificiis frequentibus oblectantur, hymnis et laudibus et dulcissimis sonis in modum caelestis harmoniae concinentibus, ut illud quod [caeleste] ⟨⟨inlectum in idola⟩⟩ est caelest*e*, us⟨u⟩ et frequentatione ⟨cultus⟩ ⟨⟨laetum⟩⟩, [[inlectum in idola]] possit [[laetum]] humanitatis patiens longa durare per tempora. Sic deorum fictor est homo.

1 Isin δ *et Aug.* : ipsi *B* : ipsa *MG* 2 *Fortasse* Osiridis ⟨coniugem⟩ 4 ex utraque natura *GL* (*ex corr.*) *et Aug.* : extraque naturam *cett.* 5 contigit *Aug.* : contingit *codd. Ascl.* 7 consecratae (*ex corr.*) *M et Aug.* : consecrata *cett.* | et *om. M et Aug.* 8 incoantur *B* : inchoentur *M* : incolantur *cett.* 10 ac propterea (h *ante* ac *eras.*; ea *post* propter *add. man. post.*) *B* : hac propterea *M* : ac propterea *cett.* 11–16 *Cap.* 27 d (consecrabuntur ... monte Libyco) *huc transposui* 11 consecrabuntur *scripsi* : distribuentur ω 19 divinitatis naturam *MG*; divinitatis naturalem *man.* 1 *B* : vim divinitatis naturalem δ 23 caeleste, usu *scripsi* : caelesti usu *man.* 2 *B et ed. Rom.*; caelestius *cett.*

from every quarter? And Isis too, the wife of Osiris,[1]—do we not know how many boons she confers when she is gracious, and how many[2] men she harms when she is angry? For terrestrial and material[3] gods are easily provoked to anger, inasmuch as they are made and put together by men out of both kinds of substance. And hence it has come about that the sacred animals are recognized as such[4] by the Egyptians, and that in the several cities of Egypt people worship the souls of the men to whom these animals have been consecrated[5] as living statues;[6] so that the cities are governed by the laws which those men made,[7] and bear their names. Thus the same animals which some cities think it right to worship and revere are in other cities held in small esteem; and this, Asclepius, is the reason why the cities of Egypt are wont to make war on one
another. Moreover, in time to come the rulers of the land will **27 d**
be made gods, and their worship will be established[8] in a city at the very border of Egypt, a city which will be founded towards the setting sun, and to which men of every race will speed by land and sea.[9]—*Ascl.* But tell me, Trismegistus, where are such deified rulers to be found in our own day?—*Trism.* Their worship is established in the great city in the Libyan mountain.—

Ascl. And these gods who are called 'terrestrial', Trismegistus, **38 a**
by what means are they induced to take up their abode among us?[10]—*Trism.* They are induced, Asclepius, by means of herbs and stones and scents which have in them something divine.[11] And would you know why frequent sacrifices are offered to do them pleasure, with hymns and praises and concord of sweet sounds that imitate heaven's harmony? These things are done to the end that, gladdened by oft-repeated worship,[12] the heavenly beings who have been enticed into the images may continue through long ages to acquiesce in the companionship of men. Thus it is that man makes gods.

[1] *Isin Osiridis* = Ἶσιν τὴν τοῦ Ὀσίριδος ⟨γυναῖκα⟩.
[2] *Quantis* = ὅσοις. [3] *Terreni* = ἐπίγειοι: *mundani* = ὑλικοί?
[4] *Nuncupari* = ὀνομάζεσθαι, which may have been wrongly substituted for νομίζεσθαι.
[5] *Consecrata* = ἀφιερωμένα. Cf. Diod. I. 83. I: περὶ τῶν ἀφιερωμένων ζῴων.
[6] *Imagines viventes* = εἰκόνες ζῶσαι.
[7] *Ita ut eorum legibus incolantur* = ὥστε κατὰ τοὺς ἐκείνων νόμους οἰκοῦνται αἱ πόλεις. [8] *Conlocabuntur* = ἱδρυθήσονται, or καθιδρυθήσονται.
[9] Viz. Alexandria. [10] *Evocatio* = ἔκκλησις.
[11] *Divinitatis naturam* = θείαν φύσιν, or τῆς θείας τι φύσεως.
[12] *Usu et frequentatione cultus* = τῃ τῆς θρησκείας χρήσει καὶ πυκνώσει?

38 b Et ne putassis fort⟨e⟩ *irr*itos effectus esse terrenorum deorum o Asclepi: dii caelestes inhabitant summa caelestia, unusquisque ordinem quem accepit conplens atque custodiens; hi nostri vero, singillatim quaedam curantes, quaedam sortibus et divinatione praedicentes, quaedam providentes hisque pro modo subvenientes, humanis amica quasi cognatione auxiliantur. ⟨Ita⟩ ⟨⟨caelestes dii catholicorum dominantur, terreni incolunt singula.⟩⟩—

39 *Ascl.* Quam ergo rationis partem εἱμαρμένη vel fata incolunt, o Trismegiste? [ante] [[caelestes dii catholicorum dominantur, terreni incolunt singula.]]—*Trism.* Quam εἱμαρμένην nuncupamus, o Asclepi, ea est [[necessitas]] ⟨⟨effectrix rerum⟩⟩ omnium quae geruntur semper sibi catenatis ⟨⟨necessita⟨ti⟩s⟩⟩ nexibus vincta⟨e⟩. Haec itaque est [aut] [[effectrix rerum]] aut deus summus, aut ab ipso deo qui secundus effectus est [deus], *e*t omnium caelestium terrenarumque rerum firmata divinis legibus disciplina. Haec itaque εἱμαρμένη et necessitas ambae sibi invicem individuo conexae sunt glutino; quarum prior εἱμαρμένη rerum omnium initia parit, necessitas vero cogit ad effectum quae ex illius primordiis pendent. Has ordo consequitur, id est textus et dispositio temporis rerum perficiendarum. Nihil est enim sine ordinis conpositione; [[in omnibus mundus iste perfectus est]] ipse enim mundus ⟨⟨vel maxime⟩⟩ ordine gestatur, vel totus

1 forte irritos *scripsi* : fortuitos ω 9 ante *seclusi* : vel (an)ne *man.* 2 *B* : aut *L* : si *F* : ante *cett.* 12 vinctae *scripsi* : vincta ω 14 et *scripsi* : aut ω 17 quarum *GF* : quorum *cett.* 18 cogit ad effectum *man.* 2 *B et ed. Rom.* : cogit adfectum *man.* 1 *B et M* : cogit affectum *vel* effectum *cett.* 21 in omnibus . . . perfectus est *hinc ad cap.* 40 b *transposui* 22 vel maxime *huc a cap.* 40 a *transposui*

13–21 'Haec itaque est . . . sine ordinis conpositione.'
Lydus *De mensibus* (Wuensch) 4. 7:

ἡ δὲ εἱμαρμένη ἐστὶ⟨ν⟩ [καὶ ἡ εἱμαρτὴ] [[ἐνέργεια]] ἢ αὐτὸς ὁ θεός, ἢ ἡ μετ' ἐκεῖνον[a] τεταγμένη ⟨⟨ἐνέργεια⟩⟩, καὶ[b] πάντων οὐρανίων τε καὶ ἐπιγείων μετὰ τῆς ἀνάγκης ⟨κατὰ θεῖον νόμον⟩ τάξις. ⟨. . .⟩ καὶ ἡ μὲν αὐτὰς κύει τὰς ἀρχὰς τῶν πραγμάτων, ἡ δὲ καταναγκάζει καὶ τὰ τέλη γίνεσθαι. ταύταις δὲ ἀκολουθεῖ τάξις [καὶ νόμος] ⟨. . .⟩. καὶ ⟨γὰρ⟩ οὐδὲν ἄτακτον.

[a] ἐκεῖνον *scripsi* : ἐκείνην *Wuensch.* [b] καὶ *scripsi* : κατὰ *Wuensch.*

And you must not suppose, Asclepius, that the operations[1] 38 b
of the terrestrial gods are to no purpose.[2] The celestial gods dwell in the heights of heaven, and there each one of them unswervingly accomplishes the part assigned to him[3] in the ordering of the Kosmos; but these our gods on earth below see to things[4] one by one, predict events by means of sacred lots and divination, foresee what is coming and render aid accordingly; they assist, like loving kinsmen, in the affairs of men. Thus the celestial gods rule over things universal; the terrestrial gods administer[5] particulars.

Ascl. But tell me, Trismegistus, what part of the government[6] 39
of the universe is administered by Destiny?[7]—*Trism.* That which we name Destiny, Asclepius, is the force by which all events are brought to pass;[8] for all events are bound together in a never-broken chain by the bonds of necessity. Destiny then is either God himself, or else it is the force which ranks next after God; it is the power which, in conjunction with Necessity, orders all things in heaven and earth according to God's law. Thus Destiny and Necessity are inseparably linked together and cemented[9] to each other. Destiny generates the beginnings of things; Necessity compels the results to follow. And in the train of Destiny and Necessity goes Order, that is, the interweaving[10] of events, and their arrangement[11] in temporal succession. There is nothing that is not arranged in order; it is by order above all else that the Kosmos itself is borne upon its course;[12] nay, the Kosmos consists wholly of order.

[1] *Effectus* = ἐνέργεια. [2] *Irritus* = μάταιος?
[3] *Ordo* = τάξις: *complens atque custodiens* = ἐκπληρῶν καὶ φυλάττων.
[4] *Quaedam . . . quaedam* = τὰ μὲν . . . τὰ δέ.
[5] *Incolunt* = διοικοῦσι. [6] *Ratio* = οἰκονομία?
[7] εἱμαρμένη *vel fata* = ἡ εἱμαρμένη alone, or ἡ εἱμαρμένη ἢ αἱ Μοῖραι?
[8] *Effectrix rerum omnium quae geruntur* = ἡ ἐνεργοῦσα πάντα τὰ γιγνόμενα?
[9] *Conexae sunt glutino* = συγκεκόλληνται.
[10] *Textus* = συμπλοκή, or ἐπιπλοκή.
[11] *Dispositio* = διάθεσις? *Rerum perficiendarum* = τῶν ἀποτελουμένων?
[12] *Gestatur* = φέρεται?

constat ex ordine. ⟨⟨Prima ergo εἱμαρμένη est, quae iacto velut semine futurorum omnium sufficit prolem: sequitur necessitas, qua ad effectum vi coguntur omnia: tertius ordo, textum servans earum rerum quas εἱμαρμένη necessitasque disponit.⟩⟩

40 a Haec ⌜ergo⌝ tria, εἱμαρμένη, necessitas, ordo, [[vel maxime]] dei nutu sunt effecta, qui mundum gubernat sua lege et ratione divina. Ab his ergo omne velle aut nolle divinitus aversum est totum; nec ira etenim commoventur nec flectuntur gratia, sed serviunt necessitati rationis aeternae, quae [aeternitas] inaversibilis, inmobilis, insolubilis est. [[Prima ergo εἱμαρμένη est, quae iacto velut semine futurorum omnium sufficit prolem: sequitur necessitas, qua ad effectum vi coguntur omnia: tertius ordo, textum servans earum rerum quas εἱμαρμένη necessitasque disponit.]]

40 b [[Haec ergo est aeternitas ⟨⟨in omnibus ⟨quibus⟩ mundus iste perfectus est⟩⟩: [[quae nec coepit esse nec desinet]] qui, fixa inmutabili⟨s⟩ lege currendi, sempiterna commotione versatur, ⟨⟨quae nec coepit esse nec desinet,⟩⟩ oriturque et occidit alternis [[saepe]] per membra, ita ut variatis temporibus ⟨⟨saepe⟩⟩ isdem quibus occiderat membris oriatur. Sic est enim rotundita⟨ti⟩s volubilis ratio, ut ita sibi coartata sint cuncta, ut initium quod sit volubilitatis ignores, cum omnia se semper et praecedere videantur et sequi.]]

40 c Eventus autem vel fors insunt omnibus permixta mundanis. ⟨. . .⟩

* * * * *

27 e ⟨⟨Et haec usque eo narrata sint. De inmortali vero et de mortali modo disserendum est: multos enim spes timorque

1–4 prima . . . disponit *huc a cap.* 40 a *transposui* 6 qui *unus* ς *et ed. Rom.*: quae *vel* que *cett.* 14–22 *Cap.* 40 b (haec ergo . . . et sequi) *hinc transposui*: *vide post cap.* 32 a (p. 352) 25 sqq.: cap. 27 e–29 b (et haec . . . stellas inluminat) *huc transposui* 25 sint *man. post. B*: sunt *cett.* | et *scripsi*: aut ω

25–6 *infra* 'de inmortali . . . . sensus interitus' = Stob. 4. 52. 47, vol. v, p. 1087 Hense:

Ἑρμοῦ ἐκ τῶν πρὸς Ἀσκληπιόν.

περὶ δὲ τοῦ ⟨θνητοῦ καὶ τοῦ ἀ⟩θανάτου νῦν λεκτέον· τοὺς γὰρ πολλοὺς ὁ θάνατος φοβεῖ ὡς κακὸν μέγιστον, ἀγνοίᾳ τοῦ πράγματος. θάνατος γὰρ γίγνεται διαλύσει[a] καμόντος σώματος, καὶ τοῦ ἀριθμοῦ πληρωθέντος ⌜τῶν ἁρμῶν τοῦ σώματος· ἀριθμὸς γάρ ἐστιν ἡ ἁρμογὴ τοῦ σώματος⌝.[b] ἀποθνήσκει δὲ τὸ σῶμα ὅταν μηκέτι δύνηται[c] φέρειν ⌜τὸν ἄνθρωπον⌝.[d] καὶ τοῦτο ἔστι θάνατος, διάλυσις σώματος καὶ ἀφανισμὸς αἰσθήσεως σωματικῆς.

Of these three, the first is Destiny, which sows the seed, as it
were, and thereby gives rise to all that is to issue from the seed
thereafter; the second is Necessity, by which all results are
inevitably compelled to follow; and the third is Order, which
maintains the interconnexion of the events which Destiny and
Necessity determine. But Destiny, Necessity, and Order, all **40 a**
three together, are wrought by the decree[1] of God, who governs
the Kosmos by his law and by his holy ordinance.[2] Hence
all will to do or not to do is by God's ruling wholly alien from
them. They are neither disturbed by anger nor swayed by
favour;[3] they obey the compulsion of God's eternal ordinance,
which is inflexible, immutable, indissoluble.

Yet chance or contingency[4] also exists in the Kosmos, being **40 c**
intermingled with all material things.[5] . . .

* * * * *

But enough of this. I must now speak of the mortal and **27 e**
immortal parts of man. The many are afraid of death, thinking

[1] *Nutus* = νεῦμα.
[2] *Lex* = νόμος: *ratio* = λόγος.
[3] *Gratia* = χάρις.
[4] *Eventus vel fors* = τύχη? or τὸ συμβεβηκὸς καὶ ἡ τύχη?
[5] *Mundana* = ὑλικά?

---

[a] διαλύσει *scripsi*: διάλυσις *codd.*
[b] *Fortasse* τοῦ ἀριθμοῦ πληρωθέντος τῶν [ ] ἐτῶν ἐφ' ἃ διαμένει (?) ἡ ἁρμογὴ τοῦ σώματος.
[c] δύνηται *Halm*: δύναται *codd.*
[d] *Fortasse* τὸν ἀνθρώπινον βίον.

mortis excruciat, verae rationis ignaros. Mors enim efficitur dissolutione corporis labore defessi, et numeri conpleti ⌜quo⌝ corporis membra in unam machinam ad usus vitales aptantur; moritur enim corpus, quando hominis vitalia ferre posse destiterit. Haec est ergo mors, corporis dissolutio et corporalis sensus interitus: de qua sollicitudo supervacua est. Sed est alia necessaria, quam aut ignoratio aut incredibilitas contemnit humana.—*Ascl.* Quid est, o Trismegiste, quod aut ignorant aut esse posse

28 diffidunt?—*Trism.* Audi ergo, o Asclepi. Cum fuerit animae e corpore facta discessio, tunc ⟨fiet⟩ arbitrium examenque meriti eius. Transiet ⟨enim⟩ in summi daemonis potestatem: isque eam cum piam iustamque perviderit, in sibi conpetentibus locis manere permittit; sin autem delictorum inlitam maculis vitiisque oblitam viderit, desuper ad ima deturbans procellis turbinibusque aeris igni et aquae saepe discordanti[bu]s tradit, u*t* inter caelum et terram mundanis fluctibus in diversa semper aeternis poenis agitata rapiatur: ut in hoc animae obsit aeternitas, quod sit inmortali sen*su* aeterno supplicio subiugata. Ergo ne his inplicemur, verendum, timendum, cavendumque esse cognosce: incredibiles enim post delicta cogentur credere, non verbis, sed exemplis, nec minis, sed ipsa passione poenarum. ⟨⟨Praescia etenim omnium rerum divinitate, pro delictorum qualitatibus, perinde ut sunt, reddentur poe̤nae.⟩⟩—*Ascl.* Non ergo, Trismegiste, hominum delicta sola humana lege puniuntur?—*Trism.* Primo, Asclepi, ⟨⟨sunt mortalia⟩⟩ terrena quae sunt omnia [[sunt

2 desolutione (vel dis- *man.* 2) *B*: desolatione *M* | *Fortasse* numeri conpleti (= τοῦ ἀριθμοῦ πληρωθέντος, *gen. abs.*) ⟨annorum ad⟩ quo⟨s⟩ **3** vitalis (-es *man. post.*) *B*: vitales *cett.* **6** sed est *man.* 2 *B*: sed et *cett.* **15** igni *BMF*: ignis *GPL* | discordantis *scripsi*: discordantibus ω | tradit ut inter *Vulcanius*: traditur inter *BMLG*: traditur ut inter *man.* 2 *B*: tradit atque inter *F* **17** rapiatur *B*: raptatur *cett.* **18** sensu *scripsi*: sententia ω **21–23** praescia . . . poenae *huc transposui, mutato verborum ordine*

it the greatest of evils, through ignorance of the truth. Death comes to pass through the dissolution of a worn-out body, and takes place at the completion of the number of years for which the bodily parts are coadjusted to form a single instrument for the discharge of the vital functions; for the body dies when it is no longer able to sustain the stress of human life. Death then is the dissolution of the body, and the cessation of bodily sense; and about this we have no cause to be troubled. But there is something else, which demands our anxious thought, though men in general disregard it through ignorance or unbelief.—*Ascl.* What is it, Trismegistus, that men do not know
of, or do not believe to be possible?—*Trism.* I will tell you, 28
Asclepius. When the soul has quitted the body, there will be held a trial and investigation of its deserts. The soul will come under the power of the chief of the daemons.[1] When he finds a soul to be devout and righteous, he allows it to abide in the region which is suited to its character; but if he sees it to be marked with stains of sin, and defiled with ⟨incurable⟩ vices, he flings it downward, and delivers it to the storms and whirlwinds of that portion of the air which is in frequent conflict with fire and water, that[2] the wicked soul may pay everlasting[3] penalty, being ever swept and tossed hither and thither between sky and earth by the billows of cosmic matter.[4] And so[5] the everlasting[3] existence of the soul is to its detriment in this respect, that its imperishable faculty of feeling[6] makes it subject to everlasting[3] punishment. Know then that we have good cause for fear and dread, and need to be on our guard, lest we should be involved in such a doom as this. Those who disbelieve[7] will, after they have sinned, be forced to believe; they will be convinced, not by words, but by hard facts, not by mere threats, but by suffering the punishment in very deed. All things are known to God,[8] and the punishments inflicted will vary in accordance with the character of men's offences.—*Ascl.* It is not true then, Trismegistus, that men's offences are punished only by human law?—*Trism.* Some parts of man, Asclepius, are mortal; that is to say,

[1] *Summus daemon* = δαιμονιάρχης. [2] *Ut* = ἵνα.
[3] *Aeternus* = ἀΐδιος. [4] *Mundanus* = ὑλικός.
[5] *Ut* = ὥστε. [6] *Sensus* = αἴσθησις.
[7] *Incredibiles* = οἱ ἀπιστοῦντες.
[8] *Praescia . . . divinitate* = πάντων γὰρ τῷ θεῷ γνωρίμων ὄντων, or something of the sort. 'All things' must here mean all men's deeds, and especially their evil deeds.

mortalia]]; tunc ea etiam, quae sunt corporali ratione viventia et
a vivendo eadem corporum ratione deficientia. Ea omnia ⟨⟨in
vita⟩⟩ pro vitae meritis aut delictis poenis obnoxia ⟨. . .⟩ tanto
post mortem severioribus subiciuntur, quanto [[in vita]] forsitan
fuerint celata, dum viverent, ⟨delicta⟩. [[Praescia etenim omnium
rerum divinitate reddentur perinde ut sunt pro delictorum quali-
29 a tatibus poenae.]]—*Ascl.* Qu*a*⟨re⟩ sunt digni maioribus poenis, o
Trismegiste?—*Trism.* Qui⟨a⟩ damnati humanis legibus vitam
violenter amittunt, ut non naturae animam debitam, sed poenam
pro meritis reddidisse videantur. Contra iusto homini ⟨. . .⟩⟩⟩

* * * * *

33 b ⟨⟨Dico nunc daemonas quos credo ⟨⟨in terra[m]⟩⟩ commorari
nobiscum, ⟨et quos . . .⟩ ⟨⟨supra nos⟩⟩, et [heroas] quos in[ter]

3 vitae *secludendum*? 3–4 *Fortasse* poenis obnoxia ⟨sunt. Inmortalia vero quae sunt, poenis⟩ tanto post mortem severioribus subiciuntur 7 quare *scripsi*: qui ω 8 quia *scripsi*: qui ω 11–3 *infra*: *cap.* 33 b (dico nunc . . . commotio) *huc transposui* 12–1 *infra*: in aeris purissima parte *scripsi*: inter aeris purissimam partem ω

---

11 *sqq.* (*cap.* 33 b). Lydus *De mens.* 4. 32 (Wuensch): ὅτι ὁ Αἰγύπτιος Ἑρμῆς ἐν τῷ λόγῳ αὐτοῦ τῷ καλουμένῳ τελείῳ φησί

τοὺς μὲν τιμωροὺς τῶν δαιμόνων, ἐν αὐτῇ τῇ ὕλῃ παρόντας, τιμωρεῖσθαι τὸ ἀνθρώπειον κατ' ἀξίαν· τοὺς δὲ καθαρτικούς, ἐν τῷ ἀέρι πεπηγότας, τὰς ψυχὰς μετὰ θάνατον ἀνατρέχειν πειρωμένας ἀποκαθαίρειν περὶ τὰς χαλαζώδεις καὶ πυρώδεις τοῦ ἀέρος ζώνας,

ἃς οἱ ποιηταὶ καὶ αὐτὸς ὁ Πλάτων ἐν Φαίδωνι Τάρταρον καὶ Πυριφλεγέθοντα ὀνομάζουσι·

τοὺς δὲ σωτηρικούς, πρὸς τῷ σεληνιακῷ χώρῳ τεταγμένους, ἀποσώζειν τὰς ψυχάς.

Lydus *De mens.* 4. 148: κατὰ τὸν Αἰγύπτιον Ἑρμῆν, ὃς ἐν τῷ λεγομένῳ τελείῳ λόγῳ φησὶν οὕτως·

αἱ δὲ παραβᾶσαι ψυχαὶ τὸν τῆς εὐσεβείας κανόνα, ἐπὰν ἀπαλλαγῶσι τοῦ σώματος, παραδίδονται ⟨τούτοις⟩ τοῖς δαίμοσι, καὶ φέρονται [κατὰ] [[τοῦ ἀέρος]] σφενδονούμεναι (legendum -νώμεναι?) [καὶ] κατὰ τὰς πυρώδεις καὶ χαλαζώδεις ⟨⟨τοῦ ἀέρος⟩⟩ ζώνας,

ἃς οἱ ποιηταὶ Πυριφλεγέθοντα καὶ Τάρταρον καλοῦσιν.

firstly, all those parts of him which are of earthy substance, and secondly, those parts of him also which live their life after the manner of the body,[1] and likewise cease from life after the manner of the body. All these parts are liable to punishment in this life, so far as the man has deserved punishment by his offences. But man's immortal part is subject to punishment after death; and that punishment is all the more severe, if his offences chance
to have escaped detection[2] during his life on earth.—*Ascl.* But 29 a
why, Trismegistus, do such men deserve severer punishment?—*Trism.* Because those who are condemned by human laws are forcibly[3] deprived of life, and so it is held that they have not yielded up their life[4] as a debt due to nature, but have paid by its loss the penalty which they deserved. But to the righteous man, on the other hand, . . .

* * * * *

I say that there are daemons who dwell with us here on earth, 33 b
and others who dwell above us in the lower air, and others

[1] Perhaps, *θνητά ἐστιν, ὦ Ἀσκληπιέ, πρῶτον μὲν ὅσα γήινα, εἶτα δὲ καὶ τὰ κατὰ τὸν τοῦ σώματος λόγον* (or *τρόπον*) *ζῶντα.*

[2] *Quanto forsitan fuerint celata* = *ἐὰν τύχῃ κρυφθέντα.*

[3] *Violenter* = *βιαίως.*

[4] *Animam* = *ζωήν*, or *πνεῦμα*?

Lydus *De mens.* 4. 32: 'Hermes of Egypt, in his *Crowning Discourse*, as it is called, says

that the daemons of punishment are present in the very matter (of the human body?), and punish men's sins according to their deserts;

that the daemons of purgation are in the air and consist of coagulated air, and that when the souls after death are striving to ascend, these daemons purge them in those strata of the air which teem with hail and fire;

and that the daemons of salvation are stationed near the lunar sphere, and bring the souls off in safety (to the place where they would be).'

aeris purissima[m] parte[m] [[supra nos]] [et] [[in terram]], ubi nec nubilis locus est nec nubibus, nec ex signorum aliquorum agitatione commotio.⟩⟩

* * * * *

29 b ⟨⟨In dei religione et in [summa] pietate praesidium est ⟨unum⟩: deus enim tales ab omnibus tutatur malis. Pater enim omnium vel dominus, et is qui solus est omnia, omnibus se libenter ostendit, non ubi sit loco, nec qualis sit qualitate, nec quantus sit quantitate, sed hominem sola intellegentia mentis inluminans; qui, discussis ab animo errorum tenebris, et veritatis claritate percepta, toto se sensu intellegentiae divinae commiscet, cuius amore a parte naturae quae mortalis est liberatus, inmortalitatis futurae concipit fiduciam. Hoc ergo inter bonos malosque dista[bi]t. ⟨Ut⟩ [unus] enim quisque pietate, religione, prudentia, cultu, et veneratione dei clarescit, ⌜quasi oculi vera ratione perspecta et fiducia credulitatis suae⌝ tantum inter homines quantum sol lumine ceteris astris antistat. [Ipse enim sol non tam magnitudine luminis quam divinitate et sanctitate ceteras stellas inluminat].⟩⟩

* * * * *

1 et interram *BM*: et in terram *PL*: et terram *GF*: et aethera *Kozio.* 2 nec nubibus *B*: *om. cett.* 12–13 distat *scripsi*: distabit ω 14–15 *Fortasse* clarescit, ⟨⟨fiducia credulitatis suae⟩⟩ quasi oculis vera ratione perspecta [et] [[ ]] tantum 14 oculis *ed. Rom.*: oculi ω 18 inluminat ω: *fortasse* exsuperat

---

4–5 'in dei religione . . . tutatur malis.' Lactantius *Div. inst.* 2. 15. 6: 'adfirmat Hermes eos qui cognoverint deum non tantum ab incursibus daemonum tutos esse, verum etiam ne fato quidem teneri.

μία inquit φυλακὴ εὐσέβεια. εὐσεβοῦς γὰρ ἀνθρώπου οὔτε δαίμων κακὸς οὔτε εἱμαρμένη κρατεῖ· θεὸς γὰρ ῥύεται τὸν εὐσεβῆ ἐκ παντὸς κακοῦ. τὸ γὰρ ἓν καὶ μόνον ἐν ἀνθρώποις ἐστὶν ἀγαθὸν εὐσέβεια.'

Cyrillus *c. Iulian.* iv. 130 E, Migne vol. 76, col. 701 A: 'γράφει δὲ ὧδί καὶ αὐτὸς (*sc.* ὁ τρισμέγιστος Ἑρμῆς) ἐν ⌜τῷ⌝ πρὸς Ἀσκληπιόν, περὶ τῶν ἀνοσίων δαιμόνων, οὓς δεῖ φυλάττεσθαί τε καὶ φεύγειν προτροπάδην·

μία δὲ φυλακή ἐστι, καὶ αὕτη ἀναγκαία, ἡ εὐσέβεια· εὐσεβοῦς γὰρ ἀνθρώπου καὶ ἁγνοῦ καὶ σεμνοῦ οὔτ' ἂν δαίμων τις κακὸς οὔτε εἱμαρμένη κρατήσαι ποτὲ ἢ ἄρξειεν. ὁ θεὸς γὰρ ῥύεται τὸν τοιοῦτον, ὄντα ὄντως εὐσεβῆ, ἐκ παντὸς κακοῦ.'

again,[1] whose abode is in the purest part of the air, where no mist or cloud can be, and where no disturbance is caused by the motion of any of the heavenly bodies.

*   *   *   *   *

(Lydus *De mens.* 4. 148:)[2] And the souls which have transgressed the rule of piety, when they depart from the body, are handed over to these daemons,[3] and are swept and hurled to and fro in those strata of the air which teem with fire and hail.

*   *   *   *   *

The one safeguard is piety.[4] Over the pious man neither evil **29 b**
daemon nor destiny has dominion; for God saves the pious from every ill. Piety is the one and only good among men. The Father and Master of all, he who alone is all things, willingly reveals himself to all men. He does not indeed enable them to perceive him as situated in a certain place, or as having certain (sensible) qualities,[5] or a certain magnitude; but he illuminates[6] man with that knowledge alone which is the property of mind;[7] whereby the darkness of error is dispelled from the soul,[8] and truth[9] is seen in all its brightness, and so man's consciousness[10] is wholly absorbed in the knowledge of God;[11] and being freed, by his ardent love of God,[12] from that part of his being which makes him mortal,[13] he is assured of his immortality in time to come. In this consists the difference between the good man and the bad. For in so far as a man is illumined[14] by piety and devotion, by knowledge[15] of God, and worship and adoration of him, . . .[16] he surpasses other men as much as the sun outshines the other lights of heaven.

*   *   *   *   *

[1] *Dico nunc daemouas* &c.: perhaps, λέγω δὲ δαίμονας οὓς μὲν μεθ' ἡμῶν οἰκεῖν ἐπὶ γῆς, ⟨οὓς δὲ⟩ ὑπὲρ ἡμῶν ⟨ἐν τῷ περιγείῳ ἀέρι⟩, οὓς δὲ κ.τ.λ.

[2] Absent in the Latin text of the *Asclepius*, but quoted from the Greek original by Lydus.

[3] Viz. the daemons who dwell in the lower air.

[4] *Dei religio et pietas* = εὐσέβεια. [5] *Qualitas* = ποιόν.

[6] *Inluminans* = φωτίζων. [7] *Intellegentia* = γνῶσις: *mens* = νοῦς?

[8] *Animus* = ψυχή? [9] *Veritas* = ἀλήθεια.

[10] Or, 'man's thought'. *Sensus* = αἴσθησις? or νοῦς?

[11] *Intellegentia divina* = ἡ θεία γνῶσις, or ἡ τοῦ θεοῦ γνῶσις.

[12] Or, 'by his ardent desire for that knowledge (*gnosis*)'. *Amor* = ἔρως.

[13] Or, 'from the mortal part of the universe'.

[14] *Clarescit* = φωτίζεται? [15] *Prudentia* = γνῶσις?

[16] Perhaps, 'and, in the assurance of his faith, beholds reality as though with bodily eyes'.

⟨*Epilogus.*⟩

40 d *Trism.* 'Dictum est vobis de singulis, ut humanitas potuit, ut voluit permisitque divinitas. Restat hoc solum nobis, ut benedicentes deum orantesque ad curam corporis redeamus: satis enim nos de divinis rebus tractantes velut animi pabulis saturavimus.'

41 a De adyto vero egressi cum deum orare coepissent, in austrum respicientes,—sole etenim occidente cum quis deum rogare voluerit, illuc debet intendere, sicuti et sole oriente in eum qui subsolanus dicitur,—iam ergo dicentibus precationem Asclepius ait voce submissa: 'O Tat, vis suggeramus patri *tuo*, e rit⟨u⟩ ut ture addito et pigmentis precem dicamus deo?' Quem Trismegistus audiens atque commotus ait: 'Melius, melius ominare, Asclepi: hoc enim sacrilegi*i* simile est, cum deum roges, tus ceteraque incendere. Nihil enim deest ei, qui ipse est omnia, aut in eo sunt omnia. Sed nos agentes gratias adoremus; hae[c] sunt enim summ*i* incensiones dei, gratiae cum aguntur a mortalibus.

10 o Tat, vis *Thomas*: o tatuis *man. pr. B*: o tati *man. post. B et cett.* | patri tuo, e ritu ut *scripsi*: patri iusserit ut ω: patri tus e ritu, ut *Reitzenstein* 13 sacrilegii *unus* ς, *Kroll*: sacrilegis *codd. cett.* 15 hae *ed. Rom.*: haec ω 16 summi *scripsi*: summae ω

12–17 'melius, melius . . . a mortalibus.' Lactantius *Div. inst.* 6. 25. 11: 'Trismegistus Hermes . . . in illo sermone perfecto, cum exaudisset Asclepium quaerentem a filio suo utrum placeret patri eius proferri tus et alios odores ad sacrificium dei, exclamavit:

"Bene, bene ominare, o Asclepi: est enim maxima inpietas tale quid de uno illo ac singulari bono in animum inducere. Haec et his similia huic non conveniunt: omnium enim quaecunque sunt plenus est, et omnium minime indigens. Nos vero agentes gratias adoremus; huius enim sacrificium sola benedictio est."'

Epilogue.

Trism. 'I have explained each of these matters to you,[1] as far 40 d
as my human powers availed, and as far as God willed and
allowed. This only remains for us to do, that we should praise
God and pray to him, and then turn our attention to the needs
of the body; for our minds have been fed full with discourse 41 a
concerning things divine.'

Having come forth from the sanctuary, they began their prayers to God, looking towards the South; for when a man wishes to pray to God at sunset, he ought to face southward, as at sunrise he ought to face eastward.[2] But when they had begun to pray, Asclepius whispered, 'Tell me, Tat, shall we propose to your father that we should add to our prayer, as men are wont to do, an offering of incense and perfumes?'[3] Trismegistus heard; and much disturbed, he said, 'Hush, hush,[4] Asclepius; it is the height of impiety to think of such a thing with regard to Him who alone is good.[5] Such gifts as these are unfit for him; for he is filled with all things that exist, and lacks nothing.[6] Let us adore him rather with thanksgiving; for words of praise[7] are the only offering that he accepts.

1 *Vobis*, plural. 2 *Subsolanus* = ἀπηλιώτης.
3 *Pigmenta* (*alios odores* Lactant.) = ἀρώματα.
4 *Melius ominare* = εὐφήμει or εὐφήμησον.
5 *De uno illo ac singulari bono* (Lactant.) = περὶ ἐκεῖνον τὸν ἕνα καὶ μόνον ἀγαθὸν ὄντα.
6 *Omnium minime indigens* (Lactant.) = πάντων ἀπροσδεής (or ἀνενδεής).
7 *Benedictio* (Lactant.) = εὐλογία.

41 b ‘Gratias tibi ⟨agimus⟩, summe, exsuperantissime; tua enim gratia tantum sumus cognitionis tuae lumen consecuti.

Nomen sanctum,
et honorandum nom*in*⟨e di⟩v⟨i⟩n*o*, quod solus d*o*⟨min⟩us es,
⟨e⟩t benedicendu*m* religione paterna, quoniam omnibus paternam pietatem et *dilect*ionem et amorem, et quaecumque est dulcior efficacia, praebere dignaris,
condonans nos sensu, ratione, intellegentia:
sensu, ut te cognoverimus;
ratione, ut te suspicionibus indagemus;
cognitione, ut te cognoscentes [[gaudeamus]] ac *l*umine salvati tuo ⟨⟨gaudeamus⟩⟩.
Gaudemus quod te nobis ostenderis totum;

1 agimus *addidit Reitzenstein* 4 nomine divino *scripsi*: nomen unum *ω*: nomine *Reitz.* 4–5 quod solus dominus es, et benedicendum *scripsi*: quo solus deus est benedicendus *ω* 6 dilectionem *Eitrem*: religionem *ω* 8 condonans *GLF*: condonas *BMP* 11 lumine *scripsi*: numine *ω*

Cap. 41 b (‘Gratias tibi’ etc.):—Papyrus magicus Mimaut (Louvre 2391) vv. 284–302; transcripsit Reitzenstein, *Archiv f. Religionswissenschaft* vii (1904), p. 393 sq. Prius ediderant Wessely, *Denkschr. der k. Akad. der Wissensch., Philol.-hist. Classe* xxxvi, Wien, 1888, Abt. 2, p. 145 sq.: Reitzenstein, *Poimandres*, 1904, pp. 151–157. Denuo edidit Reitzenstein, *Die hellenist. Mysterienrel.*, 1910, p. 113 sq. Nuper recognovit S. Eitrem, *Les Papyrus magiques grecs de Paris* (*Videnskapsselskapets Skrifter II. Hist.-filos. Klasse*, 1923, No. 1), Kristiania, p. 34 sq.

(χ)άριν[1] σοὶ οἴδαμεν, ⟨ὕψιστε,⟩[2] ψυχῇ πάσῃ καὶ καρδίᾳ[ν] πρός (σε) ἀνατεταμένῃ[ν]·[3]
⟨τῇ γὰρ σῇ μόνον χάριτι τὸ φῶς τῆς γνώσεώς σου εἰλήχαμεν.⟩[4]
⟨- - -⟩ ἄφραστον ὄνομα ⟨- - -⟩,
τετιμημένον ⟨δὲ⟩ (τῇ)[5] τοῦ θεοῦ προσηγορίᾳ, ⟨ὅτι σὺ μόνος εἶ κύριος,⟩
καὶ εὐλογούμενον τῇ τοῦ (πατρ)όϲ, ὅτ(ι)[6] π(ρὸ)ς πάντας καὶ περὶ πάντα[s][7] πατρικὴν (εὔ)νοιαν[8] καὶ στοργὴν καὶ φιλίαν, καὶ εἴ τι⟨s⟩ γλυκυτέ(ρα)[ν], ἐνεργ(είᾳ) ἐν⟨ε⟩δ⟨ε⟩ίξω,[9]
χαρισάμενος ἡμῖν[10] νοῦν, (λόγ)ον,[11] γνῶσιν·
νοῦν μέ⟨ν⟩,[12] ἵνα σὲ νοήσωμεν,
λόγον ⟨δέ⟩, (ἵν)α[13] σὲ ἐπικαλέσωμεν,
γνῶσιν ⟨δέ⟩,[14] ἵνα σὲ ἐπιγνό⟨ντες καὶ τῷ φωτί σου σωθέντες χαί⟩ρωμεν.
χα(ίρομε)ν ὅτι[15] σεαυτὸν ἡμῖν ἔδ⟨ε⟩ιξας ⟨ὅλον⟩·[16]

'We thank thee, O thou Most High[1], with heart and soul wholly uplifted to thee; 41 b

for it is by thy grace alone that we have attained to the light,[2]
and come to know thee.

We thank thee, O thou whose name no man can tell,
but whom men honour by the appellation 'God', because thou alone art Master,
and bless by the appellation 'Father', because thou hast shown in act[3] toward all men and in all things loving-kindness and affection such as a father feels, nay, yet sweeter than a father's;
for thou hast bestowed on us mind, and speech, and knowledge:
mind, that we may apprehend thee;
speech, that we may call upon thee;
and knowledge, that having come to know thee, and found salvation in the light thou givest, we may be filled with gladness.
We are glad because thou hast revealed thyself to us in all thy being;

[1] *Exsuperantissime* might stand for ὑπεροχώτατε; but perhaps it is an alternative translation of ὕψιστε.

[2] *Tantum* = μόνον? Or *tantum lumen* = τοσοῦτον φῶς, 'this great light'?

[3] The translator must have read ενεργεια (*efficacia*) as a nominative.

---

[1] χάριν *Wessely* | [2] ὕψιστε *add. Reitz.* | [3] ψυχῇ πάσῃ καὶ καρδίᾳ πρός σε ἀνατεταμένῃ *scripsi*: ψυχη πασα και καρδιαν προς . . ανατεταμενην *Pap.*: *om. Reitz.* 1910 | [4] ⟨τῇ γὰρ σῇ μόνον - - - εἰλήχαμεν.⟩ *addidi*: ⟨σῇ γὰρ χάριτι τοῦτο τὸ φῶς τῆς γνώσεως ἐλάβομεν⟩ *add. Reitz.* | [5] τῇ *Reitz.* | [6] τῇ τοῦ πατρός, ὅτι πρὸς *scripsi*: τῇ τοῦ πατρὸς ⟨προσκλήσει⟩, ὅτι πρὸς *Reitz.*: τη του . . ου οσ . π . . s *Pap*, *teste Reitz.* τη του . . ου οσ . πρ . *Pap.*, *teste Eitrem.* (*Nescio an magus perperam scripserit* θεοῦ *pro* πατρός, *et* ὅσῳ (?) *pro* ὅτι) [7] καὶ περὶ πάντα *scripsi*: και προς παντας *Pap.*: καὶ πρὸς πάσας *Reitz.* | [8] εὔνοιαν *Wessely* | [9] καὶ εἴ τις γλυκυτέρα, ἐνεργείᾳ ἐνεδείξω *scripsi*: και επιγλυκυτα . . ν ενεργ . . . ενδιξω *Pap.*, *teste Eitrem*: καὶ ἐπιγλυκυτάτην ἐνέργειαν ἐνεδείξω *Reitz.* | [10] ἡμῖν *Reitz.*: ὑμῖν *Pap.* | [11] λόγον *Reitz.* | [12] μὲν *Reitz.* | [13] δέ, ἵνα *Reitz.* | [14] δέ *add. Reitz.* | [15] ἐπιγνόντες καὶ τῷ φωτί σου σωθέντες χαίρωμεν. χαίρομεν ὅτι *scripsi*: ἐπιγνωσωμεν χα . . . . . ν οτι *Pap.*, *teste Eitrem*: ἐπιγνόντες χαίρωμεν. ⟨σωθέντες ὑπὸ σοῦ⟩ χαίρομεν ὅτι *Reitz.* | [16] ἔδειξας ⟨ὅλον⟩ *Reitz.*

gaudemus quod nos in corporibus sitos aeternitat*e* ⟨tua⟩ fueris consecrare dignatus.

Haec est enim humana sola gratulatio, cognitio maiestatis tuae.

Cognovimus te, [et] ⟨o⟩ lumen maximum solo intellectu sensibili⟨um⟩;

*cognov*imus te, o vitae ⟨humanae⟩ vera vita.

⟨⟨Cognovimus te⟩⟩, o ⟨matrix⟩ [naturarum] ⟨rerum⟩ omnium fecunda, ⟨. . .⟩ praegnatio;

cognovimus te, ⟨o⟩ totius naturae ⌊tuo⌋ conceptu plenissim⟨a⟩e [[cognovimus te]] aeterna perseveratio.

In omni enim ista oratione adorantes ⟨te solum⟩ bonum, bonitatis tuae hoc tantum deprecamur, ut nos velis servar*i* perseverantes in amore cognitionis tuae, et numquam ab hoc vitae genere separari.

'Haec optantes convert*a*mus nos ad puram et sine animalibus cenam.'

1 aeternitate tua *scripsi*: aeternitati ω: *fortasse* aeterna vita tua 5 et *om.* *F*: *seclusit Thomas* | sensibilium *scripsi*: sensibili ω 7 cognovimus *scripsi*: intellegimus ω | *Fortasse* o vita vera ⟨humanae⟩ vitae 8 cognovimus te *huc transposuit Reitz.* 9 *Fortasse* ⟨per patris im⟩praegnatio⟨nem gravida⟩ 10 plenissimae *Reitz.*: plenissimū (u *in rasura man. post.*) *B*: plenissime *cett.* 13 *Fortasse* te precamur | servari *scripsi*: servare ω 16 convertamus *scripsi*: convertimus ω

χαίρομεν ὅ(τι ἐν π)λάσμασιν[17] ἡμᾶς ὄντας ἀποθεῶ⟨σαι ἠξίω⟩(σ)ας[18] τῇ σεαυτο(ῦ . . . . .)ι̣.[19]

χάρις ἀνθρώπου πρὸς σὲ μ(ία) τὸ ⟨σὸν μέγεθος⟩ γνωρίσαι.[20]

ἐγν(ωρίσαμ)έν ⟨σε⟩, ὦ ⟨ζωὴ ἀληθὲς⟩ τῆς ἀνθρωπίνης ζωῆς·

(ἐ)γνωρίσαμε(ν, ὦ φῶς) ⟨μεγίστον⟩ ⌜ἁπάσης γνώσεως⌝.[21]

ἐγνωρίσ⟨α⟩μέν ⟨σε⟩, ὦ[ν][22] μήτρα (παντοφ)όρε[23], ἐν π̣(α)τρὸς φυτ⟨ε⟩ίᾳ̣[24] ⟨κυοῦσα⟩·

ἐγνω⟨ρί⟩σαμεν, ὦ ⟨τοῦ τὸ πᾶν ἐν⟩ σ̣τά(σει κυ⟨κ̣λ⟩ο)φοροῦντος[25] αἰώνιος διαμονή.

⟨τ⟩ούτῳ σὲ τ(ῷ̣ λόγῳ̣)[26] π̣ροσκυνήσαντες ⟨τὸν μόνον ἀγαθὸν ὄντα, παρὰ τῆς σῆς ἀγαθότητος⟩ μ(η)δεμίαν αἰτήσωμεν (χάριν πλὴν) ⟨τόδε μόνον⟩· (θ)έλησον[27] ἡμᾶς δια(τ)ηρ̣ηθῆναι ἐν τῇ σῇ γν(ώ)σ̣(ει καὶ φιλό)τητ(ι, καὶ) [τὸ] μή⟨ποτε⟩ σφαλῆναι[28] τοῦ τοιούτου (βίου).[29]

we are glad because, while we are yet in the body, thou hast deigned to make us gods by the gift of thine own eternal life.
Man can thank thee only by learning to know thy greatness.
We have learnt to know thee, O thou most brightly shining light of the world of mind;[1]
we have learnt to know thee, O thou true life of the life of man.[2]
We have learnt to know thee, O thou all-prolific Womb, made pregnant by the Father's begetting[3];
we have learnt to know thee, O thou eternal constancy of that which stands unmoved, yet makes the universe[4] revolve.
With such words of praise do we adore thee, who alone art good; and let us crave from thy goodness no boon save this: be it thy will that we be kept still knowing and loving thee, and that we may never fall away from this blest way of life.[5]

'Having prayed thus,[6] let us betake ourselves to a meal unpolluted by flesh of living things.'[7]

[1] *Solo intellectu sensibilium* = τῶν νοητῶν.
[2] This and the preceding clause are interchanged in the Greek as given in the Papyrus.
[3] *Praegnatio* (or *impraegnatio*) = φυτεία. [4] *Totius naturae* = τοῦ παντός?
[5] I.e. the bliss which is enjoyed by those who know and love God, and which Hermes and his pupils are now enjoying.
[6] Probably an aorist participle in the Greek. [7] *Animalia* = ἔμψυχα.

| 17 ὅτι ἐν πλάσμασιν *Eitrem* (ο . . . . . λασμασιν *Pap.*, *teste Eitrem*) : ὅτι ἐν σώμασιν *Reitz.* | 18 ἀποθεῶσαι ἠξίωσας *scripsi* : ἀπεθέωσας *Reitz.* : απ . θεω . ας *Pap.*, *teste Reitz.* : αποθεω . ας *Pap.*, *teste Eitrem* | 19 σεαυτοῦ θέᾳ *Reitz.* : σεαυτοῦ δυνάμ⟨ε⟩ι *vel* θελήσ⟨ε⟩ι *Eitrem*. *An* σεαυτοῦ αἰωνι⟨ότητι⟩ *vel* αἰωνί⟨ῳ ζωῇ⟩? | 20 πρὸς σέ, σοῦ τὸ μέγεθος γνωρίσαι *Reitz.* : προς σε μετὰ γνωρισαι *Pap.*, *teste Reitz.* : προς σε μ . . τọ . νωρισαι *Pap.*, *teste Eitrem* | 21 ἐγνωρίσαμέν σε, ὦ φῶς μόνῃ τῇ νοήσει αἰσθητόν (= solo intellectu sensibil*e*) *Reitz.* : . γνωρισαμε . . . . . απασης γνωσεως *Pap.*, *teste Eitrem*. *Num scribendum* ἐγνωρίσαμέ(ν σε, ὦ λ)α⟨μ⟩πὰς ⟨μέγίστη τ⟩ῆς γνώσεως (*vel* τῶν νοητῶν)? | 22 ἐγνωρίσαμέν σε, ὦ *Reitz.* : εγνωρισμενων *Pap.* | 23 μήτρα παντοφόρε *scripsi* : μήτρα κυοφόρε ⟨πάντων⟩ *Reitz.* : μητρα . . . . . . ορε *Pap.*, *teste Eitrem* | 24 ἐν πατρὸς φυτείᾳ *scripsit Reitz.*, *sed ad sequentia transposuit* : εμ π̣ . τρος φυτιαι *Pap.*, *teste Reitz.* : ε μ̣ητρος φυτιαι *Pap.*, *teste Eitrem* | 25 ὦ τοῦ τὸ πᾶν ἐν στάσει κυκλοφοροῦντος *scripsi* (*pro quo legisse puto interpretem Latinum* ὦ τοῦ παντὸς ἐν πᾶσι κυοφοροῦντος) : ωσ̣τα . . . . . . φορου . τος *Pap.*, *teste Eitrem* : ὦ τοῦ κυοφοροῦντος ⟨⟨ἐν πατρὸς φυτείᾳ⟩⟩ *Reitz.* | 26 τούτῳ σὲ τῷ λόγῳ *scripsi* : ουτος ου . . . . . *Pap.*, *teste Eitrem* : οὕτως οὖν σε *Reitz.* | 27 μηδεμίαν αἰτήσωμεν χάριν πλὴν (*vel* εἰ μὴ) τόδε μόνον· θέλησον *scripsi* : μ . δεμιαν ητησαμεν . . . . ελησον *Pap.*, *teste Eitrem* : οὐδεμίαν ἠτήσαμεν δέησιν ⟨παρὰ τῆς σῆς ἀγαθότητος (?)⟩, πλὴν θέλησον *Reitz.* | 28 ἐν τῇ σῇ γνώσει καὶ φιλότητι, καὶ μήποτε σφαλῆναι *scripsi* : εν τη ση γν . σ̣ . . . . τηι̣ . . . . το μη σφαληναι *Pap.*, *teste Eitrem* : ἐν τῇ σῇ γνώσει, παραιτηθεὶς τὸ μὴ σφαλῆναι *Reitz.* : ἐν τῇ σῇ γνώσει τῇ ἁγιωτάτῃ (?) πρὸς (?) τὸ μὴ σφαλῆναι *Eitrem* | 29 τοιούτου βίου *scripsi* : τοιούτου γένους τοῦ βίου *Reitz.*

LIST OF THE HERMETIC EXCERPTS IN

Stobaeus (Wachsmuth and Hense).	Present edition.
1. 1. 29[a]	Exc. [XXVIII]
1. 1. 30	Corp. IV. 1 b
1. 3. 52	Exc. VII
1. 4. 7[b]	Exc. XIII
1. 4. 8	Exc. VIII
1. 5. 14	Exc. [XXIX]
1. 5. 16	Exc. XIV
1. 5. 20	Exc. XII
1. 8. 41	Exc. X
1. 10. 15	Corp. IV. 10–11 b
1. 11. 2	Exc. IX
1. 18. 2	Corp. II. 1–4
1. 18. 3	Corp. II. 10–13
1. 19. 2	Corp. II. 6 b–9
1. 21. 9	Exc. VI
1. 41. 1 (a)	Exc. II B
1. 41. 1 (b)	Exc. XI
1. 41. 4	Exc. XVI
1. 41. 6 (a)	Exc. IV B
1. 41. 6 (b)	Exc. III
1. 41. 7	Exc. XV
1. 41. 8	Exc. V
1. 41. 11	Exc. XXI
1. 42. 7	Exc. XXII
1. 47. 8	Corp. X. 22 b–25
1. 47. 9	Corp. X. 12, 13
1. 48. 3	Corp. X. 16–18
1. 49. 3	Exc. XX
1. 49. 4	Exc. XVII
1. 49. 5	Exc. IV A
1. 49. 6 (and 1[c])	Exc. XIX
1. 49. 44	Exc. XXIII
1. 49. 45	Exc. XXIV
1. 49. 48	Corp. X. 7–8 b
1. 49. 49	Corp. X. 19 a b
1. 49. 68	Exc. XXV
1. 49. 69	Exc. XXVI
2. 1. 26	Exc. I
2. 8. 31	Exc. XVIII
3. 11. 31	Exc. II A
3. 13. 65	Exc. XXVII
4. 52. 47	Ascl. Lat. III. 27 e

THE ANTHOLOGIUM OF STOBAEUS

Present edition.	Stobaeus.	
Corp. II. 1–4	1. 18. 2	Hermes to Asclepius
„ „ 6 b–9	1. 19. 2	
„ „ 10–13	1. 18. 3	
Corp IV. 1 b	1. 1. 30	Hermes to Tat
„ „ 10–11 b	1. 10. 15	
Corp. X. 7–8 b	1. 49. 48	
„ „ 12, 13	1. 47. 9	
„ „ 16–18	1. 48. 3	
„ „ 19 a b	1. 49. 49	
„ „ 22 b–25	1. 47. 8	
Ascl. Lat. III. 27 e	4. 52. 47	Hermes to Ascl.
Exc. I	2. 1. 26	Hermes to Tat
„ II A	3. 11. 31	
„ II B	1. 41. 1 (a)	
„ III	1. 41. 6 (b)	
„ IV A	1. 49. 5	
„ IV B	1. 41. 6 (a)	
„ V	1. 41. 8	
„ VI	1. 21. 9	
„ VII	1. 3. 52	
„ VIII	1. 4. 8	
„ IX	1. 11. 2	
„ X	1. 8. 41	
„ XI	1. 41. 1 (b)	
„ XII	1. 5. 20	Hermes to Ammon
„ XIII	1. 4. 7[b]	
„ XIV	1. 5. 16	
„ XV	1. 41. 7	
„ XVI	1. 41. 4	
„ XVII	1. 49. 4	
„ XVIII	2. 8. 31	Hermes (no pupil named)
„ XIX	1. 49. 6	
„ XX	1. 49. 3	
„ XXI	1. 41. 11	
„ XXII	1. 42. 7	
„ XXIII	1. 49. 44	Isis to Horus
„ XXIV	1. 49. 45	
„ XXV	1. 49. 68	
„ XXVI	1. 49. 69	
„ XXVII	3. 13. 65	
„ [XXVIII]	1. 1. 29[a]	Apophthegm
„ [XXIX]	1. 5. 14	Verses

STOBAEI HERMETICA

EXCERPTUM I

Stobaeus 2. 1. 26, vol. ii, p. 9 Wachsmuth (*Floril.* 80. 9 Meineke).

Ἑρμοῦ ἐκ τῶν πρὸς Τάτ.

1 Θεὸν νοῆσαι μὲν χαλεπόν, φράσαι δὲ ἀδύνατον ᾧ καὶ νοῆσαι δυνατόν. τὸ γὰρ [ἀσώματον σώματι σημῆναι ἀδύνατον, καὶ τὸ] τέλειον τῷ ἀτελεῖ καταλαβέσθαι ⌈οὐ δυνατόν⌉, καὶ τὸ ἀίδιον τῷ ὀλιγοχρονίῳ συγγενέσθαι δύσκολον. τὸ μὲν γὰρ ἀεί ἐστι, τὸ δὲ παρέρχεται· καὶ τὸ μὲν ἀληθές ἐστι, τὸ δὲ ὑπὸ φαντασίας ⌈σκιάζεται⌉. [ὅσον οὖν τὸ ἀσθενέστερον τοῦ ἰσχυροτέρου καὶ τὸ ἔλαττον τοῦ κρείττονος
2 διέστηκε,] τοσοῦτον ⟨διέστηκε⟩ τὸ θνητὸν τοῦ θείου. ἡ δὲ μέση τούτων διάστασις ἀμαυροῖ τὴν τοῦ καλοῦ θέαν. ὀφθαλμοῖς μὲν γὰρ τὰ σώματα θεατά [γλώττῃ δὲ τὰ ὁρατὰ λεκτά]· τὸ δὲ ἀσώματον καὶ ἀφανὲς καὶ ἀσχημάτιστον καὶ μὴ ἐξ ὕλης ⌈ὑποκείμενον⌉ ὑπὸ τῶν ἡμετέρων αἰσθήσεων καταληφθῆναι οὐ δύναται. ⌈ἐννοοῦμαι, ὦ Τάτ, ἐννοοῦμαι ὃ ἐξειπεῖν ἀδύνατον· τοῦτο ἔστιν ὁ θεός.⌉

Codices Stob.: S (saeculi xi ineuntis), M (saec. xii ineuntis vel xi extremi), A (saec. xiv), B (saec. xvi).

Pseudo-Justinus *Cohortatio ad gentiles* 38 (Otto, Tom. II, *Opera Justini addubitata*, 1879): Ἑρμοῦ . . . λέγοντος· "θεὸν νοῆσαι μέν ἐστι χαλεπόν, φράσαι δὲ ἀδύνατον ᾧ καὶ νοῆσαι δυνατόν."

Lactantius *Epitome* 4. 5 (Brandt): 'Huius (*sc.* Hermae Trismegisti) ad filium scribentis exordium tale est: "Deum quidem intellegere difficile est, eloqui vero inpossibile, etiam cui intellegere possibile est: perfectum enim ab inperfecto, invisibile a visibili non potest conprehendi."'

Cyrillus *contra Julianum* 1. 31 (Migne *Patr. Gr.* 76. 549): ὁ δέ γε τρισμέγιστος Ἑρμῆς οὕτω πως φησί· "θεὸν νοῆσαι μὲν χαλεπόν . . . ὑπὸ φαντασίας σκιάζεται. ὅσῳ οὖν τὸ ἀσθενέστερον τοῦ ἰσχυροτέρου καὶ τὸ ἔλαττον τοῦ κρείττονος διέστηκε, τοσοῦτον τὸ θνητὸν τοῦ θείου καὶ ἀθανάτου."

1 ἐκ τῶν scripsi: om. S: ἐκ τοῦ codd. cett. 2 νοῆσαι μὲν Cyril., Stob. A: νοῆσαι μέν ἐστι Ps.-Just.: μὲν νοῆσαι Stob. SM: *quidem intellegere* (i.e. μὲν νοῆσαι) Lact. 2–3 ᾧ καὶ νοῆσαι δυνατόν Ps.-Just.: *etiam cui intellegere possibile est* (i.e. καὶ ᾧ ν. δ.) Lact.: εἰ καὶ ν. δ. Cyril. (Aubert): *si cui etiam intelligere possibile* (i.e. εἴ τῳ καὶ ν. δ.) Cyril. (Oecolampadius): om. codd. Stob. 3 καὶ τὸ Stob. A: τὸ γὰρ cett. | συμβῆναι Stob. A: σημῆναι Stob. codd. cett. et Cyril. 3–4 ἀσώματον . . . καὶ τὸ codd. Stob. et Cyril.: om. Lact.

STOBAEUS

EXCERPT I

An extract from the Discourses of Hermes to Tat.

To conceive God is difficult; and to describe Him is impossible, 1
even if one is able to conceive Him. For it is not easy for that
which is imperfect to apprehend that which is perfect, and it is
hard for that which is of short duration to have dealings with
that which is everlasting. The one ever is, the other passes;
the one is real, the other is but shadowed forth by sense-picturing.
So widely is that which is mortal separated from that which is
divine. And the wide interval between them dims men's vision 2
of the Beautiful. With our eyes we can see bodies; but that
which is incorporeal and invisible and without shape, and is not
composed of matter, cannot be apprehended by senses such
as ours. . . .[1]

[1] Perhaps, 'When I have in my mind a conception of this, my son', (viz. of 'that which is incorporeal', &c.,) 'I have a conception which it is impossible to express in words; and such is God' (i. e. God is incorporeal, &c., and therefore, is something that cannot be told in words).

---

4 Post ἀτελεῖ add. *invisibile a visibili* (i.e. καὶ τὸ ἀόρατον τῷ ὁρατῷ) Lact. | καταλαβέσθαι codd. Stob.: καταλαμβάνεσθαι Cyril.: *conprehendi* (i.e. καταλαμβάνεσθαι ?) Lact.: fortasse καταλαβεῖν | οὐ δυνατόν codd. Stob. et Cyril.: *non potest* (i.e. οὐ δύναται) Lact.: fortasse οὐκ εὐχερές **5** συγγενέσθαι codd Stob., Cyril. (Aub.): *sempiternum conferre* (i.e. συνενέγκασθαι ?) *cum momentaneo* Cyril. (Oecol.) | τὸ μὲν Stob. B, Cyril.: ὁ μὲν Stob. SMA **6** ἀληθές Cyril.: ἀλήθεια Stob. A: ἀληθείᾳ Stob. codd. cett. **7** σκιάζεται codd. Stob., Cyril. (Aub.): *adumbratur* Cyril. (Oecol.): fortasse σκιαγραφεῖται | ὅσῳ οὖν τὸ Cyril. (Aub.): *quantum igitur* (i.e. ὅσον οὖν τὸ) Cyril. (Oecol.): τὸ δὲ codd. Stob. **9** τοσοῦτον Cyril. (Aub.): *tantum etiam* (i.e. τοσοῦτον καὶ) Cyril. (Oecol.): τοσοῦτον ὅσον codd. Stob. | τὸ θνητὸν τοῦ θείου codd. Stob.: τὸ θνητὸν τοῦ θείου καὶ ἀθανάτου Cyril. (Aub.): *a divino et immortali mortale* (i.e. τοῦ θείου καὶ ἀθανάτου τὸ θνητόν) Cyril. (Oecol.) | Post θείου καὶ ἀθανάτου addit Cyrillus εἴ τις οὖν ἀσώματος ὀφθαλμὸς . . . μήτε ἑαυτῷ ἀνόμοιον (vide *Testim.*); quod videtur aliunde sumptum esse **10** μέση codd.: μεσηγὺ Usener: fortasse διὰ μέσου **13** μὴ B: μήτε SA: μηδὲ Meineke, Wachsm. | συγκείμενον Meineke. Fortasse μὴ ἐξ ὕλης ὑφ⟨εστὸς μηδὲ ἐκ στοιχείων συγ⟩κείμενον | Ante ὑπὸ add. καὶ A **14–15** ἐννοοῦμαι . . . ὁ θεός om. B. Fortasse ⟨τοῦτο⟩ ἐννοούμε⟨νος⟩, ὦ Τάτ, ἐννοοῦμαι ὃ ἐξειπεῖν ἀδύνατον· τ⟨οι⟩οῦτο⟨ς δέ⟩ ἐστιν ὁ θεός **15** ἀδύνατον A: οὐ δυνατόν S

EXCERPTUM II A

Stobaeus 3. 11. 31, vol. iii, p. 436 Hense (*Floril.* 11. 23 Meineke).

Ἑρμοῦ ἐκ τῶν πρὸς Τάτ.

1 Περὶ ἀληθείας, ὦ Τάτ, οὐκ ἔστι δυνατὸν ⟨κατ' ἀξίαν
εἰπεῖν⟩ ἄνθρωπον ὄντα, ζῷον ἀτελές, ἐξ ἀτελῶν συγκείμενον
μερῶν, καὶ ἐξ ἀλλοτρίων σωμάτων καὶ πολλῶν τὸ σκῆνος
⟨ἔχοντα⟩ συνεστός [τολμήσαντα εἰπεῖν]· ὃ δέ ἐστι δυνατόν
[ἢ δίκαιον], τοῦτο φημί, ἀλήθειαν εἶναι ἐν μόνοις τοῖς ἀιδίοις
2 [σώμασιν] ⟨. . .⟩ ⌈ων⌉. καὶ τὰ ⟨ἀίδια⟩ σώματα αὐτὰ ⟨μὲν
καθ' αὑτὰ⟩ ἀληθῆ ἐστι, πῦρ αὐτόπυρ [μόνον καὶ οὐδὲν ἄλλο],
γῆ αὐτόγη [καὶ οὐδὲν ἄλλο], ἀὴρ αὐτοάηρ, ὕδωρ αὐτοΰδωρ
[καὶ οὐδὲν ἄλλο]. τὰ δὲ ἡμέτερα σώματα ἐκ πάντων τούτων
συνέστηκεν· ἔχει μὲν γάρ ⟨τι⟩ πυρός, ἔχει δὲ καὶ γῆς [ἔχει]
καὶ ὕδατος καὶ ἀέρος· καὶ οὔτε πῦρ ἐστιν ⟨ἐν αὐτοῖς ἀληθὲς⟩
οὔτε γῆ οὔτε ὕδωρ οὔτε ἀήρ, οὔτε οὐδὲν ἀληθές. εἰ δὲ μὴ
τὴν ἀρχὴν ἡ σύστασις ἡμῶν ἔσχε τὴν ἀλήθειαν, πῶς ἂν
δύναιτο ἀλήθειαν ἢ ἰδεῖν ἢ εἰπεῖν; [νοῆσαι δὲ ⟨δυνατὸν⟩
μόνον ἐὰν ὁ θεὸς θέλῃ.]
3 πάντα οὖν, ὦ Τάτ, τὰ ἐπὶ γῆς ἀληθῆ μὲν οὐκ ἔστι· τῆς δὲ
ἀληθείας μιμήματα [καὶ] οὐ πάντα, ὀλίγα δέ. [ταῦτα] ⟨τὰ
δὲ⟩ ἄλλα ψεῦδος καὶ πλάνος, ὦ Τάτ, [καὶ δόξαι,] ⟨ἐκ⟩ φαντα-
4 σίας [καθάπερ εἰκόνες] συνεστῶτα. ὅταν δ' ἄνωθεν τὴν
ἐπίρροιαν ἔχῃ ἡ φαντασία, τῆς ἀληθείας γίγνεται μίμησις.
χωρὶς δὲ τῆς ἄνωθεν ἐνεργείας, ψεῦδος καταλείπεται·
καθάπερ καὶ ἡ εἰκὼν [[τὸ [[μὲν]] σῶμα]] ⟨ἡ ἐν⟩ τῇ γραφῇ
δείκνυσι ⟨⟨μὲν⟩⟩ [[αὐτὴ δὲ οὐκ ἔστι σῶμα]] κατὰ [τὴν]
φαντασίαν ⟨⟨τὸ σῶμα⟩⟩ τοῦ ὁρωμένου, ⟨⟨αὐτὴ δὲ οὐκ ἔστι
σῶμα.⟩⟩ καὶ ὀφθαλμοὺς μὲν ὁρᾶται ἔχουσα, βλέπει δὲ
οὐδέν· ⟨καὶ ὦτα,⟩ ἀκούει δὲ οὐδὲν ὅλως· καὶ τὰ ἄλλα πάντα
ἔχει μὲν ἡ γραφή, ψευδῆ δέ [ἐστι], τὰς τῶν ὁρώντων ὄψεις

Exc. II A: codices S, M, A, L, Br.

1 Ἑρμοῦ om. Br | τοῦ pro τῶν LBr | ἐκ τῶν πρὸς Τάτ om. A **2–20** περὶ ἀληθείας . . . εἰκόνες συνεστῶτα (§§ 1–3) infra leguntur post τὸν ἀεὶ ὄντα (§ 15 *fin.*) M **2** περὶ ἀληθείας om. LBr | τατον pro ὦ Τάτ L **4** μερῶν scripsi: μελῶν codd. **6** δίκαιον S: δίκαιόν ἐστι(ν) cett. Fortasse δίκαιον ⟨γὰρ⟩ ⟨⟨τολμήσαντα εἰπεῖν⟩⟩ post τοῦτο φημί **7** σώμασιν, ὧν καὶ τὰ σώματα codd. **9** αὐτὸς ἀὴρ SA¹ **9–10** ὕδωρ . . . ἄλλο Br: om. LSMA **10–13** τὰ δὲ ἡμέτερα . . . οὔτε ἀήρ: Lactant. *Div. inst.* 2. 12. 4, '(Trismegistus)

EXCERPT II A

From the Discourses of Hermes to Tat.

Hermes. Concerning reality, my son Tat, it is not possible for 1
one who is but a man to speak adequately; for man is an imperfect creature, composed of parts[1] which are imperfect, and his mortal frame is made up of many alien bodies. But what it is within my power to say, that I do say, namely, that[2] reality
exists only in things everlasting . . . . The everlasting bodies, 2
as they are in themselves,—fire that is very fire, earth that is very earth, air that is very air, and water that is very water,—these indeed are real. But our bodies are made up of all these elements together; they have in them something of fire, but also something of earth and water and air; and there is in them neither real fire nor real earth nor real water nor real air, nor anything that is real. And if our composite fabric has not got reality in it to begin with, how can it[3] see reality, or tell of reality?

All things on earth then, my son, are unreal; but some of 3
them,—not all, but some few only,—are copies of reality. The rest are illusion and deceit, my son; for they consist of mere
appearance. When the appearance flows in from above,[4] it 4
becomes an imitation of reality. But apart from the working of power from above, it remains an illusion; just as a painted portrait presents to us in appearance the body of the man we see in it, but is not itself a human body. It is seen to have eyes, and yet it sees nothing; it is seen to have ears, and yet it hears nothing at all. The picture has all else too that a living man has, but all this is false, and deceives the eyes of those who look

[1] Viz. portions of the four cosmic elements.
[2] Perhaps, 'that I do say (for it is right to speak boldly), namely, that', &c.
[3] Perhaps, 'how can we'.
[4] Or 'receives the influx ⟨of . . . ?⟩ from above'.

nostra corpora ex his quattuor elementis constituta esse dixit a deo: habere namque in se aliquid ignis, aliquid aeris, aliquid aquae, aliquid terrae, et neque ignem esse neque aerem neque aquam neque terram.' 12 *καὶ ἀέρος* S: *ἔχει καὶ ἀέρος* LABr 15 *δύναιντο* SA. Fortasse *δυναίμεθα* 17 *ὦ Τάτ* om. LABr | *ἀληθῆ* scripsi: *ἀλήθεια* codd. 17–18 *τὰ δὲ ἀληθῆ* A: *τῆς δὲ ἀληθείας* cett. 19 *καὶ δόξαι* codd.: fortasse *κατὰ δόξαν* 20 Fortasse *ὅταν μὲν γὰρ* 23 *ἡ ἐν τῇ γραφῇ* scripsi: *τῆς γραφῆς* codd. 26–6 *infra*: *καὶ ὀφθαλμοὺς . . . οὔτε νοήσομεν οὔτ' εἰσόμεθα* (§ 5 *fin.*) om. Br 27 *καὶ ὦτα* add. Flussas

ἐξαπατῶντα, τῶν μὲν δοκούντων ἀληθῆ ὁρᾶν, τῶν δὲ ὡς
ἀληθῶς ὄντων ψευδῶν.
5 ὅσοι μὲν οὖν ⌜οὐ⌝ ⟨. . .⟩, ψεῦδος ὁρῶσιν· ⟨ὅσοι δὲ . . .⟩,
ἀλήθειαν ὁρῶσιν. ἐὰν οὖν ἕκαστον τούτων οὕτω νοῶμεν ἢ
ὁρῶμεν ὡς ἔστιν, ἀληθῆ καὶ νοοῦμεν καὶ ὁρῶμεν· ἐὰν δὲ
παρὰ τὸ ὄν, οὐδὲν ἀληθὲς οὔτε νοήσομεν οὔτ' ὀψόμεθα.
7 ⟨⟨⌜οὕτως⌝ ἀληθὲς οὐδὲν εἶναι ἐν τῇ γῇ νοῶ⟨ν⟩ καὶ λέγω⟨ν⟩
[φαντασίαι εἰσὶ καὶ δόξαι πάντα] ἀληθῆ νοῶ καὶ λέγω.—
Οὐκ οὖν τὸ [τε] ἀληθῆ νοεῖν καὶ λέγειν, τοῦτο ἀλήθειαν δεῖ
6 καλεῖν ;—Τί δαί ;⟩⟩—Ἔστιν οὖν, ⟨ὦ⟩ πάτερ, ἀλήθεια καὶ ἐν
τῇ γῇ. [[καὶ οὐκ ἀσκόπως]]—Σφάλλῃ, ὦ τέκνον. ἀλήθεια
μὲν οὐδαμῶς ἐστιν ἐν τῇ γῇ, ὦ Τάτ, οὔτε γενέσθαι δύναται·
περὶ δὲ ἀληθείας ⟨ἀληθῆ⟩ νοῆσαι ἐνίους τῶν ἀνθρώπων, [οἷς
ἐὰν ὁ θεὸς τὴν θεοπτικὴν δωρήσηται δύναμιν,] [γενέσθαι]
7 ⟨οὐδὲν κωλύει·⟩ [[οὕτως ἀληθὲς οὐδὲν ἔστιν ἐν τῇ γῇ. νοῶ καὶ
λέγω. φαντασίαι εἰσὶ καὶ δόξαι πάντα. ἀληθῆ νοῶ καὶ λέγω.
—Οὐκ οὖν τό τε ἀληθῆ νοεῖν καὶ λέγειν, τοῦτο ἀλήθειαν δεῖ
8 καλεῖν ;—Τί δαί ;]] [τὰ ὄντα [δεῖ] νοεῖν καὶ λέγειν] [ἔστι δὲ
οὐδὲν ἀληθὲς ἐπὶ τῆς γῆς] ⟨⟨καὶ οὐκ ἀσκόπως⟩⟩ ⟨εἶπον ὅτι⟩
τοῦτο ἀληθές ἐστι, τὸ μὴ εἶ[δε]ναι μηδὲν ἀληθὲς ἐνθάδε.
9 πῶς ἂν καὶ δύναιτο ⟨ἀληθές τι ἐνθάδε⟩ γενέσθαι, ὦ τέκνον;
ἡ γὰρ ἀλήθειά [τελεωτάτη ἀρετή] ἐστιν αὐτὸ τὸ ἄκρατον
ἀγαθόν, τὸ μὴ ὑπὸ ὕλης θολούμενον μήτε ὑπὸ σώματος
περιβαλλόμενον, γυμνὸν φανόν, ἄτρεπτον [σεμνὸν] ἀναλλοίωτον [ἀγαθόν]. τὰ δὲ ἐνθάδε, ὦ τέκνον, οἷά ἐστιν ὁρᾷς,
ἄδεκτα [τούτου] τοῦ ἀγαθοῦ, φθαρτὰ παθητὰ διαλυτὰ τρεπτά,
10 ἀεὶ ἐναλλοιούμενα, ἄλλα ἐξ ἄλλων γινόμενα. ἃ οὖν μηδὲ
πρὸς ἑαυτὰ ἀληθῆ ἐστι, πῶς δύναιτο ἀληθῆ εἶναι; πᾶν γὰρ
τὸ ἀλλοιούμενον ψεῦδός ἐστι, μὴ μένον ἐν ᾧ ἐστι, φαντασίας
δὲ [μετατρεπόμενον] ἄλλας καὶ ἄλλας ἐπιδεικνύμενον [ἡμῖν].

1 ἀληθῆ scripsi : ἀλήθειαν codd. 3–4 Fortasse ὅσοι μὲν οὖν φαντασίας (vel φαντάσματα) ὁρῶσι, ψεῦδος ὁρῶσιν· ὅσοι δὲ τὰ ὄντα ὁρῶσιν, ἀλήθειαν ὁρῶσιν 5 ἀληθῆ LSM : ἀληθῶς A 6 ὀψόμεθα scripsi : εἰσόμεθα codd. 7–10 § 7 (οὕτως . . . Τί δαί) huc transposui 7 Pro οὕτως fortasse ⟨τούτων δ'⟩ οὕτως ⟨ἐχόντων⟩ | ἀληθὲς οὐδὲ LSMA | εἶναι scripsi : ἔστιν codd. | νοῶν καὶ λέγων scripsi : νοῶ καὶ λέγω LSMABr : νοῶ καὶ λόγῳ Trincavelli : νόῳ καὶ λόγῳ Turnebus 8 εἰσὶ LSMA : δ' εἰσὶ Br | ἀληθῆ νοῶ καὶ λέγω om. LBr | νόῳ καὶ λόγῳ Turn. 10 τί δαί SM : τί δέ LABr | ἔστιν οὖν om. Br | ὦ addidit Wachsm. 11 καὶ οὐκ ἀσκόπως hinc ad § 8 transposui 14 τὴν θεοπτικὴν δωρήσεται L : δωρήσηται τὴν θεοπτικὴν A 15–18 § 7 (οὕτως . . . Τί δαί) hinc transposui : vide post § 5 19 καὶ οὐκ ἀσκόπως huc a § 6 transposui 20 τὸ μὲν L : τὸ μὴ cett. | εἶναι Buecheler : εἰδέναι codd. 22 Fortasse ἡ γὰρ ἀλήθεια τελεωτάτη ἀρετή·

at it; they think that what they see is real, but it is really an illusion.

Those then who . . . see illusion; but those who . . . see reality.[1] 5
If then we think or see each of these things as it is, we think and see truly;[2] if we think and see them otherwise than they are, we shall neither think nor see truly. And so, when I think and 7
say that nothing on earth is real, I am thinking and speaking truly.—*Tat.* Well then, when a man thinks and speaks truly, is it not right to call that 'truth' (or 'reality')?—*Hermes.* What 6
do you infer from that?—*Tat.* If that is so, father, it follows that there is some reality even on earth.—*Hermes.* You are mistaken, my son. There is no reality on earth; it cannot come into being here below; but none the less it is possible for some men to think truly about reality; and I was not speaking unadvisedly, 8
when I said that it is true that there is nothing real here below.

How is it possible, my son, that anything real should come 9
into being on earth? For reality is the absolute and unmixed Good;[3] it is that which is not fouled by matter, nor muffled in body; it is bare of coverings, and shines with light undimmed; it is immutable and unalterable. But the things on earth, my son,—what *they* are, you can see. They are not capable of receiving the Good; they are subject to destruction and to perturbation; they are dissoluble and mutable, ever altering, and changing from one thing into another. And seeing that they 10
are not even true to themselves,[4] how could they possibly be real? Everything that changes is illusory, because it does not stay in the state in which it is, but presents appearances that vary.

[1] Perhaps, 'Those then who see mere appearances see an illusion; but those who see things as they are see reality'.

[2] The word ἀληθής may mean either 'real' or 'true'. I translate this word and its derivatives 'true', 'truly', 'truth' in some phrases of this paragraph, but 'real', 'really', 'reality' in the rest of the document. It is the double meaning of the word that gives occasion for Tat's argument.

[3] Perhaps, 'reality is the most perfect excellence; and the real is the absolute and unmixed Good'.

[4] Or 'not real even in relation to themselves'. A thing is 'untrue to itself', or 'unreal in relation to itself', when it does not continue to be what it is at a given moment.

⟨καὶ τὸ ἀληθές⟩ ἐστιν κ.τ.λ. | ἄκρατον codd. : ἀκρότατον Turnebus **23–24** ὑπὸ σώματος περιαγαλλόμενον L **25** ἀγαθόν secludi vult Meineke **25–26** ὁρᾷς ἄδεκτα LMBr : ὁρᾶσθαι δεκτὰ SA Turnebus **26** τοῦδε S: τούτου cett. **27** μηδὲ Meineke : μήτε codd. **28** πῶς ἂν δύναιτο Meineke **29** μένον Turnebus : μόνον codd. **30** ἐπιδεικνύμενον scripsi : ἐπιδείκνυται ἡμῖν codd.

16 ⟨⟨[τὸ δὲ ψεῦδος, ὦ τέκνον, φθείρεται.] πάντα δὲ τὰ ἐπὶ
γῆς φθορὰ κατέλαβε [καὶ ἐμπεριέχει καὶ ἐμπεριέξει ἡ τοῦ
ἀληθοῦς πρόνοια]· χωρὶς γὰρ φθορᾶς οὐδὲ γένεσις δύναται
⌜συστῆναι⌝. [πάσῃ δὲ γενέσει φθορὰ ἕπεται, ἵνα πάλιν
γένηται ⟨πάντα⟩.] τὰ γὰρ γιγνόμενα ἐκ τῶν φθειρομένων
ἀνάγκη γίγνεσθαι· φθείρεσθαι δὲ τὰ γιγνόμενα ἀνάγκη, ἵνα
μὴ στῇ ἡ γένεσις [τῶν ὄντων]. [πρῶτον τοῦτον δημιουργὸν
γνώριζε] [εἰς τὴν γένεσιν τῶν ὄντων.] τὰ οὖν ἐκ φθορᾶς
γινόμενα ψευδῆ ἂν εἴη, ὡς ποτὲ μὲν ἄλλα ποτὲ δὲ ἄλλα
γινόμενα. τὰ γὰρ αὐτὰ ⟨πάλιν⟩ γίνεσθαι ⟨ἀ⟩δύνατον· τὸ δὲ
18 μὴ ⟨τ⟩αὐτὸ ⟨ὂν⟩ πῶς ἂν ἀληθὲς εἴη;⟩⟩ ⟨⟨μεταβαλλόμενα δὲ
ψεύδεται [καὶ τὰ προόντα καὶ] τὰ ὄντα. ταῦτα μέντοι οὕτω
νόει, ὦ τέκνον, ὡς καὶ τῶν ψευδῶν τούτων [ἐνεργειῶν] ἄνωθεν
ἠρτημένων ἀπ' αὐτῆς τῆς ἀληθείας· τούτου δὲ οὕτως ἔχοντος,
τὸ ψεῦδός φημι τῆς ἀληθείας ἐνέργημα εἶναι.⟩⟩—
11 Οὐδὲ ἄνθρωπος ἀληθής ἐστιν, ὦ πάτερ;—Καθότι ἄνθρωπος, οὐκ ἔστιν ἀληθής, ὦ τέκνον. τὸ γὰρ ἀληθές ἐστι
⟨τὸ⟩ [καὶ] ἐξ αὑτοῦ μόνου τὴν σύστασιν ἔχον, καὶ μένον καθ'
αὑτὸ οἷον ἐστίν· ὁ δὲ ἄνθρωπος ἐκ πολλῶν συνέστηκε, καὶ
οὐ μένει καθ' αὑτόν, τρέπεται δὲ καὶ μεταβάλλεται ⟨εἰς⟩
ἡλικίαν ἐξ ἡλικίας καὶ ἰδέαν ἐξ ἰδέας [καὶ ταῦτα ἔτι ὢν ἐν
τῷ σκήνει]. καὶ πολλοὶ τέκνα οὐκ ἐγνώρισαν χρόνου ὀλίγου
12 μεταξὺ γενομένου, καὶ πάλιν τέκνα γονεῖς ὁμοίως. τὸ οὖν
οὕτως μεταβαλλόμενον ὥστε ἀγνοεῖσθαι, ⟨πῶς⟩ δύναται ἀληθὲς
εἶναι, ὦ Τάτ; οὐ τοὐναντίον ψεῦδός ἐστιν, ἐν ποικίλαις
γινομένων φαντασίαις τῶν μεταβολῶν; σὺ δὴ νόει ἀληθὲς
[τι] εἶναι [[τὸ]] μόνον ⟨⟨τὸ⟩⟩ [ἀίδιον] ⟨ἀεὶ ὄν⟩. ὁ δὲ ἄνθρωπος
οὐκ ἔστιν ἀεί· ἄρα οὐδὲ ἀληθές ἐστι, φαντασία δέ [ἐστι] τις
17 [ἄνθρωπος]. ⟨⟨φαντασίας οὖν καλεῖν δεῖ [ταῦτα] ⟨⟨τοὺς
ἀνθρώπους⟩⟩, ὦ τέκνον, εἴ γε ὀρθῶς προσαγορεύομεν [[τὸν
ἄνθρωπον]] [ἀνθρωπότητος φαντασίαν], τὸ [δὲ] ⟨μὲν⟩ παιδίον
παιδίου φαντασίαν, τὸν δὲ νεανίσκον νεανίσκου φαντασίαν,

1–11 § 16 (τὸ δὲ ψεῦδος . . . ἀληθὲς εἴη;) huc transposui 1 Fortasse τὸ δὲ ⟨φθειρόμενον πᾶν⟩ ψεῦδος, ὦ τέκνον [φθείρεται] | δὲ (ante ψεῦδος) om. MA | ταῦτα (pro πάντα) Turnebus 2 περιέχει A: ἐμπεριέχει cett. 3 ἀληθοῦς om. L | χωρὶς δὲ A: χωρὶς γὰρ cett. 3–4 Fortasse οὐδὲ ⟨εἰς⟩ γένεσιν δύναται συστῆναι ⟨τι⟩ 4–5 πάλι γένηται S 5 γινόμενα SM: γιγνόμενα cett. 7 τοῦτον LMA: τοῦτο Br: οὖν (?) τὸν S: οὖν τὸν Turnebus 8 γνώριζε S: γνώριζε ex γνωρίζεις corr. A: νόμιζε LMBr | τὰ γοῦν ἐκ A 9–10 ἄλλα γενόμενα A 10 ἀδύνατον Turnebus: δυνατὸν LSMA: οὐ δύνατον Br ex emend. 11 ταὐτὸ ὂν scripsi: αὐτὸ codd. 11–15 § 18 (μεταβαλλόμενα . . . ἐνέργημα εἶναι) huc transposui 11 δὲ

And all things on earth are overtaken by destruction; for 16
without destruction things cannot come into being. The things
which come into being must needs arise out of those which are
destroyed; and the things which come into being must needs
be destroyed, in order that coming-into-being may not stop.
The things which come into being out of destruction must
therefore be illusory, because they come to be different things
at different times. For it is not possible that the same things
should come into being again; and how can that be real, which
is not the same that it was before? Inasmuch as things change, 18
they are illusory. But at the same time you must understand,
my son, that these illusory things are dependent on Reality itself,
which is above; and that being so, I say that the illusion is
a thing wrought by the working of Reality.[1]—

Tat. But what of man, father? Is not man real?—*Hermes.* In 11
so far as he is man, my son, he is not real. For the real is that
which consists of itself alone, and continues to be such as it is in
itself; but man is composed of many different things, and does
not continue to be such as he is in himself, but shifts and changes
from one time of life to another, and from one form to another.
Oftentimes men fail to recognize their own children after a short
interval, and children likewise fail to recognize their parents.
And when a thing so changes that it is not known, how can that 12
thing be real, my son? Is it not an illusion, inasmuch as its
changes manifest themselves in varying appearances? You must
understand that that which ever is, and that alone, is real. But
man is not a thing that ever is; and therefore man is not
real, but is only an appearance. We ought then to call men 17
'appearances', my son, if we name them rightly. We ought
to call a child 'the appearance of a child', and a youth 'the

[1] I.e. the material world is an unreal appearance, but this unreal appearance is produced by God's working.

(ante *ψεύδεται*) codd.: fortasse *δὴ* **14–15** *τούτου δὲ . . . τῆς ἀληθείας* om. M **16** *ὁδὲ* A: *οὐδὲ* cett. **16–17** *ἀληθής* (bis) codd.: *ἀληθές* (bis) Hense **18** *τὸ ἐξ* Turnebus: *καὶ ἐξ* LSMABr | *μόνου* LBr: *μόνον* SMA **18–19** Fortasse *μένον οἷόν ἐστι καθ' αὑτό* **19** *ὅδε ὁ ἄνθρωπος* S **20** Fortasse *οὐ μένει ⟨οἷός ἐστι⟩ καθ' αὑτόν* | *καὶ ἐμβάλλεται* L **23** *γεγενημένου* L **26** *γινομένων* scripsi: *γινόμενον* codd. | *σὺ δὴ* scripsi: *σὺ δὲ* codd. **27** *εἶναι μόνον τὸ ἀεὶ ὄν* scripsi: *εἶναι τὸ μόνον ἀίδιον* LMBr: *εἶναι τὸ μόνον καὶ δίκαιον* SA: *εἶναι, τὸ μένον καὶ δίκαιον* Turnebus **29–4** *infra*: § 17 (*φαντασίας οὖν . . . γέρων γέρων*) huc transposui **29** *καλεῖν δεῖ* LSM: *δεῖ καλεῖν* ABr | *ταῦτα* LSMBr: *τὰ τοιαῦτα* A **32–1** *infra*: *φαντασίαν* (post *νεανίσκου* et post *ἀνδρὸς*) om LBr

τὸν δὲ ἄνδρα ἀνδρὸς φαντασίαν, τὸν δὲ γέροντα γέροντος φαντασίαν· οὔτε γὰρ [ὁ ἄνθρωπος ἄνθρωπος οὔτε] τὸ παιδίον παιδίον ⟨μένει⟩, οὔτε ὁ νεανίσκος νεανίσκος, οὔτε ὁ ἀνὴρ ἀνήρ, οὔτε ὁ γέρων γέρων.⟩⟩ ἡ δὲ φαντασία ψεῦδος ἂν εἴη [ἀκρότατον].—

13 Οὐδὲ ταῦτα οὖν, ὦ πάτερ, τὰ ἀίδια σώματα [[ἐπεὶ μεταβάλλεται]] ἀληθῆ ἐστι⟨ν⟩; ⟨⟨ἐπεὶ μεταβάλλεται⟩⟩ ⟨καὶ ταῦτα.⟩ —Πᾶν μὲν οὖν τὸ [γεννητὸν καὶ] μεταβλητὸν οὐκ ἀληθές· [[ὑπὸ δὲ τοῦ προπάτορος γενόμενα τὴν ὕλην δύναται ἀληθῆ ἐσχηκέναι·]] ἔχει δέ τι καὶ ταῦτα ψεῦδος ἐν τῇ μεταβολῇ· οὐδὲν γάρ, μὴ μένον ἐφ' αὑτῷ, ἀληθές ἐστιν. ⟨⟨ὑπὸ δὲ τοῦ προπάτορος ⟨ἄφθαρτα⟩ γενόμενα, τὴν ⌜ὕλην⌝ δύναται ἀληθῆ ἐσχηκέναι.⟩⟩—

14 ⟨⟨Τί οὖν ἂν εἴποι τις⟩⟩ ἀληθές, ὦ πάτερ [[τί οὖν ἂν εἴποι τις]];— Μόνον τὸν ἥλιον, παρὰ τὰ ἄλλα πάντα μὴ μεταβαλλόμενον, μένοντα δὲ ἐφ' ἑαυτῷ [ἀλήθειαν]. διὸ καὶ τὴν ⟨τῶν⟩ ἐν τῷ κόσμῳ πάντων δημιουργίαν αὐτὸς μόνος πεπίστευται, ἄρχων πάντων καὶ ποιῶν πάντα. ὃν καὶ σέβομαι, καὶ προσκυνῶ αὐτοῦ τὴν ἀλήθειαν, μετὰ τὸν ἕνα καὶ πρῶτον ⟨θεὸν⟩ τοῦτον δημιουργὸν γνωρίζω⟨ν⟩.—

15 Τί οὖν ἂν εἴποι ⟨τις ἀληθὲς⟩ τὴν πρώτην ἀλήθειαν, ὦ πάτερ;—Ἕνα καὶ μόνον, ὦ Τάτ, τὸν μὴ ἐξ ὕλης, τὸν μὴ ἐν σώματι· τὸν ἀχρώματον, τὸν ἀσχημάτιστον· τὸν ἄτρεπτον, τὸν μὴ ἀλλοιούμενον· τὸν ἀεὶ ὄντα.—

16 [[τὸ δὲ ψεῦδος . . . ἀληθὲς εἴη;]] Vide post § 10.

17 [[φαντασίας οὖν . . . γέρων γέρων.]] Vide post § 12.

18 [[μεταβαλλόμενα δὲ . . . ἐνέργημα εἶναι.]] Vide ante § 11.

1 δὲ (ante γέροντα) om. SMA 3–4 νεανίσκος, οὔτε ὁ γέρων γέρων, οὔτε ὁ ἀνὴρ ἀνήρ S Turnebus 6–26 οὐδὲ ταῦτα . . . ἀεὶ ὄντα (§§ 13–15) et τὸ δὲ ψεῦδος . . . ἐνέργημα εἶναι (§§ 16–18) inverso ordine habent LBr 8 γεννητὸν καὶ LSM : γενητὸν καὶ ABr | Fortasse Πᾶν μὲν οὖν τὸ γεννητὸν καὶ ⟨μεταβλητόν, πᾶν δὲ τὸ⟩ μεταβλητὸν οὐκ ἀληθές 11 ἐφ' αὑτῷ L : ἐφ' αὑτὸ MABr : ἐφ' αὑτὸ corr. ex ἐφ' αὑτῷ S 12 ὕλην codd. : fortasse οὐσίαν vel ὕπαρξιν | ἀληθῶς L : ἀληθῆ cett. 16 ἀλήθειαν eiecit Buecheler 17–19 ὃν καὶ . . . δημιουργὸν γνωρίζω om. LMABr 18 ἀλήθειαν, καὶ μετὰ Turnebus 19 γνωρίζων scripsi : γνωρίζω S Turnebus 20 εἴποι τις ἀληθὲς τὴν scripsi : εἴποι τις τὴν vult Hense : εἶναι τὴν LSMABr Turn. : εἶναι λέγεις τὴν Flussas

appearance of a youth', and an adult man 'the appearance of an adult man', and an old man 'the appearance of an old man'; for the child does not remain a child, nor the youth a youth, nor the adult man an adult man, nor the old man an old man. And appearance must be illusion.—

Tat. And what of these everlasting bodies,[1] father? Are they 13
too unreal? For they too suffer change.—*Hermes.* Everything that is subject to change is unreal; and the everlasting bodies also have in them something that is illusory, inasmuch as they suffer change; for nothing is real, which does not continue to be as it is. But seeing that they have been made indestructible by the Forefather, it may well be that the existence which they have received from him is real.—

Tat.[2] What then can we call real, father?—*Hermes.* The Sun alone; 14
because the Sun, unlike all other things, does not suffer change, but continues to be as he is. Wherefore the Sun alone has been entrusted with the task of making all things in the universe; he rules over all things, and makes all things. Him do I worship, and I adore his reality, acknowledging him, next after the one supreme God, as the Maker.—

Tat. What then, father, can be called real in the supreme 15
degree?—*Hermes.* He alone, my son, and none but He, who is not made of matter, nor embodied; who is colourless and formless; who is changeless and unalterable; who ever is.—

[1] The 'everlasting bodies' are the heavenly bodies and the cosmic elements. In § 2, the term is used to denote the elements.

[2] § 14 is inconsistent with the context; it must have been inserted by a sun-worshipper.

EXCERPTUM II B

Stobaeus I. 41. 1 a, vol. i, p. 273 Wachsmuth (*Ecl.* I. 698 Heeren).

Ἑρμοῦ ἐκ τῶν πρὸς Τάτ.

1 ἐγὼ [ὦ τέκνον] καὶ τῆς φιλανθρωπίας ἕνεκα καὶ τῆς πρὸς τὸν θεὸν εὐσεβείας ⌈πρῶτον τόδε συγγράφω⌉. οὐδεμία γὰρ ἂν ⌈γένοιτο δικαιοτάτη⌉ εὐσέβεια [ἢ] τοῦ νοῆσαι τὰ ὄντα καὶ χάριν τῷ ποιήσαντι ὑπὲρ τούτων ὁμολογῆσαι· ὅπερ διατελῶν οὐ παύσομαι.

2 Τί οὖν ἄν τις πράττων, ὦ πάτερ, εἰ μηδέν ἐστιν ἀληθὲς ἐνθάδε, καλῶς διαγάγοι τὸν βίον;—Εὐσεβῶν, ὦ τέκνον. ὁ δὲ εὐσεβ⟨εῖν ζητ⟩ῶν [ἄκρως] φιλοσοφήσει. χωρὶς γὰρ φιλοσοφίας [[ἄκρως]] εὐσεβῆσαι ἀδύνατον· ὁ δὲ μαθὼν οἷά ἐστι ⟨τὰ ὄντα⟩, καὶ πῶς διατέτακται, καὶ ὑπὸ τίνος, καὶ ἕνεκεν τίνος, χάριν εἴσεται ὑπὲρ πάντων τῷ δημιουργῷ ὡς πατρὶ ἀγαθῷ καὶ τροφεῖ χρηστῷ καὶ ἐπιτρόπῳ πιστῷ· ὁ δὲ χάριν ὁμολογῶν εὐσεβήσει.

3 ὁ δὲ ⟨⟨ἄκρως⟩⟩ φιλοσοφῶν ⟨μαθ⟩ήσεται καὶ ποῦ ἐστιν ἡ ἀλήθεια καὶ τίς ἐστιν ἐκείνη· καὶ μαθών, ἔτι μᾶλλον εὐσεβέστερος ἔσται, ⟨⟨καὶ οὐκέτι ἀποστῆναι δυν⟨ήσ⟩εται τοῦ ἀγαθοῦ.⟩⟩ οὐδέποτε γάρ, ὦ τέκνον, ψυχὴ [ἐν σώματι οὖσα καὶ] κουφίσασα ἑαυτὴν ἐπὶ τὴν κατάληψιν τοῦ ὄντως ἀγαθοῦ καὶ ἀληθοῦς ὀλισθῆσαι δύναται ἐπὶ τὸ ἐναντίον· δεινὸν γὰρ ἔρωτα ἴσχει καὶ λήθην πάντων τῶν κακῶν ψυχὴ μαθοῦσα ἑαυτῆς τὸν προπάτορα. [[καὶ οὐκέτι ἀποστῆναι δύναται τοῦ
4 ἀγαθοῦ.]] το⟨ῦ⟩το, ⟨ὦ⟩ τέκνον, τοῦτο εὐσεβείας ἐστὶ τέλος· ἐφ᾽ ὃ ἀφικ[ν]ό[υ]μενος καὶ καλῶς βιώσῃ, καὶ εὐδαιμόνως τεθνήξῃ, τῆς ψυχῆς σου μὴ ἀγνοούσης ποῦ αὐτὴν δεῖ ἀναπτῆναι.

5 ⟨. . .⟩ αὕτη γὰρ μόνη ἐστίν, ὦ τέκνον, [ἡ] πρὸς ἀλήθειαν ὁδός· ἣν καὶ οἱ ἡμέτεροι πρόγονοι ὥδευσαν, καὶ ὁδεύσαντες

Exc. II B: codices **F** (saec. xiv), **P** (saec. xv).

1 τῶν scripsi: τοῦ codd. **3** Fortasse πρὸ ⟨πάν⟩των τήνδε ⟨τὴν⟩ συγγραφ⟨ὴν προτιμ⟩ῶ **3–4** ἂν λέγοιτο δικαιότερον Usener **4** ἢ eiecit Meineke **6** εἰ μὴ δὲ P **7** εὐσεβῶν Usener: εὐσέβει codd. **8** εὐσεβεῖν ζητῶν scripsi: εὐσεβῶν codd. | φιλοσοφεῖ P **9** ἄκρως hinc ad § 3 *init.* transposui **11** εἴσεται ὑπὲρ πάντων Gaisford: ἕπεται ὑπὲρ πάντων F: om. P **13** εὐσεβήσεις P **14** ὁ δὲ ἄκρως φιλοσοφῶν μαθήσεται scripsi: ὁ δὲ εὐσεβῶν εἴσεται codd. **15** Fortasse καὶ ⟨ταῦτα⟩ μαθών **16** δυνήσεται scripsi: δύναται codd. **18** ὄντως Usener: ὄντος FP **20** ἴσχῃ P | Fortasse ἔρωτα ἴσχει ⟨τοῦ ἀγαθοῦ⟩ **21–22** ἀποστῆναι τοῦ ἀγαθοῦ δύναται P **22** τοῦτ᾽ ὦ τέκνον Meineke: τότε τέκνον FP | ἐστὶ scripsi: ἔστω codd. **23** ἀφικόμενος Meineke: ἀφικνούμενος codd.

EXCERPT II B

An extract from the Discourses of Hermes to Tat.[1]

I esteem[2] this treatise more highly than any other, on account of the benevo- 1
lence towards men and piety towards God that is expressed in it; for there is nothing that could more rightly be called piety than to apprehend in thought the things that are, and to give thanks for them to Him who made them. And this I will continue to do without ceasing.

Tat. If then there is nothing real here below, what must a man 2
do, father, to live his life aright?—*Hermes.* He must be pious, my son. And he who seeks to be pious will pursue philosophy. Without philosophy, it is impossible to be pious; but he who has learnt what things are, and how they are ordered, and by whom, and to what end, will give thanks for all things to the Maker, deeming him a good father and kind fosterer and faithful guardian; and thus rendering thanks, he will be pious.

And he who pursues philosophy to its highest reach will learn 3
where Reality is, and what it is; and having learnt this, he will be yet more pious. And thenceforward it will be impossible for him to fall away from the Good. For never, my son, can a soul that has so far uplifted itself as to grasp the truly good and real slip back to the evil and unreal; for the soul acquires a wondrous yearning for the Good, and oblivion of all evils,
when it has learnt to know its own Forefather. This, my son, 4
this[3] is the consummation of piety; and when you have attained to it, you will live your life aright, and be blest in your death; for your soul will not fail to know whither it must wing its upward flight.

. . . For this,[4] my son, is the only road that leads to Reality. 5
It is the road our ancestors[5] trod; and thereby they attained

[1] Exc. II B is evidently a continuation of Exc. II A. The two excerpts together make up a complete *libellus*. Stobaeus cut the *libellus* in two, and placed the two pieces in different parts of his *Anthologium*.

[2] This section appears to be a note on Exc. II B, written by an admiring reader.

[3] Viz. knowledge of God, the Forefather of the human soul.

[4] Perhaps, '⟨But you must begin by abandoning the body (i.e. ridding yourself of its debasing influence);⟩ for this', &c.

[5] 'Our ancestors', who once were men like you and me, but now are gods. See *Corp.* X. 5.

---

26 Fortasse ⟨πλὴν δεῖ σε πρῶτον τὸ σῶμα ἐγκαταλεῖψαι·⟩ αὕτη γὰρ κ.τ.λ. (vide § 8) | πρὸς τὴν ἀλήθειαν P   27 καὶ (post ἣν) om. F

ἔτυχον τοῦ ἀγαθοῦ. σεμνὴ αὕτη ὁδὸς καὶ ⌜λεία⌝, χαλεπὴ δὲ ψυχῇ ὁδεῦσαι ἐν σώματι οὔσῃ. πρῶτον [μὲν] γὰρ αὐτὴν ἑαυτῇ πολεμῆσαι δεῖ, καὶ [δια]στάσιν μεγάλην ποιῆσαι, καὶ ὑπὸ τοῦ ἑνὸς μέρους ⟨τὰ⟩ πλέω νικηθῆναι. ἑνὸς γὰρ γίγνεται πρὸς δύο ἡ [συ]στάσις, τοῦ μὲν ⟨ἄνω⟩ σπεύδοντος, τῶν δὲ καθελκόντων κάτω· καὶ ἔρις καὶ μάχη πολλὴ πρὸς ἄλληλα τούτων γίγνεται [τοῦ μὲν φυγεῖν βουλομένου, τῶν δὲ κατασχεῖν σπευδόντων].
7 ἡ δὲ νίκη ἀμφοτέρων οὐχ ὁμοία· τὸ μὲν γὰρ πρὸς τὸ ἀγαθὸν σπεύδει, τὰ δὲ πρὸς τὰ κακὰ κατοικεῖ· καὶ τὸ μὲν ἐλευθερωθῆναι ποθεῖ, τὰ δὲ τὴν δουλείαν ἀγαπᾷ. κἂν μὲν νικηθῇ τὰ δύο μέρη, μεμένηκεν ⟨ἐφ'⟩ ἑαυτῶ⟨ν⟩ ἠρεμα⟨ῖα⟩ καὶ τοῦ ἄρχοντος ⟨ὑπήκοα⟩· ἐὰν δὲ τὸ ἓν ἡττηθῇ, ὑπὸ τῶν δύο ἄγεται καὶ φέρεται, τιμωρούμενον τῇ ἐνθάδε διαίτῃ.
8 οὗτός ἐστιν [ὦ τέκνον] ὁ ⟨περὶ⟩ τῆς ἐκεῖσε ὁδοῦ ἀγών[ος]· δεῖ γάρ σε, ὦ τέκνον, πρῶτον [τὸ σῶμα [πρὸ τοῦ τέλους] ἐγκαταλεῖψαι, καὶ] νικῆσαι ⌜τὸν ἐναγώνιον βίον⌝, καὶ νικήσαντα, οὕτως ἀνελθεῖν.

EXCERPTUM III

Stobaeus I. 41. 6 b, vol. i, pp. 285–289 Wachsmuth (*Ecl.* I. 728–740 Heeren).

⟨Ἑρμοῦ ἐκ τῶν πρὸς Τάτ.⟩

1 [[ἐνέργειαι γάρ, ὦ Τάτ, ἀσώματοι αὐταὶ οὖσαι, ἐν σώμασίν εἰσι, καὶ διὰ τῶν σωμάτων ἐνεργοῦσι. διόπερ, ὦ Τάτ, καθότι ἀσώματοί εἰσι, καὶ ἀθανάτους αὐτὰς φῂς εἶναι· καθότι δὲ χωρὶς σωμάτων ἐνεργεῖν οὐ δύνανται, φημὶ αὐτὰς εἶναι ἀεὶ ἐν σώματι.]]

2 [τὰ γὰρ πρός τι ἢ ἕνεκά τινος γενόμενα προνοίᾳ καὶ ἀνάγκῃ ὑποπεπτωκότα.]

1 *λεία* codd.: fortasse *θεία* 3 *ἑαυτῆς* P¹ | *στάσιν* scripsi: *διάστασιν* codd. 4 *τὰ πλέω νικηθῆναι* scripsi: *πλεονεκτηθῆναι* codd. 5 *στάσις* Heeren ex cod. Vat.: *σύστασις* FP | *ἄνω σπεύδοντος* scripsi: *φυγόντος* FP 5–7 *τῶν δὲ . . . φυγεῖν βουλομένου* om. P 10 *τὸ δὲ τὴν* P 11–12 *ἐφ' ἑαυτῶν ἠρεμαῖα* scripsi (*ἐν ταὐτῷ ἤρεμα* Usener): *ἑαυτῶν ἔρημα* P²: *ἑαυτῶ ἔρημα* FP¹ 13 *τιμωρούμενον* P²: *τιμωρουμένη* FP¹ 15 *ἀγών* Usener: *ἀγωγός* FP 16 *τὸν ἐναγώνιον βίον* codd.: fortasse *τὸν ἀγῶνα τοῦτον* 17 Post *οὕτως ἀνελθεῖν* addunt codd. *νῦν δέ, ὦ τέκνον, κεφαλαίοις τὰ ὄντα διεξελεύσομαι κ.τ.λ.* (vide *Exc.* XI)

19–23 § I (*ἐνέργειαι . . . ἐν σώματι*) hinc transposui: vide post § II 24–25 Fortasse *τὰ γὰρ* [ ] *γινόμενα προνοίᾳ καὶ ἀνάγκῃ ὑποπέπτωκεν*· ⟨*αὗται δὲ διὰ τῶν θείων σωμάτων ἐνεργοῦσι.*⟩ 24 *γινόμενα* Usener

to the Good. It is a holy and divine road; but it is hard for
the soul to travel on that road while it is in the body. For the 6
soul must begin by warring against itself, and stirring up within itself a mighty feud; and the one part of the soul must win victory over the others, which are more in number. It is a feud of one against two,[1] the one part struggling to mount upward, and the two dragging it down; and there is much strife and
fighting between them. And it makes no small difference 7
whether the one side or the other wins; for the one part strives towards the Good, the others make their home among evils; the one yearns for freedom, the others are content with slavery. And if the two parts are vanquished, they stay quiet in themselves, and submissive to the ruling part; but if the one part is defeated, it is carried off as a captive by the two, and the life
it lives on earth is a life of penal torment. Such is the contest 8
about the journey to the world above. You must begin, my son, by winning victory in this contest, and then, having won, mount upward.

[1] The 'one' is mind or reason; the 'two' are *θυμός* and *ἐπιθυμία*, i.e. 'repugnance' (or self-assertion against opponents) and 'desire', which are the two forms of passion.

3 [ἀδύνατον ἀργά ποτε μεῖναι τῆς ἰδίας ἐνεργείας. τὸ γὰρ ὂν ἀεὶ ἔσται. τοῦτο γὰρ αὐτοῦ καὶ σῶμα καὶ ζωή ἐστι.]

4 [[τούτῳ τῷ λόγῳ ἕπεται τὸ καὶ ἀεὶ τὰ σώματα εἶναι. διὸ καὶ αὐτὴν τὴν σωμάτωσίν φημι ἀιδίαν ἐνέργειαν εἶναι. εἰς γὰρ σώματα ἐπίγεια διαλυτά, σώματα δὲ δεῖ εἶναι, τόπους καὶ ὄργανα τῶν ἐνεργειῶν ταῦτα, αἱ δὲ ἐνέργειαι ἀθάνατοι, τὸ δὲ ἀθάνατον ἀεὶ ἔστιν, ἐνέργεια καὶ ἡ σωματοποίησις, εἴ γε ἀεὶ ἔστι.]]

5 [[παρέπονται δὲ τῇ ψυχῇ οὐκ ἀθρόως παραγιγνόμεναι· ἀλλὰ τινὲς μὲν αὐτῶν ἅμα τῷ γενέσθαι τὸν ἄνθρωπον ἐνεργοῦσιν, ὁμοῦ τῇ ψυχῇ περὶ τὰ ἄλογα οὖσαι, αἱ δὲ καθαρώτεραι ἐνέργειαι κατὰ μεταβολὴν τῆς ἡσυχίας τῷ λογικῷ μέρει τῆς ψυχῆς συνεργοῦσαι.]]

6 [[αὗται δὲ αἱ ἐνέργειαι τῶν σωμάτων εἰσὶν ἠρτημέναι. καὶ ἀπὸ μὲν τῶν θείων σωμάτων ἔρχονται εἰς τὰ θνητὰ αὗται αἱ σωματοποιοῦσαι, ἑκάστη δὲ αὐτῶν ἐνεργεῖ ἢ περὶ τὸ σῶμα ἢ τὴν ψυχήν. καὶ αὐτῇ μέντοι τῇ ψυχῇ συγγίγνονται χωρὶς σώματος· ἀεὶ δὲ ἐνέργειαί εἰσιν, οὐκ ἀεὶ δὲ ἡ ψυχὴ ἐν σώματι θνητῷ ἐστι· δύναται γὰρ χωρὶς τοῦ σώματος εἶναι· αἱ δὲ ἐνέργειαι χωρὶς τῶν σωμάτων οὐ δύνανται εἶναι.]]

7 ἱερὸς λόγος [ἐστὶν [[ὦ τέκνον]] οὗτος].

Συνεστάναι μέν, ⟨⟨ὦ τέκνον,⟩⟩ σῶμα χωρὶς ψυχῆς οὐ δύναται, τὸ δὲ ⟨ἐνεργ⟩εῖσθαι δυνατόν.—Πῶς τοῦτο λέγεις, ὦ πάτερ;—Οὕτω νόησον, ὦ Τάτ. τῆς ψυχῆς χωρισθείσης τοῦ σώματος, ἐπιμένει αὐτὸ τὸ σῶμα. τοῦτο δὲ τὸ σῶμα παρὰ τὸν τῆς ἐπιμονῆς χρόνον ἐνεργεῖται, διαλυόμενον καὶ ἀειδὲς γιγνόμενον. ταῦτα δὲ οὐ δύναται πάσχειν τὸ σῶμα χωρὶς ἐνεργείας. ἐπιμένει οὖν ⟨ἐν⟩ τῷ σώματι ἡ ἐνέργεια, [αυ]τῆ⟨ς⟩ ψυχῆς χωρισθείσης.

8 αὕτη οὖν ἡ διαφορὰ ἀθανάτου σώματος καὶ θνητοῦ, ὅτι τὸ μὲν ἀθάνατον ἐκ μιᾶς ὕλης συνέστηκε, τὸ δὲ οὔ· καὶ τὸ μὲν ποιεῖ, τὸ δὲ πάσχει. ⟨καὶ τὸ μὲν κρατεῖ, τὸ δὲ κρατεῖται·⟩ πᾶν γὰρ τὸ ἐνεργοῦν

1–2 Fortasse ⟨τὰ γὰρ θεῖα σώματα⟩ ἀδύνατον ἀργά ποτε μεῖναι τῆς ἰδίας ἐνεργείας. το⟨ι⟩γαρο⟨ῦ⟩ν ἀεὶ ἔσται ⟨ἡ ἐνέργεια?⟩. Haec post § 10 subsequi possent | τὸ γὰρ ἐὸν F 3–8 § 4 (τούτῳ . . . ἀεὶ ἔστι) hinc transposui: vide post § 11 9–13 § 5 (παρέπονται . . . συνεργοῦσαι) hinc transposui: vide post § 11 14–21 § 6 (αὗται . . . δύνανται εἶναι) hinc transposui: vide post § 11 24 τὸ δὲ ἐνεργεῖσθαι δυνατὸν scripsi: τὸ δὲ εἶναι δύναται F: om. P 30 τῆς scripsi: αὕτη codd.

EXCERPT III

⟨From the Discourses of Hermes to Tat.⟩

A holy discourse. 7

Hermes. A body, my son, cannot hold together[1] without soul; but it is possible for it to have forces working in it, though it be without soul.—*Tat.* What do you mean by that, father?—*Hermes.* You must understand the matter thus, my son Tat. When the soul has been separated from the body, the body itself lasts on; and as long as the body lasts on, it is being acted on by forces. It is being broken up, and gradually disappearing; and the body could not undergo these processes if there were not a force at work in it. This force then stays on in the body after the soul has been parted from it.

This[2] then is the difference between an immortal body and a mortal body. 8
The immortal body consists of a single kind of matter; the mortal body does not. The immortal body acts on other things; the mortal body is acted on. ⟨The immortal body has the mastery, and the mortal body is mastered;⟩ for everything which puts forces in action has the mastery, and that which is

[1] I.e. cannot exist as an organized whole.

[2] § 8 breaks the connexion between § 7 and § 9, and must have been inserted here by error.

κρατεῖ, τὸ δὲ ἐνεργούμενον κρατεῖται. καὶ τὸ μὲν κρατοῦν, [ἐπιτακτικὸν καὶ] ἐλεύθερον ⟨ὄν⟩, ἄγει, τὸ δὲ ⟨κρατούμενον⟩, δοῦλον ⟨ὄν⟩, φέρεται.

9 ⟨κ⟩αὶ μὴν ⟨αἱ⟩ ἐνέργειαι οὐ μόνον τὰ ἔμψυχα ἐνεργοῦσι σώματα, ⟨⟨ἀλλ⟨ὰ⟩⟩⟩ καὶ τὰ ἄψυχα, ⟨τὰ⟩ ξύλα καὶ τοὺς λίθους καὶ τὰ [[ἄλλ']] ὅμοια, αὔξουσαί τε [καὶ καρποφοροῦσαι] καὶ πεπαίνουσαι, καὶ φθείρουσαι καὶ τήκουσαι καὶ σήπουσαι καὶ θρύπτουσαι, καὶ τὰ ὅμοια ἐνεργοῦσαι, ὅσα δύναται σώματα ἄψυχα πάσχειν. ἐνέργεια γὰρ κέκληται, ὦ τέκνον, αὐτὸ τοῦτο, ⟨τὸ δι' οὗ γίγνεται⟩ ὅ τί ποτέ ἐστι τὸ γιγνόμενον.

10 ἀεὶ δὲ γίγνεσθαι δεῖ [καὶ] πολλά, μᾶλλον δὲ πάντα. οὐδέποτε γὰρ χηρεύει τῶν ὄντων τινὸς ὁ κόσμος, ἀεὶ δὲ φερόμενος, ⟨ἀεὶ⟩ ἐν ἑαυτῷ κυίσκει τὰ ὄντα [οὐδέποτε ἀπολειφθησόμενα αὐτοῦ τῆς φ[θ]ορᾶς].

* * * * *

11 πᾶσα οὖν ἐνέργεια νοείσθω ὡς [ἀεὶ] ἀσώματος οὖσα, ἥτις ἂν ᾖ ἐν οἱῳδήποτε σώματι.

1 ⟨⟨ἐνέργειαι γάρ, ὦ Τάτ, ἀσώματοι αὐταὶ οὖσαι, ἐν σώμασίν εἰσι, καὶ διὰ τῶν σωμάτων ἐνεργοῦσι. διόπερ, ὦ Τάτ, καθότι ⟨μὲν⟩ ἀσώματοί εἰσι, καὶ ἀθανάτους αὐτάς φημι εἶναι, καθότι δὲ χωρὶς σωμάτων ἐνεργεῖν οὐ δύνανται, φημὶ αὐτὰς εἶναι ἀεὶ ἐν σώματι.⟩⟩

4 ⟨⟨τούτῳ τῷ λόγῳ ἕπεται [τὸ] καὶ ⟨τὸ⟩ ἀεὶ [τὰ] σώματα εἶναι. διὸ καὶ [αὐτὴν] τὴν σωματο⟨ποίη⟩σίν φημι ἀιδίαν [ἐνέργειαν] εἶναι. εἰ[ς] γὰρ σώματα ἐπίγεια διαλυτά, σώματα δὲ δεῖ εἶναι, τόπους καὶ ὄργανα τῶν ἐνεργειῶν [ταῦτα] ⟨ὑπάρξοντα⟩, αἱ δὲ ἐνέργειαι ἀθάνατοι, τὸ δὲ ἀθάνατον ἀεὶ ἔστι[ν ἐνέργεια], καὶ ἡ σωματοποίησις [εἴ γε] ἀεὶ ἔστι.⟩⟩

6 ⟨⟨αὐταὶ δὴ ⟨⟨ἀ[ι]σώματ[οπ]οι οὖσαι⟩⟩ αἱ ἐνέργειαι τῶν σωμάτων εἰσὶν ἠρτημέναι· καὶ ⟨γὰρ⟩ ἀπὸ [μὲν] τῶν θείων σωμάτων ἔρχονται εἰς τὰ θνητά [αὗται] [[αἱ σωματοποιοῦσαι]]· ἑκάστη δὲ αὐτῶν ἐνεργεῖ ἢ περὶ τὸ σῶμα ἢ τὴν ψυχήν. καὶ

1 τὸ μὲν κρατούμενον F 2 ὄν (ante ἄγει) add. Heeren | φέρεται FP: ἄγεται Meineke 3 καὶ μὴν αἱ scripsi: αἱ μὲν codd. 4 ἀλλὰ cod. Vatic.: om. FP 6 παπταίνουσαι P[1] 9 γενόμενον F 10 δεῖ om. P | καὶ om. Heeren 12–13 Fortasse οὐδέποτε ἀπολειφθησόμενος [ ] τῆς φ[θ]ορᾶς 13 φορᾶς Canter: φθορᾶς codd. 14 ἀσώματος scripsi: ἀθάνατος codd. 15 ᾖ om. P 16–20 § 1 (ἐνέργειαι . . . ἐν σώματι) huc transposui 16 ἐνέργεια F | ἀσώματον F | αὐταὶ Meineke: αὗται F: ταῦται P 17 ἐνεργοῦσι F: ἐνεργοῦσαι P 18 αὐτοὺς F | φημι Wachsmuth: φῂς FP 19 αὐτοὺς F 21–26 § 4 (τούτῳ . . . ἀεὶ ἔστι) huc transposui 22 σωματοποίησίν scripsi: σωμάτωσίν codd. | ἀιδίαν ἐνέργειαν F: ἀείδιενέργειαν P 23 εἰ Canter: εἰς FP | ἐπίγεια P[2]: ἐπίγερα FP[1]

acted on by forces is mastered. And that which has the mastery is free, and takes the lead; but that which is mastered is in servitude, and is passively borne along.

Moreover, the forces work not only in bodies that have souls 9
in them,[1] but also in soulless bodies, such as logs and stones and the like, increasing their bulk and bringing them to maturity, corrupting, dissolving, rotting and crumbling them, and carrying on in them all processes of that sort that it is possible for soulless bodies to undergo. For this, my son, is the very meaning of the term 'a force-at-work'; it signifies ⟨that by which is worked⟩ every sort of process that goes on.

And there must be going on at all times many processes, or 10
rather, every kind of process. For the Kosmos is never bereft of any of the things that are; ever in movement, it is ever breeding within itself the things that are.

* * * * *

You must understand then that every force is incorporeal, 11
whatever force may be at work in any kind of body.

For forces, my son, though they are themselves incorporeal, 1·
are in bodies, and work by means of these bodies. And so, my son, inasmuch as they are incorporeal, I say that they are immortal; but inasmuch as they cannot work apart from bodies, I say that they are always in a body.

Hence it follows that there are always bodies in existence. And 4
for this reason I say that the production of bodies must be everlasting. For if earthly bodies are dissoluble, and there must be bodies to serve as places and instruments for the working of the forces, and the forces are immortal, and that which is immortal exists for ever, then it follows that the production of bodies must go on for ever.

The forces, though they are themselves incorporeal, are de- 6
pendent on the bodies; for they come from the divine bodies,[2] and enter into mortal bodies. But each of them acts either on

[1] The writer ought rather to have said 'in bodies that *have had* souls in them'.

[2] I.e. the heavenly bodies.

---

25 ἔστι scripsi: ἔστιν, ἐνέργεια codd. 27–5 *infra*: § 6 (αὐταὶ . . . δύνανται εἶναι) huc transposui 27 αὐταὶ scripsi: αὗται codd. | δὴ scripsi: δὲ odd. | ἀσώματοι οὖσαι scripsi: αἱ σωματοποιοῦσαι codd.

αὐτῇ ⟨γὰρ⟩ [[μέντοι]] τῇ ψυχῇ συγγίγνονται, ⟨οὐ⟩ ⟨⟨μέντοι⟩⟩ χωρὶς σώματος. [ἀεὶ δὲ ἐνέργειαί εἰσιν.] οὐκ ἀεὶ δὲ ἡ ψυχὴ ἐν σώματί [θνητῷ] ἐστι, δύναται γὰρ χωρὶς τοῦ σώματος εἶναι· αἱ δὲ ἐνέργειαι χωρὶς τῶν σωμάτων οὐ δύνανται εἶναι.⟩⟩

5 ⟨⟨παρέπονται δὲ τῇ ψυχῇ οὐκ ἀθρόως παραγιγνόμεναι· ἀλλὰ τινὲς μὲν αὐτῶν ἅμα τῷ γενέσθαι τὸν ἄνθρωπον [ἐνεργοῦσι] ⟨παραγίγνονται⟩, ὁμοῦ τῇ ψυχῇ ⟨εἰσελθοῦσαι, καὶ⟩ περὶ τὰ ἄλογα ⟨μέρη ἐνεργ⟩οῦσαι, αἱ δὲ καθαρώτεραι ἐνέργειαι κατὰ μεταβολὴν τῆς ἡλικίας, τῷ λογικῷ μέρει τῆς ψυχῆς συνεργοῦσαι.⟩⟩

12 τῶν δὲ ἐνεργειῶν αἱ μέν εἰσι τῶν θείων σωμάτων ⟨ἐνεργητικαί⟩, αἱ δὲ τῶν φθαρτῶν· καὶ ⟨τῶν εἰς τὰ φθαρτὰ ἐνεργουσῶν⟩ αἱ μὲν καθολικαί, ⟨αἱ δὲ γενικαί,⟩ αἱ δὲ ⟨ε⟩ἰδικαί. [καὶ αἱ μὲν τῶν γενῶν, αἱ δὲ [τῶν μερῶν] ἑνὸς ἑκάστου.] θεῖαι μὲν οὖν εἰσιν αἱ εἰς τὰ ⟨ἀ⟩ίδια σώματα ἐνεργοῦσαι· αὗται δὲ καὶ τέλειαί εἰσιν, ὡς εἰς τέλεια σώματα. ⟨καθολικαὶ δὲ αἱ εἰς τὰ φθαρτὰ σύμπαντα·⟩ ⌜γενικαὶ δὲ αἱ δι' ἑνὸς ἑκάστου γένους τῶν ζῴων· ⟨ε⟩ἰδικαὶ δὲ αἱ εἰς ἕκαστόν ⟨⟨τι⟩⟩ τῶν ὄντων [[τι]].

13 οὗτος ὁ λόγος, ὦ τέκνον, συνάγει πάντα μεστὰ εἶναι ἐνεργειῶν. εἰ γὰρ [ἀνάγκη τὰς ἐνεργείας ἐν σώμασιν εἶναι] πολλὰ [δὲ] σώματα ἐν κόσμῳ, πλείους φημὶ εἶναι τὰς ἐνεργείας τῶν σωμάτων. ἐν ἑνὶ γὰρ πολλάκις σώματί ἐστι μία καὶ δευτέρα καὶ τρίτη ⟨. . .⟩, χωρὶς τῶν ⟨τῇ γενέσει⟩ ἑπομένων καθολικῶν· καθολικὰς γὰρ ἐνεργείας φημὶ τὰς ⟨τῶν⟩ ὄντων σωματ⟨ωτ⟩ικάς [[διὰ δὲ τῶν αἰσθήσεων καὶ τῶν κινήσεων γινομένας]]· χωρὶς γὰρ τούτων τῶν ἐνεργειῶν τὸ σῶμα συστῆναι οὐ δυνατόν. ἕτεραι δέ εἰσιν ⟨ε⟩ἰδικαὶ ἐνέργειαι ⌜ταῖς ψυχαῖς τῶν ἀνθρώπων διὰ τεχνῶν καὶ ἐπιστημῶν καὶ ἐπιτηδευμάτων καὶ ἐνεργημάτων⌝ ⟨. . .

14 . . .⟩ ⟨⟨διὰ δὲ τῶν αἰσθήσεων [καὶ τῶν κινήσεων] ⟨φανερὰς⟩ γινομένας·⟩⟩ παρέπονται γὰρ ταῖς ἐνεργείαις [κ]αὶ αἰσθήσεις, μᾶλλον δὲ ἀποτελέσματα τῶν ἐνεργειῶν ⟨αἱ⟩ αἰσθήσεις εἰσί.

15 νόησον οὖν, ὦ τέκνον, διαφορὰν ἐνεργείας ⟨καὶ αἰσθήσεως. ἡ μὲν γὰρ ἐνέργεια⟩ ἄνωθεν πέμπεται· ἡ δὲ αἴσθησις, ἐν τῷ σώματι οὖσα, καὶ ἀπὸ τούτου τὴν οὐσίαν ἔχουσα, δεξαμένη

6–11 § 5 (παρέπονται . . . συνεργοῦσαι) huc transposui 9 μέρη ἐνεργοῦσαι scripsi: οὖσαι codd. 10 ἡλικίας corr. cod. Vat.: ἡσυχίας FP | λοξῷ P¹: λογικῷ cett. 14 εἰδικαί Meineke: ἰδικαὶ FP 15 θεῖα P¹ | αἱ FP²: καὶ P¹ | ἀίδια Canter (an θεῖα?): ἴδια FP 17 γενικαὶ

the body or on the soul; for they enter into connexion with the soul also, but not apart from the body. The soul is not always in a body; it can exist apart from the body; but the forces cannot exist apart from the bodies.

The forces which accompany the soul do not all arrive at the same time. Some of them arrive at the moment of the man's birth, entering into his body together with the soul, and acting on the irrational parts of the soul; but the purer forces arrive when he reaches the age of adolescence, and co-operate with the rational part of the soul.

Of the forces at work,[1] some act on the divine bodies, and others act on 12
perishable bodies. ⟨Of those which act on perishable bodies,⟩ some are universal, ⟨some are general,⟩ and some are special. Those forces which act on the everlasting bodies are divine; and these are also perfect; for the bodies on which they act are perfect. ⟨Those forces are universal, which act on all perishable bodies together;⟩ those forces are general, the action of which extends throughout any one kind of living beings; and those forces are special, which act on an individual.

Hence it is to be inferred, my son, that all things are full 13
of forces at work. If there are many bodies in the Kosmos, I say that the forces at work are more in number than the bodies. For in a single body there are often a first and a second and a third . . ., besides the universal forces which accompany the birth of bodies. I call those forces 'universal', which bring the bodies of things into being; without them the body cannot be built up. And besides these there are special forces. . . .

. . . and made manifest by means of the sensations; for the 14
sensations accompany the forces, or rather, the sensations are effects produced by the forces.

You must understand, my son, the difference between a force 15
at work and a sensation. The force is sent down from above; but sense, which is in the body, and gets its being from the body,

[1] § 12 seems inconsistent with the context, and was probably written by another person.

---

scripsi: *μερικαὶ* codd. **18** *γένους* om. P | *εἰδικαὶ* Meineke: *ἰδικαὶ* FP **20** *σώμᾰτι* P **25** *τῶν ὄντων* scripsi: *ὄντως* codd. | *σωματωτικὰς* Usener: *σωματικάς* codd. **25–26** *διὰ . . . γινομένας* hinc ad § 14 *init.* transposui **27** *οὐ δυνατὸν* F: *ἀδύνατον* P | *εἰδικαὶ* Meineke: *ἰδικαὶ* FP **31** *αἱ* Heeren: *καὶ* FP **32** *ἀποτελέσματα* F^2P^2: *ἀποτέλεσμα* F^1: *ἀποτέλειμα* P^1 | *αἱ* add. F^2 **33** *οὖν* om. F **33–34** *καὶ αἰσθήσεως· ἡ μὲν ἐνέργεια* addidit Wachsmuth (*γὰρ* addidi): *καὶ αἰσθήσεως· ἡ μὲν* add. P^2 marg.

τὴν ἐνέργειαν φανερὰν ποιεῖ, καθάπερ αὐτὴν σωματοποιή-
σασα. διόπερ ⟨τὰς μὲν ἐνεργείας ἀσωμάτους καὶ ἀθανάτους,⟩
τὰς ⟨δὲ⟩ αἰσθήσεις καὶ σωματικὰς καὶ θνητάς φημι εἶναι,
⟨ἐπὶ⟩ τοσοῦτον συνεστώσας ὅσον καὶ τὸ σῶμα· καὶ γὰρ
συγγεννῶνται τῷ σώματι αἱ αἰσθήσεις καὶ συναποθνή-
16 σκουσι. ⟨⟨καὶ τὰ μὲν⟩⟩ ⟨θνητὰ σώματα αἴσθησιν ἔχει·⟩ τὰ
δὲ ἀθάνατα σώματα [[αὐτὰ μὲν]] αἴσθησιν οὐκ ἔχει, ὡς ἐξ
οὐσίας ⟨οὐ⟩ τοιαύτης συνεστῶτα. ἡ γὰρ αἴσθησις οὐδ' ὅλως
ἄλλου ἐστὶ [σωματικὴ] ⟨καταληπτικὴ⟩ ἢ τοῦ προσγινομένου
τῷ σώματι [κακοῦ ἢ τοῦ ἀγαθοῦ], ἢ τοῦ πάλιν αὖ ἀπογινο-
μένου· τοῖς δὲ ἀιδίοις σώμασιν οὔτε προσγίνεταί ⟨τι⟩ οὔτε
18 ἀπογίνεται· διὸ αἴσθησις ἐν ἐκείνοις οὐ γίνεται. ⟨⟨⟨αἱ γὰρ⟩
αἰσθήσεις [μέν] εἰσὶ παθητικαί [δέ], κατὰ αὔξησιν μόνον καὶ
κατὰ μείωσιν γιγνόμεναι. τὸ δὲ πάθος καὶ ⟨ἡ⟩ αἴσθησις
ἀπὸ μιᾶς κορυφῆς ἤρτηνται, εἰς δὲ τὸ αὐτὸ συνάγονται· ὑπὸ
δὲ τῶν ἐνεργειῶν ⟨ἀποτελεῖται συναμφότερα⟩.⟩⟩—
17 Ἐν παντὶ οὖν ⟨παθητῷ⟩ σώματι αἴσθησις [αἰσθάνεται]
⟨γίνεται⟩;—Ἐν παντί, ὦ τέκνον· καὶ ⟨γὰρ⟩ ἐνέργειαι ⟨ἐν⟩
πᾶσιν ἐνεργοῦσι.—Κἀν τοῖς ἀψύχοις, ὦ πάτερ;—Κἀν ⟨τοῖς⟩
ἀψύχοις, ὦ τέκνον. διαφοραὶ δέ εἰσι τῶν αἰσθήσεων· αἱ
μὲν ⟨γὰρ⟩ τῶν λογικῶν μετὰ λόγου γίγνονται, αἱ δὲ τῶν
ἀλόγων ⌜σωματικαί⌝ εἰσι μόνον, αἱ δὲ τῶν ἀψύχων ⟨. . .⟩.
18 [[αἰσθήσεις μέν εἰσι, παθητικαὶ δέ, κατὰ αὔξησιν μόνον
δὲ κατὰ μείωσιν γιγνόμεναι. τὸ δὲ πάθος καὶ αἴσθησις
ἀπὸ μιᾶς κορυφῆς ἤρτηνται, εἰς δὲ τὸ αὐτὸ συνάγονται, ὑπὸ
δὲ τῶν ἐνεργειῶν.]]
19 τῶν δὲ ἐμψύχων [ζῴων] εἰσὶ δύο ἄλλαι ⌜ἐνέργειαι⌝, αἳ
παρέπονται ταῖς αἰσθήσεσι καὶ τοῖς πάθεσι, λύπη καὶ χαρά.
χωρὶς τούτων ζῷον [ἔμψυχον] [καὶ μάλιστα] ⟨ἄ⟩λογ[ικ]ον
αἰσθέσθαι ἀδύνατον· διὸ καὶ ἰδίας ταύτας εἶναί φημι [τῶν
παθῶν ἰδέας] τῶν ⟨ἀ⟩λόγ[ικ]ων μᾶλλον ζῴων, ⟨ὡς τούτων
μᾶλλον⟩ ἐπικρατούσας. [αἱ μὲν ἐνέργειαι ⟨ἀφανῶς⟩ ἐνερ-
20 γοῦσιν, αἱ δὲ αἰσθήσεις τὰς ἐνεργείας ἀναφαίνουσιν.] αὗται
δέ, οὖσαι σωματικαί, ἀνακινοῦνται ὑπὸ ⟨τῶν αἰσθήσεων,
ἀντέχονται δὲ⟩ τῶν τῆς ψυχῆς ἀλόγων μερῶν· διὸ καὶ

4 τοσούτων P[1] | καὶ (post ὅσον) om. P 7 Post αὐτὰ μὲν add. ἀθάνατον P 9 ἄλλον P[1] : ἄλλου P[2] | σωματικὴ seclusit Heeren | καταληπτικὴ addidi : fortasse σημαντικὴ | προσγινομένου scripsi : προσγενομένου codd. 10–11 ἀπογινομένου scripsi : ἀπογενομένου codd. 11 τι add. Wachsmuth 13–16 § 18 (αἰσθήσεις . . . ἐνεργειῶν) huc transposui

receives the force and makes it manifest, giving it a bodily existence, so to speak. I say then that the forces are incorporeal and immortal, but the senses are corporeal and mortal, continuing in existence only so long as the body does; for the senses are
generated together with the body, and perish with it. And mortal 16
bodies have sense; but the immortal bodies[1] have not sense, because they do not consist of that sort of substance.[2] For sense cannot apprehend anything whatever except that which is added to the body, or that which on the other hand is taken from the body; but nothing is added to or taken from the everlasting bodies, and therefore sensation does not take place in them.
For sensations have to do with changes that befall the body, 18
and take place only in connexion with increase and decrease of the body. The bodily change and the sensation are attached to a single head, and joined in one; and both together are effected by the forces at work.—

Tat. Does sensation take place then in every body that is 17
subject to change?—*Hermes.* Yes, my son; for there are forces at work in all such bodies.—*Tat.* Even in soulless bodies, father?—*Hermes.* Yes, my son, even in soulless bodies. But there are different kinds of sense. The sensations of rational beings are accompanied by reason; those of irrational animals are merely . . .; and those of soulless things . . .

But beings that have souls in them have two other things, 19
which accompany the sensations and the bodily changes, namely, pain and enjoyment. It is impossible for an irrational animal to have a sensation without feeling pain or enjoyment; and so I say that pain and enjoyment are proper to the irrational animals rather than to men; for the irrational animals are more completely mastered by them. Pain and enjoyment, being corporeal, 20
are stirred up by the sensations, and take hold of the irrational parts of the soul; and therefore I say that both of them work

[1] I.e. the heavenly bodies.

[2] I.e. of such substance as admits of sense. The substance of which the writer holds them to consist is probably the Aristotelian 'fifth substance'.

---

13 *καὶ* (post *μόνον*) P[2]: *δὲ* FP[1] 14 *ἢ* addidit Wachsmuth 17 *αἴσθησις* F[2]P[2]: *αἴσθησιν* F[1]P[1] 18 *ἐνεργεία* P | *ἐν* add. Heeren 19 *κἂν* (bis) Usener: *καὶ* (bis) codd. | *τοῖς* add. Meineke 29 *ἄλογον* scripsi: *λογικὸν* codd. 30 *ἰδίας* scripsi: *ἰδέας* codd. 30–31 *τῶν παθῶν ἰδέας* seclusit Wachsmuth 31 *ἀλόγων* scripsi: *λοξῶν* F[1]: *λογικῶν* cett. 32 *ἐπικρατούσας* P[2]: *ἔτι κρατούσας* FP[1] 32–33 *αἱ μὲν . . . ἀναφαίνουσιν* seclusit Wachsmuth

ἀμφοτέρας φημὶ κακωτικὰς εἶναι. τό τε γὰρ χαίρειν, μεθ' ἡδονῆς τὴν αἴσθησιν παρέχον, πολλῶν κακῶν εὐθέως αἴτιον συμβαίνει[ν] τῷ παθόντι· ἥ τε λύπη, ἀλγηδόνας καὶ ὀδύνας ἰσχυροτέρας παρέχ⟨ουσα, τὸν βίον λυμαίν⟩εται. διόπερ εἰκότως ἀμφότεραι κακωτικαὶ ἂν εἴησαν.—

21 ⌜*Ἡ αὐτὴ ἂν εἴη αἴσθησις ψυχῆς καὶ σώματος*⌝, *ὦ πάτερ; —Πῶς νοεῖς, ὦ παῖ, ψυχῆς αἴσθησιν; οὐχ ἡ μὲν ψυχὴ ἀσώματος, ἡ δὲ αἴσθησις σῶμα;—⟨. . .⟩* ⌜*ἂν εἴη, ὦ πάτερ, ἡ αἴσθησις ἡ ἐν σώματι οὖσα τυγχάνει.*⌝*—Ἐὰν ἀσώματον αὐτὴν θῶμεν, ὦ τέκνον, ὁμοίαν τῇ ψυχῇ αὐτὴν ἀποφανοῦμεν ἢ ταῖς ἐνεργείαις· ταῦτα γὰρ ἀσώματα ὄντα φαμὲν ἐν σώμασιν ⟨εἶναι⟩. ἡ δὲ αἴσθησις οὔτε ἐνέργειά ἐστιν οὔτε ψυχή,* ⌜*οὔτε ἀσώματόν τι ἄλλο παρὰ τὰ προειρημένα*⌝*· οὐκ ἂν οὖν εἴη ἀσώματον. εἰ δ' οὐκ ἔστιν ἀσώματον, σῶμα ἂν εἴη. [τῶν γὰρ ὄντων δεῖ τὰ μὲν σώματα εἶναι, τὰ δὲ ἀσώματα.]*

EXCERPTUM IV A

Stobaeus I. 49. 5, vol. i, p. 322 Wachsmuth (*Ecl.* I. 806 Heeren).

Τοῦ *αὐτοῦ* (sc. Ἑρμοῦ).

[⟨*ὅτι*⟩ *ψυχὴ πᾶσα ἀθάνατος καὶ ἀεικίνητος.*]

1 *Ἔφαμεν γὰρ ἐν τοῖς γενικοῖς ⟨τὰς τῶν⟩ ⟨⟨σωμάτων⟩⟩ κινήσεις τὰς μὲν ὑπὸ τῶν ⟨φυσικῶν⟩ ἐνεργειῶν, τὰς δὲ ὑπὸ τῶν [[σωμάτων]] ⟨ψυχῶν γίνεσθαι⟩.*

2 *[φαμὲν δὲ τὴν ψυχήν, ⟨⟨ἀσώματον οὖσαν,⟩⟩ ἐξ οὐσίας τινὸς [οὐχ ὕλης] γεγενῆσθαι [[ἀσώματον οὖσαν]] καὶ αὐτῆς ἀσωμάτου οὔσης. πᾶν γὰρ τὸ γενόμενον ἀνάγκη ἔκ τινος γεγενῆσθαι.]*

3 *ὅσων μὲν οὖν ⟨σωμάτων⟩ τῇ γενέσει φθορὰ ἐπακολουθεῖ, τούτοις δύο κινήσεις παρακολουθεῖν ἀνάγκη, τήν τε ⟨γινομένην ὑπὸ τῆς⟩ ψυχῆς, ὑφ' ἧς κινεῖται ⟨τὸ σῶμα κατὰ τόπον⟩, καὶ τὴν [τοῦ σώματος] ⟨ὑπὸ τῆς φύσεως⟩, ὑφ' ἧς αὔξεται καὶ*

1 Fortasse κακωτικὰς εἶναι ⟨τοῦ ἀνθρώπου⟩ 3 συμβαίνει Heeren: συμβαίνειν FP 4 παρέχουσα, τὸν βίον λυμαίνεται scripsi: παρέχεται codd.

mischief. Enjoyment causes sensation to be accompanied by pleasure, and so forthwith becomes the cause of many evils to the man who feels it; and pain, producing intense distress and anguish, ⟨spoils a man's life⟩. It may therefore be said with good reason that both of them work mischief.

Tat. . . ., father?[1]—*Hermes.* What do you mean, my son, by 21
'sense belonging to the soul'? Is not the soul incorporeal, and is not sense a body?—*Tat.* . . . .[2]—*Hermes.* If we say that sense is incorporeal, my son, we shall be making it a thing like the soul, or the forces at work; for these, we say, are incorporeal, and are in bodies. But sense is neither force at work nor soul, . . .; it cannot therefore be incorporeal. And if it is not incorporeal, it must be a body.

EXCERPT IV A

From a Discourse of Hermes.

I said in my General Discourses, that of the movements of 1
bodies some are worked by the forces of nature, and others by souls. [§ 2][3]

All bodies then of which the coming-into-being is followed by 3
destruction must necessarily be accompanied by two movements, namely, the movement worked by the soul, by which bodies are moved in space, and the movement worked by nature, by which bodies are made to grow and to waste away, and are resolved

[1] Perhaps, 'Does sense belong both to the body and to the soul, father?'

[2] Perhaps, 'Why should not sense itself be incorporeal, father, though it is in a body?'

[3] [§ 2. 'But I say that the soul, being incorporeal, has been made of some substance which is itself incorporeal. For everything that has been made must necessarily have been made of something.']

8–9 Fortasse ⟨*Τί γὰρ οὐκ ἀσώματος αὐτὴ*⟩ *ἂν εἴη, ὦ πάτερ, ἡ αἴσθησις, εἰ* ⟨*καὶ*⟩ *ἐν σώματι οὖσα τυγχάνει;* 9 *ἡ* (ante *ἐν*) del. P[2] | *ἀσώματον* scripsi : *ἐν σώματι* codd. 10 *ἀποφαινοῦμεν* F 12 *οὔτε* Wachsmuth : *οὐδὲ* FP 15 *δεῖ* Canter : *ἀεὶ* FP

19 *ἔφαμεν* scripsi : *ἔφημεν* Wachsmuth (codd.?) 21 *ψυχῶν γίνεσθαι* addidi; vide § 3 23 *ἀσώματον οὖσα καὶ* P[1] 26 *ὅσων* P[2] : *ὅσον* FP[1] | *οὖν* F : *σὺν* P 27 *παρακολουθεῖν* FP : fortasse *παρέπεσθαι* 27–28 *γινομένην ὑπὸ τῆς* addidi (*τῆς* add. P[2] marg.) 28 *ψυχῆς* P[2] : *ψυχην* FP[1]

φθίνει, ἔτι δὲ καὶ ⟨φθαρὲν⟩ [ἀναλυθέντα] ἀναλύεται. ταύτην ὁρίζομαι τὴν κίνησιν τῶν φθαρτῶν σωμάτων.

4 ⟨. . .⟩ ἡ δὲ ψυχὴ ἀεικίνητος, ὅτι ἀεὶ ⟨ἔν τε⟩ ἑαυτῇ κινεῖται καὶ ἄλλοις κίνησιν ἐνεργεῖ. κατὰ τοῦτον οὖν τὸν λόγον ἐστὶ ψυχὴ πᾶσα ἀθάνατος, καθ⟨ότι⟩ ἀεικίνητος, ⟨ἐν ἑαυτῇ⟩ ἔχουσα [κίνησιν] τὴν αὐτῆς ἐνέργειαν.

5 ἰδέαι δὲ ψυχῶν, θεία, ἀνθρωπίνη, ἄλογος.

ἡ μὲν οὖν θεία τοῦ θείου σώματος ⟨κινητική, . . .⟩ αὐτῆς ἐνέργεια· ἐν μὲν γὰρ αὐτῷ κινεῖται, καὶ [ε]αὐτὸ ⟨δὲ⟩ κινεῖ.

6 [[ἐπὰν γὰρ θνητῶν ζῴων ἀπαλλαγῇ, χωρισθεῖσα τῶν ἀλόγων ἑαυτῆς μερῶν, ἐξελθοῦσα εἰς τὸ θεῖον σῶμα, ὡς ἀεικίνητος ἐν αὐτῷ κινεῖται, συμπεριφερομένη τῷ παντί.]]

7 ἡ δὲ ἀνθρωπίνη ἔχει μέν ⟨τι⟩ καὶ [τὸ] τοῦ θείου, συνῆπται δὲ αὐτῇ καὶ τὰ ἄλογα ⟨μέρη⟩, ἥ τε ἐπιθυμία καὶ ὁ θυμός· καὶ ⟨γὰρ⟩ αὗται [μὲν ἀθάνατοι καθότι καὶ αὗται αἱ] ἐνέργειαι τυγχάνουσιν ⟨οὖσ⟩αι, ἐνέργειαι δὲ θνητῶν σωμάτων. διὸ τοῦ [[μὲν]] θείου μέρους τῆς ψυχῆς, οὔσης ⟨⟨μὲν⟩⟩ ἐν τῷ θείῳ σώματι, πόρρω τυγχάνουσιν οὖσαι· ἐπειδὰν δὲ εἰσέλθῃ τοῦτο εἰς θνητὸν σῶμα, κἀκεῖνα ἐπιφύεται, καὶ τῇ παρουσίᾳ αὐτῶν
6 γίνεται [ἀεὶ] ⟨κακὴ ἡ⟩ ψυχή [ἀνθρωπίνη]. ⟨⟨ἐπὰν γὰρ ⟨τοῦ⟩ θνητοῦ σώματος ἀπαλλαγῇ, χωρίζεται τῶν ἀλόγων ἑαυτῆς μερῶν, εἰσελθοῦσα ⟨δὲ⟩ εἰς τὸ θεῖον σῶμα, ὡς ἀεικίνητος ⟨οὖσα⟩ ἐν αὐτῷ κινεῖται, συμπεριφερομένη τῷ παντί.⟩⟩

8 ἡ δὲ τῶν ἀλόγων συνέστηκεν ἐκ θυμοῦ τε καὶ ἐπιθυμίας. διόπερ καὶ ἄλογα ἐκλήθη τὰ ζῷα ταῦτα, στερήσει τοῦ [α]λογ⟨ικ⟩οῦ τῆς ψυχῆς.

9 τετάρτην δὲ νόει τὴν τῶν ἀψύχων ⟨ἐνέργειαν⟩, ἥτις ἔξωθεν οὖσα τῶν σωμάτων ἐνεργεῖ κινοῦσα. αὕτη δ' ἂν εἴη ἡ ἐν τῷ θείῳ σώματι κινουμένη ⟨ψυχή⟩, καὶ ὥσπερ κατὰ πάροδον ταῦτα κινοῦσα.—

3 Fortasse ⟨τῶν δὲ ἀιδίων σωμάτων κίνησις μία, ἡ ὑπὸ τῆς ψυχῆς γινομένη. . . .⟩ ἔν τε ἑαυτῇ scripsi : ἐν αὐτῇ Wachsmuth : ἑαυτῇ F (in ras.), P[1] : καὶ αὐτὴ P[2] 5 καθότι scripsi : καὶ codd. 9 μὲν γὰρ αὐτῷ FP : μὲν γὰρ αὐτῇ Wachsmuth | καὶ αὐτὸ Patritius : καὶ ἑαυτὸ FP[1] : καὶ ἑαυτὸν P[2] 10–12 § 6 (ἐπὰν . . . παντί) hinc transposui : vide post § 7 13 μέν τι καὶ τοῦ scripsi (μὲν καί τι τοῦ Heeren) : μὲν καὶ τὸ τοῦ FP 15 αυται αἱ F : αὖτα αἱ P[1] : αὐταὶ (om. αἱ) P[2] marg. 16 οὖσαι scripsi : αἱ F : om. P 18 τυγχάνουσιν οὖσαι F : τυγχάνουσαι P[1] : τυγχάνουσιν P[2] 19 ἐπιφύεται scripsi : ἐπιφοιτᾷ codd. 20 γίνεται κακὴ ἡ ψυχή scripsi : γίνεται ἀεὶ ψυχὴ (γ. ἀεὶ ἡ ψυχὴ P[2]) ἀνθρωπίνη codd. 20–21 τοῦ θνητοῦ σώματος scripsi : θνητῶν ζῴων codd. 21 χωρίζεται scripsi : χωρισθεῖσα codd.

into their elements when they have been destroyed. Thus I define the movement of perishable bodies.

. . .[1] Soul is ever in motion; for it is ever moving within 4
itself, and works movement for other things. And for this reason all soul is immortal, inasmuch as it is ever in motion, having its motive force within itself.

There are three different kinds of souls,—divine soul, human 5
soul, and irrational soul.

The divine soul is that which moves the divine body.[2] . . . its motive force;[3] it moves itself in the divine body, and it moves that body.

The human soul has in it something that is divine; but there 7
are joined to it also the irrational parts, namely, desire and repugnance. These also are motive forces, but motive forces that have to do with mortal bodies. And so, as long as the divine part of the soul is in the divine body, desire and repugnance are far away from it; but when the divine part has entered into a mortal body, they come into being as accretions on it, and it is through their presence that the soul becomes bad.
For when the soul has been released from the mortal body, 6
it is separated from its irrational parts; and it enters into the divine body, and, as it is ever in motion, it is moved in that body, being borne along in the circling movement of the universe.

But the soul of irrational animals consists of repugnance and 8
desire; and that is why these animals are called 'irrational', because they are deprived of the rational part of the soul.

And you must understand that there is a fourth kind of motive 9
force, which acts on soulless bodies. It is outside the bodies, and is operative in moving them. This must be the soul that is in motion in the divine body, and moves soulless bodies incidentally, so to speak.—

[1] Perhaps, '⟨But the everlasting bodies (i.e. the heavenly bodies) have one movement only, namely, that which is worked by soul. . . .⟩'.
[2] 'The divine body' probably means the sphere of heaven.
[3] Perhaps, 'Its motive force acts in two ways'.

---

22 εἰσελθοῦσα δὲ scripsi: ἐξελθοῦσα codd. **23** αὐτῷ F: ἑαυτῷ P: ἑαυτῇ Patr., Wachsmuth **26** λογικοῦ scripsi: λόγου P^2: ἀλόγου FP

EXCERPTUM IV B

Stobaeus I. 41. 6 a, vol. i, p. 284 Wachsmuth (*Ecl.* I. 726 Heeren).

Ἑρμοῦ ἐκ τῶν πρὸς Τάτ.

1 Ὀρθῶς ταῦτα ἀπέδειξας, ὦ πάτερ· ἐκεῖνο δὲ ἔτι με
δίδαξον. ἔφης γάρ που τὴν ἐπιστήμην καὶ τὴν τέχνην
ἐνεργείας εἶναι τοῦ λογικοῦ. νῦν δὲ φὴς τὰ ἄλογα ζῷα
στερήσει τοῦ λογικοῦ ἄλογα εἶναι καὶ κεκλῆσθαι· δῆλον ⟨δ'⟩
ὅτι ἀνάγκη κατὰ τοῦτον τὸν λόγον τὰ ἄλογα ζῷα μὴ μετέχειν
ἐπιστήμης μηδὲ τέχνης, διὰ τὸ ἐστερῆσθαι τοῦ λογικοῦ.—
2 Ἀνάγκη γάρ, ὦ τέκνον.—Πῶς οὖν ὁρῶμεν, ὦ πάτερ, τινὰ τῶν
ἀλόγων ἐπιστήμῃ καὶ τέχνῃ χρώμενα, οἷον τοὺς μύρμηκας
τὰς τροφὰς ἀποθησαυριζομένους [τοῦ χειμῶνος], καὶ τὰ ἀέρια
ζῷα ὁμοίως καλιὰς ἑαυτοῖς συντιθέντα, τὰ δὲ τετράποδα
3 γνωρίζοντα τοὺς φωλεοὺς τοὺς ἰδίους;—Ταῦτα, ὦ τέκνον,
οὐκ ἐπιστήμῃ οὐ⟨δὲ⟩ τέχνῃ ποιεῖ, ἀλλὰ φύσει. ἡ γὰρ
ἐπιστήμη καὶ ἡ τέχνη διδακτ[ικ]ά εἰσι· ταῦτα δὲ τῶν ἀλόγων
[οὐδεὶς] οὐδὲν διδάσκεται. ⟨καὶ⟩ τὰ ⟨⟨μὲν⟩⟩ [δὲ] φύσει γιγνόμενα ἐνεργείᾳ [[μὲν]] γίγνεται καθολικῇ· τὰ δὲ ἐπιστήμῃ καὶ
τέχνῃ ⟨⟨γιγνόμενα⟩⟩ [εἰδόσι] ⟨τισὶ⟩ παραγίγνεται, οὐ πᾶσι.
4 [[γιγνόμενα]] [[ὑπὸ φύσεως ἐνεργεῖται]]. οἷον οἱ ἄνθρωποι
⟨πάντες⟩ ἄνω βλέπουσιν· ⟨τοῦτο μὲν γὰρ⟩ ⟨⟨ὑπὸ φύσεως
ἐνεργεῖται·⟩⟩ οὐ πάντες δὲ ἄνθρωποι μουσικοί, οὐδὲ πάντες
τοξόται ἢ κυνηγοί, οὐδὲ τὰ ἄλλα πάντα ⟨πράττουσι πάντες⟩,
ἀλλὰ τινὲς αὐτῶν, ⟨ὅσοι⟩ τι ἔμαθον, ἐπιστήμης καὶ τέχνης
5 ἐνεργούσης. τὸν αὐτὸν τρόπον, ⟨εἰ⟩ οἱ μέν τινες τῶν μυρμήκων
τοῦτο ἔπραττον, οἱ δ' οὔ, καλῶς ἂν ἔλεγες ἐπιστήμῃ αὐτο⟨ὺς⟩
[τοῦτο πράττειν] καὶ τέχνῃ συνάγειν τὰς τροφάς· εἰ δὲ
πάντες ὁμοίως ἄγονται [[ὑπὸ τῆς φύσεως]] ἐπὶ τοῦτο καὶ
ἄκοντες, δῆλον ὅτι οὐκ ἐπιστήμῃ οὐδὲ τέχνῃ τοῦτο πράτ-
τουσιν, ⟨⟨ὑπὸ ⟨δὲ⟩ τῆς φύσεως⟩⟩ ⟨ἀγόμενοι⟩.

2 ἐκεῖνο scripsi: ἐκεῖνα codd. 4 ἐνεργείας scripsi: ἐνέργειαν codd. 5 δ' addidit Wachsmuth 9 χρώμενος P 13 οὐδὲ Meineke: οὐ FP 14 διδακτά Patritius: διδακτικὰ FP | ταῦτα scripsi: τούτων codd. 15 οὐδεὶς 'fortasse secludendum' Wachsmuth 16 καθολικῇ F: καθεκτικῇ P | τὰ δὲ Heeren: τῇ δὲ FP 17 εἰδόσι FP: εἰδικῶς Wachsmuth 19 πάντες addidit Wachsmuth 23 εἰ οἱ scripsi: ex οἱ corr. εἰ F: οἱ P 24 αὐτοὺς scripsi: αὐτὸ codd. 26 τούτῳ P 27–28 Post τοῦτο πράτ-

EXCERPT IV B

From the Discourses of Hermes to Tat.[1]

Tat. You have explained these things rightly, father; but there 1
is another thing about which I ask you to give me further instruction. You said before that knowledge and skill are forces put in action by the rational part of the soul. But now you tell me that it is because the irrational animals are deprived of the rational part of the soul, that they are irrational and are so called; and it is clear that it follows of necessity from this that the irrational animals have no portion of knowledge or skill, since they are deprived of the rational part.—*Hermes.* Yes, my son,
it necessarily follows.—*Tat.* How is it then, father, that we see 2
some of the irrational animals using knowledge and skill,—the ants, for instance, storing up their food, and the birds of the air building nests for themselves, and the four-footed beasts knowing
their own lairs?—*Hermes.* It is not by knowledge or skill, my son, 3
that they do these things, but by natural instinct. Knowledge and skill are things that are taught; but none of the irrational animals are taught to do the things you speak of. And the things that are done by instinct are done by a force that is universal in its working; but the things that are done by knowledge and skill are acquired by some, and not by all. For 4
instance, all men look upward;[2] for this is done by nature's working; but not all men are musicians, nor are all men archers or hunters; and all other such things also are done, not by all men, but by some of them, that is, by those who have learnt
to do this or that; for it is knowledge and skill that are at work.
In the same way, if some ants only did this, and others did not, 5
you would have been right in saying that it is by knowledge and skill that they collect their food; but if all of them alike are led to do this, and do it involuntarily, it is clear that it is not by knowledge or skill that they do it, but by nature's leading.

[1] Exc. IV B appears to be a continuation of Exc. IV A.

[2] That is, men stand erect with upturned face, in contrast to the beasts, which 'look downward'.

τουσιν add. codd. ἐνέργειαι γάρ, ὦ Τάτ, ἀσώματοι αὐταὶ οὖσαι, κ.τ.λ.: vide *Exc.* III

EXCERPTUM V

Stobaeus I. 41. 8, vol. i, p. 290 Wachsmuth (*Ecl.* I. 744 Heeren).

Ἑρμοῦ ἐκ τῶν [πρὸς Ἄμμωνα] πρὸς Τάτ.

1 καὶ ὁ μὲν [κύριος καὶ πάντων] δημιουργὸς τῶν ἀιδίων σωμάτων, ὦ Τάτ, ἅπαξ ποιήσας οὐκέτι ἐποίησεν οὐδὲ ποιεῖ· ταῦτα γὰρ ἑαυτοῖς παραδοὺς καὶ ἑνώσας ἀλλήλοις ἀφῆκε φέρεσθαι, μηδεν⟨ὸς⟩ ἐνδέοντα [ὡς ἀίδια]. εἰ δὲ δέονται τινῶν, ἀλλήλων δέ[ησ]ονται, οὐδεμιᾶς δὲ τῆς ἔξωθεν ἐπιφορᾶς, ⟨. . .⟩ ⌈ὡς⌉ ἀθάνατα· ἔδει γὰρ τὰ ὑπ' ἐκείνου σώματα γενόμενα τοιαύτην ἔχειν [καὶ] τὴν φύσιν.

2 ὁ δὲ ἡμέτερος δημιουργός, ἐν σώματι ὤν, ἐποίησεν ἡμᾶς, καὶ ποιεῖ ἀεὶ καὶ ποιήσει, σώματα ⟨ἔχοντας⟩ διαλυτὰ καὶ θνητά. οὐ γὰρ θέμις ἦν αὐτῷ μιμεῖσθαι τὸν ἑαυτοῦ δημιουργόν, ἄλλως τε καὶ ⟨. . .⟩ ἀδύνατον· ὁ μὲν γὰρ ἐκ τῆς πρώτης οὐσίας ἐποίησεν, οὔσης ἀσωμάτου, ὁ δὲ ἐκ τῆς γε[ι]νομένης σωματώσεως ἐποίησεν ἡμᾶς.

3 εἰκότως οὖν [κατὰ τὸν ὀρθὸν λόγον] ἐκεῖνα μὲν τὰ σώματα, ὡς ἐξ ἀσωμάτου οὐσίας γεγενημένα, ἀθάνατά ἐστι· τὰ δὲ ἡμέτερα διαλυτὰ καὶ θνητά, ὡς τῆς ⌈ὕλης⌉ ἡμῶν ἐκ σωμάτων

4 συνεστώσης. διὸ ⟨καὶ⟩ [τὸ] ἀσθενῆ ἐστι, καὶ πολλῆς ἐπικουρίας δεόμενα. πῶς γὰρ ἂν καὶ τὸ τυχὸν ἀντέσχεν ὁ σύνδεσμος ἡμῶν τῶν σωμάτων, εἰ μή τινα εἶχεν ἐπεισερχομένην τροφὴν ἐκ τῶν [ὁμοίων] στοιχείων, καὶ ὑπεσωμάτου ἡμᾶς ⟨αὕτη⟩ καθ' ἑκάστην [τὴν] ἡμέραν; καὶ γὰρ γῆς τε καὶ ὕδατος καὶ πυρὸς καὶ ἀέρος ἐπιρροὴ ἡμῖν γίγνεται, ἥτις τὰ σώματα ἡμῶν νεοποιοῦσα συνέχει τὸ σκῆνος.

5 ⟨. . .⟩ ὥστε καὶ πρὸς τὰς κινήσεις ἐσμὲν ἀσθενέστεροι, φέροντες ⟨αὐτὰς⟩ [κινήσεις] μηδὲ ἡμέρας μιᾶς. εὖ γὰρ ἴσθι, ὦ τέκνον, ὅτι εἰ μὴ ἐν ταῖς νυξὶν ἡμῶν ἀνεπαύετο τὰ σώματα, οὐκ ἂν πρὸς μίαν ἡμέραν ἀντέσχομεν. ὅθεν ἀγαθὸς ὢν ὁ δημιουργός, ⟨καὶ⟩ πάντα προεπιστάμενος, εἰς διαμονὴν τοῦ ζῴου ἐποίησε τὸν ὕπνον, ⟨φάρμακ⟩ον μέγιστον τοῦ καμάτου

1 πρὸς Ἄμμωνα verba 'ex titulo eclogae antecedentis (Ἑρμοῦ ἐκ τῶν πρὸς Ἄμμωνα, *Exc.* XV) male iterata' Wachsmuth 5 μηδενὸς scripsi: μηδὲν codd. | ὡς ἀίδια F: καὶ ἀίδια P 6 δέονται scripsi: δεήσονται codd. 7 Fortasse ὥσ⟨τε ταῦτα μὲν⟩ ἀθάνατα 14 γενομένης scripsi: γειναμένης codd. 16 γεγεννημένα F 18 διὸ καὶ ἀσθενῆ ἐστι scripsi: διὰ τὸ ἀσθενῆ εἶναι codd. 22 τὴν del. P[2] 26 εὖ F: εἶ P 28 ἀντέ-

EXCERPT V

From the Discourses of Hermes to Tat.

And the Maker of the everlasting bodies, my son, having once 1
made them, did not thereafter make them, nor does he make
them now; he gave them over into their own keeping, and having
united them to one another, left them to go their way, as things
that are in need of nothing. If they need anything, they need
one another; but they have no need of the addition of anything
from without. . . . immortal;[1] for the bodies which were made
by Him could not but be of such nature.

But the Maker by whom we men were made,[2] being himself 2
embodied, made us, and ever is and will be making us, as beings
whose bodies are dissoluble and mortal. For it was not permitted to him to imitate his own Maker, especially as ⟨. . . .
Moreover, . . . was⟩ impossible; for the Maker of the everlasting
bodies made them of the first substance, which is incorporeal,
but our Maker made us of the corporeal things that had been
made.

It is with good reason then that the everlasting bodies are 3
immortal, inasmuch as they have been made of incorporeal
substance; but our bodies are dissoluble and mortal, inasmuch
as our fabric is composed of bodies. And for this reason our 4
bodies are weak, and need much help. How could the bond
that holds our bodies together have endured even for a little
time, were it not that they receive into them nutriment which
comes from the elements, and that this nutriment renews our
bodies day by day? For we receive an influx of earth and water,
fire and air, which renovates our bodies, and holds our mortal
frame together.

. . . so that we are too weak to endure the strain of our 5
movements, and cannot bear them for one day. Be assured,
my son, that, were it not that our bodies rest at night, we could
not hold out for a single day. And so the Maker,—being good,
and foreknowing all things,—to the end that the living being
might last on, made sleep, a potent remedy for the weariness

[1] Perhaps, '⟨Those bodies then are⟩ immortal'.

[2] This second 'Maker' must be either the Kosmos or the Sun.

σχομεν Canter: ἀντέσχωμεν FP 30 φάρμακον scripsi: ὃν codd. (ὃν del. Heeren : post κινήσεως add. θελκτήριον Heeren, φάρμακον Meineke)

τῆς κινήσεως, καὶ ἐπ' ἰσότητος ἔταξεν ἑκατέρῳ χρόνον
6 [μᾶλλον δὲ τῇ ἀναπαύλῃ πλείονα]. μεγίστην δὴ νόει, ⟨ὦ⟩
τέκνον, τοῦ ὕπνου τὴν ἐνέργειαν, ἐναντίαν τῇ τῆς ψυχῆς,
οὐκ ἐλάττον⟨α δ'⟩ ἐκείνης. καθάπερ γὰρ ἡ ψυχὴ κινήσεώς
ἐστιν ἐνεργητική, τὸν αὐτὸν τρόπον ⟨ὁ ὕπνος . . .⟩. ⟨διὸ⟩ καὶ τὰ
σώματα ζῆν οὐ δύναται χωρὶς ὕπνου· ἄνεσις γάρ [καὶ
7 ἄφεσίς] ἐστι ⌜τῶν συνδέτων τῶν μελῶν⌝. καὶ ἔσωθεν ἐνεργεῖ,
σωματοποιῶν τὴν ἐπεισελθοῦσαν ὕλην, ἑκάστῳ τὸ οἰκεῖον
διαστέλλων, τὸ μὲν ὕδωρ τῷ αἵματι, τὴν δὲ γῆν ⟨τοῖς⟩ ὀστέοις
καὶ μυελοῖς, τὸν δὲ ἀέρα τοῖς νεύροις [καὶ φλεψί], τὸ δὲ πῦρ
τῇ ὁράσει. διόπερ καὶ ἥδεται ἄκρως τὸ σῶμα τῷ ὕπνῳ
ταύτην ἐνεργοῦντι τὴν ⌜ἡδονήν⌝.

EXCERPTUM VI

Stobaeus I. 21. 9, vol. i, p. 189 Wachsmuth (*Ecl.* I. 468 Heeren).

Ἑρμοῦ ἐκ τῶν πρὸς Τάτ.

1 Ἐπεί μοι ἐν τοῖς ἔμπροσθεν γενικοῖς λόγοις ὑπέσχου
δηλῶσαι περὶ τῶν τριάκοντα ἓξ δεκανῶν, νῦν μοι δήλωσον
περὶ αὐτῶν καὶ τῆς τούτων ἐνεργείας.—Οὐδ[ε]εὶς φθόνος,
ὦ Τάτ· καὶ ὁ κυριώτατος πάντων λόγος καὶ κορυφαιότατος
οὗτος ἂν εἴη. σὺ δὲ νόει [οὕτως].
2 ἔφαμέν σοι περὶ τοῦ ζῳδιακοῦ κύκλου, [[καὶ]] τοῦ ⟨⟨καὶ⟩⟩
ζῳοφόρου, καὶ τῶν πέντε πλανητῶν καὶ ἡλίου καὶ σελήνης
καὶ τοῦ ἑκάστου τούτων κύκλου.—Ἔφης γάρ, ὦ Τρισμέγιστε.
—Οὕτως βούλομαί σε νοεῖν καὶ περὶ τῶν τριάκοντα ἓξ
δεκανῶν, μεμνημένον ἐκείνων, ἵν' εὔγνωστός σοι καὶ ὁ περὶ
τούτων λόγος γένοιτο.—Μέμνημαι, ὦ πάτερ.—
3 ⟨Ἔ⟩φαμέν που, ὦ τέκνον, περιεκτικὸν τῶν ἁπάντων εἶναι

1 ἑκατέρῳ Meineke : ἑκάστῳ FP | χρόνον Gaisford : χρόνῳ FP 2 δὴ scripsi : δὲ codd. 3 ἐναντία P 4 ἐλάττονα δ' Heeren : ἔλαττον FP 5 ἐνεργητική scripsi : ἐνέργεια codd. 6 δύναται P : δύνανται F 7 τῶν (ante μελῶν) F : om. P 8 ἐπελθοῦσαν P 9 τοῖς add. Meineke 10 μυελοῖς codd. : fortasse μῦσι 12 ἐνεργοῦντι Meineke : ἐνεργοῦντος codd. | ἡδονήν codd. : fortasse ἐνέργειαν

13 sqq. Lemma et §§ 1–7 (Ἐπεί μοι . . . καὶ κοινῇ) desunt in cod. P 13 τῶν scripsi : τοῦ cod. 16 οὐδεὶς Meineke : οὐδὲ εἷς F 18 οὗτος

produced by movement; and he assigned time in equal portions
to movement and to sleep. Know then, my son, that the work 6
wrought by sleep is a great work. It is contrary to that wrought
by the soul, but of no less import; for as the soul works
movement, even so ⟨sleep works repose. And for this reason⟩
our bodies cannot live without sleep; for sleep is a relaxing
of .... Moreover, sleep works within us, building into the 7
body the matter that has entered in, and distributing to each
part of the body that kind of matter which is appropriate to it,
water to the blood, earth to the bones and marrow,[1] air to the
nerves, and fire to the organs of sight. And so the body feels
intense pleasure when sleep is doing this work.

EXCERPT VI

From the Discourses of Hermes to Tat.

Tat. In your former General Discourses you promised to 1
explain about the thirty-six Decans; I therefore ask you to
tell me about them now, and to explain their working.—*Hermes.*
I am quite willing, Tat; and of all my teachings, this will be of
supreme importance, and will stand highest among them. I bid
you mark it well.[2]

I have told you before about the zodiacal circle, which is also 2
called the animal-bearing circle, and about the five planet-stars
and the sun and the moon, and the several circles of these seven
bodies.—*Tat.* You have, thrice-greatest one.—*Hermes.* I desire
you then, in your thoughts about the thirty-six Decans also,
to bear in mind what I have told you, that so my teaching about
the Decans also may be intelligible to you.—*Tat.* I bear in mind
what you have told me, father.—

Hermes. I told you, my son, that there is a body which encloses 3

[1] Perhaps, 'bones and muscles'.
[2] Or, 'You must understand the matter thus'.

Heeren : αὐτὸς F | σὺ Meineke : εὖ F 19 καὶ transposuit Meineke
22 σε Heeren : σοι F 23 μεμνημένον Meineke : μεμνημένος F
24 γένοιτο F : γένηται Meineke 25 ἔφαμέν Meineke : φαμέν F

σῶμα. ἐννόησον οὖν [καὶ] αὐτὸ ὥσπερ κυκλοειδὲς ⟨τὸ⟩ σχῆμα· καὶ γὰρ οὕτως ἔχει τὸ πᾶν.—Τοιοῦτον ⟨τὸ⟩ σχῆμα νοῶ οὕτως ὡς λέγεις, ὦ πάτερ.—Ὑπὸ δὲ τὸν κύκλον τοῦ σώματος τούτου[ς] τετάχθαι τοὺς τριάκοντα ἓξ δεκανούς, μέσους τοῦ ⟨τοῦ⟩ παντὸς κύκλου ⟨καὶ⟩ τοῦ ζῳδιακοῦ, διορίζοντας ἀμφοτέρους τοὺς κύκλους, καὶ ὥσπερ ἐκεῖνον μὲν κουφίζοντας, τὸν ⟨δὲ⟩ ζῳδιακὸν καθορ[ιζ]ῶντας.

4 ⟨. . .⟩ ⌜συμφερομένους τοῖς πλάνησι καὶ ἰσοδυναμεῖν τῇ τοῦ παντὸς φορᾷ κατὰ τὸ ἐναλλὰξ τοῖς ἑπτά⌝· καὶ τὸ μὲν περιεκτικὸν ἐπέχειν σῶμα,—ἔσχατον γὰρ ἂν ἦν [ἐν] ⟨τῷ τάχει⟩ τῆς φορᾶς αὐτὸ καθ' αὐτὸ ὄν [τῷ πάσχειν],—ἐπισπεύδειν δὲ τοὺς ἑπτὰ ἄλλους κύκλους, διὰ τὸ βραδύτεραν κίνησιν ⟨αὐτοὺς⟩ κινεῖσθαι τοῦ ⟨τοῦ⟩ παντὸς κύκλου [ὥσπερ οὖν ἀνάγκη] [αὐτοὺς κινεῖσθαι καὶ τοῦ παντός].

13 ⟨⟨ὑπὸ δὲ τούτους ἐστὶν ἡ καλουμένη ἄρκτος, κατὰ μέσον τοῦ ζῳδιακοῦ, ἐξ ἀστέρων συγκειμένη ἑπτά, ἔχουσα ἀντίζυγον ἑτέραν ὑπὲρ κεφαλῆς. ταύτης [μὲν] ἡ ἐνέργειά ἐστι καθάπερ ἄξονος, μηδαμοῦ μὲν δυνούσης μηδὲ ἀνατελλούσης, μενούσης δὲ ἐν τῷ αὐτῷ τόπῳ, [τῆς] περὶ ⟨τὸ⟩ αὐτὸ στρεφομένης, ἐνεργούσης δὲ τὴν ⟨τοῦ⟩ ζῳ⟨ο⟩φόρου κυκλου ⟨περιφοράν. . . .⟩ παραδιδοῦσα τὸ πᾶν τοῦτο ἀπὸ μὲν [τῆς] νυκτὸς ἡμέρᾳ, ἀπὸ ⟨δ'⟩ ἡμέρας νυκτί.⟩⟩

5 νοήσωμεν οὖν καὶ τὰς τῶν ἑπτὰ ⟨. . .⟩ καὶ ⌜πάντα τὸν κύκλον⌝ ⟨. . .⟩, μᾶλλον δὲ τῶν ἐν κόσμῳ ἁπάντων ὡσπερεὶ φύλακας αὐτοὺς περιίστασθαι, [πάντα] συνέχοντας [καὶ] τὰ πάντα, καὶ τηροῦντας τὴν τῶν πάντων εὐταξίαν.—Οὕτως γὰρ νοῶ, πάτερ, ἐξ ὧν λέγεις.—

6 Ἔτι δὲ νόησον, ⟨ὦ⟩ Τάτ, ὅτι καὶ ἀπαθεῖς εἰσιν ὧν οἱ ἄλλοι ἀστέρες πάσχουσιν. οὔτε γὰρ ἐπεχόμενοι τὸν δρόμον στηρίζουσιν οὔτε κωλυόμενοι ἀναποδίζουσιν, ⟨. . .·⟩ ἀλλ' οὐδὲ μὴν ⌜ὑπὸ τοῦ φωτὸς τοῦ ἡλίου σκέπονται⌝, ἅπερ πάσχουσιν οἱ ἄλλοι ἀστέρες· ἐλευθέροι δὲ ὄντες, ὑπεράνω πάντων ὥσπερ

1 αὐτὸ F : αὐτοῦ Meineke 3 νοῶ Heeren : νῦν F 4 τούτου Heeren : τούτους F 5 καὶ add. Heeren 7 καθορῶντας scripsi : καθορίζοντας F 8 Fortasse συμφερομένους [ ] [[ ]] τῇ τοῦ παντὸς φορᾷ [⟨⟨καὶ ἰσοδυναμεῖν⟩⟩ κατὰ τὸ ἐναλλὰξ τοῖς ἑπτά] 10–11 τῷ τάχει τῆς φορᾶς scripsi : ἐν τῇ φορᾷ cod. 11 ὄν· scripsi (ὄν, τῷ τάχει Usener) : ἐν τῷ πάσχειν F 12 διὰ τὸ Heeren : διά τε F 15–22 § 13 (ὑπὸ δὲ . . . νυκτί) huc transposui 16 ἐπὰ P 17 ἡ om. P 19 τῆς seclusit Wachsmuth | τὸ add. Wachsm. 20 τοῦ add. Heeren | ζῳοφόρου Wachsm. : ζωφόρου FP | περιφοράν add. Heeren 22 δ' add. Heeren 23–24 Fortasse καὶ τὰς

all things. You must conceive the shape of that body as circular; for such is the shape of the universe.—*Tat.* I conceive its shape as circular, even as you bid me, father.—*Hermes.* And you must understand that below the circle of this body are placed the thirty-six Decans, between the circle of the universe[1] and that of the zodiac, separating the one circle from the other; they bear up, as it were, the circle of the universe, and look down on the circle of the zodiac.

. . . They retard the all-enclosing body,—for that body would 4
move with extreme velocity if it were left to itself,—but they urge on the seven other circles, because these circles move with a slower movement than the circle of the universe.

And subject to the Decans is the constellation called the Bear, 13
which is centrally situated with regard to the zodiac. The Bear is composed of seven stars, and has overhead another Bear to match it. The function of the Bear resembles that of the axle of a wheel; it never sets nor rises, but abides in one place, revolving about a fixed point, and making the zodiacal circle revolve. . . . transmitting the world from night to day, and from day to night.

Let us understand then that both the . . . of the seven planets 5
and all . . .;[2] or rather, that the Decans stand round about all things in the Kosmos as guardians, holding all things together, and watching over the good order of all things.—*Tat.*—Even so I conceive them, father, according to your words.—

And further, my son, you must understand that the Decans 6
are exempt from the things that befall the other stars. They are not checked in their course and brought to a standstill, nor hindered and made to move backwards, ⟨as the planets are;⟩ nor yet are they . . .,[3] as are the other stars. They are free, and exalted above all things; and as careful guardians and over-

[1] I.e. the outermost sphere, which is 'the all-enclosing body'.

[2] Perhaps, 'that the movements (or the circles) of the seven planets, and all other things also, are governed by the Decans'.

[3] Perhaps, 'nor yet are they ⟨deprived of their power when⟩ hidden from sight by the light of the sun'.

τῶν ἑπτὰ ⟨κινήσεις⟩ (vel *τοὺς τῶν ἑπτὰ κύκλους*) *καὶ ⟨τὰ⟩ πάντα ⟨τοῖς δεκανοῖς ὑποτετάχθαι⟩* **25–26** *συνέχοντας τὰ πάντα* scripsi (*καὶ συνέχοντας τὰ πάντα* Wachsm.): *πάντα συνέχοντας καὶ τὰ πάντα* F **30** Fortasse *ἀναποδίζουσιν, ⟨ἅπερ πάσχουσιν οἱ πλάνητες⟩*

φύλακες ἀκριβεῖς καὶ ἐπίσκοποι τοῦ παντὸς περιέ⟨ρ⟩χονται
τῷ νυχθημέρῳ τὸ πᾶν.—
7 Ἆρ' οὖν [[καὶ]] οὗτοι, ὦ πάτερ, ἔχουσι ⟨⟨καὶ⟩⟩ πρὸς ἡμᾶς
ἐνέργειαν;—Τὴν μεγίστην, ὦ τέκνον. εἰ γὰρ ἐκείνοις ἐνεργοῦσι, πῶς οὐ καὶ ἡμῖν, καὶ καθ' ἕνα ἕκαστον καὶ κοινῇ;
8 [οὕτως, ὦ τέκνον] τῶν ⟨μὲν γὰρ⟩ καθολικῶς πάντων συμ-
βαινόντων [τ]ἡ ἐνέργεια ἀπὸ τούτων ἐστίν· οἷον [ὃ λέγω
νόησον] βασιλε⟨ι⟩ῶν μετατροπαί[ων], πόλεων ἐπαναστάσεις,
λιμοί, λοιμοί, ⌜ἄμπωτις⌝ θαλάσσης, γῆς σεισμοί, οὐδὲν τούτων,
9 ὦ τέκνον, χωρὶς τῆς τούτων ἐνεργείας γίνεται. [ἔτι τε πρὸς
τούτοις νόησον] ⟨. . .⟩ εἰ γὰρ οὗτοι μὲν ἐπιστατοῦσιν ἐκείνων,
ἡμεῖς δὲ [καὶ] ὑπὸ τοὺς ἑπτά ἐσμεν, οὐ νοεῖς καὶ εἰς ἡμᾶς
τὴν[α] ἐκείνων φθάνειν ἐνέργειαν, ἤτοι ὑπ' [εις] αὐτῶν ἢ δι'
ἐκείνων ⟨ἐνεργουμένην⟩;
11 ⟨⟨ἔτι δὲ πρὸς τούτοις ⟨ἄλλο⟩ νόησον, ὦ Τάτ, ἐνέργημα
τούτων, ὅτι καὶ εἰς τὴν γῆν σπερματίζουσιν [ἃς καλοῦσιν]
⟨ἐνεργείας⟩ τινάς, τὰς μὲν σωτηρίους, τὰς δὲ ὀλεθριωτάτας,⟩⟩
10 ⟨ἃς⟩ ⟨⟨καλοῦσιν οἱ πολλοὶ δαίμονας.⟩⟩—Τίς ⟨δ' ἂν⟩ αὐτοῖς
εἴη, ὦ πάτερ, ὁ τοῦ σώματος τύπος; [τούτους οὖν] [[καλοῦσιν
οἱ πολλοὶ δαίμονας.]]—[[Οὐδὲ γὰρ ἴδιόν τί ἐστι γένος τὸ τῶν
δαιμόνων.]] Οὔτε [ἄλλα] σώματα ἔχουσιν ἐξ ἰδίας τινὸς
ὕλης, οὔτε ψυχῇ κινοῦνται ὥσπερ ἡμεῖς· ⟨⟨οὐδὲ γὰρ ἴδιόν τί
ἐστι γένος τὸ τῶν δαιμόνων,⟩⟩ ἀλλὰ ἐνέργειαί εἰσι τῶν τριάκοντα ἓξ τούτων θεῶν.
11 [[ἔτι δὲ πρὸς τούτοις νόησον, ὦ Τάτ, ἐνέργημα τούτων, ὅτι
καὶ εἰς τὴν γῆν σπερματίζουσιν ἃς καλοῦσι τάνας, τὰς μὲν
σωτηρίους, τὰς δὲ ὀλεθριωτάτας.]]
12 ἔτι καὶ ⟨ἄλλοι⟩ ἐν οὐρανῷ φερόμενοι ἀστέρες ⌜γεννῶσιν⌝
αὐτοῖς, ⟨οἱ καλούμενοι⟩ [ὑπο]λειτουργ⟨οί⟩, οὓς καὶ ὑπηρέτας
καὶ στρατιώτας ἔχουσιν. οὗτοι δὲ ὑπ' ἐκείνων ⌜μιγνύμενοι⌝
φέρονται ἐν τῷ αἰθέρι αἰωρούμενοι, τὸν τούτου τόπον ἀνα-

1 περιέρχονται scripsi : περιέχονται Wachsm. (cod. ?) 6 A verbis οὕτως ὦ τέκνον rursus incipit P; cuius in margine add. man. post. ἐκ τῶν τρισμεγίστου 7 ἡ ἐνέργεια ἀπὸ dubitanter Wachsmuth : τῇ ἐνεργείᾳ ἀπὸ codd. : τὰ ἐνεργήματα Usener 8 βασιλειῶν Heeren : βασιλέων FP | μετατροπαί Canter : μετὰ τροπαίων F : μετατροπαίων P : fortasse καταστροφαί | ἐπαναστάσεις codd. : fortasse ἀναστάσεις 9 λιμοὶ λιμοὶ P | ἄμπωτις codd. : fortasse πλημμυρίδες 10–11 ἔτι . . . νόησον seclusi (vide § 11 *init.*) : lacunam significavi. Fortasse ⟨τὰ δὲ καθ' ἕκαστον συμβαίνοντα διὰ μὲν τῶν πλανήτων ἀποτελεῖται, ὑπὸ δὲ τῶν δεκανῶν καὶ ταῦτα γίγνεται·⟩ εἰ γὰρ 11 εἰ F : οὐ P 13 τὴν scripsi : τινα codd. | ὑπ' Usener : υἱεῖς F : ἡεῖς P 15–17 § 11 (ἔτι . . . ὀλεθριωτάτας) huc transposui 17 ἐνεργείας τινάς scripsi : τάνας codd.

seers of the universe, they go round it in the space of a night and a day.—

Tat. Tell me then, father, do the Decans act on us men 7
also?[1]—*Hermes.* Yes, my son, they act on us most potently. If they act on the heavenly bodies, how could it be that they should not act on us also, both on individual men and on communities? The force which works in all events that befall men 8
collectively comes from the Decans; for instance, overthrows of kingdoms, revolts[2] of cities, famines, pestilences, overflowings of the sea, earthquakes,—none of these things, my son, take
place without the working of the Decans. . . . For if[3] the 9
Decans rule over the seven planets, and we are subject to the planets, do you not see that the force set in action by the Decans reaches us also, whether it is worked by the Decans themselves or by means of the planets?

And besides this, my son, you must know that there is yet 11
another sort of work which the Decans do; they sow upon the earth the seed of certain forces, some salutary and others most
pernicious, which the many call daemons.—*Tat.* And what is 10
the bodily form of these beings,[4] father?—*Hermes.* They do not possess bodies made of some special kind of matter, nor are they moved by soul, as we are; for there is no such thing as a race of daemons distinct from other beings; but they are forces put in action by these six and thirty gods.[5]

Moreover, there are other stars also which travel in heaven 1
and obey the Decans, namely, the so-called Liturgi,[6] whom the Decans have under their command as servants and private soldiers. The Liturgi, commanded by the Decans, are borne along floating in the aether, filling all the region of that element,

[1] I.e. 'Do the Decans act on men as well as on the planets and the other heavenly bodies?'

[2] Perhaps, 'destructions'.

[3] Perhaps, '⟨And those things also which befall men individually result from the working of the Decans;⟩ for if', &c.

[4] I.e. of the so-called daemons.

[5] I.e. by the Decans.

[6] I.e. Attendants or Ministers.

18 δ' ἂν add. Usener 19 οὖν F : οὓς P 21 ἔχουσιν scripsi : ἔχοντες codd. 22 οὔτε Meineke : οὐδὲ FP | ψυχῇ Heeren : ψυχῆς FP | κινοῦνται scripsi : κινούμενοι codd. 28 γεννῶσιν codd. : aptius esset ἀκολουθοῦσιν 29 λειτουργοί, οὓς scripsi (ὑπολειτουργούς, οὓς Usener) : ὑπολειτουργούς codd. 30 μιγνύμενοι codd. : fortasse ἀγόμενοι

πληροῦντες, ὅπως μηδεὶς ᾖ τόπος ἄνω κενὸς ἀστέρων, συγκοσμοῦντες τὸ πᾶν, ἐνέργειαν ἰδίαν ἔχοντες, ὑποτεταγμένην δὲ ⟨τῇ⟩ τῶν τριάκοντα ἓξ ἐνεργείᾳ· ἐξ ὧν [κ]αἱ κατὰ τὰς χώρας φθοραὶ γίνονται τῶν ἄλλων ἐμψύχων [ζῴων], καὶ ἡ πληθὺς τῶν λυμαινομένων ζῴων τοὺς καρπούς.

13 *[[ὑπὸ δὲ τούτους ἐστιν ἡ καλουμένη ἄρκτος, κατὰ μέσον τοῦ ζῳδιακοῦ, ἐξ ἀστέρων συγκειμένη ἑπτά, ἔχουσα ἀντίζυγον ἑτέραν ὑπὲρ κεφαλῆς. ταύτης μὲν ἡ ἐνέργειά ἐστι καθάπερ ἄξονος, μηδαμοῦ μὲν δυνούσης μηδὲ ἀνατελλούσης, μενούσης δὲ ἐν τῷ αὐτῷ τόπῳ, τῆς περὶ αὐτὸ στρεφομένης, ἐνεργούσης δὲ τὴν ζωφόρου κυκλοῦ, παραδιδοῦσα τὸ πᾶν τοῦτο ἀπὸ μὲν τῆς νυκτὸς ἡμέρᾳ, ἀπὸ ἡμέρας νυκτί.]]*

14 *μετὰ δὲ τούτους ἐστὶν ἄλλος χορὸς ἀστέρων, οὓς ἡμεῖς ⟨⟨μὲν⟩⟩ προσηγοριῶν οὐ κατηξιώσαμεν· οἱ δὲ μεθ' ἡμᾶς [μιμησάμενοι] ⟨ἐσόμενοι⟩ [[μὲν]] καὶ ⟨τ⟩ούτοι⟨ς⟩ προσηγορίας [τούτοις] θήσονται.*

15 *κάτωθεν δὲ τῆς σελήνης εἰσὶν ἕτεροι ἀστέρες φθαρτοί, ἀργοί, πρὸς ὀλίγον χρόνον συνιστάμενοι, εἰς τὸν ὑπὲρ γῆς ἀέρα ἐξ αὐτῆς τῆς γῆς ἀναθυμιώμενοι, οὓς καὶ ἡμεῖς ὁρῶμεν διαλυομένους. ⟨οὗτοι⟩ τὴν φύσιν ὁμοίαν ἔχουσι τοῖς ἀχρήστοις τῶν ἐπὶ γῆς ζῴων, ⟨ὅσα⟩ ἐπὶ ἕτερον [δὲ] οὐδὲν γίνεται ἢ ἵνα μόνον φθαρῇ, οἷον τὸ τῶν μυιῶν γένος καὶ τῶν ψυλλῶν καὶ τῶν σκωλήκων καὶ τῶν ἄλλων τῶν ὁμοίων. καθ⟨άπερ⟩ γὰρ ἐκεῖνα, ὦ Τάτ, οὔτε ἡμῖν οὔτε τῷ κόσμῳ χρήσιμά ἐστι, τοὐναντίον δὲ λυπεῖ ἐνοχλοῦντα, παρακολουθήματα ὄντα τῆς φύσεως, καὶ κατὰ τὸ περισσὸν τὴν γένεσιν ἔχοντα, τὸν αὐτὸν τρόπον καὶ οἱ ἀπὸ τῆς γῆς ἀναθυμιώμενοι ἀστέρες τὸν μὲν ἄνω τόπον οὐ καταλαμβάνουσιν,—ἀδυνατοῦσι γάρ, ὡς κάτωθεν ἀνιόντες,—πολὺ δὲ ⟨τὸ⟩ ἐμβριθὲς ἔχοντες, ἑλκόμενοι κάτω ὑπὸ τῆς ἰδίας ὕλης διαχέονται ταχέως, καὶ διαλυθέντες πίπτουσι πάλιν εἰς γῆν, μηδὲν ἐνεργήσαντες ἢ μόνον ὀχλήσαντες τῷ ὑπὲρ γῆν ἀέρι.*

16 *ἕτερόν ἐστι γένος, ὦ Τάτ, τὸ τῶν καλουμένων κομητῶν, κατὰ καιρὸν ἐπιφαινομένων, καὶ πάλιν μετὰ χρόνον ὀλίγον ἀφανῶν γινομένων, μήτε ἀνατελλόντων μήτε δυνόντων μήτε διαλυομένων· οἵτινες φανεροὶ ἄγγελοι καὶ κήρυκες καθολικῶν ἀποτελεσμάτων γίνονται μελλόντων ἔσεσθαι. οὗτοι δὲ τὸν*

1 *μηδεὶς* Heeren : *μηδὲν* FP 3 *τῇ* add. Wachsm. | *ἐνεργείᾳ* Wachsm. : *ἐνέργειαν* FP | *αἱ* scripsi : *καὶ* codd. 6–12 § 13 (*ὑπὸ . . . νυκτί*) hinc

that there may be no place in heaven that is empty of stars; and they help to maintain the order of the universe, putting forth a force that is their own, but is subject to the force put forth by the six and thirty Decans. From the Liturgi come the destructions of other living beings[1] that take place in this or that region, and the swarming of creatures that spoil the crops.

And after the Liturgi comes another company of stars,[2] to 14
which we have not cared to give names; but the men that shall live after us will assign names to these also.

And below the moon are stars of another sort,[3] perishable and 15
inert, which are so composed as to last but for a little time, rising as exhalations from the earth itself into the air above the earth; and we can see their dissolution with our own eyes. These are of like nature to the animals on earth that are good for nothing and are produced only to be destroyed, as for instance the races of flies and fleas and worms and the like. For as those creatures, my son, are in no way serviceable either to us or to the Kosmos, but on the contrary, vex and annoy us, being by-products of nature, and things the production of which is superfluous, even so the stars which rise as exhalations from the earth do not attain to the region of heaven,—for they are not able to do that, because they rise from below,—and, as they have in them much heavy stuff, they are dragged down by their own matter, and are quickly dissipated, and being broken up, they fall down again to earth, having effected nothing except a troubling of the air above the earth.

And there are stars of another kind, my son, which are called 16
comets. They appear at their appointed times, and disappear again after a little while. They neither rise nor set, nor do they suffer dissolution. They come as visible messengers and heralds to announce destined events that are about to befall mankind

[1] 'Living beings other (than men)'; i.e. beasts.
[2] Perhaps, 'comes a crowd of other stars'.
[3] Viz. shooting stars or meteors.

transposui: vide post § 4 **13** *τούτους* scripsi: *ταύτην* codd. | *ἄλλος χορὸς* codd.: fortasse *ἄλλων ὄχλος* **15** *ἐσόμενοι* scripsi: *μιμησάμενοι* codd. | *τούτοις* (post *καὶ*) scripsi (*αὐτοῖς* Meineke): *αὐτοὶ* codd. **16** *τούτοις* (ante *θήσονται*) del. Meineke **20** *ἔχουσι* scripsi: *ἔχοντας* codd. **23** *καθάπερ* scripsi: *καὶ* codd. **24** *ἐκεῖναι* F **26** *τὸ* (post *κατὰ*) om. P **28–29** *ὡς κάτωθεν ἀνιόντες* secludendum? **29** *τὸ* add. Usener **31–32** Fortasse ⟨*ἐν*⟩*οχλήσαντες* **32** *ἀέρι* F: *ἀνδρὶ* P

τόπον ἔχουσιν ὑπὸ τὸν κύκλον τὸν τοῦ ἡλίου. ἐπὰν οὖν μέλλῃ τι τῷ κόσμῳ συμβαίνειν, οὗτοι φαίνονται, ⟨καὶ⟩ φανέντες ὀλίγας ἡμέρας, πάλιν ὑπὸ τὸν κύκλον ἐλθόντες τοῦ ἡλίου ἀφανεῖς μένουσιν, ἐν τῷ ἀπηλιώτῃ φανέντες ⟨ἄλλοι⟩, ἄλλοι δὲ ἐν τῷ βορρᾷ, ἄλλοι δὲ ἐν τῷ λιβί, ἄλλοι δὲ ἐν τῷ νότῳ. μάντεις δὲ τούτους προσηγορεύσαμεν. [καὶ ἀστέρων ⌜ἤδε⌝ φύσις.]

17 [ἀστέρες δὲ ἄστρων διαφορὰν ἔχουσιν· ἀστέρες μὲν γάρ εἰσιν οἱ ἐν τῷ οὐρανῷ αἰωρούμενοι, ἄστρα δὲ τὰ ἐγκείμενα ἐν τῷ σώματι τοῦ οὐρανοῦ, συμφερόμενα δὲ [ἐν] τῷ οὐρανῷ· ἐξ ὧν δώδεκα ζῴδια προσηγορεύσαμεν.]

* * * * *

18 ὁ ταῦτα μὴ ἀγνοήσας ἀκριβῶς δύναται νοῆσαι τὸν θεόν, εἰ
δὲ καὶ τολμήσαντα δεῖ εἰπεῖν, καὶ αὐτόπτης γενόμενος
θεάσασθαι, καὶ θεασάμενος μακάριος γενέσθαι.—Μακάριος
ὡς ἀληθῶς, ὦ πάτερ, ὁ τοῦτον θεασάμενος.—Ἀλλ' ἀδύνατον,
ὦ τέκνον, τὸν ἐν σώματι τούτου εὐτυχῆσαι· δεῖ δὲ προγυμνά-
ζειν αὑτοῦ τινα τὴν ψυχὴν ἐνθάδε, ἵνα ἐκεῖ γενομένη, ὅπου
19 αὐτὸν ἔξεστι θεάσασθαι, ὁδοῦ μὴ σφαλῇ. ὅσοι δὲ ἄνθρωποι
φιλοσώματοί εἰσιν, οὗτοι οὐκ ἂν ποτε θεάσαιντο τὴν τοῦ
καλοῦ καὶ ἀγαθοῦ ὄψιν. οἷον γάρ ἐστι κάλλος, ὦ τέκνον, τὸ
⟨τοῦ⟩ μήτε σχῆμα μήτε χρῶμα [μήτε σῶμα] ἔχον⟨τος⟩.—Εἴη
δ' ἄν τι, ὦ πάτερ, χωρὶς τούτων καλόν;—Μόνος ὁ θεός, ὦ
τέκνον, μᾶλλον δὲ τὸ μεῖζόν τι ὂν ⌜τοῦ θεοῦ τὸ ὄνομα⌝.

EXCERPTUM VII

Stobaeus I. 3. 52, vol. i, p. 62 Wachsmuth (*Ecl.* I. 134 Heeren).

Ἑρμῆς.

1 δαίμων γάρ τις μεγίστη τέτακται, ὦ τέκνον, ἐν μέσῳ τοῦ παντὸς [εἱλουμένη], πάντα περ⟨ι⟩ορῶσα τὰ ἐπὶ γῆς γινόμενα ὑπὸ τῶν ἀνθρώπων. καθάπερ ⟨γὰρ⟩ ἐπὶ τῆς θείας τάξεως ⟨ἡ⟩ [πρόνοια καὶ] ἀνάγκη τέτακται, τὸν αὐτὸν τρόπον καὶ ἐπὶ τῶν

2 μέλλει F | καὶ add. Usener 3 φανέντας P 4 ἄλλοι (post φανέντες) add. Usener 5 ἄλλοι ter Heeren: ἄλλα ter codd. 8–11 ἀστέρες δὲ . . . προσηγορεύσαμεν seclusit Wachsmuth: 'antiquum glossema' Usener 10 ἐν del. Meineke 13–14 αὐτόπτης γενόμενος

in general. The comets have their abode below the circle of the sun.[1] When something is about to befall the world, they appear; and having appeared for a few days, they go back to their place below the circle of the sun, and abide invisible. Some of them appear in the East, some in the North, some in the West, and some in the South. We have named them 'prophet-stars'. [ ][2]

* * * * *

He who has not failed to get knowledge of these things is able 18
to form an exact conception of God; nay, if I am to speak boldly, he is able to see God with his own eyes, and having seen God, to be blest.—*Tat.* Blest indeed, father, is he who has seen God.—*Hermes.* But it is impossible, my son, for one who is yet in the body to attain to this happiness. A man must train his soul in this life, in order that, when it has entered the other world, where it is permitted to see God, it may not miss the way
⟨which leads to Him⟩. But men who love the body will never 19
see the vision of the Beautiful and Good. How glorious, my son, is the beauty of that which has neither shape nor colour![3] —*Tat.* But can there be anything, father, that is beautiful apart from shape and colour?—*Hermes.* God alone, my son, or rather, that which is too great to be called God.

EXCERPT VII

Hermes.

Hermes. For there is a mighty deity, my son, who is posted 1
in the midst of the universe, and watches over all things done on earth by men. For as Necessity has been set over the divine

[1] 'The circle of the sun' seems here to mean the sun-disk, i. e. the sun itself, and not the orbit or sphere of the sun.

[2] [§ 17. 'But *asteres* (stars) differ from *astra* (constellations). *Asteres* are those which float in heaven; but *astra* are those which are fixed in the body of heaven, and are borne along together with heaven; and twelve of the *astra* we have named Signs of the Zodiac'.]

[3] I.e. of the incorporeal.

---

et *θεασάμενος μακάριος* Wachsmuth : *αὐτόπτην γενόμενον* et *θεασάμενον μακάριον* FP **14** *μακάριος* (ante *ὡς*) Gaisford : *μακάριον* FP **18** *αὐτὸν* scripsi : *αὐτὴν* codd.

24 Lemma *ἑρμῆς* hic habet P^2: ad ultima verba antecedentis ex Herodoto eclogae adscriptum habent FP^1 **26** *περιορῶσα* Meineke : *περ ὁρῶσα* codd. **27** *γὰρ* add. Meineke | *ἡ* add. Heeren

ἀνθρώπων τέτακται ἡ δίκη [ταὐτὰ ἐκείνοις ἐνεργοῦσα].
2 ἐκείνη μὲν γὰρ κρατεῖ τὴν τάξιν τῶν [[ὄντων]] ⟨ἄνω⟩, ὡς θείων
⟨⟨ὄντων⟩⟩, καὶ ἁμαρτεῖν μὴ θελόντων μηδὲ δυναμένων·
ἀδύνατον γὰρ τὸ θεῖον πλανηθῆναι· [ἐξ οὗ καὶ τὸ ἀναμάρ-
τη⟨το⟩ν συμβαίνει·] ἡ δὲ δίκη τέτακται τιμωρὸς τῶν ἐπὶ γῆς
3 ἁμαρτανόντων. ἀνθρώπων γὰρ γένος ⟨ἁμαρτητικόν⟩, ἅτε
θνητὸν ὂν καὶ ἐκ κακῆς ὕλης συνεστός· [καὶ μάλιστα ἐκείνοις
συμβαίνει τὸ ὀλισθαίνειν, οἷς θεοπτικὴ δύναμις οὐ πρόσεστι·
τούτων δὲ καὶ μάλιστα ἐπικρατεῖ δίκη·] καὶ τῇ ⟨μὲν⟩ εἱμαρμένῃ ὑπόκειται διὰ τὰς τῆς γενέσεως ἐνεργείας, τῇ δὲ δίκῃ
διὰ τὰς ἐν τῷ βίῳ ἁμαρτίας.

EXCERPTUM VIII

Stobaeus I. 4. 8, vol. i, p. 73 Wachsmuth (*Ecl.* I. 160 Heeren)

Ἑρμοῦ πρὸς τὸν υἱόν.

1 Ὀρθῶς μοι πάντα εἶπας, ὦ πάτερ. ἀλλ' ἔτι με ἀνάμνησον τίνα ἐστὶ ⟨τῶν ἐν ἡμῖν ἀσωμάτων⟩ τὰ κατὰ πρόνοιαν, καὶ τίνα ⟨τὰ⟩ κατ' ἀνάγκην ὁμοίως, καὶ ⟨τὰ⟩ καθ' εἱμαρμένην.—

2 Ἔφην εἶναι ἐν ἡμῖν, ὦ Τάτ, τρία εἴδη ἀσωμάτων. καὶ τὸ μέν τι ἐστὶ νοητὸν ⟨. . .⟩. τοῦτο μὲν οὖν ἀχρώματον, ἀσχημάτιστον, [ἀσώματον,] ἐξ αὐτῆς τῆς πρώτης [καὶ] νοητῆς οὐσίας ⟨. . .⟩.

3 ἔστι δὲ [[καὶ]] ἐν ἡμῖν ⟨⟨καὶ⟩⟩ ⟨⟨ἕτερον εἶδος⟩⟩ ⟨ἀσωμάτων, . . .⟩. [τούτῳ ἐναντίαι σχηματότητες] [τοῦτο ὑποδέχεται.] τὸ γοῦν ⟨ἄλογον⟩, κινούμενον ὑπὸ τῆς νοητῆς οὐσίας, πρός τινα λόγον ⟨κινεῖται⟩, καὶ [ὑποδεχθὲν] ⟨οὕτω κινηθὲν⟩ εὐθέως μεταβάλλεται εἰς [[ἕτερον εἶδος]] [κινήσεως] [τοῦτο δὲ] εἴδωλόν [ἐσ]τι τοῦ νοήματος τοῦ δημιουργοῦ.

1 *ταῦτα* P 2 *ἐκείνη* Heeren: *ἐκεῖνα* FP 4–5 *ἀναμάρτητον* scripsi: *ἀναμαρτεῖν* codd. 6 *ἁμαρτητικόν* addidi (*ἁμαρτωλόν* add. Wachsm.) 7 *θνητῶν* P^1 | *συνεστὸς* F : *συνεστῶς* P 9 *ἐπικρατῇ* P 10 *ὑπόκειται* P: *ὑπόκεινται* F 15 *τὰ* (ante *κατ' ἀνάγκην*) add. Wachsmuth 16 *τὰτ* P^2 : *τὰ* FP^1 17 Fortasse *νοητὸν* ⟨*ἁπλῶς*⟩ vel ⟨*κυρίως*⟩ 19 Fortasse *οὐσίας* ⟨*προβεβλημένον*⟩ 20 *ἔστι* scripsi : *εἰσὶ* codd. 20–21 Fortasse ⟨*ἀσωμάτων, ἄλογον μέν, κινήσεως δὲ λογικῆς ὑποδεκτικόν*⟩ 22–23 *πρός τινα λόγον* F : *εἰσὶ δὲ καὶ ἐν ἡμῖν* P 25 *τι* scripsi : *ἔστι* codd.

order,[1] even so has Penal Justice been set over men. For 2
Necessity holds in her grasp the order of those above,[2] inasmuch as they are divine, and do not wish to err, and cannot err;—for it is impossible that that which is divine should go astray;—but Penal Justice has been appointed to punish those who err on earth. 3
For the human race is apt to err, because it is mortal, and is composed of evil matter; [ ][3] and men are subject to Destiny by reason of the forces at work in their birth, but are subject to Penal Justice by reason of their errors in the conduct of life.

EXCERPT VIII

A discourse of Hermes to his son.

Tat.[4] In all this, father, you have spoken rightly. But go on, 1
and tell me again what are the incorporeal things in us that are according to Providence, and likewise what are those that are according to Necessity, and those that are according to Destiny.—

Hermes. I told you, my son Tat, that there are in us three 2
kinds of incorporeals. The first of these[5] is apprehensible by thought alone . . . This is a thing without colour and without shape; it issues from nothing else than the primary intelligible substance.[6]

But there is also in us a second kind of incorporeal thing,[7] . . .[8] 3
For when the irrational part is moved by the intelligible substance,[9] it is moved rationally in some degree,[10] and being so moved, is at once transformed into an image of the Maker's thought.

[1] I.e. has been appointed to rule over the ordered system of the heavenly bodies. The stars *must* move as they do; they '*cannot* err'.

[2] I.e. the heavenly bodies.

[3] ['and the men most liable to slip are those who do not possess the power of seeing God; and on those men above all does Penal Justice lay her hold'].

[4] Excerpt VIII, as given in the manuscripts, is entirely meaningless. I have tried to make sense of it by freely altering the text.

[5] Viz. the mind,—that part of the soul in which reason resides.

[6] I.e. from God, or the divine Mind.

[7] Viz. that part of the soul in which the passions reside.

[8] Perhaps, 'which is in itself irrational, but is capable of being moved rationally'.

[9] I.e. by the mind.

[10] Literally, '⟨it is moved⟩ according to some reason'. And so again in § 6.

4 τρίτον δέ ἐστιν ⟨ἐν ἡμῖν⟩ εἶδος ἀσωμάτων, ὃ περὶ τὰ σώματά ἐστι συμβεβηκός. [τόπος, χρόνος, κίνησις, σχῆμα, ἐπιφάνεια, μέγεθος, εἶδος.] καὶ τούτων εἰσὶ διαφορα⟨ὶ⟩ δύο· ἃ μὲν γάρ ἐστιν αὐτῶν ἰδίως ποιά, ἃ δὲ τοῦ σώματος ⟨. . .⟩. τὰ μὲν ἰδίως ποιὰ ⌜τὸ σχῆμα, ἡ χρόα, τὸ εἶδος, ὁ τόπος, ὁ χρόνος, ἡ κίνησις⌝· τὰ δὲ τοῦ σώματος ⌜ἴδιά ἐστι τὸ ἐσχηματισμένον σχῆμα καὶ τὸ κεχρωσμένον χρῶμα, ἔστι δὲ καὶ ἡ μεμορφωμένη μορφὴ καὶ ἡ ἐπιφάνεια καὶ τὸ μέγεθος. ταῦτά ἐστι τούτων ἀμέτοχα.⌝

5 ἡ μὲν οὖν νοητὴ οὐσία, πρὸς ⟨μὲν⟩ τῷ θεῷ γενομένη, ἑαυτῆς ἐξουσίαν ἔχει, καὶ [τοῦ] σῴζει[ν] ⟨τὸ⟩ ἕτερον αὐτὴν σῴζουσα· ⌜ἔπειθ'⌝ αὐτὴ [ἡ] ⟨καθ' αὑτὴν⟩ οὖσα ὑπὸ ἀνάγκην οὐκ ἔστι[ν], ⟨⟨καὶ ἡ αἵρεσις αὐτῆς κατὰ πρόνοιαν⟩⟩ ⟨⟨γίνεται⟩⟩. ὑπολειφθεῖσα δὲ [ὑπὸ] τοῦ θεοῦ, αἱρε⟨ῖ⟩ται τὴν σωματικὴν φύσιν, [[καὶ ἡ αἵρεσις αὐτῆς κατὰ πρόνοιαν]] [τ]οὕτω δὲ ⟨τῇ⟩ τοῦ κόσμου ⟨ἀνάγκῃ ὑποπίπτει⟩ [[γίνεται]].

6 τὸ δὲ ἄλογον ⌜πᾶν⌝ ⟨. . .⟩ κινεῖται πρός τινα λόγον ⟨. . . .⟩

7 ⟨. . .⟩ καὶ ὁ μὲν λόγος κατὰ πρόνοιαν, τὸ δὲ ἄλογον κατ' ἀνάγκην, τὰ δὲ περὶ τὸ σῶμα συμβεβηκότα καθ' εἱμαρμένην. [καὶ] οὗτός ἐστιν ὁ λόγος τῶν κατὰ πρόνοιαν καὶ ⟨κατ'⟩ ἀνάγκην καὶ καθ' εἱμαρμένην.

EXCERPTUM IX

Stobaeus I. 11. 2, vol. i, p. 131 Wachsmuth (*Ecl.* I. 316 Heeren).

Ἑρμοῦ ἐκ τῶν πρὸς Τάτ.

1 Καὶ γέγονεν, ὦ τέκνον, ἡ ὕλη καὶ ⟨ἀεὶ⟩ ἦν. ὕλη γὰρ ἀγγεῖον γενέσεώς ἐστι· γένεσις δὲ ἐνεργείας τ⟨ρ⟩όπος τοῦ ἀγεν[ν]ήτου καὶ προόντος [τοῦ] θεοῦ. τὸ σπέρμα οὖν τῆς

1 ἀσώματον P 1-2 Fortasse ἃ περὶ τὸ σῶμά ἐστι συμβεβηκότα 3 διαφοραὶ Patr. : διάφορα FP 7 ἔστι δὲ codd. : ἔτι δὲ Usener 9 τούτων P : τούτῳ F 11 σῴζει scripsi : τοῦ σῴζειν codd. 11-12 αὐτὴν σῴζουσαν P[1] 12 ἔπειθ' FP : ἐπεί γ' Meineke 14 ὑποληφθεῖσα F | αἱρεῖται Meineke : αἴρεται P : αἴρεται F 15 οὕτω scripsi : τοῦτο codd. 17 Fortasse τὸ δὲ ἄλογον ⟨τῇ μὲν νοητῇ οὐσίᾳ πειθόμενον⟩ κινεῖται πρός τινα λόγον· ⟨μὴ πειθόμενον δὲ . . .⟩ 20 κατ' add. Wachsmuth.

23 ἡ ὕλη (ante γὰρ) P 24 ἀγγεῖον codd. : fortasse ἐκμαγεῖον (cf. Pl. *Tim.* 50 C) | τρόπος Heeren : τόπος FP 25 ἀγενήτου Wachsm. : ἀγεννήτου FP | τοῦ FP : del. P[2]

And there is in us a third kind of incorporeals also, namely, the attributes of our bodies. Of these there are two different classes. Those of the one class are qualities characteristic of the individual; those of the other class are . . . of the body.[1] The qualities characteristic of the individual are . . ; the . . . of the body are . . . 4

Now the intelligible substance,[2] if it has drawn near to God, has power over itself,[3] and in saving itself, it also saves the other part.[4] As long as it is by itself,[5] it is not subject to Necessity, and its choice is in accordance with Providence.[6] But if it falls away from God, it chooses the corporeal world, and in that way it becomes subject to Necessity, which rules over the Kosmos. 5

The irrational part of the soul[4] . . . is moved rationally in some degree, . . .[7] 6

. . .[8] And reason is according to Providence; that which is irrational is according to Necessity; and the attributes of the body are according to Destiny. This is my teaching concerning the things that are according to Providence, Necessity, and Destiny. 7

EXCERPT IX

An extract from the Discourses of Hermes to Tat.

Matter, my son, has come into being; but it also was always in being. For matter is a receptacle[9] in which the process of coming into being takes place; and that process is a mode of the working of God, who is without beginning, and was in being before the world began. Matter then has received from 1

1 Perhaps, 'are ⟨separable accidents⟩ of the body'.

2 I.e. the mind.

3 I.e. possesses free will.

4 I.e. that part of the soul in which the passions reside.

5 I.e. as long as it is not influenced or interfered with by the body and bodily things.

6 That is to say, the man's will is in harmony with God's will.

7 Perhaps, 'The irrational part of the soul, ⟨if it is obedient to the intelligible substance (i.e. to the rational part of the soul),⟩ is moved rationally in some degree, ⟨and is thereby brought into accord with Providence; but if it is not obedient to the intelligible substance, it is subject to Necessity.⟩'

8 Between § 6 and § 7 there must have been a passage, now lost, in which 'the attributes of the body' were spoken of.

9 Perhaps, 'a plastic mass'.

2 γενέσεως ⟨ἀπὸ τοῦ θεοῦ⟩ λα[μ]β[αν]οῦσα γέγονε. καὶ τρεπτὴ ἐγένετο, καὶ ἰδέας ἔ[ι]χε⟨ι πολλάς, ποικίλως⟩ μορφοποιουμένη· ἐφέστηκε γὰρ αὐτῇ τρεπομένῃ ἡ ⟨τοῦ θεοῦ ἐνέργεια⟩, τεχνιτεύουσα τὰς τῆς τροπῆς ἰδέας. ἀγεν[ν]ησία οὖν ⟨⟨ἡ⟩⟩ τῆς ὕλης ἀμορφία ἦν, [[ἡ]] [[δὲ]] γένεσις ⟨⟨δὲ⟩⟩ τὸ ἐνεργεῖσθαι.

EXCERPTUM X

Stobaeus I. 8. 41, vol. i, p. 104 Wachsmuth (*Ecl.* I. 254 Heeren).

Ἑρμοῦ ἐκ τῶν πρὸς Τάτ.

1 . . . ⌜ὡς καὶ⌝ περὶ τῶν τριῶν χρόνων ⌜εὑρεῖν⌝. οὔτε γὰρ
καθ' ἑαυτούς εἰσιν οὔτε συνήνωνται· καὶ πάλιν, ⟨καὶ⟩ συν-
ήνωνται καὶ καθ' ἑαυτούς εἰσιν.
2 ἐὰν ⟨μὲν γὰρ⟩ χωρὶς εἶναι τοῦ παρεληλυθότος ὑπολάβῃς
τὸν ἐνεστῶτα ⟨καὶ τοῦ ἐνεστῶτος τὸν μέλλοντα, . . .⟩.
ἀδύνατον ⟨γάρ⟩ ἐστι ⟨τὸν⟩ [σ]ἐνεστῶτα ⟨γενέσθαι⟩ εἰ μὴ καὶ
⟨ὁ⟩ παρεληλυθὼς γένηται, ⟨καὶ τὸν μέλλοντα, εἰ μὴ καὶ ὁ
ἐνεστώς·⟩ ἐκ γὰρ τοῦ ἀποιχομένου τὸ [σ]ἐνεστὸς γίνεται, καὶ
3 ἐκ τοῦ ἐνεστῶτος τὸ μέλλον [ἔρχεται]. [[εἰ δὲ δεῖ . . .
4 ἑστάναι δυνάμενος;]] καὶ [πάλιν] ὁ παρεληλυθὼς συνάπτων
τῷ ἐνεστῶτι, καὶ ὁ ἐνεστὼς τῷ μέλλοντι, εἷς γίνεται [[οὐ γὰρ
χωρὶς αὐτῶν εἰσι]] [τῇ ταυτότητι καὶ τῇ ἑνότητι καὶ] τῇ
συνεχείᾳ. ⟨⟨οὐκ ἄρ⟨α⟩ χωρὶς ⟨ἑ⟩αυτῶν εἰσι⟨ν⟩.⟩⟩
5 ⟨ἐὰν δὲ συνηνῶσθαι ὑπολάβῃς, ...⟩ οὕτω [καὶ συνεχὴς
καὶ] διεστὼς γίνεται, εἷς ὢν καὶ ὁ αὐτός, ⟨ὁ⟩ χρόνος.
3 ⟨⟨εἰ δὲ δεῖ καὶ ἐπὶ πλέον βασανίσαι, οὕτω λογισώμεθα·

1 λαβοῦσα scripsi: λαμβάνουσα codd. 2 ἔχει scripsi: εἶχε FP 3 τοῦ θεοῦ ἐνέργεια addidi ('fortasse addendum εἱμαρμένη' Wachsm.) 4 ἀγενησία Wachsm.: ἀγεννησία FP 4–5 Fortasse ἀγενησία οὖν τῇ ὕλῃ ἡ ἀμορφία ἦν

6 'Haec tam distant ab Hermeticis scriptis, ut nullus dubitem intercidisse Hermetis locum et lemma (fort. etiam initium) huius eclogae' Wachsmuth 7 ὡς P: 's et antea spat. 5 litt. F | παρὰ F | ὡς κἂν . . . εὕροις Usener 7–9 Fortasse οὔτε γὰρ καθ' ἑαυτούς εἰσιν, ⟨ἀλλὰ⟩ [οὔτε] συνήνωνται, καὶ πάλιν, ⟨οὐ⟩ συνήνωνται, ⟨ἀλλὰ⟩ [καὶ] καθ' ἑαυτούς εἰσιν 10 μὲν γὰρ addidi (γὰρ add. Heeren) 12 τὸν ἐνεστῶτα γενέσθαι scripsi: συνεστάναι FP²: συνιστάναι P¹ 12–13 εἰ μὴ . . . γένοιτο Wachsm.: fortasse ἐὰν μὴ . . . γένηται 13 παρεληλυθὸς F 14 ἐνεστὸς scripsi (ἐνεστὼς Heeren): συνεστὸς F: συνεστὼς P 15 ἔρχεται codd.: ἔχεται Usener 15–16 § 3 (εἰ . . . δυνάμενος) hinc transposui: vide post

God the germ from which has sprung its coming-into-being,[1]
and has thereby come into being. And it came into being as 2
a thing that is mutable; and it takes many forms, being fashioned
into various shapes; for in passing through its changes it is
governed by God's working, which fabricates the forms taken
by it in the course of its mutation. In respect of its formlessness
then, matter was without beginning; but in respect of God's
working on it, it has come into being.

EXCERPT X

An extract from the Discourses of Hermes to Tat.

. . . concerning the three times[2] . . . For they are neither 1
independent of one another nor united with one another; and
again, they are both united and independent.[3]

If you suppose the present time to be separate from the past 2
time ⟨and the future from the present, you will find yourself in
a difficulty. For⟩ it is impossible for the present to come into
being unless the past also has come into being, ⟨and for the
future to come into being unless the present has;⟩ for the present
issues from the past, and the future from the present. And 4
inasmuch as the past joins on to the present, and the present
to the future, they are made one by their continuity. They are
therefore not separate from one another.

⟨On the other hand, if you suppose them to be united with 5
one another, you will again find yourself in a difficulty . . .[4]⟩.
Thus it appears that, though time is one and the same throughout,
its parts are separate.

If we are to investigate the matter yet further, let us reason 3

[1] Or, 'the germ from which spring all things that come into being'.

[2] I.e. past time, present time, and future time.

[3] Perhaps, 'For they are not independent, but are united with one another; and again (in another sense) they are not united, but are independent'.

[4] Here must have followed a passage, now lost, in which reasons were given for saying that the three times are not 'united'.

---

§ 5 18 τῇ (ante συνεχείᾳ) om. P 19 οὐκ ἄρα scripsi : οὐ γὰρ codd. | ἑαυτῶν scripsi (αὐτῶν Usener) : αὐτῶν FP

τὸν μὲν παρεληλυθότα χρόνον ⌜οἴχεσθαι εἰς τὸ μηκέτι [οἴχεσθαι εἰς τὸ μηκέτι] εἶναι τοῦτον⌝, τὸν δὲ μέλλοντα μὴ ὑπάρχειν, ἐν τῷ μηδέπω παρεῖναι· ἀλλὰ μηδὲ τὸν ἐνεστῶτα ⌜συμπαρεῖναι⌝, ἐν τῷ ⟨μὴ⟩ μένειν. ὃς γὰρ οὐχ ἕστηκε⟨ν⟩ [[ῥοπήν]], ἔχων οὐδὲ κέντρου μονήν [χρόνου], πῶς ἐνεστὼς εἶναι λέγεται, ὁ μηδὲ ⟨⟨ῥοπὴν⟩⟩ ἑστάναι δυνάμενος;⟩⟩

EXCERPTUM XI

Stobaeus I. 41. I (b), vol. i, p. 274 Wachsmuth (*Ecl.* I. 702 Heeren).

1 νῦν δέ, ὦ τέκνον, ⟨ἐν⟩ κεφαλαίοις [τὰ ὄντα] ⟨πάντα⟩ διεξελεύσομαι· νοήσεις γὰρ τὰ λεγόμενα, μεμνημένος ὧν ἤκουσας.

2 (1) πάντα τὰ [ὄντα] ⟨σώματα⟩ κινεῖται· μόνον τὸ [μὴ ὄν] ⟨ἀσώματον⟩ ἀκίνητον.

(2) πᾶν σῶμα μεταβλητόν· οὐ πᾶν σῶμα διαλυτόν. [ἔνια τῶν σωμάτων διαλυτά.]

(3) ⌜οὐ πᾶν ζῷον θνητόν· οὐ πᾶν ζῷον ἀθάνατον⌝.

(4) τὸ διαλυτὸν φθαρτόν· [[τὸ]] μόνον ⟨⟨τὸ⟩⟩ ἀδιάλυτον ἀίδιον.

(5) τὸ ἀεὶ γινόμενον ἀεὶ καὶ φθείρεται, τὸ δὲ ἅπαξ γενόμενον οὐδέποτε φθείρεται [οὐδὲ ἄλλο τι γίνεται].

(6) πρῶτον ὁ θεός, δεύτερον ὁ κόσμος, τρίτον ὁ ἄνθρωπος.

(7) ⌜ὁ κόσμος διὰ τὸν ἄνθρωπον, ὁ δὲ ἄνθρωπος διὰ τὸν θεόν⌝.

[[(8) ψυχῆς τὸ μὲν αἰσθητὸν θνητόν, τὸ δὲ λογικὸν ἀθάνατον.]]

(9) [πᾶσα οὐσία ἀθάνατος·] πᾶσα οὐσία μεταβλητή· ⟨οὐ πᾶσα οὐσία φθαρτή.⟩

1–3 Fortasse τὸν μὲν παρεληλυθότα χρόνον ⟨⟨μὴ ὑπάρχειν⟩⟩ ⟨δῆλον ἐν τῷ⟩ οἴχεσθαι ⟨καὶ⟩ [εἰς τὸ] μηκέτι ⟨παρ⟩εῖναι τοῦτον, τὸν δὲ μέλλοντα [[μὴ ὑπάρχειν]], ἐν τῷ μηδέπω παρεῖναι 2 οἴχεσθαι εἰς τὸ μηκέτι bis scriptum FP: corr. edd. | τοῦτον del. Usener 4 συμπαρεῖναι codd.: fortasse ὑπάρχειν ἀπ⟨αρτιζόντως⟩ 5 χρόνου seclusit Wachsm.
7 Fortasse ⟨πρότερον μέν, ⟨⟨ὦ τέκνον,⟩⟩ διὰ πλειόνων λόγων ἐδίδαξά σε·⟩ νῦν δὲ [[ὦ τέκνον]] | ἐν add. Usener 12–13 ἔνια . . . διαλυτά seclusit Wachsm. 14 Fortasse [οὐ] πᾶν ζῷον γενητόν, οὐ πᾶν ζῷον θνητόν 15 μόνον τὸ ἀδιάλυτον scripsi: τὸ μένον ἀμετάβλητον codd. | Post ἀμετά-

as follows. The past time has departed, so that it no longer is; and the future is not in existence, in that it has not yet arrived.[1] And even the present is not . . .,[2] in that it does not abide. For seeing that the present does not stand fast, and does not abide even for an instant, how can it be said to be 'present', when it cannot stand fast for one moment?[3]

EXCERPT XI

Hermes. ⟨Hitherto, I have given you instruction by means 1
of numerous discourses;⟩ but now, my son, I will sum up in brief sentences all that I have taught you. You will understand what I say, if you bear in mind what you have been told before.

(1) All bodies are moved; only that which is incorporeal is 2
motionless.

(2) All bodies are subject to change; but not all bodies are dissoluble.

(3) . . .[4]

(4) That which is dissoluble is destructible; only that which is indissoluble is everlasting.

(5) That which is ever coming into being is ever being destroyed, but that which has come into being once for all is never destroyed.

(6) God is first; the Kosmos is second; Man is third.

(7) . . .[5]

(9) Everything that exists[6] is subject to change; ⟨but not everything that exists is destructible.⟩

[1] Perhaps, 'That the past time is not in existence, is shown by the fact that it has departed and is no longer here; and that the future is not in existence, is shown by the fact that it has not yet arrived'.

[2] Perhaps, 'is not exactly in existence', i. e. cannot, strictly speaking, be said to be in existence.

[3] Literally, 'how is it said to be "standing in", when it cannot stand even for a moment?'

[4] Perhaps, 'Every living being has come into being; but not every living being is mortal'.

[5] Perhaps, 'The Kosmos has been made by God, and Man has been made by means of the Kosmos'.

[6] I.e. every *material* thing, or body.

βλητον add. *τὸ ἀμετάβλητον* P[2] **17–18** *γενόμενον* scripsi : *γινόμενον* codd. **20–21** Fortasse *ὁ κόσμος ὑπὸ τοῦ θεοῦ, ὁ δὲ ἄνθρωπος διὰ τοῦ κόσμου* **22–23** Sententiam (8) hinc transposui : vide post sententiam (11)

(10) πᾶν τὸ ὂν κινητόν· οὐδὲ⟨ν⟩ τῶν ὄντων ἕστηκεν.

(11) οὐ πάντα [ψυχῇ] κινεῖται, πᾶν δὲ ⟨τὸ κινούμεν⟩ον ψυχῇ κινεῖ⟨ται⟩.

⟨⟨(8) ψυχῆς τὸ μὲν αἰσθητ⟨ικ⟩ὸν θνητόν, τὸ δὲ λογικὸν ἀθάνατον.⟩⟩

(12) [πᾶν τὸ πάσχον αἴσθεται·] πᾶν τὸ αἰσθ⟨αν⟩όμενον πάσχει· ⟨μόνος⟩ ⟨⟨ὁ νοῦς ἀπαθής.⟩⟩

(13) πᾶν τὸ λυπούμενον καὶ ἥδεται [ζῷον θνητόν]· οὐ πᾶν τὸ ἡδόμενον λυπεῖται [ζῷον ἀίδιον].

(14) οὐ πᾶν σῶμα νοσεῖ· πᾶν σῶμα νοσοῦν διαλυτόν.

(15) ὁ νοῦς ἐν τῷ θεῷ· [ὁ λογισμὸς ἐν τῷ ἀνθρώπῳ·] ὁ λόγος ἐν τῷ νοΐ. [[ὁ νοῦς ἀπαθής.]]

(16) οὐδ[ε]ὲν σωματι⟨κὸν⟩ ἀληθές· ⟨μόν⟩ον ⟨⟨τὸ⟩⟩ ἀσώματον [[τὸ]] [πᾶν] ἀψευδές.

(17) πᾶν τὸ γενόμενον μεταβλητόν· οὐ πᾶν τὸ γενόμενον φθαρτόν.

(18) οὐδὲν ἀγαθὸν ἐπὶ τῆς γῆς· οὐδὲν κακὸν ἐν τῷ οὐρανῷ.

(19) ὁ θεὸς ἀγαθός· ὁ ἄνθρωπος κακός.

(20) τὸ ἀγαθὸν ἑκούσιον· τὸ κακὸν ἀκούσιον.

(21) οἱ θεοὶ τὰ ἀγαθὰ αἱροῦνται· ⟨οἱ ἄνθρωποι τὰ κακὰ αἱροῦνται⟩ ὡς ἀγαθά.

(22) ⌜ἡ εὐνομία μεγάλη εὐνομία ἡ εὐνομία ὁ νόμος.⌝

(23) ⌜θεῖος χρόνος νόμος ἀνθρώπινος.⌝

(24) ⌜κακία κόσμου τρυφὴ χρόνος ἀνθρώπου φθορά⌝.

(25) πᾶν ⟨τὸ⟩ ἐν οὐρανῷ ἀμετάθετον· πᾶν τὸ ἐπὶ γῆς μεταθετόν.

(26) οὐδὲν ἐν οὐρανῷ δοῦλον· οὐδὲν ἐπὶ γῆς ἐλεύθερον.

1 τὸ ὂν . . . τῶν ὄντων codd.: fortasse σῶμα . . . τῶν σωμάτων | κινητόν scripsi : διττόν codd. | οὐδὲν P[2] : οὐδὲ FP[1] 2 ψυχῇ Canter : ψυχὴ FP | τὸ κινούμενον scripsi : ὂν codd. 2–3 Fortasse : [οὐ . . . κινεῖται] πᾶν [δὲ] τὸ κινούμενον ψυχῇ κινεῖται 3 ψυχῇ κινεῖται Canter : ψυχὴ κινεῖ codd. 4 αἰσθητικὸν Meineke : αἰσθητὸν codd. 6 αἰσθανόμενον scripsi : αἰσθόμενον codd. 7 ὁ νοῦς ἀπαθής huc a sententia (15) transposui 8–9 ζῷον θνητόν et ζῷον ἀίδιον seclusit Wachsm. | Fortasse [οὐ] πᾶν τὸ ἡδόμενον ⟨καὶ⟩ λυπεῖται 8–10 Sententiae (13) et (14): fortasse πᾶν τὸ λυπούμενον [ ] νοσεῖ· πᾶν σῶμα (vel πᾶν τὸ) νοσοῦν διαλυτόν 13 οὐδὲν σωματικὸν scripsi : οὐδὲ ἐν σώματι FP[1] : οὐδὲν ἐν σώματι P[2] | μόνον τὸ ἀσώματον scripsi : ἐν ἀσωμάτῳ τὸ πᾶν codd. 15 μεταβλητόν . . . γενόμενον om. P 18 ὁ δὲ θεὸς F 19 ἑκούσιον (post κακὸν) P[1] 20–21 'post ὡς ἀγαθὰ Meinekio addendum videtur οἱ ἄνθρωποι τὰ κακὰ αἱροῦνται ὡς ἀγαθά', Wachsm. 22–24 Fortasse (22) ἡ εὐνομία μετὰ θεοῦ ὁμόνοια· ἡ ἀνομία ⟨πρὸς θεὸν ἔρις⟩. (23) νόμος θεῖος ἀρετή· νόμος ἀνθρώπινος κακία (vel νόμος θεῖος εὐνομία· νόμος ἀνθρώπινος ἀνομία). (24) ὁ χρόνος κόσμου στροφή· ὁ χρόνος ἀνθρώπου φθορά 22 μεγάλη F : μεγάλου P : μετὰ θεοῦ Meineke | εὐνομία (post μεγάλη) codd. : ὁμόνοια Usener | ἡ εὐνομία

(10) Everything that is, is movable; nothing that is stands fast.[1]

(11) Not all things are moved; but[2] everything that is moved is moved by soul.

(8) The sensitive part of the soul is mortal; but the rational part of the soul is immortal.

(12) Everything that has sensation is passively affected;[3] mind alone is free from passive affections.[4]

(13) Everything that feels pain feels pleasure also; but not everything that feels pleasure feels pain.[5]

(14) Not all bodies are diseased; but all bodies that are diseased are dissoluble.[6]

(15) Mind is in God; and reason[7] is in mind.

(16) Nothing that is corporeal is real; only that which is incorporeal is devoid of illusion.

(17) Everything that has come into being is subject to change; but not everything that has come into being is destructible.

(18) There is nothing good on earth; there is nothing bad in heaven.

(19) God is good; man is bad.

(20) The good is voluntary; the bad is involuntary.

(21) The gods choose the things that are good; men choose the things that are bad, thinking them to be good.

(22) . . .

(23) . . .

(24) . . .[8]

(25) Everything in heaven is unalterable; everything on earth is alterable.

(26) Nothing in heaven is in bondage; nothing on earth is free.

[1] Perhaps, 'All bodies are movable; no bodies stand fast'.

[2] Possibly 'Not all . . . but' ought to be struck out.

[3] Or 'is disturbed by passion'.

[4] Or 'disturbing passions'.

[5] Perhaps, 'and everything that feels pleasure feels pain also'.

[6] Possibly (13) and (14) have grown out of a single aphorism, which might be restored thus: 'Everything that feels pain is diseased; and everything that is diseased is dissoluble'.

[7] Or 'speech'.

[8] Perhaps, (22) 'Obedience to law is unanimity with God; lawlessness ⟨is strife against God⟩'. (23) 'God's law is virtue; man's law is vice'. (24) 'For the Kosmos, time is revolving movement; for man, time is destruction.'

(ante *ὁ νόμος*) codd.: *ἡ ἀνομία* Heeren 24 *τρυφὴ* FP: *τροφὴ* Canter
25 *τὸ* (ante *ἐν οὐρανῷ*) add. Meineke

(27) οὐδὲν ἄγνωστον ἐν οὐρανῷ· οὐδὲν γνώριμον ἐπὶ τῆς γῆς.

(28) οὐ κοινωνεῖ ⟨τὰ ἐν οὐρανῷ τοῖς ἐπὶ γῆς· κοινωνεῖ⟩ τὰ ἐπὶ γῆς τοῖς ἐν οὐρανῷ.

(29) πάντα τὰ ἐν οὐρανῷ ἄμωμα· πάντα τὰ ἐπὶ γῆς ἐπίμωμα.

(30) ⸢τὸ ἀθάνατον οὐ θνητόν· τὸ θνητὸν οὐκ ἀθάνατον.⸣

(31) τὸ σπαρὲν οὐ πάντως [γ]θνητόν, τὸ δὲ [γ]θνητὸν πάντως καὶ σπαρέν.

(32) διαλυτοῦ σώματος δύο χρόνοι, ὁ ⸢ἀπὸ τῆς σπορᾶς μέχρι τῆς γενέσεως⸣ καὶ ὁ ⸢ἀπὸ τῆς γενέσεως μέχρι τοῦ θανάτου⸣· [τοῦ] ἀιδίου σώματος χρόνος ⸢ἐκ τῆς γενέσεως⸣ μόνος.

(33) τὰ διαλυτὰ σώματα αὔξεται καὶ μειοῦται· ⟨τὰ ἀίδια σώματα . . .⟩.

(34) ἡ διαλυτὴ ⸢ὕλη⸣ εἰς τὰ ἐναντία ἐναλλοιοῦται [φθορὰν καὶ γένεσιν], ἡ δὲ ἀίδιος [ἢ εἰς αὐτὴν ἢ] εἰς τὰ ὅμοια.

(35) γένεσις [ἀνθρώπου] φθορᾶ⟨ς⟩, φθορὰ [ἀνθρώπου] γενέσεως ἀρχή.

(36) τὸ ἀπογιγνόμενον ⟨καὶ ἐπιγίγνεται· τὸ ἐπιγιγνόμενον⟩ καὶ ἀπογίγνεται.

(37) τῶν ὄντων τὰ μὲν [ἐν] σώματά ἐστι, τὰ δὲ [ἐν] ἰδέαι[ς], τὰ δὲ ἐνέργειαι[ς]· [σῶμα δὲ] [ἐν ἰδίαις] ἰδέα δὲ καὶ ἐνέργεια, ⟨ἀσώματα ὄντα,⟩ ἐν σώματί ἐστι.

(38) τὸ ἀθάνατον οὐ μετέχει τοῦ θνητοῦ, τὸ δὲ θνητὸν τοῦ ἀθανάτου μετέχει.

(39) τὸ μὲν θνητὸν εἰς ἀθάνατον σῶμα οὐκ ἔρχεται, τὸ δὲ ἀθάνατον εἰς θνητὸν ⟨σῶμα⟩ παραγίνεται.

3 τὰ ἐν . . . κοινωνεῖ add. Wachsm. 7 οὐ θνητόν codd.: fortasse οὐ παθητόν 8 θνητόν . . . θνητὸν scripsi: γεννητόν . . . γεννητὸν codd. 10–15 Fortasse, inverso sententiarum ordine: (33) τὰ διαλυτὰ σώματα αὔξεται καὶ μειοῦται· ⟨τὰ ἀίδια σώματα οὔτε αὔξεται οὔτε μειοῦται (vel τὰ ἀ. σ. τὴν ταυτότητα σώζει)⟩. (32) διαλυτοῦ σώματος δύο χρόνοι, ὁ τῆς αὐξήσεως καὶ ὁ τῆς μειώσεως· ἀιδίου σώματος χρόνος ὁ τῆς ταυτότητος μόνος. Post ὁ τῆς αὐξήσεως additum puta glossema ὁ ἀπὸ τῆς σπορᾶς (ἤτοι γενέσεως) μέχρι τῆς τελειότητος: post ὁ τῆς μειώσεως additum glossema ὁ ἀπὸ τῆς τελειότητος μέχρι τοῦ θανάτου 11–12 μέχρι τοῦ ἀθανάτου P[1] 16 ὕλη codd.: fortasse οὐσία 16–17 φθορὰν καὶ γένεσιν seclusit Wachsm. 17 αὐτὴν FP: αὑτὴν Wachsm. 18 φθορᾶς (ante φθορὰ) 'sic ut vid. P corr.' Wachsm.: φθορὰ FP 20 καὶ . . . ἐπιγιγνόμενον add. Heeren 22 σώματά ἐστι scripsi: ἐν σώμασίν εἰσι codd. | ἰδέαι scripsi: ἐν ἰδέαις Canter: ἐν ἰδίαις FP 23 ἐνέργειαι scripsi: ἐνεργείαις codd. | ἰδέα Heeren: ἰδία FP 23–24 Fortasse ἰδέαι δὲ καὶ ἐνέργειαι, ⟨ἀσώματοι οὖσαι,⟩ ἐν σώμασίν εἰσι 27 μὲν (ante θνητὸν) F: δὲ P

(27) Nothing is unknown[1] in heaven; nothing is known[2] on earth.

(28) The things in heaven have no communion with the things on earth; but the things on earth have communion with the things in heaven.

(29) All things in heaven are without blemish; all things on earth are marred by blemishes.

(30) . . .[3]

(31) That which has been generated is not in all cases mortal; but that which is mortal is in all cases a thing that has been generated.

(32) A dissoluble body has two times, namely, . . . and . . .; an everlasting body has only one time, namely, . . .

(33) Dissoluble bodies increase and diminish; ⟨everlasting bodies . . .⟩.[4]

(34) . . .[5]

(35) Coming into being is the beginning of destruction, and destruction is the beginning of coming into being.

(36) That which goes out of being also comes into being; and that which comes into being also goes out of being.

(37) Of the things that are, some are bodies, some are forms, and some are forces. Forms and forces are incorporeal things, but are in bodies.

(38) That which is immortal has no part in that which is mortal; but that which is mortal has part in that which is immortal.

(39) That which is mortal does not go into an immortal body; but that which is immortal enters into a mortal body.

[1] Or 'unknowable'.

[2] Or 'knowable'.

[3] Perhaps, 'That which is immortal is not subject to passive affections (or disturbing passions); only that which is mortal is passively affected (or is disturbed by passion)'.

[4] Perhaps, (33) 'Dissoluble bodies increase and diminish; everlasting bodies neither increase nor diminish'. (32) 'A dissoluble body has two times, namely, the time during which it is increasing, and the time during which it is diminishing; an everlasting body has only one time, namely, the time of its uniform existence'.

[5] Possibly, 'Dissoluble things are changed into their opposites' (i. e. into indissoluble things, viz. the elements); 'everlasting things are changed into things like themselves' (i. e. into other everlasting things). The latter statement might be taken to mean that each of the elements is, part by part, transmuted into other elements.

(40) αἱ ἐνέργειαι οὐκ εἰσὶν ἀνωφερεῖς, ἀλλὰ κατωφερεῖς.

(41) οὐδὲν ὠφελεῖτα⟨ι⟩ [[ἐπὶ γῆς]] τὰ ἐν οὐρανῷ ⟨ἀπὸ τῶν⟩ ⟨⟨ἐπὶ γῆς⟩⟩· πάντα ὠφελεῖ⟨ται⟩ τὰ ἐπὶ γῆς ⟨ἀπὸ⟩ τῶ⟨ν⟩ ἐν οὐρανῷ.

(42) ὁ οὐρανὸς σωμάτων ἀιδίων δεκτικός· ἡ γῆ σωμάτων φθαρτῶν δεκτική.

(43) ἡ γῆ ἄλογος· ὁ οὐρανὸς λο⌐⟨ικ⟩ός.

(44) ⌜τὰ ἐν οὐρανῷ ὑπόκειται· τὰ ἐπὶ γῆς τῇ γῇ ἐπίκειται.⌝

(45) ὁ οὐρανὸς πρῶτον ⟨τῶν⟩ στοιχείων· ἡ γῆ ὕστατον ⟨τῶν⟩ στοιχείων.

(46) πρόνοια θεία τάξις· ἀνάγκη προνοίᾳ ὑπηρέτις.

(47) τύχη φορὰ ⟨ἄτακτος⟩· [ἀτάκτου ἐνεργείας ⟨προσηγορία⟩·] ⟨. . .⟩. [⌜εἴδωλον δόξα ψευδής⌝.]

(48) τί θεός; ἄτρεπτον, ἀγαθόν. τί ἄνθρωπος; [ἄ]τρεπτόν, κακόν.

3 τούτων τῶν κεφαλαίων μεμνημένος, καὶ ὧν σοι διὰ πλειόνων λόγων διεξῆλθον εὐκόλως ἀναμνησθήσῃ· ταῦτα γὰρ ἐκείνων εἰσὶ περιοχαί.

4 τὰς μέντοι πρὸς τοὺς πολλοὺς ὁμιλίας παραιτοῦ· φθονεῖν μὲν γάρ σε οὐ βούλομαι, μᾶλλον δὲ ὅτι τοῖς πολλοῖς δόξεις καταγέλαστος εἶναι. τὸ γὰρ ὅμοιον πρὸς τὸ ὅμοιον παραλαμβάνεται, ἀνόμοιος δὲ ἀνομοίῳ οὐδέποτε φίλος. οὗτοι δὲ οἱ λόγοι ὀλίγους παντελῶς τοὺς ἀκροατὰς ἕξουσιν ⟨ἀξίους⟩, ἢ

5 τάχα οὐδὲ τοὺς ὀλίγους [ἕξουσιν]. ἔχουσι δέ τι καὶ ἴδιον ἐν ἑαυτοῖς· τοὺς κακοὺς μᾶλλον παροξύνουσι πρὸς τὴν κακίαν. [διὸ χρὴ τοὺς πολλοὺς φυλάττεσθαι, ⟨ὡς⟩ μὴ νοοῦντας τῶν λεγομένων τὴν ἀρετήν.]—Πῶς εἶπας, ὦ πάτερ;—Οὕτως, ὦ τέκνον. [πᾶν] τὸ ζῷον ⟨τὸ⟩ τῶν ἀνθρώπων ἐπιρρεπέστερόν ἐστιν εἰς τὴν κακίαν· καὶ ⟨γὰρ⟩ ταύτῃ σύντροφον γίγνεται, διὸ καὶ ἥδεται αὐτῇ. τοῦτο δὲ τὸ ζῷον ἐὰν μάθῃ ὅτι γενητὸς ὁ κόσμος, καὶ ⟨ὅτι⟩ πάντα κατὰ [πρόνοιαν καὶ] ἀνάγκην

2 ὠφελεῖται scripsi: ὠφελεῖ τὰ ἐπὶ γῆς codd. 3 ὠφελεῖται scripsi: ὠφελεῖ codd. | ἀπὸ τῶν scripsi: τὰ codd. 6 φθαρτῶν P: φθαρτικῶν F 7 λογικός P²: λοξός FP¹ 8–9 γῇ ὑπόκειται P¹ | Fortasse τὰ ἐν οὐρανῷ ⟨προνοίᾳ⟩ ὑπόκειται· τὰ ἐπὶ γῆς [τῇ γῇ] ⟨ἀνάγκῃ⟩ ὑπόκειται (vide sententiam (46)) 10–11 τῶν στοιχείων bis scripsi: στοιχεῖον bis codd. 14 Fortasse ⟨τέχνη ἐνέργεια εὔτακτος⟩ 15–16 τρεπτὸν Usener: ἄτρεπτον codd. 18 εὐκόλως P: εὐθέως F 21 τοῖς (ante πολλοῖς) P: om. F 24 οὐλίγους P | ἕξουσιν scripsi: ἔχουσιν codd. 25 οὐδὲ om. P 29 τῶν

(40) The forces[1] do not work upward from below, but downward from above.

(41) The things in heaven receive no benefit from the things on earth; but the things on earth receive all benefits from the things in heaven.

(42) Heaven is receptive of everlasting bodies; earth is receptive of destructible bodies.

(43) Earth is irrational; heaven is rational.

(44) . . .[2]

(45) Heaven is the first of the elements; earth is the last of the elements.

(46) Providence is God's ordering; Necessity is subservient to Providence.

(47) Chance is a movement without order; . . .[3]

(48) What is God? A thing immutable and good. What is man? A thing mutable and bad.

If you keep in mind these aphorisms, you will easily recall the 3
fuller explanations I have given you in numerous discourses; for my previous teaching is summed up in these brief sentences.

But avoid converse with the many. Not that I wish you to 4
grudge a benefit to others; my reason for this warning is rather that the many will think you one to be laughed at ⟨if you speak to them as I have spoken to you⟩. Like welcomes like; but men that are unlike are never friends. And these discourses[4] will find few indeed that are worthy to hear them; nay, perhaps not even the few will be worthy. Moreover, my teaching has a certain 5
property which is peculiar to it; it urges on bad men to worse wickedness.—*Tat.* What do you mean, father?—*Hermes.* This is what I mean, my son. The living being called man is inclined to evil; he is brought up amidst evil, and therefore he takes pleasure in it. If then this being is told that the Kosmos has had a beginning, and that all things take place by necessity,

[1] I.e. the cosmic forces by which all things (or at least all things on earth) are moved and vivified.

[2] Perhaps, 'The things in heaven are subject ⟨to Providence⟩; the things on earth are subject ⟨to Necessity⟩'.

[3] Perhaps, '⟨skill is a force which works in good order⟩'.

[4] I.e. the 'Discourses of Hermes to Tat'.

ἀνθρώπων FP: τὸ ἀνθρώπινον Usener 30 ταύτην P 31 δὲ codd.: fortasse δὴ 32 ἀνάγκην FP: ἀνάγκῃ Gaisford

γίνεται, εἱμαρμένης πάντων ἀρχούσης, οὔ⟨τω⟩ πολλῷ ἑαυτοῦ χεῖρον ἔσται, καταφρονῆσαν μὲν τοῦ παντὸς ὡς γενητοῦ, τὰς δὲ αἰτίας τοῦ κακοῦ τῇ εἱμαρμένῃ ἀναφέρον, οὐδ' ἀφέξεταί ποτε παντὸς ἔργου κακοῦ. διὸ φυλακτέον αὐτούς, ὅπως ἐν ἀγνοίᾳ ὄντες ἔλαττον ὦσι κακοὶ [φόβῳ τοῦ ἀδήλου].

EXCERPTUM XII

Stobaeus I. 5. 20, vol. i, p. 82 Wachsmuth (*Ecl.* I. 188 Heeren).

Ἑρμοῦ ἐκ τῶν πρὸς Ἄμμωνα.

1 *πάντα δὲ γίνεται ⌜φύσει καὶ εἱμαρμένῃ⌝, καὶ οὐκ ἔστι τόπος ἔρημος προνοίας. πρόνοια δέ ἐστιν αὐτοτελὴς λόγος τοῦ ἐπουρανίου θεοῦ· δύο δὲ τούτου ⌜αὐτοφυεῖς⌝ δυνάμεις, ἀνάγκη καὶ εἱμαρμένη. ⟨καὶ ἡ μὲν ἀνάγκη . . .·⟩ ἡ δὲ*
2 *εἱμαρμένη ὑπηρετεῖ προνοίᾳ ⌜καὶ ἀνάγκῃ.⌝ τῇ δὲ εἱμαρμένῃ ὑπηρετοῦσιν οἱ ἀστέρες. [οὔτε γὰρ εἱμαρμένην φυγεῖν τις δύναται, οὔτε φυλάξαι ἑαυτὸν ἀπὸ τῆς τούτων δεινότητος.] ὅπλον γὰρ εἱμαρμένης οἱ ἀστέρες· κατὰ γὰρ ταύτην πάντα ἀποτελοῦσι τῇ φύσει καὶ τοῖς ἀνθρώποις.*

EXCERPTUM XIII

Stobaeus I. 4. 7b, vol. i, p. 72 Wachsmuth (*Ecl.* I. 158 Heeren).

⟨⟨Ἑρμοῦ ἐκ τῶν [Πλάτωνος] ⟨πρὸς⟩ Ἄμμωνα.⟩⟩

ἀνάγκη ἐστὶ κρίσις βεβαία καὶ ἀμετάτρεπτος [δύναμις] προνοίας.

1 *οὔτω* Usener : *οὐ* FP 2 *καταφρονῆσαν* Heeren : *καταφρονῆσαι* FP 3 *ἀναφέρον* Heeren : *ἀναφέρων* FP | *οὐδ'* Wachsm. : *οὐκ* FP
6 *ἄμωνα* P 7 Fortasse *πάντα δὲ ⟨κατὰ πρόνοιαν⟩ γίνεται ⟨τὰ⟩ φύσει ⟨γινόμενα⟩* | *καὶ εἱμαρμένῃ* secludendum? 10 Fortasse *⟨καὶ ἡ μὲν ἀνάγκη ἐστὶ κρίσις βεβαία καὶ ἀμετάτρεπτος προνοίας⟩* (vide *Exc.* XIII) 11 *καὶ ἀνάγκῃ* codd. : fortasse *κατ' ἀνάγκην*

inasmuch as Destiny governs all,—if he is told that, he will be far worse than he was before; for he will despise the Kosmos, as a thing that has had a beginning, and he will put off on Destiny the responsibility for evil, and so he will never refrain from any evil deed. You must therefore beware of talking to them, in order that, being in ignorance, they may be less wicked.

EXCERPT XII

From the teachings of Hermes to Ammon.

But all things come to pass . . .,[1] and there is no place destitute 1
of Providence. Now Providence is the sovereign design of the God who rules over the heavens; and that sovereign design has under it two subordinate powers, namely, Necessity and Destiny. ⟨Necessity is . . .;⟩[2] and Destiny is subservient to Providence . . .[3]
And the stars are subservient to Destiny. [ ][4] For the stars are 2
the instrument of Destiny; it is in accordance with Destiny that they bring all things to pass for the world of nature and for men.

EXCERPT XIII

From the teachings of Hermes to Ammon.

Necessity is a firm and unalterable decision of Providence.

[1] Perhaps, 'all things that come to pass by nature (that is, all events in the physical world) come to pass according to Providence'.

[2] Perhaps, '⟨Necessity is a firm and unalterable decision of Providence⟩'.

[3] Perhaps, 'in accordance with Necessity'.

[4] ['For no man can either escape from Destiny, or guard himself from the terribleness of the stars.']

---

16 Nullum hic lemma est in codd. Stob.: sed ante eclogam praecedentem 7 a (Θαλῆς ἐρωτηθεὶς κ.τ.λ.) habent codices in unum locum congregata quinque lemmata, quae videntur pertinere ad eclogas 4, 5, 6, 7 b, 7 c. Ex his quartum est Ερμου ἐκ τῶν πλάτωνος (add. marg. ἄκμωννα) F: ἑρμοῦ ἐκ τοῦ πλάτωνος. ἄκμωνα P. Inde colligit Wachsmuth eclogae 7 b (ἀνάγκη ἐστὶ κ.τ.λ.) lemma fuisse 'Ερμοῦ ἐκ τῶν πρὸς Ἄμμωνα

EXCERPTUM XIV

Stobaeus I. 5. 16, vol. i, p. 79 Wachsmuth (*Ecl.* I. 182 Heeren).

[περὶ τῆς ὅλης οἰκονομίας.] Ἑρμοῦ ἐκ τῶν πρὸς Ἀμοῦν.

1 καὶ ἡ μὲν διακρατοῦσα τὸν ὅλον κόσμον πρόνοιά ἐστιν· ἡ δὲ ⌜συνέχουσα καὶ περιέχουσα⌝ ἀνάγκη ἐστίν. εἱμαρμένη δὲ ἄγει καὶ περιάγει πάντα, κατ' ἀνάγκην ⟨ἐνεργ⟩οῦσα· φύσις γάρ ἐστιν αὐτῆς τὸ ἀναγκάζειν. [αἰτία γενέσεως καὶ φθορᾶς ⌜βίου⌝.]

2 ὁ μὲν οὖν κόσμος ⌜πρῶτος ἔχει τὴν πρόνοιαν· πρῶτος γὰρ αὐτῆς τυγχάνει⌝. ἡ δὲ πρόνοια ἐξήπλωται ἐν τῷ οὐρανῷ. ⌜διότι καὶ⌝ ⟨οἱ⟩ θεοὶ περὶ αὐτὸν στρέφονται [καὶ κινοῦνται] ἀκάματον καὶ ἄπαυστον κίνησιν ἔχοντες. εἱμαρμένη δὲ ⌜διότι καὶ ἀνάγκη⌝. καὶ ἡ μὲν πρόνοια ⟨. . .⟩ προνοεῖ, εἱμαρμένη δὲ αἰτία ἐστὶ ⌜τῆς τῶν ἄστρων διαθέσεως.⌝

⌜οὗτος⌝ νόμος ἄφυκτος καθ' ὃν πάντα τέτακται.

EXCERPTUM XV

Stobaeus I. 41. 7, vol. i, p. 289 Wachsmuth (*Ecl.* I. 740 Heeren).

Ἑρμοῦ ἐκ τῶν πρὸς Ἄμμωνα.

1 κινεῖται δὲ τὸ κινούμενον κατ⟨ὰ τὴν⟩ ἐνέργειαν τῆς [κινήσεως] ⟨φύσεως⟩, τῆς κινούσης τὸ πᾶν ⟨⟨καὶ διὰ πάντων πεφοιτηκυίας⟩⟩. ἡ ⟨μὲν⟩ γὰρ φύσις [τοῦ παντὸς] τῷ παντὶ παρέχει κινήσεις [μίαν μὲν τὴν κατὰ δύναμιν ⌜αὐτῆς⌝, ἑτέραν δὲ τὴν κατ' ἐνέργειαν]· ⟨ἡ δὲ νοερὰ οὐσία . . ..⟩ καὶ ἡ μὲν

1 ὅλης οἰκουμένης P 3–4 Fortasse ἡ μὲν τὸν ὅλον διακρατοῦσα κόσμον πρόνοιά ἐστιν, ἡ δὲ ⟨τὰ καθ' ἕκαστον⟩ συνέχουσα ἀνάγκη ἐστίν 5 κατ' ἀνάγκην ἐνεργοῦσα scripsi : καταναγκάζουσα codd. 8–9 Fortasse ὁ μὲν οὖν κόσμος ὅλος ἔχεται τῆς προνοίας· [[ ]] ἡ δὲ ⟨τῆς⟩ προνοία⟨ς ἐνέργεια πρῶτον⟩ ἐξήπλωται ἐν τῷ οὐρανῷ· ⟨⟨πρῶτος γὰρ αὐτῇ ἐντυγχάνει⟩⟩ ⟨ὁ οὐρανός⟩ 10 Fortasse διὸ[τι] καὶ 11–12 Fortasse εἱμαρμένη δὲ ⟨πάντα⟩ διοικεῖ κατ' ἀνάγκην 12 διότι codd. : διατίθησι Usener ; 'διοικεῖ vel διατάττει malim' Wachsmuth 12–13 Fortasse ἡ μὲν πρόνοια ⟨συμπάντων ὁμοῦ⟩ προνοεῖ, εἱμαρμένη δέ, ⟨ὑπηρετοῦσα τῇ προνοίᾳ, τὰ μὲν ἄστρα στρέφει ἀμεταβλήτως, τοῖς δ' ἐπιγείοις γενέσεως καὶ φθορᾶς⟩ αἰτία ἐστὶ ⟨διὰ⟩ τῆς τῶν ἄστρων διαθέσεως

15 ἄμμων P[1] 16 κατὰ τὴν scripsi : κατ' codd. 18 πεφοιτηκυίας

EXCERPT XIV

From the teachings of Hermes to Amun.

And the power which holds the whole Kosmos in its grasp 1
is Providence; but that which . . . is Necessity.[1] And Destiny makes all things move with a cyclic movement, working in accordance with Necessity; for it is the nature of Destiny to compel.[2]

. . . ⟨The working of⟩ Providence is spread out[3] in heaven; 2
. . . the star-gods circle in heaven with a movement which continues without failing and without cease. But Destiny . . . And Providence takes thought for . . .; but Destiny is the cause of . . .[4]

⟨Providence is the⟩ inevitable law according to which all things have been ordered.[5]

EXCERPT XV

From the teachings of Hermes to Ammon.

And that which is moved is moved in accordance with the 1
force exerted by Nature, which moves the universe, and permeates all things. For Nature gives movements to the universe; ⟨but the Mental Substance[6] . . .⟩. And Nature pervades the whole

[1] Perhaps, 'the power which grasps the Kosmos as a whole is Providence; but that which puts constraint on ⟨particular things within the Kosmos⟩ is Necessity'.

[2] Or 'to subject things to necessity'.

[3] I.e. is extended in time and space. Providence, regarded as a function of the incorporeal and eternal God, is one and indivisible; but its effects in the Kosmos are 'spread out'.

[4] The author's meaning might perhaps be expressed by rewriting this paragraph as follows: 'The Kosmos as a whole, then, is dependent on Providence; but the working of Providence is first spread out in heaven, for heaven is the first thing that encounters it (*i.e.* God's Providence acts on heaven more immediately than on the rest of the universe); and hence it is that the circling movement of the star-gods in heaven continues without failing and without cease. . . . Providence takes thought for ⟨all things together⟩; but Destiny, ⟨operating in subservience to Providence, works the unvarying movement of the stars, and⟩ causes ⟨the birth and destruction of things on earth by means of⟩ the arrangement of the stars.'

[5] This sentence appears to be wrongly placed.

[6] The 'Mental Substance' (or 'Mental Being') means the divine and supracosmic Mind. Perhaps, '⟨but the Mental Substance supplies to Nature the force which Nature exerts⟩'.

---

scripsi: πεφοιτήκασι κοινῇ codd. 20 Fortasse ⟨ἡ δὲ νοερὰ οὐσία τῇ φύσει χορηγεῖ τὴν ἐνέργειαν⟩ vel simile aliquid

διήκει διὰ τοῦ σύμπαντος κόσμου καὶ ἐντὸς συνέχει, ἡ δὲ ⌜παρήκει⌝ καὶ ἐκτὸς περιέχει. [[καὶ διὰ πάντων πεφοιτήκασι κοινῇ.]]

2 καὶ ἡ φύσις, πάντα φύουσα τὰ γιγνόμενα, [φυὴν] ⟨μορφὴν⟩ παρέχει τοῖς φυομένοις, σπείρουσα μὲν ⟨εἰς ὕλην⟩ τὰ ἑαυτῆς σπέρματα [γένεσις], ἔχουσα δὲ ⟨τὴν⟩ ὕλην κινητήν. κινουμένη δὲ θερμαίνεται ⟨καὶ ψύχεται ἡ⟩ ⟨⟨ὕλη⟩⟩, καὶ γίγνεται [[ὕλη]] πῦρ καὶ ὕδωρ, τὸ μὲν σθεναρὸν καὶ ἰσχυρόν, ⟨τὸ δὲ ἀσθενές, καὶ τὸ μὲν ποιοῦν,⟩ τὸ δὲ πάσχον. τὸ δὲ πῦρ, ἐναντιούμενον τῷ ὕδατι, ἐξήρανε τοῦ ὕδατος, καὶ ἐγένετο ⟨ἡ γῆ⟩ [[ὀχουμένη ἐπὶ τοῦ ὕδατος]]. περιξηραινομένων δὲ ⟨τούτων⟩, ἀτμὸς ἐγένετο ἐκ [τῶν τριῶν] τοῦ τε ὕδατος ⟨καὶ⟩ τῆς γῆς [καὶ τοῦ πυρός], καὶ ἐγένετο ἀήρ, ⟨⟨ὀχούμενος ἐπὶ ⟨τῆς γῆς καὶ⟩ τοῦ ὕδατος.⟩⟩

3 ταῦτα ⟨δὲ⟩ συνῆλθε κατὰ τὸν τῆς ἁρμονίας λόγον, θερμὸν ψυχρῷ, ξηρὸν ὑγρῷ, καὶ ἐκ τῆς συμπνοίας τούτων ἐγένετο ⟨. . .⟩.

* * * * *

4 ⟨. . .⟩ πνεῦμα [καὶ σπέρμα] ἀνάλογον τῷ περιέχοντι πνεύματι. τοῦτο δέ, ἐς τὴν μήτραν ἐμπεσόν, οὐκ ἠρεμεῖ [ἐν τῷ σπέρματι]· οὐκ ἠρεμοῦν δέ, μεταβάλλει τὸ ⌜σπέρμα⌝. μεταβαλλόμενον δὲ ⟨τοῦτο⟩ αὔξην ἴσχει καὶ μέγεθος· ἐπὶ τῷ μεγέθει δὲ [εἴδωλον] ἐπισπᾶται σχῆμα[τος], καὶ σχηματίζεται· [ὀχ]εῖτα[ι] δὲ ἐπὶ τῷ σχήματι ⟨προσδέχεται⟩ τὸ εἶδος, δι' οὗ καὶ εἰδ[ωλ]οποιεῖται τὸ [εἰδωλοποιούμενον] ⟨γινόμενον⟩. ⟨⟨τὸ δ' ἐν τῇ νηδύι ἀριθμοῖς λοχεύει καὶ μαιοῦται ⟨ἡ φύσις⟩, καὶ εἰς τὸν ἔξω ἀέρα ἄγει.⟩⟩

5 ἐπεὶ τοίνυν τὸ πνεῦμα οὐκ εἶχεν ἐν τῇ νηδύι τὴν ζωτικὴν κίνησιν, τὴν δὲ βλαστικὴν ⟨μόνην⟩, καὶ [ταύτην] ⟨ψυχὴν προσ⟩ήρμοσεν ⟨ἡ φύσις τῇ⟩ ἁρμονίᾳ, ὑποδοχὴν οὖσαν τῆς

1 ἐντὸς σέχει P 2 παρήκει codd.: fortasse ὑπερέχει 4 πάντα scripsi: πάντων codd. | μορφὴν scripsi: φυὴν codd. (Poterat scribi κίνησιν) 5–6 Fortasse τὰ [ἑαυτῆς] σπέρματα ⟨τῆς⟩ γενέσεως 6 Fortasse ⟨δυνάμει⟩ κινητήν 11 ἡ γῆ addidit Patritius 11–12 περιξηραινομένων δὲ τούτων scripsi: περιξηραινομένου δὲ codd. 12 καὶ add. Wachsm. 13 ὀχούμενος scripsi: ὀχουμένη codd. 16 Fortasse ἐγένετο ⟨τὰ σύνθετα σώματα⟩ 17 Fortasse, ⟨. . . ἔστι δὲ ἐν τῷ τῶν ζῴων σπέρματι⟩ 18 Fortasse ἐμπεσόν⟨τος τοῦ σπέρματος⟩ 19 τὸ σπέρμα codd.: fortasse τὸ τοῦ θήλεος περίττωμα (cf. Ar. *De gen. an.* 2. 3) vel simile aliquid 20 αὔξειν ἴσχει F | Fortasse μέγεθος ⟨προσλαμβάνει⟩ 21 ἐπισπᾶται σχῆμα scripsi: εἴδωλον ἐπισπᾶται σχήματος codd. 22 εἶτα scripsi: ὀχεῖται codd. 23 εἰδοποιεῖται τὸ γινόμενον scripsi (εἰδοποιεῖται τὸ εἰδοποιούμενον Usener): εἰδωλοποιεῖται τὸ εἰδωλοποιούμενον codd. 24–25 τὸ δ' . . . ἄγει huc a § 5 *fin.*

Kosmos, and holds it together within; but the ⟨Mental Substance⟩ transcends the Kosmos, and encompasses it without.

And Nature, producing all things that come into being, gives 2
form[1] to the things that are produced. She sows in matter her
own seeds;[2] and the matter which she has at her disposal is
capable of being moved. And matter, being moved by her,
is made hot and cold; and so there come into being fire and
water. The fire is strong and powerful, the water is feeble;
the fire is active, the water is passive. And the fire, being
opposed to the water, dried some of the water, and thereby
the earth came into being. And when the water and the earth
were being dried round about by the fire, there arose from
them a vapour; and so the air came into being, borne up on
earth and water. And these four elements entered into com- 3
bination according to the plan of the cosmic structure, hot
combining with cold, and dry with fluid; and from their co-
operation came into being. . . .[3]

* * * * *

. . .[4] a life-breath[5] analogous to the atmospheric life-breath 4
of the Kosmos. This life-breath, when it has been injected[6] into
the womb, is not inactive; and inasmuch as it is not inactive,
it works change in the . . .[7] And this, through the change
worked in it, grows, and acquires bulk; and thereupon, it assumes
a definite shape, and is shaped; and thereafter, it takes to itself
the species-form, whereby the thing that is coming into being
is fashioned according to its species. And after a measured
interval of time, ⟨Nature⟩ brings the fœtus to its birth, and acts
as midwife, and draws it forth into the external air.

Now the life-breath, as long as it was in the womb, had not 5
the movement of animal life, but only that of vegetable growth;
and so ⟨Nature, at the time of the birth,⟩ joined on ⟨a soul⟩ also
to the bodily structure, as a receptacle for the force which works

[1] Or possibly, 'gives movement'.

[2] Perhaps, 'She sows in matter the seeds of coming-into-being'.

[3] Perhaps, 'came into being ⟨all composite bodies⟩', *i.e.* living organisms (plants, beasts, and men).

[4] Perhaps, '⟨There is in the *semen genitale* of men and beasts⟩'.

[5] Or 'vital spirit'.

[6] Perhaps, 'when ⟨the *semen*⟩ has been injected'.

[7] Perhaps, 'in the matter supplied by secretion in the womb'.

---

transposui 27 βλαστικὴν Usener : βραστικὴν FP 27–28 καὶ ψυχὴν προσήρμοσεν ἡ φύσις τῇ ἁρμονίᾳ scripsi : καὶ ταύτην ἥρμοσεν ἁρμονία codd.

[διανοητικῆς] ζω⟨τικ⟩ῆς ⟨ἐνεργείας⟩. ⟨⟨παρεισέρπει γὰρ τῷ
πνεύματι ⟨ἡ ψυχή⟩, καὶ κινεῖ ζωτικῶς.⟩⟩ [[ἔστι δὲ αὕτη
ἀμερὴς καὶ ἀμετάβλητος, οὐδέποτε ἐξισταμένη τῆς ἀμετα-
βλησίας.]] [[τὸ δ' ἐν τῇ νηδύι ἀριθμοῖς λοχεύει καὶ μαιοῦται,
6 *καὶ εἰς τὸν ἔξω ἀέρα ἄγει.]] καὶ ⟨ἡ⟩ ἐγγυτάτω ⟨⟨⟨παρ⟩οῦσα⟩⟩*
ψυχὴ [[οὖσα]] ⟨προσ⟩οικειοῦται, οὐ κατά τιν⟨α⟩ συγγενικὴν
ὁμοιότητα ⟨παραγενομένη⟩, ἀλλὰ [τὴν] καθ' εἱμαρμένην· οὐ
γὰρ ἔρω⟨ς⟩[των] ἐστὶν αὐτῇ ⟨τοῦ⟩ μετὰ σώματος εἶναι. διὰ
τοῦτο καθ' εἱμαρμένην ⟨. . .⟩.

7 ⟨. . .⟩ *παρέχει τῷ γενομένῳ διανοητικὴν κίνησιν.*

⟨. . .⟩ *καὶ νοερὰν [ζωῆς αὐτῆς] οὐσίαν. ⟨⟨ἔστι δὲ αὕτη ἀμερὴς καὶ ἀμετάβλητος, οὐδέποτε ἐξισταμένη τῆς ἀμεταβλησίας.⟩⟩*

[[παρεισέρπει γὰρ τῷ πνεύματι καὶ κινεῖ ζωτικῶς.]]

EXCERPTUM XVI

Stobaeus I. 41. 4, vol. i, p. 281 Wachsmuth (*Ecl.* I. 718 Heeren).

Ἑρμοῦ ἐκ τῶν πρὸς Ἄμμωνα.

1 *⟨ἡ⟩ ψυχὴ τοίνυν οὐσία ἐστὶν ἀσώματος· καὶ ἐν σώματι δὲ οὖσα οὐκ ἐκβαίνει τῆς ἰδίας οὐσιότητος. τυγχάνει γὰρ οὖσα ⌜ἀεικίνητος κατ' οὐσίαν κατὰ νόησιν αὐτοκίνητος⌝, οὐκ ἔν τινι ⌜κινουμένη⌝, οὐ πρός τι, οὐ⟨χ⟩ ἕνεκέν τινος. προτερεῖ γὰρ τῇ δυνάμει, τὸ δὲ πρότερον οὐ δεῖ τῶν ὑστέρων.*

1 *τῆς ζωτικῆς ἐνεργείας* scripsi: *τῆς διανοητικῆς ζωῆς* codd. 1–2 *παρεισέρπει . . . ζωτικῶς* huc a § 7 *fin.* transposui 1 *γὰρ* P: *δὲ* F 2–4 *ἔστι . . . ἀμεταβλησίας* hinc ad § 7 transposui 5–6 *παροῦσα ψυχὴ προσοικειοῦται* scripsi: *ψυχὴ οὖσα οἰκειοῦται* codd. 6 *τινα* scripsi: *τὴν* codd. 7 *ὁμοιότητα* scripsi: *οὐσιότητα* F: *ἰδιότητα* P: *οἰκειότητα* Meineke e cod. Vatic. 8 *ἔρως ἐστὶν αὐτῇ* Patrit.: *ἐρώτων ἐστιν αὕτη* FP 10 Fortasse ⟨*ἡ δὲ φύσις ζωτικῶς ἤδη κινουμένῳ*⟩ *παρέχει* | *γενομένῳ* scripsi: *γιγνομένῳ* codd. 11 Fortasse ⟨*ὁ δὲ θεὸς ὀλίγοις τισὶ παρέχει*⟩ vel eiusmodi aliquid 12–13 Fortasse *τῆς* ⟨*τοῦ θεοῦ*⟩ *ἀμεταβλησίας*

in animal life; for ⟨the soul⟩ insinuates itself into the life-breath,
and makes it move with the movement of animal life. And 6
it is the soul which is nearest at hand that is assigned to[1] the
organism; and this soul comes to it, not because of any congenital
likeness, but according to destiny; for the soul is not impelled
by a desire to be combined with a body. For this reason, it is
according to destiny that . . .

. . . gives the man that has been born the movement of 7
rational thought.[2]

. . . also Mental Substance.[3] And Mental Substance is indivisible and changeless, never departing from its changelessness.[4]

EXCERPT XVI

From the teachings of Hermes to Ammon.

The soul then is an incorporeal substance; and even when 1
it is in a body, it does not depart from its own substantiality.[5] For it is found to be . . . self-moved,[6] not in something, nor in relation to something, nor for the sake of something. For it is prior[7] in its power, and that which is prior is not in need of the things which are posterior.

[1] Or 'is appropriated by'.

[2] Perhaps, 'And after a man has been born, ⟨and when he already possesses the movement of animal life, Nature⟩ gives him ⟨in addition⟩ the movement of rational thought'.

[3] Perhaps, '⟨And to some men God gives⟩ Mental Substance also'. The 'mind' which enters into the elect among men is consubstantial with the divine Mind, or with God himself.

[4] Perhaps, 'from the changelessness ⟨of God⟩'.

[5] This means that the soul, when embodied, is still a 'substance' (i.e. an independently existing thing), not a mere attribute of the body.

[6] Perhaps, 'For it is self-moved, being moved in the manner of an intelligible substance' (i.e. of an incorporeal thing). That is, the movement of the soul is of a different kind from that of bodies. The movement of bodies is called by this writer 'physical movement'.

[7] I.e. prior to body and attributes of body.

---

15 ἄμωνα P 16 'ἡ om. pro rubr. FP' Wachsm. 17–18 Fortasse τυγχάνει γὰρ οὖσα α⟨ὐτο⟩κίνητος, κατ' οὐσίαν [κατὰ] νοητὴν [αὐτοκίνητος] ⟨⟨κινουμένη⟩⟩ | οὖσα ἀκίνητος P 18 κατ' οὐσίαν καὶ κατὰ P 19 οὐχ ἕνεκεν Meineke: οὗ ἕνεκεν FP

2 ⌜τὸ ἔν τινι τοίνυν ἐστὶν⌝ ὁ τόπος καὶ ⟨ὁ⟩ χρόνος ⌜καὶ φύσις⌝· ⌜τὸ δὲ πρός τι ἐστὶν ἁρμονία καὶ εἶδος καὶ σχῆμα·⌝
3 τὸ δὲ οὗ ἕνεκα ⟨ταῦτα⟩, τὸ σῶμα. ἕνεκα γὰρ σώματος καὶ χρόνος καὶ τόπος καὶ φυσικ⟨ὴ κίνησις⟩· [ταῦτα δὲ κατὰ συγγενικὴν οἰκειότητα κοινωνεῖ ἀλλήλοις.] [ἐπεὶ τοίνυν τὸ σῶμα ἐδεῖτο τόπου] ἀμήχανον γὰρ [ἦν] συστῆναι σῶμα ἄνευ τόπου, [καὶ μεταβάλλεται φυσικῇ ⟨κινήσει⟩,] ἀδύνατον δὲ μεταβολὴν ⟨σώματος⟩ εἶναι ἄνευ χρόνου καὶ τῆς κατὰ φύσιν κινήσεως. [οὔτε σώματος οἷόν τε σύστασιν εἶναι ἄνευ ἁρμονίας].

4 ἕνεκα ⌜τοίνυν⌝ τοῦ σώματός ἐστιν ὁ τόπος· παραδεχόμενος γὰρ τὰς τοῦ σώματος μεταβολὰς οὐκ ἐᾷ ἀπόλλυσθαι τὸ μεταβαλλόμενον. μεταβαλλόμενον δὲ ⟨τὸ σῶμα⟩ ἀπὸ ἑτέρου εἰς ἕτερον μεταπίπτει, καὶ τῆς μὲν ἕξεως στερίσκεται, τοῦ δὲ εἶναι σῶμα οὐχί [συστατόν]· μεταβληθὲν δὲ εἰς ἕτερον, τὴν τοῦ ἑτέρου ἕξιν ἔχει. ⟨⟨τὸ σῶμα τοίνυν κατὰ διάθεσιν μεταβάλλεται·⟩⟩ τὸ γὰρ σῶμα, ᾗ σῶμα, μένει [σῶμα], ἡ δὲ ποιὰ διάθεσις οὐ μένει. [[τὸ σῶμα τοίνυν κατὰ διάθεσιν μεταβάλλεται.]]

* * * * *

5 ⟨ἕνεκ⟩α σώματος τοίνυν ὁ τόπος καὶ ὁ χρόνος καὶ ἡ φυσικὴ κίνησις.

6 τυγχάνει δὲ ἕκαστον τούτων τῆς ἰδίας ἰδιότητος· ἰδιότης δὲ [τοῦ] τόπου παραδοχή, χρόνου δὲ διάστημα καὶ ἀριθμός, ⌜φύσεως δὲ κίνησις, [ἁρμονίας δὲ φιλία,] σώματος δὲ μεταβολή.⌝ ἰδιότης δὲ ψυχῆς ἡ κατ' οὐσίαν νοη⟨τὴν κίνη⟩σις.

EXCERPTUM XVII

Stobaeus I. 49. 4, vol. i, p. 321 Wachsmuth (*Ecl.* I. 802 Heeren).

Τοῦ αὐτοῦ (*sc.* Ἑρμοῦ).

1 ψυχὴ τοίνυν ἐστίν, ὦ Ἄμμων, οὐσία αὐτοτελὴς ἐν ἀρχῇ· ἑλομένη ⟨δὲ⟩ βίον τὸν καθ' εἱμαρμένην, ⟨. . .⟩ καὶ ἐπεσπάσατο ἑαυτῇ ⟨ἄ⟩λογόν ⟨τι⟩ ὅμοιον τῇ ὕλῃ.

1 Fortasse τὸ ἐν τίνι (= τὸ ἐν ᾧ) 2 τὸ δὲ πρός τι . . . καὶ σχῆμα secludendum? 4 φυσικὴ κίνησις scripsi (vide § 5): φύσις codd. 7 φυσικῇ

. . . place and time . . .;[1] and that for the sake of[2] which 2
these things exist is body. It is for the sake of body that time 3
and place and physical movement exist; for bodies could not be constructed if there were no place for them, and bodies could not change if there were not time and physical movement.

Place exists for the sake of body; for it receives into itself 4
the changes of the body, and so prevents the thing which is changing from being destroyed. The body, when it changes, is transformed into something different, and ceases to be in the state in which it was before, but it does not cease to be a body; and when it has changed into something different, it is in the state which belongs to that different thing. The body then changes merely in condition; for the body, *qua* body, persists, but the particular condition in which it was before does not persist.

*   *   *   *[3]

It is for the sake of body then that place and time and physical 5
movement exist.

And to each of these things is assigned its own peculiar 6
property. The peculiar property of place is receptiveness; that of time is interval and number;[4] . . . But the peculiar property of soul is that sort of movement which belongs to intelligible substance.

EXCERPT XVII

From the teachings of Hermes.

Soul then, Ammon, is a substance which is self-determining 1
in the beginning; but when it has chosen that course of life which is dependent on Destiny, . . . and it takes on[5] as an appendage something irrational, which is similar to matter.

[1] Perhaps, 'That in which things are is place and time; ⟨for it is in place and time that⟩ physical movement goes on'.
[2] Or 'because of'.
[3] We may suppose that here followed two paragraphs, similar to § 4, in one of which it was shown that *time* 'exists for the sake of body', and in the other, that *physical movement* 'exists for the sake of body'.
[4] Perhaps, 'that of time is numbered (i.e. measured) interval'.
[5] Perhaps, '⟨it is embodied⟩, and it then takes on', &c.

FP: *φυσικῶς* vel *φυσικῇ* ⟨*κινήσει*⟩ Meineke   20 *ἕνεκα σώματος* scripsi (vide § 3 *init.*): *ἀσώματος* codd.   23 *παραδοχὴ* F: *παρασχὴ* P | *καὶ ἀριθμός* secludendum? An scribendum *κατ' ἀριθμόν*?   25 *νοητὴν κίνησις* scripsi: *νόησις* codd.   29 *ἄλογόν τι* scripsi: *λόγον* codd.

2 ⟨. . .⟩ ⌜ἔχοντα⌝ θυμὸν καὶ ἐπιθυμίαν. καὶ ὁ μὲν θυμός
[ὑπάρχει ὕλη. οὗτος], ἐὰν ἕξιν ποιήσῃ πρὸς τὸ τῆς ψυχῆς
νόημα, γίνεται ἀνδρεία, καὶ οὐ παράγεται ὑπὸ δειλίας· ἡ δὲ
ἐπιθυμία [παρέχεται. αὕτη], ἐὰν ἕξιν ποιήσηται πρὸς τὸν
τῆς ψυχῆς λογισμόν, γίνεται σωφροσύνη, καὶ οὐ κινεῖται ὑπὸ
3 ἡδονῆς. [ἀναπληροῖ γὰρ ὁ λογισμὸς τὸ ἐνδέον τῆς ἐπιθυμίας.] ὅταν δὲ ἀμφότερα ὁμονοήσῃ καὶ ἴσην ἕξιν ποιήσῃ,
καὶ ἔχηται ἀμφότερα τοῦ τῆς ψυχῆς λογισμοῦ, γίνεται
δικαιοσύνη· ἡ γὰρ ἴση ἕξις αὐτῶν ἀφαιρεῖ μὲν τὴν ὑπερβολὴν
4 τοῦ θυμοῦ, ἐπανισοῖ δὲ τὸ ἐνδέον τῆς ἐπιθυμίας. [ἀρχὴ δὲ
τούτων ἡ διανοητικὴ οὐσία] [καθ' αὐτὴν ἑαυτῇ οὖσα ἐν τῷ
αὐτῆς περινοητικῷ λόγῳ] [κράτος ἔχουσα τὸν ἑαυτῆς λόγον.]
5 ἄρχει δὲ ⟨τούτων⟩ [[καὶ ἡγεμονεύει]] ἡ ⟨νοητικὴ⟩ οὐσία, ⟨⟨καὶ
ἡγεμονεύει⟩⟩ ὥσπερ ἄρχων, ὁ δὲ λόγος ⟨συνακολουθεῖ⟩ αὐτῇ[ς]
ὥσπερ σύμβουλος.
6 ὁ [περι] [[νοητικὸς]] λόγος τοίνυν τῆς ⟨⟨νοητικῆς⟩⟩ οὐσίας
ἐστί· ⌜γνῶσις τῶν λογισμῶν τῶν παρεχόντων⌝ ⟨. . .⟩ ⟨ἀπ⟩εί-
κασμα λογισμοῦ [τῷ ἀλόγῳ], ἀμυδρὸν μὲν ὡς πρὸς λογισμόν,
[λογισμὸν] [[δὲ ὡς πρὸς τὸ ἄλογον,]] καθάπερ ἠχὼ πρὸς φωνήν,
καὶ τὸ τῆς σελήνης λαμπρὸν πρὸς ⟨τὸ τοῦ⟩ ἡλίου, ⟨σαφὲς⟩
⟨⟨δὲ ὡς πρὸς τὸ ἄλογον.⟩⟩
7 [ἥρμοσται δὲ θυμὸς καὶ ἐπιθυμία πρός τινα λογισμόν]
[καὶ ἀνθέλκει ἄλληλα] [καὶ ἐπίσταται ἐν ἑαυτοῖς κυκλικὴν
διάνοιαν.]

EXCERPTUM XVIII

Stobaeus 2. 8. 31, vol. ii, p. 160 Wachsmuth (*Ecl.* II. 358 Heeren).

Ἑρμοῦ.

1 ⌜ἔστι τοίνυν οὐσία καὶ λόγος καὶ νόημα καὶ διάνοια. φέρεται δὲ ἐπὶ τὴν οὐσίαν. φέρεται δ' ἐπὶ τὴν διάνοιαν καὶ δόξα καὶ αἴσθησις. ἴεται δ' ὁ λόγος ἐπὶ τὴν οὐσίαν. τὸ δὲ νόημα δι' αὐτοῦ ἴεται. ἐπιπλέκεται δὲ τὸ νόημα τῇ διανοίᾳ· ἐλθόντα δὲ δι' ἀλλήλων μία ἰδέα ἐγένοντο. αὕτη δέ ἐστιν ἡ τῆς ψυχῆς. φέρεται δ' ἐπὶ τὴν αὐτῆς διάνοιαν δόξα καὶ αἴσθησις. ταῦτα δὲ ἐπὶ τοῦ αὐτοῦ οὐ μένει.⌝

2–3 τὸ . . . νόημα codd. : fortasse τὸν . . . λογισμόν 3 δειλίας codd. : fortasse δείματος vel τῶν δεινῶν 4 ποιήσηται FP : ποιήσῃ Heeren

. . . repugnance and desire. And repugnance, if it has formed 2
a habit of will according to the thought[1] of the soul, becomes
courage, and is not led astray by cowardice.[2] And desire, if it
has formed a habit of will according to the reasoning of the soul,
becomes temperance, and is not moved by pleasure. And when 3
repugnance and desire have agreed together, and have formed
a habit of will that is well-balanced, and both of them cleave
to the reasoning of the soul, then justice comes into being; for
their well-balanced habit of will[3] takes from repugnance its
excess, and raises to equality that which is lacking in desire.
And repugnance and desire are commanded by the ⟨intelligent⟩ 5
substance;[4] this takes the lead, like a commander, and the
reason accompanies it, like a counsellor.

The reason then belongs to the intelligent substance; . . . a 6
copy[5] of reasoning, dim in comparison with reasoning, as is an
echo in comparison with a voice, and the brightness of the
moon in comparison with that of the sun, but clear in comparison with the irrational.

EXCERPT XVIII

From the teachings of Hermes.

* * * * *[6]

[1] Perhaps, 'according to the reasoning'.

[2] Perhaps, 'by fear', or 'by dangers'. [3] Perhaps, 'their unanimity'.

[4] 'The intelligent substance' means the 'Mind', i.e. the highest and divine part of the soul. The 'reason' here spoken of is the faculty of discursive reasoning, which this writer regards as a thing distinct from and subordinate to the 'Mind'.

[5] Perhaps, '⟨and opinion is⟩ a copy', &c.

[6] § 1, as given in the manuscripts, is meaningless. It may be conjectured that the author wrote something to this effect: 'There are in the soul then intelligent substance (= mind) and reason. Thought is the function of the intelligent substance; discursive-thought is the function of the reason. With thought and discursive-thought are intertwined opinion and sensation (which are functions of the irrational part of the soul). These things intermingle, and together make up a single whole. Thus is the soul composed.'

---

7 *καὶ ἴσην ἕξιν ποιήσῃ* delendum? **8** *ἔχηται* FP[2]: *ἔχῃ τὰ* P[1] **10–11** Fortasse *ἄρχει δὲ τούτων ἡ νοητικὴ οὐσία* (cf. § 5 *init.*) **11** *ἑαυτὴ* F: *ἑαυτῇ* P **11–12** Fortasse *αὐτὴ καθ' αὑτὴν οὖσα ἐν τῷ νοητῷ κόσμῳ* (cf. *Exc.* XIX. 1) **14** *αὐτῇ* scripsi: *αὐτῆς* P: *αὐτῶν* F **17** Fortasse ⟨*συνυπάρχει δὲ τῷ λόγῳ ἡ*⟩ *γνῶσις* (cf. *Exc.* XIX. 6) **17–18** *ἀπείκασμα* scripsi: *εἰκασμὸν* codd. | Fortasse ⟨*ἡ δὲ δόξα*⟩ *ἀπείκασμα λογισμοῦ* **20** *τὸ τοῦ ἡλίου* scripsi: *ἥλιον* codd. **23** *ἐπίσταται* FP: *ἐπισπᾶται* ⟨*τὴν*⟩ Wachsm. | *κυκλικὴν* FP: *ὑλικὴν* Usener **27** *φέρεται δὲ ἐπὶ τὴν οὐσίαν* F: om. P **28–29** *ἵεται* (bis) FP: *ἴεται* (bis) Canter

2 ⟨. . .⟩ ἔνθεν καὶ ὑπερβάλλει καὶ ἐλλείπει, καὶ ἑαυτῷ διαφέρεται. χεῖρον μὲν γίνεται ὅταν ἀποσπασθῇ τῆς διανοίας· ὅταν δὲ ἀκολουθῇ καὶ πείθηται, κοινωνεῖ τῷ [νοηματικῷ] λόγῳ ⌈διὰ τῶν μαθημάτων⌉.

3 ⟨. . .⟩ τὸ δὲ αἱρεῖσθαι ἔχομεν· τὸ γὰρ αἱρεῖσθαι τὸ κρεῖττον ἐφ' ἡμῖν ἐστίν, ὁμοίως δὲ καὶ τὸ χεῖρον. ⟨. . .⟩ ἀκουσίως· ἐχομένη γὰρ [αἵρεσις] ⟨ἡ ψυχὴ⟩ τῶν κακῶν πλησιάζει τῇ σωματικῇ φύσει, ⟨καὶ⟩ διὰ τοῦτο τῷ ⟨τὸ χεῖρον⟩ ἑλομένῳ εἱμαρμένη δυναστεύει.

4 ⌈ἐπεὶ τοίνυν⌉ ἡ ἐν ἡμῖν [σωματικὴ] ⟨νοητικὴ⟩ οὐσία αὐτεξούσιός ἐστιν. [ὁ περὶ νοηματικὸς λόγος.] αὕτη δ' ἀεὶ κατὰ ταὐτὰ καὶ ὡσαύτως ἔχει, ⟨⟨ἀμέτοχος οὖσα τῆς τῶν γινομένων φύσεως,⟩⟩ ⟨καὶ⟩ διὰ τοῦτο εἱμαρμένη ταύτης οὐχ ἅπτεται.

5 ⌈παραθεῖσα δὲ τὸν πρῶτον ἀπὸ τοῦ πρώτου θεοῦ διανοητικὸν λόγον προίησι καὶ ὅλον τὸν λόγον.⌉ ⟨. . .⟩ ⌈ον⌉ συνέταξε⟨ν ἡ⟩ φύσις τοῖς γιγνομένοις· τούτοις ⟨δὲ ἡ⟩ ψυχὴ κοινωνήσασα κοινωνεῖ καὶ τῆς τούτων εἱμαρμένης. [[ἀμέτοχος οὖσα τῆς τῶν γινομένων φύσεως.]]

EXCERPTUM XIX

Stobaeus I. 49. 6, vol. i, p. 324 Wachsmuth (*Ecl.* I. 808 Heeren).

Τοῦ αὐτοῦ (*sc.* Ἑρμοῦ)

1 ⟨ἡ⟩ ψυχὴ τοίνυν ἐστὶν ⌈ἀίδιος νοητικὴ οὖσα νόημα ἔχουσα τὸν ἑαυτῆς λόγον. συννοοῦσα δὲ διάνοιαν τῆς ἁρμονίας ἐπισπᾶται.⌉ ἀπαλλαγεῖσα δὲ τοῦ φυσικοῦ σώματος, αὐτὴ καθ' αὑτὴν μένει [αὐτὴ ἑαυτῆς οὖσα] ἐν τῷ νοητῷ κόσμῳ. ⌈ἄρχει δὲ τοῦ ἑαυτῆς λόγου φέρουσα ὁμοίαν κίνησιν ἐν τῷ

1 ἐλλείπει Meineke: ἐκλείπει FP 3–4 Fortasse κοινωνεῖ τῷ λόγῳ τῶν διανοημάτων 3 νοηματικῷ F: νοητικῷ P 6 'Num ἀλλ' ἀκουσίως?' Wachsm.: fortasse ⟨τὸ δὲ κακὸν⟩ ἀκούσιον 8 διά ⟨τε⟩ τοῦτο Usener 10-11 Fortasse [ἐπεὶ] ⟨μόνη⟩ τοίνυν [[ἡ]] ⟨τῶν⟩ ἐν ἡμῖν ⟨⟨ἡ⟩⟩ νοητικὴ οὐσία αὐτεξούσιός ἐστιν 10 νοητικὴ scripsi (νοηματικὴ Patrit.): σωματικὴ FP 11 Fortasse ⟨. . .⟩ ὁ περὶ ⟨αὐτὴν⟩ (διανοητικὸς?) λόγος 12–13 ἀμέτοχος . . . φύσεως huc a § 5 transposui 13 ταύτης Wachsm.: τούτου codd. 14–15 Fortasse προεθεῖσα δὲ (*sc.* ἡ νοητικὴ οὐσία) τὸ πρῶτον ἀπὸ τοῦ πρώτου θεοῦ, προίησι καὶ τὸν λόγον 15 ὃν codd.: fortasse ⟨τὸ δὲ ἄλογ⟩ον (*sc.* τῆς ψυχῆς μέρος) vel ⟨τὸ δὲ αἰσθητικ⟩ὸν 17 κοινωνεῖ καὶ τῆς τούτων εἱμαρμένης scripsi (posset scribi κ. κ. τῆς τούτων ⟨κρατούσης⟩ εἱμαρμένης): κοινωνεῖται ταῖς τούτων εἱμαρμέναις codd.

20–22 Fortasse ⟨ἡ⟩ ψυχὴ τοίνυν ⟨⟨αὐτὴ ⟨καθ'⟩ ἑαυτὴν οὖσα⟩⟩ ἐστὶν οὐσία [ἀίδιος] νοητική, νόημα (an κίνημα?) ⟨ἴδιον⟩ ἔχουσα τὸν ἑαυτῆς λόγον, συννοοῦσα δὲ ⟨τῇ⟩ θείᾳ ⟨προ⟩νοίᾳ (?). ⟨καὶ σώματι μὲν συνοῦσα, ἄλογόν τι ἀπὸ⟩ τῆς ⟨φυσικῆς⟩ ἁρμονίας ἐπισπᾶται· ἀπαλλαγεῖσα δὲ κ.τ.λ. 20 οὖσα FP[1]: οὐσία P[2]

. . . Whence it[1] both exceeds and falls short, and is at 2
variance with itself. It becomes worse when it is separated from the discursive thought; but when it follows and obeys the discursive thought, it shares with the reason . . .[2]

. . . But we have power to choose; for it is in our power 3
to choose the better, and likewise to choose the worse. . . . involuntarily;[3] for the soul, when it cleaves to evil things,[4] draws near to corporeal nature, and for this reason the man who has chosen the worse is under the dominion of Destiny.

. . . The intelligent substance in us is self-determining.[5] The 4
intelligent substance remains ever in the same state without change, not partaking of the nature of the things which come into being, and therefore Destiny has no hold on it.

. . .[6] Nature has thus co-ordinated . . . with the things that 5
come into being;[7] and the soul, when it has taken part with these things, takes part also in the Destiny by which they are governed.[8]

EXCERPT XIX

From the teachings of Hermes.

The soul then is . . .; but when[9] it has been released from I
the physical body, it abides by itself in the intelligible world . . .

[1] 'It' probably means 'the irrational part of the soul'.

[2] Perhaps, 'it shares with the reason in its (i.e. the reason's) discursive thoughts'.

[3] Perhaps, '⟨Yet men's evil actions are⟩ involuntary'.

[4] I.e. bodily or material things.

[5] Perhaps, 'The intelligent substance then is the only thing in us that is self-determining'.

[6] Perhaps, 'The intelligent substance has been emitted in the beginning from the primal God, and emits from itself the reason'.

[7] Perhaps, 'But Nature has co-ordinated ⟨the irrational part of the soul⟩ with the things that come into being'.

[8] I.e. is governed by Destiny, as they are.

[9] Perhaps the meaning of the original text may have been, 'The soul then, when it is by itself, is intelligent substance (i.e. pure mind).... When it is joined to a body, it draws to itself from the structure of the body something which is irrational; but when', &c.

---

21 *συννοοῦσα* F : *συνοῦσα* P 24–1 *infra*: fortasse *ἄρχει δὲ τοῦ ⟨μεθ'⟩ ἑαυτῆς ⟨ἄ⟩λόγου, φέρουσα ⟨εἰς αὐτὸ⟩* [[ ]] *κίνησιν ⟨⟨ὁμοίαν⟩⟩ τῷ ἑαυτῆς νοήματι [ὀνόματι], ⟨καὶ παρέχουσα⟩ ζωὴν ⟨αὐ⟩τῷ* 24 *ἐν* om. P

Exc. XIX *init.* iteratur Stob. I. 49. I c, vol. i, p. 320 Wachsmuth (*Ecl.* I. 798 Heeren), ubi legitur:

Ἑρμοῦ. ψυχὴ τοίνυν ἐστὶν οὐσία αἴδιος νοητική νόημα ἔχουσα τὸν ἑαυτῆς λόγον.

2 ἑαυτῆς νοήματι ὀνόματι ζωὴν τῷ εἰς ζωὴν ἐρχομένῳ.⌉ τοῦτο γὰρ ἴδιον ψυχῆς, τὸ παρέχειν ἑτέροις ὅμοιόν ⟨τι⟩ τῇ ⌈ἰδιότητι⌉ αὐτῆς.

3 δύο τοίνυν εἰσὶ ζωαὶ καὶ δύο κινήσεις, μία μὲν ἡ κατ' οὐσίαν, ἑτέρα δὲ ἡ κατὰ φύσιν [σώματος]. καὶ ἡ μὲν [γενικωτέρα καὶ ἡ] κατ' οὐσίαν αὐτεξούσιος, ἡ δὲ ἀναγκαστ[ικ]ή· πᾶν γὰρ τὸ κινούμενον τῇ τοῦ κινοῦντος ἀνάγκῃ ὑποτέτακται.

4 ⌈ἡ δὲ κινοῦσα κίνησις τῷ τῆς νοητικῆς οὐσίας ἔρωτι ᾠκείωται. εἴη γὰρ ἂν ψυχὴ ἀσώματος⌉ ἀμέτοχος οὖσ[ι]α τοῦ φυσικοῦ σώματος. εἰ γὰρ ⌈ἔχει σῶμα⌉, οὔτε λόγον ἔχει οὔτε νόησιν. πᾶν γὰρ σῶμα ἀνόητον· μεταλαβὸν δὲ οὐσίας, τὸ εἶναι ζῷον ἔμπνουν ἔσχε.

5 καὶ τὸ μὲν πνεῦμα τοῦ σώματός ⟨ἐστι τὸ αἰσθητικόν⟩, ὁ δὲ λόγος τῆς οὐσίας ⟨⟨ἐστὶ τὸ φρονοῦν. συνυπάρχει δὲ τῷ ⟨μὲν⟩ λόγῳ ἡ τῶν ⌈τιμίων⌉ γνῶσις, τῷ δὲ πνεύματι ἡ δόξα·⟩⟩ ⟨ὁ μὲν γὰρ⟩ τοῦ ⌈καλοῦ⌉ θεωρητικός ἐστι, τὸ δὲ [αἰσθητικὸν πνεῦμα] τῶν φαινομένων κριτικόν ἐστι. διῄρηται δὲ ⟨τὸ πνεῦμα⟩ εἰς τὰς ὀργανικὰς αἰσθήσεις, καὶ ἔστι [τι] μέρος αὐτοῦ [πνευματική] ὁρατικ⟨ὸν⟩ καὶ ἀκουστικὸν καὶ ὀσφρητικὸν καὶ γευστικὸν καὶ ἁπτικόν. τοῦτο τὸ πνεῦμα ⌈ἀνάγον γενόμενον διανοίας⌉ κρίνει ⌈τὸ αἰσθητικόν⌉· εἰ δὲ μή, φαντάζεται μόνον.

6 [τοῦ γὰρ σώματός ἐστι καὶ δεκτικὸν πάντων, ὁ δὲ λόγος τῆς οὐσίας] [[ἐστὶ τὸ φρονοῦν. συνυπάρχει δὲ τῷ λόγῳ ἡ τῶν τιμίων γνῶσις, τῷ δὲ πνεύματι ἡ δόξα.]]

7 ⟨. . .⟩ τὸ μὲν γὰρ ἀπὸ τοῦ περιέχοντος κόσμου τὴν ἐνέργειαν ἔχει, ἡ δὲ ἀφ' ἑαυτῆς.

2–3 Fortasse τῇ ογσιότητι αὐτῆς 8–10 Fortasse ἡ δὲ ⟨τὴν⟩ κατ' οὐσ⟨ί⟩α⟨ν⟩ κίνησιν ⟨κινουμένη ψυχὴ⟩ τῷ τῆς νοητ[ικ]ῆς οὐσίας ἔρωτι κινεῖται, [ ] ἀμέτοχος οὖσ[ι]α τοῦ φυσικοῦ σώματος. εἰ γὰρ ⟨μετ⟩έχει σώμα⟨τος⟩ (an εἰ γὰρ ἔχε⟨ται⟩ σώμα⟨τος ἔρωτι⟩?), οὔτε λόγον ἔχει οὔτε νόησιν 9 οὖσα Usener : οὐσία codd. 11 δὲ om. P 14 τῆς ⟨νοητικῆς⟩ οὐσίας? 14–15 ἐστι τὸ φρονοῦν . . . ἡ δόξα huc a § 6 transposui 16 καλοῦ F : καθόλου corr. in καλοῦ P. Aptius esset ὄντος 17–18 εἰς τὰ ὄργανα τῆς αἰσθήσεως? 19 ὁρατικὸν scripsi : ὅρασις codd. 20 ἀνάγον F : ἀνάλογον P | Fortasse ἀναγόμενον ⟨μὲν εἰς μετοχὴν⟩ διανοίας 21 κρίνει ⟨κατ' ἀλήθειαν⟩? 22 Fortasse ⟨τὸ μὲν πνεῦμα⟩ τοῦ σώματός ἐστι τὸ αἰσθητικόν (vide § 5 *init.*) 25 κόσμου secludendum ?

. . . For it is[1] a peculiar property of soul, that it gives to 2
other things something similar to its own . . .[2]

There are then two kinds of life and two kinds of movement, 3
one that is according to true being, and another that is according to nature.[3] And the life which is according to true being is self-determining, but the other is under compulsion; for everything that is moved is subject to the compulsion applied to it by that which moves it.

. . . not partaking of the physical body. For if . . ., it has 4
neither reason nor intelligence.[4] For all bodies are devoid of intelligence; but when a body has received a portion of true being, it becomes a living creature that has in it the breath of life.

The vital spirit[5] is that part of the body to which belongs 5
sensation; the reason is that part of the intelligent substance which has understanding. With the reason coexists knowledge of . . .; with the vital spirit coexists opinion. The reason contemplates the . . .,[6] but the vital spirit discerns appearances. The vital spirit is parcelled out among the organs of sense; there is a part of it that sees, a part that hears, a part that smells, a part that tastes, and a part that feels by touch. This vital spirit if, . . .,[7] discerns things rightly; but if not, it merely receives illusory impressions.

. . . For the vital spirit gets the force with which it works 7
from the Kosmos by which it is environed;[8] but the soul gets from itself the force with which it works.

[1] Perhaps, 'The soul rules over the irrational thing which is joined to it, bringing into that thing a movement similar to the soul's own thought, and giving life to it when it comes into life; for it is', &c.

[2] Perhaps, 'similar to its own substantive existence (or reality of being)'.

[3] I. e. that belongs to the physical or corporeal world.

[4] Perhaps, 'When the soul's movement is the kind of movement which corresponds to true being, the soul is moved by love of "intelligible substance" (i.e. by desire for that which truly is,—the incorporeal and divine), and has no part in (i. e. is not affected by) the physical body. If it takes part in the body' (or 'is mastered by love of the body'), 'it is unable to think rationally or intelligently'.

[5] Or 'life-breath'.

[6] It ought to be 'the real', or 'that which truly is'.

[7] Perhaps, 'if it is brought into connexion with discursive thought' (which is the function of the 'reason').

[8] Perhaps, 'from the atmosphere'.

EXCERPTUM XX

Stobaeus I. 49. 3, vol. i, p. 320 Wachsmuth (*Ecl.* I. 798 Heeren).

Ἑρμοῦ.

1 ἔστι τοίνυν ἡ ψυχὴ ἀσώματος οὐσία· ⟨. . .⟩. εἰ γὰρ ⟨μὴ ψυχὴν⟩ ἔχει ⟨τὸ⟩ σῶμα, οὐκέτι ἔσται [ἑαυτῆς σωστική]. πᾶν γὰρ σῶμα [δεῖται] ⟨πρὸς⟩ τὸ[υ] εἶναι δεῖται [καὶ] ζωῆς, τῆς ἐν [τάξει] ⟨ψυχῇ⟩ κειμένης.

2 παντὶ γὰρ τῷ γένεσιν ἔχοντι καὶ [μεταβολὴν] ⟨φθορὰν⟩ δεῖ ἐπακολουθεῖν. τὸ γὰρ γινόμενον ⌜γίνεται ἐν μεγέθει, γινόμενον⌝ αὔξην ἔχει· παντὶ [γὰρ] ⟨δὲ⟩ τῷ αὐξανομένῳ ἐπακολουθεῖ μείωσις, μειώσει ⟨δὲ⟩ φθορά.

3 μετειληφὸς δὲ [εἴδους] [ζωῆς] ⟨ψυχῆς⟩, ζῇ, καὶ κοινωνεῖ τοῦ εἶναι τῇ ψυχῇ. ἡ δὲ αἰτία ἑτέρῳ τοῦ εἶναι αὐτὴ πρώτως [ὂν] ἔστι. τὸ δὲ εἶναι νῦν λέγω τὸ [ἐν λόγῳ γενέσθαι καὶ] μετέχειν ζωῆς [νοερᾶς]. [[παρέχει δὲ ἡ ψυχὴ ζωὴν νοεράν.]]

4 καλεῖται δὲ ⟨ὁ ἄνθρωπος⟩ ζῷον μὲν διὰ τὴν ζωήν, λογικὸν δὲ διὰ τὸ νοερόν, θνητὸν δὲ διὰ τὸ σῶμα. ⟨ἡ⟩ ψυχὴ ἄρα [ἀσώματος], ἀμετάπτωτον ἔχουσα τὴν δύναμιν ⟨τοῦ ζωὴν παρέχειν, τῷ ἀνθρώπῳ⟩ ⟨⟨παρέχει [δὲ ἡ ψυχὴ] ζωὴν νοεράν.⟩⟩ πῶς γὰρ οἷόν τέ ἐστι λέγειν ζῷον [νοερὸν] ⟨τὸν ἄνθρωπον⟩, μὴ οὔσης οὐσίας τῆς καὶ παρεχούσης ζωήν; ἀλλὰ οὐδὲ λογικὸν οἷόν τέ ἐστιν εἰπεῖν, μὴ οὔσης [τῆς διανοητικῆς] οὐσίας τῆς καὶ παρεχούσης νοερὰν ζωήν.

5 ⟨⟨οὐκ⟩⟩ ἐν πᾶσι δὲ [[οὐκ]] ⟨ἐπὶ τὸ τέλος⟩ ἀφικνεῖται τὸ νοερόν, διὰ ⟨τὸ ἔν τισι μὴ κατὰ τὸ μέσον ἡρμόσθαι⟩ τὴν τοῦ σώματος σύστασιν [πρὸς τὴν ἁρμονίαν]. ἐὰν γὰρ ὑπερέχῃ ἐν τῇ συστάσει τὸ θερμόν, κοῦφος καὶ ἔνθερμος γίνεται ⟨ὁ ἄνθρωπος⟩· ἐὰν δὲ τὸ ψυχρόν, βαρὺς καὶ νωχελὴς γίνεται. ⟨ἡ μὲν⟩ ⟨⟨γὰρ⟩⟩ φύσις [[γὰρ]] ἁρμόζει τὴν τοῦ σώματος σύστα-

2 ἔστι . . . οὐσία codd.: fortasse ἔστι τοίνυν ἐν τῇ ψυχῇ ἡ τοῦ σώματος οὐσία | ἡ om. F 3 ἑαυτῆς σωστική F: μετ' αὐτῆς σωματική P 4 'δεῖται ante τοῦ εἶναι deleverim' Wachsm. | πρὸς τὸ εἶναι scripsi: τοῦ εἶναι codd. 7 Fortasse γίνεται ἐν μεγέθει ⟨τινί⟩, γενόμενον ⟨δὲ⟩ αὔξην ἔχει 8 παντὶ γὰρ FP: παντὶ δὲ Heeren 9 μετειληφὼς F 10 τῇ ψυχῇ scripsi (⟨διὰ⟩ τὴν ψυχήν Wachsm.): τὴν ψυχήν codd. | πρώτως scripsi (προτοῦ Wachsm.): πρώτη FP 11 ἐν λόγῳ codd.: fortasse ἔλλογον 12 παρέχει . . . νοεράν hinc ad § 4 transposui 17 νοερὸν seclusit Wachsm. 22 τὸ ἔν τισι

EXCERPT XX

From the teachings of Hermes.

The soul then is an incorporeal substance; . . .[1] For if the 1
body has not soul, it will no longer be real. For all bodies need life to make them real, and life resides in soul.

For[2] in the case of everything which comes into being, the coming-to-be 2
must be followed by destruction. For that which comes into being . . .[3] increases; and in the case of everything which increases, the increase is followed by diminution, and the diminution by destruction.

But if a body has a portion of soul, then it is alive, and shares 3
with the soul in the possession of reality. And that which is the cause of reality to another thing must itself be real in the highest degree. By 'reality' I here mean participation in life.

Now man is called 'a living being' because he is alive, and 4
'rational' because he has intelligence, and 'mortal' because of his body.[4] The soul then, retaining unchanged its power of conferring life, confers on man *intelligent* life. For how could one say that man is a living being, if there were not a really[5] existing thing that confers life on him? Nor could one say that man is rational, if there were not a really existing thing that confers on him *intelligent* life.

But the intellect is not fully developed in all men, because 5
in some men the composition of the body ⟨is not so contempered as to hit the mean.⟩ For if there is an excess of the hot element in the composition of the body, the man is rendered light-minded and fervid; if there is an excess of the cold element, he is rendered dull and sluggish. For nature contempers the com-

[1] 'Perhaps, 'The soul then is a real (or substantively existent) thing that is incorporeal; ⟨and it confers reality on the body also⟩'. Or possibly, 'The reality of the body then is in the soul (i. e. depends on the presence of soul in it); for if the body has not soul', &c.

[2] § 2 has nothing to do with the context; it appears to be a fragment placed here by mistake.

[3] Perhaps, 'For that which comes into being is of a certain size when it first comes to be, and having come to be, it increases'.

[4] The writer assumes the definition of man to be 'Man is a rational and mortal animal'.

[5] Or 'substantively'.

μὴ κατὰ τὸ μέσον ἡρμόσθαι addidi: vide § 6   25 *ὁ ἄνθρωπος* addidi (ante *γίνεται* add. *ἄνθρωπος* Wachsm.)

σιν ⌜πρὸς τὴν ἁρμονίαν⌝· ⟨⟨παραλαβοῦσα δὲ ⟨ἡ⟩ ψυχὴ ⟨τὸ σῶμα⟩ καθὼς εἴργασται, [τ]οὕτω παρέχει ζωὴν τῷ τῆς φύσεως ἔργῳ.⟩⟩

6 εἴδη δὲ τῆς ⟨τοῦ σώματος⟩ ἁρμονίας τρία, τὸ κατὰ τὸ θερμόν, καὶ τὸ κατὰ ⟨τὸ⟩ ψυχρόν, καὶ τὸ κατὰ τὸ μέσον· ἁρμόζει δὲ ⟨ἡ φύσις⟩ κατὰ τὸν ἐπικρατήσαντα ἀστέρα τῆς συγκρά[τη]σεως [τῶν ἀστέρων]. [[παραλαβοῦσα δὲ ψυχὴ καθὼς εἴργασται τούτῳ παρέχει ζωὴν τῷ τῆς φύσεως ἔργῳ.]]

7 ἡ φύσις τοίνυν ὁμοιοῖ τὴν ἁρμονίαν τοῦ σώματος τῇ τῶν ἀστέρων ⌜συγκράσει⌝, ⌜καὶ ἑνοῖ τὰ πολυμιγῆ πρὸς τὴν τῶν ἄστρων ἁρμονίαν⌝ ὥστε ἔχειν πρὸς ἄλληλα συμπάθειαν. ⌜τέλος γὰρ τῆς τῶν ἀστέρων ἁρμονίας τὸ γεννᾶν συμπάθειαν καθ' εἱμαρμένην αὐτῶν.⌝

EXCERPTUM XXI

Stobaeus I. 41. 11, vol. i, p. 293 Wachsmuth (*Ecl.* I. 750 Heeren).

Ἑρμοῦ.

1 ἔστι τοίνυν τὸ προὸν ἐπ[ι]⟨έκεινα⟩ πάντων τῶν ὄντων, καὶ τῶν ὄντως ὄντων προόν. ⌜ὂν γάρ ἐστι δι' οὗ⌝ ἡ οὐσιότης, [ἡ] καθόλου λεγομένη, κοινή ⟨ἐστι τῶν⟩ νοητῶν ⟨καὶ τῶν αἰσθητῶν⟩. ⟨. . .⟩ τῶν ὄντως ὄντων καὶ [τῶν ὄντων τῶν] καθ' ἑαυτὰ νοουμένων. τὰ δὲ ⟨αἰσθητά⟩, ἐνάντια ⟨ὄντα⟩ τούτοις, κατὰ τὸ ἕτερον πάλιν ⟨ἔστιν· οὐ γὰρ⟩ αὐτὰ καθ' ἑαυτά ἔστι. ⟨. . . ἡ δὲ⟩ φύσις οὐσία αἰσθητή, ἔχουσα ἐν ἑαυτῇ ⟨τὰ⟩ αἰσθητὰ πάντα. μεταξὺ δὲ τούτων [νοη[μα]τ[ικ]οὶ καὶ αἰσθητοὶ θεοὶ] ⟨τὰ δοξαστά⟩, τὰ μὲν μετέχοντα τῶν νοητῶν, τὰ δὲ ⟨οὔ⟩. [δοξαστὰ τὰ κοινωνοῦντα τῶν νοη[μα]τ[ικ]ῶν.]

1–3 παραλαβοῦσα . . . ἔργῳ huc a § 6 *fin.* transposui 1–2 τὸ σῶμα addidi (σῶμα add. Usener) 2 οὕτω scripsi : τούτῳ codd. 2–3 τῆς φύσεως F : τῆς κατὰ φύσεως P 5 τὸ (ante ψυχρόν) add. Patr. 6 'Num ἀστέρα delendum?' Wachsm. 7 συγκράσεως Patr. : συγκρατήσεως FP 10–11 Fortasse καὶ ⟨γὰρ⟩ ἥνωται τὰ ἐπὶ γῆς πρὸς τὴν τῶν ἀστέρων ⌜ἁρμονίαν⌝ 11 ἄστρων FP : ἀστέρων Wachsm. 12–13 Fortasse [τέλος] ⟨ἔργον⟩ γὰρ [τῆς] τῶν ἀστέρων [ἁρμονίας] τὸ γεννᾶν [συμπάθειαν] ⟨σώματα⟩ καθ' εἱμαρμένην [αὐτῶν]

15 ἐπέκεινα scripsi : ἐπὶ codd. 16 Fortasse ὄν⟨τος⟩ γὰρ ⟨τοῦ⟩ "ἔστι" δι⟨ττ⟩οῦ, ἡ οὐσιότης κ.τ.λ. : vel τὸ γὰρ "ἔστι" δίττως ⟨λέγεται, καὶ⟩ ἡ οὐσιότης 19 νουμένων P[1] 21 Fortasse ⟨καὶ ὁ μὲν ἄνω κόσμος ἐστὶν οὐσία νοητή, ἔχων ἐν ἑαυτῷ τὰ νοητὰ πάντα· ἡ δὲ⟩ φύσις 22 νοητοὶ scripsi : νοηματικοὶ codd. 23 τῶν (ante νοητῶν) Canter : τὸν P : om. F 24 νοητῶν scripsi : νοηματικῶν codd.

position of the body according to . . .;[1] and the soul, taking over the body as made by nature, thereupon confers life on the body which nature has made.

The contemperation of bodies is of three kinds, namely, that in which the hot element preponderates, that in which the cold element preponderates, and that which is in the mean; and nature contempers them according to the star[2] which has got control over the mixing of these elements. 6

Nature then makes the contemperation of the body resemble the . . . of the stars; . . . so that they are mutually affected.[3] . . .[4] 7

EXCERPT XXI

From the teachings of Hermes.

The Pre-existent[5] then is beyond all existent things, being prior even to the things which *really* exist.[6] For . . . the term 'substantive existence',[7] employed as all-inclusive, is applicable both to the objects of thought and to the objects of sense. . . . the things which really exist, and which are regarded by thought as existing of themselves. But the objects of sense are contrary to the objects of thought, and exist in the other way; for they are not existent of themselves. . . . The world of nature[8] is an existent object of sense, and contains within itself all objects of sense. 1

Intermediate between the objects of thought and the objects of sense are the objects of opinion;[9] and of these, some partake of the objects of thought, but others do not.[10]

1 Perhaps, 'according to the influence of the stars'.

2 Or 'planet'.

3 Perhaps, 'for the things on earth are united to the (system?) of the stars, so that the things on earth and the movements of the stars are mutually affected'.

4 Perhaps, 'For it is the function of the stars to generate bodies in accordance with Destiny'.

5 The restoration of § 1 that is here proposed is very doubtful; but it probably does not differ widely in meaning from what the author wrote.

6 'The things which *really* exist' are 'the objects of thought', i.e. the things apprehensible by thought alone, and not by sense.

7 Perhaps, 'For the word "exist" is used in two different ways, and the term "substantive existence"', &c.

8 Perhaps, '⟨The higher world is an existent object of thought, and contains within itself all the objects of thought; but the world of nature (i.e. the corporeal or material world)', &c.

9 More literally, 'the things opined'.

10 Opinions may be true or false. When an opinion is true, then, and then only, the 'thing opined' partakes of the reality which belongs primarily to the 'objects of thought'.

2 ⟨. . . τῶν αἰσθητῶν⟩ θεῶν· οὗτοι δὲ εἰκόνες εἰσὶ ⟨τῶν⟩ νοη[μα]τῶν ⟨θεῶν⟩. οἷον ἥλιος εἰκών ἐστι τοῦ ἐπουρανίου δημιουργοῦ [θεοῦ]· καθάπερ γὰρ ἐκεῖνος τὸ ὅλον ἐδημιούργησε⟨ν, οὕτω⟩ καὶ ὁ ἥλιος δημιουργεῖ τὰ ζῷα καὶ [γεννᾷ] ⟨τὰ⟩ φυτά [καὶ τῶν πνευμάτων πρυτανεύει].

EXCERPTUM XXII

Stobaeus I. 42. 7, vol. i, p. 295 Wachsmuth (*Ecl.* I. 754 Heeren).

Ἑρμοῦ ἐκ τῆς Ἀφροδίτης.

παρὰ τί τὰ βρέφη ὅμοια τοῖς γονεῦσι γίνεται ⸢ἢ συγγενείαις ἀποδίδοται⸣ ἐκθήσω λόγον. ὅταν νοστίμου αἵματος ἐξαφ[εδ]ρούμενον ⸢ἡ γένεσις⸣ ἀποθησαυρίζῃ γόνον, συμβαίνει πως ἐκπν[ε]εῖν ἐκ τοῦ σώματος ὅλου [μελῶν] οὐσίαν τινὰ ⟨. . .⟩ κατὰ θείαν ἐνέργειαν, ὡς [τοῦ αὐτοῦ] ἀνθρώπου γινομένου. τὸ δ' αὐτὸ καὶ ἐπὶ τῆς γυναικὸς εἰκὸς γίγνεσθαι. ὅταν ⟨οὖν⟩ καθυπερτερήσῃ τὸ ῥυὲν ἀπὸ τοῦ ἀνδρὸς καὶ ἄτηκτον γένηται, τῷ πατρὶ ὅμοι[ουμεν]ον τὸ βρέφος ἀποδειχθήσεται, ὡς τὸ ἀνάπαλιν τὸν αὐτὸν τρόπον τῇ μητρί. ἐὰν ⟨δὲ ἐπί⟩ τινος μέρους ⟨ἡ⟩ καθυπερτέ⟨ρη⟩σις γένηται, πρὸς ἐκεῖνο τὸ μέρος ἀφομοιοῦται. ⟨. . .⟩ ἔσθ' ὅτε δὲ καὶ εἰς μακρὰς γενεάς. ⟨. . .⟩ παραβάλλειν τὸ βρέφος τῇ μορφῇ τοῦ γεννήσαντος. ⟨. . .⟩ ⸢ἐκείνου⸣ ⟨τοῦ⟩ δεκανοῦ ⟨τοῦ⟩ λόγον ἔχοντος πρὸς τὴν ὥραν ἐν ᾗ ἡ γυνὴ ἐπαιδοποίει.

1 οὗτοι scripsi : αὗται codd. 1–2 τῶν νοητῶν θεῶν scripsi : νοημάτων codd. 2 ἐπουρανίου codd. : fortasse ὑπερουρανίου 3 δημιουργοῦ θεοῦ F : θεοῦ δημιουργοῦ P | ἐκεῖνα P 4 τὰ (ante φυτά) add. Patrit. 5 καὶ τῶν πνευμάτων πρυτανεύει om. F

7 τί τὰ F : τί δὲ τὰ P 7–8 Fortasse παρὰ τί δὲ τὰ βρέφη ὅμοια τοῖς γονεῦσι γίνεται ἢ συγγενέσι τισιν, ἀποδώσω [ἐκθήσω] λόγον. 9 ἐξαφρούμενον scripsi (ἐξαφρουμένου Usener) : ἐξαφεδρουμένου FP | ἡ γένεσις FP : fortasse ἡ φύσις | ἀποθησαυρίζῃ (ultima η in ras.) F : ἀποθησαυρίζει P 10 ἐκπνεῖν Meineke : ἐκπνέειν F : εἰσπνέειν P 11–12 ὡς τοῦ αὐτοῦ ἀνθρώπου γινομένου ut glossema del. Meineke : an delendum κατὰ θείαν . . . γινομένου? 12 εἰκὸς Canter : εἰς τὸ FP 13 οὖν add. Heeren | καθυπερτερήσῃ Wachsm. : καθυπερτερίσῃ FP 14 ἄτηκτον Patrit. : ἄθικτον codd. | ὅμοιον scripsi : ὁμοιούμενον codd. 16 δὲ ἐπὶ addidi (δὲ add. Wachsm.) | καθυπερτέρησις Meineke : καθυπέρθεσις FP

. . . of the gods apprehensible by sense; and these gods are images of the gods apprehensible only by thought. The Sun, for instance, is an image of the Maker who is above the heavens; for even as that supreme Maker made the whole universe, so the Sun makes the animals and the plants. 2

EXCERPT XXII

From the discourse of Hermes which is entitled APHRODITE.

How does it come about that children resemble their parents . . . ?[1] I will explain this. When . . . stores up[2] *semen* that is foamed forth from productive blood, it comes to pass that there is exhaled from the whole body a certain substance[3] . . . by[4] the working of a divine force, inasmuch as it is a human being that is being brought into existence.[5] And it is to be presumed that the same thing takes place in the case of the woman also. When then the efflux from the man is prepotent, and its vigour is not impaired, the child that is produced will be like its father; and in the same way, if the conditions are reversed, the child will be like its mother. And if there is such a prepotency in respect of some part of the body, the child comes to resemble the father or the mother in that part. . . . and sometimes even to remote generations. . . . to compare the child with the form of its father. . . . of that Decanus who had to do with the hour in which the woman was bearing[6] the child.

[1] Perhaps, 'or (resemble) certain others of their kin'.
[2] Perhaps, 'When nature (operating in the father's body) stores up', &c.
[3] Viz. the 'vital spirit' which is the living and active ingredient in the *semen*.
[4] Perhaps, 'and this substance is vitalized by', &c.
[5] This seems to imply that in the case of the lower animals there is no such intervention of a divine force.
[6] Or 'conceiving'?

EXCERPTUM XXIII

Stobaeus I. 49. 44, vol. i, p. 385 Wachsmuth (*Ecl.* I. 926 Heeren).

Ἑρμοῦ τρισμεγίστου ἐκ τῆς ἱερᾶς βίβλου ⟨τῆς⟩ ἐπικαλουμένης Κόρης κόσμου.

32 ⟨⟨Πρόσεχε, τέκνον Ὧρε· κρυπτῆς γὰρ ἐπακούεις θεωρίας, ἧς ὁ μὲν προπάτωρ Καμῆφις ⟨ἦν ἀρχηγέτης, Ἑρμῆς δὲ⟩ ⟨⟨παρὰ τοῦ πάντων προγενεστέρου Καμήφεως⟩⟩ ἔτυχεν ἐπακούσας, ⟨ἐγὼ δὲ⟩ παρὰ Ἑρμοῦ τοῦ [πάντων ἔργων] ὑπομνηματογράφου [[παρὰ τοῦ πάντων προγενεστέρου Καμήφεως]], ὁπότ' ἐμὲ καὶ ⌜τῷ τελείῳ μέλανι ἐτίμησε⌝, νῦν δὲ αὐτὸς σὺ παρ' ἐμοῦ.—⟩⟩

1 ταῦτα εἰποῦσα Ἶσις ἐγχεῖ π⟨ρ⟩ῶτον Ὥρῳ γλυκύ[ν] τι π[ρ]οτὸν ἀμβροσίας, ὃ αἱ ψυχαὶ λαμβάνειν ἔθος ἔχουσιν ⌜θεῶν⌝, καὶ οὕτως τοῦ ἱερωτάτου λόγου ἄρχεται [Ἶσις].

2 Ἐπικειμένου, τέκνον Ὧρε, τῇ τῶν ὑπο⟨κάτω⟩ [κειμένων] φύσει πάσῃ τοῦ πολυστέφους οὐρανοῦ, ⌜καὶ κατ' οὐδένα τόπον στερουμένου τινὸς ὧν νῦν ὁ σύμπας ἔχει κόσμος⌝, ἀνάγκη πᾶσα ὑπὸ τῶν ὑπερκειμένων συγκεκοσμῆσθαι καὶ πεπληρῶσθαι φύσιν πᾶσαν τὴν ὑποκειμένην· οὐ γὰρ δήπου δυνατὰ ⟨⟨τὰ κάτω⟩⟩ κοσμῆσαι [[τὰ κάτω]] τὸν ὕπερθεν [δια]κόσμον. ἀνάγκη τοίνυν τοῖς κρείττοσι μυστηρίοις εἴκειν τὰ ἐλάσσονα· κρείσσων δὲ τῶν ὑποκειμένων ἡ τῶν μετεώρων ἐστὶ [δια]τάξις, καὶ τῷ παντὶ ἀσφαλής [τε], καὶ θνητῶν οὐχ ὑποπίπτουσα διανοίᾳ.

* * * * *

1 τῆς (post βίβλου) add. Gaisford 3–9 § 32 (Πρόσεχε, τέκνον . . . παρ' ἐμοῦ) huc transposui 3 Fortasse ἐπακούσεις 6 ἐγὼ δὲ ante παρὰ Ἑρμοῦ addidi (ἐγὼ δὲ ante παρὰ τοῦ . . . Καμήφεως add. Canter) 8 Fortasse τῷ τέλει ⟨τ⟩ῷ ⌜μέλανι⌝ (μεγάλῳ?) ἐτέλεσε, vel τῇ τελετῇ τῇ ⌜μελαίνῃ⌝ (μεγάλῃ?) ἐτέλεσε 10 Ἶσις om. P 10–11 ἐγχεῖ πρῶτον Ὥρῳ γλυκύ τι ποτὸν scripsi : ἐγχεῖ ποτὸν Ὥρῳ γλυκὺν (γλυκὺ Heeren) τὸ πρῶτον codd. 11 ὃ codd.: fortasse οἷον | Fortasse αἱ ⟨μακάριαι⟩ ψυχαὶ 12 θεῶν codd.: ⟨ἀπὸ⟩ θεῶν Patrit.: delendum? An scribendum ⟨μετὰ τῶν⟩ θεῶν ⟨διάγουσαι⟩ vel simile aliquid? | Ἶσις del. Heeren 13 ὑποκάτω scripsi : ὑποκειμένων codd. 14–15 Fortasse καὶ τοῦ σύμπαντος κόσμου κατ' οὐδένα τόπον στερουμένου τινὸς ὧν χρείαν ἔχει vel simile quid 15 στερομένου P 18 Fortasse ⟨συγ⟩κοσμῆσαι | τὸν ὕπερθεν F : τῶν ὕπερθεν P 19 κόσμον scripsi: διάκοσμον codd. | μυστηρίους delendum? 20 δὲ Patrit.: δὴ F : δεῖ P 21 τάξις scripsi : διάταξις codd. 21–22 Fortasse ⌜καὶ⌝ τῷ παντὶ ἀσφαλὴς [τε] ⟨οὖσα⟩, καὶ θανάτῳ οὐχ ὑποπίπτουσα [διανοία]

EXCERPT XXIII

From the holy book of Hermes Trismegistus which is entitled KORE KOSMU.[1]

Isis. Give heed, my son Horus; for you shall hear secret 32
doctrine, of which our forefather Kamephis was the first teacher. It so befell that Hermes heard this teaching from Kamephis, the eldest of all our race; I heard it from Hermes the writer of records, at the time when he . . . ;[2] and you shall hear it now from me.—

Having thus spoken, Isis first poured forth for Horus a sweet 1
draught of ambrosia, such a draught as the souls are wont to receive . . . ;[3] and thereupon she thus began her most holy discourse:

Inasmuch as heaven with its many circles, my son Horus, 2
is placed above all the world of things below, . . . ,[4] it must be that all the world which lies below has been set in order and filled with contents by the things which are placed above;[5] for the things below have not power to set in order the world above. The weaker mysteries[6] then must yield to the stronger; and the system of things on high is stronger than the things below, and is wholly steadfast, and cannot be apprehended by the thoughts of mortal men.[7]

* * * * *

[1] I. e. 'the Eye-pupil of the Universe'.

[2] Perhaps, 'when he initiated me in the Black (?) Rites' (or possibly, 'in the great rites').

[3] Perhaps, 'such as are the draughts which souls in bliss are wont to receive when they dwell among the gods'.

[4] Perhaps, 'and the whole universe is not in any of its regions deprived of (i. e. left unprovided with) any of the things it needs'.

[5] I. e. we see that the terrestrial world is organized, and filled with living beings; and this must have been done by the celestial gods.

[6] 'Mysteries' seems here to mean supernatural powers or forces. But it might perhaps be better to write 'the weaker things'.

[7] Perhaps, 'is stronger than the things below, inasmuch as it is secure from disturbance and not subject to death'.

3 ἔνθεν ἐστέναζον ⌜τὰ κάτω⌝ φόβον ἔχοντες, ⟨. . .⟩ τὴν περικαλλῆ
⟨. . .⟩ καὶ εἰς ἀεὶ διαμονὴν τῶν ἐπικειμένων. ⌜ἦν γὰρ ἄξιον θεωρίας ὁμοῦ
καὶ ἀγωνίας⌝ ὁρᾶν οὐρανοῦ κάλλος [[θεῷ]] ⟨ἡλίῳ⟩ καταφωτιζομένου [[τῷ
ἔτι ἀγνώστῳ]], ⟨παρα⟩πλησίαν τε νυκτὸς σεμνότητα, ἐλάττονι μὲν ἡλίου
ὀξεῖ δὲ πυρφορουμένης φωτί, τῶν [τε] ἄλλων κατὰ μέρος κινουμένων ἐν
οὐρανῷ μυστηρίων τακταῖς [[χρόνων]] κινήσεσι καὶ ⟨⟨χρόνων⟩⟩ περιόδοις,
διά ⟨τέ⟩ τινων κρυπτῶν ἀπορροιῶν τὰ κάτω συγκοσμούντων καὶ συν-
αυξόντων. καὶ οὕτως ⟨ἐγένοντο⟩ φόβοι μὲν ἐπάλληλοι, ζητήσεις δὲ
ἄληκτοι.
4 καὶ ἕως ⟨μὲν⟩ ὁ τῶν συμπάντων οὐκ ἐβούλετο τεχνίτης ⟨γνωσθῆναι⟩,
ἀγνωσία κατεῖχε τὰ ξύμπαντα· ὅτε δὲ ἔκρινεν αὑτὸν ὅστις ἐστὶ
δηλῶσαι, ἔρωτα[ς] ἐνεφ[ο]ύσησε θε⟨ί⟩οις ⟨τισὶν ἀνθρώποις⟩, καὶ αὐγὴν
ἣ⟨ς⟩ εἶχον ἐν στέρνοις πλείονα ταῖς τούτων ἐχαρίσατο διανοίαις, ἵνα
⟨⟨θεὸν⟩⟩ ⟨⟨τὸν ἔτι ἄγνωστον⟩⟩ πρῶτον μὲν ζητεῖν θελήσωσιν, εἶτα ⟨δὲ
5 καὶ⟩ [ἐπιθυμήσωσιν] εὑρεῖν [εἶτα καὶ κατορθῶσαι] δυνηθῶσι. τοῦτο δ'
[ἄν], ὦ τέκνον ἀξιοθαύμαστον Ὧρε, οὐκ ἂν ⟨ἦν⟩ ἐπὶ θνητῇ σπορᾷ, ⟨εἰ μὴ⟩
ἐγεγόνει [οὐδὲ γὰρ ἦν οὐδέπω] ψυχὴ[ς δὲ τὴν] συμπάθειαν ἔχουσα[ς]
τοῖς οὐρανοῦ μυστηρίοις. τ⟨οι⟩οῦτο⟨ς⟩ δὲ ἦν ὁ πάντα ⟨γ⟩νοὺς Ἑρμῆς·
ὃς καὶ εἶδε τὰ σύμπαντα, καὶ ἰδὼν κατενόησε, καὶ κατανοήσας ἴσχυσε
δηλῶσαι [τε καὶ δεῖξαι]. ⟨. . .·⟩ καὶ γὰρ ἃ ἐνόησεν ἐχάραξε, καὶ
χαράξας ἔκρυψε⟨ν⟩ ⟨⟨ἀσφαλῶς⟩⟩, τὰ πλεῖστα σιγήσας [[ἀσφαλῶς]] [ἢ
λαλήσας], ἵνα ζητῇ ταῦτα πᾶς αἰὼν ὁ μεταγενέστερος κόσμου.
6 καὶ οὗτος ⟨μέν⟩, τοὺς συγγενεῖς θεοὺς δορυφορεῖν ⟨προσταχθείς⟩,
ἀνέβαινεν εἰς ἄστρα· ἀλλ' ἦν αὐτῷ διάδοχος ὁ Τάτ, υἱὸς ὁμοῦ ⟨⟨τούτου⟩⟩
καὶ παραλήπτωρ τῶν μαθημάτων [[τούτων]], οὐκ εἰς μακρὰν δὲ καὶ
Ἀσκληπιὸς ὁ ⟨καὶ⟩ Ἰμούθης, ὁ Π⟨τ⟩ανὸς ⟨τοῦ⟩ καὶ Ἡφαίστου [βουλαῖς],
ἄλλοι τε ὅσοι ⟨τὰ⟩ τῆς οὐρανίου θεωρίας π⟨λε⟩ίστῃ ἀκριβείᾳ ἔμελλον

1 Fortasse ⟨⟨*καὶ ἄγνωστα* [*μὲν*] *ἦν κατ' ἀρχὰς πάντα πᾶσι* ⟨*τοῖς ἀνθρώποις*⟩⟩⟩· *ἔνθεν ἐστέναζον κ.τ.λ.* (vide § 53 *init.*) | *ἐστέναζον . . . φόβον ἔχοντες* scripsi : *ἐστέναξε . . . φόβον ἔχοντα* codd. 1–3 Fortasse ⟨*ἅμα δ' ἐθαύμαζον*⟩ *τὴν περικαλλῆ* ⟨*τάξιν* (vel *ἁρμονίαν*)⟩ [ ] *τῶν ἐπικειμένων,—ἦν γὰρ ἄξιον θεωρίας* [ ],—*ὁρῶντες οὐρανοῦ κάλλος κ.τ.λ.* 3–4 *θεῷ* et *τῷ ἔτι ἀγνώστῳ* hinc ad § 4 transposui 3 *καταφωτιζομένου* scripsi : *καταφανταζόμενον* codd. 4 *παραπλησίαν* scripsi : *πλουσίαν* codd. 5 *πυρφορουμένης* scripsi : *προσφορουμένην* codd. 7 *ἀποριῶν* P | *κοσμούντων* P 8 *οὕτως ἐγένοντο φόβοι μὲν ἐπάλληλοι* scripsi : *οὗτος φόβος μὲν ἐπάλληλος* codd. | *δὲ* scripsi : *τε* codd. 9 *ἄληκτοι* P² : *ἄδεκτοι* FP¹ 12 *ἔρωτα* scripsi : *ἔρωτας* codd. Fortasse *ἔρωτα σ*⟨*οφίας*⟩ | *ἐνεφύσησε* scripsi (posset scribi etiam *ἐνέπνευσε*) : *ἐνεθουσίασε* codd. | *θείοις τισιν ἀνθρώποις* scripsi : *θεοῖς* codd. | *αὐγὴν* Canter : *αὐτὴν* FP 13 *ἧς εἶχον* scripsi : *ἣ εἶχεν* codd. 14 *θεὸν τὸν ἔτι ἄγνωστον* addidi (vide § 3) 16 *ἂν* (ante *ὦ*) om. Patrit. 16–17 *οὐκ ἂν ἦν ἐπὶ θνητῇ σπορᾷ, εἰ μὴ ἐγεγόνει* scripsi : *οὐκ ἂν ἐπὶ θνητῆς σπορᾶς ἐγεγόνει* codd. 17 *ψυχὴ συμπάθειαν ἔχουσα* scripsi : *ψυχῆς δὲ τὴν συμπάθειαν ἐχούσης* codd.

Thereupon[1] men moaned, being afraid, . . . the beautiful . . . and everlasting 3
duration of the things above. For it was . . . to see the beauty of the sky[2] when it was flooded with light by the Sun, and the well-nigh equal majesty of the night, torch-lit with light less than the Sun's, yet bright, when in their turn the other holy Powers[3] moved along their paths in heaven with ordered movements in fixed periods of time, and by certain secret effluences wrought order and growth in the things below. And thus arose fears upon fears, and ceaseless questionings.

And as long as the Craftsman who made the universe willed not to be 4
known, all was wrapped in ignorance. But when he determined to reveal himself, he breathed into certain godlike men a passionate desire to know him, and bestowed on their minds a radiance ampler than that which they already had within their breasts, that so they might first will to seek the yet
unknown God, and then have power to find him. But this, Horus my 5
wondrous son, it would not have been possible for men of mortal breed to do, if there had not arisen one whose soul was responsive to the influence of the holy Powers of heaven. And such a man was Hermes, he who won knowledge of all. Hermes saw all things, and understood what he saw, and had power to explain to others what he understood. . . .[4] for what he had discovered he inscribed on tablets, and hid securely what he had inscribed, leaving the larger part untold, that all later ages of the world might seek it.

And Hermes, having been bidden to attend on the gods to whom he was 6
akin,[5] was about to ascend to the stars; but to him succeeded Tat, who was his son, and therewith inheritor of the knowledge which Hermes had acquired; and not long after, Asclepius, also named Imuthes, the son of Ptah, who is also named Hephaistos, and all those other men who, by the will of that Providence which reigns over all, were destined to search out with the utmost

[1] This passage (§§ 3–8) is inconsistent both with the introductory passage which precedes it (§§ 32, 1, 2) and with the narrative which follows (§§ 9–70), and must have originally belonged to a different document.

There is reason to suspect that the preceding passage also (§§ 32, 1, 2) did not form part of the *libellus* which contained §§ 9–70, but was the beginning of another *libellus*, all the rest of which is lost.

[2] Perhaps, '⟨In the beginning, all was unknown to all men ;⟩ wherefore they moaned in fear. But at the same time they marvelled at the beauteous order of the things above (for it was a sight well worth their contemplation), when they saw the beauty of the sky', &c.

[3] I. e. the moon and stars.

[4] Perhaps, '⟨Yet he did not make the truth known without reserve⟩'.

[5] I. e. having been told by the gods that he must now die and go to heaven.

---

18 *τοιοῦτος* scripsi : *τοῦτο* codd. | *γνοὺς* P[2] : *νοῦς* FP[1] 20 *τε* om. P | Fortasse ⟨*οὐ μὴν οὐδ' ἀπερισκέπτως ἔδειξε*⟩ vel simile quid 22 *κόσμου* secludendum ? 23 *οὗτος* scripsi : *οὕτως* codd. 24 *ἀνέβενεν* P[1] 25 *τούτων* FP : *τούτου* Meineke 25–26 *καὶ ὁ 'Ασκληπιὸς* P 26 *ὁ Πτανὸς τοῦ* scripsi (*Πτανὸς* vel *Πτανὸς* ⟨*τοῦ*⟩ Reitzenstein) : *σπανὸς* FP[1] : *πανὸς* P[2] 27 *πλείστῃ ἀκριβείᾳ* scripsi : *πιστὴν ἀκρίβειαν* codd.

7 βουλομένης τῆς πάντων βασιλίδος ἱστορῆσαι προνοίας. Ἑρμῆς μὲν οὖν ⌜ἀπελογεῖτο τῷ περιέχοντι ὡς⌝ οὐδὲ τῷ παιδὶ παρέδωκεν ὁλοτελῆ ⟨τὴν⟩ θεωρίαν, διὰ τὸ ἔτι τῆς ἡλικίας νεοειδές. ⟨εἶπε δὲ οὕτως·⟩ "Ἐγὼ δὴ [τῆς ἀνατολῆς γενόμενος] τοῖς πάντα βλέπουσιν ὀφθαλμοῖς ⟨τοῦ νοῦ⟩ τὰ τῆς ⌜ἀνατολῆς⌝ ⟨ἐ⟩θεώρησα[ι τι] ἀειδῆ· καὶ ἐπισκοποῦντί ⟨μοι⟩ βραδέως μέν, ἀλλ' οὖν ἦλθεν ἡ ἀκριβὴς [δια]γνῶσις. ⟨. . . χρή με⟩ πλησίον τῶν Ὀσίριδος κρυφίων ἀποθέσθαι τὰ ἱερὰ τῶν κοσμικῶν στοιχείων σύμβολα, ἐπικατευξάμενον δὲ [καὶ τοὺς λόγους τούσδε εἰπόντα[ς]] εἰς οὐρανὸν ἀπελθε⟨ῖ⟩ν."

8 ἀλλ' οὐ καθῆκον ἀτελῆ τὴν ἀπαγγελίαν, ὦ τέκνον, ταύτην με[ν] καταλεῖψαι, εἰπεῖν δ' ὅσα τὰς βίβλους κατατιθέμενος ἐξεῖπε[ι]ν Ἑρμῆς. [ἐξ]εῖπε γὰρ οὕτως· "Ὦ ἱεραὶ βίβλοι, τῶν [ἀ]φθαρτῶν ⌜αἳ τετεύχαταί⌝ μου χειρῶν, ἃς τῷ τῆς ἀφθαρσίας φαρμάκῳ ⌜χορείας ἐπικρατῷ⌝, ἀσαπεῖς πάντας αἰῶνας [καὶ ἄφθαρτοι] διαμείνατε [χρόνους], ἀθεώρητοι καὶ ἀνεύρετοι γιγνόμεναι παντὶ τῷ τὰ γῆς ταύτης περ⟨ι⟩οδεύειν μέλλοντι πεδία, ἄχρις οὗ γέρων οὐρανὸς συστήματα ὑμῶν ἄξια τεκνώσηται [ἃς ψυχὰς ὁ δημιουργὸς προσηγόρευσε]. τοσαῦτα [εἰπὼν τὰς βίβλους καὶ] τοῖς ἑαυτοῦ κατευξάμενος ἔργοις, ⟨ταῖς ἀ⟩ιδίοις ⟨ἐν⟩τεμενίζεται ζώναις.

* * * * *

50 ⟨. . .⟩ ⟨⟨[πάλιν] ὁ μόναρχος σύγκλητον τῶν θεῶν ἐποίησε συνέδριον. καὶ οἱ θεοὶ παρῆσαν· καὶ [πάλιν] αὐτὸς [ταῦτα] οὕτως ἐφώνησε, "Θεοί" λέγων, "ὅσοι ⌜τῆς κορυφαίας⌝, ὅσοι καὶ ἀφθάρτου φύσεως τετεύχατε, οἱ τὸν μέγαν αἰῶνα διέπειν ἐς ἀεὶ κεκλήρωσθε, οἱ [ς αὐτὰ] ἑαυτοῖς ἀντιπαραδιδόντε⟨ς⟩ οὐδέποτε κοπιάσετ⟨ε⟩ τὰ σύμπαντα, μέχρι πότε [[τῆς]] ἀνεπίγνωστοι ταύτης δεσπόσομεν ⟨⟨τῆς⟩⟩ ἡγεμονίας; μέχρι πότε [ἀθεώρητα γενήσεται ταῦτα ἡλίῳ καὶ σελήνῃ] [[ἕκαστος ἡμῶν ἐφ' ἑαυτῷ γεννάτω]] ⟨⟨ἀργὴν⟩⟩ ⟨κ⟩αταλείψομεν [τῷ δύνασθαι] τὴν [ἔτι] [[ἀργὴν]] σύστασιν ταύτην; ἄπιστος τοῖς μεταγενεστέροις μῦθος δὴ δοξάτω ⟨τὸ⟩ χάος εἶναι. ἔργων ἅπτεσθε

2 ἀπελογεῖτο τῷ περιέχοντι ὡς codd.: fortasse ⟨⟨ὡς⟩⟩ ἀπελύετο τοῦ (σκήνους?) 3 τὸ ἐπὶ τῆς P | νεοειδὲς Patrit.: θεοειδὲς FP | δὴ scripsi: δὲ codd. 4 γενόμεμος FP: γενομένης Patrit. 5 ἐθεώρησα ἀειδῆ scripsi: θεωρῆσαί τι ἀειδεῖ FP[1]: θεωρῆσαι τῷ ἀειδεῖ P[2] | ἐπισκοποῦντί μοι scripsi (ἐπισκοποῦντι Patrit.): ἐπισκοτοῦντι FP 6 γνῶσις scripsi: διαγνῶσις codd.: an ⟨ἰ⟩δίᾳ γνῶσις? 8 ἐπικατευξάμενον F: ἐπικατατευξάμενον P | εἰπόντα scripsi: εἰπόντας FP 9 ἀπελθεῖν scripsi: ἀπῆλθεν codd. 10 με Meineke: μὲν FP 11 ἐξεῖπεν (ante Ἑρμῆς) Patrit.: ἐξειπεῖν FP 12 εἶπε (ante γὰρ) scripsi: ἐξεῖπε codd. 12–13 Fortasse Ὦ ἱεραὶ βίβλοι, ἃς διὰ τῶν φθαρτῶν τετευγμένας μου χειρῶν τῷ τῆς ἀφθαρσίας φαρμάκῳ ἔχρισεν ὁ ἐπὶ πᾶσι κρατῶν 12 φθαρτῶν scripsi: ἀφθάρτων codd. | τετεύχαταί F: τετεύχατέ P 13 χειρῶν ἃς Meineke: χείρονας FP | χορείας FP: χρίσας Meineke

exactness the truths of the heavenly doctrine. But Hermes . . .[1] did not 7
transmit the doctrine in its full completeness even to his own son, because Tat was still in his early youth. And thus did Hermes speak: 'I, even I, have beheld with the all-seeing eyes of mind the unseen things of . . .; and as I examined them, there came to me by slow degrees, but came in very deed, accurate knowledge of the truth. ⟨. . . And now, I must⟩[2] deposit hard by the secret things of Osiris these holy symbols of the cosmic elements,[3] and after speaking over them a prayer, depart to heaven.'

It is not fitting, my son, that I should leave this report unfinished; I must 8
tell you all that Hermes said when he was depositing his books. Thus did he speak: 'Ye holy books, which have been written by my perishable hands, but have been anointed with the drug of imperishability by Him who is master over all, remain ye undecaying through all ages, and be ye unseen and undiscovered by all men who shall go to and fro on the plains of this land, until the time when Heaven, grown old, shall beget organisms[4] worthy of you.' Having spoken this prayer over the works of his hands,[5] Hermes was received into the sanctuary of the everlasting zones.[6]

* * * * *

. . . the Sole Ruler summoned a council of the gods. The gods 50
came, and He spoke, and said: 'Ye gods, all ye . . . whose being[7] has been made imperishable, ye whose lot it is to bear sway over the great world for ever, and who will never grow weary of transmitting the universe from hand to hand among you; how long shall this our sovereign rule remain unrecognized? How long shall we leave this conglomerate mass inert? Let it seem to those of after times an incredible tale that there has been a Chaos. Set your hands to mighty works. Let each of you for

[1] Perhaps, 'when he was about to be released from the body'.

[2] Perhaps, '⟨That knowledge I have set down in writing; and now I must⟩', &c.

[3] I. e. the books of Hermes, written in hieroglyphs.

[4] Literally 'composite things'; that is, men, composed of soul and body. After long ages, there will be born men that are worthy to read the books of Hermes.

[5] I. e. over his books.

[6] I. e. he died, and went to dwell in heaven.

[7] Perhaps, 'all ye who are stationed on the topmost height, and whose being', &c.

---

14 *πάντας αἰῶνας* scripsi: *παντὸς αἰῶνος* codd. 15 *γῆς* Meineke: *τῆς* codd. | *περιοδεύειν* scripsi: *παροδεύειν* codd. 16 Fortasse *γέρων ⟨γενόμενος⟩* | *τεκνώσηται* FP: *τεκνώσεται* Meineke et Wachsm. 18 *κατεξάμενος* P | *ταῖς ἀιδίοις ἐντεμενίζεται* scripsi: *ἰδίαις τε μενίζεται* FP 19–3 *infra*: § 50 (*πάλιν ὁ μόναρχος . . . διάστασις ἐγένετο καὶ*) huc transposui 21–22 Fortasse *ὅσοι τῆς ⟨πάντων⟩ κορυφῆς ⟨ἐπιβεβήκατε⟩, [ὅσοι] καὶ* 23–24 *οἱ ἑαυτοῖς ἀντιπαραδιδόντες οὐδέποτε κοπιάσετε* scripsi: *οἷς αὐτὰ ἑαυτοῖς ἀντιπαραδιδόντα οὐδέποτε κοπιάσει* codd. 24–25 *ἀνεπίγνωστοι* scripsi: *ἀνεπιγνώστου* codd. | *τῆς* transposuit Usener 27 *καταλείψομεν* scripsi: *ἀπαλείψωμεν* codd. 28 *ἔτι* FP[2]: *αἰτίαν* P[1] 29 *δὴ* Wachsm.: *δὲ* FP

μεγάλων. ⟨⟨ἕκαστος ὑμῶν ἐφ' ἑαυτῷ ⟨τι⟩ γεννάτω·⟩⟩ ἐγὼ δ' αὐτὸς ἄρξομαι πρῶτος." εἶπε, καὶ εὐθέως [κοσμικῶς] τῆς ἔτι ⌜μελαίνης⌝ ἑνώσεως διάστασις ἐγένετο· καὶ⟩⟩ ⟨. . . .⟩

11 ⟨⟨καὶ ⟨μετὰ⟩ ταῦτα ἔτι εἰς τὸ περιέχον ἀτενίσας ⟨ἐ⟩φώνησεν· "Ἔστω πεπληρώμενος ὁ οὐρανὸς ἄ⟨σ⟩τρασιν ⟨. . .⟩ [ἀήρ τε καὶ αἰθήρ]." εἶπεν ὁ θεός, καὶ ἦν.⟩⟩ ⟨. . .⟩

9 ἱκανὸν δὲ τὸν μέσον ἤργει χρόνον [ἐκέκρυπτο] [[καὶ]] ἡ ⟨τῶν ὑποκειμένων⟩ φύσις, ὦ τέκνον, ⟨⟨καὶ⟩⟩ ἐτύγχανε στεῖρα, ἕως αὐτοὶ οἱ ἤδη περιπολεῖν τὸν οὐρανὸν κελευσθέντες ⟨⟨θεοί⟩⟩, τῷ πάντων [[θεῷ]] βασιλεῖ προσελθόντες, τὴν τῶν ⟨κάτω⟩ ὄντων ἡσυχίαν ἀπήγγειλαν, καὶ ὅτι δέον ἐστὶ συγκοσμηθῆναι ⟨καὶ ταῦ⟩τα [σύμπαντα] [[καὶ τοῦτο οὐχ ἑτέρου τινός ἐστιν ἔργον ἢ αὐτοῦ]]· καὶ "Δεόμεθά σου" ἔλεγον "τὰ νῦν ὄντα καὶ [ὧν] ὕστερον ⟨ἐσόμενα τίνος⟩ ἔχει χρείαν διασκέψασ⟨θαι⟩. ⟨⟨καὶ ⟨γὰρ⟩ τοῦτο οὐχ ἑτέρου τινός ἐστιν ἔργον ἢ αὐτοῦ⟩⟩ ⟨σοῦ⟩."

10 ταῦτα εἰπόντων ἐμειδίασεν ὁ θεός, καὶ εἶπε Φύσιν εἶναι. καὶ θῆλυ πάγκαλον χρῆμα ἐκ τῆς φωνῆς αὐτοῦ προῆλθεν, ὃ καὶ θεωρήσαντες οἱ θεοὶ κατεπλάγησαν· καὶ ταύτην Φύσεως ⟨ὀ⟩νόματι ἐτίμησεν ὁ θεὸς ὁ προπάτωρ. ⟨⟨καὶ τῇ [Εὑρέσει] ⟨Φύσει⟩ τὸ[ν] τῶν [τὸ] κάτω πάντων ἐχαρίσατο ἡγεμονικόν,⟩⟩ καὶ ταύτην προσέταξεν εἶναι ⟨. . . σπερμάτων⟩ γεννητικήν.

11 [[καὶ ταῦτα ἔτι εἰς τὸ περιέχον ἀτενίσας φώνησεν· "Ἔστω πεπληρωμένος ὁ οὐρανὸς ἅπασιν ἀήρ τε καὶ αἰθήρ." εἶπεν ὁ θεὸς καὶ ἦν.]]

12 ἡ δὲ Φύσις ἑαυτῇ λαλήσασα ἔγνω ὡς μὴ δέον αὐτήν ἐστι παρακοῦσαι τῆς τοῦ πατρὸς ἐντολῆς· καὶ ⟨. . .⟩.

13 [καλὴν Πόνῳ συνελθοῦσα[ν] θυγατέρα ἐποίησεν, ἣν Εὕρεσιν ἐκάλεσε.]

[τῇ δὲ ὁ θεὸς ἐχαρίσατο ⌜εἶναι⌝, καὶ χαρισάμενος.]

[διέκρινε τὰ ἤδη γεγονότα, καὶ ἐπλήρωσεν αὐτὰ μυστηρίων.]

[[καὶ τῇ Εὑρέσει τούτων τὸ κατὰ τούτων ἐχαρίσατο ἡγεμονικόν.]]

52 ⟨⟨πληρώσας δὲ τὰς [ι] σε⟨βα⟩στὰς [ιας] χεῖρας τῷ ⌜περιέχοντι⌝ τῶν ἐκ τῆς Φύσεως ὑπαρχόντων ⟨σπερμάτων⟩, καὶ τὰς

1 ὑμῶν Patr. : ἡμῶν codd. 3 μελαίνης om. P : fortasse ἀκοσμήτου (ex quo ortum puta κοσμικῶς) 4–6 § 11 (καὶ ταῦτα . . . καὶ ἦν) huc transposui 4–5 ἐφώνησεν P[2] : φώνησεν FP[1] 5 ἄστρασιν scripsi : ἅπασιν codd.

his own part bring something into being; and I myself will be the first to begin.' He spoke, and forthwith the hitherto . . . homogeneous mass[1] was separated into two parts[2]; and . . .

And thereafter, He gazed into the space around, and spoke 11
again, saying 'Let heaven be filled with stars . . .'. God spoke, and it was so. . . .

But during no small interval of time the world below, my son, 9
was inert, and remained barren; until those very gods who had already been bidden to go their rounds in heaven[3] approached him who is King of all, and told him of the stillness of the things below, and said that these things also ought to be set in order. 'We pray thee then', said they, 'to look into this, and find out what is lacking to the things that now are and shall be hereafter; for this is no one's task save thine alone.'

When they had thus spoken, God smiled, and bade Nature[4] 10
be; and there came forth from his voice a Being in woman's form, right lovely, at the sight of whom the gods were smitten with amazement; and God the Forefather bestowed on her the name of Nature. And he conferred on Nature the government of all things in the world below, and bade her be productive
of all manner of seeds. And Nature communed with herself, 12
and saw that she must not disobey her Father's bidding; and . . .[5]
And God filled his august hands with the abundance of seeds 52
which Nature supplied, and gripping the handfuls firmly, said

[1] Perhaps, 'the homogeneous mass, hitherto unorganized (or formless)'.

[2] The 'two parts' are heaven and earth.

[3] I. e. the star-gods.

[4] 'Nature' means the force which manifests itself in the production and growth of living things on earth. That force is here personified. But in this passage, the only function that 'Nature' is called on to discharge is that of producing plants.

[5] Perhaps, 'and ⟨so she brought into being the seeds of all kinds of plants⟩'.

---

7 *ἱκανὸν δὲ τὸν μέσον ἤργει χρόνον* scripsi: *ἱκανὸς δὲ ὁ μέσος ἤργει χρόνος* codd. 9 *οἱ ἤση* F | *κελευσθέντας* F | *θεοὶ* (post *κελευσθέντες*) add. Wachsm. 10 *τῷ* (ante *πάντων*) Patrit.: *τῶν* FP 12 *καὶ ταῦτα* scripsi: *τὰ* codd. | *τοῦτο οὐχ* P: *τοῦτο ὅτι οὐχ* F 14 *διασκέψασθαι* scripsi (*διάσκεψαι* Meineke): *διασκέψας* FP 19 *ταύτην* om. P 20 *ὀνόματι* Meineke: *πόματι* FP 20–21 *καὶ . . . ἡγεμονικόν* huc a § 13 transposui 21 *Φύσει* scripsi: *εὑρέσει* codd. | *τὸ τῶν κάτω πάντων* scripsi: *τούτων τὸ κατὰ τούτων* codd. 22 *καὶ ταύτῃ . . . γεννητικῇ* Meineke | *ταύτην* Patrit.: *ταύτης* FP | Fortasse ⟨*παντοίων σπερμάτων*⟩ 23–25 § 11 (*καὶ ταῦτα . . . καὶ ἦν*): vide ante § 9 28 *συνελθοῦσα* Patrit.: *συνελθοῦσαν* FP 33–34 *καὶ τῇ . . . ἡγεμονικόν* hinc ad § 10 transposui 35–5 *infra*: § 52 (*πληρώσας . . . συστάσει*) huc transposui 35 *σεβαστὰς* scripsi: *ἰσοστασίας* FP: *ὁσίας* Usener 35–36 *περιέχοντι* codd.: fortasse *περιουσίᾳ* vel *πλήθει*

δράκας καρτερῶς σφίγξας, "Λάβε" εἶπεν, "ὦ ἱερὰ γῆ, λάβε, πάντιμε, [καὶ] ⟨ἡ⟩ εἶναι γεννήτειρα μέλλουσα πάντων, καὶ μηδενὸ⟨ς⟩ ἐντεῦθεν λείπεσθαι δόκει." εἶπεν ὁ θεός, καὶ τὰς χεῖρας [οἵας δὴ θεὸν ⟨εἰκὸς⟩ ἔχειν] ἁπλώσας πάντα ἀφῆκεν [ἐν τῇ τῶν ὄντων συστάσει].⟩⟩ ⟨. . .⟩

51 ⟨οὕτω δὴ⟩ ⟨⟨ἐφάνη μὲν οὐρανὸς ἄνω συγκεκοσμημένος τοῖς ἑαυτοῦ μυστηρίοις πᾶσι, [κραδαινομένη ἔτι γῆ ἡλίου λάμψαντος ἐπάγη καὶ] ἐφάνη ⟨δὲ καὶ γῆ⟩ πᾶσι τοῖς περὶ αὐτὴν συγκεκοσμημένη[ς] καλοῖς. καλὰ γὰρ τῷ θεῷ καὶ τὰ θνητοῖς εἶναι νομιζόμενα φαῦλα, ὅτι δὴ τοῖς τοῦ θεοῦ νόμοις δουλεύειν ἐποιήθη. ἔχαιρε δὲ ὁ θεὸς ὁρῶν ἤδη ἑαυτοῦ τὰ ἔργα κινούμενα.⟩⟩

14 ⟨. . .⟩ αὐτὸς δ' οὐκέτι βουλόμενος ἀργὸν τὸν ὑπο⟨υ⟩ράνιο⟨ν⟩ κόσμον εἶναι, ἀλλὰ ⌜πνευμάτων⌝ πληρῶσαι δοκιμάσας ⟨καὶ⟩ τοῦτον, ὡς μὴ τὰ κατὰ μέσον ἀκίνητα [καὶ ἀργὰ] μένῃ, οὕτως εἰς ταῦτα ἤρξατο τεχνιτεία[ι]ς, οὐσ⟨ί⟩αις πρὸς τὴν τοῦ [ἰδίου] ἔργου ⟨ἀπο⟩τέλεσιν χρησάμενος ⟨ἐπιτη⟩δείαις. πνεῦμα γὰρ ὅσον ἀρκετὸν ἀπὸ τοῦ ἰδίου λαβών, καὶ νοερῷ τοῦτο πυρὶ μίξας, ἀγνώστοις τισὶν ἑτέραις ὕλαις ἐκέρασε· καὶ ταῦτα [ἑκάτερον ἑκατέρῳ] μετά τινων ἐπιφωνήσεων κρυπτῶν ἑνώσας, τὸ πᾶν οὕτως εὖ μάλα διεκί⟨ρ⟩νησε⟨ν⟩ [κρᾶμα], ἕως ἐπεγέλασέ τις ὕλη τῷ μίγματι λεπτοτέρα τε καὶ καθαρωτέρα μᾶλλον [καὶ διαφανεστέρα] ἢ ἐξ ὧν ἐγίνετο· διειδὴς δὲ ἦν αὕτη, ἣν
15 δὴ καὶ μόνος ὁ τεχνίτης ἑώρα. ἐπειδὴ δὲ ⟨⟨τελεσιουργηθεῖσα⟩⟩ οὔτε [ὡς ἐκ πυρὸς] καιομένη διετήκετο, οὔτε μὴν [ὡς ἐκ πνεύματος] [[τελεσιουργηθεῖσα]] [ε] ψύχει ⟨ἐπήγνυτο⟩, ἀλλά τινα ἰδιογενῆ [καὶ οἰκείαν] εἶχε [τὴν τοῦ κράματος] σύστασιν [ἰδιότυπόν τε καὶ ἰδιοσύγκριτον], ⟨ταύτ⟩ην δὴ [καὶ ἀπὸ τοῦ εὐφημοτέρου ὀνόματος καὶ τῆς καθ' ὁμοιότητα ἐνεργείας] ψύχωσιν ὁ θεὸς ἐκάλεσε⟨ν⟩ [τὴν σύστασιν]. ἐξ οὗ δὴ ἐπιπάγου μυριάδας ψυχῶν ἱκανὰς ἐγενεσιούργησε, τὸ [παρ' αὐτοῦ] τοῦ κράματος ἐπάνθουν πρὸς ὃ θέλει πλάσσων εὐτάκτως

1 σφίγξας F : σφίξας P 1–2 λάβε πάντιμε om. P 3 μηδενὸς scripsi : μηδενὶ codd. Fortasse μηδενὸς ⟨τῶν⟩ ⟨⟨ἐν τῇ τῶν ὄντων συστάσει⟩⟩ 4 δὴ scripsi : δεῖ codd. 6–12 § 51 (ἐφάνη μὲν . . . κινούμενα) huc transposui 6 ὁ οὐρανὸς P | συγκεκοσμημένος codd. : fortasse πεπληρωμένος 9 συγκεκοσμημένη Patrit. : συγκεκοσμημένοις FP | καλοῖς om. P 9–11 καλὰ γὰρ . . . ἐποιήθη secludendum? 13 ὑπουράνιον scripsi : ὑπεράνω codd. 15 μέσον scripsi : μέρος codd. 16 τεχνιτείας, οὐσίαις Usener : τεχνιτείαις οὔσαις codd. 17 ἀποτέλεσιν scripsi : γένεσιν codd. | ἐπιτηδείαις scripsi : ἱεραῖς codd. 18 νοερῷ Meineke : νοερῶς FP | τούτῳ P[2]

'Take them, thou holy Earth, take them, all-honoured one, thou that art destined to be mother of all things; and henceforward be not thou thought to come short of anything'.[1] And saying this, God opened his hands, and flung forth all that was in them. . . .[2]

Thus it was that heaven came to be seen above, equipped 51
with all its holy Powers,[3] and the earth below, equipped with all the goodly things that appertain to it. For even those things which mortals deem foul are goodly in God's sight, because they have been made subject to God's laws. And God was glad when he beheld his works[4] and saw that they were now in motion.[5]

. . . And God was no longer willing that the region next below 14
heaven[6] should be inert, but thought good to fill this region also with living beings, that the intermediate space[7] might not remain devoid of movement; and so he began to ply handicraft for this purpose, using substances suitable for the accomplishment of the work. He took of his own life-breath as much as would suffice, and blended it with intelligent fire, and mingled the blend with certain other materials unknown to men; and having fused together these ingredients, with utterance of certain secret spells, thereon he thoroughly stirred the whole mixture, until there bubbled up upon the surface of the mass a substance finer and purer than the things of which it was composed. This substance was transparent; none but the Craftsman himself could see it.
And when it was wrought up to completion, and was neither 15
liquefied by burning heat nor solidified by cold, but had a certain consistency peculiar to itself, God named it 'soul-stuff'. And out of this scum he wrought into existence many myriads of souls, moulding to his purpose in right order and due measure

[1] Perhaps, 'to lag behind any of the contents of the composite universe', i. e. any other part or region of the universe.
[2] Here probably followed a sentence in which it was said that plants sprang up on the earth.
[3] I. e. filled with stars, or peopled with star-gods.
[4] I. e. heaven and earth and all things in them.
[5] Or 'in action'; i. e. that they were no longer inert and lifeless.
[6] I. e. the atmosphere.
[7] I. e. the space between heaven and earth.

| *πῦρ* P **19** *ἀγνώστοις* Patrit.: *ἀγνώστως* FP **21** *διεκίρνησεν* scripsi: *διεκίνησε* codd. **26** *ψύχει ἐπήγνυτο* scripsi: *ἔψυχεν* codd. **28** *ἦν δὴ* FP: "*ἔνθεν δὴ* scripsi . . .; poteris etiam ⟨*ταύτ*⟩*ην δὴ*" Wachsm. **31** *ἐπὶ πάγου* FP[2] **32** *τοῦ* (ante *κράματος*) om. P | *πρὸς ὃ* F: *πρ σὀ* P[1]: *πρσ, ὃ* P[2]

τε καὶ συμμέτρως μετ⟨ὰ⟩ [ἐμπειρίας καὶ] λόγου τοῦ καθήκοντος, ὡς μηδέ τι ⟨. . .⟩.

16 ⟨. . .⟩ διαφέρειν [ε]αὐτὰς ἑαυτῶν ἦν ἀναγκαῖον, ἐπειδήπερ τὸ ἐκ τῆς κι⟨ρ⟩νήσεως [τοῦ θεοῦ] ἐξατμιζόμενον ἄνθος οὐκ ἦν ἑαυτῷ ὅμοιον, ἀλλὰ [μεῖζον καὶ] ⟨ὁλο⟩κληρότερον ἦν τοῦ δευτέρου τὸ πρῶτον καὶ τῷ παντὶ καθαρώτερον, τὸ δεύτερον δὲ ἱκανῶς μὲν ⟨ἧσσον⟩ ἦν τοῦ πρώτου [τὸ δεύτερον], πολλῷ δὲ ⟨κρεῖσσον⟩ τοῦ τρίτου [τὸ μεῖζον], καὶ οὕτως ἄχρι βαθμῶν ἑξήκοντα ὁ πᾶς ἀπήρτιστο ἀριθμός· πλὴν ὅτι γε πάσας ⟨ὁμοίως⟩ ἀιδίους εἶναι νομοθετήσας ἔταξεν, ὡς ἂν ἐκ μιᾶς ⟨γενομένας⟩ οὐσίας, ἧς μόνος αὐτὸς ᾔδη ⌜τελειῶ⌝. ⟨ταύ⟩ταις δὲ καὶ τμήματα [καὶ τ⟨α⟩μ⟨ι⟩εῖα] ἐν μεταρσίῳ διέταξε [τῆς ἄνω φύσεως] [οὐρανοῦ], ὅπως τόν τε κύλινδρον περιστροβῶσι τάξει τινὶ καὶ οἰκονομίᾳ καθηκούσῃ, καὶ τὸν πατέρα τέρπωσιν.

17 οὕτως δὴ [καὶ] ἐν τῇ περικαλλεῖ τοῦ αἰθέρος στὰς ⌜ει⌝, καὶ τὰς τῶν ἤδη οϲϲῶν ⟨ψυχῶν⟩ μεταπεμψάμενος φυλάς, "Ὦ[ς] ⟨⟨ψυχαί⟩⟩", φησ⟨ί⟩, "[πνεύματος ἐμοῦ καὶ] μερίμνης ἐμῆς [[ψυχαὶ]] καλὰ τέκνα, ἃ ταῖς ἐμαυτοῦ μαιωσάμενος χερσὶν ἤδη ⟨ἐν⟩ τῷ μ⟨έσ⟩ῳ καθιδρ⟨ύ⟩ω κόσμῳ, [λόγων ἐμῶν ὡς] νόμων τούτων ἐπακούσατε, καὶ τόπου μηδενὸς ἄλλου θίγητε πλὴν τοῦ διαταγέντος ὑμῖν ὑπὸ τῆς ἐμῆς γνώμης. εὐσταθησάσαις μὲν οὖν ὑμῖν οὐρανὸς [τε καὶ μένει πάλιν] ὁ μισθός, καὶ [ὁ διαταγεὶς] ⟨κατ⟩αστερισμός, θρόνοι τε ἀρετῆς πεπληρωμένοι· εἰ δέ τι νεώτερον παρὰ τἀμὰ πράξητε βουλεύματα, ἱερὸν [ὑμῖν] ὀμνύω [πνεῦμα καὶ] κρᾶμα τοῦτ' ἀφ' οὗπερ ὑμᾶς ἐγέννησα, ψυχοποιούς τε ταύτας μου τὰς χεῖρας, ὡς οὐκ εἰς μακρὰν δεσμοὺς καὶ κολάσεις ὑμῖν τεχνιτεύσω."

18 τοσαῦτα εἰπὼν ὁ θεὸς [ὁ κἀμοῦ κύριος] τὰ λοιπὰ τῶν στοιχείων [συγγενῆ] μίξας, ὕδωρ καὶ γῆν, ⟨⟨καὶ ζωοποιὸν

1 μετὰ scripsi : μετ' ἐμπειρίας καὶ codd. 3 αὐτὰς Meineke : ἑαυτὰς FP 4 κιρνήσεως scripsi (κράσεως Heeren) : κινήσεως codd. 5 ὁλοκληρότερον scripsi : πληρέστερον codd. 7 τὸ δεύτερον seclusi (τὸ del. Heeren) 8 τὸ μεῖζον seclusi (τὸ del. Heeren) 11 ᾔδη Usener : ἤδη FP | τελειῶ FP : τελείωμα Usener : fortasse ⟨τὴν σύστασιν⟩ τελειῶ⟨σαι⟩ | ταύταις scripsi : ταῖς codd. 12 ταμιεῖα Wachsm. (vide § 24) : ταμεῖα Patrit. : τμεῖα FP | Fortasse διέταξε⟨ν⟩ ⟨⟨οἰκονομίᾳ ⟨τινὶ⟩ καθηκούσῃ⟩⟩ 13 οὐρανοῦ del. Heeren | τόν τε κύλινδρον περιστροβῶσι obscurum : nescio an omissum sit aliquid 14 τάξει . . . καθηκούσῃ transponendum ? | An τέρπωσιν ⟨ὕμνοις⟩? 15 στάσει codd. : στὰς βάσει Usener : fortasse στὰς ἁψῖδι 16 οὐσῶν ψυχῶν scripsi : ὄντων codd. | φυλάς scripsi : φύσεις codd. 17 "Ὦ ψυχαί", φησί scripsi : ὡς φῂς FP[1] : ὦ φησὶ P[2] : "ὦ", φησί Wachsm. 18 'an ψυχαί secludendum ?' Wachsm. 19 ἐν τῷ μέσῳ scripsi : τῷ μῷ FP : τῷ ἐμῷ Meineke | καθιδρύω scripsi : καθιερῶ codd. | κόσμῳ codd. :

the stuff which formed on the surface of the mixture, and therewith speaking the fitting spell, that nothing might

But the souls necessarily differed one from another, because 16
the froth which exhaled from the mass when it was stirred together was not all of one quality. The first portion of it was more perfect than the second, and altogether purer; and the second portion was much inferior to the first, but far superior to the third; and so it went on, until the whole number of the different grades amounted to sixty. But God made a law by which he ordained that all the souls alike should be everlasting, inasmuch as they were all made of one substance, the composition of which was known to him alone. And he assigned to the souls divisions of space on high,[1] one to each grade of souls; . . .[2] that they might make the cylinder revolve[3] according to a fixed order and a fitting arrangement, and might give joy to their Father.[4]

Thereupon God took his stand in the beauteous vault of the 17
aether,[5] and summoned to him the tribes of souls that were now in being, and said, 'Ye souls, fair children of my anxious thought, whom I have brought to birth with my own hands, and whom I now station in the intermediate region of the universe, hearken to these my laws, and meddle with no place save that which is assigned to you by my decree. If you are steadfast in obedience, heaven shall be your reward; you shall be placed among the stars, and shall sit on thrones that are charged with potent forces. But if by any rash deed you transgress my ordinances, then, by this holy mixture out of which I brought you into being, and by these my soul-making hands, I swear that full soon will I construct bonds for your chastisement.'[6]

Having thus spoken, God mixed together the two remaining 18
elements, water and earth,[7] and breathed into them a certain

[1] I. e. distinct strata of the atmosphere.
[2] Perhaps, '⟨and he placed the souls in those divisions, and bade them dwell there⟩', or something of the sort.
[3] I do not know what is meant by 'the cylinder'.
[4] Perhaps, 'give joy to their Father ⟨by hymns of praise⟩'.
[5] I. e. in the highest part of the atmosphere, or on the upper surface of it.
[6] I. e. I will make bodies for you, and you shall be punished by incarnation.
[7] Fire and air had been used in making the first mixture.

---

fortasse *τόπῳ* vel *τοῦ κόσμου τόπῳ* | *λέγων* P[2] **20** *τόπου* secludendum? **22** *εὐσταθησάσαι* P[1] **23** *ὁ μισθός* scripsi : *ὁμοίως* codd. | *καταστερισμός* scripsi : *ἀστερισμὸς* codd. **24** *πράξητε* P : *πράξηται* F : *πράξετε* Patrit., Wachsm. **24–25** *βουλεύματα* om. P **27** *δεσμοὺς* P : *δεσμὸν* F

ἐμφυσήσας⟩⟩ ⟨τινὰ οὐσίαν⟩, καί τινας [ὁμοίως] κρυπτοὺς ἐπειπὼν λόγους, δυνατοὺς μέν, οὐ τοῖς πρώτοις δ' ὁμοίους, εὖ τε κιρνήσας [[καὶ ζωοποιὸν ἐνθουσιάσας]], ⟨τὸν⟩ τῷ κράματι ἐπιπλέοντα [ὁμοίως] ἐπίπαγον [εὐβαφῆ τε καὶ] εὐ[π]αγῆ γενόμενον ἔλαβε, καὶ ἐκ τούτου τὰ [ἀνθρωποειδῆ] ⟨πνεύματα⟩

19 τῶν ζῴων διέπλασε· τὸ δὲ τοῦ μίγματος λείψανον ταῖς ἤδη προκοψάσαις ψυχαῖς ἔδωκε, [ψυχαῖς δὲ ταύταις] ταῖς εἰς [χωρία θεῶν καὶ] τοὺς ἐγγὺς ἄστρων τόπους ⟨ἀναβάσαις⟩, καὶ ἱεροῖς δαίμοσι μετακεκλημένα⟨ι⟩ς, [πλάσσετε] λέγων "Ὦ τέκνα, τῆς ἐμῆς ⌜φύσεως⌝ γεννήματα, δέχεσθε τῆς ἐμῆς τεχνι⟨τεία⟩ς τὰ λείψανα, καὶ ἑκάστη τῇ ἑαυτῆς φύσει ⟨πεποιθυῖα⟩ πλασσέτω τι [παραπλήσιον]· παραθήσομαι δ' ἐγὼ [καὶ] ταῦθ' ὑμῖν παραδείγματα." καὶ λαβὼν εὖ καὶ καλῶς ⟨. . .⟩

20 [[τὸν ζῳδιακὸν συμφώνως ταῖς ψυχικαῖς κινήσεσι διέταξε κόσμον, πρὸς τοῖς ἀνθρωποειδέσι τῶν ζῳδιακῶν τὰ ἑξῆς ἀπαρτίσας οἷον ζῳδίοις, καὶ τὰς πανούργους ἐχαρισάμην δυνάμεις καὶ πάντεχνον πνεῦμα γεννητικὸν τῶν εἰς ἀεὶ μελλόντων ἔσεσθαι καθολικῶς πάντων.]]

21 ⟨. . .⟩ καὶ ἀπέστη, ὑποσχόμενος τοῖς ὁρατοῖς ἔργοις αὐτῶν τὰ ⟨ἀ⟩όρατα πνεύμα⟨τα⟩ ἐπιζεῦξαι, ⟨ἐξ⟩ουσίαν τε ὁμοιογονίας ⟨δοῦναι⟩ ἑκάστῳ, ὅπως [αὐτῷ [αὐτοῖς] ἕτερα γεννᾷ ὅμοια,] αὐτα⟨ί⟩ [τε] μηκέτι ἀνάγκην ἔχωσιν ἄλλο τι ποιεῖν ⟨παρ'⟩ ἃ ἔφθησαν ἐργάσασθαι.

22 —Τί οὖν, ὦ τεκοῦσα, ἐποίησαν αἱ ψυχαί;—καὶ εἶπεν Ἶσις· Τὸ κεκερασμένον, ὦ τέκνον Ὧρε, [τῆς ὕλης] λαβοῦσαι κατενόουν πρῶτον [καὶ τὸ τοῦ πατρὸς προσεκύνουν κρᾶμα], καὶ ὁπόθεν ἦ⟨ν⟩ συμπεπλεγμένον ἐπεζήτουν· τὸ δὲ ἦν αὐταῖς οὐκ εὔπορον ἐπιγνῶναι. ἔνθεν δὴ καὶ ὅτι ἐπεζήτησαν ἐφοβοῦντο μὴ τῷ τοῦ πατρὸς ὑποπέσωσι χόλῳ· καὶ

3 εὖ τε κιρνήσας scripsi: εὐτεκεῖν ἴσας FP (κινήσας man. 2 marg. P): εὖ τε κινήσας Wachsm. 3–4 Fortasse κράματι ἐπιπολάζοντα 4 εὐαγῆ scripsi: εὐβαφῆ τε καὶ εὐπαγῆ codd. 5 ἀνθρωποειδῆ (num ἀεροειδῆ?) seclusi: πνεύματα addidi (vide § 21 *init.*) 7 ψυχαῖς (ante ἔδωκε) om. P 9 ἱεροῖς δαίμοσι scripsi: ἱεροὺς δαίμονας codd. | μετακεκλημέναις Patrit.: μετακεκλημένας FP | 'πλάσσετε (πλάσσε τε F) suspectum; fort. λάβετε, nisi πλ. delendum' Wachsm. 10 φύσεως codd.: fortasse οὐσίας | δέχεσθαι P 11 τεχνιτείας scripsi: τέχνης codd. 12–13 δ' ἐγὼ scripsi: δέ τι FP 13–20 Fortasse λαβὼν εὖ καὶ καλῶς ⟨ἤδη ἀπηρτισμένα τὰ πνεύματα ταῖς ψυχαῖς παρέθηκε,⟩ καὶ ἀπέστη, ὑποσχόμενος κ.τ.λ. 15–19 § 20 (τὸν ζῳδιακὸν . . καθολικῶς πάντων) hinc transposui: vide post § 23 21 τὰ ἀόρατα

life-giving substance, and spoke over them certain secret spells, potent indeed, but not so potent as those which he had uttered before. These things he stirred well together; and when the scum which floated on the surface of the mixture had become translucent, he took this scum, and out of it he fashioned the
vital spirits of the animals.[1] But the residue of the mixture 19
he handed over to the souls that had by this time made progress, those souls that had ascended to the places near the stars,[2] and had been given a new name, and were called 'holy daemons'; and he said to them, 'My children, offspring of my being, take the residue left over from my handiwork, and let each of you fashion something,[3] relying on his own ability; and I will set before you as models these things which I have made'.[4] And
having taken . . . well and fairly . . . and then he withdrew,[5] after 21
promising to join to the visible works of their hands[6] the invisible vital-spirits, and to give to each of the creatures that should be made power to generate others like to itself, in order that the souls might not thereafter be obliged to make anything else beside what they made at first.—

Horus. Tell me then, mother, what did the souls make?—And 22
Isis said: When the souls, my son Horus, had received the mingled mass, they first examined it, and sought to find out of what ingredients it was compounded; but this it was not easy for them to discover. Thereupon they feared they might incur the Father's anger for having tried to find out; and they betook

[1] The writer assumes the 'vital spirit' of an animal to be a sort of gaseous and invisible body, like in size and shape to the gross and visible body.

[2] I. e. to the highest of the atmospheric strata.

[3] I. e. the body of some kind of animal.

[4] Viz. the 'vital spirits' of the animals.

[5] Perhaps, 'And he took ⟨the vital spirits of the animals, which were by this time⟩ well and fairly ⟨finished, and set them before the souls;⟩ and then he withdrew'.

[6] I. e. the gross bodies of the animals.

πνεύματα scripsi (*τὸ ἀόρατον πνεῦμα* Canter): *τὸ ὁρατὸν πνεῦμα* FP | *ἐξουσίαν* scripsi: *οὐσίαν* codd. **22** *αὐτῷ* (om. *αὐτοῖς*) Heeren: *αὐτῷ αὐτοῖς* FP[1]: *αὐτὰ αὐτοῖς* P[2] **23** *αὐταὶ* scripsi (*αὐταί τε* Meineke): *αὐτὰ τε* P: *αὐτά γε* F | *μηκέτι* scripsi: *οὐκ ἔτι* FP | *ἔχωσιν* P[2]: *ἔχουσιν* FP[1] | *παρ* add. Heeren: *ᾖ* add. P[2] **27** *λαβοῦσαι* scripsi: *τῆς ὕλης λαβόμεναι* codd. **28** *πόθεν* P | *ἦν* (post *ὁπόθεν*) Heeren: *ᾗ* FP

23 ἐπὶ τὸ πράττειν τὰ προσταχθέντα ἐτράπησαν. ἔνθεν ἐκ μὲν τῆς ἀνωτέρω ὕλης, τῆς ὑπερβολῇ κοῦφον ἐχούσης τὸν ⌜ἐπίπαγον⌝, τὸ τῶν ὀρνέων γένος ἐ[υ]μόρφουν, [[ἐν τούτῳ δ' ἡμιπαγοῦς ἤδη τοῦ κράματος γενομένου καὶ ἤδη τὴν στερεὰν πῆξιν λαβόντος τὸ τῶν τετραπόδων γένος ἔπλασσον,]] ⟨ἐκ δὲ⟩ το⟨ῦ⟩ [δὴ] ἧττον κούφου [καὶ ἑτέρας ὑγρᾶς[ιας] ⟨ο⟩ὐσίας δεόμενον εἰς διάνηξιν] τὸ τῶν ἰχθύων. ⟨⟨ἐν τούτῳ δ' ἡμιπαγοῦς [ἤδη] τοῦ κράματος γενομένου, καὶ ἤδη [[τὴν στερεὰν πῆξιν λαβόντος]] ⟨⟨κατωφεροῦς ὑπάρχοντος⟩⟩, τὸ τῶν τετραπόδων γένος ἔπλασσον·⟩⟩ ψυχροῦ δὲ ⟨γενομένου⟩ τοῦ λοιποῦ, καὶ ἤδη ⟨⟨[[τὴν]] στερεὰν ⟨⟨τὴν⟩⟩ πῆξιν λαβόντος⟩⟩ [[κατωφεροῦς ὑπάρχοντος]], τὴν τῶν ἑρπετῶν αἱ ψυχαὶ φύσιν ἐκαινούργουν.

20 ⟨ὁ δὲ θεὸς . . .⟩ ⟨⟨τὸν ζῳδιακὸν συμφώνως ταῖς φυσικαῖς κινήσεσι διέταξε [κόσμον], [πρὸς τοῖς ἀνθρωποειδέσι τῶν ζῳδί[ακ]ων τὰ ἑξῆς ἀπαρτίσας] [οἷον ζῳδίοις,] καὶ ⟨τούτῳ⟩ [τὰς] παν⟨τ⟩ουργοὺς [ἐ]χαρισάμεν⟨ος⟩ δυνάμεις [καὶ πάντεχνον πνεῦμα], γεννητικὸν ⟨ἐκέλευσεν εἶναι⟩ τῶν εἰς ἀεὶ μελλόντων ἔσεσθαι [καθολικῶς] πάντων ⟨ζῴων⟩.⟩⟩

24 [αυτ]αί δὲ ⟨ψυχαί⟩, ὦ τέκνον, ὡς ⟨μέγα⟩ τι πράξασαι, ἤδη καὶ περίεργον ὡπλίζοντο τόλμαν, καὶ παρὰ τὰ διατεταγμένα ἐποίουν· ⟨⟨τοῖς ⟨γὰρ⟩ ἐν οὐρανῷ θεοῖς ἐφιλονείκουν, ⟨ἴ⟩σης [ε]αὐτοῖς εὐγενείας [περικρατοῦσαι καὶ] ἀντιλαμβανόμενοι, ὡς καὶ αὐταὶ τοῦ αὐτοῦ [ε]τυχο⟨ῦσαι⟩ δημιουργοῦ.⟩⟩ καὶ ἤδη τῶν ἰδίων τμημάτων [καὶ ταμιείων] προήρχοντο· καὶ ⟨γὰρ⟩ ἐφ' ἑνὸς οὐκέτι ἤθελον τόπου μένειν, ἀεὶ δὲ ἐκινοῦντο, καὶ τὸ [ἔτι] ἐπὶ μιᾶς μονῆς εἶναι θάνατον ἡγοῦντο.

25 τοῦτο μὲν οὖν [φησίν], ὦ τέκνον, ⟨⟨ὡς⟩⟩ Ἑρμῆς [[ὡς]] [κ] ἐμοὶ λέγων ⟨ἔφη⟩, [καὶ] τὸν τῶν ὅλων κύριον [καὶ θεὸν] οὐκ ἐλάνθανον [ὃ] πράσσουσαι· κόλασιν δὲ αὐταῖς ἐπεζήτει [καὶ δεσμὸν ὃν τλημόνως ὑπομενοῦσι]. καὶ δὴ καὶ ἔδοξε τῷ πάντων ἡγεμόνι καὶ δεσπότῃ τὸ τῶν ἀνθρώπων σύστημα [τι]

2 τῆς (post ὕλης) Meineke: τῇ FP 2–3 Fortasse κούφην ἐχούσης τὴν σύστασιν vel simile quid 2 ἐχούσης Patrit.: ἐχούσῃ FP 3 ἐπὶ πάγον FP[1] | ἐμόρφουν P[2]: εὐμόρφουν FP[1] 5–6 ἐκ δὲ τοῦ ἧττον κούφου scripsi: τὸ δὴ ἧττον κοῦφον codd. 6 ὑγρᾶς οὐσίας scripsi (ὑγρασίας vel ὑγρᾶς οὐσίας Heeren, ὑγρασίας Wachsm.): ὑγρασίας ὐσίας F[1]: ὑγρασίας ὑγίας P[1]: ὑγρασίας οὐσίας F[2]P[2] 13 ἐκαινούνγουν F[1] 14 φυσικαῖς scripsi: ψυχικαῖς codd. 15 Fortasse κινήσεσι ⟨τῶν ζῴων⟩ | κόσμον codd.: fortasse κύκλον 16 ζῳδίων Patrit.: ζῳδιακῶν codd. 17 παντουργοὺς scripsi: πανούργους codd. | χαρισάμενος scripsi ('an χαρισάμενος?' Wachsm.): ἐχαρισάμην

themselves to doing the work they had been bidden to do.
Out of the upper part of the stuff, which was of very light con- 23
sistency, they fashioned the race of birds; and out of the part
which was less light, the race of fishes. And when the mixture
had become half-solid, and was now heavy, they fashioned out
of it the race of quadrupeds; and when what was left of it had
grown cold, and was quite solidified, the souls made of it yet
another sort of creatures, the breed of creeping things.

. . .[1] And God arranged the Zodiac in accord with the movings 20
of nature;[2] and having bestowed on it powers of all-various
working, he bade it be productive of all the animals that were
to be in all time to come.[3]

But the souls, my son, thinking that they had now done some- 24
thing great, began to array themselves in presumptuous audacity,
and transgress God's commands; for they sought to vie with the
gods in heaven, claiming nobility equal to theirs, in that the souls
themselves had been made by the same Maker.[4] And so they
now began to overstep the bounds of their own divisions of the
atmosphere; for they would not any longer abide in one place,
but were ever on the move, and thought it death[5] to stay in one
abode.

But when the souls did thus, my son, the Lord of all (so 25
Hermes said when he told the tale to me) failed not to mark it;
and he sought a way to punish them. And so the Ruler and
Master of all thought good to fabricate the human organism,

[1] § 20 was probably preceded by a passage in which it was said that God put the vital spirits of the animals into the bodies (as he had promised to do, § 21).

[2] I. e. the processes operated by nature in the bodies of the animals.

[3] I. e. all that were to be born after the making of the first specimen (or pair) of each kind. (It was commonly thought that births were effected by the influence of the Signs of the Zodiac.)

[4] I. e. by God, by whom the star-gods also had been made.

[5] I. e. an intolerable thing.

FP[1]: '*ἐχαρίσατο*, ni fallor, P[2]' Wachsm. **20** *αἱ δὲ ψυχαί* scripsi: *αὗταί τε* codd. **22–24** *τοῖς . . . δημιουργοῦ* huc a § 53 (p. 486) transposui **23** *ἴσης αὐτοῖς* scripsi: *τῆς ἑαυτῶν* codd. | *περικρατοῦσαι καὶ* seclusi (an secludendum *καὶ ἀντιλαμβανόμενοι*?) **24** *καὶ αὐτὰ τοῦ* P | *τυχοῦσαι* scripsi: *ἔτυχον* codd. **26** *οὐκ ἔτι ἤθελον* P: *οὐκ ἤθελον* F **27** *ἔτι* (ante *ἐπὶ*) seclusit Wachsm. **28–29** *ὡς Ἑρμῆς ἐμοὶ λέγων ἔφη* scripsi: *Ἑρμῆς ὡς κἀμοῦ* (*κἀμὲ* P[2]) *λέγων* FP **30** *ἐλάνθανον* Heeren: *ἐλάνθανεν* codd. | *πράσσουσαι* scripsi: *ὃ πράσσουσιν* codd. **32** *ἡγεμόνι καὶ* secludendum? | *τὸ* F: *τὸ* eras. ex *τῷ* P | *σύστημα* (om. *τι*) P[2]: *συστήματι* FP[1]

τεχνήσασθαι, ὅπως ἐν τούτῳ τὸ τῶν ψυχῶν διαπαντὸς γένος κολάζηται.

26 *Τότε δὴ μεταπεμψάμενος ἐμέ, φησὶν Ἑρμῆς, εἶπεν "Ὦ ψυχῆς ἐμῆ⟨ς⟩ ψυχὴ καὶ νοὸς ἱεροῦ ἐμοῦ νοῦ⟨ς, . . .⟩."*

27 ⟨. . . εἶπεν ὁ θεός·⟩ "Ἄχρι ποῦ στυγνὴ φύσις ἡ τῶν ὑποκειμένων ὁρᾶται; ἄχρι πότε τὰ ἤδη γεγονότα [ἀργὰ] μένει [καὶ] ἀνεγκωμίαστα; ἀλλ' ἄγε δή μοι τοὺς ἐν οὐρανῷ θεοὺς ⟨κάλεσον⟩ πάντας ἤδη" [εἶπεν ὁ θεός, ὦ τέκνον, ὥς φησιν Ἑρμῆς]. οἱ δὲ ⟨ὡς⟩ ἦλθον πρὸς ⟨τὸ⟩ ἐπίταγμα, "Ἀπίδετε" εἶπεν "εἰς τὴν γῆν καὶ πάντα τὰ χαμαί· ⟨. . .⟩" οἱ δὲ ἐν τάχει [καὶ εἶδον καὶ] ἐνόησαν ἃ ἐβούλετο ⟨ὁ⟩ δυνάστης, καὶ εἰπόντι ὑπὲρ τῆς τῶν ἀνθρώπων γενέσεως

28 συνέθεντο. ⟨ἐπερωτῶντος δὲ⟩ [εἴ τι παρ'] ἕνα ἕκαστον τί δυνατός ἐστι παρασχεῖν τοῖς μέλλουσι γίγνεσθαι, ἔλεγεν Ἥλιος "⌜Ἐπὶ πλέον⌝ λάμψω." ὑπισχνεῖτο Σελήνη [τὸν] μετὰ τὸν Ἡλίου δρόμον φωτίσαι· ἔλεγε δὲ καὶ προπεπαιδοποιηκέναι [φόβον καὶ] σιγὴν καὶ ὕπνον [καὶ τὴν μέλλουσαν αὐτοῖς ἔσεσθαι ⟨π⟩ανωφελῆ μνήμην]. Κρόνος ἀπήγγειλεν ἤδη πατὴρ γεγονέναι [καὶ] δίκης καὶ ἀνάγκης. Ζεὺς ἔλεγεν "Ὡς μὴ παντάπασι πολέμοις ⟨ἀπόλητ⟩αι τὸ φῦλον τὸ ἐσόμενον, ἤδη αὐτοῖς [καὶ τύχην καὶ ἐλπίδα καὶ] εἰρήνην γεγέννηκα." Ἄρης ἀγωνίας ἔλεγεν ἤδη καὶ ὀργῆς καὶ ἔριδος πατὴρ εἶναι. Ἀφροδίτη οὐκ ἐμέλλησεν, ἀλλὰ εἶπεν "Ἐγὼ δὲ πόθον αὐτοῖς, ὦ δέσποτα, καὶ ἡδονὴν ἐπιζεύξω καὶ γέλωτα [ὡς μὴ χαλεπωτάτην αἱ συγγενεῖς ψυχαὶ τὴν καταδίκην ὑπομένωσιν] [ἐπὶ πλέον κολάζωνται]." ἐτέρπετο, ὦ τέκνον, [ἐπὶ πλέον]

29 ⟨ὁ πατὴρ⟩ Ἀφροδίτης ταῦτα λεγούσης. "Ἐγὼ δέ", εἶπεν Ἑρμῆς, "[καὶ] ⟨συνετὴν⟩ ποιήσω τὴν ⟨τῶν⟩ ἀνθρώπων φύσιν [ἔφη], καὶ σοφίαν αὐτοῖς [καὶ σωφροσύνην καὶ πειθὼ] καὶ ἀλήθειαν ⟨π⟩αραθήσω· καὶ οὐ παύσομαι [τῇ εὑρέσει συνών] [ἀλλὰ καὶ τῶν ὑπὸ ζῳδίων τῶν ἐμῶν γινομένων ἀνθρώπων] εἰσαεὶ τὸν θνητῶν βίον ὠφελ[ησ]ῶ⟨ν⟩, [ζῴδια γὰρ [[τὰ]] ἐμοὶ ἀνέθηκεν ὁ πατὴρ καὶ δημιουργὸς ⟨⟨τὰ⟩⟩ ἔμφρονα [γε] καὶ νοερά,] καὶ τότε πλέον, ὅταν ἡ ἐπικειμένη αὐτοῖς τῶν ἀστέρων κίνησις σύμφωνον ἔχῃ τὴν ἑνὸς ἑκάστου φυσικὴν ἐνέργειαν." ἔχαιρεν [ὁ θεὸς] ὁ δεσπότης [κόσμου] ταῦτα ἀκούσας, καὶ προσέταξε γίγνεσθαι φῦλον τὸ ἀνθρώπων.]

30 *⟨. . .⟩ ἐγὼ δέ, φησὶν Ἑρμῆς, ἐπεζήτουν ὕλην, τίνι δέον*

1 *τεχνίσασθαι* P 4 *ἐμῆς* Patrit.: *ἐμὴ* FP | *ψυχῆς ἐμῆς ψυχὴ καὶ* secludendum? | *νοὸς ἱεροῦ ἐμοῦ νοῦς* scripsi (*νοῦς ἱεροῦ ἐμοῦ νοῦ* Wachsm.): *νοῦς ἱερὸς ἐμοῦ νοῦ* codd. 6 *τὰ εἴδη γεγονότα* P | *ἀλλά τε δῆμοι* P^1 7 *κάλεσον* add. Usener: an ⟨*καλείτω τις*⟩? 8 *ὡς* (ante *ἦλθον*) add. Heeren 9 Fortasse *καὶ εἶδον* ⟨*τὴν τῶν κάτω ἐρημίαν*?⟩ *καὶ ἐνόησαν* 10 *ὁ* P^2: om. FP^1 11 *συνέθεντο* P^2: *συνήθοντο* P^1: *συνήσθοντο* F | *ἕνα ἕκαστον* scripsi: *εἴ τι παρ' ἑνὸς ἑκάστου* codd. | *τι* (ante *δυνατός*) FP^1: *τις* P^2 13 *μετὸν* F | *Ἡλίου* scripsi: *ἥλιον* codd. 14 *προπεπαιδοπεποιηκέναι* P 15 *πανωφελῆ* Meineke: *ἀνωφελῆ* FP | *καὶ* om. Heeren 16 *πολέ-*

to the intent that in it the race of souls might through all time
suffer punishment. 'And thereon', said Hermes, 'he sent for 26
me, and said, "Thou soul of my soul, and mind of my holy
mind, . . .[1]"

. . . And God said,[2] 'How long shall the world below be gloomy to look 27
on? How long shall the things that have been made remain with none
to praise them? Come now, summon to me forthwith all the gods in heaven.'
And when they had come in obedience to his command, 'Look down', said
God, 'on the earth and all things there below, ⟨and see how . . .⟩'. And
the gods quickly understood[3] what their Sovereign wished to do; and when
he spoke of the making of man, they agreed. And God asked each of them 28
in turn, 'What can you provide for the men that are about to be made?'
Then the Sun said, 'I will shine . . .'[4] The Moon promised to give light
after the Sun had run his diurnal course; and she said also that she had
already given birth to Silence and Sleep. Kronos[5] announced that he had
already become father of Penal Justice and Necessity. Zeus[6] said, 'In order
that the tribe that is about to be may not be utterly destroyed by wars, I have
already begotten Peace for them'. Ares[7] said he was already father of
Struggle, Anger, and Strife. Aphrodite[8] delayed not, but said, 'And I,
Master, will attach to them Love and Pleasure and Laughter'. And the
Father was glad, my son, at what Aphrodite said. 'And I', said Hermes,[9] 29
'will make mankind intelligent; I will confer wisdom on them, and make
known to them the truth. I will never cease to benefit thereby the life of
mortal men; and then above all will I benefit each one of them, when the
force of nature working in him is in accord with the movement of the stars
above.' And the Master was glad[10] when he heard these words; and he gave
command that mankind should come into being.

. . . 'And I', said Hermes, 'sought to find out what material 30

[1] Perhaps, '⟨make bodies in which the disobedient souls may be imprisoned⟩', or something to that effect.

[2] This passage (§§ 27–29) must be an extract from another document. The gods who speak in the council are the seven planets.

[3] Perhaps, 'quickly saw ⟨the desolation of the earth⟩, and understood'.

[4] Perhaps, 'I will shine upon them in the day-time, and . . .'.

[5] I. e. the planet Saturn. [6] The planet Jupiter. [7] The planet Mars.

[8] The planet Venus. [9] The planet Mercury.

[10] Perhaps, 'was yet more glad'.

μοις ἀπόληται scripsi: *πολεμῆσαι* codd. **17** *τὸ ἐσόμενον* Patrit.: *τὸ ἐσομένων* P: *τῶν ἐσομένων* F **19** *ἐμέλησεν* F **21** *ὑπομένωσιν* scripsi: *ὑπομένουσαι* codd. | *ἐπὶ πλέον* seclusit Wachsm. **22** *ὁ πατὴρ* addidi ('addiderim *ὁ θεός*' Wachsm.) | *τάδε* P | *καὶ* del. Heeren **23** *τῶν* add. Heeren | *ἔφη* FP: *εὐφυῆ* Heeren et Wachsm. **24** *παραθήσω* scripsi: *ἀναθήσω* codd. **26** *ὠφελῶν* scripsi: *ὠφελήσω* codd. **26–27** Fortasse *ζῷα γὰρ ἐμοὶ ἀνέθηκεν ὁ πατὴρ καὶ δημιουργὸς τὰ ἔμφρονα καὶ νοερά* (*sc. τοὺς ἀνθρώπους*) **27** *γε* FP: *τε* Meineke | *ἢ* Wachsm.: *καὶ* FP **27–28** Fortasse *ἡ τῶν ἐπικειμένων αὐτοῖς ἀστέρων κίνησις* **29** Fortasse *ἔχαιρεν* ⟨⟨*ἐπὶ* (vel *ἔτι*) *πλέον*⟩⟩ (vide § 28 *fin.*) **30** *τὸ* (post *φῦλον*) F: *τῶν* P **31** Fortasse ⟨*'Εμὲ δή, φησὶν 'Ερμῆς, ἐκέλευσεν ὁ θεὸς τὰ σώματα πλάσαι·*⟩ *ἐγὼ δὲ ἐπεζήτουν ὕλην* vel simile quid

ἐστὶ χρήσασθαι. καὶ παρεκάλουν τὸν μόναρχον· ὁ δὲ ταῖς ψυχαῖς προσέταξε τοῦ κράματος τὸ λείψανον δοῦναι. καὶ λαβὼν εὗρον αὐτὸ παντελῶς ξηρόν. ἔνθεν πολλῷ [πλείονι τοῦ δέοντος] ἐχρησάμην ⟨εἰς⟩ κατάμιξιν ὕδατι, ⟨οὕτ⟩ως ⟨δὲ⟩ τὴν τῆς ὕλης σύστασιν νεαροποιήσας[θαι] [ὡς ἔκλυτον παντάπασιν καὶ ἀσθενὲς καὶ ἀδύνατον τὸ πλασσόμενον εἶναι] [ὡς μὴ πρὸς τῷ συνετὸν εἶναι ἔτι καὶ δυνάμεως ᾖ πεπληρωμένον] ἔπλασα· καὶ καλὸν ὑπῆρχέ ⟨⟨μου τὸ ἔργον⟩⟩, καὶ ἐτερπόμην βλέπων [[μου τὸ ἔργον]]. καὶ [κάτωθεν] ἐπεκαλεσάμην τὸν μόναρχον θεωρῆσαι· ὁ δὲ καὶ εἶδε καὶ ἐχάρη, καὶ τὰς ψυχὰς ἐκέλευσεν ἐνσωματισθῆναι.

31 αἱ δὲ τότε πρῶτον [[στυγνάσασαι]] κατακρίτους ἑαυτὰς μαθοῦσαι ⟨⟨⟨ἐ⟩στύγνασαν⟩⟩. [ἐθαύμασα οὖν] ⟨λέξω δέ σοι⟩ καὶ τοὺς τῶν ψυχῶν λόγους.

32 [[πρόσεχε, τέκνον Ὧρε, κρυπτῆς γὰρ ἐπακούεις θεωρίας, ἧς ὁ μὲν προπάτωρ Καμῆφις ἔτυχεν ἐπακούσας παρὰ Ἑρμοῦ τοῦ πάντων ἔργων ὑπομνηματογράφου, παρὰ τοῦ πάντων προγενεστέρου Καμήφεως, ὁπότε με καὶ τῷ τελείῳ μέλανι ἐτίμησε, νῦν δὲ αὐτὸς σὺ παρ' ἐμοῦ.]]

33 ὅτε γάρ, ὦ [θαυμαστὲ] παῖ μεγαλόδοξε, ἔμελλον ἐγκατα-
κλείεσθαι τοῖς σώμασιν, αἱ μὲν [γὰρ] αὐτῶν αὐτὸ μόνον
ὠδύροντο καὶ ἐστέναζον, ⟨⟨αἱ δὲ ⟨καὶ ἀντε⟩πάλαιον,⟩⟩ [καὶ]
ὅνπερ τρόπον τῶν [γεγονότων] θηρίων τὰ ἐλευθέρ⟨ι⟩α δό[υ]λοις
πονηρῶν [μελήσει] τῆς συνήθους [καὶ φίλης] ἀποσπώμενα
ἐρημίας ⟨ἐπιχειρεῖ⟩ μάχεσθαι [καὶ στασιάζειν] [καὶ οὐχ
ὁμονοεῖν] πρὸς τοὺς κρατήσαντας αὐτῶν [καὶ στασιάζειν]
[ἀλλὰ καί, ἐὰν τύχῃ περιγενόμενα, θανάτῳ παρα⟨δί⟩δω[σου]σι
τοὺς αὐτοῖς ἐπιβάλλοντας]. [[αἱ δὲ παλαιῶν]] [ἔτριζον δίκην
34 ἀσπίδων.] ὀξὺ δὲ κωκύσασα ἑτέρα, [καὶ πρὸ τῶν λόγων ἱκανὰ
κλαύσασα,] καὶ πολλάκις ἄνω τε καὶ κάτω [τοὺς ⟨οἵ⟩ους
ἔτυχεν ἔχουσα] μεταφέρουσα ⟨τοὺς⟩ ὀφθαλμούς, "Οὐρανέ,
τῆς ἡμετέρας" εἶπεν "ἀρχὴ γενέσεως, ⟨⟨περιλαμπῆ τε
[ὀφθαλμοὶ θεῶν] ἄστρα, καὶ [[φῶς]] ἡλίου καὶ σελήνης ⟨⟨φῶς⟩⟩
ἀκοπίαστον·⟩⟩ αἰθήρ τε καὶ ἀήρ, καὶ τοῦ μονάρχου [θεοῦ]
[χεῖρές τε καὶ] ἱερὸν πνεῦμα, [[περιλαμπῆ τε ὀφθαλμοὶ θεῶν
ἄστρα καὶ φῶς ἡλίου καὶ σελήνης ἀκοπίαστον,]] τὰ τῆς
ἡμετέρας ⌜ἀρχῆς⌝ σύντροφα· ὡς [ἀπάντων] ⟨⟨μεγάλων τε καὶ
λαμπρῶν⟩⟩ ἀποσπώμενα⟨ι⟩ ἄθλια πάσχομεν. ⌜πλέον οὐδ'
ὅτι⌝ ἀπὸ [[μεγάλων τε καὶ λαμπρῶν]] [καὶ] τοῦ ἱεροῦ περι-

I was to use;[1] and I called on the Sole Ruler, and he commanded the souls to hand over to me the residue of the mixture.[2] But when I received it, I found that it was quite dried up. I therefore used much water for mixing with it; and when I had thereby renewed the liquid consistency of the stuff, I fashioned bodies out of it. And the work of my hands was fair to view, and I was glad when I looked on it. And I called on the Sole Ruler to inspect it; and he saw it, and was glad; and he gave order that the souls should be embodied.'

Then first did the souls learn that they were sentenced; and 31
gloomy were their looks. I will tell you what the souls said;
listen, my glorious son. When they were about to be shut up 33
in the bodies, some of them wailed and moaned, just that and
nothing more; but some there were that struggled against their
doom, even as beasts of noble temper,[3] when they are caught
by the crafty tricks of cruel men, and dragged away from the wild
land that is their home, strive to fight against those who have
mastered them.[4] And another shrieked, and again and again 34
turning his eyes now upward and now downward,[5] said, 'O thou
Heaven, source of our being, and ye bright-shining stars, and never-failing light of sun and moon; and ye, aether and air, and holy life-breath of Him who rules alone,[6] ye that have shared our home; how cruel it is that we are being torn away from things so great and splendid! . . . We are to be expelled from the holy atmosphere, and a place nigh to the vault of heaven,

[1] *Sc.* in making the bodies in which the souls were to be imprisoned.

[2] Perhaps, 'he gave command that the residue of the mixture should be handed over to me'. (It is the *second* mixture that is meant.)

[3] E. g. lions or elephants.

[4] Perhaps, 'And others writhed like asps'.

[5] I. e. looking at heaven and earth by turns.

[6] God's 'life-breath' is the atmosphere.

1–2 *ταῖς ψυχαῖς* secludendum? **4** *εἰς κατάμιξιν* scripsi : *κατὰ μῖξιν* (*κατὰ μίξας* P^{2}) codd. | *οὕτως δὲ* scripsi : *ὡς* codd. **5** *νεαροποιήσας* scripsi : *νεαροποιήσασθαι* codd. **7** *πρὸς τὸ* P **15–19** § 32 (*πρόσεχε . . . ἐμοῦ*) hinc ad initium excerpti transposui **16** *καμῆφις* F : *καμήφης* P **22** *αἱ δὲ καὶ ἀντεπάλαιον* huc a v. 28 transposui | *καὶ ἀντεπάλαιον* scripsi : *παλαιῶν* F : *πλέον* P **23** *ἐλευθέρια* scripsi : *ἐλεύθερα* codd. **23–24** *δόλοις πονηρῶν* scripsi (an *δόλοις πονηροῖς*?) : *δούλοις πονηρῶν* FP^{1} : *δούλοις πονηροῖς* P^{2} **24** *μελήσει* F : *μελλήσει* P | *καὶ φίλης* F : *τε καὶ φίλης* P **26** *καὶ στασιάζειν* FP : om. edd. **27** *παραδίδωσι* scripsi : *παραδώσουσι* codd. **28** *τοὺς* P^{2} : *τοῖς* FP^{1} **28–29** *ἔτριζον δίκην ἀσπίδων* seclusi (an scribendum *αἱ δὲ ἐλύγιζον δίκην ἀσπίδων*?) **30** *οἵους* scripsi : *ὡς* codd. **31** *φέρουσα* P **37** *ἀρχῆς* codd. : fortasse *φύσεως* | *ὡς* scripsi : *ὧν* codd. **38** *ἀποσπώμεναι* P^{2} : *ἀποσπώμενα* FP^{1} **38–39** *πλέον οὐδ' ὅτι* F : *πλέον δ' ὅτι* P : 'num *πλέον δ' ἔτι*?' Wachsm. : an *πλὴν οἶδ' ὅτι*?

χύματος καὶ ⟨τόπου⟩ πλησίου ⟨τοῦ⟩ πόλου καὶ [ἐπὶ] τῆς
μακαρίας [μετὰ θεῶν] πολιτείας εἰς ἄτιμα καὶ ταπεινὰ οὕτως
35 ἐγκατειρχθησόμεθα σκηνώματα. [[τί ταῖς δυστήναις ἡμῖν
ἀπρεπὲς οὕτως πέπρακται; τί τῶν κολάσεων τούτων ἄξιον;]]
οἶαι τὰς δειλαίας ἡμᾶς [ἁμαρτίας] ⟨ἀνάγκαι⟩ περιμένουσιν·
οἷα [διὰ τὰ πονηρὰ τῶν ἐλπίδων] πράξομεν, ἵνα τῷ [ὑδαρεῖ
36 καὶ] ταχὺ διαλύτῳ σώματι πορίζωμεν τὰ ἐπιτήδεια. ⟨οἱ⟩
ὀφθαλμοὶ [τὰς οὐκέτι τοῦ θεοῦ ψυχὰς] χωρήσουσιν ὀλίγον,
καὶ [[παντελῶς μικρὸν]] τῷ ἐν τούτοις ⟨τοῖς⟩ ⟨⟨κύκλοις⟩⟩ ὑγρῷ
[καὶ] [[κύκλων]] ⟨⟨παντελῶς μικρὸν⟩⟩ τὸν ἑαυτῶν πρόγονον
οὐρανὸν ὁρῶσαι στενάξομεν ἀεί. [ἔστι δ' ὅτε] καὶ ⟨βλέποντες
δ'⟩ οὐ βλέψομεν ⟨⟨ἄντικρυς⟩⟩· [ἔνθ⟨εν⟩ Ὀρφεύς "τῷ λαμπρῷ
βλέπομεν, τοῖς δ' ὄμμασιν οὐδὲν ὁρῶμεν·"] ἀθλίαι⟨ς⟩ γὰρ
κατεκρίθη ⟨ἡ⟩μῖν ⟨σκότος⟩. [καὶ τὸ βλέπειν ἡμῖν οὐκ
[[ἄντικρυς]] ἐχαρίσθη, ὅτι χωρὶς τοῦ φωτὸς ἡμῖν τὸ ὁρᾶν οὐκ
ἐδόθη.] [⌜τόποι⌝ τοίνυν καὶ οὐκέτ' εἰσὶν ὀφθαλμοί.] ὡς δὲ
καὶ τῶν συγγενῶν φυσ[σ]ώντων ἐν ἀέρι πνευμάτων ἀκού⟨ου⟩σαι
τλημόνως οἴσομεν ὅτι μὴ συμπνέομεν αὐτοῖς· οἶκος ⟨γὰρ⟩
ἡμᾶς ἀντὶ τοῦ μεταρσίου κόσμου τούτου ὁ βραχὺς περιμένει
37 καρδίας ὄγκος. ⟨⟨τί ταῖς δυστήναις ἡμῖν [ἀπρεπὲς οὕτως]
πέπρακται [τί] τῶν κολάσεων τούτων ἄξιον;⟩⟩ [[ἀεὶ δὲ
ἀπολύσας ἡμᾶς ἀφ' ὧν εἰς οἷα κατέβημεν ἀπολεῖ τὸ λυπεῖσθαι.]] ⟨ὦ⟩ δέσποτα καὶ πάτερ καὶ ποιητά, [εἰ] ⟨διὰ τί⟩
ταχέως οὕτως σῶν ἔργων ἠμέλησας; [[διάταξον ἡμῖν τινας
ὅρους.]] ἔτι κἂν βραχέων ἡμᾶς ἀξίωσον λόγων [ἕως ἔτι δι'
ὅλου τοῦ περιφανοῦς ἔχομεν βλέπειν κόσμου]. ⟨⟨διάταξον
ἡμῖν τινας ὅρους ⟨τῆς κολάσεως⟩·⟩⟩ ⟨⟨[α]εἰ δὲ ⟨. . .⟩,
ἐπιλήσας ἡμᾶς ἀφ' ⟨οἵ⟩ων εἰς οἷα κατέβημεν ἀπόλγε το⟨ῦ⟩
λυπεῖσθαι.⟩⟩"

38 ἐπέτυχον, τέκνον Ὧρε, αἱ ψυχαὶ ταῦτα εἰποῦσαι· παρῆν
γὰρ [καὶ] ⟨ὁ⟩ μόναρχος, καὶ [[τάδε]] ἐπὶ τοῦ τῆς ἀληθείας
καθίσας θρόνου, ταῖς δεηθείσαις ἐφώνησεν ⟨⟨τάδε⟩⟩· [λόγοι
τοῦ θεοῦ.] [["Ἔρως ὑμῶν, ψυχαί, δεσπόσει καὶ Ἀνάγκη·
οἵδε γὰρ μετ' ἐμὲ πάντων δεσπόται καὶ ταξίαρχοι.]] Ψυχαὶ

1 τόπου πλησίου τοῦ scripsi: πλουσίου codd. | ἐπὶ FP[1]: ἀπὸ P[2] 1–2 Fortasse τῆς ⟨ἐκεῖ⟩ μακαρίας πολιτείας ⟨ἐκπεσοῦσαι?⟩ 2 καὶ ταπεινὰ (aut ἄτιμα καὶ) secludendum? 3–4 τί ταῖς . . . ἄξιον hinc ad § 37 *init.* transposui 5 οἶαι scripsi: ὃ καὶ FP[1]: ὅσαι P[2] | ἁμαρτίας FP[1]: ἁμαρτίαι P[2] 6 οἷα scripsi: ὅσα P: ὅσαι F 6–7 οἷα . . . ἐπιτήδεια secludendum? 8 ὀλίγον Meineke: ὀλίγα FP 9–10 καὶ τῷ ἐν τούτοις τοῖς κύκλοις ὑγρῷ παντελῶς μικρὸν scripsi: καὶ παντελῶς

and from the blissful life we lived there, and to be imprisoned
in habitations mean and base as these.[1] Poor wretches that we 35
are, what hard necessities await us! What hateful things we shall
have to do, in order to supply the needs of this body that must
so soon perish! Our eyes will have little room to take things 36
in; we shall see things only by means of the fluid which these
orbs contain; and when we see Heaven, our own forefather,
contracted to small compass,[2] we shall never cease to moan.
And even if we see, we shall not see outright; for alas, we have
been condemned to darkness. And when we hear the winds,
our kinsmen, blowing in the air, deeply shall we grieve that we
are not breathing in union with them. For dwelling-place, instead
of this world on high, there awaits us a man's heart, a thing of
little bulk. Unhappy we! What have we done to deserve such 37
punishments as these? O Master, thou that art our Father and
our Maker, why hast thou so soon ceased to care for the works
of thy hands? Even yet hold us of some account,[3] though it be
but little. Ordain some limits to our punishment; and if . . .,[4]
make us forget what bliss we have lost, and into what an evil
world we have come down, and so release us from our sorrow.'

Thus spoke the souls, my son Horus; and they obtained that 38
which they sought. For the Sole Ruler came, and took his seat
on the throne of truth, and spoke in answer to their prayer,
saying: 'Ye souls, all ye that do obeisance to my unageing

[1] I.e. in earthly bodies.

[2] An object cannot be seen by bodily eyes unless an image of the object enters the eye or is formed it it; the image (of the sky, for instance) which presents itself to our sight must therefore be small enough to be contained within the eye.

[3] Or, 'permit us to plead with thee'.

[4] Perhaps, 'and if the sentence is irrevocable'.

μικρὸν τῶν ἐν τούτοις ὑγρῶν καὶ κύκλων codd. | An secludendum τῶν ἐν τούτοις ὑγρῶν καὶ κύκλων? **11** στενάξωμεν F **12–13** ἔνθεν Ὀρφεὺς . . . ὁρῶμεν seclusit Heeren **12** ἔνθεν Meineke: ἔνθ' FP **13** ὅμασιν P **13–14** ἀθλίαις γὰρ κατεκρίθη ἡμῖν σκότος scripsi: ἄθλιαι γὰρ κατεκρίθημεν codd. **15** ἐχαρίσθη Canter: ἐχωρίσθη FP **16** τόποι FP: ὀπαὶ Heeren: πόροι Meineke **17** φυσώντων Wachsm.: φυσσώντων FP | ἀκούουσαι scripsi: ἀκοῦσαι codd. **18** συμπνέομεν F: συμπνέμεν P **20–21** τί ταῖς . . . ἄξιον huc a § 35 transposui **23** δέσποτα καὶ secludendum? | εἰ F: καὶ P **27** εἰ δὲ scripsi: ἀεὶ δὲ FP: ἀλλ' Meineke: fortasse εἰ δὲ ⟨ἀμετάθετος ἡ καταδίκη⟩ vel simile quid **28** ἐπιλήσας Wachsm.: ἀπολύσας FP | οἵων scripsi: ὧν codd. | ἀπόλυε τοῦ Usener: ἀπολεῖ τὸ FP **30** ταῦτα scripsi: τάδε codd. **31** ὁ add. Heeren **32–33** Titulum λόγοι τοῦ θεοῦ habent FP: om. edd. **32** λόγοι codd.: fortasse λόγος **34** δεσπόται καὶ P: δεσπόται τε καὶ F

[δὲ], ὅσαι τὴν ἀγήρατόν μου σκηπτουχίαν θεραπεύετε,
⟨⟨ἐπέγνωτε δή⟨π⟩ου[ν] ὡς διὰ τὰ πρόσθεν πραχθέντα ὑμῖν
κόλασιν ταύτην ὑπομένετε [τὴν ἐνσωμάτωσιν].⟩⟩ ἴστε ⟨γὰρ⟩
ὡς ἕως μὲν ἀναμάρτητοι ἦτε, τὰ ⟨πλησίον⟩ τοῦ οὐρανοῦ
ᾠκεῖτε χωρία· ⟨ἐπ⟩εὶ δ' ἄρα τις ὑμῶν [τινος] ἤγγισε[ι]
μέμψις, ⟨⟨σπλάγχνοις καταδικασθεῖσαι⟩⟩ θνητοῖς, καὶ αὐταὶ
⟨τὸν τούτοις⟩ προσμεμοιρα[σ]μένον χῶρον [[σπλάγχνοις κατα-
δικασθεῖσαι]] ἐνοικήσετε, ⟨ὅπου⟩ ⟨⟨Ἔρως ὑμῶν [ψυχαὶ]
δεσπόσει καὶ Ἀνάγκη· οἵδε γὰρ μετ' ἐμὲ ⟨τῶν κάτω⟩ πάντων
39 δεσπόται καὶ ταξίαρχοι.⟩⟩ ⟨⟨ἀλλ' οὐκ [δὲ] εἰκῇ καὶ ὡς
ἔτυχεν ἐνομοθέτησα τὰς μεταβολὰς ὑμῶν· ἀλλ' ὡς ἐπὶ τὸ
χεῖρον ⟨. . .⟩ εἴ τι [δια]πράξετε ἄσχημον, οὕτως ἐπὶ τὸ
βέλτιον, εἴ τι βουλεύ⟨σ⟩εσθε τῆς ἑαυτῶν γενέσεως ἄξιον. ἐγὼ
γὰρ [καὶ οὔτις ἕτερος] ἐπόπτης αὐτὸς [καὶ ἐπίσκοπος] ἔσομαι·⟩⟩
κἂν μὲν ᾖ ὑμῶν μέτρια τὰ αἰτιάματα, τὸν ἐπίκηρον τῶν
σαρκῶν [συν]δεσμὸν καταλιποῦσαι πάλιν ἀστένακτοι τὸν
ἑαυτῶν ⌜οὐρανὸν⌝ ἀσπάσεσθε· εἰ δ' ἄρα τινῶν μειζόνων
ἁμαρτημάτων ἔσεσθε ⌜ποιητικαί⌝, [οὐ μετὰ τέλους καθήκοντος]
τῶν πλασμάτων προελθοῦσαι ⌜οὐρανὸν⌝ μὲν οὐκέτι οἰκήσετε,
οὐδ' αὖ σώματα ἀνθρώπων, ⟨εἰς⟩ ζῷα δ' ἄλογα μετα⟨βᾶσαι,
χαμαὶ⟩ πλανώμεναι ⟨τὸ⟩ λοιπὸν διατελέσετε."

40 τάδε εἰπών, ὦ τέκνον Ὧρε, πάσαις αὐταῖς ⌜ἐχαρίσατο
πνεύματα⌝, καὶ πάλιν ἐφώνησεν· "[[Ἄλλους δὲ εἰκῇ καὶ ὡς
ἔτυχεν ἐνομοθέτησε τὰς διαβολὰς ὑμῶν, ἄλλως ἐπὶ τὸ χεῖρον
εἴ τι διαπράξετε ἄσχημον, οὕτως ἐπὶ τὸ βέλτιον εἴ τι
βουλεύεσθε τῆς ἑαυτῶν γενέσεως ἄξιον· ἐγὼ γὰρ καὶ οὔτις
ἕτερος ἐπόπτης αὐτὸς καὶ ἐπίσκοπος ἔσομαι.]] [[ἐπίγνωτε δὲ
οὖν ὡς διὰ τὰ πρόσθεν πραχθέντα ὑμῖν κόλασιν ταύτην
41 ὑπομένετε τὴν ἐνσωμάτωσιν.]] ⟨. . . ἀρχ⟩ὴ τοίνυν [διαφορὰ]
[τῆς] παλιγγενεσίας ὑμῖν ἔσται ἡ τῶν σωμάτων [ὡς ἔφην]
διαφ⟨θ⟩ορά, [εὐεργεσία δὲ] καὶ ⟨τῆς⟩ πρόσθεν εὐδαιμονία⟨ς
ἀνανέωσις⟩ ἡ διάλυσις· τυφλωθήσεται δ' ὑμῶν ἡ φρόνησις,
[ἐάν τι ἀνάξιον ἐμοῦ δόξητε πράσσειν,] ὥστε φρονεῖν τὰ

1 θεραπεύεται P[1] 2–3 ἐπέγνωτε . . . ἐνσωμάτωσιν huc a § 40 *fin.* transposui 2 ἐπέγνωτε scripsi: ἐπίγνωτε codd. | δήπου scripsi (δὴ οὖν Wachsm.): δὲ οὖν FP 3 τὴν (ante ἐνσωμάτωσιν) F: καὶ P 4 ἦτε scripsi: ἐστε codd. 5 ᾠκεῖτε scripsi: οἰκήσετε FP[2]: οἰκήσεται P[1] | ἐπεὶ scripsi: εἰ codd. | ἤγγισε scripsi: ἐγγίσει codd. 7 προσμεμοιραμένον scripsi: προσμεμοιρασμένον codd. 8 ἐνοικήσεται P[1] 9–10 Fortasse οἵδε γὰρ [μετ' ἐμὲ] ⟨τῶν κάτω⟩ πάντων [δεσπόται καὶ] ταξίαρχοι (an secludendum οἵδε . . . ταξίαρχοι?) 10–14 ἀλλ' . . . ἔσομαι huc a § 40

sovereignty, you have learnt, methinks, that it is by reason of the deeds which you have done before that you have to endure this punishment. For you know that, as long as you were sinless, you dwelt in the places nigh to heaven; but now that blame has come upon you, you have been condemned to imprisonment in the organs of mortal bodies, and must yourselves dwell in the region assigned to them. And in that region Desire and
Necessity will be your masters; for it is they that, after me, 39
are masters and captains of all things below. Howbeit, not at random have I ordained the changes of your state; but as your condition will be changed for the worse if you do aught unseemly, so will it be changed for the better if you resolve on action worthy of your origin. I myself will keep watch on you; and if the charges against you shall be but slight, you shall be released from the deadly bondage of the flesh, and, freed from sorrow, shall greet again your home above. But if you shall be found guilty of any greater sins, in that case, when you quit your bodily frames, you shall not thereafter dwell in . . .,[1] nor yet in human bodies, but you shall be transferred into the bodies of beasts, and shall thenceforth continue to wander upon earth.'

Having said this, my son Horus, God gave . . . to[2] all the 40
souls; and then he spoke again, and said, '. . . The destruction 41
of your bodies then will be the starting-point for a rebirth, and their dissolution, a renewal of your former happiness. But your minds will be blinded, so that you will think the contrary, and

[1] MSS., 'in heaven'. But the sense required is 'in the atmosphere'.
[2] Perhaps, 'assigned bodies to'.

transposui 10 ἀλλ' οὐκ Patrit.: ἀλλ' οὐδὲ Canter: ἄλλους δὲ FP 10–11 καὶ ὡς ἔτυχεν secludendum? 11 ἐνομοθέτησα Patrit.: ἐνομοθέτησε F: ὀνομοθέτησε P | μεταβολὰς (vel διανομὰς) Meineke: καταβολὰς Heeren: διαβολὰς FP | ἀλλ' ὡς Patrit.: ἄλλως FP 12 Fortasse ⟨ἡ μεταβολὴ γενήσεται⟩ 12–13 Fortasse ἐάν τι πράξητε . . . ἐάν τι βουλεύσησθε 12 πράξετε scripsi: διαπράξετε F: διαπράξητε P 13 βουλεύσεσθε Meineke: βουλεύεσθε F: βουλεύεσθαι P 14 καὶ ἐπίσκοπος del. Meineke 15 ᾖ Meineke: ἦν FP | αἰτιάματα Patrit.: αἰτιώματα FP 16 δεσμὸν scripsi: σύνδεσμον codd. | ἀστένακτον P: an ἀστενακτί? 17 ἑαυτῶν F et P marg.: ἐπ' αὐτὸν P | ἀσπάσεσθαι P 18 ἔσεσθαι P | ποιητικαί codd.: fortasse ὑπόδικοι 19 προσελθοῦσαι P | οἰκήσεται P[1] 20–21 μεταβᾶσαι, χαμαὶ πλανώμεναι scripsi: μεταπλανώμεναι codd. 21 τὸ add. Heeren 22–23 ἐχαρίσατο πνεύματα codd.: fortasse διέδωκε σώματα 23–27 ἄλλους . . . ἔσομαι hinc ad § 39 transposui 27–29 ἐπίγνωτε . . . ἐνσωμάτωσιν hinc ad § 38 transposui 29 ἀρχὴ scripsi: ἡ codd. 30 ἡ τῶν om. P 31 διαφθορά scripsi: διαφορά codd. 31–32 εὐδαιμονίας ἀνανέωσις scripsi: εὐδαιμονία codd. 32 Fortasse ἡ ⟨τοῦ πλάσματος (vel συστήματος)⟩ διάλυσις | ἡμῶν P 33–1 *infra*: φρονεῖν τὰ ἐνάντια καὶ secludendum?

ἐναντία, καὶ τὴν μὲν κόλασιν ὡς εὐεργεσίαν ˹ὑπομένειν˺, τὴν δὲ εἰς τὰ βελτίονα μεταβολὴν ⟨ὡς⟩ ἀτιμίαν [τε] καὶ ὕβριν. αἱ δικαιότεραι δ' ὑμῶν καὶ τὴν εἰς τὸ ˹θεῖον˺ μεταβολὴν ἐκδεχόμεναι ⟨. . .⟩"

42 ⟨. . .⟩ εἰς μὲν ἀνθρώπους, βασιλεῖς δίκαιοι, φιλόσοφοι γνήσιοι, κτίσται καὶ νομοθέται, μάντεις [οἱ] ἀληθεῖς, [ῥιζοτόμοι γνήσιοι], ἄριστοι προφῆται θεῶν, μουσικοὶ ἔμπειροι, ἀστρονόμοι νοεροί, οἰωνοσκόποι σαφεῖς, ἀκριβεῖς θύται, καὶ ὁπόσοι ἔς τι καλῶν κἀγαθῶν ἄξιοι. εἰς δὲ πτηνά, ἀετοί, διότι οὐδὲν ⟨οὗτοι⟩ τῶν ὁμογενῶν οὔτε ˹ἐκβοήσουσιν˺ οὔτε θοιν[ησ]ῶνται, ἀλλ' οὐδὲ [πλησίον τούτων] ζῷον ἕτερον ἀσθενέστερόν τι αὐτῶν ἀδικεῖν ˹ἀφεθήσεται˺· ἐνδικωτάτη γὰρ ἡ τῶν ἀετῶν φύσις [μετελεύσεται]. εἰς δὲ τετράποδα, λέοντες· ἰσχυρὸν γὰρ τὸ ζῷον, [καὶ φύσεως ἔτυχεν ἀκοιμήτου τρόπῳ τινι,] καὶ φθαρτῷ σώματι τὴν ἀθάνατον γυμναζόμενον φύσιν· οὔτε γὰρ κάμνουσιν οὔτε κοιμῶνται. εἰς δὲ ἑρπετά, δράκοντες, δυνατὸν ὅτι τὸ ζῷον, καὶ μακρόβιον, ἄκακόν τε, καὶ φιλάνθρωπον οὕτως ⟨ὥσ⟩τε ⟨ἐνί⟩ους καὶ τιθασεύεσθαι, καὶ ἰὸν οὐκ ἔχει, ⟨ν⟩εάζει δὲ καὶ γηράσαν, καθάπερ φύσις ἡ θεῶν. ἐν δὲ νήχουσι, δελφῖνες· συμπαθ[ησ]οῦσι γὰρ [καὶ] τοῖς εἰς πέλαγος ἐμπίπτουσιν οὗτοι, καὶ το⟨ὺς⟩ μὲν ἐμπνοῦς διακομί⟨ζ⟩ουσιν εἰς γῆν, τῶν δὲ τελευτησάντων οὐδ' ὅλως ποτε ἅπτονται, καίτοι φιλοβ⟨ο⟩ρωτάτου πάντων ὄντος τοῦ τῶν ἐνύδρων γένους.

τοσαῦτα ὁ θεὸς εἰπὼν ἀόρατος [νοῦς] γίγνεται.

43 τούτων οὕτως γενομένων, τέκνον Ὧρε, ἰσχυρότατόν τι ἀπὸ γῆς ἀνίσταται πνεῦμα, ἀκατάληπτον μὲν περιοχῇ σώματος, δυνάμει δὲ φρονήσεως ὑπερ⟨έ⟩χον, [ὃ] [[καίπερ εἰδὸς ὑπὲρ ὧν ἐπυνθάνετο]] τὸ σῶμα [[μὲν]] κατ⟨ὰ⟩ τύπον ἀνδρὸς περικείμενον, καὶ καλὸν ⟨⟨μὲν⟩⟩ καὶ σεμνοπρεπὲς ὄν, ὑπερβυλῇ δὲ ἄγριον καὶ

1 ὑπομένειν codd.: fortasse ὑπονοεῖν (an τὴν μὲν κόλασιν ὡς εὐεργεσίαν [ ] ⟨προσίεσθαι⟩, τὴν δὲ ε. τ. β. μεταβολὴν ὡς ὕβριν ⟨φεύγειν vel φοβεῖσθαι⟩)? 2 τε seclusi (an secludendum ἀτιμίαν τε καὶ?) 3 καὶ (post ὑμῶν) F: κατὰ P 3–4 καὶ . . . ἐκδεχόμεναι secludendum? | θεῖον codd.: fortasse βέλτιον 5 Fortasse ⟨αἱ εὐγενέσταται (vel βασιλικαὶ) ψυχαὶ⟩ εἰς μὲν ἀνθρώπους ⟨εἰσελθοῦσαι γίγνονται⟩ 5–6 Fortasse βασιλεῖς δίκαιοι καὶ κτίσται καὶ νομοθέται, φιλόσοφοι γνήσιοι 6 οἱ F: ἡ P: seclusit Wachsm. | ῥιζοτόμοι γνήσιοι aut delendum aut transponendum | ἄριστοι codd.: fortasse πιστοὶ | θεῶν secludendum? 7 Fortasse οἰωνοσκόποι σαφεῖς, ⟨ῥιζοτόμοι?⟩ ἀκριβεῖς [θύται] 8 ἔς τι Usener: ἐστὲ codd. | ἄξιαι codd.: 'num ἄξιοι?' Wachsm. 9 ἐκβοήσουσιν FP: ἐκσοβήσουσιν Wachsm.: fortasse ἐξωθ[ησ]οῦσιν | θοινῶνται scripsi: θοινήσονται codd. 10 αὐτῶν scripsi: αὐτοῦ FP | ἀφεθήσεται codd.: fortasse ἐφίενται 10–11 ἐνδικωτάτη scripsi: ἐνδικωτέρα FP 11 ἡ τῶν ἀρετῶν φύσις P 13 κάμνουσιν Patrit.: κάμνωσιν FP 15 οὕτως . . . τιθασεύεσθαι secludendum? | ὥστε ἐνίους scripsi: τε οὖν FP | τιθασεύεσθαι scripsi: τιθασευθήσεται codd. | οὐκ ἔχει scripsi: οὐχ ἕξει codd. 16 νεάζει scripsi (νεάσει Wachsm.): ἐάσει FP 17 συμπαθοῦσι scripsi:

will regard the punishment[1] as a boon, and the change to a better state[2] as a degradation and an outrage. But the more righteous[3] among you, those who look forward to the change . . .'

⟨Souls of the noblest kind,⟩[4] when they enter human bodies, become righteous kings, founders of cities, and lawgivers, genuine philosophers, true diviners, trustworthy prophets, skilled musicians,[5] sage astronomers,[6] men that find sure omens in the flight of birds, priests exact in the rites of sacrifice,[7] and all kinds of men that are of high worth in any sort of work. When such souls enter the bodies of birds, they become eagles; because eagles neither drive away other creatures of their kind[8] nor devour them, and do not seek to wrong any other sort of animal that is weaker than themselves; for eagles are most righteous by nature. When they enter the bodies of quadrupeds, they become lions; for the lion is a strong beast, and one that trains itself to imitate with its mortal body the immortal nature of the gods, inasmuch as lions are never tired, and never sleep. When they enter the bodies of reptiles, they become dragons; for the dragon is a powerful animal, and long-lived; and it is harmless, and so friendly to man, that some dragons are even tamed by men; it has no venom; and it renews its youth when it has grown old, resembling the gods in this. And among the fishes,[9] such souls are dolphins; for dolphins take pity on men who fall into the sea; they convey the man to land if he is still alive, and they never even touch him if he is dead, though the race of fishes is voracious beyond all others. 42

And having thus spoken, God vanished from their sight.

When[10] these things had come to pass as I have told you, my son Horus, 43
there arose from the earth a mighty spirit, named Momus, who had a body of enormous bulk, and a mind of surpassing power. This spirit was clothed in a body of manly form; he was comely and stately to look on, but exceeding

[1] I. e. your life in the body.

[2] I. e. death.

[3] Possibly, 'the more right-thinking'.

[4] This paragraph has evidently been taken from another document, and inappropriately tacked on to God's speech to the souls.

[5] Perhaps the kind of music meant is chiefly the singing of hymns to the gods.

[6] Or 'astrologers'.

[7] Or possibly, 'unerring herbalists'.

[8] I. e. other birds.

[9] Or 'when they are in fish-bodies'.

[10] This passage (§§ 43–48) is another account of the making of men, and is inconsistent with the story told in §§ 24–41. Perhaps the words 'When these things . . . my son Horus', and the phrase 'as soon as he saw the souls entering into their bodily frames', were added to the passage by the man who inserted it into the *Kore Kosmu*.

συμπαθήσουσι codd. **17–18** *τοὺς μὲν ἐμπνοῦς* scripsi : *τὰ μὲν ἔμπνοα* codd. **18** *διακομίζουσιν* scripsi : *διακομιοῦσιν* codd. **19** *ἅπτονται* scripsi : *ἅψονται* codd. | *φιλοβορωτάτου* Meineke : *φιλοβρωτάτου* P : *φιλοβρωτάτου* (sed *ω* corr. in *ο*) F : *φιλοβορωτοτάτου* P[2] | *ὄντος* scripsi : *ἐσομένου* codd. **20** *ἀόρατος* scripsi : *ἄφθαρτος νοῦς* codd. **21** *τι ἀπὸ* F : *τε ἀπὸ* P **22** Fortasse *πνεῦμα ⟨ᾧ ὄνομα Μῶμος⟩* | *περιοχῇ* P[2] : *περιοχῆς* FP[1] | *ὑπερέχον* Meineke : *ὑπάρχον* codd. **23** *εἰδὸς* Wachsm. : *εἶδος* FP | *μὲν* (post *σῶμα*) om. Patrit. | *κατὰ τύπον* Meineke : *καὶ τύπον* FP

πλῆρες φόβου· ὃ δὴ παραυτίκα τὰς ψυχὰς εἰσιούσας εἰς τὰ πλάσματα θεωρῆσαɴ [αν], ⟨⟨καίπερ εἰδὸς ὑπὲρ ὧν ἐπυνθάνετο,⟩⟩ "Τίνες" ἔλεγεν "οὗτοι
44 καλοῦνται, ὦ Ἑρμῆ, θεῶν ὑπομνηματογράφε;" εἰπόντος δὲ "Ἄνθρωποι", [ἔφης] ἔφη "Ὦ Ἑρμῆ, τολμηρὸν ἔργον ποιῆσαι τὸν ἄνθρωπον, περίεργον ὀφθαλμοῖς ⟨⟨μέλλον⟨τα⟩ εἶναι⟩⟩, καὶ [λάλου γλώσσης] ἀκουστικὸν [[μᾶλλον εἶναι]] [[καὶ]] τῶ⟨ν⟩ αὐτῷ μὴ προσηκόντων, ⟨⟨καὶ⟩⟩ λίχνον ⟨γεύσει, καὶ . . .⟩ ὀσφρήσει, καὶ μέχρι πάντων τῷ [τῆς ἁφῆς] ἁπτικῷ μέλλοντα καταχρᾶσ⟨θ⟩αι. τοῦτον ἀμέριμνον καταλεῖψαι κέκρικας, ὦ γενεσιουργέ, τὸν ὁρᾶν μέλλοντα τολμηρῶς τῆς φύσεως τὰ καλὰ μυστήρια; ἄλυπον ἐᾶσαι θέλεις τοῦτον, ⟨τὸν⟩ καὶ μέχρι [τῶν] περά⟨τω⟩ν γῆς τὰς ⌜ἑαυτοῦ⌝ μέλλ[ησ]οντα πέμπειν ἐπινοίας;
45 ⟨⟨εἶτα [οὐ καὶ μέχρις οὐρανοῦ περίεργον ὁπλισθήσο⟨ν⟩ται τόλμαν οὗτοι;] οὐκ [ἀμερίμνους] [ἐκτενοῦσιν] ἐπ[ε]ὶ [καὶ] τὰ στοιχεῖα [τὰς ψυχὰς αὐτῶν]⟩⟩ ⟨⟨τολμηρὰς ἐκτε[ι]νοῦσι χεῖρας;⟩⟩ ῥίζας φυτῶν ἀνασκάψουσιν ἄνθρωποι, καὶ [ποιότητα⟨ς⟩ ἐξετάσουσι χυλῶν,] λίθων φύσεις ἐπισκοπήσουσι· καὶ διὰ μέσον ἀνατεμ[ν]οῦσι τῶν ζῴων τὰ ἄλογα, οὐ μόνον ⟨δὲ ταῦτα⟩, ἀλλὰ καὶ ἑαυτούς, ⟨π⟩ῶς ⟨. . .⟩ ἐγένοντο ἐξετάζειν θέλοντες, ⟨⟨καὶ τίς ἐνδοτέρω τῶν [ἱερῶν ἀδύτων] ⟨. . .⟩ φύσις ὑπάρχει.⟩⟩ [[τολμηρὰς ἐκτείνουσι χεῖρας]] [καὶ μέχρι θαλάσσης καὶ] τὰς αὐτοφυεῖς ὕλας τέμνοντες [μέχρι καὶ] [[τῶν πέραν]] διαπορθμεύ⟨σ⟩ουσι[ν ἀλλήλους] ⟨θάλασσαν⟩ ἐπὶ ζήτησιν ⟨⟨τῶν πέραν⟩⟩ [[καὶ τίς ἐνδοτέρω τῶν ἱερῶν ἀδύτων φύσις ὑπάρχει]]. ⟨⟨⟨ὀρύσσοντες μέτ⟩αλλα [καὶ τούτων] τὴν ἐσχάτην [τῷ θέλειν] ⟨τῶν ὑπογείων⟩ ἐρευνήσουσι νύκτα.⟩⟩ ⟨⟨ἔτι μέτρια ταῦτα·⟩⟩ ⟨καὶ⟩ τὰ [μέχρις] ἄνω διώξουσι, παρατηρῆσαι βουλόμενοι τίς οὐ⟨ρα⟩ν⟨οῦ⟩ καθέστηκε κίνησις. [[ἔτι μέτρια ταῦτα.]] [λείπει γὰρ οὐδὲν ἔτι πλὴν γῆς τόπος ἔσχατος.] [[ἀλλὰ καὶ τούτων τὴν ἐσχάτην τῷ θέλειν
46 ἐρευνήσουσι νύκτα.]] μηδὲν οὖν ἐμπόδιον ἔχωσιν οὗτοι, ἀλλὰ [τῷ τῆς ἀληθείας ἀγαθῷ μυηθῶσι καὶ] τοῖς χαλεποῖς μὴ βιασθέντες τοῦ φόβου κέντροις ἀμερίμνῳ βίῳ ⟨ἐν⟩τρυφήσωσιν; [[εἶτα οὐ καὶ μέχρις οὐρανοῦ περίεργον ὁπλισθήσεται τόλμαν; οὗτοι οὐκ ἀμερίμνους ἐκτενοῦσιν ἐπεὶ καὶ τὰ στοιχεῖα τὰς ψυχὰς αὐτῶν;]] δίδαξον ἐντεῦθεν ⌜ἐρᾶν τοῦ τί βουλεύεσθαι⌝ ⟨. . .⟩ [ἵνα ἔχωσι καὶ τῆς ἀποτυχίας τὸ χαλεπὸν φοβηθῆναι,] ἵνα τῷ τῆς λύπη⌝ δακνηρῷ δαμασθῶσι, τῶν ἐλπιζομένων ἀποτυχόντες. χρεωκοπείσθω [τῶν ψυχῶν] αὐτῶν τὸ περίεργον [ἐπιθυμίαις καὶ φόβοις καὶ λύπαις καὶ ἐλπίσι πλάνοις]. ἐπάλληλοι τὰς ψυχὰς αὐτῶν [ἔρωτες] νεμέσθωσαν ἐλπίδες ποικίλαι [ἐπι-

2 θεωρῆσαν, "τίνες" Wachsm.: θεωρῆσαι ἄν τινες FP | ἔλεγεν Heeren: ἔλεγον FP 3 ὑπομνηματογράφε Heeren: ὑπομνηματογράφοι FP 4 ἔφης (ante ἔφη) del. Heeren 5 μᾶλλον FP: μέλλοντα Wachsm. 6 τῶν Patrit.: τῷ FP | λίχνον Patrit.: λίχνων FP 7 Fortasse ⟨τρυφερὸν⟩ ὀσφρήσει | καταχρᾶσθαι Heeren: καταχρᾶσαι P: καταχράσαι F 9 τολμηρῶς

fierce and terrible. And as soon as he saw the souls entering into their bodily
frames, he asked (though he well knew the answer to his question), 'What
are these creatures called, Hermes, you record-writer of the gods?' 'They 44
are called *men*,' said Hermes. Then Momus said, 'Hermes, you are doing
a rash thing in making man; for he is like to be a creature that sees with
inquisitive eyes, and hears things he has no right to hear, and indulges greedily
his sense of taste, and makes voluptuous use of his sense of smell,[1] and misuses
to all extremes his sense of touch. Tell me, you that are the author of his
being, is it your settled purpose to leave him free from care, this being that
is going to look with audacious gaze upon the beauteous mysteries of nature?
Is it your will to let him be exempt from sorrow, this man that is going
to send forth his designing thoughts to the very ends of the earth? And if so, 45
will not men put forth audacious hands against the elements? They will dig
up roots of plants, and investigate the properties of stones. They will dissect
the lower animals,—yes, and one another also,—seeking to find out how they
have come to be alive, and what manner of thing is hidden within ....[2] They
will cut down the woods of their native land,[3] and sail across the sea to seek
what lies beyond it. They will dig mines, and search into the uttermost
darkness of the depths of the earth. And all this might be borne, but they
will do yet more: they will press on to the world above, seeking to discover
by observation the laws of movement of the heavens. Are they then to meet 46
with no impediment? Shall they never be overpowered by the cruel stings
of fear, and shall they luxuriate in a life exempt from cares? Teach them
henceforth to ....[4] ⟨Make them . . . ,⟩ that they may fail to get the things
they hoped for, and be subdued by the pangs of grief. Let their presumptuous
eagerness be disappointed of its expectations. Let their souls be a prey

[1] This probably refers to the use of scents and unguents.
[2] Perhaps, 'is hidden beneath the outer flesh'. [3] *Sc.* to build ships.
[4] Perhaps, 'to keep their designs within the limits of what is fitting for them'.

---

secludendum? **10** *μέχρι περάτων* scripsi (*μέχρι τῶν περάτων* Wachsm.): *μέχρι τῶν πέραν* FP | *τὰς ἑαυτοῦ* Heeren: *τὰ σεαυτοῦ* FP | *μέλλοντα* scripsi: *μελλήσοντα* codd. **11–12** *εἶτα . . . ψυχὰς αὐτῶν* huc a § 46 transposui **11** *καὶ* om. P | *ὁπλισθήσονται* Heeren: *ὁπλισθήσεται* FP **12** *ἐπὶ* Heeren: *ἐπεὶ* FP | *καὶ* (ante *τὰ στοιχεῖα*) om. Heeren **13** *ἐκτενοῦσι* Heeren: *ἐκτείνουσι* FP | *ἀνασκάψουσιν* F: *ἀνακάμψουσιν* P **14** *ποιότητας* scripsi: *ποιότητα* codd. | *καὶ* (ante *διὰ*) secludendum? | *μέσου* scripsi: *μέσον* F: *μέσων* P **15** *ἀνατεμοῦσι* Heeren: *ἀνατέμνουσι* FP **16** *πῶς* scripsi: *ὡς* codd. | Fortasse *πῶς ⟨ἔμψυχοι⟩ ἐγένοντο* **16–17** "*καὶ τίς . . . ὑπάρχει* num post *θέλοντες* transponenda?" Wachsm. **16** Fortasse *ἐνδοτέρω τῶν σαρκῶν* **19** *διαπορθμεύσουσι θάλασσαν* scripsi (*διαπορθμεύσουσιν ἀλλήλων* Heeren): *διαπορθμεύουσιν ἀλλήλους* codd. **20** *ὀρύσσοντες μέταλλα* scripsi: *ἀλλὰ* codd. **21** *καὶ τούτων* F: *καὶ τοῦτον* P | *ἐρεύνησιν* P **23** *οὐρανοῦ* Canter: *οὖν* FP **25** *ἔχωσιν* F: *ἔχουσιν* P **26** *ἀληθείας* F: *ἀλυπίας* P **27** *ἐντρυφήσωσιν* scripsi (an scribendum *ἐντρυφῶσιν*?): *τρυφήσωσιν* FP **27–29** *εἶτα . . . ψυχὰς αὐτῶν* hinc ad § 45 *init.* transposui **27** *οὐ* (post *εἶτα*) Canter: *οὗ* FP **29** *τοῦ τί* F: *τουτὶ* P | Fortasse *⟨μηδὲν π⟩έρα[ν] τοῦ π⟨ροσήκοντος⟩ βουλεύεσθαι* **29–30** *ἵνα ἔχωσι . . . φοβηθῆναι* seclusit Wachsm. **32** *περίεργον* codd.: fortasse *περισσὸν ⟨τῆς . . .⟩* | *πλάνοις* Heeren: *πλάνης* F: *πλάν* (supra *ν* superscr. *s*) P

θυμίαι], ποτὲ μὲν ἐπιτυγχάνουσαι, ποτὲ δὲ ἀτευκτοῦσαι, ἵνα αὐτοῖς καὶ ⟨τὸ⟩ τῆς ἐπιτυχίας ἡδὺ δέλεαρ ᾖ εἰς ἄθλησιν τελειοτέρων κακῶν. ⌜βαρείτω πυρετὸς αὐτούς, ἵνα ἐκκακήσαντες κολάσωσι τὴν ἐπιθυμίαν.⌝"

47 [λυπῇ, τέκνον Ὧρε, τάδε ⟨ἀκούων⟩; ⟨⟨καταπλήσσῃ⟩⟩ ἑρμηνευούσης σοι τῆς τεκούσης [οὐ θαυμάζεις] [οὐ] [[καταπλήσσῃ]] πῶς ὁ τάλας ἄνθρωπος ἐβαρήθη; ⟨ἔ⟩τι δεινότερον ἐπάκουσον.]

48 ἐτέρπετο Μώμου ταῦτα λέγοντος Ἑρμῆς· ἐλέγετο γὰρ οἰκείως αὐτῷ τὰ εἰρημένα. [[καὶ ταῦτα ἔπραττεν ὅσα περ εἰρήκει]] [λέγων] "⟨Ὦ⟩ Μῶμε", ⟨ἔφη,⟩ [ἀλλ' οὐκέτ' ἀργὴ γενήσεται [πνεύματος θείου] φύσις ἡ τοῦ περιέχοντος.] [εἶπε γὰρ εἶναί με ταμίαν καὶ προνοητὴν ὁ τῶν συμπάντων δεσπότης.] [[ἐποπτετῆρα τοίνυν τὰ γῆς ἔσται τῶν ὅλων ὀξυδερκὴς θεὸς Ἀδράστεια.]] ⟨. . .⟩ καί τι κρυπτὸν ὄργανον ἐγὼ τεχνάσομαι, ἀπλανοῦς καὶ ἀπαραβάτου ⌜θεωρίας⌝ ἐχόμενον, ᾧ [τὰ ἐπὶ γῆς] ἀναγκαίως δουλαγωγηθήσεται πάντα τὰ ⟨τῶν ἀνθρώπων⟩ ἀπὸ γενέσεως ἄχρι φθορᾶς ἐσχάτης [[ἔχον τὴν ἀποτελουμένων πῆξιν]]· πεισθήσεται δὲ τῷ ὀργάνῳ τούτῳ καὶ τὰ ἐπὶ γῆς ἄλλα πάντα." εἶπεν Ἑρμῆς [ἐγὼ δὲ] ταῦτα τῷ Μώμῳ, ⟨⟨καὶ [ταῦτα] ἔπραττεν ὅσα περ εἰρήκει.⟩⟩ καὶ ἤδη τὸ ὄργανον ἐκινεῖτο· ⟨⟨ἐπόπτε⟨ι⟩[τη]ρα [τοίνυν τὰ γῆς] ⟨δ' ἐπ⟩έστη τῶν ὅλων ὀξυδερκὴς θεὸς Ἀδράστεια,⟩⟩ ⟨⟨ἔχο⟨υσα⟩ τὴν ⟨τῶν⟩ ἀποτελουμένων πῆξιν.⟩⟩

49 ταῦτα δὲ ὡς ἐγένετο, καὶ ἐνεσωματίσθησαν αἱ ψυχαί, [καὶ ἐπαίνου ὑπὲρ τῶν γενομένων αὐτὸς ἔτυχεν,] ⟨. . . .⟩

50 [[πάλιν ὁ μόναρχος σύγκλητον τῶν θεῶν ἐποίησε συνέδριον. καὶ οἱ θεοὶ παρῆσαν, καὶ πάλιν αὐτὸς ταῦτα οὕτως ἐφώνησε, "Θεοί" λέγων, "ὅσοι τῆς κορυφαίας, ὅσοι καὶ ἀφθάρτου φύσεως τετεύχατε, οἳ τὸν μέγαν αἰῶνα διέπειν ἐς ἀεὶ κεκλήρωσθε, οἷς αὐτὰ ἑαυτοῖς ἀντιπαραδιδόντα οὐδέποτε κοπιάσει τὰ σύμπαντα, μέχρι πότε τῆς ἀνεπιγνώστου ταύτης δεσπόσομεν ἡγεμονίας; μέχρι πότε ἀθεώρητα γενήσεται ταῦτα ἡλίῳ καὶ σελήνῃ; ἕκαστος ἡμῶν ἐφ' ἑαυτῷ γεννάτω. ἀπαλείψωμεν τῷ δύνασθαι τὴν ἔτι ἀργὴν σύστασιν ταύτην. ἄπιστος τοῖς μεταγενεστέροις μῦθος δὲ δοξάτω χάος εἶναι. ἔργων ἅπτεσθε μεγάλων, ἐγὼ δ' αὐτὸς ἄρξομαι πρῶτος." εἶπε, καὶ εὐθέως κοσμικῶς τῆς ἔτι μελαίνης ἑνώσεως διάστασις ἐγένετο· καὶ]]

51 [[ἐφάνη μὲν οὐρανὸς ἄνω συγκεκοσμημένος τοῖς ἑαυτοῦ μυστηρίοις πᾶσι· κραδαινομένη ἔτι γῆ ἡλίου λάμψαντος ἐπάγη, καὶ ἐφάνη πᾶσι τοῖς περὶ αὐτὴν συγκεκοσμημένοις καλοῖς. καλὰ γὰρ τῷ θεῷ καὶ τὰ θνητοῖς εἶναι νομιζόμενα

to a succession of varying hopes, sometimes fulfilled and at other times frustrated, so that even the sweetness of attainment may be but a bait to lure the wretches on to more unmitigated miseries. . . .'[1]

Hermes was pleased by what Momus said; for it was said in friendliness 48
to him.[2] 'Momus,' said he, '. . . and I will devise a secret engine,[3] linked to unerring and inevitable fate, by which all things in men's lives, from their birth to their final destruction, shall of necessity be brought into subjection; and all other things on earth likewise shall be controlled by the working of this engine.' So said Hermes to Momus; and he did even as he had said. And when the engine began to work, the keen-eyed goddess Adrasteia took her stand above to supervise the whole, having in her hands the confirmation of all that was wrought by the working of the engine.

And when these things had come to pass, and the souls had 49
been embodied, . . .[4]

[1] Perhaps, 'Let them be scorched by the flame of desire, that so they may lose heart, and be (the more severely?) punished'.

[2] Perhaps, 'for he thought there was good reason in it'.

[3] Viz. the system of the stars.

[4] Between § 49 and § 53 might perhaps be placed § 47: 'Are you grieved, my son Horus, when you hear this? Are you dismayed, when your mother describes to you the miseries by which unhappy man was oppressed? You must hear something yet more terrible.'

---

1 *ἀτευκτοῦσαι* Meineke: *ἀπευκτοῦσαι* FP **2** *ἡδὺς* P | *εἰς ἄθλησιν* secludendum? An scribendum *ἵνα* [*αὐτοῖς*] . . . *δέλεαρ ᾖ τοῖς ἀθλίοις*? **2–3** Fortasse *καιέτω αὐτοὺς τὸ πῦρ τῆς ἐπιθυμίας, ἵνα . . . κολασθῶσι* **6** *ἔτι* scripsi: *τὸ* codd. **7** *οἰκείως* codd.: fortasse *εἰκότως* vel *ἐπιτηδείως* **9** *οὐκέτ' ἀργὴ* Usener: *οὐκ ἐναργῆ* FP **10** *με ταμίαν* Canter: *μετὰ μίαν* FP | Fortasse *ταμίαν* ⟨⟨*πνεύματος θείου*⟩⟩ | *προνοητὴν* F: *προνοητικὴν* P | Fortasse *προνοητὴν* ⟨*τῶν ἐπὶ γῆς*⟩ **13** *θεωρίας* codd.: fortasse *ἀνάγκης* | *ἀναγκαίως* om. Heeren, nescio an recte **14** *ἐσχάτης* secludendum? **16** *εἶπεν* Patrit.: *εἶπον* FP | *ἐγὼ δὲ* del. Heeren **17** *ἐπόπτειρα* Meineke: *ἐποπτετῆρα* FP **18** *δ' ἐπέστη* scripsi: *ἔσται* codd. | *ἔχουσα* scripsi: *ἔχον* codd. | *τῶν* (post *τὴν*) add. Wachsm. **19** *ἀποτελουμένων* codd.: fortasse *ἀποτελεσμάτων* **20** *ἐνεσωματίσθησαν* Canter: *ἐνεσηματίσθησαν* P: *ἐνεμβατίσθησαν* F **21** *ἔτυχεν* Heeren: *ἔτυχον* FP **22–34** § 50 (*πάλιν ὁ μόναρχος . . . ἐγένετο καὶ*) hinc transposui: vide post § 8 (p. 460) **35–2** *infra*: § 51 (*ἐφάνη . . . κινούμενα*) hinc transposui: vide ante § 14 (p. 464)

φαῦλα, ὅτι δὴ τοῖς τοῦ θεοῦ νόμοις δουλεύειν ἐποιήθη. ἔχαιρε δὲ ὁ θεὸς ὁρῶν ἤδη ἑαυτοῦ τὰ ἔργα κινούμενα.]]

52 [[πληρώσας δὲ τὰς ἰσοστασίας χεῖρας τῷ περιέχοντι τῶν ἐκ τῆς φύσεως ὑπαρχόντων, καὶ τὰς δράκας καρτερῶς σφίγξας, "Λάβε," εἶπεν, "ὦ ἱερὰ γῆ, λάβε, πάντιμε καὶ εἶναι γεννήτειρα μέλλουσα πάντων, καὶ μηδενὶ ἐντεῦθεν λείπεσθαι δόκει." εἶπεν ὁ θεός, καὶ τὰς χεῖρας, οἵας δεῖ θεὸν ἔχειν, ἁπλώσας πάντα ἀφῆκεν ἐν τῇ τῶν ὄντων συστάσει.]]

53 [καὶ ἄγνωστα μὲν ἦν κατ' ἀρχὰς παντάπασι.] νεωστὶ γὰρ αἱ ψυχαὶ καθειρχθεῖσαι [καὶ τὴν ἀτιμίαν μὴ φέρουσαι] [[τοῖς ἐν οὐρανῷ θεοῖς ἐφιλονείκουν, τῆς ἑαυτῶν εὐγενείας περικρατοῦσαι καὶ ἀντιλαμβανόμεναι, ὡς καὶ αὐταὶ τοῦ αὐτοῦ ἔτυχον δημιουργοῦ,]] ἐστασίαζον· καὶ ⟨οἱ κρείσσονες⟩, τοῖς λειπομένοις ἀνθρώποις ὀργάνοις χρώμενοι, ἐποίουν αὐτοὺς ἑαυτοῖς ἐπιτίθεσθαι καὶ ἀντιτάσσεσθαι, καὶ πολεμεῖν ἀλλήλοις. καὶ [οὕτως ἡ [μὲν] ἰσχὺς κατὰ τῆς ἀσθενείας μέγα ἠδύνατο, ὥστε] οἱ ἰσχυροὶ τοὺς ἀδυνάτους καὶ ⌜ἔκαιον⌝ καὶ ἐφόνευον, καὶ [κατὰ τῶν ἱερῶν] τοῦτο μὲν ζῶντας ⟨ἠνδραπόδιζον⟩, τοῦτο δὲ καὶ νεκροὺς ἔρριπτον ⟨ἀθάπτους⟩ [κατὰ τῶν ἀδύτων].

54 ⟨⟨πολλοῦ δὲ ἤδη γενομένου τοῦ κακοῦ,⟩⟩ [ἕως] ἀγανακτήσαντα τὰ στοιχεῖα τῷ μονάρχῳ θεῷ ἐντυχεῖν ἐδοκίμαζον ὑπὲρ τῆς τῶν ἀνθρώπων ἀγρίου πολιτείας· [[πολλοῦ δὲ ἤδη γενομένου τοῦ κακοῦ]] [τὰ στοιχεῖα] ⟨καὶ⟩ τῷ ποιήσαντι αὐτὰ [τῷ θεῷ] προσελθόντα τοιούτοις λόγοις [ὑπὲρ μέμψεως] ἐχρήσαντο.

55 καὶ δὴ ⟨⟨τὸ πῦρ, πρῶτον⟩⟩ ⟨γὰρ⟩ [καὶ] εἶχε τὴν τοῦ λέγειν ἐξουσίαν [[τὸ πῦρ πρῶτον]], "Δέσποτα" [δὲ] ἔλεγε "καὶ τοῦ καινοῦ τούτου κόσμου τεχνῖτα, ⟨οὗ⟩ καὶ [[κρυπτὸν]] ⟨⟨σεβαστὸν ⟨τὸ⟩ ὄνομα⟩⟩ ἐν θεοῖς καὶ ⟨⟨κρυπτὸν⟩⟩ [[σεβαστὸν ὄνομα]] [μέχρι νῦν ἅπασιν] ἀνθρώποις, μέχρι πότε [ὦ δαῖμον] ἄθεον καταλεῖψαι τὸν θνητῶν βίον προ[ς]αίρεσιν ἔχεις; ⟨⟨οὐκ ἐῶσί με ⌜μένειν⌝ εἰς ὃ πέφυκα, παραχαράσσοντες οὐ καθηκόντως τὸ ἄφθαρτον·⟩⟩ ⟨⟨μ⟨ι⟩αίνομαι γάρ, ὦ δέσποτα, [μέχρι νῦν,] καὶ ὑπὸ τῆς τῶν [γενομένων] ἀνθρώπων [ἀθέου] τόλμης
56 σάρκας ἀναγκάζομαι τήκειν.⟩⟩ ἀνάδειξον ἤδη σεαυτὸν χρή-
[ματι]ζοντι τῷ κόσμῳ, καὶ τοῦ βίου τὸ ἄγριον λῦ[η]σον. [[εἰρήνῃ χάρισο νόμους τῷ βίῳ. χάρισαι νυκτὶ χρησμούς.

For when the souls had but recently been imprisoned, they 53
began to quarrel among themselves; and the stronger men used
the weaker as tools, and made them attack each other, and array
themselves in hostile ranks, and make war on one another. And
the strong ... [1] and slew the powerless; and they enslaved the
living, and cast out the dead unburied.

But when the mischief had grown great, the Elements were 54
indignant, and resolved to make petition to God, who rules alone,
concerning the savage conduct of mankind. And they approached
their Maker, and addressed him as follows.

Fire was permitted to speak first, and said, 'Master, and 55
Fabricator of this new universe, thou whose name is revered
among the gods and hidden from men, how long is it thy purpose
to leave the life of mortals godless? These men do not let me
render the services for which my nature fits me; they put a false
and unmeet stamp on my imperishable being. I am polluted,
Master, and by men's audacity I am forced to consume human
flesh. Reveal thyself at once to the world that needs thee, and 56

[1] Perhaps, 'tortured' or 'mutilated'.

3–9 § 52 (*πληρώσας . . . συστάσει*) hinc transposui: vide post § 13 (p. 462) **12–14** *τοῖς . . . δημιουργοῦ* hinc ad § 24 (p. 470) transposui **15** *λοιπομένοις* P | *χρώμενοι* scripsi: *χρώμεναι* codd. **16–17** *καὶ πολεμεῖν ἀλλήλοις* secludendum? **19** *ἔκαιον* codd.: fortasse *ᾔκιζον* | *κατὰ τῶν ἱερῶν* seclusit Wachsm. **21** *κατὰ τῶν ἀδύτων* del. Heeren **22–23** *ἀναγκαστήσονται* P **24** *ὑπὲρ . . . πολιτείας* secludendum? **26** *τῷ θεῷ* del. Usener **30–31** 'an *κρυπτὸν* et *σεβαστὸν* inter se mutanda?' Wachsm. **33** *προαίρεσιν* Heeren: *πρὸς αἵρεσιν* FP **33–37** *οὐκ . . . ἄφθαρτον* et *μιαίνομαι . . . τήκειν* huc a § 56 *fin.* transposui **34** *με* scripsi: *τε* codd. | *μένειν* codd.: fortasse *ὑπηρετεῖν* **35** *μιαίνομαι* Canter: *μαίνομαι* FP **37** *ἀνάδειξον* scripsi: *ἀνάτειλον* codd. **37–38** *χρῄζοντι* Usener: *χρηματίζοντι* codd. **38** *λῦσον* scripsi (an ⟨*κατά*⟩*λυσον*?): *μύησον* codd.

πλήρωσον καλῶν ἐλπίδων πάντα.]] φοβείσθωσαν ἄνθρωποι τὴν ἀπὸ θεῶν ἐκδικίαν, καὶ οὐδεὶς ἁμαρτήσει. [ἐπαξίους ἁμαρτημάτων μισθοὺς ἂν ἀπολάβωσι⟨ν οἱ ἁμαρτόντες⟩, φυλάξονται οἱ λοιποὶ τὸ ἀδικεῖν.] [φοβηθήσονται ὅρκους, καὶ οὐδὲ εἷς ἔτι ἀνόσιον φρονήσει.] ⟨⟨εἰρήνην χαρισάμενος τῷ βίῳ [χάρισαι νυκτὶ χρησμούς] πλήρωσον καλῶν ἐλπίδων πάντα·⟩⟩ ⟨καὶ⟩ μαθέτωσαν εὐεργετηθέντες εὐχαριστῆσαι, ἵνα [χαῖρον] [παρὰ λοιβαῖς] παρὰ θυσίαις ὑπηρετ⟨οῦν⟩ ἐγὼ τὸ πῦρ [ἵν'] εὐώδεις ἀτμοὺς ἀπ' ἐσχάρας προπέμψω σοι. [[μαίνομαι γάρ, ὦ δέσποτα, μέχρι νῦν, καὶ ὑπὸ τῆς τῶν γενομένων ἀνθρώπων ἀθέου τόλμης σάρκας ἀναγκάζομαι τήκειν.]] [[οὐκ ἐῶσί τε μένειν εἰς ὃ πέφυκα, παραχαράσσοντες οὐ καθηκόντως τὸ ἄφθαρτον.]]"

57 ὁ δὲ ἀήρ "Καὶ αὐτὸς θολοῦμαι, δέσποτα," ἔλεγε, "[καὶ] ἀπὸ ⟨τῆς ἐκ⟩ τῶν νεκρῶν [σωμάτων] ἀναθυμιάσεως, νοσώδης τέ εἰμι, καὶ ⟨⟨οὐκέτι⟩⟩ ὑγιεινός [[οὐκέτι]]· ἐφορῶ τε ἄνωθεν οἷα μὴ θέμις ὁρᾶν."

58 ὕδωρ ἑξῆς, ὦ παῖ μεγαλόψυχε, τὴν τοῦ λέγειν εἶχεν ἐξουσίαν, καὶ ἔλεγεν οὕτως· "Πάτερ [καὶ θαυμαστὲ ποιητὰ πάντων] αὐτογόνε [δαῖμον] καὶ τῆς διὰ σὲ πάντα γεννώσης ποιητὰ φύσεως, ἤδη ποτὲ [ὦ δαῖμον] [[ἀεὶ]] ῥεῖθρα [ποταμῶν] ⟨τἀμὰ⟩ καθαρὰ πρόσταξον εἶναι· [ἢ] ⟨⟨ἀεὶ⟩⟩ γὰρ ἀπολούουσι ποταμοὶ καὶ θάλασσαι τοὺς φονεύσαντας [ἢ] ⟨καὶ⟩ δέχονται τοὺς φονευθέντας."

59 γῆ παρῆν περίλυπος ἑξῆς, καὶ ⌜τάξομαι τῆς ἀπὸ τῶν λόγων⌝, ὦ παῖ μεγαλόδοξε, οὕτως λέγειν ἤρξατο· "Βασιλεῦ καὶ ⟨⟨πάτερ⟩⟩, τῶν οὐρανίων πρύτανι [καὶ δέσποτα] ἁψίδων, ⟨καὶ⟩ στοιχείων ἡμῶν ἡγεμὼν [[πάτερ]] τῶν σοι παρεστώτων, ἐξ ὧν [αὐξήσεως καὶ μειώσεως] ἀρχὴν ἔχει τὰ πάντα, εἰς ἃ καὶ πάλιν καταλήγοντα ἀναγκαίως ὀφειλόμενον τέλος ἔχει· [ἀλόγιστος, ὦ πολυτίμητε, καὶ ἄθεος] [[ἀπ' ἀνθρώπων ἐπ' ἐμὲ χορὸς ἔπεστι]] [χωρῶ δ' ἐγὼ καὶ φύσιν πάντων] ⟨⟨στοιχείων τιμιωτέραν τῶν ἄλλων τὴν γῆν [μετ]ἐποίησας·⟩⟩ αὐτὴ γάρ, ὡς σὺ προσέταξας, καὶ φέρω πάντα καὶ [τὰ φονευθέντα] δέχομαι.

60 ἀτιμοῦμαι δὲ ἤδη· [ὁ ἐπὶ πάντων] [[ὁ ἐπιχθόνιός σου κόσμος

2 ἁμαρτήσει Patrit. : ἐκαρτήσει FP : ἐγκακήσει Meineke 4 φοβηθήσονται codd. : fortasse φοβείσθωσαν 5 εἰρήνην χαρισάμενος scripsi : εἰρήνῃ· χάρισο νόμους FP 6 ἐλπίδων secludendum ? 7 πάντα F : πάντα corr. ex πάντων P 8 ὑπηρετοῦν ἐγὼ scripsi : ὑπηρετήσω codd. 9 ἀτμοὺς F :

put an end to the savagery of human life. Let men be taught to fear the penal justice of the gods, and then no man will sin. Bestow peace on mankind, and thereby fill the world with goodly hopes; and let them learn to give thanks to thee for thy benefits, that so I, the Fire, may render service at their sacrifices, and send up fragrant vapours to thee from the altar-hearth.'

Then spoke Air, and said, 'I too, Master, am made turbid 57
by the reek which rises from the corpses, so that I breed sickness, and have ceased to be wholesome; and when I look down from above, I see such things as ought never to be seen'.

Next, my magnanimous son, Water was given leave to speak, 58
and spoke thus: 'O Father, self-begotten, and Maker of Nature, that power which generates all things to give thee pleasure, it is high time for thee to give command that my streams be kept pure; for the rivers and seas are ever washing off the defilement of the slayers, and receiving the corpses of the slain.'

Next Earth stood forth, in bitter grief; and . . .,[1] my glorious 59
son, she thus began: 'O King and Father, President of the over-arching spheres of heaven, and Governor of us, the Elements, that stand before thee, us out of whom all things get their beginning, and into whom they are resolved again when they cease to be, and reach their end, paying a debt that must be paid;[2] thou didst make Earth more highly honoured than the other Elements; for it is I that, as thou hast commanded, both
bring forth all things and receive them back into me. But now, 60

[1] Perhaps, 'when she in turn was given leave to plead'.

[2] Perhaps, (omitting the words 'and reach . . . be paid') 'out of which all things (i.e. all organized bodies) are formed by composition when they begin to be, and into which they are resolved again when they cease to be'.

αὐτὰρ P **15** τῆς ἐκ addidi (τῆς ἀπὸ add. Usener) **16** οἷα scripsi: ὅσα codd. **17** μὴ Heeren: με FP¹: οὐ P² marg. **20** αὐτόγονε Meineke: αὐτόγενε FP¹: αὐτογενὲς P² | δαῖμον om. Patrit. | καὶ τὴν διὰ P¹ | διὰ σὲ secludendum? **25–26** Fortasse ἀξιουμένη (vel ἀξιωθεῖσα) καὶ αὐτὴ λόγου ('num ἀξιουμένη τῆς ἀπολογίας?' Wachsm.): τἀξίωμα τῶν ὅλων ('desiderium omnium elementorum') coni. Usener **28** ἡμῶν ἡγεμὼν codd.: fortasse ἡμῶν δέσποτα **30** καταλήγοντα codd.: fortasse διαλυόμενα | ἀναγκαίως codd.: fortasse ἀνάγκῃ (an secludendum ἀναγκαίως ὀφειλόμενον?) **31–32** ἀπ' ἀνθρώπων . . . ἔπεστι hinc ad § 60 transposui **32** καὶ φύσιν πάντων codd.: fortasse τὰ φύσει ⟨γιγνόμενα⟩ πάντα **32–33** στοιχείων . . . ἐποίησας huc a § 61 transposui **33** ἐποίησας scripsi (an scribendum ἐμὲ ἐποίησας?): μετεποίησαν codd. **34** Fortasse σὺ ⟨⟨ὁ ἐπὶ πάντων⟩⟩ προσέταξας | τὰ φονευθέντα seclusi (an scribendum [τὰ] διαλυθέντα?) **35–1** *infra*: ὁ ἐπιχθόνιός . . . οὐκ ἔχει hinc ad § 61 transposui *πεπληρωμένος θεὸν οὐκ ἔχει]] ⟨⟨. . . ἀπ' ἀνθρώπων ἐπ' ἐμὲ ⌜χορὸς⌝ ἐπέστη⟩⟩. πάντα γάρ, ὃ φοβηθῶσιν οὐκ ἔχοντες, παρανομοῦσι· καὶ κατ' ἐμῶν, ὦ κύριε, ⌜τενόντων⌝ ⟨πεδίων⟩ πάσῃ πονηρᾷ τέχνῃ ⟨φονευόμενοι⟩ καταπίπτουσι, καταβρέχομαι δὲ πᾶσα διαφθειρομένω⟨ν⟩ σωμάτων χυλοῖς.*

61 *ἐντεῦθεν, κύριε, ⟨ἐπεὶ⟩ [καὶ] τοὺς οὐκ ἀξίους ἀναγκάζομαι χωρεῖν, χωρῆσαι θέλω μεθ' ὧν φέρω πάντων καὶ θεόν. ⟨μέχρι πότε⟩ ⟨⟨ὁ ἐπιχθόνιός σου κόσμος, ⟨θνητῶν⟩ πεπληρωμένος, θεὸν οὐκ ἔχει ;⟩⟩ χάρισαι τῇ γῇ, κἂν [οὐ] ⟨μὴ⟩ σεαυτόν, οὐ γὰρ σὲ χωρεῖν ὑπομένω, ⟨ἀλλὰ⟩ σαυτοῦ ⟨γέ⟩ τινα ἱερὰν ἀπόρροιαν. [[στοιχείων τιμιωτέραν τῶν ἄλλων τὴν γῆν μετεποίησαν.]] [μόνῃ γὰρ αὐχεῖν τῶν ἀπὸ σοῦ πρέπει τὰ πάντα παρεχούσῃ.]"*

62 *τοσαῦτα μὲν τὰ στοιχεῖα εἶπεν· ὁ δὲ θεός, ἱερᾶς [ἐν τῷ λέγειν] φωνῆς τὰ σύμπαντα πληρώσας, "Πορεύεσθε," εἶπεν, "ἱερὰ καὶ μεγάλου πατρὸς ἄξια τέκνα, καὶ κατὰ μηδένα τρόπον νεωτερίζειν ἐπιχειρεῖτε, μηδὲ ἀργὸν τῆς ἐξ ὑμῶν ὑπηρεσίας τὸν σύμπαντά μου κόσμον καταλείπετε. ἑτέρα γὰρ ἐν ὑμῖν τις ἤδη ⟨κατοικήσει⟩ τῆς ἐμῆς ἀπόρροια φύσεως, ὃς δὴ καὶ ὅσιος ἔσται τῶν πραττομένων ἐπόπτης, καὶ ζώντων μὲν κριτὴς ἀμεθόδευτος, φρικτὸς δ⟨ὲ⟩ [οὐ μόνον ἀλλὰ καὶ τιμωρὸς] τῶν ὑπὸ γῆν τύραννος· [καὶ] ἑκάστῳ δὲ τῶν ἀνθρώ-*

63 *πων ἀκολουθήσει ⌜διὰ γένους⌝ μισθὸς ἐπάξιος." καὶ οὕτως ἐπαύσατο τῆς ἐντυχίας τὰ στοιχεῖα [[τοῦ δεσπότου κελεύσαντος]] καὶ ἐχεμυθίαν εἶχεν· καὶ ⟨⟨τοῦ δεσπότου κελεύσαντος⟩⟩ ἕκαστον αὐτῶν τῆς ἰδίας ἐξουσίας ἐκράτει [καὶ ἐδέσποζε].—*

64 *καὶ ἐκ τούτου εἶπεν Ὧρος· Ὦ τεκοῦσα, πῶς οὖν τὴν τοῦ θεοῦ ἀπόρροιαν ἔχειν εὐτύχησεν ἡ γῆ ;—καὶ εἶπεν Ἶσις· Παραιτοῦμαι [[γένεσιν ἱστορεῖν]] [[οὐ γὰρ θεμιτὸν]] σῆς σπορᾶς καταλέγειν ἀρχήν, ὦ μεγαλοσθενὲς Ὧρε· ⟨⟨οὐ γὰρ θεμιτὸν⟩⟩ [ὡς μήποτε ὕστερον εἰς ἀνθρώπους ἀθανάτων ⟨δι⟩έλθῃ γένεσις] θεῶν ⟨⟨γένεσιν ἱστορεῖν⟩⟩· πλὴν ὅτι γε ὁ μόναρχος θεός, ὁ τῶν συμπάντων [κοσμοποιητὴς καὶ] τεχνίτης, τῇ ⟨γῇ⟩ τὸν μέγιστόν σου πρὸς ὀλίγον ἐχαρίσατο πατέρα*

1–2 *ἀπ' ἀνθρώπων . . . ἐπέστη* huc a § 59 transposui 2 *χορὸς* codd. : fortasse *θόρυβος* | *ἐπέστη* Meineke : *ἔπεστι* FP 2–3 Fortasse *ὃ γὰρ φοβηθῶσιν οὐκ ἔχοντες, πάντα παρανομοῦσι* 5 *διαφθειρομένων* Usener : *διαφθειρομένη* codd. | *σωμάτων* codd. : fortasse *πτωμάτων* | *χολοῖς* P 7 *μεθ' ὧν φέρω πάντων*

I am dishonoured; . . .[1] has risen up against me from mankind. Having naught to fear, they commit all manner of crimes; slaughtered by every sort of cruel device, men fall dead on my plains, O Lord, and I am soaked through and through with the juices of rotting corpses. Henceforward, Lord, since I am forced 61
to contain beings unworthy of me,[2] I wish to contain, together with all the things which I bring forth, God also. How long shall thy terrestrial world, peopled with mortals, have no God? Bestow upon Earth, if not thy very self,—that I ask not, for I could not endure to contain thee,—yet at least some holy efflux from thee.'

Thus spoke the Elements; and God filled the universe with 62
the sound of his holy voice, and said, 'Go your ways, my holy children, that are worthy of your great Father; make no attempt to violate my laws, and leave not my universe bereft of your services. Another[3] shall now come down to dwell among you, an efflux of my being, who shall keep holy watch on men's deeds. He shall be judge of the living,—a judge that none can deceive,—and a terrible king of the dead; and every man shall meet with such retribution as his deeds deserve.' Thereon the Elements 63
ceased from their entreating, and kept silence; and at their Master's bidding, each of them continued to wield the power committed to him.—

Thereupon Horus said: Tell me then, mother, how did Earth 64
attain to the happy lot of receiving the efflux of God?—And Isis answered: Mighty Horus, do not ask me to describe to you the origin of the stock whence you are sprung;[4] for it is not permitted to inquire into the birth of gods. This only I may tell you, that God who rules alone, the Fabricator of the universe, bestowed on the earth for a little time your great father Osiris

[1] Perhaps, 'trouble' or something of the sort.
[2] I.e. men.
[3] Viz. Osiris.
[4] I.e. to explain to you how your father and mother came into being.

secludendum? | φέρων P 10 σαυτοῦ F: ταυτοῦ P | γέ add. Meineke | ἱερὰν secludendum? 11–12 στοιχείων . . . μετεποίησαν hinc ad § 59 transposui 12 τὰ (ante πάντα) codd.: fortasse τῇ 15 πορεύεσθαι P 16 μεγάλου secludendum? 17 ἀργὸν codd.: fortasse ἄμοιρον | ὑμῶν scripsi: αὐτῶν FP (αὑτῶν Wachsm.) 18 καταλείπητε F: καταλίπητε Meineke | ἑτέρα codd.: fortasse ἕτερος 25 εἶχεν scripsi: εἶχον codd. 33 διέλθῃ scripsi: ἔλθῃ codd. 35 τῇ γῇ scripsi (γῇ Usener): τὶ codd.

Ὄσιριν καὶ τὴν μεγίστην θεὰν Ἶσιν, ἵνα τῶν πάντων δεομένῳ ⟨τῷ⟩ κόσμῳ βοηθοὶ γένωνται.

65 οὗτοι, ⟨τοῦ θ⟩είου τὸν βίον [ἐ]πληρώσαν⟨τες⟩, [οὗτοι] τὸ τῆς ἀλληλοφονίας ἔπαυσαν ἄγριον.

⟨⟨οὗτοι [παρ' Ἑρμοῦ μαθόντες ὡς τὰ κάτω συμπαθεῖν τοῖς ἄνω ὑπὸ τοῦ δημιουργοῦ διετάγη] [τὰς] πρὸς κάθετον ⟨ὁμολογούσας⟩ τοῖς ἐν οὐρανῷ μυστηρίοις ἱεροποιίας ἀνέστησαν ἐν γῇ.⟩⟩

⟨⟨οὗτοι⟩⟩ τεμένη ⟨τοῖς⟩ προγόνοις θεοῖς [[αὐτοὶ]] καὶ θυσίας καθιέρωσαν· [νόμους] οὗτοι καὶ τροφὰς θνητοῖς καὶ σκέπην ἐχαρίσαντο.

66 "οὗτοι τὰ κ υπτά", φησὶν Ἑρμῆς, "τῶν ἐμῶν ἐπιγνώσονται γραμμάτων πάντα καὶ διακρινοῦσι, καὶ τινὰ μὲν ⌜αὐτοὶ κατασχῶσιν⌝, ἃ δὲ καὶ πρὸς εὐεργεσίας θνητῶν ⌜φθάνει⌝, ⟨ἐν⟩ στήλαις καὶ ὀβελίσκοις χαράξουσιν."

67 [οὗτοι πρῶτοι δείξαντες δικαστήρια] [[εὐνομίας τὰ σύμπαντα καὶ δικαιοσύνης ἐπλήρωσαν.]]

οὗτοι, δεξιᾶς καὶ πίστεως ἀρχηγέτην [γενόμενοι καὶ] τὸν μέγιστον θεὸν Ὅρκον εἰσαγαγόντε⟨ς⟩ εἰς τὸν βίον, ⟨⟨εὐνομίας τὰ σύμπαντα καὶ δικαιοσύνης ἐπλήρωσαν.⟩⟩

οὗτοι, ⟨⟨τὸ φθόριμον τῶν σωμάτων ἐπιγνόντες,⟩⟩ τοὺς παυσαμένους τοῦ ζῆν ὡς δέον ἐστὶ[ν] [[ἐδίδαξαν]] περιστέλλειν ⟨⟨ἐδίδαξαν⟩⟩.

οὗτοι, τὸ τοῦ θανάτου ζητήσαντες αἴτιον, ἔγνωσαν ὡς τοῦ ἔξωθεν ⟨⟨εἰς τὰ τῶν ἀνθρώπων πλάσματα⟩⟩ ⟨εἰσελθόντος⟩ πνεύματος φιλυποστρόφου τυγχάνοντος [[εἰς τὰ τῶν ἀνθρώπων πλάσματα]] ⌜ἐὰν ὑστερήσῃ ποτέ, ἀνάκτησιν οὐκ ἔχουσαν ἐργάζεται λ[ε]ιποθυμίας.⌝

οὗτοι, τὸ περιέχον ὅτι δαιμόνων ἐπληρώθη παρὰ Ἑρμοῦ μαθόντες, ⟨. . . ἐν⟩ κρυπταῖς στήλαις ἐχάραξαν.

68 οὗτοι [μόνοι], τὰς κρυπτὰς νομοθεσίας τοῦ θεοῦ [παρὰ Ἑρμοῦ] μαθόντες, [τεχνῶν καὶ ἐπιστημῶν καὶ ἐπιτηδευμάτων ἁπάντων εἰσηγηταὶ] τοῖς ἀνθρώποις ἐγένοντο [καὶ] νομοθέται.

1 τῶν πάντων secludendum? | δεομένῳ Canter: δεομένων FP 3 τοῦ θείου scripsi: βίου codd. | Fortasse τὸν ⟨ἀνθρώπινον⟩ βίον | πληρώσαντες scripsi: ἐπλήρωσαν codd. 5–8 οὗτοι . . . ἐν γῇ huc a § 68 transposui 6–7 πρὸς κάθετον ὁμολογούσας scripsi: προσκαθέτους FP 9 τοῖς addidi (an secludendum προγόνοις?) | αὐτοὶ (post θεοῖς) codd.: οὗτοι Meineke | καὶ θυσίας secludendum? 10–11 οὗτοι καὶ τροφὰς . . . ἐχαρίσαντο secludendum? 13 κατάσχωσιν F: καταχώσουσιν Usener: num αὐτοὶ κατασχό⟨ντες ἐννοήσου⟩σιν? 14 φθάνει codd.: fortasse τείνει 17 ἀρχηγέτην scripsi: ἀρχηγέται codd. 18 εἰσαγαγόντες scripsi: εἰσηγάγοντο codd. 20 τὸ φθόριμον τῶν σωμάτων ἐπιγνόντες huc a § 68 transposui: sed hic quoque postea

and the great goddess Isis, that they might give the world the help it so much needed.

It was they that filled human life with that which is divine,[1] and 65
thereby put a stop to the savagery of mutual slaughter.

It was they that established upon earth rites of worship which correspond exactly to the holy Powers in heaven.

It was they that consecrated temples and instituted sacrifices to the gods that were their ancestors, and gave to mortal men the boons of food and shelter.

'They',[2] said Hermes, 'will get knowledge of all my hidden writings,[3] 66
and discern their meaning;[4] and some of those writings they will keep to themselves, but such of them as tend to the benefit of mortal men, they will inscribe on slabs and obelisks.'

It was they that introduced into men's life that mighty god, 67
the Oath-god, to be the founder of pledges and good faith; whereby they filled the world with law-abidingness and justice.

It was they that, noting how corpses decay, taught men the fitting way to swathe the bodies of those who have ceased to live.

They sought to discover the cause of death; and they found out that the life-breath,[5] which has entered from without[6] into men's bodily frames, is apt to return to the place from which it came, and . . .[7]

It was they that, having learnt from Hermes that the atmosphere had been filled with daemons,[8] inscribed . . .[9] on hidden slabs of stone.

It was they that, having learnt God's secret lawgivings, became 68
lawgivers for mankind.

[1] Or 'with religion'.

[2] § 66 is certainly out of place here; it may possibly have been intended to stand at the end of the speech of Hermes in § 8. In that case, 'they' would mean the men of after times who were destined to find and read the books of Hermes.

[3] Or 'all the secret lore taught in my writings'.

[4] Or perhaps, 'and will divide them into two parts'.

[5] Or 'vital spirit'. [6] I. e. from the atmosphere.

[7] Perhaps, 'and if a man runs short of it, he swoons; ⟨but if he loses it entirely,⟩ he cannot get it back, ⟨and so he dies⟩'.

[8] Possibly altered from 'is full of daemons'.

[9] Perhaps, 'inscribed the names of the daemons' (or 'forms of words for invoking the daemons').

---

additum videtur **23** *αἴτιον* scripsi: *ἄγριον* codd. **25–26** Fortasse *ἐὰν ⟨μὲν⟩ ὑστερήσῃ ποτὲ ⟨αὐτοῦ ὁ ἄνθρωπος, κατέχεται⟩ ⟨⟨λιποθυμίᾳ⟩⟩, ⟨ἐὰν δὲ παντάπασιν ἀποστερηθῇ,⟩ ἀνάκτησιν οὐκ ἔχων ⟨ἀποθνήσκει⟩* vel eiusmodi aliquid **26** *ἔχουσαν* FP: *ἔχον* P^2 | *λιποθυμίας* scripsi: *λειποθυμίας* codd. **27** *ἐπληρώθη* codd.: fortasse *πεπλήρωται* **27–28** Fortasse ⟨*τὰ ὀνόματα* (vel *τὰς ἐπικλήσεις*) *αὐτῶν ἐν*⟩ *κ. σ. ἐχάραξαν*

[[οὗτοι, παρ' Ἑρμοῦ μαθόντες ὡς τὰ κάτω συμπαθεῖν τοῖς ἄνω ὑπὸ τοῦ δημιουργοῦ διετάγη, τὰς προσκαθέτους τοῖς ἐν οὐρανῷ μυστηρίοις ἱεροποιίας ἀνέστησαν ἐν γῇ.]]

οὗτοι [[τὸ φθόριμον τῶν σωμάτων ἐπιγνόντες]] τὸ ⌜ἐν ἅπασι τέλειον⌝ τῶν προφητῶν ἐτεχνάσαντο, [ὡς μήποτε ὁ μέλλων θεοῖς προσάγειν χεῖρας προφήτης ἀγνοῇ τι τῶν ⟨δε⟩όντων,] ἵνα φιλοσοφίᾳ μὲν [καὶ μαγείᾳ] ⟨τὴν⟩ ψυχὴν τρέφῃ, σώζῃ δ' [[ὅταν τι πάσχῃ]] ἰατρικῇ ⟨τὸ⟩ σῶμα ⟨⟨ὅταν τι πάσχῃ⟩⟩.

69 ταῦτα πάντα ποιήσαντες, ὦ τέκνον, Ὄσιρίς τε κἀγώ, τὸν κόσμον πληρέστατον ἰδόντες ⟨ἀγαθῶν γενόμενον⟩ [[ἀπῃτούμεθα λοιπὸν]] ὑπὸ τῶν τὸν οὐρανὸν κατοικούντων, ⟨⟨ἀπῃτούμεθα λοιπὸν⟩⟩ ⟨. . .⟩. ἀλλ' οὐκ ἦν ἀνελθεῖν πρὶν ⟨ὕμνῳ⟩ ἐπικαλέσασθαι τὸν μόναρχον, ἵνα δὴ ⌜καὶ τῆς θεωρίας ταύτης⌝ πλῆρες τὸ περιέχον γένηται, αὐτοί τε εὐπαράδεκτοι [εὐτυχήσωμεν] ⟨ποιησώμεθα⟩ τὴν ἀνάβασιν. [χαίρει γὰρ ὕμνοις ὁ θεός.]—

70 Ὦ τέκουσα, εἶπεν Ὧρος, κἀμοὶ χάρισαι τὴν τοῦ ὕμνου ἐπίγνωσιν [ὡς μὴ ἀμαθὴς ὑπάρχω].—Καὶ εἶπεν Ἶσις, Πρόσεχε, παῖ.

EXCERPTUM XXIV

Stobaeus I. 49. 45, vol. i, p. 407 Wachsmuth (*Ecl.* I. 980 Heeren).

Ἐν ταὐτῷ.

1 Σὺ δέ, ὦ παῖ μεγαλόψυχε, εἴ τι θέλεις ἕτερον ἐπερώτα.—καὶ εἶπεν Ὧρος· Ὦ πολυτίμητε μῆτερ, εἰδῆσαι θέλω πῶς γίγνονται βασιλικαὶ ψυχαί.—καὶ εἶπεν Ἶσις· Ἡ γιγνομένη, τέκνον Ὧρε, περὶ τὰς βασιλικὰς ψυχὰς διαφορὰ τοιαύτη τίς ἐστιν. [ἐπεὶ γὰρ] τόποι τέσσαρές εἰσιν ἐν τῷ παντί, οἵτινες ἀπαραβάτῳ νόμῳ καὶ ⟨βασιλικῇ⟩ προστασίᾳ ὑποπίπτουσιν, ὅ τε οὐρανὸς καὶ ⟨ὁ⟩ αἰθὴρ καὶ ὁ ἀὴρ καὶ ἡ [ἱερωτάτη] γῆ. καὶ ἄνω μέν, ὦ τέκνον, ἐν οὐρανῷ θεοὶ κατοικοῦσιν, ὧν ἄρχει

1–3 οὗτοι . . . ἐν γῇ hinc ad § 65 transposui **4–5** τὸ ἐν ἅπασι τέλειον codd. : fortasse τὸ ἐν ἅπασιν ὠφέλιμον ⟨ἔθνος⟩ **6** δεόντων scripsi : ὄντων codd. **13–14** καὶ τῆς θεωρίας ταύτης codd. : fortasse [καὶ] τῆς εὐφωνίας (vel εὐλογίας) [ταύτης] **14** εὐπαράδεκτοι scripsi : εὐπαράδεκτον codd. (an scribendum [εὐπαράδεκτον] εὐτυχήσωμεν τὴν ἀνάβασιν ?)
26 ἀπαραβάτῳ νόμῳ καὶ secludendum ? **27** ὁ add. Heeren

It was they that devised the . . .[1] of the prophet-priests, to the end that these might nurture men's souls with philosophy, and save their bodies by healing art when they are sick.

When we had done all this, my son, Osiris and I, perceiving 69
that the world had been filled with blessings by the gods who dwell in heaven, asked leave to return to our home above. But we were not permitted to return until we had invoked the Sole Ruler with a hymn, so that the atmosphere might be filled with . . .,[2] and we ourselves might be well received above when we ascended.—

Mother, said Horus, grant to me that I too may learn that 70
hymn.—And Isis said, Hearken, my son.[3]

EXCERPT XXIV

In the same book.[4]

Isis. 'But if you wish to ask any further question, my 1
magnanimous son, ask on.'—'My honoured mother,' said Horus, 'I wish to know what is the origin of kingly souls.'—And Isis said, 'My son Horus, the distinction by which kingly souls are marked out is as follows. There are in the universe four regions, which are subject to law that cannot be transgressed, and to kingly presidency; namely, heaven, the aether, the air, and the earth. Above, my son, in heaven, dwell gods, over whom, as

[1] Perhaps, 'the order of the prophet-priests, which is helpful to men in all things'. Or possibly, 'the initiation' or 'the training of the prophet-priests'. (The word 'prophets' probably here means Egyptian priests.)

[2] Perhaps, 'with the music of our voices', or 'with the sound of our song of praise'.

[3] Here followed the hymn.

[4] I. e. 'This piece occurs in the same book from which *Exc.* XXIII was taken'.

μετὰ καὶ τῶν ἄλλων πάντων ὁ τῶν ὅλων δημιουργός· ἐν δὲ
τῷ αἰθέρι ἀστέρες, ὧν ἄρχει ὁ μέγας φωστὴρ ἥλιος· ἐν δὲ τῷ
ἀέρι ψυχαὶ [δὲ μόναι], ὧν ἄρχει σελήνη· ἐπὶ δὲ τῆς γῆς
ἄνθρωποι [καὶ τὰ λοιπὰ ζῷα], ὧν ἄρχει ὁ ⟨ἀεὶ⟩ [[κατὰ καιρὸν]]
βασιλεύς· γεννῶσι γάρ ⟨⟨κατὰ καιρόν⟩⟩, ὦ τέκνον, [βασιλεῖς]
2 ⟨ἄνθρωπον⟩ οἱ θεοὶ ἐπάξιον τῆς ἐπιγείου (ἡ)γ⟨εμ⟩ονίας. καί
εἰσιν οἱ ⟨ἄλλοι⟩ ἄρχοντες τοῦ ⟨ἐν οὐρανῷ⟩ βασιλέως ἀπόρροιαι·
ὧν ὁ μᾶλλον ἐκείνῳ πλησίον, οὗτος καὶ τῶν ἄλλων βασιλικώ-
τερος. ὁ μὲν γὰρ ἥλιος, καθὸ ἔγγιόν ἐστι τοῦ θεοῦ, τῆς
σελήνης ἐστὶ μείζων καὶ δυναμικώτερος· [ᾧ δευτερεύει ἡ
σελήνη καὶ κατὰ τάξιν καὶ κατὰ δύναμιν·] ⟨ἡ δὲ σελήνη ....⟩
3 καὶ ὁ [μὲν] ⟨ἐπὶ γῆς⟩ βασιλεὺς τῶν μὲν [ἄλλων θεῶν]
⟨δ᾽ ἀρχόντων⟩ ἐστὶν ἔσχατος, πρῶτος δὲ ἀνθρώπων. καὶ
μέχρις ὅτου ἐπὶ γῆς ἐστι, τῆς μὲν ἀληθοῦς θε[ι]ότητος
ἀπήλλακται, ἔχει δὲ ἐξαίρετόν τι παρ⟨ὰ τοὺς ἄλλους⟩
ἀνθρώπους, ὃ ὅμοιόν ἐστι τῷ θεῷ· ἡ γὰρ εἰς αὐτὸν κατα-
πεμπομένη ψυχή [ἐξ ἐκείνου] ἐστι⟨ν ἐκ⟩ [τοῦ] χωρίου ὃ
ὑπεράνω κεῖται ἐκείνων ἀφ᾽ ὧν εἰς τοὺς ἄλλους καταπέμπονται
ἀνθρώπους.

4 καταπέμπονται δὲ ἐκεῖθεν εἰς τὸ βασιλεύειν διὰ δύο ταῦτα
αἱ ψυχαί, ὦ τέκνον· αἱ ⟨μὲν⟩ [γὰρ] καλῶς καὶ ἀμέμπτως
δραμοῦσαι τὸν ἴδιον ἀγῶνα, καὶ μέλλουσαι ἀποθεοῦσθαι, ἵνα
κἀν τῷ βασιλεύειν ⟨εἰς⟩ τὴν τῶν θεῶν προγυμνασθῶσιν ἐξου-
σίαν· αἱ ⟨δέ⟩, θεῖαί τινες ἤδη οὖσαι, καὶ ἐν μικρῷ τινι
παραθεμιστεύσασαι τὸν [ἐν] θε⟨ῖ⟩ον γνώμονα, ἵνα [μὴ] κόλασιν
μὲν ἐν τῷ ⟨ἐν⟩σεσωματίσθαι ὑπομένωσι [δι᾽ ἀδοξίαν καὶ
φύσιν], μηθὲν ⟨δὲ⟩ ὅμοιον ταῖς ἄλλαις πάσχωσιν [ἐνσωματι-
σθεῖσαι], ἀλλ᾽ ὅπερ ⟨προ⟩εῖχον λελυμέναι, τοῦτο καὶ δεθεῖσαι
⟨προ⟩έχωσιν.

5 αἱ μέντοι περὶ τὰ ἤθη τῶν βασιλευόντων γιγνόμεναι
διαφοραὶ οὐκ ἐν τῇ τῆς ψυχῆς φύσει κρίνονται, πᾶσαι γὰρ
θεῖαι, ἀλλ᾽ ἐν τῇ τῶν δορυφορησάντων αὐτῆς τὴν κατάβασιν

3 δὲ μόναι F : μόναι P : δαιμόνιαι Meineke 6 ἄνθρωπον οἱ θεοὶ ἐπάξιον scripsi : βασιλεῖς οἱ θεοὶ ἐπαξίους codd. | ἡγεμονίας scripsi (μονῆς Usener) : γονῆς codd. 7 τοῦ ἐν οὐρανῷ βασιλέως scripsi (θεοῦ βασιλέως Usener) : τοῦ βασιλέως codd. 8 οὗτος P : ἐκεῖνος F | καὶ ὁ τῶν ἄλλων P 10 ἐστὶ μείζων scripsi : ἐπὶ μείζων FP[2] : ἐπιμείζων P[1] | δυναμικώτερον P 11 Fortasse ⟨ἡ δὲ σελήνη τοῦ κάτω ἄρχοντος⟩ 14 θεότητος scripsi : θειότητος codd. 15–16 παρὰ τοὺς ἄλλους ἀνθρώπους scripsi (παρ᾽ ἀνθρώπους Meineke) : παρ᾽ ἀνθρώποις FP 21 μὲν Usener : γὰρ codd. 22 ἀγῶνα Meineke : αἰῶνα codd. 24 δὲ add. Heeren | ἐν scripsi : ἐπὶ codd. (An ἐπὶ μικρόν τι?)

over all else likewise, rules the Maker of the universe; in the aether dwell stars, over whom rules that great luminary, the Sun; in the air dwell souls, over whom rules the Moon; and upon earth dwell men, over whom rules he who is king for the time being; for the gods, my son, cause to be born at the right time
a man that is worthy to govern upon earth. The other rulers[1] 2
are effluxes of Him who is king in heaven; and among them, he who is nearer to Him is more kingly than the others. The Sun, inasmuch as he is nearer to God, is greater and mightier than the Moon; ⟨and the Moon is mightier than the earthly
king.⟩ He who is king on earth is the last of the four rulers, 3
but the first of men. As long as he is on earth, he has no part in true deity;[2] but as compared with other men, he has in him something exceptional, which is like to God; for the soul which is sent down to dwell in him comes from a place which is situated above the places whence souls are sent down to dwell in other men.[3]

Now souls are sent down thence to reign as kings, my son, 4
for these two reasons. Souls that have well and blamelessly run their appointed race, and are about to be transmuted into gods, are sent down to earth in order that, by reigning here as kings, they may be trained to use the powers which are given to gods; and souls that are already godlike, and have in some little thing transgressed God's ordinances, are sent down to be kings on earth in order that they may undergo some punishment in being incarnated, and yet may not suffer in like measure with the rest, but in their bondage may still retain the same pre-eminence which they enjoyed while they were free.

The differences in the characters of kings are not determined 5
by the nature of their souls (for all kingly souls are godlike), but by that of the angels and daemons that have escorted the

[1] I. e. the Sun, the Moon, and the earthly king.
[2] I. e. he is not a god.
[3] I. e. comes from a higher stratum of the atmosphere.

25 *θεῖον* scripsi: *ἔνθεον* codd. | *μὴ* seclusit Wachsm. 26 *ἐνσεσωματίσθαι* scripsi: *σεσωματίσθαι* codd. 27 *δὲ* add. Heeren | *ταῖς ἄλλαις* scripsi: *τοῖς ἄλλοις* codd. | *πάσχωσιν* Heeren: *πάσχουσιν* FP 28 *προεῖχον* scripsi: *εἶχον* codd. | *λελυμένα* P¹ | *τοῦτο καὶ θεῖσαι* P¹ 29 *προέχωσιν* scripsi: *ἔχωσιν* codd. 30 *τὰ ἤδη τῶν* F 31 *φύσει* scripsi: *κρίσει* codd. 32 *ἐν τῇ τῷ* P¹ | *κατάβασιν* scripsi: *κατάστασιν* FP

ἀγγέλων καὶ δαιμόνων. αἱ γὰρ τοιαῦται καὶ ἐπὶ τοιαῦτα κατερχόμεναι δίχα προπομπῆς καὶ δορυφορίας οὐ κατέρχονται· οἶδε γὰρ ἡ ἄνω δίκη τὴν ἀξίαν ἑκάστῳ νέμειν, κἂν ἐκ τῆς
6 εὐημερούσης χώρας ἀπωθῶνται. ὅταν οὖν οἱ κατάγοντες αὐτὴν ἄγγελοι καὶ δαίμονες, τέκνον Ὧρε, πολεμικοὶ ὦσι, ⟨τότε καὶ αὐτὴ πολεμεῖ·⟩ [τούτων ⟨γὰρ⟩ περικρατεῖ[ν] τῆς γνώμης ἡ ψυχή [ἔχει ἣ] ἐπιλαθομένη τῶν ἑαυτῆς ἔργων, μόνων δὲ μεμνημένη [τούτων μέχρι] τῶν ⟨ἀπὸ⟩ τῆς [ε] ἱερᾶς συνοδίας προσγεγονότων·] ὅταν δὲ εἰρηνικοί, τότε καὶ αὐτὴ [τὸν ἴδιον δρόμον] εἰρηνοποιεῖται· ὅταν δὲ δικαστικοί, τότε καὶ αὐτὴ δικάζει· ὅταν δὲ μουσικοί, τότε καὶ αὐτὴ ᾄδει· ὅταν δὲ φιλαλήθεις, τότε καὶ αὐτὴ φιλοσοφεῖ. ὡς γὰρ ἐξ ἀνάγκης αἱ ψυχαὶ αὗται τῆς τῶν καταγόντων περικρατοῦσι γνώμης· πίπτουσι γὰρ εἰς τὴν ἀνθρωπότητα τῆς μὲν ἰδίας φύσεως ἐπιλαθόμεναι [καὶ παρόσον μακρὰν αὐτῆς ἀπέστησαν], μεμνη⟨μέ⟩ναι δὲ τῆς τῶν κατακλεισάντων αὐτὰς διαθέσεως.—

7 Καλῶς, εἶπεν Ὧρος, [ἅπαντα] ⟨ταῦτά⟩ μοι ⟨ἐξήπλωσας⟩, ὦ τεκοῦσα· πῶς δὲ εὐγενεῖς γίγνονται ψυχαί, οὐδέπω μοι διηγήσω.—[Πῶς γίγνονται εὐγενεῖς ψυχαί.] Ὃν τρόπον ἐπὶ γῆς, ὦ τέκνον Ὧρε, εἰσί τινες πολιτεῖαι διαφέρουσαι ἀλλήλων, οὕτως καὶ ἐπὶ τῶν ψυχῶν ἐστι. καὶ αὗται γὰρ τόπους ἔχουσιν ὅθεν ὁρμῶσι, καὶ ἡ ἀπὸ τοῦ ἐνδοξοτέρου τόπου ὡρμηκυῖα εὐγενεστέρα ἐστὶ τῆς μὴ οὕτως ἐχούσης. ὅνπερ γὰρ τρόπον ἐν ἀνθρώποις ὁ ἐλεύθερος εὐγενέστερος εἶναι δοκεῖ δούλου,—τὸ γὰρ [[ἐν ταῖς ψυχαῖς]] ὑπερέχον καὶ βασιλικὸν δουλοποιεῖ⟨ται⟩ τὸ ὑπερεχόμενον ἐξ ἀνάγκης,— οὕτω δή, ὦ τέκνον, καὶ ⟨⟨ἐν ταῖς ψυχαῖς⟩⟩ ⟨ἔχει⟩.—

8 ⟨Πῶς, ὦ τεκοῦσα⟩, ἀρρενικαὶ καὶ θηλυκαὶ γίγνονται ψυχαί;—[Πῶς ἀρρενικαὶ καὶ θηλυκαὶ γίγνονται ψυχαί.] Αἱ ψυχαί, ὦ τέκνον Ὧρε, ὁμοφυεῖς εἰσιν ἑαυταῖς, καθάπερ ἐξ ἑνὸς οὖσαι χωρίου, ἐν ᾧ αὐτὰς διετύπωσεν ὁ δημιουργός, καὶ οὔτε εἰσὶν ἄρρενες οὔτε θήλειαι. ἡ γὰρ τοιαύτη [διάθεσις] ⟨⟨διαφορὰ⟩⟩ ἐπὶ σωμάτων γίγνεται, καὶ οὐκ ἐπὶ

2 προπομπῆς καὶ (vel καὶ δορυφορίας) secludendum? 3–4 An κἂν ἐκ . . . ἀπωθῶνται transponendum, ut legatur post οὐ κατέρχονται? 4 ἀπωθῶνται Wachsm.: ἀποθῶνται FP 6 περικρατεῖ scripsi: περικρατεῖν codd. 7 ἔχει ἣ seclusi ('ἣ deleverim' Wachsm.): an scribendum ἔχεται, deleto περικρατεῖ? | ἐπιλαθομένη F: ἐπιλαθομένους P | ἔργων codd.: fortasse ἐνεργειῶν 8 μόνων scripsi: μᾶλλον codd. | μεμνημένη F: μεμνημένοι P | ⟨ἀπὸ⟩ τῆς ἱερᾶς Usener: τῆς ἑτέρας codd. 2 φιλαλήθεις P: φιλαλήθης F 15 ἐπιλαθόμεναι Patrit.: ἐπιλαθόμενοι FP | ἐπέστησαν P 16 μεμνημέναι scripsi: μέμνηται FP 17 ἐξήπλωσας

soul on its way down to earth. For souls that are of this quality,[1]
and come down to earth for this purpose,[2] do not come down
without escort and attendance; for the Justice that rules on high
knows how to assign to each his due, even though they be
exiled from the Happy Land. And so, my son Horus, when 6
the angels and daemons who bring the kingly soul down from
above are warlike, then that soul wages war; when they are
peaceful, then it maintains peace; when they are disposed for
judicial work, then it sits in judgement; when they are given
to music, then it sings; when they are truth-lovers, then it
pursues philosophy. For these souls, as of necessity, cling to
the temper of the angels and daemons who bring them down
to earth; for when they sink into the condition of man, they
forget their own nature, and bethink them only of the disposition
of those who have shut them up in the body.'--

'Mother,' said Horus, 'you have full well explained these 7
things to me; but you have not yet told me what is the origin
of *noble* souls.'—*Isis*. 'Just as on earth, my son, there are certain
grades of social standing which differ one from another, even so
it is with the souls. For the souls also have certain places
whence they come; and the soul which has come from a more
glorious place is nobler than one that is not thus exalted. For
just as among men the free man is held to be nobler than
the slave, because that which is of superior and kingly nature
necessarily enslaves that which is inferior, even so it is, my son,
in the case of the souls.'—

Horus. 'Tell me, mother, what is the origin of *male and female* 8
souls.'—*Isis*. 'The souls, my son Horus, are all of one nature,
inasmuch as they all come from one place, that place where
the Maker fashioned them;[3] and they are neither male nor
female; for the difference of sex arises in bodies, and not in

[1] I. e. that are godlike.
[2] I. e. to reign as kings there.
[3] Viz. the atmosphere.

---

addidi (ἐδήλωσας add. Heeren) **19** Titulum Πῶς . . . ψυχαί habent FP **20** πολιτεία P **21** ἀλλήλων codd.: fortasse τῶν ἄλλων **23** ὡρμηκυῖα scripsi: ὁρμηκυῖα codd. **24** ἐν (post τρόπον) scripsi: ἐπ' codd. **25** Fortasse τὸ γὰρ [[ ]] ⟨τῇ φύσει⟩ ὑπερέχον **25–26** καὶ βασιλικὸν secludendum? **26** δουλοποιεῖται Usener: δουλοποιεῖ codd. **27** καὶ ἐν ταῖς ψυχαῖς ἔχει scripsi (καὶ ⟨ταῦτ' ἔχει⟩ Heeren: καὶ ⟨ἐπὶ τῶν ψυχῶν ἐστιν⟩ Wachsm. **28** πῶς, ὦ τεκοῦσα addidi (πῶς δὲ ὦ τεκοῦσα add. Wachsm.) **29** Titulum Πῶς . . . γίγνονται ψυχαί (ψυχαί om. F) habent FP **30** ὦ om. FP^2 **31** διετύπωσεν P^2: διατυποῦσαι P^1: διατυποῦται F

9 ἀσωμάτων. ἡ δὲ [[διαφορὰ]] ⟨αἰτία⟩ τοῦ τὰς μὲν ⟨τῶν ἀρρένων⟩ ⟨ὀ⟩βριμω[δεσ]τέρας εἶναι, τὰς δὲ ⟨τῶν θηλειῶν⟩ εὐαφεῖς, ⟨. . .⟩ ⌜ὁ ἀήρ ἐστι, τέκνον Ὧρε, ἐν ᾧ πάντα γίγνεται· ἀὴρ δὲ ψυχῆς ἐστιν⌝ ⟨. . .⟩ αὐτὸ τὸ σῶμα ὃ περιβέβληται, ὅπερ στοιχείων ἐστὶ φύραμα, γῆς καὶ ὕδατος καὶ ἀέρος καὶ πυρός. ἐπεὶ οὖν τὸ μὲν τῶν θηλειῶν σύγκριμα πλεονάζει μὲν τῷ ὑγρῷ καὶ ⟨τῷ⟩ ψυχρῷ, λείπεται δὲ τῷ ξηρῷ καὶ ⟨τῷ⟩ θερμῷ, παρὰ τοῦτο ἡ εἰς τοιοῦτον πλάσμα συγκλειομένη ψυχὴ δίυγρος γίγνεται καὶ τρυφερά, ὥσπερ ἐπὶ τῶν ἀρρένων τὸ ἐναντίον ἐστιν εὑρεῖν· ἐν γὰρ τούτοις πλεονάζει μὲν τὸ ξηρὸν καὶ τὸ θερμόν, λείπεται δὲ τὸ ψυχρὸν καὶ ⟨τὸ⟩ ὑγρόν, ⟨καὶ⟩ διὰ τοῦτο αἱ ἐν τοιούτοις σώμασι ψυχαὶ τραχεῖαι καὶ ἐργατικώτεραί εἰσι.—

10 Πῶς γίγνονταί [αἱ] ψυχαὶ συνεταί, ὦ τεκοῦσα;—καὶ ἀπεκρίθη Ἶσις· [Πῶς γίγνονται αἱ ψυχαὶ] Τὸ ὁρατικόν, ὦ τέκνον, περιβέβληται χιτῶσιν. ὅταν οὗτοι οἱ χιτῶνες πυκνοὶ ὦσι καὶ παχεῖς, ἀμβλυωπεῖ ὁ ὀφθαλμός· ἐὰν δὲ ἀραιοὶ καὶ λεπτοί, τότε ὀξυωπέστατα βλέπει. οὕτως καὶ ἐπὶ τῆς ψυχῆς· ἔχει γὰρ καὶ αὕτη ἴδια περιβόλαια, ἀσώματα, καθὸ καὶ αὐτὴ ἀσώματός ἐστι. τὰ δὲ περιβόλαια ταῦτα ἀ⟨έ⟩ρος ⟨χιτῶνές⟩ εἰσι τοῦ ἐν ἡμῖν. ὅταν οὗτοι ὦσι λεπτοὶ καὶ ἀραιοὶ καὶ διαυγεῖς, τότε συνετὴ ἡ ψυχή ἐστιν· ὅταν δὲ τοὐναντίον πυκνοὶ καὶ παχεῖς καὶ τεθολωμένοι, [[τότε]] ὡς ἐν χειμῶνι, ⟨⟨τότε⟩⟩ ἐπὶ μακρὸν οὐ βλέπει, ἀλλὰ τ⟨οσ⟩αῦτα ὅσα παρὰ ποσὶ κεῖται.—

11 καὶ εἶπεν Ὧρος· Διὰ τίνα οὖν αἰτίαν, ὦ τεκοῦσα, οἱ ἔξω τῆς ἱερωτάτης ἡμῶν χώρας ἄνθρωποι [ταῖς διανοίαις] οὐχ οὕτως εἰσὶ συνετοὶ ὡς οἱ ἡμέτεροι;—καὶ εἶπεν Ἶσις· Ἡ γῆ μέσον τοῦ παντὸς ὑπτία κεῖται, ὥσπερ ἄνθρωπος, ⟨πρὸς⟩

1–4 Fortasse ἡ δὲ αἰτία . . . ⟨οὐχ⟩ ὁ ἀήρ ἐστι, τέκνον Ὧρε, ἐν ᾧ [ ] ⟨οὔπω ἐνσωματωθεῖσα ᾤκει (?) ἡ ψυχή, ἀλλὰ⟩ αὐτὸ τὸ σῶμα ὃ περιβέβληται 2 ὀβριμωτέρας scripsi : βριμωδεστέρας codd. 5 στοιχείων Patrit. : στοιχεῖον FP 10 ἐν scripsi : ἐπὶ codd. 12 Fortasse τραχύτεραι 14 γίγνεται P 15 Titulum Πῶς γίγνονται (γίγνεται P) αἱ ψυχαὶ (deest συνεταί) habent FP 16 Fortasse ⟨καὶ⟩ ὅταν ⟨μὲν⟩ 17 ἀμβλυωπεῖ Canter : ὀξυωπεῖ FP : οὐκ ὀξυωπεῖ P[2] 18 καὶ βλεπτοὶ P[1] | βλέπει Meineke : βλέπουσιν FP 19 ἔχει γὰρ ἔχει γὰρ P[1] 19–20 ἀσώματα . . . ἀσώματός ἐστι secludendum? 20–21 ἀέρος χιτῶνές scripsi : ἀέρες P[2] : ἄρες FP[1] 21 εἰσι τοῦ ἐν ἡμῖν scripsi : εἰσὶν οἱ ἐν ἡμῖν codd. | Fortasse ⟨καὶ⟩ ὅταν ⟨μὲν⟩ 23–24 Fortasse ὡς ⟨ὁ ἀὴρ⟩ ἐν χειμῶνι 24 τοσαῦτα scripsi : ταῦτα codd. 25 παρὰ ποσὶ Patrit. : παρὰ πᾶσι FP 27–28 οὐχ οὕτως Heeren : οὐκ ὄντως codd. 29 κεῖται P : κεῖται καὶ κεῖται F

incorporeal beings. And the reason why the souls of males 9
are more robust, and those of females delicate, . . . the body itself, in which the soul is enwrapped.[1] The body is a mixture of the elements, that is, of earth, water, air, and fire; and so, since the body of the female has in its composition an excess of the fluid element and the cold element,[2] and a deficiency of the dry element and the hot element,[3] the result is that the soul which is enclosed in a bodily frame of this nature is melting[4] and voluptuous, just as in males one finds the reverse; for in males there is an excess of the dry element and the hot element, and a deficiency of the cold element and the fluid element, and hence it is that the souls in male bodies are rougher and more energetic.'—

Horus. 'Tell me, mother, what is the origin of *intelligent* 10
souls?'[5]—Isis replied, 'The organ of sight, my son, is wrapped in membranes; and when these membranes are dense and thick, the eye sees but dimly, but if they are rare and thin, it sees with the greatest keenness. And even so it is in the case of the soul. For the soul also has certain wrappings of its own, which are incorporeal, inasmuch as the soul itself is incorporeal. These wrappings are coats made of the air that is within us.[6] When these coats are thin and rare and transparent, then the soul is intelligent; but when on the other hand they are dense and thick and muddied, as the outer air is in stormy weather, then the soul cannot see far, but sees only what is close at hand.'—

And Horus said, 'Why is it then, mother, that the men who 11
dwell beyond the borders of our most holy land[7] are not so intelligent as our people are?'—'The Earth', said Isis, 'lies in the middle of the universe, stretched on her back, as a human

[1] Perhaps, 'the cause of the fact that the souls of males are more robust, and those of females delicate, is ⟨not⟩ the air, my son, in which ⟨the soul dwelt before it was embodied, but⟩ simply the body in which the soul is enwrapped' (that is to say, this difference in incarnate souls results, not from any difference in the air in which the souls resided before their incarnation, but from a difference in the bodies in which they are incarnated).

[2] I.e. of water and air.

[3] I.e. of earth and fire.

[4] Or 'soft'; more literally, 'diluted'.

[5] Or 'how do souls become intelligent?'

[6] Or 'layers of the air that is within us'.

[7] I.e. Egypt.

οὐρανὸν βλέπουσα. μεμέρισται δὲ καθ' ὅσα μέρη ὁ ἄνθρωπος
μερίζεται· [⟨ἐμ⟩βλέπει δ' [ἐν] οὐρανῷ καθάπερ πατρὶ ἰδίῳ,
ὅπως ταῖς ἐκείνου μεταβολαῖς καὶ αὐτὴ [τὰ ἴδια] συμμετα-
βάλλῃ·] καὶ πρὸς μὲν τῷ νότῳ τοῦ παντὸς κειμένην ἔχει τὴν
κεφαλήν, πρὸς δὲ τῷ ἀπηλιώτῃ ⟨τὸν⟩ δεξιὸν ὦμον, ⟨πρὸς δὲ
τῷ λιβὶ τὸν εὐώνυμον,⟩ ὑπὸ ⟨δὲ⟩ τὴν ἄρκτον τοὺς πόδας, [τὸν
δὲ εὐώνυμον ὑπὸ τὴν κεφαλὴν τῆς ἄρκτου,] τοὺς δὲ μηροὺς ἐν
12 τοῖς μετὰ τὴν ἄρκτον [τὰ δὲ μέσα ἐν τοῖς μέσοις]. καὶ
τούτου σημεῖόν ἐστι τὸ τοὺς μὲν νοτιαίους τῶν ἀνθρώπων καὶ
ἐπὶ τῇ κορυφῇ ⟨τῆς γῆς⟩ οἰκοῦντας εὐκορύφους ⟨⟨εἶναι⟩⟩ καὶ
καλλίτριχας, τοὺς δὲ ἀπηλιωτικοὺς πρὸς μάχην προχείρους
[[εἶναι]] καὶ τοξι[α]κούς,—[αἰτία] ⟨κρείττων⟩ γὰρ τούτοις ἡ
δεξιὰ χείρ ἐστι,—τοὺς δ' ἐν τῷ λιβὶ ⌜ἀσφαλεῖς⌝ εἶναι καὶ ὡς
ἐπὶ τὸ πλεῖστον ἀριστερομάχους [καὶ ⟨ἐν⟩ ὅσοις ἄλλοι τῷ
δεξιῷ μέρει ἐνεργοῦσιν, αὐτοὺς τῷ εὐωνύμῳ ⌜προστιθεμένους⌝],
τοὺς δὲ ὑπὸ τὴν ἄρκτον [πρός τινα] ⟨. . .⟩ τοὺς πόδας, καὶ
ἄλλως εὐκνήμους. [τοὺς] ⟨οἱ⟩ δὲ μετὰ τούτους καὶ μικρῷ
πόρρω [τὸ νῦν Ἰταλικὸν κλίμα καὶ τὸ Ἑλλαδικόν], πάντες
δὴ οὗτοι καλλίμηροί εἰσι καὶ εὐπυγ[ον]ότεροι [ὥστε τῇ τοῦ
κάλλους τῶν μερῶν τούτων ὑπερβολῇ καὶ τοὺς ἐνταῦθα
ἀνθρώπους καταβαίνειν πρὸς τὴν τῶν ἀρρένων ὁμιλίαν.]
13 πάντα δὲ ταῦτα τὰ μέρη ⟨τῆς γῆς⟩, πρός ⟨τινα μὲν ἐνεργὰ
ὄντα, πρὸς δὲ⟩ τὰ ἄλλα ἀργά [ὄντα], ἀργοτέρους ⟨τὴν νόησιν⟩
ἤνεγκε καὶ τοὺς ἀπ' αὐτῶν ἀνθρώπους. ἐπειδὴ δὲ ἐν τῷ
μέσῳ τῆς γῆς κεῖται ἡ τῶν προγόνων ἡμῶν ἱερωτάτη χώρα,
τὸ δὲ μέσον τοῦ ἀνθρωπίνου σώματος [μόνης] τῆς καρδίας
ἐστὶ σηκός, τῆς δὲ ψυχῆς ὁρμητήριόν ἐστι⟨ν ἡ⟩ καρδία, παρὰ
ταύτην τὴν αἰτίαν, ὦ τέκνον, ⟨οἱ⟩ ἐνταῦθα ἄνθρωποι τὰ μὲν
ἄλλα ἔχουσιν οὐχ ἧττον ὅσα καὶ πάντες, ἐξαίρετον δὲ τῶν
πάντων νοερώτεροί εἰσι [καὶ σώφρονες], ὡς ἂν ἐπὶ καρδίας
⟨γῆς⟩ γενόμενοι καὶ τραφέντες.

14 ἄλλως τε, ὁ μὲν νότος, ὦ παῖ, δεκτικὸς ὢν τῶν ἐκ τοῦ
περιέχοντος συνισταμένων νεφῶν, ⟨. . .⟩. αὐτίκα γοῦν καὶ

1 μεμέρισται scripsi: μεμερισμένη FP[2]: μεμερισμένοι P[1] | καθ' ὅσα μέρη Wachsm.: καὶ ὅσα μέλη FP | ὁ (ante ἄνθρωπος) om. P 2 μερίζεται scripsi: μελίζεται codd. | ἐμβλέπει δ' Heeren: βλέπει δ' ἐν FP 3–4 συμμεταβάλλει P 5 τὸν (ante δεξιὸν) add. Heeren 5–6 πρὸς δὲ . . . εὐώνυμον add. Heeren 6 τὴν ἄρκτον scripsi (τῆς ἄρκτου Heeren): τὰς ἄρκτους FP 10 καὶ καὶ F 12 τοξικούς P[2]: τοξιανούς FP[1]: fortasse τοξεύ⟨ειν δει⟩νούς | τούτοις scripsi: τούτων codd. 13 ἀσφα-

being might lie, facing toward heaven. She is parted out into as many different members as a man; and her head lies toward the South of the universe, her right shoulder toward the East and her left shoulder toward the West; her feet lie beneath the Great Bear,[1] and her thighs are situated in the regions which follow next to the South of the Bear. Evidence of this may be 12
seen in the fact that the men of the South, who dwell where the top of Earth's head lies, have the tops of their heads well developed, and have handsome hair; the men of the East are apt for battle, and are good bowmen, because in them the right hand is the stronger; the men of the West are . . ., and for the most part fight with the left hand; and those who live beneath the Bear have strong [2] feet, and sturdy legs as well. And those who come next after them, and dwell a little farther from the North,[3] all these have comely thighs and well-shaped buttocks. Now all these parts of the earth are active in some respects, 13
but sluggish in all else, and the men whom they produce are somewhat sluggish in intelligence. But the right holy land of our ancestors lies in the middle of the earth; and the middle of the human body is the sanctuary of the heart, and the heart is the head-quarters of the soul; and that, my son, is the reason why the men of this land, while they have in equal measure all other things that all the rest possess, have this advantage over all other men, that they are more intelligent. It could not be otherwise, seeing that they are born and bred upon Earth's heart.

And there is another reason also. The South, my son, being 14
receptive of the clouds which are formed by condensation from the atmosphere, ⟨. . .⟩. Indeed, it is said to be in consequence

[1] I.e. in the far North.
[2] Or possibly 'swift'.
[3] That is, in or about the latitude of Italy and Greece.

λεῖς εἶναι codd.: exspectes ἐναντίως διακειμένους 14 ἐν ὅσοις scripsi: ὅσον codd. 15 προστιθεμένους codd.: fortasse [πρός τι] ⟨χρ⟩ωμένους 16 Fortasse ⟨ταχεῖς⟩ τοὺς πόδας 17 ἄλλως Patrit.: ἄλλους codd. 18 πόρρω codd.: fortasse πορρωτέρω | κλῆμα F 19 δὴ Wachsm.: δὲ FP | εὐπυγότεροι Barth: εὐπωγονότεροι FP 20 μερῶν Canter: μηρῶν FP 22 τὰ (post ταῦτα) om. P | μέρη Heeren: μέλη FP 24 καὶ secludendum? | ἀπ' αὐτῶν scripsi (ἐπ' αὐτῶν Heeren): ἀπ' αὐτῆς FP 25 γῆς om. P[1] | κεῖται om. P | ἡμῶν Patrit.: ἡμῖν FP 27 ἐστιν ἡ scripsi: ἐστι codd. 28 οἱ add. Heeren 30 καὶ σώφρονες seclusi (an scribendum καὶ φρονιμώτεροι?) 31 γενόμενοι P[2]: γενάμενοι FP[1] 33 Lacunam signavit Meineke

διὰ τὴν οὕτως αὐτῶν γενομένων ἐκεῖ⟨σε⟩ [κ] ἀνακομιδὴν ἐκεῖθεν
ῥεῖν λέγουσιν καὶ τὸν ἡμέτερον πο⟨ταμόν⟩, λυομένης ἐκεῖ τῆς
⌜πάχνης⌝. ὅπου δ' ἂν ἐμπέσῃ νεφέλη, τὸν ὑποκείμενον
ἤχλυσεν ἀέρα, καὶ τρόπον τινὰ καπνοῦ κατέπλησε· καπνὸς
δὲ ἢ ἀχλὺς οὐ μόνον ὀμμάτων ἐστὶν ἐμπόδιον, ἀλλὰ καὶ νοῦ.
ὁ δὲ ἀπηλιώτης, ὦ μεγαλόδοξε Ὧρε, τῇ σύνεγγυς τοῦ ἡλίου
ἀνατολῇ θορυβούμενος καὶ ἐκθερμαινόμενος, ὁμοίως δὲ καὶ ὁ
ἀντικείμενος τούτῳ λὶψ μετέχων τῶν αὐτῶν κατὰ δυσμάς,
⟨οὐκ⟩ [οὐδεμίαν] εἰλικρινῆ ⟨τὴν⟩ [ἐπι] σύνεσιν ποιοῦσι τῶν
παρ' αὐτοῖς γεννωμένων ἀνθρώπων· ὁ δὲ βορέας τῇ συμ-
φύτῳ ψυχρίᾳ ἀποπήσσει μετὰ τῶν σωμάτων καὶ τὸν νοῦν
15 *τῶν ὑπ' αὐτὸν ἀνθρώπων. τὸ δὲ μέσον τούτων, [εἰλικρινὲς*
ὂν καὶ] ἀτάραχον ⟨ὄν⟩, καὶ ⟨αὐτὸ καθ'⟩ ἑαυτὸ προ[λ]έχει, καὶ
τοῖς ἐν αὐτῷ ⟨γεννωμένοις⟩ [πᾶσι]· τῇ γὰρ συνεχεῖ ⟨εὐ⟩η-
μερ[ιμν]ίᾳ ⟨συνετοὺς⟩ γεννᾷ. καὶ ⟨ἀλλοφύλους δὲ⟩ κοσμεῖ
καὶ παιδεύει· καὶ ⟨γὰρ⟩ μόνον ⟨ὅ⟩σοις ⟨⟨ἐρίζει⟩⟩, τοσούτους
[[ἐρίζει]] καὶ νικᾷ, καὶ [[ἐπιστάμενον τὴν ἰδίαν]] νική⟨σα⟩ν,
ὥσπερ σατράπην ἀγαθὸν τοῖς νενικημένοις [καὶ] ⟨⟨ἐπιστήμην
[ον] τὴν ἰδίαν⟩⟩ ἐπιδίδωσι.—
17 *Καὶ τοῦτό μοι, κυρία μῆτερ, ἔκθου· παρὰ ποίαν αἰτίαν ἔτι*
ζώντων ἀνθρώπων ἐν ταῖς μακραῖς νόσοις καὶ ὁ [λόγος καὶ
αὐτὸς ὁ] λογισμὸς καὶ αὐτὴ ἡ ψυχὴ ἔσθ' ὅτε βλάπτεται;—
καὶ ἀπεκρίθη Ἶσις· Τῶν ζῴ[ντ]ων, ὦ τέκνον, τὰ μὲν ᾠκείωται
πρὸς τὸ πῦρ, τὰ δὲ πρὸς τὸ ὕδωρ, τὰ δὲ πρὸς ἀέρα, τὰ δὲ
πρὸς γῆν, τὰ δὲ πρὸς τούτων δύο ἢ τρία [τὰ δὲ καὶ πρὸς τὰ
ὅλα]· ⟨καὶ⟩ πάλιν αὖ τὰ μὲν ἀπηλλοτρίωται τοῦ πυρός, τὰ δὲ
τοῦ ὕδατος, τὰ δὲ τῆς γῆς, τὰ δὲ τοῦ ἀέρος, τὰ δὲ δύο τούτων,
18 *τὰ δὲ τριῶν [τὰ δὲ τῶν ὅλων]. οἷον ἀκρὶς μέν, ὦ τέκνον, καὶ*
πᾶσα μυῖα φεύγει τὸ πῦρ, ἀετὸς καὶ κίρκος καὶ ὅσα ὑψι-
πετ⟨έστ⟩ερά ἐστι τῶν ὀρνέων φεύγει τὸ ὕδωρ, ἰχθύες ἀέρα καὶ
γῆν, ὄφις τὸν ἀέρα τὸν εἰλικρινῆ ἀποστρέφεται· φιλοῦσι δὲ

1 *ἐκεῖσε ἀνακομιδὴν* scripsi : *ἐκεῖ κατακομιδὴν* codd. 2 *ποταμὸν λυομένης* Meineke (*ποταμὸν πολυομένης* Patrit.) : *πολυομένης* FP 2–3 Fortasse *λυομένης ⟨εἰς ὄμβρον?⟩ ἐκεῖ τῆς συστάσεως ⟨τῶν νεφῶν⟩*? 3 *πάχνης* F : *τέχνης* P | *ὑποκείμενον* scripsi : *ἐπικείμενον* codd. 4 *κατέπλησε* scripsi : *κατεκόμισε* codd. 4–5 *κάπνος δὲ ἢ ἀχλὺς* codd. : fortasse *ἀχλὺς δὲ* 5 *ὄμματων* edd. : *ὀνομάτων* FP 6 *σύνεγγυς* scripsi : *συνεχῇ* F : *συνεχεῖ* P 9 *οὐκ* scripsi : *οὐδεμίαν* codd. (an *οὐδ' ἐκεῖνοι*?) | *τὴν σύνεσιν ποιοῦσι* scripsi : *ἐπίστασιν ποιοῦνται* codd. | *τῶν* (ante *παρ' αὐτοῖς*) om. P 10 *γενομένων* P 10–11 *συμφύτῳ* Usener : *συμφώνῳ* codd. 11–12 *νοῦν τὸν ὑπ'* F 13 *ἀτάραχον ὄν* scripsi : *εἰλικρινὲς ὂν καὶ ἀτάραχον* codd. *αὐτὸ καθ' ἑαυτὸ* scripsi (*αὐτὸ* Wachsm.) : *ἑαυτῷ* FP | *προέχει* Wachsm. :

of the conveyance of the clouds to the southern region when they have thus been formed, that our river[1] flows from that quarter, the . . . being there broken up.[2] Now wherever a cloud arrives, it makes the air below it misty, and fills it with smoke, so to speak; and smoke or mist is an obstruction not only to the eyes, but also to the mind. And the East, my glorious son, is troubled and overheated by the rising of the sun in close proximity to it; and likewise its opposite, the West, is affected in the same way at the sun's setting; and thus both the East and the West cause the intelligence of the men born in those regions to be wanting in clearness. And the North, with the cold that belongs to it by nature, freezes the minds as well as
the bodies of the men who live beneath the northern sky. But 15
the country which lies in the middle[3] is undisturbed, and is consequently superior both in itself and in the men born in it; for in virtue of the continual serenity of its climate, it produces men of high intelligence. And it disciplines and educates men of other races also; for it is the only land that is victorious over all competitors, and having won the victory, it bestows on its defeated rivals the gift of its own knowledge, as a king might send a good satrap to govern a conquered province.'—

Horus. 'Explain to me this also, my lady mother; why is it 17
that in long[4] diseases, though the man is still alive, the reason and the soul itself is sometimes disabled?'—Isis replied, 'Among animals, my son, there are some that have an affinity to fire, some to water, some to air, some to earth, and some to two or three of these elements; and again, some of them are alien to fire, some to water, some to earth, some to air, some to two
of the elements, and some to three. For instance, the locust, my 18
son, shuns fire, and so does every kind of fly; the eagle, the falcon, and all high-flying birds shun water; fishes shun air and earth; and snakes avoid pure air. And on the other hand,

[1] I. e. the Nile.
[2] Perhaps, 'the clouds being there (*sc.* in the South) dissolved in rain'.
[3] I. e. Egypt.
[4] Perhaps, 'great' or 'grievous'.

προλέγει FP **14–15** *εὐημερίᾳ* scripsi: *ἀμεριμνίᾳ* codd. **15** *συνετοὺς* addidi (an *συνετωτέρους* ?) **16–17** *ὅσοις ἐρίζει, τοσούτους καὶ νικᾷ* scripsi: *τοῖς τοσούτοις ἐρίζει καὶ νικᾷ* codd. **17** *νικῆσαν* scripsi: *νίκην* codd. **18** *σατράπην ἀγαθὸν* scripsi: *σατράπης ἀγαθὸς* codd. | *ἐπιστήμην* scripsi: *ἐπιστάμενον* FP **21–22** *λόγος καὶ αὐτὸς ὁ* seclusi (*καὶ αὐτὸς ὁ λογισμὸς* om. Heeren) **23** *ζῴων* Meineke: *ζώντων* F: *ζῶν τῶν* P **29–30** *ὑψιπετέστερα* Gaisford: *ὑψιπέτερα* FP

τὴν μὲν γῆν οἱ ὄφεις καὶ ὅσα ἕρπει, τὸ δὲ ὕδωρ τὰ [κι]
νη⟨κ⟩τὰ πάντα, τὸν δὲ ἀέρα τὰ πτηνά [ἐν ᾧ καὶ πολιτεύεται],
τὸ δὲ πῦρ ὅσα ὑπερπετῆ ἐστι καὶ ἐγγὺς ⟨ἡλίου ἔχει⟩ τὴν
δίαιταν. [οὐ μὴν ἀλλὰ καί τινα τῶν ⟨ἄλλων⟩ ζῴων φιλεῖ τὸ
πῦρ, οἷον αἱ σαλαμάνδραι· ἐν γὰρ τῷ πυρὶ καὶ φωλεύουσιν.]
19 *⟨. . .⟩ ⌜ἕκαστον γὰρ τῶν στοιχείων περιβολή ἐστι τῶν*
σωμάτων.⌝ πᾶσα οὖν ψυχή, ἐν τῷ σώματι οὖσα, βαρεῖται
καὶ θλίβεται τοῖς τέτταρσι τούτοις. [καὶ γὰρ εἰκός ἐστι καὶ
ταύτην τισὶ μὲν τούτων τέρπεσθαι, τισὶ δὲ ἄχθεσθαι.] διὰ
τοῦτο οὖν οὐκ ἔχει ⟨ἐντ⟩αῦθα τὴν ἀκροτάτην εὐδαιμονίαν,
ἀλλ' ὡς ἂν φύσει θεία οὖσα κἀν τούτοις οὖσα ⌜μάχεται⌝·
καὶ νοεῖ, ἀλλ' οὐχ ὅσα ἂ⟨ν⟩ ἐνόησεν ἀσύνδετος οὖσα σώματι.
ἐὰν μέντοι [καὶ] τοῦτο σάλον λάβῃ καὶ ταραχὴν ἤτοι ἀπὸ
νόσου ἢ ⌜φόβου⌝, τότε καὶ αὐτὴ ὥσπερ ἐν βυθῷ ⟨πεσὼν⟩
ἄνθρωπος ἐπικυμαίνεται, καὶ οὐδὲν ⟨ἀνθ⟩ισταμένη φέρετ⟨αι⟩.

EXCERPTUM XXV

Stobaeus I. 49. 68, vol. i, p. 458 Wachsmuth (*Ecl.* I. 1070 Heeren).

Ἑρμοῦ λόγος Ἴσιδος πρὸς Ὧρον.

1 *Θαυμαστῶς, εἶπεν Ὧρος, ἕκαστά μοι διηγήσω, ὦ μέγα*
δυναμένη τεκοῦσα Ἶσι, ὑπὲρ τῆς θαυμαστῆς ψυχοποιίας τοῦ
θεοῦ, καὶ θαυμάζων διατελῶ· οὔπω δέ μοι ἀπήγγειλας ποῦ
τῶν σωμάτων ἀπολυθεῖσαι χωροῦσιν αἱ ψυχαί. βούλομαι
οὖν καὶ τῆς θεωρίας ταύτης μύστης γενόμενος εὐχαριστῆσαι
2 *σοὶ μόνῃ, ἀθάνατε μῆτερ.—καὶ εἶπεν Ἶσις· Πρόσεχε, παῖ·*
ἀναγκαιοτάτη γὰρ ζήτησις αὕτη· ⟨⟨[μύστης] ⟨ἐγὼ⟩ δέ, [ὥσπερ]
τῆς ἀθανάτου φύσεως καὐτὴ [τυγχάνουσα] ⟨μετέχουσα⟩, καὶ

2 *νηκτὰ* P²: *κινητὰ* FP¹ | *ᾧ* Heeren : *οἷς* codd. | *ἐν . . . πολιτεύεται* seclusit Meineke 3 *ἡλίου ἔχει* addidi : *ἔχει* add. post *δίαιταν* Heeren, post *ἐγγὺς* Wachsm. 5–6 Fortasse [*καὶ*] *φωλεύουσιν* ⟨*αὗται*⟩ 6 Fortasse *ἑκάστου γὰρ τῶν στοιχείων* ⟨*ἀπηλλοτρίωται ἡ ψυχή . . .*⟩ 8 Fortasse [⟨*οὐ μὴν τοῖς ὅλοις·*⟩ *καὶ γὰρ κ τ λ.*] 10 *ἐνταῦθα* scripsi : *αὐτῆς* FP 11 *τούτοις* codd. : fortasse *ἀλλοτρίοις* vel *ἀνοικείοις* | *μάχεται* codd. : fortasse *ταράσσεται* 12 Fortasse *νοεῖ* ⟨*τρόπῳ τινί*⟩ vel ⟨*μέχρι τινός*⟩ | *ἂν* Heeren : *ἃ* FP (an delendum *ἃ*?) | *σώματι* Usener : *σωμάτων* FP 13 *τοῦτο* scripsi : *καὶ ταῦτα* codd. | *καὶ ταραχὴν* secludendum? An

snakes and all creeping things love earth; all animals that swim love water; the birds love the air; and fire is loved by all creatures that fly high and spend their lives near the sun.[1] . . .[2]
Every soul therefore, as long as it is in the body, is weighed 19
down and oppressed by these four elements. For this reason then the soul does not enjoy perfect happiness here on earth, but is perturbed, inasmuch as it is divine by nature and is hemmed in by the elements; and it is intelligent to some extent, but not so intelligent as it would have been if it were not bound up[3] with the body. But if the body is storm-tossed and perturbed by disease or . . ., then the soul too is tossed upon the waves, like a man that has fallen into the deep sea, and is swept along unresisting.'

EXCERPT XXV

Written by Hermes: a discourse of Isis to Horus.

'Wondrously', said Horus, 'have you, my mighty mother Isis, 1
described to me in all details the wondrous making of souls by God, and my wonder ceases not; but you have not yet told me where the souls go when they are released from their bodies. I desire therefore to be initiated in this doctrine also, and to
give thanks for that to you alone, my immortal mother.'—And 2
Isis said, 'Give heed, my son; for this inquiry is most needful; and I, who am myself participant in the being of the Immortals,

[1] E. g. by eagles.

[2] Here must have stood a sentence in which it was said that the human soul is in like manner alien, not to one or more of the elements only, but to all the four elements.

[3] Or perhaps, 'as it was when it was not bound up'.

---

legendum [καὶ] ταραχθὲν? 14 φόβου codd.: fortasse ἄλλου τινός 14–15 ὡσπερεὶ βυθῷ ἀνθέρικος Meineke et Wachsm. 15 ἀνθισταμένη φέρεται scripsi: ἑσταμένον φέρει codd.
16 ὥρου πρὸς ἶσιν P 19 ποῦ codd.: ποῖ Meineke 22 ἀθάνατος P 23–2 *infra*: μύστης . . . ὡς δὴ huc a § 4 transposui 23 ὥσπερ seclusi (an scribendum ὡς [περ]?)

ὡδευκυῖα διὰ τοῦ πεδίου τῆς ἀληθείας, διεξελεύσομαί σοι τῶν ὄντων τὸ καθ' ἕκαστον, ἐκεῖνό σοι φήσασα πρῶτον, ὡς δὴ⟩⟩ ⌜τὸ συνεστὸς καὶ μὴ ἀφανιζόμενον χῶρον ἔχει⌝ ⟨. . .⟩.

3 ἀλλ' ὧδε γὰρ ἐρεῖ ⟨τις, ὡς δὴ⟩ [λόγος ἐμός] [Ποῦ τῶν σωμάτων ἀπολυθεῖσαι διατρίβουσιν αἱ ψυχαί] [οὐ γάρ, ὦ θαυμαστὲ καὶ μεγάλου πατρὸς Ὀσίρεως μέγα τέκνον] [[ἀκρίτως]] [καὶ ὁρμηδὸν] τῶν σωμάτων προελθοῦσαι εἰς ἀέρα ἀναχύνονται [τε] ⟨⟨ἀκρίτως⟩⟩ καὶ διασκεδάννυνται μετὰ τοῦ ἄλλου ἀπείρου πνεύματος· εἶτα οὐκέτι δύνασθαι πάλιν τὰς αὐτὰς οὔσας εἰς ⟨⟨ἄλλα⟩⟩ σώματα παλινδρομῆσαι, [[ἀλλὰ]] οὐδὲ εἰς ἐκεῖνον ἔτι τὸν χῶρον [εἶναι], ὅθεν ἦλθον τὸ πρότερον, ἀναστρέφειν, καθάπερ οὐδὲ τὸ ⌜λαμβανόμενον ἐκ τῶν κάτω ἀγγείων⌝ ὕδωρ εἰς τοὺς αὐτοὺς τόπους ὅθεν ἐλήφθη ⌜ἐπέχειν⌝ ἐστὶ δυνατόν, [ἀλλ' οὐδ' ⌜αὐτὸ παραυτίκα λαμβανόμενον καὶ χεόμενον τὴν ἰδίαν λαμβάνει χώραν⌝], πλὴν ἀναμίγνυται τῷ παντὶ τοῦ ὕδατος χύματι.

4 ἀλλ' οὐκ ἔχει οὕτως, ὦ μεγαλόφρων Ὧρε· [[μύστης δὲ ὥσπερ τῆς ἀθανάτου φύσεως καὐτὴ τυγχάνουσα, καὶ ὡδευκυῖα διὰ τοῦ πεδίου τῆς ἀληθείας, διεξελεύσομαί σοι τῶν ὄντων τὸ καθ' ἕκαστον, ἐκεῖνό σοι φήσασα πρῶτον, ὡς δὴ]] τὸ ⟨μὲν γὰρ⟩ ὕδωρ σῶμά ἐστιν ἄλογον, ἐκ πολλῶν συγ⟨κε⟩κριμένον παρατεθλιμμένων εἰς χύσιν, ἡ δὲ ψυχὴ πρᾶγμα ἰδιοφυές, τέκνον, [καὶ βασιλικόν,] καὶ ἔργον τῶν τοῦ θεοῦ χειρῶν τε καὶ νοῦ, ⌜αὐτῷ θ' ἑαυτῷ⌝ εἰς νοῦν ὁδηγούμενον. τὸ τοίνυν ἐξ ἑνὸς καὶ οὐκ ἐκ ⟨π⟩ολλῶν ἀδύνατον ἑτέρῳ ἀναμιγῆναι· ὅθεν δεῖ καὶ τὴν πρὸς τὸ σῶμα αὐτῆς σύνοδον [ἁρμονίαν θεοῦ] ὑπὸ ἀνάγκης γενομένην εἶναι.

5 ὅτι δὲ οὔτε εἰς ἕνα καὶ τὸν αὐτὸν τόπον ⟨πᾶσαι⟩ χυδαίως, οὔτε εἰκῇ καὶ ὡς ἔτυχεν [[ἀλλὰ]] ἑκάστη, ⟨⟨ἀλλὰ⟩⟩ ἐπὶ τὴν ἰδίαν ἀναπέμπεται χώραν, φανερὸν καὶ ἐξ ὧν ἔτι ἐν τῷ σώματι οὖσα [καὶ τῷ πλάσματι] πάσχει ⟨καὶ⟩ [γὰρ] παρὰ τὴν
6 ἰδίαν φύσιν ⌜πεπαχυμμένη⌝. [ἀλλὰ καὶ] πρόσ⟨σ⟩χες ⟨γάρ⟩, ὦ περιπόθητε Ὧρε, τῷ λεγομένῳ ὁμοιώματι. φέρε γὰρ εἰς ἓν καὶ τὸ αὐτὸ συσχετήριον ἐγκεκλεῖσθαι ἀνθρώπους τε, καὶ ἀετοὺς καὶ περιστερὰς καὶ κύκνους καὶ ἱέρακας καὶ χελιδόνας

3 Fortasse τὸ ⟨μὲν⟩ συνεστὸς καὶ ⟨διαλύεται, τὸ δὲ⟩ μὴ ⟨συνεστός⟩, ἀφανιζόμενον, χῶρον ἔχει ⟨εἰς ὃν ἀπέρχεται. . . .⟩ 4 λόγος ἐμός codd. : fortasse [Λόγος πέμπτος] 4–5 Titulum Ποῦ . . . ψυχαί habent FP 5 οὐ γάρ codd. : fortasse σὺ γάρ 6 θαυμαστὲ καὶ secludendum? 9 εἶτα FP[1] : ὥστε P[2] marg. 11 οὐδὲ scripsi : μηδὲ codd. | εἶναι seclusit Heeren

and have journeyed through the Plain of Truth, will describe to you in all particulars the things that are. I begin by saying that . . .[1]

But perhaps some one will say that when the souls go forth 3
from their bodies, they are indistinguishably diffused in the air, and are dispersed throughout the boundless atmosphere, and that they cannot thereafter retain their identity and come back again to dwell in other bodies, nor yet return to the place from which they came before; just as it is impossible that the water . . .[2] should return to the same place from which it was taken, but it is mingled with all the mass of flowing water.

But in the case of the soul, high-minded Horus, it is not so. 4
Water is a body, an irrational thing, composed of many ingredients crushed into fluidity; but the soul, my son, is a thing of peculiar nature, a thing that has been made by the hands and mind of God, and is guided . . .[3] on the way that leads to Mind. And that which consists of one thing only and not of many[4] cannot be mingled with anything else. Hence it follows that the union of the soul with the body must have been effected by compulsion.

Souls, when they quit the body, are not all sent promiscuously 5
to one and the same place; nor is each of them sent to some place at random and by chance; but each soul is sent to its own proper place. This you may clearly see from what befalls the soul even when it is still in the body, and is . . .[5] against its
proper nature. Give heed, well-beloved Horus, to the similitude 6
which I am about to set forth. Suppose that in one and the same enclosure there are shut up men, and eagles and doves

[1] Perhaps, 'that which is composite is broken up and destroyed, but that which is not composite (is not destroyed, but) has a place to which it goes when it disappears from our sight'. (The body is composite; the soul is not composite.)

[2] Perhaps, 'which is poured out from a vessel'.

[3] Perhaps, 'by God himself'.

[4] Viz. the soul.

[5] Perhaps, 'weighed down', or 'fast bound'.

12–13 λαμβανόμενον ἐκ τῶν κάτω ἀγγείων codd. : fortasse ἐκχεόμενον ἐξ ἀγγείου 13 ἐπέχειν codd. : fortasse ἔτι ⟨ἀνατρ⟩έχειν 14–15 καὶ χεόμενον om. P 15 ⟨ἀνα⟩λαμβάνει Meineke 17–20 μύστης . . . ὡς δὴ hinc ad § 2 transposui 21–22 συγκεκριμένον παρατεθλιμμένων scripsi : συγκριμάτων παρατεθλιμμένον (παραθλιμμένον P) codd. 23 τε om. P 24 αὐτῷ θ' ἑαυτῷ codd. : fortasse αὖθίς τε ὑπ' αὐτοῦ 25 ἐκ πολλῶν scripsi : ἐξ ἄλλου codd. 26 δεῖ Heeren : δὴ FP 27 γενομένην εἶναι codd. : fortasse γεγονέναι 30 ἔτι FP² : ἐστιν P¹ 31 γὰρ seclusit Heeren 32 πεπαχυμένη F : fortasse βεβαρυμμένη vel πεπεδημένη | πρόσσχες scripsi : πρόσχες codd. 33 Fortasse ⟨τούτῳ⟩ τῷ [λεγομένῳ] 34 συγχετήριον P¹

καὶ στρουθοὺς καὶ μυίας, [[καὶ ὄφεις]], καὶ λέοντας καὶ παρδάλεις καὶ λύκους καὶ κύνας καὶ λαγωοὺς καὶ βόας καὶ ποίμνια, ⟨⟨καὶ ὄφεις,⟩⟩ καί τινα τῶν ⸢τῆς κοινότητος ἐχομένων⸣ ζῴων, οἱονεὶ φώκας καὶ ἐνύδρεις καὶ χελώνας καὶ τοὺς ἡμετέρους κροκοδείλους· ἔπειτα τούτους, ὦ τέκνον, ⟨πάντας⟩

7 ὑπὸ μίαν ῥοπὴν ἀπολυθῆναι τοῦ συσχετηρίου. ⟨οὐ⟩ πάντως τραπήσονται οἱ μὲν ἄνθρωποι εἰς [τε] ἀγορὰς καὶ στέγας, ὁ δὲ ἀετὸς εἰς τὸν αἰθέρα, ὅπου καὶ φύσιν ἔχει διαιτᾶσθαι, αἱ δὲ περιστεραὶ εἰς τὸν πλησίον ἀέρα, οἱ δὲ ἱέρακες ὑπεράνω τούτων· αἱ δὲ χελιδόνες οὐχὶ ὅπου ἂν οἰκῶσιν ἄνθρωποι, οἱ δὲ στρουθοὶ περὶ τὰ καρποφόρα τῶν δένδρων, οἱ δὲ κύκνοι ὅπου ἔξεστιν αὐτοῖς ᾄδειν, αἱ δὲ μυῖαι περὶ αὐτὴν τὴν γῆν, τοσοῦτον αὐτῆς ἀπέχουσαι ὅσον ἀναβῆναι δύνα[ν]ται ἀνθρώπων [τῇ] ὀσμή;—ἀνθρωπόλιχνον γὰρ ἰδίως, ὦ τέκνον, ἐστὶν ἡ μυῖα, καὶ χαμαιπετές·—οἱ δὲ λέοντες καὶ παρδαλεῖς οὐκ ἐπὶ τὰ ὄρη, οἱ δὲ λύκοι ἐπὶ τὰς ἐρημίας, οἱ δὲ κύνες κατ' ἴχνος ἀνθρώπων, λαγωοὶ δὲ ⟨εἰς⟩ δρυμούς, καὶ βόες ⟨εἰς⟩ αὐλιστήρια [πεδία], καὶ εἰς τὰς νομὰς τὰ ποίμνια; οἱ δὲ ὄφεις εἰς τὰ μύχια τῆς γῆς; φῶκαι δὲ καὶ χελῶναι μετὰ τῶν ὁμοίων εἰς βάθη καὶ νάματα, ὡς μὴ πεδιάδος γῆς στέροιντο μηδὲ τοῦ συγγενοῦς ἀπολειφθεῖεν ὕδατος, ἑκάστου εἰς τὴν οἰκείαν χώραν ὑπὸ τοῦ ἔνδον κριτηρίου ἀνατρεπομένου;

8 οὕτως ἑκάστη ψυχή, καὶ ἀνθρωπευομένη καὶ ἄλλως ἐπιγειζουσα, οἶδεν ὅπου πορευτέον αὐτῇ ἐστι· πλὴν εἰ μή τις τῶν Τυφωνίων, ὦ τέκνον, παρελθὼν λέγοι ὅτι δυνατὸν ταῦρον μὲν ἐν βυθῷ, ἐν ⟨δὲ⟩ ἀέρι χελώνην διαζῆν. εἰ δὴ τοῦτο πάσχουσι σαρκὶ καὶ αἵματι βεβαπτισμέναι, ὡς μηδὲν παρὰ τάξιν πράσσειν κἂν κολάζωνται,—κόλασις γὰρ αὐταῖς ἡ ἐνσωμάτωσις,—πόσῳ πλέον [βαπτισμοῦ καὶ] ⟨τῆς⟩ κολάσεως ⟨ἀπολυθεῖσαι⟩, καὶ ἐλευθερίας ⟨τῆς⟩ ἰδίας μετασχοῦσαι;

9 ⟨. . .⟩ ἔχει δὲ ἡ ⟨τῶν⟩ ⟨⟨ἄνω⟩⟩ διάταξις [ἡ ἱερωτάτη] οὕτως. [ἤδη ποτέ [[ἄνω]], ⟨ὦ⟩ μεγαλοφυέστατε παῖ, βλέπε] [ψυχῶν διατάξεις.] τὸ ἀπ' οὐρανοῦ κορυφῆς μέχρι σελήνης θεοῖς

3 Fortasse γῆς ⟨τε καὶ ὕδατος⟩ [κοινῶς?] ἐχομένων 6 οὐ add. Meineke 9–12 οἱ δὲ ἱέρακες . . . αἱ δὲ χελιδόνες . . . οἱ δὲ στρουθοὶ . . . οἱ δὲ κύκνοι . . . αὐτοῖς ᾄδειν (et supra καὶ κύκνους καὶ ἱέρακας καὶ χελιδόνας καὶ στρουθοὺς) secludenda? 10 ὅπου om. F 13–14 δύναται ἀνθρώπων ὀσμή scripsi : δύνανται ἀνθρώπων τῇ ὀσμῇ codd. ('an αἱ ὀσμαί?' Wachsm.) 17–18 λαγωοὶ δὲ . . . πεδία (et supra καὶ λαγωοὺς καὶ βόας) secludenda? 17 εἰς *bis* add. Meineke 18 πεδία FP[1] : καὶ πεδία P[2] 21 ἕκαστον P 22 ἀνατρεπόμενα P[2] 23 ψυχὴ ἡ καὶ P 24 ὅποι Meineke | ἐστιν αὐτῇ P 26 ἐν δὲ

and swans and hawks and swallows and sparrows and flies, and lions and leopards and wolves and dogs and hares and cows and sheep, and snakes, and some of the amphibious animals, such as seals and otters and tortoises and the crocodiles of our own country; and suppose, my son, that all these creatures are released from the enclosure at one moment. Will not the men 7
be sure to betake themselves to market-places and houses, and the eagle to the upper air, which is its natural abode, and the doves to the lower air not far from earth, and the hawks to a higher region than the doves? Will not the swallows make their way to the dwellings of men, and the sparrows to the neighbourhood of fruit-trees, and the swans to places where they are free to sing? Will not the flies seek places close to the ground, only so far above it as the scent of men can rise? For the fly, my son, is peculiarly greedy for human flesh, and is a grovelling creature. Will not the lions and leopards betake themselves to the mountains, and the wolves to uninhabited places? And will not the dogs follow at men's heels, and hares go to coverts, and cows to farmsteads, and the sheep to the pastures? Will not the snakes creep into holes in the earth? And will not seals and tortoises and the like seek hollows and flowing waters, that they may neither be deprived of dry land nor suffer want of the water that is congenial to them? For each of the creatures is sent back to its own place by that thing within it by which its action is determined.[1] And even so does 8
every soul, whether incarnated as a man or dwelling on earth in some other shape, know whither it must go; unless indeed, my son, some follower of Typhon[2] were to step forth and tell us that it is possible for a bull to live in the deep sea, and a tortoise in the air. If then it is so with the souls when they are immersed in flesh and blood, and if they do nothing against God's ordering even when they are undergoing punishment,—for incarnation is a punishment inflicted on them,—will they not much more act thus when they are released from this punishment, and have obtained the liberty which belongs to them by nature?

. . . And the arrangement of the things above the earth is as 9
follows. The space from the topmost height of heaven down

[1] I. e. by its own instinct. [2] I. e. some perverse opponent.

P²: ἐν P¹: καὶ ἐν F 29 πόσῳ scripsi: πόσου codd. 30 ἀπολυθεῖσαι coni. Wachsm.

καὶ ἄστροις καὶ τῇ ἄλλῃ προνοίᾳ σχολάζει· τὸ δὲ ἀπὸ σελήνης, ὦ τέκνον, ἐφ' ἡμᾶς ψυχῶν ἐστιν οἰκητήριον.

10 ἔχει μέντοι ἐν ἑαυτῷ [ὁδὸν] ⟨κίνησιν⟩ ὁ [τοσοῦτος] ἀήρ, ὃν ἄνεμον καλεῖν ἔθος ἐστὶν ἡμῖν, [ἴδιον] [μέγεθος ἐν ᾧ] ⟨ἣν⟩ κινεῖται πρὸς ἀνάψυξιν τῶν ἐπιγείων· ὃ δὴ καὶ ὕστερον ἐρῶ. κατ' οὐδένα μέντοι τρόπον πρὸς ἑαυτὸν κινούμενος ἐμπόδιον γίγνεται ψυχαῖς· κινουμένου γὰρ τούτου ἔξεστι ψυχαῖς ἀναΐσσειν καὶ καταΐσσειν, ὡς ἂν τύχῃ, ἀδιακωλύτως. ῥέουσι γὰρ δι' αὐτοῦ ἀμιγῶς καὶ ἀκολλητί, ὡς δι' ἐλαίου ὕδωρ.]

11 τὸ δὲ διάστημα τοῦτο, ὦ τέκνον Ὧρε, μοιρῶν μέν ἐστι γενικῶν τεσσάρων, ⟨ε⟩ἰδικῶν δὲ χωρῶν ἑξ⟨ήκοντα. καὶ τῶν μοιρ⟩ῶν ἡ μὲν ἀπὸ γῆς ἄνω χωρῶν ἐστι τεσσάρων, ὡς τὴν γῆν κατά τινας λόφους καὶ ἀκρωρείας [ἀνατεῖναι καὶ] φθάνειν ἄχρι τοσούτου· ὑπὲρ γὰρ ταύτης αὐτὴν ἀναβῆναι ⟨εἰς⟩ [τὸ] ὕψος οὐκ ἔχει φύσιν. ἡ δ' ἀπὸ ταύτης δευτέρα ἐστὶ χωρῶν ὀκτώ· ἐν αἷς γίγνονται ἀνέμων κινήσεις. [πρόσεχε, παῖ· ἀρρήτων γὰρ ἐπακούεις μυστηρίων γῆς τε καὶ οὐρανοῦ καὶ παντὸς τοῦ μέσου [ἱεροῦ] πνεύματος.] ὅπου ⟨δὲ⟩ ἡ τοῦ ἀνέμου κίνησις, ⟨ἐκεῖ⟩ καὶ ἡ τῶν ὀρνέων πτῆσις· ὑπὲρ γὰρ ταύτης οὔτε [[ἀὴρ]] κινεῖται ⟨ὁ⟩ ⟨⟨ἀὴρ⟩⟩ οὔτε ζῷον βαστάζει. ἔχει μέντοι παρὰ τῆς φύσεως ταύτην τὴν ἐξουσίαν ὁ ἀὴρ οὗτος, ὥστε καὶ ἐν ταῖς ἰδίαις ὀκτὼ χώραις καὶ ἐν ταῖς τῆς γῆς τέτταρσι περιπολεῖ⟨ν⟩ μεθ' ὧν ἔχει ζῴων, τῆς γῆς εἰς τὰς

12 [ἑ]αυτοῦ ἐπαναβῆναι ⟨μὴ⟩ δυναμένης. ἡ δὲ τρίτη χωρῶν ἐστιν ἑκκαίδεκα, ἀέρος λεπτοῦ καὶ καθαροῦ πλήρης. ἡ δὲ τετάρτη ἐστὶ δύο καὶ τριάκοντα, ἐν αἷς ἐστι λεπτότατος καὶ εἰλικρινέστατος ἀὴρ καὶ διαυγής. ⟨. . .,⟩ διορίζων ⌜ἐφ' ἑαυτοῦ⌝ τοὺς

13 [ἄνω] οὐρανούς, ἐκπύρους ὄντας τὴν φύσιν. καὶ ἔστιν ἡ διάταξις αὕτη κατ' εὐθυτενῆ γραμμὴν ἄνωθεν κάτω [ἀκολλητὶ] [τὴν φύσιν], ὡς εἶναι μοίρας [γενικὰς] μὲν τέσσαρας, [διαστηματικὰς δὲ δώδεκα,] χώρας δὲ ἑξήκοντα. ἐν δὲ ταῖς χώραις ταύταις, ἑξ⟨ήκοντα⟩ οὔσαις τὸν ἀριθμόν, οἰκοῦσιν

1 καὶ ἄστροις καὶ τῇ ἄλλῃ προνοίᾳ secludendum? 3 ἑαυτοῦ P | ⟨κίνησιν⟩ scripsi: fortasse ⟨κίνησιν ἰδίαν⟩ (vide [ἴδιον] ante μέγεθος) 5 ὃ δὴ codd.: fortasse ⟨περὶ⟩ οὗ δὴ 7 ἔξεστι scripsi: ἐξὸν codd. | καὶ καταΐσσειν om. P 10 εἰδικῶν Meineke: ἰδικῶν FP | ἑξήκοντα Canter: ἓξ FP 10–11 καὶ τῶν μοιρῶν scripsi: ὧν codd. 12 ἀκροτηρίας P 13 ταύτης scripsi: ταύτας codd. 15 ὀκτώ Canter: ἢ F (debebat scribi η′, quo significatur ὀκτώ): om. P 16 Fortasse ἐπακούσεις 21 ὀκτὼ Heeren: ἢ (pro η′) FP 22 περιπολεῖν Patrit.: περιπολεῖ FP | μεθ' . . . ζῴων secludendum? 23 αὐτοῦ Heeren: ἑαυτοῦ FP | μὴ add. Canter 26 διαυγής Usener: δι' αὐτῆς FP | καὶ διαυγής secludendum? | Fortasse ⟨. . . ὁ κύκλος τῆς σελήνης,⟩ διορίζων | ἐφ' ἑαυτοῦ codd.: fortasse ἀπ' αὐτοῦ

to the moon is reserved for gods and stars, and for Providence[1] in general; but the space from the moon down to us on earth, my son, is the dwelling-place of souls.

Howbeit,[2] the air has a movement of its own, which we are wont to call wind, a movement which serves for the refreshment of things on earth; about that I will speak later on. But the air in no way impedes the souls by its own movements; for while the air is in motion, souls are free to dart through it upward and downward, as it may chance, without any hindrance; they flow through it without mixing with it or adhering to it, just as water flows through oil. 10

And this space,[3] my son, consists of four main regions, and sixty subdivisions. Of the four regions, the first extends upward from the earth, and contains four subdivisions; and so far up does the earth reach in some hilly and mountainous places; for such is the nature of the earth, that it cannot rise above the first region. The second region contains eight subdivisions; and in these eight subdivisions take place movements of winds. And where there is movement of wind, there birds can fly; but above this region, the air is not in motion, and does not bear the weight of any living creature. Howbeit, such is the power given by nature to the air of this second region,[4] that it goes to and fro, together with the living creatures contained in it,[5] not only in the eight subdivisions which properly belong to it, but also in the four which are adjacent to the earth; but the earth cannot rise into the eight subdivisions which belong to that windy air. The third region contains sixteen subdivisions, and is full of fine pure air. The fourth region contains thirty-two subdivisions; and in them is air which is fine and pure in the highest degree, and perfectly translucent. ⟨. . . the sphere of the moon,⟩ the boundary between the air and the heavens, which are fiery by nature. 11

12

This arrangement extends in a straight line from the top to the bottom[6] of the atmosphere; there are four regions, and sixty subdivisions. And in these subdivisions, which are sixty in number, dwell the souls, each in that subdivision for which 13

[1] I. e. the divine powers by which the world is governed.
[2] § 10 appears to be an extract from another document.
[3] Viz. the space between the lunar sphere and the earth.
[4] I. e. the windy air, or the wind.
[5] I. e. the birds.
[6] Or rather, 'from the bottom to the top'.

(*sc.* ἀπὸ τοῦ ἀέρος) 28 Fortasse κάτωθεν ἄνω 31 ἑξήκοντα Canter: ἕξ FP

αἱ ψυχαί, ἑκάστη πρὸς ἣν ἔχει φύσιν, μίας μὲν καὶ τῆς αὐτῆς συστάσεως οὖσαι, οὐκέτι δὲ τιμῆς· ὅσῳ γὰρ ἑκάστη τῶν χωρῶν ἀπὸ γῆς ὑπερβέβηκε⟨ν⟩ [τῆς] ἑτέρας, τοσούτῳ καὶ ⟨αἱ⟩ ἐν αὐταῖς ψυχαὶ ⟨ἡ⟩ ἑτέρα τὴν ἑτέραν καθ' ὑπεροχὴν λείπει[ν], ὦ τέκνον. [χώρα καὶ ψυχή.]

14 τίνες μὲν οὖν εἰς ἑκάστην τούτων ἀναλύουσι ψυχαί, ἐντεῦθέν σοι πάλιν, ὦ μεγαλόδοξε Ὧρε, καταλέγειν ἄρξομαι, ἄνωθεν ἐπὶ τὰ πρόσγεια τὴν τάξιν ποιουμένη.

EXCERPTUM XXVI

Stobaeus I. 49. 69, vol. i, p. 463 Wachsmuth (*Ecl.* I. 1082 Heeren).

Περὶ ἐμψυχώσεως καὶ μετεμψυχώσεως.

1 Τὸ μεταξὺ γῆς καὶ οὐρανοῦ κεχωρίσται, τέκνον Ὧρε, πρὸς μέτρον καὶ ἁρμονίαν. αἱ δὲ χῶραι αὗται ὑπὸ τῶν προγόνων καλοῦνται ὑφ' ὧν μὲν ζῶναι, ὑφ' ὧν δὲ στερεώματα, ὑπὸ δὲ ἑτέρων πτυχαί. ἐν δὲ ταύταις φοιτῶσιν αἵ τε ἀπολελυμέναι τῶν σωμάτων ψυχαὶ αἵ τε μηδέπω ἐνσωματισθεῖσαι. ἑκάστη δὲ τούτων, ὦ τέκνον, κατὰ τὴν ἀξίαν καὶ χώραν ἔχει, ὥστε τὰς μὲν θείας καὶ βασιλικὰς ἐν τῇ ὑπεράνω πάντων κατοικεῖν, τὰς δὲ ἐλαχίστας κατὰ τιμήν, καὶ [τὰς ἄλλας] ὅσαι εἰσὶ χαμαιπετεῖς, ἐν τῇ ὑποκάτω πάντων, τὰς δὲ μέσας ⟨ἐν⟩ τῇ μέσῃ.

2 αἱ μὲν οὖν εἰς τὸ ἄρχειν καταπεμπόμεναι, ὦ τέκνον Ὧρε, ἐκ τῶν ὑπεράνω ζωνῶν καταπέμπονται· αἳ καὶ λυθεῖσαι εἰς τὰς αὐτὰς ἢ καὶ ἔτι ὑπεράνω ἀνέρχονται, πλὴν εἰ μή τινές [ε]τι εἶεν ⟨παρὰ⟩ τὴν ἀξίαν τῆς ἑαυτῶν φύσεως καὶ τὴν τοῦ θείου νόμου παραγγελίαν πεπραχυῖαι· ⟨ταύτ⟩ας γὰρ ἡ ἄνω πρόνοια πρὸς μέτρον τῶν ἁμαρτημάτων εἰς τὰς ὑποκάτω

3 αἱ add. Heeren 4 An ψυχαὶ ἑτέρα [τὴν] ἑτέραν? 4–5 λείπει Heeren: λείπειν FP 5 χώρα καὶ ψυχή delevit Heeren 6 ἑκάστην scripsi: ἑκάτερα codd.

13 τε Meineke: γε FP 14 τε P²: γε FP¹ 16 χώραν Meineke: χῶρον FP | ὥστε Meineke: ὥς γε FP 17 κατὰ τιμὴν Canter: κατατεμεῖν FP 19 ἐν add. Meineke 21 αἳ (ante καὶ λυθεῖσαι) secluden-

it is suited by its nature. The souls are all constituted alike, but they are not equal in rank; in proportion as one subdivision stands above another in distance from the earth, in the same proportion does a soul that is in the one subdivision surpass in eminence, my son, a soul that is in the other.

I will now begin afresh, most glorious Horus, and tell you 14
in succession what souls go to each one of the subdivisions when they depart from life on earth. I will speak of the subdivisions in order, beginning with the highest, and ending with places close to earth.'

EXCERPT XXVI

Concerning the incarnation of souls, and their reincarnation in other bodies.[1]

Isis. 'The space between earth and heaven is parted out into 1
divisions, my son Horus, according to a system of measured arrangement. These divisions are variously named by our ancestors, some of whom call them 'zones', others 'firmaments', and others 'layers'. They are the haunts of the souls that have been released from their bodies, and likewise of the souls that have not yet been embodied. And each of the souls, my son, resides in one division or another according to its worth. Godlike and kingly souls dwell in the highest division of all; the souls that are of lowest rank, and all that are wont to grovel, dwell in the lowest division; and the souls of middle quality dwell in the middle division.

Those souls then, my son Horus, which are sent down to earth 2
to bear rule there, are sent down from the highest zones; and when they are released from the body, they return to the same zones, or even to a place yet higher, excepting those of them that have done things unworthy of their own nature, and transgressed the commandments of God's law. These souls the Providence which rules above banishes to the lower divisions

[1] There is nothing about reincarnation in this Excerpt.

dum? 22 καὶ ἐπὶ P[1] 22-23 τινές τι Meineke : τινες ἔτι FP 23 παρὰ add. Heeren 24 ταύτας γὰρ scripsi : ἅσπερ F : ἅπερ P

χώρας ἐξορίζει, ὥσπερ καὶ τὰς ὑποδεεστέρας δυνάμει τε καὶ ἀξίᾳ ⟨. . .⟩ ἐκ [γὰρ] κατωτέρων ἐπὶ [μείζονας καὶ] ὑψηλοτέρας ἀνάγει.

*   *   *   *   *

3 ⟨. . .⟩ εἰσὶ γὰρ ⌜ἄνωθεν οἱ⌝ ⟨. . .⟩, δορυφόροι ὄντες τῆς καθόλου προνοίας, ὧν ὁ μὲν ψυχοταμίας, ὁ δὲ ψυχοπομπός· καὶ ὁ μὲν ψυχοταμίας ⟨. . .⟩ ψυχῶν, ὁ δὲ ψυχοπομπὸς ἀποστολεύς τε καὶ διατάκτης τῶν ἐνσωματουμένων [ψυχῶν]· καὶ ὁ μὲν τηρεῖ, ὁ δὲ προίησι κατὰ γνώμην τοῦ θεοῦ.

4 ⌜τῷ οὖν λόγῳ τούτῳ, ὦ παῖ, καὶ τῇ ἄνω τῶν πραγμάτων ἐξαλλαγῇ καὶ⌝ ἐπὶ γῆς ἐστιν ἡ φύσις, [[πλάστρια]] ⟨⟨σκηνοποιὸς⟩⟩ [γὰρ] οὖσα, καὶ [[σκηνοποιὸς]] ⟨⟨πλάστρια⟩⟩ ⟨τῶν⟩ ἀγγείων εἰς ⟨ἃ ἐμ⟩βάλλονται αἱ ψυχαί. παρεστᾶσι δὲ δύο ἐνέργειαι καὶ αὐτῇ, μνήμη καὶ ἐμπειρία. καὶ ἡ μὲν μνήμη ἔργον ἔχει τοῦτο, ὅπως ἡ φύσις [τηρῇ καὶ] περικρατῇ τοῦ [τε ἑκάστου] τύπου ⟨τοῦ⟩ ἐξ ἀρχῆς καταβεβλημένου, καὶ τοῦ παρα⟨δείγ⟩ματος τοῦ ἄνω ⟨εἰκὼν⟩ γίγνηται ⟨. . .⟩· ἡ δὲ ἐμπειρία, ὅπως πρὸς ἀνάλογον ἑκάστης τῶν καταβαινουσῶν ψυχῶν εἰς τὸ ⟨ἐν⟩σωμα[κ]τισθῆναι καὶ τὸ πλάσμα [ἐνεργῇ καὶ] γένηται, καὶ ταῖς μὲν ὀξέσι τῶν ψυχῶν ὀξέα γένηται καὶ τὰ σώματα, ταῖς δὲ βραδέσι βραδέα, ταῖς δὲ ἐνεργέσιν ἐνεργῆ, καὶ ταῖς νωθραῖς νωθρά, καὶ ταῖς δυναταῖς δυνατά, καὶ ταῖς δολίαις δόλια, καὶ ἁπαξαπλῶς ἑκάσταις κατὰ τὸ εἰκός.

5 ⟨. . .⟩ οὐ γὰρ ἀσκόπως πτηνὰ μὲν ἐπτίλωσε⟨ν ἡ φύσις⟩, [[λογικὰ δὲ περισσαῖς καὶ ἀκριβεστέραις αἰσθήσεσιν ἐκόσμησε,]] τετραπόδων δὲ τὰ μὲν κέρασι, τὰ δὲ ὀδοῦσι, τὰ δὲ ὄνυξι καὶ ὁπλα⟨ῖ⟩ς ἐκαρτέρωσε. τὰ δὲ ἑρπετὰ ⌜εὐχαίτοις⌝

2 Lacunam post ἀξίᾳ signavit Wachsm. 4 Fortasse ἄνω θεοὶ ⟨δύο . . .⟩ 5 ψυχοταμίας Patrit.: ψυχοτομίας FP 6 Lacunam post ψυχῶν statuit Heeren: ψυχῶν ⟨οὐκέτι ἐνσεσωματωμένων τηρητής ἐστιν⟩ coni. Meineke: fortasse ⟨φύλαξ ἐστὶ τῶν ἄνω κατοικουσῶν⟩ ψυχῶν 7 ἀστολεύς P^1 | ἐνσωματουμένων scripsi: ἐνσωματωμένων FP: ἐνσεσωματωμένων Meineke et Wachsmuth: fortasse ⟨ἀεὶ⟩ ἐνσωματουμένων 8 προίησι Meineke: πρόεισι FP 9–10 Fortasse ὁμόλογος δὲ τούτοις, ὦ παῖ, καὶ τῇ ἄνω τῶν πραγμάτων ⟨οἰκονομίᾳ κατ'⟩ ἐπαλλαγὴν ⟨ἀντίστροφος⟩ ἐπὶ γῆς ἐστιν ἡ φύσις 10 ἐστιν ἡ P^2: ἐστι· μὴ FP^1 12 εἰς ἃ ἐμβάλλονται scripsi: εἰσβάλλονται (ἐν οἷς βάλλονται P^2 marg.) codd. | παραστᾶσι P | δυ' P 13 μνήμη (post μὲν) Patrit.: γνώμη FP 14 τηρῇ P: τηρεῖ F | περικρατεῖ F 16 παραδείγματος scripsi: φυράματος codd. | εἰκὼν γίγνηται scripsi (γίγνηται εἰκών Meineke): γίγνεται FP | Fortasse ⟨τὸ πλασσόμενον⟩ post γίγνηται 17 πρὸς ἀνάλογον codd.: fortasse πρὸς ἀναλογίαν vel [πρὸς] ἀνὰ λόγον 18 ἐνσωματισθῆναι scripsi (σωματισθῆναι Patrit.): σῶμα κτισθῆναι FP | ἐνεργεῖ P 18–19 ἐνεργῇ καὶ

according to the measure of their sins, even as it raises up from lower to higher divisions souls that are inferior in power and dignity, . . .[1]

* * * * *

. . . For there are . . .,[2] who are attendants of the Providence 3
that governs all. One of them is Keeper of souls; the other is Conductor of souls. The Keeper is he that has in his charge the unembodied souls; the Conductor is he that sends down to earth the souls that are from time to time embodied, and assigns to them their several places. And both he that keeps watch over the souls, and he that sends them forth, act in accordance with God's will.

. . . upon earth is Nature,[3] who is the maker of the mortal 4
frames, and fashioner of the vessels into which the souls are put. And Nature also[4] has at her side two Powers at work, namely, Memory and Skill. The task of Memory is to take care that Nature adheres to the type that has been established from the first,[5] and that the body which she fashions on earth is a copy of the pattern on high; and the task of Skill is to see that in each case the frame that is fashioned is conformable to the soul that comes down to be embodied in it,—to see that lively souls have lively bodies, and slow-moving souls slow-moving bodies; that energetic souls have energetic bodies, and sluggish souls sluggish bodies; that powerful souls have powerful bodies, and crafty souls crafty bodies; and in general, that every soul gets such a body as is suitable for it.

. . . For it is not without purpose that Nature has provided 5
birds with plumage, and has given force to quadrupeds by arming some with horns, and some with teeth, and some with claws or hoofs. And to the reptiles she has given soft bodies, flexible

[1] Perhaps, '⟨if they have lived good lives on earth⟩'.

[2] Perhaps, 'there are, in the world above, two gods'.

[3] Perhaps, 'And in agreement with these, my son, and working in reciprocation as a counterpart to the administration of things in the world above, is Nature upon earth'.

[4] I. e. as well as Providence. The two assistants of Nature on earth correspond to the two attendants of Providence on high.

[5] I. e. the race-type, the generic form of this or that kind of animal.

---

seclusit Wachsm. 19–23 *καὶ ταῖς μὲν ὀξέσι . . . κατὰ τὸ εἰκός* secludendum ? 21 *ἐνεργῇ* P[2] : *ἐναργῇ* FP[1] 24 *ἀσκόπως* FP[2] : *ἀσκέπτως* P[1] 26 *δὲ* (post *τετραπόδων*) P[2] : *μὲν* FP[1] 27 *ὀπλαῖς* P[2] : *ὀπλᾶς* F : *ὀπλᾶς* P[1] | *ἑκατέρωσε* P | *ἑρπετὰ* Heeren : *ἕρποντα* FP | *εὐχαίτοις* codd. : *εὐκάμπτοις* Meineke : 'fort. *ἀσχέτοις*' Wachsm. : fortasse *ἑλικτοῖς* vel *εἰκτικοῖς*

σώμασι καὶ [εὐ]ὑποχωρητ⟨ικ⟩οῖς ἐμαλάκυνε, καὶ ὅπως μὴ τῇ τοῦ σώματος ὑγρότητ⟨ι⟩ τέλεον ἀσθενῆ ⌜διαμένῃ⌝, ὧν μὲν τὰ στόματα [καὶ τοῖς] ὀδοῦσιν ἐχαράκωσεν, ὧν δὲ τοὺς ὄγκους αὐξήσασ⟨α⟩ δύναμιν περιέθηκεν. [οὕτως τὰ μὲν τῇ τοῦ θανάτου εὐλαβείᾳ ⟨. . .⟩ ἰσχυρότερα τῶν ἄλλων.] τὰ δὲ νηκτά, δειλὰ ὄντα, ἐνοικεῖν ἔδωκε στοιχείῳ ἐν ᾧ τὸ [φῶς] ⟨πῦρ⟩ οὐδετέραν ὧν ἔχει δυνάμεων ἐνεργεῖν ἰσχύει· ⟨ἐν⟩ γὰρ ὕδατι τὸ πῦρ οὔτε φαίνει οὔτε καίει· ἕκαστον δὲ αὐτῶν [ἢ φολίσιν ἢ ἀκάνθαις] ἐν ὕδατι νηχόμενον φεύγει ὅπῃ ἂν θέλῃ, τὴν ἰδίαν περιβεβλημένον δειλίαν, καὶ σκεπαστήριον ἔχον εἰς τὸ μὴ ὁρᾶσθαι τὸ ὕδωρ. ⟨⟨λογικὰ δὲ περισσαῖς καὶ ἀκριβεστέραις αἰσθήσεσιν ἐκόσμησε,⟩⟩ ⟨. . .⟩.

6 εἰς γὰρ ἕκαστον τῶν σωμάτων τούτων καθ' ὁμοιότητα ἐγκλείονται αἱ ψυχαί, ὥστε εἰς μὲν ἀνθρώπους χωρεῖν τὰς κριτικάς· εἰς δὲ πτηνὰ τὰς ⌜ἀπανθρώπους⌝· εἰς δὲ τετράποδα ⟨τὰς⟩ ⌜ἀκρίτους⌝, νόμος γὰρ ἐκείνοις ἐστὶν ἡ ἰσχύς· εἰς δὲ ἑρπετὰ τὰς δολίας, οὐδὲν γὰρ αὐτῶν ἐξ ἐναντίου ἐπεξέρχεται τοῖς ἀνθρώποις, λοχήσαντα δὲ καταβάλλει· εἰς δὲ [τὰ] νηκτὰ τὰς δειλάς, καὶ ὅσα⟨ι⟩ τῶν λοιπῶν στοιχείων ἀπολαύειν ἀνάξια⟨ι⟩ τυγχάν⟨ου⟩σι.

7 γίγνεται μὲν οὖν καὶ ἐν ἑκάστῳ ⟨γένει⟩ εὑρεῖν ζῷον τῇ ἰδίᾳ φύσει ⌜μὴ καταχρώμενον⌝.—Πῶς [πάλιν], ὦ τεκοῦσα; εἶπεν Ὧρος.—καὶ ἀπεκρίθη Ἶσις· Ὥστε ἄνθρωπον μέν, ὦ τέκνον, τὸ κριτικὸν ὑπερβῆναι, ⟨πτηνὸν δὲ . . .,⟩ τετράπουν δὲ τὴν ἀνάγκην παραλλάξαι, ἑρπετὸν δὲ τὸ δόλιον ἀπολέσαι, καὶ νηκτὸν τῆς δειλίας καταφρονῆσαι [καὶ πτηνὸν τῆς ἀπανθρωπίας ἐκπεσεῖν].

[[καὶ τὰ μὲν περὶ τῆς διαθέσεως τῶν ἄνω καὶ τῆς καταβάσεως αὐτῶν καὶ τῆς σωματουργίας τοσαῦτα.]]

8 συμβαίνει δέ, ὦ τέκνον, ἐν ἑκάστῳ εἴδει ⟨ἀνθρώπων⟩ εὑρίσκεσθαι [καὶ γένει τῶν προκειμένων] βασιλικάς τινας ψυχάς. [[καταβαίνειν δὲ καὶ ἄλλας ἀλλοίους, τὰς μὲν διαπύρου τὰς δὲ ψυχρὰς τὰς δὲ ὑπερηφάνους τὰς δὲ πραείας τὰς δὲ βαναύσους τὰς δὲ ἐμπείρους τὰς δὲ ἀπείρους τὰς δὲ ἀργὰς τὰς δὲ ἐνεργεῖς τὰς δὲ ἄλλο τι ἄλλως οὔσας. συμβαίνει δὲ τοῦτο

1 ὑποχωρητικοῖς scripsi : εὐυποχωρήτοις FP[2] : ἐνυποχωρήτοις P[1] | μὴ τῇ scripsi (μὴ ἡ Wachsm.) : μήτε FP 2 ὑγρότητι scripsi : ὑγρότης codd. | διαμένῃ codd. : fortasse γίνηται 3 καὶ τοῖς seclusi (an scribendum καρτεροῖς?) 4 αὐξήσασα scripsi : ὀξύνας codd. 4–5 οὕτως . . . ἄλλων seclusi ('haec aut manca aut interpolata' Wachsm.) 5 Fortasse εὐλαβείᾳ

and yielding; and that their pliancy may not make them utterly helpless, she has placed in the mouths of some of them a palisade of teeth, and has given strength to others by increasing their bulk. And the fishes, which are timid creatures, she has made to live in that element in which fire cannot put in action either of its two powers; for in water fire neither shines nor burns; and every fish, swimming in water, flees whither it will, protected by its own timidity, and having the water for a shelter to hide it from sight. But rational animals[1] Nature has equipped with senses more perfect and more accurate than those which she has given to other creatures, . . .

For the souls are shut up in bodies of this kind or that, each 6
soul in a body that is like it; so that those souls which possess the faculty of discernment enter human bodies; those which are flighty enter bird-bodies; those which are . . .[2] enter quadruped bodies, for quadrupeds obey no law but that of force; those which are crafty enter reptile bodies, for reptiles never attack men face to face, but lie in ambush, and so strike them down; and those which are timid, and all souls that are unworthy to enjoy the other elements,[3] enter fish-bodies.

But in each kind of living creatures may be found some that 7
do not act according to their natural dispositions.'—'Tell me, mother,' said Horus, 'what do you mean by that?'—Isis replied, 'A man, my son, may transgress the law laid down by his power of discernment; ⟨a bird may . . .;⟩ a quadruped may avoid compulsion; a reptile may lose its craftiness; and a fish may rise above its timidity.

And it comes to pass, my son, that in every class of men there 8

[1] I. e. men. [2] Perhaps, 'violent'.
[3] I. e. to live in any other element than water.

⟨ἀσφαλῆ, τὰ δὲ τῷ ὄγκῳ⟩ ἰσχυρότερα 5–6 Fortasse τοῖς δὲ νηκτοῖς, δειλοῖς οὖσιν, ἐνοικεῖν ἔδωκε⟨ν ἐκεῖνο τὸ⟩ στοιχεῖον 7 ἰσχύει· ἐν γὰρ Patrit.: ἰσχύειν γὰρ FP¹: ἰσχύει· καὶ γὰρ ἐν P² 9 φεύγῃ F 10–11 εἰς τὸ μὴ δρᾶσθαι secludendum? 15 ἀπανθρώπους codd.: ἀνεδράστους Usener (vide § 15) 16 τὰς (post τετράποδα) add. Heeren | ἀκρίτους codd.: fortasse ἀκρατεῖς 18 τὰ (ante νηκτὰ) del. Wachsm. 19 δειλίας P¹ | ὅσαι scripsi: ὅσα codd. | ἀπολαύει F 20 ἀνάξιαι τυγχάνουσι scripsi: ἀνάξια τυγχάνει codd. 21 γένει addidi (εἴδει add. Wachsm.) 22 μὴ καταχρώμενον codd.: μὴ καταρκούμενον Meineke: fortasse μηκέτι χρώμενον 25 ἑρπετὸν Wachsm.: ἑρπετὰ FP 28–29 καὶ τὰ . . . τοσαῦτα hinc ad § 13 *init.* transposui 30 ἑκάστῳ ἔδει P¹ 32-3 *infra*: καταβαίνειν . . . ψυχῆς hinc ad § 10 transposui

παρὰ τὴν τῶν τόπων θέσιν ὅθεν εἰς τὸ ἐνσωματισθῆναι καὶ θάλλονται αἱ ψυχαί. αἱ μὲν γὰρ ἀπὸ βασιλικοῦ διαζώματος
9 καταπηδῶσι τῆς ὁμοιοπάθους βασιλευούσης ψυχῆς.]] πολλαὶ γάρ εἰσι βασιλεῖαι· αἱ μὲν γάρ εἰσ⟨ι⟩ ⌜ψυχῶν αἱ δὲ σωμάτων,⌝ αἱ δὲ τέχνης ⟨κ⟩αὶ [δὲ] ἐπιστήμης, αἱ δὲ αὖ τῶν ⟨⟨καὶ [ἑαυ]τῶν⟩⟩. —Πῶς πάλιν; εἶπεν Ὧρος [[καὶ ἑαυτῶν]].—Οἷον, ὦ τέκνον Ὧρ⟨ε⟩, ἀπογεγονότων [ἤδη ψυχῶν] μὲν ⟨βασιλεὺς⟩ Ὄσιρις ὁ πατήρ σου, [σωμάτων] ⟨ζώντων⟩ δὲ ὁ ἑκάστου ἔθνους ἡγεμών· [βουλῆς δὲ ὁ πατὴρ πάντων·] καὶ καθηγητ⟨ικ⟩ῆς ὁ τρισμέγιστος Ἑρμῆς, ἰατρικῆς δὲ [ὁ] Ἀσκληπιὸς ὁ Ἡφαίστου. [ἰσχύος δὲ καὶ ῥώμης πάλιν Ὄσιρις, μεθ' ὅν, ὦ τέκνον, αὐτὸς σύ· φιλοσοφίας δὲ Ἀρνεβεσχῆνις· ποιητικῆς δὲ πάλιν [ὁ] Ἀσκληπιὸς ⟨ὁ καὶ⟩ Ἰμούθης.] καθόλου γάρ, ὦ τέκνον, εὑρήσεις, ἐὰν ἐξετάσῃς, πολλοὺς [καὶ] πολλῶν ἄρχοντας καὶ
10 πολλοὺς πολλῶν βασιλεύοντας. ἀλλ' ὁ μὲν πάντων κρατῶν, τέκνον, ἐκ τῆς ὑπεράνω χώρας ἐστίν, ο⟨ἱ⟩ δὲ τῶν κατὰ μέρος ⟨. . .⟩. ⌜ἐκείνην ἔσχε τὴν ἀφ' οὗ τόπου ἐστὶν βασιλικωτέραν⌝. ⟨⟨ϲυμβαίνει[ν] δὲ ⟨εὑρίσκεσθαι⟩ καὶ ἄλλας ἀλλοίας, τὰς μὲν διαπύρου⟨ς⟩ τὰς δὲ ψυχράς, τὰς δὲ ὑπερηφάνους τὰς δὲ πραείας [τὰς δὲ βαναύσους], τὰς δὲ ἐμπείρους τὰς δὲ ἀπείρους, [[τὰς δὲ ἀργὰς]] τὰς δὲ ἐνεργεῖς ⟨⟨τὰς δὲ ἀργάς⟩⟩, τὰς δὲ ⟨κατ'⟩ ἄλλο τι ἀλλοίας οὔσας· συμβαίνει δὲ ⟨καὶ⟩ τοῦτο παρὰ τὴν τῶν τόπων θέσιν ὅθεν εἰς τὸ ἐνσωματισθῆναι κα[ι]θάλλονται αἱ ψυχαί. οἱ μὲν γὰρ ἀπὸ βασιλικοῦ διαζώματος καταπηδήσ⟨α⟩ντες ⌜ὁμοιοπάθους⌝ βασιλεύουσιν [ψυχῆς]⟩⟩·
11 [[διαζώματος τετευχότες πυρὸς ἐργάται γίγνονται καὶ τροφῆς]] [οἱ δὲ ἀπὸ ὑγροῦ ἐν ὑγροῖς διαζώμασιν] οἱ δὲ ἀπὸ ἐπιστημονικοῦ καὶ τεχνικοῦ περὶ ἐπιστήμας καταγίγνονται καὶ τέχνας, ⟨οἱ δὲ ἀπὸ ἐνεργοῦς⟩ ⟨⟨διαζώματος ⟨κα⟩τεληλυθότες [πυρὸς] ἐργάται γίγνονται καὶ τροφεῖς,⟩⟩ οἱ δὲ ἀπὸ ἀργοῦ ἀργῶς καὶ ἐπιρρεμβῶς διαζῶσι. πάντων γὰρ τῶν ἐπὶ γῆς,

4 εἰσι Patrit. : εἰς FP | εἰς ψυχῶν αἱ δὲ σωμάτων codd. : fortasse εἰσιν ἰσχύος καὶ ῥώμης 5 καὶ (post τέχνης) scripsi : αἱ δὲ codd. | αἱ δὲ αὖ τῶν καὶ τῶν Usener : αἱ δὲ αὐτῶν FP 6 καὶ ἑαυτῶν (post Ὧρος) FP : del. Usener 7 Ὧρε Meineke : ὡς FP | ἀπογεγονότων Meineke : ἐπιγεγονότων FP | 'ὁ om. P' Wachsm. (sed utrum ὁ ante πατήρ an ὁ ante ἑκάστου, non liquet) 9 καθηγητικῆς scripsi : καθηγητὴς codd. 13 ὁ καὶ (ante Ἰμούθης) addidi (ὁ add. Patrit.) 14 ἐξετάσῃς Canter : ἐξετάζῃς codd. 14–15 ἄρχοντας καὶ πολλοὺς πολλῶν secludendum? 16 ὑπεράνω ⟨πάντων⟩? | οἱ δὲ scripsi : ὁ δὲ codd. | τῶν κάτω μέρος F 17 Fortasse ⟨ἐκ τόπων κατωτέρων⟩ post μέρος 18–25 συμβαίνει . . . βασιλεύουσιν ψυχῆς huc a § 8 transposui 18 συμβαίνει

are found some souls that are kingly. For there are many kinds 9
of kingship; there are kingships of . . .,[1] and kingships of art and science, and of divers other things also.'—'Again I ask,' said Horus, 'what you mean?'—*Isis*. 'For instance, my son, your father Osiris is king of men that have passed away, and the ruler of each nation is a king of living men; and thrice-greatest Hermes is king of the art of teaching; and Asclepius the son of Hephaestus is king of the art of medicine.[2] For, to speak generally, you will find, my son, if you look into the matter, that there are many who rule as kings, and many departments
over which they rule. But he who has mastery over all,[3] my son, 10
comes from the highest division of the atmosphere, and those who have mastery over this or that department . . .[4] And it comes to pass that other souls also[5] are found to differ in quality; some are fiery and some cold, some haughty and some meek, some skilful and some unskilful, some active and some inactive, and others differ in other ways. And these differences also result from the positions of the places whence the souls plunge down to be embodied. For those who have leapt down from a kingly
zone reign upon earth as kings; those who have come from 11
a zone of science and art are occupied with sciences and arts; those who have come from a zone of industry become workers, and provide food by their labour; and those who have come from a zone of inactivity live idle and desultory lives. For the

[1] Perhaps, 'of political power'.

[2] ['And Osiris again is king of might and strength, and after him you yourself, my son; and Har-neb-eschenis is king of philosophy; and Asclepius again, he who is also called Imuthes, is king of the art of poetry.']

[3] I. e. the supreme political ruler (e. g. the Roman emperor).

[4] Perhaps, '⟨come from places high up, but below the highest of all⟩'.

[5] I. e. others besides the kingly souls.

---

scripi : *καταβαίνειν* codd. | *ἀλλοίας* scripsi : *ἀλλοίους* codd. **19** *διαπύρους* P[2] : *διαπύρου* FP[1] | *διαπύρους τὰς δὲ ψυχρὰς τὰς δὲ* secludendum? **20** *τὰς δὲ βαναύσους* seclusi : ⟨*τὰς δὲ ἐλευθερίους*⟩ *τὰς δὲ βαναύσους* Meineke **22** *ἀλλοίας* scripsi : *ἄλλως* codd. **23–24** *καθάλλονται* Heeren : *καὶ θάλλονται* F : *καὶ βάλλονται* P[1] : *καταβάλλονται* P[2] **24** *οἱ μὲν* scripsi : *αἱ μὲν* codd. | *ἀποβατικοῦ* F **25** *καταπηδήσαντες* scripsi : *καταπηδῶσι τῆς* codd. | *βασιλεύουσιν* scripsi : *βασιλευούσης* F : *βασι* et lac. 5 litt. P[1] : *βασιλικῆς* P[2] **27** *διαζώμασιν* FP : *διαζῶσιν* Canter **28** *καὶ* (ante *τεχνικοῦ*) om. P | *τεχνικοῦ* scripsi (*τεχνιτικοῦ* Meineke) : *τεχνίτου* FP | *καταγίνονται* F : *γίγνονται* P **29** *κατεληλυθότες* scripsi : *τετευχότες* codd. **30** *τροφεῖς* Heeren : *τροφῆς* FP : fortasse ⟨*ἀνθρώπων*⟩ vel ⟨*πόλεων*⟩ *τροφεῖς*

ὦ τέκνον, [διὰ λόγου καὶ ἔργου πραττομένων] ἄνω εἰσὶν αἱ πηγαί, μέτρῳ καὶ σταθμῷ ἐπιχύνουσαι ἡμῖν τὰς ⌜οὐσίας⌝· καὶ οὐκ ἔστιν ὃ μὴ ἄνωθεν καταβέβηκε.
12 καὶ πάλιν ἀνέρχεται ⟨πάντα ἐκεῖσε ὅθεν⟩ [ἵνα] κατέβη. —Πῶς [πάλιν] λέγεις τοῦτο, ὦ τεκοῦσα; παράδειξον.—Καὶ ἀπεκρίθη Ἶσις [πάλιν]· Τῆς παλινδρομίας ἐναργὲς τοῦτο σημεῖον τοῖς ζῴοις ἐνέθηκεν ἡ ἱερωτάτη φύσις· τοῦτο γὰρ ὃ σπῶμεν ἄνωθεν ἐξ ἀέρος πνεῦμα, τοῦτο πάλιν ἄνω πέμπομεν, ⟨ὅθ⟩εν ἐλάβομεν. καὶ εἰσίν, ὦ τέκνον, τούτου τοῦ ἐνεργήματος τεχνίτιδες ἐν ἡμῖν φῦσαι· αἳ ἐπειδὰν μύσωσι τὰ δεκτικὰ [ἑαυτῶν] τοῦ πνεύματος στόματα, τότε ⟨αὐτοὶ⟩ ἡμεῖς οὐκέτι ὧδέ ἐσμεν, ἀλλ' ἀναβεβήκαμεν.

13 ⟨⟨καὶ τὰ μὲν περὶ τῆς διαθέσεως τῶν ἄνω καὶ τῆς καταβάσεως αὐτῶν [καὶ τῆς σωματουργίας] τοσαῦτα.⟩⟩ προσεπιγίγνεται δέ, ὦ παῖ μεγαλόδοξε, καὶ ἕτερά τινα ἡμῖν ἐκ τῆς τοῦ φυράματος συσταθμίας.—Τί δέ ἐστιν, Ὧρος εἶπε, τὸ φύραμα τοῦτο, ὦ τεκοῦσα;—Σύνοδός ἐστι καὶ κρᾶσις τῶν τεσσάρων στοιχείων, ἐξ ἧς [κράσεως καὶ συνόδου] ἀναθυμιᾶταί τις ἀτμός, ὃς περιειλεῖται μὲν τῇ ψυχῇ, διατρέχει δὲ ἐν ⟨τῷ⟩ σώματι, ἀμφοτέροις μεταδιδοὺς [τουτέστι τῷ σώματι καὶ τῇ ψυχῇ] τῆς ἰδίας ποιότητος· καὶ οὕτως αἱ διαφοραὶ τῶν ψυχικῶν καὶ σωματικῶν ⌜ἐναλλοιώσεων⌝
14 γίνονται. εἰ μὲν γὰρ κατὰ τὴν σωματικὴν ⌜διάπηξιν⌝ πλεονάσειε τὸ πῦρ, τὸ τηνικαῦτα ἡ ψυχὴ θερμὴ τὴν φύσιν ὑπάρχουσα καὶ ἕτερον θερμὸν προσλαβοῦσα [ἐκπυρωδεστέρα γενομένη] ποιεῖ τὸ ζῷον ἐνεργότερον καὶ θυμικόν [τὸ δὲ
15 σῶμα ὀξὺ καὶ εὐκίνητον]. εἰ δὲ πλεονάσειεν ὁ ἀήρ, τὸ τηνικαῦτα [καὶ] κοῦφον καὶ πηδητικὸν καὶ ἀνέδραστον γίνεται

1 *πραττομένων* scripsi : *πραγμάτων* codd. 2 *ἡμῶν* F | *οὐσίας* codd. : fortasse *ἀπορροίας* 4 *κατέβη* scripsi : *καταβῇ* codd. 5 *παράδειξον* secludendum? 6 *ἐνεργὲς* F 7 *ἐνέθεικεν* F 7–8 *ὃ σπῶμεν* Wachsm. (*ὃ πνέομεν* Heeren : *ᾧ ζῶμεν* Meineke) : *ὡς τὸ μὲν* P : *ὡς τὸ μὴ* F 8 *τοῦτο* codd. : *τὸ αὐτὸ* Usener 9 *ὅθεν ἐλάβομεν* scripsi : *ἵνα λάβωμεν* codd. 10 *τεχίτιδες* P[1] | *μύσωσι* Canter : *μισῶσι* FP 11 *δεκτηκὰ* P 13–14 *καὶ τὰ . . . τοσαῦτα* huc a § 7 *fin.* transposui 14 *αὐτῶν* codd. : fortasse *τῶν ψυχῶν* 16 *ἐκ τῆς* scripsi (*ἐκτὸς ⟨τῆς⟩* Wachsm.) : *ἐκτὸς* codd. 17 *τοῦτο ὦ* P : *τοῦτ' οὖν* F 19–23 Fortasse *ὃς περιειλεῖται [μὲν] τῇ ψυχῇ, [διατρέχει δὲ ἐν ⟨τῷ⟩ σώματι, ἀμφοτέροις] μεταδιδοὺς ⟨αὐτῇ⟩ [τουτέστι τῷ σώματι καὶ τῇ ψυχῇ] τῆς ἰδίας ποιότητος· καὶ οὕτως αἱ διαφοραὶ τῶν ψυχ[ικ]ῶν [καὶ σωματικῶν ἐναλλοιώσεων] γίνονται* 19 *ὃς περιειλεῖται* P[2] : *ὡσπερεί· εἱλεῖται* F : *ὥσπερὰ εἱλεῖται* P[1] 20 *τῷ* add. Wachsm.

sources of all earthly things, my son, are on high; those sources pour forth . . .[1] upon us by fixed measure and weight; and there is nothing that has not come down from above.

And all things go back again to the place whence they have 12
come down.'—*Horus.* 'What do you mean by that, mother? Give me an example.' Isis answered, 'A manifest sign of this return of things to their source has been placed in living beings by most holy Nature. Our life-breath, which we draw from above out of the air, we send up again to the place whence we received it. We have in us bellows-like organs, my son, by which this work is done; and when these organs have closed the apertures through which the life-breath is taken in, then we ourselves abide no longer here below, but have gone up on high.[2]

Of the arrangement of the things above, and of their descent[3] 13
to earth, I have now said enough. But there are added to us, my glorious son, other qualities also, which result from the proportions in which things are combined in the mingled mass of the body.'[4]—'But tell me, mother,' said Horus, 'what is this "mingled mass"?'—*Isis.* 'It is a combination and mixture of the four elements; and from it there is exhaled a vapour, which envelops the soul, and is diffused in the body, imparting to both something of its own quality; and thus are produced both the differences between one soul and another, and the differences
between one body and another.[5] If there is an excess of 14
fire in the composition of the body, in that case the soul, being hot by nature and having more heat added to it, makes
the living creature more active[6] and spirited. If there is an 15
excess of air, in that case the creature comes to be light and

[1] Perhaps, 'their influences'.
[2] I. e. we are dead, and our souls have returned to their places in the atmosphere.
[3] Perhaps, 'of the descent of the souls'.
[4] I. e. the proportions of the several elements of which the body is composed.
[5] Perhaps, 'a vapour, which envelops the soul, and imparts to it something of its own quality; and thus are produced the differences between one soul and another'.
[6] Perhaps, 'in that case [ ] the living creature is made more active'.

20–21 *τουτέστι . . . ψυχῇ* seclusit Meineke 22 *καὶ* (post *ψυχικῶν*) F: *καὶ τῶν* P | *ἐναλλοιώσεων* codd.: fortasse *ποιοτήτων* 23 *αἱ μὲν γὰρ* P¹ | *διάπηξιν* codd.: potius esset *σύγκρασιν* vel *σύστασιν* 24–26 *τὸ τηνικαῦτα . . . γενομένη* secludendum, et legendum *ποιεῖ⟨ται⟩ τὸ ζῷον*? 25 *προσλαμβοῦσα* P 26 *γενομένη* Patrit.: *γεναμένη* FP | *ἐνεργότερον* P²: *ἐπεργότερον* FP¹ | *καὶ θυμικόν* om. P

16 τὸ ζῷον καὶ ψυχῇ καὶ σώματι. εἰ δὲ τὸ ὕδωρ πλεονάσειε, τὸ
τηνικαῦτα [καὶ] τὸ ζῷον τῇ μὲν ψυχῇ γίγνεται εὔ[χ]ρουν [καὶ
εὐφυὲς] καὶ εὐπερίχυτον, ἱκανῶς τε τοῖς ἄλλοις ἐπιπεσεῖν
καὶ κολληθῆναι δυνάμενον, διὰ τὸ πρὸς τὰ ἄλλα [ἑνωτικὸν
καὶ] κοινωνικὸν τοῦ ὕδατος· [ἐφιζάνει] ⟨ἑνοῦται⟩ γὰρ πᾶσι, καὶ
πολὺ μὲν ὂν ⟨⟨καὶ περιλαβὸν⟩⟩ εἰς ἑαυτὸ[ν] ἀναλύει [[καὶ
περιλαμβάνει]], ὀλίγον δ' ὑπάρχον καὶ καταδὺ[σα]ν ἐκεῖνο
γίγνεται ᾧ ἐμίγη. τὰ μέντοι σώματα ὑπὸ τῆς πλαδαρότητος
καὶ χαυνότητος εἰς περίσφιγξιν οὐ ⟨συ⟩νάγεται, ἀλλὰ μικρᾷ
τινι [νόσου] ἀφορμῇ λύεται [καὶ τοῦ ἰδίου συνδέσμου κατ'
17 ὀλίγον ἐκπίπτει]. εἰ δὲ τὸ γεῶδες πλεονάσειε, τὸ τηνικαῦτα
ἀμβλεῖα [μὲν] τοῦ ζῴου ἡ ψυχὴ γίνεται, οὐκ ἔχουσα τὴν
[σωματικὴν] ⟨ἰδίαν⟩ ἀραιότητα εὔλυτον, [οὐδὲ ⸢τοῦ δι' οὗ⸣
⟨ἐκ⟩πηδῆσαι ⟨δύνα⟩ται, πεπαχυ⟨σ⟩μένων τῶν αἰσθητικῶν
μερῶν, ἀλλ' ἔνδον μένει παρ' ἑαυτῇ,] ⟨ἀλλὰ⟩ ὑπὸ [βάρους καὶ]
⟨τῆς⟩ πυκνότητος ⟨τοῦ . . .⟩ πεδηθεῖσα· τὸ δὲ σῶμα στερεὸν
μέν, ἀλλὰ ἀργὸν καὶ βαρύ, καὶ μετὰ βίας ὑπὸ τῆς προαιρέ-
18 σεως μετακινούμενον. εἰ δὲ σύμμετρος γένοιτο ἡ πάντων
⟨σύ⟩στασις, τότε τὸ ζῷον θερμὸν ⟨μὲν⟩ εἰς πρᾶξιν, κοῦφον δὲ
εἰς κίνησιν, ⸢εὔκρατον⸣ δὲ εἰς ⸢ἀφήν⸣, ⸢γενναῖον⸣ δὲ εἰς πῆξιν
27 κατασκευάζεται. ⟨⟨[αὐ]τὸ μὲν γὰρ [τὸ] γεῶδές ἐστιν ἡ τοῦ
σώματος πῆξις, τὸ δὲ ὑγρὸν ἡ ἐν τούτῳ ἐστὶν εἰς ⸢συμπαγίαν⸣
περίχυσις, τὸ [γὰρ] ⟨δὲ⟩ ἀερῶδές ἐστι τὸ ἐν ἡμῖν κινητικόν,
καὶ τούτων πάντων διεγερτικὸν τὸ πῦρ.⟩⟩

19 ὅσα οὖν [τῷδε τῷ λόγῳ] κεκοινώνηκε πλείονος μὲν πυρὸς καὶ πνεύματος, ⟨ὀλίγου δὲ ὕδατος καὶ γῆς,⟩ ταῦτα ἀπωρνέωται, καὶ ἄνω παρ'
20 ἐκείνοις πολιτεύεται τοῖς στοιχείοις ἐξ ὧν καὶ ἐγένετο. ὅσα δὲ πλείονος
μὲν πυρός, ὀλίγου δὲ πνεύματος, ὕδατος δὲ ⟨μετρίου⟩ καὶ γῆς ἴσης, ταῦτα

2 μὲν (vel τῇ μὲν ψυχῇ) secludendum? | εὔρουν Meineke: εὔχρουν FP | καὶ (ante εὐφυὲς) P: τε καὶ F 3–4 ἐπιπεσεῖν καὶ secludendum? 5 καὶ κοινωνικὸν om. P 6 ἑαυτὸ P²: ἑαυτὸν FP¹ 7 ὑπάρχειν P¹ | καταδὺν scripsi ('num καταδυθὲν?' Wachsm.): καταδῦσαν FP¹: καταδύσον P² 8 πλαδωρότητος P¹ 9 οὐ συνάγεται scripsi: οὖν ἄγεται FP¹: ἴσως οὐκ ἄγεται P² marg. 10 συνδέσ P¹ 10–11 καὶ τοῦ ἰδίου . . . ἐκπίπτει seclusi (an secludendum τὰ μέντοι σώματα . . . ἐκπίπτει?) 13 τοῦ δι' οὗ codd.: fortasse τοῦ ἰδίου ⟨τόπου?⟩ 14 ἐκπηδῆσαι δύναται scripsi: πηδήσεται codd. | Post πηδήσεται add ‡ οὐκ ἔχουσα τὴν σωματικὴν ἀραιότητα ‡ P | πεπαχυμμένων Wachsm.: πεπαχυμένων FP 15 μερῶν Usener: μελῶν FP: fortasse ⟨τοῦ σώματος⟩ μερῶν 16 Fortasse πυκνότητος ⟨τοῦ ἀτμοῦ vel τοῦ φυράματος⟩ 16–18 τὸ δὲ σῶμα . . . μετακινούμενον secludendum? 19 σύστασις Meineke: στάσις FP 20 εὔκρατον δὲ εἰς ἀφήν codd.: fortasse εὐπερίχυτον (vel εὔρυτον) δὲ εἰς συναφήν | γενναῖον codd.: fortasse στερεὸν | δὲ εἰς πῆξιν P²: διαθῆξιν FP¹ 21–24 § 27 (τὸ μὲν

flighty and unsteady in soul and body alike. If there is an excess 16
of water, the result is that the creature's soul flows freely and
diffuses itself readily, and is highly capable of flinging itself
on things and cleaving to them, because water has the power
of associating with things. For water unites with all things;
and when there is much water, and it envelops a thing,[1] then
it dissolves that thing into itself; but when there is only a little
water, and it sinks into the thing,[2] then it is transmuted into
that with which it is mingled. And such bodies,[3] being flaccid
and spongy, are not tightly knitted together; a little thing is
enough to cause their dissolution. If there is an excess of the 17
earthy element, in that case the result is that the creature's soul
is dull, because, though the soul itself is a thing of rare consistency, it cannot easily get free,[4] but is hampered by the density
of . . . ;[5] and the body is solid, but inert and heavy, and cannot
be put in motion by the will without a strong effort. But if all 18
the four elements are combined together in fit proportions, then
the creature is so made as to be ardent in action, light of
movement, . . . in . . . ,[6] and solid in structure. For the earthy 27
element is that which makes the body solid; the watery element
is that in it which makes it diffuse itself so as to unite with
things; the airy element is that in us which causes movement;
and all these are roused to action by the fire in us.

All creatures then[7] that have had assigned to them large portions of fire 19
and air, and small portions of water and earth, have become birds; and they
live their lives on high, in the region of those elements of which they are
chiefly made. All those that have had put into them much fire, a little air, 20
and a moderate portion of water and of earth, have become men. And in

[1] For instance, when a lump of earth is thrown into a large tank of water.

[2] For instance, when a drop of water falls on a large mass of earth.

[3] I. e. human or animal bodies in which there is an excess of water.

[4] The Greek which I have here cut out is probably an appended note to this effect: 'the soul cannot leap forth from its seat within the body, because the bodily sense-organs (through which alone an embodied soul can go out to communicate with the external world) are thick and dense; (and so) it remains within and stays by itself.'

[5] Perhaps, 'the density ⟨of the body⟩', or 'the density ⟨of the vapour exhaled from the mingled mass of the body⟩'.

[6] Perhaps, 'apt to flow forth so as to unite with things'.

[7] This paragraph (§§ 19–23) is inconsistent with what precedes, and must have been written by another person.

γὰρ . . . τὸ πῦρ) huc transposui | *τὸ μὲν γὰρ* scripsi : *αὐτὸ μὲν γὰρ τὸ* codd. **22** *συμπαγίαν* codd.: fortasse *συναφὴν* **23** *δὲ* (ante *ἀερῶδές*) Meineke : *γὰρ* FP **24** *διενεργητικὸν* P **27** Fortasse ⟨*τὸ πλέον*⟩ *ἐγένετο*

ἀπηνθρώπισται· καὶ τῷ ζῴῳ τὸ περισσὸν τοῦ θερμοῦ εἰς σύνεσιν ἐτράπη.
ὁ γὰρ ἐν ἡμῖν νοῦς θερμόν τι χρῆμά ἐστιν, ὃ καίειν μὲν οὐκ οἶδε, διαδύνει
21 δὲ [κατὰ] ⟨διὰ⟩ πάντων [καὶ ἐπίσταται]. ὅσα δὲ πλείονος μὲν ὕδατος,
πλείονος δὲ γῆς, [μετρίου δὲ] ⟨⟨ὀλίγου δὲ⟩⟩ πνεύματος καὶ [[ὀλίγου δὲ]]
πυρός, ταῦτα ⟨ἀπο⟩τεθηρίωται· τῇ δὲ τοῦ θερμοῦ παρ[ι]ουσίᾳ ἀλκιμώτερα
22 γέγονε τῶν ἄλλων. ὅσα δὲ γῆς ⟨μὲν⟩ καὶ ὕδατος [ἴσων] ⟨πλείονος⟩
κεκοινώνηκε, ⟨πνεύματος δὲ μετρίου, πυρὸς δὲ οὐδενός,⟩ ταῦτα ἀφηρ-
π⟨έτ⟩ωται· καὶ τῇ ⟨μὲν⟩ τοῦ πυρὸς στερήσει ἄτολμα γέγονε καὶ ἀπαρρη-
σίαστα, τῇ δὲ τοῦ ὕδατος [[κοινωνίᾳ]] ⟨περιουσίᾳ⟩ [ψ] ὑγρὰ ἐγένετο, τῇ δὲ
τῆς γῆς βαρέα καὶ νωθρά, τῇ δὲ τοῦ πνεύματος ⟨⟨κοινωνίᾳ⟩⟩ ⌜εὐκίνητα εἰ
23 προαιρέσει τὸ κινεῖσθαι⌝. ὅσα δὲ πλείονος μὲν ὑγροῦ, ὀλίγου δὲ ξηροῦ,
⟨πυρὸς δὲ καὶ πνεύματος οὐδενός,⟩ ταῦτα ἀπιχθύωται· καὶ τῇ μὲν τοῦ
θερμοῦ καὶ ἀέρος στερήσει δειλά ἐστι καὶ ⟨κατ⟩αδυτ⟨ικ⟩ά, τῇ δὲ τοῦ
ὑγροῦ περιουσίᾳ καὶ τῇ τοῦ γεώδους παρ[ι]ουσίᾳ ἐν ⌜λελυμένῃ γῇ καὶ⌝
ὕδατι διὰ τὸ συγγενὲς κατοικεῖ.

24 ⌜καὶ πρὸς μὲν τὴν τοῦ ἑκάστου στοιχείου μοῖραν καὶ τῆς μοίρας τὴν περιοχὴν καὶ τὰ σώματα ἡλικιάζεται καὶ πρὸς τὴν ὀλιγομετρίαν τὰ λοιπὰ ζῷα μεμετροποίηται πρὸς ἐνέργειαν τὴν ἑκάστῳ τῶν στοιχείων οὐσιομετρίας⌝.

25 καὶ ἔτι ⟨τόδε⟩, ὦ παῖ περιπόθητε, λέγω, ὅτι [ἐκ ταύτης τῆς οὕτω συστάσεως] [ἡ κατὰ τὴν πρώτην σύνοδον γενομένη κρᾶσις καὶ ὁ ἐκ ταύτης ἀναθυμιώμενος ἀτμός] ἐφ᾽ ὅσον ⟨μὲν τὸ φύραμα⟩ τὴν ἰδίαν τηρεῖ ποιότητα, ὥστε τὸ μὲν [θερμὸν] ⟨πῦρ⟩ ἕτερον μὴ λαβεῖν θερμόν, [καὶ] ⟨μηδὲ⟩ τὸ [[ἀερῶδες]] πνεῦμα ἕτερον ⟨⟨ἀερῶδες⟩⟩, μηδὲ τὸ ὑγρὸν ἑτέραν ὑγρασίαν, μηδὲ τὸ γεῶδες ἑτέραν πυκνότητα, τὸ τηνικαῦτα τὸ ζῷον ὑγιαίνει· ἐπὰν [γὰρ] ⟨δὲ⟩ μὴ οὕτως μένῃ, ὦ τέκνον, ἐφ᾽ οἷς ἔσχεν ἐξ ἀρχῆς μέτροις, ἀλλ᾽ ἤτοι πλεονάσῃ τούτω⟨ν τι

3 διὰ Gaisford: κατὰ codd. 5 ταῦτ᾽ ἀποτεθηρίωται Meineke: ταῦτα τεθηρίωται FP²: ταῦτε θηρίωται P¹ | παρουσίᾳ scripsi: περιουσίᾳ codd. 6 ὕδατος ἴσον P 7–8 ἀφηρπέτωται Wachsm. (ἀφηρπετώθη Meineke): ἐφειρπώθη FP 9 ὑγρὰ scripsi: ψυχρὰ codd. 10–11 εἰ ⟨ἐν⟩ προαιρέσει Meineke (an εἴ ⟨ποτε⟩ προαιρεῖται κινεῖσθαι?) 13 καταδυτικά scripsi: ἄδυτα FP: αὐτὰ Usener: ἀδύνατα Meineke 14 παρουσίᾳ (post γεώδους) Wachsm.: περιουσίᾳ codd. 14–15 ἐν λελυμένῃ γῇ καὶ ὕδατι codd.: fortasse ἐν ὕδατι διαλελυμένην ἔχοντι γῆν vel simile quid 16–19 Fortasse huiusmodi aliquid: καὶ πρὸς μὲν τὴν [τοῦ] ἑκάστου στοιχείου μοῖραν καὶ τῆς μοίρας τὴν ⟨ὑ⟩περ[ι]οχὴν ⟨αἵ τε ψυχαὶ⟩ καὶ τὰ σώματα ⌜ἡλικιάζεται⌝ (ἠλλοίωται?) ⟨τῶν ἀνθρώπων⟩, καὶ πρὸς τὴν ὀλιγομοιρίαν· (an hinc transponenda verba καὶ πρὸς τὴν ὀλιγομοιρίαν et post τῆς μοίρας τὴν ὑπεροχὴν collocanda?) τὰ ⟨δὲ⟩ λοιπὰ ζῷα ⌜μεμετρο⌝ (ἀσύμμετρα?) ποιεῖται πρὸς ⌜ἐνέργειαν⌝ (ἀναλογίαν?) τῆ⟨ς ἐ⟩ν ἑκάστῳ (sc. ζῴῳ vel ζῴων γένει) τῶν ⟨ἀνωφερῶν?⟩ στοιχείων ὀλιγομοιρίας 19 οὐσιομετρίας F: οὐσιομετρίαν P 20–21 For-

man, the excess of the hot element has been turned into intelligence. For the mind in us is a hot thing; it has no power to burn, but it penetrates all things. All creatures that have in their composition much water, much 21
earth, and a little air and fire, have become four-footed beasts; and the presence of the hot element in them[1] makes them more pugnacious than the other animals.[2] All those that have had put into them much earth and water, 22
a moderate portion of air, and no fire, have become reptiles. The absence of fire causes them to be lacking in boldness and openness; the excess of water makes them soft and supple;[3] the excess of earth makes them heavy and sluggish; and the fact that they have some air in them makes them . . .[4]
All those that have in them much of the fluid element, a little of the dry 23
element, no fire, and no air, have become fishes. The absence of fire and air makes them timid, and apt to dive into the depths;[5] and the excess of the fluid element and the presence in them of some earth cause them to live in water that has some earth dissolved in it, by reason of their affinity to these two elements.

* * * * * *[6] 24

And this also I tell you, my well-beloved son, that as long as 25
the mingled mass of the body keeps its own quality unchanged,—as long as the fire in it receives no access of heat, the air no access of anything of airy nature, the water no access of fluid, and the earthy element no access of density,—so long the creature is in health; but when it does not keep unchanged the original proportions of its several elements, but one of them is either increased or diminished,—I do not mean an increase

[1] I. e. the fact that they have in them some fire, though only a little.

[2] I. e. than those that still remain to be spoken of, viz. the reptiles and the fishes.

[3] More literally, 'fluid' or 'yielding to pressure'. (The MSS. give 'cold'.)

[4] Perhaps, 'makes them capable of moving easily (or quickly) if at any time they choose to move'.

[5] They tend downward, because they have in their composition no portion of either of the two light and 'upward-tending' elements.

[6] § 24: possibly, 'And the souls and bodies of men vary according to the apportionment of each element, and according as the portion assigned is in excess or is deficient; but the lower animals are so made that they are unevenly adjusted, and more or less so in proportion to the deficiency of the upward-tending elements (fire and air) in the composition of each kind of animal'. If this, or something like it, was the meaning, § 24 may have been intended to stand next after §§ 18 and 27.

---

tasse *ἐκ* [*ταύτης*] *τῆς* ⟨*τ*⟩*ούτω*⟨*ν*⟩ *συστάσεως* (an *τῆς οὕτω* ⟨*γενομένης*⟩ *συστάσεως*?) **21–22** *ἡ κατὰ . . . ἀτμὸς* seclusi (vide § 28 *init.*) **23** *τηρεῖ ποιότητα* scripsi: *τηροῦσιν ἰδιότητα* codd. **24** *μηδὲ* Meineke: *καὶ* FP **25** *ὑγρασίαν* P²: *ἐργασίαν* FP¹ **27** *δὲ* P²: *γὰρ* FP¹ | *οὕτως* secludendum? **28** *ἔσχεν* om. F | *τούτων τι ἢ ἐλαττωθῇ* scripsi: *ταῦτα* codd.

ἢ ἐλαττωθῇ⟩, οὐκ ⸢ἐνεργείᾳ [λ] λέγω τὴν περιοχήν⸣, οὐδὲ τῇ κατ' αὔξησιν γινομένῃ μεταβολῇ [τοῦ γένους καὶ] τῶν σωμάτων, ἀλλὰ τῇ [ὡς προέφημεν] συστατικῇ τῶν στοιχείων κράσει, ὥστε τὸ μὲν θερμὸν ἐπὶ πλέον αὐξηθῆναι ἢ [ἐπὶ πλέον] ἐλαττωθῆναι, τὰ δὲ ἄλλα ὁμοίως, ⟨τὸ⟩ τηνικαῦτα [οὕτως] νο⟨σ⟩εῖ τὸ ζῷον.

26 [ἐπὰν γὰρ οὕτως διατεθῇ τό τε θερμὸν καὶ τὸ ἀερῶδες, ἃ δὴ σύσκηνά ἐστι τῆς ψυχῆς, τότε ἐν ⸢ἀλληγορίαις⸣ καὶ ἐκστάσεσι γίγνεται τὸ ζῷον.]

[πεπύκνωται γὰρ τὰ στοιχεῖα δι' ὧν διαφθείρεται τὰ σώματα.]

27 [[αὐτὸ μὲν γὰρ τὸ γεῶδές ἐστιν ἡ τοῦ σώματος πῆξις, τὸ δὲ ὑγρὸν ἡ ἐν τούτῳ ἐστὶν εἰς συμπαγίαν περίχυσις, τὸ γὰρ ἀερῶδές ἐστι τὸ ἐν ἡμῖν κινητικόν, καὶ τούτων πάντων διεγερτικὸν τὸ πῦρ.]]

28 ὥσπερ οὖν ὁ ἐκ τῆς πρώτης συνόδου καὶ κράσεως τῶν στοιχείων γιγνόμενος ἀτμός [καὶ ὡσανεὶ ἔξαψις καὶ ἀναθυμίασις], ὁποῖος [ε]ἂν ᾖ, παραμιγεὶς τῇ ψυχῇ, ἄγει [ε]αὐτὴν εἰς ἑαυτόν, [ὡς ἂν ἔχῃ φύσεως, εἴτε σπουδαίως εἴτε μή], ⟨οὕτω
29 καὶ . . .⟩. τῇ ⟨μὲν⟩ γὰρ ἐξ ἀρχῆς ⟨. . .⟩ [πρὸς αὐτὸν οἰκειότητι καὶ συντροφίᾳ] ἐπιμένουσα ἡ ψυχὴ τὴν τάξιν διατηρεῖ· ὅταν δὲ ἐπιπροσγένηται ἤτοι τῷ ὅλῳ συγκράματι ἢ καὶ [μέρεσιν ἢ] μέρει ⟨τινὶ⟩ αὐτοῦ ἔξωθέν τις πλεία⟨ν⟩ μοῖρα τοῦ προκαταβεβλημένου, ⟨τό⟩τε ⟨⟨μεταλλοιούμενος⟩⟩ [[καὶ]] ὁ ἐντεῦθεν [[μεταλλοιούμενος]] ⟨γιγνόμενος⟩ ἀτμὸς μεταλλοιοῖ ⟨⟨καὶ⟩⟩ [ἤτοι] τὴν τῆς ψυχῆς διάθεσιν [ἢ τὴν τοῦ σώματος].

30 [τὸ ⟨μὲν⟩ γὰρ πῦρ καὶ τὸ πνεῦμα, ἀνωφερῆ ὄντα, ἐπὶ τὴν ψυχήν, ὁμ[οι]όχωρον αὐτοῖς ὑπάρχουσαν, ἀνατρέχει, τὸ δὲ ὑγρὸν καὶ τὸ γεῶδες, κατωφερῆ ὄντα, τῷ σώματι, ὁμοέδρῳ ὄντι, ἐφιζάνει].

1 ἐνεργείᾳ λέγω Canter: ἐνεργεῖ ἀλλ' ἐγὼ FP[1]: οἶμαι οὐ λέγω P[2] marg. | Fortasse οὐ τῇ τοῦ περιέχοντος ἐνεργείᾳ λέγω 3 Fortasse ἀλλὰ τῇ [ ] συστάσει καὶ ⟨⟨κράσει⟩⟩ τῶν στοιχείων | προέφημεν FP: προέφαμεν Patrit. 5 τὸ add. Meineke 6 οὕτως seclusit Meineke | νοσεῖ P[2]: νοεῖ FP[1] 10–11 Fortasse πεπύκνωται γὰρ ⟨. . .⟩ τὰ ⟨κατωφερῆ⟩ στοιχεῖα ⟨. . . νόσοι ?⟩ δι' ὧν διαφθείρεται τὰ σώματα 12–15 § 27 (αὐτὸ . . . πῦρ) hinc transposui: vide post § 18 18 ἂν Heeren: ἐὰν FP | ὁποῖος ἂν ᾖ seclusit Wachsm. | αὐτὴν Meineke:

or diminution caused by the operation of the environment,[1] nor by that change in bodies which takes place in the course of growth,[2] but an increase or diminution that results from an alteration in the mixing of the elements of which the body is composed,—when, I say, the hot element, or one of the other elements, is increased or diminished, then the creature is diseased.

Now just as the vapour that is produced by the first coming **28**
together and mixing of the elements in the body, whatever the quality of that vapour may be, mingles with the soul and assimilates it to itself, even so . . .[3] As long as the soul continues **29**
to be in its original condition, it maintains its good order unimpaired; but when either the mixed mass as a whole, or some one part of it,[4] receives, by subsequent addition from without, a portion of one of the elements larger than that which was originally assigned to it, then there is an alteration in the vapour thence produced, and the altered vapour alters the condition of the soul.'[5]

[1] E. g. such an increase in the heat of the body as takes place when a man warms himself before a fire.

[2] When the body grows, the *quantity* of each of the elements of which it is composed increases: but in healthy growth, the *proportions* of the several elements to one another remain unaltered.

[3] Perhaps, '⟨even so every alteration in the quality of the vapour causes a corresponding alteration in the quality of the soul⟩'.

[4] There may, for instance, be an increase of fire in some one limb or organ of the body; there would then be inflammation of that limb or organ.

[5] § 30, which here follows in the MSS., appears to be an extract from another document; and it is possible that § 26 is another fragment of that same document. The two together might be translated thus:

§ 26: 'For when the hot element and the airy element, which are lodged in the same habitation as the soul, are put into this condition, then the living being falls into (distraction?), and comes to be beside itself. . . .' § 30: 'For the fire and the air, being upward-tending elements, run up to the soul, the place of which is the same as (or 'is similar to') their place; but the fluid element and the earthy element, being downward-tending elements, settle down on the body, the abode of which is the same as (or 'is similar to') their abode'.

ἑαυτὴν FP 19 *σπουδαίως* Usener : *σπουδαῖος* FP 20 Fortasse *ἐξ ἀρχῆς* ⟨*διαθέσει*⟩ 20–21 *πρὸς αὑτὸν ἰδιότητι* F 21 *τάξιν* codd. : fortasse *εὐταξίαν* 23 *πλείων* Patrit. : *πλείω* FP 24 *τότε* Meineke : *τὲ* FP 28 *ὁμόχωρον* scripsi : *ὁμοιόχωρον* codd. 29–30 *ὁμοέδρῳ ὄντι* scripsi : *ὁμοιέδρῳ ὄντι* P[2] : *ἐμῶεδρόοντι* FP[1]

EXCERPTUM XXVII

Stobaeus 3. 13. 65, vol. iii, p. 467 Hense (13. 50 Meineke).

Ἑρμοῦ ἐκ τοῦ Ἴσιδος πρὸς Ὧρον.

ἔλεγχος γὰρ ἐπιγνωσθείς, ὦ μέγιστε βασιλεῦ, εἰς ⌜ἐπιθυμίαν⌝ φέρει τὸν ἐλεγχθέντα ὧν πρότερον οὐκ ᾔδει.

EXCERPTUM XXVIII

Stobaeus 1. 1. 29 a, vol. i, p. 34 Wachsmuth.

Θαλῆς, ἐρωτηθεὶς τί πρεσβύτατον τῶν ὄντων, ἀπεκρίνατο· Θεός, ἀγέννητον γάρ.

Σωκράτης, ἐρωτηθεὶς τί θεός, εἶπε· Τὸ ἀθάνατον καὶ ἀΐδιον.

Ἑρμῆς, ἐρωτηθεὶς τί θεός, εἶπεν· Ὁ τῶν ὅλων δημιουργός, σοφώτατος νοῦς καὶ ἀΐδιος.

EXCERPTUM XXIX

Stobaeus 1. 5. 14, vol. i, p. 77 Wachsmuth (*Ecl.* I. 174 Heeren).[1]

[Περὶ εἱμαρμένης·] [Ἑρμοῦ.]

ἑπτὰ πολυπλανέες κατ' Ὀλύμπιον ἀστέρες οὐδὸν
εἱλεῦνται, μετὰ τοῖσιν ἀεὶ περινί⟨σ⟩σεται *αἰών·*
νυκτιφανὴς Μήνη, στυγνὸς Κρόνος, Ἥλιος ἡδύς,
⌜παστοφόρος⌝ Παφίη, θρασὺς Ἄρης, εὔπτερος Ἑρμῆς,

2 ἐπιγνωθεὶς A 2–3 ἐπιθυμίαν codd. : fortasse ἐπιστήμην
4–5 Cf. Clem. Alex. *Strom.* 5. 97 : ἐρωτηθεὶς γέ τοι ὁ Θάλης τί ἐστι τὸ θεῖον, "Τὸ μήτε ἀρχὴν" ἔφη "μήτε τέλος ἔχον".

[1] Iteratur hoc carmen sine nomine auctoris in Anthologia Graeca (Planud. p. 494) Append. nr. 40 Jacobs.

Catal. codd. astrol. Graec. III (Mediolan.) 5. F 100, nullo auctoris nomine: Εἰς τοὺς ἑπτὰ πλανήτας καὶ τὰς ἐν ἡμῖν δυνάμεις καὶ πάθη· Ἑπτὰ πολυπλανέες . . . κόσμος ἀπείρων. Quae iterantur *ib.* cod. 21. F 106 r., et cod. 24. F 19 v. Empedocli adscribuntur versus eidem *ib.* cod. 28 F 57 (*tit.* τοῦ αὐτοῦ (*sc.* Ἐμπεδοκλέους) πλανωμένων σφαῖρα ἐν ἡρωικοῖς μέτροις) et cod. 30. F 4.

EXCERPT XXVII

Written by Hermes: an extract from the Discourse of Isis to Horus.

For a refutation, great king, when it has been recognized, brings him who has been refuted into ...[1] of things which he did not know before.

EXCERPT XXVIII

Hermes, when some one asked him what God is, said: 'The Maker of the universe, Mind most wise, and everlasting'.

EXCERPT XXIX

[*Written by Hermes.*]

There are seven wandering stars which circle at the threshold of Olympus, and among them ever revolves unending Time. The seven are these; night-shining Moon, and sullen Kronos,[2] and glad Sun, and the ...[3] Lady of Paphos,[4] and bold Ares,[5] and swift-winged Hermes,[6] and Zeus,[7] first author of all births,

[1] Perhaps, 'knowledge'.
[2] The planet Saturn.
[3] Perhaps, 'all-productive'.
[4] The planet Venus.
[5] The planet Mars.
[6] The planet Mercury.
[7] The planet Jupiter.

---

10 *περὶ εἱμαρμένης* FP: del. Wachsm. 12 *μετὰ τοῖσιν ἀεὶ δ' ἐπινήσεται* FP: *καὶ τοῖσιν ἀεὶ κανονίζεται* Anth.: *μετὰ τοῖσι δ' ἀεὶ περινίσσεται* Jacobs
13 *νυκτιφανεὶς* P¹ | *στυγνὸς κρόνος* Anth., P² marg.: *νυκτὸς* FP¹
14 Fortasse *παντοφόρος* | *εὔπτερος* P², Anth.: *εὔσπερος* FP¹

καὶ Ζεὺς ἀρχιγένεθλος, ἀφ' οὗ φύσις ἐβλάστησεν.
οἱ δ' αὐτοὶ μερόπων ἔλαχον γένος, ἔστι δ' ἐν ἡμῖν
Μήνη, Ζεύς, Ἄρης, Παφίη, Κρόνος, Ἥλιος, Ἑρμῆς.
τοὔνεκ' ἀπ' αἰθερίου ⌜μεμερίσμεθα⌝ πνεύματος ἕλκειν
δάκρυ, γέλωτα, χόλον, γένεσιν, λόγον, ὕπνον, ὄρεξιν.
δάκρυ μέν ἐστι Κρόνος, Ζεὺς ⌜δὴ⌝ γένεσις, λόγος Ἑρμῆς,
θυμὸς Ἄρης, Μήνη δ' ἄρ' ὕπνος, Κυθέρεια δ' ὄρεξις,
Ἠέλιος δὲ γέλως· τούτῳ γὰρ ἅπασα ⌜δικαίως⌝
καὶ θνητὴ διάνοια γελᾷ καὶ κόσμος ἀπείρων.

1 *ἀρχιγένεθλος* P[2] : *ἀρχίγεθλος* FP[1] 2 *ἔλαχον* FP : *ἐλάουσι* Anth. 3 Fortasse Ζεύς, Ἄρης, Παφίη, ⟨⟨Μήνη⟩⟩ 4 *μεμορήμεθα* Meineke 5 *δράκρυ* P | *χόλον* F : *χολὴν* P, Anth. 6 *δράκρυ* P | *δὴ* Anth. : *ἡ* FP : *δ' ἡ* Jacobs | Fortasse *γένεσις δὲ* Ζεύς 7 *κυθαίρεια* F : *κυθέρια* P 8 *δὲ* Anth. : *τε* codd. Stob. | Fortasse *τούτου γὰρ ἅπασα δι' αὐγὰς*

from whom Nature has sprung. To those same stars is assigned the race of men; and we have in us Moon, Zeus, Ares, the Lady of Paphos, Kronos, Sun, and Hermes. Wherefore it is our lot to draw in from the aetherial life-breath[1] tears, laughter, wrath, birth, speech, sleep, desire. Tears are Kronos; birth is Zeus; speech is Hermes; anger is Ares; the Moon is sleep; Aphrodite is desire; and the Sun is laughter, for by him . . .[2] laugh all mortal minds, and the boundless universe.

[1] I.e. from the aether, which is the life-breath of the universe.
[2] Perhaps, 'for by reason of his radiance'.

FRAGMENTA

1. Tertullianus *De anima* 33.

(Mercurius Aegyptius dicit) animam digressam a corpore non refundi in animam universi, sed manere determinatam, uti rationem patri reddat eorum quae in corpore gesserit.

2. Cyprianus (?) *Quod idola dii non sint* 6.

Hermes quoque Trismegistus unum deum loquitur, eumque incomprehensibilem adque inaestimabilem confitetur.

3. Lactantius *Div. inst.* 1. 6. 4.

(Mercurius Trismegistus deum appellat) dominum et patrem.... Ipsius haec verba sunt: *ὁ δὲ θεὸς εἷς. ὁ δὲ εἷς ὀνόματος οὐ προσδέεται· ⸢ἔστι γὰρ ὁ ὢν ἀνώνυμος⸣.*[1]

Lact. *Epit.* 4. 4.

(Hermes deum) dominum et patrem nuncupat, eumque esse sine nomine, quod proprio vocabulo non indigeat, quia solus sit.[1]

4. Lact. *Div. inst.* 1. 7. 2.

(Mercurius Termaximus) non modo *ἀμήτορα*, ... sed *ἀπάτορα* quoque appellat deum, quod origo illi non sit aliunde. Nec enim potest ab ullo esse generatus qui ipse universa generavit.

Div. inst. 4. 13. 2.

Ipse enim pater deus, quoniam parentibus caret, *ἀπάτωρ* atque *ἀμήτωρ* a Trismegisto verissime nominatur, quod ex nullo sit procreatus.

Epit. 4. 4.

Nec habere (deum) ullos parentes, quia ex se et per se sit.

5. Lact. *Div. inst.* 1. 11. 61.

(Trismegistus), cum diceret admodum paucos extitisse in quibus esset perfecta doctrina, in his Uranum Saturnum Mercurium nominavit, cognatos suos.

Epit. 14. 3.

Trismegistus, paucos admodum fuisse cum diceret perfectae doctrinae viros, in iis cognatos suos enumeravit Uranum Saturnum Mercurium.

[1] Fortasse *ὁ δὲ θεὸς εἷς. ὁ δὲ εἷς ⟨⟨ὢν ἀνώνυμός⟩⟩ ⟨ἐστιν⟩· ὀνόματος ⟨⟨γὰρ⟩⟩ οὐ προσδεῖται, ⟨ἐπεὶ μόνος⟩ ἐστί* [[ ]].

FRAGMENTS[1]

1. The soul, when it has quitted the body, does not flow back into[2] the soul of the universe, but remains separate,[3] that it may be called to account by the Father for the deeds which it has done in the body.

2. There is one God; he is beyond comprehension[4] and beyond appraisement.

3. God is called Master and Father.—God is one. And he that is one is nameless; for he does not need a name, since he is alone.

4. God is without father and without mother; for he has been generated by none but himself.

5. There have been very few men that have had perfect knowledge.[5] Among those few are my kinsmen Uranos, Kronos, and Hermes.[6]

[1] Notes on the Fragments will be found among the notes on *Testimonia* in vol. iv.

[2] I. e. is not reabsorbed into.

[3] ἀφωρισμένη.

[4] ἀκατάληπτος?

[5] γνῶσις? Knowledge *of God* must be meant.

[6] The Hermetic writer here makes Hermes Trismegistus the teacher speak of another Hermes, whom he perhaps assumes to have been the teacher's grandfather, as in *Ascl. Lat.* III. 37.

6. Lact. *Div. inst.* 2. 8. 48.
(Trismegistus praedicat) divina providentia effectum esse mundum.

7. Lact. *Div. inst.* 2. 8. 68.
Ut Hermes ait, mortale inmortali, temporale perpetuo, corruptibile incorrupto propinquare non potest.[1]

8. Lact. *Div. inst.* 2. 10. 14.
(Hermes) non tantum hominem ad imaginem dei factum esse dixit a deo, sed etiam illut explanare temptavit, quam subtili ratione singula quaeque in corpore hominis membra formaverit, cum eorum nihil sit quod non tantundem ad usus necessitatem quantum ad pulchritudinem valeat.[2]

9. Lact. *Div. inst.* 2. 14. 6.
(Diabolum) Trismegistus daemoniarchen vocat.[3]

10. Lact. *Div. inst.* 2. 15. 6.
ἡ γὰρ εὐσέβεια γνῶσίς ἐστιν τοῦ θεοῦ.

11. Lact. *Div. inst.* 4. 7. 3.
αἴτιον δὲ τούτου [τοῦ αἰτίου] ἡ τοῦ [θε] ἀγενήτου [ἀγαθο] βούλησις, οὗ τὸ ὄνομα οὐ δύναται ἀνθρωπίνῳ στόματι λαληθῆναι.

Epit. 37. 8.
Hermes ait non posse nomen eius (*sc.* dei filii) mortali ore proferri.

12. Lact. *Div. inst.* 4. 7. 3.
ἔστιν γάρ τις, ὦ τέκνον, ἀπόρρητος λόγος, σοφίας ὁσίοΥ ⟨μ⟩εστόc, περὶ τοῦ μόνου κυρίου πάντων καὶ προεννοουμένου θεοῦ, ὃν εἰπεῖν ὑπὲρ ἄνθρωπόν ἐστιν.

Ib. 4. 9. 3.
esse ineffabilem quendam sanctumque sermonem, cuius enarratio modum hominis excedat.

13. Lact. *Div. inst.* 4. 8. 5.
(Hermes dicit deum) *αὐτοπάτορα* et *αὐτομήτορα.*

14. Lact. *Div. inst.* 7. 9. 11.
(Spectationem dei) Trismegistus *θεοπ⟨τ⟩ίαν* rectissime nominavit.

[1] Vide Herm. *ap.* Stob. *Exc.* I. [2] Vide *Corp.* V. 6.
[3] Vide *Ascl. Lat.* III. 28.

6. The world has been made by God's providence.

7. That which is mortal cannot draw near to that which is immortal, nor that which is for a time to that which is everlasting, nor that which is corruptible to that which is incorruptible.

8. Man has been made by God in the image of God. God has fashioned with consummate skill each member of man's body; every one of the members is perfectly adapted both for use and for beauty.

9. The ruler of the daemons.

10. For piety is knowledge of God.

11. And the cause of this is the will of Him who is without beginning, whose name cannot be spoken by human lips.

12. For there is, my son, a secret doctrine, full of holy wisdom, concerning Him who alone is lord of all and . . .,[1] whom to declare is beyond the power of man.

13. God is his own father and his own mother.

14. Seeing God.

[1] 'and preconceived (?) God'. Cf. *Fr.* 17.

15. Lact. *Div. inst.* 7. 13. 3.

Hermes naturam hominis describens, ut doceret quemadmodum esset a deo factus, haec intulit: ⌜καὶ τὸ αὐτὸ⌝ ἐξ ἑκατέρων φύσεων, τῆς τε ἀθανάτου καὶ τῆς θνητῆς, μίαν ἐποίει φύσιν τὴν τοῦ ἀνθρώπου, τὸν αὐτὸν πῇ μὲν ἀθάνατον, πῇ δὲ θνητὸν ποιήσας. καὶ τοῦτον φέρων ἐν μέσῳ τῆς θείας καὶ ἀθανάτου φύσεως καὶ τῆς θνητῆς καὶ μεταβλητῆς ἵδρυσεν, ἵνα ⌜πάντα⌝ μὲν ὁρῶν ⌜πάντα⌝ θαυμάζῃ.[1]

16. *Abammonis ad Porphyrium responsum*[2] 8. 6 a.

τὸ δὲ πῶς ἔχει, δεῖ διὰ πλειόνων ἀπὸ τῶν Ἑρμαϊκῶν σοι ⟨ὑπο⟩μνηματων διερμηνεῦσαι. δύο γὰρ ἔχει ψυχάς, ὡς ταῦτά φησι τὰ γράμματα, ὁ ἄνθρωπος· καὶ ἡ μέν ἐστιν ἀπὸ τοῦ πρώτου νοητοῦ, μετέχουσα καὶ τῆς τοῦ δημιουργοῦ δυνάμεως, ἡ δὲ ἐνδιδομένη ἐκ τῆς τῶν οὐρανίων περιφορᾶς, εἰς ἣν ἐπεισέρπει ἡ θεοπτικὴ ψυχή.[3]

17. *Ib.* 10. 7.

⌜αὐτὸ δὲ⌝ τἀγαθὸν τὸ μὲν θεῖον ἡγοῦνται[4] τὸν προεννοούμενον θεόν, τὸ δὲ ἀνθρώπινον τὴν πρὸς αὐτὸν ἕνωσιν, ὅπερ Βίτυς ἐκ τῶν Ἑρμαϊκῶν βίβλων μεθηρμήνευσεν.

18. Iamblichus *apud* Proclum *in Tim.* 117 D (Diehl).

Ἰάμβλιχος ἱστόρησεν ὅτι καὶ Ἑρμῆς ἐκ τῆς οὐσιότητος τὴν ὑλότητα παράγεσθαι βούλεται.[5]

19. Zosimus Panopolitanus i. 4.

τοὺς τοιούτους δὲ ἀνθρώπους ὁ Ἑρμῆς ἐν τῷ περὶ φύσεων ἐκάλει ἄνοας, τῆς εἱμαρμένης μόνον ὄντας πομπάς, μηδὲν τῶν ἀσωμάτων φανταζομένους,[6] μηδὲ αὐτὴν τὴν εἱμαρμένην τὴν αὐτοὺς ἄγουσαν δικαίως ⟨ὑπολαμβάνοντας⟩, ἀλλὰ [τοὺς] δυσφημοῦντας αὐτῆς τὰ σωματικὰ παιδευτήρια, καὶ τῶν εὐδαιμόνων αὐτῆς ἐκτὸς ⟨μηδὲν⟩ ἄλλο φανταζομένους.[7]

[1] Fortasse ἵνα [παν] τὰ μὲν ο⟨ὐ⟩ράν⟨ια⟩ [πάντα] θαυμάζῃ, ⟨τὰ δὲ ἐπίγεια θεραπεύῃ⟩.

[2] I.e. 'Iamblichus *De mysteriis*'.

[3] εἰς ἣν . . . ψυχή secludendum?

[4] *Sc.* οἱ Αἰγύπτιοι.

[5] Vide *Abammonis resp.* 8. 3 g (*Testim.*).

[6] Fortasse ἐννοοῦντας.

[7] Vide *Corp.* IV. 4 et 7.

15. . . . Out of those two things, the immortal and the mortal, God made this one thing, man, making him in one respect mortal and in another respect immortal. And him God took and placed between that which is divine and immortal and that which is mortal and mutable, that he might behold the things of heaven with wondering reverence,[1] ⟨and tend the things of earth⟩.

16. Man has two souls. One of them comes from the first Intelligible,[2] and partakes of the power of the Demiurgus; the other soul is put into the man by the revolution of the heavenly bodies, and into this latter soul enters subsequently the soul which is able to see God.[3]

17. The divine Good is . . . God;[4] the good of man is union with God.

18. Materiality is brought into existence out of substantiality.[5]

19. Those men who are devoid of mind are merely led along in the train of Destiny. They have no conception of anything incorporeal, and they do not rightly understand the meaning of Destiny, that very power by which they are led; they complain of the bodily discipline which she imposes, and they do not recognize any other kind of happiness than that which she confers.

[1] MSS., 'that, beholding all things, he might admire all things'.
[2] I. e. from the first or highest part of the incorporeal world.
[3] I. e. the first-mentioned of the two souls.
[4] MSS., 'the God who is preconceived (?)'. Cf. *Fr.* 12.
[5] This probably means that matter is not an independent entity, but is derived from the immaterial world,—or in other words, issues from God.

20. Zosimus i. 5.

ὁ δὲ Ἑρμῆς καὶ ὁ Ζωροάστρης τὸ φιλοσόφων γένος ἀνώτερον τῆς εἱμαρμένης εἶπον,[1] τῷ μήτε τῇ εὐδαιμονίᾳ αὐτῆς χαίρειν— ἡδονῶν γὰρ κρατοῦσι—, μήτε τοῖς κακοῖς αὐτῆς ⌜βάλλεσθαι⌝,[2] πάντοτε ἐν ἀϋλίᾳ ἄγοντας.

21. Zosimus i. 7.

ὁ μέντοι Ἑρμῆς ἐν τῷ περὶ ἀϋλίας διαβάλλει [καὶ] τὴν μαγείαν, λέγων ὅτι οὐ δεῖ [τὸν πνευματικὸν ἄνθρωπον] τὸν ἐπιγνόντα ἑαυτὸν [οὔτε] διὰ μαγείας κατορθοῦν τι, ἐὰν καὶ κακὸν νομίζηται, μηδὲ βιάζεσθαι τὴν ἀνάγκην, ἀλλ' ἐᾶν ὡς ἔχει φύσεως [καὶ κρίσεως] πορεύεσθαι. ⌜δὲ διὰ μόνου τοῦ⌝ ζητεῖν[3] ἑαυτὸν καὶ θεὸν ἐπιγνόντα κρατεῖν ⟨. . .⟩[4] [τὴν ἀκατονόμαστον τριάδα], καὶ ἐᾶν τὴν εἱμαρμένην ὃ θέλει[ν] ποιεῖν τῷ ἑαυτῆς πηλῷ, τουτέστι τῷ σώματι. καὶ οὕτως, φησί, νοήσας καὶ πολιτευσάμενος ⟨. . .⟩.

22. Ephraim Syrus.

23. Didymus *De Trinitate* 757 B: Cyrillus *c. Julianum* 556 A.[5]

οὐ γὰρ ἐφικτόν ἐστιν ⌜εἰς ἀμυήτους⌝ τοιαῦτα μυστήρια ⌜παρέχεσθαι⌝.[6] ἀλλὰ ⟨. . .⟩[7] τῷ νοΐ ἀκούσατε. ἓν μόνον ἦν [φῶς νοερὸν] [πρὸ φωτὸς νοεροῦ] καὶ ἔστιν ἀεί, νοῦς ⌜νοὸς φωτεινός⌝.[8] καὶ οὐδὲν ἕτερον ἦν ἢ ἡ τούτου ἑνότης. ⟨οὗτος⟩, ἀεὶ ἐν ⟨ἑ⟩αυτῷ ὤν, ἀεὶ τῷ ἑαυτοῦ [νοΐ καὶ] φωτὶ καὶ πνεύματι πάντα περιέχει. — — —[9] ἐκτὸς τούτου οὐ θεός, οὐκ ἄγγελος, οὐ

[1] Fortasse τὸ δὲ φιλοσόφων γένος ὁ Ἑρμῆς [καὶ ὁ Ζωροάστρης] ἀνώτερον τῆς εἱμαρμένης εἶπεν.

[2] βλάπτεσθαι?

[3] Fortasse δε⟨ῖ⟩ δὲ μόνον [τοῦ] ζητεῖν.

[4] Fortasse ⟨τῶν παθῶν⟩ vel ⟨τοῦ ἀλόγου⟩.

[5] αὖθίς τε (Ἑρμῆς). . . ἀποφθέγγεται τοιάδε Didymus: λέγει . . . Ἑρμῆς ἐν λόγῳ τρίτῳ τῶν πρὸς Ἀσκληπιόν Cyril.

[6] Fortasse οὐ γὰρ ἐ. ἐ. τοῖς ἀμυήτοις τ. μ. παραδέχεσθαι.

[7] Fortasse ⟨ἐντεταμένῳ⟩.

[8] Fortasse νοῦς, νοεροῦ φωτὸς ⟨ἀρχή vel πηγή⟩.

[9] καὶ μεταξὺ ἄλλων ἐπάγει Didymus: καὶ μεθ' ἕτερά φησι Cyril.

20. Philosophers are above Destiny; for they find no joy in the happiness she gives, since they hold pleasures in subjection; and they are not harmed by the ills she inflicts, because they dwell at all times in the immaterial world.

21. He who has learnt to know himself ought not to set right by means of magic anything that is thought to be amiss, nor to use force to overcome necessity,[1] but rather to let necessity go its own way according to its nature. A man ought to seek to know himself and God and hold his passions in subjection, and to let Destiny deal as she wills with the clay which belongs to her, that is, with his body. And if a man thinks thus and behaves thus, . . .

22. Ephraim Syrus, *Refutations of Mani, Marcion, and Bardaisan*, edited and translated by C. W. Mitchell, A. A. Bevan, and F. C. Burkitt, vol. ii, p. xcix.

'Hermes taught that there was a Bowl, filled with whatever it was filled with, and that there are Souls excited by desire, and they come down beside it, and, when they have come close to it, in it and by reason of it they forget their own place. . . . Hermes teaches that the souls desired the Bowl.'

23. *From the third of the Discourses of Hermes to Asclepius.*

For it is not possible for the uninitiated to have such holy secrets told to them. But hearken ye with attentive mind. There was and ever is one thing alone, even Mind, the source of intellectual light; and beside the unity of this one thing, there was nothing else in being. This Mind, ever existing in itself, ever encompasses all things with its own light and spirit. ——— There is no god, nor

[1] 'Necessity' is the working of Destiny or natural law; and to employ magic is 'to use force to overcome necessity'.

δαίμων, οὐκ οὐσία τις ἄλλη· πάντων γάρ ἐστι κύριος καὶ πατήρ [καὶ θεὸς] ⌈καὶ πηγὴ καὶ ζωὴ καὶ δύναμις καὶ φῶς καὶ νοῦς καὶ πνεῦμα⌉, καὶ πάντα ἐν αὐτῷ καὶ ὑπ' αὐτόν ἐστι.

24. Didym. *ib.* 756 B: Cyril. *ib.* 556 B.[1]

εἰ μὴ πρόνοιά τις ἦν τοῦ πάντων κυρίου ὥστε με τὸν λόγον τοῦτον ἀποκαλύψαι, οὐδὲ ὑμᾶς τοιοῦτος ἔρως κατεῖχεν ⟨ἂν⟩ ἵνα περὶ τούτου ζητήσητε· νῦν δὲ ⟨. . .⟩. ⟨. . .⟩ τὰ λοιπὰ τοῦ λόγου ἀκούετε. τούτου τοῦ πνεύματος, οὗ πολλάκις προεῖπον, πάντα χρῄζει· τὰ πάντα γὰρ ⌈βαστάζον κατ' ἀξίαν τὰ πάντα⌉ ζωοποιεῖ καὶ τρέφει, καὶ ἀπὸ τῆς ἁγίας πηγῆς ἐξήρτηται, ⌈ἐπίκουρον πνεύμασι⌉ ⟨. . .⟩[2] *καὶ ζωῆς ἅπασιν ἀεὶ ὑπάρχον, γόνιμον ἓν ὄν.*

25. Cyril. *ib.* 9

⟨καὶ ἑτέρωθι (sc. φησὶν Ἑρμῆς)·⟩ Εἴ τῳ οὖν ἀσώματος ὀφθαλμός, ἐξερχέσθω τοῦ σώματος ἐπὶ τὴν θέαν τοῦ καλοῦ, καὶ ἀναπτήτω καὶ αἰωρηθήτω, [καὶ] ⟨μὴ⟩ σχῆμα, μὴ χρῶμα [μὴ ἰδέας] ζητῶν θεάσασθαι, ἀλλ' ἐκεῖνο μᾶλλον τὸ τούτων ποιητικόν, τὸ ἥσυχον καὶ γαληνόν, τὸ ἑδραῖον, τὸ ἄτρεπτον, ⌈τὸ αὐτὸ πάντα καὶ μόνον⌉,[3] *τὸ ἕν,*[4] *τὸ αὐτὸ ἐξ ἑαυτοῦ, τὸ αὐτὸ ἐν ἑαυτῷ, τὸ ἑαυτῷ ὅμοιον*[5] *[ὃ μήτε ἄλλῳ ὅμοιόν ἐστι μήτε ἑαυτῷ ἀνόμοιον].*

26. Cyril. *ib.* 549 C, D.

καὶ πάλιν ὁ αὐτὸς (sc. Ἑρμῆς)· Μηδὲν οὖν, περὶ ἐκείνου [πώποτε][6] *τοῦ ἑνὸς καὶ μόνου ἀγαθοῦ ἐννοούμενος, ἀδύνατον εἴπῃς· ἡ πᾶσα γὰρ δύναμις αὐτῷ*[7] *ἐστιν. μηδὲ ἔν τινι αὐτὸν διανοηθῇς εἶναι, μηδὲ πάλιν [κατ'] ἐκτός τινος· αὐτὸς γὰρ ἀπέραντος ὢν πάντων ἐστὶ πέρας, καὶ ὑπὸ μηδενὸς ἐμπεριεχόμενος πάντα ἐμπεριέχει. ⟨. . .⟩ ἐπεὶ τίς διαφορά ἐστι τῶν σωμάτων πρὸς τὸ ἀσώματον, καὶ τῶν γενητῶν πρὸς τὸ ἀγένητον [καὶ τῶν ἀνάγκῃ ὑποκειμένων πρὸς τὸ αὐτεξούσιον] [ἢ τῶν*

[1] Ἑρμοῦ Τρισμεγίστου ἐκ ⌈τῶν πρὸς Ἀσκληπιὸν λόγων τριῶν⌉· ἐρομένου τινὸς ⌈τὸν ἀγαθὸς δαίμονα⌉ περὶ τοῦ τρισαγίου πνεύματος, ἔχρησεν οὕτως cod. Didym.: ὁ αὐτὸς ἐν τῷ αὐτῷ τῶν πρὸς Ἀσκληπιόν, ὡς ἐρομένου τινὸς περὶ τοῦ θείου πνεύματος, φησὶν οὕτως Cyril.

[2] Fortasse ⟨αἴτιον φωτὸς⟩.

[3] τὸ αὐτὸ πάντα καὶ μόνον secludendum?

[4] Fortasse τὸ ἓν ⟨πάντα ὄν⟩. [5] Fortasse τὸ ἑαυτῷ ⟨μόνῳ⟩ ὅμοιον.

[6] Fortasse Μηδὲν οὖν ⟨μηδέποτε⟩, περὶ ἐκείνου [ ] τοῦ ἑνὸς κ.τ.λ.

[7] αὐτῷ scripsi: αὐτὸς Aub.

angel, nor daemon, nor any other being, that is outside of Him; for He is Lord and Father of all . . .,[1] and all things are in Him and subject to Him.

24. *From the third of the Discourses of Hermes to Asclepius.*

If it had not been ordained by the providence of Him who is Lord of all that I should reveal this doctrine, ye would not have been possessed by such passionate desire to seek the truth concerning this; but as it is, ⟨. . .⟩.—Hearken ye to that which I have yet to tell. Of this spirit, concerning which I have many times spoken before, all things have need; for . . . it gives life and sustenance to all things. It is dependent on[2] the holy source, . . . being ever ⟨the cause of light (?)⟩ and life to all things, inasmuch as it is the one thing that is fecund.

25. If any man then has an incorporeal eye, let him go forth from the body to behold the Beautiful, let him fly up and float aloft, not seeking to see shape or colour, but rather that by which these things[3] are made, that which is quiet and calm, stable and changeless, . . . that which is one,[4] that which issues from itself and is contained in itself, that which is like nothing but itself.

26. Say not then, in your thought concerning Him who alone is good, that anything is impossible; for to Him belongs all power. And think not that He is in anything, nor again that He is outside of anything; for He is limitless himself, and is the limit of all things; He is encompassed by nothing, and encompasses all things. . . . For in what do bodies differ from that which is incorporeal, and things which have come into being from that which is without

[1] Perhaps, 'and source of life and light and spirit'.
[2] Perhaps, 'It flows forth from'.
[3] *Sc.* shaped and coloured (i.e. bodily) things.
[4] Perhaps, 'that which, being one, ⟨is yet all things⟩'.

ἐπιγείων πρὸς τὰ ἐπουράνια, καὶ τῶν φθαρτῶν πρὸς τὰ ἀίδια]; οὐχ ὅτι τὸ μὲν αὐτεξούσιόν ἐστι, τὰ δὲ ἀνάγκῃ ὑποκείμενα;[1] ⟨. . .⟩ τὰ δὲ κάτω, ἀτελῆ ὄντα, φθαρτά ἐστιν.[2]

27. Cyril. *ib.* 552 D.

ὁ δὲ τρισμέγιστος Ἑρμῆς οὕτω φθέγγεται περὶ θεοῦ· Ὁ γὰρ λόγος αὐτοῦ προελθών, παντέλειος ὢν καὶ γόνιμος καὶ δημιουργ⟨ικ⟩ός, ἐν γονίμῳ φύσει πεσών [ἐπὶ γονίμῳ ὕδατι], ἔγκυον τὸ ὕδωρ ἐποίησε.[3]

28. Cyril. *ib.* 552 D.

καὶ ὁ αὐτὸς (*sc.* Ἑρμῆς) αὖθις Ἡ οὖν ⌜πυραμίς⌝, φησίν, ⌜ὑποκειμένη τῇ φύσει καὶ τῷ νοερῷ κόσμῳ⌝· ἔχει γὰρ ἄρχοντα ἐπικείμενον ⟨τὸν⟩ δημιουργὸν λόγον τοῦ πάντων δεσπότου, ὃς[4] μετ' ἐκεῖνον πρώτη δύναμις, ἀγένητος, ἀπέραντος, ἐξ ἐκείνου προκύψασα, καὶ ἐπίκειται καὶ ἄρχει τῶν δι' αὐτοῦ δημιουργηθέντων.

29. Cyril. *ib.* 553 A.

καὶ πάλιν ὁ αὐτός (*sc.* Ἑρμῆς), ὡς ἐρομένου τινὸς τῶν ἐν Αἰγύπτῳ τεμενιτῶν, καὶ λέγοντος "διὰ τί δέ, ὦ μέγιστε Ἀγαθὸς Δαίμων,[5] τούτῳ τῷ ὀνόματι ἐκλήθη ἀπὸ τοῦ πάντων κυρίου;"[6] φησὶ "καὶ ἐν τοῖς ἔμπροσθεν εἶπον· σὺ δὲ οὐ συνῆκας; ⟨ἡ⟩ φύσις τοῦ νοεροῦ αὐτοῦ λόγου [φύσις] ἐστὶ γεννητική.[7] [τοῦτο ὥσπερ αὐτοῦ ἡ γέννησις ἢ φύσις ἢ ἔθος ἢ] ⟨σὺ δὲ⟩ ὃ θέλεις αὐτὸ⟨ν⟩ καλεῖν κάλει, τοῦτο μόνον νοῶν, ὅτι τέλειός ἐστι[ν ἐν τελείῳ] καὶ ἀπὸ τελείου, ⟨καὶ⟩ τέλεια ἀγαθὰ ἐργάζεται, καὶ δημιουργεῖ[8] καὶ ζωοποιεῖ. ἐπειδὴ οὖν τοιαύτης ἔχεται φύσεως, καλῶς τοῦτο προσηγόρευται."

[1] τὰ . . . ὑποκείμενα scripsi: τὸ . . . ὑποκείμενον Aub.

[2] Fortasse ⟨τὰ μὲν γὰρ ἄνω, τέλεια ὄντα, ἀίδιά ἐστι,⟩ τὰ δὲ κ.τ.λ.

[3] Fortasse ὁ γὰρ λόγος αὐτοῦ προελθών, . . . ⟨καὶ⟩ ἐν (vel ἐπὶ) γονίμῳ φύσει (*sc.* τῇ τοῦ ὕδατος) πεσών [ ], ἔγκυον τὸ ὕδωρ ἐποίησε.

[4] Fortasse τὸν [δημιουργὸν] τοῦ πάντων δεσπότου λόγον, ὃς κ.τ.λ.

[5] Fortasse Ἀγαθοδαῖμον.

[6] Fortasse ἐκλήθη ⟨ὁ⟩ [ἀπὸ] τοῦ πάντων κυρίου ⟨λόγος⟩.

[7] Fortasse ἡ φύσις τοῦ . . . λόγου [φύσις] ἐστὶν ⟨ἀγαθῶν⟩ γεννητική.

[8] Fortasse καὶ ⟨πάντα⟩ δημιουργεῖ.

beginning? Is not the difference this, that the one[1] is self-determining, and those other things[2] are subject to necessity? . . ., but[3] the things below, being imperfect, are perishable.

27. For God's Word, who is all-accomplishing and fecund and creative, went forth, and flinging himself upon the water,[4] which was a thing of fecund nature, made the water pregnant.

28. . . .;[5] for it[6] has over it as ruler the creative Word of the Master of all. That Word is, next after Him, the supreme Power, a Power ungenerated, boundless, that has stooped forth from Him;[7] and the Word presides over and governs the things that have been made through him.[8]

29. But tell me, great Agathodaimon, why was he[9] called by this name[10] by the Lord of all?[11]—I have already told you; did you not understand? The nature of His intellectual Word is generative.[12] You may call him[13] what you will, provided that you understand this, that he is perfect and issues from one that is perfect, and that he works perfect goods, and makes and vivifies all things. Since then he is of[14] such a nature, he is rightly called by this name.

1 *Sc.* that which is incorporeal and without beginning.
2 *Sc.* bodies, things which have come into being.
3 Perhaps, '⟨For the things above, being perfect, are everlasting,⟩ but'.
4 I.e. the primal chaos of water out of which the world was evolved.
5 The sense of this corrupt clause was probably something like 'The material world is subject to intelligent government'.
6 *Sc.* the material world.
7 I.e. has issued from the supreme God and looked down on things below.
8 I.e. the world which the supreme God has made by the agency of his Word.
9 *Sc.* God's Word.
10 The 'name' spoken of must have been a name which signified something like 'He who is perfect, and whose works are perfectly good'.
11 Perhaps, 'why was the Word of the Lord of all called by this name?'
12 Perhaps, 'generative ⟨of goods⟩'.
13 *Sc.* God's Word.
14 Literally, 'holds on to' or 'pertains to'.

30. Cyril. *ib.* 553 A, B.

καὶ ὁ αὐτὸς (*sc.* Ἑρμῆς) ἐν λόγῳ πρώτῳ τῶν πρὸς Τὰτ διεξοδικῶν οὕτω λέγει περὶ θεοῦ· Ὁ τοῦ δημιουργοῦ λόγος, ὦ τέκνον, ἀίδιος, αὐτοκίνητος, ἀναυξής, ἀμείωτος, ἀμετάβλητος, ἄφθαρτος, ⌈μόνος⌉[1] ἀεὶ ἑαυτῷ ὅμοιός ἐστιν, ἴσος δὲ καὶ ὁμαλός,[2] εὐσταθής, εὔτακτος, εἷς ὢν [ὁ] μετὰ τὸν προεγνωσμένον[3] θεόν.

31. Cyril. *ib.* 588 A.

ἔφη γὰρ οὗτος (*sc.* Ἑρμῆς) ἐν ⌈τῷ⌉ πρὸς Ἀσκληπιόν·[4] Καὶ εἶπε, φησίν, Ὄσιρις· "εἶτα, ὦ μέγιστε Ἀγαθὸς Δαίμων,[5] πῶς ὅλη ἡ γῆ ἐφάνη;" καὶ εἶπεν ὁ μέγας Ἀγαθὸς Δαίμων· "κατὰ ⌈τάξιν⌉ καὶ ἀναξήρανσιν, ὡς εἶπον. καὶ ⟨γὰρ⟩ τῶν πολλῶν ὑδάτων κελευσθέντων ἀπὸ τοῦ ⟨. . .⟩[6] εἰς ἑαυτὰ ἀναχωρῆσαι, ἐφάνη [ὅλη] ἡ γῆ, ἔμπηλος[7] καὶ τρέμουσα· ἡλίου δὲ λοιπὸν ἀναλάμψαντος, καὶ ἀδιαλείπτως διακαίοντος καὶ ξηραίνοντος, ἡ γῆ ἐστηρίζετο ἐν τοῖς ὕδασιν, ἐμπεριεχομένη ὑπὸ τοῦ ὕδατος."
— — —[8] 588 B. ἡλίου δὲ πέρι πάλιν ὧδέ φησι· Καὶ εἶπεν Ὄσιρις "ὦ [τρὶς] μέγιστε Ἀγαθὸς Δαίμων,[5] ⟨πόθεν ἐφάνη ὁ μέγας οὗτος ἥλιος;" καὶ εἶπεν ὁ μέγας Ἀγαθὸς Δαίμων "ὦ Ὄσιρι,⟩ ἡλίου γένναν βούλει ἡμᾶς καταλέξαι [πόθεν ἐφάνη]; ἐφάνη προνοίᾳ τοῦ πάντων δεσπότου."

32. Cyril. *ib.* 588 A.

καὶ μὴν καὶ ἑτέρωθι (*sc.* ἔφη Ἑρμῆς)· Ὁ πάντων δημιουργὸς καὶ κύριος ἐφώνησεν οὕτως, "ἔστω γῆ [καὶ φανείτω στερέωμα]·" καὶ εὐθέως ἀρχὴ τῆς δημιουργίας γῆ ἐγένετο.

33. Cyril. *ib.* 588 B.

καὶ ⟨ὁ⟩ αὐτὸς (*sc.* Ἑρμῆς) ἐν τῷ πρὸς τὸν Τὰτ διεξοδικῷ λόγῳ πρώτῳ φησίν· Ὁ δὲ πάντων κύριος εὐθέως ἐφώνησε τῷ ἑαυτοῦ ἁγίῳ [καὶ νοητῷ] καὶ δημιουργικῷ λόγῳ "ἔστω ἥλιος"· καὶ ἅμα τῷ φάναι, τὸ πῦρ,[9] [τῆς][10] φύσεως ἀνωφεροῦς ἐχόμενον,

[1] Fortasse μόνιμος.
[2] ἐστιν ἴσος δὲ καὶ ὁμαλός secludendum?
[3] Cf. ὁ προεννοούμενος θεός, *Fr.* 12, 17, 36.
[4] Fortasse ἐν τῷ ⟨τρίτῳ (?) τῶν⟩ πρὸς Ἀσκληπιόν.
[5] Ἀγαθοδαῖμον?
[6] Fortasse ⟨πάντων κυρίου⟩.
[7] Fortasse ⟨τὸ μὲν πρῶτον⟩ ἔμπηλος.
[8] Fragmentum 32 hic interponit Cyrillus.
[9] Fortasse καὶ ἅμα τῷ ⟨εἰπεῖν⟩ ἐφάνη ⟨ὁ ἥλιος⟩· τὸ ⟨γὰρ⟩ πῦρ κ.τ.λ.
[10] Fortasse ἅτε.

30. *From the first of the Explanatory Discourses of Hermes to Tat.*

The Word of the Maker, my son, is everlasting, self-moved, without increase or diminution, immutable, incorruptible, . . . ;[1] he[2] is ever like to himself and equal to himself, equable, stable, well-ordered; after the supreme God[3] he stands alone.

31. *From one of the Discourses of Hermes to Asclepius.*[4]

And Osiris said, 'Tell me next, most great Agathodaimon, how did all the land come forth?' And the great Agathodaimon said, 'It came forth by . . .[5] and drying up, as I told you. For when the many waters were bidden by the ⟨Lord of all⟩ to go back into themselves, then the land came forth. At first it was muddy and quivering; but afterwards, when the sun shone forth, and scorched and dried it without cease, the land was firmly fixed amid the waters, being encompassed by the water.— — — And Osiris said, 'Tell me, most great Agathodaimon, ⟨whence did this great sun come forth?' And the great Agathodaimon said, 'Osiris,⟩[6] do you wish me to describe the origin of the sun? The sun came forth by the providence of Him who is Master of all'.

32. The Maker and Lord of all spoke thus, 'Let earth be' [ ];[7] and straightway earth came into being, and so began the making of the world.[8]

33. *From the first of the Explanatory Discourses of Hermes to Tat.*

And straightway the Lord of all spoke with his own holy and creative speech,[9] and said, 'Let the sun be'; and even as He spoke, ⌜Nature drew to herself with her own breath⌝ the fire, which is of upward-tending nature,—that fire, I mean, which is unmixed and

[1] Perhaps, 'abiding'. [2] *Sc.* God's Word.

[3] MSS., 'the foreknown God'. [4] Cf. *Fr.* 23 and *Fr.* 24.

[5] Perhaps, 'by separation' (*sc.* of earth from water).

[6] 'Whence . . . Osiris': omitted in the Greek text, but preserved in Oecolampadius's Latin translation.

[7] ['and let a firmament appear'].

[8] Cyril does not say from what *libellus* he took this extract; but its verbal similarity to *Fr.* 33 makes it probable that it was taken from the same document as that, viz. *the first of the Explanatory Discourses of Hermes to Tat.*

[9] Or 'spoke to his own holy and creative Word'?

λέγω δὴ τὸ ἄκρατον καὶ φωτεινότατον καὶ δραστικώτατον καὶ γονιμώτατον,[1] ἐπεσπάσατο ⌜ἡ φύσις τῷ ἑαυτῆς πνεύματι⌝,[2] καὶ ἤγειρεν εἰς ὕψος ἀπὸ ⟨τοῦ⟩ ὕδατος.

34. Cyril. *ib.* 588 C.

εἰσκεκόμικε γὰρ (Ἑρμῆς) τὸν θεὸν λέγοντα τοῖς κτίσμασιν· Ἀνάγκην δὲ ὑμῖν τοῖς ὑπ' ἐμὲ περιθήσω ταύτην τὴν διὰ τοῦ λόγου μου ὑμῖν ἐντολὴν δεδομένην· τοῦτον γὰρ νόμον ἔχετε.[3]

35. Cyril. *ib.* 920 D.

ἔφη δέ που . . . Ἑρμῆς περὶ τοῦ πάντων ἀριστοτέχνου θεοῦ· Καὶ γὰρ ὡς ⌜τέλειος⌝[4] καὶ σοφὸς τάξιν [καὶ] ἀταξίᾳ ἐπέθηκε, ⟨. . .⟩ ἵνα τὰ μὲν νοερά, ὡς πρεσβύτερα καὶ κρείττονα, προεστήκῃ καὶ τὸν πρῶτον τόπον ἔχῃ,[5] τὰ δὲ αἰσθητά, ὡς δεύτερα, [ἵνα] τούτοις ὑποστήκῃ. τὸ οὖν κατωφερὲς [τερ] ὂν [τοῦ νοεροῦ] καὶ βρῖθον λόγον ἐν ἑαυτῷ σοφὸν ἔχει [δημιουργικόν]· ὁ δὲ λόγος [αὐτοῦ] οὗτος δημιουργικῆς ἔχεται φύσεως, γόνιμος ὑπάρχων καὶ ζωοποιός.

36. Pseudo-Anthimus § 15.

οὗτος γὰρ (*sc.* ὁ Τρισμέγιστος) μετὰ τὸν πρῶτον θεὸν περὶ τοῦ δευτέρου λέγων οὕτως ἔφη· Εἰσόμεθα τόν ⟨τε⟩ προεννοούμενον θεὸν ⟨καὶ τὸν δεύτερον⟩, ὃς τὰ πάντα μὲν ἐκείνου ὅμοια βουληθέντος ἔχει,[6] δυσὶ δὲ λείπεται, τῷ εἶναι ἐν σώματι καὶ ὁρατὸν ὑπάρχειν.

37. Shahrastani.

[1] Fortasse φύσεως ἀνωφεροῦς ἐχόμενον [λέγω δὴ τὸ ἄκρατον] καὶ φωτεινότατον ⟨ὂν⟩ κ.τ.λ.

[2] Fortasse ἐπεσπάσατο [ἡ φύσις] (*sc.* ὁ πάντων κύριος) τῷ ἑαυτοῦ πνεύματι.

[3] ἕξετε?

[4] Fortasse τεχνικός.

[5] καὶ τὸν πρῶτον τόπον ἔχῃ secludendum?

[6] Fortasse ὃς τὰ μὲν ⟨ἄλλα⟩ πάντα ἐκείνου βουληθέντος ὅμοια ἔχει.

most luminous and most active and most fecund,—and raised it up[1] aloft from the water.

34. God said to the beings that He had made: 'And on you that are subject to me I will impose as an irresistible constraint this commandment that has been given you by my speech; this you shall have as your law.'

35. For God, as being ⌜perfect⌝[2] and wise, imposed order on disorder, . . .[3] that so the things of mind, as being prior and mightier, might preside and hold the first place, and the things perceptible by sense, as being secondary, might be placed under them. And so that which is downward-tending and heavy has in it a wise Word; and this Word is of creative nature, being fecund and life-giving.

36. We shall know both the God who is preconceived (?),[4] and the second God,[5] who, by the will of the first God, is like him in all else, but fall short of him in two respects, namely, in that he is in a body, and in that he is visible.

37. Shahrastani (*Haarbrücker* ii, p. 81).

'Concerning ⌜Adsîmûn⌝ (Agathodaimon), the philosophers hand down the tradition that he said "that the first principles were five. namely, the Creator, Reason, Soul, Space, and ⌜Void⌝,[6] and that the composite things came into being thereafter".[7] But this is not reported of Hermes'.

[1] Perhaps, 'and even as He spoke, the sun appeared. For He (i.e. God) drew to himself with his own breath (or spirit) the fire, which is of upward-tending nature and is most luminous and most active and most fecund, and raised it up', &c.

[2] Perhaps, 'skilful'.

[3] Perhaps, ⟨'appointing his Word to govern the material world'⟩, or something to that effect.

[4] The meaning of this phrase is doubtful; but the God denoted by it is the first or supreme God. Cf. *Fr.* 12, 17, and 30.

[5] I. e. the Kosmos.

[6] Perhaps rather, 'and Time'.

[7] Probably taken from a Greek *Hermeticum* in which the teacher was Agathos Daimon.